A Comprehensive Study of Education

A Comprehensive Study of Education

SECOND EDITION

S. SAMUEL RAVI
Visiting Professor
R.P.A. College of Education
Mamoottukadai, Tamil Nadu

PHI Learning Private Limited
Delhi-110092
2026

In fond memory of ***Shri Asoke K. Ghosh*** *(October 1942 – February 2024), Founder Chairman and Managing Director of PHI Learning, whose vision endlessly inspires.*

The Legacy Continues....

Published by Pushpita Ghosh, PHI Learning Private Limited, Rimjhim House, 111, Patparganj Industrial Estate, Delhi-110092 and Printed by Multi Colour Services, 92, DSIDC Sheds, Okhla Industrial Area, Phase-I, New Delhi-110020.

₹1395.00

A COMPREHENSIVE STUDY OF EDUCATION, Second Edition
S. Samuel Ravi

ISBN-978-93-91818-28-9 (Print Book)
ISBN-978-93-91818-29-6 (e-Book)

The success of education is in differentiating man
from illiterates in character and deeds,
and in developing a casteless, secular and democratic outlook,
and in making people useful for society and nation;
of course, in the greatness of human values.

— S. Samuel Ravi

CONTENTS

UNIT III : INDIAN AND WESTERN PHILOSOPHERS

UNIT IV : EDUCATIONAL SOCIOLOGY

PREFACE

Most welcome with immense pleasure to make use of the second edition of A COMPREHENSIVE STUDY OF EDUCATION for new educational thoughts, philosophies and principles in the complicated and polluted materialistic world. The present edition is more comprehensive than the previous one and very useful for researches, seminars, discussions, debates and conferences in the contemporary educational society. It is needless to say that the new edition contains almost all topics/study materials prescribed in various universities in India and foreign countries. So, it not only meets the requirements of students, teachers, professors, scholars, researchers and readers but also for curriculum constructors, educational policy makers, peace makers, counsellors and educationists in the emerging educational, philosophical, psychological and sociological world. Moreover, it is presented in simple and effective language in such a way to be used and grasped easily by all categories of readers in graduate, postgraduate and research levels.

The second edition contains 59 chapters wherein eighteen topics are new ones, i.e., Agencies of Education, Education for 21st Century, Curriculum for Modern Society, Awakenism, Humanism, Eclectic Tendency in Education, Progressive Education, Sarvepalli Radhakrishnan, John Heinrich Pestalozzi, Bertrand Russel, Karl Marxian Education, Socialisation of Child, Education for New Social Order, Education and Politics, Religious Education, Education for Peace, Education for Human Rights, and Education for Social Pollution. I gratefully acknowledge my heartfelt thanks for your reception and accordance to the new edition. Also welcome the users to buy this book at any cost but must avoid taking photo copy at any price. In fact, it is a real investment that makes you wealthy, healthy and happy. Wish you all the best in all endeavours.

S. Samuel Ravi

PREFACE TO THE FIRST EDITION

I, with great pleasure, greet the readers who are interested in understanding the comprehensive idea of education. This book would take you to the world of new education. In fact, A Comprehensive Study of Education is an earnest attempt to provide the readers with a thorough understanding of the various concepts of education. As it is an outcome of two decades of work of the author as an academician in different educational and research institutions, its contents are qualitatively as well as quantitatively different from other books on education available in the market. In fact, this book has been prepared in such a way that its leaves may be turned to change your thoughts and its words may be perused to mould and shape yourself to become a model pedagogue and better future citizen of the world. Therefore, this book can be used as a powerful tool to bring about the desirable changes in the society. Moreover, concepts such as education, philosophy, educational philosophy, educational sociology, social change, social mobility, social stratification, economics, national integration and international understanding have been interpreted and explained according to the present situation. Hence, this book will be of great use to the lecturers, teachers, students, researchers and social activists at the B.Ed., M.Ed., and M.Phil. levels.

Further, this book has been written according to the syllabus prescribed by the Indian universities for undergraduate and postgraduate degree courses in education. It provides an exhaustive treatment of the subject in a very lucid and cogent manner, so that the educators and educands can grasp the subject completely and clearly. I hope that this book can be used as a reference book also as it would meet the requirements of people who are interested in entering the world of education.

S. Samuel Ravi

ACKNOWLEDGEMENTS

I gratefully remember the great people my beloved parents Mr. S. Selvamony, Mrs. M. Dhasammal who yielded me to the world with social qualities. Rev. Fr. G. Alphones for his valuable help in my physical and intellectual growth, Socrates, Confucius, Buddha, Mahavir, Jesus Christ, St. Paul, Mohammed Nabi, Guru Nanak, Abraham Lincoln, Karl Marx, Thomas Alva Edison, Rabindranath Tagore, Mahatma Gandhi, Swami Vivekananda, Radhakrishnan, Jiddu Krishnamurti, Mahakavi Bharathiyar, Kaviyarasar Kannadhasan, Rousseau, Froebel, Pestalozzi, Montessori, Ivan Illich John Dewey and the classical, neoclassical and modern economists like Adam Smith, Alfred Marshal, Lionel Robbins, J.B. Say, David Ricardo and John Maynard Keynes who made me think the world and education differently.

Express the gratitude to Dr. A.J. Bensam, Dr. J. Prem Kumar, Mr. Friederich Rajasekhar, James College of Education, Karungal, Dr. B. William Dharmaraja, Dr. G. Rexlin Jose, Department of Education, M.S. University, South India, Prof. R. Wilson (Late) Bethlahem College of Education, Karungal, Dr. G. Samuel George, Immanuel Arasar College of Education, Nattalam, Prof. D. Christian Babu, Dr. S. Dawn Dharma Roy, Mr. J. Jayahar Joseph, Dr. S. Linsa Ratna Lal, Dr. P. Jegan Babu, Paloor K. Francis, and Prof. Adlin Selvaraj, N.M. Christian College, Marthandam, Prof. Daisy David, Lashmipuram College of Arts and Science, Lakshmipuram, Monday Market, Dr. R. Francis, Dr. T. Praveendhar, Mr. M. John Milan Sandee and Mr. R. Murugan, R.P.A. College of Education, Mamoottukadai, Dr. C. Bright, Holy Trinity College of Education, Melpalai, whose supports, suggestions helped me a lot in preparing the book usefully.

Immensely thankful to Dr. Kappiyarai V. Rayappan (Socialist and writer), Mr. S. Johnson, Head Master, Salvation Army Hr. Sec. School, Nager Coil, Mr. C. Augustin (Chennai) and Manan Vilai Maru. G. Nelson whose encouragements have made me this much.

Convey my thanks to Mr. R.K. Ratheesh Lynd, Mr. A. Selvin Singh, Mr. C. Austin Prabu, Mr. M. Baiju, Mr. H. Starwin, Vazhuthalampallam P. Raja Perinba Dhas and Jenisha who computerised the manuscripts superbly.

Gratefully indebted to Mr. Asoke K. Ghosh, Chairman and Managing Director, and the entire editorial and production team of PHI Learning, Delhi for their co-operation, guidance and suggestions to make the my efforts in the book form and publish it to be used in the international level to create a new epoch in the educational world.

S. Samuel Ravi

UNIT I

MODERN CONCEPT OF EDUCATION

CHAPTER 1

MEANING AND NATURE OF EDUCATION

INTRODUCTION

Education is the most important and powerful instrument invented by mankind to shape and mould himself in a desirable manner. Any modification brought about in the behaviour of an individual, as a result of his interaction with the environment, constitutes learning. The history of the world proves that education has been the root cause for any change which takes place in the social, cultural, spiritual, political and economic aspects of human life. It is education, which not only transforms the human animal into a rational human being, but also prepares and develops him to survive and adjust with surroundings so as to lead his personal as well as social life successfully. Therefore, we may say that education is anything which the individual acquires through formal or non-formal organizations in the form of certificates or training by which his personality is prepared and developed to undertake any sort of task and adjust himself with the varying environments in order to fulfil his basic necessities and objectives of life. It is discerned from this statement that education has become one of the basic necessities of human life, like food, clothing and shelter. Today, life is education and education is life. Hence, no distinction can be made between life and education under any circumstances.

In fact, education is part and parcel of human life. Generally, human life consists of biological, sociological, spiritual and cultural aspects. The biological aspects of human life can be sustained by food, shelter and reproduction. This aspect of life is found common in almost all biotic organisms. But the sociological, spiritual and cultural aspects of life are found in human life alone. It is the only aspect which differentiates mankind from all other living organisms on the earth. Therefore, the sociological aspects of human life should be given due consideration. They can be achieved and developed only through the medium of education. Lock has aptly remarked, "Plants are developed by cultivation and men by education". Hence, we may conclude that as shelter is essential for biological life, so is education for sociological life. In short, man's goals become impossible to achieve in the absence of education.

MEANING OF EDUCATION

Education is a dynamic as well as comprehensive concept, which has a very wide connotation. Since education is related with human life, it is very difficult to ascribe a single meaning to it. The concept of education is like a diamond, which appears to be of different colours when seen from different angles. It is like the concept of the proverbial elephant and the blind man. Various people—a philosopher, psychologist, sociologist, biologist, priest, professor, teacher, shopkeeper, merchant, politician, an artisan, educator, economist and others seem to have their own concept and meaning of education according to their own outlook in life and past experiences. However, the meaning of the word "education" can be understood from its roots in four Latin words, that is, *Educare, Educere, Educatum* and *Educo* (Figure 1.1).

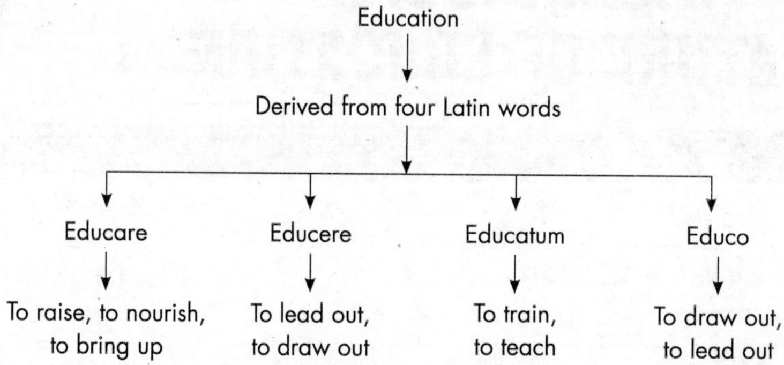

FIGURE 1.1 Derivation of education.

Educare: The term 'education' has been derived from the Latin word *Educare* which means "to nourish", "to bring up", "to raise". So, the meaning of the word "education" is to bring up children physically and mentally.

Educere: This is another Latin word from which the word 'education' is derived. The word *educere* implies "to draw out", "to lead out", "to bring forth". Hence, 'education' means bringing forth or leading out the inner power of the child, that is, drawing out what is inside the child.

Educatum: Latin word *educatum* denotes "to train", "to teach". Thus, education implies the act of training or teaching the child.

Educo: The origin of the word 'education' is considered to be the combination from *E* and *Duco*. *Duco* means "I lead" and *E* stands for "out of". So, education means to draw out or lead out the internal power of man. This is similar to the meaning of the word *educere*.

Thus, education is the drawing out of the inner capacities of the individual and develops his personality to the full extent through training or teaching and extra-curricular activities.

NARROW AND WIDER MEANINGS OF EDUCATION

In order to understand the concept of education, educational thinkers have interpreted and classified the meaning of education into two main categories, namely, narrow and wider concept of education.

Narrow Meaning of Education

The narrow meaning of education usually implies imparting information, giving instruction, schooling, training, making people literate, teaching, preparing for a trade or vocation. In the narrow sense, education is confined to school, college and university instructions. The scope of education is very narrow here. Education starts when the child gets admission in the school and ends when he leaves school, college or university. The following definitions of some renowned educationists make the narrow meaning of education more clear.

S.S. Mackenzi: "In the narrow sense, education may be taken to mean any consciously directed effort to develop and cultivate powers".

James Drever: "Education is a process in which and by which the knowledge, character and behaviour of the young are shaped and moulded".

G.H. Thompson: "The influence of the environment on the individual with a view to producing a permanent change in his habits of behaviour, of thoughts and attitude".

John Stuart Mill: "The culture which each generation purposefully gives to those who are to be its successors, in order to qualify them for at least keeping up and if possible for raising the level of improvement which has been attained".

However, in the narrow sense, we may state that education is anything acquired from formal institutions in the form of certificates or training which enables the individual to carry out a particular task. The following points bring out the meaning more clearly.

- Education is provided through planned institutions like schools, colleges and universities.
- Education is a deliberate, conscious and systematic influence exerted by the matured person (teacher) on the immatured (student).
- Education is limited to the teaching of readymade materials.
- Education is intentional rather than incidental.
- Knowledge is the accumulated experience of the human race.
- Education is regarded as synonymous with instruction.

Wider Meaning of Education

In this view, education is a life-long process which starts from the womb and ends in the tomb. It becomes the sum total of experiences and knowledge that the child receives inside and outside the school, through the study of different subjects, through various activities, through the library, the museum, the playground, the workshop or through other agencies. Thus, in a wider sense, education is more than teaching or instruction. Education is regarded as synonymous with the act of living. Accordingly, education is not confined to schools, colleges or universities alone. From the wider meaning of education, we get a new life from education and the life gives us new education. It includes all the knowledge and experiences acquired during infancy, childhood, adolescence, youth, adulthood, through any agency of education namely, school, home, society, church, industry, market, hotel, hospital, etc. The wider concept of education has been interpreted by some eminent educationists in the following ways:

S.S. Mackenzi: "In the wider sense, education is a process that goes on throughout life, and is promoted by almost every experience in life".

M.K. Gandhi: "By education, I mean, the all-round drawing out of the best in child, man—body, mind and soul".

W.H. Kilpatrick: "From the broad point of view, all life thoughtfully lived is education".

Dumvile: "Education, in its widest sense, includes all the influences which act upon an individual during his passage from cradle to the grave".

Edward Thring: "Education is the transmission of life by the living to the living".

John Dewey: "Education is the development of all those capacities in the individual which enable him to control his environment and fulfil his possibilities".

T. Raymont: "Education is a process of development from infancy to maturity, the process by which, he adapts himself gradually to various aspects of physical, social and spiritual environment".

In the widest sense, we may define education as something which is a life-long process of acquiring knowledge through formal or non-formal organizations in the form of certificates or training by which the personality of the individual is prepared and developed to undertake any task and adjust himself with the varying environments in order to achieve the goals in life. A pupil gets one fourth of education from his educator, another fourth by his own intellectual efforts, next fourth from his fellow students and the rest, in the course of time, through life and experience. The wider concept of education is not just the teaching and learning of the three R's (reading, writing and arithmetic)

The wider meaning of education includes the following features:

- Education is a life-long process, from infancy to old age or from womb to tomb.
- This type of education is acquired through formal, informal and non-formal agencies of education.
- It consists of the development of four H, i.e., head, heart, hand and health.
- Life and education cannot be separated from each other.
- All experiences are said to be educative.
- Education is synonymous with the act of living.
- Education includes all aspects of human life—cultural, domestic, economic, geographical, political, religious and social.

INDIAN AND WESTERN MEANING OF EDUCATION

The term "education" has been widely discussed and interpreted by different thinkers, philosophers and educationists with reference to its aims, functions and implications. It is a very comprehensive as well as a complex idea. Hence, divergent opinions and views have been expressed by the Indian as well as the Western thinkers about education in different ages with reference to their philosophies, needs and tempo of the social order.

Meaning of Education in India

According to the ancient Indian educational thinkers, the term *shiksha* has been derived from the Sanskrit verbal root *shas* which means "to discipline", "to teach", "to instruct" or "to control". Thus, *shiksha* means education which denotes the act of teaching, training or instructing. Another term, *vidya* has also been derived from a Sanskrit verbal root, *vid. Vid* refers to education which implies knowledge. Hence, disciplining the mind and imparting knowledge, by controlling and teaching the child, are the basic meanings of education.

We find four words—*siksha, adhyayana, vinaya* and *prabodha* in the Indo-Aryan literature. These words correspond to the modern word 'education'. *Siksh* is found in the Vedic hymns which means "to learn to recite". The word *adhyayana* found in the Brahmanic Upanisadic and Sutra literature denotes *to go near* and express the views of pupils going to some Guru (teacher) for education. In the institution, *upanayana* is the ceremony which refers to *taking near,* i.e., parents in the ancient period took their children to the Guru (teacher) for their education. The term *vinaya* denotes to *lead out* in a particular way. It emphasises the drawing out or leading out and development of the inborn powers of the child. The fourth term *prabodha* is used by the famous poet Kalidas to express the outcome of education. *Prabodha* implies 'awakening' or 'enlightenment' which is created in the child through teaching and learning.

Indian thinkers have placed special emphasis upon the development of spiritual aspect of education. Swami Vivekananda says, "Religion is the inner most core of education". In the words of A.S. Altekar, "Education has always been regarded in India as a source of illumination and power which transforms and enables our nature by the progressive and harmonious development of our physical, mental, intellectual and spiritual powers and facilities". Education was used as an instrument to enable the individual to rise above and to attain the truth, the beautiful and the good. In fact, education in India passes through four *ashramas* into which human life has been divided. The first stage *brahmacharya ashram* is considered as the life of education and preparation. The second stage *Grahastya* is the life of the householder in which an individual has to execute his social responsibilities. The third stage, *vanaprastha,* is the life of retirement and meditation for which he has to withdraw himself from the worldly life. The last stage is *sanyasa* in which an individual cuts off all social and family ties and leads a holy life to attain salvation.

Meaning of Education in the West

The meaning of education in the West is found in Plato's work. According to him, "education is a life-long process starting from the first year of childhood and lasting to the very end of the life". He also points out in his book *Republic* that true education will have the greatest tendency to civilize and humanise the people in their relation to one another and to those who are under their protection. Education has been taken as a process of inculcating values. He says, "Now I mean by education that training which is given by suitable habits to the first instincts of virtue in children". His views have been widely accepted in the West as well as in the East.

Western Educational Philosophers have generally accepted that the growth of the human child is the essence of education. In the words of Robert R. Rush, "Education is the enhancement or enrichment of personality and the embodiment of universal values". Thus, education is the process of development which means the gradual and continuous progress of mind and body. Through this development, the child acquires: (a) the knowledge of the environment by which he is surrounded; (b) the necessary motor control to fulfil his individual needs; (c) linguistic abilities to enable him to converse; and (d) knowledge of individual and collective relationships. The development of all these elements begins at home. The task of the educator is to encourage it while the child is at school.

According to the Western educational thinkers, education is a deliberate and organized activity through which the physical, intellectual, aesthetic, moral and spiritual potentialities of the child are developed. It enables the individual as a member of society to lead the fullest and richest life on the earth and attain Moksha (reaching God or liberation) in the world to come after death.

DEFINITIONS OF EDUCATION

"Education" has been defined by philosophers, thinkers and educationists in different ways according to their philosophy of life gained out of their past experiences. Since, education is related to time and space, philosophers and thinkers, from Socrates to John Dewey in the West and Yajnavalkya to Jiddu Krishnamurti in the East have defined it differently.

Indian Views on Education

Rig Veda: "Education is something which makes a man self-reliant and selfless".

Upaṇishads: "Education is that whose end product is salvation".

Bhagavad-Gita: "Nothing is more purifying on earth than knowledge".

Yajnavalkya: "Education is that which makes a man of good character and useful to the world".

Panini: "Human education means the training which one gets from nature".

Kautilya: "Education means training for the country and love for the nation".

Kannada: "Education means development of self-contentment".

Sankaracharya: "Education is the realization of the self and attainment of Moksha (liberation)".

Guru Nanak: "Education is self-realization and service of the people. It enables an individual to win victory over the five enemies—lust, anger, greed, infatuation and ego (*kam, krodh, lobh, moh, ahankar*)".

Dayanand: "Education is a means for character formation and righteous living". To him, an educated person is healthy and an uneducated person is suffering from the disease of ignorance.

Swami Vivekananda: "Education means the manifestation of the divine perfection, already existing in man".

Tagore: "Education means enabling the mind to find out that ultimate truth which emancipates us from the bondage of the dust and gives us the wealth, not of things but of inner light, not of power but of love, making this truth its own and giving expression to it". In short, "The widest road leading to the solution of all our problems is education".

Mahatma Gandhi: "By Education, I mean an all-round drawing out of the best in the child and man—body, mind and spirit".

Aurobindo: "Education is helping the growing soul to draw out that is in itself".

Radhakrishnan: "Education means training the intellect, refinement of the heart and discipline of the spirit".

Zakir Hussain: "Education is the process of the individual mind getting to its full possible development to realize absolute moral and intellectual value".

Jiddu Krishnamurti: "Education in the true sense is helping the individual to be mature and free, to flower greatly in love and goodness".

Humayun Kabir: "Education is a dynamic process which in its totality changes with the changing situations and developing circumstances. It enables man to realize higher values of life which are essential for him to become *roof and crown* of all creations".

P.C. Bannerji: "Education is the development of the power of adaptation to an everchanging social environment".

A.P.J. Abdul Kalam: "Education is one that fosters capacities such as spirit of enquiry, creativity, entrepreneurial and moral leadership, which are central to nation building in a democracy. We need education which develops in our children these capacities and makes them autonomous learners who are self-directed and self-controlled".

However, the meaning of education has been changing from time-to-time and place-to-place. Today, we may define education as anything by which the individual prepares and develops himself to undertake any sort of task and adjust to the varying environments for the purpose of attaining his goals of life. It is a very comprehensive definition of education, which reflects a complete picture of the present system of education in the emerging Indian society. Thus, education is the process of gaining those experiences, knowledge and training which prepare the individual for personal, social, spiritual, cultural, aesthetic, political and economic life.

Western Views on Education

Socrates: "Education means the bringing out of the ideas of universal validity which are latent in the mind of every man. It is dispelling error and discovering truth".

Plato: "Education is the capacity to feel pleasure and pain at the right moment. It develops in the body and in the soul of the pupil all the beauty and all the perfection which he is capable of".

Aristotle: "Education is the creation of a soundbody. It develops man's faculty especially his mind so that he may be able to enjoy the contemplation of supreme truth, goodness and beauty of which perfect happiness essentially consists".

Comenius: "All those who are born as human beings need education because they are destined to be real men, not wild beasts, dull animals and clumps of wood".

Rousseau: "Education of man commences at his birth before he can speak, before he can understand, he is already instructed. Experience is the fore runner of precept. It is the development from within".

Kant: "Education is the development in the individual of all the perfection of which he is capable".

Pestalozzi: "Education is natural, harmonious and progressive development of man's innate powers".

Froebel: "Education is unfoldment of what is already enfolded in the germ. It is the process through which the child draws out his internal potentialities. It is the cultivation of awareness, love and independence in the child".

John Dewey: "Education is the development of all those capacities in the individual which will enable him to control his environment and fulfil his possibilities".

T. Raymont: "Education is a process of development from infancy to maturity, the process by which he adapts himself gradually in various ways of his physical and spiritual environment".

James Drever: "Education is a process in which and by which knowledge, character, and behaviour of the young are shaped and moulded".

Bossing: "Education is conceived to be the adjustment of man to his environment, to the end that most enduring satisfaction may accrue to the individuals and to the society".

Adams John: "Education is a conscious and deliberate process in which one's personality acts upon another in order to modify the development of the other by the communication and manipulation of knowledge".

T.P. Nunn: "Education is the complete development of the individuality of the child so that man can make an original contribution to human life according to the best of his capacity".

Ruskin: "Education does not mean teaching the people what they do not know. It means teaching them to behave as they do not behave".

Thompson: "Education is the influence of the environment on the individual with the view to producing a permanent change in his habits, behaviour, thought and attitude".

Ross: "Education is the development of valuable personality and spiritual individuality".

Brown: "Education is the consciously controlled process whereby changes in behaviour are produced in the person and through the person within the group".

William James: "Education is fitting the individual to his physical and social environment".

Huxley: "Education is fashioning the will of the individual to enable him to move in harmony with nature".

Montaigne: "Education is cultivating manners, behaviour, and judgement than bare and mere liberal learning".

Herbert Spencer: "Education is preparing for complete living".

Emerson: "Education means controlling mind".

Milton: "Education is that which fits a man to perform justly, skilfully and magnanimously all the offices, both private, and public of peace and war".

Redden: "Education is the deliberate and systematic influence exerted by the matured person (educator) upon the immatured (educand) through instruction, discipline and harmonious development of physical, intellectual, aesthetic, social and spiritual powers of the human being, according to individual and social needs and directed towards the union of the educand with his creator as the final end".

FACTORS OF EDUCATION

The data of education comprises five factors namely, the child, heredity, environment, explosion of knowledge and time.

Child: The child is the foremost important factor in education. Each child is different from the other in physical, mental and social abilities as well as in his interests, aptitudes and attitudes. Hence, his natural development is possible only according to his innate powers. The full development of the child necessitates proper and comprehensive knowledge of his nature.

Heredity: The heredity of the child is the combination of mental and physical characteristics. It constitutes the basis of education. The maximum possible development of the child depends upon the potential existing in his innate and inherited qualities. Education can be imparted to a child only according to his inherited qualities. It is not possible to make a child an artist if he has not inherited any aesthetic interest or inclination. Thus, the basis of education is formed by inherited characteristics.

Environment: The environment is the third important constituent of education. Every child is born in a family at a particular place and time. So, the upbringing and development of each child takes place in a physical and social environment which plays a vital role in his development. The environmentalists hold the view that as the child gradually comes into contact with the material and social environments, his innate tendencies flower out and his behaviour starts to change step-by-step. They believe that education is a process based on and conditioned by the environment in which the child is brought up. For example, it is the environment which makes a child musician, an artist, a teacher, a policeman, a lawyer, etc.

Explosion of knowledge: It is fourth factor of education. Continuous growth of knowledge, expansion of experiences, emergence of new subjects, inter-relationship of disciplines and development of science, technology and arts have widened the area of education. New thinking, creativities and discoveries have increased the scope of education. As the world is dynamic, education also changes and grows accordingly based on the needs, of society. Now, technical, oriented scientific study and vocational tendency determine the factors of education in market economy.

Time: This is the fifth important factor of education which determines specific activities indulged in by the child during the process of his development. Education should correspond and suit the mental level of the child, otherwise it will mar his mature development and create complexes. Therefore, education to be really effective should correspond to its plans and programmes according to the growth of the child.

CHARACTERISTICS OF EDUCATION

From the Indian as well as Western concepts of education, we come to descry the nature of education as given below:

Life-long process: Education is the sequence of learning through the medium of experience which is acquired through formal, non-formal and informal institutions, and continues upto death.

Dynamic process: Education is related to human life which will never be static, but always dynamic. Therefore, the nature of education changes according to the changing needs of time, place and society. In the words of John Dewey, "Education is the process of living through a continuous reconstruction of experiences".

Individual development: Education is the process of individual development. The all-round development of an individual has seven dimensions, that is, physical, mental, aesthetic, moral, spiritual, social and economic development. It is education which coordinates these seven dimensions of the individual and makes him get rid of animal instincts and be a civilized man. J.S. Mill says, "Whatever helps to shape the human being, to make the human being, what he is or to hinder him from being what he is not—is a part of his education".

Develops child's innate power: Education is not a thing to be inserted into the mind of the child from outside, but it helps to develop his innate capacities through outside experiences of the environment. If the child has the faculty of speech, he can become a good speaker with the help of education. Thus, education provides every person with the opportunity of developing his innate power according to his capacities. Gandhi remarks, "By education, I mean, an all round drawing out of the best in child and man—body, mind and spirit". The Western philosophers such as Pestalozzi and Froebel have emphasised the development of the child's innate power as the characteristic of education.

Modifies behaviour: Education helps the individual to bring about a desirable change in his behaviour. In fact, the behaviour of an educated individual is better than that of an uneducated man. If not, the education of the individual will be incomplete and he will be called as a literate rustic. Ruskin says, "You need not educate a man by telling what he knows, but by making him what he is not". Prof. Drever has rightly remarked, "Education is a process in which and by which knowledge, character and behaviour of the young are shaped and moulded".

Social adjustment: Education is an important tool which helps the individual in making adjustment with the social environment, that is, with the parents, relatives, friends, teachers and other members of the society. Human personality cannot be balanced unless he is able to adjust himself with every field. Through the process of education, the child is taught to adjust himself according to the environment.

Bi-polar process: John Adams calls education a bi-polar process. In this process, there is a constant interaction between the teacher and the taught and the impact of personalities like two poles interacting with each other. Ross writes, "Like a magnet, education has two poles, it is a bi-polar process". As such, education becomes a conscious and deliberate process in which one personality acts upon another in order to modify the development of the other by the communication and manipulation of knowledge. It means, the direct application of the educator's personality to the personality of the educand through 'shared activity' or sharing experiences. Thus, education is a bi-polar process in which both the teacher and the student are equally important. In other words, if the teacher instructs, the child follows, if he gives, the student receives in fact the teacher moulds and modifies the behaviour of the child so that the latter develops his personality (Figure 1.2).

Adams has also pointed out the subjective and objective sides of the process of education. Education becomes subjective when the learner does not question the educator. On the other hand, education becomes objective when the learner understands the motives of the educator and questions him or even opposes him and applies his own reasoning.

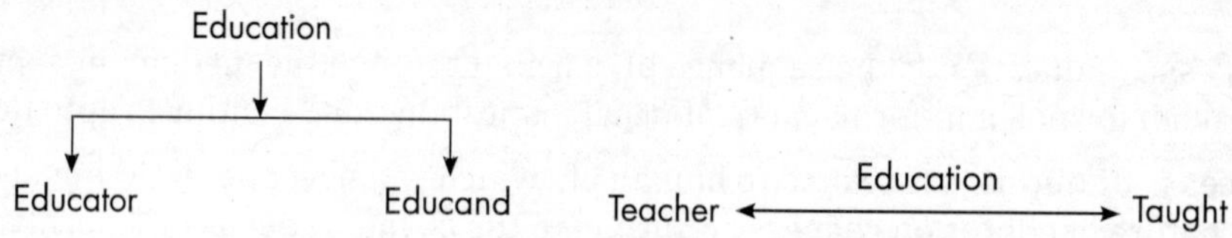

FIGURE 1.2 Education—bi-polar process.

Tri-polar process: Education is also regarded as a tri-polar process involving the interaction of the personality of the educator with that of the educand in a social setting which modifies the behaviour of the educand. John Dewey believes that the process of education cannot even be thought about without social environment. According to him, "All education proceeds by the participation of the individual in the social consciousness of the race". A system of education becomes incomplete in the absence of social environment. J.E. Adamson proposes the tri-polar theory of education. According to him, the whole environment of the individual becomes the source of education (Figure 1.3).

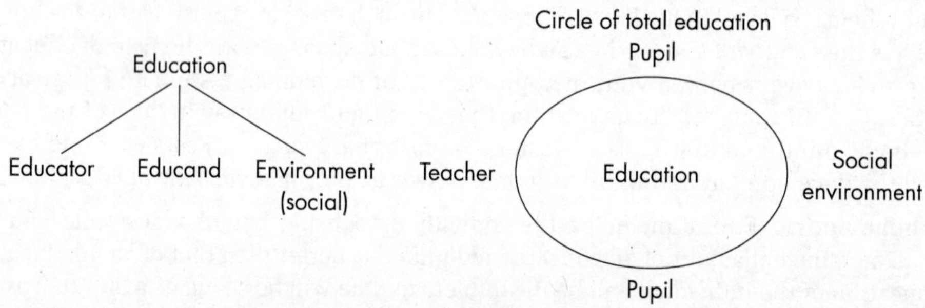

FIGURE 1.3 Education—tri-polar process.

The pragmatists consider man as a social animal and he learns everything while living in the society. So, social environment is the third dimension which influences the personality of the child. In this way, the process of education consists of three poles—(i) teacher, (ii) child, and (iii) society. Hence, the teacher consciously designs and plans educational experiences in the light of social environment and directs the child's instincts, urges, impulses and tendencies towards the socially desirable channels. The three poles (teacher, child and society) should actively participate in the process of education so that education system could be completed successfully.

Multi-polar process: The present education is a sum total of information, knowledge, experiences, and training received from or by the influence of socio-natural environments, books, or non-book materials. As such education has become a multi-polar process and it is not confined only to the teacher, parent, relatives and friends, but living and non-living things. In fact, a child receives education when he comes across the people of different categories living in happiness, sickness, poverty and sadness.

Direct and indirect processes: Education is said to be a direct process when the teacher and the taught are in direct contact. It is an indirect process when pupils receive education (non-formal and informal) from a distance.

Enrichment of experiences: It is regarded as an important characteristic of education. Generally, every individual has his own range of experiences which can be directed towards the goal of life through the process of education. Thus, education enriches human experiences which maybe right or wrong.

Goal attainment: The main feature of the concept of education is helping the individual to fulfil his goals in life. It maybe put forth thus: Education is anything by which the personality of the individual is developed and prepared to undertake any task and adjust with surroundings in order to fulfil his basic necessities and objectives of life. In short, education is anything which satisfies our needs and fulfils our desires.

Theoretical and practical in nature: The social, religious, moral, cultural, economic and intellectual knowledge can be acquired from the theoretical and practical forms of education through school, college or university, training centres and social institutions such as, churches, temples and mosques. Thus, education provides both theoretical as well as practical knowledge.

Demand of modern age: We consider that education is one of the basic necessities of life like food, clothing and shelter, because it seems to be very important for sociological life as shelter is for biological life. Sociological life is very important to develop national integration and international understanding in the minds of younger generation. The need for education in agricultural, industrial, technical and professional fields has been increasing. As a result, adult education, social education, women education, population education, environmental education, etc. have emerged in order to meet the demands for different professionals in the modern age.

Scientific nature of education: The modern age is a scientific age. Education is mostly based on science and technology. In fact, in the whole life of man, school, college and university have become laboratories of education. Education induces the desire to undertake researches in many topics pertaining to different aspects of human life in social, political, religious, moral, cultural, economic and aesthetic areas. The nature of education is artistic in nature. In this sense, education helps to design the personality of the child. The teacher is an artist who moulds the child into a better, purer and nobler person. Education helps the child in acquiring knowledge, integrated growth, social and economic efficiency in order to lead his life in the scientific age successfully.

Instrument of social change: Education is a powerful instrument for social reconstruction. It brings about a remarkable change in social, political, cultural, religious, moral, spiritual, scientific, economic, and aesthetic aspects of human life. No change occurs in any society in the absence of education. Hence, education is the most important invention of mankind by which the society is being shaped and moulded in a desirable way. Social change is one of the important characteristics of present education.

TYPES OF EDUCATION

Education is far wider and more inclusive than schooling. We acquire education from our experiences outside the school. R.C. Lodge says, "All experience is said to be educative. The bite of a mosquito, the taste of water melon, the experience of falling in love, of flying in an aeroplane, of being in a storm in a small boat—all such experiences have a direct educative effect on us". Thus, education includes all the influences which act upon an individual during his passage from cradle to grave. This wider meaning of education includes all the meanings attached to different types of education.

Generally, we have three types of education on the basis of scope and meaning namely, formal, informal and non-formal education.

Formal education: This type of education is consciously and deliberately planned and imparted in educational institutions like school, college or university in order to modify the behaviour of the individual. It is provided according to certain rules and regulations through co-curricular activities, planning of monthly or yearly programmes, time of opening, time of teaching the subjects and time of closing. It follows a well-defined and systematic curriculum, method of teaching, textbooks and discipline. This type of education is given in a well-organized way by the teachers who are qualified and trained and able to bring about all-round development of the child according to the needs of the individual and the society. It prepares the child for examination and provides him certificates or degrees.

Informal education: There is no specialised agency to impart this type of education. It is not pre-planned or deliberate but it is a spontaneous and quite incidental. The child gets this education, consciously or unconsciously, while he moves and lives in the community. He goes on learning, throughout his life, through the medium of experiences which maybe pleasant or unpleasant. The press, the family, the community and the playgrounds are some of the agencies of informal education. Usually, this kind of education takes place at home, in the temple, mosque, church, gurudwara, social agencies, public place and in the political meetings. Every person plays the role of a teacher as the occasions demand. This kind of education is also to be long process and it takes place whenever people learn, work and live together. In other words, such education takes place in the social environments. It is entirely different from both formal and non-formal education. That is, no time table, curriculum, classroom teaching, examination and rules and regulations.

Non-formal education: Non-formal education is one of the modern types of education which falls in between formal and informal education as a life-long process. It is more elastic and the pupil who drops out of the school or those employed, without proper education, illiterate, financially poor, housewives, residing a long distance away from educational institution, and who want to improve their skill can make use of this kind of education.

Definitions of non-formal education: A number of definitions of non-formal education are as follows:

Bremwork: "Non-formal education differs from formal education from the proximity to immediate action, work and the opportunity to put learning to use".

Philip H. Combs: "Non-formal education is a residual category. It includes all organized systematic educational activity carried on outside the formal education".

McCall: "Non-formal education is the entire range of learning experiences outside the regular graded school system".

Henderson: "Non-formal is far wider and more inclusive than school which imparts wider experiences out of school".

Harbuism: "Non-formal education is the only means of filling the gap between the 'schooled' and 'unschooled' population"

Paulston: "Non-formal education includes any structured systematic, non-school education and training activities of relatively short duration, where sponsoring agencies seek concrete behavioural changes in fairly distinct target population".

International education commission: "Non-formal education is a life-long process and it emphasized the informal and non-formal education for those who left education at certain stage of life and now they have felt the necessity".

Characteristics of non-formal education: The prominent characteristic of non-formal education are as follows:

Free from formal education: Non-formal education is free from all rules and regulations that followed in formal education system. It is non-formal education in which attendance of students is not compulsory. It provides freedom for the students in selecting the subjects and time for the study. In fact, learning takes place in the students according to their interest, ability and needs.

Open system: It is an open system of education which is flexible and out of rigid rules and regulations. This type of education is open to all irrespective of their castes, creeds, colours, place, etc. Admission is not made on the basis of mark and money, but educational qualification.

Organized education: It is an organized and systematised education like formal education with fixed curriculum and examination.

Life-long process: It is a life-long process integrated with life and work. It is based on the life and environment of the individual.

Intended for all ages: It is meant for all age groups. People of any sections of society and at any stage can pursue their education through non-formal system.

Suitable alternative: It is useful and a suitable alternative to formal education. It is a panacea for those who abandon their education and reside in places where higher educational opportunities are not available and they can fulfil their desire for education. It helps them to learn while they earn.

Means of filling the gap: Harbuism says, "Non-formal education is the only means of filling the gap between the 'schooled' and unschooled population". It falls between the formal and informal education.

Universalisation of education: Non-formal education brings about universalisation of professional, vocational and technical education. It also meets the requirements of higher education of people who could not get the opportunity in their early stages.

Self-motivational: Non-formal education is naturally self-motivational. The growth of a learner motivates him to pursue higher education under non-formal education which makes him confident and self-reliant.

Main agencies involved: Multiple agencies are involved in the process of non-formal education. For instance, mass media, open schools, open universities, directorate of distance education, etc. act as the agencies through which non-formal education is imparted at national and international levels.

Adoptability: Non-formal system of education adopts suitable curriculum and methodologies so that it fulfils the requirement of the learners.

Sources of Different Types of Education

Every type of education has its sources or agencies by which the individual and the society are educated and trained in such a way as to lead a meaningful life as a civilized man in the world (Figure 1.4).

Types of Education

Formal	Non-formal	Informal
School	Distance education	Family
College	Summer institutes	Relatives
University	Radio-broadcast	Friends
Training institutions	Television, Computer	Society
Religious institutions	Open university	Playground
Museums, Libraries	Public library	Press, Studio
Art galleries	Adult literacy	Film, Tour
	Satellite programme	Markets

FIGURE 1.4 Circle of total education.

EDUCATION DIFFERENTIATED FROM RELATED TERMS

School is one of the formal agencies for imparting systematic education. As a result, both school and education go together. Ross says, "The schools are devised by civilized man for the purpose of aiding in the preparation of the young for well-adjusted and efficient membership of society". According to T.P. Nunn, "The school must be thought of primarily not as a place of learning where certain knowledge is learnt but as a place where the young are disciplined in certain form of activity". Some people think that education is related only to schools, colleges and universities. But there is a lot of difference between education and schooling.

TABLE 1.1 Formal and Non-formal Education

Sl.No.	Differences	Formal Education	Non-formal Education
1.	Scope	Limited and narrow	Unlimited and Vast
2.	Learner	Learners who are in a position to attend full time	Learners who have dropped their education at school or college and who want to improve their qualification
3.	Aim	Get certificates or degrees for a job or self-employment	Increase knowledge and skills to improve personality
4.	Place	School, college, university or other training institutions	No specific place—factory, open space, farm, library, may also be held at school or college (Correspondence Course)
5.	Age	Minimum age is prescribed	No age limit
6.	Grade	Students are treated as group (classwise)	Students are not grouped except distance education
7.	Curriculum	Rigid and fixed	Not fixed except in distance education
8.	Textbooks	Prescribed textbooks	Usually, no prescribed books
9.	Examination	Held at regular intervals; written and oral tests consist of essay and short answer questions	Normally no examination except distance education which conducts non-semester examinations

(Contd...)

TABLE 1.1 Formal and Non-formal Education (*Contd...*)

Sl.No.	Differences	Formal Education	Non-formal Education
10.	Teacher	Teacher occupies an important place in the educational process (full-time basis)	Has limited role and plays the role of friend, philosopher and guide (part-time basis)
11.	Teaching methods	Direct teaching methods, face-to-face teaching	Radio, computer, television, very little face-to-face teaching
12.	Status	Usually high status	Usually low status
13.	Period	Limited to a period of 'being taught' imparted in educational institution	Life-long process, integrated with life and work
14.	Entry	Fixed points of entry and exist. Age and qualification for admission are prescribed	Flexible points of entry and exist, re-entry and re-exist can be made throughout the life of the individual
15.	Nature of education	Employment-oriented	Maximising human potentialities
16.	Discipline	Strict discipline as well as flexible	Self-imposed or inner discipline. There is no forced discipline.
17.	Principle	Works on the principle of weeding out failures	Works on the universal principle. Success through learning satisfaction
18.	Expense	It is more expensive	Comparatively less expensive
19.	Utilization	It does not utilise all human resources	It utilises maximum human resources
20.	Dependency	The child should entirely depend on teachers and schools for his education	Students need not depend on teachers or institutions (except distance education)
21.	Media	It does not utilise different media for educating the children	It utilises different media to educate the people

Source: K.K. Bhatia and C.L. Narang, *Philosophical and Sociological Bases of Education.*
Yadav and Yadav, *Education in Emerging Indian Society.*
S.S. Wadwa, *Education in Indian Society.*

TABLE 1.2 Formal and Informal Education

Sl.No.	Differences	Formal Education	Informal Education
1.	Scope	Its scope is limited and narrow	Its scope is very vast
2.	Age	It starts and ends in a prescribed age	No age limit for this education
3.	Aim	It has a definite aim of getting knowledge and certificate	It has no definite aim
4.	Place	Education is provided in an Institution	No definite place for such education
5.	Planning	It is pre-planned and well organized	It is not planned and systematically organized education
6.	Course	It has a definite course to be covered in a definite period	No definite course to be finished in the given period
7.	Lessons	Education is imparted through formal lessons	No formal lessons to be followed in imparting education

(*Contd...*)

TABLE 1.2 Formal and Informal Education (*Contd...*)

Sl.No.	Differences	Formal Education	Informal Education
8.	Strain	There is a lot of mental strain in learning	No strain involved in learning
9.	Awareness	Teacher and taught are aware of the process through which education is imparted	There is no awareness or consciousness
10.	Organization	It is organized by government or non-government	There is no such organization
11.	Curriculum	Fixed timetable and curriculum are followed	No fixed timetable and curriculum to be adopted
12.	Teaching method	Teaching is done face-to-face between educator and educand a number of methods are followed	There is also face-to-face contact but teaching methods are not followed
13.	Evaluation	Work of the student is evaluated from time-to-time as steps are taken (if necessary) for further improvement	Not possible to evaluate the performance of the pupil
14.	Teacher	Qualified and trained teachers are required to impart education	Education can be received from any person. No training or experience is needed
15.	Rules	Strict rules and regulations are followed in the educational process	There are no rules and regulations to be in force
16.	Degree	It provides certificates or degrees after evaluating the performance of the child	No certificate or diploma or degree awarded
17.	Discipline	Students are expected to under go strict discipline	No discipline. Learners are forced to learn without any hindrance
18.	Learning period	Period of learning at school or college is fixed	It is a life-long process which has no end or beginning and integrated with human life
19.	Nature of education	This kind of education is unnatural	This kind of education is natural
20.	Source of education	The child gains education through curricular activities and subjects	The child gains education through experiences or social contacts

Source: K.K. Bhatia and C.L. Narang, *Philosophical and Sociological Bases of Education.*
Yadav and Yadav, *Education in Emerging Indian Society.*
S.S. Wadwa, *Education in Indian Society.*

TABLE 1.3 Education and Schooling

Sl.No.	Differences	Education	Schooling
1.	Meaning	It is a comprehensive term	It has narrow meaning used to define a specific term
2.	Scope	Its scope is wide, covering all-round growth and development of the individual	The scope of schooling is limited and close ended
3.	Duration	It is a life-long and continuous process	It has limited duration and it ends after 10 or 12 years
4.	Coverage	It includes all types of education—formal, informal and non-formal education	School covers formal education only

(*Contd...*)

TABLE 1.3 Education and Schooling (*Contd...*)

5.	Aims	Physical, mental, social, spiritual, moral, aesthetic development	Mental development is the only aim of schooling
6.	Nature	Education is a natural process	Schooling is an artificial process
7.	Place	Places of education include home, educational institutions, market, business place, religious institution, hospitals, library, museums, radio, computer, television etc.	School is the only place for schooling. (Primary, Middle, High and Higher Secondary Schools)
8.	Curriculum	Generally, curriculum of education is not pre-determined except formal education which emphasises curriculum	The act of school is pre-determined and fixed. It is limited to specific subjects and activities
9.	Agents	The agents of education are teacher, parents, relatives, friends, neighbours etc.	Teacher is the only agent who plays the most important role in schooling
10.	Teaching methods	A number of teaching methods are followed according to the needs of the pupil and the nature of subjects. Informal education adopts conversation debate and lecture methods. Today, we apply software as well as hardware technology in the educational process	Definite and fixed methods of teaching are adopted. Generally, lecture, dictation, demonstration, textbooks, experiments, projects and question answer methods are in usage
11.	Discipline	Social discipline and social control in education except informal education	Discipline is maintained in schooling for which instruction is provided
12.	Relation	There is formal and informal relations between the teachers and the pupils	Formal relations between the teacher and the taught
13.	Evaluation	A comprehensive set of evaluation tools are used to assess the pupils' performance	Evaluation is made on the basis of student's performance in tests and examinations
14.	Practicality	Place for more practicality than theoreticality	Place for maximum theoreticality and minimum practicality
15.	Results	The results of education are good citizens and cultured people. There is no place for certificates or degrees except formal and non-formal education	The results of schooling are literate people. Certificates are issued to the students who pass in the relevant examinations

Comparison of Education and Training

Training is a part of education. It means to attain skill or proficiency in a specific field. For example, after passing BA, BSc, or MA, MSc, one has to get training in education (DTEd or BEd) to become a teacher. Similarly, a doctor has to take training in a hospital after getting MBBS or BAMS, or BHMS, or BDS examination for becoming an efficient doctor. Education develops the personality of an individual whereas training prepares him to be successful in the task that he undertakes.

TABLE 1.4 Education and Training

Sl.No.	Differences	Education	Training
1.	Scope	The scope of education is wide which covers all-round development of an individual	The scope of training is very narrow which is meant for specific purpose. It develops professional competencies
2.	Aim	The total development of physical, mental, moral, social, spiritual aesthetic aspects of the learners	Developing proficiency in a specific or particular skill to do a job efficiently
3.	Duration	Duration of education is as long as the history of mankind. It continues from womb to tomb	Duration of training is fixed. It maybe for a week, a month, a year or some years.
4.	Sources	Learning takes place in almost all places–home, hospital, hotels, hostels and political, social, religious and educational institutions.	Training is provided in hospital, workshop, some colleges, industries and training centres etc.
5.	Knowledge	Education provides both theoretical and practical knowledge	It bestows more importance to practical knowledge
6.	Curriculum	Curriculum of education is broad and it is not pre-determined except formal education. It relates to all aspects of life	Curriculum of training is in narrow and fixed. It relates to development of proficiency in specific skills
7.	Teaching methods	Different methods of teaching are followed according to the interests of pupils and the nature of subjects	Limited methods of training are adopted proceeding from one skill to another. They are practical in nature. Training in specific skill requires specific method
8.	Teacher	Teachers are well-versed in their subject areas. No teacher for informal education	Only trained, well-experienced and skilled persons are required to impart training
9.	Discipline	The stress is laid on social discipline. All people should adjust in life according to the circumstances	The stress is laid on strict discipline. Training does not socialise a person, but it develops discipline
10.	Motivation	Social prestige is the source of inspiration in education	The source of motivation in training is economic aspect
11.	Rules	It does not follow rigid rules and regulations except in formal education	Training has rigid and systematic rules and regulations
12.	Outcome	Knowledge, certificates or degrees and good citizens are the outcome of education	Trained up individuals to carry out the task skillfully is the outcome of training
13.	Types	It is of three types: formal, informal and non-formal education	It is of two types: pre-service and in-service training
14.	Evaluation	In education, evaluation of an individual is done on the basis of his social adjustment	In training, evaluation of an individual is done on the basis of his efficiency in skill (performance of the individual)
15.	Availability	Education is available to all on payment of cash except informal education. (Huge amount is collected in school, college and university)	Training maybe available at free of cost when it is offered by the government or management to their workers, but not applicable to all categories

Source: K.K. Bhatia and C.L. Narang, *Philosophical and Sociological Bases of Education.*
Yadav and Yadav, *Education in Emerging Indian Society.*
S.S. Wadwa, *Education in Indian Society.*

Comparison of Education and Instruction

Instruction brings about behavioural changes in the individual. It is necessary in learning because through this knowledge is developed. But all aspects of personality that is, knowledge, affection (feeling) and activity (doing) are developed through education. Conversations and discussions take place in the process of instruction in which arguments are given and conclusions are drawn. Instruction is a part of education. It is related to understanding in which discrimination is made between what is true and what is false. In the words of Dr. R.A. Sharma, "Instruction is the process of influencing learners towards some goals". According to Robertson, "Instruction in the class and education ends only with life". Education differs from instruction in its scope, meaning, method, curriculum etc. Let us see the difference between education and instruction (Table 1.5).

TABLE 1.5 Education and Instruction

Sl.No.	Differences	Education	Instruction
1.	Scope	The scope of education is wide which is the full development of all the innate powers of a child	Its field is narrow and is limited to the teaching of specific subjects
2.	Meaning	The meaning of education is very comprehensive which develops the child physically, mentally, socially, spiritually, emotionally and aesthetically	Instruction means the inculcation of predetermined dozes of knowledge into the mind of a child to achieve mental development only
3.	Duration	It achieves tctal personality development in the child. It prepares the child to survive and adjust with surroundings	Only intellectual development by giving the knowledge of specific subjects which helps the child in passing examinations
4.	Period	Education continues from birth to death	It continues upto the time, the child receives education in the school
5.	Type of knowledge	More importance is given to practical knowledge	Theoretical knowledge has been given more importance
6.	Place	Education is imparted through formal, informal and non-formal education	Instruction is provided only in formal education
7.	Curriculum	It includes all subjects and activities which are related to life	Fixed subjects and time. Teacher has to teach them in the given time
8.	Method	Different methods of teaching are adopted according to the needs and interests of the pupil	Lecture method, question answer method is followed in order to complete the syllabus on time
9.	Role of teacher	In education, the role of a teacher is subsidiary	The role of a teacher is more important
10.	Role of child	Education is always child centred. The place of child is central, pivotal and of prime importance. The interests, capacities and needs of the child are taken into considerations	The role of child is secondary. Instruction neglects the interests, inclinations and capacities of the child
11.	Preparation	Education prepares the child for real life	Instruction prepares the child to pass in examinations

(Contd...)

TABLE 1.5 Education and Instruction (*Contd...*)

Sl.No.	Differences	Education	Instruction
12.	Self-learning	Education enables the child for self-learning. It can be applied to solve the problems in future life	Instruction encourages cramming or rote memory which cannot be applied to meet the challenges of life successfully
13.	Motivation	Social prestige is the source of inspiration in education	Securing good marks in the subject is a source of motivation for the child
14.	Evaluation	In education, pupils are evaluated on the basis of their performance	Tests and examinations are the important tools by which pupils are evaluated
15.	Final outcome	The outcomes of education are good citizens, cultured individuals and developed nation	The outcomes of instruction are pupils with basic knowledge and well-versed in their subjects and fields of activity

Source: K.K. Bhatia and C.L. Narang, *Philosophical and Sociological Bases of Education.*
Yadav and Yadav, *Education in Emerging Indian Society.*
S.S. Wadwa, *Education in Indian Society.*

MODERN CONCEPTS OF EDUCATION

An attempt has been made here to grasp the modern concept of education by a comparative study of the old and modern concepts of education. With the help of this comparative study, we discern the following differences between the old and the new concepts of education:

Meaning of education: The modern concept of education seeks to develop or train the child according to his interests, inclinations, capacities and needs in a social environment. Education, according to the old concept, was taken to mean as a process to thrust readymade knowledge into the mind of a child considering it to be an empty vessel. In short, modification of individual behaviour was the meaning of the old concept of education whereas the present education develops and prepares the personality of the individual to survive and adjust with the surroundings. Thus, the meaning of the modern concept of education is based on philosophical, psychological and sociological aspects.

Aim of education: The aim of ancient education is centered around the mental, spiritual and moral development of the child. It prepares the child to lead a holy life for salvation. Ancient education and its aims were entirely based on ancient philosophy of idealism which held faith in the eternal values and the spiritual world. On the contrary, modern educationists, philosophers and thinkers lay stress on the development of physical, mental, spiritual, social, vocational, moral, emotional and aesthetic aspects. Thus, the aim of modern education is to bring about a total development in the child and attain social efficiency and dynamism. Today, the aim of education is to bring about social and economic development, build up national integration, develop international understanding and prepare world citizens for the progress of the whole world.

Curriculum: The ancient curriculum included and emphasised those subjects and activities promoting mental, spiritual and moral development. The subjects prescribed in the curriculum were not integrated and they were rigid and mostly confined to classroom activities and experience. While constructing the curriculum, interests, inclinations, capacities and needs of the child were not taken into consideration. On the other hand, modern curriculum is flexible, varied and progressive according to the conditions of the ever changing and growing needs of the child and the modern society. It bestows importance on both theoretical and practical knowledge which is confined to classroom and outside school activities and experiences. It includes co-curricular and extra-curricular activities in order to bring out a whole personality development in the child.

Teaching methods: Old methods of teaching laid stress on cramming and it stimulated rote memorisation. Different philosophers and educationists advocated different methods of teaching according to their own interests and the nature of subjects. They recommended lecture, discussion and question answer methods. But the modern educationists and philosophers not only condemn the ancient methods of teaching, but introduce various lively and effective methods according to the interest, inclination and capacities of the child and also the nature of subjects. They follow play way, learning by doing, learning by experience, project method, observation, experimental method, problem solving, travelling etc. These modern methods of teaching stimulate motivation, interest and attention of the child and develop fellow-feeling and cooperation in him, which is essential for community living.

Discipline: Ancient system of education emphasised the use of rod and punishment to enforce obedience and discipline in children. Freedom was restricted to the child. Control and strict discipline were recommended by the ancient educationists. They adhered to the Biblical verse "Spare the rod spoil the child" while punishing the child. But this type of corporal punishment and enforcing discipline through repression has been vehemently criticised by all modern educationists. They advocate self-discipline and social discipline, leading to natural obedience. They stand in favour of providing freedom to the child which enables him to grow in the natural environment.

Examination: The old system of education encouraged essay type questions which led to cramming and rote memorisation. Written test was conducted to evaluate the mental development of the child. On the contrary, modern educationists have given up the old pattern of evaluation and developed modern techniques to evaluate as well as examine the achievement of the child. Such techniques include objective tests, short answer tests, progress reports, cumulative records, interviews and practical performances.

Agencies of education: Ancient educationists regarded that school was the only agency for educating the children. According to modern views all formal, informal and non-formal agencies are imparting education. The non-formal agencies play a vital role in the universalisation of education.

Teacher: In ancient education, teachers occupied the most important position in the educational process. They were respected as co-workers of God, were called 'Guru' and placed next to God. But in modern times, a teacher is considered as friend, guide and philosopher. However in the post modern society, the status of teachers has come down because of their poor quality and the mushroom growth of profit oriented educational institutions.

Child: According to the ancient concept of education, a child played a subsidiary role and had been treated very strictly. He was a passive recipient of whatever the teacher instructed. Education was teacher and curriculum centred. But the modern system of education is child centred. The curriculum is constructed and methods of teaching are followed according to the interests, inclination, capacities and the needs of child. The child is freely allowed to interact actively with the teacher and his classmates to achieve effective learning which promotes his own development and that of the society.

School: In the ancient period, school was the only source to educate the child. It served as a shop for selling education (knowledge). It adopted rigid rules and regulations, pre-planned and fixed curriculum and methods of teaching. Teachers were concerned with the input and bothered little about the output. On the contrary, modern educationists regard school as a miniature of society emphasising more on output in comparison with input. It is a place where social qualities are cultivated and developed in the child.

Education as a discipline: According to the ancient concept, education was meant for only getting knowledge and training to lead a holy life. But now education is a separate discipline of deep study, investigation and research like other disciplines—Physics, Chemistry, Mathematics, Economics etc. Today, it is a very important process of human development in all fields of human activities.

SCOPE OF EDUCATION

Scope of education refers to the breadth, range, extent, comprehensiveness and variety of learning experiences to be provided in the educational process. Education is a life-long process. In fact, everyday and every minute step-by-step we learn from every source of formal, non-formal and informal organizations. Hence, the scope of education is very wide and long. It is as wide as the world and as long as the history of mankind on the earth. In this sense, the entire life of an individual comes under the purview of education. That is, the aesthetic, cultural, social, spiritual, mental, physical and vocational development of the individual is involved. The following subject matter maybe included under the scope of education.

Educational philosophy: The meaning, nature, purpose and content of education of a country is largely determined by the philosophy of that country. Philosophy of education emerged as one of the separate and newest disciplines in the twentieth century. Educational philosophy is the combination of philosophy and education. They are related like flower and its fragrance. Under this title, various philosophical thoughts and their influence on education and life are studied. Philosophy determines all aspects of education—meaning and nature of education, aims, curriculum, method of teaching, nature of textbook, nature of discipline, role of a teacher and school environment. Thus, educational philosophy is the philosophy applied in the field of education for solving various issues related to it.

Educational sociology: Sociology of education maybe defined briefly as a study of relation between education and society. Education is an activity which goes on in the society. Hence, the aims, curriculum, methods of teaching, nature of discipline etc. depend on the nature of the society in which it functions. We study the society and its impact on education, and the impact of education on culture and society. The sociological basis is merged with education in order to achieve the objective of socialisation of an individual through education. This branch of study deals with the aim of education, methods of teaching, curriculum, administration, school environment and nature of discipline.

Educational psychology: Psychology has been considered as one of the most influencing factors which affect the process of education in different ways. The child faces a number of problems related to education and development. The solution to his problems requires to be sought out with the help of psychology. Educational psychology studies various stages of physical, social, mental and emotional development of a child. Learning theories of psychology are applied in the teaching–learning environment for making the learning possible. It also deals with the problems related to personality, intelligence, memory adjustment and understanding of a child. The teachers at present should be equipped with those psychological skills which are needed for the successful guidance of learning adjustment and growth of the child.

Educational technology: This branch of study helps the teacher to achieve the most with the least possible time, energy and resources by applying various teaching techniques. The mind of the child is a growing organism. Hence, the teachers follow different techniques of teaching based on the nature of the subject matter or psychology of the learning process. The way of presenting the lesson is essential to develop the interest and attention of the pupils.

Educational administration: Administrative functions are concerned primarily with the material facilities and the operation of the schools. The supervisory functions are related with improving the learning situation. Success of the process of education depends entirely on the efficient administration. In this regard, principles of educational administration, supervision and control of schools, appointment of teaching and non-teaching staff, qualifications and duties of teachers and evaluation of school performance are studied, and reforms and changes are made for the effective performance.

Educational measurement and evaluation: The evaluation work is a supplement to the whole educational process. Under this division, we study why and how evaluation in education is done, how much degree of achievement maybe guaranteed for success and how much degree of error in measurement is acceptable.

Comparative education: Comparative education helps us to modify, reform, reorient and improve our own educational system in the light of the system followed in foreign countries. It is a study of cross cultural comparison to the structure, operation, methods, aims and achievements of various educational systems and practices of different countries of the world.

Special education: Special education refers to the methods of imparting education to deviant groups of the society—handicapped or backward and talented or superiors. The relative importance of special and integrated education is also studied under this division.

History and problems of education: History of education comes under the scope of education in which we study the nature and patterns of education from the ancient period to the twenty-first century and their related problems. As a result, we understand the gradual development of education during different periods. It helps us to find out a suitable system of education according to the changing needs of the society.

Other fields of study: Education plays a dynamic role in any dynamic society. As a consequence, new subjects of studies are coming under the jurisdiction of education. Some of them are (i) Education in the Emerging Indian Society; (ii) Non-formal Education; (iii) Professional and Technical Education; (iv) Library Education; (v) Education and Vocational Guidance; (vi) Audio–Visual Education, (vii) Basic Education, (viii) Environmental Education; (ix) Health Education; (x) Measurements, Evaluation and Statistics; (xi) Fundamental of Teaching Practice; (xii) Socially Useful Productive Work.

Since the scope of education is very wide, it is not possible on the part of the individual to become perfect in all fields of education. Therefore, students will have to specialise themselves in different fields of education based on their needs and interests.

IMPORTANCE OF EDUCATION

Education is the wealth of the nation and power of the people. The garden of life will be colourless and without fragrance in the absence of education. It is education which fashions and models man to become fit for society and differentiates him from all other biotic organisms in the earth. Aristotle says, "Educated men are as much superior to uneducated as the living are to the dead". Education has become an essential virtue for man to live and lead a civilized life. Diogenes is of the opinion that, "Education is a controlling grace to the young, consolation to the old, wealth to the poor and ornament to the rich". Education makes man perfect. Dayanand says, "Educated person is healthy and uneducated person is suffering from disease of ignorance". It is true that this world would have been enveloped in the darkness of ignorance, if it had not been illuminated by the light of education.

The host of scientists, philosophers and educators has explained the needs and importance of education in a rational and scientific way. They present the following cogent arguments in favour of education as the most essential factor for human development:

Biological necessity: Education is a biological necessity for man. He is not an animal which learns all that is necessary for his future life. For instance, a calf needs no training to run or jump after its birth. A kitten very soon learns how to catch mice without education. But a human child would die if not properly attended to. In fact, the new born infant is a helpless human being and he learns to protect himself from harm only with the help of others. He will remain motionless, speechless and will not struggle for existence in the absence of proper instruction and training. As he grows older, he is influenced by formal, informal and non-formal agencies of education, which develop his physical, mental, emotional, social and vocational feelings. In this way, education develops in the child a sense of maturity and responsibility by bringing in him the desired changes according to the needs and demands of an ever changing society. Thus, education develops the individual like a flower, which spreads its fragrance all over the environment.

Sociological necessity: Animals learn a few tricks and tasks from their parents and become self sufficient. But it is different in the case of a human child. He has to assimilate a vast treasure of cultural heritage which cannot be transmitted to him biologically. The things learnt by one generation do not automatically pass on to another or ensuing generation. Hence, for each generation education is a must otherwise, human race would lapse into barbarism. The acquisition of knowledge, skill, attitude, character, aesthetic sense, moral sense, and creativity by humanity makes education a sociological necessity for the preservation, protection, and promotion of culture. The demands on education are greater than it had been in the past to make justice, peace, well-being and progress as the main characteristics of modern civilization.

Economic necessity: Education is a powerful tool which turns man into a manpower. It not only improves the working efficiency but also increases the productivity of the individual. In other words, it enables the individual to find any sort of task or job or self employment, which helps to stand on his leg. In short, it prepares the people for life. It is seen in the present society that people give more importance to the study of those subjects like Science, Medicine, Law, Engineering, Computer and Technical Courses and Management which makes them self-sufficient and vocationally efficient. In this way economic needs of the individual can be met only by different types of education. Therefore, education is considered as an important wealth next to health.

Global necessity: Modern inventions and discoveries in communication and transports have shrunk the world into a 'small village' called global village. As a result, an Indian, a German or an American is not considered as a member of his country alone but he is a citizen of the world. This trend can be developed among the citizens of the different countries only through the medium of education. In fact, education develops broad mindedness, removes narrowness, and leads to a global thinking that is, 'live together'. In this regard, education is more important than any other wealth.

Human capacity for learning: By nature a human child possesses a unique capacity for learning. He possesses potentialities for speech, thinking, reflection, judgement, scientific curiosity and other traits. These potentialities need to be developed through training and education for a long period. On the other hand these capacities will be dormant, unused and undeveloped in the absence of education.

Impressionability of the child: Experience can be acquired by the human being during his adult life. We attach importance to the early life for imparting education. This is because a child's mind is more elastic and impressionable during the earlier years than during adulthood. In the absence of proper training and education in the early years, habit formation in the adult becomes a problem. Hence, imparting right education during childhood should be emphasised.

Economic development and national-international understanding: The economic development of a country is determined by its human resource development which is influenced by the quality of education available to them. Education plays a vital role in economic development, which can be achieved through world peace, freedom, justice, safety for all, equalisation of education, population control etc. Education strengthens national integration and fosters international understanding which are essential for the progress of a nation. Education also helps us to invent and discover, new machines, tools, and medicines which increase the production of goods and services, and prevent the people from diseases. Thus, education is essential in all walks of human life. As education is one of the basic necessities for individual and social life, we place it next to food, clothing and shelter. We can conclude that shelter is essential for biological life as education is for sociological life.

CONCLUSION

Education is the matchless weapon which fashions and models the mankind socially, culturally, spiritually, aesthetically, vocationally and economically fit for existence in the earth. It is the widest road leading to find out solutions for the problems of individuals and helping them reach their destination. Hence, education is considered as one of the basic and most important necessities of human life. In fact, all types of education namely, formal, non-formal and informal are very essential in the modern age to bring about proper growth and development of the individual and the society. Therefore, we can conclude with the words of Comenius, who says, "All who are born as human beings need education because, they are destined to be real men, not wild beasts, dull animals and clumps of woods". Today education plays a very important role for biological, sociological, spiritual, cultural, aesthetical and economical aspects of human life.

CHAPTER 2

FUNCTIONS OF EDUCATION

INTRODUCTION

The functions of education are to help in the growth of a helpless young animal into a happy, moral and efficient human being. In fact, the main concern of education is the development of man. Since education is an integral part of human life, its field is very vast and complex. It includes all activities and experiences which prepare the individual for life. We know that, the nature of such activities changes according to time and circumstance and even from country-to-country. As a result, no fixed meaning of education, its functions and aims can be determined for all countries in the world. That is why, different scholars, thinkers, and educationists differ about the meaning of education, its functions and aims.

MEANING, FUNCTIONS AND AIMS OF EDUCATION

It is very difficult to differentiate between the meaning of education, its functions and aims as these three factors are so closely interrelated with one another. However, we can say, "what is education" is the meaning of education; "what education does" is the function of education; and "what education should do" is the aim of education. The main function of education is to prepare and develop the child for future life. In the words of John Dewey, "Education is not the preparation for life, but life itself." According to Daniel Webster, "The function of education is to discipline feelings, to control emotions, to stimulate motivations and to develop religious sentiments". We consider that the function of education is what it performs to the individuals and the society to control the environment for their better living as social beings.

M.L. Jack has stated that though there is plenty of work for education, its prime task is to transform original evil into acquired good. The main theme of education is to enable the child to think for himself, to respect hard work, to have good fellowship, to have taste and sense of eternal realities. Ralph Borsodi considers the function of education as "the humanization of mankind". In fact, education has to discharge a number of functions towards the individual as well as towards the society. The functions of education have been classified under three heads namely:

- General Functions of Education
- Functions of Education in Human Life
- Functions of Education in National Life

General Functions of Education

All-round development of a personality: All round personality development of the child is very essential for a balanced and harmonious development which enables him to lead personal as well as social life successfully. Hence, the main function of education is bringing about development in the physical, mental, spiritual, social, cultural, emotional and aesthetical aspects of the individual. When emphasising this function, Mahatma Gandhi has stated thus, "By education, I mean, an all round drawing out of the best in the child and man—body, mind and soul." It is an undeniable fact that a healthy mind lies only in a healthy body, and body alienated from soul is dead. Likewise, a healthy life lies only in the balanced development of the child.

Development of innate powers: Almost all educationists and psychologists consent that each child is endowed with some inherent tendencies (innate powers) like love, affection, curiosity, reasoning, imagination and self respect. Hence, the important function of education is to develop these powers in the child in order to prepare him for the future life. According to Pestalozzi, "Education is a natural, harmonious and progressive development of man's innate powers". Prof. Ross also emphasises this function of education by saying "Education consists in leading out the innate knowledge, virtues, and powers of the child, making the potential actual".

Modification of behaviour: Another important function of education is to develop the moral qualities in the child and build his character in order to modify his behaviour in a desirable way. In this regard, education transforms the behaviour of a person from 'instinctive behaviour' to 'human behaviour'. Prof. Drever says, "Education is a process in which and by which the knowledge, character and behaviour of the young are shaped and moulded". In the words of Dr. Johnson, "It is education which makes the man, a good man or a bad man according to its contents, its nature and its methods".

Sublimation of instincts: Every infant is born with some basic instincts which direct and mould his activities. Hence, the function of education is controlling, redirecting, and sublimating the inborn instincts in a desirable way. Otherwise the child will not be able to behave properly in the society. Without education, such transformation will not take place in the child. Daniel Webster has rightly remarked, "Through education, the feelings are to be disciplined, the passions are to be restrained, true and worthy motives are to be inspired".

Preparation for adult life: The function of education is to prepare the individual for the future life. The responsibilities of the child increase with age. When he grows up, he needs a job to support himself and his family. He is expected to develop a good social relation with his relatives, friends, neighbours, and the people at large. The vocational and social efficiencies are taught to him through formal, informal and non-formal education. According to T.P. Nunn, "Education is the complete development of individuality so that a man makes an original contribution to human life according to the best of his capacity". As the child is the father of man, he has to perform social, political, and domestic duties in future. For this, education prepares him to lead a responsible life in the society. According to John Dewey, "Education is not preparation for life, but life itself. It is the process of living through a continuous construction of experiences which develop all those capacities in the individual, which will enable him to control his environment and fulfil his responsibilities". We can, therefore, say that the function of education is preparing and developing the personality of an individual to undertake any kind of task and to adjust to his environment for achieving his basic necessities and objectives of life.

Enrichment of experiences: This is said to be an important function of education in the modern age. In fact, every individual has his own range of experience which may or may not be useful. But such experiences are directed towards the goal of life only through the process of education.

Character building: Character building or formation is an important function of education. An individual is evaluated by the society on the basis of his qualities. That is why Swami Vivekananda says, "We want that education by which character is formed".

Inculcation of social feelings: Man is a social animal. He has to live in a society. This is because, he has to develop himself in and through the society. He has to help others in the society in which he lives. For this purpose, inculcation of social feelings in the child is essential. It is education which alone can inculcate the social feelings, spirit of social service and social qualities such as love, fellow feeling, kindness, cooperation, sympathy and sacrifice in children through various social activities in the school environments. Thus, development of social feeling among the children has become the main function of education.

Development of good citizenship: Generally, the child, in his childhood, is selfish and wants the satisfaction of his desires only. It is not good for a country. So, the child should be transformed into a good dynamic citizen. The qualities of good citizenship are a sense of responsibility, fellow feeling, cooperation, love, service, leadership, honesty, patriotism and a sense of duty. It is the function of education to develop these qualities in the head and heart of the children and make them good citizens.

Social reform: Education is regarded as an important tool to bring about social reforms and social progress. Without education, the world would have been enveloped in the darkness of ignorance, superstition, illiteracy and social evils. In fact, education eradicates all blind beliefs, useless traditions and evil customs which mar and bar the progress and development of the society.

Preservation of culture and civilization: Education helps us in the preservation of culture and civilization, and it transmits them to the next generation. An individual is born in a society where there are various cultures, traditions and religious ideals. Culture influences the values and progress of the individuals. So, each nation is proud of its cultures and traditions. Since culture, tradition and civilization are valuable; they should be preserved, promoted, and transmitted to the succeeding generation for the betterment of human life. In this respect, the functions of education are to preserve our culture, tradition and civilization for the present generation, and transmit them for the next one.

National security: National security is very important to strengthen a country. Education develops patriotism and other necessary qualities in the individuals so that they are prepared to sacrifice all their belongings, even their lives, to protect and honour their nations. Thus, today it has become an important function of education to impart the necessary training for the inculcation of the noble sentiments of patriotism, nationalism and sacrifice. H. Mann has described this function of education in his words, "Education is our only political safety". In short, the function of education is building up a powerful country. The general individual functions of education are to develop a balanced and integrated human being. Moreover, these functions enable the child to become a useful member of the society. In this regard, we may remember the words of Pandit Jawaharlal Nehru, who says, "Education is supposed to develop an integrated human being and to prepare young people to perform useful functions for society and to take part in collective life".

Functions of Education in Human Life

All philosophers, psychologists and thinkers of the world have tried to set the goal of human life. They find that every individual has an inner urge to make his life happy. For this, he tries to achieve vocational social, spiritual efficiencies, which give him happiness at the physical, social and spiritual levels. So, the functions of education in human life are to accomplish and achieve human welfare.

Education as growth: John Dewey considers the outstanding function of education as growth. He says, "Since growth is the characteristic of life, education is all one with growing, it has no end beyond itself". According to a famous trio, "education is life" "life is growth" and hence "education is growth". The child is immature at birth and often behaves like an animal. So, he has to be trained for effective group-life and adaptation to human environments. Education refines and culturises. That is why Redden says, "Education is the deliberate and systematic influence, exerted by a matured person upon the immatured, through instruction, discipline and harmonious development of physical, intellectual, aesthetic, social and spiritual powers of the human being, according to individual and social needs". A child can develop and grow naturally without any education or training. But Pestalozzi says "when you carelessly leave the earth to nature, it bears weeds and thistles". Similarly, if we leave the education of the child to nature alone, he will develop only confused impressions on his senses and the desirable changes may not be brought about in him. Education is a process of growth in which the child is helped to foster his hidden potentialities. The development of a child's talents, powers, interests and ambitions take place in his physical, mental, moral, social, aesthetic, spiritual and emotional aspects. Thus, growth must be for the whole organism of the child and it is a continuous process. It is the end product of education which facilitates adjustment to human environments. In this way, education functions as the means for the natural harmonious growth of a child.

Education as direction: The physical and social environments of the child stimulate him for activities which maybe desirable or undesirable. Therefore, the child should be directed properly in a desirable way. Direction is "fixation of the activity into a proper response by elimination of unnecessary and confusing movements". Educating the child means directing and developing his gifts of natural instincts, tendencies and innate capacities properly. Taneja says, "Educative process is nothing but directing the children to have worthy interests in the various phases of life". According to Froebel, "Education is the progressive development of child's innate qualities." Thus, the main function of education is to direct the undeveloped capacities, attitudes, interests, urges and needs of the child into the most desirable avenues. This direction of education has been beautifully emphasised in the Vedic prayer "Lead me from untruth to truth, from darkness to light, and from mortality to immortality". Education in all respects helps the child to ascend from darkness to light, poverty to prosperity and from frailty to health.

Adaptation to environment: Teaching of adaptation and adjustment to the environment is another important function of education in human life. Hence, this function of education is important in the modern times. We become maladjusted in the society whenever we fail to get what we desire. Maladjustment leads to decay and destruction. So, education is essential for life and existence. According to Bossing, "The function of education is conceived to be the adjustment of man to his environment to the end that the most enduring satisfaction may accrue to the individual and to the society". Therefore, we can state that the function of education is what it performs to the individuals and the society to adjust themselves with the environment for their better life.

Modification of social environment: A healthy social environment is necessary for the growth of the individual in the proper direction. Education inculcates good habits in a human being, which enables him to modify his environments according to his needs and requirements. This is the dynamic function of education in the age of struggles and strives due to diversities of religion, race, caste, language and habits of living. These diversities create social and racial tensions which in turn lead to communal conflicts vitiating the whole atmosphere. These become obstacles to national integration and economic development. Moreover, man is a social animal who cannot live in isolation and his individuality can find fullest expression only in a social environment. Therefore, it is the function of education to modify the behaviour of the individual and change social environments by resolving tensions and promoting unity in diversity in order to make human life happy.

Making man civilized: Man is a mere two-legged animal and he often behaves like one during infancy and childhood. Education reforms the child by educating him about how to behave towards different people in different ways. This makes the whole human society civilized. Thus, the function of education is to civilize and enlighten the individual so as to make a cultured and civilized human being out of him. For this purpose, rules of conduct and norms of ethics are being taught to him through formal and informal education.

Satisfaction of needs: Every individual has several needs to be satisfied for the purpose of existence and making life happy. The needs are biological, sociological, psychological, intellectual, economic, aesthetic, ethical and spiritual. Education develops the capacities in the individual to find solutions to these needs. In this regard, we may state that education prepares and develops the individual to undertake any sort of task and fulfil his basic necessities of life. Thus, education functions as a powerful instrument by which all our needs are satisfied.

Achievement of self-sufficiency: Self-sufficiency makes human life happy. Therefore, every individual wants to be self-sufficient in every aspect of life. Education makes him self-reliant and self-supporting. It inculcates in him the sense of self-sufficiency, independence, and service for the society he is in. The function of education is to make the individual self-sufficient and lead a happy life. Swami Vivekananda has rightly remarked "We want that education by which one can stand on one's own feet".

Maximisation of human welfare: Man is not satisfied with food, clothing and shelter alone. His wants are unlimited, but the means which satisfy them are very limited. Education helps him to maximise his welfare with the available resources. A man maybe rich or poor, but his aim is to get the maximum utility or benefit at minimum cost. Education enhances the intellect of the individual which enables him to maximise his welfare. In the modern world, the function of education is the maximisation of human welfare.

Achievement of material prosperity: The world is both spiritual and material. Today, more emphasis is given to the material aspects. In fact, man wants to attain more and more material prosperity than spiritual prosperity. Education determines the economic or materialistic prosperity of an individual. More education means more material prosperity. In todays materialistic age the function of education should be the achievement of material prosperity.

Vocational efficiency: Education provides us various kinds of vocational and professional knowledge. This makes the individual self-reliant and self- supporting. Education increases vocational efficiency, which in turn increases the productivity of an individual. The increase in production increases his income, which again increases his satisfaction. The function of education is to help the individual to choose a vocation of his choice according to his talents and temperament. This leads to economic freedom which is the way to achieve happiness in the modern world. According to Dr. S. Radhakrishnan, "To help students to earn a living is one of the important functions of education". This is true of the modern society because education is meant for economic satisfaction and happiness in life. In other words, we acquire education in the form of certificates or training and skills, by which we are prepared and developed to undertake any sort of task which yields income for our existence.

Reconstruction of experiences: Education is the preparation for life through life's experiences. In other words, "Education is the transmission of life by the living to the living". According to John Dewey, "Education is the process of living through continuous reconstruction of experiences". Every man undergoes a number of experiences when he comes in contact with the physical and social environment (fellow-being). He classifies and consolidates those experiences which are conducive to his welfare and progress, and eliminates those experiences which are superfluous. Education is the only process through which such classification and consolidation of experiences can be reconstructed for human welfare. Thus, the function of education is the continuous re-organization and reconstruction of the past and the present experiences for future generation.

Prevention of mankind from evil and vices: The function of good education is the prevention of mankind from being defiled by evils and vices. In fact, this is the age of materialism, in which the individual lusts for more and more wealth, such greed leads him astray. Today, we can find evils and vices of all sorts reigning all over the world. As a result, human life is beset with pitfalls and dangers all round. Education is the light which removes the prevailing darkness of evils and vices. The quality of an individual depends on the quality of education which he receives and the quality of the teacher by whom he is taught.

Imparting practical knowledge: Modern world has become a complex world due to knowledge explosion. Theoretical knowledge of various spheres of human thoughts and activities is available to the individual. But such knowledge will not be effective unless it is given practically. This is because today's citizens need practical efficiency in work. Therefore, education should impart theoretical as well as practical knowledge to the students so that an all-round personality development in them can be achieved. The function of real education is to provide more and more practical work. In the words of Swami Vivekananda, "You have to be practical in all spheres of work. The whole country has been ruined by masses of theories".

From these explanations, we can say that education plays a very important role in human life. The functions of education in human life are to prepare and develop the child for a blissful life. This fact can be discerned from the statement of University Education Commission (1948–1949) which observes, "Education according to the Indian traditions is not merely a means of earning a living; nor it is only a nursery of thoughts or a school for citizenship. It is initiation into the life of spirit, a training of human souls in the pursuit of truth and the practice of virtue. It is a second birth, *divitya janma*".

Functions of Education in National Life

Various politico-economic, socio-cultural, philosophical, psychological and geographical factors have developed a new system of education, which has a very vital role in our national life. In fact, education transforms the Indian society from the medieval and traditional to the modern pattern. Kothari Commission has rightly remarked, "The destiny of India is being shaped in her classrooms".

There is an intimate relationship between the life of the individuals and the life of a nation. This is because an individual cannot be separated from his nation. Therefore, national progress depends upon the handwork, energy, selflessness, uprightness, and devotion of the individual. According to Maclever, "The quality of the nation is the quality of the social units whose common life it is—if the fuel is poor, how can the flame be bright". Education creates citizens who show the qualities of dynamic leadership and sense of responsibility towards their nation. Let us list the main functions of education in Indian society.

Training for leadership: The most important function of education is to develop leadership qualities among the growing generation for the uplift of the nation in all aspects. The successful functioning of democracy needs efficient, experienced, developed and dynamic leaders, who decide and construct policies in every field of national activities and progress. Education produces ablest leaders in political, social, spiritual, cultural, educational, economic, scientific, medical, industrial and other fields. The quality and development of a nation depends on the leadership quality of the individual who guides and leads the nation in the path of progress and prosperity. The function of education is, thus, providing training for leadership and developing the qualities needed for effective and efficient leadership. For this purpose, educational institutions provide an atmosphere in which the students are encouraged to participate in various kinds of co-curricular activities.

Inculcation of civic and social values: The nation is valued on the basis of her quality in a democratic set up. Such democracy can be established through civic and social values. It is education through the medium of which civic and social values are imparted to the younger generation. The ideals and values strengthen democracy and reconstruct society. A multi-religious country like ours should promote a tolerant study of all religions so that its citizens can understand each other better and live amicably together.

Inculcation of civic and social duties: In a democratic country, all citizens should perform their duties and obligations towards the nation for maintaining its progress and prosperity. In the words of Dr. Zakir Hussain, "In a democratic society, it is essential that individal should cheerfully share the responsibility of making the life of society a better life, both morally and materially". Hence, one of the important functions of education is to make the younger generation understand their rights and duties, and discharge their responsibilities to the best of their capacity as dynamic citizens of this country.

National development: There is a direct relationship between education and national development. The development of a nation depends on the quality of her population, which is largely determined by education. That is why it is said that education is the corner stone of national development. This function of education can be achieved by making education mass-based and relating with for increasing productivity. Education applies scientific productive processes and emphasises vocationalisation to produce more and more wealth, which determines the progress and prosperity of a nation. It helps to produce scientists, technologists, doctors, lawyers, engineers, professors, teachers whose contribution in the agricultural, industrial and tertiary sectors promotes our economy. In short, education is the backbone of political, social, cultural and economic development.

National integration: National integration is an essential factor for national peace, security, and prosperity. Unity in diversity is the meaning and nature of national integration. Ours is a country where we have diversities of religions, languages, castes, cultures, locations, and modes of living. These are also the stumbling blocks to national integration as they create dissensions and conflicts in our national life. Often the dissensions and conflicts cause huge losses of property and human lives. Therefore, these diversities should be brought under check and social, political, provincial, linguistic, economic, cultural and religious unity should be developed and strengthened. Education can help us to attain unity in diversity by inculcating a feeling of oneness in all the people irrespective of all their differences. Pandit Jawaharlal Nehru rightly says, "The question of integration covers in a sense almost everything in life. Above all, it covers education. This is basic". In the words of Dr. S. Radhakrishnan, "If India is to remain free united and democratic, education should train people for unity and not localism, for democracy and not dictatorship". According to Prof. Nurul Hassan, "Education should be responsive to the new milieu of socio-economic changes. It should also inculcate among people a sense of integrity and unity of the country".

Emotional integration: Emotional integration is the prerequisite for national integration. India is a country of diversities and differences which create narrow feelings in almost all spheres of national life. Such feelings develop hatred, enmity, jealousy and rivalry. They become the cause for conflicts and riots resulting in huge loss of property and human lives. The evils which pollute the human minds should be shunned by the creation of unity, harmony and emotional integration. In order to unite the nation and make it powerful, the development of emotional integration among varied culture groups becomes inevitable in Indian society. So, the development of emotional integration is essential for promoting feelings of tolerance, fellow feeling, cooperation and adjustment. These are the main functions of education in the Indian society. Pandit Jawaharlal Nehru says, "By emotional integration I mean the integration of our minds and hearts, the suppression of feeling of separation".

Training in morality: Morality is a self-imposed discipline which is guided by spiritual values. This is a valuable treasure of every nation. In fact, a high sense of morality develops the character of a nation and serves as a guiding light in our life. Education is the only means to inculcate moral and spiritual values and train the children in moral behaviour and moral activities. It is regrettable that we have fallen from the high moral values and ideals of conduct, which our country greatly honoured in the ancient times. Therefore, it has fallen upon education to preserve and promote high moral values and ideals by citing the examples of priests, prophets, history of national and religious leaders and justice-loving rulers so as to bring honour to our nation in today's world.

National discipline: Education promotes national discipline, which is essential for the growth and development of a country. India is a vast democratic country which requires national discipline to maintain her freedom. The Secondary Education Commission Report has emphasised the need for national discipline. It says, "A democracy cannot function successfully unless all the people—not merely a particular section—are trained for discharging their responsibilities and this involves training in discipline". Hence, our educational system should be shaped in such a way so as to promote national discipline at all levels in all citizens of the states for the success of democracy. Dr. S. Radhakrishnan remarks, "The success of democracy in Asia depends on our will to remain in discipline and sacrifice our personal interests".

Supply skilled manpower: Increasing productivity is one of the aims of Indian Education Commission (1964–1966). In order to achieve this aim of education, we need a number of skills and techniques to perform various types of productive and non-productive tasks. For this, skilled and semi-skilled workers are supplied by formal, informal and non-formal educational institutions. Thus, we may state that education is acquired from womb to tomb through formal or non-formal organizations, in order to obtain certificates and degrees or skills, by which his personality is prepared and developed to undertake any sort of mental or manual task. In this way education helps to supply manpower required for all sectors of the economy. In fact, even an illiterate man increases his value and vocational efficiency, when he acquires some technical skill and engages himself in any task for which he is capable. In modern times, an important function of education is the production of scientists, engineers, technologists, industrialists, doctors, professors, teachers, administrators, traders, lawyers, bankers, musicians, artisans, artists, sportsmen, mechanists, typists, clerks etc., to ease the ever-increasing demand for different types of manpowers.

Promotion of social efficiency: Social efficiency is the prerequisite for prosperity and economic growth of a nation. That is, the welfare of a country depends on its social efficiency, which in turn depends on individual efficiency. The efficiency of the individual depends on the standard of education created for him. John Dewey remarks that the aim or function of education is to bring about "Social Efficiency". According to Prof. Bagley of America, "A socially efficient individual is he who is self-reliant and does not depend upon the income of others. He does not interfere with the activities of others but helps to promote social welfare". Alfred Adler says, "The only worth while achievements of man are those which are socially useful". Education is the medium through which in service training in medical, engineering and teaching professions or apprenticeship in trade, technical and industrial works are imparted to promote the social efficiency of the individual.

Priority to national interests: The function of education in national life is giving priority to national interests which promote the citizens of the country. The records of our old history display the sacrifice of our national leaders for the freedom, integrity, security and honour of our nation. In fact, the real function of education in national life is to emphasize qualities of sacrifice, service, patriotism, nationalism, secularism and democratic feelings and inculcate them in the child through its various activities and programmes.

Development of environmental awareness: This is one of the most important functions of education in modern times not only at the national level but also in the international level. The unceasing growth of population, industrialisation and urbanisation demands the application of new science and technology to increase the production of goods and services resulting in environmental pollution and crisis. Environmental degradation is the greatest problem which threatens not only the present generation but also the generations of the future. When man interferes in the rules and functions of Nature for his selfish interests, his environment gets disturbed. Thus, man creates unfavourable conditions for himself. It has been threatening the survival of man himself and other living organisms. In this juncture, the function of education is to create awareness in matters of population and environment, by inculcating in the child the need to preserve Nature in all its glory.

CONCLUSION

From the given functions of education, we can say that education has a predominant role in individual, social and national life. "If a democracy like ours is to survive, education must, without a single exception, perform all the functions mentioned here". Moreover, the general functions and the individual functions of education in human and national life should be studied collectively. In short, all functions of education add up to "man making" and "nation making".

CHAPTER 3

AIMS OF EDUCATION

INTRODUCTION

Education is an art of living, closely associated with human life. In the words of Aristotle, "Every art does something good. Education is an art. It is to be seen what good is done by education to man and society". Education is a very comprehensive term having different meanings and multiple aims. In fact, man always develops new ideas, tries them out and rejects or modifies them in the light of experience and knowledge. As a result, no aim can be final and it is changed by the influence of time, conditions and needs of the individual and the society. Hegel declares, "There is no philosophy but only philosophies". It is a universally accepted fact that every educational aim is an expression of a philosophy of life. We have a number of aims in education due to the complexity of human character.

MEANING OF AIM

All activities in the universe can be classified under aimed and aimless. Education is said to be a living activity and a social necessity. So, it must have some aim to make its activity, effective. What is the aim or the goal or the objective of this activity? It is sure that this kind of question will arise in the minds of the literate and the illiterate or even sometimes in an expert in the field of education. Hence, it has to be answered clearly and precisely, particularly when everyone is confused about education. Generally, *aim* is a predetermined goal which inspires the wilful activities of an individual till it is achieved. John Dewey defines "An aim implies an orderly activity, in which the order consists of the progressive completion of a process". He believes that a systematic activity is always directed to some goals which influence each step taken in the desired direction for achieving some end. The word *orderly* denotes the systematic nature of the activity. The word *ordered* refers to the direction implied in the activity. Thus, aim is that which gives a sense of order and direction to "an activity". In the words of John Dewey, "Aim is a foreseen end which gives direction to a certain activity or motivates human behaviour". In short, we can say that aim is the steering wheel by which the vehicle called '**education**' can be directed in a possible and a desirable way.

Importance of Aims in Education

Education is a purposeful and planned activity. Therefore, its various aims have been emphasised by scholars, philosophers, educators, psychologists and sociologists in all ages. To have an aim is to act with meaning, unlike an automatic machine. The importance of educational aims lies in the fact that they give foresight to the educational planners. In fact, there can be no educational activity without an aim. Educational practices at all times have been determined by the accepted educational aims. Professor B.D. Bhatia says, "Without the knowledge of aims, that educator is like a sailor who does not know his goal or his destination and the child is like a rudderless vessel which will be drifted along somewhere ashore". The aims of education have changed in the present age, as they function as a light for the blind, a stick for the crippled and literacy for the illiterate. The importance of aims in education has also been emphasised in the encyclopedia of modern education. According to it "Education is a purposeful and ethical activity. Hence, it is unthinkable without aim". Therefore, we observe that the aim of education is like the blood of man without which it becomes a dead process that yields nothing.

NEED FOR AIM

Education is related to human life; It is life itself. Hence, it should grow and for that it should have certain aims in itself. In fact, it needs aim in the same way as a plant needs sunlight, water, air and fertilizer, and man needs water, air, food, dress and shelter.

Aims provide direction to our efforts: John Dewey says, "An aim is a foreseen end that gives direction to an activity or motivates behaviour". Our efforts can be directed properly only if we have information about aims. The aim of education provides light for the teacher and the students to direct their efforts in the proper direction.

Aims provide action to the teachers: The aims of education activate the teachers to work shoulder-to-shoulder with one another, and make it a joint enterprise. The whole educational planning in the school will be reduced to a muddle in the absence of consensus with regard to aims of education.

Aims assess outcomes of educational process: Aims of education help us to look back and review the results of educational activities. Such assessment of the educational system can be done after fixing the aims of education. An aim is the tool with which one can measure the success or failure of work done in the school and the achievements of the young scholars.

Aims allow us to act intelligently: Aims of education allow us to act intelligently and with a meaning in anything that we do. Thus, aims enable us to know what we are doing and why we are doing. In fact, aims save us from waste of time and energy, and help us to be wise.

Aims make school administration efficient: Educational aims help the school officials in organizing, equipping and administering the school efficiently. They also help in various aspects of school management such as proper selection of teachers, curriculum planning, well-equipped library and desirable planning of co-curricular activities.

Aims change human life in the technological age: In the scientific and technological age, human life has become very complex and it faces many problems. As a result of technological development, urbanisation and industrialisation, we come across social, economic, political, moral, cultural, educational and religious changes. These changes cannot be faced by us unless we are trained to adjust with them. Therefore, aims of education should be changed according to the changing needs of the modern society.

Aims help to evaluate school organization: We need aims in education to evaluate the school organization. In fact, educational aims provide answers to the questions such as, is the curriculum proper? Has the selection of teachers been done on the basis of experience and ability? Whether the school has proper infrastructure like buildings, laboratories, playgrounds, libraries and other facilities? The evaluation of the whole educational system can be done with the help of aims of education.

Aims impart guidance to the teachers: Educational aims guide the teachers in the teaching–learning process. They exalt the status of the teachers in the society as social engineers and nation builders. Aims help them to create an atmosphere in the school in which students are encouraged to take part in various activities so that they can develop their social efficiency.

Aims promote national integration and international understanding: The development of national and emotional integration and international understanding will be impossible if education is without aims. International understanding and national integration are inculcated in the children only when they possess the knowledge of the aims of education. Through these aims, they are mentally prepared for international understanding and national integration.

Aims increase national development: The development of a nation depends on education. Therefore, national development should be one of the objectives of education. The educational system of a country can be successful only if it caters to the needs of national development. As a result, we find every system of education aiming at national development. For example, when the aim of education is increasing agricultural production and vocational efficiency, it will become the aims of national development.

Aims help us to apply the right method of teaching: Different methods are being applied for imparting education to the child. But the most suitable method is chosen only with the help of educational aims. In fact, the aims of education help us to select a method of teaching not only according to the nature of subjects but also bearing in mind the age, interests and aptitude of the pupils. Without aims, teaching–learning will not be effective and fruitful.

Aims modify environments: We need aims in education because it is powerful in bringing about desirable changes in society through modifying the human behaviour. As education is closely associated with human beings, any change in human life takes place as a consequence of change in aims of education. Thus, aims of education change in accordance with time, place and circumstances and they prepare the people to be fit in the changing environments.

Aims prepare the child for life: The aims of education prepare the child for adult life and make him stand on his own feet. Today's education aims at fostering vocational and social efficiency in the child. Vocational efficiency and social efficiency are the main aims of education through which the individuals can have a meaningful and useful life in the earth.

Aims develop democracy: We live in a democratic country. Hence, democratic feelings should be developed and strengthened in the younger generation. It is possible only through the aims of education. The educational aims foster fellow feeling, cooperation, brotherhood, tolerance, love and sympathy, which are the basic foundations of democracy. The aims of education direct the school to undertake various group activities and programmes, which provide an atmosphere in which teachers, parents, pupils, educationists and the public share their joint responsibilities.

Aims preserve our culture: Aims of education help to preserve, promote and transmit our culture and civilization, which are the values in human life. If we find no such aims in education, our culture will be destroyed and there will be no progress in society. Thus, educational aims are essentially needed to propagate and promote our ancient culture so that national feelings can be protected and strengthened.

CRITERIA OF A GOOD AIM

An aim is a predetermined goal, which inspires the wilful activities of an individual after careful thinking and proper planning till it is reached. Every man must have an aim to achieve something in life. In the words of Prof. Tyron Edwards, "High aims form high character and great objects bring out great minds". Therefore, aim should be constructed on the basis of certain good criteria so that it can be purposeful. John Dewey, the greatest exponent of pragmatic philosophy of education has outlined the characteristics or criteria of good aim in his famous book *Democracy and Education*.

Related to real life: Good aims are related to the situations of life. They are born in real life and they should grow out of those situations. Thus, aim must be related to the life needs and aspirations of the people. For instance, the aspirations of the Indians in the constitution are to establish a democratic, socialistic, secular, republic with social justice. Therefore, aim of education should reflect the aims of national, social and individual lives.

Flexible: Good aims are flexible. The aim, which is suitable under one situation, maybe found unsuitable in another situation. So, aims should be flexible enough to meet the demands of the circumstances of life. John Dewey says, "The value of legitimate aim lies in the fact that we can use it to changed situations".

Represent various activities: A good aim always represents a span of diverse activity which constitutes the core of education. In fact, human beings are busy with various types of activities. A good aim should try to highlight all the special and purposeful activities as a part of the educative process. It is necessary that aims of education should correspond, on the one hand, to the existing needs and on the other hand, be supported by the prevailing philosophy of life. It must also depend on the psychology of learning and development.

Defined in operational terms: As far as possible the aim must be defined in operational terms and it should not be stated in a general and abstract way. For example, the aim of education should be either vocational development or spiritual and moral development. Absence of a definite aim would lead to confusion to formulate steps for realising the aim of education.

It should have a terminal point: The aim must always have a terminal point and it should be defined in such a way that after a stage, there must be termination of activities. For instance, after the completion of BA, BSc, BCom, or BBA courses, a student may ask "what next?" Then he may answer himself, "Let me take up MA, MSc, MCom or MBA." Further, he will have to ask "what next?". He may find odd jobs or take up MPhil, Ph.D, or BEd. Thus, an aim should have a terminal point.

It must emerge out of existing conditions: Good aims of education must emerge out of the social, economic and political conditions of a given group of people at a particular point of time. For example, the Secondary Education Commission emphasised the development of citizenship and development of leadership qualities as the important aims of education. These were based on the existing conditions of India after her independence. Kothari Commission considered national development as an important aim of education.

FACTORS DETERMINING THE AIMS OF EDUCATION

Education is a living process which rests on many pillars such as geographical, philosophical, political, social, economic, moral and cultural environments. As a result, we have a number of factors which contribute to the determination of educational aims. These factors touch almost every phase of human life.

A.K.C. Ottaway has stated, "Education is an activity which goes on in a society and its aims and methods depend on the society in which it takes place". The important factor, which determines the aims of education are discussed in the succeeding lines.

Philosophy of life: The prevailing philosophy of life is the most important factor of determining educational aims. Professor Whitehead says, "One of the subject matters of education is life". Hence, aims of education should have a close relationship with the prevailing philosophy of life and the views of eminent thinkers and philosophers about the nature of reality. The idealistic view of life regards spirituality and God as the supreme reality. According to this view, education aims at self-realisation and exaltation of human personality or unfolding of the latent potential in the child. The naturalists believe that the external physical existence is real and instincts, emotions and feelings of man are his real self-realisation. On the basis of this view, education aims at self-expression. The pragmatists consider life as a process of socialisation of an individual. Therefore, education should aim at enabling the individual to control his environment and fulfil his possibilities.

Psychological factor: Psychologists have different views about human nature. In fact, it is composed of heterogeneous elements, rational and non-rational, intellect, emotions, man's animal self and his spiritual self. Educational aims, therefore, have often been decided keeping in view one or the other element, which comprises human nature. Thus, aims of education have been decided on the basis of the concept of human nature. From the psychological point of view, idealists want that education should aim at unfolding the divine in the child and man. But naturalists consider that education should aim at developing 'self-expression' in the child. Pragmatists think that education should aim at the development of the social efficiency in a child.

Geographical factors: Geographical factors play an important role in deciding the aims of education from the ancient period. For example, education in Sparta aimed at developing physical strength, courage, endurance and obedience in order to train the Spartan youth to protect the state from foreign aggression. The same aim was emphasised in Germany and Italy to make the countries strong enough to face the World War. India emphasises spiritual and vocational aims of education to enable its citizens to stand on their own feet and lead a holy life.

Political factors: The political factors like democracy, totalitarianism, communism, socialism, mixed economy, capitalism and fascism go a long way in determining the aims and the system of education. As a result, there are different aims of education. The history of the world has proved that the political factors or ideologies have a great impact in determining the aims of education. For example, India is a democratic country where democratic values are emphasised. Therefore, education aims at the development of democratic values. In other words, its aims are to develop the full personality of each individual irrespective of caste, creed and religion. On the other hand, there is no place for individual development in a communist society.

Economic factors: The aims of education are influenced by economic factors. Formal education is possible in an economy where production exceeds consumption. The aim of education predominates bread and butter when an individual is basically concerned with earning a livelihood. For example, our country had to increase the production of goods and services as the consequence of the growth of population, urbanisation and industrialisation. In this condition, the important aim of education is increasing productivity. This objective of education has also been emphasised by the Indian Education Commission during 1964–1966, in order to make our nation self-sufficient in production. In this way, educational aims have been determined by the economic factors.

Social factors: These factors also play a considerable role in determining the educational aim in the scientific age. The tremendous explosion of science and technology has created intricate problems of social adjustment among the individuals. Therefore, new emphasis has been placed on literacy and social activities through re-organizing the curricula at all stages. The new forces in the social structure of the Indian Society have provided a fresh incentive for educationists to frame new aims for education.

Religious factors: Religion is an important factor which affects the aims of education in our country. For instance, the Brahmanic system of education, the Buddhist education and the Mohammedian education were dominated by religion. In the same way, the aims of education in the Western countries were influenced by Protestant and Catholic religions. In fact, the development of moral and spiritual values has been fixed as the aim of modern education.

Cultural factors: The aims of education of a country are also influenced by its cultural factors. We know that every country has its own cultures and it wants to preserve, promote and transmit the culture for the benefit of the succeeding generations. Education is the only instrument by which our culture can be preserved, promoted and transmitted, for the progress of mankind. As a result, preservation, promotion and transmission of cultural heritage, have become important aims of present education.

Environmental factors: Environment also plays a significant role in determining the aims of education in the recent years. Environment constitutes everything that surrounds us. Since we are a part of it, the study of environment and its crisis has drawn the attention of educationists, thinkers, political leaders, scientists, social reformers, workers and illiterates. The detrimental growths of population, deforestation, industrialisation and urbanisation have been the causes of environmental degradation, which is harmful to all living organisms. In this condition, every child should have knowledge of his environment and its crisis, and how to overcome it. Education is the only source through which environmental awareness and measures to control the environmental crisis can be inculcated in the child's mind. Thus, the development of environmental awareness is an important aim of education in the industrialised society.

Knowledge factors: Explosion of knowledge in science and technology has a great impact on education and it is one of the determinant factors of educational aims. Education, all over the world, has become science oriented due to the explosion of science and technical knowledge. Therefore, the study of modern science and technology and mathematics is being emphasised in almost all stages of education. The government provides liberal grants and scholarships in order to encourage the study of modern science for the progress of our country. The Indian Education Commission has stressed the study of science and mathematics while formulating the aims of education in India. As a result, the study of science and technology has been an important aim of our present education.

INDIVIDUAL AND SOCIAL AIMS OF EDUCATION

So, far, we have seen the meaning, need, importance and the determining factors of educational aims. From these, we know that education, and its aims are closely related to human life which varies with time, place and circumstances. In fact, educational aims vary from country-to-country and even in the same country with its political, social, spiritual, aesthetic and economic conditions. It is a burning question before the educationists whether education should aim at the training and development of individualistic or socialistic nature. The educationists, who think that individual development is greater than that of the society, emphasise the individual aim of education. On the other hand, the educationists, who consider the importance of society, insist on the social aim of education. Individual and social aims of education are quite often regarded as opposed to each other. But in the final analysis we might arrive at the conclusion that the development of individuality, apart from social setting is a meaningless pursuit. In fact, these are the two sides of the same process. The educational system of

Greece and Rome raised an issue that is still very important in the present situation. "Should education train good individuals or good citizens? Are the social needs in education more important than the needs of the individuals? Which of the two, the individual or the society should occupy the foreground of the picture?". An individual is born with certain potentialities and natural endowments. It is the task of the educator to develop him into a distinct individual. But this kind of development does not take place in a vacuum. In this condition, we must decide whether the individual or the society should occupy the first place in education. In other words, we have to decide whether the individual owes his existence to the society or the society exists for the individual. Let us now consider both the aims of education in their most extreme forms.

INDIVIDUAL AIMS OF EDUCATION

Meaning of individual aim: Individual aim of education denotes the training and development of the individual according to his or her interests, abilities and specialities. Therefore, maximum opportunities should be made available to each individual for realising his physical, moral, intellectual and spiritual possibilities without any hindrance. Individuality is the ideal of life. "Schools of every type fulfil their purpose in so far as they foster to the free growth of individuality, helping every boy and girl to achieve the highest degree of individual development of which he or she is capable in and through the life of a society". The protagonists of this aim assert that the individual should be in the forefront of the picture. They believe that social institutions—such as the family, the church, the school and the state—exist for the betterment and improvement of the individual.

The Greek philosophers and ancient literatures lay stress on the individual aim of education. In the words of Plato, "It is for the good of the state that the individual should be allowed to develop along the line of his own greatest powers". During the modern age, educationists like Rousseau, Pestalozzi, Froebel, Gandhi, John Dewey, Kant and Nunn stress the development of the individuality of the child as the aim of education.

Kant: "Education is the development in the individual of all perfection of which he is capable".

Pestalozzi: "Education is the natural, harmonious and progressive development of man's innate powers".

Aristotle: "Education is the creation of a sound mind in a sound body".

Montessori: "Education is the active help given to the normal expansion of the life of the child".

Froebel: "Education is the unfoldment of what is enfolded in the germ. It is the process by which the child brings out his internal potentialities.

Narrow and Wider Meanings of Individual Aim

Narrow meaning of individual aim: Individual aim is known as self-expression. The narrow meaning of individual aim is based on the philosophy of naturalism, which stresses that education should develop the unique individuality of a child in accordance with his instincts. Sir Percy Nunn is the chief supporter who holds that the central aim of education is the autonomous development of the individual. According to him, "Nothing good enters into the human world except in and through the free activities of the individual men and women and that the educational practice must be shaped to accord with this truth". Thus, the individual aim emphasises self-expression, all-round development or natural development of the child according to his interests, inclinations capacities and needs.

Wider meaning of individual aim: It is known as self-realisation. Psychology emphasises the wider aspect of the development of individuality. The educationists and psychologists believe that each individual is born with his own peculiar and distinct innate tendencies and capacities. Hence, the aim of education is to develop each individual fully according to his interests, inclinations, aptitudes, capacities and needs. Nunn reinforces this aim by saying "Education should help the child to make his original contribution to the variegated whole of human life as full and as truly characteristic as his nature permits". He also believes that if an individual is cut off from the society, he cannot develop himself in any way. According to Nunn, "Individual aim of education does not deny or minimise the responsibility of man to his fellows, for individual life cannot develop only in terms of his own nature and that is social as truly as self regarding".

VIEWS IN FAVOUR OF INDIVIDUAL AIMS

The development of individuality of the child as the primary individual aim of education has been emphasised by all types of thinkers—naturalists, biologists, psychologists, spiritualists and progressivists. The supporters of the individual aim consider that the individual should be in the forefront of the picture.

Views of naturalists: The naturalists as well as educationists such as Rousseau, Comenias, Pestalozzi and Nunn believe that education should be "according to nature". The central aim of education is the autonomous development of the individual. According to Rousseau, "True education is something that happens from within the individual; it is an unfolding of his own latent powers". Nunn is of the view that education must secure those conditions where every individual is allowed to have a free play of his personality. He is free to develop his inherent powers and, thus, realise the highest potentialities of self. In short, education should be in accordance with the nature of the individual.

Views of biologists: The biologists believe that every individual is unique. In fact, every child is born in the world as a new product. We cannot change his nature just as we cannot change the colour of his eyes. Hence, education should be meant for the individual. It is to enable the individual to survive and lead a complete life. Professor G. Thompson says, "Education is for the individual; its function being to enable the individual to survive and live out its complete life. Education is imparted to preserve the individual life. Community exists for the individual not individual for the community. Community being the means and the individual being the end, education should not set the means over the end. Education is given for the sake of individual, with a view to save him from destruction". Therefore, the individual and not the society should be the centre of all educational efforts and activities. The history of the world shows that the repression of individuality is the cause of the occurrence of many dangerous consequences. For example, during the two World Wars, people were engaged in economically unproductive activities of organized destruction due to the repression of individuality.

Views of psychologists: Psychologists have proved that children differ from one another in interests, aptitudes, tastes, needs and capacities. According to them, no two children are alike in their inborn capabilities. Therefore, it is not desirable to follow a uniform curriculum and teaching methods for a large number of children. If they are forced to follow a rigid curriculum, textbooks and teaching methods, tension, stress, and strain will occur. As a result, a broad based, flexible curriculum teaching methods and suitable textbooks should be followed according to the interests, inclinations, aptitudes, capacities and needs of different children. The psychologists and educationists, who advocate individual aim of education, emphasise on the development of the innate potentiality and unique individuality of each child according to his nature.

Views of progressivists: The progressivists are of the view that "the progress and advancement of individuals is due to the influence of great individuals born in different periods and places of history". They are great scientists, inventors, explorers, religious and political leaders, social reformers and philosophers. In fact, the activities of Jesus Christ, Buddha, Mohammed Nabi, Plato, Aristotle, Socrates, Guru Nanak, Swami Vivekananda, Raja Ram Mohan Roy, Mahatma Gandhi, Sri. Narayana Guru, Karl Marx, Lenin, Abraham Lincoln, St. Paul, Martin Luther King and Martin Luther have made the world a better and a happier place to live in. The progressivists also believe that if the individual is fully developed, the society is automatically developed. Therefore, the school atmosphere should pay much attention to the growth of individuality, helping every boy or girl to achieve the highest degree of his or her individual development. The individuals create the society and preserve, purify, promote and transmit its culture to the oncoming generation. So, progressivists emphasise the development of individuality as the aim of education. The individuality of the child has been described by Khalil Gibran as:

> "Your children are not your children
> They are the sons and daughters of life's longing for itself
> They come through you but not from you
> And though they will be with you yet they belong not to you
> You may give them your love but not your thoughts
> For they have their own thoughts
> You may house their bodies but not their souls
> Which you cannot visit, and even in your dreams,
> You may strive to be like them, seek not to make them like you
> For life goes not backward, not tarries with yesterday"

Views of spiritualists: The moralists are of the view that spiritual progress and self-realisation are individual processes. According to them, every individual is a separate entity and responsible for his own actions, whether good or evil, depending on the way he has been trained. Therefore, the aim of education is to lead the individual to self-realisation. In the words of Swami Vivekananda, "Man is potentially divine. The goal is to manifest this potentiality from within, by controlling nature—external and internal through education". Goethe says, "No one can be like another but every one can be like the highest". How is that to be? Let every one be perfect in himself". Since the spiritual development of man is an individual process, the development of his individuality should be the aim of education.

Views of democrats: The democrats stress on the dignity and freedom of all individuals. Man should be educated as a man because his nature is human. Otherwise, it will do harm to him and also to the society of which he is a member. Every democratic country emphasises the development of good citizens. Good citizens can be developed from good persons. This depends on the quality of education that they receive. Hence, the aim of education should be the development of the innate potentialities and qualities of initiative, enterprise and self-reliance in the individuals. The individual should be given maximum freedom to express his natural endowments.

VIEWS AGAINST INDIVIDUAL AIMS

The individual aims of education are not exempted from criticism. The extreme form of individual aims is undesirable. Those who support the social aim of education have criticised the individual aims vehemently.

Isolated individual: The first limitation of individual aim is that it isolates the individual from the society. T. Raymont says, "An isolated individual is only a figment of imagination". We cannot think of an individual living and developing in isolation from society". Supporting this view, John Dewey remarks, "As a social being, he is a citizen, growing and thinking in a vast complex of interactions and relations". He does not exist anywhere on the surface of the earth. Even Nunn, the greatest champion of individual aim believes that individuality develops only in a social atmosphere where it can feed on common interests and common activities.

Indiscipline, conflicts and crises: The individual aim of education provides unlimited and unrestricted freedom to the individual which makes him a man of arbitrary decisions and reckless actions. Unrestricted freedom will motivate him to do whatever he wants. It makes the pupil self-centred, selfish and indisciplined. These factors develop conflicts, crises and tension, resulting in social disintegration.

Inapplicable to real life: Individual aim emphasises the individual development of the child according to his interest, inclination, capacities, aptitudes and needs. But it is not possible to formulate aims and construct curriculum and teaching method for each child. Even the richest country of the world cannot meet the expenses in such a system of education. Hence, it is inapplicable in educational theory and practice of real life.

Emphasis on innate potentialities: The biologists lay stress on the autonomous development of individuality. They ignore the influence of socio-cultural environments and insist only on the innate potentialities. If education fails to inculcate cultural values in the child's mind which are transmitted to the next generation, human values will start to decay. Hence, socio-cultural environment should be considered as an essential factor for individual development.

Individualism leads to autocracy: Individual aim of education encourages the individual to be self-centred and proud. Such a tendency might develop immoral behaviour and unhealthy attitudes in the child. For instance, dictators and despots such as Mussolini, Hitler, Zia-ul-Haq and Stalin had feelings of superiority complex and self-conceit. The encouragement to individualism will make the society suffer.

Anti-socialism: Naturalists stand in favour of the autonomous development of the individual. This provides him with maximum freedom, which will result in defiance of social norms, rules and code of conduct. A few people will enjoy all the benefits and exploit the rest for their own welfare and prosperity. In short, individualisation will promote capitalists, monopolists and a corrupt society.

Disregard for morals: The individual differences of children have been emphasised as an important aim of education. In this condition, it will be very difficult to develop love, sympathy, sacrifice, service, cooperation, fellow-feeling, brotherhood and other values in the children.

Disregard man's social nature: Each man is a social animal. Therefore, the aim of education is not the development of individuality but the enrichment of his personality with the cooperation of society. It is education, which must transform the child from an individual being to a social being so that he can be fit to live in the society. It is essential for the individual to adjust with others for a successful life.

Against spiritual nature: The critics of individual aim consider that the individual, left to himself, is an animal, selfish and indisciplined. It is believed that the conflict between individualism and socialism is that between a man's lower animal nature and higher spiritual nature. This animal instinct of man leads him to the state of primitive barbarism, which is against the spiritual nature of man.

Individual's greatness in society: The great men of the world like Jesus Christ, Buddha, Mohammed Nabi, Guru Nanak, Swami Vivekananda, Mahatma Gandhi, Abraham Lincoln, Rousseau, Isaac Newton,

Albert Einstein, Marconi, Thomas Alva Edison, Michael Faraday, Mother Teresa and Abdul Kalam were great because they assimilated the rich legacy of their own country. They gave their individual self to make the society liveable and civilization progress. Thus, the contributions of great men were not isolated from the society. Their rich heritage of thoughts, wisdom and action were developed and preserved by others in society, which worked against some social background. From this fact, we discern that the very basis of their great contribution is social.

SOCIAL AIMS OF EDUCATION

The protagonists of social aim of education oppose the individual aim and advocate that the state or society is superior to the individual. Society is real, and the individual is only a means. So, the individual has to work for the welfare and prosperity of his society. They believe that man is a social being and he cannot live without a society. If he is cut off from the society, it will be very difficult for him to remain alive. This is because the society alone puts forth its own claim on education as the be-fall and end-all of educational activities. Herbert Spencer lays the foundation of sociological thinking in education by saying, "Complete living is the aim of education". This is a two-fold philosophy behind the sociological thinking in education.

- State or society is the source of all human values. The individual accepts the social ideas as his own, and
- The individual realises his best by being socialised.

Narrow and Wider Meaning of Social Aim

Narrow meaning of social aim: The extreme type of social aim of education is equated with state socialism. According to this concept, "the state is an idealised metaphysical entity over and above the individual citizen, superior to him in every way, transcending all his desires and aspirations". Here the liberty of the individual is totally curtailed and he is subordinated to the state by socialising all aspects of his individual life. This is because, society is the reality and the individual is nothing more than a throb in the pulse. The individuality of the individuals flows only from the society. Therefore no individual can dream of his individual identity and he must strive for the good of the society. The individual has to sacrifice everything, even his life, for the good and the welfare of the state. It means that he cannot have a wish of his own but live for the society. In short, Fascist says "Everything by the state, everything for the state and everything of the state". Hence, the state should frame the aim of education, construct curriculum, formulate teaching methods and textbooks in such a way to curb the sense of identity and individualism.

Historical evidence of social aim: The concept of individual subordination to the welfare of the state is not a new concept. Its traces are found in ancient Sparta, Greece, Germany, Italy and Roman Catholic doctrines.

Ancient sparta: Sparta is the most perfect example of a socialistic state where strict discipline was observed to control the sense of individualism. The state policy was "each man was born, not for himself, but for his country". As Sparta was surrounded by powerful neighbours, she had to prepare soldiers, for which military training was emphasised and individual freedom of thought and action was totally discouraged. The aim of whole education was an exercise of obedience to the state authority.

Nazi Germany: Germany is another example of the socialistic state. In 1806, Germany was defeated by Napoleon at Jena. Professor Fitche of Jena University remarked, "It is education alone, which can save us from all the evils by which we are oppressed". The social aim of education was seen in the educational system of Hitler. The German philosopher, Hegel, says, "An individual has no individuality of his own save what he derives from the state. The state is the real person the real entity which has will". The extreme slogan of social aim is (fascist army says), "Everything of the state, everything for the state and everything by the state". On the basis of this slogan, the system of German education was designed before the two World Wars to exalt statecraft and soldiery to produce a fascist army. T.P. Nunn remarks, "The state is conceived of an idealized metaphysical entity, over and above the individual citizens, superior to him in every way, transcending all his desires and aspirations. It is an embodiment of all reasons and justice". School to the University should be used as an instrument of engraining these notions into the soul of the pupils". An individual was expected to develop unquestioning loyalty and obedience to the Nazi party. The only aim of education was to achieve the goal of the state.

Fascist Italy: Italy also followed and developed the social aim of education against the democratic philosophy of education. It developed fascism and used the individual as means to achieve the ends of the state. Its aim of education was not to equalise educational opportunities but was the identification of the individual with the interest of the state.

Roman catholic doctrine: The Pope, the spiritual head of the Roman Catholic Church, claimed absolute loyalty, obedience and submission from the members of the Catholic Church. The Pope was the embodiment of power and authority. The aim of education was to make people subordinate to the church and develop loyalty and unquestionable obedience to the Pope.

Wider meaning of social aim: In the wider sense, social aim means making the individual socially efficient for a democratic society. The aim of education is to enable the individual develop himself fully to be compatible with the interests of the society. John Dewey and Bagley, the chief exponents of liberal social aim of education, believe that education should attempt to secure social efficiency by the positive use of individual power and capacities in social occupations. A socially efficient individual would be able to control his environment and earn his livelihood. Dewey says, "All education proceeds by the participation of the individual in the social consciousness of the race". Therefore, a truly educated man is he who is vocationally fit and independent, culturally refined and morally above an animal being."

John Dewey and Bagley think that the social aim of education means to bring about "social service" and "social efficiency". Professor Bagley in his book *Education Values* has mentioned three characteristics of a socially efficient individual, namely, (i) economic efficiency, (ii) negative morality and (iii) positive morality. Economic efficiency means ability to pull one's own weight in the economic life. Negative morality means unwillingness or reluctant to sacrifice one's own desire when their gratification would interfere with the economic efficiency of others. Positive morality means willingness to sacrifice one's own desire when their gratification would contribute directly or indirectly to social progress. A socially efficient individual is not a parasite on any member of the society but a good citizen to understand and appreciate the world. He is prepared to sacrifice his own desires if they are harmful to others. In short, a socially efficient individual is one who is physically strong, intellectually sharp, spiritually enlightened, culturally refined, vocationally self-sufficient and morally well-disciplined. Hence, education should be planned and organized in such a way so as to enable the individuals for achieving "Education for Citizenship", "Education for Social Service" and "Education for Social Efficiency".

VIEWS IN FAVOUR OF SOCIAL AIMS

Social nature of man: Man is born and brought up in the society. As a social being, he thinks of his own welfare and that of the society. He may have to sacrifice everything, even his life for the welfare and prosperity of the society in which he is a member.

Socialisation of individual: The individual is selfish in his infancy and childhood. He behaves like animals. When he grows, he acquires socialisation through his contact with family members, relatives, friends, neighbours, and people at large in the society. He satisfies his physical, psychological and social needs through socialisation in the company of his fellow beings. Social aim of education is essential for socialisation of the individuals.

Development of personality: The all-round development of the individual's personality is possible only in a social environment. Nunn, the supporter of individual aims, believes that individuality develops only in a social atmosphere where it can feed common interests and common activities. J. B. Baldwin says, "Personality cannot be expressed in any but social terms".

Peace, justice and security: Only a well-knit social organization can create the atmosphere of peace, justice and security. These are essentially needed for a good social life.

Salvation through social service: Some philosophers such as Swami Vivekananda and Mahatma Gandhi, have given great importance to social service in human life. They believe that service to mankind is service to God. Swami Vivekananda emphasises that we should see God in people. Service to mankind would unite us with God and help us to attain salvation.

VIEWS AGAINST SOCIAL AIMS

Like individual aim, social aim of education is also subjected to criticism for its extreme forms.

Un-psychological: Social aim is un-psychological as it neglects the individual differences of children. Without considering the capacities, interests and needs of the individuals, it prepares them to fulfil the needs and requirements of the society. As a result, the creative powers of the individuals are suppressed.

Individual-non-entity: Education for the personality development of the individual is neglected. Social aims leave no place for the individual personality to flourish. At the same time, it curbs the free and natural development of the individuality of the child. Education aims at the development of the whole man but the social aim totally neglects this aspect of education.

Hindrance to individual development: The social aim is against the individual aim in supporting freedom for the individual. As far as this aim is concerned there is no room for liberty and freedom for the child to express his personal views. Strict discipline leads the individual to revolt against the unreasonable dictates of the society.

Lack of development in arts and literature: The development of art and literature is possible only when the individual gets liberty and initiative. Only then, he can take efforts for this purpose. But this aim has no room for freedom and there is no scope for the development of any art or literature.

Encouragement of narrow nationalism: Social aim states that education is society-centred, and it develops narrow-mindedness. Literary education is confined to the praise of the nation and it prepares the people to sacrifice themselves for the sake of the society. It develops narrow-minded citizens who say, "My country—right or wrong" and encourages a frame of mind, which is dogmatic, unscientific and hence unprogressive.

Wrong use of educational agencies: Social aim considers that social goods are superior to the individual. Hence, all formal and non-formal agencies of education are exploited for the purpose of social development and the individual, together with his needs and requirements, is neglected.

Lack of intellectual and moral development: Social aim ignores the development of the individual. The desires and aspirations of the individual are oppressed. He has to work for the good of the state. Under this condition, intellectual and moral development of the individual becomes very difficult.

Individual-a tool of the government: The extreme notion of all powerful nations ignores the legitimate interests, desires and needs of the individual, and suppresses his creative powers. It uses education to make the individual only a tool of the government. The duty of the individual is to be obedient and loyal to it.

Harmful to democracy: This aim proves to be harmful in a democratic country like India. In fact, the ruling political party tries to interpret this aim in terms of its own ideology without caring for the sentiment of others. So, education becomes an instrument of struggle for political power. The result is that the interest of one particular group is considered to be superior even to the common good of all human beings. Thus, the sociological purpose of education is defeated.

One-sided education: Social aim insists on the development of citizenship qualities and social-efficiency only. There is no room for intellectual, physical, aesthetic, spiritual and artistic development of individuals. One-sided education will not bring about total personality development in the individual and it will stunt the growth and development in other aspects of human life.

SYNTHESIS BETWEEN INDIVIDUAL AND SOCIAL AIMS

From the given descriptions of the individual and social aims of education, we can discern their extreme forms that both the aims are one-sided, undesirable, and not conducive either to the individual development or to the development of the society. These two types of aims maybe opposed to each other if stretched out to their extreme forms. But if their sharp edges are rounded off, they become complementary in nature. The individual is essential to the society and the society is necessary to the individual. Development of the individual and the society is a cooperative process. The development of one leads to the development of each other. They are mutually supplementary, complementary and independent. In fact, neither the individual nor the society can exist without each other. In the words of John Adam, "Individuality requires a social medium to grow. Without social contacts we are not human".

An individual who is cut-off from all social obligations and deprived of all social life is like a bird without wings. A number of questions emerge in our minds when we analyse the individual and the society separately. They are: How can an individual earn his bread and fulfil other necessities of his life? With whom does he communicate? Who will give recognition to his achievements? Who will educate him? Where will he find a job? etc. Hence, an isolated individual is a dream, and a non-existing entity. On the other side, imagine a society without individuals who are responsible for pushing its wheel of progress forward. The society is insignificant and it is something which stands in the air in the absence of individuals. Social medium is necessary for the development and growth of the individual. Without social contacts we are not humans. In the same way, individuals are indispensable for the progress of the society. Since an individual is a part of the society and the society is made up of individuals, true aim of education cannot be other than the highest development of the individual as a member of the society. Socialisation and the development of individuality should go hand-in-hand in the process of education. In fact, neither can be fostered without the other. Individual and society are the two ends of life.

The nature of each child is both social and individual. He has got his own thoughts and aspirations but these are inspired by others. Individuality is not a private possession, but this is the means through which real good can enter the world. The good of all is the good of each. Therefore, instead of being regarded as isolated entities, the individual and the society should be considered as functionally related to each other. That is, the individual is acting on the society and the society is reacting on the individual. According to J.S. Ross, "There is always an interaction between the society and the individual. No individual can develop in a social vacuum. An individual can only develop in a progressive society and society can only make progress with developed individuals. This circle cannot be broken". Let the education burn the individual flame, feeding it with the oil of society, let the light of this flame illuminate the social horizon, shedding away all the prevailing darkness.

GENERAL AIMS OF EDUCATION

Education is a dynamic concept and a life-long process, which has multiple aims and activities. On the basis of changing values and ideals and ever-growing needs of the individual and the society, different philosophers, educationists and social reformers have formulated various aims of education.

Knowledge Aim

Socrates, Aristotle, Dante, Comenius, Francis Bacon and other philosophers have professed that knowledge is an important aim of education. Knowledge has been widely accepted as the aim of education since the time of sophists, in 400 BC. Knowledge gives power to the weaker intellect, and satisfies the hunger of the stronger intellect and gives harmony to the normal human curiosity. Intellectual training is a byproduct of gaining knowledge about all that concerns human life. Bacon and Comenius want, "all knowledge for all". Socrates says, "Knowledge is power by which things are done". He also says, "One who had true knowledge could not be other than virtuous". Cicero says, "As a field, however fertile, cannot be fruitful without cultivation, neither can a mind without learning".

Knowledge is for the sake of knowledge and that is the reason why common people receive education. The teacher imparts knowledge to children. Bookish knowledge is sought for and given a high priority in the society. In the wider sense, knowledge means *mental development*. It is the development of all mental powers namely, thinking, reasoning, discrimination, judgement and memory in a discipline. True knowledge cooperates with activity in making the life of an individual quite happy and successful.

Arguments in favour of knowledge aim: Some of the favourable arguments are as follows:

- Knowledge is an instrument of education. It is the medium of tripolar activity—the teacher, the pupil and the social environment.
- It helps the individual to attain peace, happiness and comfort which are essential for human development and progress.
- It enables the individual to succeed in material life.
- It helps the individual to control his thoughts, feelings and actions in a desirable way.
- It aids the individual to adjust with the varying environments.
- It increases the vocational efficiency in the individual.
- It is the basis for moral behaviour. From the teachings of great philosophers we find slogans such as "know thy-self", "knowledge is virtue", "ignorance is sin" and "knowledge is power".
- Mental development enables the individual to utilise his capacities and powers for his own development and the welfare of the society.
- It enables the society to grow by transmitting social and cultural heritages to the succeeding generation through education.
- It helps the individual to improve his standard of living and have a small size family.

Arguments against knowledge aim: Some of these argument are as follows:

- Lee Farrar says, "Knowledge without common sense is folly, without method, it is waste, without kindness it is fanaticism, without religion it is death. With common sense it is wisdom, with method it is power, with charity it is beneficence, with religion it is virtue and life and peace".
- It ignores the physical development of the individual. It is essential to lead a successful life. In fact, a sound mind lives in a sound body.
- Bookish knowledge helps the individual in passing examinations only.
- It does not develop the capacity to face the problems of life boldly.
- Mechanical superficial knowledge spoils books, methods and even examination. Adam says, "Schools are knowledge shops and the teachers are knowledge mongers".
- Knowledge may feed the intellect but will starve the soul.
- Knowledge aim emphasises the study of book materials rather than the child.
- Knowledge for the sake of knowledge becomes an end in itself. Professor Whitehead says, "A merely well informed person is the most useless bore on God's earth". Therefore, education should give knowledge to make the individuals socially efficient, economically competent and morally sound so that they may live a fuller and richer life.
- Mahatma Gandhi points out that "Man is neither mere intellect, nor the gross animal body, nor head nor soul alone. A proper and harmonious contribution of all the three is required for the making of the whole and constitutes the true economics of education".
- This aim makes the scope of education very narrow and limited.

Cultural Aim

Culture stands for something ripened and cultivated as against the raw, crude and unrefined nature of man. It means to cultivate, grow, develop and expand from a crude life into a beautiful and graceful human personality. E.B. Taylor defines culture as, "that complete whole which includes knowledge, belief, art, morals and laws, custom and any other capabilities and habits, acquired by man as a member of society". The earlier scholars emphasised the material aspect of culture representing the word civilisation. But the present trend is to emphasise the non-material aspects like moral habits, art, language, literature and religion which add dignity and grace to human life.

The word "culture" has been interpreted variously in different countries at different times. Some countries consider "culture" as synonymous with love for music, dancing, literature and refined social behaviour. Some regard smoking, drinking, gambling and free sex as items of culture. There are some countries where it is interpreted in terms of ways of living, varieties of entertainment, general behaviour and standard of fine arts in society. John Dewey says, "Education is the cultivation of powers which join freely and fully in shared or common activities". Thus, culture is a very broad term, which means the cultivation of the best that has been thought and said in the world since its creation. A cultured person is one whose personality is refined, whose aesthetic tastes are developed and one who lives a socially useful and desirable life. Human race has a rich heritage in the form of traditions, manners and customs, which is called **culture**. Our culture should be conserved, and transmitted to the next generation through formal, informal and non-formal education. Such activities bring the child towards a better and happier future. Cultural aim of education includes the inculcation of noble ideas, arts, language and literature, religion, attitudes and patterns of behaviour.

Arguments for cultural aim: Some of the favourable arguments of cultural aim of education are as follows:

- It helps us to know the cultural heritage of our past by which we can adorn our present life.
- It makes an individual well-versed in music, dancing and fine arts and helps him to spend his leisure in a profitable and appropriate way.
- It purifies and modifies the animal behaviour of the child and makes him a real human being in his conduct.
- It stimulates and develops the heart and the mind, and makes human life happy and joyful.
- Culture helps the individual to achieve harmonious adjustment with the environment.
- It trains the individual to be a cultured person, who gives up narrow ideas and selfish interests and becomes a person of high ideas and noble objectives.
- Culture satisfies men and women when they try to form better habits of thoughts and action, which helps in the establishment of a future society.

Arguments against cultural aim: These arguments are listed as follows:

- It can be good only at the time of peace, joy, economic prosperity, and social harmony. But when mankind is caught in poverty, unemployment, disease, loss and communal conflicts cultural education will be unprogressive.
- It may feed the upper class people and make them happy. But it will downgrade the common man who is busy in earning his livelihood.
- It is difficult to decide what should be included and emphasised in cultural education. This is because of the diversity in the cultural traditions of different people in the world, even so in our country. For instance, Western materialistic culture and Eastern spiritual culture can never go hand-in-hand. In India, the cultural traditions of Punjab are different from those of Bihar or Tamil Nadu. Now the question is, which of these two should education aim at? Or which of these cultural traditions should be preserved and promoted by education?
- It emphasises the glories of the old culture and values and ideals which are undesirable in modern society. The present generation is not interested in the old cultures and traditions.
- Some countries consider free mixing with the opposite sex, dancing, singing, smoking and gambling as culture. If they are emphasised and included in cultural aim of education, the entire society will face great harm and eventual decay and destruction.
- Cultural training is misused by persons who are in power as indoctri- nation, enforced discipline and other acts of chauvinism. The boys and girls indulge in aristocratic refineries and social mannerisms. This may lead to aversion for manual work and dignity of labour. This is one of the differences between a public school and a matriculation school.
- Too much love of one's culture creates a false sense of egoism, superiority complex and conflicting attitudes among children resulting in emotional disintegration and national discord.

Character-Building Aim

Character building is an ancient aim of Greek and Indian education. Plato, Herbert, Swami Vivekananda, Mahatma Gandhi, Dewey and Bertrand Russell have emphasised character building as an important aim of education. Plato remarks, "Nothing should be admitted in education which is not conducive to the promotion of character". The man-making aspect of education also reveals the underlying idea of character formation. Character building is the supreme aim of education, which determines the development of the individual as well as the society. That is why Swami Vivekananda says, "We want that education by which character is formed". Herbert remarks "The one and the whole work of education maybe summed up in the concept of morality". Gandhi observes, "The end of all knowledge must be building up of character".

"Character", in the ethical sense, is an inner consistency and unity which gives steadfastness and dependability to a man's conduct. Aristotle finds two tendencies in man. That is, the passionate and brutal tendency, and the intellectual and human tendency. By character education, Gandhi meant to develop courage, strength and virtue. The aim of character-building education consists in the conquest of higher intelligence over the lower impulses. Character has two facets—the one which is personal and the other which manifests itself in our relationship with society. It is the product of daily, hourly actions, words and thoughts, such as forgiveness, unselfishness, kindness, sympathies, charities, sacrifices for the good of others and struggles against temptation. Good acts and habits are the basis of good character which is the product of innate endowment, influence of environment and constant introspection. John Good Land has pleaded, "The central task of education for elementary school is to develop men of good will who do not cheat, or steal or kill; universal individual who value as one both self and mankind".

Mrs. Indira Gandhi, in her convocation address at Vishva Bharathi University in 1966 remarked, "Let us not measure the quality of our education by the statistics of pass, failure and wastage, however, important these figures may be as official records. The quality of education must be reflected in the quality of life, in its value and grace". R.W. Emerson has described the man of character as:

Not gold, but only men can make
A people great and strong—
Men who for truth and honour's sake
Stand first and suffer long
Brave men, who work while others sleep
Who dare while others fly
They build a nation's pillars deep,
And lift them to the sky

From these lines, we can conclude that money, power, cleverness is not necessary even health is not the one thing required but character alone is essential and education must develop it. John Dewey believes that "establishing of character is a comprehensive aim of school instruction and discipline".

Arguments for moral aim: The arguments in favour of moral aim are as follows:

- Ancient Indian and Greek idealists have emphasised the highest ideals such as truth, beauty and goodness for the formation of a good character.
- A man of good and strong character is respected by society.
- This aim saves humanity from conflicts, decay and destruction.
- Strength of good moral character enables the individual to achieve success in all fields of life.
- A strong character is an asset not only to its owner but also to the whole society. It purifies one's thoughts, words and deeds.
- A bad man's character is very pernicious (Kant).
- The teacher's concern is to cultivate, not the wealth of muscle, nor fullness of knowledge, nor refinement of feeling, but strength and purity of character. (T. Raymont).
- Education is the training of character to fit the students to participate creatively as citizens (Secondary Education Commission).
- This aim helps in nation building and national integration.
- The development of the individual as well as of the soceity depends upon moral ideals and values.

Arguments against moral aim: Some of these arguments are as follows:

- This aim does not prepare an individual to earn his livelihood.
- A man who possesses good character generally despises others as low and mean.
- Moralists and men of character are generally out of touch with real conditions of society and human life. They are labelled as ignorant and foolish.
- Formation of character is possible at the cost of suppressing the basic instincts. This may lead to the formation of mental complexes and strains.
- All individuals are not in favour of moral education.
- It emphasises the moral side and neglects the physical, mental, social, aesthetical and economic factors which are very essential for one's personality development.
- It is very difficult to interpret correctly the meaning of right character and wrong character. What is right for one person maybe wrong for another. Therefore, the teacher should inculcate in the child only those virtues, which are highly respected and valued by the society.

Spiritual Aim

The idealists regard that the only aim of education is to develop the spirituality of an individual. Spiritual aim of education has been emphasised in the ancient Indian philosophy. Great men like Buddha, Guru Nanak, Aurobindo, Swami Vivekananda, Tagore, Mahatma Gandhi, Dayanand, Kant, Burton, S. Radhakrishnan and Froebel advocate the spiritual aim of education. As a result, "Education for Spiritualism" has become an important slogan along with "Education for Vocation", "Education for Citizenship", "Education for Social Efficiency" and "Education for Democracy". Ancient Indian educators defined education as a means for spiritual development and salvation. Dr. S. Radhakrishnan says, "The aim of education is neither national efficiency nor world solidarity but making the individual feel that he has within himself some thing deeper than intellect, call it spirit, if you like" Kant is of the view that a life without religion is incomplete and so is morality. E.D. Burton says, "Religion and education are natural allies. Both recognize and have to do with spiritual as over against an exclusive attention to the physical and material. Both seek to emancipate man". The spiritual aim of education maybe summed up in the words of Finlay, who says, "Material progress is a good thing; social and political reforms are even more valuable, both to the race and the individual; their final worth lies in the aid they afford to spiritual life".

Arguments in favour of spiritual aim: These arguments are as follows:

- The spiritual aim of education saves the individual as well as the society from disaster, destruction, exploitation, selfishness, aggression and hatred.
- It enables the individual to lead a holy, peaceful and happy life.
- It fosters love, kindness, sympathy, compassion and affection, which strengthen human relationship.
- It helps the individuals to shun evil, corruption and greed.
- It makes a real and a cultured man.
- Knowledge alone can never produce a moral code of living, nor ensure salvation for mankind.
- Education must have five principal aspects related to five principal activities of human being namely, the physical, the vital, the mental, the psychic and the spiritual, in order to make it a complete process.

Arguments against spiritual aim: Some of these arguments are as follows:

- Spiritual or religious education leads to an attitude of escapism, renunciation of the world and absolute inaction.
- Theoretical knowledge of spiritual values such as truth, ahimsa, love and compassion is not enough, because a practical approach is healthier than a theoretical one.
- The existence of different religions with different ideals and beliefs confuses the individual.
- Too much emphasis on spiritual education may lead to communal riots which may affect the development and progress of the individual and the society.
- It will lead to the division of society on the basis of religion.
- This aim of education is not suitable for an underdeveloped country where common man is busy in earning his livelihood.
- It is also not desirable in a multireligious country where the development of secularism is more important for social progress and national integration.

Vocational Aim

The individual life as well as the social life was very simple in the past. This is because the son usually adopted the vocation of his father without any specialised training from outside home. But, with the great advancements in the field of science technology and industrialisation, parents are too busy in offices, fields, factories or institutions to find any time to impart the necessary education and training to their children in the vocation. Thus, earning a livelihood has become difficult in the modern world. That is why some educationists such as Mahatma Gandhi and John Dewey emphasise that the aim of education should be vocational. It means that education should help an individual to earn his livelihood. They stress that education should be utilitarian rather than ornamental. Therefore, we may say that, "Education is anything by which the individual should be prepared and developed to under take any sort of task for the fulfillment of his basic necessities of life". In fact, parents send their children to schools so that they receive education, which enable them to earn their livelihood.

Education will become useless if it makes the individual a parasite on others even for the fulfilment of his basic needs of life. Hence, the chief aim of education should be to provide vocational education to each child, so that, he is able to solve his economic problems without any difficulty. Thus, education is a means for economic satisfaction and a happy life. Vocational aim in education is derived from sociological approach to education. In fact, the present trend lays much emphasis on social efficiency through vocational efficiency. So, the knowledge gained must be functional and applicable to the problems of the individual and social life. In the words of John Dewey, "Education with vocational aim will balance the distinctive capacity of the individual with social service". Since vocational aim of education emphasises the problems of earning for the fulfillment of economic needs of the individual, we may call this aim as *Bread and Butter Aim, Blue Jacket Aim* and *White Collar Aim.*

Arguments in favour of vocational aim: Some of these arguments are as follows:

- Vocational aim of education makes the individual self-sufficient. Self sufficiency is a great source of satisfaction, self-confidence, mental freedom and moral strength. Economic efficiency is the first characteristic of social efficiency. A satisfied person can spread satisfaction in society. Plato says, "It is the business of education to discover what each person is good at and to train him in the mastery of that mode of excellence because such development secures the fulfilment of social needs in the most harmonious way".

- Vocational education strikes a balance between economic and industrial progress. It prepares students for a useful life and useful occupation. In the words of Mahatma Gandhi, "True education ought to be a kind of insurance against unemployment".
- Vocational aim of education reduces emphasis on verbalism and mere intellectual domination. For instance, Mahatma Gandhi introduced basic education. Pestalozzi, Froebel, Rousseau, John Dewey and modern progressive educationists advocate vocational education to increase the productive, technical and vocational efficiency of the students.
- This aim makes education a purposeful activity. A child learns efficiently when he is engaged in a purposeful activity. All purposeful activities lead to efficiency and help to achieve practical skills. Mahatma Gandhi says, "It is utterly a false idea that intelligence can be developed only through book learning. In fact, the quickest development of the mind takes place if manual work is made the intellectual means of training". The Indian Education commission is in favour of introducing work experience in all schools.
- Vocational education is suitable for children with lower intelligence. In fact, children who face difficulty in receiving academic education can learn more intelligently through vocational education and training.
- Vocational aim in education bridges the gulf between the upper class and the lower class by providing equal vocational education in the centres of learning.
- It results in the creation of engineers, scientists, industrialists, technologists, doctors and nurses, who are the backbone of the economic development of a country.
- Vocational education provides the individual with social status and social prestige.
- It helps the individual to eradicate illiteracy, ignorance, superstition, dependency and poverty.
- All advanced countries such as America, Germany, Japan, England and France emphasise vocational aim of education. In these countries, vocational guidance and training are provided to the school children. This is very essential for the socio-economic development of a country.

Arguments against vocational aim: These arguments are as follows:

- It does not meet all the requirements of human life. Man does not live by bread alone. He has to develop physically, socially, intellectually, morally and spiritually. Therefore, vocational aim is not a complete aim of education.
- Vocational education makes our outlook narrow. It may produce good doctors, scientists, mechanics, electricians, engineers but not necessarily good men.
- Vocational aim may not provide peace and happiness to the individual.
- It may lead to conflicts, jealousies and competitions in the capitalist society.
- The education is illiberal which aims at the acquisition of wealth or bodily strength apart from intelligence and justice. In fact, mere vocational education will not make an individual a true human being full of moral, spiritual and social qualities. He maybe a good doctor or nurse or engineer but he may not be a good human being because he lacks moral and social qualities. Therefore, vocational aim of education is also one-sided, which does not bring about total personality development in the individual.

Harmonious Development Aim

The child is naturally blessed with a number of powers and capabilities. Development of all these powers of the child should be harmonious in order to produce a well-balanced personality. So, developing one or two powers at the expense of other's capacities is undesirable and it may become a cause for maladjustment in society. As a consequence, a number of modern educationists support the idea of all-round harmonious development of personality as the true aim of education. Rousseau, Pestalozzi and Mahatma Gandhi have emphasised this aim of education. This aim is based on the psychological foundations which assert that each child is born with some innate tendencies, aptitudes and capacities. By harmonious development aim of education, we mean that all aspects of the child's personality namely physical, mental, emotional, spiritual, social, moral and aesthetic should be developed harmoniously. Pestalozzi, the greatest champion of the harmonious development aim, says "The sole aim of education is the harmonious development of the faculties and disposition which make up personality". He emphasises the development of 3 H's—head, heart and hand—as the essence of all the educational activities. In the words of Pestalozzi, "Education is the natural, harmonious and progressive development of man's innate powers". Mahatma Gandhi has also the same view, and he says, "By education, I mean, an all round drawing out of the best in child and man—body mind and spirit". According to him development of physical, intellectual and spiritual side of an individual's personality constitutes the meaning of true education. Rousseau, another supporter of this aim, says, "The spontaneous development of our organs and faculties constitutes the education of nature". Now this aim of education has been widely accepted by all.

Arguments in favour of development aim: Some of the favourable arguments are as follows:

- This aim is entirely based on the psychological foundations.
- It removes one-sidedness of education and pays attention to all the aspects of development.
- It brings about a harmonious personality development by developing all the innate tendencies of the child in a balanced way.
- This aim broadens the nature of curriculum and includes almost all the aspects which develop the personality harmoniously.
- The curriculum based on this aim includes subjects which are important, useful and relevant for bringing about a harmonius development in the child.
- It enables the child to adjust with the varying environments.
- It promotes a spirit of social service and a feeling for the welfare of the society and national integration and development.
- Secondary Education Commission remarks, "No education is worth the name which does not inculcate the qualities necessary for living graciously, harmoniously and efficiently with one's fellow men".
- Mahatma Gandhi says, "A proper and harmonious combination of body, mind and spirit is required for making the whole man and constitutes the true economics of education".
- Painter says, "The end of education is complete human development".

Arguments against development aim: These arguments are as follows:

- The term "harmonious" is vague. What standard of development of various capacities would be ideally harmonious? No standard criteria are available to measure whether the harmonious development of an individual has been achieved or not? Is it the maximum development of the full faculties of man? No individual is master of all trades. Hence, this aim is not clear and definite.
- We are living in an age of specialisation. So, the individuals have to be allowed to develop the best in them for which they are best suited.
- It is psychologically unsound. In fact, harmonious development of all individuals is impossible as each child has his own distinct innate tendencies.

- This is practically impossible because a country cannot provide all sorts of education and training to all children in all fields.
- It creates educational limitations by putting equal stress on physical, mental, emotional, spiritual, moral and aesthetic aspects of the child. If so, what type of curriculum is needed? How much weightage on each subject is to be given? How is the whole scheme (development of head, heart and hand) to be put through?
- It enables the child to achieve a little knowledge about any subject but it cannot make him master in all.
- The true meaning of harmonious development does not consist in making an athlete-cum-scholar-cum-artist-cum-saint-cum-everything. The true meaning lies in the development of that aspect or specific ability, whether artistic or scientific which is more powerful than others, to the fullest extent.

Citizenship Aim

Socialists, scholars, and educationists have laid great emphasis on training for citizenship as an aim of education. They believe that creation of true, honest and dynamic citizens is most essential for the development of a democratic country. Good and dynamic citizens should have mental, moral and social qualities, which strengthen democracy. Therefore, education should be constructed in such a way that it should develop these qualities in each child according to his inclinations, aptitudes and capacities. Such education enables the individual to grasp the problems of society with a clear understanding of his duties and responsibilities. In fact, a fully developed individual will be a really dynamic, resourceful, enterprising and responsible citizen. Hence, citizenship aim of education has been emphasised in almost all democratic countries in the modern age. In the words of Horne, "Citizenship is man's place in the state".

Argument for citizenship aim: Some of the arguments in favour of citizenship aim are as follows:

- Education prepares the individual to discharge his duties, amicably, honestly and fruitfully.
- It develops the individual for the meaningful participation in social and political life.
- Democracy is a way of life. So, all must know this way of living.
- Education for citizenship gives full knowledge to the individual to be aware of the political and social process.
- It develops a useful character, which is essential for democratic living.
- Success of democracy depends on the citizenship aims of education.
- It impresses on the child the value of having organized relations with his fellow citizens.

Argument against citizenship aim: These arguments are as follows:

- It leads to narrow nationalism or chauvinism.
- It does not help the individual to be self-sufficient.
- This aim of education has no value in the scientific world.

Complete Living Aim

Herbert Spencer, an eminent educationist and philosopher of the nineteenth century, has expounded "complete living" as the true aim of education. He is a social philosopher and he tries to make educational aims concrete and utilitarian. In fact, he wants that education should enable an individual to face all problems in life. He arranges the aims of complete living in the order of their survival value to the individual and to the society. Education must strive to achieve the following survival values in order to fulfil the aim of complete living:

- Teach the art of self-preservation.
- Teach one how to earn one's living and secure the necessities of life.
- Prepare the pupils to perform social and political responsibilities.
- Impart knowledge about bearing and rearing children who carry the message of the previous generation.
- Prepare one to utilise one's leisure by enjoying the refinements of culture, art, literature and the like.

Herbert Spencer has divided human activities into five categories according to their value and importance (Table 3.1).

TABLE 3.1 Human Activities and Subjects.

Activities	Subjects
Self-preservation	(a) Physiology (b) Hygiene (c) Physics and Chemistry
Prepare to earn a living	(a) Mathematics (b) Biology (c) Sociology and Physics
Bearing and rearing child	(a) Physiology (b) Domestic Science and (c) Psychology
Perform social and political activities	(a) History (b) Politics and (c) Economics
Prepare to use leisure life with	(a) Art (b) Music (c) Poetry taste and feeling

Arguments for complete living aim: Some of the arguments in favour of complete living aim are as follows:

- It is not one-sided and narrow like the other aims of education.
- It brings about an overall personality development.
- It prepares the individual to face all the eventualities of life.
- It emphasises science, cooperation, social, political and utilitarian aspect for social progress.
- It emphasises the fulfilment of all the needs of life.

Argument against complete living aim: These arguments are as follows:

- There is no place for religious, moral and spiritual education.
- Full attention to be given to physical and mental development
- The life after death has not been considered.
- It is un-psychological, because it prescribes the same curriculum for all children, irrespective of their nature, aptitudes and capacities.
- It prepares the child for adult life. Rousseau remarked, "What are we to think of that barbarous education which sacrifices the present to future".
- Physical and material sciences are difficult for children to learn at an early stage.
- The static aim of education is useless in a dynamic society.

Physical Development Aim

Some educationists have laid stress upon the development of the body. They believe in "sound mind in a sound body". So, they insist on physical development as an important aim of education. This aim of education has been emphasised since the ancient age in many countries. Sparta, in ancient Greece, gave top priority to this aim in its educational system. Plato stressed on this aim in his scheme of education. Rousseau also emphasised the importance of physical development and he insisted on free physical drills, sports and outdoor activities. In the words of Rabelais, "Without health life is not life, It is only a state of languor and suffering, an image of death". According to this statement, education should develop sound and handsome physique of all children".

Arguments for physical development aim: These arguments are as follows:

- Physical robustness keeps an individual fit, to achieve a joyful life.
- Physically strong citizens make their country strong.
- This aim is based on "sound mind in sound body".
- Dr. Johnson says, "To preserve health is a moral and religious duty, for health is the basis of all social virtues".
- Swami Vivekananda says, "Physical and mental development of the child promotes national growth and a fearless and physically well developed citizens of tomorrow". He remarks that power is life, weakness is death and he advocates football playing, in place of the Bhagavad-Gita, for the child.
- Rousseau says that a feeble body makes a feeble mind and all wickedness comes from weakness.

Arguments against physical development aims: Some of these arguments are as follows:

- Mere physical development is not enough to achieve the all-round development of the child.
- Physical development leads to the neglect of mental development.
- This aim makes education narrow and limited.
- Physical development makes the individual proud and tyrannical.
- Modern psychologists prove that a sound mind infuses health and zest in the body.
- There is no place for moral, social and spiritual education.
- This aim will enable the individual to mar himself and the society by indulging in characterless action.

Leisure Utilisation Aim

In modern times, leisure utilisation is considered as one of the aims of education. This is because science and technology have brought out so many efficient inventions and varieties of time-saving gadgets so that an individual finishes his daily work in a very short time and gets a lot of leisure time. Now the problem is what does an individual do with his leisure time? For answering the question, some educationists advocate leisure utilisation as an aim of education. It enables the individual to spend his leisure time fruitfully. Ranganath remarks, "Leisure is, time that unoccupied with work forced by physical, economic, hygienic and spiritual necessities". Utilisation of the leisure time, becomes a concern and an all-encompassing obsession.

Arguments for leisure utilisation aim: Some of the arguments in favour of this aim are as follows:

- Prepares children for creative activities by which they learn efficiently.
- Increases intellectual development.
- Helps the individual to utilise his leisure usefully.
- Prevents the individual from wasteful and harmful activities.
- Makes human life very peaceful and joyful.
- Develops emotional and artistic faculties in the child.
- Promotes the habits of distance learning in the individual.

Arguments against leisure utilisation aim: These arguments are as follows:

- It enables the individual to make the best use of leisure time alone. But he cannot use this aim to solve the problems of life.
- It is not suitable for many people who live in industrial countries where they find no leisure time.
- It is useful for a few people who are well-settled in life.
- This is not a regulated education and there is no room for an all-round personality development.
- This is not suitable in a democratic, under-developed country such as India where the masses are occupied and worried about their livelihood.
- It does not improve the work efficiency of an individual.
- People who are interested in art, music, poetry, and education can make use of their leisure for which this aim of education is not necessary to be considered.

Adjustment Aim

Man is a social being and he cannot live as a recluse. Therefore, he is always engaged in a struggle with his environmental conditions or surrounding situations of nature and society. For this reason, some educationists emphasise adjustment aim as an important aim of education. They believe that this aim of education inculcates capacity in the individual to adjust himself to the ever-changing environment. In fact, we can conclude that education is anything by which the individual is prepared and developed to undertake any sort of task and trained to adjust with the varying environment for attaining the purpose of his life. The individual who is unable to adjust with the environment would decay and disappear.

Arguments for adjustment aim: The arguments in favour of this aim are as follows:

- It develops the capacity in the individual to adjust with the varying environments.
- Adjustment promotes human survival and development.
- Maladjustment with the environment mars one's life.
- A socially adjustable person generally will have the spirit of social service.
- This aim of education is essential for the progress of a country.

Arguments against adjustment aim: Some of these arguments are as follows:

- It makes the scope of education very narrow and limited.
- The only purpose of education is not just to develop the capacity for adjustment.
- It does not fulfil all the requirements of the individual and the society.
- It is difficult to develop the adjustable qualities among the people of different characters and economic status.
- It is not applicable to human life which has love, pity, compassion and sacrifice.

Self-expression Aim

Individualists advocate self-expression as the aim of education. It signifies free and natural development according to one's interests, inherent tendencies and capacities. Froebel believes that abilities of man remain dormant in the child and it is the function of education to arouse and express them. He says, "Education is the process by which the child brings forth his internal potentialities". Man is creative in nature. His geniuses, hopes, desires, aspirations, pattern of outlook and thought can be understood only through his expression. His emotions are revealed through his activities. Hence, modern educationists give attention to the self-expression of the pupil through the medium of his free activity. In order to bring about the inner capacities of the pupil, the function of education must be aimed at giving expression to those activities which help the pupil to realise himself. For this, the pupil should have both freedom of body and freedom of mind.

Arguments for self-expression aim: Some of the arguments in favour of this aim are as follows:

- Self-expression is the inborn instinct of a child.
- It is psychologically sound. It helps the child to develop his basic instincts.
- Suppression of instincts is harmful and leads to mental disorders.
- Self-expression bestows peace, happiness and bliss to the individual.
- It enables the child to develop his personality.

Arguments against self-expression aim: These arguments are as follows:

- Self-expression cannot be taken as the only aim of education.
- Neither the individual nor the society wants everything to be expressed.
- Sorakin proves that the number of mental patients has increased by 45% in countries where sex freedom has been allowed.
- It is against social discipline and decorum. Raymont says, "Free self-expression is bound, in the long run, to defeat its own purpose".
- It destroys the rights of others. As Pinckard says, "True liberty consists in the privilege of enjoying our own rights, not in the destruction of the rights of others".
- The basic instincts of a child are animal in nature. Free expression is the license for the child to behave as an animal.
- This aim of education is very narrow and limited.

Self-realisation Aim

Educationists who are in favour of idealistic philosophy have emphasised self-realisation as the main aim of education. Self-realisation means to understand nature, human beings, God and their relationship. Aim of self-realisation means to provide the actual form to the highest potentialities and powers of the spirit. Self-realisation enables the child to realise his real being in the earth. Thus, the aim of education is self-realisation associated with idealism. Swami Vivekananda remarks, "Education is the realization of divine perfection already existing in man". Sankaracharya observes, "Education is the realization of the self". In the words of James S. Ross, "The aim of education is to enable man to become his truest self". In fact, they advocate this aim of education so as to inculcate high moral qualities and spiritual ideas in the child.

Arguments for self-realisation aim: Some of these arguments in favour of this aim are as follows:

- Self-realisation brings happiness, peace and bliss in human life.
- It helps to purify, mould and sublimate the basic instincts.
- It develops high moral qualities and spiritual ideas in child.
- It helps the child to transform himself from his animal instincts.
- It elevates the individual as well as the society to a higher level of glory.
- It brings about physical, mental, moral, social and spiritual development in the child's personality.
- It promotes perfection of individuality.

Arguments against self-realisation aim: These arguments are as follows:

- It gives too much emphasis on the religious aspect of life.
- It ignores the practical aspect of life completely.
- It makes education remain incomplete because it does not prepare the child for a better life.
- There is no place for physical development and vocational efficiency.
- It is also one-sided, narrow and limited.

CHANGING AIMS OF EDUCATION IN INDIA

India has been famous for its philosophy and education. Indian philosophies play a vital role in influencing the aims of education. In fact, we have different aims of education in ancient, medieval and British periods. This is the outcome of the impact of different philosophies on education. It will be useful to have a cursory glance at the aims of education in both ancient and modern India. Ancient period included Vedic, Brahmanic and Buddhist periods.

Aims of Education in Vedic Period (Birth of Indian Civilization to 1400 BC)

India was predominantly a land of religion. Hence, religion had a great impact on all the aspects of life. It was an integral part of man's life from his birth to death. It was closely associated with education through which moral, spiritual and religious values were inculcated in the child. Dr. Altekar says, "The objective of education in Vedic period was worship of God, a feeling for religious formation of character, fulfilment of public and civic duties, an increase in the social efficiency or skill and the protection and propagation of national culture".

Physical development: It was believed by the Vedic people that a strong body had a strong mind. They realised that a strong body was necessary in religious and worldly life. A student remained a Brahmachari upto the age of twenty five and lead a very disciplined life.

Mental development: The physical development was followed by intellectual development. Possession of knowledge was considered absolutely necessary. Therefore, knowledge of the four Vedas—Rig Veda, Sama Veda, Yajur Veda and Athar Veda was emphasised.

Moral and spiritual development: Vedic education emphasised the development of moral and spiritual faculties in man. Before starting education, the child had to fast for purity, reciting regular prayers in the morning and evening. Various religious festivals were observed in the homes and ashrams which infused in children a spirit of piety and religion.

Inculcation of civic and social duties: Vedic people believed that an educated person should perform his duties in different domains of life cooperatively, creatively and enthusiastically. For this, the child was taught to become social-minded and devoted to social service giving up selfishness and narrow-mindedness. A sense of duty towards family members relatives, friends and people at large was also promoted in children.

Sublimation of basic instincts: Man is basically instinctive by nature. He is a slave of instincts, which are embedded in his psyche and when he is obsessed by his senses, he adopts a wrong path. Education aims at sublimating these instinctive tendencies in order to control over materialistic tendencies and centre them upon the spiritual world.

Character formation: Indian philosophers believed that the inculcation of moral qualities was essential to form a strong character. Therefore, education aimed at developing the values of self-restraint, self-confidence, discipline, sympathy, cooperation and love through religious discourses of gurus and saints.

Promotion of social efficiency: Vocational and technical education was imparted to children to make them socially useful. Brahamans and Kshatrias performed the duties of the rulers. Shudras worked as philosophers for the upliftment of the society. Common man carried on his family vocation. It led to the general progress and happiness of society and there was no problem of unemployment.

Cultural preservation: Aim of Vedic education was to preserve and propagate the cultural heritage. In those days knowledge and skills were transmitted to the succeeding generation through the medium of schools known as gurukuls. Dr. Altekar says, "Education is the chief means of social and cultural continuity and it will fail, in its purpose if it did not teach the rising generation to accept and maintain the best traditions of thought and action and transmit their heritage of the past to the future generation".

Emphasis upon knowledge and experience: Dr. R.K. Mukerjee, opines that the aim of education was not merely reading but the subjective assimilation of knowledge and experience. Students displayed their knowledge obtained through discussions conducted in a concourse of scholars in gurukuls.

Immediate and ultimate aim: The most immediate aim of ancient education was to prepare the people of different castes for their actual needs of life. On the other hand, the ultimate aim was the preparation for life in this world and beyond it.

Aims of Education in Brahmanic Period (1400 BC—600 BC)

Self-control: Brahmanic education aimed at giving practice to the students the control over their senses in order to have simple living and high thinking. Self-control was essential to achieve success in social and moral life.

Character development: Brahmans believed that the right behaviour or morality was the highest Dharma. So, Brahmanic education aimed at developing moral virtues such as honesty, loyalty, tolerance, fellow-feeling, truthfulness, justice, sincerity, self-control and temperance in the child for promoting social efficiency.

Personality development: Brahmanic education advocated an all-round development of a child's personality. Hence, education aimed at physical, mental, social, emotional, moral and religious development. Attempts were also made to develop self-confidence, self-restraint, discrimination and judgement so as to bring out total personality development in the child.

Generation of social awareness: Brahmanic education aimed at generating sociability or social awareness by developing socially efficient individuals— who were ready to sacrifice their own desire if it was harmful to others or social progress.

Preservation of knowledge and culture: Brahmans regarded education as the most potent means to preserve and transmit their culture to the rising generation. Hence, Brahmanic education aimed at preserving and transmitting knowledge, belief, art, morals, law and custom to the succeeding generation.

Inculcation of civic and social duties: Like Vedic education, Brahmanic education emphasised the inculcation of civic and social duties as an aim of education. It prepared the child to give up selfishness and narrow-mindedness and to become social-minded to discharge civic and social duties.

Infusion of piety and religiousness: According to B.D. Bhatia, "The study of Vedas and moral development had been the dominated aims in the Brahmanic system of education. Education was regarded as a means of inculcating such moral habits as strict obedience to elders, truthfulness, honesty and temperance". Thus, Brahmanic education stood in favour of infusing piety and religiousness among the students.

World brotherhood: Brahmanic education aimed at developing a worldly brotherhood by preparing the ideas of love, truth, non-violence, peace and welfare of humanity.

Preparation for life: The aim of Brahmanic education was to prepare the child for existence, that is, enabling the child to live.

Propagation of purity: Brahmans considered education as the best of all divine gifts. To attain salvation, purity was propagated by education. Thus, propagation of purity became an important aim of Brahmanic education.

Aims of Education in Buddhist Period (500 BC)

Professor B.D. Bhatia says, "Buddhistic education was primarily monastic in its own outlook and contents. It aimed at the religious development of the individual". The aim of Buddhist education was based on idealistic point of view. The Buddhist philosophy had shown a way of purging sorrow, which was called the **way of Nirvana**. Buddhism popularised the way of Nirvana in the Eightfold path. The Eightfold path leads to a good, pure, pious and noble life. Education helps to follow eight paths by which Nirvana can be achieved.

Samma dithi (right knowledge): The first aim of Buddhist education was to provide man with the right knowledge. True knowledge helped man to perceive the real world.

Samma sankalp (right intention or right will): Right knowledge did not end the suffering, unless man led a life in accordance with knowledge. So, man should be determined to give up hatred, indulgence in sensuous objects and stop being involved in any kind of violence. In this way, the aim of Buddhist education was to develop the right intentions or will in man.

Samma vacha (right speech): The aim of Buddhist education was to enable man to have control over his speech. He should avoid unpleasant and foul language and should not speak ill of others.

Samma kamant (right conduct): Buddhist education aimed at controlling actions of man and doing good to others. Education should develop the right conduct which comprised non-violence, truth, non-stealing and control over senses.

Samma aieet (right living or vocation): Buddhism advocated right living by adopting the right vocation depending on one's own interests, disposition and skills. He should never deviate from discharging his duties which he had chosen. Thus, aim of Buddhist education was to prepare a person to feed himself and his family.

Samma vyayam (right effort or exercise): In fact, a person might deviate from his right path of life, despite having the right knowledge, because of basic instincts or as a result of past experience. Therefore, Buddhist education aims at preaching the right knowledge and right will.

Samma sati (right mindedness or memory): The aim of Buddhist education was to make a person recall what he had learnt so that he would not relapse into ignorance again. Even right knowledge would fade away if not recalled from time-to-time.

Samma samadhi (right meditation or concentration): After developing the given mentioned paths of Nirvana, a person is qualified to enter into the state of right meditation to attain Nirvana, the ultimate goal of human life. In short, Buddhist education aimed at preparing a person for right meditation to attain Nirvana.

Moral development: Buddhist education aimed at moral and spiritual development of the individual. The pupils were taught to lead a life according to the Eightfold code of conduct. Satya and Ahimsa were the directive principles of Buddhist education.

Transmission of culture: Conservation and transmission of the Buddhist philosophy and Indian cultural heritage was the important aim of education. The "Bhikshus" studied the Buddhist philosophy and practised the same in their lives, and taught it to others.

AIMS OF EDUCATION IN MEDIEVAL INDIA

Aims of education in the medieval period were entirely different from those of ancient times. Medieval period comprises Muslim and British periods.

Aims of Education in Muslim Period

Propagation of Islam: The spread of Islam was regarded as a religious and sacred duty. So, the first aim of Islamic education was to propagate Islamic religion in India. To attain this aim, 'Maktabs' and 'Madarsas' were established at different places where 'Quran', Islamic history and rituals were taught in order to impart Islamic knowledge.

Spread of knowledge: Muslim theologians believed that Nijat (Salvation) could be achieved through education. Hence, the aim of Islamic education was to impart Islamic ideas and values of life.

Extension of islamic kingdom: Muslim rulers wanted to extend their empire, language, caste, religion and culture in our country. Therefore, Islamic education aimed at imparting the Muslim children the art of warfare (diplomacy) to extend the Islamic kingdom.

Development of morality: The aim of Islamic education was to develop a particular type of morality based on Islamic doctrines. Muslim children were taught religious books, ideals of morality and how to live a pious life.

Formation of character: Hazrat Mohammed believed that man could prosper only by his good character for which appropriate type of education was a must, because Islamic tenets say that a man with a poor character would be burnt in the hell fire.

Propagation of shariyat: Shariyat means a code of Islamic laws and rules of conduct to be followed by Muslims. The aim of Islamic education was to propagate the Shariyat to children, kings, officers and common people.

Preparation for material well-being: Islamic education also aimed at preparing the people for material life. Muslim youth were given training in several practical arts and skill, and vocational education to promote their material and moral welfare.

Aims of Education During British Rule

The British system of education was based on politics. In the words of Lord Macaulay, "Education was meant to develop a class of persons, Indians in blood and colour, but English in taste, in opinion, in morals and in intellect".

Spread English education: According to Macaulay, the chief aim of education was to spread English education through English as the medium of instruction.

Consolidation of British empire: The British system of education aimed at consolidating the British Empire with a view to strengthen the British rulers in India.

Recruitment of clerks: The aim of British education was to recruit cheap clerks to run their offices. The British rulers taught the native Indians in order to use them as clerks in English offices.

Propagation of English culture: British rulers established schools for Indian children where English was the medium of instruction. In this way British education aimed at spreading English culture and ways of the living in the minds of the upper class Indians.

Propagating craze for English articles: Through the English medium of education, British the developed a craze for English books, English literature, English clothes and English articles for daily use. Thus, British education aimed at creating an appetite for English materials in the school children.

Preparation of interpreters: The aim of British education was to prepare a class of Indians who could interpret English laws for courts in India.

Translation of Indian literature: British rulers wanted to get the Indian religious books and important literature translated into English. Thus, the aim of British system of education was to produce the translators so that they could enjoy the beauty of our literature.

Aims of Education in Modern India

India became an independent country on August 15, 1947. At that time, she (India) had about 85% of illiterate people. Therefore, the government of India appointed three commissions under the chairmanship of Dr. S. Radhakrishnan, Dr. A. Lakshman Swami Mudaliar and Dr. S. Kothari to bring about quantitative as well as qualitative improvements in education. Pandit Jawaharlal Nehru stressed on education to make the foundation of the country strong. He said, "Great changes which have taken place in the educational system must be in keeping with them. The entire basis of education must be revolutionised".

Aims of Education: University Education Commission (1948–1949)

Dr. S. Radhakrishnan examined the prevalent situation of education and recommended some aims of education to modify our educational system. They are as follows:

- Development of leadership
- Preservation and transfer of culture
- Vocational education
- Human and spiritual training
- Development of democratic qualities
- Development of international understanding
- Development of character
- Social development

Aims of Education: Secondary Education Commission (1952–1953)

Dr. A Lakshman Swami Mudaliar, the then Vice-Chancellor of Madras University in 1952, studied very deeply the educational problems of that time and presented some aims of secondary education in 1953.

Development of democratic citizenship: The most important aim of secondary education is the development of qualities of democratic citizenship among the children. In fact, the success of the democracy and the progress of the country depend on the citizens of the country. Therefore, the aim of secondary education is to develop the democratic values such as discipline, co-operation, sympathy, equality and tolerance in the child.

Improvement of vocational efficiency: The secondary schools emphasise crafts and productive work which are needed for economic development. Therefore, education aims at providing the child agricultural, technical and commercial courses to increase his vocational efficiency.

Development of personality: The secondary education commission realised the importance of mental development along with the physical, moral, social and spiritual development of the individual. So, the secondary education aims at bringing out balanced development through co-curricular activities such as, art, craft, music, dancing and similar hobbies.

Development of patriotism and international understanding: The aim of education is to develop the feeling of patriotism among the students by preparing them to sacrifice their interests for the sake of the country. They should also be taught to inculcate international understanding in them, as they are members of the entire world.

Development of leadership: The aim of secondary education is to train the youth to develop their leadership qualities in the social, political, religious, industrial and cultural fields.

Aims of Education: Indian Education Commission (1964–1966)

The educationists of our country were appointed as the members of the commission under the chairmanship of Dr. Daulat Singh Kothari. About this commission Dr. S. Radhakrishnan says, "It is my earnest desire that the commission should survey all aspects of educational system at all levels and impart suggestions that may help the educational system in progressing at all levels". The Kothari Commission is a landmark in the history of Indian education. It aims at surveying the entire field of education and suggesting for its reconstruction according to our national goals. It states, "No reform is more urgent than to transform education to endeavour to relate it to the life needs and aspirations of the people and thereby make it a powerful instrument of social, economic, and cultural transformation, necessary for the realization of our national goals". For this purpose, the commission suggested the following aims of education:

Increasing productivity: This commission aims at making education related with productivity to increase national income through science education, work experience, vocationalisation and application of science in productive process.

Achieving social and national integration: India is a land of diverse social groups. Therefore, the aim of achieving social and national integration is very essential. This aim can be achieved by various programmes or steps through education such as: (a) common school systems; (b) social and national services; (c) appropriate language policy; and (d) promotion of national consciousness. (For details refer to Unit VI, Indian Education Commission, National Objectives of Education) (pp. 786–799).

Accelerating the process of modernisation: The present century has seen great advancement in scientific and technical knowledge as a result of knowledge exploration. This needs a radical change in the educational system not with imparting of knowledge but with the awakening of curiosity, the development of proper interests, attitudes and the building up of such essential skills, as independent study and capacity to think and judge for oneself to become a responsible member of a democratic society. Therefore, the aim of education is to accelerate the process of modernisation to spread education, to produce educated and skilled citizens and to train adequate and competent intelligentsia.

Cultivation of social, moral and spiritual values: The national system of education aims at cultivating social, moral and spiritual values in the child. For this purpose, both the central and the state government should introduce education in social, moral and spiritual values in all institutions under their control. The privately managed institutions should also be expected to adopt such education. Some periods should be reserved and instruction should be given to the teacher for this kind of education. The commission also suggests that the University Department of Comparative Religions should show special concern about this aspect of education. India is a secular democratic country where different religions flourish. So, it is necessary to promote a tolerant study of all religions, which will help its citizens to understand one another and make them live together amicably.

CONCLUSION

It is the first time that we have an integrated picture of Indian education in all its wide and diverse dimensions. The commission lays stress on making education a vehicle of national reconstruction that leads our teeming millions to social, economic, political and moral emancipation. Addressing the 29th Annual Convocation of Utkal University on 8th April 1978, Mr. Morarji Desai, the Late Prime Minister of India, said, "Education system should be recasted in a way whereby the young men are equipped with a spirit of enquiry to distinguish between right and wrong and capacity to stick to truth and to avoid false hood and stay away from doing wrong things". These words outline the main aims of education in the present India.

CHAPTER 4

AGENCIES OF EDUCATION

INTRODUCTION

Education is a life-long process which goes on directly or indirectly in the social organisations and natural environments. It is the sum total of experiences that the child and man receive inside and outside the educational institutions through the study of different subjects, various activities and through the library, museum, playground and workshop or through other agencies. So, education is not confined to schools, colleges, universities and institutions. It is a process which takes place in the society by the society and for the society. According to R.C. Lodge, "All experiences are educative process. The bite of mosquito, the taste of water melon, the experience of falling in love, of flying an aeroplane, of being in a storm in a boat—all such experiences has a direct educative effect on us". Thus, education includes all the influence which acts upon an individual during his passage from cradle to grave. It is a fact that educational institutions provide a part of life's education, experience and knowledge, Counts says that the school is but one among many educational agencies. Raymont observes that teachers are not the only educators and schools and college are not the only educational institutions. The other institutions, though good or ill, are unquestion ally educational in their effects. It is true that of all education we receive, we learn one-fourth from our teachers, one-fourth from books, one, fourth from our colleges and the one-fourth from the overall environment. Thompson says that the whole of the environment is the instrument of man's education. The instruments such as family, state, school, mass communication, peer groups and religious institutions are called agencies of education.

WHAT IS AGENCY?

Agency is a word which has been derived from the English word 'agent' which means a person or thing that acts or exerts power. The meaning of agency is a group of people who are workers and work as representatives or active in the form of means. Hence, agencies of education are those factors, which exercise an educational influence on the child and man. According to B.D. Bhatia, "Society has developed a number of special institutions to carry out the functions of education. These institutions are known as the agencies of education". So we can define agencies of education as all those social groups and organisations which help the children and other members of the society, directly or indirectly, in the matter of education.

Classifications of Educational Agencies

The agencies of education may be broadly classified on the basis of personal and informal agencies (Table 4.1); active and passive agencies; and Brown's classification.

TABLE 4.1 Classification 1: Personal and informal agencies

Personal Agencies	Informal Agencies
Schools	Family and society
Colleges	Workshop places
Universities	Market places
Institutions	Fairs
Research centres	Exhibition
Industrial centres	State
Television (Education related)	Pear group
Cinema (Value education)	Cinema
Radio	Television (Through varied programmes other than education)
Pictures	Relatives
Libraries	Neighbours
Laboratories	Computer with internet
Sports and games	Newspaper

Formal Agencies of Education

The formal agencies of education are organised systematically with aims, curriculum, methods of teaching, working hours, textbooks and rules and regulations as the formal are deliberately planned to bring about specific influence on the child, they are called **intentional mode of education**.

Merits: The formal agencies of education have definite and specific objectives, learning experiences desire behavioural changes together with measuring and valuation techniques. In the words of John Dewey, without formal education, it is not possible to transmit all the resources and achievements of a complex society. It also opens a way to a kind experience which would not be accessible to the young if they are left to pick up their training in informal association with others. It means that the aims of the society and the state are realised through the medium of these agencies. The preservation and transmission of culture from one generation to another can be made possible through the formal agencies of education. In fact, the education given to the child through these agencies is not possible informing one.

Demerits: The formal agencies of education have certain demerits in its practices. Education imported by formal agencies is often merely bookish. Therefore, there is a social and artificial devoid of realisation of life and society. It is planned under rigid conditions and strict discipline which make the whole environment dead and lifeless. It emphasises interpretation of words and phrases and often neglects the real sprit underlying the centre. It promotes rote memorisation without understanding and inserting such bookish knowledge into the minds of children. These agencies are not competent to provide complete education, but prepare the child for examination. John Dewey rightly observes that "formal education easily becomes remote and dead, abstract and bookish, what accumulated knowledge exists in low grade societies is at least put into practice". But, in advanced culture much which has to be learnt is stored in symbols. It is far from translation into familiar acts. There is the standing danger that the material of formal education will be merely the subject matter of schools isolated from the subject matter of life experiences.

Informal Agencies of Education

The informal agencies of education are those institutions or groups which influence the child incidentally in a direct or individual way. They have no formal organisation or pre-planned programmes of these agencies are wider and more comprehensive than educational objectives because it begins at birth and continues throughout life. They play a very important role in providing education about the language, of the dialect, living, eating, dressing and traditional customs and traditions. John Dewey, the renounced educationist of America, is of the opinion that these agencies can prove very helpful in developing the power of imagination and intelligence which serve as that basis for school education. The family, the play group, youth clubs and neighbours are some of the informal agencies of education. Education through these agencies, is imbibed incidentally and naturally by the students own initiative and efforts. Therefore, John Dewey calls it incidental, natural and important. The unconscious influence of informal agencies is very stable and it affects every fibre of human body, mind and soul.

Merits: The informal agencies make education a life-long process. It is imparted naturally and incidentally in a free atmosphere that is without any rigid control and direction. It leads to self-intact, self-planning, self-picking and self-choosing in the social environments. John Dewey remarks, "The child is informally educated by living with others and the very process of living together educates. It enlarges and enlightens experiences, it stimulates and enriches imaginations. It creates responsibility, accuracy and vividness of statement and thought".

Demerits: No well-organised education can be provided through these agencies, and, nothing is definite and determined in such type of education. Consequently, they often impart vague knowledge and information. So, whatever education and experiences obtained through informal agencies suffer from lack of systematisation, the scientific and material life has become much complex and complicated that it needs to provide education in a well-organised manner. The education of arts, science, techniques and industrial education and vocational training is not positive through informal agencies. Moreover, children may learn and develop harmful attitudes and habits such as drinking, smoking and chewing intoxicants, stealing, killing and disrespecting the elders, parents and teachers. These undesirable behaviour and activities pollute the young generation and society.

Formal and Informal Agencies of Education

Like the two sides of a bulk, formal and informal agencies strive for the complete development of the child. They are complementary supplementary helpful to each other. The co-ordination between the two is very necessary for the balanced development of the child. In fact, the education received from the family is the basis of school education because mother is the first teacher of the child. There is also the impact of relatives and social groups on the child. But, the problems of society and nation such as population explosion, terrorism, corruption, poverty, unemployment and a number of anti-social activities can be mitigated through providing well-organised formal education. Therefore, schools should provide equal opportunities to the education of students according to their interest, tendencies and needs. The success of the schools depends upon the co-operation of informal agencies. Hence, the recognition of school and family should be alike, Sir Godfrey Thomson observes that the whole of the environment is the instrument of man's education in the widest sense. But, in that environment, certain factors are distinguishable as being more particularly concerned with the home, the religion, the community, the state and the mass media which have a great impact on the development and character formation in the child.

Non-Formal Agencies

The non-formal agencies of education neither came in the category of formal or informal education. These are those groups or organisation in which provisions are made for the education of children and adults who could not get education in the formal agencies of education. Open learning institutions (Indra Gandhi Open University) and the agencies offering correspondence education and adult-education are some of the non-formal agencies.

The active agencies have a great educational influence in the human beings. In fact, education takes place (behavioural changes) through imitation in the socio-natural environments. The interaction is a two-way process in which individual influencing the individual or group and vice-versa. For example, the teacher has an impact on the students in school and in turn the students also have impact on him. Thus, the social group receive impact on another in one form or the other. The active agencies are very important from the educational point of view.

TABLE 4.2 Classification 2: Active and passive agencies of education

Active Agencies	Passive Agencies
Family	Cinema
School	Newspaper
Community	Magazines
Religion	Radio
Workshop	Television, Internet
Institutions	Marketplace
Social clubs	Railway station
Peers	Journal
Relatives	Library
Neighbours	Tape recorder
Playground	Hospitals
Dancing halls	
Amusement centres	

On the other hand, education impacted through positive agencies is a one-way process. Such agencies influence the individual but are not influenced by him. In other words, only the learner is affected but the other side is not affected. For instance, the student may learn from these agencies but they cannot have any impact on the agencies of education. These are not alternatives of the teachers, and the double cannot be removed through them. In fact, these agencies are actually not the agencies of education but only a means of education. Newspapers, journals, radio, television, library and cinema are the agencies of education but they are powerful means which have a great impact on the people.

Brown's Classification: According to Professor Brown, the educational agencies can be classified into four categories.

Formal agencies: The formal agencies institutions set up by the society are to discharge exclusive educational functions for the acquisition of knowledge and bringing about changes in the behaviour of learners. Schools, art galleries, recreation centres and religious institutions are the examples of formal agencies.

Informal agencies: It includes those agencies which have formed not for the exclusive purpose of providing education, but, they consciously or unconsciously, directly or indirectly and incidentally have an impact on the child. The family, playground, peer, neighbours, commercial centres are informal agencies of education.

Commercial agencies: The commercial agencies such as television cinema, radio, video, tape recorder, dancing halls, theatre and newspaper are need for providing education. They directly or indirectly have an impact on the people.

Non-commercial agencies: These are service institutions meant for social welfare. Sport, clubs, youth welfare clubs, society and guiding, women welfare centres and child welfare centres are some of the examples.

DIFFERENT EDUCATIONAL AGENCIES

Family

Family is the oldest basic and fundamental unit of human society. It is an important agency of education and has been exercising an everlasting and immediate influence on the behaviour, character, conduct and personality of its members. It consists of the husband, wife and children together with all the young and old dependents. They are related to one another in one way or the other. So it may be regarded as small social groups consisting of a few related persons. According to Young and Mack, "The family is the oldest human group and the basic one. While the particular forms society to society, the central foci of family activities everywhere are child-rearing and initial induction of the child into the culture of a given society, in short socialisation." Thus, family is the first social institution where a child learns his first lesson of living, working, helping, co-operating, adjusting and caring each other. Each family has its own distinct habits of clothing, eating, thinking, talking and living. This culture is preserved and transmitted by each family from one generation to another in different ways.

The educationists, philosophers, sociologists and scholars relate family to education.

Comenius: The first six year of the child is the school of mother's knee.

Rousseau: Mother is the true nurse and father is the true teacher.

Pestalozzi: Family is the centre of love and affection, the best place for education and the first school of the child.

Vinoba Bhave: In a sound system of education, home should become school and school home.

Mazini: A child learns the first lesson of citizenship from the kins of the mother and the protection of the father.

Lari:. At all the levels of educational history, family is the main agency of the education of the child.

Henderson: The education of the child starts from his home, what he sees the world done by other individual's, he imitates the same and takes part in it. At that time, he is being educated informally.

Raymont: The home is the soil in which spring up those virtues of which 'sympathy' is the common characteristics. It is here that the child learns the difference between generosity and meanness, self-less and selfishness, justice and injustice, truth and non-truth, hard work and laziness. It is the place where these habits are developed first of all in him.

EDUCATIONAL FUNCTIONS OF FAMILY

Family is the first social institution in which education for the child begins with intimacy, contacts of parents, brothers, sisters, grand parents and relatives. The male child imitates his father to develop leadership qualities whereas the female one takes up the work of a householder. It is family only through which the economic, social, spiritual, cultural, aesthetical and educational needs of the child are met in the world.

Physical development: Family is the role educational agency in which the child is properly cared and brought up. Child is saved from being ill and given training to lead a well-organised life. He is given the knowledge of cleanliness and sanitation, to eat, in time. To sleep in time, to wake up in time, playing with similary members in the natural environment makes the child. Thus, the family takes full precautions about the health of the child.

Mental development: According to Pestalozzi, the child is born with certain inborn tendencies or powers. The mental development of the child takes place with the help of many experiences in the family. For example, language skill, creative thinking and memory power and reasoning capacity can be developed in the child through providing suitable opportunities in the family. Recitation of stories, songs, riddles and mathematics strengthen the mind.

Moral development: Family can inculcate and develop morals such as give and take policy, loyalty, obedience, honesty, mercy, truthfulness, and benevolence. This is because the behaviour of family is central for moral development of the child.

Character development: As a good tree yields good fruits, a good family develops good character such as speaking truth, doing honesty, keeping punctuality, obeying elders, parents and teachers. in the child. Moreover, observing good and useful deeds and words, and practicing these values are the virtues of character formation. Thus, character formation is essential for personal and social life. It is in the family where these virtues originate and foster in the early childhood. In other words, it is a cradle where character of the child takes up roots at the age of six and other institution develop it further.

Social development: Like school, family is also a miniature society in which the child learns the social values namely, sympathy, empathy, love, co-operation, tolerance, adjustment, responsibility, brotherhood, friendship, justice and unity. These values are very essential in socialising the child and preparing him for personal and social life. They can be learnt and practised first in the family and then in the society.

Spiritual development: India is a religion dominated country. The people have reverence and faith in one religion or the other. Children see their elders performing religious activities and observing important religious days and they too are attracted towards such matters. They become aware of the values and recognition of religion. Religion develops moral behaviour and human values such as love, affection, sympathy, empathy, compassion, kindness, fellow-feeling, co-operation, and adjustment in the child. Family plays a vital role in inculcating religious faith and belief in the child.

Cultural development: Cultural development is an essential part of the total education of the child. The child receives those sacraments and experiences of the family. For example, the family inculcate in him the language, customs and traditions, ways of eating and dressing, style of living, mixing with others, courtesy, patriotism and behavioural pattern of the family. It is only through family that the foundation of cultural development is laid in the social environment. As India is a country of diverse language, cultures and religions, the family share plays an active role to develop the spirit of liberalism in the child.

Emotional development: The real education of the child begins not intellectually but emotionally. Lack of good follow feeling and unity among the family members affect the emotional makeup of the child. At the same time, the family with good atmosphere in human relationship can develop emotion such as kindness, sympathy, tolerance, compassion, affection and adjustment in the child.

Vocational development: The role of family cannot be underestimated in the vocational development of the child. This is true in many areas where vocational development is possible only in the family through providing some sort of training in agriculture, industry and service sectors. For instance, metal and wood works like making jwelles and toys. In fact, the child learns these vocations from his parents and brothers. It is important to say that the training on many vocations, small scale industries and self-employment are obtained directly or indirectly from the family.

Personality development: Family is the platform for all-round personality development. The child develops socialisation by developing democratic and secular outlook. It prepares him for social life. As family consists of men and women, it can develop healthy attitude towards sex, the child receives the basic education, the 3 R's, reading, writing and arithmetic in the lap of mother and develop those qualities which make him fit for life.

Can the Family Do It?: The successful implementation of the educational functions of family entirely depends upon the quality of parents and family members. Parents having good character and humanistic tendency can create appropriate environment for the child's development and growth. The divorced or separated or illegal sexual brother brawl and problematic parents cannot discharge fruitful educational functions or parental responsibility. A prostitute mother or an illegal father can not make conducive for their children. In face, the father who goes back to corruption, illegal contact, printing fake certificates and currencies, raping, killing, swindling, cheating, stealing, terrorism and intoxicants pollute the whole family and society. A child who belongs to such family suffers physically, mentally and socially. On the other hand, only those families are literate, conscious, well-behaved and have liberal attitudes. But, most of the present families pollute the child and fail to inculcate those values in him which make him a man for individual as well as social life. Swami Dayanand has rightly remarked that blessed is the family whose parents should be godly and learnt to unite the child. In the words of the Indian educationist Saiyidain, "The education of man depends on the environment that he enjoys. If the environments are based on good customs and traditions of the family, they will spread beautiful influence on his ideas and development and his education will be useful not only to him but to the whole community". As family determines the quality of society and nation, its members should be neat and clean in words, thoughts and actions and refrain from anti-social activities. This is so good for child and father. It implies that father should be father and son should be son, then there will be family and if any collapse or gap in it, it will degrade the quality of man and relationship in all respects.

COMMUNITY

The word 'community' combines 'com' and 'munis'. Com means togetherness and munis indicates 'to serve'. It means live and serve together. So, community is a group of people in a geographical piece of land having common ways of living and sharing experiences. In short, it is groups of many families having own natural, geographical, social, cultural and political limits. It may be in village, a town, a state, a nation and the world level.

DEFINITIONS OF COMMUNITY

Davis. K: "A community is the smallest territorial group that can embrace all aspects of social life".

Ogburn and Nimkoff: "A community may be thought of as the total organisation of social life within a limited area".

Bogardus: "A community is a small group with some degree of we feeling and living in a given area".

Alwin Goods: "A community is a primary group resulting from social contacts, largely direct of those residing in a small area".

Brownell: "Community is meant a small diversified group of people, male and female with different skills and abilities living together as kin-neighbours".

Cook and Cook: "Community is an organised way of life within a geographical area. It is in more detail population aggregate in habiting a de-limitable area, sharing historical heritage, possessing of a set of basic institutions, participating in a common life, conscious of local unity and able to act together in solving problem which involve public interest".

EDUCATIONAL FUNCTIONS OF COMMUNITY

Community is one of the very effective and powerful agencies of education. It is much bigger than the family from every educational point of view. This is because community has a great impact on the family. The child comes out of the four walls of the family, contacts with the other members of the community. It gets knowledge and experience by initiating them. In fact, community is the very important agency in performing active role in the expansion of education.

Educational development: Community strives for provision of education at village or city level. It establishes different types of schools in rural and urban areas to make educated society. Many communities establish their own communal schools to train their children to lead a better life.

Physical development: The community organises local bodies such as parks, gardens, health hospital and sports games and gymnasiums. The children make use of facilities to enjoy their leisure in the fresh light, and air to do physical exercises. These local bodies help the children head to keep them strong. In fact, these sources influence the physical development of the child.

Mental development: The enlightened communities have reading rooms and libraries for children and adults. The arrangements of exhibitions, cultural programmes, debates, meetings on national days provide a healthy environment for the mental development of the child.

Social development: Community play a vital role in developing social values in the child. The spirit of social services is developed through social values like sympathy, co-operation, fellowship, tolerance, sacrifice, adjustment and brotherhood. It helps to link the children belonging to different socio-economic background and prepares them for social life. In fact, community exerts a great influence on the social development of the child.

Cultural development: Community is a group of many families and each family has its own of culture. For instance, life style, religious, belief and faith, customs and tradition vary from one family to another. The culture of one family influences another in a community. This is because of the imitation character. As a result, the language style, manners, behaviours and life patterns easily spread from one child to another. Thus community is a vehicle of transmitting and preserving culture for generations.

Character formation: The second environment has a great influence in the character formation of the child. It is seen that a child may become best or worst because of the influence of the community. Honouring parents, respecting elders, keeping neat and tidy, speaking truth, behaving politely and living honestly depend on the community in which the child lives.

Political knowledge: The community imparts political lessons to the child. Political community leaders arrange political meetings and conference to highlight principles and policies. The political speeches have a great influence on the child and develop leadership qualities.

Vocational development: Community is the source of vocational choices and development of the child. The child observes the different vocations followed by the community members. So, he learns about advantages, disadvantage and nature of various vocations. It enables him to choose the right vocation for future life.

Personality development: The community provides a lot of opportunities which help the child achieve all round personality development. Radio, television, theatres, picture house, museums, zoos, libraries, playground and clubs are the various community resources which play important role in shaping the personality of child.

Thus, community influence the education of the child formally, informally and incidentally, According to Crow and Crow, "A community cannot expect something for nothing. If it wishes its young people to serve their community well, it must provide whatever educational advantages are needed by the young people, individually and collectively to prepare themselves for that service".

The State

The state is one of the most important active informal agencies of education. Raymont observes that education may be conducted by all or any of the three means, firstly by voluntary efforts with a view to making profit, secondly by voluntary efforts arising from philanthropic or religious motives, thirdly by the agency state. State is a well-organised association of human beings which came into existence to carry out the function of all the social institutions effectively. According to Kandel, "state is an organised political community with government recognised by people". In the words of Garner, state is a community of persons, more or less, numerous, permanently occupying a definite portion of a territory independent and so of a foreign control and possessing an organised government to which the inhabitants render a habitual obedience.

Educational functions of the state plays very important role in the provision and universalisation of education. Education is completely centred with the results that all aspects of teaching place of school location and discipline, are all guided and supervised by the central government in a totalitarian state. On the other hand, the democratic state distributes its power among citizens by decentralisation. As a result, the state provides more and more opportunities to the citizens to plan and execute education policies for better development.

NATIONAL SCHEME OF EDUCATION

Each state constructs a national scheme of education, keeping into consideration on the multifarious needs of the citizens. It contracts a comprehensive scheme of education with the help of educationists and ministers. It provides equal educational opportunity without discriminations to the citizens on the basis of colour, caste, sex as well as economic and social status.

Training in Citizenship: A democratic state provides political, social, cultural and economic training to the citizens to enable them grow into dynamic, resourceful and national-minded individuals. Training in citizenship is given by the way of film shows, military demonstrations, radio programmes, magazines, newspapers and television, social training are given through various social services and programmes like national social service, National Cadet Corps and Red Cross Society. Moreover, cultural training is given through national tours, national fairs, clubs, museums and picture galleries, economic training is given by imparting useful productive work and vocational and technical training.

Universalisation of Education: Education for all is the responsibility of each welfare state. The state provides universal, compulsory and free education up to a certain level. Thus, the state fulfils the basic needs of its citizens.

Financing of Education: Financing of education is one of the social responsibilities of the welfare state. It requires huge amount of financial resources. The state can also meet such requirements and provide education at free of cost.

Establishment of Educational Institutions: The state establishes schools, colleges and universities to provide different types of education and indirectly runs them through various autonomous and voluntary bodies, such as SCERT, DIET and CBSE.

Adult Education: The state plays an important role in providing education for uneducated and illiterate adults. It establishes a number of centres at district level to eradicate illiteracy and poverty through adult education programmes.

Attract Public Towards Education: More opening of schools or colleges cannot be effective in providing education. This is because most of the people are socially, culturally and economically disadvantaged. It is the responsibility of the state to provide education to all by offering infrastructural facilities, stipends, scholarships, uniforms, free-meals, educational loans and free transport. These facilities will attract the people towards education in the Indian society.

Training to Teachers: The state establishes teacher training institute and colleges to produce effective and efficient teachers to provide quality education and discharge the duties and responsibilities sincerely.

Supply Standard Books at Low Price: It is the state which takes efforts to provide standard books at reasonable price. The state should take the whole responsibility of supplying textbooks at low price up to the certain standard of education.

Scouts and Guides Training: The state encourages the provision of scouts and guides training to teachers and students, which inculcate values such as cooperation, fellow feeling, patriotism, punctuality and responsibility. For instance, one week scouts and guides training is made compulsory for the prospective teachers and it is an integral part of teacher education in India.

Red Cross and First Aid Training: It is very essential on the part of the state that it should provide opportunity to train up teachers and students in first aid and Red Cross procedure so as to prepare them to help the needy and helpless during natural hazards and accidents.

Control and Direct Education: Each state exercise controls/determines the aims, curriculum and methods of teaching evaluation procedures and conduct of school activities according to the local conditions. It punishes the defaulting educational institutions and guides to run them on the right track.

Establishes Board and Committee: The state organises boards and committees for the development of educational institutions and provision of quality education at regional and national levels. The committees and boards determine the arms, curriculum, methods, the examination and evaluation system.

Appointing Committee: The state appoints commissions of enquiry to know about the working diffidences and drawbacks of educational institutions and suggest various measures for their improvement and progress. For example, the university education commission and Kothari education commission were the contribution of state to modify the whole education system in India.

Encouraging Research: The state encourages fundamental and action research in all areas of education. For instance, the bodies such as UGC, ICSR, NCERT and SCERT provide adequate funds, facilities and resources to conduct research and publish the findings. Thus, the state ensures that the research finds application in various educational programmes and projects.

SCHOOL

School is one of the most important formal agencies of education. It plays a very significant role in discovering, moulding and developing the innate capacities, attitudes, habits and ideas of the children. In the words of S. Balakrishnan Joshi, "A well conducted school is a happy home, a sacred shrine, asocial centre, a miniature society, and a bewitching Brindavan, all beautifully blended into a synthetic structure".

Meaning and Definitions of School

Etymologically the word school is derived from the Greek word "Skhole" which means leisure. The leisure places were used for self-development in ancient Greece. These places came to be known as school where teachers give specific dozes of curriculum during a fixed time under a pre-planned system.

J. S. Ross: "Schools are institutions devised by civilised man for the purpose of aiding in the preparation of the young for well-adjusted and efficient members of society".

John Dewey: "School is a special environment where ascertain quality of life and certain types of activities and occupations are provided with the objectives of securing the child's development along desirable lines".

Ottaway: "School is a social invention to serve society for the specialised teaching of young".

Educational Functions of School

School is the first organised learning centre for the child. It is the place of transmitting teachers' behaviour, knowledge and experiences to the students. Hence, school discharges many educational functions.

Mental Development: Mental or intellectual development is the most important function of a school. The mental power of the child is developed through various exercises like speaking, reading, writing, memorising, reciting, understanding and expressing. Such exercises enable the child to think freely, clearly and logically which will strengthen his mental power.

Social Development: School is a miniature society in which children belonging to varied castes, religion, region, socio-economic backgrounds and culture sit, learn and play together. So, it provides opportunities to inculcate social values like we feeling, brotherhood, cooperation, sympathy, tolerance and adjustment by organising students union, social service camps and celebrating and observing national and religious days.

Physical Development: As plant grown in the gardens child grows in the school. Jesus Christ said 'Man lives not by bread done but words'. The entire environment of school should be such that it leads to the physical well-eing of the children. Learning in the natural environment and playing in the open air conducive for the physical development of child.

Emotional Development: This is one of the educational functions of the school. School must be artistic with garden, flower plants, beautiful natural objects, neat and clean buildings and campus, quality teachers, learning freedom and taste and fully decorated classrooms. Moreover, trips, tours, exhibitions, bales and cultural programmes should be organised to stimulate emotional and aesthetic sense of children. It festers the high ideas of human life.

Cultural Development: School provides various opportunities for cultural development of the child. School is a place where children of varied culture learn together. As a result, culture of give and take policy, respecting elders and teacher, food and language style, dressing and behaviour are transmitted easily from one child to another in the social environment. Thus, school is the centre for preserving and transmitting culture from the present generation to the future one.

Vocational and Industrial Development: School acts as the centre for vocational development. It provides training on embroidery, tailoring, shop and flower-making and technical or industrial training with a view to preparing the child for life. For instance, higher secondary school includes several programmes and activities like work experiences and vocation subjects.

Citizenship Development: It is school which develops the quality of citizenship in the child. Such quality helps the child to become active and responsible citizen imbibed with the quality of leadership leading the society and nation in the path of progress.

Character Formation and Development: The important formal function of school is to develop the child morally and socially. School organises various social activities and programmes which enable them to acquire firm and noble character.

Spiritual Development: Religious instruction is given to the child in most of the schools. It inculcates and develops spiritual feeling. In India, many private schools impart religious education, which help the child develop spiritually.

Democratic Development: School brings about all round personality development in the child. It also develops democratic values. The democratic values or qualities such as equality, freedom, justice, and tolerance and human values like affection, sympathy, honesty, dutifulness, compassion, kindness and fellowship are taught to the child through teaching value and democratic-oriented subjects.

RELIGIOUS INSTITUTIONS

Religion is one of the most universal characteristics of human life. It influences behaviour of the individuals. In fact, people have a way of life in accordance with certain beliefs, moral and spiritual values. Religion is a faith and belief shown in rituals, ceremonies and worship in the name of god for blessings. It also signifies purity of heart, feelings and actions together with spiritual development. It is not merely an intellectual imagination but it is sum of all desirable social, moral and spiritual values embodied in people's conduct and character.

The word 'religion' is a combination of two Latin words namely '*Re*' and '*Legere*' which mean to bind back or establish connection. It signifies those moral bonds of love, sacrifice and social service which hold the human community together. Thus, the essence of true religions is love, affection, sympathy, co-operation, tolerance, sacrifice, fellow-feeling, honesty, truthfullness, functionality and responsibility which shape human behaviour and form character. Ginsbert has rightly stated, "Religion establishes a double bond, one between man and God and the other between man and man as children of God."

Meaning and Definitions

Religion is a doctrine of faith on God and God's world. People have heterogeneous faith and belief in terms of God and divinity.

Bertrand Russell: 'Religious' is based on faith—a firm belief in something for which there is no evidence.

Ginsbert: Religion is the dynamic belief in and submission to God or to God's on whom man feels dependent.

White: Religion is a vision of something which stands beyond, behind and within people.

Herald Haffding: The essence of religion is faith in the conservation of values.

Kant, Immanuel: Religion is the recognition of all our duties as divine commandments.

Dawson: Wherever and whenever man has a sense of dependence on external powers which are concerned as mysterious and higher than men's own, there is religious.

EDUCATIONAL FUNCTIONS OF RELIGIOUS INSTITUTIONS

Schooling begins with religious education in most of the countries. Religion influences directly as well as indirectly. So, school imparts religious spiritual songs and prayers and insists pupils to the beliefs and practices with a view to forming desirable character and ultimately prepare the child for holy life. The idealistic philosophy emphasises the development of spiritualism in the child through education. It indicates that there is a close relationship between religion and education. According to Burton, religion and education are close and real friend. Both are related to spiritualism in contact to physical and material phenomenon. Both try to free the human being not from his physical surrounding but try to free him from the slavery to physical environment. The religious values modify the human behaviour and make him superior. In fact, proper placing of religion in the system of education provides opportunities for spiritual development and character formation.

Moral and Spiritual Values: Religious education does not aim at teaching the way of worship or practice of specific rituals and ceremonies. But, it inculcates those moral and spiritual values which make the child pure in thoughts and actions.

Man-making Education: Religious education plays important role in man-making processes. As religion is part of general education, it directs the child in the right path of life. The life based on religious values makes man important in the society.

Develop wider Attitude: The teaching of religious education changes the child in his/her attitude and social outlook. The feeling of I and selfishness disappears and the we-feeling and fellowship emerges. It trains the child to think uncertainty of life develop global thinking and prepare him for meaningful life.

Character Formation: The end of all religions is character formation. Religion teaches the child what is good and bad and which is essential for better life. The man of good character can enjoy the life happily and peacefully. The religious values like love, affection, truthfulness, honesty, sacrifice, dedication, forgiveness, honour, parents respect elders and do not adulterate, lie, steal, and kill are good ideals for character formation in the child.

Democratic Outlook: Religious education emphasises that all human beings are equal in creation. No one is either superior or inferior to others. It establishes relationship between man and god and between man and other human beings. Thus, it develops the feeling of oneness in diversity.

Cultural Development: Religious education preserves and promotes culture from one generation to another. The lifestyle, faiths, belief and behaviour and deeds based on high ideas of religion which highly influence the family community and school. Hence, it becomes an integral part of life and education.

All-round Personality Development: Religious education includes high ideas and all activities which bring about all-round personality development in the child. It ensures independent self-reliance and self-confident personalities.

Redirect and Sublimate Instincts: Religious education helps the child to purify his thoughts and actions. It contracts or sublimates the undesirable instincts and redirects them into desirable behaviour to be used for the progress of the individual and society.

Peer Group: Peer is a group of boys and girls having equal rank in terms of age, qualification and experiences. It is also one of the informal agencies which provide education. It is a process of exchanging ideas, knowledge and experience among the equal aged and knowledge persons.

EDUCATIONAL FUNCTIONS OF PEER GROUP

Peer group plays vital role in changing the behaviour, interest and attitudes of the children.

Social Development: The word 'I' has become meaningless in the social life and 'we' is more important than anything in the society. Friendship, co-operation, tolerance, give-and-take policy, affection, brotherhood and sacrifice are values which prepare the peer group for integrated social life.

Physical Development: Organising games and sports among the peer group leads to the physical development. Group games help in not only physical development but also cultural development.

Cultural Development: Culture of the individual and community is easily transmitted from one person to another through free contact in the social environment. In fact, they prepare themselves to adjust and accept the faith, belief and lifestyle of others because of closeness and affection.

Humanistic Development: Peer group develops the quality of humanism, friendship and affection included the feeling of sacrifice, sympathy, compassion, kindness and helping one another. These values lay foundation for humanism.

Mental Development: Sharing of ideas, knowledge and experiences, widen the scope for intellectual development and creativity. Peer group provides opportunity for intellectual development through acquisition of knowledge, exchange of thoughts using arguments and rational thinking.

Vocational Development: The peer group discusses the nature and problems of different vocations and job. It enables the child to choose the right job according to his interest and ability. It also helps to develop the vocational efficiency in which the child is interested.

Leadership Quality: Leadership quality is developed in the peer group. It helps develop the personality to lead, direct guide the group.

MASS MEDIA

Mass media such as newspaper, radio, television, and film improve the quantity and quality of education. These are very important in transmission and expansion of education. Most of the mass media serves as the agency of distance education. The socio-economic and environmental problems such as population explosion, inflation, unemployment, poverty, evils of intoxicants, environmental pollution and degradation are analysed in the mass media. Thus, it develops socio-economic and environmental awareness in the people and prepare them for better life.

Newspaper

It carries daily information occurred throughout the world. It highlights political, economic and social activities and matters related to agricultures and industries and environment and price level of important products. Short stories, novels, poems, riddle and knowledge-oriented information given in the newspaper and journals are important and useful educative sources. Moreover, information-related rainfall, time of sunrise and sunset, time of trains, banking activities and share markets, release of films, government programmes and various local, national and international news keep the people with up-to-date with information and knowledge. Newspaper and journals help and encourage the students and scholars to exhibit their talents in the written form. Thus, printed materials occupy predominant role in human life.

Radio

It is also used as informal agency for the propagation and exhibition education throughout the state country and world. George Washington remarks radio is not an addition to education. It is something to be placed on top of education. Rather radio is education. In the words of F. Wittis, "I feel happier in thinking that the education given through Akashvani is solid and stable and is just like a drama. Its contribution is that it creates a very appropriate environment towards education on a very large scale. In short it is a powerful, important and useful aid in the field of education. The lesson presented through radio is properly planned and interesting. The services of skilled and experienced teachers are utilised maximum level with the help of Akashvani. Hearing music, songs, stories and drama is very interesting and help to make use of leisure fruitfully. It broadcast current information without delay. It develops the qualities of listening and understanding the information and also language style.

Television

Television is the most powerful and important means of education in the scientific information knowledge world. It is the best means for distance education, and educational advertisement. It is the combination of two English words 'tele' means far away and 'vision' means to look. So, it is known as 'Doordarshan' in Hindi. It is a highly educative process because the lessons of Doordarshan are well-planned and prepared by the subject experts. So, the learning process of education becomes simple and easier. The maximum number of students gets advantages of the services of good and trained teachers. Social, economic, political, related issues are presented through television, which enable the people to understand the situation of country and abroad. Thus, television is the best audio-visual aid in the field of education.

Films

Films were integrated part of human life as it was the only source of entertainment for the rich and the poor about three decades ago. In fact, people gave importance to films, because they were story-centred focussing social or cultural or religious ideals and values. It was worthy to be watched with the family together. But most of the present films are just violence and obscene centred and it is not carry any values to be practised in life. It teaches to kill and escape from punishment. How to love and elope with lovers. How to swindle and evade from cases? How to disrespect the officials or politician, or parents and create a bad image in the society. Nothing to be learnt from films but only wasting time and money. However, it has a great impact on the peoples' life especially youths.

- It transmits the culture of one state or country to another.
- It develops communication skill.
- It develops listening skill.
- It helps to change language and lifestyle.
- It develops creativity and new thoughts.

It cannot be denied that historical films for children and films related to country and values are useful to bring about desirable changes in the child and society.

CONCLUSION

Whether these agencies are educating the child in a right way? This question stops the mind a little minute. The answer may be Yes. How can it be yes? It will be yes, if the father is good, teacher is good, community is good, priest or pastor is good, film producer is good, film song writer is good and politician is good. Lust on money, woman and wine instigate father (man) to steal, sex illegally and corruptive in the society. He cannot be a worthy father or pastor, or teacher or politician. Most of the families, teachers, peer groups and films pollute the character of the child. In fact, all these agencies aim at money-making not at man-making and nation-making. As Osho said, children are the expression of sexual obscene. So, the world is not destroyed in atom bomb but by sexual obscene. It is true that homo sex or marriage, drinking and smoking, prostitution, illegal sex and eve-teasing in the sight of children affect the whole life atmosphere. Religious institutions use various tactics and God for employment and income. So, the soul of spiritualism is encovered with the skin of materialism. Community and peer group are the mixture of best and worst people. So, character formation is meaningless in the materialistic world. Film focuses obscenity and violence. Hence, all agencies should take utmost care of children for which they should be effective and worthy agencies. The agencies of education directly or indirectly influence the development of child. It may be desirable or undesirable behaviour which depend on the quality of family, teacher, pastor, community, peer group, films and the social environment. Deviation of bricks in the building affects the whole building and makes it useless. Likewise, the parents, teachers, politicians and priests who deviate from their position and character will affect the whole human society. As Confucious says, father should be father, son should be son and government should be government, then only there will be good family and society.

CHAPTER 5

EDUCATION FOR 21ST CENTURY

INTRODUCTION

Of course, the 21st century is entirely different from the earlier ones in the spiritual, cultural, social, economic and political life. This is so because, the present generation is mostly influenced by the materialism, obscene-violent based mass media and a number of undesirable and contemptible activities. As a result, this century faces a lot of challenges such as value and environmental crises, corruption, poverty and unemployment which make the human life, unhappy unhealthy and peace-less. In fact, the characterless generation, quality less parents, teachers, officials and politicians pollute the socio-natural environments. At the same time, the invention of advanced technology has made life simple and comfortable and shrinked the broad world in to a small global society. So, all people are treated as world citizens where caste, religion, region and culture are meaningless but man is more important than anything in the social environments. Hence, the children should be given equal opportunities in education, employment and income for better life. In fact, we need a new philosophy of education and life to meet the challenges and difficulties in the mass media based materialistic global society.

New Philosophy of Education: A new philosophy of education is very important to prepare the child for personal national and global life. As such, it should include a new epistemology of knowledge and learning, a new code of ethics, a new code of politics, a new economic, new socio-cultural and spiritual life. An International Symposium and Round Table convened by UNESCO (1989) emphasised on the philosophy of education needed for a meaningful life in the challenged 21st century.

A New of view of Knowledge: The new epistemology of knowledge and learning emphasise the new of view of knowledge throughout the educational systems, which develop rationalism and intuitive approaches in the child. This is because acceptable and desirable traditional culture has gone into the mass media based polluted society. Therefore, we must develop a knowledge of multi-cultural life. For this purpose, the present educational system needs to promote several areas of knowledge and approaches for making life successful in the ever challenging world.

A Greater Integration of Knowledge: The prevailing education has increased the fragmentation of knowledge into meaningless and irrelevant units. In fact, it has failed to solve the problems of life. In other words, there is no integration between education and human life. That is why it produces many characterless and unemployable generations. Hence, we need a new approach of education to life, which enables the child to find solutions for problems and challenges at local, national and global levels.

A life-long learning: Education is a life-long process because every individual receives a type of education from birth to death. Moreover, new thoughts, inventions and researches have increased the areas of knowledge and new subjects. So one should keep on learning to have up to date knowledge in all fields which make him fit in the ever changing society.

A Change in Educational System: The educational philosophy includes a change or shift from for conformity to promote creativities and innovativeness,

- From competitiveness to co-cooperativeness.
- From national viewpoint to global one.
- From emphasising the private benefits of learning to the public benefits of learning.
- From stress community
- Develop a sense of service for healthy and happy life.

Education for All: It emphasises provision of educational opportunities to all and not for some or a few.

Care for All: We need a new approach of education to realise social justice through the empowerment of disadvantaged people to enable them to seek solutions to their economic problems and develops innovative behaviour.

A New Code of Ethics: The present generation has gone to the extent of money making and social pollution. So, the educational philosophy for 21st century emphasises a new code of ethics for peaceful, stress less and happy life. It emphasises the people to realise and practice various ethics such as corruption violent obsence and drugs free human beings. Be happy peaceful healthy, honest, dutiful, responsible and globalist one, and avoid jealous, killing, suicide, illegal sex, prostitution, drugs and other contemptible activities causing social pollution and social hazards. Let us be the man of principles models and useful to the family, society and world.

A New Code of Political and Economic Approaches: We suffer from disguised democracy and lack of quality leaders. The number of principles political functionaries do not know social needs but use politics for contemptible activities and money making. It develops narrowism and neglects human welfare. Hence education should prepare the children for good leadership, communication and secular-democratic outlook. Moreover, inequality found in the income distribution and variation in education in terms of useless different boards of education must be removed and social justice maintained in all respects. There should be a national system of education and equal pay for equal one.

NEW SYSTEM OF EDUCATION

A new system of education is very important to face the challenges and meet the requirements of the international community emerged in 1990's. UNESCO appointed an International Commission on Education for the Twenty-first century (1993–96) under the Chairmanship Jazques Delors (France) and fifteen educationists belonging to India, China, France, Jamaica, Japan, Jordan, Korea, Mexico, Poland, Portugal, Senegal, Slovenia, United States, Venezuela and Zimbabwe.

The commission pointed out a list of major tensions which the world faces in the 21st century between:

- The global and local levels.
- The universal and individuals
- Tradition and modernity.
- Long-term and short-term considerations.
- Need for competition and concern for equal opportunities.
- Explosions of knowledge and capacity to assimilate.
- Spiritualism and Materialism.

Meaning of Education for 21st Century

Education is a comprehensive term because it has different meanings in the dynamic-globalised society. In fact, it was the teaching of 3 R's (Reading, Writing and Arithmetics) Later it was meant for training, and development of 3 H's (Hand, Heart and Head). The great educationists of 18 and 19th centuries considered it as source of 5R's (Reading, Writing, Arithmetics, Reasoning and Research). Modern educationalists like John Dewer and Mahatma Gandhi regarded education as a source of socio-economic life. But the education for 21st century is regarded as a source of individual, social and global life. It is acquired from formal non-formal institutions and social environments. As such education is what that prepares for the child for socio-economic, cultural, spiritual, aesthetic and political life at personal social, national and international levels.

The prevailing education produces characterless generations who lack secular-democratic outlook, communication skills and leadership qualities. As a result, materialistic outlook, in human and contemptible activities, narrowism, selfishness, philosophy of use and throw life have been the characteristics of present generation. In fact, education is study of arts, science, technical and professional subjects based on curriculum for certificates and degrees.

Definition of education: (21st Century): We may define education as "Anything one leans from books, non-book materials and socio-natural environments for knowledge, certificates and training which prepare for all aspects of life". In short, education is anything which makes human life better in all respect at all levels. It provides a comprehensive meaning and definition for education based on the requirements of ever challenging global society. Moreover, it includes all aspects of learning materials which are useful to one's life. As such, education becomes a life-long process received from all sources.

AIMS OF EDUCATION IN THE 21ST CENTURY

The present educational system, aims at cash making through privatisation and creation of inequalities in terms of different curriculum, English and fake advertisements. In fact, it has failed in character formation. This is mainly because of the impact of meaningless, obscene violent based mass media, socially undesirable contemptible activities, intoxicants, characterless parents, teachers and politicians on the children are more than examination and certificate oriented money making education. However, based on the definition of education for 21st century we emphasise the aims which are vitals for peaceful, healthy and happy personal, social and global life.

Comprehended the Nature of Life

The most important aim of education is to enable the child to grasp himself/herself and the nature of human life. The great philosopher Socrates rightly said, "Know thyself, Lack of understanding of oneself and death is the causes of problems in one's life". In fact, each child should understand his duties and responsibilities in the social environments and also life is fall of ups and downs and nothing is permanent. Life may be short or long but make it useful, happy and peaceful. Don't compare you with rich or poor one but lead as it is. If you say yourself zero you will be hero in all if you think you are hero you will be zero in all. If you say you know 'nothing' you will be a man of knowledge and wisdom. If you say 'I know all', you will be a noddy. So you learn yourself to lead a simple and humble life. It is not possible for anyone who fails to understand the reality of life. Weather rich or poor, literate or illiterate, white or black man or women young or old, upper castes or lower one's all are equal because when one alive others say or use one's name or designations and one becomes body on the occasion of death. So the child should understand his/her strength and weakness and develop positive ideas and deeds which are good to self and society. Hence, nothing is proud of human life and important we are not better than great people who are living still. In other words, most of us live like animals become parents of one or two children educate them arrange marriage and leave the earth. This is the nature of human life.

Comprehend the Socio-natural Environment

The second aim of education for 21st century is helping the children savvy the socio-natural environments. Social environment refers to the human beings their relationships and man-made things. On the other hand, natural environment refers to anything which is the basis for all existence of human and non-human things. This is because learning or education takes place when the child contact the social environments and listen the nature. Man depends on social and natural environments for his biological, physical, sociological, political and economic needs. So, each child should learn to maintain amicable relationship with families relatives neighbours and society and take care of natural resources for sustainable development. This is very important because nature is a source of life of all living things. Hence it should be protected preserved and conserved for future generations. Moreover, prepare the child to prevent natural and social pollutions for better life.

Communication Skills

This is very essential because the present generation is very poor in oral, written and reading skills. It is regrettable that the higher educational and training institutions produce corers of graduates and post graduates of all arts and science, Engineering, professional and technical/vocational students who lack in subject knowledge and communication skills. So, they become unemployable educated people who retard the economic growth and development of the country. Effective communication skills of Jawoharlal Nehru, Mahatma Gandhiji and Sardar Vallabai Patel set India free from the British government and created an integrated India. Effective communication skill of Jesus Christ created a huge throng who accompanied him. He himself said, *"There is life in my words"*. In fact, His words are food and life. It is very essential to prevent war, violence and conflicts. Moreover, it is a source of leadership. Hence, it should be developed in the children through proper education and training for making effective leaders thinkers and administrators in the complicated global society.

Development of Capacities

Education for the 21st century is expected to develop enough capacities in the children to oppose and prevent social pollution such as inequalities in income and education, corruption, illegal sex, intoxicants, raping of innocent girls and women killing, suicide unemployment poverty prostitution and other contemptible and undesirable activities which affect individual, family and society. The present teachers think of salary increment, promotion and transfer and have failed to think of their qualities and responsibilities in the man-nation making processes. The educationists, educational administrators and teachers have defeated the purpose of real education and aim at producing mark/grade oriented certificate/degree for holders for higher fees and salaries. As such, there is no humanity in the society. It is very urgent that we should prevent the obscene violence based media which pollute the human beings and turn them least to animals. But no one worries about the impact of such mass media. It is more dangerous than nuclear weapons. Film producers demand actress to act nakedly for crores of money. They never think about their wives daughters and sisters. Showing nakedness cannot make the children and society better, but pollute everything and push in to darkness. Hence, education should develop awareness about the mass media and develop capacities in the child to protect the society and the environment from such pollution.

Promotion of Book Culture

One of the most important aims of education is to promote book reading culture in the child. It is seen that the present generation is lazy and wastes their time and money on unnecessary things and addict to obscene films, violence, internets, cell phone-based entertainments or engage in gossips and back biting or wandering aimlessly. Such media and activities spoil the character of child and make life meaningless. At the same time, reading good books not only increases knowledge, experience and skills which are vital to overcome complicated challenges crossed in the ordinary business of life but also develops desirable activities and makes them fit for personal, social and global life. Mahatma Gandhi says that book is the best teacher and it teaches better than teachers. In fact, good books are not only sources of knowledge but also successes of life. That is why educationists and philosophers emphasise self-learning or auto-learning. A pregnant lady can produce best child if she read holy books, biography of great leaders and social reformers. On the other hand, if she/husband watches obscene violence based media will give birth to socially undesirable child. It is very regrettable that teachers, parents and the society have failed to promote the book culture which is very essential in the knowledge oriented challenged life. Hence, this aim should be imbibed in the child.

Secular-Democratic Outlook

It is another important aim of education in the 21st centuries. To integrate diverse population. This is because families, education, religion politics and social environments have failed to bring about secular- democratic outlook which is essential for non-discriminated and healthy life. The government of India emphasise caste and religion and develops inequalities. In fact, human beings are stratified in different criteria like caste, religion, sex, politics, language, education, socio-cultural and economic status. So, it is essential to bring about unity in diversities to make the nation strong, healthy and peaceful. It requires the development of secular democratic outlook in the children. Such outlook enables them to accept the fact that man for man not for any deviating and discriminating forces.

Prepare for Global Life

Education always aims at preparing the child for social, cultural, spiritual, political and economic life. The world has become a global society where one earth and one sky for all citizens. Hence, the children should be prepared to think act and work globally. As such, education has four pillars that is, learning to know, learning to do, learning to live and learning to be better. So, the child should acquire knowledge from socio-natural environments, books and different types of education throughout their life. They should do or apply or implement the knowledge to overcome the challenges and make their life useful and successful. They would learn to adjust, understand and accept others for living together. Finally they should be prepared to enjoy happy, peaceful life. Thus, the aim of education is to prepare the child to live better at all levels.

Technical Skills

This is a mechanical world where modern technologies play vital role in domestic, agricultural, industrial and communicational activities. Now we use various machines, tools, gadgets and devices to make our life simple and comfortable. So every child should have a sufficient technical knowledge and skills to live successfully. As such, the present education should foster technical knowledge and skills.

Development of Research Attitudes

Generally, students join research studies for the sake of money making and employment oriented degrees. As a result, research becomes a meaningless one. Most of them are not original or old thesis in new titles and jackets. In fact, research scholars and guides are poor in research activities. Many professors guide for money or illegal activities or name sake. Students carry out research for degrees and employment. Broadly speaking, it is bought and sold in colleges and universities. However, research is very essential to analyse the local, national and global socio-economic and cultural issues and seek solutions and also find out cause effects of various factors and their relationships in the socio-natural environments. Hence, the development of research attitudes in the students is quite inevitable in complicated, materialistic and multi-minded societies.

Formation of Desirable Character

The present education always aims to prepare the child for marks/grade oriented certificates/degrees to be produced for employment and income. So, it is materialistic one where culture and character is meaningless. Moreover, people do not know what is character and culture. Both are different but acquired from education and social environments. Some character and cultures are socially desirables and acceptable because they are useful and important and harmless to individual and social life whereas socially undesirable and contemptible activities pollute the individual and society.

The Practices of contemptible activities such as illegal sex, prostitutions naked dances homosexuals, homo marriage, corruption, rapping of innocent girls and women, smoking, drinking, watching obscene violence based mass media, wearing tightly transparent or sexy dresses, killing, chewing intoxicants affect and pollute the social environments (Social pollution). On the other hand, practices of good and socially desirable character/cultures such as truthfulness, patience, co-operation, love, affection, sympathy, empathy, friendship, patriotism, equality, kindness etc should be encouraged and developed as for as possible for better life and environments.

CHANGING OF FORMAL EDUCATION AT DIFFERENT LEVELS

Primary Level Education

Acquiring Basic Skill: Education should strengthen the basic knowledge of reading, writing and arithmetic's and also develop the ability to express oneself in mother tongue or any other language.

Scientific Knowledge: This is very essential to prepare the child for scientific world. The need for receptivity to science opens the door to the 21st century and scientific and technological upheavals.

Socialise the Child: The number of children has decreased to one or two in a nuclear family system. They have no brother or sister to play with them. Moreover, their parents have no time to spend with them. At this juncture, the school is mini society which should socialise the child for co-operative life, fellowships and unity.

Secondary Level Education

Learning Throughout Life: Education should make learning a life-long process in order to live with up to date knowledge. It enables the child to overcome ever increasing challenges and problems in the complicated society.

Philosophy and Religion: Opportunities should be provided to learn the philosophies of life and various religious principles. Such studies include human values, ethics and moral life. Moreover, they differentiate human beings from animals. It helps the child to discern the uncertainly of human life and prepare them for moral, spiritual and ethical life.

Language: Students should be provided opportunities to learn many languages at regional or state, national and international levels. So that, they can be proficient in one or two languages which are essential for national and international life. However such studies should be given on optional basis. It develops language skills and employment opportunities.

Higher learning Techniques: Debates, conferences and seminars should be organised frequently in order to develop languages and subject skills. It also helps to foster human values such as co-operation, adjustment, tolerance, understanding and fellowship etc.

Book Culture: Reading habits have been decreasing due to the influence of various entertainments and obscene violent based mass media. In fact, youngsters are addicted to intoxications and live aimlessly. So, they neglect the importance of book reading. Such culture is very essential not only to be fit in knowledge society and prepare for global life. Above all, it makes people happy and peaceful.

University Level Education

Research and Teaching: University is the centre of higher education and research. It should produce skilled and talented students with leadership qualities and communication skills. It encourages research on current, social-economic, political, cultural and environmental issues. Research should be original not for degree sake and money making but for problems solving and face the challenging society.

Publication: University should produce quality books on every branch of knowledge/subjects based on curriculum and requirements of the society. Such books should be marketed at national and international levels.

Learned Better Citizens: It is regrettable that Indian Universities produce quality less and unemployables graduates, post graduates and research scholars. Such candidates are very poor in language and subjects, but they get employment easily in the education and other departments not based on their talents but on money and recommendations of higher officials. As a result, university has lost its academic and professional qualities. This trend should be changed to produce a better learned generation for global thoughts and life.

REFORMATION OF EDUCATION AND SOCIETY

A child receives education nor only from books, non-books and teacher oriented ones, but also from the socio-natural environments. In other words, learning occurs in all times and all places. So it is a life-long process. He/she learns more from the society than from books and teachers. So his/her character is highly influenced by the social environments, which is polluted with a lot of socially contemptible and undesirable activities. Moreover privatisation of education aims at money making through fake advertisements and English medium. It widens in equality between the rich and poor, and rural and urban areas. Hence, we cannot produce or expect better generations in the 21st and ensuing centuries unless a great reformation is brought about in politics, education, religion and society for all reasons.

Education: Meaning, nature and purpose of education should be changed according to the requirements of the 21st century. A uniform and national system of education is a must and should be followed in a country except mother tongue or at least a state level. Otherwise, education itself causes in equality in the children and society. Education is meant for better personal, social and cultural life and understanding, adjustment, acceptance and strengthens for global life. However, a separate education should be given to mentally physically challenge ones.

Curriculum: It should be dynamic and flexible according to the growth of children and requirements of the society. Above all, it includes those subjects and activities which enable the child for life in all respects. As such, it should develop knowledge, skill, vocational efficiency, and communication skills to face the challenging society. In fact, language skill are very important for the development of all other skills. A society or state opposes the study of other regional and global languages due to lack of efficiency in its mother tongue, ignorance, lack of flexibility and broad outlook. It is not good for a growing global society where understanding others, adjustments and fellow feelings are very important for global life. As our country is the united states of India, we should include and encourage the study of regional and national language (Hindi). This is good for a healthy social environments and national integration. In short, global thoughts, global life and vocational efficiency are expected to be developed in all children for four 'H'—Head, Heart, Hand and Health.

Examination and Valuation

Examination is the measuring scale of rote memorization of students from primary to university education. It encourages the students to memorise the book materials or write anything whether relevant or irrelevant for scoring high marks or grade at college and university levels. As they are studying only for examination, they will be very poor in subject knowledge and forget everything in a very short period. Valuation is very poor because most of the teachers or professors are very poor in subject and language. Mark or grade is based on the number of pages or answer sheets. If valuation is strictly done the percentage of students who pass in the examination will be 10 to 20 percent liberal and poor valuation produces various degree holders who fail in the competitive examinations. A part from written examinations, communication skills and vocational or professional efficiency should be examined through direct interviews. Worst valuation produces worst teachers who produce worst students. This trend should be changed as for as possible.

Teachers

Teachers should be better than the students in knowledge, subjects, language and character. They may be very poor in all aspects at the time of appointments but they should be developed and modified to be deserved for teaching profession. It is a noble profession but polluted by their socially undesirables and contemptible activities. They should be polite, honest and free from all bad habits. And avoid sitting, cheating and mobiling in the class room. They should discharge their duties and responsibilities not to be criticised by the students and society but remembered for ever. They should provide and create more and more opportunities to develop the communication skills and leadership qualities and prepare them for global thoughts and life. They should develop secular democratic and international outlook in the students.

Institution

Educational institutions are mini societies where students from various places with different cultures and characters learn together. As such, the institutions must be the centres for learning and developments. All discriminations in the name of castes, colours, gender, creeds, religions, regions and socio-economic status should be avoided and develop human values and book culture. All are equal by birth have rights to learn, earn and live with freedom and liberty. The institutions should have all facilities which are essential for the growth and development of students in all aspects.

Discipline

Social discipline should be developed in the students. Avoid all types of punishments because they live in the polluted and intoxicated society Moreover, students learn more from the families, societies and obscene violence based mass media than from the books and teachers. Most of the teachers and parents are worst in character and aim at money making. As such students live in the socio-natural pollution where strict discipline may mislead their life. So the teachers should be better guide, philosopher, counsellor and friends to their students. However, teacher's character and teaching of spiritual and moral values with practical experiences may develop desirable discipline in them.

Governments

The role of government is very essential to make education meaningful and useful, and prepare the citizens for 21st and ensuing centuries. It is highly deplorable that lack of leadership qualities and principle less politics make the government worst and worst. It encourages crimes and criminals by promoting the production of drugs and intoxicants and enjoys at the cost of privatization of education. In fact, the present governments never think of the impact of intoxicants and obscene-violence based mass media on students, family and society. As a result, education is meant for certificates, employment and money not for man-nation making and global life. The government and educational authorities demand to produce cent percent results. So, any body can get pass mark. Consequently, fake literate and researchers are found in materialistic and polluted society.

- Privatisation of education should be controlled.
- Production of intoxicants must be prohibited.
- Salary of teachers should not be increased because such cost is non-productive in the mass media world.
- There is no increment for additional studies degrees.
- Avoid corruption for certificates and employment
- Create opportunities for learning regional, national (Hindi) and international languages on optional basis.

CONCLUSION

We may suggest various ideas to improve and modify the educational systems for 21st century. But everything will be futile in the absence of quality governments, educational authorities, useful researchers and good society. In fact, everything is polluted for money by money and of money. It is very difficult to bring about change in the intoxicated society. Alcoholic and tobacco intoxicants and artificial drugs obscene-violence based mass media, divorce, prostitution, separation, killing, raping of innocent girls and women, chronic diseases, suicide, poverty and unemployment make human life stress and stress and peace into pieces. Hence, we strongly advocate that education for 21st century must be centred on character formation, humanism and vocation-profession making for better life. Education for all, employment for all and earn based on the nature and time of work. Finally, we should remember the powerful words of Jesus Christ if the salt loses its savour with what could it be salted. Similarly if education loses its quality in man making or character formation with what could it be made one? Let us learn, those activities which are socially good and useful for life and give up those which are undesirables and contemptible in the polluted society. This is education and life for the 21st century.

CHAPTER 6

CURRICULUM FOR MODERN SOCIETY

INTRODUCTION

Curriculum plays a vital role in the formal education offered in schools, colleges, universities and institutions. It is the most important tool which directs and guides education in a meaningful way. In other words, it helps to achieve the goals of education and life. In fact curriculum determines the quality of education. As such, curriculum construction and development is very important in the dynamic society. As child grows and society changes, curriculum should be modified and developed according to the requirements of the individual, society and country. So, it should include all aspects of activities (practices) or works, theories and exercises which are essential to prepare the children for personal, social and national life. It should also include various issues which retard the progress of the individual and society. It enables the child to challenge or face the problems in the materialistic society. Curriculum displays what are the activities should be taught or practiced in different stages of education. So, it may be regarded as wheels which facilitate the smooth running of education in all levels. Above all, it should socialize the child and develop secular-democratic outlook and global thinking or broad minds. Accordingly, curriculum should be constructed and developed in the complicated society.

MEANING OF CURRICULUM

Curriculum is a comprehensive term derived from the Latin word implying an athletic ground. It is the ground through which the student should pass in order to reach a definite goal. In fact, it is a race course in the field of education. As a person runs to win the race, a child should undergo various experiences to run through the curriculum and win the educational prizes/degrees. Hence, curriculum is that path over which a child/student runs to achieve the aim of education. In short, it refers to the syllabus or course of study which determines the limits of various subjects/knowledge to be gained in different levels/states of child. Broadly speaking, curriculum is a set of all those activities and experiences which the child undergoes in and outside the class according to his/her interests and needs. As such, it is the sum total of efforts which influence the learning whether in the class room on the playground or out of school, college, university or institution. So, it includes the overall experiences and knowledge that student receives through the manifold activities that go in the educational institutions—in the class room, library, laboratory, workshop, playground and in the numerous informal contacts among the teachers and students. Thus, the whole life of the educational institutions becomes curriculum which touches / influences the life of students at all stages. Hence, it includes those experiences and activities which provide the students with the knowledge and skill they require in facing the various situations of their life.

DEFINITIONS OF CURRICULUM

Curriculum is a comprehensive term defined in different ways.

Cunningham: "Curriculum is a tool in the hands of the artist (teacher) to mould his material (pupil) according to his ideal (objective) in his studies (school)".

Monroe: "Curriculum includes all those activities which are utilized by the school to attain the aims of education".

Froebel: "Curriculum should be conceived as an epitome of the rounded whole of the knowledge and experience of the human race".

Crow and Crow: "The curriculum includes all the learner's experiences in or outside school that are included in a programme which has been devised to help him develop mentally, physically, emotionally, socially, spiritually and morally".

Laswell: "The curriculum is made up of everything that surrounds the learner in all his working hours".

Horne, W.W.: "The curriculum is that which the pupil is taught. It involves more than the acts of learning and quiet study. It involves occupations, productions, achievement, exercise and activity".

We may define curriculum as, "It is the aggregation of theoretical knowledge and practical experiences and skills that the students expected to acquire from in and out of educational institutions". Therefore, it is a set of subject matters, activities and exercises based on the interest, needs and abilities of the students.

NATURE OF CURRICULUM

The salient features/nature of curriculum can be stated as below:

- It is comprehensive one includes syllabus, co-curricular and extra-curricular activities practiced in and out of educational institutions.
- It is prepared by educational authorities and well experienced faculties or a committee appointed by the governments based on the requirements of students and society.
- It is dynamic one changing based on the needs of the students, society and country. For instance, scientific study and vocational education and activity centred education have been given due importance in the contemporary society.
- Curriculum is changed due to the selection and arrangements of content for different stages of education in the materialistic primary, secondary, higher secondary and college levels.
- The contents of curriculum vary from state to state or country to country levels.
- It is flexible to include vocational subjects and scientific-technological studies.
- It promotes secular, democratic and international outlook in the child.
- It relates the academic subjects with real life activities and prepare the children for life in all respects.
- It encourages researches and investigation which expands the boundaries of knowledge and skills.

- A comprehensive curriculum inspires the children to develop all round personalities.
- It inculcates in children the human values such as honesty, kindness, sympathy, compassion, co-operation, tolerance, and brotherhood etc.
- A good curriculum promotes creative and constructive abilities in the children in conformity with different stages of development based on their needs, abilities and dynamic tendencies.
- It integrates the various achievements and experiences of great personalities in science, medicine, religion, politics, economics, education and history.

PRINCIPLES OF CURRICULUM CONSTRUCTION

Educationists and philosophers have stated various views about the fundamental principles of curriculum constructions. Education is meaningful and useful if it is based on curriculum. So, curriculum construction should have some principles which are mentioned below:

Principles of Utility: This is the basic principle of curriculum construction in the knowledge and complicated society. So, the curriculum should include those subjects, activities and experiences which are useful to the personal, social and national life of children. As such, there is no place for irrelevant and useless material in the curriculum. Such materials needs to be removed and replaced by6 useful, important and relevant ones for man-making and nation-making in the polluted social environments.

Principles of Proper Pattern of Conduct: According to Crow and Crow, the main principle of curriculum construction is that through education the child should be able to adopt the desirable pattern of behavior in different circumstances. Naturally, man is a social animal and he should be humanized with proper pattern of conduct. In the words of Crow and Crow, "The curriculum should be so framed that it may help the children in the achievement of wholesome behavior patterns. So, it should contain those subjects, activities and experiences that inculcate in the children social and moral qualities and shape courteous behavior towards others. In fact, all activities in social, political, economical, cultural, spiritual and moral environment constitute the behavior or conduct of human beings. Hence, the aim of education is to teach them how to behave in different situations.

Principle of Synthesizing of Play and Work Activities: It is seen that some educate the children through play whereas others through work. Most of the educationists support that curriculum should aim at achieving a balance between the both play and work. There is difference between work and play. So, parents want to engage their child in work instead of allowing him/her to play all the time. Naturally, the child is inclined to playing. So, this principle emphasizes the inter relation of play and work activities. As such, learning activities and experiences should be included in the curriculum and made so much interesting so that the child gains knowledge and experiences in playing and working activities. T.P. Nunn rightly remarks, "The school should be thought of not as a knowledge monger's shop but a place where the young are disciplined in certain forms of activity".

Principle of Synthesising all Activities of Life: Accordingly, curriculum should include all activities, subject, skills and experiences which are relevant to actual life of the child. It enables every child to perform a great variety of activities in the personal and social life. Hence the curriculum should not neglect any form of activity related to any aspect of life. So, the curriculum should be comprehensive child may requires in later life.

Principle of Individual Differences: This principle stresses the curriculum for child-centred education based on individual differences. Naturally, people differ in respect of their ages, intelligence, needs, interests, aptitudes, attitudes, abilities, skills, knowledge and activities. As these differences are innate, curriculum should be designed so as to provide opportunity for comprehensive and complete development to widely differing individuals. As such, curriculum construction should be child-centred education in all respects.

Principle of Flexibility: Another basic principle of curriculum construction is that it should be flexible. It should accommodate the development and changes take place in science, technology, engineering and medical fields, and help the children prepare for modern life. So, it would be adequate for all times and in all places. Hence, it becomes necessary to reshape the curriculum frequently in order to incorporate the latest developments.

Principle of Creativity: Naturally, man has creative and constructive powers. So, one of the aims of education is to develop the creative faculty of the child. Raymont rightly remarks, "Curriculum should be suited to the needs of today and future, there must be a positive bias towards definite creative subjects". Hence curriculum should have a prominent place for those subjects and activities which develop the creative and constructive capacities and abilities of the children as far as possible.

Principle of Variety of Experiences: The innate complexity of man with many facets of his personality requires a variety of knowledge and experiences which enable him to survive in the polluted socio-natural environments. So, one kind of curriculum cannot develop all faculties of the child. As such, the curriculum must have variety at every level of his / her growth and development. Hence, it should include the literary and academic subjects as well as varied human experiences and activities which a child receives in and out of educational institutions and through various informal contacts with the teachers and colleagues. The Secondary Education Commission of India states that there should be enough variety and elasticity in the curriculum to allow for individual differences and adaptation to individual needs and interests.

Principle of Cultural Preservation: This principle emphasis the preservation and transformation of culture and civilization. So, the curriculum should include cultural and civilization oriented subjects, activities and experiences. This kind of education enables the child to understand and practice the ancient culture which are important in the social life.

Principle of making Leisure Useful: Utilisation of leisure gainfully is one of the problems of many people in the modern society is seen that such people have no plan to spend their leisure meaningfully. So, education is not only meant for employment or work but also making leisure useful and pleasurable. Hence, a variety of social, artistic and sporting activities should be included in the curriculum to put the leisure in constructive and pleasant one.

Principle of Community Life: Generally curriculum is based on the principle that school and community life must be intimately related to each other. Moreover, educational institution is only a miniature form of community. Hence, full consideration of local needs and issues should be kept in mind while constructing curriculum. It should include all those activities, social beliefs, altitudes, traditions and problems of the community life which enables the children to understand them and discharge their responsibilities towards them. The Secondary Education Commission of India remarks, "The curriculum should be vitally and organically related to community life". This would develop social qualities which is essential for community life.

Principle of Development of Democratic Values: The construction of curriculum in a democratic society emphasise the development of democratic values and qualities in the child. So, it should be designed with activities and experiences which promote democratic behavior and feelings in the child. The programme devised in the educational institutions should lead to the development of socio-democratic qualities which enable the child to participate in democratic life. This is the chief consideration in shaping the curriculum for primary, secondary and higher education.

Principles of Problem Solving: Education is not only meant for employment and income but it should enable the educands to face various issues and problem and find out suitable solutions and achieve harmonious adjustments in the changing social environments of life. Hence, the curriculum contains subjects and activities which should be forward looking to solve problems and challenges faced in the present and future life.

Principle of Correlation: The unrelated fragments and unconnected subjects/units destroy the importance of curriculum and the purpose of education. Hence, the principle of curriculum is to keep various units interrelated so as to make the teaching learning process effective, successful and meaningful.

AIMS OF CURRICULUM CONSTRUCTION

The aims of education can be achieved and realized through curriculum construction. Hence, aims and objectives of curriculum are making education a meaningful and important process for individual and national developments. Curriculum contains what should be taught, practiced and exercised at different levels of education offered in schools, colleges and universities. Hence, curriculum is framed with aims and objectives which vary from time to time and place to place based on the requirements of the individuals and society.

Establish Relationship between Education and Society: Formal education is offered in educational institutions like school, college and university. The society (children) receives education from these institutions which depend on well structured curriculum. Thus, curriculum establishes relationship between education and society. In fact, curriculum contains various socio-economic and environmental issues and solutions to overcome them. As such, the aim of curriculum is to link education with society. In other words, it establishes a relationship between education and children (society).

Incorporate Current Issues in Education: Incorporation of current issues is another aim of curriculum. For instance, it includes the problem of population, growth, socio-environmental pollution, terrorism, unemployment, poverty, dowry, violence etc. Moreover, it accommodates new subjects' activities and experiences. This aims makes curriculum a dynamic and flexible one.

Activate Educational Practices and Activities: The remarkable aim of curriculum is to activate the various practices, activities and experiences in the educational institutions. As such, it makes education a meaningful and useful process which develop the personality of child and prepare him/her in all aspects of life.

Attain Educational Goals and Objectives: Education has varied goals and objectives which can be attained through curriculum. This is because curriculum reflects the aims of education in different ages. In fact, as the aims of education changes, the contents of curriculum changes according to the needs of the individuals and society. So, we have varied subjects, activities and experiences offered in different types of education. Thus, curriculum helps to attain the educational and social goals.

Design the Study Materials and Activities: This is also considered as an important aim of curriculum. It is seen that curriculum designs or includes various subjects, activities, experiences and exercises based on the age of children and the level of education in order to make learning interesting and successful.

Directs and Educational Activities: The aim of curriculum is to direct the educational activities successfully. In fact, it decides what should be included and taught and practiced in educational institutions meant for primary, secondary and higher education. As such, it makes education a purposeful activity.

Prepare Child for Life: Education is centred around curriculum and vice-versa. So, the aim of curriculum is to prepare the child for personal and social life, and adjust to the complicated environments. That is why, the content of curriculum includes the study of values, science, vocations, arts and technology. This comprehensive curriculum prepares the child for life in all possible ways.

Create a Suitable Environment to the Child: Another aim of curriculum is to create a suitable and useful environment to the child for a balanced development. In other words, the environment must assist the pupils in achieving maximum possible development of his faculties, abilities and capabilities.

Synthesis the Branches of Knowledge and Experiences: Curriculum is an important tool in synthesizing various branches of knowledge. It helps the child to acquire comprehensive knowledge in various fields and activities. Thus, the aims of curriculum is to integrate the theoretical and practical experiences which are essential to the physical, mental, spiritual, social and economic development of the child.

Develop and Expands Knowledge: Curriculum aims at the expansion and development of education. It is possible through curriculum which incorporates philosophical, psychological, sociological, scientific, historic, political, economic and technological knowledge. As such, curriculum widens the area of studies in the modern society.

Synthesis Subjects and Life: The aim of curriculum is to arrange and provide those subjects, activities and experiences which are related to the life of child. So, it satisfies the general and specific requirements of the child.

Curriculum is a tool by which the educational aims are achieved through schools, colleges, universities and institutions. Hence, curriculum and education go hand to hand to make the individual and society better in all respects.

BASES OF CURRICULUM

Curriculum is a means to achieve the aims of education which is based on philosophical, psychological, sociological, ecological and scientific views. Therefore, construction of curriculum depends upon these bases and aims of education. In fact, there are differences found in curriculum according to the varying aims of education determined by different aims and philosophies of education such as idealism, realism, naturalism and pragmatism. It is also influenced by psychological, sociological, scientific and ecological factors.

Aims of Education Based Curriculum: Aims of education are the most important bases of curriculum construction. In fact, changes in the aims bring about changes in curriculum construction. For example, If education aims at spiritual development of the child, curriculum would contains the study of different religions. If it aims at vocational efficiency of the child, it would include various occupational activities and practices. If it aims at scientific development, it would give priority to the study of science subjects and practices. Moreover, if it aims to character formation of the child, the curriculum would contain the study of moral and ethical values. Thus aims of education play very important role in curriculum construction.

Philosophy Based Education: It is seen that the formation of curriculum is based on the philosophy of education. In other words, educational philosophy influences the construction of curriculum at all stages of education. In fact, philosophy determines the goals of education and life achieved through curriculum. So, changes in philosophical ideologies due to changes in the goals of life and education from time to time and place to place changes the construction of curriculum so as to meet the requirements of individuals and society in the materialistic society. As such there is an intimate relationship between philosophy and curriculum. So, the shape and contents of curriculum should be changed to suit the prevailing ideologies and fulfil the needs of the individuals and society. For instance, the present day curriculum is entirely different from ancient times. It is seen that idealistic construction of curriculum includes those subjects and activities which enable the child to achieve spiritual, mental, cultural, development and character formation. Curriculum based on realism includes physical, science for actual life because it believes in reality and materialism. At the same time, naturalistic curriculum is child centred based on individual differences, interest, abilities, capacities and needs of the child. So, the curriculum contains games, sports, physics, psychology, material science, language, geography, history, mathematics, chemistry and biology. The pragmatic curriculum emphasizes the principles of utility and creativity. So, it recommends those subjects and activities which are useful to life and develop creativity of the child.

Psychology Based Curriculum: As education is child centred, the construction of curriculum depends on the psychological principles. It is the fact that the child develops through various stages and with different interests needs impulses, urges, capacities, creativities, and talents. Accordingly, curriculum should be flexible and accommodating various subjects, creative activities and useful experiences. Such kind of curriculum helps the child to achieve balanced developments. Thus psychological bases assist to construct the curriculum effectively.

Sociological Based Curriculum: Education is meant for individuals and society. Hence, sociological based construction of curriculum is very useful and important to analyse social as well as national issues such as population explosion, unemployment, poverty, inflation, terrorism, communal conflicts, dowry, eve-teasing, human trafficking, raping, illegal sex, homo-marriage and a lot of anti-social/ undesirable activities and find out the remedies to solve or overcome problems which affect the progress of the individuals and society. So, the curriculum should include those topics/subjects, activities and experience which deals with such issues, and ways and means to mitigate them for man-making and nation-making.

Scientific Based Curriculum: The modern life is mostly influenced by science and technology. This is because the invention and discoveries of materials and medicines make our life real, comfortable and easy. Hence, study of science, technology and engineering should be given utmost importance at all levels of education. It enables to reconstruct the curriculum based on the requirements of the society and scientific and technological developments. Accordingly, the present curriculum incorporates those subjects, activities and experiences which develop scientific outlook, creativity and rational thinking in the child.

Socio-environmental Based Education: The modern society is suffering from both social and environmental pollution and degradation which make human life unhappy, unhealthy and peaceless and the natural environments loss its qualities and quantities cause extinction of plants, birds, animals and lot of microorganisms. It affects the life of people and sustainable development of nature. Moreover, man pollutes man through killing, suicides, raping, illegal sex, dowry, obscene-violence centred mass media, corruption, inequality, intoxicants, and community conflicts. So, life has become tension, frustration and peaceless. At this juncture, education is meant for environment protection, sustainable development through environmental studies, environmental education, environmental engineering, environmental economics and environmental protection Acts, and man-making and nation-making through secular, democratic values, social pollution and the measures to control I, national integration and international understanding. As such, the present curriculum should contain those subjects, activities, knowledge and experiences which impart knowledge and skills to keep the man and environment from socio-environmental pollution and degradation. Thus, socio-environmental pollution and degradation occupy an unique place in the reconstruction of curriculum meant for all levels and stage of education.

TYPES OF CURRICULUM

There are various types of curriculum based on the requirements of individuals and society and different stages and nature of education in the vocational, scientific and technological oriented world. However, a few types of curriculum have been prescribed briefly in the subsequent passages.

Subject Centred Curriculum: This type of curriculum is known as book centred curriculum. It gives more importance to the study materials than the children. It is found common in general subjects. It is unpsychological ignoring the ability, capacity, interest and needs of children. It is not flexible but rigid one which is not suitable in everchanging/dynamic society. It never brings about the wholesome personality development in the child. It does not promote democratic feelings secular outlook and creative thinking. However, it aims to knowledge development. It's contents are definite and predetermined meant for rote memorization. It facilitates examination and testing. It encourages reading and writing only.

Experience Centred Curriculum: Curriculum embodies all the experiences of the past and present are utilized by the school to attain the aim of education. Accordingly, various subjects included in the curriculum not intended for study or rote learning but to convey the experiences of various kinds which are useful for the child. As such, curriculum does not mean only the academic subjects taught in the school, but it includes the totality of experiences that the child receives through various activities going on in the school, class room, library, laboratory, workshop, playgrounds and informal contacts between teachers and pupils. According to Crow and Crow, the curriculum includes all the learner's experiences in and outside school which enable the child to develop mentally, physically, emotionally, socially, spiritually and morally. So, the aim of curriculum is to provide experience to the pupil so that he may achieve complete development.

Activity Centred Curriculum: This type of curriculum emphasizes activities. John Dewey believes that a child will develop interest in useful and purposeful activities. In fact, the combination of subject matters, activities and experiences constitutes a pupil's school life. So, curriculum involves occupation, production achievement, exercise and activity. In short, activity centred curriculum enables the child to learn by doing.

Child Centred Curriculum: This kind of curriculum gives more importance to the child than subject studies. It is based on the interest, abilities and talents of the child. Montessori, Method, Kinder Garten and project method are using child centred curriculum to impart education, training and exercise which enable the children to develop their personalities in a harmonious way.

Craft Centred Curriculum: This type of curriculum makes learning interested and useful. Curriculum is craft centred emphasizing various crafts such as drawing, dying, spinning, painting, weaving, woodwork, leather work, metal work etc. The craft centred curriculum includes related subject matters and experiences.

Correlated Subject Curriculum: There is a correlation among the science subjects and activities. It is also found among humanities. So, correlated subjects centred curriculum incorporates the study of physics, chemistry, biology and mathematics together. And emphasizes the study of history, Economics, Political Science and Administration together. This type of curriculum combines the related subjects and activities together. So, the child would receive a comprehensive knowledge in arts or science or engineering subjects.

Care and Optional Centred Curriculum: This type of curriculum includes some subjects is essential and compulsory or core subjects for study at secondary or higher education level. And a few subjects are incorporated in the curriculum for study on optional basis. The study of basic subjects is known as core-curriculum is necessary and compulsory for all students. But, out of optional subjects, students are free to choose any one or more subjects according to their interests, needs and capacities. This type of curriculum is followed in American educational systems. So, many subjects are taught together which are child centred and provide practices and life experiences to face personal and social problems.

MERITS OR IMPORTANCE OF CURRICULUM

Achievement of Educational Aims: Curriculum is the most important tool which helps to achieve the aims of education. It accommodates various subjects and activities to achieve different educational aims based on the requirements of individual and society. In fact, it would be impossible to do anything systematically and successfully in the absence of curriculum.

Determines Teaching and Learning: It is very necessary to determine the body of knowledge and skills to be acquired by the students, at different levels of education. It is also important to determine the amount of teaching to be done by the teachers. Hence, curriculum is must in order to implement the educational programmes properly in different schools, colleges and universities. In fact, it determines the amount of teaching and learning in an academic year.

Dissemination of Knowledge: Curriculum comprises of various subjects, activities and experiences. As a result, the student can acquire a quantity of knowledge. Moreover, curriculum prepared for different levels of education help the student achieve mental development.

Expansion of Various Studies: Curriculum is flexible and accommodates various subjects on current achievements and developments. As such, it widens the area of studies which create new branches of knowledge or disciplines.

Purposeful Activity: Curriculum makes education a meaningful and purposeful activity meant for the personal, social and national life of the children in all respects. In fact, education will be meaningless in the absence of well constructed curriculum.

Shaping Education in Desirable Way: Curriculum provides a desirable shape to education according to the levels of students and needs of the society. In fact, it includes those topics/subjects, which deals with current social and national issues. As such, it keeps education a living organism.

Prepare for Employment and Income: Education through constructive curriculum prepares the students for all sorts of employment and make it a source of income for many people. In fact, curriculum is constructed with various subjects, activities and experiences in such a way to produce employable human resources in terms of certificate/degree holders and skilled ones.

Creation of Research Minds: The construction of curriculum for higher level of education encourages and develops interests in the research fields.

Basic for Formal Education: This is one of the most important merits of curriculum. In fact, facilitates the smooth functions of academic institutions. As such, it fulfils the aims of education and institutions. In other words educational institutions cannot function in the absence of curriculum.

DEMERITS OF CURRICULUM

Curriculum is very important to make educational activities effective and successful one. However, it is not free from criticism or drawbacks. Let us see them briefly.

Narrow Based Curriculum: Curriculum has been constructed to prepare the children for examinations that is book learning. It ignores the natural interest, abilities and needs of the students to challenge various issues and problems faced in their real life. In fact, it is subject and activities centred not life centred one. As such there is no difference between literate and illiterate in character and deeds in the materialistic society.

Emphasise Theoretical Knowledge: Curriculum meets the educational requirements through emphasizing bookish and the theoretical knowledge. It is just meant for examination, and degrees/ diplomas, or certificates without proper practical knowledge related to life. As such, curriculum becomes one sided neglects the development of various creativity and leadership qualities.

Difficulties of Teaching and Learning: Modern curriculum is constructed with overcrowded subjects to satisfy the needs of subject specialists. As a result it contains more and more subject contents, which create the problem of teaching and learning in a particular period. In fact, both teacher and student feel it a burden and strain imposed on them. It is the fault of educational authorites, academic experts and governments.

No Relation between Education and Life: Curriculum suggests various subjects and activities which are not related to life of the child. In fact, academically highly qualified person fails to overcome or solve even small problems or issue which he/she faces in the ordinary business of life. So, instead of emphasizing the study of subjects in the academic institutions, curriculum should provide opportunities to discuss the current personal and social issues and means and ways to face them without making the situation worst. It is highly deplorable that educated addict to many mistakes and wrong doings (social pollutions) more than the uneducated ones. The biggest but non-answerable question in the society is Are you educated one?

Neglecting Individual Differences: Curriculum is unpsychological ignoring the individual differences, interests, intelligence, abilities and talents. These are very essential while constructing curriculum. But the existing curriculum imparts same subjects, activities and experiences to all children. As such curriculum cannot be child centred one.

Examination Oriented Curriculum: The sole aim of curriculum is to prepare the students for specific examinations. It keeps teachers and students be busy in cutting some materials required from the examination point of view. So, it does promote reading habit and help the children to acquire a comprehensive knowledge of the specific subjects and activities.

Lack of Technical and Vocational Subject: The regrettable drawbacks of curriculum is the lack of technical and vocational subjects in the arts and science studies offered at secondary and higher education levels. This is true because most of the degree holders remain unemployed due to lack of technical and vocational skills. Such sort of education is very essential to prepare the child for economic life. So, both technical and vocational education should be included in the curriculum meant for education in all possible ways.

Lack of Character Formation and Values: Curriculum contains various subjects and experiences with moral and ethical values. But such curriculum is meant for examination and not for real life. Hence, the teachers teach and the students learn them for examination where there are no importance is given to learn and practice moral values. Even if, it is taught along with other subjects. Students and teachers treat as a part of general studies. As a result, character of the young generation is going down and number of criminals and crimes are increasing in the polluted society. Therefore, curriculum and teacher emphsise moral values in practical life. Above all, teacher should be a model to their students who are influenced by various learning sources in the intoxicated society.

Lack of Uniformity in Curriculum: There are different Boards of education at state and central or national levels which influence the construction of curriculum at different levels meant for same aged children. As such, it is possible to achieve balanced development in the children studying under different boards of curriculum.

Lack of Experts to Construct Curriculum: Curriculum is flexible and subjected to be changed according to the requirements of human resources of the country and the world. Lack of experts affect the construction of curriculum containing various subject matters, and experiences which make education meaningful and useful for life in all respects in the contemporary society. Moreover, addition or deletion of one or more topics does not mean reconstruction of curriculum but it should reflects the personal national and worldwide needs.

CONCLUSION

Curriculum is a powerful tool which enables to achieve goals of education at all levels and stages of individuals and society. It should be modified and developed by incorporating social, economic, political, environmental issues and values. Such curriculum brings about wholesome personality development in the child. Moreover, curriculum should contain those subjects, activities and experiences which foster vocational efficiency, secular-democratic outlook, leadership qualities, and social, ethical and moral values for man and nation making and to live and work together at global level. Hence, the present curriculum directs and leads education towards the destination of three principles—equality, liberty and fraternity and reach the top of one man and one world. So, there is no conflicts but peace and happiness everywhere should be ultimate peak of life and education. It is highly deplorable that most of people of the present day are still in the darkness of ignorance, superstitions, selfishness and narrow minds.

UNIT II

EDUCATION AND PHILOSOPHY

CHAPTER 7

EDUCATIONAL PHILOSOPHY

INTRODUCTION

Philosophy is the mother of all sciences and arts, including education. Therefore, the study of philosophy becomes necessary to discern the nature of education. It is because philosophy provides answers to all the ultimate questions vis-a-vis education. Fichte says, "The art of education will never attain complete clearness without philosophy". In fact, philosophy is a sun around which all the aspects of education rotate. It gives direction to education by providing certain guidelines. In this way, philosophy is regarded as the cornerstone for the foundation of education. Gentile is very right when he remarks that the process of education cannot proceed on right lines without the help of philosophy. Now let us concentrate on what is philosophy? What is education? What is educational philosophy? And what is the relationship between philosophy and education?

MEANING OF PHILOSOPHY

The word "philosophy" has been derived from two Greek words—*philos* and *sophia*. The term *philos* means love. The concept *sophia* means wisdom. Therefore, philosophy means *love of wisdom*. It refers to the search for wisdom, truth or fact and the relationship among ideas. The man who engages himself in this effort is called a **philosopher**. In the words of Plato, "He who has a taste for every sort of knowledge and who is curious to learn and is never satisfied may be justly termed a philosopher".

DEFINITIONS OF PHILOSOPHY

Different philosophers have defined the term philosophy according to their own mature reflection and thinking. The following definitions make it clear for us to understand philosophy:

Raymont: "Philosophy is an unceasing effort to discover the general truth that lies behind the particular facts, to discern also the reality that lies behind appearances".

Henderson: "Philosophy is a search for a comprehensive view of nature, an attempt at a universal explanation of the nature of things".

Aristotle: "Philosophy is a science which investigates the nature of being, as it is in itself".

Plato: "Philosophy aims at knowledge of eternal nature of things".

Bertrand Russell: "Philosophy like all other studies, aims primarily at knowledge".

Fichte: "Philosophy is the science of knowledge".

Brightman: "Philosophy may be defined as the attempt to think truly about human experience as a whole and to make our whole experience intelligible".

Radhakrishnan: "Philosophy is a logical enquiry into the nature of reality".

Harold Titus: "A person's philosophy is the sum of his fundamental beliefs and convictions".

R.W. Seller: "Philosophy is a persistent attempt to gain insight into the nature of the world and of ourselves by means of systematic reflection".

Marcus Tullius Cisero: "Philosophy is the mother of all arts and the true medicine of mind".

Aristotle: "Philosophy is a science, which discovers the real nature of supernatural elements".

V.R. Taneja: "Philosophy being a mother of discipline, all arts and sciences look to it for the solution of their problems".

Kant: "Philosophy is the science and criticism of cognition".

Prem Nath: "Philosophy is open-mindedness cultivated through the rigorous discipline of the mind".

However, from these definitions, we may define thus "philosophy is the truth or wisdom gained out of human knowledge and experience as a consequence of his interaction with the enfolded facts of nature". It is clear that philosophy is an attempt to answer the ultimate questions of life. It also means the search for knowledge, wisdom, and the relationship between the variables and their impact on nature. Thus, it is an attitude towards human life and universe where the effort is made to search for truth on the basis of logical enquiry.

KINDS OF PHILOSOPHY

We know that Philosophy is a deep and comprehensive subject. It does not end with love of wisdom; but it goes beyond to find relationships and discover implications. It helps us to understand the importance of all human experiences and activities. Hence, the areas or the scope of philosophy is very vast. It can be divided into three areas, kinds or divisions. They are metaphysics, epistemology and axiology.

Metaphysics: Metaphysics is the first division of philosophy which deals with the nature of reality. The questions such as what is the nature of the universe we live in? What is reality? What is soul? What is God? etc. are discussed under Metaphysics. It has the following parts:

Theology It is concerned with the theological aspects of philosophy. That is, it is about the presence of God and His nature etc.

Ontology It deals with the ultimate reality—the nature of existence.

Cosmology It is the study of the problems connected with origin and imposition.

Cosmogony It is the theory concerning the origin and development of the universe—the creation of the world.

Philosophy of self It refers to the philosophical interpretation of the self. For example, "Who am I?" is the first question before every man. This leads to all other questions about man and his nature.

Eschotology It is a philosophical doctrine which studies the last or final matters as death and the life after death.

Epistemology: This is the second division of philosophy that deals with the theory of problem of knowledge. Questions such as, how do we get knowledge? How does a man know what is real? What are the sources of knowledge etc. are analysed under epistemology. Thus, it explains the nature of knowledge, origin of knowledge, types of knowledge, methods of knowledge, limits of knowledge, validity of knowledge and the sources of knowledge. The naturalists believe that knowledge can be gained through senses whereas the idealists believe that knowledge can be acquired through spiritual experiences. Pragmatists believe that knowledge is acquired through project method and experimentation.

Axiology: Axiology is the third area of philosophy which studies values philosophically. Here, the questions such as what are the higher values of life? What are the principles of life? How do they support the view of reality? What are the importance of developing values such as truth, beauty and goodness in life? How can we preserve these values? etc. are explained. Axiology studies three areas namely, logic, ethics and aesthetics.

Logic: Logic deals with the rules and techniques of reasoning. It applies the scientific method of enquiry through inductive and deductive methods. Logical thinking, imagination or supposition and investigation are considered under this part of philosophy.

Ethics: It is known as moral philosophy. It deals with judgement of rightness and wrongness, goodness and badness, virtues and vices. In short, it deals with the principles of conduct which help to judge whether an action is good or bad.

Aesthetics: It is concerned with beauty. It analyses beauty and ugliness, their characteristics and the standards of measuring the two concepts that is taste and appreciation. Thus, the scope or areas of philosophy is very wise and it includes the knowledge of the entire universe.

MEANING OF EDUCATION

Defining the term 'education' is a difficult task as it is like a diamond which appears to be of different colours when seen from different angles. It is believed that the word "education" has been derived from the Latin words, *educare* meaning 'to bring up' or 'to nourish', *educere* meaning bring forth or draw out and *educatum* meaning the act of teaching or training. The origin of the word 'education' is derived from *E* and *duco*. The word *E* denotes *out of* and *Duco* implies *I lead*. Therefore, *educo* means "lead out of" or "bring out of" the latent potentialities of the child. In short, education means bringing about a desirable behaviour in human beings. In the words of Prof. James S. Ross, "Education consists of leading out the innate knowledge, virtues, and powers of the child, making the potential actual".

DEFINITIONS OF EDUCATION

Philosophers and educationists have defined the term 'education' according to their knowledge, experiences and the needs of their society. As a result, different definitions have been put forward by them. A few of them are stated here with a view to making the meaning of education more clear.

Aristotle: "Education is the creation of a sound mind in a sound body".

Pestalozzi: "Education is the natural, harmonious and progressive development of man's innate powers".

Froebel: "Education is the unfoldment of what is already enfolded in the germ. It is the process through which the child develops his innate qualities".

John Dewey: "Education is the process of living through a continuous reconstruction of experiences. It is the development of all those capacities in the individual which will enable him to control his environment and fulfil his possibilities".

Raymont: "Education is a process of development from infancy to maturity, the process by which he adapts himself gradually in various ways of his physical and spiritual development".

James Drever: "Education is a process in which and by which knowledge, character and behaviour of the young are shaped and moulded".

Swami Vivekananda: "Education is the manifestation of divine perfection already existing in man".

Tagore: "Education is that which makes one's life in harmony with all existence and thus enables the mind to find out that ultimate truth which gives us the wealth of inner light and love and gives significance to life".

Mahatma Gandhi: "By education I mean an all round drawing out of the best in child and men—body, mind and spirit".

Sri Aurobindo: "Education is helping the growing soul to draw out that is in itself".

From the definitions of philosophy and education we can conclude the fact that the common subject of both philosophy and education is "man". So, the study of man and life is more important than the study of any other organisms in the earth.

MEANING OF EDUCATIONAL PHILOSOPHY

Educational philosophy is the branch of general philosophy, which answers educational questions such as aims, curriculum, method of teaching role of a teacher, discipline, evaluation and so on. We can say that the application of philosophy in the field of education to solve various educational issues is regarded as educational philosophy. In fact, educational philosophy is that philosophy which provides answers to the educational issues of why to educate (aim), whom to educate (child), who to educate (teacher), where to educate (school), what to educate (curriculum), how to educate (methods), when to educate (motivation) and so on. Thus, it is the educationist's approach to solve educational problems by referring to the philosophy of society.

DEFINITIONS OF EDUCATIONAL PHILOSOPHY

G.E. Patridge: "In a very deep sense, it is quite as responsible to say that philosophy is based upon education, as education is based upon philosophy".

John Dewey: "Educational philosophy is the most significant phase of philosophy, for it is through the process of education that knowledge is obtained".

We may define educational philosophy thus; "It is the application of philosophical principles in the educational practices which directs the process of education towards the aims of human life". In short, educational philosophy relates philosophy to life through the medium of education.

SCOPE OF EDUCATIONAL PHILOSOPHY

The scope of educational philosophy is the study of all those aspects or schools of philosophy, which are important from the educational point of view. Educational philosophy includes areas such as aim of education, curriculum, methods, teacher, child, textbooks, school, discipline, evaluation, supervision and administration. Let us analyse the scope of educational philosophy to devise various programmes of activities for the development of both the individual and the society.

Aims: Educational philosophy helps in determining the aims of education. An educator is helpless in arriving at the aims of education if he lacks the knowledge of related circumstances and problems.

Curriculum: Educational philosophy provides adequate support to the educator while he is engaged in formulating the subject contents for the young members of the society. It means that curriculum must have sound philosophical support, so that young learners can build an epistemological philosophy.

Methods of teaching: The scope of educational philosophy includes different methods of teaching. The method of teaching must have philosophical support, so that teaching can be very effective and attractive. Philosophy determines a suitable method of teaching according to the interests and abilities of the child.

Teacher: The role of teacher in the process of teaching is determined by educational philosophy. The teacher occupies an important place in idealism, whereas the position of the teacher is secondary in naturalism. It is educational philosophy that indicates the position of the teacher in different times. The teacher is regarded as the friend, philosopher, and guide in pragmatism.

Child: Child has an important place in naturalism whereas it has a secondary position in idealism. Thus, the role of the child in school is determined by educational philosophy. So, scope of educational philosophy answers the questions such as—what is the existence of the child. What is the existence of school? Is the child meant for the school or the school for the child? Many more similar questions fall within the scope of educational philosophy.

Textbooks: The scope of educational philosophy provides guidelines in preparing textbooks according to the age, interests, attitudes and abilities of children, and also the growing needs of the society.

Discipline: Educational philosophy maintains discipline among the children in order to bring out all-round development in them. The scope of educational philosophy includes self-control, freedom and social discipline that are implemented in different schools of thoughts.

OBJECTIVES OF STUDYING EDUCATIONAL PHILOSOPHY

It is educational philosophy that makes education a dynamic and life-long process. Hence, the study of the objectives of educational philosophy has become an important aspect in the modern times:

- The most important objective of studying educational philosophy is to find solutions for various educational issues.
- The purpose of studying educational philosophy is to make education according to the need based life and society.
- The aim of educational philosophy is to determine the aim of human life, that is, aim of survival.
- The objective of studying educational philosophy is to produce better citizens by fostering democratic attitudes in behaviour.
- Make the teaching–learning process more effective and attractive according to interests, inclinations and abilities of the child.
- Discern the different philosophies and choose any one of them to lead a fruitful life in the society.

- Expand our knowledge and experiences, and implement them in the educational practices.
- Bring out an all-round personality development in child and prepare him to stand on his own feet.
- Make education flexible in order to achieve the goals of a country—national integration, international understanding and globalization.
- Develop education as a powerful instrument to bring about social, cultural, political and economic change in a society.

NEED AND IMPORTANCE OF EDUCATIONAL PHILOSOPHY

Educational philosophy is the cornerstone of the foundation of education. It provides direction to education by assigning certain guidelines. Education is a dynamic and life-long process. Hence, the responsibilities of the teacher have increased further. The system of education also has to be changed in accordance with the changing environment of the society. Therefore, the knowledge of educational philosophy has become more important in these days.

Objectives of life: Educational philosophy is important to get the knowledge of the objectives of human life. Everybody wants that he/she should do something in life. He gets such knowledge or aim through the medium of educational philosophy. In this regard, educational philosophy helps him to achieve the objectives of his life.

Selection of proper life philosophy: There are different educational philosophies to solve educational issues. The study of different educational philosophies help us to select proper life philosophy or ideology that solves our problems relating to education and life.

Aims of education: Educational philosophy is more important to determine the aims of education. It gives guidelines to change the aim of education during different periods. Self-expression is the aim of education under naturalism, whereas it is self-realisation in idealism and social efficiency in pragmatism.

Curriculum: We get knowledge about formulating a curriculum through the study of educational philosophy. With the help of educational philosophy, a teacher comes to know why naturalism give emphasis to science subjects and why idealism give importance to religious subjects? Thus, educational philosophy is important to construct a curriculum based on the needs of society.

Method of teaching: Educational philosophy is very important to adopt suitable method of teaching and make classroom teaching effective and attractive. We get the knowledge of different methods of teaching, that is, 'learning by doing' in naturalism, 'Lecture method' in idealism and 'experimental method' in pragmatism. With the help of educational philosophy, we can choose suitable methods of teaching according to the nature of subjects and school environment.

Discipline: Idealism advocates strict discipline and self-control whereas naturalism emphasised freedom and natural discipline, and pragmatism stressed social discipline. These disciplines are known from the study of different educational philosophies. Hence, knowledge of educational philosophy is essential to follow a desirable discipline.

Personality of teacher: Educational philosophy is necessary to get knowledge about the personality or quality that a teacher should possess. It is educational philosophy that considers teacher as a friend, philosopher guide, and social engineer. It also determines the importance of his role in the modern world.

Student: The role of students in the educational process is determined by educational philosophy. With the help of educational philosophy, we get knowledge pertaining to the role of students in the schools. Students get secondary importance in idealism whereas they get primary importance in naturalism.

Measurement: Educational philosophy provides knowledge to the teacher to know the criterion that he should use or apply to evaluate the growth and performance of the students. He can adopt any criteria to measure or evaluate the students (physical, intellectual, spiritual, social and moral development) with the help of educational philosophy.

School administration: The knowledge of what kind of school administration we should adopt is determined by educational philosophy. Educational philosophy helps to establish a school in democratic or totalitarian system. In these days, the school administration is done in a democratic setup. This is based on educational philosophy.

Teacher and student: Through educational philosophy, we get knowledge about the relationship between the teacher and the student. There is a close relation ship between the teacher and the student in pragmatism and idealism whereas it is limited in naturalism.

Educational problems and solutions: We are facing new problems everyday. They are even more in the educational field. This is because of the advancement of science and technology. Now new visual aids, communication etc. are utilised in the society, which have a great impact on educational practices. Thus, educational philosophy helps us to solve the growing problems by using new ideology according to the nature of environments.

RELATIONSHIP BETWEEN PHILOSOPHY AND EDUCATION

Philosophy and education are integrally and interdependently related to each other. Practically, it is very difficult to separate them. In the words of J.S. Ross, "Philosophy and education are like the two sides of the same coin; one is implied by the other; the former is the contemplative side of life, while the latter is the active side". Both philosophy and education are related like flower and fragrance, skeleton or flesh and blood. In short, they are two flowers of one stem and two sides of a coin.

Philosophy without education is blind.
Education without philosophy is cripple.

If education is the physical body, philosophy is its soul. The very existence of education is due to philosophy and in the same way the existence of philosophy is due to education. Education is a plant on which the flower of philosophy blooms. From these words we can discern that there is a very close relationship between philosophy and education. Fichte says that the art of education will never attain complete clearness in itself without philosophy. In the words of Gentile, "To educate children without concerning ourselves with the subtle problems of philosophy means a failure to understand the precise nature of education". In fact, the nature of education cannot be understood in the absence of philosophy. Hence, both are essential to grasp each other and they function together to achieve the goals of human life.

Philosophy determines the direction of education: Education is a conscious dynamic and purposeful process. It is an integral part of life. Hence, it needs proper guidance and supervision. Philosophy determines the goals of life. It provides suitable and effective guidance and supervision for education to achieve that goal. In other words, philosophy gives direction to education. In the light of philosophy, education moves towards its goal. How should education play its role? Is social development possible through education? It is philosophy that answers these questions. In the words of Rusk, "Philosophy formulates what it conceives to be the end of life education offers suggestions how this end is to be achieved".

Education is the means for propagation of philosophy: Education is the active side of the coin. It acts as the most powerful tool in propagating the philosophical ideology. A philosopher is a constant seeker after truth. He should not withdraw himself entirely from reality and live in an 'ivory tower'. He should propagate his philosophy in order to convert others to his beliefs. Only then he can become a true philosopher. After realising the truth, he should use education for teaching people what to believe. Education is used by the philosophers for the purpose of ideological propagation.

Education is the practical side of philosophy: The function of philosophy is to formulate the aims and the functions of education. In fact, education is the practical side of philosophy, which makes education a dynamic process and answers all problems related to it. In the words of Adam, "Education is the dynamic side of philosophy. It is the active aspect of philosophical belief, the practical means of realising the ideals of life". Education cannot even be imagined without philosophical principles like wise philosophical principles are lifeless without the help of education. For example, the introduction of the 10+2+3 system of education and craft education are the consequence of philosophical views. Thus, philosophy equips us with thoughts and these thoughts are put into practice by education.

Great philosophers are great educationists: The great philosophers of all times, from Plato upto the present day, have also been great educators. Great Western philosophers such as Socrates, Plato, Locke, Rousseau, Spencer, Froebel, Dewey, H.G. Wells, Bertrand Russell, A.N. Whitehead, Aldous Huxley, Aristotle, and Comenius were great educators. Modern Indian philosophers such as, Mahatma Gandhi, Zakir Hussain, Swami Vivekananda, Sri Aurobindo, Gurudev Tagore, Dayananda and Radhakrishnan were great educationists of their times. The history of education proves that all philosophers have been great educators. J.S. Ross says, "The great philosophers have also been the great educators". John Locke, a philosopher of the seventeenth century of England, stated that a mind is capable of finding truth only when trained specifically to think.

Political philosophy determines education: Political philosophy has an inseparable relation with education. It means that there is always a philosophy working behind any politics. In the words of K. Kshatriya, "If education is a philosophy in action, so also is politics. Political systems are the last resort to the outcome of philosophical positions". India is a democratic country which believes in a democratic way of thinking. This way of thinking is reflected in the field of education. The dictatorship of Sparta Germany and Italy can be found in the field of education. A different form of education can be seen in communist countries.

Philosophy determines various aspects of education: All the problems of education are the problems of philosophy. That is why, Gentile says, "Education without philosophy would mean a failure to understand the precise nature of education". It is because philosophy determines both the aim of life and the aim of education. It helps to construct curriculum according to the needs of the individual and the society. The influences of philosophy can also be seen in the conception of methods of teaching, the role of teachers, discipline, textbook, school administration, evaluation, selection of subject matter, and the role of students etc. J.S. Ross remarks, "From every angle of the educational problems comes the demand for philosophical basis of life and education".

Modern philosophers have impact on education: The World Wars and consequent destruction in the twentieth century have resulted in less faith in mere intellect in the application of modern science and technology. Humanism, faith in higher principles and values of life, character development, and emotional integration have received greater impetus. In order to develop these qualities new schools of philosophy that aimed at synthesising science and religion were evolved. The present age is the age of reunion. Hence, this is the period of synthesising both philosophy and education. In fact, modern philosophy develops social discipline and democratic attitude in the child's behaviour through education.

Philosophy provides answers to ultimate questions: Philosophy performs the functions of methodical interpretation of educational problems on the criterion of philosophy. It is a deep study which converts philosophy into a metaphysics, ethics, logic or a combined subject. Bertrand Russell says that philosophy is born out of the effort to give answers to the ultimate question of education. Therefore, the ultimate question of philosophy is the ultimate question of education. Butler states that philosophy is a guide to educational practice. Education as a field of investigation yields certain data which serve as a basis for philosophical judgement.

Philosophy shapes the aspects of education: Generally, there are two aspects of education, namely theoretical and practical education. It is philosophy that determines how much emphasis should be provided to either of these aspects of education. This view is reflected in the present system of education. In other words practical education is assigned great importance in science and technology.

IMPACT OF PHILOSOPHY ON EDUCATION (RELATION OF PHILOSOPHY WITH EDUCATION)

Philosophy is the mother of all arts including education. Hence, a study of philosophy is very helpful in understanding the following practices and trends in education:

Philosophy and educational values: Philosophy has given a rational and logical shape to educational values such as accountability to man and unseen good, honest and impartial attitudes towards all humans, purification of souls, independent thinking etc. by giving answers to 'How and Why' questions. These values are important for the mental development of the child along with his spiritual development.

Philosophy and science education: Science is the systematic knowledge based on observation and experimentation and conclusions are drawn on the basis of the data collected. The relationship between facts and events, and respective cause and effects are established with the help of the available data. Then, conclusions are presented in the form of principles and theories. Philosophy also does the same job. The scope of science is limited to the physical world but the scope of philosophy is the entire universe, both seen and unseen. Science interprets only the natural phenomenon of a thing, but philosophy elaborates the supernatural phenomenon also. Both philosophy and education are related in research activities.

Philosophy and aim of education: Philosophy is the determining force for laying down the aims of education. The aims of education are related to the aims of life. The aims of life are determined by the philosophy of that time. They change with the changing philosophy of life. In the words of Bode, "Unless we have philosophical understanding of life and some guiding philosophy, education will be meaningless". According to Ross, "The educational aims and methods are corollaries of philosophical doctrines". Idealism recommends self-realisation as the aim of education whereas it is self-expression in naturalism and socialisation in pragmatism. John Dewey says that philosophy is concerned with determining the ends of education. In the modern age different countries have different aims of education according to their philosophy. In democratic countries such as India, England and America, freedom, equality, fraternity, and justice are the main aims of education. In communist countries like China and Russia the aims of education is to make the individual useful and subservient to the interest of the nation. Bode says that unless we have some guiding philosophy in the determination of aims, we will get nowhere at all. Education is a purposeful activity. Hence, it is unthinkable without aims. It is philosophy that makes education a purposeful activity by determining the directions and aims of education.

Philosophy and curriculum: In the words of K.G. Saiyidain, "The curriculum is primarily an aid in the process of adjusting the child to the environment in which he functions from day-to-day and in the environment in which he will have to organize his activities later". Curriculum maybe deemed as the practical side of philosophy. It is the means through which we realise the aims of education. The philosophy of a country at a particular time determines the curriculum in which such subjects, activities and experiences are included which meet the emerging demands of the society. Various philosophies such as realism, humanism, idealism, naturalism, pragmatism have influenced curriculum in varying degrees. For example, the naturalists included various subjects and activities in the curriculum based on the interests, experiences and activities of the child. They advocated physical sciences and direct experiences. Idealists stressed an ideal life. They recommended subjects like Ethics, Logic, Literature and Humanities in the curriculum. The pragmatists supported utilitarian, flexible and correlated curriculum.

The High Schools of America stress the study of automobile repair, electronics and aeronautics to fulfil the needs of a technological society. Similarly, the use of calculator and computers forms an important part of school curriculum in the United States, India and other countries. The contents of Indian education include materials on developing the values of secularism, socialism and democracy to produce better citizens.

Philosophy and method of teaching: The process of education cannot proceed on right lines without the help of philosophy. In the absence of an adequate philosophy of life, the method of teaching followed by the teacher may repel the students from the subjects. It is, therefore, that there is a close relationship between philosophy and method of teaching. Every philosopher formulates his own methods of teaching according to his own philosophy. So, we have different methods of teaching propounded by different philosophical thoughts. According to the philosophy of idealism, question—answer method, lecture method, discussion method, debates and discussions are the most suitable methods of education. Naturalists recommend various new methods of teaching like learning by doing, learning by self-experience, direct experience, Dalton plan, Heuristic method, play-way method and Montessori method. They emphasise the child-centred method of teaching. Pragmatists advocate project method, problem-solving method, experimental method, group activities and socialist techniques. Through the process of teaching methods, the teacher establishes contact between the child and the subject matter. When philosophy changes, method of teaching also changes.

Philosophy and textbooks: A good textbook must reflect the prevailing values of life fixed by philosophy. Textbooks are important instruments through which the aims of education are realised. As a curriculum is influenced by the philosophy of times, so also the textbooks are affected by the prevailing philosophy of the day. Therefore, the textbooks should reflect the ideology, ideals and values of society. The government should keep an eye on the production of books for children. Standard books of utility for children should be made available and undesirable books should be discouraged and banned from production and circulation. Hence, textbooks need special care and attention. Moreover, textbooks must be written in accordance with the philosophy of the time, cultural, social and political background of a society. Naturalists, idealists and realists give importance to pictures in the textbooks in order to arouse interest in the students.

Philosophy and teacher: Every teacher is a philosopher. Education takes place through the interaction between the teacher and the taught. So, the teacher has to play an important role in shaping and moulding the ideals, habits, manners, tastes and ways of life, and above all the character and personality of the students. For this purpose, a teacher should know fully well the needs of the children and the demands of the society. He must keep in mind that his own beliefs, ideas and principles of behaviour have a powerful impact on the development of children. Hence, he must possess a good understanding of all philosophies of life and choose the best from them to form his own philosophy. The teacher is the backbone of the entire process of education. So, he should have high ideals, morals, and spiritual values together with a sense of national responsibility for national prosperity and international goodwill.

Each philosophy determines the place of the teacher differently in the teaching–learning process. For example, the naturalists stress that 'Nature' is the best teacher. The teacher is the observer of students. He should never interfere with the free activities of children. Here, they give secondary importance to the teacher. The idealists advocate that teacher is the pivotal point in the process of education. The teacher was called Guru and was placed before God. According to the pragmatists, the teacher is a friend, a guide, a philosopher. He should not impose anything on the pupil. He should provide opportunity to the students to undertake experiments and researches. In all cases, the teacher is guided by a particular philosophy of education. Gentile rightly says that to educate children without concerning themselves with philosophy means a failure to understand the precise nature of education.

Philosophy and students: Philosophy determines the place of students in the process of education. It is about the relationship between the teacher and the students. Idealists give secondary importance to students. The duty of a student is to realise himself. He should give his teacher the status of 'Guru'. But naturalists give primary importance to the students. Students enjoy full freedom to develop themselves naturally. Nature is the best teacher and allows the child to learn in the laps of 'Nature'. Pragmatists want the students to become useful members of the society. Therefore, the spirit of equality, freedom and fraternity should be given importance in education. In the words of John Locke, "The mind of a child is a clean slate on which many impacts can be made". The modern philosophies stress that the student should be given opportunity for independent development.

Philosophy and discipline: Philosophy determines the nature and form of discipline observed in educational institutions. Discipline reflects the philosophy of life. In other words, despotic and authoritarian governments enforce rigid discipline while democratic countries give more or less freedom of action to children in schools. Prof. Adam has discussed three forms of discipline on the philosophical basis.

Repressionistic discipline This type of discipline is based upon despotic and authoritarian ideologies. The child is repressed by the despotic attitude of the teacher. There is no freedom for children at all. Children should abide by the rules and regulations of the school without questioning why physical punishment, or creating a sense of fear is used as a means to enforce disciplinary rules. Idealists followed the repressionistic discipline in order to develop good behaviour in the child, so that he could lead a holy life for salvation.

Impressionistic discipline This type of discipline is based upon self-discipline. It is believed that no child is good or bad in behaviour and his behaviour can be shaped by teachers who come in contact with him. The impression of the teacher's lofty character and good conduct influence the school environment. There is no need for corporal punishment or creating a sense of fear in the minds of the children. Love, sympathy and affection transform the feelings and actions of children for better channels. Realists advocated this type of discipline.

Emancipatory discipline This type of discipline is based on naturalism. Naturalists advocate full freedom for the child. This freedom develops him like the flower of a plant. Here the child is allowed to learn by the laws and rules of natural consequences. So, nothing is dictated to him from outside. It enables the child to develop his thinking and reasoning power naturally. Here, the problem before us is which type of discipline should a school follow? It is determined by the prevailing philosophical foundation of the society where the school functions. Idealists have faith in rigorous type of discipline, which develops self-discipline. Realists support the concept of discipline based on love and sympathy. Naturalists believe that the child can be kept in discipline through nature. If the child makes a mistake, he would be punished by nature. Pragmatists have faith in social discipline. They are not in favour of unlimited freedom to the child. They maintain discipline by keeping the child busy in group activities. Modern concept of discipline gives maximum freedom to child and it provides opportunities to have self-control, coexistence and the inner discipline, based upon the democratic ideology and social philosophy.

Philosophy and school building: Philosophy determines the type of school building, and the place where it should be built. It provides answers to the questions such as what type of school building should be there? And where should the school building be built? Naturalism recommends that school building should be far away from the hue and cry of the cities. It should be built in the natural environment. They also stress that the school should have playgrounds, open spaces, workshops and laboratories. Pragmatists give importance to workshops and laboratories in the school so that social discipline can be developed among the children. Idealists clain that an ideal school must have four departments, that is, faculty or vedic department, literary department, cultural department and personality department. Modern philosophers stress that school is a miniature of society that should have adequate buildings, appropriate laboratory, playgrounds, workshops and open space, library, first aid facilities etc.

Philosophy and evaluation: Evaluation becomes the dynamic side of philosophy. Without philosophy, evaluation is a boat without a rudder. Evaluation becomes philosophy when ideas of sense of responsibility are added to performance. For instance, when a teacher is found guilty for the poor performance of his students, he maybe punished for this reason. Naturalists evaluate the physical and mental activities of the child. Idealists evaluate the spiritual and moral development of the child. Pragmatists measure the social adjustment of the child. In the philosophy of realism, social and scientific points of view are examined. Thus, different philosophies help the educationists to evaluate the performance of students and teachers in order to ascertain the maximum utilisation of resources and develop a sense of responsibility among all individuals concerned.

Philosophy and supervision: There are many questions before us today like what is supervision? What is the purpose of supervision? What points should be kept in mind while supervising? For such questions, we seek answers with the help of philosophy. It is philosophy that gives answers relating to these questions. Naturalists supervise whether the development of the child is taking place in the free environment. Idealists supervise the discipline of the child and the teacher at every step very minutely. He should inculcate certain good qualities in him. Pragmatists check whether the social development of the child is taking place in the group. Realists supervise the development of child from different angles.

Philosophy and school administration: Philosophy tells us under whose leadership the administration of the school should be and who should have control over education—State or the

Centre. Individualistic philosophy prefers education under the control of voluntary organizations. The socialistic ideology is of the opinion that education should be under the full control of the state. Philosophy also tells us what type of principal should be there for the administration of the school. The management of the school would be democratic in the society that has faith in democratic ideology.

Philosophy contributes to gigantic tasks such as establishment of schools, management of schools, finance, supervision and organizing co-curricular activities in schools.

Establishment of schools: Decision to establish a school is taken after analysing the specific needs of the society concerned. Then the place is selected keeping in view of the aims of education set by the society. After this, physical facilities are arranged. The inner and outer decoration of the school is made according to the aesthetic sense of the local people.

Management of schools: The philosophers should decide whether the school should be run by the government or by a private management committee. The role of management is very important to frame the policies regarding the appointment of teachers and admission of students. For example, if the management committee has idealistic views of life, it will appoint teachers who give importance to spiritual and moral values and thoughts.

Finance: If a school is to be established in a poor locality, the state will have to face the financial responsibilities of the school. But a school can be established without the state or outside help if people of a particular area are rich and they are willing to contribute for the development of education. Hence, the philosophers take decision regarding who should meet the financial needs of the school in a society.

Supervision: Supervision and control is the fourth aspect of educational administration. Through this process the maximum utilisation of physical and human resources are ascertained. Honest and unbiased attitudes make this process a success and corrupt behaviour will spoil the whole process.

Co-curricular activities: The nature of co-curricular activities is decided by the philosophy of those who are engaged in educational administration.

CONCLUSION

We cannot escape from philosophy of life and education. Philosophy represents a system of thought which education embraces in the content of instruction; philosophy offers an outlook on life which is fostered or developed through education in the child. Philosophy presents a way of life; education is an understanding of and a preparation for it. So, all educational questions are ultimately questions of philosophy. As a consequence, education becomes incomplete without philosophy. Hence, we can say that philosophy, life and education are intimately linked with one another. In fact, philosophy leads and education follows the path shown by philosophy.

CHAPTER 8

IDEALISM

INTRODUCTION

Idealism is the most ancient thought in the world of philosophy. It has many forms, and deals with certain basic questions of human life. Idealism shifts the emphasis from the natural or scientific fact of life to the spiritual aspects of human experience. It assumes that knowledge acquired through the activity, creativity and exercise of the mind is more important than the knowledge acquired through the senses. It means that idealism recognises ideas, feelings and ideals rather than material objects. It emphasises that human development should be according to moral, ethical and spiritual values through which man acquires knowledge of unity in diversity.

PROTAGONISTS OF IDEALISM

Idealism is an old philosophy represented by great philosophers such as Plato, Socrates, Descartes, Spinoza, Comenius, Berkley, Fichte, Hegel, Kant, Gentile, Schelling, Pestalozzi, Froebel, Kapil, Green, W.T. Harris, Mahatma Gandhi, Rabindranath Tagore, Swami Vivekananda, Guru Nanak, Dayananda, Aurobindo Ghosh and S. Radhakrishnan. They have accepted and developed idealistic views and applied them in the field of education.

MEANING OF IDEALISM

The words 'idea', 'ideology' and 'idealism' come into the vocabulary of philosophy from the Greek word *ideain* meaning to see something figuratively. The term *idealism* is the combination of the words—'Idea' and 'Ism'. It is the synonym of the English word 'Idealism'. Idealism maybe derived from 'ideas' or 'ideals'. In other words, idealism is born out of Plato's *Theory of Ideas*. According to this doctrine, the ultimate supremacy is of ideas. The real word is 'ideaism' but the letter "I" added to aid in the pronunciation and, hence, it is known as **Idealism**.

Idealism is known as **spiritualism**. It holds that the spiritual world is more important than the material world that is destructible and mortal. But the spiritual world is a world of ideas, feelings and ideals which reveal the reality of mind and soul. Idealists believe that there is nothing beyond the spiritual world and spiritual values. According to them, these values are immortal and true. Man's spiritual nature is considered to be the very essence of his being. Idealism emphasises the study of man more and more because he is empowered with higher intellectual powers and shows greater levels of intelligence and discrimination. Ross says, "Human personality is of supreme value and constitutes the noblest work of God". In this way, in idealistic philosophy, the highest place is acquired by the study of human personality. The essence of idealism has been admirably explained briefly in the words of G.T.W. Patrick. He says that the idealists refuse to believe that the world is a great machine. They deny the supreme importance of matter, mechanism and the conservation of energy which is thought to define our world. They feel that somehow certain sciences, such as psychology, logic, ethics and aesthetics have to do with things basal and intrinsic, that they are quite as much a key to nature's secrets as are physics and chemistry. They believe that the world has a meaning, a purpose, perhaps a good, and that there is a kind of inner harmony between the heart of the universe and the soul of man, such that, human intelligence can pierce through the outer crust of nature and penetrate to its inner being, at least in some measure.

In short, idealism is a philosophical position which adheres to the view that nothing exists except as an idea in the mind of man. Ideas or human values are more important in human life than anything else. They believe that ideas are eternal and unchanging.

DEFINITIONS OF IDEALISM

The meaning of idealism can be made more clear with the help of some important definitions put forward by eminent scholars.

D.M. Dutta: "Idealism holds that ultimate reality is spiritualism".

H.B. Titus: "Idealism asserts that reality consists of ideas, thoughts, minds, or selves rather than material objects and forces".

J.S. Ross: "Idealistic philosophy takes many and varied forms, but the postulate underlying all this is that mind or spirit is the essential world stuff, that the true reality is of a mental character".

Brubacher: "Idealists point out that it is mind that is central in understanding the world. To them nothing gives a greater sense of reality than the activity of the mind engaged in trying to comprehend the world".

Horne: "Educational philosophy of idealism is an account of man finding himself as an integral part of a universe of mind".

Rusk: "Idealism contends that the material and physical universe known to science is an incomplete expression of reality that it exists but to subserve and requires to complement it a higher level of reality, a spiritual universe".

FEATURES OF IDEALISM

Idealism is an ancient philosophy. It has the following principles that reveal its characteristics. The true reality consists in ideas. Ideas are more important in human life than anything else. Some of these ideas are as follows:

- God is the source of all creations found in the world.
- God is the source of all knowledge.
- Spirit and mind constitute reality.
- Man is the best creation of God. He is an incarnation of God, his Creator.
- Man is a spiritual being and there is a spiritual power in him.

- Our wisdom or mental attitude is the means of attaining the knowledge of truth.
- Material or physical universe is not real and is perishable.
- The soul and God are true. They are indestructible and immortal.
- Spiritual values are eternal, absolute and unchanging.
- Spiritual world is more important than the material world.
- Idealism exalts human personality.
- Man is not the creation of his environment like the animals.
- Reality is to be found in a man's mind rather than in material nature.
- Wisdom or intellectual enlightenment is the source of attaining true knowledge.
- Truth, goodness, beauty are the eternal values which are essential qualities of human beings.
- Idealism believes in unity in diversity.
- It gives more importance to moral and spiritual education in general education.
- Study of man's nature and his mind is more important than the study of material universe.
- Man needs some encouragement or light in the face of darkness.
- Idealism prepares the child for holy life.
- What is ultimately real is not the object itself but the ideal or idea behind it.
- It divides the world into two forms—material and spiritual. Material world is unreal because it is mortal; but the spiritual world is real and immortal.
- It gives a great importance to man, the supreme work of God. He has higher power that is intelligence, by which he can mould and modify his surroundings and circumstances according to his needs.

FORMS OF IDEALISM

The idealistic philosophers have understood the philosophy of idealism in different ways. As a result, various forms of idealistic principles have emerged. They are as follows:

Personalistic idealism or subjective idealism: Berkley is the exponent of the personalistic philosophy of idealism. He accepts only the existence of mind. Even attributes and qualities are mental. They will be subjective, that is, each one considers an object in one's own way and defines it. Thus, attributes, which are transformed into objects, are very much personal in nature. Here we observe the attributes only.

Absolute idealism: Fitche and Hegel are the exponents of the idealistic philosophy of absolute idealism. They consider that only self (soul) is the absolute reality. In the physical world, all events are governed by some absolute laws. Therefore, only the absolute laws are real. Progress in the world is the outcome of thesis antithesis and synthesis. The process of progress goes on till we reach the absolute truth by synthesising thesis and antithesis.

Objective idealism: Plato is the originator of the philosophy of objective idealism. He is of the opinion that reality of spirit is not because it is realised by some but it is independent of realisation. If God is real, he will always remain real whether or not anybody considers him real. Independent existence of reality is the source of all souls. According to objective idealism "There is no God without world and there is no world without God".

Phenomenal idealism: Kant is the exponent of phenomenal idealism. According to him the knowledge that we have acquired about physical or metaphysical world is not actually and absolutely real. It is only the phenomenon of the reality. Original or absolute reality cannot be known, as it is beyond our capacities. For instance, God, heaven, or hell actually cannot be known by anybody.

IDEALISM IN EDUCATION

Plato introduced the idealistic philosophy in the field of education. The study of man and his mind is given great importance because human personality is considered as a worthy subject for study. In the words of Emerson, "Man is everything, environment is nothing". Rusk remarked, "Education is expected to enlarge the boundaries of the spiritual realism". Idealists like Plato, Pestalozzi and Froebel consider education to be a process which leads one to the highest moral conduct and deepest spiritual insight, that is, truth, goodness and beauty. Education works as a link between the individual mind and the spiritual environment. According to Ross, "The function of education is to help us in our exploration of the ultimate universal values so that the truth of the universe may become our truth and give power to our life".

IDEALISM AND AIMS OF EDUCATION

Idealism has influenced every sphere of education. It prescribes certain fundamental aims of education that are directly influenced by the aims and principles of life. Since idealism believes human personality to be the most important, it wants education to aim at the development of human personality and the attainment of self-realisation. Horne says, "The end of ends, the goal of goals, according to idealism, is the increasing realisation of the absolute idea for the individual, society and the race". Idealism has given us very lofty aims of education as follows:

Self-realisation: Idealism gives much importance to self-realisation as the main aim of education. According to idealism, man is the most beautiful and powerful creation of God. Hence, the idealists lay great stress on the exaltation of human personality or self-realisation. Adam has given great importance to self-realisation and the development of human personality. In this context, Indian philosophers have given some definitions. For example, Shankaracharya says, "Education is the realisation of the self"; Swami Vivekananda states, "Education is the realisation of divine perfection already exiting in man". Aurobindo Ghosh remarks, "Education helps the growing soul to draw out that is in itself". Self-realisation involves full knowledge of the self. The Western philosophers also emphasise the same aim of education. James S. Ross says, "The aim of education is to enable man to become true himself". According to Aristotle, "Education develops man's faculty, especially his mind so that he may be able to enjoy the contemplation of supreme truth, goodness and beauty in which perfect happiness essentially consists". Hence, the first aim of education, according to idealism, is to take the self of the individual higher and higher till self-realisation is achieved.

Universal education: Education is the birthright of every man. According to Idealism, education should be universal in nature. The idealists believe that every man is, equally, the noblest work of God. So, every individual must be given the fullest opportunities to realise his/her highest potentialities. In order to achieve this aim of education, idealists are in favour of universalisation of education. It may help to establish an ideal society in the country. Thus, idealism wants to lead man towards the betterment of society. Hence, the universalisation of education has become an important aim of this philosophy.

Spiritual development: Idealists give greater importance to spiritual values than to material attainments. According to them, the aim of education is to develop the child mentally, morally and above all spiritually. The teacher should organize education in such a way as to develop the child spiritually. Professor Rusk says, "Education must enable mankind through its culture to enter more and more fully into the spiritual realm and also enlarge the boundaries of spiritual realm".

Physical development: The physical well-being of the individual is the important aim of idealistic education. It is an undeniable fact that spiritual exaltation is not possible without being physically fit. So, physical aspects of education should be taught with general education without which personality development cannot be achieved. According to James Ross, "The health and fitness of the body must receive attention, for, without such health and fitness, the pursuit of spiritual values is seriously handicapped".

Preparation for holy life: Idealists emphasise that education should create such condition and provide an environment which are conducive to develop the children spiritually and prepare them to lead a holy life. A holy life full of piety and good ideals will lead towards spiritual development and self-realisation. Froebel has rightly stated, "The objects of education is the realisation of a faithful, pure, inviolable and hence holy life". So, the aim of idealistic philosophy is to prepare the child for a holy life.

Intellectual development: The aim of idealistic philosophy of education is the mental and intellectual development of the child. It may enable the child to achieve the highest aim by developing his creative power and control, and adjust with his environment. Intellectual development is essential to undertake appropriate jobs and occupations available in the society.

Moral development: Moral development is another important aim of education. Idealists have attached great importance to the moral development of the child. Such development enables the child to distinguish between right and wrong. It helps the child to follow what is right and reject what is evil. Only the citizens endowed with the quality of morality can make the society progressive with peace and security. Therefore, idealistic education aims at the development of morality. Dr. Prem Nath states, "The process of education must lead to the deepest spiritual insight and to the highest moral and spiritual conduct".

Preservation and transmission of culture: Idealists believe in preserving and enriching our cultural environment. A man is incomplete without culture. So, idealism wants the growth of cultural development in the child. Man is the only being endowed with a keen and penetrating intellect, intelligence and an enormous capacity for assimilating knowledge. In fact, man's achievements in the realm of science, art and culture are of great intrinsic values. Our cultural heritage is of immense value and worth which belongs to the whole humanity. In the process of education our culture is preserved, developed and transmitted to all corners of the world. Thus, the aim of education, according to idealism, is to acquaint the child with the cultural heritage so that he can conserve, promote and transmit it to the rising generation.

Development of inventive and creative powers: Man can change the force of nature so that it could suit his own needs. It means that he should change and modify his physical environment according to his requirements. For this purpose, education must foster the inventive powers of man which will ensure his mastery over the materials given to him.

Simple living and high thinking: Simple living and high thinking is an important aim of idealistic education. It is the mind that should be developed and trained, and controlled in order to lead a simple life with high thinking. It implies that gaudy and fashionable clothes and rich living mean nothing in the end.

Development of unity in diversity: Idealistic education wants to develop the feeling of unity among human beings. It is in favour of making one a complete man at the national level. It is education that should mould the people in such a way that they would be willing to sacrifice their individual interest for social interest. Education provides knowledge that generates the feeling of unity in diversity. This aim of idealistic education has become very relevant in these days to foster national integration and international understanding.

Cultivation of truth, beauty and goodness: The aim of idealistic education is to cultivate spiritual values in the individuals. The pursuit of the highest ideals, that is, truth, beauty and goodness should be encouraged more and more in the child so that he achieves self-realisation. These three values determine three types of human activities—intellectual, aesthetic and moral.

IDEALISM AND CURRICULUM

Curriculum is a means to realise the aim of education. The realisation of the aims of education is impossible in the absence of a curriculum. While structuring a curriculum, idealists give more importance to thoughts, feelings, ideals and values than to the child and his activities. Therefore, a curriculum should be concerned with the whole humanity and its experiences. Idealism stresses three highest values, that is 'truth', 'goodness' and 'beauty'. These three values determine four types of human activities—intellectual, moral, aesthetic and physical. Hence, great importance is given to subjects such as humanities, languages, social sciences, physical sciences, ethics, metaphysics, religion, and aesthetic activities like art and poetry.

Idealism does not ignore physical activities because without health and fitness, the pursuit of spiritual values is seriously hampered. So, idealists feel that physical education is essential. The study of hygiene and physiology and the practice of physical skills, gymnastics, and athletics must form an integral part of the school curriculum.

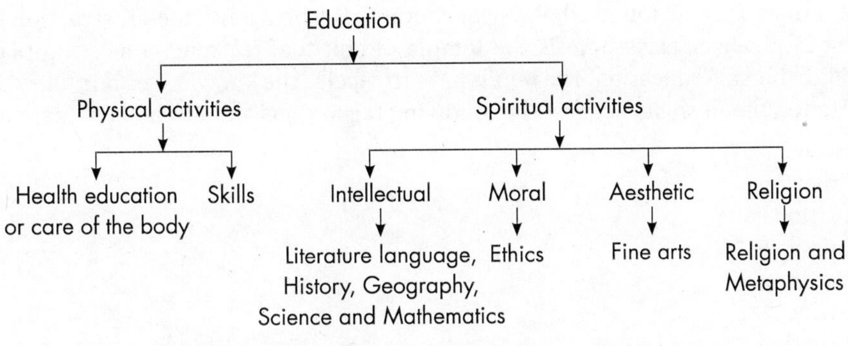

FIGURE 8.1 Views of J.S. Ross about curriculum.

According to idealistic philosophy, a curriculum should be so constructed and developed as to enable the child to develop the skills of knowing, willing and doing. For instance, the teaching of different subjects will develop the knowing faculty of the mind, the teaching of arts, music, dance and drawing will develop the willing faculty, and the teaching of science will develop the doing capacity of the mind. The development of knowing will help the child to discover the truth, the development of willing will enable him to realise beauty and the development of doing will make him competent in physical and material activities. Several schemes of curricula have been propounded by different idealists such as Plato, Herbert, T.P. Nunn and James S. Ross.

Plato's scheme: According to him, the aim of life is to realise God and this is possible by pursuing high ideals namely truth, beauty and goodness. These can be attained by three types of activities, that is, intellectual, aesthetic and moral. Hence, he gives importance to subjects like language, literature, history, geography, mathematics, science etc. which are taught for intellectual training. arts, music, poetry etc. are taught for aesthetic training and religion, ethics, metaphysics, etc. are taught for moral and spiritual training.

Herbert's scheme: According to him, the idealistic aim of education is the promotion of moral values. So, he gives priority to subjects like literature, history, arts, music, poetry, political economy to promote moral values and ideals and secondary place to science subjects.

T.P. Nunn's scheme: According to him, a school should promote and maintain morality and the historical tradition to preserve and keep its achievements. Hence, Nunn emphatically advocates those activities and subjects which reflect the highest creations of human mind and involve the noblest expressions of human ingenuity and creative intelligence. He classifies human activities in two groups. He puts physical, social, moral and religious activities in the first group. Idealists need physical education, culture, sociology, ethics and religion to study. He places literary and aesthetic subjects in the second group. Idealists also need arts, literature, music, handicraft, history, geography, science and mathematics to study.

IDEALISM AND METHODS OF TEACHING

In idealism there is no specific method of teaching. The idealists follow different methods of teaching according to their own interests and the demand of the situation. According to idealism, any teaching method can be chosen keeping in view the demand of the situation and the educational aims. Socrates used question–answer method. Plato emphasised discourse method and Aristotle advocated inductive-deductive method. Descartes employed the device of simple to complex method. Pestalozzi insisted on observation method. Froebel followed play-way method. Herbert advocated Instruction method.

According to idealists, classroom is the temple of spiritual learning, a meeting place of human minds and a place for self-education. The pupils have to receive the knowledge and ability to understand themselves. Hence, the idealists suggest the following techniques and methods of teaching:

1. Narration,
2. Explanation,
3. Exposition,
4. Questioning,
5. Discussion,
6. Play-way,
7. Observation,
8. Practice and Repetition.

Butler has rightly stated, "Idealists consider themselves as creators and determiners of methods, not devotees of any one of these methods".

IDEALISM AND TEACHER

The place of the teacher in idealism is very high. His role is very important and glorious in the educational process. The teacher enjoys a place of prestige and respect in education. His place is next to God. He carries the child from the darkness of ignorance and superstition to light. In short, he guides the students to find the way to reach God. He must assume the role of a Guru. He should understand the pupils thoroughly. He should possess a high standard of behaviour. He should have a deep knowledge in his subject. Gentile says, "Teacher is a spiritual symbol of right conduct". Therefore, the teacher should guide the students with love, affection and sympathy. Froebel states, "The school is a garden, the teacher is a cautious gardener and the child is a tender plant. The plant can grow no doubt without help but a good gardener sees that the plant grows to the finest possible perfection". Thus, idealists have given a very respectable and honourable position to a teacher. According to J.S. Ross, "The Naturalists maybe contented with briars, but the Idealists want to find roses".

IDEALISM AND STUDENT

Idealistic philosophy gives more emphasis to ideas or thoughts, whereas it provides secondary place to the child in the educational process. The idealist believes that the child is a limited soul and he has to be made an unlimited soul through appropriate and regular instruction, so that he may attain immortality. B.B. Bogoslovasky remarks, "The student is a finite person growing when properly educated into the image of an infinite person". The idealists consider the child to be under the teacher. The students should obey the dictates of their teacher. They should have the qualities of respect, the feeling of dedication, a liking for meditation, regularity, taking of less food and sleep, carefulness in speech, utmost wisdom, and respect towards their teacher. There should be cordial relations between the teacher and the taught.

IDEALISM AND DISCIPLINE

Idealists want to keep the child under discipline. They punish him when he does anything wrong. No reward is given for doing good deeds because doing good is the prerequisite for spiritual development. Idealists believe that there can be no spiritual development in the child without discipline. So, they are not in favour of free discipline. Self-insight and self-analysis are the main disciplinary factors. The habit of self-discipline is also developed by impressing the child with the exemplary conduct and behaviour of the teacher. Idealists recommend a sympathetic control over the undesirable activities of the child. They grant regulated liberty to the child for his spiritual development. They should also inculcate the qualities of humility, respectfulness and subservience in the minds of pupils. Thomas and Lang have rightly stated, "Freedom is the cry of Naturalists while discipline is that of Idealists". Thus, discipline is the slogan of idealists.

IDEALISM AND SCHOOL

The school of the idealists is based on the principles of simple living and high thinking. It is a place where the capacities of logical thinking, reasoning and evaluating the child are progressively sublimated and developed by teachers. It is the meeting place of the souls of the teachers and students. It plays the role of a leader and reformer for society through its students and teachers. Idealists want to develop the qualities of patriotism, humanity, devotion to God, religiousness in the students through teachings of the lives of great men, and prayers. School is a temple of spiritual learning, a meeting place of human mind and a place for self-education and self-realisation. An idealistic school is based on an ideal imagination through which the educational process can proceed in a well-mannered way.

CONTRIBUTIONS OF IDEALISM TO EDUCATION (IMPACT OF IDEALISM ON EDUCATION)

The idealistic philosophy has influenced every society and brought remarkable changes in the field of education. The contribution of idealism in education has drawn the attention of modern educationists and philosophers. Now let us concentrate on its contribution to educational theory and practice.

Aim: The contributions of idealism from the points of view of aims, are of a very high order and unique. Idealism has helped in the determination of educational aims. The aim of education is personality development through self-realisation and creation of an ideal society. Such aim has helped to a great extent in the construction of curriculum and teaching techniques. In order to develop spiritual and moral qualities, religious and moral education have been given great importance in Indian schools. This aim of education is based on the idealistic philosophy.

Teacher: Idealism has given the teacher a place of pride and respect. It stresses the ideal character of the teacher. It is very important in order to bring about a desirable change in the behaviour of students. It tells us how the teacher ought to be in the society and spells out the qualities which he should possess. Idealism has raised the feeling of respect towards the teacher. This view has been in practice in Indian schools.

Child: Idealism has recognised the individuality of the child, and it tries to stimulate his creative potentialities. Idealists want to develop the eternal values in the child. These views of idealism have been adopted by most of the educational systems in framing curriculum and methods of teaching.

Teacher-student relation: Idealists advocate intimate relationship between the teacher and student. In order to develop this affinity between the two, the ratio of teacher-student is being reduced today. This reflects the influence of idealism in modern education.

Discipline: Idealism has emphasised self-discipline and has put it into practice. The discipline based on impressionistic type of discipline was accepted by all modern philosophers. Indian philosophers such as Mahatma Gandhi and Swami Vivekananda advocated the concept of self-discipline. Even today, emphasis is given to self-discipline. Idealists want to develop the personality of the child through the medium of self-discipline to find fine roses.

Universalisation of education: Idealists are in favour of universalisation of education so that an ideal society maybe formed. Education must be provided to every individual in order to make him move forward towards social welfare. Now this view has been accepted by all philosophers, educationists and political leaders. Education has become the birthright of human beings. Today, universalisation of education is one of the objectives of educational policies of India.

Historical importance: Idealism has historical importance. It has been supported by many great philosophers and educationists both of the East and the West. The reason is that it determines the path of educational philosophers and gives them inspiration. Moreover, many educational schemes and plans have had their beginning in idealistic philosophy.

MERITS OF IDEALISM

- Idealism is the most ancient and comprehensive philosophy and its contributions to educational thought is solid and profound.
- Idealism has given a higher place to mental and spiritual qualities than to the physical world so that men can lead a peaceful and contented life. Thus, the aim of education is the perfection of the individual.
- Idealism leads to the spiritual insight and to the highest moral and spiritual conduct.
- Idealism lays stress on self-realization, which is essential to acquire knowledge relating to the spiritual world.
- It guides us to a simple living and high thinking.

- Idealistic philosophy prepares us for both heavenly life and life in the earth.
- Idealism provides a significant place to the teacher and places him next to God in the educational process.
- Idealism contains the highest knowledge that of self, or divine cosmic or spiritual life that leads to the freedom of mind.
- Idealism gives importance to the development of human personality which results in a fresh look at human relations in teaching.
- It makes the educational institutions, places for learning and creating values like, truth, beauty and goodness which will lead to the development of the moral character of the child.
- Idealism determines the path of many educational philosophers. It has been supported by great philosophers of the world who have put it into educational practices.
- Idealistic philosophy emphasises religious studies in order to foster character development in the child.
- Idealism warns against the views of treating the human being as a machine.
- Idealism holds that every man must receive a chance to be educated. It emphasises universalisation of education to form a better society.
- Idealistic philosophy provides clear and direct guidelines to determine the aims of education, curriculum, role of teacher etc.

DEMERITS OF IDEALISM

- The aims of idealistic education are abstract, a figment of imagination and impracticable, and are difficult to achieve in this functional world.
- Idealism neglects the psychological nature of the child and is inclined towards spiritualism.
- Idealism ignores material world and stresses on the spiritual world. This philosophy becomes imaginary and does not work in the modern scientific world.
- Idealistic philosophy assigns too much importance to teachers and places them next to God. It asserts that the teacher gives the child second birth. It treats the child as slave.
- Idealism leads to a rigid and often totalitarian social order. The child is kept under strict discipline.
- Idealists follow different methods of teaching according to their own interests. They fail to have a significant method of teaching.
- Idealists regard the highest values such as truth, beauty and goodness as permanent and immortal. But in reality, they are not absolute and may change with time and environment.
- Idealism pays less attention to physical, industrial, social and electronic environment, which are essential for achieving socio- economic developments.
- Idealists do not take note of the individual differences and special abilities of pupils.
- Idealistic philosophy emphasises humanities and neglects the study of science and technology which occupy a very significant role in modern education.
- Idealistic method of teaching and curricula are teacher centred. They neglect the attitude, interest and ability of the child while constructing curriculum and teaching.
- Idealism leads the child to depend on his teacher, and books for knowledge, and it stresses on cramming and rote memory.

CONCLUSION

Idealism occupies an important place in the field of education and its contributions are valuable and useful to bring about necessary reforms and changes in the policy of education. This philosophy has become a milestone which determines the way for the solution of educational problems of the present and future educationists. Idealistic education is essential for the peaceful living of human being and is devoted to social good and national welfare. The present world is full of stresses, strains, conflicts, envies and material struggles. In this juncture, idealistic educational philosophy is necessary to create spiritual environment, which will make the life of humanity happy. This philosophy can make a creative contribution to the educationists to overcome the various problems in Indian education. Hence, this philosophy of education can play an active role in making education more purposeful.

CHAPTER 9

REALISM

INTRODUCTION

In the realm of Indian philosophy, the doctrine of realism has been quite evident since the time of Vedas. In fact, the descriptions of natural phenomenon and objects are found in the Vedas. Moreover, Buddhism and Jainism advocate realism of the material world. According to them, this world perceived by senses is the ultimate reality. Thus, realism is not a new concept or school in the scene of philosophies. Professor D.M. Dutta has rightly remarked that "The realistic attitude, however, is not a new one in philosophy. "Realists say "Realism is the instinctive belief of man and it is, therefore, as old as man". The doctrine of idealism is found in the Western philosophy since the time of Aristotle. However, it is believed that realism developed as a doctrine of philosophy during the seventeenth century. This is because this philosophy emerged as a protest against idealism and development of scientific knowledge. During this century, monasticism, scholasticism, renaissance, reformation and humanism appeared as powerful movements in Europe. Such movements transformed the attitudes, beliefs, behaviour, needs and conducts of people. At the same time, idealistic philosophy and education emphasised the spiritual world and failed to inculcate those capacities in the child which would enable him to face the problems of life. Moreover, new researches and techniques of production affected every field of life and they created an urge to modify or remove old beliefs and traditions and stressed scientific outlook. Thus, the impact of science and technology on materialism turned against the philosophy of spiritualism or idealism and developed a new philosophy 'Realism', which gave rise to a new realistic outlook on life, material phenomenon and material things. In this way, realism became a complete and deliberate philosophical thought and received a distinct status in the philosophical world in the nineteenth century. Lastly, the rapid development of science and technology in the twentieth century made it a distinct philosophy, which has great influence on educational principles and practices.

CHIEF PROTAGONISTS OF REALISM

Aristotle, a Greek philosopher is regarded as the profounder of realism. John Locke, an English philosopher gave new impetus to it. Erasmus, Rabelias Milton, Lord Montaigne, Mulcaster, Francis Bacon, Ratke, Comenius, Whitehead and Bertrand Russell are the chief exponents of this philosophy.

MEANING OF REALISM

Let us be clear about the meanings of terms such as real, reality and realism. The word 'real' means, actual or the existing. It refers to things or events that exist in their own right as opposed to that which is imaginary or fictitious. Thus, real refers to what is? Reality is the state or quality of being real or actually existent in contrast with what is mere appearance. Etymologically, realism means 'about a thing' or 'concerning some object'. It is an angle of vision according to which things as we see and perceive are realities. It is the philosophy which holds the view that knowledge only through senses is true. It indicates that what we see and perceive by our own senses is real and the true entity of the world. Realism accepts the existence of real things only. According to it, physical world alone is 'objective' and 'factual' which can be accepted as it is whereas personal feelings and wants are 'subjective', 'subordinate' and 'secondary'. Hence, this philosophy is called **objectivism** and a realist is called a **physical realist, a materialist, a positivist** or **believer in naturalism**. Realism looks at human beings as it would look at other material objects. In short, it is the philosophy which believes in the independent existence of the world and all objects having their own unique properties, and disregards everything subjective, personal and emotional except the study of psychology from the behaviourist point of view. Thus, realism and objectivism are metaphysical theories concerned with the existence of things. In fact, realism is a philosophy of common sense and also the philosophy of science.

DEFINITIONS OF REALISM

Realism is the doctrine about the objects of our senses that exists independently, of their being known or perceived by the mind. However, the following definitions put forward by the philosophers make the meaning and nature of the term 'Realism' yet clearer.

Swami Ram Tirth: "Realism means a belief or theory which looks upon the world as it seems to us to be a mere phenomenon".

J.S. Ross: "The doctrine of realism asserts that there is a real world of things behind and corresponding to the objects of our perception".

Butler: "Realism is the reinforcement of our common acceptance of this world as it appears to us".

Good: "Realism is the doctrine that objective reality or the material universe exists independently of conscious mind, its nature and properties are being affected by being known".

Brown: "The main contention of realism is that all things or the objects of external world are real and their existence is independent of their perceiver. Even if there is no body to be there objects, even then they exist".

PRINCIPLES OF REALISM

Realism took different forms in the seventeenth, eighteenth and nineteenth centuries and developed as a distinct philosophy in the twentieth century due to the development of scientific knowledge. This philosophy has the following basic principles:

Study of the world: "Realism is a philosophy away from the world of ideas or spiritualism. It is concerned with the study of the world we live in".

Nature is the real world: According to Realism, the real world is the world of nature. There is no world other than that we live in. It also believes that there is no life beyond this. Thus, realists have no faith in eternal world and life. In the words of James S. Ross, "Realism simply affirms the existence of an external world and is therefore the antithesis of subjective idealism".

Existence of object: The naïve realists believe in the existence of objects irrespective of our knowledge of them. In fact, scientific realism accepts this notion, but according to its thoughts, concerning the objects, they are based on the mind. It also states that everything which exists in the universe is matter or energy or matter in motion.

Senses are the doors of knowledge: Like naturalists, Realism believes that senses are the gateways of knowledge. It means that the impressions and sensations which result from our contacts with external world through our senses result in knowledge. According to Bertrand Russell, "I contend that ultimate constituent of matter are not atoms ... but sensation. I believe that the stuff of our mental life consists wholly of sensations and images".

Theory of organism: Realism believes that conscious and unconscious thing form an organism. According to it, mind is the function of organism. In the words of Whitehead, "The universe is a vibrating organism in the process of evolution. Change is the fundamental features of this vibrating universe. The very essence of real actuality is process. Mind must be regarded as function of the organism".

Opposition of idealism: There is no place for imagination in realism. Realism denies the existence of God, soul, heaven and hell. It emphasises the scientific realities of matter. And it believes that the things we see and perceive are real.

Man is a part of material world: Realism considers man as a part of material world. It is because man is endowed with sense organs and the mind through which he attains the knowledge of the real world.

Emphasis on experiment: Realism gives more importance to experimentation and observation. Hence, this philosophy does not accept any experience as true unless it is analysed and classified with the help of scientific methods.

Emphasis on applied life: Realism is of the opinion that spiritual world cannot be understood by means of senses. It believes that the existence of God, soul and spiritual values are the creations of man's imagination. Hence, importance should be given to physical and material existence. This philosophy stresses the physical and material facts of the present life. This is because such material only promotes human welfare and happiness. According to Rusk, "The aim of new realism is to expound a philosophy which is not inexistent with the facts of common life and with the development of physical science".

Natural laws: Realism believes that all physical phenomenon of the universe operate according to some vast plan of the nature, which is known as natural laws. Realists regard the natural laws as ultimate truth. True knowledge can be acquired by observing accurately the natural law at work.

FORMS OF REALISM AND ITS IMPACT ON EDUCATION

The idea of Realism emerged as a protest against idealism but the development of scientific knowledge and researches made it a distinct philosophy. Consequently, we have five different forms of realism. Each realistic form has a unique importance and impact on education. Let us discuss the various forms of realism and their contribution to education briefly (Figure 9.1).

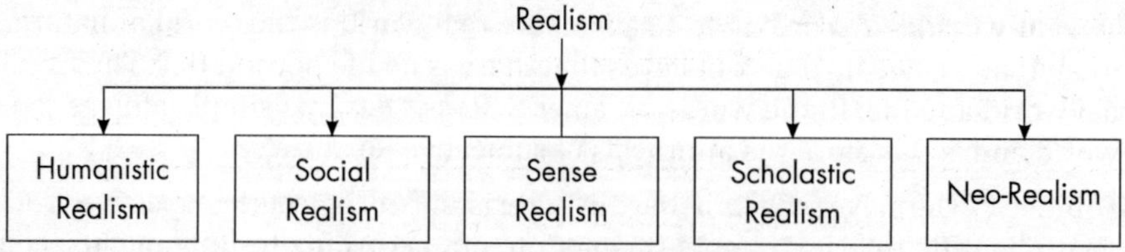

FIGURE 9.1 Forms of realism.

Humanistic Realism

Humanistic realism developed in the fifteenth century. This form of realism was propounded by Erasmus (1466–1536), Rabelias (1483–1553) and John Milton (1608–1674). It came into prominence after the period of renaissance. The protagonists of humanistic realism believed that education should be realistic. They felt that only such an education can promote human welfare. For this purpose, they advocated the study of Greek and Roman literatures. According to them, literature alone contained all essentials for success and happiness in life. In fact, Erasmus, John Milton and Rabelias believed that the study of Greek and Roman literatures was very essential to make human life happy and successful.

Main Tenets of Humanistic Realism: These are as follows:

1. Realism interprets knowledge in simple terms.
2. It makes a direct study of man and things.
3. It considers man as a physical part of reality.
4. It considers that study of Greek and Roman literatures is of great importance.
5. It believes that the study of literature can promote human welfare and happiness.

Let us see the views of protagonists of humanistic realism:

Erasmus (1466–1536): Erasmus, a resident of England, opposed the unrealistic educational system and favoured broad and liberal education. According to him, "knowledge seems to be of two kinds, that of things and words. That of words comes first, but that of things is more important".

Rabelias (1483–1553): Rabelias, a French scholar, favoured liberal education. He condemned the idealistic academic and theoretical type of education. He stressed the physical, social, religious and moral education. He advocated knowledge of things. According to him, education should prepare the individual to face all problems of life with courage and solve them successfully. He considered that practical knowledge of environment is necessary. He, therefore, advocated the reorganization of curriculum and brought out changes in the methods of teaching. In fact, he prescribed scientific and psychological methods and techniques in order to make the teaching interesting. According to him, the aim of education is to make practical life better.

Milton (1608–1674): Milton, a great poet, a man of literature, a great philosopher and an educationist, favoured humanistic realism. His educational ideas are found in his book Tracts of Education. According to him education should give knowledge of things and objects. He gave importance to physical education and suggested walking and touring for physical health and well beings. He opposed the education of masses and presented a plan of education for the child from 12–21 years. The curriculum for the first two years should include the study of Latin, Grammar, Mathematics, Geometry and Morality. After it, education for next four years (14–18) should include the study of Agriculture, Physiology, Handicrafts, Natural Philosophy and Geography. The curriculum designed for the groups of 19–21 years should include the study of Bible, Hebrew, Greek, Roman, Saxon, Economics, Political Science, History, Poetry and Law. As Milton was a religious man, he wanted that education should impart knowledge about God and foster a life of Him in the child. He was in favour of complete and liberal education and against mere academic education. In his view, education is a very comprehensive term which develops practical efficiency in the child. He himself says, "I call, therefore, a complete and generous education which fits a man to perform justly, skillfully and magnanimously all the offices, both private and public, at peace and war".

Social Realism

The aim of this philosophy is to make human life happy and successful by fulfilling the needs of society. Therefore, the upholders of social realism were against isolated life of man and condemned cramming. They gave full importance to society and the social environments. Moreover, they opposed academic and bookish knowledge and advocated for education which was useful to life and practical in nature. In fact, they wanted that education should promote the working efficiency of the individuals. According to them, all learning should take place in company with others. So, they included the study of geography, history, arithmetic, law, diplomacy, warfare, horse-riding, dancing, and gymnastic exercises in the curriculum and believed that such studies should develop social qualities in the child. Moreover, they prescribed travelling, touring, observation and experiences in order to make education effective and useful. James S. Ross says, "The social realists, looking askance at bookish studies, stressed the value of direct studies of man and things having in mind chiefly the upper class, they advocated a period of travel, a grand tour which give real experience of the varied aspects of life"

Let us see the views of different protagonists of social realism:

Lord Montaigne (1533–1592): Michael de Montaigne, a famous French educationist, represented socialistic realism which aimed at making a child a worldly man. He criticised bookish knowledge and supported the idea to make knowledge practical and utilitarian. Thus, the purpose of education is to develop intelligence and self-discrimination in the child so that they can lead their life smoothly and successfully. Therefore, he opposed knowledge for the sake of knowledge and advocated knowledge to be useful for social life. He condemned cramming, learning by experiences and expressionistic discipline. He prescribed tours and journeys for the child. According to him, children should learn first their own mother tongue, then language of the neighbours and all Greek and Latin languages. About the methods of teaching, Montaigne says, "A boy should not so much memorise his lesson as practice it. Let him repeat it in his actions". He suggested that moral knowledge should be gathered from the biographies of great persons.

John Locke (1632–1704): Locke, a famous English educationist, described his educational thoughts in his famous book Some Thoughts Concerning Education. According to him, education should inculcate and foster in the child virtue, wisdom breeding and capacity to learn. He gave importance to the physical, moral and intellectual development of the child. As Locke was an individualistic philosopher, he opposed the education of masses. He believed that the mind of a child is a clean slate on which only experiences write. Therefore, education by private tutor should impart in a pleasant and lively method of teaching, which must stimulate motivation and interest in the child. According to him, education should be imparted through the mother tongue. He recommended the inclusion of those subjects in the curriculum, which are individually and socially useful. He considered experience as an important source of knowledge.

Sense Realism

Sense realism is also known as **scientific realism**. It developed as a form of realism in the seventeenth century. Several discoveries made by philosophers, educationists and thinkers concluded that senses are the gateways of knowledge. Thus the term *sense realism* has been derived from the basic belief that knowledge comes primarily from the senses. This ideology has a great impact on modern educational philosophies. In fact, the protagonists of this philosophy believed that knowledge comes through senses, not from words. Therefore, the child's ears, nose, eyes, mouth and skin should be freely used to the maximum in the education. In other words, without exercising sense organs of the child, no knowledge can be gained. Hence, training in sense perception received the highest attention in the process of education. Since all knowledge originates from the external nature, education should adopt real and effective methods instead of artificial techniques. Further, they believed that truth can be gained by observation and contact between senses and external objects. This is the natural way of education, which provides more and more opportunities to the child to observe and study natural phenomenon and come in contact with external natural objects through his senses. It enables the child to gain the knowledge of natural objects, natural phenomenon and natural laws.

Impact of sense realism on education: Some of these impacts are as follows:

1. Mother tongue should be the medium of instruction.
2. Observation and contact with nature is the way of gaining truth and knowledge.
3. Emphasises the study of scientific subjects in place of literature and humanities.
4. Education should be child centred.
5. Senses are the gateways of knowledge, which requires proper exercises through the process of education.
6. Importance is given to useful and practical education.
7. Deductive method is more important than inductive method.
8. Teaching should be done in the free environment.

Let us look at the views of the main protagonists of sense realism

Mulcaster (1530–1611): Richard Mulcaster, an English educationist who worked as a Headmaster in different schools for 37 years, stressed the importance of physical and intellectual development of the child. He was against the current system of education during his period. According to him, education should be scientific and a natural process. He emphasised the training of senses as real education and stood against memorization. He advocated child-centred education which should be given through the medium of mother tongue. He stressed the great importance and use of psychological methods of teaching. Therefore, he gave importance to mother tongue, reading, writing, music, painting and other subjects at the primary level and scientific subjects at the secondary level. The teacher should have a sound knowledge of the method of teaching. Above all he says, "The end of education and training is to help nature to perfection".

Francis Bacon (1562–1623): Francis Bacon, a famous man of literature, a writer and a philosopher, also condemned bookish education and tried to make it practical. He gave prime importance to the study of Nature, which is the source of knowledge and secondary importance to philosophy, literature and language. This is because he believed that the aim of education, that is, making the child useful for society, cannot be achieved by the prevailing system of education. Hence, he wanted to re-organize the whole process of education and introduced inductive method of teaching. As a result, the child is free to observe and experiment by means of his senses, which reduces the importance of Aristotelian deductive method. Thus, he is known as a greater supporter of the inductive method in science. Francis Bacon says, "The object of all knowledge is to give man power over nature".

Ratke (1571–1625): Ratke, a German philosopher, supporter of sense realism, considered education as a process of development of the child according to his nature. He advocated the following principles:

1. Education should be imparted through mother tongue.
2. Teaching should be done in the free environment.
3. One thing should be taught at a time.
4. Follow nature.
5. Nothing should be learned by rote
6. First things, then words.
7. No repression.
8. Knowledge through senses.
9. Uniformity of all things.
10. Object knowledge should be acquired by direct experience and experiment.

Comenius (1592–1671): Comenius, a resident of Moravia and supporter of sense realism, considered that the ultimate end of man is eternal happiness. For this purpose, he wanted to make education child-centred, moral-centred and God-fearing centred. He believed in the principle of universal education. He opinioned that even the poor should receive proper education. According to him, knowledge comes not only through the senses but through man's intelligence and divine inspiration. He advocated natural method of education and believed that the inductive method of Bacon is insufficient. He propounded the following rules regarding the methods of teaching:

1. Teaching methods should be simple.
2. Suitable textbooks should be followed.
3. Only useful knowledge should be given to the child.
4. Teaching should be done very effectively.
5. Mother tongue should be the medium of instruction.
6. Parts of material should be taught step-by-step in a sequence.
7. General rules of teaching should be explained.
8. Subject matter should be discussed very clearly.
9. Purpose of reading material should be told to the child.
10. Teaching should be continued till learning is achieved.

Comenius opposed any form of repression and physical punishment. He advocated a synthesis of educational psychology, educational organization and educational methodology. His educational thoughts were later accepted and developed further by Rousseau, Pestalozzi and Herbert. In fact, the contribution of Comenius to education and philosophy is great and it has been a root to the modern education.

Scholastic Realism

Scholastic realism developed as an important form of realism. It is the Western philosophy ascribed to Roman Catholics. This philosophy gave importance to the study of eternal truth over world objects. According to scholastic realism, the study of eternal truth should have hold over object of world around us. In the words of Brubacher, "The educational philosophy of scholastic realism is fundamentally dualistic". In fact, as it recognises an order of natural as well as that of the supernatural things, it is considered as dualistic philosophy. For example, in scholastic realism, God is central and Nature is His manifestation.

This philosophy believed that morality is an essential element of religion. Hence, religion is the main spring of ethics and social morality.

Neo-Realism

Neo-realism has more importance in the field of philosophy and science than in education. In the words of Rusk, "The positive contribution of neo-realism is the acceptance of the methods and results of modern developments in physics". This ideology believed that like other rules and procedures, rules and procedures of science are also unchangeable and valid only in certain conditions and circumstances. Alfred Whitehead and Bertrand Russell are considered as the Chief exponents of neo-realism and they emphasised both education and science.

Whitehead (1861–1947): Whitehead, an English philosopher and mathematician, recommended not only the study of scientific subjects, but gave due weightage to arts and humanities, language and literature. He believed that the consciousness and unconsciousness and movable and immoveable are each organism. So, education should provide the child full knowledge of an organism. He states, "When you understand all about the sun, all about the atmosphere, all about the rotation of earth which takes place at cognitive level, but you may still miss the radiance of the sun set, which is a 'feeling' component and takes place at 'affective level'".

Bertrand Russell (1872–1970): Bertrand Russell, a great philosopher, educationist, intellectual thinker and supporter of neo-realism, believed that senses are the doors of knowledge. According to him, education should come by means of senses. He, therefore, emphasised the sensory development of the child. He advocated the method of analysis and classification, and accepted liberal education as the ideal one, but no place for religious education. He stressed the study of physics and opposed the kindling of emotional exuberance in the child. In the words of Russell, "First and foremost, there must be as little emotional strain as possible in connection with the acquisition of knowledge . . . emotional strain is the chief cause of harmful fatigue".

REALISM IN EDUCATION

Realism entered the field of philosophy and education as a protest against over-emphasis on spiritualism, bookish knowledge, sophisticated and abstruse curricula of idealism. It considered that education should be closely related with the realities of life in all conceivable aspects. In the words of John Milton, "I call a generous and complete education which fits a man to perform justly, skillfully and magnanimously all the offices both private and public, at peace and war". According to this philosophy, education should try to give all those skills and knowledge to the individual which are necessary for a happy living in the society. It also believed that whenever education loses its touch with human life and its problems, at those junctures, realism surfaces in education and starts exerting its influence on different aspects of it.

CHARACTERISTICS OF REALISTIC EDUCATION

The realistic education has the following features:

Scientific education: Realistic education emphasises the study of science subjects in the place of academic and artificial education. It believes that scientific subjects make education useful and purposeful. Therefore, the supporters of realism advocate the inclusion of scientific subjects such as physics, chemistry and biology in the curriculum which gave birth to naturalism.

Present life: This is the second characteristic of realistic education which makes the present life of the child important. In fact, this philosophy gives more importance to the preparation of child for present life. Realists believe that this world is real, and nothing beyond it. Hence, education should prepare the child to solve the present problems and help him lead a better life. According to this philosophy, the present life of the child should be the centre of all educational activities. In short, preparing the child for present life is an important aim of realistic education.

Experiment and experiences: Realistic education gives more importance to experiments, experiences and application of knowledge learnt. It lays great stress on learning by doing, by developing creativity and urge of practical works which enable the children to solve their immediate problems and prepare them to lead a successful life.

Against bookish knowledge: Realistic education is against academic, theoretic and bookish knowledge because they develop rote memory and encourage cramming. Knowledge gained in this way does not enable the child to understand the realities of external things and natural phenomenon. Moreover, such knowledge cannot solve the problems faced by the child. According to realists, education should inculcate in the child an understanding of both the things and the environment. That is why "Not words but things", has been the slogan of realistic education. In fact realistic education promotes intelligence and a sense of judgement which is impossible in the bookish education.

Freedom of child: Realistic education realises the importance of child. Therefore, it gives full freedom to the child, within limits, which enables him to develop his personality according to his innate tendencies. According to realists, limited freedom in the learning environment enables the child to acquire more knowledge and experiences. They believe that freedom encourages the child to proceed from ignorance to knowledge slowly but surely through his own efforts and self-discipline.

Training of senses: Realists advocate self-learning through senses which ought to be trained. According to them, senses are the doors of knowledge. Experience is the touch-stone of what is real; "Seeing is believing". Therefore, senses of the child should be trained and developed in a right way.

Importance to individuality and sociability: Realistic education gives equal importance to the individuality and sociability of the child. In fact, the aim of realistic education is to prepare the child for individual as well as social life. In the words of Bacon, "Realistic education develops the individual on the one hand and on the other hand tries to develop society through the development of social consciousness and sense of service in the child". Thus, realistic education contributes to individual as well as social development.

Mother tongue is the medium: This is said to be an important characteristics of realistic education. According to realists, all education should be given to the child through his mother tongue. It enables the child to understand the natural objects and phenomenon better.

No punishment: Absence of punishment is another important characteristic of realistic education. Realists condemn the repression and punishment given to the child. Thus, there is no place for punishment or reward in realistic education.

Limited religious education: As we know, realism emerged as a protest against idealism which believes in God, spiritual world, heaven and hell. But realistic education denies the existence of God and the world beyond this. However, realists like John Milton and Comenius pay less attention to the study of religion and make education God-centred.

Child-centred education: This is also considered as an important feature of realistic education. In fact, sense realists such as Comenius and Mulcaster make education child-centred. According to Mulcaster, the aim of education is physical and mental development of the child. Therefore, education should be child-centred which enables the child to achieve the fullest development according to his innate tendencies.

Vocational education: Realists hold the view that education should have practical utility for the child. Since livelihood is the main problem of life, realism gives due importance to vocational education. As a result, education has become activity-centred. Thus, the inclusion of vocational education makes the realistic education as a distinct philosophy.

REALISM AND AIMS OF EDUCATION

The most important aim of realistic education is the preparation of child for a happy and integrated life. Broadly speaking, realistic education is constructed and developed to achieve the fullest development of the child. For this purpose let us explain the important aims of realism in educational principles and practices.

Preparation for a happy and successful life: Preparing the child for a happy and successful life is the first and most important aim of realistic education. It means that education should enable the child to solve his problems of life successfully and lead a happy life. According to the American educationist, Franklin Bobit, happiness of life maybe achieved by undertaking the following activities through the medium of education:

1. Activities concerned with language
2. Activities concerned with hygiene
3. Citizenship activities
4. Ordinary and social activities
5. Leisure activities
6. Activities of mental health
7. Religious activities
8. Activities concerning race-preservation
9. Vocational behaviour
10. Vocational activities. Thus, the child should be provided complete knowledge of society and trained in the external nature, social organization and social environments.

Preparation for practical life: The second aim of realistic education is preparing the child for real and practical life. Realists believe in the reality of knowledge of external material world gained through senses. Therefore, the child should be prepared for real and practical life of material world. Thus, it is considered as one of aims of realistic education.

Train the senses: Realistic education aims at training the senses of the child through appropriate experiences. It is believed that proper training of senses enables the child to the achieve fullest development. According to the Realists, the child will not have a perfect knowledge about the external world unless his senses are trained and developed properly. Since senses are the gateways of knowledge and experiences, realistic education aims at the development of senses of the child through various activities.

Develop physical and mental powers: Development of physical and mental powers is another aim of realistic education. Realists believe that physical organs as well as mind of a man constitute an organism composed of matter. Therefore, they give very importance to the development of physical and mental powers of the child through education. In fact, realists consider that such powers help the child to develop intelligence, discrimination and judgements, by which he is able to solve the problems of life.

Relating the child to nature and social environment: Realists consider man as a part of material as well as social world. Hence, the child should be related both to the external nature and social environment. As a result, realistic education aims at providing the child knowledge of the society and the external nature. It is believed that such acquaintance of the child with nature and social environment enables him to lead a happy and successful life.

Develop vocational efficiency: According to the realists, the child should be trained for vocational pursuit, so that he can prepare himself to meet the problems of livelihood. Hence, this ideology insists that developing vocational efficiency should be one of the aims of education. This aim makes education craft-centred.

CURRICULUM

Realists include those subjects and activities in the curriculum which enable the child to achieve the fullest development of his innate powers. In fact, the curriculum designed for realistic education prepares the child to solve the problems of life and lead a happy and successful life.

Subjects for study: Realists prescribe different subjects and activities according to the interest and needs of the child and the society. However, they emphasise the study of science subjects, such as physics, chemistry, biology, astrology and physiology in the place of language, literature and humanities.

Vocational subjects: Realists aim at preparing the child for practical life which includes the problems of livelihood. So they include the study of handicrafts and knowledge of farming in the curriculum.

Utilitarian subjects: Exponents of realism believe that knowledge for the sake of knowledge and art for the sake of art are meaningless. The curriculum should include those subjects which are necessary for individual and social life. They neglect the study of literature, religion, art, dance, music, etc.

Study of language: Realists give due importance to the study of mother tongue and include language studies in the curriculum. They believe that study of language enables the child to read, write and conduct all types of social interactions. But the study of literature finds no prominent place in the curriculum because of its less practical utility.

Travelling and tours: Realists encourage travelling and tours and include such activities in the curriculum with a view to establish a direct contact between the child and the nature. They believe that learning by travelling and tours are the powerful means of education, by which the child gets direct experience.

METHODS OF TEACHING

The most important aim of realistic education is to prepare the child for real and practical life. According to it, realists change the system of education and introduce new methods of teaching. In fact, they adopt various techniques in the teaching–learning process on the basis of subjects and interests of the child. However, most of the realists advocate the following methods in order to achieve the fullest development of the child:

Inductive method: Francis Bacon, one of the famous realists, introduced inductive method in the process of education. This method enables the child to generalise the truth from a particular fact. According to this method, the object is shown to the child first and then its interpretation is given. This method enables the child to observe and experiment by means of his senses. It encourages self-learning to a great extent.

Deductive method: Comenius is another realist who advocates this natural method of education and considers that the inductive method of Bacon is insufficient. It enables him to arrive at a particular truth from general principles. Thus, this method develops the reasoning capacity in the child.

Observation method: Realists consider the observation method as one of the learning techniques through which the child gets direct experiences. According to them, the child should be trained for real life. For this purpose, all senses should be involved in the learning process. Hence, observation method should be adopted and encouraged so as to increase the strength of mind, knowledge and experiences.

Experimental method: Realistic education aims at preparing the child for practical life. In fact, realistic education prepares the child to face the problems of livelihood. For this purpose, it emphasises the study of science subjects in the place of art, language, literature and humanities. The study of science subjects can be made effective only through experimental method.

Travelling and tours: Realists believe that learning by direct experience is the powerful means of education. That is why, John Milton advocated travelling for learning and John Locke stressed the importance of tours. In fact, they discourage rote memorisation and bookish knowledge and advocate learning by observation and experience, and follow the principle of correlation between various subjects of study.

REALISM AND TEXTBOOKS

Realists like Comenius advocate the study of science subjects and consider that such subjects prepare the child for real and practical life. As a result, they introduce scientific methods of teaching instead of bookish knowledge and rote memorisation. Therefore, they consider that textbooks should not be a work of mere theory, but it should be the combination of theoretical as well as practical knowledge and experiences. According to them, the book prescribed for language and literature should be simple and natural.

REALISM AND TEACHER

Realists give importance to the personality of the teacher in the process of education. Practically, the role of the teacher is neither as high nor important as idealists consider and nor so negligible as naturalists speak out, but the teacher is important. According to the realists, the teacher should have full knowledge of the subject content and the needs of children. He should tell children about the scientific discoveries, researches and inventions in various fields of knowledge. He should engage himself in research and experimentation. Moreover, the teacher should encourage the child to observe and experiment the natural objects and phenomenon. It enables the child to find out new facts. Realists suggest the training of teachers before they engage in teaching. He should make a selection of subject matter according to the interest of the student.

REALISM AND STUDENT

Realists give due importance to the development of children. They advocate child-centred and craft-centred education in order to achieve the fullest development of the child according to his innate tendencies. The requirements of the child are taken into consideration at the time of curriculum construction and selecting the teaching methods. Realists consider the student as part of the world and so he should learn to adjust to the environment. Moreover, they want the student to remain in close touch with the harsh realities of life.

REALISM AND DISCIPLINE

The school should be organised in such a way that the child should learn self- discipline by controlling his feelings and desires and perform his duties. Comenius, desires to treat the child with affection and sympathy. So realists allow considerable freedom to the child. They believe that discipline is essential to prepare the child for useful life. For this purpose, they include moral and religious education in the curriculum. In short, realism emphasises a synthetic form of impressionistic and emancipatory discipline according to the natural and social procedures.

REALISM AND SCHOOL

There are different views about the nature of school among the realists. This is because some realists, like John Locke, feel that there is no need for school and they prescribe wide travelling tours, and teaching by tutors, whereas realists like, John Milton, Francis Bacon, Comenius and Ratke emphasise the importance of school and class teaching. However, they want that the school should be organised on the basis of needs of the child and the demands of the society. In fact, they regard school as a mirror of the society reflecting its true state of affairs. Hence, the school should have well-furnished and equipped aids and devices for effective observation and experimentations, and include all activities going on in the society. According to them, school is the only agency which helps the child to achieve the fullest development and provides vocational education to prepare him for real life. In the words of Comenius, "Schools are true foregoing places of men, which should be like the laps of mothers, full of affection, love and sympathy". In short, school is a socially well-named institution and mirror of the society.

CONTRIBUTION OF REALISM TO EDUCATION

The impact of realistic philosophy has been reflected in every principle and practice of education. Its influence is great on practical education due to overemphasis on the study of natural sciences. In fact, the teaching of natural sciences developed in Europe in the seventeenth century and in America in the eighteenth century. England and German schools insisted religious education and mother tongue as the medium of instruction. As a result, technical and vocational education have become a common feature of the present education. The following changes in educational principles and practices are considered to be the contribution of realism to education.

Widens the scope of education: Realists have widened the scope of education in order to bring out a balanced personality development in the child. In fact, they include scientific subjects, technical subjects, social sciences, humanities and literature in the curriculum.

Education for practical utility: Realists regard that education should have practical utility. It means education should include those subjects and activities which prepare the child for real and practical life. It enables him to solve the problems of life and makes life happy and successful.

Practical education: The realist insists the practical nature of education which has been the root of empirical, experimental and practical method followed in the present system of education.

Vocational education: According to the realists, education imparted to the child should prepare him for livelihood. For this purpose, they advocate and include the study of handicrafts and agricultural farming in the curriculum. The idea of vocational education has a great influence on modern education and changed it according to the needs of the individual and society.

Methods of education: Realists have modernised the teaching–learning process by applying different methods of teaching, for example, inductive and deductive method, debate and discussion, observation, learning by experiences, travelling and tour, heuristic method, sense training and experimentation in place of bookish knowledge. "First objects and then their exposition" are the watch words of the realists. They stress integrated knowledge through co-curricular activities.

Child-centred education: Realists consider that education should be given according to the needs of the child and demands of the society. Hence, they advocate child-centred education and change the method of teaching according to the requirements and interests of the child.

Proper discipline: Realists favour impressionistic and emancipationistic type of discipline in place of repressionistic discipline. In fact, they believe that school discipline should be developed in the child through love, affection, sympathy and understanding. According to them, repression and coercion affect the environment of the school and balanced growth of the child.

Little freedom for child: Realists allow the child to enjoy little freedom against idealism. In this regard, realism is the first philosophy which favours the child's freedom in the school environment. They believe that little freedom will encourage the child to involve in all activities which prepare them for personal as well as social lives.

Science education: Realists emphasise the study of science subjects, such as, physics, chemistry, biology and neglects literature, music, dance and art. According to them, only science subjects have practical utility which develop a scientific outlook in the child.

Senses training: Realists believe that senses are the gateways of knowledge. Therefore, senses should be trained properly in order to observe, experiment and understand the natural objects and phenomenon clearly and comprehensively.

Emphasis on objectivity: Realism lays emphasis on objectivity. It is on account of the efforts of this school of thought that teachers encourage students to analyse the subject matter objectively. In fact, realists want the child to understand the words only through objects.

MERITS OF REALISM

- Realism emphasises the study of science subjects. It is essential for individual and social development.
- Realism advocates the child-centred education. It enables the child to achieve the fullest development according to his needs and interests.
- It is in favour of the limited freedom for the child. Freedom enables the child to develop himself naturally.

- It introduces a number of teaching methods such as inductive, deductive, experimental, observation and travelling methods according to the nature of subjects and interests of the child.
- It opposes the idealistic philosophy and prepares the child for the present life.
- It emphasises the vocational education with a view to meet the livelihood of the child.
- It includes those subjects and activities which are useful to the child and the society.
- It enables the child to solve the problems of life and lead a happy and successful life.
- It reduces the importance of bookish knowledge and rote memory and develops the scientific outlook in the child.
- It widens the scope of education by including various subjects and activities.
- It regards the school as a socially planned institution and a mirror of the society.
- It advocates impressionistic and emancipatory discipline which are conducive for learning.
- It develops the curriculum according to the utility and needs of the child and the society.
- It believes in the importance of material world and individual and social development.
- It considers that senses are the gateways of knowledge.

DEMERITS OF REALISM

- It ignores meditation and yoga which are considered to be the sources of getting knowledge.
- It neglects the study of social sciences and literature which are essential to aesthetical development, promotion and transmission of our culture.
- It gives excessive importance to the knowledge of objectivity. But objective and subjective are relative terms. No scientists claim absolute objective. In fact, knowledge and ignorance is subjective and objective. It ignores imagination, feeling, emotion and sentiments which are important facts of individual and social lives.
- It believes that the science subjects alone prepare the child for a happy life. But some sort of training in ethics and religion are necessary for a happy and successful life.
- It lays great stress on the physical world and neglects the spiritual world which prepares the child for a happy life.
- It emphasizes material aspects and neglects the development of social efficiency.
- It gives less importance to the role of a teacher in education.

CONCLUSION

Realism is a well-developed philosophy and its contribution to education, though it suffers from certain limitations, is unique and undeniable. This philosophy provides a new light and wisdom which brings about remarkable changes in the educational principles and practices. In fact, change in the scope and aims of education, development of diversified curriculum, introduction of new teaching techniques, giving importance to sense training, advocating little freedom for the children, developing self-discipline through love and sympathy, and introduction of vocational education for a happy life have been the remarkable outcome and contribution of realistic trends of education.

CHAPTER 10

NATURALISM

INTRODUCTION

Naturalism is the oldest philosophy of the Western world. It is a materialistic philosophy which has been playing an important role in the field of education. Naturalism is also known as **materialism** on the basis of the premise that the universe is matter. It believes that reality and nature are identical and that beyond nature, there is no reality. "Material world is the real world". It means that nature is everything. Nothing is before, behind and beyond 'Nature'. The ultimate reality is of 'Nature'. Naturalism is a distinct philosophy, which does not believe in sentimentalism, spiritualism and supernaturalism. According to Prof. V.R. Taneja, "The naturalists see things as they are. They want to apprehend reality as it is in its own nature. They want to develop the self, which is influenced by reality". Naturalism believes that nature alone contains the normal and the final answer to all philosophical problems pertaining to education.

PROTAGONISTS OF NATURALISM

J.J. Rousseau is considered as the champion of naturalism. Among the chief exponents of naturalism are Aristotle, Comte, Hobbes, Bacon, Nunn, Darwin, Lamark, Huxley, Spencer, Shaw, Butler, Democritus, Epicurus, Johnson, Tagore and Neil. They advocate the doctrine of naturalism and apply its principles in the field of education in order to find solutions for various problems.

MEANING OF NATURALISM

Naturalism lays emphasis on the nature in every field of education. It is a philosophy which considers nature as everything and denies the existence of any spirit. It accepts nature to be the ultimate and complete reality and those who accept this view are regarded as *naturalists*. This philosophy does not believe in the existence of God. The term 'Nature' in naturalism stands for the totality of objects and events in space and time. Human life is a part of the scheme of nature. Naturalism applies natural laws to the entire gamut of human experiences, material, rational or spiritual. It gives importance to the 'matter' and the physical world.

DEFINITIONS OF NATURALISM

The term 'naturalism' has been defined by different philosophers and educationists in very clear terms.

George Hayward Joyee: "Naturalism is a system whose salient characteristic is the exclusion of whatever is spiritual or indeed, whatever is transcendental of experience from our philosophy of nature and man".

James Ward: "Naturalism is the doctrine that separates nature from God, subordinates spirit to matter and sets up unchangeable laws as supreme".

R.B. Perry: "Naturalism is not science but an assertion about science. More specifically, it is the assertion that scientific knowledge is final, leaving no room for extra scientific and philosophical knowledge". In other words, "Naturalism is the philosophical generalization of science. It applies the theories of science to the problems of philosophy".

Hocking: "Naturalism is metaphysics which considers nature as the whole of reality. It excludes what is supernatural or of other world".

Thomas and Lang: "Naturalism is opposed to Idealism, subordinates mind to matter and holds that ultimate reality is material world".

Rusk: "Naturalism is a philosophical position adopted by those who approach philosophy from purely scientific point of view".

J.S. Ross: "Naturalism is a term loosely applied in educational theory to systems of training that are not dependent on schools and books but on the manipulation of the actual life of the educated".

According to an Indian thinker, "Naturalism is a system that views man and universe, as physical, mechanical, biological and geological".

FORMS OF NATURALISM

The naturalists have propounded four forms of naturalism. Let us analyse them briefly here:

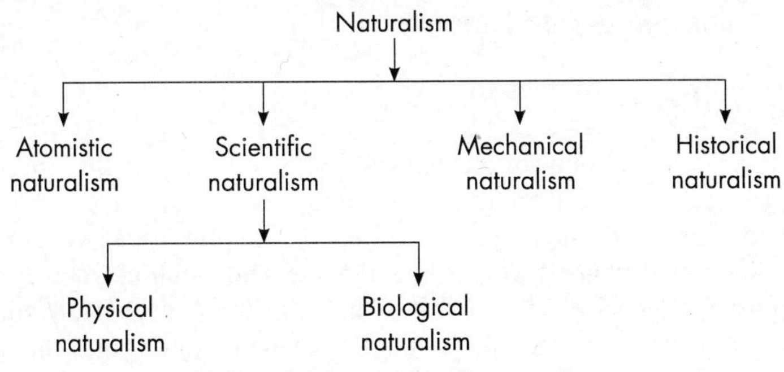

FIGURE 10.1 Forms of naturalism.

Atomistic Naturalism

The atomistic naturalism is the oldest form of naturalism. Epicurus and Democritus are the chief exponents of this philosophy. According to this philosophy, when we go on dividing or discussing a thing, a situation arises when further division or discussion is not possible. This ultimate individual unit is known as **atom**. The universe is composed of such atoms which are different from each other in colour, form, shape and quality. Democritus states further that heavy atoms fall more quickly than the lighter ones and begin to unite with each other on the way. Thus, according to them, the creation of the universe is a natural process in which there is no role of any metaphysical power.

Scientific Naturalism

This type of philosophy of naturalism emerged in the period during which scientific experiments were going on at a fast speed. Scientific experiments prove that heavy and light atoms fall with the same velocity. Materials divided atoms into electron, proton and neutron. The ultimate unit of substance for them is not atom but energy of electric or electronic power. According to this form of naturalism, Nature has been created by this energy. As far as explanations are concerned, scientific naturalism is totally against the philosophy of atomistic naturalism. But the derivations of these forms of naturalism are almost similar.

Physical naturalism: This is the sub-title of scientific naturalism. Physical naturalism attaches greater importance to the external materials phenomena than the conscious human beings. In other words, this philosophy is related to external nature and it discusses the world in terms of matter. It has no faith in morality, freedom of will and the inner nature of human mind. According to this philosophy, nature and matter are the same things and there is no difference between nature and consciousness. It accepts the laws of physical science as supreme. This philosophy has not got much importance in the field of education.

Biological naturalism: This is another subdivision form of scientific naturalism based on the evolution theory of Darwin. Man is the supreme product of this process of evolution. The advocates of this philosophy believe that heredity has a powerful influence on the nature and temperament of an individual human being. Biological naturalism emphasises the development of man's natural impulses, natural propensities and inborn tendencies. Darwin puts forward three principles to explain this philosophy. First is adaptation to the environment, that is, each species has to gain adjustment in order to live. Second is struggle for existence, that is, one has to struggle to live. The third principle is survival of the fittest, that is, only the fittest survive, others decay and die out. This form of naturalism has a great influence on the process of education.

Mechanical Naturalism

Herbert Spencer is the main exponent of mechanical philosophy. According to him, the world is like a huge machine which gets its form through matter and motion. Man is considered as a tiny part of this huge machine and is himself a small machine. This philosophy therefore, aims at training man as a good machine, and keeping it in good working conditions. The machine goes on moving without any mental or spiritual power. Since man is also a part of this huge machine, his movement is also governed by external stimuli or forces of nature. Similarly, matters keep on moving and changing and this change is governed by the laws of physical science. The mechanical naturalistic philosophy has given rise to the development of modern psychology which emphasises the importance of conditioned responses and the effective principle of learning by doing.

Historical Naturalism

This philosophy considers that wealth is real and it is essential for human survival. According to this philosophy, human history is the history of man's struggle on this earth. The main cause which motivates all struggles is the accumulation of wealth. This is because wealth is real and its accumulation is a natural phenomenon. This philosophy has led to the rise of the communist philosophy in the twentieth century.

PRINCIPLES OF NATURALISM

Belief in nature: Nature is great and powerful and delimits all the capacities of an individual human being. There is no reality beyond nature. Everything is nature and nature is everything. Naturalism regards nature as the ultimate reality. W.E. Hocking states that naturalism denies the existence of anything beyond nature, behind nature, before nature other than nature. Natural light or air is more important than artificial light or air. According to naturalism, nature is the only source of all knowledge.

Man—a supreme product: Naturalists consider man as the supreme creation of nature. He maybe termed as the supreme and superior animal.

Belief in science: Naturalism stresses the study of science subjects only. It believes that scientific knowledge is real and final. According to the naturalists the knowledge which is obtained from experience and experimentation is real.

Belief in material: The real world is the material world and the material world is the real world. It is so because the matter can be experienced by our senses. But the soul, spirit or God cannot be experienced by our senses. Therefore, they are not real. Naturalists believe only in what is real.

Man—a machine: The universe or world is a huge machine. Man is also a part of this huge machine and a complete machine in himself.

No faith in soul: Naturalists do not have any faith in soul or spirit. According to them, God, soul, mind, heaven, hell, freedom of will, moral values, prayer and wonders are illusions. Human life is interpreted in terms of matter only.

Unchangeable laws of nature: Laws of nature which govern the whole universe are unchangeable. They explain all the events and occurrences of the world.

Nature is good: Naturalists believe that nature is good and society is full of evils. They think that everything that comes to us from nature is good but it degenerates in the hands of man.

Equality: According to the naturalists, in the natural order of things all human beings are equal.

Nature of values: All values are created in terms of specific needs and purposes. They are the outcome of the conditions of human life.

Man creates society: Naturalists advocate the development of the society. They regard man as a social animal. He must live in the society. He creates society to fulfil his requirements. He adjusts and changes the environment according to his needs.

Senses—gateway of knowledge: Naturalists believe that all knowledge comes through the senses, that is, eye, ear, nose, tongue and skin. Knowledge acquired through these senses is more lasting than that acquired through books.

Heredity and environment: Naturalists regard that both heredity and environment have a vital role in influencing the personality of a man. A good psychological environment is essential for a man to adjust himself in the society.

NATURALISM IN EDUCATION

Naturalism in education means putting the child at the centre of all educational processes. Natural laws will be the teacher to teach the child according to his own nature. The nature of a child is two-fold, physical and biological or psychological nature. Physical nature is external which includes the laws of nature and psychological nature is internal which includes the basic instincts, impulses, tendencies, capacities and other inborn potentialities of the child. Naturalists emphasise the fact that the external laws of nature should correspond and coincide with the internal nature for the natural development of the child. It means that the child should be given full freedom to develop his innate tendencies and natural capacities.

The credit of introducing naturalism into education goes to Comenius and Francis Bacon but Rousseau and Herbert Spencer have brought this movement to the zenith. They advocate the re-organization of education in such a way that all shackles of formalism verbosity and snobbery should be broken, and the development of the child must continue according to his inherent nature, needs and inborn propensities. Rousseau and Herbert Spencer put the child at the central position of educational process and declared that nature should be regarded as the best teacher and that natural facts are the agencies and means of education of the child according to nature. In the words of Ross, "Education is merely the fostering of natural development, and true education takes place when the nature, power and inclinations of the child are allowed to develop freely with a minimum of guidance". Monroe says, "Education is the process of development into an enjoyable rational, harmoniously balanced, useful and hence natural life". The application of naturalistic philosophy in the field of education has enabled it to be child- centred as well as scientific.

CHARACTERISTICS OF NATURALISTIC EDUCATION

Back to nature: "Back to Nature" and "Follow Nature" are the watch words of naturalism for effective education. According to the naturalists, the best teacher for a child is Nature. Hence, education should be provided in the natural environment in order to develop the child according to his nature. Rousseau declares, "All things are good as they come from the hands of the author of nature, every where they degenerate in the hands of man".

Negative education: Negative education is an important feature of naturalistic education. Rousseau regards that the child is good; but it is the society that makes him bad. So, he advocates that the first education should be purely negative. According to him, the child should not be taught the principles of truth and virtue but be guarded against vice and error. James S. Ross is right when he says, "A negative education does not mean a time of idleness, far from it. It does not give virtue; it protects the child from vice. It does not inculcate truth, it protects from error. It disposes the child to take the path that will lead him to truth when he has reached the age to understand it, and goodness, when he has acquired the faculty of recognizing and loving it". In other words, it consists not in teaching virtue or truth, but in preserving the heart from vice and the mind from error. Rousseau says, "I call a negative education one that tends to perfect the organs that are the instruments of knowledge and the endeavours to prepare the way for reason, by the proper exercise of the senses".

Progressive manner of education: Naturalistic education believes that a child is a child and not an adult. As a child, he is a dynamic individual who develops gradually. According to the mental and physical growth of the child, the curriculum is also developed progressively. It means that the load of the curriculum is distributed according to the age and mental level of a child. The child's development passes through four stages, that is, infancy, childhood, adolescence and adulthood. Each stage has its own needs and problems. Education should meet these needs and develop the capacity to solve those problems. Rousseau says, "Nature wills that children should be children before they are men. If we seek to pervert the order, we shall produce forward fruits without ripeness and flavour".

Oppose bookish knowledge: Naturalists oppose the academic knowledge and verbalism of books. They regard the mere cramming of Greek and Latin literature, as artificiality, snobbery and mere show. Hence, they emphasise that real education should be according to the nature of the child through the development of natural interests and activities.

Self-learning: Naturalists lay stress on self-learning. To them all education, even the one in the early childhood, should be self-learning or learning by doing. The child should be given the opportunity for learning through his own experiences in the lap of nature.

Central position of child: Naturalism puts the child at the centre of the educational process. Naturalists are of the view that education is meant for the child. So, education is organized in such a way that the child learns by his own activities, observations and experiences without any guide.

Freedom: Naturalistic education allows full freedom for the child to develop himself according to his inherent nature, needs and inborn propensities. He is given all opportunities to observe and experience the matter that exists before him. The child should be put under no restraints, no interferences, no difficulties and no confusions. Rousseau exhorts, "God makes all things good. Man meddles with them and they become evil".

Training of senses: Naturalists emphasise that sense organs are the gateways to knowledge. They believe that knowledge acquired through the senses is real. Thus, sense organs need the training to discharge their function with efficiency. Rousseau says, "Education should prepare the way for reason by the proper exercise of senses".

Materialistic education: Naturalists lay stress only on materialistic education. They neglect spiritual education which is of no use for a child. To them, wealth (matter) is everything as it alone can provide the child pleasure and comforts.

Scientific education: This is one of the notable principles of naturalistic education. Naturalists consider scientific knowledge as real and final. So, they give importance only to science subjects and believe that such subjects prepare the child to contribute to scientific inventions and discoveries which in turn bring comforts to his life.

NATURALISM AND AIM OF EDUCATION

Self-expression: The aim of naturalistic education is self-expression and self-preservation. Spencer holds that self-preservation is necessary to continue and maintain one's existence. Hence, education aims at acquainting a person with the laws of health and enabling him to earn to live and training him to preserve and maintain life.

Protection of human machine: The protection of man as a human machine is an important aim of naturalistic education. Naturalists regard the whole universe as a huge machine. Man is a part of this huge machine. Hence, education should make the individual work very effectively. J.S. Ross says, "Education should make the human machine as good a machine as possible by attending to its constitutions by elaborating it and making it capable of more and more complicated tasks".

Attainment of present and future happiness: Herbert Spencer believes that education should aim at preparing and training the man to secure present and future happiness. McDougall asserts that happiness and misery come according to natural consequences. Hence, he emphasises the emancipating, moulding and guiding of the basic impulses of the child to attain natural progress and natural development.

Struggle for existence: The aim of naturalistic education is to equip the individual to struggle for existence and ensure his survival. It should help children to adjust themselves physically and mentally to their environment and to the changing circumstances of life.

Adaptation to environment: Naturalists hold that the aim of education is to enable an individual to live in harmony with its surroundings. Teaching the child the art of adjustment can ensure his health and happiness.

Improvement of racial gains: The aim of naturalistic education is that education should conserve and transmit the cultural heritage and develop it further. Bernard Shaw remarks that along with transmission of physical traits, racial experience should also be transmitted. James S. Ross rightly remarks, "Education is the preservation, the handling and the enhancement of the racial gains generation by generation".

Autonomous development: According to T.P. Nunn, "Autonomous development of man" should be the aim of education. The aim of naturalistic education is to ensure complete development of individuality without any interference by the society.

Redirection and sublimation of human instincts: Man's instincts are the guiding force and the basis of all conducts. It is, therefore, the aim of education that there should be the redirection and sublimation of these instincts towards socially useful work.

Natural development: According to the naturalists, the natural development of the child should be the aim of education. Rousseau has emphatically declared that, education should develop the child according to his inborn tendencies, interests, inclinations, aptitudes and capacities in a free environment and, thus, make him physically healthy and strong. In short, the aim of education is to put away all barriers and provide the child with maximum opportunity for his natural development.

Education according to nature: The aim of naturalistic education is to provide education according to the nature of the child. In other words, it should be according to the child's tendencies, capacities, instincts, likes and dislikes. According to Munroe, "Education finds its purpose, its process and its means wholly within the child life and the child-experiences". Rabindranath Tagore pleads that education should take place entirely according to the nature of the child.

NATURALISM AND CURRICULUM

The naturalists do not advocate a fixed curriculum. They consider the child as an important part of education. Thus, the curriculum must be child-centred so that he may have maximum opportunity for his natural development according to his inborn tendencies, interests, inclinations, aptitudes and capacities. As a result, the child may lead a happy life by fulfilling his present and future needs. In naturalistic education, every child is given the right to determine his own curriculum. He is expected to learn directly from nature through personal experiences. However, various naturalists have constructed curricula according to their perception of the aim of education and the needs, interests and abilities of the child.

Science: Naturalists lay emphasis on science subjects such as physics, chemistry, biology, arithmetic, zoology, botany and other scientific subjects. In their view literature, language, art etc. are subsidiary subjects. Rusk says that subjects related to science should be included in the curriculum. Huxley also gives emphasis on the study of science.

Mathematics: Mathematics and languages are included in the curriculum in order to facilitate the understanding of other subjects.

Social studies: History and social studies have been given importance to grasp the past experience of the race.

Physical education: Naturalists lay stress on physical education and health training, and home science also.

Herbert Spencer recommends various subjects such as chemistry, physics, mathematics, biology, agricultural science, home science, psychology, health and hygiene, history, economics, sociology, political science, music, painting, language, literature, carpentry etc.

NATURALISM AND METHOD OF TEACHING

Naturalists revolt against the traditional methods and bookish system of education. They want to keep the child active in the process of education. They follow different methods of teaching according to the interests, capacities and aptitudes of the child.

Learning by doing: Naturalists believe that direct experience is the best teacher. Rousseau opposes the rote method of learning on the ground that knowledge acquired through actual doing or actual experience is permanent. He says, "Give your scholar no verbal lessons; he should be taught by experience alone. Teach by doing whatever you can; Book knowledge should be as little as possible". He has a faith that the child can learn better by direct experience, that is, learning by doing.

Direct method: Naturalists advocate this method in teaching language. Here chalk and talk procedure is followed.

Heuristic method: This method is emphasised in the teaching of science and mathematics in order to prepare the child to solve problems and involve himself in discoveries and inventions.

Observation and excursion: History and geography are taught with practical exercises through actual excursion and observation.

Play-way method: This method is suitable to the nature of the child. It is also a direct experience that makes learning more interesting. Play-way method is regarded as the most natural and suitable method of creative education. Dr. Prem Nath says, "Play way is a staple method of naturalistic education". It creates the spirit of joyful and spontaneous activity.

Learning through senses: Naturalists believe that senses are the gateways of knowledge. Hence, senses should be trained and utilised fully. Rousseau wants the maximum utilisation of senses.

Self-government, self-effort and co-education: The naturalists recommend open air schools, self-government in schools and the establishment of co-education in educational institutions. Self-government will provide a direct experience of social life. The co-educational system will develop the right type of family and community life.

Learning through participations: Naturalists advocate this method of teaching to develop a better human society. A child requires social learning to enable him to take part in social activities.

Other methods: Apart from the above methods, naturalists adopt Dalton Plan, kindergarten, excursion method, montessori method, experimentation and textbook method so as to bring about a natural development in the child.

NATURALISM AND TEACHER

According to the naturalists, "Nature is the only supreme teacher". The teacher comes only next to the child in the educational process. The teacher should not interfere in the natural development of the child. He should not impose upon the child anything under his own will or authority. The teacher should behave sympathetically and affectionately towards the children.

Nature—supreme teacher: Naturalists consider Nature as the best teacher. They believe that whatever comes from Nature is good and that the society is evil. So, the child can develop normally and naturally when he lives in the lap of nature.

Teacher—the observer: According to the naturalists, the place of teacher in education is "behind the scenes". A teacher is merely an observer or spectator of the natural development of the child. The role of a teacher is to facilitate the process of child growth as well as learning.

Understand about child: Naturalists apply the maxim "know thy pupil" in naturalistic education. Hence, the teacher must understand the child and in no way interfere with his development. According to Rabindranath Tagore, "To teach the child, a teacher ought to have and realize the child in himself".

Teacher—the stage setter: As naturalism accords the teacher only a secondary position in teaching, a teacher is best only as the stage setter. He has to supply material, provide an ideal environment and create conditions conducive to the natural development of the child. According to Prof. Rusk, "A teacher is only a setter of the stage, a supplier of materials and opportunities, a provider of an ideal environment and creator of conditions conducive to the natural development of pupils".

Teacher—the gardener: The role of the teacher is like that of a gardener who prepares for the earth for the proper growth of plants. A teacher should create a conducive learning environment in the class for the natural development of the child.

NATURALISM AND STUDENT

Naturalists consider the child as the 'hero' in the drama of education. They state that education is for the child rather than the child for the education. They emphasise the fact that a child should be treated as a child and not an adult. At the time of birth, the child is fully free from evils. But later the society and the environment vitiate and corrupt him. So, the child should be kept away from the ills of society. He should be provided education in a free and natural environment. The child gets precedence over the teacher in this ideology.

NATURALISM AND DISCIPLINE

Naturalists give full freedom to the child to perform and learn whatever he likes. Freedom is the slogan of naturalism. They do not advocate any sort of punishments for the child. Since nature is his teacher, it gives him punishments for his mistakes. Therefore, no external punishment is desirable.

Discipline by natural consequences: Natural consequences are those experiences which the child receives by following an activity. Spencer observes, "When a child falls or runs its head against the table, he suffers pain, the remembrance of which tends to make him more careful, and by repetition of such experiences, he is eventually disciplined into proper guidance of his movement". At the same time Spencer wants that this principle should not be applied during infancy. He says "A three year old child playing with an open razor cannot be allowed to learn by this discipline for the consequences may be serious".

No punishment: Naturalists believe that the child is essentially good and pure. Hence, they are not in favour of any sort of punishment for the child. According to them, Nature will punish the child if he contravenes the law of Nature. Thus, he will learn by the natural consequence of his actions. In the words of Rousseau, "Children should never receive punishment. Freedom and not power is the greatest good".

Full freedom: Naturalists stand in favour of allowing full freedom for the child. It helps the child to learn and do what he likes and develop naturally.

Free society: The school should provide an environment which is conducive for the free development or growth of a child. So, the whole school should be organized as a free and natural society where pupils learn how to lead and how to follow.

Naturalists assume that the child has no knowledge of good and bad, but he suffers pain when he makes a mistake, and pleasure when he does something right. Thus, he gets reward or punishment for his actions.

NATURALISM AND SCHOOL

According to naturalists, Nature is the best teacher and its lap is the best school. The school environment should be completely free, flexible and without any rigidity. It should be helpful for the free and natural development of the child. It should be situated in the lap of Nature, far away from cities. There should not be any fixed time table and ready dozes of knowledge. There should be no provision for punishment. Naturalists are in favour of co-education in educational institutions. Such a school develops the feeling of self-learning and self-discipline. It does not want to burden the child with examinations.

CONTRIBUTION OF NATURALISM TO EDUCATION (IMPACT OF NATURALISM ON EDUCATION)

The contribution of naturalistic education to modern education has been unique. This philosophy makes the teaching–learning process more effective and attractive.

New psychological methods: Naturalism has given an impetus to new psychological methods in education. Self-expression, 'Follow-Nature', 'Learning by doing', 'Auto-Education', 'Play-Way' techniques are some of the important contributions of naturalistic philosophy. These techniques have blazed a new trail in the field of education and they make the teaching and learning process very simple and attractive. Modern philosophers, educationists and psychologists over the world now apply these psychological methods in their fields.

Importance of child: Naturalists consider the child as the gift of nature. According to them, the child is good and pure. He has been regarded as the 'hero' in the drama of education. Thus, this philosophy has given primary importance to the children in all stages of education. Today, children (students) decide the success or failure of educational industries.

Development of child psychology: Naturalists for the first time emphasised the development of the child according to his natural tendencies, needs, aptitudes, and capacities. This view of naturalism has given rise to the development of child psychology. It leads to the emergence of psychological, sociological and scientific tendencies in the field of modern education.

Study of society and sociology: This philosophy attaches much importance to the study of man. As a result, people start to study the impact of society and environment on man and vice-versa. Thus, naturalism gives birth to the scientific study of society and social process. Sociology is gaining ground as a scientific study of modern times.

Rise of democracy: Rousseau emphasises three guiding principles for man, that is, liberty, equality and fraternity which had long been denied to humanity by despotic rulers and religious leaders. These powerful principles of naturalism forced the people to rise against the existing socio-political system. This led to the flowering of democracy which in turn ushered in a new era of equalisation of educational opportunities in Switzerland and America like India.

Experience-centred curriculum: Naturalists shift from a subject-centred curriculum to an experience-centred curriculum. In fact, this is a 'must' in modern life. Modern life needs various experiences to be given to the child through co-curricular activities so that he would be educated and trained to face life squarely and solve all its problems successfully.

Freedom: Naturalists advocate unrestrained freedom for the natural development of the child. They emphasise the principle of discipline through natural consequences. The emergence of naturalism was a logical outcome of the repression of the child in the period of Rousseau. The child used to be punished severely and kept under the control of teachers. This strict discipline was discarded because of the influence of naturalism. As a result, now the child enjoys full freedom to learn and do whatever he likes. Thus, freedom for the child is the chief contribution of naturalism to modern education.

Place of educational institutions: Naturalists insist that educational institutions should be established in natural surroundings. According to this philosophy, schools should be situated in the lap of Nature, far away from cities and free from environmental pollution such as noise pollution and air pollution. Nature is more suitable for learning. This view needs to be followed at the time of construction of educational institutions in our country.

New movement in education: Naturalists have given birth to new movements. New types of educational institutions have come up in recent years. Institutions like the summer school of A.S. Neil, Vishvabharathi of Rabindranath Tagore, Kindergarten schools of Froebel, Montessori schools have come into existence as a result of the influence of naturalism in education.

Favour of co-education and residential school: The naturalists want to protect the educand from evils. For this purpose, they favour residential schools so that the environment of the educands who reside in hostels attached to the school can be maintained on a healthy level. They also advocate co-education because it develops more natural attitudes in boys and girls towards family and community life. Now coeducational system has become common in all stages and types of education.

MERITS OF NATURALISM

Naturalism is accepted as one of the important schools of philosophy of education. This philosophy differs from all other philosophies in its meaning and objectives. It has the following merits, which are laudable and useful in the world of education.

- It gives the child a very important place in the educational process. It treats a child as child and not as an adult. The child is good and pure at the time of birth.

- It considers Nature as the best teacher in whose company the child learns better. Society is full of evils.
- It lays stress on the psychological development of the child in the lap of Nature.
- It considers individual interests, aptitude, inclination, needs and capacities while structuring the curriculum.
- It introduces different methods of teaching techniques such as play-way, observation, learning by doing, etc. which occupy an important place in modern education.
- It assigns importance to science subjects, which are real. It prepares and encourages the child to engage in experimentation, discoveries and inventions.
- It considers man as a social animal and he has to build societies to meet his requirements. Individual life is not possible on the earth.
- It advocates full freedom for the child for his natural development. It motivates the child to acquire more knowledge in the natural environment.
- It revolts against old, traditional methods and bookish system of education, based on the rote method.
- It gives direct inspiration to the concept of psychological, sociological and scientific education.

DEMERITS OF NATURALISM

Though the naturalistic philosophy has many merits, it is not free from criticism. Several defects in this philosophy have been pointed out by different thinkers and educationists.

Unsatisfying aim of education: Naturalists concentrate on natural environment and natural development of the child. If the child is developed according to his nature in the laps of Nature only, the child will become unsocial with no feeling of social service. Thus, the aim of naturalistic education is one sided and unsatisfactory.

Neglects spiritual world: Naturalism ignores the spiritual world and considers the material world only. For balanced development of the child, it requires knowledge of both the spiritual and the material worlds. The material attitude of the people makes them selfish which is dangerous for a society.

Neglects future: Naturalism lays stress on solutions for only the present needs and problems of an individual and neglects his future needs and problems. It has failed to prepare the child for the future life.

Neglects moral and spiritual values: Naturalism advocates no concern for spiritual values and the remote future. But these values are essential for the balanced development of a child. Education is futile if it avoids moral and spiritual values.

Neglects books: Naturalists neglect the bookish system of education. We cannot neglect the treasure of knowledge contained in the printed materials. They insist that the education of the child should be based on his activities and his life experiences. But these activities and experiences cannot bring about the total development of a child's personality. Therefore, the role of books in the education system cannot be ignored.

Emphasis on science subjects: Naturalists emphasise scientific education. Naturalist like Spencer has given priority to scientific subjects and only a secondary place to humanities in the curriculum. In fact, both are equally important and essential in the development of a child's personality.

Unlimited freedom to child Naturalism advocates unrestricted freedom for the child to develop himself naturally. This may lead to self-assertion resulting in arbitrary behaviour without any consideration for others. This is undesirable, and harmful to the child. Full freedom will never exist in a civilized society. "A child cannot be given a long rope to hang himself".

Little role for teacher: Naturalism minimises the role of the teacher in the educative process. A teacher is an observer, a sympathetic guide and helper in structuring experiences for the child. This attitude is not considered very healthy and desirable in modern democratic countries where various social, moral, and spiritual qualities are to be inculcated among children by the educational processes. Even in the electronic age, a teacher occupies an important place in the teaching–learning process.

Unappealing principles of discipline: The principle of discipline by natural consequences is quite unsuitable and very often harmful. For instance, lighting of a matchstick without proper guidance may start a conflagration of a gigantic magnitude. Thus, this principle appears very unjust, hazardous, rash and unhealthy.

Ignores the development of society: Naturalism emphasises individual development ignoring the society which is equally important. The development of an individual maybe achieved with the close cooperation and development of the others. They are like the two sides of the same coin. But this philosophy has failed to emphasise the development of the society.

CONCLUSION

The contribution of naturalism is significant in the progressive modern educational thought and practice. All the modern methods of teaching techniques owe their origin to this school of philosophy. The psychological basis of child-centred education, the emphasis on freedom and self-expression in learning, the revolt against the traditional educative process and the recognition of the importance of the child in the process of education have brought about a renaissance in the field of modern education. This philosophy has developed a scientific attitude in man. It has also made teaching more enjoyable, useful, real, effective and attractive. It has given inspiration to the concept of psychological, scientific and sociological education. In short, we can say that naturalism has made a creative, unique and unprecedented contribution to education by revolting against the old and traditional methods of educative process and bookish system of education. The present educational world is moving ahead with modern technology in the twenty-first century. Paul Monroe has rightly remarked, "Naturalism has given direct impetus to the clear formation of the psychological and scientific conception of education".

CHAPTER 11

PRAGMATISM

INTRODUCTION

The Roman Catholics perpetrated inhuman cruelties upon the protestants and the reformists in Europe in the sixteenth and seventeenth centuries. As a result, thousands of the oppressed migrated from Europe to America for freedom, safety and peace. Some years later the spirit of Industrial Revolution in Europe reached the shores of America and it affected the migrants who had to confront new problems and difficulties due to the changed environment. Their old ideals and values were incapable of meeting and solving the new problems. This generated in them a new type of thinking to solve the emerging problems. The new mode of thinking led them to new types of activities and new ways of learning by doing and by consequences and experiences. They judged the events on the basis of their consequences. They selected and used only those activities which were found good and useful to solve their problems of life. In this way, the pragmatic philosophy was conceived in the nineteenth century and its influence is growing in all areas of human life and development even today. The circumstances and compulsions of life led the Americans to evolve this new ideology as it suited their ever changing needs of life. This philosophy is known as the **gift of American philosophy** which has made a very deep impact on the education of the twentieth and the twenty-first centuries.

PROTAGONISTS OF PRAGMATISM

The chief exponents of pragmatism are Charles S. Peirce, William James, Schiller, John Dewey, Margaret H. Mead and W.H. Kilpatrick.

MEANING OF PRAGMATISM

The term 'pragmatism' first appeared in 1878 in "How to Make Our Ideas Clear", an article of Charles Sanders Peirce. The word *pragmatism* has been derived from a Greek word *pragma* which means 'to do', 'to make', 'to accomplish', and 'to act'. Therefore, the words 'activity', 'action', 'practice', 'doing', 'making' and 'accomplishing' etc. are used to refer to pragmatism. Some scholars think that the word 'pragmatism' has been derived from the Greek word *pragmatikos* which means 'practicability' or 'utility'. According to this school of thought, practice comes first and theory afterwards. Thus, action gets priority over thought. Everything is tested on the touchstone of experience. It emphasises action rather than thought. The basic assumption of this philosophy is whatever is learnt in education ought to be useful for the individual in his social life.

Pragmatism is also known by various names such as "practical philosophy", "utilitarian philosophy", "experimental philosophy". "philosophy of instrumen-talism" and "philosophy of consequentialism". Archie J. Bahm calls it "down to earth philosophy" and "cash value philosophy".

DEFINITIONS OF PRAGMATISM

Pragmatism is the modern ideology of education which has been defined by different philosophers.

James B. Prett: "Pragmatism offers us a theory of meaning, a theory of truth of knowledge and a theory of reality".

Arnold Reid: "Pragmatism is an 'activity', 'engagement', 'encounter' based on the concept of practice or workability of an idea or theory".

William James: "Pragmatism is a temper of mind, an attitude, it is also a theory of the nature of ideals and truth, and finally it is a theory about reality".

J.S. Ross: "Pragmatism is essentially a humanistic philosophy, maintaining that man creates his own values in the course of activity, that reality is still in the making and awaits its part of completion from the future, that to an unascertainable extent our truth are man-made products".

Prem Nath: "The nature of pragmatism is naturalistic, its duration is scientific and practicable and its aim is social and humanistic".

Will Durant: "Pragmatism is the doctrine that truth is the practical efficacy of an idea".

FORMS OF PRAGMATISM

Humanistic pragmatism: This form of pragmatism believes in the welfare of humanity. It is concerned with human needs, aspiration and satisfaction. According to humanistic philosophy, "whatever fulfils our purpose, satisfies our desire, develops our life is true". This ideology emphasises that only those things and activities which satisfy human beings are true.

Experimental pragmatism: According to experimental pragmatism only those ideas or things are true which can be verified and proved by experiments. This ideology believes, "whatever can be experimentally verified is true or what works is true". It assigns more emphasis on personal experiences and ignores social experiences.

Nominalistic pragmatism: According to medieval European nominalistic philosophy, "a universe is only a name". Whenever we make any experiment, the prospective results start coming to our mind. Nominalistic pragmatism believes that these results of our experiments are always particular and concrete. There are many names of one thing. For example, 'water' in English, is 'Paani' in Urdu and 'Thannir' in Tamil and 'Jal' in Hindi. But meaning is the same. Thus, this form of philosophy bestows emphasis on the material form of the ideas and names them.

Biological pragmatism: According to this form of pragmatism, the power or capacity of human being is valuable and important. It enables him to adjust himself to the environment and change his environment according to his needs and requirements. It believes that knowledge is an instrument for enabling the human organism to make a better environment for himself. This philosophy is known as Instrumentalism which is very dominant in modern times. John Dewey is the chief exponent of this ideology.

PRINCIPLES OF PRAGMATISM

Revolt against traditionalism and absolution: Pragmatism is a revolt against the existing beliefs such as idealism and naturalism. This ideology gives emphasis to the practicability of things and activities. It believes that truth is that which works in practical situations. According to Pragmatism, "whatever fulfils one's purposes, satisfies one's desire, and develops one's life is true". In fact, this philosophy is a mid-way between naturalism and idealism.

Truth changes: According to pragmatists truth always changes. They believe that what is true today may not necessarily be true tomorrow, what is true to one, may not necessarily be true or good to others, what is true to India may not necessarily be true to England or America and so on. Thus, truth is not absolute or predetermined for all times to come. It changes with the changes in person, place, time or circumstances. In the words of John Dewey, "Truth is made just as health, wealth and strength are made in the course of experience".

No ultimate values: The main principle of pragmatic philosophy is that it has no ultimate values. Values such as truth, goodness and beauty are only man-made products. They are not fixed and they emerge only in the individual social-flow of events. In the words of John Dewey, "Values are as unstable as the forms of clouds. They keep on changing from time-to-time and reality is still in the process of making. Ideal ends are remotely connected with immediate and urgent conditions".

Thought is subordinate to action: Pragmatic philosophy bestows supreme position to action. It considers that activity is more important than ideas. In other words, ideas should be born out of activities. According to this school of philosophy, "Practice comes first and theory afterwards".

Faith in democracy: Pragmatism has deep faith in democracy. An individual can realise the maximum development of his personality only in a social context. Therefore, he should acquire the qualities of social skills. The spirit of sharing one's experiences develops an understanding of other people and their attitudes towards him. Pragmatists hold the view that life, education, and democratic process are all rolled into one.

Faith in flexibility: Pragmatists have strong faith in flexibility. They believe that nothing is fixed and final in this world. Everything grows, changes and develops in course of time. In other words, the world is changing and everything is under a process of transformation. Human life is also changing. This flexibility brings out progress and development in the society.

Faith in present and future: According to pragmatism, each individual has to solve the problems of his present and future life. Hence, the present and the immediate future are of great values to him than the past. They hold that it is of no use to think and talk about what is dead and gone.

Faith in pluralism: Pragmatists uphold pluralism. About the absolute reality, there are three views and beliefs, that is, monoism, dualism and pluralism. Experience is the test of truth. Man's experiences provide the validity of an idea or thing. There are many pragmatic truths. Rusk says, "Naturalism reduces everything to life, idealism to mind or spirit. Pragmatism sees no necessity for seeking one fundamental principle of explanation. It is quite content to admit several principles and accordingly pluralistic". In short, pluralism refers to the different views that people have on a particular thing.

Faith in experimentation: Pragmatism is also known as experimentalism. Human life is like a laboratory wherein each individual undertakes various experiments to solve the problems of his life. No judgement is possible before an experiment is tested by experience. In the words of William James, "The cash value of truth is in experimental terms". C.S. Peirce calls it, "The laboratory habit of mind".

Faith in manpower: Pragmatists bestow a great importance upon the power of man. They have faith in manpower such that a man can create an environment which is useful, beneficial and conducive to his own development and the welfare of the society. Man himself determines the goals for his present life.

Faith in experience: Pragmatists lay stress on experience. Truth, goodness and beauty are accepted if they work. They say that only human experience is reliable. Human experiences and purposes are the determining factors of values and life.

Principle of utility: Pragmatism is a utilitarian philosophy. It believes that anything which bestows satisfaction is useful or which helps in the growth of man is useful. In other words, only those ideas or things are true or right which have a utility for man. According to William James, "It is true because it is useful". Whatever has utility is real.

Reality still in the making: This philosophy holds that reality is not readymade. It is still in the making. The world is still in the process of formation and development of theories for reality. Man is to aid this process of formation of theories to such an extent that all the needs and requirements of human beings are fully satisfied. The great pragmatist William James says, "For naturalism, reality is readymade and complete from all entities, while for pragmatism it is still in the making and awaits its parts of completion from the future".

Faith in practical philosophy: According to pragmatism, true philosophy is one that helps in the solution of the practical problems in life. It says, "Philosophy is thinking what to do in a life situation and it is brought into existence when problems occur". In other words philosophy is anything which is practical to find solution for problems occurring in life.

Instrumentalism: Pragmatists believe that ideas are only tools and instruments. These are the sources or means to gain practical knowledge. According to this belief, "a thinker is a manipulator and not a beholder. Ideas or thoughts enlarge their scope by testing themselves on practical issues".

Interaction with environment: Pragmatism believes that growth of population takes place because of its interaction with environment. Man tries to adjust himself to his environment and this results in his growth.

Social values: Man is born in a society and he lives there. So, his existence without a society is meaningless. Hence, pragmatists give more importance to social values and ideas than individual values and ideals. They consider freedom, equality, tolerance, responsibility and justice as social values.

Knowledge is a by-product of action: Pragmatism holds the view that the reconstruction of experience is knowledge. Such knowledge can be acquired through imagination and experimentation or action.

Problems motivate truth: According to this philosophy, man undertakes various experiments to solve the problems which occur in the course of his growth and development. Hence, the success of an experiment is the search for truth. Thus, problems are the motivating force for the search of truth.

Rejection of authoritarianism: The pragmatic philosophy rejects or opposes all types of authoritarianism whether in government or religion or education. It has a firm faith in the doctrine of democracy.

PRAGMATISM IN EDUCATION

Pragmatism emerged as the twentieth century revolution against the nineteenth century rationalism, dogmatism, universalism, monoism, and dualism. The credit of introducing pragmatism into education goes to two social thinkers namely, William James and John Dewey. Pragmatism has promoted a new consciousness and awakening in the field of modern education. According to John Dewey, "The real value of a thing lies in its utility for human welfare". Since education contributes to human welfare and progress, it will be more useful and purposeful. The pragmatists have two fundamental beliefs; the first is that no principle or idea is valid and true for all times. The second belief is that the real value of a thing lies in its utility and usefulness for human welfare. On the basis of these beliefs, they hold the view that no educational process can be regarded as final and useful for all times to come. It changes according to the changing needs and circumstances of the society. Education prepares man to test knowledge or truth on the basis of its usefulness by activity or experience in a social environment to solve his social problems. Pragmatists believe that human beings create their own ideals and values through various activities and experiences. According to these philosophers, education is not the dynamic side of philosophy, but philosophy itself evolved from education. Education is not the preparation of man for his life but it is life itself involving experience, experimentation and free thinking. In the words of John Dewey, "Education is the process of reconstruction of experiences, giving it a more sociological value, through the medium of increased individual efficiency".

CHARACTERISTICS OF PRAGMATIC EDUCATION

Since pragmatism is a practical and utilitarian school of philosophy, it has influenced education to the maximum extent. Hence, the study of the characteristics of pragmatism has become important from the educational point of view.

Education as life: Pragmatists firmly believe that education is life itself. Education provides a child more and more opportunities to undertake various activities and experiments through which real knowledge can be gained. As a result, he creates his own values and ideals that make his life better and comfortable.

Education as growth: According to pragmatists, education is a dynamic and progressive process in nature according to the changing circumstances of life. John Dewey says, "Growth is the real function of education". In other words, man and society are growing and accordingly their needs are growing and changing. So, education has to grow in order to meet the needs and requirements of human beings. Pragmatists believe that each child is born with inherent tendencies, aptitudes and capacities. It is education which should develop these inherent qualities of a child to create his own values which equip him to face all problems of life at various times and different situations.

Education as reconstruction of experiences: John Dewey says, "Education is a process of continuous reconstruction of experiences". Pragmatists stress that real knowledge is gained by experiments and experiences conducted by the child himself. One experience leads to another and then to many others. Thus, the process of reconstruction of experiences goes on till the final truth is gained. These experiences enable the child to develop his personality to adjust with other people in the society in a more democratic way. Thus, educative process has no end and it goes beyond itself. In short, education means more education.

Education as a social process: Man is a social animal and he lives in the society. He is integrally related to all human beings. He should, therefore, be educated through the medium of society so as to develop the desirable social qualities in him. This is also because he gains more and more knowledge through personal experiences than he gets from books. Hence, it is the function of education that it should teach him the give and take process and make him aware of his social obligations. Brubacher points out the two basic principles of pragmatic education. The first is that education has a social function and the second, it must provide social experience to the child. In the school, the educand must be trained to become useful in a democratic pattern of life. Pragmatists emphasise the importance of social values. In the words of John Dewey, "Education is the social continuity of life". The education of the child through the medium of society promotes his welfare and happiness.

Education as a responsibility of state: Education is the birthright of each individual in a democratic country. Hence, it is the whole responsibility of the state to provide education to all its citizens. Pragmatists stress the fact that the state should take the responsibility of providing education to each child by which he is prepared to meet the problems and challenges of life successfully.

Education as freedom: Pragmatic education works on the principle of democracy which infuses in a child a sense of freedom, initiative, equality and also a sense of responsibility. It insists that freedom should be given to the child for the development of his all-round personality.

Education as development of philosophy of education: Pragmatists believe that the aim of education is a comprehensive practical education based on the philosophy of liberal education. This aim of education is to achieve intellectual, moral, aesthetic, physical and spiritual development in the educands. Education must be comprehensive and aim at developing the child to achieve a better social adjustment.

Education as humanitarianism: Pragmatic education aims at creating humanitarian values in every sphere of education. Education of all kinds should aim at evolving human values through adopting suitable methods of teaching aims of education, curriculum etc.

Education as democracy: Pragmatists want to utilise education to create democratic values and ideals in educands. A democratic society stresses the importance of equality, liberty and fraternity. It is education which should be evolved in such a way as to prepare the educands for a democratic and social life.

Education as human personality: Pragmatic philosophy attaches the greatest importance to the human personality. According to this ideology, human personality is considered as the most significant element in the process of education. Education must be paedocentric, based on the natural activities and inclinations of the child in order to make him capable of adapting to the social environment.

PRAGMATISM AND AIMS OF EDUCATION

In the words of Brubacher, "The progressive education has no fixed aims or values in advance. Educational aims, no matter how well authenticated by the past, are not to be projected indefinitely into the future. In a world rendered precarious and contingent by a compound of the novel and the customary, educational aims must be held subject to revisions as one advances predetermines into the future. If education has any general aims in the light of which their successive revisions can take place, it is only the pupil's growth. But growth itself has no end beyond further growth. In other words, education is its own end". Pragmatists do not believe in fixed, predetermined, ultimate and general aims of education. According to them, the aims of human life always change with the changing times, places and circumstances. As a result, no specific aim of education can be predetermined. There should, therefore, be different aims of education for different children for different times and circumstances. In the words of John Dewey, "Education has no aims, only persons have aims". However pragmatist philosophy stresses a few aims of education which maybe listed as follows:

More education: The aim of pragmatic education is more education. It means that education is the development of knowledge. Every part of learning leads to another. Thus, the educative process has no end beyond itself.

Creation of new values: According to pragmatism, the creation of new values to meet the needs of the individual and the new social demands are the aims of education. In the words of J.S. Ross, "The general educational aim of the pragmatist is just the creation of new values. So, the main task of the educator is to put the educand into a position of developing values for himself".

All-round development: The essential aim of education is to direct the impulses, interests, and abilities towards the satisfaction of the felt needs of the child in his environment. The individual develops his personality in terms of his physical, intellectual, social, moral and aesthetic aspects.

Growth: This is the ultimate aim of pragmatic education. Growth means the growth of "inner sight". The growth takes place through mutual interactions and changing social order, and it is possible in a democratic society. According to John Dewey, "Life as growth and education is a process of growth of man and society". Thus, the chain of growth and more growth continues.

Social efficiency: Socialisation of an individual is the core aim of pragmatic education. According to pragmatism, education is the development of social efficiency in the child. In other words, education should prepare the child for social life. Therefore, pragmatists suggest cooperative learning, and social discipline, and co-curricular and extra-curricular acitivities which socialise the child. Thus, the aim of pragmatic education is to develop social efficiency in the child and make him a dedicated and able citizen for the nation.

Personal and social adjustment: Pragmatic education wants to develop in the child a dynamic and adaptable mind to enable him to adjust and control his environments successfully according to the changing scenario. In the words of John Dewey, "Pragmatic education is the development of all those capacities in the individual which will enable him to control his environment and fulfil his possibilities".

Leads to democracy: The pragmatic aim of education is to create a democratic environment in the society. Kilpatrick is correct in saying, "Our school rooms must become living democracies that in a democracy, it is self directing personalities that we try to build, the kind that can carry forward life even more successfully in the developing world, and that the progressive development of a better life for all men is the basis out of which morality and moral conduct arise". So, education must create the environment for democracy to flourish, which enables the individual to determine his belief and fulfil his needs.

PRAGMATISM AND CURRICULUM

Pragmatism advocates a useful, flexible, dynamic active and correlated curriculum. It prescribes a broad and flexible type of curriculum including all experiences that the children acquire in the classroom, on the playground, in the laboratories and libraries and various social relationships. Pragmatists believe that the aims of life cannot be definite. Any change in the aims of human life brings about changes in the aims of education. As a result the curriculum goes on changing to meet the changing needs of the society. So, all the subjects should be included in the curriculum to fulfil the needs and solve the problems of life. They follow certain principles in the field of curriculum development.

Principle of utility: Utility is the only watchword of pragmatism. Pragmatists are utilitarians who believe that utility lies in facilitating human adjustment and adaptation. Therefore, only those subjects, activities and experiences are included in the curriculum which should be useful to the present needs and immediate future expectations of the child. At the elementary stage, reading, writing, arithmetic, nature study, drawing, and handwork should be prescribed. At a later stage, practical subjects such as language, physical training, hygiene, social studies, physical sciences and mathematics should be included in the curriculum. Agriculture for boys and home science for girls is prescribed. Vocational and technical education are included in the curriculum in order to enable the child to stand on his own feet.

Principle of interest: Curriculum should be based on the interest, aptitudes and tastes of the child. It means that only those subjects, activities and experiences should be included in the curriculum in which the child takes interest. John Dewey has mentioned four varieties of interests namely, (a) Interest in conversation, (b) interest in investigation, (c) interest in construction and (d) interest in creative expression. On the basis of the principle of interest, reading, writing, counting (arithmetic), arts, craftswork and natural sciences are taught at the primary level.

Principle of experience: Pragmatism emphasises the importance of practical work and experiences. Hence, the curriculum should consist of purposeful social activities and experiences to promote original thinking in the child. These activities or experiences help the child to fulfil his needs along with the fulfillment of the needs of the society. This will make the children good citizens and men of high moral character.

Principle of integration: According to this principle, the instruction in various subjects should be given through one activity. It means that all the subjects should be taught through their interrelations. Subject-wise, independent teaching will not result in integration. Hence, the watertight division of the subjects should be avoided. "Instead of working at separate subjects, the public should be encouraged to draw freely upon all knowledge that is relevant to the activity in which he happens to be engaged". This principle insists that the curriculum should be based on the principle of correlation.

Principle of flexibility: Pragmatism advocates a changeable curriculum. It should not be static or rigid, but it should go on changing according to the needs and situation of the child, so that new knowledge and experiences maybe included in it. John Dewey believes that the curriculum cannot be fixed in advance and it should be according to the needs and requirements of the child. It should be made flexible, proper and relevant according to the times also.

Principle of child centredness: Pragmatism accepts the child as an important pivot of education. Therefore, it provides proper attention to individual differences and the interests of the child in the curriculum. According to this philosophy, the curriculum should be based on the interests, abilities, aptitudes and the needs of the child. Moreover, the curriculum should take into account the successive stages of a child's development. From the psychological and scientific point of view, pragmatists want curriculum to be always child-centred.

Principle of life-centredness: According to pragmatic philosophy, curriculum is the mirror of life. The curriculum should be life-centred and child-centred. As far as possible, the curriculum should include only those subjects and activities which can be related to the child's pattern of life. It enables the child to become capable of solving problems and meet the compulsory needs of life.

PRAGMATISM AND METHODS OF TEACHING

Pragmatism opposes the traditional methods of teaching. It does not believe in any fixed method of teaching. According to the pragmatists, "Education is not so much teaching the child things he ought to know, as encouraging him to learn for himself through experimental and creative activity". However, they introduce child-centred, scientific, psychological and active methods of teaching. Their main methods of teaching are project method and problem-solving methods. Let us explain the methods of teaching advocated and followed by the pragmatists.

Learning by doing: The pragmatists believe that the child learns best when he performs acts related to particular subjects. The child is spontaneously active by nature. Therefore, the child should be acquainted with facts while he is engaged in activity related to those facts by which he can develop his own natural abilities and qualities. Thus, the child learns best through his activities. In the words of Ryburn, "Experience (experiment) is the truest and best master and one too, whose lessons we never forget". Knowledge acquired through actual doing or actual experience is far more permanent than knowledge acquired through words.

Project method: It is a direct outcome of the philosophy of pragmatism. Through this method, a problem is posed and a situation is created. The pupils find a solution after trying out various possibilities. They develop an insight, foresight and various other skills. In the words of Kilpatrick, "A project is a whole-hearted, purposeful activity proceeding in a social environment". In the project method, the educand is presented with a problem in the form of a project. He makes the best effort to try to put this project into practice. It is posed in the form of a problem; the child is inspired to solve the problem. Most of the problems are related to day-to-day life, and the solution to such problems requires more than just mental activity.

Experimental method: Knowledge is gained through experimentation. The pragmatists want their pupils to think and act for themselves, to do rather than to know, to originate rather than repeat. Thus, they want the pupils to test and verify any idea to find the reality.

Purposive process of learning: Pragmatism emphasises self-learning through self-effort. It means that the method of teaching should provide conducive experiences and productive practical activities for the benefit of the child to face boldly and successfully the problems and challenges of modern life.

Problem-solving method: This is another method of teaching introduced by pragmatists. A number of problems are put before children and teaching is done through problems. The child gets knowledge to solve the practical problems of life. This method is related to the life of the pupils and enables them to tackle problems that occur in natural situations.

Integrated approach of teaching: All subjects are taught in a correlated and integrated manner to make knowledge a single unit. This method of teaching is most effective and brings about the correlation and integration of all subjects, activities and experiences. It implies that all knowledge and experiences are to be coordinated in human terms. The child is ever active— continuously doing things. While doing, he is learning, while learning, he is doing. Thus, all activities are correlated and integrated.

PRAGMATISM AND DISCIPLINE

Pragmatists advocate social discipline based on the child's interests, activities, and his sense of social responsibility. The merging of play with work will develop interest and a sense of purpose in the child to do his work with joy and eagerness. This mental condition will infuse in him seriousness, sincerity and consideration for others. He will also foster self-confidence, self-reliance, cooperation, sympathy and fellow-feeling for others. These social qualities develop in him a sense of discipline and moral obligation towards the self and others. The pragmatist emphasises social discipline through participation in cooperative activities in the school society. This participation enables the child to imbibe virtues such as tolerance, mutual respect, sympathy, initiative and service of humanity. In the words of John Dewey, "Out of doing things that are to produce results and out of doing in a social and cooperative way, there is born a discipline of its own kind and type".

Discipline does not mean a simple obedience to rules or commands imposed from outside. Blind obedience is the negation of democracy. Hence, all educators have to create discipline to evoke a sense of social responsibility in the child. Social responsibility helps the educand to become disciplined and this discipline helps him in successfully performing all personal and social tasks. The pragmatic educationist constantly experiments with a view to discovering new ways to create real discipline in the school. As a result, many new methods have been developed.

PRAGMATISM AND TEACHER

The educator is the most important element in the school's social environment. His role is necessary for the development of the child. By coming into contact with the educator, the educand can develop a set of very desirable and useful social habits, attitudes and interests.

Teacher—an experimentalist: From the pragmatic educational point of view, a teacher must be a practically trained, socially efficient, professionally talented, and intelligent with vision and foresight. He must be an experimentalist to create learning situations and stimulate the child's activities. He puts the child in the position of a discoverer and experimenter.

Teacher—a friend and a guide: According to pragmatism, teacher is a friend, philosopher, counsellor, helper and a guide for the child. He should maintain a cordial relationship with his educands. He should provide education to the child in the social environment in order to develop social interests, attitudes and habits for the welfare of the society. John Dewey says, "I believe that every teacher should realize the dignity of his calling".

Teacher adopts hands-off policy: Pragmatism adopts 'hands-off' policy. The teacher serves in the capacity of helper, guide, and arranger of experiences. The function of the teacher is to assist the child when he is in difficulty to guide his general development in the light of a superior wisdom which the child does not yet possess.

Teacher should know the child and society: The teacher is expected to have knowledge about the interests of his taught and a full understanding regarding the conditions and situations of changing society.

Teacher—a model: It is essential for the educator to present a good model in his own behaviour to create an atmosphere of cooperation and brotherhood. He is not to impose anything on the child. But he should be a model to the child in order to develop the desirable qualities.

PRAGMATISM AND STUDENT

Pragmatists consider the child as an important constituent of educational process. The child has educational freedom to decide his own aims, goals and purposes independently. The educands get education in the social environment. They have opportunities to develop three aspects of personality, that is, biological, psychological and social aspects.

PRAGMATISM AND SCHOOL

In the sight of pragmatists, school is a social institution where the child acquires real experiences of actual life. John Dewey describes a school as a 'miniature society' in which the child gets real experiences to act and behave according to his interests, aptitudes, and capacities. According to pragmatists, the school is also a living laboratory providing knowledge to the students in the social environment. The school is an institution which socialises the child and prepares him for social change. It is not a centre of education alone but it is also a community centre of various activities and experiences. In the words of John Dewey, "School should be the true representative of society". In fact, school is the embryo of the community. It acts as an instrument for the preservation and promotion of the world culture.

CONTRIBUTION OF PRAGMATISM TO EDUCATION

The contribution of pragmatism is of considerable importance in the field of education. It has brought about revolutionary changes in modern education.

Democratic outlook: Pragmatism has deep faith in democracy. The democratic outlook of pragmatism is needed in the present world. The democratic values such as fellow-feeling, tolerance, cooperation, liberty, equality, etc. are essential for the progress of society. Pragmatic education develops a democratic way of learning through purposeful and cooperative projects and activities which foster the democratic values among the students.

Social efficiency: Socialisation or social efficiency is a very significant concept put forth by pragmatism. It is the main aim of pragmatic education and leads to the development of vocational efficiency and feelings of social and national service in the child. The development of social efficiency has had a great impact on the modern education.

School–a miniature society: Pragmatists name the school as a "miniature society". In fact, the school and the society are complementary to each other. The school provides education according to the needs of the society and seeks help from the society for its growth. In this way, the school has become a community centre. This view is widely accepted by the philosophers and educationists of the modern world.

Child-centred education: Pragmatists advocate the child-centred education based on the interests, aptitudes and capacities of the child. It helps the child to develop his personality according to his will. The pragmatic approach is neither teacher-centred, nor examination-centred, nor curriculum-centred, but pupil-centred.

Utility education: Pragmatic education prepares the child to live in the society. Whatever we do, it must have utility. The school provides learning experiences and skills which will be useful to the child in future.

Social discipline: Pragmatism emphasises social discipline through free, purposeful and cooperative activities organized in the schools. These activities are helpful in controlling indiscipline. This kind of social discipline has become popular in the present educational system.

Equal importance to teacher and the taught: Pragmatism assigns equal importance to the teacher and the child in the educative process. The teacher has been accepted as the creator of social environment, harbinger of social progress, friend, helper, guide, counsellor and philosopher of the child. It also gives equal importance to the child and his personality development through life-centred subjects, activities and experiences in the free environment.

New techniques of teaching: The pragmatists introduce new methods of teaching techniques to make the teaching and learning process more effective and attractive. This philosophy has emphasised various teaching techniques like project method, problem-solving method, activity method and experimental method. These methods of teaching have a great impact on the present world of education.

Optimistic attitudes: Pragmatism emphasises the qualities of freedom, initiative expression, conducive experiences, congenial environment, purposeful creativity and development of human values. These progressive and optimistic attitudes are essential for the progress of a democratic society.

New life in education: Pragmatists have revolutionised the process of education to a very great extent. As a result, new concepts such as "new education" "progressive education" an "activity-centred curriculum" have come into existence. These concepts have changed the very norms of education and transformed education into a powerful tool for the establishment of a democratic world.

MERITS OF PRAGMATISM

- Pragmatic philosophy is very useful and practicable in any society where values and ideas are changing very fast and education has to catch up with it.
- It gives direction to modern philosophers and educationists to frame educational policies in accordance with the varying environments.
- It prepares the pupil for the present and the future life by providing opportunities for developing vocational and social efficiencies (skills).
- It applies various teaching techniques (experimental) by which the child becomes an inventor or discoverer.
- It constructs a child-centred curriculum on the basis of the abilities, interests, aptitudes and inclinations of the child.
- It develops a flexible and adaptable mind in the child to create new values and ideas for an unknown future.
- It saves the child from the burden of education which is too much centred on books.
- It insists on the principle of integration and correlation of all subjects or knowledge in the curriculum.
- It is a scientific philosophy that gives great importance to science subjects and other activity-oriented subjects.
- This philosophy prepares the child to learn skills and attitudes which are required of him to live as a useful member in the society.

DEMERITS OF PRAGMATISM

Negation of eternal truth: According to idealism, truth is truth. It does not and cannot change. But pragmatists believe that truths or eternal values change according to the change in circumstances, time and place. What is true today may not necessarily be true tomorrow. They stress on the fact that whatever fulfils one's purposes satisfies one's desires and develops his life is true.

Ignores spiritual values: Pragmatists ignore the existence of spiritual values. But such values are essentially required for peace of mind and completeness in life. In fact, human values, welfare, peace, happiness and satisfaction cannot be achieved without spiritual values.

Emphasis on material world: This philosophy bestows too much importance on the physical world. It mars human values and society. People prefer to seek wealth for the present life. It pollutes the human environment and leads to a peaceless and struggle-torn life. It also widens the gap between the haves and the have-nots.

No fixed aim of education: Pragmatic philosophy suffers in the absence of clear-cut aims of education. Education without aims cannot play its role efficiently and will achieve nothing.

Negation of the past: Pragmatists emphasise the present and future, and neglect the past. The knowledge of our past is essential to grasp the greatness of our ancient culture. We cannot understand the present without the knowledge of the past and we cannot predict anything in the future unless we know the present thoroughly. The knowledge of the past, therefore, cannot be neglected.

Against formal education: Pragmatic education is against formal education. It believes that all knowledge and experiences can be acquired through direct personal experiences. It is impossible to gain all knowledge through direct experiences. Hence, both personal experience and formal education are very necessary to acquire all knowledge.

Difficulty in curriculum construction: Pragmatists believe that all knowledge can be acquired from the experiences of life. But it is very difficult to select a project and construct a curriculum so as to gain all knowledge from life experiences.

Heavy demands on teacher: Pragmatism puts heavy demands on the teacher. Only a few resourceful and gifted teachers maybe able to cope with the demands of teaching in an environment set up under pragmatic conditions.

Academic freedom and mismanagement: Pragmatism provides academic freedom to every school which will eventually lead to mismanagement and disorganization in schools. Therefore, it is not advisable in India where national integration is the crying need in every field of activity.

Negation of humanities: There is no place for humanities and cultural activities in the pragmatic scheme of education. The absence of religious and moral education in the curriculum will lead to the starvation of the soul which will be the cause of the detrimental to culture in the long run.

COMPARISON OF IDEALISM, NATURALISM AND PRAGMATISM

Chief Exponents

Idealism: Mahatma Gandhi, Rabindranath Tagore, Dayanand, Swami Vivekanand, Aurobindo, Shankaracharya, Socrates, Plato, Descartes, Spinoza, Barkley, Kant, Fichte, Green, Hegel, Gentile, Schopenhauer and Schilling.

Naturalism: Rabindranath Tagore (Tagore is an idealist as well as a naturalist), Aristotle, Comte, Hobbes, Rousseau Francis Bacon, Darwin, Lamarck, Huxley, Herbert Spencer, Bernard Shaw and Samuel Butler.

Pragmatism: John Dewey, Kilpatrick, C.B. Pearce, William James, Schiller and Margaret H. Mead.

Fundamental Principles

Idealism: Believes in God. Spiritual perfection is a must to reach Him. Trust in the spiritual world. Spiritual values are supreme and universal. Values are predetermined. It is a monistic concept. Spiritual world is real world.

Naturalism: No faith in God and spiritual world. Nature is everything. Material world is the real world. No supreme values other than matter. Physical world is supreme and universal. It is also a monistic concept.

Pragmatism: Believes in man. The power of man is supreme. Spiritual principles are not universal. They change according to the changing conditions of time and circumstances. Values are man-made and they are not predetermined. This is based on psychological principles. It is a pluralistic concept.

Principles of Education

Idealism: Principles of education are entirely based on spiritualism and ethics. Importance is given to mental development. Teacher and curriculum-centred education. Book learning and rote method are emphasised. Individual and society are valued.

Naturalism: Principles of education are based on psychology. It emphasises the basic instincts, interests and tendencies of the child. It is a child-centred education. It is against book learning. The individual is considered and valued. It is a progressive and a dynamic ideology.

Pragmatism: Principles of education are based on psychology and science. It assigns importance to experiment and practice. Child is the centre of all educational activities. It neglects book learning. Sociability is emphasised and valued. It is a progressive, dynamic and changeable ideology.

Meaning of Education

Idealism: It considers education to be the spiritual need.

Naturalism: According to naturalism, education is a biological need.

Pragmatism: To the pragmatists, education is a social need.

Aims of Education

Idealism: Self-realisation or personality exaltation. Spiritual development. Realisation of Truth, Beauty and Goodness. Preservation and transmission of culture. Conversion of inborn nature into spiritual nature. Preparing the child for a holy life and develop his intelligence and rationality.

Naturalism: To perfect the human machines. To attain present and future happiness. Preparation for the struggle of existence. Adaptation to environment. Improvement of racial gains. Natural and autonomous development.

Pragmatism: Aims of education are not predetermined. They change with the time and needs of the society. Getting more education, creation of new values, social development, and harmonious development are the tentative aims of education.

Curriculum

Idealism: Idealistic curriculum is constructed and developed according to ideals and eternal values. Humanistic subjects like social science are emphasised. The subjects included in the curriculum are religious and spiritual studies, ethics, language literature, sociology, geography, history, music and fine arts.

Naturalism: Naturalistic curriculum is formulated on the basis of basic instincts, aptitudes and tendencies of the children. Science subjects take precedence over humanities. The subjects included in the curriculum are games and sports, physical science, physiology, health, culture, material sciences and biological sciences.

Pragmatism: Pragmatic curriculum is based on the subjects of utility. Social subjects form the main body while others are secondary. The main subjects emphasised are health, hygiene and science, physical culture, history, geography, mathematics, home science, science and agriculture.

Methods of Teaching

Idealism: No fixed method of teaching. Different idealists have adopted different methods of teaching. Since, education is teacher-centred, they advocate various methods according to their interest and the nature of curriculum. They follow question answer method, conversation, discussion, lecture, book study and argumentation.

Naturalism: Naturalists emphasise learning by doing, learning by Self- experience and learning by play. They adopt the following methods of teaching—observation, play-way, dalton plan, heuristic, montessori and kindergarten methods.

Pragmatism: Pragmatists have emphasized the principles of purposive process of learning, learning by doing and by experience, project method, experimental method and method of integration.

Discipline

Idealism: Freedom is restricted. Idealism gives support to self-discipline at all costs.

Naturalism: Freedom is the slogan of naturalism. It is in favour of establishing discipline through natural consequences.

Pragmatism: Pragmatists develop self-discipline through group activities. They advocate social discipline with limited freedom.

Students

Idealism: It provides only secondary position to the child in the educational process.

Naturalism: It gives the child primary importance in the educational process. It says child is the "hero" in the drama of education.

Pragmatism: Pragmatists bestow equal importance on both the teacher and the students.

Teacher

Idealism: Idealists consider that the teachers are the co-workers of God. They give top priority to the teachers in the educational process. Teacher as a gardener knows best as to how to care and develop a child like a plant.

Naturalism: Naturalists regard that nature is the best teacher. They give secondary importance to the teacher. The place of the teacher is behind the curtains. He has to set the stage for the child.

Pragmatism: Pragmatists give importance to the teachers. Teachers are considered as friends, philosophers and guides. They are social engineers or agents of social change. They are the creators of social environment so that the child learns to create new values for the future.

School

Idealism: Idealists hold that school is the only place for regular and effective education. The school is based on the principle of "simple living and high thinking". It is an ideal form of pleasing and joyful activities for children.

Naturalism: Naturalists recommend a school in the lap of nature far away from the hue and cry of the cities. The school should have a natural and free environment for the child so that he can develop himself naturally.

Pragmatism: For the pragmatists the school is a laboratory for experiments to be done by children. They consider the school to be a mini-society where the social efficiency of the child is developed.

In spite of the many similarities and dissimilarities among these schools of thought, they are complementary to one another and guide us to make the educational system effective and relevant. Therefore, we can conclude with the words of Swami Vivekananda, "The end of all education, all training should be man-making".

CONCLUSION

Pragmatism plays a very creative and productive role in the field of education. It gives birth to new thoughts, by which educational system can be made more purposeful and useful. This philosophy has influenced thinkers from all over the world. We can consent with Dr. Prem Nath when he says that synthesis of idealism and pragmatism is the best approach to education.

CHAPTER 12

EXISTENTIALISM

INTRODUCTION

Existentialism is a post-World War philosophy that originated out of the frustration and horrors of the two World Wars. It is an undeniable fact that the two World Wars had deprived man of his essential humanity. As a consequence of this, existentialism, a new philosophy, came into existence. Existentialism maybe described as the philosophy of the twentieth century. This youngest philosophy prefers man to nation, body to intelligence and physical world to nature. In fact, it opposes industrial age, science and technology which have made man a tool in the hands of industrial society and political system. Existentialism believes that everything should serve man and vice-versa. This philosophy has been propounded against philosophies such as idealism, Marxism, realism, naturalism and pragmatism. But it is very difficult to find its roots in any of the ancient philosophies. This philosophy can be considered as a bridge between religion and the life of the twenty-first century.

The problem of "Being and Existence" has loomed large in the minds of the philosophers, saints and seers. Hence, the philosophers of the East and the West of the ancient as well as modern times have all been seriously preoccupied by the problem of existence. In fact, no philosopher can avoid considering the ontological problems and, at bottom, they all are existentialistic. Now, some questions may emerge in our mind as to how is the modern existentialist is different from the ancient ones? And why do we call other philosophies existentialism? As far as modern existentialism is concerned, unlike other philosophies, it deals more with the problem of becoming than the problem of being, more with particulars than universals, with existence than essence. As Soren Kierkegaard, the father of modern existentialism, puts it the chief concern of an existentialist Christian is not the knowledge of rules and principles of Christianity but "how am I to become a Christian". The non-Christian or atheist existentialists substitute the word "authentic being" for the term Christian. In this way the existentialists have emphasised 'action' and 'choice' and of knowledge and explanation and replaced the question of what by how.

HISTORICAL DEVELOPMENT OF EXISTENTIALISM

Attempts have been made to trace the beginning of existentialism in the Greek philosophy. This is because the entire philosophical doctrine of the West is an appendix on Socrates. The existentialists have considered Socrates to be the first existentialist because of his statement, "I am and always have been a man to obey nothing in my nature except the reasoning which upon reflection appears to me to be the best". But an analysis of the Socrates Philosophy proves that Socratic method maybe existentialistic by nature. The central idea of Western philosophers such as Socrates, Plato, Aristotle and Spinoza is "essence precedes existence". According to them, essences are ideas, values, ideals and thoughts. But this view has been opposed by the existentialists. According to Dr. S. Radhakrishnan, "Existentialism is a new name for an ancient method". In the words of J. Blackham "Existentialism appears to be reaffirming in modern idiom the protestant or the stoic form of individualism, which stands over against the empirical individualism of the renaissance or of the modern or of Epicurus as well as over against the universal system of Rome or of Moscow or of Plato ... It is a contemporary renewal of one of the necessary phases of human experience in conflict ideals which history has not yet resolved".

Historically, the philosophy of existentialism developed out of the horrors and frustration due to the two World Wars. After the World Wars, people wrote stories, novels and plays in order to highlight the consequence of these wars such as despair, death, sufferings, anxiety, anguish, horror, dread, persecution, frustration and human sacrifice. In the words of Ralph Harper, "Tragedy, death, guilt, suffering all force one to appraise one's total situation much more than do happiness, joy and success, and innocence, since it is in the former that momentous choices must be made". This type of writing has influenced a group of philosophers who are spread all over Germany, France and Italy. These countries had witnessed social crises. Social upheavals set many thinkers such as Karl Jasper and Martin Heidegger in Germany, and Gabriel Marcel and Jean Paul Sartre in France thinking.

Soren Kierkegaard, a Danish philosopher is considered as the founder of the philosophy of existentialism. He wrote in protest against Hegalianism and its impact on the culture of the West. He turned his philosophical genius against the industrialised society and institutionalism, which had reduced the individuality of the people to almost nothingness by bringing emphasis on science and technology. He points out, "The individual loses his authentic reality when he is swallowed up by history, by associations, by the public, or by the age in which he lives". He raised his voice against all the schools of philosophy and his views were supported by all other existentialists. All the existentialists were against rationalisation, universalisation and generalities of philosophy.

PROTAGONISTS OF EXISTENTIALISM

Existentialism is a modern philosophy which is primarily built upon the works of the contemporary scholars of the nineteenth and twentieth centuries. The chief exponents of this philosophy are Soren Kierkegaard, Friedrich Nietzsche, Jean Paul Sartre, Karl Jasper, Reinhold Niebuhr, Gabriel Marcel, Buber and Tillich, Russell Martin, Heidegger, Dostoyevsky, Abbagnano, Berdyaev and Albert Camus.

MEANING OF EXISTENTIALISM

The term 'existentialism' has been derived from two German words ex-sister meaning "which stands out" or "which emerges". From the etymological meaning of existentialism, it is understood that it is a philosophy which emerges out of the problems of life. Marshall has rightly pointed out that "philosophy is a counsellor in crisis". The basic concept of existentialism is "existence precedes essence". Plato holds the view that we are living in a world of essence—ideas and values. The main purpose of our life is to discover its essence. The self is a universal essence, which has been accepted by the majority of the Western philosophers. But Sartre states that "existence precedes essence". It means that, first of all, man exists, turns up, appears on the scene and only afterwards defines himself. Man, as the existentialist, is undefinable, because in the beginning he is nothing. Only later he would be something and he himself would have made what he would be. "Not only is man what he conceives himself to be but he is also what he wills himself to be after this thrust towards his existence. Man is nothing other than what he makes himself. This is the principle of existentialism".

Existentialism is a philosophy of reaffirming and regaining the lost status of man in the advanced scientific and technological society. Therefore, this philosophy is considered as a theory of individual meaning which asks each man to ponder over the reason for his existence. It is true in the modern society that man, the creator of science, himself becomes a victim of his own creation and feels like a mere cog in a highly mechanical system. As a result, this philosophy reasserts the superiority of man and the importance of individual. In fact, it is concerned with the perennial problems of life and in particular with the inevitability of death, the reality of choice, the experience of agony of the ecstasy of love. Thus, existentialism tries to understand the human conditions and the basic structure of man's existence so as to raise the status of the individual.

DEFINITIONS OF EXISTENTIALISM

Existentialism, like idealism, naturalism and pragmatism, has been made a distinct philosophy in the twentieth century. The following definitions give us a clear meaning and characteristics of this philosophy and its impact on education.

Fernandes: "Existentialism is a type of philosophy which endeavours to analyse the basic structure of the human existence and calls to be awareness of their existence on its essential freedom".

Titus: "Existentialism emphasises human existence that is the distinctive quality of individual person rather than man in the abstract or nature and the world in general".

Guru Dutt: "Existentialism is an attempt to reach the inmost core of human existence in a concrete and individual fashion".

EXISTENCE—FROM BIRTH TO DEATH

Existentialists advocate the idea that the existence of a person means his period from birth to death. In the words of Heidegger, "There was nothing before birth and would be nothing beyond death. In between we have been thrown into a social life and the characteristics of this social life are the contingent circumstances of our life. This contingency is often characterised by experiences of dread, horror, anguish, solitude, bewilderment, uncertainty and finally limited by death". The word 'existence' has been discussed by Alexander Koyre as "We are there: I am there such as I am; and I neither know why nor how; the only thing I know, truly and inexorably". Heidegger's "Being and Time" is an exposition of this view, in which he has remarked "That some day I am going to die. And that is what limits all my possibilities and my future. My future is limited, and I know it—that is my situation in the world. I know that my existence is precarious and short, and that I can lose it. This is the only thing that I have, and I can lose at any moment; that is why there is the substratum of anxiety, fear and anguish". Among all the living beings, man alone knows that some time he will die. The contemporary existentialist philosophy views man as participating in a world of things and events, and encountering other men. The meaning of human existence is that it is man's nature to exist—"to stand out into reality, to participate in being, to be present to all that is".

FUNDAMENTALS OF EXISTENTIALISM

Existentialism cannot be considered as a school of philosophy such as idealism, naturalism, pragmatism and other schools of traditional philosophy. This is because the existentialists do not like it and they make contradictory and inconsistent statements which are fundamental to existentialism.

Karl Jasper: "Renounce your world and you will return to it".

Heidegger: "Analyse death to understand life".

Kierkegaard: "You are a free man if you accept God".

Sartre: "You are a free man if you deny God".

Nietzche: "God is dead and we have killed him you and I. Is it not the greatness of this dead too great for us? Must not we ourselves become Gods simply to be seen worthy of it".

Dostoyevsky: "If God did not exist, everything would be possible".

ASSUMPTIONS OF EXISTENTIALISM

- The centre of existence is man rather than truth, laws, principles or essence. Man is characterised by decisions, will and choice.
- Man is a supreme organism. He should not be exploited in the interest of the society or the nation. Society or political system is a must but society should not give secondary place to man. Society is for man and not vice-versa.
- This philosophy is limited to time. According to this philosophy the struggle for existence was there when man was first evolved and it continues even today. Man tries to become victorious at all costs.
- Man is the maker, and therefore, the master of culture. He develops an ultimate concern for his life and the condition in which it is placed. This will assist him in understanding the predicament of his existence in the world. Man cannot be 'taught' what the world is about. He must create this for himself.
- Man is not alone in the world. He is connected to other men. He communicates with others. Life is seen as a gift. Man is free to choose commitments in life; in his choice, he becomes himself. He is an individual who is different from other persons. The real living person is more important than any statement we can make about him. His existence is more important than his essence.
- Existence does not mean mere living. It rather means complete, strong, self-conscious, responsible and progressive life of man.
- Existentialism believes that man cannot accept the readymade concepts of existence forced upon him. He is a free agent capable of shaping his own life and choosing his own destiny.
- The existentialists consider that each man has the responsibility of creating his own values and in doing so, he is choosing freedom and responsibility. In fact, all knowledge of truth and value will flow from his self-knowledge only.
- The mechanical and industrial life of today has snatched individual freedom from man and hence he is deprived of the realities of life.
- The scientific and technological world forces man to lead a solitary and frustrated life full of anxieties, fear and guilt. This philosophy tries to remove the frustration, fear, sense of guilt and worries of man by recognising his individuality and providing secondary place to technological progress.

CHARACTERISTICS OF EXISTENTIALISM

It is clear from the above assumptions that in existentialism, human person and his freedom are given great importance. According to existentialism, personal growth and development can take place through the individual's own efforts and none can help him in this regard. Hence, the practical problems of living are invested with great values and importance. Let us see the chief characteristics of existentialism.

Criticism of idealism: Existentialism has emerged and developed as a reaction against idealism. According to idealism, a human person is essentially an expression of some underlying spiritual or psychic element, which is of universal character. In this way, all men are fundamentally same and share with each other the universal character. But the existentialists criticise the idealist's contention about the universal element and man's good being subject to general good. They consider the search for essence a mistaken pursuit. According to the existentialists, it is not the essence but existence which is real.

Criticism of naturalism: The existentialists criticise the philosophy of naturalism. The naturalists believe that life is subjected to physio-bio-chemical laws which, in turn, are subject to the universal law of sensation. The law of sensation states that whatever happens is due to the antecedent causes and there is no event which can appear suddenly without some causes. If this law is universally operative there can be no human freedom of action. Human acts are as mechanical as the actions of an animal. Existentialists consider this as an anathema. They stoutly defend the freedom of man. According to Sartre, man is so free that he is fearful of his freedom.

Criticism of scientific philosophy: The existential philosophers are also critical of scientific conceptualism. Science abstracts from the immediate data and brings them under some universal laws or general rules, whereas, according to existentialists, all abstraction is false, reality is in the immediate data only. Furthermore, with the tremendous progress in science and technology, rapid industrialisation and urbanisation have taken place. As a consequence, crowded towns rise up in which an individual is lost. Everything is done or happened on a large scale and all personal values, individual likes and dislikes are altogether lost. The existentialists, therefore, oppose scientific philosophy and culture. They believe that any true philosophy must be grounded in axiology or theory of values and not in epistemology or theory of knowledge. The existentialists condemn both historicism and the scientific philosophy.

Born of despair: Due to the unparalleled progress of science and technology, huge industrial complexes and townships have sprung up. Hence, everywhere man is losing touch with nature. In fact, with the growing application of technology and consequent increase in the mechanisation of life, there is a growing despair in the minds and hearts of men. The worth of human efforts is decreasing and the life is becoming like a raft on the open sea which is carried hither and thither without any definite direction. As a result, a sensitive mind finds itself lost and forlorn. The existentialists analyse and describe these human predicaments and find a way out of these. According to this philosophy, if man allows himself to be overwhelmed by misery, pain and apparent hopelessness of the situation, he would sink into apathy and cynicism. Thus, existentialist philosophy is born out of human despair.

Value of human personality: Existentialists recognise the paramount of the human personality. According to them, man is the centre of the universe and nothing else is equal to it. The basic feature of human personality is his freedom—unfettered and unrestrained. Anything which obstructs the growth and development of the individual must be discarded. In this way, the existentialist writers, artists and thinkers have expressed their views uncompromisingly and waged great battles for securing these freedoms for men.

Importance of subjectivity: According to the Danish philosopher Soren Kierkegaard, truth is subjectivity; objectivity and abstraction are hallucinations. The existentialists are extremists who believe that only the immediate feeling or apprehension reveals the truth and that abstraction in any form or manner vitiates the truth and reality. The immediate experience or feeling about which the existentialists talk is the direct experience by individuals of things like conflict, divisiveness, pain, anguish, anxiety, suffocation etc. The various existentialists have tried to describe experiences such as spiritual crisis, sexual crisis, marital crisis, value crisis etc. They believe that all human values are based on subjective experience. According to existentialism the origin of values is not in the social situation but in the personal insight.

No construction of philosophical system: The ancient philosophers tried to present philosophies which embraced all the problems of God, soul, space, time, physical world, its origin and evolution etc. and developed a theoretical system. But the existentialists distrust system making and theorisation. They believe that the true aim of philosophy is action and not theory. That is why they do not cogitate over traditional problems.

Relation of individual and world: The existentialists are not satisfied with the traditional explanations to the problem of the relationship between individual and the world. If we believe in the one universal element called the absolute whose manifestation is everything, the individual has no value per se and is not free. The worth of man is underivable from any universal element. The existentialist's account of man is neither mystical nor philosophical. Man and the world both are unbound and free. According to the existentialists, man should be the centre of all values and activities. Because of this, their view can also be called anthropocentrism.

Emphasis on the problem of inner conflict: The central problem of the modern, highly complex world is not ideological but practical. It is to inspire in men a sense of responsibility and freedom. In order to develop this sense, the process of communication is facilitated. This is because the world peace cannot be accomplished by raising slogans. We, therefore require individuals who are free, communicate freely and above all, respect theirs as well as other's personalities. The peace is possible if and only if there is peace in each heart, if each man is free from the inner conflicts, if each can be free from the desire to subject others to his will. Due to this reason, the existentialists attach great importance to the problem of inner conflict.

Man is the centre of existence: Existentialists believe that man is the centre of existence rather than truth, laws, principles or essence. Man is characterised by decisions, will and choice. Science and rational thinking cannot grasp or explain it. As he is the maker and master of culture, he can impose a meaning on his universe. He is free and has other alternative but to be free. The world offers him opportunities and ideal possibilities and what he chooses and what he rejects is absolutely his own choice. Freedom enables him to shape and mould his own world as he likes.

EXISTENTIALISM AND EDUCATION

Existentialism is a new philosophy which has not developed any specific educational programme comparable to other philosophies. It has very little to offer as a philosophy of education. George Keller remarks, "Existentialists do not carry their doctrine into practical theory or policy for school behaviour". In other words, the philosophy of existentialism has not displayed any particular interest in education. It is not a philosophy for revealing the truth, reality and values of the objective of the world. It is a doctrine discussing the existence of self. A man becomes considerate to the personality of others only on the basis of subjectivity.

MEANING OF EDUCATION

Education, according to this philosophy, is to give special importance to individuality of man in education and to develop the self of all individuals. Existentialists define education on the basis of their own experience. In a broad sense "education is that which helps an individual to realise the best he is capable of". Education, therefore, should help an individual to realise the "facticity" (contingency) of his existence and to face the categories of this facticity— dread, anguish, anxiety and fear so as to help him to meet death with pleasure. Education for happiness is a dangerous doctrine. There can be no happiness without pain and no ecstasy without suffering. The slogan of existentialists is education for adjustment to human sufferings, misery, anguish and the dreadful responsibilities of adult life. They advocate "education for death". This is a new kind of education as compared to the idea of other philosophers who advocate education for life, complete living, happiness and freedom.

AIMS OF EDUCATION

Existentialists stress the following aims:

- Existentialists believe in the concept of individual difference from the psychological point of view. Education should help the individual to make him human. So, the aim of education is to educate each and every individual of the society in order to develop his insight and feeling for the development of his innerself.
- The aim of education is to develop an awareness among the students about freedom in life and develop their thinking power.
- To develop the ability of perseverance and tolerance in man so that he may live and adjust in the modern world without compromising his individuality and subjectivity.
- Acquainting man with his destination, by giving him understanding of his being and ultimately lead him to the heavenly abode.
- The aim of education is the realisation of inner truth in modern man who is full of anxieties, frustrations, fears and guilts. His individuality is being corrupted and he feels that he is lonely, though in a crowd. Education should help him to realise his subjective consciousness.
- The essential aim of education is humanitarian and humanist by fostering uniqueness in man. Education should develop the individual physically, mentally, emotionally and spiritually.
- To develop self-observation, power among pupils for making them into one who lives and makes decisions about what he will do and be.

CURRICULUM

The existentialists have not prescribed curriculum for educating the pupils. But they stress that education should always be child-centred allowing full freedom to him for his natural development on the basis of his interest, ability and needs. Therefore, the pupil must choose his own curriculum related to the immediate social, economic, political and other problems which he will have to face during his lifetime. However, the existentialists give more importance to humanities, social sciences, ethics and religion. They believe that these subjects help man to keep more closely to himself than science. They oppose scientific, industrial and technical environment as they do not allow the individuality of man to develop for inner realisation and for achieving peace and happiness.

Ralph Harper has given the following ideas about curriculum in existentialism: 1. Everybody must be taught certain things—reading, writing, arithmetic, history, etc. 2. The pupil is not the one to decide what he should learn. This is the prerogative of the teachers. It is not injurious to be made to learn arithmetic or reveal the Bible or the Odyssey. 3. The human mind always works in certain ways and therefore, it is essential for man to learn logic, as it leads to truth.

Jean Paul Sartre and Martin Heidegger consider humanistic study as more valuable than scientific subjects. This is because such subjects, help to understand human sufferings, anguish, anxiety and death, and remain more closely to himself. Humanities deals with subjective knowledge, but science deals with objective knowledge. Self-knowledge precedes universal knowledge. Hence, there must be a provision for self-knowledge in the curriculum.

METHOD OF TEACHING

Existentialists stand in favour of the Socratic method of teaching. That is, they advocate the method of asking questions, refining answers, asking more questions and pushing the issues until some acceptable conclusion is reached. In this method, knowledge and wisdom are gained through personal relationships between the teacher and the pupil. They give emphasise on individual attention. Hence, pupils prefer home education to school education. In this system, the personal touch and living relationship between the Acharya and Brahmachari constitutes education. This method gives the pupils maximum freedom to learn according to their own inclinations and to develop the creative activity in them. Education for creativity is of utmost importance to the existentialists. They stand against group methods of teaching. About the method of teaching of existentialists, George Kneller has stated, "The existentialists favour Socratic method, not so much because it involves 'induction' or the collection and analysis of all available evidence; not because of its complementary process of 'definition' whereby general values are reached from particular instances, but chiefly because it is a method that tests the inner life as a stethoscope sounds the heart".

ROLE OF THE TEACHER

According to the existentialists the teacher creates an educational situation in which the student may establish contact with himself; become conscious of it and achieve self-realisation. For this purpose, the teacher should have an experience of self-realisation, so that he maybe capable of guiding the students in this process. He cannot impose upon children his own ideas, ideals, ideologies and values. He should facilitate his students to think about life. This philosophy advocates that the teacher–student relationship will be more personal and interactive. He should initiate the act of education as an authentic man. He should be sympathetic towards his students and treat them as free individuals. He must be sensitive and enter into the emotional life of the children.

DISCIPLINE

Existentialists give more importance to the students without lessening the importance of the teacher. They are against the practice of giving incentives, rewards or punishment to the pupils. Here, students are given full freedom to develop their selves by changing their extroversion into introversion. They can achieve self-realisation under the guidance of their teacher. Children are trained in such a manner that they do not become selfish, autocratic or irresponsible due to their subjectivity. The subjectivity of children will lead them to understand the subjectivity of others. According to existentialism, to be a man is to be free. Such freedom brings about a happy and pleasant life.

RELIGIOUS EDUCATION

Existentialism is actually a link philosophy between religion and the modern age. The modern scientific age has made man a machine and a tool in the hands of science and political groups. It has been lessening the interest of man in religion at a fast rate. In this juncture, this philosophy tries to bring man closer to religion without compromising the scientific and industrial progress. In fact, the existentialists lay emphasis upon religious and moral education. Religious education gives the individual an understanding of his existence in the cosmos. It shows the religious path of self-realisation which makes him capable of utilising faith in self-development. The only difference between existentialism and religion is that existentialism advocates a deep faith of man in the preservation and progress of his being. This philosophy approves individual progress. On the other hand, religion advocates social being or progress instead of individual being. The existence of the individuals maybe compromised when social being is considered important.

EDUCATIONAL IMPLICATIONS OF EXISTENTIALISM

- The primary aim of education is the making of a human person as one who lives and makes decisions about what he will do and be. Human existence and the value related to it is the primary factor in education. The knowledge of knowing oneself, social relationship and biological development are the essential parts of becoming a human person.
- The school should provide an atmosphere where the individuals can develop in a healthy way. Children learn better when relieved from intense competition, harsh discipline and fear of failure. Encouragement and acceptance by teachers foster trustworthiness and sense of security among the children. This will help the child to understand his own needs and values and take charge of the experiences for changing them.
- All school subjects and activities should present existential situations for teaching and the development of human being. The two most prominent of these are literature and arts.
- The teacher should facilitate the development of originality and creativity by providing a climate as well as basic skills and tools which make exploration possible. The teacher must build positive relationship between himself and his students. It indicates the role of teacher and his activities, the subject matter to be studied and the way this subject matter is to be approached by the students.
- The teacher is an observer or guide. He initiates the act of education through his personal influences. He is very active and welcomes challenges to his ideas from the students.
- Democratic ideas must pervade the school environment in which the students grow. Children come to share in the mutual respect for the value of work and the creativity of man. Self-government, pupil participation in planning and the encouragement of a free environment characterise the school.
- Concern and respect for the individual student should be the main interest of the school. Education in the contemporary, industrial and technological society may well be cleansed and strengthened by emphasis on man for himself.

CONTRIBUTION OF EXISTENTIALISM TO EDUCATION

Existentialism has emerged and developed as a reaction against the contemporary social, economic and political situation, in which man has lost himself. This philosophy has widely influenced art and literature. It stands against war in politics and it advocates peaceful and happy life. Let us concentrate on the contribution of existentialism in the field of education.

Total development: The existentialists have aimed at total development of personality through education. According to existentialism, education should aim at the whole man by developing his character and self-realisation. That is, education should develop the individual physically, mentally, emotionally and spiritually.

Subjective knowledge: The present age of science and technology has made too much of objective knowledge. As a result of it, the term subjective has come to mean unreal, nonsense, ignorant and irrelevant. The existentialists point out that the subjective knowledge is more important than objective knowledge. They hold that truth is subjectivity. It is a human value. Reduction of values to facts has led to widespread loss of faith in values. Therefore, along with the teaching of science and mathematics, the humanities, art and literature should be given a suitable place in the curriculum at every stage of education. This is considered to be an important contribution of existentialism in the field of education.

Importance of environment: The present industrial, economic, political and social environment is valueless and develops confusion, corruption, tensions and conflicts. Therefore, the existentialists seek to provide an environment for self-development and self-consciousness. This environment in the school requires contribution from humanities, art and literature, which will help in the development of individuality in the educand.

MERITS OF EXISTENTIALISTIC PHILOSOPHY

- The twenty-first century has made man materialistic and selfish. So, he has lost himself in the industrial and material progress around him. At this juncture, existentialist philosophy is very much needed.
- The individuality of man has been completely neglected in the industrial and military world. He has become a tool in the hands of science and technology. It is existentialism that recognises the individuality of man and all-round development of his personality.
- Man is very much dynamic and progressive. His interest in the objective world has very much increased, but has made him leave his religion aside. This philosophy brings man close to religion again.
- Existentialism wants to make man perfect and subjective, which enables him to realise the sufferings of others on the basis of self-realisation. For instance, the feeling of hunger is felt only when a person is hungry.
- Existentialism helps the individual to lead a peaceful and pleasant life by making him a complete man.

DEMERITS OF EXISTENTIALISTIC PHILOSOPHY

Existentialist's revolt against intellectualism has its own demerits. This is because the existentialist method of teaching maybe useful in moral and religious education. But, it cannot workout in the education of science and technology. This philosophy suffers from the following drawbacks:

- Existential aim of education is one-sided like naturalism and idealism. This philosophy is considered as the old wine in a new bottle.
- This philosophy stresses on humanities, art and literature. It has also become one-sided, by neglecting science and technology.
- The existentialists forget that a very important aim of education is earning one's living. Therefore, the utilitarian purpose of education has been neglected.
- This philosophy has failed to discuss the values properly.
- Existentialistic idea of absolute freedom is not acceptable in the modern social setup.
- Existentialism is far from being satisfactory as a complete philosophy of education.
- The educational methods in existentialism appear to be impractical and inapplicable in an industrial society.
- It requires a good deal of time and effort on the part of the teacher to develop an individual relationship with the students for having a close understanding of their personalities.
- Terminologies used such as 'being' 'meaning', 'person', and 'Existence' in existentialism are not very clear.
- Negligence of objectivity and overemphasis on subjectivity make the philosophy only a game of arguments. That is why, this philosophy has not gained popularity so far.

CONCLUSION

Existentialism is a modern philosophy primarily built upon the works of the contemporary scholars of the twentieth century. The philosophy of existentialism is a protest against mass society, mass religion, mass education and mass communication. It lays emphasis on the individual but not his environment. We may find that the philosophy of existentialism has both merits and demerits. Even though we cannot deny that it is a growing young philosophy. The basic question that existentialism possess is—can a society emerge in which each individual takes personal responsibility for the laws he obeys, the conventions he consents to, the values he appreciates for his own life? The answer to such a question can be sought by taking cognisance of the implications of existentialism to education. It attaches great importance to the study of history, literature, philosophy and art which relate to the development of student's personality.

CHAPTER 13

AWAKENISM

INTRODUCTION

Awakenism is a modern philosophy introduced in the 21st century with a view to modernise the educational principles and practices to modify the human behaviour better in the materialistic society. It is a philosophy which develops awareness in the people and prepares them to make a casteless, secular and democratic society. It is possible only through the medium of right education imparted by right teachers at right time with right curriculum using right methods.

There are philosophies which provide guidelines for education and life, and make it effective process in the dynamic world, but the philosophies such as Idealism, Naturalism, Pragmatism, Realism and Humanism are very useful and important to frame the educational principles and practices, and redeem the people from the bondage of superstitious faith and beliefs and the grip of poverty, ignorance, unemployment, illness and instigate them to involve in a lot of anti-social activities. The great educationists like Swami Vivekananda, Mahatma Gandhi, Rabindranath Tagore, Sri Aurobindo Ghosh and Jiddu Krishnamurti vehemently criticised the educational system prevailing in India for forcing the pupils to score maximum marks in the examination and failing to foster human values and character formation. This is because the governments, educationists and teachers have failed to practice such educational philosophy in the man-making process. In fact, they use everything for money making through mark, and English-oriented commercialisation of education.

BACKGROUND OF THE PHILOSOPHY

The undesirable social activities and lack of human values give birth to the ideas of Awakenism. In fact, the present education has not brought about desirable changes in the behaviour if the individual. It is seen that there is no difference between literates and illiterates in words and deeds. Idealistic philosophy of education insists spiritual world and prepares the child to lead holy life and attain Mokhsha (Salvation). Thus, it believes that there is life after death. On the other hand, pragmatic philosophy of education emphasises materialistic world that is prepare the child for present life. So the human life has become a pendulum between spiritual and material worlds. Thus, people have become more selfish than before and seek God for materialistic blessing and healthy and happy life. But they experience a lot of problems in life due to lack of understanding themselves and uses education for getting certificates and degrees and employments. In fact, there is no place for values and character formation.

Moreover, after the advent of characterless teachers, priests and politicians, education, religion and politics have turned in to sources of employment and income for large mass. Such people pollute the social and natural environments. In fact, man is a machine in the materialistic world. He uses caste, religion, language and region to differentiate the human beings. Too much emphasize on caste, religion, regional language, region and money making and narrowism pollute the whole human society. Further, corruption prostitution intoxicants, terrorism, printing fake certificate and currencies, robbing, stealing, killing, committing suicide, raping and lack of desirable and socially acceptable character affect the whole human beings. At present, most of the people involved in any one or two contemptible practices with a view to make them rich and happy. Ultimately they get tension, pressure unhappiness and lot of diseases or die until death. Hence, it is quite inevitable to awake and lead the people to come out of the grip of caste, religion, language, region and lust on materialism and understand the essence and uncertainty of human life and make life happy and peacefully.

MEANING OF AWAKENISM

The Philosophy: "Awakenism" is a combination of two words '*awaken*' and '*ism*'. It has been derived from the English word 'awaken' which means conscious, aware or rising. The word conscious implies being conscious of uncertain life and meaningless emphasize on regional language caste, religion and language and impacts of anti-social activities on man and environment. Aware indicates being aware of how one behaves in words and deeds which may affect others and nature. Rising refers to get out of superstitious faith, anti-social activities and addiction to the consumption of intoxicants. And 'ism' means ideas or views. Hence, it is the view or idea or principle of awareness or consciousness about anything which pollute the man and society. Therefore, Awakenism is concerned with study and application of those principles and practices which develop an awareness or consciousness in the people about anything which separate or stratify and pollute them. In short, this philosophy aims at creation of individual and society free from caste, religious fundamentalism and anti-social activities and developing democratic outlook in which all are equal and the sons of the world.

DEFINITION OF AWAKENISM

This philosophy is of two broad views about the present education. As such, the term education is very comprehensive in meaning, nature and aims in the socio-economic complicated society. So, we can define the awakenistic education in two ways. Accordingly, the first view—Education is anythings which influence the child and man directly or indirectly in the socio-natural environments and determining positive or negative behaviour or character in personal, social, cultural and economic life. Another view—education is any things meant for socio-economic status by certificates/degrees and employments. Thus, we may define awakenistic education as it is education which aims at developing awareness about the materialistic society where man is more important than money. This philosophy believes that too much emphasis on money makes man and life meaningless but causes social pollution.

PRINCIPLES OF THIS PHILOSOPHY

- Man is not an evaluation of any animal. He is different from ape. He is one of the living species in the natural environment. So no man is superior or inferior to others in the biological process of life.

- He creates caste, gods, religion language and money which differentiate himself. But he is more important than anything in the earth.
- He alone believes in gods and life after death but there is no realty.
- He is controlled and measured by money than man.
- Whatever the religion or faith may be, diseases and death are common to all human beings.
- Language is the most powerful weapon which alone differentiate the whole human beings. The region wise politicians cheat the people in the name of languages to rule the state or country but man is more important than language and one can use any language to express one's feelings and thoughts.
- Struggle or conflicts in the name of religion, caste, language or region is meaningless and vain but separate the humans and cause loss of life and properties.
- Climate and culture (faith and belief) differ from region to region, country to country and even time to time. But, man has to understand and adjust everything or adaptive to the changing social and natural environments, so as to make his life happy, healthy and peaceful.
- It believes that terrorism cannot be solution to any problems but causes fearness and great loss to life and properties.
- It is against corruption, prostitution, illegal sex, killing, raping, suicide, robber, divorce or separation, production and consumption of intoxicant, weaken the people physically, mentally, culturally, socially and economically.
- Corruption may make man rich in short period but causes a great loss to his generations.
- Strength and prosperity of a country do not lie in atomic power or in the words of politicians but in people's character and labour.
- Most of the parents spend their time, energy and money for the welfare of their children but fail to be a role model in words and deeds and creates characterless and money minded generations.
- Religion may be good if it is practiced for the welfare of human beings especially needy and downtrodden people.
- The presence of God can be realised only in sacrifice, sincerity, helping, truth, affection and sympathy.

SIGNIFICANCE OF AWAKENISM

There is no compromise in the present education which has failed or slipped from man-making and is emphasising money-making, developing corruptive society and producing characterless generations in the market economy. Money is given more importance than any thing but it has no value in the absence of man. However, everything measured in terms of money in the materialistic society. Education prepares doctors, engineers, pastors, teachers and the workers of different categories. They can earn more and more but enjoy less and less. Moreover, obscene-violance based mass media and intoxicant substances pollute the whole human society. Infact, they produce characterless generations and make human life meaningless. The present generations study or read only for certificates/degrees not for language , knowledge and ultimately life. It is very easy how to commit suicide or kill others but very hard to know how to survive and make life happy and peaceful in the complicated materialistic society. According to this philiosophy, education is not meant for degrees and employments but for life with socially desirable characteristics. In this juncture, awakenlism is essential to be aware of oneself and the reality of human life.

It is highly deplorable that there is difference between teachers and students, pastors and church members, rich and poor, literate and illiterate, Hindus and Muslims or Christians and higher castes and lower ones in characters and deeds. Money controls every thing including man also. But they have failed to think the negative aspects of life in the polluted society. So, the awakenistic philosophy is very important and useful to the peaceless and healthless people in the disease and weakness centered society, and enable the people to enjoy life with what at hands.

The people of today run after money, gold, land, lad or lady, cigarettes and drugs. And they are ready to do any thing for obtaining these objects. Lack of reading, predominant of ignorance, lust for materialism and the impact of worldly pleasure govern/guide/control many people where education is helpless and useless, and develop aversion over life. As it is so, every one should prepare him/her to live happily. Awakenistic education is quit inevitable one to foster those useful thoughts, human values and deeds which make man happy, healthy and peaceful. No wealth, religion , caste, language can make man to lead such life. But spotless smiling, kindness, adjustments, helping, and understanding of addressless life and uncertainty of demise make man free from tension, frustration and undesirable/ contemptible behaviours. So, the teachers, scholars, educationists, readers and thinkers should understand this philosophy and apply it in the complicated practical life.

AWAKENISM AND EDUCATION

Education is the root cause for all changes take place in every field of life. It has brought about some desirable changes such as increase in production employment income and standard of living and undesirable changes like corruption and materialistic outlook and anti-social activities due to the advent of characterless generations and cast, religious and regional based fundamentalists. This is because learning is not only taking place in educational institutions but also in the social environments. So the entire educational system should be modified with a view to change the behaviour faith and belief of human beings and make them grasp the nature and importance of life. In this regard, Awakenism plays important role in making education an effective process for man making and nation building in the post-modern society.

MEANING OF EDUCATION

According to Awakenism, Education is anything acquired from the socio-natural environments which enable the child to work and live together. Awakenistic education is influenced by the curriculum prescribed for study and one's parents, teachers, priests or Poojari, relatives, friends and other socio-environmental factors. It makes education a comprehensive process which includes all those theoretical and practical aspects for one's balanced development based on the interest and capacity of the children. Thus, education is the development of Awakenism for making casteless, secularist and democratic society wherein man is the most supreme powerful in activating all except the natural process.

EDUCATIONAL PHILOSOPHY OF AWAKENISM

- Education is not merely meant for obtaining certificates and degrees but it should be the source of knowledge, employment, income and life.
- Education of an individual or child is not only influenced by school or college education but also by his parents, teachers, relatives and society.

- Education instead of emphasizing rote memorisation, it should give importance to thinking, creativities and communications.
- School or College is the centre for all round personality development which enable the student to find employment in any organisation or self-employment. That is, education is meant for economic life.
- Education should enable the student to fight against the production of intoxicants and caste and religions fundamentalism.
- Education is not meant for mark scoring but for man-making—men of character.
- Most valuable and important thoughts of different religions should be displayed in college or school premises.
- Education is not wasting time, energy and money on a particular subject but it should enable one to understand one self and reality of life and prepare for global life.
- Education is meaningful if it differentiate the learners form illiterate in character and deeds.
- Education should be given to all according to the interest and ability to utilise the human resources maximum level. The present education causes tension, pressure and suicide. So avoid stress, restless teaching, daily test, but create a conducive atmosphere of learning in schools and colleges.

AIMS OF EDUCATION

The present education prepares the child for materialistic life in which money is more important than man. But, this philosophy considers that man is more important than anything in the world.

Enable the man understand himself: The present man fails to understand himself and his life. This is a great tragedy of human life. In fact, he is proud of his caste, religion, region, language and economic status, but fails to understand the uncertainty of life and certainty of death. As a result he gives very important to the material world and develops selfishness and neglects human values. Most of us do not know what we do, but interested in finding ill of others and criticised them. It is not good for the healthy social environment. So this philosophy aims at helping the child to understand himself and the purpose of human life.

Realise the supremacy of man: Everything behind man except nature. It is man who has created gods, castes, religions languages and money. He uses them to stratify and differentiate or separate himself. In fact man uses them to show himself that he is better or more important than others who belong to other than his caste, religion and language. Nothing is important than man. But everything weakens human society. So the second aim of education is to realise the supreme of man in the earth.

Make casteless society: Casteism affects unity and strength of human society. It is the creation of mankind but it stratifies himself. No caste is superior or inferior to other one belong to different castes do not differ in character. In fact, whatever the caste may be socially desirable and undesirable activities are found in all people. Moreover casteism develops inferiority or superiority complex. Birth is the beginning and death is the end of human life which is common to all where cast system is meaningless. If anyone sticks on one's caste people for survival is impossible in the multi-faced society. In fact, people belong to one caste depend on others who belong to other castes so it is education which should eradicate the place for caste in the academic register and make the society a casteless one.

Develop Secular and Democratic Outlook: People are ready to fight for their gods and religions but not ready to observe a word. This is the trend of religious fundamentalists. It is seen that the religious based institutions never paves the way for secularism but develops enmities among them. Religion is created by, for and of man. No religion is free from mistake. However, man is more important than Gods and religions. Whatever the religious faith may be diseases and death are common to all. Democracy is misused in Indian society and it can be seen in gender, education, employment and inequalities. In fact, commercialization of education, politics and religion make democracy a disguised one in the state or central elections. It is not good for the welfare of the country. So the awakenistic education aims to develop secular and democratic outlook in the people.

Character and Culture Formation: The Indian education always stresses character formation and cultural development of the child. But character and culture have become meaningless words in the materialistic society. In fact, the present people do not distinguish what is character or culture and what is not in the intoxicated world. Smoking cigarettes, drinking brandy or wine and chewing tobacco, illegal sex, prostitution, killing, stealing and raping were treated as worst character and culture but now it has become life style and culture. It is highly deplorable that the present generation use one hand for smoking or holding cell phone and other hand for driving vehicle or taking tea and smoking cigarettes together. Moreover, wearing half naked or transparent dresses, corruption, prostitutions, suicide, murdering, raping and homosexual or homo marriage makes man inferior to animals.

These are the cultures found among the people. Educated people are not excepted from this phenomena. However, values are very important to make human life happy and useful in the materialistic world. So the development of desirable or socially acceptable character and culture is one of the important of awakenistic aims of education in the Indian society.

Produce Employable Human Resources: This is one of the most of aims of Awakenistic education. Thousands of trained or untrained graduates or postgraduates/higher secondary educators are not employed because of their poor subject knowledge, language and communication skills or lack of any vocational skill. In fact, holding diploma degrees or certificates does not mean that a person is qualified to be employed in government/Private/corporate sectors. So this Philosophy advocates that 3R's (Reading, Writing, and Arithmetic) communication and any one or two vocational trainings are essentials components of education to produce employable people.

Develop Global Outlook: The scientific development comparable advantages of agricultural and production of the world countries prove that no society or no nation can stand on its own leg for existence and development. More over, the national hazards such as tsunami, earthquake, volcano or fire, flood and famine in one region or country affects all parts of the world. Culture and character may be different but the whole human society is one. So, we are one and learn to live and work together not for the progress of the one country bur for the progress of the whole world with international outlook. This is essential to eradicate war, maintain peace, avoid jealous, expand mutual financial assistance, reduce poverty and unemployment and control inflation and achieve national as well as international growth. So this tendency should be the aim of present education for global awakenism.

CURRICULUM

This philosophy advocates a comprehensive curriculum. It includes the study of those subjects, languages, practices and experiences which prepare the child to challenge the socio-natural problems and make casteless and secular society.

1. The study of social science mathematics, language, hygiene and vocational training should be imported at high school level.
2. Study of science subject mathematical language work experience, political science, economics, sociology should be taught at higher secondary level.
3. History may be taught as optional subject at all levels of education and training in order to acquire knowledge about the past and present episodes which are important to foster leadership qualities, democracy, nationalism and international outlook. Generally history of the past, no body proves or disproves it. Moreover, it does not develop creativity or rational thinking in the child. It may be taught only to understand the past and changes that take in the society. So weekly two hours may be reserved for teaching history.
4. About 18 Indian languages are in use at regional, state and national levels. As a result, no one speaks either pure Tamil or Telugu or Punjabi or Bengali. In fact, inter-state culture is found in all states which affects purify of spoken and written languages. At the same time, every language is superior or inferior to other language. However, man cannot be separated from his mother tongue as it equals to his mother's milk. Emphasis on mother tongue develops narroawism and the politicians cheat the people in the name of language. It is a global society so in which people of one state or country lives in another state or country for education, employment and income. So this Philosophy advocates the study of one's mother tongue, neighbour states language national and international languages on optional basis so that a child belongs to Tamil Nadu (South India) can choose any three languages that is at regional or national and international levels. The Government of Tamil Nadu cheats its people by insisting regional language and neglecting national language Hindi. Learning many languages develops internationlistic outlook in the child and helps to become proficiency in any language in which he/she is interested. Therefore, this philosophy advocates the study of at least there language on optional basis but not compulsory
5. Instead of including more and more subjects child may be given opportunity to develop communication skill and prepare him to be employable in any sectors. And also included those subjects which foster casteless, secular and democratic outlook and human values in the child.
6. Avoid the inclusion of many topics in a particular subject. But these papers which are related to life and essential for subject sake and useful to the society may be included for study.
7. Work experience, useful productive work or any type of vocational training, should be made compulsory at higher secondary and degree level with view to make education purposeful and increase employment opportunities.

METHODS OF TEACHING

Direct Experience: Direct experience makes learning permanent and understanding easy and simple in the socio-natural environment.

Learning by Doing: It increases the practical experiences in the life related problems. It makes learning clear independent and simple. This method encourages and develops creativity.

Auto Learning: This is knowledge explosion age in which the area of every discipline increases and ever changing. So it is not possible to learn everything with the help of teachers in a short period. So auto learning is the best method used in higher learning techniques like conference, seminar, symposium and workshop. And advise the students to utilise library resources.

Book Culture: Encourage the students to develop book culture for knowledge, experience and various skills which enable them to overcome the challenges in the complicated society. Moreover good book is the best teacher. So, teachers should advise and encourage the students to visit the library for references, assignments and project works.

Tour

This method is the best for acquiring knowledge related to nature and man. So student should be encouraged to visit not only naturally as well as historically important places but also visit general and mental hospitals, homes of mentally and physically challenged people, leprosy ward and prisons. Such tours makes the students realise the suffering of human beings and the importance of the sacrifice compassion, sympathy, help and neglect caste, religion and regionalism.

TEACHERS

This philosophy considers teachers as secondary role in the teaching learning process. This is because books and non-book materials teach the students more than an ordinary teacher. However teachers should be model in character, knowledge and guidance but most of the teachers lack character knowledge and memory power. However, their role is important in primary and secondary education. Since most of the admissions in matriculation and colleges are made on the basis of merit and money in private educational institutions. Teacher's role is limited in teaching. Moreover teacher depends on guides which available in the market at school level and internet facilities at college level. The present teachers forget the meaning and responsibility of their profession. Most of them think that sitting and reading is teaching but they fail to explain, evaluate, guide and lead them properly. They should not use cell phone and chat with others while class is going on and avoid sitting at the time of examination. They should have clean habits and never allow the students and society to degrade them, in character and performance. They should think of social and economic conditions and sufferings of people working in agriculture, business and shops and living in slums. They may not teach but they should be example in life. As a teacher he/she should have memory power to teach the subject without holding hints or books in the class. If he does so, students should be allowed to use hints in the examination.

STUDENTS

This is a materialistic world in which everybody is selfish easy going and seeking monetary benefits. So students should develop their personality with available resources in the educational, social and natural environments either the guidance of teacher or parents or neighbours. They should not spare time but spend it on useful deeds. Today effective reader will be tomorrow's leader or creator should be slogan of every students. They should develop knowledge communication and character to be useful to society and nation. Every student should be taught to utilise their time, energy and money for achieving balanced development in educational institution.

EXAMINATION

The present education is examination oriented one. It is a tool to measure or evaluate the performance of students and educational achievements. Most of the teachers do not evaluate the answer scripts properly due to lack of key answer and laziness. As a result academically and average students score high marks in examination. Moreover teachers in the examination hall do not supervise properly and most of them sit on the chair and use cell phone or standing out of the hall and either using cell phone or chatting with other teachers. It encourages the students to copy other answer sheet it can be corrected by proper attention of the institutional heads. Key answer should be given for correct valuation. So examination system and evaluation method should be reformed in such away to ensure the performance of the students righteously.

NATIONAL SYSTEM OF EDUCATION

There should be a national system of education except mother tongue to enable and deserve the students to face the labour market at national and international level. Role of the government in education is more important than in encouraging the production of intoxicants and spoil the students. It should controls the monopoly of higher education which increase the cost and reduce the quality of education. Moreover, Board of Education such as CBSE, BSE and Matriculation Board follows different educational systems which differentiate the students quantitatively as well as qualitatively. The adoption of national educational system not only makes education uniform in all states and the leads to national integration. Further, the government should avoid the provision of fund, to research scholars under Faculty Improvement Program (FIP) scheme and increment for those who produce certificate from the Directorate of Distance of Education. This is because most of the present researches are not problem oriented but they are useless and purposeless. It is undertaken for monetary benefits not for quality development in subject knowledge.

CONCLUSION

Awakenism in all children is very essential in the caste-religious fundamentalism and materialistic society. Application of this Philosophy in education not only changes the educational system but also makes it effective and useful tool to bring about a casteless secular and democratic outlook. It also develops human values and eradicate unemployment, poverty and inequality. Man is the creator of Gods spiritual world, heaven and hell, religion, caste, language and money. So this philosophy opposes the creations which control or makes man inferior in the earth. Man is everything and nothing is behind him except the nature. As all the men are equal in birth and death, let us live for one another and oppose any thing which separate caste, religion or region and weaken smoking, chewing, drinking, corruption, prostitution, illegal life, raping, suicide, murdering and print fake certificate and currencies. At least, let us differentiate the literate from illiterate in words and deeds for making better society.

CHAPTER 14

HUMANISM

INTRODUCTION

Jesus Christ is the greatest humanist who preached and practiced human values throughout his life. He has shown compassion, sympathy and empathy upon the sick, poor and needy ones. He always emphasized the human values such as brotherhood, affection, fellow-feeling, compassion, kindness and internationalism. Moreover, the ideas of humanism are found in Upanishads and Bhagavad-Gita. As such, the concept of humanism is the oldest one, but it took a philosophical form in the eighteenth century. However, its importance and influence in education are realized in the nineteenth and twentieth centuries. This philosophy is very important in the 21st century because it is the modern age where materialism, monetarism, mechanisation and commercialization have a great impact on human society. As a result, human and spiritual values have become meaningless and everything for money, of money and by money. In short, money is more important than man and human life has become use and through one. It is highly regrettable that present education is meant for certificates and degrees for employment and it has failed to foster human values. Consequently, human life is unhappy, unhealthy and peaceless. That is why, humanists emphasize the study of humanism and preach the human values for man making, character formation and personality development. So, the study of humanism has been given due importance in the philosophical field. Moreover, it influences the educational principles and practices in the materialistic society. The chief exponents of Humanistic philosophy are like Aulis Gallous Confucius, Gautama Buddha Cicero, Zoroaster, Lao Tzu, Anaxagoras, Thales, Xenophanes Epicures, F. I. Niethammer, George Voigt, Burckhardt Thomas Paine, Hegelians, Petrarch and Davies.

BACKGROUND OF HUMANISM

The word **Humanism** has been derived from the Latin concept ***humanitas*** which means benevolence towards one's fellow humans. Aulis Gillis a Latin Grammarian (125–180A.D) says that humanities is commonly used for philanthropy or kindness and benevolence towards one's fellow human beings. However, Cicero (106–43 B.C) defined and popularised the term humanitas to settle disputes and live together in harmony. During the French Revolution in France and later in Germany, humanism referred to an ethical philosophy centered on mankind without attention to the supernatural power. Historically, Bavarian Educational Commissioner Friedrich Immanuel Niethammer coined (1808) the term **Humanism** to describe the new classical curriculum and offer it to German secondary schools. The word **Humanism** entered in the English language in 1836 and it gained universal acceptance in 1856 when George Voigt, German historian and philosopher, used humanism to describe Renaissance humanism, which flourished in the Italian Renaissance to revive classical learning. Greek philosophers stress human-centered philosophy in the linguistic and cultural disciplines.

The humanistic ideas are also found in Upanishads and Bhagavad Gita. The seers maintained that man is a soul, beyond mind, intellect, body and sense organs. The soul is doer, knower and enjoyer. It is eternal and beyond life and death. So, Upanishads emphasizes the integral relation between Man, Nature and God. This trinity may he called integral humanism and the community is humanity. Thus Upanishads identified humanity with divinity in the universe. This reality is expressed in the trinity which is metaphysical, epistemological and axiological reality. Bhagavad Gita is known as the essence of the Upanishads, which also maintains an integral relationship between man, God and the universe. According to Bhagavad-Gita, the humanistic ideas can be achieved by knowledge, devotion and action. In fact, it preaches integral humanism—a synthesis of hedonism and asceticism for external actions and inner peace, knowledge and devotion, individual liberation and consolidation of society. All Indian philosophers have emphasized integral humanism which is essential for life.

The philosophy of Confucius (551–479 B.C) contains several humanistic traits placing a high value in human life. The Greek philosophers like Thales of Miletus and Xenophanes explained the humanistic philosophy. Muslim thinkers also pursued humanistic, rational, and scientific discourses for knowledge, meaning and values. In fact, the medieval Islamic writings on love, poetry, history and philosophical theology show the humanistic ideas of individualism, occasional secularism, skepticism and liberalism. According to George Makdist, Renaissance humanism has its roots, in medieval Islamic thoughts including the humanistic attitude towards classical language.

The scholars like Jacob Grimm, J.R.R. Tolkien, E.O. G. Turville and Petre have identified a stream of humanistic philosophy in the Icelandic sages. The German historian George Voigt (1827–91) identified Petrarch as the first Renaissance humanist who is known as father for discovery of classical texts and his personal commitment found in the ancient literature and philosophy. It was in Leonardo Bruni's (1369–1444) time that the word humanism came into use in the subjects such as grammar, rhetoric poetry, moral philosophy and history. The renaissance scholars associated with humanism were religious, but inveighed against the abuses of the church. So, secular humanism was introduced in the 19th century. The modern secular humanism grew with the development of an important split between reason and religion. The rationalization of the 18th century philosophies and the radical, historical based German 19th century Biblical criticism of the Hegelians, David Friedrich Strauss and Ludwig Feuerbach brought about the first political inspiration in French and projects humanity as the hero of liberty, and second the German philosophical thoughts, which seek the totality and autonomy of knowledge and stress understanding rather than freedom as the key to human fulfilment and emancipation. These two themes set the boundaries of different types of humanism in the 19th century. According to Feuerbach, "The human being is a good to humanity" or "God is nothing other than the human being to himself".

The British Humanistic Religious Association was organized in 1853 in London. Felix Adler (America) turned the term ethical culture into Ethical humanism in 1877. F.C.S. Schiller labeled his work humanism referred to the pragmatic philosophy and shared with William James in 1920. Charles Francis Palter founded (1929) the first humanist society of New York with an advisory board of including Julian Huxley, John Dewey, Albert Einstein and Thomas Mann. The American Humanist Association was organized in 1941. It joined (2004) other groups such as agnostics, atheist and free thinkers to create the secular coalition in America advocating the separation of church and state for the acceptance of non-theistic Americans.

Thus, human centered ideologies have been popular among the philosophers and religious leaders since at least 1500 B.C when the Greek philosophers understood the world through the lens of human reasons and abilities rather than through the super natural working of God. Zoraster and Lao Tzu developed the similar philosophy in the East. Anaxagoras, a famous teacher of Socrates, used scientific enquiry to gain knowledge about the outer space and the nature of the universe. He hypothesized that this universe has always existed as small fragments in a chaotic mass. This materialistic view led him to a death sentence in Athens that sent him into exile. It is Cicero (106–43 B.C.E) who coined the term humanitas which distinguishes human beings from all other creatures—the ability to reason, to speak, and to create law that allow them to live in peaceful societies. In 1808, humanism was primarily used in English to note education—the revival of clerical learning. Ultimately, humanism came to refer to a specific ethical philosophy of mankind. In fact, it has become a distinguished philosophy which centered on human values, need and abilities, purposely distanced from the supernatural in influencing the education practices.

MEANING OF HUMANISM

The literal meaning (Etymology) of the term **Humanism** is taken from the word **Humaniora** which means study of human body and surrounding nature. In this sense, humanism regards man as the measure of all things. He is the dispenser of his own destiny. He is the architect of his own fortune. Encyclopedia of Social Sciences gives the meaning of humanism as "It is characteristically human, not supernatural, that which belongs to man not to external nature; that which raises man to his greatest height or gives him, as a man, his greatest satisfaction". Thus, humanism is a philosophy of life that considers the welfare of mankind. It is a philosophical and ethical stance which embraces the value and agency of human beings. It is a progressive philosophy that, without theism or other super natural beliefs, affirms our ability and responsibility to lead ethical lives of personal fulfilment that aspire to the greater good. So it is a rational philosophy informed by science, inspired by art and motivated by compassion. Broadly speaking, it is a democratic and ethical life stance which affirms that human beings have the right and responsibility to give meaning and shape to their own lives. It stands for the building of a human society through the ethics based on human and natural values in a spirit of reason and free enquiry. As such, it is an approach to life based on reason and our common humanity recognizing that moral values are proposal founded on human nature and experience along.

DEFINITIONS OF HUMANISM

A few scholars, humanists, philosophers and educationists have defined the term humanism. According to American Humanism Association, "Humanism is a concept or idea which has faith in people, in all humanity and in science as a means of attaining truth. It is also a quest for the ethical and spiritual values of life through philosophy, science, arts and literature".

In the words of Prof *K.G. Saiyidain*, "Humanism is a belief in his infinite worth, his unlimited potentialities his right to over reverence and affection, his status as an end and not merely as a means for working out the ends of others. Man is entitled to this respect, not because of his wealth or ability or power but because of his being an image of God."

According to *Nicholas Hans*, "Humanism implies both a human and humane approach to educational problems; human in the sense that human nature and human interests should not be suppressed by religion in favour of an ascetic ideal and a narrow dogmatic interpretation of the world. Humanism in the sense that the nature of the child. Its growing mind should not be suppressed by cruel school discipline and rigid methods of instruction. In its original meaning humanism meant the liberation of reason from the shackles of dogmas and a critical study of nature and humanity through the observation of actual facts."

We may define ,"Humanism is a human centred philosophy of everything for man, of man and by man emphasizing human values for man-making, character formation and personality development to create a healthy, happy and peaceful life".

PRINCIPLES OF HUMANISM

Humanism is a distinguished philosophy developed with some unique principles as given below:

- It believes that human experience and rational thinking provide the only sources of both knowledge and moral code to live by.
- It rejects the ideas of knowledge reveal to human beings by god or in special books.
- There are no super natural beings.
- The material universe is the only thing that exists.
- Science provides the only reliable source of knowledge about the universe.
- We live only this life. There is no other life and no such thing as reincarnation
- It believes in the principle of unity through diversity.
- Human beings can live without religious beliefs.
- Man is more important than anything in the universe.
- Human beings derive their moral code from the lessons of history, personal experience, social contacts and thoughts.
- It believes that science never will be able to explain the ultimate origin or destiny of the universe.
- It drives the goals of life from human needs and interests rather than from theological or ideological abstractions.

FEATURES OF HUMANISM

We can draw out the salient features of Humanism.

- **Producing educated men:** One of the main targets of humanism is to produce broadly educated and intellect men. Such men and women are well accomplished, well informed and they are able to express themselves in liberal arts and other cultural pursuits.
- **Pursuit of excellence:** The main purpose, mission or field of activity is the pursuit of excellence. Human pursuit of excellence is the key to the larger good of humanity. It is the goal of humanistic philosophy.
- **Ethical and moral values:** Humanism has faith in ethical and moral values. Educational decisions should be based on liberal education and scientific rationalism.
- **Man is the measure:** Humanism regards man as the measure of everything in the universe. Accordingly, man is more important than anything in the earth.
- **Educational institutions shaping human beings:** Humanism assigns grate responsibility to educational institutions. Educational institutions have the responsibility of shaping men and women in to the individuals of high character. Education should mould their abilities and their ideas in such a way that they become desired members of the society.
- **Realisation of spiritual ideals:** Humanism lays stress on realizations of spiritual ideals. Man can achieve the spiritual realm by making the proper use of his intellect. Truth, goodness,

beauty, humility, sympathy and will to work for human welfare are the qualities which are the ideals of Humanism.

- **Man has supreme power:** This philosophy believes that man has supreme power to control anything except nature is the doer, creator and destroyer with the use of his knowledge, experience and needs.

TYPES OF HUMANISM

The humanistic philosophy is a dynamic one. It has different forms like ethical, evolutionary, life stance, non-theistic, rationalistic and scientific skepticism. It shows that humanists have different views from time to time and place to place based on their knowledge, experience and thoughts.

Historical Humanism

Historical humanism is that kind of humanism different from the rhetorical and civic humanism of renaissance. It has been developed out of idealistic philosophy and traditional thoughts. It has dominated the conception of liberal education in the Western societies. In fact, its roots can be traced in the Greek philosophical thoughts. It supports democratic institution which truly works for the good of human society. In other words, it stands for the welfare and progress of all individuals. So it emphasizes human values and regards man as the measure of all things. This humanistic ideology is found in the writings of Plato, Aristotle, Charles Darwin, Milton, Bacon, Schiller and many others. Plato says, "True education civilizes and humanizes man in their relation to one another and those who are under their protection". Aristotle says, "Sound mind in a sound body". He regards the body one the mind as equally important in the concept of education. Milton, English poet and humanist, rightly observes, "I call a complete and generous education that which fits a man to perform justly, skilfully and magnanimously all offices both private and public of peace and war".

Scientific Humanism

This is the product of modern science and technology. It combines humanistic attitudes with scientific temper. It broadens human outlook and develops sympathetic approach and common welfare. We cannot ignore science and technology when we are taking long leaps forward in the ever changing materialistic society. At the same time science must be used to refine culture and bring about the welfare of human society This is the true spirit of scientific humanism, so it deals with educational and human problems in a scientific and rational manner. In fact, it prepares the human wind to know the world and adopt it as for as possible to suit one's own needs . As such, it gives no place to super naturalism. Man is the measure of every thing and posses rational thinking and super natural power. In fact, man is the central core of reality. Above all, this humanism makes no distinct in between man and man on the basis of nationality, race, sex, language, education and economic status. However, it recognizes human abilities scholarship as the means of human welfare.

Secular Humanism

This is a philosophy or life stance embracing human reason, secular ethics and naturalism . It believes that human beings are capable of being ethical and moral without religion or belief in deity. However, it does not mean that man is either inherently good or bad nor does, but he is supreme to nature. As such, it is a comprehensive one rejecting supernatural claims, but lead by human reason, metaphysical naturalism, altruistic morality and justice.

The International Humanist and Ethical Union (IHEU) is the world union of humanist, rationalist, irreligious, atheistic, bright, secular, ethical culture, and free thought organizations. The "Happy Human" is the official symbol of the IHEU as well as being regarded as a universally recognized symbol for secular humanism. According to the IHEU, "Secular humanism is a democratic and ethical life stance, which affirms that human beings have the right and responsibility to give meaning and shapes to their own lives". It stands for the building of a more human society through an ethic based on human and other natural values in the spirit of reason and free inquiry through human capabilities. It is not theistic, and it does not accept supernatural views of reality.

Religious Humanism

Religious humanism is an integration of humanist ethical philosophy with congregational but non-theistic ritual and community activity center on human needs, interest and abilities. It opposes secular humanism "Religious humanists" are non-superstitious people who nevertheless see ethical humanism as their religion, and who seek to integrate humanist philosophy with congregational rituals based on human values needs, interests, and abilities. The practitioners of religious humanism did not officially organize under the name of "humanism" until the late 19th and early 20th centuries, but non theistic religions paired with human-centred ethical philosophy have a long history. A unified Ethical culture movement was first founded in 1876; its founder, Felix Alder, was a founder member of the free Religious Association of Ethical culture as a new religion that would retain the ethical message at the heart of all religions. Ethical culture was religions. Ethical culture was religious in the sense of playing a defining role in pepol's lives and addressing issues of ultimate concern. The religious humanists in the united states represent organizations such the American Ethical union and describe themselves as "ethical humanists or humanists". At the same time secular humanists and religious humanists organize together as part of larger national and international groupings, and differentiate themselves primarily in their attitude to the promotion of humanist thinking.

NEED AND IMPORTANCE OF HUMANISM

We can justify the need and importance of humanism in the following grounds:

- Man is measured in terms of money/wealth, but man is more important than anything in the earth.
- This is a materialistic society where there is no room for human values.
- This is a scientific world in which life is fast and man is a machine.
- This is a socially polluted society in which there are lot of contemptible and undesirable activities which affect human health, wealth and happy life.
- The present man suffers from lack of love, affection, kindness and other human values.
- The scientific and materialistic values reduce spiritual values.

Scientific World: This is a scientific world where there are no spiritual and human values. In the words of Burton Clark, "Modern man is clearly in a second scientific one. The first revolution centered on the stream engine and spinning machines and put machine in the place of muscles. The second revolution centers on atomic energy, automation, computers and chemical materials. It greatly magnifies technically produced energy, changes processing methods, alters the materials on which men and machines work, and often substitutes machines for human thought and control. Although we have been sliding in to a technological age on the basis of accumulated techniques produced by the first scientific revolution, we are now in for technology with a vengeance. Through its ramifying effects—technology alters nearly all institutions. Hence, we need this philosophy.

Lack of Knowledge: Most of the people live behind the mass media. There is no practical knowledge to lead the life smoothly. Technological changes have directly affected the operations of school through the introduction of a variety of new teaching and administrative techniques. From an educational standpoint automated classroom systems for teaching compliment skills, language laboratories, scientific materials, audio-visual equipments and a host of related development have made teaching an increasingly specialized activity. Education has narrowed down its social and spiritual significance. It also requires the need and importance of this philosophy.

Neglecting Personality Development: We may enjoy a comfortable life in the scientific world. But there is no personality development. This is an apparent outcome of mechanicals. The aims, outlook, approach, instructional techniques, role of the teacher and the school have undergone a complete change. Education is deeply concerned with equipping an individual to be a specialist with a totally changed outlook from humanism to mechanicals. Present individuals are more of a machine and less of a human being. He is a living machine and moves or works day and night as a body devoid of tender spirit that drinks in the sea of piety. His education is not liberal but technical. The personality development is essential to solve individual and social problems.

Pull out of Self-centeredness: There is no sacrifice for others but everything self-centered. It is not good for social life. Humanism alone can pull man out of his self-centeredness and an attitude of false pleasure-seeking. Prof. K.G. Saiyidain rightly remarks "Man's life should not be self-centered like the lightning which revolves round itself and fails to illumine the word". Modern man is busy in adoring his outer personality, whereas his soul is being starved. Modern education has surrendered its aesthetic heritage. Mechanicalism is the crux of the new age. Today, man is surrounded all around with machines, scientific equipment and push-button appliance. He is the lord of lord and even claims to do wonders and perform miracles. At the same time, he has attained the capacity to reduce the magnificent buildings and human-creations along with humanity, to ashes, pieces and skeletons. In fact, the modern man has become a slave to the machines. His health, his job, his security, his production and consumption of goods, and his education now are dependent on huge impersonal forces, locked up in the materialistic and polluted environments.

Social Pollution: Humanism is essential to realize human values and make human life better. It is regrettable that the present generation suffers more from social pollution than environmental pollution. For example, prostitution, divorce, separation, raping and killing of innocent girls and women, murdering, suicide, robbing, printing fake currencies and certificates, lack of love, affection, patriotism and other human values. So this philosophy is important to make human life happy and peaceful.

HUMANISM AND EDUCATION

Humanism applied to education aims at producing a complete man in all respects. Milton, a true humanist, pleaded for 'a complete and generous education' which would produce men who would carry out "justly, skillfully and magnanimously" a responsibilities of life. Tagore inspired by Descartes and Locks also wanted to revive humanistic tradition in education. Humanistic education is essentially the exaltation of human personality.

AIMS OF EDUCATION

According to Humanists, the humanistic education should aim to produce complete man for social, cultural, political, aesthetical and economic life. So they state the aims of education as given below:

Man-making: Humanistic education aims at man making. It means that man should be secular, rational and scientific one.

Train the faculty of reason: The most important aim of education is to train the faculty of reason. The world in which man lives can be known by the proper exercise of reason. Reason distills truth and truth gives right direction to man's activities in the social environments. nature.

Cultivation of intellect: Cultivation of intellect is a complementary aim for training faculty of reason. It is important "not just as a means to an end but more significantly as an end in itself. It is the educational summum bonum (A type of drink)". This is also essential to realize human values in the materialistic society.

Liberation from dogmas and superstition: Once the faculty of reason is trained, human minds is set fee from the chains of dogmas and superstition. A mind thus liberated becomes the caretaker of human values of truth, goodness, beauty, humility, sympathy etc. Humanist education fulfils this aim.

Development of Perfect personality: Humanist education aims at development of all round best personality. Only such a person can perform his responsibility to the public, state and self in a just and magnanimous manner. This aim is very important to prepare the man for social, cultural, spiritual, moral and economic ljfe.

Abundant Life: The aim of humanist education is life and more abundant life. Human happiness is the goal of humanism. It is abundant life which can give happiness. Education must equip man to lead abundant life. In fact, its purpose is to increase efficiency and happiness of human beings.

Team Spirit: Humanistic education aims to foster team spirit and cooperation through play way method. Community programs prepare the children for cooperative life. This aldo develops unity in diversity.

Welfare of entire humanity: The happiness and welfare of the entire humanity is the concern of humanist. So, humanist education should develop culture and peace. As an extension of this humanist education should aims to cultivate the values for life among children to respect life, promote human rights, fundamental freedom, right to sovereignty and development, tolerance and equality between man and man, man and women.

HUMANISTIC CURRICULUM

Humanists advocate liberal and extensive curriculum which includes, science, arts, humanities, moral and religious subjects for all types of knowledge and experiences. Moreover extra-curricular activities are for the development of social virtues. So the humanist curriculum includes those studies which would ignite the mind of children. A humanist education believes that it is the pupil who comes first or gets priority, method and theory later. The great academician J.B Florin advocated that philosophy and the sciences ought to be made the principal subjects of study for young persons. He classified all subjects of instruction in to three groups.

- Relation of man to nature,
- Relation of man to himself,
- Relation of man to other men.

In fact, humanistic curriculum includes humanities and applied science. The essence of human nature is its rational character. Broacher is of the view that in selecting the material for curriculum, the rational humanist would prefer to choose "the essentials". Since it is not possible for the school to include everything which meets this criterion, there must be a further hierarchy of values. "The subjects with the greatest rational content, of course, are liberal arts, and among liberal arts, the humanities. These are best exemplified in 'the great' books of our culture."

J. B. Florin's scheme of curriculum includes in the first group (Relation of Man to Nature) all branches of Mathematics, Physics, Chemistry, Astronomy, Natural history, Applied sciences etc., in the second group (Relation of Man to Himself) Latin, French, Italian, Grammar, Logic, Rhetoric, Poetry, Drawing, Music etc. And in the third group (Relation of Man to other man), subjects like History – ancient and modern, Politics, Economics and Biographies.

HUMANISTIC TEACHING METHODS

Humanistic Pedagogy recognizes two orders of learning. The first is the inherent and essential order of the subject matter itself. Teaching methods should help the learner to discover this order and move along, step by step. And the second order of learning takes its cue from the nature of the learner himself. The teacher starts with the experience available in the child and commences with the concrete and particular. The humanist teacher may use discussion method, cooperative play, understanding and reproduction as essential techniques of teaching. There is little scope for rote memorization. Humanists always emphasize the teaching methods based upon human psychology. So the teacher should teach according to the principles of child psychology, developmental psychology and educational psychology. Education should be provided through mother tongue for originality and creativity. However, national and international languages should be taught at higher stages so as to encourage human communication at global level.

Teacher

Humanism assigns an important place to the teacher. It regards the teacher as a versatile person, endowed with the qualities of head and heart. Humanistic teacher would believe that knowledge at its best comes through the faculty of reason. Reason is the anchor of the intellect. Humanist teacher believes that intellect is the fountain head of knowledge. Humanism expects a teacher to be endowed with such traits of personality as insight and imagination, instruction, clarity and reason. Such qualities alone would activate the intellect of the teacher. Such a teacher would guide the pupil in attaining an all-round personality.

School

According to humanist, the school organization should be democratic in which the management, the teacher and the students can take part in all activities. It should be organized in such a way to develop responsibility, liberty, equality and fraternity. So the school administration should be liberal and democratic one.

Discipline

Humanist wants self-discipline based on freedom. They encourage peaceful relation so that boys and girls may help in the establishment of peace upon the earth. The school should follow rational and secular rules and regulations, Humanist synthesis, nationalism and internationalism. Universities should encourage the development of all aspects of cultural. Regional universities should preserve national culture and encourage mixing of students from different countries to create an International cultural atmosphere. We can see two humanism universities in India—one is Rabindranath Tagore's Shanti Niketan (West Bengal) and other is Sri Aurobindo's International University, Arovilla, (Pondicherry). Humanistic discipline gives ample support to the dignity and worth of the individual. It does not believe in suppression of child's emotions. The use of authority should be rational, based on sympathy and humanitarian reasoning. The child should be educated to control himself through self-imposed conditions of good conduct.

CONCLUSION

The educational implementations of humanism reveal that it is the best blue print for planning future education. It is the solid basis for the development of values and culture. So humanism as a philosophy odd education is not an end in itself. It is a philosophy which respects the fundamentals of humanity. Its educational concept is for social welfare through positive social changes seen and as yet unforeseen. Humanistic education prepares the younger generation not only in terms of skills but in terms of character, perspective and a personality capable of adapting to new situations. Therefore, technological advancement and human understanding must be combined; otherwise we create mechanical monsters which may threaten our survival. At this juncture, humanistic philosophy of education would be accepted and required in all countries.

CHAPTER 15

ECLECTIC TENDENCY IN EDUCATION

INTRODUCTION

Blend of different philosophies is called eclectic tendency. Pandit Jawaharlal Nehru has outlined indirectly the idea of eclectic tendency in education. He delivered it in his speech in Moulana Azad Memorial lecture that education is supported to develop an integrated human being and to prepare the young people to perform useful function for society and to take part in cooperative life. But, when the society is changing now and then, it is difficult to know how to prepare and what to aim for. So, it needs to make educational philosophy most modern so as to meet the needs of present day society through a harmonic 'synthesis' between all the conflicting factors in educational philosophies and tendencies. A smooth synthesis of all major philosophies develops an eclectic tendency in education. The implication of eclectic tendency is more important than a single philosophy in post modern education and life. This is because it is the synthesis of those aims, principles and activities which are found in different philosophical ideologies, but useful to the individual and society.

MEANING OF ECLECTIC TENDENCY

The function or synthesis and pleading of diverse philosophies is known as 'Eclectic Tendency'. It is a tendency which seeks to achieve a harmonious synthesis between all the conflicting factors in educational philosophies and tendencies. According to Munroe, "The eclectic tendency is that which seeks the harmonisation of principles underlying in various tendency and realisation of educational practices". It is the process involving and putting of various views from different philosophies together into one comprehensive whole and applied in educational practices. Thus, it implies finding harmony among the various philosophies theories and using it in man-making process. In other words, it is the combination of emphasising spiritual world and life. Naturalism stresses the natural development of child and pragmatism selects those ideas and activities which suit the changing society. Thus, eclectic tendency is found in the modern educational principles and practices.

CHARACTERISTICS OF ECLECTIC TENDENCY IN EDUCATION

- It synthesizes the important and useful ideologies of major philosophies.
- It changes the educational principles and practices according to the changing environment.

- It develops a broad outlook and large heartedness.
- It fosters the attitudes of appreciation and acceptance of various conflicting views.
- It prepares the individual and society to lead a life of adjustment and understanding.
- It creates an environment in which one learns to disagree without disagreeables.
- It makes education a complete process.

NEED FOR ECLECTIC TENDENCY

We have different philosophical ideas and principles which influence every aspect of human life. So, the synthesis of all philosophical thoughts are essential to develop all round personality of a child and a man. Moreover, we hive in a modern society of various cultures, ideologies and beliefs. At the same time, scientific and technological development, global thinking, democratic outlook, feeling, thinking and human values leave aside differenced and conflicts. It is possible only through the function of eclectic tendency which emphasises attitude of appreciation and acceptance of various cultures and civilisation. These inspire children to lead a life of smooth adjustment, broader outlook, large heartedness, sympathy, tolerance, co-operation and fellow feeling among all the citizens of the world. Hence, the need for eclectic tendency can be justified on the following grounds.

No Philosophy is Complete in Itself: No single philosophy is complete in itself, and it cannot be applied in all situations. For example, idealism emphasises child-centred education and natural growth in free environment and pragmatism stresses vocational development and social efficiency. It is seen that ideas and principles of one philosophy is different from another. So, single philosophy is incomplete and it does not bring about desirable changes in the personality development, but synthesis of all philosophies is essential to make educational principles and practices effective and meaningful in the man-making and nation-making process. Therefore, synthesis and the function of diverse ideologies are needed to develop adjustment, co-operation and fellow feeling in varied cultural and ideological people.

Dynamic World and Dynamic Thought: This is a dynamic world in which everything changes according to the aims of human life. So, it is not safe. It is stick to one degree, creed, belief or philosophy; some ideas of philosophy may be true today but it may not be true tomorrow. According to Gaind and Sharma, "We live in an age in which dogmatic adherence of a single principle or philosophy might be harmful. It is therefore, instead of adhering to rigid and fixed for ever ideologies, it requires eclectic tendency for acquiring dynamic outlook and mental flexibility to change our behaviour in the changing conditions on demand". Thus, it emphasises the need for eclectic tendency in education and life.

Harmonising the Different Philosophies: Eclectic tendency in philosophical world is quite unavailable to harmonise the difference found in different educational philosophies. The synthesis of general philosophy of education contains the useful and acceptable features of different philosophies and tendencies in education. It is a harmonious philosophy which makes education a complete process and develops unity in diversity for co-operative thought and life.

Education is not Based on One Philosophy: The modern education is not based on one philosophy but different philosophies. So, it needs eclectic tendency which is gaining wider and wider appreciation and acceptance in individual and social life. It reflects a harmonious synthesis of all those dynamic ideals, principles and activities on which various tendencies have had their influence in different times. Hence, we need eclectic tendency in education and life.

Different Philosophies Stress the Same Views: Almost all educational philosophies uphold the dignity of an individual and respect for human personality. So, education aims at child development, and child becomes the centre of education. All the major philosophies believe that mind is a powerful force and significant in the human life. Idealists regard mind as something which creates its own objects, and discovers its own laws. Thus, mind and spirit constitutes reality. According to Naturalist, there is an impact of environment on mind; pragmatists mind is a functional behaviour). Thus, dignity of the individual and powerful force of mind is generally accepted by all philosophies which caused the emergence of eclectic tendency.

ECLECTIC TENDENCY IN MODERN EDUCATION

Aim of Education: The aims of modern education are individual development and social efficiency which are correlative aspects of any educational programmes in the eclectic tendency.

Principles of Education: The eclectic tendency has seven principles of education. The principle commands education a fundamental process, health, competence in family, civic and vocational, social efficiency, worthy use of leisure, ethical, character and global thinking.

Curriculum: Curriculum of modern education is flexible and useful. It is constructed based on the ever-changing needs of society, broad based, diversified and many-sided, nearly all philosophies recommend humanities, history geography, science, art and various activities, moreover, all philosophies of education condemn verbalism, and recommended different activities.

Method of Teaching: Philosophies advocate those methods which are interested for the child, for instance, education through direct experiences activities and observation are given due importance in the post modern society. In other words, learning through activities founds in all philosophies.

Importance of Subject Specialists: The curriculum of modern education prescribes broad and varied subjects and activities. So, one teacher cannot teach all subjects. Hence, specialists are appointed to teach every subject or a group of allied subjects these days.

Teaching is a Profession: Today teaching is regarded as a profession. Teachers are working for definite pay and other allowances.

Training of teacher: Eclectic tendency emphasises the provision of training to teacher. It believes that education is an art. It is not possible for a person to impart the teaching process successfully. In short, teacher requires training to have psychological knowledge and develop their personality.

Role of teacher: Eclectic tendency gives importance to teachers and considers them as friend, philosopher and guide in the educational practices.

Secular Form of Education: Education was imparted by the religious institutions in the ancient and medieval times. With the influence of eclectic tendency, the modern education has become secular and materialistic one.

Place of School: The function of school is to prepare dynamic citizens to participate in the social activities and group life. So, school is a miniature society which aims at socialising the child. It is the centre for the child to acquire all round personality development.

Discipline: Modern education condemns repression or compulsion of any kind of discipline given to the child. It supports free discipline. It believes that discipline through knowledge and knowledge through experience. So, it stimulates a sense of self-discipline among children for individual and social life.

Education Policy: Eclectic tendency stresses the importance of education for all. Consequently, each state follows the policy of free, compulsory and universal education. It enables all citizens to meet their basic educational needs, which is essential for existence.

Comprehensive Education: Eclectic tendency makes education a comprehensive process. The concept of child-centred education, respect for personality, sympathy with the child, value of love in discipline and development of human values and vocational efficiency and international outlook make the scope of education wider and meaningful in the materialistic world.

CONCLUSION

The best approach of modern education is eclectic tendency. It is the process by which the gist of all philosophies are studied, accepted and applied to achieve integrated personality development in the child. The application eclectic approach is helpful in solving different problems concerning education. It is a healthy sign that the present system of education is being organised, oriented, developed and planned in the light of electric approach. In fact, the trend of philosophical psychology, sociology, scientific and spiritual tendencies have sufficiently influenced the educational policies, principles and practices. It can be seen that the philosophies are inter-dependent exclusively in complex materialistic world. So, instead of contracting, they complement each other in the interest of man-making and nation-making. Eclectic tendency in education enables the child to achieve balanced integrated and co-ordinated personality. Hence, the dominant characteristics of all philosophies should be faced into unity giving rise to the theory of education which will meet the needs of the day and satisfy loftiest aspirations of the human race. We conclude the eclectic tendency in education with the words of Gaind and Sharma, "This tendency draws inspiration from various sources and borrow from each what might be useful under the present situation and fuse them so as to give them a form in which the distinctive individuality of each is merged in the collectively of the whole without losing sight of the value termed eclectic and is the characteristics of the present trends in education".

CHAPTER 16

PROGRESSIVE EDUCATION

INTRODUCTION

Progressive education is a movement that took form in European and American countries during the late 19th century as a reaction to the alleged narrowness and formation of traditional education. Its objective is to educate the 'whole child that is to attend the physical, emotional and intellectual growth'. The progressive school is considered as a laboratory in which the child should take active part that is, learning thorough doing. The theory was that a child learns best by actually performing tasks associated with learning creative and manual arts gained importance in the curriculum and the children should be encouraged towards experimentation and independent thinking. As such, progressive education is regarded as a protest to the traditional education as well as a vision of child centred and quite alive to the social implications of education. In fact, it aims to standardization of education and regimentation of mind.

PROTAGONISTS OF PROGRESSIVE EDUCATION

Progressive education is based on pragmatism, a philosophical movement that began in the United States in the 1870s. Its contributors are Charles Sanders Peirce, William James, John Dewey, and Ferdinand Canning and Scott Schiller. These pragmatists have been inspired by the works of Francis Bacon's scientific method, David Home's ideas of naturalism, Tomas Reid's direct realism, and Immanuel Kant's idealism. Others who influenced progressive education include John Locke, Jean-Jacques Rousseau, Johann Heinrich Pestalozzi, and Friedrich Frobel. While related ideas of progressive education are seen internationally in the schools of Maria Montessori in Italy, Olive Decroly in Belgium, Leo Tolstoy in Russia, and Janusz Korcrak in Poland, among others, this introduction provides a perspective in the context of American Progressive education. William Heard Kilpatrick is one of the most influential advocates of progressive education.

MEANING OF PROGRESSIVE EDUCATION

The term progressive education, "first used sporadically in the 1880s has appeared as a generic term in educational literature for over a century, usually with a commonly understood or misunderstood meaning. Progressive education is a response to the traditional methods of teaching. It can be defined as, "An educational movement which gives more values to experience than formal learning. As such, it is based more on experiential learning that concentrates on the development of talents in the child. In short, it is based on the belief that students learn best in real-life activities with other people".

QUALITIES OR FEATURES OF PROGRESSIVE EDUCATION

Progressivists believe that education should focus on the whole child rather than on the contact of the teacher. Progressive education is based on the belief that students learn best in real life activities with other people. So, a progressive teacher should provide not only reading and drills but also real world experiential activities that relate to the actual lives of the students. As such, the typical slogan of this education is "Learning by doing".

- It emphasizes learning by doing-projects, expeditionary learning and experiential learning.
- It is based on integrated curriculum focused on thematic units.
- It is the integration of entrepreneurship into education.
- It leads to group work and development of social skills.
- The goals of learning is understanding and actions.
- It opposes rote knowledge but emphasizes knowledge of experiential life-related activities.
- It encourages collaborative and co-operative learning projects.
- It is meant for social responsibility and democracy.
- It is highly personalized education accounting for each individual's goals.
- It is the integration of community service and learning projects into daily curriculum.
- It selects the subject content based on what skills needed in the future society.
- It reduces the importance of text books in favour of varied learning resources.
- It is a dynamic and comprehensive education.
- It assess the students by the evaluation of their projects and productions.

AIMS OF PROGRESSIVE EDUCATION

Progressive education began with the pioneering work of Francis W. Parker in the 1870s, and gained popularity through the writings of John Dewey and adoption by the Progressive Education Association as a movement to improve the lives of individuals. The movement focuses on the three elements: (1) quality of family and community life, (2) instruction tailored to educate everyone, and (3) create a culture where everyone shares in the benefits of science and the pursuit of arts. Progressive education has always represented different things to different people. For example, social settlement workers viewed progressive education as a means to transform the school into a community center for social education, while Pgrarian reformers envisioned a means to educate children on the joys and possibilities of farm life. John Dewey and his daughter Evelyn (1915 / 1962) vividly documented the variety of progressive schools such as the Marietta Johnson School of Organic Education in Alabama and the neighbourhood-oriented programs in Indianapolis. They argued for adjusting education to society through a new kind of education appropriate to a democratic society that equips everyone to live intelligently, making for a better and richer society. Thus, the different meanings of progressive education for different group of people makes sense.

Therefore, there are five groups of educationists with different aims of progressive education. For one group, the progressive education movement meant a society devoted to human worth and excellence through highly individualistic pedagogy where schools encourage children to freely develop their uniquely creative potential. A second group (Elsie Ripley Clapp) advocates for school activities directed at social and economic regeneration of local communities. George S. Counts and his followers were a third group, who sought to build a new social order through political reform. Eugene Randolph Smith and a fourth group of progressive educators concentrated on reorganizing and enlivening the traditional school studies. Finally, the fifty group, including John Dewey, regarded the progressive education movement as an expression of experimentalism emphasizing scientific method, naturalism, and social planning.

TENETS OF PROGRESSIVE EDUCATION

Aims of progressivism provide a vision or goals for education. Tenets are the principle ideas for achieving the vision regardless of the means with which to pursue the aims. The progressive education movement has never been precisely defined by the progressives whereas prominent connotations are linked to child-centeredness, guided by concepts of interest, freedom, and self-activity, a psychology of learning by doing, and a social philosophy that stresses individual worth and cooperation over competition.

Bode remarks, the progressive school cultivates an atmosphere of activity and freedom which is all its own. In academic language, the progressive school is a place where children go, not primarily to learn, but to carry on a way of life.

According to Washburne (1952), progressive education is not easy to define, simply because it is always changing This is because it is a school, which progresses beyond the description. In other words, progressive education is continuously progressing; it is alive and growing with no fixed creed, no unchanging body of knowledge, and no specific method to be applied. Just as science and society are constantly changing, progressive education adapts to the progress of science and humanity. As our knowledge of how students learn, develop, and mature improves, so does progressive education in providing experiences that help students to develop their abilities and interests, to understand their unique role in the changing world, and to view their own well-being as inseparable from that of others.

At the suggestion of Marietta Johnson, between late 1918 and early 1919, Stanwood Cobb convened a small group of leaders carrying on experimental programs and their supports to prepare for the formation of the Association for the Advancement of Progressive Education (renamed in 1931 as Progressive Education Association). As the founder of the School of Organic Education in Fairhope (Alabama) Johnson implemented the unconventional ideas about education, which included no examinations, no homework, and no possibility of failure. Another leading pioneer in the group was Eugene Randolph Smith, first headmaster (1912–1922) at the Park School in Baltimore, Maryland, and later headmaster of the beaver Country Day School in Brookline, Massachusetts. Smith recognized that what children needed was an education that helps an individual to develop an understanding of life, and the character and the power of thinking and doing that will help him to live richly, to use his abilities wisely and fully, and to be a useful and constructive member of his community. The group, with mostly a synthesis of the ideas from Johnson and Smith, crafted seven tenets/principles of progressive education.

Freedom to Students for Natural Development: Progressives emphasise the provision of freedom to students for their natural development. Accordingly, students should manage their conduct according to the social needs of the community rather than by arbitrary rules and be provided with opportunities for initiative and self-expression in an environment rich with interesting and freely available materials.

Interest Motivates in All Works: They believe that interest of the students motivates them in all works. Therefore, students interest should be satisfied and developed through the direct and indirect experiences with the world activities, application of knowledge and integration of subjects, and consciousness of achievement.

Teacher is guide: According to progressive education the teacher should serve as guide only, not as a task master. As such they should be facilitators of small classes by encouraging student use of their senses; training students to observe and make judgements; mostly guiding students to use various sources of information, including lived experiences and books; providing support for student reasoning about acquired information; and expressing forceful conclusions reached logically.

Scientific Study of Student Development: The development of students should be studied/ analysed scientifically. According to progressive education student assessment should not be limited to grades but should include both objective and subjective reports on the physical, mental, moral, and social attention on the all-important work of student development rather than simply teaching subject matter.

Greater attention to Personality Development: According to progressive education, greater attention should be given to all that affect the whole personality development of the students. So, health of the student should be the first priority of schools by providing adequate space for movement, good light and air, clean and well-ventilated buildings, and easy access to and frequent use of adequate playgrounds and the outdoors for physical development.

Cooperation of School and Home: Progressives want the cooperation between school and home to meet the requirements of student's life. Therefore, parents and teachers should intelligently cooperate to provide as much of the natural interest and activities for practical experience, to include homemaking and healthful recreation for both boys and girls. All, if not most, student studying should be done at school, and extra-curricular studies should be at school or home to dissipate unnecessary energy. Parents should know what the school is doing and why and ways to effectively cooperate. teachers should help parents develop a broad outlook on education and provide help by making school resources available.

Progressive School is Educational Movement: Progressives belive that progressive school is a leader of educational movement, carrying new ideas useful for life. According to them, the school should be a laboratory of new ideas—which, if warranted, are encouraged – and lead movements in education, combined with the best of the past, and added to the sum of educational knowledge, rather than schools being ruled by tradition alone.

CONTENTS OF EDUCATION OR CURRICULUM

Progressive educationists oppose the traditional curriculum. They believe that such curriculum disintegrates the individual because it insists mainly on subject-matter learning. It leads to rote memorisation which prepares the students for examination from certificate or degree point of view. There is no place of thinking and creativity. Therefore, progressives like to have a curriculum consists of experiences of actual living. According to them, "Learning takes place when any part or phase of experience, once it has been lived, stays on to affect pertinently further experience. We learn what we live and in the degree that we live it. Therefore, no ready made curriculum should be given to the teacher and the pupil. However, it should include all aspects of daily living for practical, social, moral, vocational, aesthetical, physical and intellectual developments".

A progressive curriculum is based on the interests of the child. Moreover, the learning sessions should be organized around problems and questions that allow the students to explore difficult issues in theory and practice which would engage them in active learning inquiry and problem solving in the complicated life. The progressive curriculum are varied multiage approach and experiential related to life activities.

PROGRESSIVE SCHOOL

Progressive education is based on the belief that students learn best in real-life activities with other people. As such, it is different from the traditional philosophic and methods of teaching. It focuses on students and how they learn in the social environments. Progressive school classrooms create an environment for learning. The children feel at home and comfortable to learn according to their needs abilities. Therefore, the advocates of progressive education do not encourage the establishment of school into distinctly separate classes in the traditional manner. They believe that the mechanics of school organization like the division of education into pre-school, elementary, primary, secondary and higher secondary may spoil the purpose and function of the school. According to them, the school alone will not be able to develop significant whole personalities. This is because they believe that other social and voluntary organization must cooperate with the efforts of the school in educating children. So, progressive education requires the entire community should be organized so that every individual can get necessary help and guidance for achieving an integrated personality.

PROGRESSIVE TEACHER

The protagonists of progressive education have a great faith in the teacher who are the most important agency of education. Teachers make the school interesting and useful by planning leassion and provoking curiosity in the children. As a result, students can learn actively and interact one another and develop social qualities. So the teacher should be a facilitator, guide, director and philosopher in creating and conducive environment for learning. He should encourage the students to use a wide variety of activities to learn by hands on projects and discovery.

MERITS OF PROGRESSIVE EDUCATION

The concept of progressivism has modified the philosophy, meaning, aims, curriculum and methods of teaching of education. Progressive education has emerged out of the pragmatic philosophy of John Dewey. It is against to the traditional education that stresses the teacher-centred learning, rote memorization and evaluation of students by their examinations. Progressive education is important and useful which develop the 'whole' in child which prepares him/her for life.

- Progressive education enables the students to learn mostly through experiences, collaboration and play.
- It creates a conducive for learning with freedom.
- It turns the students into creative and logical thinkers in the knowledge world.
- It is child-centred education based on their abilities and interest in learning through activities.
- It is life-centred education which enables the students to solve many problems and difficulties.
- It is based on activities related to life experiences and interaction with others.
- It makes education a dynamic and comprehensive one in the ever-changing society.

- It is meant for whole personality development of the students in social, cultural, moral, physical and mental aspects.
- It develops social skills, teamwork, creativity, critical, thinking, cooperation and independence in the child.
- It prepares the child to lie in a democratic society by teaching the importance of participation in school activities and personal and social life.
- It develops a love of education and make it a life long one.

DISADVANTAGES OF PROGRESSIVE EDUCATION

Progressive educators believe that traditional schools are rigid and do not model real life, so it may be better than the traditional ones to prepare the child for personal and social, life at regional, national and international levels. However, it is not free from some demerits.

- It shift the teacher from teaching the students to watching them how they learn in the practical life.
- There is no standard way of teaching or learning a concept. Students should learn themselves.
- This type of education is not suitable for socially and economically backward children or countries.
- It is the substitute for book learning, but best book enriches the mind and strengthen the body. So, students would not gain the amount of practice of literary knowledge which is also essential for life and human relationship.
- This kind of education may be useful to the students in the long run and give them a reason to love learning in the scientific-technological oriented knowledge world.
- It is not an educational philosophy which forms a 'utopian' concept. In fact, it is an approach and pervades in all tendencies of education in recent years.

CONCLUSION

The idea of progressive education is viewed as "a pedagogical movement that emphasizes student-centred learning experiences and that incorporates aspects such as learning by doing, valuing diversity, integrated curriculum, problem-solving, critical thinking, collaborative learning, social responsibility, democracy, and life-long learning". It means different things to different people. In fact, some progressive education schools focus on learning by projects and others focus on social justice, the important common feature is the situation of learning within a social, community, or political context that some progressive educators may more broadly use to actively promote critical pedagogy and democratic education. However, it has a great impact on the educational theories and practices in the modern society. It is seen that progressive schools adopt activity-based, child-centred education according to the interest, abilities and talents of the students. As it is found as advanced educational approach, it may be implemented through out the world. Moreover, it makes education a dynamic and comprehensive on practical experiences related to life in the complicated materialistic society.

UNIT

III

Indian and Western Philosophers

CHAPTER 17

RABINDRANATH TAGORE
1861–1941

INTRODUCTION

Rabindranath Tagore, is considered as one of the makers of modern India. He is one among the contemporary Indian philosophers of education who revolted against the British system of education. His education philosophy is based on the ideas of Western thinkers like Rousseau and belief on the ancient Indian vedas. He contributed a lot of great ideas to the modification and development of the Indian education system. It cannot be denied that he has raised the status of India at the international level and has become a great son of the soil through his unique achievements in the field of literature, art and education. Therefore, his name will ever shine like a star in the galaxy of philosophers and educationalists.

LIFE OF RABINDRANATH TAGORE

Rabindranath Tagore, the founder of Vishwa Bharathi, a great poet, philosopher, dramatist, novelist, painter, actor, rishi, guru, patriot, social reformer and educator, was born on May 6, 1861, at Kolkata, in a most cultured and creative family of Brahma Samajists. He was the fourteenth and the youngest son of Maharshi Debendranath and grandson of Dwarkanath Tagore. His father Debendranath Tagore was a great leader of Brahma Samajist organization. Rabindranath Tagore received his early education at home. He was taught sanskrit, Indian philosophy and astronomy by his father. He gained higher education from the Bengal Academy but he left the academy before the completion of his course because of its dull and rigid nature of education. He recorded his own impressions regarding his early education. The masters and pundits who were charged with my education soon abandoned the thankfull task. The teachers realised that this boy could not be dragged into the ancient path of education. He was sent to St. Xavier's School, Kolkata. He did not like the prevailing system of education. Therefore, he reacted against it and developed a hatred for it. He studied a number of subjects including physiology, language, mathematics etc. through private arrangements. He was sent to England in 1877 for receiving education in law. He did not like this subject and returned to India before the completion of the course. During his stay in England, he developed his proficiency in English language and literature which made him a famous writer in the world of literature.

Rabindranath Tagore was a gifted child and at the age of eight, he composed verses in Bengali. He wrote poems, short stories, novels and plays. He was taken by his father on tours to Himalayas and also abroad (USA, USSR, Japan and England) which developed in him a faith in the brotherhood of man and spiritual unity of humanity. He was a great lover of nature and became a painter. He was awarded the Nobel Prize for literature in November 1913 for the English Version of his famous book *Gitanjali.* He was also conferred the honorary degree of Doctor of Literature by the Calcutta University in December 1913. The British Government conferred on him 'Knighthood' in 1915. As Tagore was a great patriot, he returned the Knighthood to the British government in protest against the great tragedy of Jallianwala Bagh massacre in 1919.

He established a school known as **Shantiniketan Ashram** at Bolpur, 93 miles away from Kolkata, in 1901. This school became the famous Vishwa Bharathi, an International University, on September 22, 1921. The aim of this university was to bring about a synthesis between the Eastern and the Western cultures. Tagore, the great apostle of truth, goodness, beauty, (Satyam, Sivam and Sundaram) peace and universal brotherhood passed away on August 7, 1941. On his death, the syndicate of the university of Kolkata placed on records his services to India: "Through him India has given her message to mankind, and the unique achievements in the fields of literature, philosophy, education and art have won imperishable fame for himself and have raised the status of India in the estimation of the world".

TAGORE'S PHILOSOPHY OF LIFE

Tagore was a great lover of nature. His family environment created in him a great reverence for religion and the cultural heritage of India. His extensive travels to different countries of the world and his contacts with people of different countries developed in him a faith in the brotherhood of man and the spiritual unity of humanity. These factors played a significant role in the formulation of his philosophy. We can see the philosophy of Tagore in the expression of his thoughts. He had a vision in his life which maybe considered as his *darshan* or philosophy.

Indian in spirit: Tagore was greatly influenced by the Indian philosophers, vedas, and upanishads. He studied them deeply and lived according to them. He pleaded for spiritual harmony and salvation of the soul in accordance with the doctrines of Indian philosophy.

An idealist: Tagore had never put much stress on physical or material world. He assigned a lot of emphasis to self-realisation through fulfilling the dharmas. His advice was "let us find God, let us live for the ultimate truth which emancipates us from the bondage of the dust and gives us the wealth, not of things but of inner light, not of power, but of love". Tagore believed in the existence of God who pervades in the entire universe and directs the destinies of all. In the words of Dr. S. Radhakrishnan, "The soul of ancient India is mirrored in Tagore's writings. It embodies all the ancient ideals of religion, philosophy and art".

A realist: Tagore was a realist and he wanted to revive the traditional culture of our country. He also had faith in truth, goodness and beauty which never perished. In the words of Tagore, "Our education should be in full touch with our complete life, economic, intellectual, aesthetic, social and spiritual, and our educational institutions should be in the very heart of our society".

A naturalist: Tagore was a great lover of Nature and he bestowed a very important place to Nature. He said, "Education divorced from Nature has brought untold harm to young children". Tagore, therefore, wanted human beings to have close communication with the natural surroundings. In Nature he visualised the manifestation of God.

A spiritualist: Tagore was born in a rich family of Brahma Samajists. So, he was brought up in the spiritual tradition of India. As a result, he stressed on the spiritual upliftment of man, the development of spiritual powers and divine potentialities. In the words of Tagore, "The one abiding ideal in the religious life of India has been mukti, the deliverance of man's soul from the grip of self, its communion with the Infinite Soul in the passing moment of life".

An individualist: Tagore was an individualist, believing in the rights, freedom and potentialities of the individual. To him every individual is different from another and is unique. So, he held fast to the theory that every individual should be given freedom to develop in his own way according to his natural endowments. There is an external unity between the individual and the creator. His individualism was not meant to be cut off from the rest of the society but based on the unity of mankind.

A humanist: Tagore was the prophet of humanity. He regarded the human race as one and there is reality in it. He was against untouchablility. According to him, "Reality is human and truth is human". He had implicit faith in the fundamental unity of mankind and human brotherhood.

A patriot: Tagore was a great patriot and he had a hatred for the imperialism of the British Government. He was so pained and stirred by Jallianwala Bagh massacre in 1919, that it induced him to return the knighthood to the British Government as a mark of protest. He wrote to the Viceroy of India, "The time has come when badges of honour make our shame glaring in their incongruous context of humiliation". In fact, he tried to free his motherland from political subjection for which he participated in "Swadeshi Movement" and wrote the Indian National Anthem.

An internationalist: Tagore is known as an ardent prophet of world humanity. He is considered as the champion of internationalism. According to him, "a judicious synthesis between the contributions of the East and the West will solve the world problems". He became a citizen of the world by extending the hospitality of Shantiniketan without limit and irrespective of the boundaries of politics, race and religion. His "Vishwa Bharathi" has a separate department to study the cultures of different countries. Today, Vishwa Bharathi University stands for the development of international knowledge and understanding.

Harmony with all things: Tagore believed that harmony is the basic principle of life on the earth. It is the law of the universe and the basis of man's thoughts and achievements. Tagore writes, "I cannot help believing that my Indian ancestry has left in my being the legacy of its philosophy, the philosophy which speaks of fulfillment through our harmony with all things". This harmony maybe interpreted in three ways that is harmony with nature, harmony with human surroundings and harmony in international relationships. Our life should be in harmony of all existence.

EDUCATIONAL PHILOSOPHY OF TAGORE

The educational philosophy of Rabindranath Tagore is based on his general philosophy related to life and the experience which he acquired from the prevailing educational institutions and Nature. He was dissatisfied with the existing system of education and he developed an aversion for it. He considered the then educational institutions as, "Educational factories, lifeless, colourless, disassociated from the context of the universe, within bare white walls, staring like eye balls of the dead. This is so because it ignored our own customs, traditions, conventions, manners, ideologies, morals and spirituality. It provided information and knowledge for the intellectual growth and it neglected the aspects of human growth". He further says, "Education is a permanent part of the venture of human life. Educational institution is like hospital where a treatment is administered to cure the ignorance of students and it is the place for the natural expression of their mind".

Harmony with all things: Tagore believed that the real education is that which makes one's life in harmony with all existence. Hence, the primary object of an educational institution is to bring the child in perfect tune with the symphony of response between life and world and to find the balance of their harmony. According to him, "The highest education is that which does not merely give us information but makes our life in harmony with all existence". He interpreted the harmony in three ways, that is, harmony with Nature, harmony with human surrounding and harmony in international relations. His educational philosophy is based on four fundamentals namely, naturalism, humanism, internationalism and idealism. On the basis of these philosophies, Tagore accounted the functions of education. They enable us to realise that "to live as a man is great, requiring profound philosophy for its ideals, poetry for its expression and heroism for its conduct".

Freedom: Tagore stressed on the freedom of mind, freedom of heart and freedom of will for spontaneous self-expression of emotional outbursts of feelings, impulses and instincts. He was in favour of giving maximum freedom to children so that they would be like the kite as it soars in the vast sky. According to him, "Education has its only meaning and objects in freedom— freedom from ignorance about the laws of universe and freedom from passion and prejudice in our communication with the human world". As a naturalist, Tagore advocated freedom for children and he was in favour of natural surroundings.

Creative self-expression: Tagore condemned the excessive dominance of intellectualism in education. He felt that mere intellectual development cannot bring about an all-round personality development. Therefore, education should take place through some activities and direct experiences for promoting creative self-expression. He said, "Hand work and arts are the spontaneous overflow of our deeper nature and spiritual significance". Tagore recommended the teaching of leather work, art, craft, music, drama, drawing, painting, dancing and other creative pursuits for the creative self-expression of the students.

Active communication with Nature and man: Tagore emphasised that the child should be brought up in direct contact with Nature. He insisted that education should be imparted in natural surroundings with all its beauty, colours, sounds and forms so that the child may understand Nature and its relation to human life. According to him, Nature is the manuscript of God. There is a spiritual relationship between Nature and God, Nature and man and hence man and God. Nature provides the child with satisfaction of mind and peace of soul which are essential for his spontaneous development and natural growth. Thus, his concept of naturalism stands for love and harmony with all that exists in nature. He declared, "We should have, the gift to be natural with Nature and human with human society". In fact, he wanted the child to be educated in the laps of Nature far away from towns and provided opportunities for social contacts in order to develop a sense of social service. Next to Nature, the child should be brought into touch with the stream of social contacts that is communion of man with man.

Internationalism: Tagore stood for the unity of mankind. He believed in unity in the diversity of races and nations. He translated his idea of harmonious development of the human race into Vishwa Bharathi, an international university. This university still remains the symbol of world culture, international understanding and broad humanism. According to Tagore, "Vishwa Bharathi acknowledges India's obligation to offer to others the hospitality of her best culture and India's right to accept from others their best". The main ideals of Viswa Bharathi, the fourth central university, are "to establish intimate relationship between the East and the West, to promote inter-cultural, inter- social understanding and to strive for the unification of mankind". Ours is the goal of building a greater India in which Hindu, Muslim and Christian, the dark-skinned and the white-skinned will all find their place.

BASIC EDUCATIONAL THOUGHTS OF TAGORE

- Mother tongue should be the medium of instruction by which our mind is awakened and quickened to learn as far as possible.
- The child should be given opportunities to enjoy full freedom during his education so that he may achieve his natural growth.
- The child should be provided opportunities for self-expression and creative activities.
- The child should be brought up and educated in the laps of Nature far away from the environment of towns and cities.
- The child should be provided opportunities for social contact in order to develop in him a sense of social services.
- Foreign education cannot be the basis of national education. It never awakens in us our national spirit.
- National education should be closely connected with national life.
- Indian child should get Indian education so that our children will come to know about national ideals, values and culture.
- The child should be acquainted with our philosophy and culture through national education.
- Education should bring about an all-round development of a child's personality—mentally, physically, socially, economically, morally and spiritually.
- Indian philosophy and social ideals should find a place in the curriculum by which our culture is preserved, promoted and transmitted to the succeeding generations.
- The child should be encouraged to learn from original sources because knowledge acquired from original sources is the best.
- Children should not be forced to acquire bookish knowledge which leads them to the rote method and makes them dull and dependent on their teacher for learning.
- Children should be bestowed full freedom to live in a natural environment, wherein, they can learn by doing or engaging themselves in practical activities.
- Education is a vehicle of social reform. It should prepare the child to serve humanity and develop international brotherhood.
- Education should not train children to become successful farmers, clerks or craftsman, but it should develop them to be complete human beings.
- Schools should be reformed by creating in them an atmosphere which is conducive for learning.

MEANING OF EDUCATION

Tagore described education as a "reformatory and expansive process which seeks to unfold all that is good and noble to the individual". The highest education is that which does not merely give us information but makes our life in harmony with all existence. He further says, "Education is a permanent part of the venture of life. It is not like a painful hospital treatment of curing students of the malady of their ignorance, but it is the formation of health and the natural expression of their minds". He conceived education as a dynamic, living and closely associated with life.

Education is the process of development of human personality, development for complete manhood, for enlightenment and self-realisation. Tagore defined education as, "The highest education is that which does not merely give us information but makes man's life in harmony with all existence". It enables the mind to find out the ultimate truth which emancipates us from the bondage of the dust and gives us the wealth not of things, but of inner light, not of power, but of love". He had a belief that

"The widest road leading to the solution of all our problems is education". In short education not only imparts information and knowledge to us, but also promotes love and fellow feeling between us and the living being of the world.

AIMS OF EDUCATION

Tagore was not an educationist in the academic sense. He had not written any books on education. He, however, expressed his educational ideals either directly or indirectly in his numerous writings and speeches. Let us refer to the aims of education as recommended by him.

Physical development: Tagore condemned the existing system of education which partially exercised the intellect only to the entire neglect of the body. He insisted that the first aim of education should be to develop the child physically. He also believed that a healthy mind lives in a healthy body. Hence, he gave more importance to healthful living and physical development. He prescribed various physical activities such as swimming, diving in ponds, climbing on trees, plucking flowers and fruits, and games and sports for the physical development of the child.

Moral and spiritual development: Tagore was an idealist. Therefore, he stressed inner discipline, peace, tranquility, a simple way of life and naturalness. He emphasised the power of self-determination, attainment of inner freedom, an inner power and enlightenment. He wanted children to know the importance of mutual cooperation, sociability, tolerance, courtesy, self-discipline and inner freedom to promote their moral and spiritual development. To him, man belongs to two worlds, one of which lies within and the other outside. Education should lead to the satisfaction of mind and the peace of soul.

Mental or intellectual development: Tagore equally emphasised the development of the power of thinking and the power of imagination of the mind. He condemned bookish teaching and prescribed more and more activities and experiences in natural surroundings. Education shall cultivate the power of acquiring ideas through self-effort and develop scientific knowledge and scientific outlook in the mind of the child.

Harmonious development: The aim of education is to bring about harmonious development in the child. Tagore had given great importance to sociability and human feelings. It led to the harmonious development of all human faculties. The purpose is to attain complete manhood. Tagore established a synthesis between individual development and the development of the society. He believed in an inner harmony among man, Nature and God. In the words of Tagore, "The fundamental purpose of education is not merely to enrich ourselves through the fullness of knowledge, but also to establish the bond of love and friendship between man and man".

Individual development: Tagore was an individualist and he gave importance to individual development. To him, the child is more important than all kinds of books, educational rules and teachers. So, he opposes the crushing of a child's individuality by traditional, rigid and lifeless rules. He emphasised that the child should be saved from the burden of dead books, and imposed discipline and allowed all initiative and self-experiencing for his individual development.

Social development: Tagore considered society to be an essential medium for the individual freedom and development of the child. He, therefore, gave maximum importance to community activities and social service in his educational plans. According to him social service is a bond which knitted the human beings into communities and communities into nation and so on. Thus, education brings about a synthesis between individual and society.

Development of national feelings: Tagore was a patriot and he respected Indian culture. He expressed patriotism in his poems and writings through which he made Indians gain an emotional oneness. For this purpose, education should aim at imparting to children respect and love for the healthy traditions of their motherland.

Development of international understanding: Tagore was regarded as the champion of international understanding and world peace. He stood for international knowledge, universal brotherhood and international harmony. In the words of Tagore, "Mankind must realise a unity, wider in range, deeper in sentiment, stronger in power than ever before". He established the Vishwa Bharathi University as a synthesis between the East and the West, to promote inter-cultural, inter-social understanding and to strive for the unification of mankind.

Development of tolerance: This is an important aim of education. Tagore stressed on the teaching of religious toleration to children. He wanted the children to be trained to live peacefully, amicably and cheerfully in the company of others having different faiths.

Economic development (utilitarian aim): Tagore emphasised the utilitarian aim of education. He did not want education to be cut off from the daily life of the people. It means the aim of education should be related to our economic life and wants. According to him, knowledge has two departments: one is pure knowledge, the other is utilitarian knowledge. Education should be imparted to the village folks so that they may become practically efficient in all respects for earning their livelihood. Thus, the real aim of education is to develop men and women to fulfil the needs of the country. Tagore says, "One of the main aims of education is to prepare the individual for the service of the country".

CURRICULUM

Tagore wished to develop the complete man. He criticised the existing curriculum which was purely academic and not according to the needs of the child. He advocated a comprehensive curriculum with a view to developing an individual physically, mentally, morally, socially and spiritually to the utmost limits. His curriculum consisted of subjects, activities and actual life experiences. It must be based on the problems of society and realities of life. Tagore clearly says, "Our education should be in full touch with our complete life, economic, intellectual, aesthetic, social and spiritual and our education institutions should be in the very heart of our society connected with it by the living bonds of varied cooperation". He emphasised various subjects and co-curricular activities.

Subjects: Tagore minimised bookish knowledge. He gave importance to language, literature, history, geography, nature study, science, philosophy, religion and psychology.

Activities: Tagore emphasised various activities and occupation in the curriculum in order to develop vocational efficiency in the child activities like, drawing, dancing, music, arts, excursions, painting, collection of different objects, singing, sports, games and cooking (for girls), designing, sewing, cutting, knitting and gardening.

Actual living and community service: Tagore realised the need for social development. He, therefore, emphasised community services, doing manual labour and participation in community activities in the programme of education. His view is reflected at his Shantiniketan, wherein, life is practical, full of vigour and sense of service. It makes everyone an active member of the community. Tagore suggested various subjects and activities and to put them into practice in the hope that the child after receiving such education would be in a position to discharge his responsibilities successfully as a member of the society.

METHODS OF TEACHING

Tagore totally opposed and criticised the dull and mechanical methods of teaching prevailing in his time. He also boldly condemned the bookish, and examination oriented teaching. According to him, the real life and natural surroundings should be the basis of teaching. He insisted that the mother tongue must be the medium of instruction. Tagore recommended the following methods of teaching:

Teaching while walking: Tagore believed that teaching while walking is the best method of education. Education imparted in the classroom will not influence the mind and body of the child, when he is sitting idle. He remains passive, inactive and inert. At the same time, if the teacher walks while teaching, the class will keep its mind alert, awake and grasp matters easily.

Activity method: Tagore followed the activity principles and advocated constructive and creative activities. According to him, activity should be the basis of all methods of teaching. The child is active by nature and wants to learn through different activities (climbing trees, jumping, shouting etc.) and experiences.

Heuristic method: This method is popular at Shantiniketan. Tagore was in favour of the heuristic method of teaching which makes an individual a discoverer. It is a useful method for teaching science and mathematics.

Direct experience: Education in nature is knowledge through direct experience. Bookish knowledge is second-hand. Direct experience is a very simple method of teaching. A child learns best when he is face-to-face with nature and natural surroundings such as trees, birds, mountains, rivulets, ocean, sky etc. Excursions, tours, outings and walks are the best means of educating children.

Debate and discussion method: Tagore advocated debate, discussions and question–answer methods as very effective and attractive while teaching. He suggested that the learners should be encouraged to take active part in debate and discussions. It must be based on real problems of life. Here, every topic is taught through debate and discussion methods of teaching.

DISCIPLINE

Tagore was against the principle of strict and harsh discipline followed in the prevailing system of education. According to him, "The object of education is the freedom of mind which can only be achieved through the path of freedom".

No suppression of the child: Tagore did not like the child to be suppressed by an authority. He was in favour of giving maximum freedom to the child. According to him, a child should not grow under the shadow of suppression by the teacher. He says, "The teacher is present only to stimulate and guide, but it is the child who is to choose and react according to his natural inclination".

Sympathy for the child: Tagore had a great sympathy for the child. He says, "Teachers only deserve to be teachers who are patient and tolerant". He wanted the teacher to have genuine love and sympathy for the child. Teachers should consider the children innocent and treat them with great love, affection and sympathy.

Self-discipline: Tagore was in favour of self-discipline and for this he gave emphasis to social environment, ideal teacher's love, sympathetic behaviour, organization of cultural activities and freedom to work. He believed that an individual can practice self-discipline in the social environment.

Freedom: Tagore opposed the provision of punishment for the development of the inner feeling of the child. He was of the opinion that only the freedom of will should be the aim of education, which can be achieved only by following the path of freedom. Therefore, all the efforts of the school should lead the children towards freedom.

Brahmacharya: Tagore wanted the students to follow Brahmacharya to develop discipline in them. Brahmacharya includes controlling of senses, leading a simple and natural life and being pure in all dealings. Students should clean their bodies, act as per the rules and instructions, behave in a humble manner, be lovers of beauty and have faith in the world brotherhood, cultivate an outlook for the acquisition of both worldly and spiritual knowledge, and keep away from any condemnable action.

TEACHERS

According to Tagore, "Only man can teach another man". So, he assigns a very prominent place to the teacher in the education of the child. The teacher should treat the child with great love, affection, sympathy and consideration. He must know the child thoroughly. Tagore also says, "He who has lost the child in himself is absolutely unfit for the great work of educating the children". He further says, "Only he can teach, who can love". The greatest teachers of men have been lovers of men. The real teaching is a gift. It is a sacrifice, it is not a manufactured article of routine work, and because it is a living thing, it is the fulfillment of knowledge of the teacher himself". Tagore emphasised that a teacher must have a receptive mind and a learning attitude in order to inspire others. For this, Tagore says, "A teacher can never truly teach unless he is still learning himself. A lamp can never light another lamp unless it continues to burn its own flame". Hence, a teacher is a learner first and a learner last. The teacher should provide a conducive environment for the child to engage himself in useful and constructive activities, instead of emphasising book learning. The teacher should also be busy kindling the creative capacities of children to keep them busy with constructive activities and experiences.

SCHOOL AND STUDENT

In the sight of Tagore, a school lays the seeds for the development of man. A free atmosphere is better than classroom teaching. According to him, traditional school was like a "prison house". It was more like a pigeon-hold box. The time spent had been thoroughly wasted. Therefore, a school should have a natural harmonious, free, open and simple atmosphere to provide education for the children. Education is a bi-polar process where students and teachers play their respective roles. A school becomes complete only through students. Tagore had the opinion that the child should be treated as a child and not as an adult. The subconscious mind of the child is more important than the active mind. He emphasises three important principles, that is, freedom, fullness and vastness for the education of the student.

CONTRIBUTION OF TAGORE TO EDUCATION

Tagore was an idealist, realist, naturalist and worshipper of Indian culture. He had travelled all over the world and wanted everybody to see the world through education. In this way his thoughts were very broad, and contribution to education was worthwhile.

Religious education: Tagore was against religious education imparted as a part of formal education. He believed that religious education cannot help to have an experience of the spiritual world, but, it can be gained by living in the world. In his own words, "True religiousness lies in gladly recognizing the values of man as man". To him, the service of mankind is the best service to God. He believed that serving the poor and uplifting the backward is the way to realise God. Hence, religious education should be imparted in a natural atmosphere of piety.

Mass education: Tagore felt that poverty and the ills and maladies of the country are due to lack of education. He, therefore, laid stress on the need for mass education. For this purpose, he suggested two ways—education has to be made compulsory and free up to the primary and secondary levels and secondly, arrangements to be made for adult education. These types of education should be given through the medium of mother tongue.

Rural education: Tagore assigned maximum emphasis on rural education. He wanted that there should be no difference between rural and urban areas. He used to say that service of the country should begin with reforms in villages. For this purpose, compulsory free education and adult education have to be given in rural areas.

Women education: Tagore emphasised the need for women's education. In the times of Tagore, women had been confined within the four walls of the house. They had been deprived of education during the Brahamanic period. Tagore realised the importance of women's education and prepared an outline for their educational management. He classified knowledge into two departments, that is, pure knowledge (academic) and utilitarian knowledge. He stressed that pure knowledge should be made available to both men and women equally. He was of the opinion that women should be taught home science so as to enable them to perform the roles of wives and mothers better.

Vocational education: Tagore believed that the poverty of our country can be eradicated through actions only. He, therefore, assigned more importance to vocational and industrial education. As a majority of our population lives in the village, they depend on agriculture, small scale and cottage industries. Hence, he gave maximum importance to agriculture and practical arts. At the same time he assigned an equal status to science subjects.

National and international education: Tagore was not only a nationalist but an internationalist also. He wanted to inculcate the sprit of nationalism and internationalism in students through education. He stood for the unity of mankind and international brotherhood. In order to develop nationalism and internationalism, he prepared a comprehensive curriculum. His curriculum included games and sports, social service, student self-rule, fine arts, national and international languages, literature and culture of the East and the West.

NOTE ON SHANTINIKETAN

Tagore was a great educational practitioner. In fact, he gave a practical shape to his educational ideas in the form of an educational institution which he established in 1901 at Bolpur, 93 miles north of Kolkata, far away from the hustle and bustle of the city life. He named it "Shantiniketan"—the abode of peace. It has an environment of joy and freedom, love and peace, sympathy and nobleness of spirit. In his words, "The school was a work of art and not a pedagogical laboratory. This school had all the characteristics of a garden school, 'Ashram' and 'Gurukul'. This school was functioning under the direct supervision of Tagore. Here, education is imparted in the lap of natural surroundings.

Objectives of Shantiniketan

- Develop and educate the child in the lap of Nature.
- Provide spiritual training to the students.

- Educate the children in the atmosphere of freedom and love.
- Propagate both Eastern and Western culture.
- Create a contact between the teacher and the taught like parents and children.
- Impart knowledge through mother tongue.
- Foster vocational and social efficiency in the child.
- Develop nationalism and internationalism so as to bring about unity in diversity and develop the spirit of world humanity.
- Provide a natural, harmonious, free, open and simple atmosphere in the school for spiritual, intellectual and physical development of child.
- Train up the children to have simple living and high thinking.

Characteristics of Shantiniketan

- It has all the characteristics of a garden school, 'Ashram', and 'Gurukul'.
- It is situated amidst natural surroundings with a fine display of Nature's own beauty with its varied gifts of colours, flowers, fruit, and birds combined with the joy of her mornings and the peace of her starry nights.
- It is a co-educational and residential institution.
- It is a community school meant for all children regardless of caste, creed, place, sex and colour.
- It imparts knowledge through mother tongue.
- It provides training in sewing, book-binding, weaving, and carpentry.
- It includes drawing, art and music in the curriculum as an integral part of education.
- It provides adequate opportunities for choosing their hobbies and occupations.
- It is a self-governing institution having a dairy farm, post office, hospital, workshop and court (students hold their own courts).
- There is a close personal contact between the teacher and the taught. They live like parents and children.
- It is based on the concept of freedom of the mind. The children are free from dos and don'ts.
- It has a well-furnished library.
- The school has a place for manual labour.
- As an idealist, Tagore follows the guiding principle of simple living and high thinking at his Shantiniketan.
- Classes and meetings are held in the open, under the trees or in the verandas except on rainy days.
- It provides an environment after the fashion of ancient 'tapovana'— forest school mentioned in the upanishads.
- Students receive individual attention at Shantiniketan.

Homely Atmosphere at Shantiniketan

It is a residential hermitage where teachers and students live together. They reside on the premises, eat, drink and sleep together irrespective of caste and creed. Simple and less expensive food is taken. The students perform most of their own work like drawing water from the well, keeping their room tidy, and washing their clothes. Thus, Tagore experimented his philosophy of simple living and high thinking.

Religious and Spiritual Atmosphere at Shantiniketan

Tagore wanted the emancipation of man from material bondages with the assistance of religious and spiritual education. For this, he made provision for the study of the ideas of the Hindus, the Buddhists, the Jains, the Islamic, the Sikhs, Christians and other religions of the East and the West. His primary objective in opening Shantiniketan was not teaching but living a life in God. Tagore saw spiritual nature in natural facts. So, he established his school in a natural environment which was the best means for spiritual progress.

Natural Atmosphere at Shantiniketan

Shantiniketan is a garden school where students receive education in the open air and under the shades of the trees. Thus, the whole life of the school is in outdoors. Students enjoy the flowers of the spring and the harvest of autumn, the heat and the dew, storm and rain and the quiet moonlight at night. Thus, Tagore created a *tapovana*, the forest hermitage, where the students and teachers lead a life of truth in the natural beauties of the forest.

Organization of Classes at Shantiniketan

The activities of Shantiniketan begin at 4.00 A.M. All regular classes are over by noon. Indian painting, Indian dancing, music, physical training etc. are taught in the afternoon session. Creative work in literature and art are encouraged. Good behaviour, respect for others, orderliness, modesty, cleanliness are practiced in order to develop a sense of discipline.

Daily Activities at Shantiniketan

Early morning at 4.30 A.M., a group of student singers would go around the ashram and wake up the students. After waking up, the students would clean their rooms and take up physical exercises. Then they take bath. Before sunrise, they meditate for ten minutes under the trees. After this, they take their breakfast. From 8.00 A.M. to 11.30 A.M., students are engaged in hard work. They take lunch at 12.00 noon. Then they are engaged in preparing lessons, group discussions, games and other creative activities. They devote a few minutes for meditation before sunset. After this they take dinner. At night, students are engaged in music, songs, dancing, dramatics, story telling and other artistic activities. They go to bed at about 9.30 P.M. while the choir boys sing once again. Thus, the daily activities at Shantiniketan begin with song and end with song.

VISHWA BHARATHI

Shantiniketan ashram was turned into the Vishwa Bharathi, the international university at Shantiniketan on December 22, 1921. It was made the fourth central university by the Central Government of India in 1951. The word Vishwa Bharathi is composed of two words. In Sanskrit, the word *Vishwa* means 'world' and *Bharathi* means 'Culture'. Thus, the name Vishwa Bharathi indicates a place of universal knowledge and world culture. The motto of this university or the aim of Tagore is "Yatra Viswham Bharathi Ekamidam", that is, where the whole world meets in one place. Through the Vishwa Bharathi as a whole, the poet and the seer sought to establish a relationship between the East and the West, to promote inter-cultural and inter-social amity and understanding and fulfil the highest mission of the present age—the unification of mankind.

Today, 'Vishwa Bharathi' is known not only all over the world, but it also attracts scholars from different parts of the world. Tagore has observed, "I have formed the nucleus of an International University, as one of the best means of promoting mutual understanding between the East and the West. It was intended to be 'Treasure of Light' not only for India but also for the world". He wanted to extend by degrees the scope of this university on simple lines until it comprehended the whole range of Eastern culture—the Aryans, Semitic, Mongolian and others. Its object will be to reveal the Eastern mind to the world.

Objectives of Vishwa Bharathi

Tagore had five main objectives on the basis of which he established the Vishwa Bharathi University:

1. To teach different cultures of the East, especially those that originated in India or found shelter within her shores.
2. To establish "The Institute of Rural Reconstruction" in order to lay the foundation of a happy and contented human life in the villages.
3. To establish a living relationship between the East and the West, to promote inter-cultural and inter-social amity and understanding and fulfil the highest mission of the present age—the unification of mankind.
4. To bring up our pupils in inseparable association with Nature.
5. To strengthen the fundamental conditions of world peace through the establishment of free communication of ideas between the East and the West.

Features of Vishwa Bharathi

1. The institution that bore the name of Vishwa Bharathi was founded with the call that man had to be set free not only in Nature but also in society.
2. The greatest distinction of the school is the direct and immediate emotional contact of pupils with their teachers and with external nature.
3. A speciality of the institution is that it wants to bring up the pupils in close association with Nature. The aim is to bring about an all-round development of individual personality through harmonious union of the spirit with the environment.
4. It wants to hold before the world the ideal of the universality of man.
5. The centre of culture should not only be the centre of the intellectual life of India, but the centre of her economic life as well.
6. It is one of the best means of promoting mutual understanding between the East and the West.
7. It is in a position to cooperate with the culture of Europe and synthesise all the different cultures of Asia.

Constituents of Vishwa Bharathi University

Indian Government has given recognition to Vishwa Bharathi as a full-fledged Central University. It has three departments namely, Shantiniketan school, University and Institute of Rural Reconstruction. Some other constitutents of this university are as follows:

- ***Sisu bhavan*** (nursery school).
- ***Path bhavan*** (school section—Matriculation Examination).
- ***Shiksha bhavan*** (higher secondary).
- ***Vidya bhavan*** (college of graduate and postgraduate studies and research). Here research facilities in Sanskrit, Hindi, Pali, Prakrit, Arabic, Persian, Urdu and Bengali Literature and in Indian philosophy, Buddhism, and Indian mysticism are available.
- ***Vinya bhavan*** (college of teaching). Here the teachers of the future are trained in a systematic way.
- ***Kala bhavan*** (college of fine arts and crafts). Here the students devote themselves to the learning of fine arts like painting etc.
- ***Sangeet bhavan*** (college of dance). Learning of music and dance.
- ***Siriniketan*** (department of rural reconstruction). Knowledge about the rural life is imparted in the department. The problems of the pupils are discussed here and their solutions are found.
- ***Siksha satra*** (rural high school).
- ***Silpa sadana*** (college of industrial training). Students learn about industries such as tailoring, needlework etc.
- ***Cheena bhavan*** (school of languages). It is concerned with Indian, Chinese, Tibetan studies etc. It has a big library.
- ***Hindi bhavan*** Research and Study of Hindi is carried out here.
- ***Islamic research school*** It is devoted to the Islamic research.

Life in Vishwa Bharathi University

Vishwa Bharathi is a residential university where all the students reside in the premises along with their teachers. They have to get up at five in the morning. After bath, they worship or pray. Everyone is ready for work by 6.30 a.m. in the summer. They take breakfast after two hours of work. The regular classwork is over by noon. Cultural subjects such as music, dancing, painting, physical training and games are carried out in the afternoon. All students draw water from the well, wash their clothes, and sweep their rooms. Students visit the neighbouring villages and hold night classes for the poor and the low castes. Perfect discipline is maintained everywhere to create a family atmosphere in the University.

CONCLUSION

Tagore is the greatest prophet of educational renaissance in modern India. He waged a ceaseless battle to uphold the highest educational ideas before the country, and conducted educational experiments at his own institutions, which made them living symbols of what an ideal should be. He has given the message to mankind, the message of unity of mankind, internationalism, brotherhood of man and service to humanity, illiterates, sufferers and the backward. He is a great philosopher of the twentieth century whose philosophy is the outcome of his educational experiments. Tagore has made Vishwa Bharathi a temple of Indian cultural awakening and a centre for international education from where India gives a message of humanity to the whole world. It is the living symbol of Tagore's philosophy, life and education. Tagore is not with us, but his great personality would remain present in the Vishwa Bharathi. Dr. S. Radhakrishnan says, "Tagore is a symbol of the understanding spirit of man who lifted the hearts of mankind and of height, we aspire for the new society and a new civilization".

CHAPTER 18

MAHATMA GANDHI 1869–1948

INTRODUCTION

Mohandas Karamchand Gandhi is known as **Mahatma**, a practical philosopher who wanted to establish a free and casteless society with no exploitation and racial discrimination. His contribution to educational principles and practices has a great impact on the whole humanity. This is because his educational philosophy is based on the history of his life and experiments in India and Western countries. His ideas on the concept of education have widened the meaning, nature and scope of education so as to bring about all-round personality development in the child. He has expanded the process of education by making it both religious and craft-centred, which prepares the child for spiritual as well as the material world. According to him, "Education ought to be for the children a kind of insurance against unemployment". Thus, he has changed education into a purposeful activity for spiritual, physical, intellectual and economic development. As a result modern education has certainly incorporated most of his ideas even today.

LIFE OF MAHATMA GANDHI

Mahatma Gandhi, father of the Indian Nation, the apostle of peace, truth and non-violence, great educator, leader, practical philosopher, statesman, writer and socio-political reformer of the modern India, was born on October 2, 1869 in a very respectable family at Porbandar in Kathiawar of Gujarat. His father Karamchand Gandhi was the Dewan (Chief Administrator and Chief Revenue Officer) of Rajkot and Porbandar. His mother Putli Bai was a saintly woman who had a strong influence on his life. Gandhi was slow, shy and hesitant at school. He passed his matriculation examination in 1887. Later, he pursued his higher education in Samaldas College at Bhavanagar, but he could not stay there because of the dull and monotonous environment of the college. On the advice of his best friend, he sailed for England on September 4, 1887 to study law. He was allowed to leave for England on promise that he would not touch meat, wine and women during his stay. He got an opportunity to peruse *The Holy Bible and Light of Asia*, and came into contact with Anne Besant when he was in England. He returned to India after passing the law examination in 1891 and he started his practice at Rajkot and Mumbai. But he did not succeed in his profession as a lawyer. In 1893, he got an opportunity to go to South Africa in connection with a civil law case of an Indian company. He stayed in South Africa for about twenty years and it brought about a turning point in his life. He found that the Indians were treated like animals. He completely devoted himself to the service of the people through *Satyagraha* and *Ahimsa*. He decided to adopt Brahmacharya in 1906 to serve the humanity better.

He returned to India in 1914 and started taking active part in the Indian National Congress, and organized a non-violent struggle against the British rule in India. He established the Sabarmati Ashram at Ahmedabad in 1917 for propagating Harijan upliftment, village industries, social reforms and launching of creative programmes for national upliftment. The Ashram was the centre for politics, economic reforms and spiritual upliftment. He started his Civil Disobedience Movement after the massacre of Jallianwala Bagh in Amritsar in 1919. The period from 1919 to 1947 was a period of struggle, imprisonment, sacrifice, tortures and sufferings. During this period, he organized independence struggles, strikes, and satyagrahas and started many movements to set free our nation from the hands of the British Government. He was successful in the attainment of independence for the country on August 15, 1947 by following the path of truth, non-violence and peace.

Mohandas Karamchand Gandhi was the champion of our freedom movement. He devoted his life for this mission and incessantly worked for the uplift of the million of downtrodden poverty stricken, half-naked and semi-starved masses of India. Gandhiji wanted to establish a casteless society with no exploitation and racial discrimination. However, communal riots broke out across the country after the independence of India. It engulfed the lives and properties of millions. Gandhi tried his best to pacify the people and put an end to this merciless and terrible carnage. His efforts for communal peace and harmony enraged one fundamentalist named Nathu Ram Godse who shot the apostle of peace and non-violence to death on January 30, 1948. This is the black day in the history of India. The whole world was plunged into deep and indescribable grief. Thereafter, this great soul was known as the **Mahatma** or the **Father of the Nation**.

GENERAL PHILOSOPHY OF GANDHI

Gandhi was influenced by the teachings of his mother Putli Bai, Lord Buddha, Lord Mahavir and also by the ancient Hindu philosophical monographs. He learnt the concept of Ahimsa from the Upanishads, Buddhism and Jainism. The *Bhagavad-Gita* inspired him to become a *Karma Yogi*. He also learnt self-realisation from the *Bhagavad-Gita*. Gandhi was much influenced by the teachings of Christianity and Islam. He was very much impressed by the noble and simple life of Jesus Christ. He liked one impressive sentence in the Bible, that is, "Hate the sin, and don't hate the sinner". He learnt the value of Satyagraha and non-violence from the Christian teachings. Tolstoy's, *The Kingdom of God is Within You* was another source of inspiration to Gandhiji. From Ruskin, Gandhiji learnt three basic principles: (a) The good of man is to be found in the good of all; (b) The work of barber is as good as that of a lawyer, both being the means to earn one's livelihood; and (c) The farmer, labourer or any other individual who is doing physical labour must be given due importance. He learnt from Ruskin the principle of dignity of labour. He learnt, "The concept of Civil Disobedience" from Henry David Thoreau, an American philosopher. Gandhi was a versatile philosopher cum statesman. Some of his prominent philosophical doctrines are belief in god, truth, love, ahimsa and brotherhood of man. Let us see his general philosophy of life.

Belief in god: Gandhi believed in the Almighty God. He says, "God cannot be bound in any definition. We can only experience Him but cannot see Him. To me God is Truth and Love. God is the source of light and life". According to him, "God is changeless, that holds all together, that creates, dissolves and recreates".

Truth: God for Gandhi is truth and truth is God. He used to say, "I have no God to serve but Truth". The denial of truth means the denial of God, and hence, the denial of all that is good in life. Gandhi advocated truth in all his personal and social dealings.

Ahimsa: Gandhi believes that Ahimsa is the only means to the realisation of truth and God. For Gandhi, truth and ahimsa are the two sides of the same coin. Truth and ahimsa are so intertwined that it is practically impossible to disintegrate and separate them. Gandhi says, "Ahimsa is complete absence of ill will against all that lives. In its dynamic condition, it means conscious suffering. Non-violence is its active form, good will towards all life. It is pure love". According to him, "The only certain means of knowing God is Non-violence, Ahimsa and Love."

Love: Gandhi advocates that the only true religion of man is the religion of love. He says, "To see the universal and all prevailing spirit of truth face to face, one must be able to love the nearest of creation as oneself". His love is not limited to only individual, society or nation, but he is the supporter of universal love. He adopted truth ahimsa and love as the basis of his life.

Fearlessness: Mahatma Gandhi emphasises the fact that without fearlessness, it is practically impossible to practice truth and ahimsa. A coward cannot adhere to these principles of truth and ahimsa. According to him, "Fearlessness connotes freedom from all external fear—fear of disease, bodily injury and death, or dispossession or of losing one's nearest and dearest, of losing reputation or giving offence, and so on".

Brotherhood of man: Mahatma Gandhi has deep faith in the gospel of the brotherhood of man. His motto is "Thou shalt love thy neighbour as thyself". His dream is the establishment of a universal community of free persons without radical discrimination and artificial barriers of caste, colour, creed, wealth and power.

Satyagraha: The practical application of non-violence, truth and love is Satyagraha. It is the method of securing a right by personal suffering and not inflicting injury on others. It is to achieve a change of heart by self-suffering based on truth and non-violence. In the words of Gandhi, "So, the doctrine came to mean vindication of truth, not by infliction of suffering on the opponent but on one's self".

Service to humanity: Mahatma Gandhi believes that God is the temple of humanity. He devotes his entire life in the service of humanity, because it is the only way to see him in his creation. He states, "I shall work for an India in which the poorest shall feel that it is their country, . . . an India in which all communities shall live in perfect harmony. In such a society even the women shall enjoy the same right as men".

Ram rajya: Mahatma Gandhi tries to establish Ram Rajya which he identified with justice, peace, happiness and welfare of all.

Individual as a spiritual being: Mahatma Gandhi believes in the spiritual essence of all human beings. As an idealist he says "What though we have different bodies but we have one soul. The rays of the sun are many through refraction, but they have the same source. All humanity is, therefore one. All are brothers".

Useful citizen: Mahatma Gandhi tries to create a society in which the government may guarantee freedom, justice and fraternity for all. He wants that each individual should be trained to be a useful citizen, shouldering responsibilities and fulfilling duties he owes to the society.

Economic equality: Mahatma Gandhi realised that industrialisation leads to mass production, overprofits, exploitation, accumulation of wealth, evils of capitalism, poverty of the workers, loss of personal joy of the workers and loss of skill of the craftsman. He also knew that the growing industrial society is cutting at the roots of the economic prosperity of village communities. He, therefore, despises industrialisation which makes the rich richer and the poor poorer. He is in favour of decentralisation of capital, promotion and distribution of wealth and income among the masses, absence of competition, cooperation, and encouragement of the native skill of the craftsman.

EDUCATIONAL PHILOSOPHY OF GANDHI

Gandhi has synthesised the educational philosophies of idealism, naturalism and pragmatism. His educational philosophy is the outcome of his long experience in politics, social and economic life of the country and the world. The basic principles of Gandhi's philosophy of education are summarised as follows:

- Education for each child up to 14 years of age should be free, compulsory and universal.
- All education should be imparted to the child through the medium of his mother tongue.
- English should not be given any importance in the education of a child, that is, no place for English in the curriculum.
- Mere literacy cannot be equated with education. It should develop human values in the child.
- Education should enable the child to realise the ultimate truth (God) through non-violence and purity of means.
- Education should develop all the powers of the child so as to fit him into the community of which he is an integral part.
- Education should develop the total personality of the child, that is, education should aim at achieving harmonious development of his mind, body and soul.
- Education should create vocational efficiency in the child in order to prepare him to earn his living. Hence, craft education should be emphasised in the curriculum and it should be correlated with the local industries.
- Education should create useful, responsible and dynamic citizens to fulfil the duties they owe to the society.
- Education (*Basic Education*) should purify the heart and mind of the people and create a society free from all exploitations and aggressions.
- A child should also be given gainful work experiences through practical training without which theoretical knowledge is useless.
- The school should be a place for activity and all work experiences should be given to the child so that he may gain economic self- reliance for his life.
- Education should inculcate universal moral values in the child for achieving any success in the field of education.

FEATURES OF GANDHIAN EDUCATIONAL PHILOSOPHY

Dr. M.S. Patel contests the claim of Green that Pestalozzi was the starting point of modern educational theory and practice. He says that this maybe true so far as the Western education is concerned. An impartial study of Mahatma Gandhi's educational teaching will reveal that he is the starting point of the modern educational theory and practice of the East. Gandhian philosophy of education is relevant to our country. Let us see the main features of his educational philosophy.

New concept of education: Mahatma Gandhi interprets education as the development of human personality. The scheme of education is life-centred. Thus, education is life and life is education. It really provides opportunities for the development of an all-round personality and it prepares the child for effective and successful living.

Education for new social order: Mahatma Gandhi tries to make education an instrument of social change and social reconstruction. He wants to establish a new society—a classless as well as casteless society by mass education based on the principles of truth and non-violence in personal and social life.

Education for ideal citizenship: Basic education aims at giving the citizens of the future a keen sense of personal worth, dignity and efficiency, which strengthens in them the desire for self-improvement and social services in a cooperative community.

Phychologically sound: Mahatma Gandhi's educational Philosophy is psychologically sound. The whole structure of his basic education is child-centred. In fact, child is the centre of education.

Sociologically sound: Mahatma Gandhian scheme of education inculcates 'we-feeling', cooperative activity and fosters group life and builds social qualities. It provides better understanding of social life and its problems.

Practical nature of education: Gandhi wants to impart education to the child through the medium of craft education or practical education. In the words of Gandhi, "Craft is taught not for craft's sake but for opening up avenues of creative self-expression, practical work and learning by doing".

Sound teaching methods: The techniques of correlation are sound methods of teaching. Mahatma Gandhi correlates every knowledge with craft or life. It has brought about a great revolution in Indian thinking.

Solution for unemployment: Mahatma Gandhian educational philosophy is economically sound in the sense that it emphasises craft education which leads to self-sufficiency—the crying need of today. It enables the child to earn his livelihood and helps to solve unemployment problems.

Equality in education: Mahatma Gandhi stands for free and compulsory education for all boys and girls irrespective of their caste, creed, location and economic status.

Education for national development: Mahatma Gandhi's educational philosophy aims at rural and urban development by developing vocational efficiency in the child. The upliftment of the rural people improves the economic conditions of the country.

PUBLICATIONS OF GANDHI ON EDUCATION

Gandhi is a great educator, a social reformer and a famous writer. He has published a few books on education aimed at bringing about the socio- economic development of our nation by changing the system of education.

1. An autobiography
2. All men are my brothers
3. All are equal in eye's of God
4. Towards new education
5. India of my dreams
6. My religion
7. Character and nation building
8. Prayer
9. Village industries

10. Village swaraj
11. Way to communal harmony
12. Truth is God
13. My non-violence
14. Key to health
15. Essence of Hinduism
16. Social service, work and reform
17. Ramanama
18. Satyagraha in South Africa
19. Panchayat Raj
20. Message of Gita

GANDHI'S VIEWS ON EDUCATION

The educational views of Gandhi are based on idealistic, naturalistic and pragmatic backgrounds. Gandhi viewed education as a powerful instrument of social reconstruction. He gave practical shape to his educational philosophy.

MEANING OF EDUCATION

Gandhi is of the view that education should develop the body, mind and heart. He changes the 3R's (reading, writing and arithmetic) to 3H's (hand, head and heart). Hence, the function of education is to develop the hand, head and heart. In his own words, the definition of education is "By education I mean an all-round drawing out of the best in the child and man—body, mind and spirit". According to Gandhi, "Literacy is neither the beginning nor the end of education. This is only a means through which man or woman can be educated". He wants that type of education which should develop all capacities of the child in such a way as to produce a complete human being.

AIMS OF EDUCATION

Gandhi's educational aims are more comprehensive. His aims of education have been classified into two categories namely, immediate and ultimate aims.

Immediate aims of education: This category has been further divided into the following:

Vocational aim: The most important and immediate aim of education is self- support. Gandhi wants education to help the child to become self-supporting in the later life. Education must enable every individual to earn his living and stand on hiss own feet. Mahatma Gandhi says, "You impart education and simultaneously cut at the root of unemployment".

Cultural aim: Education must make a child Indian in behaviour and attitude. Gandhi regards culture as the foundation, the primary thing and an essential part of education. He says, "This culture should show itself in smallest details of your conduct and personal behaviour; how you sit, how you walk, how you dress etc. Inner culture must be reflected in your speech, the way in which you treat visitors and guests and behave towards one another and your teachers, and elders". It should be the quality of one's soul, pervading all aspects of human behaviour.

Character aim According to Mahatma Gandhi: "The end of all knowledge should be the building up of character—personal purity". He considers it as the most important aim of education. Character building includes the cultivation of moral values such as courage, strength of mind, righteousness, self-restraint, service of humanity, truth, non-violence, Brahmacharya, non-stealing, non- taste, renunciation and fearlessness. These are more important than literacy. In the words of Gandhi, "Students have to search within and look after their personal character. Purity of personal life is an indispensable condition for building a sound education".

All-round or perfect development aim: Mahatma Gandhi wants to develop the whole man through education. All-round development—body, mind and soul are essentially needed for economic, social, spiritual and intellectual progress. He emphasises three H's to train the head, heart and hand of the child instead of the three R's, for achieving perfect development. In his magazine 'Harijan' of September 11, 1937 he writes, "The real education is that which fully develops the body, mind and soul of children". Thus, by education he means an all-round drawing out of the best in child and man— body, mind and soul.

Liberation aim: The aim of education is to liberate the body, mind and soul. Education should lead to freedom from political, economic, intellectual and spiritual slavery. The liberation of the soul from worldly pursuits is more important than other freedoms. Mahatma Gandhi remarks, "Spiritual freedom alone can initiate an individual into the higher life of the spirit".

Training leadership aim: The children of today will be the citizens of tomorrow. They should be trained in such a way as to enable them to take up leadership in political and social activities. Success of democracy depends on good leaders. The quality of leaders depends on the training which they get through education. Hence, education should produce good leaders to shoulder responsibilities in a responsible way.

Labour dignity aim: Mahatma Gandhi bestows more importance to manual work. He insists that all individuals should do some manual work, which is the aim of his basic education. No study is superior or inferior to other studies. But the students must learn the dignity of labour.

Ultimate aims of education: Some of the important aims in this category are as follows:

Self-realisation aim: Mahatma Gandhi emphasises self-restraint, self-realisation, self-insight and self-analysis. The highest aim of education is self-realisation. He says, "I had realised that the training of the spirit was a thing by itself. To develop the spirit is to build character and to enable one to work towards the knowledge of God and self-realisation". He wishes every child to grow into a divine human by realising godliness in his self.

Individual and social aim: The aim of education for Gandhi is both social and individual, that is, he lays equal emphasis on the individual and social aims of education at different times. He wants individual perfection and a new social order based on "Truth and Non-violence". We cannot think of social good without the individual and vice-versa. According to him, if the individuals are good, the society is bound to be good. In this way, Gandhi synthesises the individual and the social aims of education.

CURRICULUM

Mahatma Gandhi advocates a complete overhauling of the curriculum. He prescribes productive craft as the curriculum of instruction in order to achieve the objectives of education. In his words, "The whole process of education should be imparted through some handicraft or industry". He emphasises that education should be related to the environment of the child and the needs and aspirations of the society. In order to meet those needs and create a classless society, Gandhi frames an activity-centred curriculum.

Basic craft: A direct relationship between knowledge and life is maintained through craft education. Everything is taught to the child through the medium of crafts so that he is made to be an earning member of the society. A number of crafts such as agriculture, spinning, weaving, gardening, wood art, leather work, book binding, potteries, fisheries and home science have been recommended.

Mother tongue: Mahatma Gandhi believes that proper education can be imparted through the mother tongue. Therefore, teaching of mother tongue should be the foundation of all education. According to him mother tongue alone could acquaint the child with the social heritage, aspirations, ideas, ethical and moral values of the country. In the words of Mahatma Gandhi, "I must cling to my mother tongue as to my mother's breast, in spite of its short comings. It alone can give me the life giving milk".

Practical mathematics: Mathematics should be taught to develop the capacity of the students to solve ordinary numerical and geometrical problems. The study of practical mathematics includes arithmetic, algebra, geometry and measurements etc.

Social studies: The curriculum should find a place for social studies to inculcate the right attitude and values in the students. It includes the study of history, geography, civics, economics and current events. These subjects develop civic efficiency, a sense of nationalism and a love for international understanding.

General science: In order to promote intelligence and scientific outlook among students, general science such as botany, zoology, physiology, hygiene, chemistry and home science are taught.

Music and drawing: Music and drawing should be included in the curriculum in order to create in the students a real interest in education.

Health science: In order to develop a healthy atmosphere among the students, cleanliness, exercises, games and plays have been emphasised in the curriculum.

Hindustani: It is a combination of Hindi and Urdu. Today our national language is Hindi. For those whose mother tongue is not Hindi, it should be made a compulsory subject with a view in developing national integration.

Moral education: Moral development is one of the aims of education. It includes moral education, social service and social functions as the main and essential basis of educational development.

Flexible curriculum: Curriculum should be flexible and it should change according to the interests of the teachers and the students, and local needs. Instead of the 3 R's, the curriculum should stand for 3 H's. Hence, curriculum should be flexible and it must be in accordance with the growth of science and technology.

Methods of Teaching

The teaching method in the Gandhian scheme of education can be deduced from his *Basic Education*. He wants education to be given to the child through the medium of craft. He, therefore, emphasises learning by doing and the techniques of correlation between knowledge and craft. He says, "The brain must be educated through the hand". Thus, he always advocates the practical method of teaching.

Correlation: Mahatma Gandhi stands for the principle of correlation. He wants all knowledge to be correlated with craft. This will encourage self- activity and improve the practical efficiency of the students.

Teach through craft: Craft is the centre of the Gandhian scheme of education. Hence, everything should be taught to the child through the medium of craft. According to Gandhi, "The brain must be taught through hand". Manual training produces articles which are saleable or marketable to fetch an income. This is the self-supporting aspect of education.

Teach through mother tongue: Mahatma Gandhi insists that all education should be imparted to the students through the medium of their mother tongue. The teaching of subjects in mother tongue makes the process of education natural and meaningful.

Activity method: Mahatma Gandhi is not in favour of bookish knowledge. He believes that the child learns better through activity method than through reading printed materials. Therefore, he advocates that education should be provided through creative and productive activities.

Learning by doing: Like naturalists, Gandhi believes that learning by doing is one of the best methods of teaching by which the child grasps the subject matter quickly. Before the teaching of alphabet, art training should be provided so that the students can learn better. Learning–doing and doing–learning should go hand-in-hand.

Learning by living: All learning should take place not only by doing, but also by living and self-experiences in varying environments. Gandhi recommends manual work, play, games, and social services, in this regard.

Lecture, question and discussion methods: Mahatma Gandhi advocates the lecture method, question–answer method and discussion method to impart theoretical knowledge, particularly social studies. He emphasises these techniques in order to make the teaching process effective.

Teacher

Mahatma Gandhi is a great teacher himself. He wants the right type of teachers dedicated to their profession to teach the young. He says, "I always felt that the true textbook for the pupils is his teacher". Further he remarks, "The politician may succeed in his purpose even though he lacks character, but a pupil's teacher cannot do without character. If he lacks, he will be like salt without its savour". So, the teachers must be well trained and proficient, men of knowledge, and full of faith, character and nationalistic feelings zeal and enthusiasm. They are responsible for shaping the future of their students. Teachers should be men of action and devotion, and ready to serve the illiterate masses.

Discipline

Mahatma Gandhi's discipline is based on self-control in mind, thought and action. Self control refers to inner discipline or self-discipline. Discipline should spring from within. In the words of Gandhi, "The student's mind must not be caged. This does not mean that they are not subject to discipline. No school can be run without it. But discipline has nothing to do with artificial restraint upon students' all-round growth". Therefore, Gandhi is against the corporal punishment given for the child. He also states that if the boys and girls do not learn discipline in their school days, money and time spent on their education is a national loss. His concept of discipline is in tune with social discipline generating "we feeling" among the individuals. Mahatma Gandhi has given us the concept of "voluntary discipline" which is a synthesis of freedom and internal control. He wants the children to be prepared to accept the appropriate discipline and training.

School

School, according to Gandhi, is a place for enquiries, experiments and discoveries. It is a community centre, as well as a cradle for future citizenship. It is a place from where the individuals achieve physical, intellectual, social, cultural, moral and spiritual development. He emphasizes the view that there should be different community activities organised in the school in order to develop cooperation between the school and community.

CONTRIBUTIONS OF GANDHI TO EDUCATION

Free and compulsory education: Mahatma Gandhi wants free and compulsory primary education for all boys and girls between the ages of 7 and 14. Elementary education up to matriculation should be minus English. He advocates that the state should shoulder the responsibility of school education and finance it.

Mass education: Mahatma Gandhi regards illiteracy to be a very big curse which curbs the progress of our country. In order to deliver the country from this curse, he assigns a lot of emphasis on mass education, adult education and women education. Mass education can be achieved in two ways, that is, providing free and compulsory primary education to all children up to the age of 14 years, and providing adult education. The responsibilities of education for the illiterates rest on the society. Social leaders, social organizations and students should accomplish this great task. The curriculum of adult education should include the tasks of cleanliness, health care and intellectual, moral, vocational and social development.

Co-education: Mahatma Gandhi accepts the possibility of co-education. He believes that at the primary level and at the higher level, provisions for co-education can be made, but for adolescents, co-education is not appropriate. He has given freedom to every society to opt for co-education or decide against it depending on their environment.

Women education: Mahatma Gandhi has a firm belief that education of little boys and girls could be more effectively handled by women than by men. Since women are the best creation of God, they must be given education. He is of the opinion that the education of boys cannot be complete unless equal emphasis is laid on the provision of education for women. Gandhi says that women have the functions of a wife, mother and builder of the society. In order to discharge her responsibilities, along with the 3 R's, women must acquire education in the domestic affairs, like bringing up children, nursing, cleanliness and hygiene and knowledge of civilization and culture. Gandhi suggests that women should be kept away from music and dancing which excite sex. In his words, "My greatest hope is in women. They want a helping hand to lift them out of the hell in which they have been kept".

Religious education: Mahatma Gandhi has strong faith in God and religion. He believes that the effective means of development of a personality and character is the study of religion. In fact, religion is the way of life. He observes, "Life without religion is life without principle, life without principle is a ship without rudder, and a ship without rudder will be tossed about from place to place and never reach a destination". Hence, religious education should be imparted to the child through virtues like truth, peace, love, justice and non-violence. This is because Gandhi is not in favour of giving instructions in a particular religion. He considers all religions equal. He fears that India is a multi-religious country where religious education may give a boost to communalism. Therefore, he emphasises the general principles of all the religions and moral education in his curriculum. He believes that the service to the mankind is the true and highest religion.

Medium of instruction: Mahatma Gandhi observes that the medium of instruction should be in one's mother tongue. According to him, "All education should take place through the medium of mother tongue". He believes that mother tongue makes the process of education natural and meaningful. He is against English to be made as the medium of instruction. Referring to English medium, he remarks, "It has sapped the energy of the nation. It has shortened the lives of the pupils. It has estranged them from the masses. It has made education unnecessarily expensive". The foreign medium has made our children practically foreigners in their own land. It is the greatest tragedy of the existing system of education. As English is being the medium of instruction we have lost all our originality. He says, "To inflict English on children is to stunt their natural growth and perhaps to kill originality in them". In fact, we have become birds without wings.

Craft-centred education: Mahatma Gandhi wants to impart education through the medium of some craft, that is, all the subjects should be taught around some craft. It is education through craft. According to him, "The process of education should be imparted through some handicraft or industry". He writes, "The core of my suggestion is that handicrafts are not to be taught merely for productive work but for developing the intellect of the pupils". He insists that the brain of the child must be educated through the hand.

Self-supporting education: Mahatma Gandhi realises that the government cannot fully finance the education of the teaming millions of India. He also feels that the educational system introduced by the foreigners in India is expensive and it is a big burden for poor countries like India. Therefore, Mahatma Gandhi formulates a new scheme called Basic Education. It is not only work-centred but also self-supporting. Earn while you learn is the feature of this basic education. In the words of Mahatma Gandhi, "Our rural education ought to be made self supporting, if it is to be compulsory". Accordingly, when the child completes his school education at the age of 14 years, he should be able to earn his livelihood in the society.

National education: Mahatma Gandhi has formulated a new system of education keeping in mind the prevalent situation in India. It is his suggestion that every youth should devote one year to social service or service to the country by making craft as a centre of education. This is national education suitable for the whole country. The crafts could be changed in relation to the local needs. Thus, curriculum may differ from region-to-region.

Comprehensive education: Mahatma Gandhi visualises a very broad based concept of education. In fact, he wants to bring about an all-round personality development through education. Therefore, he emphasises the training of three H's (head, hand and heart) instead of three R's (reading, writing and arithmetic). According to him, "True education is that which draws out and stimulates the spiritual, intellectual and physical faculties of the child".

GANDHI'S BASIC EDUCATION (WARDHA SCHEME)

Gandhi realised that the British system of education was unreal and outdated. He stated, "The present system of education is not only wasteful but positively harmful. It does not meet the requirements of the country in any shape or form. English has been made the medium of education in all the highest branches of learning, and it has created a permanent bar between the highly educated few and the uneducated many". He, therefore, said, "Let us now cry a halt and concentrate on educating the child properly through manual work not as a side activity but as a prime means of intellectual activity".

Origin of Basic Education

The word 'Basic' has been derived from the word 'Base' which means the bottom or the foundation of a thing upon which the whole thing rests or is made. The education is called basic because:

1. It is based on ancient Indian Culture.
2. It lays down the minimum educational standards which every Indian child is entitled to receive without any distinction of caste or creed.
3. It is closely related to the basic needs and interests of the child.
4. It makes use of the native potentialities of the child.
5. It is intimately related to the basic occupations of the community.
6. It is for the common man of the country, who is the foundation and back bone of our national life.
7. It comes first in the primary period of our education.

The principle of non-violence is the basis of basic education. Through basic education, Mahatma Gandhi wants to develop qualities which are necessary for building a non-violent society. It is against exploitation and centralisation. He finalised the basic system of education in1937 at Wardha under the Chairmanship of Dr. Zakir Hussain. This scheme of education is known as the **Wardha Scheme** or the **Basic National Education**. The aim of basic education is to build a non-violent society.

Principles of Basic Education

- It is education for a just social order.
- It is co-education where boys and girls should be taught together.
- Education is imparted through craft and manual work.
- Work should be entrusted to each student after ascertaining his/her inclination.
- All education should be imparted to the child through the medium of his or her mother tongue.
- General knowledge should be taught to the child as soon as he is able to understand things.
- The child should be trained to draw geometrical figures before he learns to write (for good handwriting).
- The child should be trained to read before he is able to write.
- It is a self-sufficient education.
- Children should not be compelled to learn anything.
- Indian child should learn Hindustani (Hindi–Urdu) as a national language.
- Education should be related to life activities and experiences.
- Free and compulsory education for all boys and girls between the ages of seven and fourteen.
- It prepares the child for future life by providing some vocation.
- It is based on freedom for children but under discipline.
- English should find a place in the syllabus only as a language. It is a language for international communication and commerce.
- A boy or a girl of sixteen years should know sewing and cooking.
- Huge and costly buildings are not necessary for education.
- Teachers must get enough salaries to maintain themselves. They need to have big salaries. They should be animated by a spirit of service.
- The child acquires a general knowledge of world history, geography, botany, astronomy, arithmetic, geometry and algebra.

- Dignity of labour.
- It builds the correlation between the knowledge and life.
- It provides mass education and spiritual training.
- External examinations should be abolished. The day-to-day work of the students should be the determining factor.
- Textbooks should be avoided as far as possible in basic education.

Scheme of Basic Education

The working hours of a school under the scheme of basic education is 5½ hours. It could roughly be classified as shown in Table 18.1.

TABLE 18.1 Activity Scheme of Basic Education

	Minutes
Basic craft and correlated subjects	150
Physical Activities	10
Mother tongue teaching	40
Art	40
Arithmetic	20
Social Studies and General Science:	60
Recess	10

Time distribution might vary from craft-to-craft (spinning and weaving, carpentry, agriculture, fruit and vegetable gardening, leather work and any other craft), but in no case the time allotted to the basic craft should exceed the above estimation. The school should work for 288 days in a year. Each school should have attached to it a plot of land big enough for garden and a playground.

Tenets or Fundamentals of Basic Education

Free and compulsory education: Education should be free and compulsory for all boys and girls for eight years. It means education for which parents will not have to pay any fees and for which they must send their children to school. Gandhi believes that primary education is the minimum education that must be available to all. In the words of Gandhi, "I think we can postpone the question of higher education for some time; but the problem of primary education cannot be postponed even for a minute". He suggests that girls maybe withdrawn at the age of twelve if their guardians so desire. Thus, the first pre-requisite of his scheme is to extend the torch of knowledge to all.

Craft-centred education: Education in the basic system is imparted to the child through the medium of craft or industry. Gandhi writes, "The core of my suggestion is that handicrafts are not to be taught merely for productive work but for developing the intellect of the pupils". He says, "The brain of the child must be educated through his hand". According to Zakir Hussain committee, "Modern educational thought is practically unanimous in commending the idea of educating children through some suitable forms of productive work. This method is considered to be the most effective approach to the problem of providing an integral all-sided education". In the words of Zakir Hussain, "Children want to do and undo, break and mend things. This is how Nature educates them". Hence, the whole process of education should be imparted through some handicrafts.

Education through mother tongue: Mahatma Gandhi emphasises the ideas that all education should be given to the child only through his mother tongue. He believes that a good knowledge of mother tongue is necessary for developing precision of thought. According to Zakir Hussain Committee, "The proper teaching of the mother tongue is the foundation of all education. Without the capacity to speak effectively and to read and write correctly and lucidly, no one can develop precision of thought or clarity of ideas. Moreover, it is a means of introducing the child to the rich heritage of his people's ideas, emotions, and aspirations and can therefore, be made a valuable means of social education".

Self-supporting aspects of education: "Earn while you learn and learn while you earn" is another fundamental feature of basic education. The self-supporting aspect of education has a special significance in an economically backward country like India. Gandhi feels that the educational system introduced by the foreigners in India is expensive. He, therefore, introduces the basic education that aims at preparing the child to earn while he learns. Thus, at the end of the period of basic education the individual becomes self-reliant and self-supporting.

Learning by doing: This is the educational method of basic education. Gandhi believed that children acquire the knowledge of the formal school subjects through purposeful activities in basic education. Therefore, he condemns bookish knowledge, that is, 'Chalk' and 'talk' method of teaching. He always insists that the brain should be educated through the hand—learning by doing. In fact, he wants that school must be the place for "doing things".

Integrated knowledge: Basic education treats knowledge as an integrated or correlated whole. Curriculum is built around three integrally related centres, namely, physical environment, social environment and craftwork. Thus, all knowledge is integrated with related subjects and life.

Cult of non-violence: Mahatma Gandhi affirmly believes that the cult of non-violence is the panacea for all evils. So, true education must be imparted through non-violence. This is the central idea of Gandhi's scheme of education. He rightly says, "We cannot, will not think of exploitation and we have no alternative but this plan of education which is based on non-violence". According to Mahadev Desai, "The idea of self supporting education cannot be divorced from the ideological background of non-violence. Non violence is the panacea for all evils".

Relationship with life: Education should be related to life, that is, the subjects taught in the school should be correlated with the child's life. In short, education is to be directed to the needs of life. Gandhi believes that knowledge must come through concrete situations. The subject matter must be correlated with craftwork, life problems, physical and social environment of the child.

Ideal citizenship: The scheme of basic education is based on three factors namely, worker, citizen and parent. Through education we must produce good citizens rather than productive citizens and certainly not parasites. Ideal citizenship is very important for modern India to become democratic in the social, political, economic and cultural life of the country.

Ideal co-operative community: The cornerstone of basic education lies in the activities and the community life of the school. Thus, basic education aims at developing the ideas of mutual understanding and the habits of cooperative and mutually helpful living among the students through its various practical and constructive programmes. It strengthens in them the desire for self-improvement and social service in a cooperative community.

Freedom for the teacher and the taught: In basic education, the teacher gets many opportunities to make experiments, think for himself and put his ideas and plans into action. Here, discipline implies an intelligent use of freedom.

Social equality: Basic education creates a social order in which there is no unnatural division between 'haves' and 'have-nots'. Everyone is assured of the right to freedom. Free and compulsory primary education is given to all irrespective of caste, creed, sex, location and economic status.

National education: Basic education is not meant for rural areas alone. It is intended to be imparted in both rural and urban areas. It is a plan of national education for the whole country. Keeping in view the educative possibilities of a craft in relation to local needs, the curriculum may differ from region-to- region. But the basic principles of life are the same everywhere.

Syllabus for Basic Education

Basic crafts: Spinning and weaving, carpentry, agriculture, fruit and vegetable gardening, leather work, book binding, pottery and fisheries.

Mother tongue: The child should be trained to speak effectively and to read and write correctly and lucidly. The proper teaching of mother tongue is the foundation of all education without which no one can develop precision of thought or clarity of ideas.

Mathematics: It is taught to develop in the pupil the capacity to solve numerical and geometrical problems arising in connection with his craft and with his home and community life. It includes arithmetic, algebra, geometry and measurements.

Social studies: History, geography, economics, civics and other social sciences.

General science: Agriculture, zoology, biology, chemistry, physics, and home science.

Drawing: Drawing the observed material, drawing plants, animals and man. Designing, scale drawing, graphs and pictorial graphs.

Music: Teach the pupils a number of beautiful songs. The child's natural sense for rhythm should be developed by teaching him to keep his own time by beating with the hand. The best and most inspiring songs should be selected for the artistic interpretation of some healthy and elevating theme.

Hindustani: Hindustani is a compulsory subject in the school curriculum. This is the combination of Hindi and Urdu languages spoken in Hindustani- speaking areas. The study of Hindustani will be compulsory during the fifth and sixth years of school life in non-Hindustani-speaking areas.

Merits of Basic Education

Compulsory free education: This is most necessary as far as India is concerned where millions are living in poverty. At this juncture, imparting free and compulsory education to all boys and girls, between the age of seven and fourteen, eases the financial burden of the parents.

No wastage: It means that there is no failure and all pass in the scheme of basic education.

Ideal citizenship: During the course of basic education, children acquire traits of citizenship and learn to solve the problems of their future life.

Close to life: Basic education has close relationship with life. Education is directed towards the needs of life. The subjects taught and the activities or experiments done through crafts in the school are correlated with life.

Productive education: Craft is the centre of basic education. Education is imparted to the child through some handicrafts or productive activity. This type of education prepares the individual to become self-reliant and self-supporting.

Mother tongue: This is another merit of basic education by which subjects can easily be understood. A good knowledge of the mother tongue develops precision of thoughts.

Progress of Indian languages: Basic education promotes Indian languages. It is against English. It lays stress on Hindi and other regional languages through the medium of which all education can be provided to the child. It helps in the progress of Indian languages.

Child-centred education: Basic scheme of education treats the child as the centre of education. He is imparted knowledge through some activity of self-aspiration. It lays great emphasis on the individual interest of the child.

Ideals: The scheme of basic education has been arranged systematically in such a way that it fosters in the child several ideals such as, democracy, socialism, secularism, nationalism, patriotism etc.

Consonance with environment: The scheme of basic education started in the rural atmosphere, that is, in the natural environment which forms the basis of this education. As a result, education has perfect consonance with the geographical, economic and social conditions of the country.

High principles: Gandhi's basic system of education is built on the basis of high principles namely, truth and non-violence which influence and inspire the people of our country.

Trained teachers: The teachers who are trained in subjects and crafts are appointed for the benefit of the child.

Freedom: Basic education provides intellectual freedom to the teachers and the taught.

Demerits of Basic Education

Concept of basic education is not made clear: Most of our educationists, educational administrators and teachers are in a state of confusion in understanding the concepts and fundamentals of basic education. As a result of this, the government of India does not take any step to implement it and the general masses fail to grasp the significance of basic education.

Based on unsound psychological foundation: Basic education has completely ignored the development of the tender mind of the child. It forces the child to learn a craft before he is twelve. Moreover, it is cruel to make the child earn during the stage when he ought to be playing and enjoying himself.

Not accepted by the rich: The rich and learned people oppose basic education and send their children to a public school or to an English medium school.

Not suitable for urban people: This scheme of education is useful only in the villages and not good for the urban population.

No correlation between craft and education: It is impossible to establish any natural and real correlation between craft and all other subjects. In fact, all subjects cannot be taught through the medium of some basic craft. For instance, social sciences can be taught through books most effectively.

Industrialisation of education: Basic education gives great emphasis to productive activity through which the child is taught various subjects. Thus, the scheme of this education is abused. Schools could become cottage industries and the children the means of earning money.

Not accepted by muslims: The Muslim community feels that basic education is against their culture due to the ideology of 'Ahimsa'.

Faulty timetable: Basic education puts a heavy burden of work on the children of tender age. It pays more attention to craft and neglects other subjects. R.K. Singh says, "In a basic school only two third or half of the normal time is given to academic education, the rest being taken up by crafts. The timetable for academic subjects comes after the craft work. As a result, students sometimes may not find time to take up academic work seriously".

Expensive education: The scheme of basic education takes up a lot of the student's time. It increases the cost of education. So, the basic education is expensive.

Neglects higher education: Basic education is only primary education and it has not given any importance to higher education. As a result of this, secondary education and higher education suffer. Much attention has been paid to the improvement of primary education at the cost of higher education.

Neglect of the child: In a hurry to pay more attention to craft, it has neglected the child. It may arrest the child's spontaneous development.

Ignores religious education: There is no place for religious education in the curriculum prescribed for basic education.

Lack of trained teachers: Basic education requires trained teachers to impart education through the medium of some craft or industry. But most of the teachers who teach in the school are not trained for this type of education.

Absence of books: Suitable textbooks to teach in accordance with the requirements of basic education are not made available. Mahatma Gandhi is against bookish knowledge.

Artistic and aesthetic sides neglected: These aspects are neglected in some of the basic schools. Children produce very little artwork. The appreciation of beauty of art is neglected.

Matriculation minus english: Basic education is provided in mother tongue; English should not be taught to the students up to the matriculation stage. This attitude creates aversion for this education.

Lack of research: Research activities are not encouraged in the scheme of basic education.

We cannot deny that Mahatma Gandhi's Basic Education is subjected to a number of unfavourable criticisms. Though it has many shortcomings, it was implemented in several states of India during the British rule, and throughout the country after independence. But the importance given to basic education has declined due to the development of science, technology and knowledge explosion. In fact, this scheme of education is suited to the needs, genius, cultural, social, political and economic backgrounds of the Indians. It is true that this type of education prepares and develops the individual to stand on his own feet. Therefore, the government and other agencies should implement this scheme properly so that our country can achieve the desired ends in the reconstruction of a new social order and in bringing true socialism with some necessary changes and orientation. No doubt, vocationalisation of education is the means by which chronic problems such as unemployment, poverty, and illiteracy could be eradicated from the Indian society.

CONCLUSION

Mohandas Karamchand Gandhi has secured a unique place in the galaxy of the great teachers who have brought fresh light to the field of education. Among the contemporary philosophers of India, Mahatma Gandhi stands supreme as a practical philosopher. He has successfully synthesised different philosophies of education and emerged as an idealist, naturalist and pragmatist. He is regarded as a true Indian, man of God, practical philosopher and a man of masses. He stands for freedom, self-realization, spiritual development, learning by doing, education through life experiences and activities. Dr. M.S. Patel rightly remarks, "Gandhi's philosophy of education is naturalistic in its setting, idealistic in its aims and pragmatic in its methods and programme of work". An impartial study of Mahatma Gandhi's educational teaching will reveal that he is the starting point of modern educational theory and practice of the East. In fact, his system of education can be described as 'new', 'epoch making', 'original' and 'revolutionary' which brings about social, moral, spiritual and economic changes in human life.

CHAPTER 19

SWAMI VIVEKANANDA
1863–1902

INTRODUCTION

Swami Vivekananda, a practical saint of modern India, wanted to revive the ancient vedic wisdom and succeed in re-establishing the glorious traditions of great India. As he had immense faith in the dignity of man and his well being, he preached and practiced the gospels of truth, righteousness, renunciation, brotherhood of man and the realisation of God throughout his life. He was also one of the contemporary Indian philosophers who revolted against the imposition of British system of education in India. He criticised such education on the ground that it is not related to India's culture and pointed out that it brings about an external change without any profound inner force. So he emphasised the new ideas such as mass education, physical education, religious education, vocational education and women's education based on the Indian culture and the needs of the society. He is the first great personality who realised the importance of women in national development and raised his voice in favour of women's freedom and education. He is also regarded as the champion of physical education because he always emphasised such education to make man strong. As his mission was to strike a balance between the spirituality of the East and the materialism of the West, this great soul is known as a **world teacher** and a great educationist of the twentieth century.

LIFE OF SWAMI VIVEKANANDA

Swami Vivekananda, a great teacher as well as practical saint of modern India, was born in a Bengali Kshatriya family on January 12, 1863 in Kolkata. His real name was Narendranath Dutta. His father Vishwanath Dutta was a famous lawyer in Kolkata High Court. He helped the poor and the needy. Swami Vivekananda's mother Bhuvaneshwari Devi was a pious lady. The atmosphere at home was indeed religious. He inherited a religious temperament and far sighted intelligence from his parents. He was sent to school at the age of five. He studied history, literature and Indian philosophy. Herbert Spencer and J.S. Mill were his favourite philosophers and Wordsworth was his favourite poet. He passed the matriculation examination at the age of 16 and joined the Presidency College. There he studied both Indian and Western philosophies. He led a simple and pure life. He practiced brahmacharya, and always remained engrossed in prayers, worship and meditation. The principal of his college Mr. Heasty once remarked, "Narendranath Dutta is really a genius. I have travelled far and wide, but I have never yet come across a lad of his talents and possibilities even in German

Universities among philosophical students". One day Mr. Heasty introduced Narendranath to the famous spiritual leader Shri Ramakrishna Paramhamsa. Narendranath remained in close contact with Swami Ramakrishna Paramhamsa for more than six years. Shri Ramakrishna inspired him to lead the life of a monk and spread the light of India throughout the world. Three days before the death of Ramakrishna (1886), he appointed Narendranath as his successor and gave him the title 'Swami Vivekananda'. At the time of his appointment, Shri Ramakrishna said, "Today I have become penniless after giving you everything that I have. The power that I have inculcated in you through yoga would be instrumental in you performing great works. After accomplishing this task only you would go there from where you have come". After Shri Ramakrishna's death, Swami Vivekananda established Ramakrishna Mission and preached throughout his life in Asia, Europe, England and America the teachings of Ramakrishna. He set out for the Himalayas in 1890 and wandered there for 2 years. In 1892, he reached Kanniyakumari and visited the sacred shrine of the goddess. He jumped into the sea and reached a rock. He started meditation there. He then reached Chennai where the people were impressed by his personality. They collected funds to send him to America to participate in the Vishva Dharma Sammelan in September 1893. He introduced to the world Indian religion, culture and philosophy. As a consequence, the unknown monk of India suddenly leapt to fame and gained international attention at the Parliament of Religions held in Chicago in 1893. He travelled on foot and saw the naked form of India. He, therefore, wanted to establish a society of strong and self-reliant Indians. With this mission, he rendered meritorious service to the motherland. He preached the gospel of international brotherhood and left for his heavenly abode on July 4, 1902 at the age of 39.

GENERAL PHILOSOPHY OF LIFE

Great vedantist: Swami Vivekananda is a great vedantist and a true follower of Ramakrishna Paramhamsa. He believes that Vedanta is perfectly impersonal and eternal. According to him, "The Dvaita, the Vasistadvaita, and the Advaita are the different expressions of the Vedanta". In fact, these are the different methods of attaining unity with God.

God is supreme: Swami Vivekananda describes God as supreme power and omniscient. He is of infinite existence, infinite knowledge and infinite bliss. He is present in man.

God and man: Swami Vivekananda believes that man is the incarnation of God. He finds the manifestation of God in man. According to him, "Each soul is a star. Man is potentially divine". Since God is present in man, the worship of man is the true worship of God. The ultimate goal of human life is to attain wonderful unity with the creator.

Equality of all religion: Swami Vivekananda has a firm faith that all different religions of the world lead to the attainment of unity with the Creator. He thinks that every religion is progressive and has many good points. He advocates that no religion is inferior or superior to another. The goal of all religions is reaching God through spiritualism and brotherhood.

Faith in man: Swami Vivekananda has immense faith in the greatness of mankind. Man is the supreme temple of God. He says, "The only God to worship is the human soul in the human body. Of course, all animals are temples too, but man is the highest, the Taj Mahal of temples. If I cannot worship in that, no other temple will be of any advantage". He further remarks, "If you cannot see God in the human face, how can you see in the clouds or in the images made of dull, dead matter, or in mere fictitious stories of your brain? I shall call you religious from the day you begin to see God in men and women". He who loves, lives and he who is selfish, is dying.

Universalism and spiritual brotherhood of man: Swami Vivekananda believes that all men are equal and they are the creation of God. Hence, there is a spiritual brotherhood of man which makes the world a family of nations. He says, "No one can be happy until all are happy". He preaches the brotherhood of man and fatherhood of God. He asks, "If you cannot worship your brother, man, the manifestation of God, how can you worship a God who is un-manifested?".

Science and spirituality: Swami Vivekananda interprets the vedanta along the lines of a scientific analysis. He believes that both vedanta and science maintain common principles.

Goals of life: Swami Vivekananda states that material prosperity is not the reality and it is not the goal of our life. According to him, the real happiness lies neither in the body, nor in the mind, but in life without dependence, in life absolutely free from any bondage. Happiness through dependence on sense gratification is temporary and false, and is like a sugar coated bitter pill. In other words, dependence is misery and independence is absolute, joy and bliss. Thus, reality is freedom from material prosperity. The goal of life is freedom. And freedom is attained by work, worship and knowledge.

Fourfold path: Swami Vivekananda presents the fourfold path of work that is, work, worship, contemplation, and knowledge for the attainment of freedom and liberation. In his lectures on karma yoga, bhakti yoga, raja yoga and janana yoga, he makes a scientific analysis of the diverse means of attainment of the spiritual goal.

Patriotism: Swami Vivekananda himself is a true patriot. He develops a deep spirit of patriotism in every Indian. He asks all the communities to forget the points of difference, disharmony and strife, and to hear the gentle voice of the motherland. He commands them to remove all the weakness to root out priest raft and orthodoxy, and to work for the economic upliftment of the country through trade, commerce and agriculture.

Optimism and strength: Swami Vivekananda develops in his mind an undaunted strength and deep optimistic faith. He calls men "lions on the face of the earth" and exhorts them to behave like lions. He gives the call to his country men thus, "Be a hero, always say, 'I have no fear'. Tell this to everybody, 'Have no fear'. To him fear is sin, fear is hell, fear is unrighteousness, and fear is wrong life". He says, "Strength is life, weakness is death: Strength is felicity, life is eternal and immortal, weakness is constant strain and misery. Weakness is death. Let positive, strong, helpful thoughts enter into your brains from the very childhood". He remarks that a cowardly, sad and indifferent person can do nothing in his life. Only the brave can uplift the world. He therefore, asks his country men, "Stand up, be bold, be strong, . . . you are the creator of your destiny". In fact, one who is afraid of nothing will do marvelous work.

Service and sacrifice: Swami Vivekananda believes that human development is possible through service and sacrifice. He says that unless people are ready to serve their fellow beings and sacrifice their lives for the sake of others, peace and prosperity will not be achieved in the society. Hence, service and sacrifice of humanity is the prime object of life.

BASIC PRINCIPLES OF EDUCATIONAL PHILOSOPHY

Swami Vivekananda has been ranked among the greatest educationists of the world. His philosophy of education is a reflection of his general philosophy of life, which is built upon the bedrocks of vedanta. He criticises the existing system of education. In fact, he has brought about a great revolution in the fields of Indian education and touched almost all aspects of it.

- All knowledge is in the human mind. He has to uncover and develop it by his own efforts.
- The infinite library of the universe is in our minds.

- Study of books alone is not education.
- Religious education should be imparted through sweet impressions and the fine conduct of the teacher, not through books.
- Education should be imparted according to the nature of the child and his natural propensities.
- Concentration is the key to all knowledge for which the practice of Brahmacharya is necessary.
- Knowledge of Western technology and industrial education is a must for the progress of the country.
- Real education is that education which prepares a man for the struggle for survival in the world, and it is not just passing examination and getting degrees.
- Purity of thoughts, speech and deed is self-discipline, developed through meditation and concentration.
- Education should develop the child physically, mentally and spiritually.
- Education should foster spiritual faith, devotion and self-surrender in the individual through service and sacrifice.
- Boys and girls should be given the same type of education.
- Women should be imparted religious education so that they can facilitate character formation in their children.
- Education should develop character, mental power, intelligence and inculcate self-confidence together with self-reliance in the taught.
- The subjects included in the curriculum should promote the material and spiritual advancement of a child.
- Mass education should be formulated and launched with a view to eradicate illiteracy, ignorance and poverty.
- Teacher should be a friend, philosopher and guide. He should bring out the latent knowledge of the child by inspiration and motivation.
- There should be an intimate relationship between the teacher and the students.
- Human development is possible only through service and sacrifice. It is essential for achieving peace and prosperity in the society.
- Human life is a constant struggle between the strong and the weak. Every individual should prepare himself for this struggle and face all the challenges boldly and confidently with the help of education.

MEANING AND DEFINITION OF EDUCATION

Education is not the mass of information which is inserted into the minds of the children by force. In the words of Swami Vivekananda, "If education means information only, then libraries could be the greatest saints of the world and encyclopedia would become seers and rishis". It is not just passing examinations or receiving degrees. In fact, it is a life-long process which prepares a man for his struggle for existence by making him self-reliant and developing his character and intelligence.

Swami Vivekananda has defined education thus, "It is the manifestation of divine perfection already reached in man". He further observes, "The education which does not help the common mass of people to equip themselves for life, which does not bring out strength of character, a spirit of philosophy and the courage of a lion—is it worth the name? Real education is that which enables one to stand on one's own legs". These words of Swami Vivekananda give a very practical concept of education. In other words, real education is meant for character formation, and intellectual and vocational development in the child.

MAIN INGREDIENTS OF EDUCATION

Education as manifestation of perfection: Swami Vivekananda's philosophy of education reflects his general philosophy of life. In his own words, "Education is the manifestation of the divine perfection already existing in man. Knowledge is inherent in man, no knowledge comes from outside, it is all inside, what we may say a man knows, should in strict psychological language be what he discovers or unveils". Like fire in a piece of flint, knowledge exists in the mind. Man discovers it with the guidance of his teacher.

Education as self-development: Swami Vivekananda believes that education is a process of development. The child can educate himself. According to him, "you cannot teach a child any more than you can grow a plant". The plant develops its own nature. Education should help the child to grow in a proper way. He says, "Men must teach themselves. The child teaches himself. Your duty is to afford opportunities and to remove obstacles". Thus, the teacher should remove the hindrances which come in the way of self-development.

Real education: Real education is that which prepares a man for the struggle for existence. It prepares a man for social services, develops his character and finally imbues him with the spirit and courage of a lion. It is not simply passing examinations and getting some degrees. In the words of Swami Vivekananda, "We want that education by which character is formed, strength of mind is increased, the intellect is expanded and by which one can stand on one's own feet".

Education as a natural growth of the child: Swami Vivekananda thinks that each child is naturally growing and teaching himself. Nothing should be forced on the children. They should be left free to carve out their own path. Kindness and encouragement will help their growth.

Education is based on a child's need: Swami Vivekananda thinks that every soul is the soul of God. It is therefore, the responsibility of the teacher to help and serve the children and impart to them education according to their needs and tendencies. Swami Vivekananda advises the teachers to come down to the level of the students—their mental abilities and so on.

Universal education: Swami Vivekananda is a great champion of universal education. He wants education to be universalised as it is the birthright of every human being. It is a biological, social, spiritual and economic necessity. Therefore, education must be provided to all people. He says, "India lives in cottages, education must reach them". If the poor boy cannot come to education, education must go to him. In the words of Swami Vivekananda, "I consider that the great national sin is the neglect of the masses, and that is one of the causes of our downfall". He also observes "No amount of politics would be of any avail until the masses of India are once more well educated, well fed and well cared for".

Concentration of mind: Concentration is the only valid method to attain knowledge. The very essence of education is the concentration of mind and not the collection of facts. Swami Vivekananda says, "If I had to do my education once again, and had any voice in the matter, I would not study at all. I would develop the power of concentration and detachment, and then with perfect instrument. I could collect facts at will". The treasure house of knowledge can be opened only through the key of concentration. One should not measure education by the number of books one has read, but measure it in terms of concentration, which one has attained.

Brahmacharya: Brahmacharya means chastity in thoughts, words and deeds. It is the best way to attain concentration. It is essential to acquire knowledge. This will lead to concentration, which is the source of education. Swami Vivekananda believes that by observing strict brahmacharya, all learning can be mastered within a very short time.

National system of education: Swami Vivekananda advocates a national system of education based on the needs and requirements of the country. He believes that the national system of education helps to improve the condition of our people. In his "Rousing call to the Nation" he has given great importance to a system of education based on our national needs, problems, aspirations and the general role of the country in the world's perspective. On the basis of this view, he has laid the foundation for mass or universal education connected with the general upliftment of the people.

Religious education: Swami Vivekananda considers religion as the backbone of the society, the central theme of life and the inner most core of education. The gospel of the vedas and upanishads is, "Arise, awake and stop not till the goal is reached". He tries to make this gospel the guiding principle of education. The religious education imparted to the children should include the lives of great saints of all lands. No particular religion should be followed and taught while providing religious education in educational institutions. Religion must be a living experience with oneself. He says, "One must enter into heart of religion, that is, one must realize it in one's own life". All religion must be accepted and only their essential spirits should constitute the religious education to be given to children.

Women's education: Swami Vivekananda is considered as a great champion of women's education. He had seen in America and Western countries how women were highly educated and trained, worked shoulder-to-shoulder with men. But in India, they are totally neglected and controlled by men. He feels that there can be no hope of well-being of the country unless the condition of the women is improved. In the words of Swami Vivekananda, "All nations attain greatness by paying proper respect to women. That country and that nation which does not respect women, has never become great nor will ever be in future. There is no hope of rise for that country or family where women live in sadness". He remarks, "Only those nations progressed in the world that had respect for the women and gave them a chance to get education". He stresses that daughters should be brought up and educated with as much care and attention as the sons. He wants to provide a type of education that may make women fearless and brave, which may form character and enable them to face the realities of life boldly. He recommends the study of history, puranas, housekeeping and the arts for the development of an ideal character. He also cites, as example, the ideal lives of great Indian women such as Sita, Ahalya Bai, Mira Bai and Queen of Jhansi. His opinion is that the upliftment of women must come first and only then there can be any real greatness for the country. Finally, he observes, "To the women of this country I would say exactly what I say to the men. Believe in India and in our Indian faith. Be strong and hopeful and unashamed".

Mere book learning is not education: Swami Vivekananda stands against bookish knowledge and the existing system of education. According to him, true education is that which develops the will and enables the child to realise the divinity latent in him. Hence, education must include those activities which develop the infinite energy, zeal, courage and patience in man. He believes that mere bookish knowledge is not enough for achieving development in the above-stated aspects.

Secular education: Swami Vivekananda has great regard for all religions. He says, "All religion must be respected and only their essential spirits should constitute the religious education to be given to children. He speaks about the diversity of his faith: "I go to church, I go to mosque and I go to any temple". Further he remarks, "Let us take in all that has been in the past, enjoy the light of the present and open every window of the heart for all that will come in the future. Salutation to the prophets of the past, to the great ones of the present and to that comes in the future".

Physical and health education: Swami Vivekananda is greatly concerned about the proper care of the body and the healthy development of one's physique. He advises thus; "Be strong, my young friends". You will be nearer to heaven through football than through the 'Gita'. Freedom, physical freedom, mental freedom and spiritual freedom are the watchwords of the Upanishads. "Strength is goodness. Weakness is sin". He clearly says, "Make your nerve strong. What we want is muscles of iron and nerves of steel".

Vocational education: Swami Vivekananda stresses the practical aspect of life because he wants to make education self-supporting in all respects. He believes that it would be better if the people got industrial and technical education so that they might find work and earn their livelihood. Vocational education not only makes the people economically independent but also makes their nerve strong and helps them achieve economic and material prosperity. He has written, "It would be better if people are given some technical education, so that they do not wander here and there in search of a job, but engage themselves in some occupation and make both ends meet". Therefore, he gave equal importance to the study of Western technology and engineering. He believed that this was essential for the economic prosperity of India.

AIMS OF EDUCATION

Swami Vivekananda has summed up the aims of education in two words—"man making". In the words of Swami Vivekananda, "The ultimate aim of all education and all training is man making". Thus, education aims at bringing about an all-round development in an individual. He further says, "Blessed are the men and women whose minds are centered on the acquisition of knowledge, who possess sweet and amicable tempers, who cultivate truthfulness and other similar virtues, who are engaged in altruistic work as prescribed by the Vedas".

Making a man perfect: The aim of education is to make a man perfect by diagnosing the perfection which is already latent in him. It means that all material and spiritual knowledge is already present in man but it is covered with a veil of ignorance. Education of the right type should aim at removing the veil of ignorance and bring him to the best level of self-actualisation.

Creating self-confidence and self-realisation: Man should have full confidence and self-realisation in himself, and strive to reach the highest goal of his life. Education must provide self-knowledge, which brings material prosperity and freedom from the bondage of worldly existence. A man can attain perfection and achieve the glory of life through self-analysis and self- insight. Swami Vivekananda says, "Faith in our self and faith in God ... this is the secret of greatness". Education must aim at this kind of knowledge of the self and at the creation of self-confidence and self-realisation.

Physical development: Swami Vivekananda remarks that the aim of education is producing men of iron muscles and steel nerves to promote national development and produce the fearless, and physically well-developed citizens of tomorrow. He has glorified physical power. In his words, "Power is life and weakness is death". He emphasises the fact that the people must know the secrets of making the body strong, and they should also convey this knowledge to others. He believes that teaching the child football instead of the Gita makes him strong and takes him to the heaven.

Mental development: Stressing the need for the mental development of the child, Swami Vivekananda wants education to enable the child to stand on his own leg. Mental development can be achieved and promoted by the study of vedanta and modern science. He says, "We want that education by which the strength of mind is increased and the intellect is expanded by which one can stand on one's own feet".

Moral and character development: The greatness of the people of a country is measured by its moral development and character formation. So, Swami Vivekananda emphasises the practice of brahmacharya for building a strong character leading to purity in thoughts, words and deeds. He says, "We want that education by which character is formed". He stresses that what is needed by us today is men and women endowed with the quality of character. Education is not meant for information but for life building, man making, character making and assimilation of ideas. Hence, fostering moral development and formation of character in child should be the aims of our education.

Spiritual development: Without spiritual development, we cannot experience the highest power. Swami Vivekananda believes that spiritual development is possible only through social service and fostering world brotherhood feeling. Both moral and spiritual development, make the child perfect and prepare him to lead a holy life.

Spirit of renunciation: Swami Vivekananda tries to foster the spirit of renunciation in the individuals through the medium of education so that they will not become selfish and will work for the welfare of others. It is the aim of education to inculcate in man the fellow feeling. According to him, "We are all debtors to the world and the world does not owe us anything. It is a great privilege for one to be able to do something to the world". It does not mean total renunciation of the world.

Personality development: Personality is the influence or impression one creates on others. In the words of Swami Vivekananda, "Personality is two thirds and intellect and words are only one third in making the real man". The science of yoga develops the personality. It is education by which yoga should be imparted to the child for the growth and strength of personality. According to him, "The end of all education, all training should be man making".

Service to mankind: The aim of education is serving God in man. Swami Vivekananda says, "If you want to find God, serve man". He believes that it is not the God in symbols and images that we find and worship in temples. It is the God in the sick, the poor, the miserable, the ignorant and the downtrodden that we should worship. In fact, there is no other worship more important than the service of mankind and there is no religion greater than services.

Promotion of universal brotherhood: Swami Vivekananda stands for the unity of mankind and universal brotherhood. Education, therefore, must promote this feeling that the soul is the same in all humans. He says, "Through education, we should gradually reach the idea of universal brotherhood by flinging down the walls of separation and inequality. In every man, in every animal, however, weak or miserable, great or small, resides the same omnipresent and omniscient soul. The difference is not in the soul, but in manifestation". We should live with love by considering all the living beings of the world as members of one family like we give cooperation to one another in a small family and like an individual sacrifices his own interests for the interests of the others during emergency.

Vocational aim or practical side of life: Swami Vivekananda wants everyone to stand on his own legs by developing the capacity to earn his own bread and salt and lead a comfortable life. It is education, which should prepare the children for this life. He considers that a system of education is worthless which ignores the practical aspects of life. Therefore, he suggests the establishment of workshops and practical arts to solve the problems of hunger and unemployment in our country. Once he remarked, "The education remains or may not remain—there is nothing to gain or lose from it. It would be better if people are given some technical education, so that they do not wander here and there in search of a job, but engage themselves in some occupation and make both ends meet". For that he recommends the study of agriculture and technical subjects.

Development of nationalism and internationalism: Swami Vivekananda is not only a great patriot and a nationalist but also a great internationalist. He stands for the harmony and good relationship of all nations. According to him, one of the aims of education is the development of national feelings and internationalism. He says, "I am thoroughly convinced that no individual or nation can live by holding itself apart from the community of others". Education therefore should inculcate in the child the feeling that "Every Indian is my brother. Indians are my supreme soul. The gods and goddess of Indian are my God. Indian society is a swing of my childhood, flower garden of youth and crutches of old age".

Preparation of bold citizens: The aim of education is the preparation of bold citizens by strengthening the body and mind. Swami Vivekananda realises that fear is the main cause for all social and individual problems. It is education which should remove this fear and make the citizens bold and brave to face the challenges of life.

Scientific and technological progress: Swami Vivekananda believes that material, technological and scientific progress are essential to prepare the child for survival in this world. He advocates teachings of Western science and technology for the prosperity and fulfillment of the basic necessities of human life.

Development of unity in diversity: The true aim of education is to develop a oneness of feeling between the material and the spiritual worlds. If there is any distinction, it is because of the illusion. Education must remove this illusion and develop an insight in the people so that they can realise unity in diversity.

CURRICULUM

Though Swami Vivekananda has not prescribed any typical curriculum to be followed in teaching, he has advocated only those subjects and activities, which foster material welfare along with spiritual development.

Study of vedanta: Swami Vivekananda emphasises the study of vedanta, religion, upanishad and philosophy in the curriculum in order to bring about spiritual development in the child.

Study of common and regional language: Swami Vivekananda is in favour of a common language for the unity and integrity of the country. He is of the opinion that all education must be provided in the regional languages or mother tongue of the child.

Study of Sanskrit: Swami Vivekananda recommends the study of Sanskrit in order to preserve and transmit our cultural heritage and past greatness. He considers Sanskrit as the source of all Indian languages.

Study of arts: Swami Vivekananda includes arts in education . He believes that art is an essential part of human life.

Study of social sciences: Swami Vivekananda advocates the study of history, economics, geography, psychology, home science and political science, in order to achieve material progress.

Study of physical exercises: Swami Vivekananda stands for that education which makes human body strong with iron muscles and steel nerves. According to him, "power is life and weakness is death". He, therefore, stresses the study of social sciences with games, sports and physical exercises (yoga) for physical development.

Study of vocational subjects: Swami Vivekananda is in favour of the study of vocational subjects such as agriculture, industrial and technical subjects in order to develop vocational efficiency in the child so that he could become economically self-sufficient.

METHODS OF TEACHING

Swami Vivekananda is in favour of the ancient Indian system of educational organization based on the criteria of learning by sitting at the feet of the *acharya*, *guru* or the teacher. There is a close contact between guru (teacher) and his disciples (students) for better discipline of mind and body. He recommends the following methods of instruction:

Practice of yoga: Yoga should be practiced to control the fleeting mental faculties and emotions.

Observing meditation: Observing deep meditation and concentration is the source for the development of mind.

Brahmacharya: Brahmacharya is necessary for developing the power of concentration. Swami Vivekananda believes that all learning can be mastered within a very short time by observing strict brahmacharya. It is the source of all education.

Lecture and discussion: Swami Vivekananda recommends this method of teaching to teach science, social science, vedanta and philosophy.

Guidance and counselling: This method of instruction is emphasised to lead the child in the right path. Individual guidance by the teacher is essential and helpful to remove doubts which the child has about any subject.

Self-learning: Swami Vivekananda observes that a child educates itself. The teacher spoils everything by thinking that he is teaching. All knowledge is within man and it requires only an awakening, and that alone is the work of the teacher. The child may learn to apply his intellects for the proper use of his hands, legs, eyes, ears. The teacher should act as a guide and helper.

Travel: Swami Vivekananda recommends travel as a method of teaching. He suggests that pupils and teacher should undertake travelling in order to gain knowledge from the world outside. This method enables us to share our vedanta, upanishad and philosophy with the people of other countries.

PLACE OF TEACHER

Provider of suitable environment: Swami Vivekananda emphasises the fact that education should be child-centred. Like a plant, a child grows by his own inner power naturally. Hence, the function of the teacher is to remove obstacle in the way of the self-development of the child and help him in making the potential actual. The main duty of the teacher is to provide a suitable environment for the all-round development of the child.

Teaching like worshipping: Like Rousseau and Froebel, Swami Vivekananda believes in the freedom of the child in the field of learning. The teacher should allow freedom and teach the students in a proper manner. It means that the teacher should consider teaching a sacred duty.

A true teacher: Swami Vivekananda states that the true teacher is one who can immediately come down to the level of the student, and transfer his soul to the student's soul and see through and understand his mind. Only such a teacher can really teach and no one else.

Teacher as a guide: The teacher is a friend, philosopher and guide of the student. He is a tyagi imparting knowledge to the child.

Quality of the teacher: Swami Vivekananda lays stress on the personal life and character of the teacher. According to him, the personal life of the teacher is more important than the knowledge he possesses so that he can impart in the child all good things. Only a dedicated and selfless person can be a good teacher. He must have love and sympathy for his children. He should be pure in speech and deeds.

PLACE OF CHILD

The child is the centre in the process of education. Each child is the storehouse of all knowledge, because he is getting such gifts from nature. Therefore, he should be encouraged to discover his inner knowledge. In the words of Swami Vivekananda, "The child is the greatest book that ever was or will be. Until the inner teacher opens all outside teaching is in vain".

DISCIPLINE

Swami Vivekananda emphasises child-centred education in which the child is provided full freedom for activity and self-learning. The child is bestowed with full opportunities and suitable environment to develop himself naturally. Each child is his own teacher having latent knowledge in his mind. The task of the teacher is only to help, guide and inspire the child in order to bring out the inner knowledge of his pupils.

CONTRIBUTIONS OF SWAMI VIVEKANANDA TO EDUCATION

Spirit of humanism: Swami Vivekananda interprets vedantic philosophy to mean that the worship of God is service to mankind. He wants education to lead us to the goal of realising God through love of humanity, self-sacrifice and work for the upliftment of mankind.

Free and compulsory mass education: Swami Vivekananda is a great champion of free and compulsory mass education. He stresses the ideas that education should be universalised and it must be provided to cottages because India lives in them. He remarks that neglecting mass education is a great national sin and it is one of the causes of our downfall.

National system of education: Swami Vivekananda is in favour of a national system of education based on the needs and requirements of the country. A national system of education should include a study of India's philosophy, culture, arts, religion, history and languages. The scheme of studies should be built around it.

Women's education: Swami Vivekananda feels that there can be no hope for the well-being of the country unless the condition of the women is improved. He desired proper education and training for all women who in turn should be prepared to work for the economic, social and educational reforms of the country. They should become leaders and be placed in higher positions in order to function effectively in society.

Insist on Western science and technology: He emphasises the teaching of modern science and technology for prosperity and progress and to meet all the basic necessities of life.

Character development education: He lays stress on character development education. He believes that the greatness of the people of a country is measured by their character. He says, "We want that education by which character is formed".

Attack on castism and untouchability: Swami Vivekananda points out that all men are equal as they are created by God. The spiritual brotherhood of man makes the whole world into a family. Hence, there would be no place for casteism and untouchability among the people.

Liberal outlook in education: He recommends a unique and outward look in education through learning English, Western science and technology, travel to other countries, organizational methods, commerce and religious studies.

Ramakrishna Mission: The greatest contribution of Swami Vivekananda in the educational and social sphere is the establishment of Ramakrishna Mission in 1899. The Ramakrishna Mission has opened many centres all over India in order to preach the teachings of Ramakrishna and render social services for the welfare of our nation.

Vedanta society: Swami Vivekananda established the vedanta society in San Francisco for spreading the message of vedanta and Indian culture and philosophy within and outside India.

NOTES ON MAN-MAKING EDUCATION

Swami Vivekananda saw the 'Divine' in the poor whom he called **Daridra Narayan**. His vision denotes the direction of 'Man-making' education, that is, it is education, which should foster a spirit of services. It means the poor and the needy should be helped to uplift themselves. In the words of Swami Vivekananda, "The end of all education, all training should be man-making". In short man-making education underscores the great importance of the famous words—Help, Assimilation, Harmony and Peace. Education should develop these qualities in man in order to bring about character development and vocational development.

Elements of Man-making Education

The chief elements of Swami Vivekananda's man-making education are based on the vedantic philosophy of his life. The concept of man-making education is a very comprehensive concept built up with the following chief elements, on the basis of which our educational system should be directed and shaped:

1. Every individual should understand that the ultimate goal of human life is to attain "Unity with the creator".
2. Service to man is equated with devotion to God because God resides in every human heart. Hence, man should foster the spirit of service to his fellow beings.
3. Man should develop an attitude of respect for all religions. He should understand that the essential elements of all religions are the same, and no religion is superior or inferior to other religion.
4. Man should imbibe love for all and hatred for none, because love is the highest good of all religions.
5. Man should attain the knowledge of science and spirituality.
6. Man must develop a rational attitude in life.

Aim of Man-making Education

Character development: Man-making education implies that education should build character. Education is an instrument for human betterment. The basis of all systems social or political, rests upon the goodness of man. No nation is great or good because its parliament enacts this or that, but because, its men are great and good. That is why, Swami Vivekananda stresses on character formation in the man-making process. Further, he wants to strengthen the mind and expand the intellect of the child through education. This is because he believes that character, strong mind and sharp intellect prepare the child for better life. He further says, "If you really want to judge the character of man, look not at his great performances watch a man do his most common actions. Those are indeed the things which will tell you about the real character of other great men". Therefore, character development is the first aim of man making.

Develop the spirit of social service in man: The second aim of man-making education is providing education for the development of the spirit of social service in man. Swami Vivekananda's wide travels in India have given him first-hand knowledge of the socio-economic conditions of the people of our country. He is deeply distressed by the utter poverty and backwardness of the people. He remarks, "So, long as the millions live in hunger and ignorance, I hold every man a traitor who, having been educated at their expense, pays not the least heed to them . . . I call him a 'Mahatma' who feels for the poor. Let these people be your God—think of them, work for them". Thus, the most important aim of man-making education is inculcating the spirit of selfless service in man.

Mental development: The third aim of man-making education is developing a strong mind. Mental development is very essential to enable the child to stand on his own leg.

Rational development: The rational development of man enables him to believe in the unity of all religions. Such rational attitude in man is very important to develop a noble character in him, which is the purpose of man-making education.

Curriculum on Man-making Education

Swami Vivekananda recommends that for man making, the curriculum should synthesise the knowledge and wisdom of the East and the West. He bestows great importance on the physical development of the individual for which purpose he includes physical education as an integral part of the curriculum.

Methods of Instruction in Man-making Education

Swami Vivekananda believes that a child educates itself. The task of the teacher is only awakening the latent knowledge, which is in the child. The teacher has to guide the child to apply his intellects for the proper use of his hands, legs, ears, eyes and nose. Swami Vivekananda advocates those methods of instruction which develop the reasoning power of the child. He has suggested the following methods of instruction for man making:

- The child educates himself and all knowledge is within him. So, a teacher has to help the child to apply his intellects for the proper utilisation of his organs and senses.
- The method of teaching should be modified according to the needs and interests of the taught.
- Positive suggestions encourage learning. Negative thoughts weaken them. Therefore, positive suggestions should be provided in the instruction in order to make the learning process more effective.
- Concentration is the best method of learning and it is the key to the treasure-house of knowledge. The essence of education is the concentration of mind, not the collecting of facts.
- The method of observing brahmacharya is essential for developing the concentration of mind. It can be achieved and developed through purity in thoughts, speeches and actions.
- The learner or the taught must have great power of endurance.
- The learner should be able to control the internal and external senses.

- The learner should have faith in himself. It enables him to imbibe knowledge effectively.
- The pupil should inculcate the attitude of respecting the 'guru' or the teacher.
- Travel broadens our horizon and enables us to share our culture, philosophy, vedanta and knowledge with others.
- Purity in thoughts, speech and action is absolutely necessary in the taught and in the teacher to make teaching learning process more effective and meaningful for the development of the child.
- Frank and open discussion on all topics of study between the teacher and the taught should be fostered for learning and intellectual development.

Role of Teacher in Man-making Education

Swami Vivekananda says, "Education is a personal contact with the teacher". There would be no education without the personal life of a teacher. It is the personality of man that really impresses us and not merely his words. The words and thoughts contribute only one-third and the personality is two- thirds in the making of the real man. For man making, the teacher should come down to the level of the students and transfer his soul to the student's soul. The teacher should be a friend, philosopher, guide and a *tyagi* for creating a real man. Swami Vivekananda wants the teacher to provide the proper environment for the child to grow naturally.

Women's Education in Man-making

Swami Vivekananda believes that there is no scope for the progress of a family or a country where the women are not educated and are leading a pitiable life. He also believed that the countries and the nations which do not respect women have never become great, nor will ever be in future. He, therefore, advocates women's education and attaches great importance to all types of education and training which may uplift women's lives. He wants to give them such education as will make them fearless and help them acquire the spirit of valour and heroism to face the realities of life bravely. In order to foster the above qualities in women, Swami Vivekananda recommends various subjects and activities, such as history, housekeeping, arts, sewing, upbringing of children, household duties, worship, meditation and the puranas.

Mass Education in Man-making

For man making, Swami Vivekananda insists that education must reach every home. He says, "If the poor boy cannot come to education, education must go to him". He observes, "No amount of politics would be of any avail until the masses in India are once more well-educated, well-fed, and well-cared for". "If we want to regenerate India, we must work for them through free and compulsory mass education".

Physical Education in Man-making

In man-making process, Swami Vivekananda emphasises physical education. According to him, "Strength is goodness, weakness is sin. Power is life and weakness is death". According to him, people must know the secrets of making the body strong and they should also convey this knowledge to others. He very emphatically declares, "You will be nearer to Heaven through football rather than through the Bhagavad-Gita".

Vocational Education in Man-making

Swami Vivekananda includes vocational education in man-making education. He wants that education which would develop vocational self-sufficiency in man. He says, "It would be better if the people got technical education so that they might find work and earn their livelihood". Swami Vivekananda recommends the study of Western science and technology to increase the vocational efficiency which is essential for man-making.

Religious Education in Man-making

For man making, Swami Vivekananda assigns great importance to religious education. He says that without spiritual development we cannot experience the highest power. So, everything that is good in all religions must be studied. All religions teach us the love of God which lead us to a holy life.

Health Education in Man-making

Swami Vivekananda includes health education in man-making education for the betterment of human life. He is not satisfied with an education that merely looked into the development of the mind. He pays greater attention to the proper and healthy development of human body. He always advises the young people to be strong and produce healthy youngsters to build a powerful nation. In order to fulfil the dream of man making, Swami Vivekananda, asks every educated young man to go from village-to-village and make the people understand their real condition, rouse them from misery and advise them how to improve themselves and their lives. Man-making education develops such individuals who are ethically sound, intellectually sharp, physically strong, religiously liberal, socially efficient, spiritually enlightened and vocationally self-sufficient. Swami Vivekananda founded the Ramakrishna Mission which is engaged in the task of man-making through its multifarious activities. It has opened several educational institutions, libraries, reading rooms, hospitals and dispensaries for man making. Hundreds of selfless workers of the mission are working for the upliftment of the masses.

CONCLUSION

Swami Vivekananda is a great educationist and he occupies a very prominent place among the Indian thinkers. He calls for that education which is man making and nation building. He stresses on free and compulsory mass education and women's education. He stands for a national system of education and is against casteism and untouchability. He is in favour of secularism, socialism and democracy. On the basis of these three pillars, a country is developed through the medium of education. He became a teacher of love; of the love of God flowing into the service of man; of faith flowing into works and both for giving character which is manliness and manliness which is spirituality. In the words of Jawaharlal Nehru, "Rooted in the past and full of pride in India's prestige, Swami Vivekananda was yet modern in his approach to life's problems and was a kind of bridge between the past of India and her present. His mission was the service of mankind through social service, mass education, religious revival and social awakening through education". It is seen from his writings, speeches and actions that he has suggested a relevant and meaningful system of education based on the needs of modern India.

CHAPTER 20

SRI AUROBINDO GHOSH 1872–1950

INTRODUCTION

Sri Aurobindo Ghosh, occupies a very important position among the contemporary Indian philosophers of education due to his wide knowledge of East and West, ancient and modern system of education. He has presented an integral philosophy of education through his 'ashram' at Pondicherry. Here, experiments are conducted to evolve a new system of education which maybe adopted for the reconstruction of Indian education. He considers the fulfilment of *swadharma* as the law of life and wants that every individual in a nation should fulfil his *swadharma*. Hence, the purpose of education is to prepare the individual to serve their nation and humanity. His education philosophy in the field of modern educaton is very important.

LIFE OF SRI AUROBINDO GHOSH

Sri Aurobindo Ghosh, a famous sage, poet, patriot, philosopher and an educationist, is known by the name Aurobindo, was born on August 15, 1872 in Kolkata. The word 'Aurobindo' means 'Lotus' in sanskrit. His father Dr. Krishan Dhan Ghosh loved the Western culture and he wanted his son to grow up into a fake Englishman. So, Aurobindo was sent to England at the age of seven and he lived there for 14 years. He got education in London and Cambridge, and he became a master in English, Greek and Latin. He passed the Indian Civil Service Examination in 1890 but he could not appear for the horse-riding test. As a result, he was disqualified for the job and he returned to India in 1893.

Aurobindo studied sanskrit language and literature in India and served as an adviser and sometimes as secretary to the Maharaja for fourteen years in the princely state of Baroda. He became a professor of English at Baroda College. He learnt Bengali, Gujarati and Marathi, and delve deeply in the culture and philosophy of India. He practiced yoga in 1904. As per the instruction of the Indian National Congress, he became the principal of Bengal National College (now Jadavpur University) at Kolkata. After the Bengal Partition (1905), Aurobindo resigned from his job and became an active freedom fighter. He launched the journals *Vande Matram, Karma Yogi, Dharm* and the Bengali daily *Yugantar* to propagate his revolutionary ideas and arouse intense feelings of nationalism among the people of India. His political and nationalistic sentiments were expressed through his writings and fiery speeches. The British Government arrested Aurobindo and put him in Alipore Jail for a year in connection with the Alipore Bomb Case in 1908. When he was in jail, he spent most of his time in yoga, meditation and the study of the Gita, philosophy and spiritual literature.

Once he was in Alipore jail, he realised the presence of God in a dream. After his release from the prison, he shunned all his political activities immediately and returned to Pondicherry for penance and spiritual advancement. He spent his retired life at his ashram in Pondicherry. He became a yogi and devoted his time to yoga and meditation. He preached his philosophy of dharma, education, spiritual advancement and brahmacharya across the country. He had set up an international ashram and International Centre of Education at Pondicherry and started several educational and social activities. He established Auroville as a city of universal culture for international cooperation and human unity. Aurobindo propounded his major philosophy and published it in *Arya* a new journal in English from 1914 to 1921. Aurobindo, the great saint, passed away on December 5, 1950. His demise put an end to a glorious chapter in the spiritual history of India.

AUROBINDO'S GENERAL PHILOSOPHY OF LIFE

Sri Aurobindo's philosophy of life is based on an experienced integralism. It is a synthesis of idealism, realism, naturalism and pragmatism. His life began with psychic experiences connected with his political, philosophical and poetic life. The general philosophical ideas of Aurobindo are found mostly in his weekly newspaper "karma yoga".

Corner stone of Indian thought: Jnana (knowledge), Bhakti (devotion) and Karma (work ethics) are the three cornerstones upon which the Indian philosophy of life has been built. Those who resort to Jnana, Bhakti and Karma can walk on the divine path. Aurobindo stood against the exclusive emphasis on them. He did not want to deprive the individual of the variety of life. He believed any such emphasis resulted in the lopsided development of a personality. He felt that there should be a combination of India's genius consisting of spirituality, creativeness and intellectuality. Spirituality is indeed the master key of the Indian mind, the sense of the infinite is native to it. The first age of India's greatness was a spiritual age when she sought passionately for the truth of existence through the intuitive mind and through an inner experience and interpretation of both the psychic and the physical existence. Aurobindo had a great faith in the creativeness of India. "For three thousand years at least... India has been creating abundantly, incessantly and lavishly with an inexhaustible many sidedness republics and kingdoms and empires; philosophies and cosmogonies and sciences; creeds, arts and poems ... systems of yoga, arts spiritual, arts worldly, ... the list is endless and in each item there is about a plethora of activity". The third pillar of India's genius is its strong intellectuality. In the words of Aurobindo, "the greatness of Indian culture depends on its strong intellectuality. It is at once austere and rich, robust and minute, powerful and delicate, massive in principle and curious in detail.

Integral approach to Indian thought: Aurobindo wanted to discover integration in Indian thoughts. He also wanted to see life as a whole. As he wanted to strike a balance between the multicoloured shades of life, he turned to the Gita. He says that there is a fellowship between God and man. The fellowship with God can be achieved by disinterested action (Nishkan Karma) in society, never-ending meditation, self-forgetting devotion and feeling a kind of unity of all things in God.

Synthesis and understanding: The basic principle of Aurobindo's philosophy of life is the synthesis and understanding of life and the universe. He believed that the Gita preserves a proper balance in the world of knowledge, devotion and work. In the words of Aurobindo, "He in whom all three meet and become one entirety". He is the supreme being, the "Purushothama". Swami Sivananda says, "Aurobindo is the consummate expression of the Indian spirit of synthesis".

Unity of truth: Aurobindo arrived at the concept of the basic unity of truth by synthesising the views in Indian thoughts. He observes, "First of all, there is undoubtedly a truth, one and eternal, which we are seeking, from which all other truth derives, by the light of which all other Truth finds its rightful place in the total scheme of knowledge".

Supermind: This is the keyword of Aurobindo's philosophy. He believes that the mind of man is imperfect and is not in a position to understand the integral truth. Only the supermind can have an understanding of the integral truth. Aurobindo remarks, "Man will become a super mind. Super mind will have a super mental consciousness. Consciousness of Sat-Chit-Anand: Truth, Self, Bliss : Truth, Beauty, Goodness".

Superman: Man becomes a superman when he attains a supermind. He surrenders himself completely to the will of God and becomes a superman. Aurobindo aimed at the integral man. The superman is the integral Man, the ideal man who makes an ideal society.

Purna Yoga: Aurobindo thought that there is a wide gulf between the ordinary mind and the super mind. He tried to integrate them into a single whole through purna yoga (Figure 20.1). He believed that purna yoga helps man to realise the supreme, the Purushothama. According to him, "All life is "Yoga". In the words of Aurobindo "The very first lesson in this yoga is to face life and its trials with a quiet mind, a firm courage and an entire reliance on the Divine Shakti". According to Aurobindo, "An unconditional surrender to God is the first step of Yoga". In fact, Aurobindo's yoga aims at the creation of divinity in the whole man. The education of the mind is stressed in order to achieve the aim of yoga.

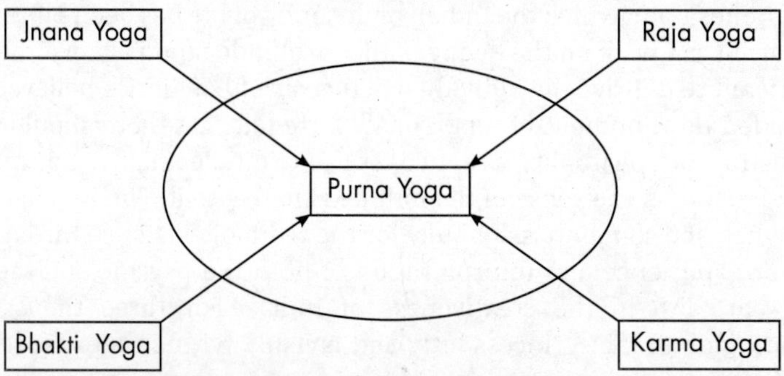

FIGURE 20.1 Types of yoga.

Life: Aurobindo was of the opinion that life is universal and it is imperishable. According to him, "Life is a form of cosmic energy, a dynamic movement or current of it, positive or negative, a constant act or play of the force which builds up forms, energises them by an unceasing process of disintegration and renewal of their substances".

Rebirth: Aurobindo had a deep faith in the philosophy of rebirth. According to him, birth and death are a predetermined process in the scheme of evolution. In the words of Aurobindo, "All the secrets of circumstances of rebirth center around the capital need of the soul, the need of growth, the need of experience, that governs the line of its evolution and all the rest is accessory".

Law of karma: Aurobindo believed that man is the maker of his own fate. But the heredity and environment are determined by the present and past actions of man. He found continuity between different births. In this way he believed the doctrine of karma. However, karma does not determine the fate of soul.

Evolution of man: Aurobindo was of the opinion that the individual is in the continuous process of evolution to attain the union of the individual soul with the supreme soul. According to him, "Life is not for life alone, but for God. There is an inner law and meaning for all things depending on the supreme". This is the inner law, which guides, regulates and controls the universe, and propels it into action.

Experienced integration: Aurobindo's philosophy is the result of his concept of "experienced integration". It is an integral approach to solve various problems of human life. It is a synthesis of the idealism, realism, naturalism and pragmatism of the East and the West and of the old and the new.

Spiritualism: Aurobindo was a spiritualist. He regretted the neglect of spiritual elements, which is responsible for the decay of human societies. He says, "The radical defect of all civilization has been the neglect of the spiritual elements".

AUROBINDO'S PHILOSOPHY OF EDUCATION

Aurobindo Ghosh is a true yogi, a great philosopher and an eminent educationist. He starts his life as a political thinker but very soon he becomes a spiritual integralist. He shows mankind the way to the highest spiritual growth. His philosophy of education directly emerges from his philosophy of life based on spiritual penance, practice of yoga and brahmacharya. He believes that any education, which involves all the three factors, will definitely develop man to the fullest extent. The journey of his life is a unique experience in harmonising the two important ends of existence, that is, spirit and matter. He tries to translate these ideals into a system of education through his Pondicherry ashram school now grown into Auroville—a city of universal culture. According to Aurobindo, real education is that which provides a free and creative, environment to the child by developing his interests, creativity, mental, moral and aesthetic senses. Finally, they lead to the development of his spiritual powers.

Study of mind: The true basis of education is the study of mind. Any system of education that ignores the study of mind hampers the intellectual growth. Therefore, the study of human mind is basic to education. The human mind consists of four layers, namely, chitta, manas, buddhi, and intuition. Chitta is the store house of memory. This passive memory is automatic and needs no training. The active memory requires training and improvement. Manas or the power of mind is the second layer of the mind. It is regarded as the sixth sense. Intellect or buddhi is the third layer of mind and works at the higher level. There are two kinds of intellect that is right hand mind and left hand mind. Right hand mind judges, images, memories, observe commands and manipulates. Left hand mind is the source of analytical faculties—distinguish, compare, classify, generalise, deduce, infer and conclude. Intuition is the fourth layer of mind having a "direct vision of knowledge". "It brings to man those brilliant messages from the unknown, which are the beginning of his higher knowledge". Therefore, an ideal teacher should try to develop this intuitive power in the people.

Focal points: Aurobindo considers the man, the nation or people and the universal humanity as the three focal points. True education should take them into account.

Development of spirit: Aurobindo advocates the national system of education on a spiritual basis. True education will be "an instrument for this real spirit in the mind and body of the individual and the nation".

Development of real man: The important business of education is to bring out the real man. Therefore, education should aim at the development of all the faculties of the child to make him a real man. It can be done by promoting the powers of observation, memory, reasoning, etc.

Education according to child's nature: Aurobindo believes that education must be provided to the child according to his mental aptitudes and psychological needs. He wants and advocates child-centred education.

Freedom for child: Aurobindo wants education to be child-centred. He, therefore, advocates perfect liberty for the child. This is because he believes that the child can acquire the best knowledge if his mind is trained in a free atmosphere without any hindrance. He also advises that hard things should not be brought into the child's experience.

Development of consciousness: Education should foster consciousness in the students by bringing out or developing the latent powers of the child.

Brahmacharya: Aurobindo lays great stress on brahmacharya. In fact, he wants brahmacharya to be the main foundation of education.

Physical purification: Aurobindo bestows great importance on moral education for physical purification. He wants the child to habituate himself to the right emotions, the noblest associations, the best mental, emotional and physical habits through moral education. The teacher should impart the moral training to the students by his personal example, daily conversation and extensive reading of good books.

Religious education: Aurobindo is of the opinion that without religious overtones in education there will be corruption and anarchy in the country. He believes that the essence of religious education is to prepare the student to live for God, for humanity, for country, for others and for himself.

Training of senses: Like Western philosophers Rousseau, Pestolazzi and Froebel, Aurobindo believes that the senses are the gateways of knowledge. So, the senses of the child should be trained in a proper manner. Such training helps the child to grasp the soul of education.

Subjects of education: Aurobindo is in favour of child-centred education. Therefore, he recommends those subjects which are of interest to the students and are related to their lives.

Emphasis on mother tongue: Aurobindo wants mother tongue as the medium of all instruction. He believes that the child could learn better if the education is imparted to him through the medium of his mother tongue.

BASIC PRINCIPLES OF AUROBINDO'S EDUCATION

- Education should be child-centred.
- There should be perfect liberty for the child.
- Education should be related to the life of the child.
- Education should be according to the mental aptitudes and psychological needs of the child.
- Education should be imparted through the medium of mother tongue.
- Education should bring out the latent powers of the child.
- Education should help to achieve the physical purification of the child.
- Education should develop consciousness.
- Education should train the senses of the child.
- The basic foundation of education should be brahmacharya.
- Education should develop the soul substance of an individual.
- Education should develop all faculties of the child in order to make him a complete man.
- Religious education should be a part of education to prevent corruption in the country.

MEANING OF EDUCATION

Aurobindo Ghosh comes out against the educational system of his time. He believes that education should be according to the mental and spiritual needs of the children and the demands of the country. It means that education should lie in accordance with the changing and growing needs of our real as well as modern life. Thus, education should create dynamic citizens so that they may be able to face the present challenges and meet the needs of the modern complex life with ease. In the words of Sri Aurobindo, "Education to be true must not be a machine made fabric but a true building or living evocation of the powers of the mind and spirit of human being". According to Aurobindo, "Education is helping the growing soul to draw out that is in itself". In other words, education should bring out the latent powers of child to make him a complete man. N.C. Dowsett has summerised Sri Aurobindo Ghosh's philosophy of education thus, "the meaning of the word education is to bring forth the inner, hidden, latent, dormant, potential secret within every human being, secret because, it is not of senses but of the inner truth of being and because it is that most unknown pan of the being which has yet to evolve to its full stature".

AIMS OF EDUCATION

Acquire knowledge: The aim of education is helping the child to acquire knowledge. According to Aurobindo, knowledge should be the latest and related to the different fields such as literature, culture, science, politics etc.

Physical purity: Physical purity and development of the child is the main aim of education. This is because it is the body which should perform all religious obligations. Aurobindo insists that without physical purity and development, spiritual development is not possible. In fact, physical purity and development are the two bases upon which the edifice of spiritual development is built.

Training of senses: The aim of education is to train all the senses namely, hearing, speaking, listening, touching, smelling and tasting. As senses are the important sources of knowledge, they should be trained properly so that nerve, chitta and manas become pure. Education is the only process through which the senses of the child can be trained to the fullest extent in order to acquire more knowledge.

Develop logical faculty: Aurobindo believes that logical faculty plays a very significant role in the education of the child. He has mentioned three steps for the training and development of the logical faculty, that is, drawing inferences, making success and failures and causes of success and failures. The first step of logical faculty involves the encouragement of the child to draw inferences from the facts and enable him to trace the causes and effects, which lead to the drawing of inferences. The second step of logical faculty is to enable the child to mark success and failures. This enables him to draw inferences in a logical manner. The third step is to enable the child to notice the causes of success and failure of a particular experiment.

Mental development: Mental development means the development of all mental faculties such as memory, thinking, reasoning, imagination, discrimination, special relationship and generalisation. The aim of education is to develop these faculties harmoniously.

Development of morality: Moral and emotional development are the essentials needed for the child to foster the right attitude in him. In the absence of these developments, mental development will become harmful to human progress. Aurobindo, therefore, emphasises the fact that the hearts of children should be trained and developed through education to show extreme love, sympathy and consideration for all living beings. The teachers should be a role model for the child to develop morality.

Development of conscience: Aurobindo has remarked four levels of conscience—chitta, manas, intelligence and intuition. The duty of the teacher is to help the child in the development of all these levels of conscience harmoniously.

Spiritual development: Aurobindo believes that every human being has some element of divinity in him. The teacher should bring it out, then nourish it through yoga exercises and brahmacharya. According to Aurobindo, "The chief aim of education should be to help the growing soul to draw out that in itself which is best and make it perfect for a noble use".

Self-realisation: Aurobindo believes firmly that self-realisation should be the aim of education. In fact, self-realisation enables the individual to realise his real being. Therefore, this is the ultimate meaning of life on the earth.

Development of potentialities: Aurobindo believes that every child has some latent physical, mental and spiritual potentialities. Hence, he considers the development of such hidden potentialities as one of the aims of education. Here, the task of the teacher is to draw out these potentialities in a harmonious way and turn the child into a complete man or real man, i.e., superman.

CURRICULUM

Aurobindo suggests all those subjects and activities, which the students are interested in. The subjects and activities included in the curriculum should possess creativity and educational expression. Thus, the curriculum is constructed in such a way as to develop the inner potential of the child and turn him into a super human being. Aurobindo has prescribed the following five principles of curriculum construction.

1. Curriculum should be interesting for the child.
2. Curriculum should include all subjects and activities which promote mental and spiritual development of the child.
3. The subjects of a curriculum should be able to motivate the child to learn.
4. Curriculum should activate the creative potentialities of the child in order to develop him into a real man.
5. Curriculum should motivate the children towards the attainment of up-to-date knowledge of the whole world.

On the basis of these above principles, Aurobindo includes the different subjects and activities in the curriculum for the different stages of education and types of education for the proper growth of the learners.

Primary stage: Mother tongue, English, French, Literature, National History, Art, Painting, General Science, Social Studies and Arithmetic.

Secondary stage: Mother tongue, English, French, Arithmetic, Art, Physics, Chemistry, Biology, Physiology, Health Education and Social Studies.

University stage: Indian and Western Philosophies, History of Civilization, English Literature, French Literature, Sociology, Psychology, History of Science, Physics, Chemistry, Zoology, Botany, International Relations and Integration.

Vocational education: Arts, Paintings, Photography, Sewing, Sculptural drawings, Typing, Shorthand, Cottage Industries, Carpentry, Mechanical and Electrical Engineering, Nursing, Indian and European Music, Dramatisation and Dancing.

Physical education: Physical training, games, gymnastics, preventive medical care and health education.

Mental education: It is meant for the development of the powers of the child's mind. It includes the study of Language, Mathematics, Social Science and Applied Sciences.

Psychic and spiritual education: Spiritual and psychic values such as love, truth, faith in God, strength of mind and heart are stressed .

International education: Universal love, sympathy, fellow feeling and international understanding are the main features of this education.

Moral education: The pupils should be guided to cultivate: (a) Right emotions; (b) noble habits; (c) right associations; and (d) right actions to develop morality among them. Moral training should be supplemented by the application of Raja Yoga. This type of training purifies the mind and the body.

Vital education: It includes various activities such as student participation in music, fine art, dance, drama, craft and ballet.

METHODS OF TEACHING

Freedom to child: Freedom to the child enables him to acquire more and more knowledge by his own efforts. Any restriction imposed on the child will retard his natural growth and development. So, the teacher should act only as a helper and guide and stimulator for the natural development of the child.

Love and sympathy for the child: The teacher should treat the child with utmost love, sympathy and kind consideration. This will reduce the tension felt in learning and promote the natural development of the child.

Mother tongue: Education through mother tongue enables the child to grasp and understand even the most difficult subjects. Hence, the medium of instruction should be in mother tongue.

Child-centred education: Education should always be child centred. The teacher should study the varied interests of his pupils before he provides education to them. This will encourage and motivate the learners to acquire more and more knowledge.

Self-experience: Self-learning experiences should be provided to the child. This type of learning is very useful for his future life.

Learning by doing: Aurobindo believes that learning by doing is the best method of learning. This method places great emphasis on the activities of the pupils. Here, the bookish knowledge is supplemented by experimentation.

Group learning or co-operative learning: The teaching–learning process is a cooperative process. Therefore, there must be a learning based on the cooperative activities of teacher and children.

Nature of child: Naturally each child has been gifted with some mental and spiritual potentialities. Education should develop these gifts in the child by developing his inner capacity.

Education according to 3 A's: The mind of the child is a great vehicle for acquiring knowledge. So, the mind has to be consulted in his growth. According to Aurobindo, education should be provided to the child according to three A's namely, age, ability and aptitude. For this purpose, the teacher should adopt the methods of teaching according to the age and nature of the child. He should know the ability and aptitude of his students before he imparts education to them. Aurobindo emphasises this aim of education because every child has something divine in him. It is education which should discover and develop the divine qualities in the child.

Lead child from near to far: The child should be educated from the known to the unknown and from what he is to what he shall be. It is to work from the near to the far. All new knowledge must be built around the child's daily experiences directly connected with his environment—local as well as national. The past is our foundation, the present is our material and the future will be our aim and summit. Thus, the past, present and future should go hand-in- hand towards the progress of the individual.

PLACE OF TEACHER

The teacher occupies a very important role in the process of education. He is an embodiment of self-control, humility, spiritual equality between man and man. In the words of Aurobindo, "Teacher is a man helping his brothers, a child leading children, a light kindling other lights, an awakened soul awakening other souls, at the highest a power of presence of the divine calling to him other powers of the divine". He also remarks, "One must be a saint and a hero to be a good teacher. One must become a great 'yogi' to be a good teacher". According to Aurobindo, "The teacher is not an instructor or task master; he is a helper and guide. His business is to suggest and not to impose. He does not actually train the pupil's mind, he only shows him how to perfect his instruments of knowledge and helps him and encourages him in the process. He does not impart knowledge to him. He shows him how to acquire knowledge for himself. He does not call forth the knowledge that is within. He only shows him where it lies and how it can be habituated to rise to the surface".

The teacher is not only an instructor but a helper and a guide for the pupils. He should not impose anything on the learners. He should stimulate the child in order to develop him naturally. The role of the teacher will always be appreciated if he can prepare the child to serve the suffering humanity and eradicate the evils, which are obstructing the progress of society and humanity.

PLACE OF CHILD

According to Aurobindo, nature has bestowed different human beings with different capacities and powers. Therefore, education should develop in the child whatever has already been endowed to him by God. In this regard, he says, "The child is a soul to find them, to find himself, to grow into their maturity, into a fullness of physical and vital energy and utmost breadth, death and height of his emotional, his intellectual and his spiritual being". Thus, each human being is self-developing. But the parents and the teachers should help him achieve the fullest development. He believes that the child has his own inherent capacities and special abilities. So, he has assigned a special place to the child in the teaching–learning process. Hence, education should satisfy the needs and interests of the child. This will enable the child to develop his personality fully according to his powers. Aurobindo observes, "The idea of hammering the child into the shape desired by the parents or teacher is a barbarous and ignorant superstition. There can be no great error than for the parents to arrange before hand that his son shall develop particular qualities and capacities. To force the nature to abandon its own *Dharm* is to do permanent harm, mutilate its growth and deface its perfection".

DISCIPLINE

Aurobindo is in favour of full freedom for the child to express himself and act without any restriction imposed on him. The teacher should not interfere in the self-experience of his pupils. Aurobindo believes that the child has his own interests and potentialities. So, the purpose of education is to develop these divine gifts fully and turn the child into a superman. For this purpose, the child should be provided full freedom. The freedom of the child enables him to develop his latent capacities and helps him to acquire more knowledge.

CONTRIBUTIONS OF AUROBINDO TO EDUCATION

National system of education: Aurobindo saw that the people of India were moving away from spiritualism to materialism. Consequently, the inherent divine light in them was decreasing. So, he felt that Indians need such education which develops the power of our mind based on Indian culture. The national system of education should have right relation with life, need and soul of our nation. In fact, national system of education is the way to achieve national integrity and preserve and promote our culture and tradition.

Child centred-education: Though Aurobindo was an idealist, he favoured child-centred education. According to him, education should be based on the mental aptitudes and psychological needs of the child. In short, education should develop his personality according to his innate powers. This view is accepted and practiced by all educators of the east and west.

Moral education: Aurobindo believed that physical development of the child leads to corruption and dishonest life. So he gave importance to the study of moral education. According to him, "The wildness and recklessness of many youngsters are only the over-flowing of an excessive strength, greatness and nobility. They should be purified, not discouraged". Today, most of the educational institutions include moral education as an integral part of general education.

Religious education: Aurobindo was an idealist in nature. So, he gave more importance to the spiritual development of the child. Religious education enables the child to achieve such development. According to him, "To live for God, for humanity, for country, for others, for oneself in these". Hence, religious education should be imparted not through preaching but by practice of religious life. In fact, religious education has become an impart of school instruction.

Physical education: Aurobindo realised the importance of physical education and believed that such education aimed at the perfection of the body, its health, strength and fitness. According to him, "If our seeking is for a total perfection of the being, the physical part of it cannot be left aside, for the body is the material basis, the body is the instrument which have to use". Thus, he gave more importance to the physical development of the child. The same idea is insisted in all educational institutions.

Education of yoga: Aurobindo believed that taking up yoga will to lead man to perfection. So, education without yoga is insufficient. It means a complete education needs the help of yoga. According to him, "Yoga is life, which bridges the gap between ordinary man and superman". It strengthens the power of mind. Thus, the study of yoga becomes an integral part of life and finds an important place in the present education.

Education of mind: Aurobindo believed that man's mind is imperfect and it is not in a position to understand the integral truth. Hence, it requires the development of intellect through increasing concentration on attention. He regarded the steady and long practice as the way to the development of the power of double and triple of multiple concentration. As the mind of the child is the great vehicle of acquiring knowledge, it should be consulted in his growth. According to him, "The first thing the teacher has to do is to accustom the pupil to concentrate attention". This enables the child to observe, compare, remember and judge various class of objects. Today the development of mind has been emphasised through brahmacharya, meditation and yoga.

Education of senses: Like naturalists, Aurobindo believed that the child gathers knowledge and experiences for his mental development through his senses of sight, hearing, touch, smell, taste and understanding. So the training of senses should be the most important type of early education of the child. In fact, he stressed on the training of six senses—eyes, ears, nose, mouth, skin and mind. It is accepted that senses are gateways of knowledge and importance is given to the development of senses.

Medium of instruction: Like other Indian philosophers, Aurobindo felt that education should be imparted to the child through the medium of his mother tongue. According to him, "Other languages can be mastered only after getting a sound knowledge in one's mother tongue. The mastery of mother tongue enables the educand to understand the literature, history of his country and the life around him". This is particularly by true about the early education of the child.

Freedom of the child: Though Aurobindo was an idealist, he advocated the freedom of child. He gave a special place to the child in the teaching–learning process. He wanted that the child should be treated with love, affection and sympathy. Such freedom enables the child to achieve the fullest personality development according to his talents and capacities. Freedom of the child is recognised and implemented in educational practices.

International education: The main features of Aurobindo's education are universal, love, sympathy, fellow feeling and international understanding. He put these ideas into practice in his World University Centre at Pondicherry, where men and women of all countries can live together in peace and harmony above all creeds, politics and nationalities. For this purpose, he included the study of International Relations and Integration in the curricular prescribed for University Education. Such studies have become important in fostering internationalism.

Comprehensive curriculum: Aurobindo is a distinguished philosopher and educationists who prescribed a number of different subjects and activities in the curriculum according to the age, abilities and needs of the child. In fact he prescribed varied curriculum according to primary, secondary, higher secondary and university stages of education with a view to prepare the child for life. The present educationist also formulates and follows different curriculum on the basis of development of the child.

Methods of teaching: Like Naturalists, Aurobindo introduced new methods in the teaching–learning process. He stressed on the cooperative activities of the teacher and the taught. Teacher from the known to the unknown from the near to the far or from that which is to that what shall be and teach according to the three A's (age, ability and aptitude) were his notable teaching techniques that have been implemented by the modern educators.

Importance to teacher: Teacher occupied a very important role in Aurobindo's integral education. He should be an embodiment of self-control, humility, and spiritual equality between man and man. According to him, "Teacher should be a saint and a hero to be good teacher". Teacher should be a friend, philosopher and guide of the child. These concepts are accepted by the educators of the world.

Education through practical experiences: Aurobindo introduced different science subjects and activities in order to educate the child through practical experiences. He believed that education through practical experience develops the powers of imagination, creativity and the nature of enquiry in the child. Such experiences enable the child to solve the problems of life. Thus, education given through practical experiences is very effective and interesting, and it has a unique importance in teaching technical, vocational and science subjects.

NOTES ON AUROBINDO'S INTEGRAL EDUCATION

Meaning of Integral Education

Integral education is that education in which the human body, mind and intellect are combined together to form a magnificent machine. We can call it a machine for want of a better word and it is superior to any other equipment built by man. According to Aurobindo, "Integral education is that which helps to bring out full advantage, makes ready for the full purpose of life and scope of all that is in the individual man, which at the same time helps him to enter into his right relation with life, mind and soul of the people to which he belongs and with the great total life, mind and soul of humanity of which he himself is a unit and his people or nation, a separate and inseparable member". He is a great supporter of the national system of education and he realises that this is the source of national reconstruction. This view is contained in his system of integral education. In this way, integral education should have the following four chief points:

Chief Points of Integral Education

Education must integrate the human body, mind and soul to serve its real purpose.

Strengthening body and mind: Integral education should strengthen the physical and mental aspects through the study of science and technology. Education through science and technology makes the material basis stronger, complete and more effective for the manifestation of the spirit.

Five principal aspects of integral education: Aurobindo's idea of integral education is the idea of complete education. He says that education to be complete must have five principal aspects relating to the five principal activities of human being—the physical, the vital, the mental, the psychic and the spiritual.

Four major aspects of truth: Integral education should have four major aspects of truth, namely, love, knowledge, power and beauty. In the words of Aurobindo, "The truth we seek is made of four major aspects: love, knowledge, power and beauty. These four attributes of truth will spontaneously express themselves in our being. The psyche will be the vehicle of true and pure love, the mind that of infallible knowledge and the body will be the expression of a perfect beauty and a perfect harmony".

The vehicles of love, knowledge, power and beauty: Integral education of Aurobindo spells four vehicles for the four aspects of Truth.

Education of physical being (tapasya of beauty): Physical education is an important component of integral education. The physical body will be the expression of a perfect beauty and a perfect harmony. Hence, education should be directed towards the realisation of four important goals, namely,

1. To discipline and control the physical functions.
2. Harmonious development of the body and physical movements.
3. Rectification of defects and overcoming physical limitations.
4. To awaken the body consciousness.

One has to undertake physical exercises to achieve the first three goals, and to achieve the fourth goal one has to draw upon multiple faculties. The spiritual discipline, service, bhakti, yoga, games and sports, asanas and pranayama are considered to be the most important tools to control the restlessness of the body and to achieve concentration. Physical education is also essential for controlling the sex drives.

Education of vital being (tapasya of power): Education of the vital being is an important part of the concept of integral education. Vital education lays emphasis on the observation of impulses, energies and desires of the vital being of man. As a result, the pupils get an opportunity to understand both the inner world and the world outside. The second aspect of the vital being is the utilisation of the sense organs which helps an individual to receive knowledge. Therefore, senses like, sight, hearing, smell, touch, taste and mind should be trained. To get a training to be an aesthetic personality, one should give up bad habits and develop human habits, emotions and their associations. Aurobindo advises that training of the senses should be the first care of the teacher.

Education of mental being (tapasya of knowledge): Since the human mind is the vehicle of infallible knowledge, education must build its power to make it an excellent medium of knowledge. The mind has to be made silent and attentive in order to receive knowledge and manifest it. By yoga one acquires mastery of the mind and reaches a region higher than the mind, which we call knowledge. This helps in the gradual liberation from ignorance. Mental education has three fold functions: (i) to gather old knowledge; (ii) to discover new knowledge; and (iii) to develop the capacity to use and apply the knowledge acquired. The pupil develops cognition, ideas, intelligence and mental perceptions through the application of his knowledge. As we have already mentioned, the mind has four levels—chitta, manas, buddhi and intuition.

Education of psychic being (tapasya of love): Psychic being is the psychological centre of man. It is the vehicle of true and pure love. The function of education is to enable man to become conscious of this psychological centre which is the key to an integral personality. Love is made of desirable feelings and emotions, directed towards whole-hearted clarity and goodwill towards others and communion with the Divine. Psychic education enables an individual to see his soul and helps him to grow in freedom according to its inner nature. It supports the vital, the physical and the mental being so that an individual understands life and himself.

Two-fold Bases of Integrated Education

Aurobindo has mentioned two bases for integrated education:

- Individuality is one whole
- Humanity is one.

Individuality is one Whole: This can be divided into the following categories:

Harmonious development: The individuality of man constitutes body, mind and soul which have their significances when they are harmoniously developed. An individual's intellectual development must be developed in relation to his moral, emotional and spiritual nature and vice-versa. A balanced and harmonious development of all the aspects of human personality—cognitive (knowledge), conative (skills) and affective (attitudes and values) moulds an individual into an integrated individual.

Socio-economic-political integration: Education should aim at developing the individual as an economic, political and social being, in order to train him as a productive and disciplined member of the society.

Different aspects of 'self' but self is one: We may distinguish in man the different aspects of his being, mental, intellectual, ethical, practical, aesthetic, physical and the like. But all these have been as powers of a "self" that manifests through them and yet they are not all the 'self'.

No concentration on academic perfection alone: The study of the mind is essential to understand the innate power of the child. Any system of education which concentrates on academic perfection of the child, disregarding his mind, hampers intellectual growth. Hence, concentration on academic perfection of the child and the study of his mind are necessary to produce an integrated mind.

Humanity is one: Aurobindo immerses himself in vedanta and yoga. He developed synthesis between the East and the West instead of finding conflict between them. He also synthesises 'Spirit' and 'Matter', 'Science' and 'Vedanta' in order to see the oneness of humanity.

Objectives of Integral Education

Aurobindo's integral education has the following objectives:

Recovery of old spiritual knowledge: Integral education should aim at the recovery of the old spiritual knowledge experienced in all its splendour, depth and fullness.

New forms of philosophy and literature: The second objective of Aurobindo's integral education is to let the spiritual knowledge flow into new forms of philosophy, literature, art, science etc.

Synthesis of a spiritualised society: The aim of integral education is to strive for a great synthesis of a spiritualised society. According to Aurobindo, the existing problems must be dealt within the light of the Indian spirit.

Stages of Integral Education

There are five stages in the integral education related to the principal activities of the human beings. The five stages of integral education succeed each other in a chronological order for the growth of the individual (Figure 20.2). But the five stages must continue, complementing each other, till the end of life.

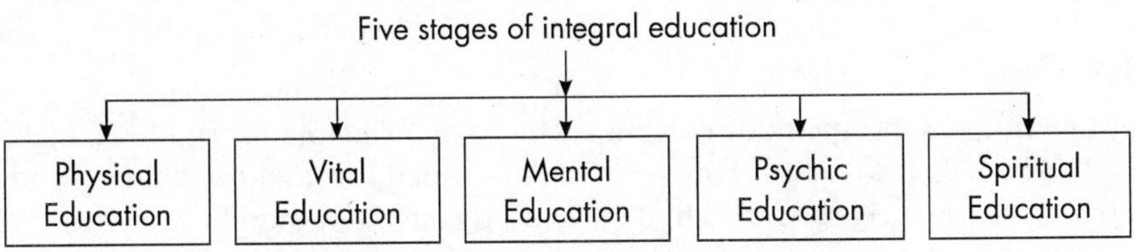

FIGURE 20.2 Stages of integral education.

Physical education: It includes physical training, games, gymnastics, balanced diet, preventive medical care and health education. For total harmonious and integrated development of the body, physical discipline, by controlling various parts of the body and freedom from diseases, must be obtained.

Vital education: It includes student participation in music, fine art, dance, drama, craft and ballet for the development and utilisation of senses so as to eventually control them. Learning by doing is the guiding principle of this education.

Mental education: It includes various academic studies such as languages, mathematics, social sciences, applied and pure sciences and so on for the development of attention and concentration, development of the capacity to expand and enrich the mental horizon and development of reasoning power to accept the desirable thoughts and reject the undesirable ones.

Psychic education: It includes the study of spiritual and psychic values like love, truth, faith in God, and strength of mind and heart. Psychic education is related to yoga. It is education which includes the development of non material values.

Spiritual education: This education leads to eternal bliss. This is the highest level of education called super-mental education. This stage is reached after one develops physical, vital, mental and psychic elements. It requires deep and intensive insight and persistent efforts.

Measures for Achieving the Ends of Integral Education

Role of teacher in integral education: The teacher has a unique place in integral education. He is not an instructor or task master. He is a helper and guide. His business is to suggest ways for the natural development of the child.

Discipline in integral education: Aurobindo stresses the significance of free environment under the guidance of the teacher. Maximum freedom should be given to the child for the development of the psychic being. The students should be allowed to choose their own subjects and develop the areas of interests.

Moral training in integral education: Moral principles should be provided to the child through the personal example of the teacher. It should be based on practical opportunities. Moral training should be given through yoga.

Faith in the potentialities of child in integral education: Generally every child possesses hidden potentialities. The teacher must have an immense faith in the capacity of the child. His task is to bring it out and help develop it so as to turn the child into a complete man.

Physical education in integral education: The human body is the means of fulfillment of dharma. Therefore, the aim of integral education is the development of the physical part of the body and it cannot be left aside.

Principles of teaching in integral education: The basic principle of true teaching is that nothing can be taught. The knowledge is within the child. It is revealed through swadharma and swabhav. The second principle of teaching is that the child should be consulted in his own growth. The chief aim of education is to help the growing soul to draw out that which is hidden and make it perfect for the best use. The third principle of teaching is teaching the child from the known to the unknown. That is, all new knowledge must be built around the child's daily experiences directly connected with his environment.

Curriculum in integral education: Curriculum in integral education system includes the five basic elements of 'being' the physical, the vital, the mental, the psychic and the spiritual. The integral education system emphasises a flexible, interest based and environment based curriculum so that the child achieves the utmost possible perfection of himself and contributes his maximum to humanity as a whole.

The concept of integral education is a remarkable contribution of Sri Aurobindo. We must understand the inter-relationship among the different elements within man, the nation and the universal humanity. We must also see the synthesis among these elements in order to grasp the concept of integral education.

AUROBINDO ASHRAM AT PONDICHERRY (AUROBINDO INTERNATIONAL CENTRE OF EDUCATION)

Sri Aurobindo's Ashram school was established near the sea-shore at Pondicherry in 1943. It started functioning with twenty children of Aurobindo's disciples. It expanded gradually from a primary school to a full- fledged high school. The Ashram is intended to provide an environment of peace and harmony. There are both residential and day students. The Ashram school was inaugurated in 1952 by the Mother [Sri Aurobindo's close spiritual collaborator, Mirra Richard (1878–1973) a French women, was known as "The Mother". She played an active role in the merger of the French pockets in India, and according to Sri Aurobindo's wish helped to make Pondicherry a seat of cultural exchange between India and France] as the "Sri Aurobindo International University Centre". But it came to be known as "Sri Aurobindo International Centre of Education" from 1959 onwards. In this way, the growth of Ashram is like that of an organism. It has developed with many departments and services, workshops, farms and with a number of commercial and industrial undertakings.

Nature of International Centre of Education

The centre of international education is meant to be the cradle of the new world. The life of the children is related to the life led in the Ashram. It aims at divine human life in the light of the teaching of Aurobindo and the Mother. There is a continuity of education from the kindergarten till the end of studies. A student is required to stay at the centre for 10 to 15 years. He may continue to live if he likes after his studies. This centre provides everything needed for the free growth of the child according to nature without any compulsion whatsoever. A child should not be brainwashed or indoctrinated through false propaganda.

The international centre of education provides opportunities to develop unity in diversify which is very essential for national integration and international understanding. The students and the teachers of this institution are from different parts of India and other countries of the world. They live and work together, irrespective of their race, caste, creed, colour, sex and religion. Most of the Indian languages are taught here. The culture of different countries is accepted here to promote racial unity and develop a synthetic organisation of all nations. Their attire, games and sports, exhibitions and films are used extensively for the purpose of encouraging unity in diversity.

Objectives of International Centre of Education

1. Evolve a system of education for making it dynamic and ideal for society.
2. Organise an environment which may provide inspiration and facilities for the exercise and development of the five aspects of personality—the physical, the vital, the mental, the psychic and the spiritual.
3. Emphasise the unity of all knowledge.
4. Develop the sense of oneness of mankind.
5. Devise and prepare for the role of India to play in the formation of the new international harmony.

Curriculum at the International Centre

1. Psychic and spiritual studies.
2. Academic subjects.

3. Physical and health education.
4. Cultural activities like art, music, dance and drama.
5. Vocational Training.
6. Education for International understanding.

Principles of Integral Teaching and Learning at International Centre

Sense training: Sense training is developed through observation of natural phenomenon under the guidance of the teacher.

Developing power of investigation: Observation plays an important role in developing the power of investigation.

Training of memory: Training of memory and mind is done by equipping the students to note the similarities and dissimilarities.

Training in making judgements: The sense training, power of investigation, and training of memory and mind provide suitable training in making judgements.

Training of logical faculty: Training of logical faculty depends on ascertaining correctness of facts, collecting accurate data and sifting the facts by eliminating the false elements.

Training of imagination: Training of imagination depends on forming current images, developing the power of creative thinking, and training in appreciating the existence of truth, goodness and beauty of soul in the existing things.

Training of languages: Training of language is given through appropriate methods of teaching and also through concrete things.

Free environment: Aurobindo advocates the significance of free environment under the guidance of the teacher so that the child develops freely by choosing its own subjects and activities.

The Mother of International Centre of Education says, "The aim of this center is to help individuals to become conscious of the fundamental genius of the nation to which they belong and the same time to put them in contact with the modes of living of other nations so that they may know and respect equally the true spirit of all the countries upon the earth. For all world organizations to be real and to be able to live, must be based on mutual respect and understanding between nation and nation as well as between individual and individual".

AUROVILLE

Auroville, "The City of Dawn" five miles away from Pondicherry was inaugurated by the Mother (Mira Richard, a French Woman) on February 28, 1968. It is a landmark in the history of Aurobindian education. The Charter of Auroville was signed by children from 121 countries who poured soil from their respective lands into a lotus shaped urn symbolising the unity of the human race. Auroville aims at searching for a new education in a new society. It is the city of twenty-first century man. The environment of Auroville was organized with the aim of humanising the people living there by synthesising their nations, ideologies, knowledge, culture etc. The city has four zones namely cultural, industrial, residential and educational. They represent the four important activities of human life.

According to the Charter of Auroville, "Auroville belongs to nobody in particular. It belongs to humanity as a whole and is conceived as "the City of Human Unity". But to live in Auroville, one must be a willing servitor of the Divine consciousness. Auroville will be the place of an unending education, of constant progress and youth that never ages.

Juile Medlock writes in The Sunday Standard, "Attracting much favourable attention to India all around the world these days is the unique new project underway in South India, just outside of Pondicherry—the building of Auroville as a city of universal culture in international cooperation and human unity".

It is a World University Centre, a university in which continuing education from infancy to old age will be offered. The Auroville project has the support of the Indian Government and of UNESCO. The purpose of the project is to create a universal town where men and women of all countries can live together in peace and harmony, above all creeds all politics and all nationalities. UNESCO has invited its member-states to participate actively in the building of the new town, stressing that "It will add a new dimension to UNESCO's activities for the promotion of international co-operation and understanding and well-being, together with the values of different cultures and civilizations in a harmonious environment with integrated living standards which correspond to a man's physical and spiritual need". Auroville wants to be the bridge between the past and the future, and will be a site of material and spiritual development for a living embodiment of an actual human unity.

CONCLUSION

Aurobindo is a great philosopher, educationist, nationalist and a yogi. His contribution to the field of education is very unique. He stresses child-centred education and allows maximum freedom to the child for his natural development. He integrates the Western philosophy with the Indian one. He accepts the teacher as a helper, guide and instructor. The bases of his philosophy of education are spiritual faith, brahmacharya and yoga practices. His philosophical ideas lead us from materialism to spiritualism. He preaches the ideals and values of Indian culture based on brahmacharya, yoga, concentration and meditation. His preaching helps an individual to attain the full development of his body, mind and soul in a harmonious way. The philosophy of Sri Aurobindo Ghosh is a unique one in the field of Indian education. He wants to make the Indian soceity good and happy by making the individuals good through education. In the words of Dr. R. S. Mani, "His views on education reveal that Sri Aurobindo Ghosh was one of the most eminent and distinguished educationists of our country".

CHAPTER 21

JIDDU KRISHNAMURTI
1895–1986

INTRODUCTION

Jiddu Krishnamurti is an outstanding intellectual thinker and a great philosopher of India in the twentieth century. Since he was one among those contemporary Indian philosophers who stood against the traditional system of education and refused to follow Indian philosophical schools and any of religious cults, he became a unique philosopher. In fact, he condemned vehemently the ineffectiveness of the present education in fostering love, sympathy, rational thinking and humanism in the child. As he was deeply interested in education and schools, he established eight schools in different parts of the world. His educational ideas were found in his book, *Education and Significance of Life* (1973). His eternal message is, "First understand the purpose of life—the purpose of this individual existence. Understand what it is towards which you are thriving. Then utilize every emotion, every thought to strengthen you". Krishnamurti observed that the man who can split the nation, but has no love in his heart, becomes a monster. The exclusive creation of technique has produced scientists, mathematicians and engineers, who have no understanding of the process of life. Emphasis on efficiency without understanding what life means, brings about misery and chaos in the world.

LIFE OF KRISHNAMURTI

Jiddu Krishnamurti, an intellectual thinker, a great philosopher, a popular writer and speaker on philosophical, spiritual and educational subjects, was born on May 11, 1895 in an orthodox brahmin family of Madhanapalli town in Andhra Pradesh. He is known as J.K. Murti and is matched with Dr. S. Radhakrishnan and Pandit Madan Mohan Malaviya. According to Bernard Shaw, "Jiddu Krishnamurti is the most handsome person". Aldox Huxley described him as "the man of supremely pure and healthy mind among Indians". Mrs. Annie Besant announced that "Krishnamurti would be the vehicle of the world teacher". In all respect, he is a unique individual and the most enlightened intellectual of the twentieth century.

Jiddu Krishnamurti's parents Narainiah and Sanjeevamma named him Krishnamurti after the Lord Krishna. Though, Krishnamurti's family was a Telugu speaking brahmin, his father was a member of the Theosophical Society. Krishnamurti was very fond of his mother Sanjeevamma who passed away when he was ten. As his father was a Tahsildar, he had a transferrable job. This naturally affected Krishnamurthi's schooling. Moreover, he hated school and book learning. In fact, he was not interested in studies but was a keen observer and would stand for long stretches at a time watching trees and clouds or squat on the ground, gazing at plants and insects. About his school, he wrote in his memoir as, "I cannot say I was particularly happy at school, for teachers were not very kind and gave me lessons that were too hard for me. I enjoyed games as long as they were not rough, as I had very delicate health". However, he had a unique temperament of thoughtful nature with a habit of quiet observation.

Mrs. Annie Besant, the president of the Theosophical Society, invited Narainiah and his sons (Krishnamurti and his brother Nityanand) to Adyar in Chennai. Here, Krishnamurti got well acquainted with Mrs. Annie Besant and understood a simplified definition of theosophy. Theosophy is the study of God, beliefs, values and theories attached to a religion. Academically, Krishnamurti was dull and found it difficult to concentrate on books and examination. So, Annie Besant and Leadbeater tried their best to inculcate education in the traditional method, but they failed in their attempts. But, under the care of Annie Besant and the influence of the Theosophical Society, he became a staunch theosophist. He was unique since he boldly refused to follow any traditional Indian philosophical school and anyone of the religious cults.

At the age of 15, Krishnamurti accompanied Mrs. Annie Besant, to England in 1911 and stayed there for a decade (1911–1922). He enjoyed most the theatres he was taken to see the plays such as 'The Prisoner of Zenda, The Julius Caesar and Macbeth in the London. He made three unsuccessful attempts to pass matriculation examination in London University. He was contrary to any genuine learning and believed that religious cults retard the search of truth or God. He embarked in a series of lectures, meetings and discussions around the world relating to his duties as the head of the 'order of the star' the patronage of theosophical society. He gave his first speech in London in 1911. In the meantime, a legal dispute arose between Annie Besant and Narainiah for the guardianship of Krishnamurti. It ended when he was sent to Europe and was brought up under the care of Lady Emily Lutyeas. Besant saw in Krishnamurti all potentials of becoming the World Teacher. Therefore, she provided all the necessary facilities and conditions for his development. He wrote a book *Education As Service* in 1912 in which he described the life of a school where love and rules inspire the child to grow into noble adolescents under the fostering care of teachers who feel the greatness of their vocation. In 1922, Krishnamurti left for California with his brother Nityanand who suffered from lung disease and died there on December 23, 1925. Death of Nityanand transformed the whole life of Krishnamurti and he started thinking about the very basis of all existence on this earth.

Krishnamurti had an unusual spiritual experience which brought in him a turning point and made him a world spiritual leader. Besant appointed him as the seventh disciple and announced that Krishnamurti would be the vehicle of the world teacher. Krishnamurti, the Prince of Wales of the Theosophical Society, became the most important man of the theosophical circles all over the world. The young spiritual teacher, wherever he went, was received with great honour. At the silver jubilee celebration of the Theosophical Society at Adyar in Chennai on December 28, 1925, he pronounced the great elements of divinity that he himself expressed under a great banyan tree in a Hindu temple of Bharat Samaj that "we are all expecting God who will be an embodiment of all nobility, full of sympathy and happiness for all". He spoke about his ceaseless struggles in search of truth in his famous radio talk on August 2, 1927. He went on a world tour during 1928–29 and delivered lectures at various places in America and Europe. Krishnamurti declared himself as a teacher of humanity and decided to act for setting man free from ignorance, illusion, fear and blind belief. Thus, his life has been an eternal voyage of self effluent light across the infinite of void of dimly perceptible darkness of finite space setting aflame the widening souls surrounding admits dust of spiritual existence. He said that truth is a pathless land. Man cannot come to it through any organization, through any creed, through any dogma, priest or ritual, not through any philosophical knowledge or psychological techniques. He has to find it through the mirror of relationship, through the understanding of the contents of his own mind, through observation and through intellectual analysis or introspective dissection.

Krishnamurti's new vision and consciousness continued to develop and reached a climax in 1929, which made him to denounce all organized belief, the nation of 'gurus' (teacher) and teacher student–relationship. He began to disassociate himself from the Theosophical Society and its teachings and practices, but he maintained cordial terms with some members and ex-members throughout his life. Thus, he not only denied the role of the world teacher but closed down the "order of the Star" that made him famous also. He left the Theosophical Society and returned all the money and wealth to the donors. He himself expressed, thus "I want to free man from chains and fear, I am not finding a new religion. My only purpose is to free man completely".

The great intellectual thinker Krishnamurti gave lots of discourses on religion, philosophy and education to large gatherings in Australia, England, Holland and North and South America. He established several centres in various countries for philosophical studies. In 1985, he spoke to an invited audience at the United Nations in New York where he was awarded the United Nations Peace Medal. He visited India in December 1985, holding a number of farewell talks and discussions. His talk included the fundamental questions about the new concern related to the recent advancement in science and technology, and the way they affected mankind. Annie Besant considered him as her new 'Guru'. Many of the theosophists became his followers and did not mind the division in the Theosophical Society.

Jiddu Krishnamurti who was a powerful speaker on philosophy and religion had extraordinary courage of conviction to say without fear what he thought best. In his last talk on January 4, 1986 in Chennai, he again invited the audience to examine the effect of technology in the nature of life and meditation and the nature of creation. This great man breathed his last on February 17, 1986, due to deterioration of his physical body from pancreatic cancer. His remains were cremated and scattered by his friends and the former associates in India, England and America where he had spent most of his life. His mind lives on even today, energetic and bright as always in the world of philosophy, religion and education.

GENERAL PHILOSOPHY OF JIDDU KRISHNAMURTI

Jiddu Krishnamurti is a great thinker who enriches the philosophical and cultural tradition of India. The most significant quality of Krishnamurti's philosophy of life is that it is not influenced by social, political, spiritual and economic ideology. He has great courage in rejecting all the rubbish in the name of religion and advise men to investigate truth without submitting their mind to conditions. He speaks on life and problems associated with it in an orthodox manner. According to him, one must realise that there is no security in the past, present or future. With this conviction, one can find out that it is possible to live without any guidance control, or without any effort psychologically. The mind must remain free to find the truth and not to conform to any pattern of authority. He pleads that one should live a life without any fixed pattern, without goal, without any idea of the future and life without conflict. For this, one has to learn to live with 'what is' that which is taking place. One must live with it, without any thought of transforming it or going beyond it, without trying to control things. In his view, man should not waste his energy in controlling, suppressing, resisting and in trying to escape, but all that energy would be used in living with the existing conditions.

Krishnamurti expresses his reaction to the existing conditions of life, social relations and human behaviour not as a saint or philosopher but as an intellectual fully awakened to natural and social environment. He does not prescribe any doctrine or pattern of life to live happily but suggests that we should live with the mind completely free from the blind idea of past or future. This is the undeniable fact that most of human energy and resources are being spent in preparation for war and in terrorising others. People spend the rest of the time in unconstructive or non-productive work. It is seen that most people in cities spend almost 50 hours a week before the television boxes. It decreases their social works and fruitful exchange of views, and changes human relationship. He questions that in such condition what good can be expected. He is extremely disturbed at the disorder of the world marked by corruption, conflict and uncertainty. He considers fear as one of the greatest problems in the world. It is mainly caused by the thought of tomorrow. In fact, people talk of what will happen in future and get into their trap and get frightened. A practical man destroys himself when he thinks about the future. So. Krishnamurti asks us to enjoy the present life.

It is practically seen that most of the people need shelter or friends to depend on, otherwise they have fear. Krishnamurti says that the sensitivity dependence on others and fear are interrelated. According to him, when there is dependence, there is inner desire of freedom. In his own words, "Freedom means freedom from fear. It means freedom from any form of resistance. Freedom means a movement without isolation. It means having no resistance at all". Moreover, he says that when there is freedom, there is love. Freedom and love show us when to cooperate and when to not. This is not an act of choice, because choice is the result of confusion. Further, he says that lamenting over the existing conditions is mainly caused by our relationship with things, people, property and ideas. There are divisions in the name of nations, religions, economic, social and political relations. Thus, the whole world has been broken up outwardly as men are broken inwardly. According to him, "this outer fragmentation is the manifestation of the human being's inner division". It is true that all our life is determined by our mind, brain, feelings and actions of the past. Therefore, there must be a radical change of the mind and the heart to live sanely in this world. Here, change is not a movement from known to unknown but it is a progress from being a sinner to being a saint or progress from one illusion to another.

As the most unconventional thinker, Krishnamurti freely expressed his views on a variety of issues and problems. In fact, all the problems of daily life require serious consideration that attracted his attention. The problem ranges from pleasure, love, art, beauty to death. It is a fact that every human being is engaged in seeking pleasures in life. The pleasure maybe derived from possession of things, political or economic power, sex or domination. According to him, "Pleasure is gratification, satisfaction, indulgence, entertainment and stimulation". Pleasure is not happiness and the latter is not sought but it comes uninvited. He feels that if one pursues happiness, he can escape from unhappiness. Intelligence cannot be separated from ending unhappiness or getting happiness. According to Krishnamurti, knowing oneself is the ending of sorrow. The most significant elements in all sufferings are self-pity and attachment. Hence, for ending sorrow, we must know ourselves as we are. In fact, when there is a light of understanding, sorrows come to an end.

The greatest tragedy of our life according to Krishnamurti, is that we never think, never enquire the meaning of our living. He is of the opinion to find out the full meaning of our life, and not be afraid of anything including death that comes at the end of life. Our life is a constant battle with problems that have occasional moments of relief, but the struggle goes on. He believes that the person who does not waste his life in conflicts and worries will have full energy and clarity. He considers death as the end of all that one knows, of all one's attachments, of one's bank accounts, of all one's attainments—there is a complete ending. Though the thought of living and death go together, we are only afraid of death and ask about life after death. It is hard to know what living itself is, because, there is thought of life before death and life after death.

Krishnamurti points out the problems of the present generation such as, children are by and large disrespectful to their parents, they do not listen, nor do they care about what is said to them. In short, they refuse to follow the pattern of thinking of their parents. There are the new phenomena found all over the world due to a serious defect in the method of upbringing, the education and training and is imparted to children. In fact, most of us want children to follow the path which their forefathers, parents and teachers have advocated for them. This tendency can never develop the personality of a child in a healthy manner. He wants that we should create a new generation who are not afraid, who do not conform to the past and who are equipped with intelligence. For this purpose, we attach great importance to the cultivation of the mind.

According to Krishnamurti, a religious life which implies the denial of pleasures and beauty of nature, as the most religious leaders and saints have preached, is a false view. He believes that those who talk of religion torture themselves in that belief. The belief insists that the only way to reality or God is through self-denial. Krishnamurti considers it as a distortion of religion. He says that those who preach religious doctrines should distinguish between the world life of pleasure and religious life—denial of pleasures and beauty of nature. According to the religious doctrine, a man is called worldly when he lives a full life of pleasure and sorrow in the society. Hence, all social reformers patriots and idealists are worldly people. But Krishnamurti says, "We cannot live without matter and life is not possible without persons and things. What is important is the totality of life. A religious life in the real sense is concerned with the whole and not with the particular. When we divide the religions from the worldly we create conflict. A life of conflict is not a religious life". Our religious tradition considers God as the creator, sustainer and destroyer of the world. It binds our mind with belief which makes us prisoners of belief. Since God is not perceived, each man creates his own image of God. In the words of Krishnamurti, "God is the illusion which we worship, and the non-believer creates the illusion of another god which he worships—the state or some utopia or some book which he thinks contain all truth". He states that if we want to be religious, we must free ourselves from the concept of God and its illusion. This is due to two reasons—firstly, people who do not believe in God do good to others whereas those who believe in God kill others for their belief or any other reasons and secondly, religions have played havoc during the whole course of human history.

According to Krishnamurti, people who believe in God, hope that He will protect from all evils and come to rescue them in times of difficulty. Thus, uncertainty and insecurity in the ever-changing world create fear as the basis of beliefs in the divine presence. According to him, "Belief comes from fear which is the most destructive thing. One must be free of fear and of belief. Belief divides people, makes them hard, makes them hate each other and cultivate war". Fear or belief in the mind makes man incapable of understanding the 'truth'. He also says that the inner feelings of emptiness, poverty, sensitivity and insufficiency instigate man to mentally depend on invisible power.

We may summarise the philosophical ideas of Jiddu Krishnamurti thus:

- Truth does not reside in dark premises of temples nor in lighted places of organized society, nor religious scriptures or customs and conventions.
- Down with all temples, churches and all religious organizations for worship of God, and follow none.
- To be religious, we must free ourselves from the concept of God and its illusion.
- God is the illusion which we worship. We are in despair which creates hope and hope produces belief in God.
- Belief comes from fear and is the most destructive thing. Fear and belief in the mind curb man from understanding the 'truth'.

- Fear is one of the greatest problems and it destroys people when they think about the future.
- Freedom means freedom from fear and any form of resistance.
- We do not perceive God. Hence, each man creates his own image of God.
- The greatest tragedy of our life is that we never think, never enquire the meaning of our life.
- Death means the end of all that one knows, of all one's attachments, of one's bank accounts, of all one's attainments—there is a complete living.
- There should be no thought of reformation as it has no end. We should forget to reform the world.

KRISHNAMURTI'S VIEWS ON INDIAN EDUCATION

Jiddu Krishnamurti is a unique individual who regenerates the human mind in a revolutionary manner. His contribution to philosophy and education is very deep and comprehensive which has brought about a remarkable change in the principles of education. He analyses the prevailing system of education in the Indian society and condemns its ineffectiveness in solving the problems of life. He has pointed out the following short comings of the Indian education:

- The traditional education fails to develop independent thinking in the child.
- It leads to dullness of mind and heart.
- It develops fear in one's mind and heart.
- It fails to develop creativity in the child.
- It does not enable to understand the higher and wider significance of life.
- It prepares the child to gain vocational efficiency or get a better job.
- It ignores the aesthetic, cultural and social development of the child.
- It has made examinations and degress as the criteria of education and intelligence.
- It has developed cunning minds which avoid vital human issues.
- It makes the child subservient, mechanical and thoughtless.
- Technical education emphasises technical knowledge which is necessary but without understanding the total process of life that becomes a means of destroying man.
- It awakens us intellectually, but leaves us incomplete, stultified and uncreative.
- It denies freedom for the child. In the absence of freedom, natural growth of the child is not possible.
- Education leads to competition and mutual destruction where people get jobs and earn money but no humanity and moral values.
- It trains the individual to seek personal gain and security, which is the ultimate goal of industrial security.
- It does not help the child to achieve freedom from worries and tensions.

Jiddu Krishnamurti not only denounces the traditional Indian education but also the present technical education. According to him, "present day education is a complete failure because it has overemphasised technical studies. In overemphasising technique, we destroy man. To cultivate capacity and efficiency without understanding life, without having a comprehensive perception of the ways of thought and desire, will only make us increasingly ruthless, which is endanger war and jeopardize our physical security". He says that such education has produced doctors, scientists, mathematicians, bridge builders and space conquerors but they do not understand the total process of life. Moreover, he says, "Technical knowledge however necessary, will in no way resolve our inner, psychological pressures and conflicts; and it is because we have acquired technical knowledge without understanding the total process of life and technology has become means of destroying ourselves. The man who knows how to split the atom but has no love in his heart becomes a monster". Thus, our technical knowledge and progress is fantastic, but it has only increased our powers of destroying one another, and there is starvation and misery in every land, we are not peaceful and happy people.

He regards education as, it is, at present, in no way encouraging the understanding of the inherited tendencies and environmental influences which condition the mind and heart and sustain fear, and therefore, it does not help us to break through these conditions and bring about an integrated human being. Any form of education that concerns itself with a part and not with the whole of man inevitably leads to increasing conflict and suffering. Further, he says that education emphasises theoretical aspects only. In the words of Krishnamurti, "Modern education, in developing the intellect, offers more and more theories and facts, without bringing about the under-standing of the total process of human existence. We are highly intellectual, we have developed cunning minds, and are caught up in explanations. The intellect is satisfied with theories and explanations, but intelligence is not and for the understanding of the total process of existence, there must be an integration of the mind and heart in action. Intelligence is not separate from love".

EDUCATIONAL PHILOSOPHY OF KRISHNAMURTI

Jiddu Krishnamurti stands as one of the great educators in the series of the Western and Eastern educators. His educational philosophy is unique and different from that of all Indian and Western philosophers. In fact, he ransacks the prevailing system of Indian education and condemns it vehemently, and gives education a new shape by changing its meaning and aims. He makes education a comprehensive process against that education which puts emphasis on technical and vocational education. According to him, education should help the individual to understand the total process of life through self-observation and find out everlasting values which make him a peaceful and a happy man. He, therefore, emphasises the need for implementing right education to bring out a new social order based on love, affection and intelligence. He wants that education should cultivate an integrated outlook on life. For this purpose, he advocates integral education. It means education should encourage self- observation and the experience of life as a whole. He believes that an integrated individual is one who is capable of dealing with life as a whole. According to him, a wise man observes himself and knows himself; the knowing himself is the beginning of wisdom and the ending of sorrows. Knowing oneself is easy to say but practically, it needs patience and determination where education is required. We may point out the following ideas related to education from Krishnamurti's philosophy:

- True education is that which should help the individual to mature and free to bloom greatly in love, goodness and intelligence.
- Education should help man to be free from his own ambitions.
- Education should foster love and kindness in the child, which makes life peaceful and happy.
- Education should develop a tendency of creativeness.
- Modern education does not develop the child to love one another. Love alone may lead one to understand the significance of life.
- Good teachers should be enlisted to develop a good educational system.
- Man is not a machine, and cannot be adjusted in a perceived structure of things.
- Education should help the individual to discover the everlasting values which enable him to observe himself and understand the whole process of life.
- Only dedicated teachers can play an important role in the enlightened society.

- Condition of parents, teachers and society prevents the flowering of the mind and heart of the child.
- The teacher needs to understand the unique quality of every individual and then educate them accordingly.
- There should be no basic difference between the atmosphere of the home and the school so that the child can be protected from worries and tensions.
- Proper guidance facilities should exist in the school.
- A small school should be maintained through the spirit of self- sacrifice.
- There should be a cordial relationship between the teacher and the taught.
- Teacher should not give importance to certificates and rewards but stress on academic excellence through intrinsic motivation.
- Knowledge is a series of actions and reactions that our minds have stored based on the past experiences.
- Real education is possible only through small school.
- A big school with hundreds of children is just like an industry where interests of the child are neglected. Such school gives under importance to co-curricular activities just to impress the parents and public.
- We should not educate our fellow beings to conform themselves to others' ways of thinking and ways of life.
- We have to give full freedom to the child to reach his maximum growth which maybe individually satisfying and socially desirable.
- The co-curricular activities of the school should be conducted in a democratic manner in which all teachers and students should be made obligatory. No child should be deprived of an opportunity to do something related to the group in the school.

MEANING OF EDUCATION

Education in the true sense is helping the individual to mature and be free, to flower greatly in love and goodness. It is not to transmit the existing values in the minds of children, but enable them to think critically and rationally. Krishnamurti says that it is education which should help the people to discover the lasting values so that they do not merely be inclined to formulas or repeat slogans. It should also help them to break down our social and national barriers instead of emphasising them, for they breed antagonism between man and man. Education is the essence of learning which is the very movement of intellect, not from a book but from the observation of the world and learns what exactly is happening without theories, prejudices and values in education. Krishnamurti says as an advise to the young student that to be really educated means not to conform, nor to imitate, not to do what millions are doing. If you feel like doing that, do it . But be awake to what you are doing. Education lies in helping people to feel free from the mundane bondage, guiding people to love each other and feeling pride in helping others. In the process of real education, there should be complete freedom so that minds are used to their higher capacity. Education should provide full opportunity so that children can express themselves and live in this world a life of intelligence and sanity. In the words of Krishnamurti, "Education helps us to be sane, non-mechanical and intelligence".

AIMS OF EDUCATION

The purpose of education is not to produce mere scholars, technicians and job hunters, but integrated man and woman who are free of fear, for only between such human beings can there be enduring peace.

The beginning and the end of education is understanding life and ourselves. Education is flowering in goodness; goodness cannot flower in the field of fear. So, fear should not be the instrument of education. It is not a matter of reading a lot of books, passing examinations and getting a job, it extends from the moment we are born to the moment we die which means education is a life-long process. Hence, the aim of education is to help man to be free from his own ambitions. It implies that education should help the child grow without fear to the best of his capacities and talents that lead to understand life as a whole. Thus, the aim of education is to help us to discover the lasting values and develop scholars and technicians and also to create men and women who are free from fear. Krishnamurti wants that education should prepare the young generation for a new type of free living. In other words, one of the most important tasks of education is to develop a child into such a perfect person who could perceive life in its completeness. According to him, "education should help the child in facing the world in a totally different and intelligent way, knowing to earn a livelihood, knowing all the responsibilities, the miseries of it all". In short, the aim of education is helping the child to observe himself and understand the purpose of human life.

CURRICULUM

Jiddu Krishnamurti founded eight schools in different parts of the world. He lectured in India, England, Holland, Australia and North and South America on various topics related to religion and education. He was deeply interested in education and schools. Based on his experiences, he said that teachers should not give importance to certificates and degress but stress on academic excellence through intrinsic motivation. Therefore, he said that teaching should include a wide range of activities like art and craft, dance and music, dramatic and debates, sports, yoga, swimming, gardening, athletics and work experiences in order to provide an all-round development of the child.

METHODS OF TEACHING

Krishnamurti has given various suggestions to impart the right kind of education through the right kind of teaching. He believes that illusion takes the place of reality in the absence of right kind of teaching. As a consequence, the individual is ever in conflict within himself and therefore, there is conflict in his relationship with others which is society. One teaches because one sees that self-knowledge alone, and not the dogmas and rituals of organized religion, can bring about a tranquil mind and that creation, truth. God comes into being only when He, 'me' and the 'mine' are transcended. Hence, the right kind of teaching should include certain methods, such as:

1. The method should not teach the child 'what to think' but 'how to think'.
2. The method should provide freedom for the child which enables him to think for himself.
3. The method employed in teaching should enable the child to study the subject thoroughly.
4. Questioning and critical thinking are needed to be made a part of the instructional process.
5. Teaching and learning is a two-way process in which the teacher and the student should form an equal partnership. It means that the teacher should strive to motivate the students to take learning and at the same time he should take some learning from the student.

ROLE OF TEACHER

The teacher should be fully educated in order to understand the real purpose of human life. He must help each pupil to discover his inner psychological resources and realise his weakness, and develop his individual strength. For this purpose, he has to create the right environment through affection as well as patience. Krishnamurti believes that problematic teachers develop only problematic children, so such teachers should be resolved. The teacher has to encourage creative intelligence of his students. For the true teacher, teaching is not a technique, it is his way of life, like a great artist, he would starve rather than give up his creative work. Unless one has this burning desire to teach, one should not be a teacher. According to him, if we have dedicated ourselves to the right kind of education, we do not create barriers between home life and the life at school for we are concerned with freedom and intelligence of the child. Hence, the teacher should consider equally the children of rich and poor and regard each child as an individual with his particular temperament, heredity and ambition. In the words of Krishnamurti, "as long as the teaching is considered as a profession or means of earning livelihood, the teacher cannot dedicate himself in teaching". In fact, teaching should be considered as a worship, the child as a deity and the school a temple. For this purpose, only dedicated teachers are needed to play an important role in the enlightened society. The teacher should not regard himself merely as an instrument for imparting knowledge but a person who is concerned with the task of leading students to a way of life according to their resources. Hence, the teacher should not impose his beliefs, manners and ideologies on the student. Here the task of the teacher is not to teach 'what' to think, but to teach 'how' to think and act.

True teacher: Krishnamurti stresses the pen picture of a true scholar or teacher. According to him, "An educator is not merely a giver of information he is one who points the way to wisdom, to truth. Truth is far more important than the teacher. To create a new society, each one of us to be a true teacher, which means that we have to be both the pupil and the master, we have to educate ourselves". The true teacher is not he who has built upon impressive educational organization nor he who is an instrument of the politicians nor he who is bound to an ideal, a belief or a country. The true teacher is inwardly rich and, therefore, asks nothing for himself, he is not ambitious and seeks no power in any form, he does not use teaching as a means of acquiring position, or authority, and, therefore, he is free from the compulsion of society or the control of government. Such teachers have the primary place in an enlightened civilisation, for true culture is founded, not on the engineers and technicians but on the educators.

Integrated educator: Human beings must be integrated, but the main problem is how to develop an integrated individual when he comes out of the present world crisis. Therefore, the educator himself must obviously be integrated. For this purpose, the right kind of education is of the highest importance, not only for the young but also for the older generations. Krishnamurti says that if we love our children we will see that whether they have the right kind of educators.

Observer of the child: The teacher should observe the child at his play, study and in his different moods to understand him. He should not project anything on the basis of his own prejudices, hopes and fear or mould the child to fit the pattern of his desires. We are constantly judging the child according to our personal likes and dislikes, we are bound to create barriers and hindrances in our relationship with him and in his relationship with the world. Therefore, the teacher should be a keen observer of the child before he inculcates education.

Source of intellectual development: The right kind of education consists of understanding the child as he is without imposing upon him any idea of what we think that he should be. If teacher is of the right kind, he will not depend on a method of teaching but will study each pupil and provide education according to his needs and interests. He should not thrust his faith, beliefs, ideas or dogmas on his children. However, the role of teacher is very important and he is the source of intellectual development from which the child gains knowledge and experience which prepares him for a happy and peaceful life.

PLACE OF SCHOOL

Krishnamurti believes that the integrated personality development of the children can be achieved in school. This is possible only when the number of students in the class is limited. He also believes that mass instruction is a suicidal technique to the development of the child's individuality. The interests of children are generally neglected in a big school. Moreover, the headmaster of the school cannot take upon the responsibility of all the children. Therefore, a small school should be maintained through the spirit of self-sacrifice. According to Krishnamurti, "A big school with hundreds of children is just like a big industry, a big government office, or a big bank that aims at completing certain routine work in a mechanical manner". In fact, real education maybe given only through a small school where the teacher can pay compassionate attention to each and every child. It enables the teacher to take the children under his care. The headmaster should associate with his co-workers for the smooth functioning of the school. Freedom should be given to the students to discuss educational matters. There should be provision for proper guidance in the schools so that the child could gain the confidence and cooperation of the teachers. The school should understand the hereditary and environmental factors of each child. Such understanding will reveal the background of the child. It needs individual attention and guidance. There should be a feeling of equality and cooperation. The school should enable the child to discover what he is interested in, so that he will be educated in the real sense of the term. It is not possible in a big school where the principal or manager has great interest in pump and show the parents and public by overloading the children with heavy homework and a big load of text and notebooks. Moreover, big schools give under importance to co-curricular activities just to impress the parents and public.

STUDENT

Like Western and Eastern philosophers, Jiddu Krishnamurti believes that every individual is unique in his approach to learning. The teacher needs to understand the unique quality of his students and then educate them appropriately. In fact, every child has different potentials—some in academics, others in sports, still others in art. Therefore, the teacher should observe the child and then arrive at his own conclusions. Krishnamurti suggests that a student council should be formed to discuss matters related to the well-being of the whole group.

DISCIPLINE

Jiddu Krishnamurti believes that discipline makes the student subservient to the system of education and life. According to him, freedom never comes through discipline. He considers family quarrels, defective nourishment, lack of adequate rest or some hidden fears as causes of indiscipline. Hence, discipline maybe an easy way to control children. But it does not help them in understanding the problems which are closely related to their lives. He believes that reward and punishment maybe helpful in upholding a system but it is an applying force which is not desirable. But education, worthy the name, is not possible where the child should be motivated by any reward or punishment. However, he is of the opinion that individual attention and assistance enable the children to keep themselves disciplined. According to him, obedience has no place in the right kind of education. A better discipline can be developed in small school through a cordial informal and affectionate relationship between the teacher and the taught. The teacher should be a model to the taught. It means that the teacher himself should be fearless if he wants to make the child fearless. He himself should understand the importance of freedom before giving freedom to the child. The headmaster should invite political, religious leaders and social reformers to his school in order to advertise their achievements.

CONTRIBUTIONS OF KRISHNAMURTI TO EDUCATION

Though Jiddu Krishnamurti, was a great educator and philosopher, he never tried to pose himself as a reformer of education or society. But his works and lectures proved him to be a man of great intellectual personality. He is a practical thinker who established nearly a dozen co-educational schools and put his educational ideas into practice for the betterment of society. About ten percent of the seats in his school were reserved for non-paying pupils. Krishnamurti used to visit his schools in India and abroad every year for discussion with students and teachers. This revealed how much attention he paid to the development of school and the betterment of the students. Thus, it cannot be denied that Krishnamurti is one of the greatest educators and a distinguished philosopher of the world. In fact, his philosophical ideas have a great impact on educational principles and practices and give a new shape to the system of Indian education. We may summarise the educational contribution of Jiddu Krishnamurti under a few headings.

New meaning to education: Krishnamurti is disturbed at the disorder all over the world marked by corruption, conflict and uncertainty. Moreover, people who do not believe in God are also do good to others and those who believe in God kill others for their beliefs. There is no freedom and fearness in human life. In our search for knowledge, we are losing love and humanity. These truths have changed his thoughts and made him to give a new meaning to education. According to him, "Education in the true sense is helping the individual to be mature and free, to flower greatly in love and goodness". It means that education is the preparation of fearless child with love and goodness.

Real education: Krishnamurti emphasises real education and believes that it alone can help people to be free from the mundane bondage. According to him, wrong education leads to narrowness and self-deception. Real education is that which has to create new values, which should develop the child as much as it is possible. He believes that only right kind of education brings freedom in which love and goodness can bloom. In fact in the absence of real education our civilization of the past will be destroyed.

Integral education: Krishnamurti emphasises integral education in place of traditional Indian education. He believes that without an integrated understanding of life, our individual and collective problems will only deepen and extend. Hence, the purpose of education is the production of integrated man and woman who are free of fear. According to him, understanding of life is understanding ourselves and that is both the beginning and the end of education. It means education is not merely acquiring knowledge, gathering and correlating facts, it is to see the significance of life as a whole. In fact, integral education develops the capacity of the individual to face challenges. It is the only education which cultivates right relationship between individuals and between individuals and society.

Aims of education: Krishnamurti changes the aim of education from spiritual, cultural and vocational development to the development of love and goodness in the child through real education. According to him, aim of education is not just a matter of reading lot of books, passing examination and getting a job, but it is to help man to mature and be free, to flower greatly in love and goodness. Therefore, the aim of education is to help a child grow without fear to the best of his capacities and talents that enables him to solve the problems of life. Another aim of education is to help the child to discover the lasting values which enable to understand his whole life.

Life and education: The present education has made us afraid of new experiences. Therefore, we are compelled to show false respect to tradition and authorities. Some people desire to protest and revolt. The search for realising the importance of life is the real significance of education. The present education encourages only corruption and self-defensiveness which does not create love for one another. The search for truth and importance of life should be the significance of education.

Education and world peace: Krishnamurti opines that wrong values, such as corruption, selfishness, nationalism, dishonesty, conflicts of life are the causes of universal crisis. It is due to the non-acceptance of the existing conditions. Modifications in one's own notions, feelings and activities are necessary for resolution of a crisis. He says that world peace would dawn when we begin to think creatively for others. According to him, nationalism, consciousness of one's caste, class and religion are the bases of conflicts or crises. In fact, the present education teaches one to hate others and consider oneself superior to others. Therefore, he advises that the government and religious control of education should not be encouraged or allowed as they fail to maintain in the world. According to Krishnamurti, "There can be no world peace as long as education is controlled by either the government or religion". This trend can be seen in the present education system.

Teacher: According to Krishnamurti, "Only that person who himself is fully educated can faithfully perform the task of a teacher". If the teacher is of the right kind, he will not depend on a method but will study each child. Such study will help the teacher to mould the child in a desirable manner. He says, "we are not dealing with mechanical devices that can be quickly repaired but with living being (children) who are impressionable, volatile, sensitive affairs and affectionate. So we (teachers) should have a great understanding about our strength have a great understanding about our strength of patience and love in order to deal with them". The great task of the teacher is to develop integrated individuals. The teacher who wants to teach should understand the meaning of teaching. Problematic teachers are not able to behave in a normal manner with their children. A fearless person alone can be sensitive and prone to learn various things and bring out new things out of the old ones. The teacher should not regard himself merely as an instrument for imparting knowledge but a person who is concerned with the task of leading students to a way of life according to their resources. A devoted teacher will help the child to reach his maximum growth. Thus, the place and task of a teacher is very important in the education of a child.

School: Krishnamurti regards school as a big industry or big bank that aims at completing certain routine work in a mechanical manner. Big school gives under importance to co-curricular activities just to impress the parents and the public. In such schools, the interests of children are generally neglected. Moreover, the headmaster or teacher of the school cannot take upon the responsibility of all children. Krishnamurti, therefore, advises that there should be a limited number of students in a classroom, so that the individual personality development can be given more importance. The idea of Krishnamurti indicates the present situation of both government and private schools.

Freedom for the child: Like other philosophers, Krishnamurti emphasises freedom for the child. According to him, freedom enables the child to grow free and fearless. Such growth in the child helps him to flower greatly in love and goodness. Maximum growth of the child can be achieved only through freedom. It enables the child to understand himself and life as a whole. This view is widely accepted and followed in all types of education in eastern and Western countries.

Students and their individuality: Krishnamurti believes that every student is unique in his approach to learning. According to him some in academics, others in sports, still others in art. The integrated personality development of the child is possible through school. Therefore, the school should be small having a limited number of students in order to give individual attention, for the welfare of each child.

Guidance: Krishnamurti insists that necessary guidance should be given to all needy children. The purpose of guidance is to make the child acquire a capacity of self-directiveness. The school should help the child to develop his varying interest through appropriate guidance so that he becomes an educated in the real sense of the term and finds solutions to the problems of life.

Method of teaching: Krishnamurti's concept of teaching method is progressive in nature. According to him "One teaches because one sees that self knowledge alone". Hence, students should be treated as an equal partner. Critical thinking needs to be developed through instructional process. Students should be discouraged to accept the statement, and taught not 'what' to think but 'how' to think. The method that we follow should allow the child freedom and enable him to think for himself. Today, the development of creative thinking is an important aspect of education.

CONCLUSION

Jiddu Krishnamurti is known as J.K. in the field of education and philosophy. He is an outstanding intellectual thinker of the twentieth century who enriched the principles of education. In fact, Krishnamurti's conception of methods of teaching, school, organization, role of teacher, real education, integral education, education for world peace, role of students and discipline in truly progressive nature widens the scope of education. Moreover, his approach to the development of an integrated personality through integral education makes him a distinguished philosopher and is highly commendable by almost all thinkers. However, he maybe considered as the first educational thinker who states the failure of education in bringing out world peace. He has highlighted the picture of present school and education in the emerging Indian society. In the words of Jiddu Krishnamurti, "Today's education prepares us for various professions and vocations that can only contribute to our miseries and illusions. True education not only trains the mind to take up various vocations but also educates the mind. Education should develop love and understanding among people and does not promote industrialization that has the potential to annihilate others. Education should help us to learn the permanent values of life and develop creativity".

CHAPTER 22

SARVEPALLI RADHAKRISHNAN 1888–1975

INTRODUCTION

Dr. Sarvepalli Radhakrishnan is known as a great Philosopher, a great teacher, a scholar par excellence, a creative genius, a great humanist, a spiritualist, a man of vision, a man of mission, a man of principles, an idealist, an orator with the gab, an original thinker, a prolific writer, chairman of university of education commission, and the second President of India. He is one of the greatest educationists and makers of modern India. He not only enlightens our nation but also the whole world by his outstanding personality, philosophy and intellectual ideas. He shines like a luminous star in the galaxy of intellectuals. He is the torch-bearer of the Indian education. He influences the social, philosophical, economical, cultural, political spiritual and educational aspects of modern India. It is quite natural that philosophers have never been kings and kings have never been philosophers. But he is the only philosopher who has been the President of India and Indian Ambassador to Russia. As a great Philosopher he is equally an authority in the Western and Eastern thoughts. In fact, he is an authority of the modern world in religion, culture and philosophy. His contribution to the field of education, philosophy, religion, culture and science are very important, unique and immortal. He loves the teaching profession first and those who studied under him still remember him with gratitude for his great qualities as a teacher. Dr S Radhakrishnan is a superman in the educational, philosophical, spiritual and cultural scenarios.

LIFE AND WORKS OF DR. RADHAKRISHNAN

Dr. Saravepalli Radhakrishnan one of the most distinguished twentieth-century scholars of comparative religion and philosophy, renowned professor, able administrator, successful diplomat, famous statesman and ardent patriot of India, was born to the parents of Sarvepalli Veerasami and Seethamma Devi on 5th September 1888 at Sarvepalli, near Thiruttani, Tamil Nadu, South India in a Telungu Niyogi Brahmin Hindu family. He studied primary education at K.V. Hign School, Thiruttani and moved to the Hermanburg Evangelical Lutheran Mission School (1896) Thirupati and Government High Secondary school, Walajapet Vellor District (South India). He had been awarded scholarships throughout his academic life. He joined Voorhees college, Vellore and later moved to Madras Christian College, Chennai for higher education and graduated in 1906, and continued there for Postgraduate study in Philosophy. He submitted a project on 'The Ethics of the Vedanta and its metaphysical presuppositions'. It was charged that the Vedanta system had no room for ethics. Professors William Meston and Dr Alfred

George Hogg commended his M.A. Dissertation. Radhakrishnan said, "The Christian teachers of Indian culture criticised and disturbed faith and shook the traditional props". The challenge of Christian critics, impelled him to take up a study of Hinduism and find out what is living and what is dead in it. This led him to carry out a critical study of Indian Philosophy and religion and a life-long defence of Hinduism against un informed Western criticism. He commended professor Hogg as 'My distinguished teacher' and one of the greatest Christian thinkers we had in India. Prof William Skinner, Principal of Madras Christian College, gave a testimony saying "Radhakrishnan is one of the best men we have had in recent year" which enabled him to get the first job in the Department of Philosophy at Madras Presidency college in April 1909–1919. He became the professor of Philosophy in the university of Mysore (1918–1921). Aushutosh Mukherjee appointed him at the University of Kolkata (West Bengal) to occupy the King George V Chair of mental and moral science in 1921–1931. He represented the University of Calcutta at the Congress of the universities of the British Empire (June 1926) and the international congress of Philosophy at Harvard University (Sep. 1927). Dr. S. Radhakrishnan was invited to occupy the post vacated by principal J. Estlin Carpenter. So, he had an opportunity of teaching comparative religion to the students of Manchester college of Oxford University in 1927. He was Knighted by George V for his service to education in June1931. He was appointed as the Vice-Chancellor of Andhra University (1931–1936). He taught Eastern Religion and Ethics at Oxford University in 1936. He was elected as a fellow of All Souls College (Oxford University) in 1939. He was invited by Pandit Madan Mohan Malaviya to be Vice-Chancellor of Banaras Hindu University (1937–1948).

After the independence of India he represented the country at the UNESCO and later served as Ambassador of India to the Soviet Union of Russia during 1949–1952. He won the hearts of Russian leaders by his sweet learned and impressive behaviour. The government of India appointed him as the chairman of the University Education Commission (1948). He became an elected member of the Constituent Assembly of India (1952) and was the First Vice President of the country (1952–1962). He was honoured with the highest civilian award–Bharat Ratna in 1954 for his contribution to education, religion, culture and philosophy. There after he was elected as the second President of India (1962–1967). His students wanted to celebrate his birthday. As Dr. Radhakrishnan loved the teaching profession first, he wanted to celebrate such a day as 'Teachers day'. Since then, his birthday has been observing as teachers' day. He also received the order of Merit in 1963 and the Templeton Prize in 1975. He devoted his retired life to the philosophical pursuits. This great philosopher, statesman and President of India left this earth peacefully due to heart failure on 17th April 1975.

PHILOSOPHY OF RADHAKRISHNAN

Dr. S. Radhakrishnan's Philosophy is idealism which includes logic, ethics, aesthetics and metaphysics—Metaphysics is concerned with the ultimate nature of things. It comprises of two main aspects—oncology and epistemology. Science studies the different facts of expertises where as philosophy develops the meaning and explanations of experience as a whole philosophy has an explanatory and descriptive sides, and a metaphysical and an empirical sides. As such, it studies experience in a concrete form and reveals the order. It is a sustained attempt to comprehended the universe as a whole . It co-ordinates and interprets all aspects of experience, the reports of scientists, the intuitions artists and the insights of saints. It offers him the opportunity to comprehend life and vision of the realities of living. Therefore, his philosophy does not deviate from the truth of existence According to him, the functions of philosophy is to order life and guide human actions. It enables life and broadens the outlook. In other words, philosophy gives an insight in to the meaning of life. It means that life has a purpose, ideals and values. These are the dynamic forces which provide direction to life and help to achieve the goals. There are values which transcend man and society. The proper ends of life is inherent in the very nature of the universe morally obligate man to discover, recognise and accept the supremacy of values, and regulate his behaviour accordingly. It is an expression of the absolute reality Dr. S. Radhakrishnan explains that the absolute is God, Man's inborn feeling is God. In fact, his quest for truth, his striving for perfection, his longing for goodness, his craving for beauty, all his hopes ideals and aspiration prove his essential divine nature. But he is a complex multi-dimensional being. He is not only spirit but also has mind, life and body. These multiple sides of his nature are not contradictory. Thus, he is indivisible, so nothing in him can be rejected. Dr. S. Radhakrishnan believed that everything in the man is the expression of the divine. Therefore, he considers the end of man is let the sprit in him, permeates his whole being, his soul flesh and affection man attains his deepest self by losing his selfish ego.

Matter and Sprit: Matter and spirit are the important themes of Radhakrishnan's Philosophy. However, the development of science and technology have made some erroneously to believe that matter is the most important thing in our life. But a little scrutiny reveals the omnipotence of the human spirit and not of matter. It shows the superiority of the human mind. We are not merely a part of nature. This is because there is non-natural element in us which exceeds the quality and potentiality of matter. The non-natural element refers to the spirit of man. It is the spirit which is responsible for all achievements in the world. In fact, the spirit of man which controls matter. Man is a spiritual being and the frontier of mystery. It is he himself that can reach the frontier and make a break-through. If he realises this, then he can rid himself of his lower passions and rise to his truer nature. But some kind of crudeness (deep down) does not allow the man to settle down in an atmosphere of freedom from fear. Men may be nuclear geniuses but they remain ethical dwarfs. The spectacular achievements smother the spiritual breath of mankind. Man is afraid of his brother and lives in an atmosphere of distrust and fear.

Divinity of Human Soul: Dr. S. Radhakrishnan believes in the divinity of human soul. The world over the unleashed tendencies which crush the human spirit and degrade and dehumanise the mind are on the rampage. It is seen that humanity has been forced to become a robot, so the human mind surrenders its humanity and makes itself as an object lapses into rigidly routine and does not understand the boundless possibilities located in the creative side of human nature. It is then that man becomes victim of necessity, dialectical, mechanical, historical or even providential. But there is no such thing as God dictating the future events. He considers as we are the co-workers with divine spirit. According to him, the divine uses human beings. So every individual has this eternal spark as a creative element. If we overlook it, we are untrue and unfaithful to our own education and, humanity. Therefore, the spiritual nature of man, or the essential divinity of the human soul should be given utmost reverence. It is the divine in man which is behind the apparatus of body, mind, heart and intellect. As such, it is the ray of the celestial light which propels man towards complete fulfilment. Religions also emphasis the divinity of human soul. Our spiritual being is inward and, therefore, it derives its strength from within and not from without. Hence, we need to get back to the shrine of inward solitude and not get back to the shrine of inward solitude and not get lost in the worldly turmoil of materialism. This is essential for the renewal of our sprit. In fact, man is not satisfied with what he is, for he longs to become better and nobler. As a result, he seeks and aspires. However, he can make himself the instrument of higher purpose through detachment and renunciation. It proves that there is no such thing as inevitability as far as human beings are concerned. Man is not a helpless toy in the hands of the great cosmic forces. The inevitable spirit within him triumphs over the gravitational downward pull of circumstances.

Place of Religion: Religion has a place of crucial importance in the educational and philosophical thoughts of Dr. S. Radhakrishnan. He believes that the way of religion is the remaking of man, a complete integration of his being. This is because it introduces an entirely new sense, a totally new set of values. Radhakrishnan defines religion as the insight into the nature of reality (*darsana*) or experience of reality (*anubhava*). Experience is the responsibility of the whole personality the integrated self to the central reality. According to him, religion is the self-manifestation of the ultimate reality in man. It is the awareness of our real nature in God. It is a strenuous endeavour to apprehend truth. It holds that man exists on the level of super nature. The function of religion is to the evaluation of man into his divine nature, develop awareness and intensity of understanding and bring about a better, deeper and more enduring adjustment in life. It commands man to make change in his own nature and to let the divine in him manifest it. He states that hearing (*Sravana*) reflection (*manana*) and disciplined meditation (*nididhyasana*) respectively are the three stages of religious life, and one has to rise from one stage to another. As such, religion is not doctrinal conformity or ceremonial piety but it is personal encounter of the individual with the supreme (God). There was a time when it was assumed that a man could not be true believer in his own religion unless he also believed that all other religious were false. Many wrongs were penetrated in the name of religion. Therefore, he believes that teaching of sectarian creeds to children, instead of developing in them the spirit of brotherly love, generates narrow group loyalties and sows the seed of future strife.

Secular Concept of State: Radhakrishnan has faith in the secular philosophy. Secularism does not mean the neglect of religion. In other words, it is not indifferent to religion but respect for all faiths, and respects everything which man holds sacred and anything worthy or reverence. The fundamental principles of the constitution of India call for spiritual training. So all people are equally entitled to freedom of conscience and the right to freely profess, practice and propagate religion. However, there is no state religion, which otherwise would have meant of becoming partial to any one religion.

Religion and Science: Radhakrishnan believed that emphasis on religions does not be little the role of science in our life. Science and religion are not opposed to each other because both seek truth. According to him, the quest of truth is the quest of God. However, religion and science represent the two dimensions of the human being the rational and the spiritual. Therefore, there is a need for co-ordination and integration. Human despair, depression and fear of fratricidal wars appear on the scene only when science as the pursuit of knowledge turns in to power and is used as a weapon of tyranny and exploitation by power seekers and selfish men. Radhakrishnan remarks, "Struggling as we are with the fateful horizons of the atomic age. The achievements of science have induced our minds a mood of despair, making us feel like homeless exiles, caught in a blind machine". This cannot be counted as the failure of science it is in fact, the failure of man. The fundamental problem remains whether science will be used in future for peace, prosperity and the profound increase of Joys of mankind or for destruction, devastation and desolation. What is wrong is not the scientific discoveries or technological achievements but the outlook of man with his cult of power and selfish motives. In fact , men sometimes become unmindful of their implication and social consequences. He further says that 'The powers of science can be considered safe in the hands of those who have great reverence for human feelings and tenderness that colour the daily existence of our life'. So any system of education must not forget that knowledge and feeling are equally important ingredient of human life.

Ethics: According to Radhakrishnan, evil is a negative conception, lack of good, and all conflicts are between good and better bad and worse. It is due to one's free will and God permits it because He does not interface with the human choice. Suffering is not punishment but the reward of fellowship, an essential accompaniment of all endeavours. The goal of the world process is a harmonious unity and therefore, moral life is the enrichment of life that is the outcome of the recognition of others. Moral is a form type of life where we have significance and social values. It is the current brand of social custom and one who deviates from it is immoral. Immorality is considered as an ethical value in the next generation. Life is a great adventure and not a set scheme. So no progress is possible if moral rules are considered as *sacrosanct*

Aesthetics: Radhakrishnan considers art as the expression of experience in some media. The experience is clothed in different forms which appeal to the emotion through the senses. The relation between the experience and the medium is closer in some forms of arts such as in poetry than in others. The experience is released afresh by means of the work of art and the enjoyer becomes the sharer of creator's mind. According to him, 'Art is the form of knowledge, a disclosure of the deeper reality of things, and an imitation of inner reality'. So the aim of art is to capture the inner and inform the spirit. It is by integrating the insight or spiritual intuition that the artist attains to the power of artistic expression. Therefore, arts do not much represent as suggest, do not so much produce reality as create aesthetic emotion.

EDUCATIONAL VIEWS OF DR. RADHAKRISHNAN

Dr. Radhakrishnan is an idealistic philosopher but his educational thoughts are influenced by the pragmatic philosophy. So his educational philosophy is not only idealistic but also pragmatic one. We may point out his educational Philosophies as:

- Education is the instrument for social economic and cultural change.
- It should be utilised properly for social and national integration and increasing productivity.
- Education is not only in knowledge and skill but it should help us to live with others.
- The right kind of education could solve many problems of society and country.
- Education helps us to see the other world, the invisible and intangible world beyond space and time.
- It gives us a second birth to realise what we have already in us.
- It should develop the minds of students a love of sustained thinking, adherence to truth and the power of resistance to popular sentiments and mob passion.
- Education is not meant for loving knowledge but for its practical utility.
- Education helps the children for natural development and prosperity.
- It is based on the principles of universal love and humanity, mutual help and co-operation, self-sacrifice and self-abnegation.
- It should emphasise the acquisition of technical skills which are essential in the modern society.
- All powers and knowledge are within the man. So heart can be refined and purified through appropriate education and also the spirit.
- Education dispels ignorance and enlightens the individual.
- It is neither book learning nor memorising facts and figures.
- It is not accumulation of words or stuffing mind with countless information unrelated to life and world.
- It is also not memorisation of thoughts of others in foreign language and reproducing those in examination to get diplomas and degrees for white collar jobs.
- It is the assimilation of values and ideas for man-making, character forming and life building.
- Education which does not inculcate spiritual feelings in students is not true.

MEANING AND DEFINITION OF EDUCATION

Dr. Radhakrishnan's concept of education is the harmonious blending of the positive views of Eastern and Western culture and Philosophy. So his definition of Education is very far and wide, and yet more comprehensive which is essential to the modernised global life and society. In fact, his educational philosophy is based on the principles of universal love and humanity, mutual help and co-operation, self-sacrifice and self-abnegation. As such, the meaning of education includes everything for personal, social, cultural, economic and aesthetical life. He defines "Education as the instrument for social, economic and cultural changes". In other words, education is a powerful instrument which should properly be used for social and national integration, increasing productivity and fostering human values. It is possible through a balanced growth of the individual with knowledge skill and wisdom. More over, he states that the real meaning of education is to emancipate the individual from ignorance, evils and narrowism. So we need education of the wholeness—mental, physical intellectual, spiritual and economic life. This is because Dr. Radhakrishnan has been influenced by the Eastern and Western philosophers like Swami Vivekandanda, Rabindranath Tagore, Sri Aurobindo Ghosh, John Dewey Pestalozzi etc.

FUNCTIONS OF EDUCATION

The comprehensive definition of Dr. Radhakrishnan emphasise various functions of education which are very important and useful for man-making, character formation, national integration, worldly brotherhood, co-operative living and spiritual development. In short, education for life-building at personal, national and global levels.

Training of Intellect, Heart and Spirit: Dr. Radhakrishnan affirmly believed that education is said to be complete. It must be humane, it must include not only the raining of the intellect but also the refinement of the heart and the disciplined spirit. According to him, "No education can be regarded as complete if it neglects the heart and the spirit". This is because all knowledge and powers are within the man. So, the first and foremost function of education is to train and develop them properly.

Turning to Humanism: Naturally man is a social animal but selfish one living in ignorance, superstition and polluted environments. More over no country in the world can hold its place of primacy and perpetuity. At this juncture, what counts is the moral contribution, we make to human welfare. Therefore the function of education is turn the social animal in to relational one and develop the qualities of charity in judgement and companion for people who are suffering. He says, if we adopt such an approach, the tension of the world will diminish rapidly.

Democratic Outlook: It is very essential for happy, healthy and peaceful life in the diversity. The cause of democracy is the cause of individual of the free spirit of man with its spontaneous inspiration and endeavour. Every man whose thoughts and feelings are not silted up has his own inner possession, which belongs to him alone, his holy shrine, which he has won for himself. When an individual is trained to appreciate his own holy being, he will develop a chastity of mind and spirit and approach with inner trembling another's sanctuary. According to him, intolerance is basically unchastely. If we do not give this spiritual direction to our education, it will fail in its purpose. Hence, the function is to develop secular based democratic outlook through training the students for freedom and unity not for localism and for democracy not for dictatorship.

Developing Scientific Spirit: This is another important function of education. According to Radhakrishnan, it is education which should increase productivity. It is possible only through the development of science and technology. Therefore, the spirit for inquiry, curiosity, intellects, dedication, imaginative power and talents in the pursuit of science and rejects all clichés of thoughts sterile styles and social manners which hamper the individual aims and efforts. Moreover, scientific spirit is important to strengthen the minds of young people and redeem the society from ignorance, laziness, and superstitious faith and beliefs.

Inculcating Human Values: Dr. Radhakrishnan emphasises the inculcation of human values through proper education. He remarks, 'Education should develop a universal love and humanity, mutual help and co-operation, self-sacrifice and self-abnegation.' The present man though standing on the earth, stretches out to hold stars. In fact, he knows everything to fly in the sky and swim in the water except how to walk and live in the earth. There is nothing wrong about science and technology what is wrong is the use we make of it. Man has lost his values in the materialistic and polluted society. As a result, there is a great deal of intellectual and technical skill but the ethical and spiritual vitality is at a low ebb. Man's completeness results from the pursuit of truth and its application to improve human life, the influence of what is beautiful in nature, man and art, and spiritual development and its embodiment in ethical principles.

Developing Spiritual Values: Dr. Radhakrishnan, naturally idealistic philosopher, was influenced by Hinduism. So, he wants to import spiritual values as an integral part of education. According to him, education is the means by which we can tide up our minds, acquire information and spiritual values. He further, says that education without spiritual values fail in its purpose and it is not true. Therefore, it is considered as an important function in the materialistic society.

Searching for Integration and Truth: This is one of the most important functions of education. Education should prepare the students to search for the integration of human beings. This is because we must know the world and have an idea of the general plan of the universe and search for truth to be conscious of our moral and social obligation. He remarks when we attain truth, our burden are lightened and our difficulties are diminished. In fact, it lights up our path way with the radiance of Joy.

Developing Capacity for Discernment: According to Dr. Radhakrishnan, education is not only meant for the acquisition of information but also develop the capacity for discernment. It is true that judgement is more important than cleverness. This is because today we have many men who are clever but not many who are up right in the social moral, cultural and economic life. Therefore, the function of education is to cultivate respect, for purity which is essential in daily life and administration so that we can weed out corruption and clear up the nation.

Developing the Spirit of Enquiry: He further says that we should develop the spirit of enquiry and dedication to the pursuit of science and technology. This is so because we are misled in to the participation in non-academic endeavour. So, we waste our years in colleges in trivialities and inanities. Moreover, we have enough material but it is not guided property. Hence, the function of education is to inculcate the spirit of enquiry in the mind of young.

Training People for Freedom: Dr. Radhakrishnan advocate freedom for the people through education. He says, if we twist the minds of the young out of shape, they will be danger to society. The future of democracy in Asia depends on our willingness to submit to discipline and undergo personal sacrifice. If India is to remain free united and democratic educational institutions should train people for freedom, not for obedience, for unity and not localism, for democracy and not dictatorship. Our young should have a sense of purpose. Hence, this is considered to be one of the functions of present education.

Training for Self-discipline: He remarks that education should train the young to the best possible all round living in the individual and social levels. So it is education that must make them intelligent and good citizens. He wants that they must observe spontaneously, those unwritten laws of decency and honour felt by good men but not enforced by any statute.

Preserving Spirit of Youth: It is considered as an important function to protect the spirit of youth. In the words of Dr Radhakrishnan, "Unless we preserve the spirit of youth, keep an open mind and change our blind belief and practice, we cannot endure. India has endured for centuries, it is because she has kept spirit of youth." She can keep alive only if she does not idolise her institutions, does turn them into ends in themselve.

AIMS OF EDUCATION

Generally, Indian Philosophers are similar in educational philosophy principles and aims. However, they are unique important and useful for shaping better man and society. They emphasise the social, spiritual, cultural economic and aesthetic life. So the aim of all education is man-making. Dr Radhakrishnan stated various aims of education in his occasional speeches and writings.

Personality Development: A satisfactory system of education aims at a balanced growth of the individual, based on knowledge and wisdom. It can be gained by the study of literature, Philosophy and religion. Moreover, education should develop a love of sustained thinking, adherence to truth and the power of the resistance to popular sentiments and mob passion in the students. So, the guiding motto of education system should be the development of personality.

Character Formations: Socially desirable character should be formed in the minds of people. Dr Radhakrishnan advocates character building and considers it as an important aim of education. According to him, character of a man is the aggregate of the tendencies of his mind or sum total of the impressions created by his speech and action. He says, that character is destiny necessary in every walk of life. He further states that education is incomplete if it does not initiate in the child, the values of love, truth, goodness and beauty. He feels that his aim is the key to all education.

Prevention and Transmission of Culture: According to Radhakrishnan, "Culture is transformation of one's being to produce sweetness of temper, sanity of mind and strength of spirit". Therefore, he attaches great importance to the cultural aspects of education. Man has created his culture at a great cost of time and labour. So, a country enriched in culture is advanced in many aspects. He believes that it is education which preserves, enrich transmits and modifies the culture of a country. Now culture has become meaningless in the materialistic society.

Development of Spiritual Values: Dr. Radhakrishnan has given a right place to education for developing spiritual values among the people. According to him, education which does not inculcate spiritual feelings in the students is not true one. He, further says that without a spiritual bent of mind, the physical and intellectual development of a person remains stunted. This situation is detrimental to the progress of mankind. Hence, the human development should not be confused with the acquisition of mechanical skills or intellectual information. He suggests to develop human attitude and manly spirit through the refinement of heart and fostering of good habits.

Develop New Ideas: Dr. Radhakrishnan remarks, "The university education should generate new ideas and discard those which prevent the growth of the nation. New ideas are necessary to rise above superstitions of achieving progress". Therefore, the aim of university education is to imbibe good culture and accept new values for an all round development of the individual.

Longing for Higher Values: The educational and training institutions produce a number of technicians who are without conscience and tastes. Moreover, there is moral vacuum in them, so the aim of education is to develop constructive thoughts for the poor and the suffering, show chivalry and respect woman, faith in brotherhood regardless of race, colour, nation, religion, love of peace and freedom and dislike cruelty.

Develop Scientific Attitude: This is an era of science and technology where man himself is a machine. Therefore, education should enable the child develop talents to create, discover and invent something new, novel and useful. Moreover, science and technology are basic needs of human life used for productive works. At this juncture, we should know to operate and apply science and technology. So education should develop spirit for inquiry and dedication to the pursuit of science and technology.

Strengthen National Integration: India is a country of united states where many cultural people live together. So, strengthening of national integration is very important and is the basic need of India and the aim of education. Religious education, mass education, programmes like social services, community living and observing national days, have been emphasized for the development of nationalism in the child.

International Understanding: Dr. Radhakrishnan considers international understanding as an important aim of education. He advocated the creation of new world order, growth of world community and world citizenship. Therefore, he emphasises education as a means for creating international understanding and mutual cohesion among the people across the border.

Develop Vocational Efficiency: He is also a pragmatic philosopher emphasising education for the development of vocational efficiency. He believes that this aim of education enables the child to attain certain skills which will make him economically sufficient. He feels that by increasing his own income through involvement in farms and factories can increase the wealth of nation. So he advocates imparting vocational courses as an aim of education.

Giving Second Birth and Self-realisation: According to Dr. Radhakrishnan, education should aim at bringing the man nearer to God, through the study of various subjects. And enabling him to realise what he has in him. The true aim of education is to prepare the man for second birth or born again into world of spirit and freedom through silence, dedication, truth, love, sacrifice, simple living and high thinking. He wants that education which helps the people see the other world, the invisible and intangible world beyond space and time. He also wants to establish a classless society in order to bring equality between man and man and develop universal brotherhood through education.

CURRICULUM

Dr. Radhakrishnan is an idealist and pragmatist so his curriculum is based on idealistic and pragmatic thoughts.

Subjects: According to Dr. Radhakrishnan curriculum must be related to life. So, he wants the students to study a number of subjects such as literature, language, philosophy, science, ethics, politics, theology, geography, history, economics, agriculture, natural science, civics, mathematics, arts, music, fine arts, vocational/professional subjects, sports and physical education, Yoga and religion.

Language: Dr. Radhakrishnan recommends' to study three languages that is, mother tongue/regional or state language, federal language-Hindi and link language- English. He also emphasises the study of Sanskrit because it is essential to understand indigenous culture and the noble ideas described in Vedas and Upanishads, the Bhagavad-Gita and other scriptures.

Intellectual Development: He suggests to study History, Geography, Economics, Mathematics, Philosophy and religion for the intellectual development of society and human races.

Spiritual and Economic Development: He includes the study of religion and spiritual education, moral education vocational courses women education, and mass education in the curriculum for socio-economic and spiritual development.

Curriculum for Women: Dr. Radhakrishnan recommends to include the subjects such as literature, history, science, religion, ethics, *puranas*, housekeeping, arts, sewing, domestic work, home science, child rearing, worship, Yoga and meditation meant for women which are useful to them for their specific duties in life. He believes that no society can progress satisfactorily with the backwardness of women race.

METHODS OF TEACHING

Dr. Radhakrishnan is the great teacher who advocates no fixed method of teaching for acquisition of knowledge. He emphasises two things—What to Teach? and How to teach? What to teach refers to the content/Subject and How to teach? refers to Methodology. A teacher must know these things which are equally importance to make the teaching effective. Dr. Radhakrishnan has given great importance to observation, experiments, discussion, learning by meditation, Textbook method, seminar and tutorial system, (Brings teacher and taught closer). He wants to teach moral values through real and living examples. He recommends imitation method to teach industrial subjects. He advocates regular practice in Yoga and meditation. According to him, intuition, reasoning and self-knowledge are the sources of knowledge. He remarks method of teaching cannot be lecture and demonstration. It should be question answer and discussion methods. These methods provide adequate opportunities to the students for conversation, debate discussion and exchange of opinions and thoughts with the teachers. He also wants the students to come closer to society and nature to understood the life and reality.

DISCIPLINE

Dr. Radhakrishnan believes that lack of self-control deteriorates the standards of scholarships character and integrity of students. Discipline is very important for Yoga and spiritual activities. In other words, Yoga and meditation are not feasible without discipline. According to him, discipline leads to self-realisation. He wants the students to be trained to approach life's problems with fortitude, self-control and a sense of balance. So, there should be adequate provision for games and other corporate activities. Thus, he gives much importance to discipline in the progress and growth of the students.

TEACHERS

Dr. Radhakrishnan always emphasises the importance of teacher in teaching process. He says, 'Teacher is the corner stone of the arch of education'. He further remarks, really without quality and effective teacher, the educational institution, curriculum, teaching aids and educational planning are meaningless. He views on an 'ideal teacher' contrary to many of the common teaching practices. A true teacher always helps us to think for ourselves in the new situations which arise, widen our knowledge and help us to see clearly. So, a good teacher must know how to arouse the interest of the pupils in the field of study for which he is responsible. He must himself be a master in the field of study and he in touch with the latest development in the subjects. According to him, teacher must himself be a fellow traveller in the exciting pursuit of knowledge. He believes that teachers are removers of spiritual blindness. So, teacher is also called 'Guru'. Guru is a combination of two words, 'Gu' means darkness and 'ru' means to remove. As such, teacher should bring the children and society out of ignorance of darkness and superstition. Moreover, they are the reservoirs of new spirit of adventure in the intellectual, social and political matters.

RELEVANCE OF DR. RADHAKRISHNAN'S THOUGHT IN INDIA AND WORLD (CONTRIBUTION OF RADHAKRISHNAN TO EDUCATION) IN 21ST CENTURY

Dr. Radhakrishnan's contribution to education has exclusive and exceptional one. In fact, he has made a solid and splendid contribution to the modern India and world.

Report of University Education Commission: Dr. Radhakrishnan's greatest contribution to education is his reports recommending to cover a wide range of subjects, academic standards, status and salaries of teachers, declining of jobs from degrees, religious education, medium of instruction and reservation of seats for the backward people. All recommendation were not implemented but he caused to the establishment of university grants commission with sustained benefits to the autonomy and development of Indian universities.

Emphasise Character and Moral Values: The present education suffers from the crisis in character and loss of moral values. Radhakrishnan emphasises the development of character and moral values.

Combination of all Educational Philosophies: Educational thoughts of Dr. Radhakrishnan are the combination of idealistic, realistic, humanistic, pragmatic and existentialistic philosophies. So his educational thoughts fulfil the aims of education and help to achieve all round development of the child for social, spiritual, cultural, economic, and aesthetical life.

Free and Compulsory Education: He strongly advocates free and compulsory education to all children irrespective of their castes, creed, gender and socio-economic status. This view has been accepted by all committees and commissions, and implemented in the country.

Unity in Diversity: India is a multi-racial, multi-lingual, multi-political and multi-cultural country. She is a united states of India which stands in unity in diversity. So, he emphasises tri-lingual system at regional (Mother Tongue), national (Hindi) and international (English) levels. He believes that it will help in solving various problems arise in recent time. However, the regional or state-wise government opposes it to exploit the people in Tamil Nadu (South India). This is a curse to the state due to ignorance and politics.

Universal Literacy: Universalisation of education is the logical and inevitable requirement for the progress of the country. So, no child whether poor or lower should be deprived of the opportunities in education. Radhakrishnan advocates inclusive education with special emphasis on the changing the facts of women and the deprived sections of society through education.

New ideas for National Development: The ideology of Radhakrishnan about education for democracy is very germane and his thoughts of self-development, man-making and self-expression are the three important educational attempt for individual and national development.

Education solves Problems of Society: Radhakrishnan believes that right kind of education could solve many problems of the society and the country. Education can be turned into powerful instrument for making peace and solving problems at all levels.

Development of Human Qualities: Radhakrishnan remarks, 'Students are very much interested in using science and technology in various spheres of life. As a result, human qualities are degraded day-by-day and education has become meaningless in fostering human values'. According to him, science helps us to build up our outer life, but another discipline, is necessary to strengthen and refine the living spirit. He, further, says that 'though we have made enormous progress in knowledge and scientific inventions, we are not above the level of past generations in ethical and spiritual life'. So, he emphasises spiritual education for fostering moral values, faith in God, good manners, honesty and fellow-feeling. This is great relevance for the present time particularly in the age of science and technology.

Development of Vocational Efficiency: He lays emphasize on the development of vocational efficiency in the students. For this he suggests to introduce, agriculture as a subject in rural schools, and open agricultural colleges and rural universities. It is deplorable that the present educational system is unable to develop new enterprises and employment for the youth. At this juncture, Dr Radhakrishnan's thoughts on vocational education is quite relevant and useful for economic life.

National Integration: This is one of the basic needs of India. So Dr. Radhakrishnan considers national integration as one of the important aims of education. He emphasis religious education, mass education, social services community living, and study of social sciences for the development of nationalism. At the same time, the present education has a very little impact on adult's mind to tolerate and pay regards to other's faiths and beliefs. So the views of Dr. Radhakrishnan are very much relevant to strengthen national integration.

International Understanding: He advocates the development of international understanding as an important aim of education. So, he emphasises the creation of new world order, growth of world community and world citizenship. He believes that education is a means for creating international understanding and mutual cohesion among the people across the world. Moreover, it is essential to fight against various socio-economic and environmental issues like terrorism, environmental pollution, poverty, unemployment and diseases. According to him, it is education which creates a sense of fellow feeling, cohesion and attitude of sharing among the students. This is a global society where culture is international and science is cosmopolitan. Thus, his views and recommendation are quite praise worthy and note worthy in the world families.

Teacher-Taught Relationship: The teacher-student relationship is diminishing in the present educational scenario due to student indiscipline fighting with the teachers/students at the time of student council/election and examination. So the sound educational environment becomes polluted one. Dr. Radhakrishnan emphasis the close and cordial teacher-taught relationships to make education effective and possible. But, no cordial relationship between them in the profit oriented privatisation of educational industries and materialistic society. The availability of textbooks, guides and lack of quality teachers and commercialisation of education have widened the gap between the teacher taught relationship. However, the educational thoughts of Radhakrishnan highlight the importance of teacher-student relationship in the educational exchange.

Preservation and Transmission of Culture: Radhakrishnan wants to preserve the rich traditional culture of the country. He also recommends it as an important aim of education. However, it has become meaningless in the obscene-violence based mass media and intoxicant world. There is a rapid socio-economic change in the materialistic society. Radhakrishnan's educational thoughts are good enough for realising the present scenario of Indian society and other countries.

Supporting All Views: Dr. Radhakrishnan supports in favour of scientific and practice-oriented society, child-centered education, activity oriented education, job-oriented education, life-centred and community-based education, which are important to prepare the child for life.

Method of Teaching: Dr. Radhakrishnan emphasis almost all methods of teaching he himself is a great teacher. Observation experiments, discussion, learning by meditations textbook method, seminar, tutorial system, close to nature, and society, Yoga and meditation, intuition, question- answer are quite useful methods for all levels of education.

Democracy and Classless Society: He believes that the success of democracy very much depends upon education. Narrow politics are working for their own benefits. But Radhakrishnan's views on democracy and politics are very much significant because he wants to establish a classless society without exploitation, corruption, ill-feeling, inequality etc. Politics is a branch of ethics, it should promote human welfare and happiness. Thus, his educational thoughts are highly useful to create a better world for better life.

BOOKS OF RADHAKRISHNAN

Dr. S. Radhakrishnan is a prolific writer and published many books on philosophy and education.

- The Ethics of Vedanta and its Metaphysical Presuppositions (MA Thesis) Published in 1908
- The Philosophy of Rabindaranath Tagore (1918)
- Resign of Religion in contemporary Philosophy (1920)
- Indian Philosophy (1 Volume) highlighting the philosophy of Vedas and the Upanishads Bhagavad-Gita, Realism of Jainism and Idealism of Buddha and Buddhist philosophy (1923).
- Indian Philosophy (2 Volume) describes the six systems of Nyaya Vaisheshika, Samkhya Yoga Mimanusa, Vedanta, Vaishnava—Shaiva Shakta systems of Theism (1926–1927).
- The Hindu View of Life (1926).
- The Idealist View of Life (1932).
- East and West in Religion (1931).
- Eastern Religions and Western Thoughts (1939).
- Future of Civilisation (1941).
- The Religion We Need (1942).
- Education and Society (1947).
- The Bhagavad-Gita—An Introductory Essay (1948).
- The Dhammapada (1950).
- The Principal Upanishads (1953).
- The Recovery of Faith (1956).
- Brahma Sutra (1957).
- Fellowship of the Spirit
- On Nehru
- The Concept of Man
- My Search for Truth.
- Freedom and Culture
- A Source Book in Indian Philosophy (1957).
- Religion, Science and Culture (1968).

CONCLUSION

Dr. Sarvepalli Radhakrishnan is a multi-dimensional creative genius in the twentieth century. He has provided a great contribution in all diverse field of life. In fact, his creative contribution can be seen in the philosophical, educational social, diplomatic and political fields. He is a great exponent of Hindu philosophy and boom of the educational Philosophy. His educational thoughts on the meaning, functions, aims, curriculum method of teaching, discipline and the role of teacher are very relevant in the 21st Century. In the words of Pandit Jawaharlal Nehru, "Radhakrishnan has served his country in many capacities. He is a great teacher from whom all of us have learnt much and will continue to learn. It is India's peculiar privilege to have a great philosopher, a great educationist and a great humanist as her President. That in itself shows the kind of man we honour and respect. He further remarks, "Wherever he went his words brought comfort to the people, and his own wisdom brought people nearer to each other". Aldus Hurley says, 'Dr. Radhakrishnan is the master of words and no words'. It refers to his ability to express the most abstruse thoughts of Philosophy in such a fine language that it becomes comprehensible to all. Prof. H.N. Moorhead says, 'Dr. Radhakrishnan has the rare qualification of being equally versed in the great European and the not less great Asiatic tradition which may be said to hold in solution between them the spiritual wisdom of the world, and of thus speaking as a philosophical bilinguist upon it.' George P. Conger rightly remarks, 'Among the Philosophers or time, no one has achieved so much in so many fields as has Sarvepalli Radhakrishnan'. In fact, Dr. Radhakrishnan has been highly appraised by Paul Arthur Schillpp saying, would it be possible to find a more excellent example of a living bridge between the East and the West than Professor Radhakrishnan. Now let us observe the Golden words of Dr. Radhakrishnan, "Our education should encourage the development in its members fearlessness of mind, strength of conscious and integrity of purpose. If we claim to be civilised, we must develop thought for the poor and the suffering, chivalrous regard and respect for woman, faith in human brother hood regardless of race , colour, nation or religion, love of peace and freedom, abhorrence of cruelty and ceaseless devotion to the claims of justice". He himself left the office of the President saying in the valedictory address. Our slogan should be not power at any price, but service at any cost. This great personality is no more in the world, but the volumes of work done and left us will inspire the human civilisation forever. In fact, he messages for India as well as for the world will make him immortal and the future generations will get inspiration through his life dedicated to learning and service of humanity. As he lives in our hearts, his thoughts vibrate in our mind. Dear teachers, professors, politicians we unfortunately enter the field of education and politics not because of our quality. We may be poor in teaching and ruling but remember not power at any price but service at any cost. Dear, at least don't exploit the children (demanding gifts on teacher's day) and society in his NAME. We are worthless to spell his NAME. However, let us learn from Dr Radhakrishnan and work for the welfare of India and World.

CHAPTER 23

JEAN JACQUES ROUSSEAU 1712–1778

INTRODUCTION

Rousseau is the first man in the world who brought about a remarkable change in the social and political structures of many countries through his sound educational ideas. In fact, his thought-provoking ideas such as liberty, equality and fraternity caused the modification of political systems and the development of sociological tendency in education. As he has revolutionised our thinking in so many ways, he is considered as the father of civilization. He has introduced a new theory and practice of education through his writings on religion, society, marriage, education and government. He has highlighted the evils of society and wanted to reform it by modifying the process of education according to the needs and interests of individual and society. He is the pioneer of making education into practical process by introducing trade, business, leather work, and embroidery as livelihood. He is the chief exponent of naturalism which has a great impact on modern education. The introduction of new teaching techniques and giving importance to the study of natural sciences make him a distinguished philosopher and place his name in the top among the educationists.

LIFE OF ROUSSEAU

Jean Jacques Rousseau, the first man in the history of mankind to preach the gospel about common man, a great educator of the eighteenth century, the champion of modern education, the most important naturalistic philosopher, a powerful thinker, father of French Revolution and an apostle of individual liberty, was born in the small city of Geneva in 1712. He lost his mother soon after his birth and was brought up by his father. He received his early education at the hands of his father who was a poor watch maker and a private tutor. His father was quite ignorant of the art of bringing up his son. Therefore, Rousseau fell into bad habits for which he was generally, very severely, beaten in the school. As a result, by nature he became vehemently opposed to this inhuman practice. He developed a tendency of sentimentality and sensuality. He left the school at the age of twelve and tried different sorts of occupation, but he failed in all. He was wandering from one place to another and met different types of people, and learnt to sympathise with the poor.

One day he became very tired and hungry because of his aimless wanderings. A priest Savoyard Vicar took him to his home and fed him. This incident shaped the life and character of Rousseau. He became familiar with the existing social and philosophical problems. The writings of Hobbes, Locke,

Montaigne, Pascal, Fenelon Voltaire, Leibnitz, Descartes, Kepler, and Newton influenced him very deeply. His mind was occupied with problems concerning 'education' and 'government'. After a number of journeys, a desultory study of Catholicism, music, and a survey of all sciences, he tried his hands at various professions like those of a private tutor, music teacher, secretary, composer and dramatist. He settled in Paris in 1741 and became a writer.

Rousseau was particularly influenced by the poverty and sufferings of the people. He hated the society for the evils and wanted to reform it. In his publications, he condemned the existing institutions and portrayed the oppression and corruption in the society. He declared, "Everything is good as it comes from the hands of the author of the nature, but everything degenerates in the hands of man". He bestowed the slogan, "Return to Nature" (Back to Nature or Follow Nature). He wrote, "Man is born free and everywhere he is in chains". His work *Emile* revolted against the canons of society. France and Switzerland banned this book and burnt it in many places. He earned the displeasure of the French authorities. As a consequence, Rousseau had to live in exile for many years. After 11 years, he returned from England to France and wrote his last book entitled *Confessions*. He was very much disgusted and disappointed by the political authorities of France and Switzerland. Rousseau, the most influential political as well as educational philosopher, died in 1778 due to a sudden attack of thrombosis which many believed to be a suicide. But his profound thoughts such as liberty, equality and fraternity inspired the French Revolution in 1789. The insurrection not only exalted the fame of Rousseau but also brought about a remarkable change in the socio-economic and political conditions of several countries.

PHILOSOPHY OF ROUSSEAU

The philosophy of Rousseau emerges as a revolt against the artificial and autocratic society. He advocates the idea that there should be a "Natural State", a "Natural Man", and a "Natural Civilization". According to him, cities are the graves of civilization. So, his philosophy is termed as *Naturalism*. He believes that "everything" is good as it comes from the hands of the author of nature, but everything degenerates in the hands of man". He further indicates that a child is essentially good but his contact with society makes him bad. In his book *Social Contract*, he writes, "Man is born free but everywhere he is in chains". He emphatically states that man himself is responsible for his miseries and sorrows. Therefore, the human society should give up the present artificial mode of life and go back to nature for forming a natural man, a natural state and a natural civilization in order to regain the old vitality and happiness. According to Rousseau the slogan, "Return to Nature" is the panacea for all evils.

In the field of politics, he emphasises the concepts of liberty, equality and fraternity. He revolts against traditional education and raises his voice to free the child from the tyranny of strict discipline and the artificiality of school environment and stereotyped methods of teaching. He wants men to be free from the bondage of society by educating them, not for citizenship but for manhood. Thus, his philosophical ideas combine his political, social and educational ideologies. It is the outcome of three factors namely the state of time, extremely varied experiences of life, and his impulsive and emotional nature, which influence and shape the philosophy of Rousseau.

ROUSSEAU'S THREE CONCEPTS OF NATURE

Rousseau is the most important naturalistic philosopher. So, he wants the people to live according to nature and follow the order of nature in education. According to him, 'Nature' has several connotations, but he has stated three concepts of nature.

Nature as "endowment"—innate tendencies: According to Rousseau, education comes to us from nature, from men and from things. He regards nature as equivalent to endowment. He believes that the best learning takes place when the child is free to develop and grow according to his natural impulses. Nature is the spontaneous development of the innate disposition of the child. Rousseau says, "When I want to train a natural man, I do not want to make him a savage and to send him back to the woods, but living in the whirl of social life ... he should not let himself be carried away by the passions and prejudices of man. Let him see with his eyes and feel with his hearts". So, education must start from the child's instinctive tendencies.

Nature—isolation from society: Rousseau believes that nature is good and everything; but society is negative which drags the child away from nature. According to him, society is an artificial and unnatural product which is full of evils. So, the child should be saved and isolated from the evil influences of society. He wants the child to be brought up in the lap of nature, that is, in contact with the beauties and wonders of nature, away from social influence. It means non-social education—a preventive education which is not based on traditions and formalities of society. Thus, nature is defined as "negative to society".

Natural phenomena—living according to nature: Rousseau is of the opinion that the child must be given education in a natural environment. He wants the child to live according to nature in accordance with the rational principles of the universe. Since Rousseau is a great lover of nature, mountains, streams, ocean, sunrise, sunset, solitude and country life, he recommends contact with hills, streams, plants, birds, trees, animals, stones and physical forces of all kinds. He believes that one becomes a natural man automatically when he is brought up and taught in the natural environment.

ROUSSEAU'S PHILOSOPHY OF EDUCATION

Education according to nature of child: Rousseau believes that education is the only remedy to shun the evil influences of society. He, therefore, advocates that the child is the centre of gravity. According to him, the nature of a child should determine the nature of teaching rather than a logical order of subject matters, which is suited only to the adult mind. He emphasises the dictum that the child should be treated as child not as an adult. Hence, the child should be provided with real, vital and concrete experiences.

Education according to different stages of child: Rousseau spells out how the child should be provided education. In his book Emile, he regards Emile as an imaginary male child, and divides his scheme of education according to his different stages of growth. According to him, childhood has its own way of seeing, thinking and feeling. There is time for every kind of teaching and we ought to recognise it. The different stages of child are infancy (0–5 years), childhood (5–12 years), adolescence (12–15 years) and youth (15–18 years). Hence, the construction of curriculum and the methods of teaching should be in accordance with the different stages of the child.

Education from nature, man and things: According to Rousseau, the education of the child comes from nature, from man and from things. Education from nature means the internal development of our organs as a consequence of our relationship with our physical environment. Education from men means we are taught to make use of that development through our relationship with our social environment. Education from things is the acquisition made by our own experiences with the objects which surround us. Rousseau says that harmony in education is possible by subordinating the education of men and things to that of nature because we have no control over nature. So, we have to ensure cooperation of these three factors for imparting the ideal education.

Education a process of guidance: Rousseau believes that education is the process of guidance by the teacher, but it is not instruction by the teacher. According to him, the art of teaching consists in making the pupil wish to learn. His concern is to educate the child to live his life.

Negative education: Rousseau was the first man to stress on negative education. He states, "The most dangerous period in human life lies between birth and the age of twelve. Hence, education from five to twelve should be negative effort by the educator who should leave the child to learn how to use time wisely. Negative education is the preparation against the social condition in which the child lives. It consists not at all in teaching virtue. But it shields the child's heart from vices and his mind from errors.

ROUSSEAU'S CONCEPT OF EDUCATION

The educational views of Rousseau are considered to be new and modern. They are meant to relieve the child from strict discipline, artificial school, social environment, undue control, and rigid methods of teaching. According to Rousseau, education should aim at the fullest development of the child's innate potentialities and powers in a natural environment. He has defined education thus: "It is a process of development into an enjoyable, rational, harmoniously balanced useful and hence natural life". It means the natural development of organs and powers of the child. Education as such is a life-long process. He states, "To live is not merely to breathe, it is to act, to make use of our organs, senses, our faculties and of all those parts of ourselves, which give us the feeling of an existence".

AIMS OF EDUCATION

The aim of education is to help the child to remain alive. According to Rousseau, "Life is not merely to breathe but it is to act and to make use of our organs, senses and faculties which give us the feeling of our existence". In other words, life is to live, to work, to develop and to properly utilize the various parts of the body, the sense organs and the various other powers of the body to make the child a real human being.

Physical development: Rousseau feels that a strong physique is essential to develop the child into a healthy and wholesome personality. A feeble body makes a feeble mind. He says that we are born weak and we want strength. We are poor and we want help and so on. Thus, whatever we do not have is to be given by education. And, this is the ultimate aim of education.

Development of senses: Rousseau believes that senses are the gateways of knowledge. So, development or training of senses is the important task of education. It is education which helps the child to attain pleasure by using his organs and senses and by applying his strength.

Development of innate faculties: The aim of education is to help the child to develop his innate faculties in a natural way and in the natural environment. To establish harmony between man, objects and nature, a child's natural impulses and instincts must be particularly attended to.

Intellectual development: The aim of education is to develop the child to the fullest for his complete and happy living. So, Rousseau stresses on the importance of intellectual development during one's childhood. To achieve intellectual development, he has recommended physical sciences, language, mathematics, history and geography.

Learning trade: The aim of education is to prepare the child to live his life. For this purpose, the child must learn a trade, a mechanical art and manual labour. This can give him a living.

Development of social and moral values: The aim of education is to lead the child to become a member of the society and an ideal head of the family. Rousseau emphasises moral and spiritual education during youth in order to prepare the child to lead a good life.

AIM OF EDUCATION AT DIFFERENT STAGES OF CHILD

The aims of education, according to Rousseau, change at different stages of the child's development, because each stage has different tastes, interests, needs and stresses. Therefore, the aim of education should be changed in accordance with the growth of the child.

Infancy: Infancy begins at birth and continues upto five years. During this period, development and strengthening of every part of the body is essential so that the child can grow up healthy and strong. Rousseau held the opinion "All wickedness comes from weakness. The child should be made strong so that he will do nothing which is bad". So, he has suggested providing the infant full freedom to engage in playing and exercising his body. Thus, education aims at physical development during infancy.

Childhood: This stage lasts from five to twelve years. It is the period of development of the child's sense organs through experience and observation. Hence, the aim of education is to help the child to observe and experience various things in nature and develop his sense organs.

Adolescence: At this stage (12–15 years) education aims at developing adolescent personality through hard work, guidance and study of various subjects. Since the aim of education is intellectual development, Rousseau recommends subjects like, physical sciences, language, mathematics, history and geography.

Youth (15 to 18 or 20 years): The aim of education during this stage is the development of emotions and sentiments that is the training of the heart. The development of sentiments leads to the development of moral and social qualities in the youth. Rousseau reiterated that moral and religious education should be imparted to the youths so as to prepare them to lead a good life. Thus, education aims at preparing the youth to become a member of society and an ideal head of the family.

ROUSSEAU'S CONCEPT OF CURRICULUM

Rousseau divides his whole programme of education on the basis of the development stages of humans. In his book *Emile*, he divides his scheme of education (curriculum) into five stages. The curriculum for the first four stages is in accordance with the developmental stages of Emile and his felt needs. The fifth stage is meant for the education of Sophy—an imaginary girl to become an ideal wife of Emile. Rousseau has prescribed different subjects and activities on the basis of infancy, childhood, adolescence and youth of Emile and Sophy.

Education for infancy (0 to 5 years): Rousseau recommends negative education during infancy. At this stage instead of teaching subjects, attention should be given to the development of the child's body and his sense organs. His dress should be comfortable so that he does not have any difficulty in the free movement of his body organs. He should be allowed to play with whatever things he likes without any force from outside, and wander about freely in the countryside. His play things should be simple, natural like leaves, plants, flowers, fruits, stones etc. and not expensive toys. The child should be brought up by his mother and he should be given due protection.

Education for childhood (5 to 12 years): Rousseau opposes the use of any textbook for educating the child. The child should be given training to learn everything through observation and experience.

Rousseau suggests various activities by way of training, for the development of the mind, and the power of reasoning through negative education. The child should be given full freedom to use his senses in the natural environment. His eyes should be trained to measure height, weight, distance, colour and size. Music educates his ears, flowers train his nose, weather educates his skin and so on. Rousseau's advice for this stage is, "Exercise the body, the organs, the senses and powers, and keep the soul lying fallow as long as you can".

However, geometry maybe taught during this stage. Moral education should not be given as long as the child does not understand the meaning of "morality". But a little of moral education maybe given through activities. Rousseau opines that the child will learn his morality by the natural consequences of his own actions.

Education for adolescence (12 to 15 years): This is a good period of intellectual development during which the child should be taught various subjects and activities. It is a suitable time for work, instruction and enquiries. Rousseau prescribes a formal curriculum consisting of physical sciences, languages, mathematics, music, painting, woodwork and social sciences. He opines that the study of science will enhance the curiosity of the child his inclination towards research, invention and self-education. Painting helps the pupils to train the muscles and eyes. Handicrafts help to develop the ability to work. Rousseau wants to teach Emile industrial exchange and professional experience in banking and transportation to prepare him to earn his livelihood. He recommends for reading the book Robinson Crusoe, a study of life according to nature.

Education for youth (15 to 20 years): During this stage, the child is expected to grow emotionally, aesthetically, socially and morally to adapt himself to the conduct and interest of others. Rousseau wants Emile to get training in moral and religious education about his relations with his fellowmen and develop moral qualities such as benevolence, kindness, service and sympathy. He suggests that moral education should be given through activities and occupations and not through lectures on ethics. Travel through different countries is recommended for knowing the world, their languages and modes of life in the neighbouring countries. The youth should visit hospitals, prisons and orphanages in order to see the evils and miseries of the society directly and gain first hand knowledge. Sex instruction during youth consists of direct moral exhortation on chastity.

Education for women: Since men and women differ from each other, Rousseau prescribes a separate curriculum for the education of female, Sophy (imaginary girl of Rousseau). He mentions in his Emile that men should be strong and active; the women should be weak and passive. According to him, "Men are born to serve, women are born to please". Woman is simply supplementary to the nature of man. The aim of women's education is "To be pleasant in his sight to win his respect and love, to train him in childhood, to tend him in manhood, to counsel and console, to make his life pleasant and happy, these are the duties of women for which she should be taught while she is young". He remarks, "An illiterate woman is the plague of her husband, her children, her family her servant and everybody". So, he recommends to provide education in reading and writing to make them efficient to keep their body healthy and adorn themselves. In this respect, they should learn housekeeping, sewing, embroidery, weaving and get religious education too. They should also learn singing, dancing and other accomplishments.

METHODS OF TEACHING

Rousseau is against the artificial and harsh methods of teaching which repressed the natural inclinations and tendencies of the child. He recommends simple and direct methods of instruction according to the nature of the child.

Direct experience and observation: Rousseau favours direct experience and observation methods of education to develop the sense organs and reasoning capacity of the child. He urges children to acquire "experience before expression" and "objects before words". He says, "Let the child learn nothing from books which they can learn from experience". He believes that geography could be learnt by observation of natural phenomena. He says, "Give your scholar no verbal lesson. He should be taught by experience alone".

Learning by doing: Rousseau stands against the rote method of learning and believes that knowledge acquired through actual doing or experience is far more permanent than knowledge acquired through words. In the words of Rousseau, "Teach by doing whenever you can and only fall back upon words when doing is out of the question". Rousseau insists on practical education rather than theoretical one. He opines that long lectures bore the child and blunt his appetite for new things. Hence, instead of delivering long lectures to the child, it is better to give him the opportunity to act for himself.

Play-way method: Rousseau maintains, "Education should be practical rather than oral. The child should not read through books. He should stop reading words". For Rousseau, education to the child should be provided by play. He feels that work or plays are all one for the child. His games are his work; he knows no difference. He should be allowed to play or work and explore the environment in whatsoever way he likes and he will learn it that way.

Heuristic method: Rousseau recommends Heuristic method of teaching in order to prepare the child to become a researcher and discoverer. It is the method of discovery and problem solving in subjects like natural science and mathematics. Heuristic method of teaching prepares the child to find out new things.

Example is better than precept: This method is recommended to impart moral education. Rousseau believes in the principle that example is better than precept. The teacher should set an example of moral behaviour instead of lecturing on morality to the child and opportunity maybe provided to him to practise virtue.

ROLE OF TEACHER

Rousseau assigns only a secondary place to the teacher in the educative process. The teacher has a limited role in imparting education to the child. He is not regarded as an instructor but only a guide. The most important task of the teacher is to motivate the child to learn by exploiting his innate tendencies. He should have a profound understanding of the child's nature and be able to control his emotional reactions in a proper manner. He should not impose any rules of control or his willingness upon the child. He should allow the child perfect freedom and guide him properly to live in the natural environment.

DISCIPLINE

The function of education is to foster natural development in the child. Therefore, Rousseau advocates complete freedom with a minimum guidance and wants total absence of any restraints on the child. The child should be left in the free environment so that he can develop his natural powers. There is no place for giving punishment or reward. Since nature is a great teacher, there will be natural discipline. Rousseau assumes that the child has no knowledge of good and bad, but he suffers pain when he makes mistakes and pleasure when he does something right. For instance, if Emile breaks the window of the bedroom, he should not be punished by his tutor but let him sleep in the room with the broken window and the cold which follows will teach him not to break windows. This is natural punishment through which the child will learn better discipline.

SCHOOL ORGANIZATION

Rousseau objects to the system of school education. He believes that the child is born innocent and pure, but he is defiled and distorted by the defective environment of the school. He, therefore, suggests that it is better to separate the child from his parents, to take him away from school, and leave him in the natural environment. Because in natural surroundings, the child will himself look after the development of his actual abilities. In fact, the location of school should be in natural surroundings, away from the city.

ROUSSEAU'S CONTRIBUTION TO EDUCATION

Rousseau, the father of modern educational theory and practice, has influenced many great educators of the nineteenth and twentieth centuries. He occupies a very prominent place in the world of education. In the words of R.H. Quick, "Rousseau did in the world of ideas what the French Revolutionists afterwards did in the world of politics; he made a clean sweep and endeavoured to start afresh". He is regarded as the apostle of individual liberty, equality and fraternity. Let us discuss his contribution in the field of modern education.

Pioneer of modern education: Rousseau is the forerunner of modern educational psychology. He provides new directions and new dimensions to education which is quite suitable to the child—his temperament, needs, inclinations and capacity. Thus, the aim of education is to foster the innate potentialities of the child in a natural way. This is an important contribution of Rousseau. Modern psychology and education are fully based on his findings. He initiated the psychological movement in education by emphasising the importance of individual differences, the psychology of growth, learning by doing, child's native interest and tendencies, motivation, play- way and activity principle.

Discovery of unfolded traits of the child: Rousseau is the first great educator to discover and recognise the traits of childhood. He divides the stages of a child's growth and finds out the distinctions and independence of each stage. According to him, each stage has its own characteristics and needs. In his own words, "Childhood has the ways of seeking, thinking and feeling peculiar to itself: nothing can be more foolish than to substitute our ways to them". This concept of Rousseau was put into practice by Pestalozzi and Froebel, who stressed on the child-centred education based on the child's needs, interests, inclinations, tendencies, impulses, instincts and his nature.

Redeemer of social evils: Rousseau is the champion of individual liberty. He succeeds in freeing the individual from the chains of artificial, social setup and educational environment. He delivers the child from the torture of the teacher and the society. He is eloquent on the "Right of Man", "Right of Childhood" against social evils. This eloquent philosophy of Rousseau has created a new epoch in the field of education and politics.

Introducer of new methods of teaching: Rousseau advocates and introduces new teaching techniques which have been accepted and implemented by modern educators. He suggests the modern method of problem solving saying "put problems before the child and let him solve them himself. Let him know nothing because you have told him but because he has learnt it himself. Let him not be taught science, let him discover it". His emphasis on direct experience, practical activities, learning by doing, no verbal lesson, problem solving, discovery, and heuristic approach prove a landmark in the methodology of teaching.

Founder of sound educational principle: According to Rousseau true education comes by judgement and reasoning rather than memory. The judgement and reasoning is based on first hand experiences of man, nature and things. He says that a subject should be taught by direct experience. He advocates that the child should be taught through concrete things rather than abstract signs and symbols. In his words, "In general, never substitute the sign for the thing itself, save when it is impossible to show the thing". Thus, he becomes the founder of sound educational principles having a great impact on modern education.

Supporter of free and positive discipline: Rousseau stands in favour of free and positive discipline which holds true even today. He condemns punishment and opposes imposition of any rules which destroy the originality and intellectual interest of the child. He recommends maximum freedom for the child so that he may develop in the natural environment. In the words of Rousseau, "Let the child move freely in nature and learn from his own personal experience and actual participation in day-to-day life activities". Moral education should be given through examples at an appropriate stage.

Forerunner of sociological basis of education: Rousseau lays the foundation of sociological tendency in modern education. His happy blending of individual and social training serves as a base for democratic education. His emphasis on moral and emotional development and sense training gives a sociological basis to education. Democratic concepts such as liberty, equality and fraternity of Rousseau have a great impact on both education and politics.

Introducer of vocational training: Rousseau is the first to propose introduction of vocational training as part of general education. In fact, the present day emphasis on vocational education is the outcome of his contribution. His stress on learning a trade has brought about a remarkable change in the educational field. Modern educationists such as Pestalozzi, Mahatma Gandhi and Vivekananda have emphasised the value of craft in education. Thus, Rousseau's vocational ideas have broadened the principles of education.

Creator of child-centred education: Rousseau is the first educator to give a prominent place to the child in the educative process. He has stressed on that education should start with the child as the base. It should cater to the child's needs, interests, inclinations, instincts and his future. A sympathetic approach to the children motivates them to learn the subjects. This fundamental idea inspires all educators and thus education has become child centred.

Advisor of physical activities: Rousseau states that the positive education in childhood comprises physical and sensory training. He remarks, "A feeble body makes a feeble mind. All wickedness comes from weakness. A child is bad only because he is weak: make him strong and he will be good". He further says, "Cultivate your pupil's intelligence and give his body constant exercise, make it strong and healthy, in order to make him good and wise; let him work, let him do things, let him run and shout, let him be strong and he will soon be a man of reason". His views are accepted by almost all educators and philosophers, and are being implemented in education.

NEGATIVE EDUCATION

The term negative education denotes Rousseau's aversion for the formal educational system in the society. He regarded it unnatural and against the nature of the child. He believed that everything is good as it comes from the author of Nature but it degenerates in the hands of man. He also had the opinion that the child is good, but society makes him bad. He, therefore, advocated negative education to protect the child against the evil influences of the society. Negative education consists not in teaching virtue or truth, but in preserving the heart from vice and the mind from error. According to him, negative education is a sort of preventive education for life, rather a preparation against the social conditions in which the child lives. It does not give virtue, it protects from vice; it does not inculcate truth, it protects from error. It disposes the child to take the path that will lead him to truth, when he has reached the age to understand it. Since the most dangerous period in human life lies between birth and the age of twelve, education from five to twelve should be largely negative by leaving the child to learn how to lose time wisely. Hence, negative education means allowing the child to move freely in nature so that he is able to perfect the organs of his body, which are the instruments for acquiring knowledge and protecting the heart of the child from the evil ways of the society.

Characteristics of Negative Education

No positive education: Formal education or positive education should not be given in the childhood. The child should be allowed freely to learn and develop himself in the lap of nature. Hence, there is no need for the tutor to teach reading and writing during the childhood, i.e., from five to twelve years.

No time saving: Childhood is a period when the child should not save his time but he should lose it wisely. The child should run, jump, play all day long which will strengthen the organs of his body and enable him to acquire more knowledge. So, time lost in play and recreational activities in the childhood is not lost but profitably gained.

No book learning: There is no place for books in negative education. Rousseau is against the bookish knowledge which means learning by rote. He says, "I hate books because they are a curse to children. They teach us to talk only that which we do not know". He advocates that the child should think for himself and learn with his own efforts. He further says, "Instead of making the child stick to his books, I keep him busy in the workshop; his hands will work to the profit of his mind".

No habit formation: Rousseau says, "The only habit which the child should be allowed to form is to contract no habit at all". Young children should not be made slaves of rigid habits. They should be left free in all their activities. He wants to form natural habits in the child.

No moral education: There is no place for direct moral instruction in negative education. The mind of the child is not matured enough to receive positive and direct moral education. Rousseau says, "Much more harm than good is done by your ceaseless preaching and moralizing". According to him, let the child be left free to act and learn what is right or wrong by the consequences of his own actions.

No traditional methods of teaching: Rousseau hates traditional and formal education which imparts bookish knowledge under strict discipline. Negative education is given to the child in the play-way and activity method, direct experience and observation, learning by doing and heuristic method. He says, "Give me a child of twelve who knows nothing at all. At fifteen I will restore him to you, knowing as much as those who have been under instruction from infancy, with the difference that your scholar only knows things by heart while mine knows how to use his knowledge".

No formal discipline: Rousseau advocates free and positive discipline for children in negative education. According to him, let the children suffer from the natural consequences of their own actions without the intervention of human beings. In this way they will set themselves right. For instance, "If a child breaks motor rules, let him pay fine and learn not to do so again".

Individual instruction: Negative education emphasises individual instruction. The individuality of the child is recognised by the teacher. Hence, the instruction given to the child is based on his interest, instincts, and capacity.

Allow the child to follow his natural impulses: Negative education allows the child to follow his natural impulses to attain natural development. Rousseau says, "Speak to him of duty or obedience; he will not know what you are talking about; bid him do something, he will pay no attention. Give him no orders at all, absolutely none. Do not even let him think that you claim any authority over him". Rousseau asserts that the child should follow his natural impulses.

Back to nature: Negative education of Rousseau insists that the child returns to nature which is good and pure, and learns from it. It is believed that nature is the best teacher for providing negative education to the child, so that he may grow in the natural environment.

Criticisms of Negative Education

Rousseau's negative education suffers from the following drawbacks:

1. It neglects books and media which play a vital role in making the teaching–learning process more effective and attractive.
2. It is difficult to find naturalistic surroundings which are quite suitable for negative education and natural growth.
3. It ignores the formation of habit in the child which is essential for making a complete or perfect man.
4. Absolute freedom given to the child is a myth and is harmful. We cannot allow the child to have a taste of poison and suffer the natural consequences of his action.
5. It assigns very little importance to the teacher in the educative process. He should not impose any rules or authority on the child, but he should guide him to learn from nature.
6. Education is more comprehensive and dynamic. Hence, physical nature alone is not sufficient for providing it.
7. It is against the formal system of education which has a vital part in the modern scheme of education.
8. Negative education has no fixed aim of education and it is meant for only children up to the age of twelve.
9. It ignores the future by preparing the child for the present life, that is, earthly life.
10. It neglects spiritual education and the spiritual world, but pays a great deal of attention to the material world.

ROUSSEAU'S EMILE

Rousseau is a great thinker as well as writer. Some of his famous writings are: (i) The Progress of Arts and Science (1750); (ii) The Origin of Inequality Among Men (1953); (iii) The New Heloise a Romance (1759); (iv) Social Contract (1762); and (v) Emile or Concerning Education (1762). *Emile* is the most important book in which Rousseau has expounded his educational ideas. He states that education comes from nature, man and from things. The purpose of the book *Emile* is to showcase education in Nature's way by bringing the man nearer to nature. Rousseau himself says, "The introduction of a specific boy is only an expository device for expounding a universal system of education".

The *Emile* is a treatise on education cast in the form of a novel in which there are three characters, that is, Emile—an imaginary male character, Tutor— teacher of the imaginary boy Emile, and Sophie—

an imaginary female character who is destined to be the mate of Emile. Emile consists of five parts on training and education. Part I deals with the infant (0–5). Part II is about childhood (5–12), Part III relates to adolescence (12–15), Part IV deals with youth (15–20) and Part V deals with education of girls.

Rousseau condemned the society for its evils and demanded that the child follow Nature which is everything and good. His *Emile* is a book of richness, power, and wisdom. It offers protection against traditional education which is unsound, unreal and unprogressive, and favours bookish knowledge and strict discipline. At the same time his book insisted on freedom for the child, respect for his individuality faith in his goodness, proper regard for his natural inclinations and interests, motivation, play way and recreational activities. The book created a revolutionary awakening in the field of politics and education. So, *Emile* was criticised vehemently in the parliament of Paris and it was burnt publicly. The Government of France ordered the arrest of Rousseau.

So, he left for Switzerland. The reading of *Emile* was also forbidden by the Archbishop of Paris. Emile had a great effect on thought and action which had brought about a remarkable change in the field of education in the eighteenth and nineteenth centuries. It has been the basis for the philosophical and sociological foundation of education developed by modern educators like Gandhi, Tagore, Froebel, Pestalozzi, Basedow, Herbert and John Dewey. Lord Morley has described the value of 'Emile' thus: "It touched the deeper things of character. It filled parents with a sense of the dignity and moment of their task. It cleared away the accumulation of clogging prejudices, and obscure inveterate usage, which made education one of the dark formalistic arts. It admitted floods of light and air into the tightly closed nurseries and school rooms. It effected the substitution of growth for mechanism ... It was the character of youthful deliverance".

One eminent educationist commenting on the importance of the book says, "There is no book in the world, so worthy of commendation as that in which there is traced a plan of education. Read or re-read the Emile, observe all that we are doing, the manner in which we train the child and conduct his instruction and you will be convinced that our master is Rousseau". In the words of H. Payne, "The Emile has justly been called the Gospel of childhood. If it had no other claims to consideration, it would deserve the homage of parents and teachers by reason of that sacredness with which it invites the personality of every child".

CONCLUSION

Rousseau is the founder of the grand ideas liberty, equality and fraternity, rights of man and rights of childhood. These ideas have had a profound influence on the educational theory and practice. His provocative thoughts and naturalistic philosophy have rendered a direct impetus to the formation of psychological, sociological and scientific education. The educational doctrines of Rousseau have been put into practice by the later educators of the nineteenth and twentieth centuries such as Tagore, Mahatma Gandhi, Pestalozzi, Herbert, Froebel, John Dewey and Basedow. Munro has rightly remarked, "Rousseau was the forerunner of so many, who have followed in the trails; he blazed through the forest until now they have become the broad highway of common travel". He is regarded as the champion of naturalism for advocating ideas like "Natural State", "Natural Man" and "Natural Civilization". In the words of Ross, "Rousseau occupies an important place among the Western educators for his two-fold ideas of the Rights of Man and the Rights of Childhood. He is regarded as the father of French Revolution". In the words of Napoleon, "Without Rousseau, the French Revolution would not have occurred. When his ideas were applied to education, it created a new epoch also". He is to modern education what Plato was to ancient education.

CHAPTER 24

JOHN HEINRICH PESTALOZZI 1746–1827

INTRODUCTION

Pestalozzi was one of the greater reformers of education found in his periods. In fact, among the great educators, he, appeared a man afflicted with new educational ideas. He practiced them, in his book 'Swan song' by teaching his own child Jacobi. His educational views are found in his writings- Leonard and Gertrude (1781), How Gertrude Teaches Her Children (1801). The Swan Song (1813) and his letters on Early education (1818). The book How Gertrude Teaches Her Children is a manual for mothers. It contains some exercises for children. It also provides a systematic psychological theory which is useful in educational practices.

LIFE OF PESTALOZZI

Pestalozzi a great swiss educator, philosopher and writer was born at Zurich, Switzerland in 1746 He lost his father, a physician at the age of five, so he was brought up by his mother. He hated the Latin school at Zurich as it lacked in realism but enjoyed college education at the Collegiums Humanities and Collegium Earolinum. He engaged in several professions like law and politics, and failed in all he took up agriculture and developed a farm at Neuh, Where he began his first experiment in education.

He turned the farm house into a refuge for destitute children. He found that their natural need is to be active and in born powers lead to self support at their early ages. Therefore, he combined education, moral regeneration and practical training with agriculture and handicrafts, and taught the children by means of conversation on all kinds of topics. He was in charge of poor children and felt the need for new approach to education. But, he closed the farm school due to financial constraints.

However, he established a school at Burgdorf and a boarding school at Yerdum and conducted his experiments there also. The school ran harmoniously with its natural and relaxed environment attracted the attention of educators. In fact the method of teaching was also highly appreciated by them. A letter of appreciation from the school examiners and inspectors reveals his effort as "All that you hoped from your method of teaching has been realised. You have shown that what powers already exist in even the child. In what way are these powers to be developed, and how each talent must be sought out and exercised in such a way as to bring it to maturity. The astonishing progress made by your young pupils in spite of their many differences of character and dispositions, clearly show that every child is good for something in a truly psychological manner. Your teaching has brought to light the foundation on which all instruction must be based, if it is ever to be of any real use, it also shows that from the tender age, and in a very short time, a child's mind can attain a wonderful breadth of development which must make its influence felt, not only during his few years of study but throughout his whole life".

Thus Pestalozzi set up a philanthropic institute for destitute children in 1764. He engaged in writing books from 1780 to 1818. Most of his books are very popular and expressed his educational ideas and practical experiences gained from school life. The great intellectual thinker and educator of the Europe passed away in 1827.

PESTALOZZI EDUCATIONAL PHILOSOPHY

The educational Philosophy of Pestalozzi is mostly similar to that of Rousseau. In fact, he was greatly influenced by the later. So Pestalozzi emphasised the natural development of the child in a free atmosphere. At the same time, he did not accept the views of Rousseau in all aspects. This is because he observes whenever you carelessly leave the earth to nature it bears weeds and thistles, whenever you leave the education of your race to her, she has no further than a confused impression of the sense that it is not adopted to your power of apprehension not to that of child in the way that is need for the best instruction. According to Pestalozzi, education depends on the inner development of the child. So it should not be imposed from outside. He believes that the principle of education should be discovered through observation and experiments. The success of the teacher depends upon teaching based on the interest of the child. He view, that child hood is the most important period in a person's education. The aim of education is helping the child achieve all round development in knowledge, skills, capacity and ability. Hence, the teacher should not only know various subjects but should also be conversant with the best teaching methods.

Meaning of Education

According to Pestalozzi, "Education is natural harmonious and progressive development of man's innate powers". In other words, it is the natural progressive and harmonious development of all the powers and capacities of human beings.

Aims of Education

The meaning and aims of education include those aspects which prepare the child to achieve a harmonious development in intellectual and vocational fields. According to Pestalozzi, the purpose of education is the harmonious development of the innate powers of the child. So the aim of all instruction is and can be noting but the development of human nature by harmonious cultivation of its powers, talents, and the promotion of manliness of life. Hence, the aims of education include,

- Balanced and integrated growth of child.
- Develop the child's innate potentialities and capacities and
- Prepare the child self sufficient and for better life.

CURRICULUM

According to Pestalozzi, the curriculum should be framed on the basis of individual as well as social needs. Moreover, it should be based on activity and experience so as to enable the child to develop his inner potentialities harmoniously. So, he framed a comprehensive curriculum which contains subjects such as Arithmetic, Geography, History, nature study, Drawing music, physical education and agriculture.

The activities and experiences at Yerdun school include drawing, writing, singing physical exercises, group recitations, model making, collections, map making and field trips. The well constructed curriculum for lower and upper classes are shown below:

No.	Lower Class	Hours	No.	Upper Class	Hours
1	Nature Study	2	1	Natural History	2
2	Description of Products of art	2	2	Technical Work	2
3	Geography	2	3	Arithmetic	6
4	Knowledge of the Country (Walking)	2	4	Geometry and Drawing	4
5	Mental arithmetic	6	5	Language	4
6	Drawing	4	6	Singing	3
7	Reading and Language	6	7	Religion	9
8	Singing	3			
9	Religion	6			
	Total	33			30

These are the three classes for primary, lower and upper education for children under 8, between 8 and 11 and between 11 and 18 years old.

METHODS OF TEACHING

He wanted to Psychologies education to bring about natural development in the child. He said, I wish to Psychologies education instead of bookish learning. In fact, he laid stress on sense training and object lesson. His methods of teaching include the following aspects.

Sense Perception: Like Russeau, Pestalozzi believed in the importance of sense perception in learning. In fact, observation is the key note of his methods of teaching. According to him, "man's knowledge must be found in sense impression".

Medium of Play: Pestalozzi believed that children express their natural drive through play. It is essential for physical and mental development of the child.

Emphasis on Concrete Teaching: He placed much emphasis up on the real objects in teaching learning situation. He opposed the artificial method of teaching like memory and preferred "words" to "thing"; He advised that teach not by words that you teach by things.

Direct Experience: Like naturalists, Pestalozzi considered direct experience as the best method of learning.

TEACHER

Pestalozzi believed that nature teaches better than men. However, he realised the importance of teacher in teaching learning. So he felt the need of training the teachers to have the knowledge of child psychology. It enables the teachers to know the need and interest of the child and prepare lesson planning. He established a Teacher Training School at Yerdun to provide training to the teachers and implement his educational ideas. He wanted the teachers to take the place of parents and show immense love for children.

DISCIPLINE

Pestalozzi stressed the discipline based on love and affection. He opposed corporal punishment of learners. According to him, the child's trust in his teacher, their love and gratitude which should take the place of rules and discipline.

ANSCHAUUNG OF PESTALOZZI

Anschauug is a Swiss concept for which there is no equivalent word in English. English and American writers use this term to convey the same ideas of immediate awareness, direct acquisition, direct appreciation, concrete experience, personal contact, firsthand experience, face to face knowledge and the direct impact of things and persons. Pestalozzi believed that anschauung is the basis of the knowledge and experience. It comprises the spontaneous appreciation of moral actions and direct realisation of situations. In short, ansehauung is a method of instruction 'teaching' by experience'.

Three Principles of Anschauung:

- Teaching children to look upon every object that is brought before them as a unit, that is separated from those with which it is connected,.
- Teaching children the form of every object, that is its size and proportions.
- Making children immediately acquired with all the words and names descriptive of objects known to them.

Techniques of Instruction: According to Pestalozzi, the technique of instruction should be directed to the primary faculties of counting, measuring, and speaking. It provides a basic knowledge about the object.

- Appreciation of form should be developed through drawing which enables the child to get knowledge of proportion and use slate and pencil in making tiny letters.
- Pestalozzi reduced language to words or names for language teaching. He says, "I always put the picture before the eye, they sought for a word, for the picture".

School: He emphasises the model school like a home for the child. The teacher should act like a father He should set himself an example in all activities. According to Pestalozzi, just as co-operation and mutual understanding govern a good house. So these ideals should be applied to the school.

Vocational Education: Pestalozzi stresses the necessity of vocational education to prepare the child for better life.

CONTRIBUTIONS OF PESTALOZZI TO EDUCATION

Philosopher like Fichte R. Rusk Marlow Ediger and Carool Atkinson and Eurgene T Maleska have pointed the contribution of Pestalozzi to educational thoughts and practices.

The great German Philosopher Fichte observes that the type of education developed by Pestalozzi would regenerate the nation. He contributed to education through a basic of idea that it consists of guiding children into a natural and orderly unfolding of their innate capacities.

R. Rusk Points out the salient features of Pestalozzi's educational contribution

- Anschauung is the common starting point of all instructions.
- Teaching should follow an orderly sequence
- Formulation of a psychological based method of teaching.
- Recognition of the practical and emotional aspects of personality.
- Laying the basis of elementary school system.
- Reinforcing democratic tradition in education.

Marlow Ediger summarised the contribution of Pestalozzi to education as

- Reality rather than abstraction should be in evidence in the school curriculum in initial child learning.
- The Semi-concrete (Model and illustration) should follow realistic concrete experiences.
- Students should master each step of learning prior to progressing to the next ordered activity or experience.
- Physical punishment of Pupils should be eliminated and discipline is based on love and gratitude
- The use of senses like touch, smell, taste, hearing and sight is vital in learning.

Marrlow Ediger also noted that Pestalozzi opposed the educational practices of his times:

- Rote learning of contents without understanding.
- Drill and practice without developing pupils interest in ongoing activities and practices.
- Survey approaches in teaching-learning situations without students attaining depth knowledge in the subject.
- Physical punishment of students without emphasising students enjoying activities and experiences.
- Forced discipline upon students without developing spontaneous quality behaviour with in them.

Carroll Akinston and Eurgene T Maleska mentioned in the Story of Education (1962) as Pestalozzi insists that the natural instincts of a child should provide for learning. He considered cooperation and sympathy rather than compulsion or physical punishment as means to achieve discipline. Based on the influence of Rousseau, he believes that in free expression would allow the child to develop his natural powers. Since, it is nature that gives the drive to life, he maintains that the teacher's responsibility is to adapt instruction to each individual according to his particular changing unfolding nature as required at the various stages of his development. Pestalozzi looks upon the child as a unity made of moral physical and intellectual powers all of which can be developed harmoniously through education.

LIMITATION OF PESTALOZZI'S EDUCATIONAL PRINCIPLES

- Pestalozzi always insists on beginning instructions with the elements of experiences. But he does not provide idea of the elements of experiences.
- His instruction is not suitable for advanced stages of education.
- There is no definite curriculum so instruction is done on disconnected topics at random basis.
- He believes that nature teaches better than man but it is not possible to all subjects and in all situations.
- He emphasises the use of concrete object in teaching. This is not possible in all teaching of activities and experiences.

CONCLUSION

John Henrich Pestalozzi is one of the greatest educational Philosophers. He gives a new comprehensive meaning to education to bring about a harmonious development in the child and prepare him for better life. He allows maximum freedom and opposes corporal punishment and rote learning with a view to help natural development of the child. His greater contribution in education is the introduction of analysis method of instruction on psychological basis, using objects senses, play and grouping (Grouping the children based on individual difference). His educational thoughts and practises influenced Froebel, Montessori and Herbart who laid strong foundation for Psychological based education which is essential for natural harmonious and balanced development of the child. Moreover, he attached great importance to a good home with a good mother and considered the school as transformed home. In fact, Pestalozzi, a genuine teacher, who translated the ideas of Rousseau in the actual field of education.

CHAPTER 25

FROEBEL
1782–1852

INTRODUCTION

Friedrich August Froebel, a German Philosopher, whose contribution to education created a new epoch in the history of teaching methodology applied for education of young children in his kindergarten schools. In fact he has given a tinge of philosophy to the educational principles and methods of early childhood education. Therefore, his kindergarten has been declared by far the most original, attractive and philosophical form of infant development. The kindergarten system of education is highly acclaimed all over the world by both the educators and parents alike. Moreover, his educational ideas have been recognised as the effective ways to deal with a highly "teachable moment" in the life of the child. He has assigned the role of plants and their garden to children and teachers in his scheme of education. The introduction of play- way method in the teaching–learning process makes Froebel an outstanding educationist and philosopher.

LIFE OF FROEBEL

Friedrich Wilhelm August Froebel, best known to the world as a great educator, philosopher, founder of the kindergarten system of education and the father of the sociological trend in education, was born in Oberweisback, a small village in South Germany on April 21, 1782. He lost his mother when he was only nine months old. His father married again when Froebel was four years. He never paid much attention to Froebel and his step mother treated him very unfairly. As a result, Froebel became a neglected child and his childhood days were very unhappy. So, his maternal uncle pastor Hoffman took pity on him and admitted him in a school when he was ten. He stayed with his uncle for about four years with some peace and comfort. As he was considered a dunce in the school, he left the school and became an apprentice to a forester. He came into intimate contact with nature and spent his time in the forest where he received his real education. The religious influence of his father and maternal uncle and the contact with nature cultivated in him a spirit of mysticism and idealism. He also developed an intensive sympathy for children and spent his life for promoting their lives. As he was interested in the study of natural science, he joined the University of Jena at the age of 18, but he could not pursue his education for want of finance. He was profoundly influenced by the idealistic philosophy of Fichte, Kant and Schilling during his university days.

After leaving the university, he began to study architecture at Frankfurt. There he developed a close association with Dr. Grunner, Director of a model school, who founded that Froebel could become an excellent teacher. So, he persuaded Froebel to join the school. He felt as happy as a fish in the water or a bird in the air. In order to become a teacher, Froebel paid a visit to Pestalozzi's institution at Yverdun, where he learnt as well as taught for two years. There he disagreed with the ideas of Pestalozzi and found himself unfit for school teaching which made him resign from the job. He joined the Gottimgen University in 1811 in order to obtain university education in natural science, but he did not succeed here too. Then he joined the military to fight against the aggression of Napoleon. This military service gave him an understanding of the true spirit of discipline and united action. He left the service after three years and become a curator in Berlin Museum. As he was interested in education, he did not like to continue in this for long.

Froebel established a small school in 1816 at Griesheim and he transferred it later on to Keihan where he developed his own principles and methods of instruction. Play and artwork were the main features of this school. He published his famous book, *The Education of Man* in 1826 in which he states that the true method of education consists in considering the mind of the child as a whole in which all the parts work together to produce harmonious unity. He started many schools in Germany. The Government of Germany did not take kindly to the revolutionary ideas of Froebel and conducted an enquiry into the working of his institutions. The enquiry produced a favourable report, "I found here a closely united family of some sixty members held together in mutual confidence and every member seeking the good of the whole—The aim of institution is by no means knowledge and science merely, but free self-active development of the mind from within".

Froebel had to face financial difficulties in continuing his task in Germany. So, he shifted his work to Switzerland in 1830. The Government of Switzerland appreciated his work and sent their teachers to him for training. Thereafter, he moved to Burgdorf where he became a superintendent of an orphanage. As he continued the task of training teachers, he became concerned about the non-availability of education to children in the preschool age. Then he returned to Germany in 1836 and established his first kindergarten in 1837 in the village of Blankenburg. Froebel devoted his life to discovering and devising an apparatus for kindergarten. But the government of Germany did not subscribe to the ideas of Froebel and prohibited him from establishing any school. This rejection hurt him so much that he could not rid himself of the agony till the very end of his life. Froebel, the lover of child education and the father of kindergarten, passed away on June 21, 1852 in poverty, misery and agony. His grave has been marked by a slab with a cube, a cylinder and a sphere on it. Though he died, yet he lived for the child. This great aim and purpose of his life is summed up in his famous saying, "Come, let us live for our children".

PHILOSOPHY OF FROEBEL

Froebel is a great educator as well as a great philosopher. He is religiously influenced by his father and maternal uncle, and philosophically influenced by the well-known idealistic philosophers like Fichte, Kant and Schilling. Therefore, the philosophical views of Froebel are mainly based on idealism. The principles of his philosophy are outlined as under.

Principle of unity in diversity: As an idealist, Froebel believes in God and he views the whole universe as one, a gift from God. With this faith, he formulates the principle that there is unity of man, nature and God. Men must be aware of the absolute unity of the Universe. The real purpose of education is "to expand or develop the life of an individual until it comprehends this existence through participation in all-pervading spiritual activity". In his book The Education of Man he remarks, "The whole world—the All, the Universe—is a single organism in which an eternal uniformity manifests itself". Life is the union of the spiritual with the material. God is one of the grounds of all things. God is the all comprehending, the all sustaining. God is the essential nature, the meaning of the world. All things, animate or inanimate, originate from God. Man and nature are one. There is unity in diversity and diversity in unity. In the words of Froebel, "All things have come from the Divine Unity (God) and have their origin in the Divine unity. All things live and have their beings in and through the Divine Unity. The Divine affluence that lives in each thing is the essence of each thing". The unity is three-fold,

Unity of substance: There is only one substance from which all things come.
Unity of origin: There is one source, that is God, from which all things come.
Unity of purpose: All things strive towards perfection, i.e., God.

Principle of development: The principle of continuity or development is based upon the first principle of the law of unity. Frobel advocates balanced and unified development of body, mind and soul. He believes that life is ever changing and growing. This development should take place from within and strive towards unity. Such development should not be unnatural and artificial, and it should always be according to natural and inner laws. It can be produced only by the exercise of faculty-physical, mental or spiritual. He says that each child is born with some innate tendencies, which inspire him to realise God. Such innate tendencies of the child should be exercised for the development of the mind and body. Effective development takes place when the exercise arises from the child's own activity. Froebel rightly says, "Each individual must develop from within self service and freedom, in accordance with the eternal law". He observes that full development comes only by spontaneous self-activity.

Principle of self-activity: Froebel convinces that real growth and development of the individual is possible only through self-activity. He emphasises 'play' as the most suitable medium of self-activity. Any forced activity is artificial and unnatural. He allows full freedom to the child through self-composed actions. 'Play' is the purest and the most spiritual activity of man. It gives joy, freedom, contentment, inner rest and peace within the world. This spontaneous activity leads to a balanced and unified development of body, mind and soul.

Principle of development in social setting: Froebel stands in favour of the development of the child in the social setting. He advocates individual integration and social cohesion. He remarks, "No community can progress while the individual remains behind". According to him, true education of the individual is only possible when its relationship with the education of the whole society is realised. This is because he believes that the individual is not apart from the life of the society.

Principle of symbolism: Froebel is of the view that there is a connection between mind and matter. The connecting force diffuses itself freely and equally in all directions. The material resultant of such centrifugal forces is a symbolic sphere. It is different from all other forms, yet contains all of them, it is formless yet the most perfect form. This principle of symbolism underlines the choice of his gifts to be presented to the children to play with.

Principle of kindergarten: The basic principle of kindergarten is that it is a miniature society for young children. According to Froebel, "kindergarten is the nursery for future citizens, the teacher is the gardener and the students are tender plants". It inculcates in the children the sense of socialisation and self- realisation. Like the gardener, the teacher is to look after the little human plants and water them to grow into beauty and perfection. He believes that a child and a plant are similar in the process of growth and development. The plant grows from within according to the seed that is within, in the same way the child grows from within.

MEANING OF EDUCATION

According to Froebel, education is growth from within. It is a development by which an individual realises that he is one of the all-encompassing unities. He defines, "Education is unfoldment of what is already enfolded in the germ. It is the process by which the child develops his innate powers". It means that education is to unfold the child's innate powers and it awakens his spiritual nature, which unites him with God. He also remarks that education should lead and guide the child to clearness, concerning himself and in himself, bringing him face-to-face with Nature and unite with God. Education lifts the child to knowledge of himself and of the mankind, to knowledge of God and of nature and to the pure and the holy life.

EDUCATIONAL THOUGHTS OF FROEBEL

Froebel attaches great importance to education in the child's early life. His philosophy of education is the outcome of his experiences, which he acquired from his school founded for the young children.

Object of education: The object of education is the realisation of the faithful, pure, inviolable, and hence, holy life. The divine essence of man should be unfolded, brought out, lifted into consciousness and man himself raised into free, conscious obedience to the divine principle that lives in him and to a free representation of this principle in his life. Education should lead and guide man to clearness concerning himself and in himself, to face with nature, and to unite with God.

Programme of education: Froebel has given different programmes of education for different stages of development. Infancy is a period of sensory development. So, only sense organs should be used to acquire any sort of knowledge. Childhood is a period during which the child makes his innate tendencies, external thought, activities, attention, watchfulness and action. Now the actual education begins. Objects are identified with their names and words are uttered clearly. Play-way can be an important method of instruction. Adolescence is a period in which external is made internal. A child perceives many things in his environment, he thinks over them and internalises them. Now child-centred education is needed. Froebel says, "If activity brings joy to the child, the work will give delight to the boy". Here interest in product is created. Through various activities, the child will mostly solve his practical problems in life.

Curriculum: Froebel recommends various subjects to be taught to the child during the adolescence period. They are drawing, painting, gardening and nature study. He wants to teach these activities along with formal subjects like religion and philosophy, natural sciences, mathematics and languages. All the subjects should possess internal unity and a high degree of correlation.

Methods of education: Froebel's methods of teaching are based on four basic principles:

Principle of self-activity: It means those activities which a child does in accordance with his own interest. Nothing is imposed from outside.

Principle of learning by games: Child takes much interest in play activities and games. So, curriculum should be organized through games.

Principle of sociability: Self-activities should be expressed in a good social environment through group plays to develop sociability. Group plays develop mutual love, sympathy, cooperation and fellow feeling along with the feeling of competition among them.

Principle of freedom: Froebel advocates full freedom to the child for the expression of activities and educational development.

Discipline: Froebel's concept of discipline is self-discipline learned through self-activities. There should not be any outside interference, compulsion and control. The child should be educated in a free atmosphere under social discipline. Such discipline should be maintained through group activities and team works.

Social aspects of education: Froebel lays stress on the social aspect of education. He is of the opinion that social institutions such as the home, the school, the church and the state etc. act as agencies for individual development from which unity in diversity is realised.

Child-centred education: Like Rousseau, Froebel is in favour of child-centred education. According to him, education should be in conformity with the child's nature and needs.

Totality of educational endeavour: Man needs his senses, and emotions as well as reasons to realise the divining character of the universe. As they are the windows of the soul, Froebel emphasises the totality of educational endeavour.

Relatedness of all education: The educator should lead the child through such situations which will help him to relate his experiences organically one with another. It will help the child to realise his own personal unity and the unity inherent in the diversity of life.

Child's mind as a living whole: In the words of Froebel, "The true method of education consists in considering the mind of the child as a living whole in which all the parts work together to produce harmonious unity".

Creativeness of childhood: Froebel believes that the child possesses his own creativeness. So, an adult has no right to feel superior or inferior to children. The task of an adult is first to understand the child and then guide him accordingly.

Play and activity: According to Froebel, "Play is the purest, most important activity of man at this stage. It gives joy, freedom, contentment, inner rest and peace with the world". It is the most important phase in the spontaneous development of the child, because it allows him to exercise harmoniously all his physical emotional and intellectual qualities. Play is for the child as ethical as devotion to his work is for the adult. Froebel has given seven gifts to children to play with.

Place of songs in education: Froebel has given fifty play songs in his book, Mother and Nursery Songs which plays an important role in education. He devises songs, gestures and construction as the chief means of stimulating the imagination of the child.

Role of teacher in education: Froebel bestows a very important place to the teacher in education. The teacher is like a gardener who carefully nurses and protects children in order to secure their full and free development in desirable ways.

Education of preschool child: There are two reasons for Froebel to concentrate particularly on the education of the preschool child. One is psychological. Froebel reveals as astounding insight into the importance of the early experiences of childhood for future personality development. His close contact with Pestalozzi, and Herbert, led him naturally to emphasise the importance of preschool education. The other reason is sociological. Froebel's period was the period of Napoleanic wars and their destructive influences resulting in capitalism and a series of social revolutions. He saw that the children were imperiled in all these crises. Such critical circumstances forced him to reform the elementary school as the basis for the reconstruction of mankind, and fight for the establishment of kindergarten schools.

FROEBEL'S KINDERGARTEN

Froebel is known to the world by his kindergarten—the garden of children established at Blankenburg in 1837. It has brought great name and fame to him in the field of education.

Meaning of kindergarten: 'Kindergarten' is a German word which means the garden of children or a small state for children. According to Froebel, "Kindergarten, is a miniature state for young children". In fact, it is the home for children to play freely by which they express themselves and develop their personalities. According to Froebel, "School is the nursery of future citizens, the teacher is the gardener and the students are tender plants". Like the gardener, the teacher is to look after the little human plants and water them to grow into beauty and perfection. He discovers the fact that there is a great similarity between a child and a plant in the process of their growth and development. The plant grows naturally from within according to the inner fertility of the seed. In the same manner, the child grows from within according to the innate tendencies, which he possesses.

Environment of the kindergarten: The lovely atmosphere of kindergarten is freedom, peace, play and joyful living. It inculcates in the child the sense of socialisation and self-realisation. Froebel's kindergarten is a school without books and without fixed intellectual tasks for children. But the training consists of songs, gestures etc. and construction is given along with the use of language to foster self-activity, creativeness, social cooperation and concrete expression. The songs, gestures and construction are connected as a whole, that is, when a story is told or read, it is expressed in song, dramatised in movement and gestures, and illustrated by construction form in blocks, paper, clay or drawing. This process develops the imagination and thought of the child. It helps the child to train up his hands and limbs, his eyes and other senses in order to do certain things.

Objectives of the Kindergarten

1. Provide the children employment in agreement with their whole nature.
2. Strengthen the bodies of children to be physically fit.
3. Exercise their senses which are the gateways of knowledge.
4. Engage their awakening mind through their senses in order to make them acquainted with nature and their fellow creatures.
5. Guide a right heart and affections, and to lead them to the original ground of all life.

In the words of Froebel, "The objective of a kindergarten is to give the children employment in agreement with their whole nature, to strengthen their bodies, to exercise their senses, to engage their awakening mind and thorough their senses to make them acquainted with the nature and their fellow creatures. It is specially to guide the heart and the affections, and to lead them to the original ground of all life, to unity with themselves".

Characteristics of Kindergarten

Froebel realised the needs and the paramount importance of childhood and opened the first kindergarten as an institution of children from age 4 to 6, at Blankenburg in 1837 to protect them from the destructive influences of Napoleonic wars, capitalism and a series of social revolutions. The important features of the kindergarten are:

Self-activity: This is the dominant idea underlying kindergarten. Self-activity directs the growth of the child along the lines of racial development. It is self-realisation through which the child comes to know of his own nature as well as the life around him. Then he unites and harmonises his individual spirit with the spirit of humanity. Self-activity not only fills the gap between knowledge and action but also provides freedom, contentment, peace of mind and bliss. This activity can be imparted and promoted in three ways through songs, gestures and constructions. About this self-activity an inspector remarks, "Self- activity of the mind is the first law of institution, the kind of instruction given here does not make the young mind a strong box into which, as early as possible kinds of coins of the most different values and coinage such as are now current in the world are stuffed, but slowly, continuously, gradually and always inwardly that is, according to a connection found in nature of the human mind, the instruction steadily goes on without any ticks from the simple to the complex, from the concrete to the abstract, so well adapted to the child and his needs that he goes as easily to his learning as to his play".

In order to make the self-activity effective, the following conditions should be kept in mind:

1. Self-activity should not be vague.
2. It should be a sublimated or controlled activity.
3. Social atmosphere should be created to secure meaningful activities.
4. Self-activity may take the form either of work or play.

Creativeness: Froebel believes that every man's mind or soul and heart is inseparable, but it is made of independent parts. Mind and soul express themselves through physical activity and expression. Education will be futile if it does not change thinking into action. In fact, every child is creative by nature. If he is given some materials, he will try to create new forms at once. In the words of Zakir Hussain, "Children want to do and undo, break and mend things. This is how nature educates him". Therefore, creativeness in the child should be encouraged and developed through education.

Social participation: Froebel believes that man is essentially a social animal who should live in the company of other persons. So, he emphasises the social aspect of education and advocates that home, school, church, vocation and the state should provide all opportunities to children for social participation. This kind of social participation helps the child to develop his physical, intellectual, social and moral aspects.

Child-centred education: Education according to the nature of the child is an important feature of the kindergarten. It emphasises the fact that education should be imparted in accordance with nature and needs of the children in an atmosphere of freedom. This view of Froebel leads us close to the naturalistic tendencies of modern education.

Activity method: Education is imparted to the child in the kindergarten through activity methods. Froebel advocates various activity methods such as games, collection, gardening, drawing, building shelters and boats and creating boxes etc. These activities facilitate free and unobstructed and natural development of the child. This character of the kindergarten takes us near to the naturalistic and pragmatic philosophies of education.

Freedom and growth: Freedom, joy, peace, play and love are the salient features of the kindergarten. It maybe said to be a home for children for joyful living and learning. There is no external restraint and bodily punishments. It is a garden where plants grow freely. In the same way kindergarten is the garden of children where they can grow freely.

CURRICULUM

Froebel prescribes different types of curriculum according to the different stages of a child's development. He advocates sensory development in infancy, and play in childhood. Instruction and education becomes curriculum centred in boyhood. His curriculum consists of both activities and subjects. The curriculum which is followed in the kindergarten has the following five divisions:

1. Manual work
2. Religion and religious instruction
3. Natural science and mathematics
4. Language
5. Arts and objects of arts

Teaching Procedure in the Kindergarten

Froebel's kindergarten is a miniature state for children in which, they can move freely and joyfully. He is in favour of the spontaneous development of the children through self-expression. Therefore, he prescribes neither books nor a fixed curriculum. The entire programme or education is imparted to the children only through songs, gestures and construction. It makes education a joyful experience. For example, when a topic is taught, it is expressed in a song, dramatised in movements and gestures and finally demonstrated by constructive work form in blocks, clay, paper, drawing or any other materials. In this way, "thoughts are stimulated, imagination vivified, hands and eyes trained, muscles coordinated, and moral nature strengthened". Thus, teaching procedure in the kindergarten involves teaching through songs, gifts and occupation.

Teaching through songs: Songs are the most important means through which education is imparted in the kindergarten. All songs, therefore, about the common objects of life are included in the daily school programme. The songs selected and included by Froebel relate to nursery games and they satisfy the physical, mental, social, moral and spiritual needs of the children. Songs are arranged in accordance with the development of children. Each song has three parts namely, (i) a motto for the mother's guidance; (ii) a verse for singing; and (iii) a picture for illustrating the verses. Besides this kind of fifty play songs, Froebel devises many nursery rhymes likes "Jack and Jill", "Humpty Dumpty" and "Cyndrella". These type of rhymes enable the child to use his senses, limbs and muscles and to become familiar with the objects around him.

Teaching through gifts and occupations: Froebel lays stress on various activities and plays in the kindergarten. For this purpose, he devises different gifts and occupations. He regards them very essential for nursery education. Gifts are educational toys presented to the child in a definite order without changing their forms. Sphere comes first followed by crystal, cube, cylinder etc. Full freedom is given to the child to handle them in the way he likes. Such activities connected with these gifts are called occupations. Gifts are materials in the form of wooden balls of different colours, wooden spheres, cubes and cylinders of different types and sizes. Gifts are also in the shape of wooden squares, triangles, tables, sticks, and rings. Occupations include activities like construction with paper, clay, wood and other materials. The activities are paper folding, clay moulding, cardboard works, wood carving, mat making, basket making, embroidery, drawing, sewing etc. The purpose of these gifts and occupations is to enable the child to utilise his senses of sight and touch, and to give him an idea of size, form, and surface and to develop the number sense and artistic consciousness.

Froebel has devised about twenty gifts for the complete education and training of children. But only the first seven gifts are now usually called by his name.

Gift 1: It consists of red, yellow, blue, orange, green and purple coloured wooden balls, contained in a box. The occupation consists in rolling them. The child rolls them about in play. This gift and occupation develops in the child the idea of colour, materials, motion and direction.

Gift 2: It consists of a sphere, a cube, and a cylinder made of hard wood. Occupation is playing with these gifts. This gift and occupation helps the child to notice the differences, that is, a cube is stable, a sphere is mobile and cylinder is both stable and movable.

Gift 3: It is a big wooden cube, divided into eight smaller equal cubes. With these gifts, the child learns to construct a number of useful artistic forms such as benches, steps, doors, bridges etc. This gift also enables the child to gain an elementary idea of addition and subtraction.

Gift 4: It is also a large cube divided into eight oblong prisms. Length of each cube is twice the breadth and the breadth is twice the thickness. This gift enables the child to construct different kinds of buildings and patterns.

Gift 5: A large cube is divided into twenty seven small cubes. Three of which are again divided diagonally into halves and three into quarters. This gift trains the child to construct beautiful forms and patterns. It also enables him to learn form and number.

Gift 6: It is a big cube divided into eighteen whole and nine small oblong blocks. This gift is useful in designing and teaching numbers.

Gift 7: It is a set of square and triangular wooden tablets in two colours. This gift is useful for the child to exercise in algebra, geometry, trigonometry and drawing.

Other gifts consist of materials such as stick laying, perforating, paper cutting, threading of beads, mat making, embroidery, basket making, wirework, drawing and modelling.

Teaching through play: Froebel introduces the play-way method of teaching in the kindergarten for the growth and development of the child. He discovers and stresses on the educational value of play. He remarks, "Play is the characteristic activity of childhood. It is the highest phase of child- development—of human development in this period. It is through play that the child discloses his real self and clearly indicates his interest". Therefore, Froebel gives a prominent place to play activities in the kindergarten. He utilises play for cultivating in the child the habits of action, feeling and thinking and for developing courage, instincts and motivation. Teaching through play enables the child to train and develop his senses, which are the gateways of knowledge. The following song can be taught through play using Gift 1 (see gifts and occupation).

Oh, see the pretty ball
So sound so soft and small
The ball is round and rolls each way,
The ball is nice for baby's play

ROLE OF TEACHER IN KINDERGARTEN

Froebel compares the growing children with plants. He, therefore, demands that the teacher acts as a gardener and asks him to let the children grow and develop in accordance with their natural endowments. In the words of Froebel, "The tree germ bears within itself the nature of the whole tree, so the development and formation of the whole future life of each being is contained in the beginning of its existence". Therefore, the teacher should be a passive person. He has to suggest suitable occupations when gifts are assigned to children. He is also required to demonstrate certain activities to them. He has to sing songs so that the child can form appropriate ideas and develop his capacities. Moreover, the teacher should inculcate values like love, sympathy, humility, cooperation and obedience to elders.

Discipline in Kindergarten

Froebel loves the children much and stands against external restraint and bodily punishment. According to him, discipline is not a set of rules and regulations imposed upon children. Discipline, in the kindergarten, is of the protective and cooperative type based on love, goodwill and mutual understanding. He advocates the inculcation of self-control which is inner discipline leading to outer discipline. Therefore, the child should be trained to develop self-control or inner discipline through spontaneous and play activities, games and stories, arts and crafts, gifts and occupations. Froebel stresses that woman should be trained for training children at this stage.

Merits of Kindergarten

- It bestows great importance to preschool or nursery education for children between the age group of 3 and 6.
- It emphasises the significance of play in early education.
- Froebel broadens the concept and scope of school as a social institution, where the children learn the virtues of cooperation, sympathy, fellow feeling and responsibility.
- The gifts and occupations of the kindergarten have brought about a new approach to the method of education.
- Froebel's kindergarten makes children creative workers.
- Kindergarten emphasises the necessity for the study of the child's natural instincts and impulses.
- Kindergarten provides sufficient scope for activities.
- Gifts and occupations used in the kindergarten provide training for the development ofsenses.
- The nature study helps to develop love for nature and world in the mind of thestudents.
- It is a child-centred education though the importance of the curriculum is neglected.
- The child will not lose interest till the end.
- The spiritual atmosphere, freedom, love, joy, peace and contentment are the nature of kindergarten and they are essentially needed for the physical, mental, social, cultural and spiritual development.

Demerits of Kindergarten

- Froebel lays too much stress on the inner development of the child. He ignores the environment and the adaptation of the child to his environment.
- The songs prescribed by Froebel are out of date. They cannot be utilised in all schools. They should be changed according to the changing environment and the needs of the children.
-
- The gifts of Froebel are formal in nature and meant for sense training. The order of presentation of gifts is arbitrary. Modern schools employ scientific devices for the training of senses.
- There is little correlation in the teaching of various subjects. Nature study is taught in isolation.
- There is too much stress on socialisation. Individual attention is neglected which has been stressed by modern educationists and psychologists.
- It requires sufficient training on the part of teacher to frame new songs and device new techniques.
- The excessive emphasis on play in education detracts the child from serious learning and makes education meaningless.

- The symbolism involved in gifts is also too difficult to be understood by immature brains.
- Educating children through gifts and occupations may cost much time and energy.
- Though Froebel's kindergarten is suitable for nursery education how can this method be applicable in the scientific age, when knowledge doubles?

MEANING OF PLAY-WAY METHOD

The term 'play-way' was introduced in educational fields by Caldwell Cook. He associated learning with spontaneity freedom and laughter through play activity. The play-way method is considered as complementary to the activity method which is recognised as the language of the child. In fact, the child can express his behaviour through play rather than language. Moreover, play makes the child a balanced self, physically, mentally and emotionally. Hence, there can be no growth in the child without action or play. Froebel uses several activities or plays in his kindergarten for the development and growth of the child. This method is known as **Play-way method** in teaching–learning process. The meaning and significance of the term 'Play-way' has been derived from the word 'play'. In the words of Froebel, "Play is the purest, most spiritual activity of man at this stage (childhood) and at the same time, typical of human life as a whole—of the inner, hidden natural life in man and all things. It gives, therefore, joy, freedom, contentment, inner and outer root, peace with the world. It holds the source of all that is good. The plays of childhood are the germinal leaves of all later life".

Froebel has given seven gifts to children to play with. Play-way method envisages that all works should be done in the spirit of play. It is quite different from the normal meaning of the word play, which is considered as a form of physical activity. Play-way in the kindergarten is a means for the cognitive, and effective development of the child in intellect, skills and feelings.

Five Kinds of Play

1. Play leading to recreation and construction activities.
2. Play for imaginative development.
3. Play for developing cooperation.
4. Play for the development of character.
5. Play for learning 3 R's—reading, writing and arithmetic.

Principles of Play-way Method

- Principle of growth and development of the child through play.
- Principle of self-development under the guidance of the teacher.
- Principle of self-activity and self-expression through play.
- Principle of spontaneity through play.
- Principle of freedom, happiness and joy in play activities.
- Principle of unity and socialisation through group activities.
- Principle of aesthetic appreciation.
- Principle of creativeness and drawing out using gifts and occupations.
- Principle of discipline through love, sympathy and mutual understanding.
- Principle of sense training through gifs and occupation.
- Principle of concrete to abstract ideas about unity while playing with gifts.
- Principle of learning 3R's through songs, gifts and occupations.

Gifts, Occupations, Songs, Gestures and Construction in Play-way

Froebel stresses on the place of activity and play in his kindergarten. He devises suitable gifts to provide activities. The gifts suggest some form of activity, and occupations are the activities suggested by the gifts. The order of the gifts is devised in such a way as to lead the child from the activities and thought of one stage to another.

Froebel has found an organic relationship between play, songs, gestures and construction. He considers them as three coordinate forms of expression in the child. What the child learns is first expressed in a song, then it is dramatised or expressed in gesture or movement, and finally illustrated through some constructive work. These activities provide exercise to the senses, limbs and muscles of the child. In this way, the child achieves a balanced development in physical, mental and social aspects.

Play-way and Songs

Froebel has given fifty play songs in his book, *Mother and Nursery Songs.* He uses these songs in his kindergarten, which enable the child to use his senses, limbs and muscles and to familiarise him with the surroundings. The child begins to use language through these songs. Each song is followed by gesture or movement. The selection of the songs is determined by the teacher in accordance with the needs and development of the child. Each song contains three parts namely,

- A motto for the guidance of mother or teacher.
- A verse accompanied by music.
- A picture illustrating the song.

Here is a specimen of the drill song.

Let us have a drill today
March along grand array
And whoever steps the best
Shall be captain over the rest
And lead us on our way.

Role of Teacher in the Play-way

Froebel attaches great value to the guidance of the teacher. According to him, the child can be stimulated to achieve certain ends through spontaneous activities only if he is properly directed and influenced by the teacher. Therefore, the teacher should play the role of a gardener who looks after the tender plants. He has to provide an environment of joy, peace, freedom and love which are essential for the natural growth of the child. For this purpose he has to plan his work very carefully and demonstrate the play-way activity.

The teacher should behave like a friend, guide and philosopher while presenting the gifts and demonstrating different activities. He should not remain passive but see whether the games introduced are educationally useful and effective. For instance, when a cube is presented, the teacher may sing the following song:

Eight corners, and twelve edges see,
And faces six, belong to me;
One face behind; and one before;
One top; one bottom, that makes four
One at the right, at left side one,
And that counts six, if rightly done.

FROEBEL'S CONTRIBUTIONS TO MODERN EDUCATION

Froebel has created a new epoch in the field of education by establishing the kindergarten for small children. His contribution to educational theory and practices is highly valuable and useful to bring about a radical change in the child's development. The kindergarten system has become very popular in Europe. It has reformed the shape of nursery schools throughout the civilized world. He loved the children and lived for them. He also invites us to love our children and live for them. In fact, Froebel has shown the right road to the modern educators and thinkers for further development of education and the child.

Emphasis on nursery education: Froebel has given great importance to the preschool education of infants. He says, "All school education was yet without a proper initial foundation and until the education of the nursery was reformed, nothing solid and worthy could be attained". The present educators accept the views of Froebel and fully recognise the importance of the education in the early years. Today, we can come across a number of schools catering to the needs of the child, which is due to Froebel's pathbreaking theory. Thus, his educational theory and practices have been recognised as the most significant step towards the education of the infant.

Self-activity in education: Froebel is the first educator to make self-activity as the basis of education. He says that the children are not only receptive of knowledge they are also very active in expression. So, they should be allowed at the preschool stage to see, handle, arrange, rearrange, make and unmake things themselves. The present school has become a place of activity and joy for children. 'Learning by doing' is an important slogan of the present day. We provide many activities to the students to satisfy their instincts of construction, manipulation curiosity and acquisition.

Respect for child's individuality: Froebel lived for children, worked for children and died for children. He is the first educator who realised the value of discovering and developing individuality early in one's life by means of initiative, execution and cooperation in the educational process. This view of Froebel has had a great impact on modern education. In fact, modern educators recognise the child's individuality and work on it by means of the child's own initiative and effort. They consider the school as a "temple where they are to pay homage to the individuality of the child".

Learning through arts and crafts: Froebel is an early supporter of the inclusion of manual work in the school curriculum. He believes that a human child needs to preserve his body by securing food, clothing and shelter and to uplift himself spiritually. So, the child is made to create and construct things with his own labour and effort. He says, "Manual work is a necessary condition for the realization of the child's personality". And he adds, "The young, growing human being should be trained early for creation and productive activity". To achieve his views, he includes various arts and crafts like, drawing, painting, woodwork, leatherwork, clay modelling, paper cutting, cardboard work and embroidery in the preschool education. As a result, great stress is laid on learning through arts and crafts as in the basic education propagated by Mahatma Gandhi.

Emphasis on sense training: Like naturalists, Froebel also believes that senses are the gateways to knowledge. Therefore, he insists on sense training instead of verbal instruction to sharpen the intelligence of the pupils. In this respect, he is regarded as the forerunner of Maria Montessori. Moreover, he introduces gifts and occupations to train the senses of children. With these gifts, he gives the child the idea of shape, form, colour, size and number. Now instead of the gifts the child gets audio-visual aids as an integral part of its education.

Education through play: Froebel introduces play-way techniques–in the teaching learning process of education. He believes that play is the highest phase of self-development. This doctrine of play-way method has been accepted by every educator. It is now the case of modern education. Today progressive modern schools teach children through songs, movements, gestures, dramatisation, handwork, project methods and experimental and creative activities based on play-way.

Sociological aspects of education: Froebel says, "The good results of all true education depend on the careful fostering and development of this feeling on the part of the child that he is a whole and yet also a part of the life around". He gives due recognition to the sociological aspect of education by which children develop the power of doing things in a social atmosphere. Modern progressive trends in democratic education need the development of primary virtues like cooperation, sympathy, fellow feeling and sharing of responsibilities in children. In this regard, Froebel is considered as the father of sociological trend in education.

Nature study in education: Froebel stresses the necessity for the study of a child's nature, his instincts and impulses. He advocates the nature study so as to enable the child to understand the world in which he lives and to develop habits of careful observation. Thus, nature study is meant to realise the presence of the all-pervading Divine spirit in the natural phenomena. He includes nature study in the school curriculum for the moral and religious uplift of the child. Today nature study has become popular in schools.

Women teacher in nursery stage: It is due to the influence of Froebel that women teachers are considered to be more suited for the task of instruction at the pre-primary or pre-basic stage of teaching at the nursery stage.

New conception of school: Froebel's kindergarten is a little world in which responsibility of the children is shared by all. The individual rights of the children are respected by all. Above all, brotherly sympathy is fostered and voluntary cooperation is practised in the kindergarten. Therefore, his school is an ideal society, which is indeed a new concept.

CONCLUSION

It has been accepted worldwide that Froebel is the champion of modern educational practice, the exponent and ardent lover of child education. His educational philosophy of kindergarten has proved a landmark in the history of teaching methodology. In fact, his kindergarten system of education aims at the complete development of the child. We can conclude by saying, "It is by far the most original, attractive and philosophical form of infant development, the world has yet seen". The eternal message of Froebel, the founder of kindergarten system of education, is "Come! Let us live for children".

CHAPTER 26

JOHN DEWEY
1859–1952

INTRODUCTION

John Dewey remains as one of the greatest educational thinkers of modern times. He is a great educator whose contribution to education makes him to be remembered for all times throughout the world. Though he was born in a poor family, he became very popular on the basis of his works and great deeds for the development of educational system. He is the chief exponent of pragmatism which emphasises practical aspects of education. He is the philosopher of the twentieth century which is dominated by science, technology, engineering, industrialism and democracy. His approach to the problems of life is original and practical, and he has offered sound solutions for them. Indeed Dewey's contributions to modern educational theory and practices are highly useful to the society.

LIFE OF JOHN DEWEY

John Dewey, the greatest of the pragmatists, the most intellectual philosopher, a great educationist and a great thinker of the present age, was born at Burlington, in Vermont, a small town in New England, USA in 1859. He was brought up in a rural environment and used to meet and talk to people who visited his father's shop. He received his primary education in his native place. He obtained his degree from the University of Vermont in 1879. Then he joined John Hopkins University for higher education. There he studied philosophy under George S. Morris and Charles S. Pierce, political and institutional history under Herbert B. Adams, and psychology under G. Stanley Hall. He obtained PhD in philosophy in 1884. He became lecturer in the Department of Philosophy in Minnesota, Michigan and Chicago Universities.

He founded a laboratory school in the Chicago University in 1896 and it made him world famous. All his educational theories were tested in the school. His concepts of education were modified and clarified in the light of his practical experience in running the school. In1904, he adorned the chair of the Head of the Department of Education and Philosophy in Columbia University, New York.

During his stay in Columbia, he was invited by different countries of the world such as Japan, China, Turkey and Russia for advice and suggestions regarding the organization of education there. He visited the University of Peking to deliver a lecture on education and philosophy. In 1919, he delivered a series of lectures at the Imperial University of Tokyo. These lectures were published in a book, *Reconstruction in Philosophy*. The National Government of Turkey asked him to draw up a report on the reorganization of national schools in Turkey. He was a great scholar as well as a prolific writer. He has written about fifty books and more than 800 articles on philosophy, education, politics and sociology. Many of his writings have been translated into various foreign languages. He was highly influenced by Hegel, William James and Herbert, Spencer. John Dewey, a great contributor in the field of education and philosophy, passed away in 1952.

JOHN DEWEY'S EDUCATIONAL PHILOSOPHY

Dewey's educational philosophy is based on the evolutionary concepts of Darwin and pragmatism. His philosophical doctrine and educational ideology reflect the influence of the industrial revolution, the change of population, the rapid growth of the machine era and the domestic ideal. Dewey believes that there are two sides to the educative process—the psychological and the sociological. The goal of education cannot be achieved in the absence of these educative processes. The psychological side is the study of the child with his interests, instincts, endowments and inclinations. Thus, it forms the basis of all education. But the sociological side is the social environment, in which the child is born, lives and grows for society. Education is progress, both for the individual and the society. It is a bi-polar process consisting of the psychological and the sociological elements. Dewey's educational philosophy has been named as 'Experimentalism', 'Functionalism', 'Instrumentalism', 'Operationalism', 'Practicalism', 'Pragmatism' and 'Progressivism'.

Pragmatism: John Dewey is a pragmatist. Therefore, experience forms the core of his educational philosophy. Dewey wants to test everything including any idea, hypothesis, faith or religion by how it works and the consequences thereof. Educational experiences should be measured by the degree and extent to which they cater to the actual needs of the individual and the society. Its results are accepted if they are useful to the society and otherwise rejected.

Social utility: According to John Dewey, school is a miniature society. So, the needs of the society should be taken into consideration. School becomes the natural part of the society if it reflects the natural inclinations and activities of the child. The school should make the society free from evils.

Social change: Dewey believes that social change is a natural phenomenon. No society can remain static for a long time. Everything changes as time changes. So, education is also changing according to the changing needs of the society.

Social discipline: Dewey's concept of social discipline is reflected in a democratic society. To him, the purpose of school discipline is the cultivation of social attitudes, habits and ideas of conduct in the children through the conjoint activities organized in the school.

Child centredness: Dewey wants education to be child centered so that every child can have the full opportunity and freedom to develop himself according to his needs, interests and ability.

Self experience: Dewey is also an experimentalist. According to him, every idea should be tested or experimented before it is accepted. So, he wants the child to discover the truth by using reflective enquiry and experimentation. He believes that whatever is truth is useful and whatever is useful is truth.

Universal education: According to Dewey, education aims at the development of the individual personality. So, it should not be restricted to only a particular section of the society. Every individual must be provided equal opportunities to develop his personality through education. For this purpose, education should be universalised and made available to all.

Democracy is the philosophy of education: Dewey states that democracy is the political and moral philosophy of education. He believes that the barriers of caste, colour, religion, language etc. have divided humanity. But it is education that can break such barriers and develop democratic values. The essence of education is the extension of shared areas of meaningful action which is the essence of democracy. In this way education establishes a happier and nobler world.

Education relates individual with society: It is education through which an individual is trained to make the best citizen growing and thinking in a vast complex of interactions and relationships. In this sense a school is regarded as a 'society in miniature'. A child can neither grow in solitude nor in natural surroundings. Hence, an individual must live both in natural environment and human (social) environment in order to attain his proper growth for which education is quite inevitable.

Education based on scientific method: Science and scientific method is the significant feature of Dewey's educational philosophy. According to him, knowledge and thinking is the process of experience and experimentation. Therefore, it is the education of, by, and for experience that leads to experimental methods of teaching.

DEWEY'S CONCEPT OF EDUCATION

All education progresses by the participation of the individual in the social consciousness of the race. This process begins unconsciously almost at birth and continually shapes the individual's powers, saturating his consciousness, forming his habits, training his ideas and arousing his feelings and emotions. Education is the process of reconstruction of experience, giving it a more socialised value through the medium of increased "social efficiency". According to John Dewey, "Education is the development of all those capacities in the individual which will enable him to control his environment and fulfil his responsibilities".

FUNCTIONS OF EDUCATION

John Dewey has described the following as functions of education:

Education is growth: The real function of education is growth. This growth must be wise and economical, and directed towards a desirable end. The end of growth is more growth and the end of education is more education. What the child learns in the class makes him grow. Dewey says, "The process of education is a continuous process of adjustment, having as its aim at every stage an added capacity of growth". Thus, the purpose of educational effort is to facilitate the changing and growing personality of an individual. The teacher therefore, should help the child to develop his instincts and capacities by providing him opportunities and problems which will make him think and find solutions. In this way the power of thinking and the mind grows. It will develop the capacity of the child for further thoughts.

Education is life: The function of education is not a preparation of life but, it is life itself. In the words of Dewey, "Life is a by-product of activities and education is born out of these activities". The child lives in the present and the future is unknown, and meaningless to him. Therefore, pupils should be made active participants in the social and community life of the school and trained to lead a cooperative and helpful life outside. They should be encouraged to face actual life problems in the school in order to gain varied experiences. In this respect, school is an extension of home, which provides life experiences to the child only through the medium of education. Hence, education is life itself.

Education develops social efficiency: The important function of education is developing social efficiency in the child by transforming him into a social human being. Dewey says, "What nutrition and reproduction are to physiological life, education is to social life". Man is essentially a social being who draws energy, strength, knowledge, experiences and attitudes in a social medium. Through education, he is developing reasoning in social relations, cultivating social virtues. Thus, the function of education is teaching the child give and take policy and making him aware of social obligation. In fact, right education helps the child to adjust himself to the social environments. Social efficiency includes economic and cultural efficiency. Dewey technically calls it socialisation of an individual. In this sense, education maybe called a social process, which is the fundamental method of social progress and individual uplift.

Education reconstructs experiences: Dewey stresses the point that experience is the source of knowledge. Education is the process of the reconstruction of experiences giving them a more socialised value through the medium of individual efficiency. One experience leads to further experiences and each new experience calls for the revision or modification or rejection of the previous experience. The continuity of experience helps man to grow physically, mentally, socially and morally. The true function of education is the progressive development and enrichment of the child's experience and enhancement of his native powers. In the words of Dewey, "Education is by experience, for experience and of experience". Hence, the function of education lies in creating suitable conditions for the promotion of continuity of experiences. It is only experience which increases knowledge and modifies the child's behaviour through the medium of education.

AIMS OF EDUCATION

John Dewey has set no fixed aim for education. He believes that physical and social environments are always changing. Therefore, the aims of education must be changed and they cannot be fixed for all times to come. He stands against the traditional aims of education—such as moral, spiritual, physical and intellectual of eighteenth and nineteenth centuries. He wants education to cater to the present needs of the child rather than the future which is unknown to him. He, therefore, suggests that educational aims must be restated and reformulated in the light of the rapid social and economic changes in the present day life. However, he has stated the following aims of education in order to prepare the child for the present life.

Create values: Man creates values which are related to time and space. Education facilitates the creation of new values. It is possible to develop democratic values and ideals in the child only through education.

Maximum growth: Education aims at providing the conditions for a better, complete and harmonious growth. That is, education should help to develop the child's innate potentialities according to his interests, abilities and needs.

Social efficiency: Education is basically concerned with the production of a socially efficient individual. This means that social qualities should be developed in the child through various cooperative and group activities organized according to his own traits.

Make child as experimentalist: Dewey is an experimentalist and he wants every child to be an experimentalist or a discoverer. Therefore, the aim of education is to enable the child to discover the truth and cultivate the habit of experimentation.

Prepare child for life: According to Dewey, education is life itself. Pragmatic education is basically practical. Hence, education aims at preparing the individual for the present and the immediate future life, and fulfilling his requirements.

Besides the above aims of education, John Dewey has also given priority to the social aims of education. Let us point out some important social aims prescribed by him.

- Reform and reconstruct the society through education.
- Enable the individual to adjust to the changing social environment.
- Develop the child fully according to his interests, abilities and needs.
- Create social efficiency in the children.
- Develop democratic values and ideals in the child.
- Provide educational opportunities to all citizens.
- Instil the habit of experimentation in children.
- Remove social evils and make the society good—a good place for living.
- Enable the child to discover the truth himself so as to prepare the child to stand on his own feet.

SCHEME OF EDUCATION

Dewey outlines a definite scheme of education and divides the period of elementary school life of the child into three namely, play period, period of spontaneous attention and period of reflective attention according to the stages of the mental development of the child.

Play period (4 to 8 years): In this period, the child studies the life and occupations at home. Then he learns about the larger social and community activities on which his home life depends. During this period, he also learns reading, writing and geography.

Period of spontaneous attention (8 to 12 years): The child learns to solve the practical problems of life. He understands the difference between means and ends. In this period or stage, he should be taught social studies in order to make him understand how man could achieve his purposes under various conditions in different periods of history.

Period of reflective attention (12 years onwards): At this stage, the child is grown up enough to raise new problems and find out solutions to overcome them. He acquires definite skills and arts to mould himself as a useful and efficient member of the society.

Thus, subjects, activities and experiences are integrated into one whole process which makes education quite meaningful and purposive. As a result, the individual would attain every sort of efficiency and become a successful member of the society.

PRINCIPLES OF CURRICULUM

Dewey's curriculum is neither a scheme of studies nor it is a list of subjects but, it is an entire range of human activities and experiences. In his opinion "purposeful activity and a curriculum comprising standard factors of social life, would give the children more interest and insight, through the functioning of intelligence and will, in the achievement of self-control and the appreciation of social values". He includes occupational, moral, aesthetic and moral education in the curriculum. He recommends that this education should be given through practical experiences not through "chalk and talk lessons" in the classroom. Curriculum is determined by the psychological aspects of the child's interest, instinct, ability and need, and the sociological aspects of creating an atmosphere in the school which would allow the child to take an active part in the social awakening of his group.

Let us list the principles of curriculum in order to grasp the nature and purpose of it.

Utility: The curriculum imposed on the child must have utility. It should help to develop the desire to talk and exchange ideas for discovery, creation and artistic expression. It should be designed in such a way that it should include the teaching of reading, writing, counting, manual skill, science, music, and arts.

Flexibility: The curriculum must be flexible and not predetermined and rigid. Every society is dynamic and the needs of the child are also changing and growing. So, the curriculum should be capable of accommodating the changing needs of the child and the society.

Nature of child: The curriculum should be based on the child's interests, inclinations and abilities during the various stages of his development.

Social efficiency: The curriculum should include those subjects and activities which make the child socially efficient and democratic in his behaviour. This means that it should enable the child to get fully adjusted in the society.

Experimentation: The curriculum should foster the habit of self-experience and experimentation in the child. It should present problematic situations before him and he should find solutions to these problems through activities and experimentation.

Related to life: Education is life itself. Therefore, the curriculum should include only those subjects and activities which are related to the child's pattern of life at that particular stage.

METHODS OF TEACHING

The different methods of teaching followed by the teachers in the centres of learning are either based upon the nature of the subject matter or the psychology of the learning process to attract the interest and hold the attention of the students. Dewey is a successful educational psychologist who has presented many novel and useful ideas on educational methods in his two books namely *How We Think* and *Interest and Effort in Education*. Let us list out his ideas on the teaching methods.

Learning by doing: The child learns best when he himself performs actions related to particular subjects. Dewey says that all learning must come as a by- product of actions and never as something learned directly for its own sake. In the teaching process, the teacher should provide learning situations and create suitable environment and the child will learn by doing.

Direct experience: If learning is to be moral and sound, it must come forth as the result of the normal and direct experience of the child. According to Dewey, the child learns effectively through observation and direct experience. The function of the school is to provide an environment and improvise activities for learning through the use of child's senses.

Integrated approach: Dewey stresses on integration between the child's life, his activities and the subjects he studies. The subjects taught to the child should be arranged around his activities to which he is accustomed. In this way his learning becomes compact, useful and systematic.

Individual approach: The method of teaching should be according to the interest, inclination and ability of the child. In fact, each child is unique and different from his fellow flock. Therefore, the educator must understand the interest and capacity of the child before organizing the activities which are useful to him. That is, teach a child according to his level of understanding and specific interest.

Collective approach: Dewey is of the opinion that in a democratic educational pattern, the child should be made to participate in collective activity which makes the learning more effective and useful, and helps to develop social efficiency in him. The teacher should assign various types of programmes to the children to be completed by them collectively. This kind of teaching method creates social discipline among the learners.

Project method: Dewey recommends projects to be used as a teaching technique. A project is a purposeful activity proceeding in a social environment. This method lays emphasis on the pupil's purpose, needs, interest, self-activity and participation in the entire process of teaching. Dewey suggests that problematic situations should be provided to children in and around the classroom. But it should not be too ambitious and beyond the pupil's capacity to accomplish.

Experimental method: Dewey emphasises the fact that all learning must come as the by-product of experimentation. He wants to test everything before finally accepting it. According to him, experimental method is in tune with the heuristic method through which all ideas and hypotheses are tested to discern whether they are true and useful to society.

DISCIPLINE

Dewey stands against the traditional system of strict discipline. He advocates free discipline, self-discipline and a social discipline. The main purpose of social discipline is the cultivation of social attitudes, habits, and ideals of conduct in the pupil through the conjoint activities of the school which has been organized as a community. This type of discipline can be created out of free, purposeful and creative activities which reflect a democratic society. Dewey believes in free discipline based not on punishment and rewards, but it is through cooperative and shared activities for the realisation of certain definite purposes. The role of the teacher is to provide a right kind of environment (due freedom) in the school so that the child may find ample scope to develop himself as a responsible member of the society.

ROLE OF TEACHER

As Dewey himself is a practical teacher of great repute, he assigns considerable importance to the educators in teaching activities. The teacher has to observe, plan and encourage the activities of the pupils and provide natural environment and experiences. In this way, the teacher is a friend, a guide, a helper and a philosopher. He holds the great responsibility of guiding the young not only in the habits of democratic cooperation but also towards the highest intellectual pursuits and the fullest aesthetic experiences. He is not a lecturer, not a policeman and not a supervisor to the children. He should not impose his will or authority on the pupils. He should pay constant attention to the individual differences, and allow them freedom to think and develop their natural impulses. A teacher must be professionally trained and an efficient person to discharge his duties successfully. Dewey says, "Teaching may be compared to selling commodities. No one can sell unless some one buys. In the initiative with the learner, the teacher is a guide and director".

DEWEY'S CONCEPT OF SCHOOL

School is a specialised institution: The school is regarded as an enlarged home or specialised institution which provides specially controlled environment. Here, the child learns the habits of obedience, faith, skills, regularity, hardwork, cooperation, sacrifice, fellow feeling, patience and discipline. This will enable the child to meet his social obligations. The teacher plays the same role as the parents at home.

School is a miniature society: The school is an idealised society considered as a miniature society. It is an activity school where opportunities are provided to the child to construct his experiences under the scientific guidance of teachers. It is a place where the children learn to live life. The child learns by doing and by actual participation in purposeful and intelligent activities such as cooking, sewing, woodwork, weaving and other vocations. Thus, the school as a miniature society provides various types of social, economic, and moral experiences of practical utility.

School is a social institution: School life is a part of social life. It is, therefore, necessary that the school should grow gradually out of the home life. School is a place where the real meaningful activities of the child are simplified, purified and balanced for the purpose of children so that they are initiated into the social life. In fact, the school is a small community within the larger community.

CONTRIBUTION OF DEWEY TO MODERN EDUCATION (IMPACT OF DEWEY ON EDUCATION)

John Dewey is an original and intellectual thinker, next to Plato. He is a great philosopher and a practical teacher because he is a great educationist. No philosopher before him has intimately identified philosophy and education. He is the first man to provide a systematic treatment of "philosophy and education". His educational philosophy has had a very significant and lasting influence on modern educational theory and practices.

Impact on democracy in education: The great contribution of John Dewey is the inculcation of democratic values and social responsibilities which are the important aims of education. Dewey insists on developing these qualities in the child through providing educational opportunities to all. It is democracy, which breaks down the social, national, religious and economic barriers between man-and-man, group-and-group and nation-and-nation. Thus, democracy stands for universalisation of free and compulsory education. The idea of free and compulsory education from 6–14 years in India has been derived from the thoughts of John Dewey. It has been made the seventh fundamental right under the 91st Amendment of the Constitution in 2001 by amending article 45(A) and 21 of Indian Constitution.

Impact on curriculum: Dewey has given a new concept of life-centred and experience-centred curriculum according to the interests, inclinations, abilities and needs of the child. The impact of Dewey's ideas on the subjects to be included in the curriculum leads to the introduction of skill subjects into modern curricula with special importance to various kinds of games.

Impact on teaching methods: The impact of Dewey's ideas is seen in the methods of education in recent times. His activity and self-experience and the methods of teaching are very much recognised today. The project method, experimental method, problem-solving method and the idea of learning by doing have been very influential in the development of modern educational practices and techniques.

Impact on project method: It is the practical outcome of Dewey's educational philosophy. This method is based on "learning by doing and experiencing". It encourages pupils to learn through self-effort and creative activity in real life situations. In modern days, this method has become very popular in the world of education. In fact, modern educationists have accepted this method as an important method of learning and have implemented it in school, college and university education.

Impact on psychological and sociological aspects of education: The psychological and sociological aspects of education is Dewey's most significant contribution. It has had a great impact on the world of modern education. He has established an organic relationship between the individual and the society which is the basis for democratic movement in education. Today, education is a social medium and the school is a social institution in which children are trained to live and work together.

Impact on discipline: The concept of positive discipline, self and social discipline stressed by Dewey has influenced modern education. He believes that social discipline can be developed through creative activities and democratic citizenship. According to him, the school is an idealised society, a social institution, an extension of home and miniature society. Hence, the whole structure of educational setup has been changed. It has created a new avenue for modern progressive education that encourages the pupils towards social activities.

Impact on modern thoughts: Dewey is a great philosopher of the present dynamic age which is dominated by the forces of science, technology, industrialism and democracy. As a result, we find freedom, happiness and friendliness in schools. He has given a new progressive outlook to education and calls it "life itself", that is, education is life. He has glorified every aspect of education that he touches. His thought-provoking ideas on educational philosophy are echoed in every corner of the world of education.

CRITICISM OF DEWEY'S EDUCATIONAL THOUGHTS

Though Dewey's ideas on educational principles have a great impact on the modern educational theory and practices, they are subjected to criticism on many grounds. Let us bring them out here.

Not accepting the eternity of truth and values: Dewey believes that all values and truths are not eternal. They are subjected to change in course of time. According to him, values and truths have utility only in a particular set of circumstances and are related to time and space. Hence, his principle of pragmatism itself becomes only relatively true because it does not accept truth as something permanent. But it is not applicable to all values and truths.

Materialistic bias: Dewey stands against the idealist philosophy. At the same time, he wants to realise the democratic ideals of freedom, fraternity and equality through education. It is difficult to understand how this can be done unless he accepts an idealistic basis for his system of education.

Absence of aim of education: Dewey has failed to set a particular aim to be achieved through education. He says that education is life itself, and it is not feasible to determine any objectives for it. This view is criticised by many scholars and they believe that education can progress only when it has some definite aim and objective. Hence, the aims of education must be defined vividly.

Emphasis on individual differences: Dewey has always emphasised child-centred curriculum and child-centred method of education. Modern psychologists concur with the fact that the curriculum of education and method of teaching must be according to the interest, inclination, ability and need of the child. But it is impossible to construct a curriculum and teaching method for each child on the basis of his interest, inclination and ability. In fact, it is not possible to eliminate many complex and difficult subjects from the curriculum only because the student is not interested in them.

Limitation of learning by doing: Dewey rejects the experience of others and believes in self-experience. This idea is not acceptable to realists because many facts known to an individual are acquired from another person and it is impossible for one individual to experience every fact known to him. In fact, the educand may benefit from the experience of his teacher, parents and colleagues.

Religious education is neglected: Dewey's concept of education assigns importance to the materialistic world and it ignores religious education. But religious education is essential to make the heart of man pure and protect him from the corrupt society.

Impracticability of project method: The project method of learning is the scientific method of teaching which is not suitable for all situations. It is not possible to apply project method in all aspects of literature and social studies. Thus, it has limited utility.

Heavy burden on teacher: Dewey's educational principles lay a heavy responsibility on the teacher. He assigns an important place to the teacher in the educative process. The teacher is considered as a friend, a guide, a philosopher and a helper. He must be a resource person, a professionally trained and efficient person to discharge his duties successfully.

Emphasis on present and neglects future: According to Dewey, education is life itself. Education must cater to the present needs of the child rather than the future because the child is not interested in the unknown future. It is, therefore education which should prepare the child to live life in the present and the immediate future. Thus, Dewey gives great importance to the present and ignores the future.

Emphasis on practicalism: Dewey insists that all ideas or hypotheses should be tested or experimented before being accepted. He assigns more emphasis to practicalism and neglects the theoretical aspect of studies. But it is not possible to test all ideas and put them into practice.

CONCLUSION

John Dewey is a great intellectual thinker and philosopher. His bold and new thoughts have brought about a revolutionary change in the modern educational theory and practices. His ideas and findings have ruled and guided the educational world for more than half a century. No doubt that Dewey is a source of inspiration to many thinkers, educationists and philosophers of the East and the West. Today, he stands in the top rank of the educators of the world. In the words of R.R. Rusk, "In education we cannot but be grateful to John Dewey for his great services in challenging the old static cold storage ideal of knowledge and in bringing education more into accord with the actualities of present day life". Prof. Ulich has summed up the contribution of John Dewey in these words "Dewey's work encourages an experimental and scientific attitude. It shows what men can achieve if they rely on their reason and courage instead of clinging to their prejudice". Regarding the work of John Dewey, Irwin Edman (Ed) in '*John Dewey: His Contribution to American Tradition* (1955)' has observed, "The breakdown of the violation of school from society, of book learning from vital experience, of the individual from his environment—the extent to which schools and colleges have removed these seperations is a measure of the direct impact of refreshing reconstruction of Dewey's thinking".

CHAPTER 27

BERTRAND RUSSELL
1872–1970

INTRODUCTION

Bertrand Russell was an English philosopher, great educator, versatile, genius thinker, writer and speaker in the intellectual world. In fact, he was one of the most creative minds of the 20th century. His researches, insights and thoughts have made valuable contribution to the fields of mathematical logic, epistemology, history, political philosophy, education and life. He has written more than twenty books and several papers related to these subjects. He has also written two books—on Education (1926) and Education and social order (1932) and a few papers on Education. His contribution to Education and philosophy earned him imperishable fame in the respective fields.

LIFE OF BERTRAND RUSSELL

Bertrand Russell, great intellectual thinker and creative writer, was born in Monmouth Shire, in United Kingdom, in 1872. He lost his parents at the age of four and was brought up by his grandparents. He was profoundly influenced by his grandmother. He was tutored at home till the age of 18, and then he joined Trinity College Cambridge for higher education. Later on, he worked as a professor in some institutions. He won Nobel Prize for literature in 1950. He established a school at Sussex (1927), where he experimented his educational ideals. His works on Education and social order have created stir in the educational world. He dedicated his life to the cause of international peace and amity. He is a fine example of pragmatic approach in the contemporary times of the philosophy of education. Bertrand Russell, the outstanding great scholar, breathed his last in 1970.

PHILOSOPHY OF RUSSELL

The philosophy of Bertrand Russell has been called 'Logical Automism'. He was an eminent mathematician, and he developed his philosophy of logical atomism as a consequence of his deep and penetrating studies in the mathematical philosophy. According to him, the objects are concepts and propositions in logical analysis whereas memories, thoughts, emotions and other philosophical processes in psychological analysis. The main object of logical analysis is to discover the fundamental elements of the universe. It follows the logical atoms philosophy which atoms a point in analysis where further analysis is not possible. In other words, logical atom is the irreducible element of logical analysis. He observes, "The reason that I call my doctrine logical atomism because the atoms that I wish to arrive at as the sort of last residue in analysis are logical atoms and not physical atoms".

The logical atomism believes that logical analysis is a method of discovery. According to him, we can learn about the fundamental elements of the universe by using the techniques of logical analysis. So, the task philosophy is the discovery of the basic elements of the universe. This is possible through the analysis of the gross object. He firmly believes in the efficiency of the logical analysis to reveal reality. According to him, it is most appropriate means of discovery. However, it may not be, practically, a very fertile method in philosophic inquiry, but undoubtedly there is no theoretic difficulty or problems in its application to philosophy. He deals with the creative tendencies of the individual and society. He believes that creativity can be expressed in a democracy and free atmosphere. But, it is the opposite of positive tendencies which are major source of evil in social institutions. So, he wanted family, marriage, education, religion, state and other human institutions should be guided by creative tendencies and not by possessive tendencies. According to him, happiness is the result of by expression of creativity. So he suggests the reconstruction of social institutions and organisation in a way to realise maximum expression of creativity.

From his philosophy, we can understand that he emphasises on the creative aspect of man. The proper development of creative instinct of man can bring about the desired satisfaction in human life. He believes in reasoning and wanted to test all existing belief, on the basis of logic. He opposes atomic weapons, and is an ordain supporter of human welfare.

EDUCATIONAL THOUGHTS OF RUSSELL

The educational thoughts of Bertrand Russell are very comprehensive, which change the meaning, nature and aims of education.

Meaning of Education

According to him, "Education is the process of perfection of the human being". It means that education is not only the process of the transmission of external information, but it aims at the broad cultivation of the mind leading to awareness of man's place and developing in the society and universe.

Aims of Education

Bertrand Russell has pointed out the following aims of education:

All-round development: The most important aim of education is to help the child to achieve all-round development. It includes the development of vitality, courage, sensitive and intelligence.

Vitality: It increases health, happiness and also develops the capacity of hard work. It is based on the physical and mental health. Hence, the school should provide all opportunities for the development of vitality.

Courage: This is a part of all round of development of the child. Fear weakens the body and mind, but courage helps both to be stronger. In fact, a courageous person can live without fear. So, school should develop the quality of courage the welfare of the children.

Sensitiveness: It is in the nature of children. It should be developed through proper education. Such development takes place in praise, hate, contempt, affection, sympathy and empathy. In fact, sympathy and affection make the outlook of the children wider and help to develop desirable qualities. So the aim of education is inculcating and developing desirable sensitiveness in the child.

Intelligence: This is very essential to understand one's own self, and develop curiously. It is a source of all round development. So, education should develop knowledge curiosity and wisdom through the expression of creativity.

Character formation: According to Bertrand Russell, all-round development of the child depends on the character formation.

Acquisition of skill: The aim of education is acquisition skill, which is necessary for the provision of the techniques, goods and services to help in making life happy and comfortable.

Student welfare: Russell says, welfare of students should be the ultimate aim of education.

Intellectual virtues: He calls the techniques of obtaining knowledge as intellectual virtues 'The techniques include curiosity, open-mindedness, patience, industry, exactness, concentration and observation. Education should aim at the development of these virtues for intellectual development.

World peace and Internationalism: According to Russell, the aim of education should be to develop world peace and internationalism. In fact, he vehemently opposed nationalism as says nationalism is undoubtedly the most dangerous vice of our times for more dangerous than drunkards or drugs or commercial dishonesty. He believes that development and civilisation cannot continue unless the virulence of nationalism is abated in the human minds.

World citizenship: The man's vital need of the near future will be the civilisation of a vivid sense of citizenship of the world. So, education should not only grow internationaly, but should be the cultivation of international outlook and broad mindedness.

CURRICULUM

Russell recommended a general and compulsory curriculum for children upto fourteen years. According to him, curriculum should include ancient literature, modern language, mathematics, science, music, dance and geography. He also prescribed two types of curriculum for students aged between 15 to 18. Specialised curriculum for meritorious and advanced students and general curriculum for mediocre and less intelligent students should be introduced and practiced in school. The teaching of agriculture at this stage is essential and the curriculum should include humanities, mathematics, ancient, literature anatomy, physiology, hygiene and civics. He considered science as utilitarian subject, as it provides our daily necessaries and pleasures of life. However, he advocated that a synthetic view of curriculum along with science, literature, history, music, and fine arts should be taught to bring about all round development in the child.

He also advocated sex education for children along with other subjects, to prevent mental abnormalities caused by sex taboos. He was against religious education in school, and nourished strong views of religious neutrality. He favoured various co- curricular activities in school to develop self-control, parents and teachers can associate themselves with their wards in sport activities to promote mutual relationship, dance music, agriculture and play are co-curricular activities.

METHOD OF TEACHING

Bertrand Russell advised to apply psychological methods in teaching-learning process; it means teaching method should be based on interest of the child. So, he advocated Montessori method of teaching for the education of children. He also pleaded for play- way method, and favoured learning by doing and story-telling method. He advocated dramatic method in teaching history, geography, foreign language and literature.

Teacher

According to Russell, the teacher should not be expected to flatter or prejudice either of the mob or of the officials. It should be the business of the teacher to stand outside. The strife of pasties and endeavour to in still into the young, the habit of impartial inquiry, leading them to judge issue on their merits, and to be on their guard against accepting ex-parte, statements at their face value. The teacher should have sound knowledge of the subjects. He should as well-prepared and motivate the students to learn. He should have sympathy. Teacher requires only affection and patience for his students. According to him, the right sort of training should be given together with a degree of sympathy and patience. Thus, Russell recognised the role of teacher in teaching and the development of child.

Students

Russell emphasised the active participation of students in the learning process. The students may be given guidance and opportunities for developing their individual potentialities. In fact, he gave utmost importance to the child and his/her development through proper education.

Discipline

Russell was in favour of providing freedom to the children. He believed that if children are subjected to rigorous discipline it may lead to mental tension. The effect of compulsion in education is that it destroys originality and intellectual interest in the child. However, he never supported unrestricted freedom or rigorous discipline. He always said the right discipline is not in external, but in habits of mind, which lead spontaneously to desirable rather than undesirable activities. He further said that children who are forced to eat require a loathing for food, and children who are forced to learn acquire a loathing for knowledge.

Beacon Hill School

Bertrand Russell established a school at Beacon Hill Petersfield in 1927, to study the problem of educating their own children. It functions with Russell as head master and Dors Russell as head mistress with twenty boys and girls between 4 and 11 years. The children were taught games, but not football, cricket and hockey. Russell disapproved punishment and opposed corporal punishment under any circumstances. According to him, every time a child is slapped a complicated turmoil of conflicting passion is aroused. But, on the contrary he never believed that children should be left entirely uncontrolled. They should be encouraged to realise that they have duties to others and society. So learning is essential to enable them to play their part in the world.

PRINCIPLES OF EDUCATION

According to Bertrand Russell, education for children should start at the age of six. At this stage, the aim of education should be to develop curiosity, creativity and natural skill of the child. So, the most important traits required for the children are curiosity and freedom from prejudice, faith in the personality of knowledge, perseverance intense, durable and voluntary attention, patience and realism in the ideas, words and action. Education must be interesting according to the stages of child, so the teacher should have sympathy and be a philosopher and guide for the natural development of the students.

Scheme of Education

Bertrand Russell constructed the scheme of education based on four stages of child's development:

- ♦ Nursery School Stage – up to 5 years old
- ♦ Elementary Stage – 6 to 10 years old
- ♦ Secondary Stage – 11 to 14 years old
- ♦ Higher Secondary Stage – 15 to 18 years old
- ♦ University Stage – Above 18 years old

Nursery school stage: Early development of the child should be entrusted to nursery school. So, Russell advocated nursery education for the children of rich and poor families, city and village on free and compulsory basis. The aim and function of such education is to develop healthy habit in children. The teacher should have the knowledge of psychology, physiology, and hygiene (medical science) to help in the physical development of child. Russell considered kindergarten and montessori schools as the ideal for nursery education.

Elementary stage—Primary education: This education starts at the age of six. So, care should be taken to provide education according to the individual peculiarities of the children. They should develop the ability of reading and writing during the first 2 years. A study of history, geography and general knowledge may be given in the first year and study of mathematics may be postponed to the age of seven years. The teaching of science, mathematics, algebra, geometry, physics, chemistry, biology and classical language should be taught between the age 12 and 14 years.

Secondary/Higher secondary education: Bertrand Russell considered education at this age as a sort of specialisation. So, he has classified curriculum into three groups namely,

(a) Classical language
(b) Mathematic and science
(c) Modern humanities

He recommended these subjects of the study for the intellectual development of the child. Moreover, he advocated a pleasing school environment and full of activities to make the child participate actively in the teaching-learning process. Science and Mathematics are correlative subjects, but may be taught separately. He was of the view that the student must learn any one these special groups at the age of 18.

University education: According to Russell, university education should be for those who are really talented, able and interested to pursue higher education. He advocated admission test for entrance in higher education. The main aim of university education is to expand knowledge and research and to prepare the trained men and women for various vocation.

Teacher

The research work should aim at welfare of the humanity and progress of the world. The teacher should encourage the students to study books for knowledge. He should guide them in studies and evaluate their abilities. He should be free from financial worries and get sufficient leave for the enrichment of their knowledge.

School Organisation

Bertrand Russell advocated for both day and residential schools. He wanted that the school should be organised on democratic basis. The child may select these schools on the basis of his/her circumstances health, age, household conditions, nature and interests. The parents can select a suitable school for their children.

CONTRIBUTIONS OF BERTRAND RUSSELL TO EDUCATION

Bertrand Russell was a great scholar philosopher and writer. His unique contribution to education is that he has constructed a comprehensive scheme of education according to the different stages of child. Following are the main points of his education:

- Aim of education is to help the child achieve all round development and maximise human welfare.
- He emphasised the inclusion of utilitarian subjects in the curriculum for the wise use of leisure.
- He opposed nationalism and develops internationalism through education and practices.
- He advocated psychological-based education in teaching and learning process.
- He favoured freedom in education and oppose corporal punishments.
- He gave importantance to character formation and generation of human beings who have health, generosity, vigour and joy.
- He planted for the recognition of the rights of the individual in education.
- He advocated mass free and compulsory education for the proper development of human beings.
- His nursery education is quite justified in all countries.
- His advises for restricted admission of student is higher education based on ability, interest and merit. (But, this is not practiced in Indian educational institutions.)

The educational philosophy of Bertrand Russell may be criticised on the following grounds.

- He opposed the state control of education.
- This view is not suitable for Indian society.
- It is seen that privatisation of education exploits the people, and degrade its quality.
- He favoured sex education.
- This is not suitable to Indian society, because it misguides the teachers and students. In fact, it weakens them sexually and leads to wrong life.

CONCLUSION

The contribution of Bertrand Russell to education and philosophy has created a great impact on the present education. In fact, he made a happy synthesis of all the conflicting views. Moreover, he pleaded for universal free and compulsory education for all. He condemn the narrowism and nationalism, and advocated internationalism. He also emphasised child-centred education based on psycho-analysis. He gave importance and respect to the role of teacher in education. Prof. V.P. Verma in his book 'Studies in the Philosophy of Education' has observed that Bertrand Russell is important in the history of educational thought because he has made an active and energetic proposal from the intellectual stand point, which is a great service to democratic community. It is concluded that Russell achieved world reputation as one of the greater thinkers of all times through his life and inspirational writings in education and philosophy.

CHAPTER 28

MARIA MONTESSORI 1870–1950

INTRODUCTION

Maria Montessori is the first woman who entered the world of education through his intimate association with the education and development of the mentally challenged children. Her contribution to the education of early childhood, especially mentally challenged children, has revolutionised the world of education. In fact, almost every civilized country feels, in some measure, the impact of her unique method of teaching young children. The world read with astonishment of the almost incredible doing of those slum children in the first Casa dei Bambini (children's home) in Rome. Her efforts and dedication in making the mentally challenged children into normal children in teaching 3 R's through didactic apparatus have brought imperishable fame to her in the history of education. It was seen at the time of her demise when tributes to her life-long labour on behalf of the child appeared in the press from every parts of the world. In fact, her selfless sacrifice and dedication has developed hope and courage in the life of mentally challenged children, which made her to be ranked among the forerunners of great educators. Today, Montessori method flashes like a comet across the educational horizon.

LIFE OF MONTESSORI

Dr. Maria Montessori, the originator of the montessori method, a famous educationist and the first Italian lady doctor, was born on August 31, 1870 in Italy. She wanted to become an actress and for this purpose she actually joined a dramatic school. Then she decided to become an engineer, but after her schooling she changed her mind and decided to become a doctor of medicine. But no woman was admitted to the medical college in those days. So, she used a ruse to get herself admitted to a medical college. She signed herself as M. Montessori in the application form. The authorities admitted her thinking she was a man. In this way, she became the first Italian lady to get the degree of Doctor of Medicine. This reveals her talent and ability.

Montessori worked as a professor of anthropology in the University of Rome from 1900 to 1907. It was here that she got an opportunity to supervise a ward of mentally challenged children. She studied those children very intensively and reached the conclusion that mental deficiency was due to the dullness of senses. After scrutinising the mentally deficient children, she derived the following facts:

- The mental deficiency of the children results from the dullness of the senses.
- Marvellous results could be achieved through sense training.

- Better results could be achieved if sense training is given in the education of the normal children.

She felt that training of sense organs could achieve marvellous results. So, she developed her own method of instruction through practical experimentation. In 1907 she was appointed as a supervisor of schools by the Director of Roman Association for Good Building. There she had to look after the education of children between the age of 3 and 7, and who were neglected by their parents. Like a true scientist, she studied these children deeply and developed a novel method of teaching through sense training. Her method attracted the attention of the whole world. She was invited by many countries like England and America to demonstrate her method. Though she was a doctor by qualification, she entered the field of education through her interest in mentally deficient children.

She studied child psychology and established a school for children. She named her school, Casa dei Bambini or children's house. She used a self- learning and self-correction apparatus known as Didactic apparatus. The government of Italy appointed her as the inspectress of Infant Schools in 1922. She began to train the teachers in her method. Teachers from several countries from Europe including England came to Italy for training. Montessori left for Holland and founded a school there. She came to India in 1939 and remained here up to 1946. During her stay in India, she gave training to teachers according to her method. Her headquarters is in Chennai. She spent some time in India in 1950–51 and returned to Holland in 1951. Dr. Maria Montessori, champion of education for the mentally deficient children, breathed her last in 1952.

MEANING OF EDUCATION

According to Montessori, "Child is a body which grows and a soul which develops—these two forms, physical and psychic have an eternal front, life itself". She wants each child to develop himself from within and not from without. Education should guide the process of unfolding the hidden powers of the child. In her words, "Education is the active help given to the normal expansion of the life of the child". She says that every child is different from others, physically as well as mentally. So, the child's individuality must be respected and not suppressed through collective teaching. Each child should be bestowed individual attention and allowed to grow at his own pace.

PRINCIPLES OF MONTESSORI METHOD (EDUCATIONAL THOUGHTS OF MONTESSORI)

After graduation in medicine, Montessori was in-charge of the training of mentally challenged children. She taught a number of such children to read and write so efficiently by adopting her special method and her previous experience acquired from the infant schools in Rome. The montessori system became an 'education by touch'. Only the methods, which Montessori adopted to educate and train up the muscles and sense organs of the mentally challenged children is known as montessori method.

Development from within: According to Montessori, the source of education of a child is within himself. Each child has got his own peculiar interest, aptitude, capacities and endowment. Education should help the child to unfold his individuality from within himself. In her words, "If any educational act is to be efficacious, it will be only that which tends to help towards the complete unfolding of the child's individuality. The child has a body which grows and a soul which develops". So, after recognising the physical and mental differences of the individuals a suitable environment should be provided to the child so as to enable him to grow and develop the potentialities that he has within him.

Freedom or liberty: Montessori is of the opinion that freedom or liberty is the birthright of every individual. She insists that there should be no interference in the way of the child's growth and development. She stands for full freedom which is essential for the spontaneous development of the child. In the words of Montessori, "The school must permit the free, natural manifestations of the child if he is to be studied in a scientific manner". She believes that freedom and self-discipline in the school ensure proper development of children.

Self-education or auto education: Montessori believes that self-education is the best method by which the child can learn in his own way and at his own speed. According to her, self-education is the only true education and it should be without any interference from outside. For self-education, she recommends the use of didactic apparatus which controls every error and helps the child to correct himself automatically. Even dull and challenged children can receive education with the help of this apparatus. In fact, it is a substitute for teacher and keeps the children busy at learning the powers of movements, reading, writing and arithmetic, and duly conforms to the psychological steps of association, recognition and recall.

Sense training: According to Montessori, senses are the gateways of knowledge. They occupy an important role in a child's education. The acquisition of knowledge depends on the training given to the senses. She believes that mental deficiency is due to the dullness of senses. Therefore, we should approach the child's mind through sense training. She realises that the senses are very active between the ages of 3 and 7, and that the maximum learning takes place during this period. Sense training, enables the child to recognise weight, colour, sound, temperature, touch, smell, size and forms. Thus, sense training enables the child to be sensible and serves as the key for intellectual development.

Motor efficiency of muscular training: Montessori lays stress on the muscular training as part of the early education of the child. She believes that such a training facilitates various activities such as writing, drawing, speaking, cleaning, sweeping, washing, combing etc. In fact, walking, running, jumping etc. depend on muscular training.

Individual teaching and development: Individualistic instruction based on the physical and mental levels of the individual is the keynote of Montessori's philosophy of education. This is because she believes that collective teaching suppresses the individuality which is essential for the growth and development of the child. She treats each child as a separate individual and recommends individual teaching according to the child's physiological readiness to learn. In this way education of the children should depend on their mental development.

Reverence for the child: According to Montessori, "The child is God". Her school is the temple and the aim of the temple is to help the child in his growth and development. It needs to reform the methods of education and instruction for the regeneration of man. Thus, she assigns a very significant place to the child in the educative process.

No material rewards and punishments: Montessori feels that rewards and punishments are incentives of unnatural or forced effort. She says that the development that takes place in the child should not be out of any reward or punishment, but it should be natural. Therefore, all rewards or punishments should be shunned in order that they will not curb or interfere in the natural development of the child.

Reverence for the teacher: Montessori has given an important place to the teacher in the process of teaching and learning. She replaces the word teacher by the word 'directress'. She wants the teacher to direct the child and not to teach. Her motto is, "I must diminish to let the child grow".

No fairy tales: Montessori feels that fairy stories tend to confuse the children. Moreover, such tales hinder them in the process of adjusting themselves to the real world. She, therefore, eliminates fairy tales from the curriculum prescribed for the young children.

PRACTICES OF MONTESSORI METHOD IN CHILDREN'S HOUSE

Montessori established a school in 1907 called Casa dei Bambini means children's house. It is the place where children are taught in a homely atmosphere and provides them everything necessary to develop in their own way. The children's house has many rooms for study, assembly, lunch, rest, manual work, gymnasium, bathing and lab. They are equipped and furnished according to the needs of the children and the spirit of the montessori method. Tables, chairs, sofas, and cupboards are provided. The children keep their didactic apparatus in the cupboard and their things in a little drawer. The blackboards are fixed on the wall. The children use them to draw or paste pictures, as they wish. The students are provided with flowers, toys, pictures, indoor games etc. Low tables, chairs, spoons, knives, tumblers etc. are placed in the lunch room. The children are provided with their own little shelfnes in which they keep soaps and towels for the purpose of washing. There is a small garden where the children can enjoy the open air, play, work, take rest or sleep. They can also eat their lunch there. A pedometer and a weighing machine are used in the children's house to measure the height and weight of the students. Didactic apparatus is used to provide sensory training, motor training and teaching language and arithmetic.

EXERCISES IN CHILDREN'S HOUSE (PRACTICES OF MONTESSORI METHOD)

There are three types of exercises or practices given to the children below the age of six in the montessori school, that is, children's house.

- Exercises in practical life,
- Exercises in sensory training, and
- Didactic exercises for 3 R's.

Exercises in practical life: The pupils are given freedom in the children's house to exercise themselves for practical life. They are trained to wash their hands, sweep their rooms, dust and clean the furniture and arrange them as they like, clean their nails, brush their teeth, dress and undress, wash their clothes, polish their shoes and comb their hair. They learn to lay tables, hang up their clothes, use washstands with small pitchers and basins and use their soaps and towels. Thus, the children take turns in various household duties and learn by imitation to overcome the difficulties that they face. Montessori devises gymnastic exercises to develop the coordinated movements of the child. Enthusiasm and delight, fellow feeling and mutual aid are the characteristics of the children learning the jobs. Muscular education and training is given through ascending and descending stairs without holding on, walking, sitting, holding objects and handwork. In this way the child learns to walk in straight lines and balance himself properly.

Exercises in sense training: Montessori assigns greater importance to sensory training than learning or thinking. So, she uses a device called didactic apparatus to sharpen the pupil's sense and accelerate learning. Varied materials such as blocks, cylinders, paper, cabinets, coins, tables, chair, pencil, pen, wools of different colours, boxes, balls, cubes, rods and water of different temperature are meant to provide the perception of size, form, colour, touch, smell, hearing, weight, height etc. The sense of touch is developed by presenting water in different temperature and sand papers of graded roughness. Perception of size is developed through handling a series of wooden cylinders of varying heights and diameters. Sense of hearing is developed through cylindrical sound boxes containing pebbles and other sound-producing materials. Sense of weight is taught through pieces of wood of varying weights. Perception of colour is trained through a graded series of coloured wooden blocks and papers. The process of learning through the didactic apparatus involves the three psychological steps of association, recognition and recall which are the basic principles of self-education (Table 28.1).

TABLE 28.1 Sensory Apparatus: Purpose and Type

Sl. No.	Purpose	Apparatus (material used)
1.	Perception of size	Series of wooden cylinders varying in heights, blocks varying in sizes, rods varying in lengths.
2.	Perception of form	Geometrical insets in metal, wood, or the shapes of the insets drawn on paper, cards.
3.	Perception of colour	Series of coloured woods, papers, tablets etc.
4.	Discrimination in weight	Tablets of wood, similar in size but different in weight.
5.	Discrimination in touch	Highly polished surface and sand paper surface is used
6.	Discrimination in sound	Cylindrical sound boxes containing different substances.
7.	Discrimination in temperature	Water of different temperature.
8.	Tactful activity	Train him to discriminate differences in weight and temperature keeping his eyes closed.

Exercises for teaching language and arithmetic: Montessori believes that muscular skill in children is very easily developed through the teaching of writing rather than reading. She is of the view that writing is a purely mechanical activity, and reading partly intellectual. Didactic apparatus is used to impart language and arithmetic teaching. The children are taught reading, writing and arithmetic only after the sensory training.

MONTESSORI'S DIDACTIC APPROACH

The word 'didactic' means learning with pleasure. Didactic apparatus is a concrete material used to educate the young children who are mentally challenged. This is a great contribution of Montessori by which learning becomes joyful.

Principles of Didactic Approach

The Didactic apparatus is meant to translate the educational philosophy of Montessori into action. It is based on certain principles. Let us list them here:

- Development of the child from within.
- Individual difference of children.
- Reverence for the teacher as directress.
- Reverence for the child.

- Learning by doing and self-discipline.
- Freedom and individualistic teaching.
- Senses and muscular training.
- Auto education or self-learning.
- No rewards and punishments or interferences.
- No place for fairy tales or exclusion of mystery stories.

Didactic Apparatus for Teaching 3 R's

Montessori believes that self-education is the best method by which a child can learn in his own way and at his own speed, without any interference from outside. She recommends the use of didactic apparatus to control every error and help the child to correct himself automatically. Thus, didactic apparatus is a substitute for teacher which enables even the dull and challenged children to receive education.

After sensory training, children are taught reading, writing and arithmetic. Montessori suggests that writing should be started before reading. In this regard, she depends on the psychological principles of "Transfer of Training". She says, "Preparatory Movement could be converted and reduced to a mechanism by means of repeated exercise, not in the work itself, but in that which prepares for it".

Teaching of Writing

There are three factors involved in the procedure of teaching of writing. They are recognising the form of letters, learning phonetic sounds and manipulating the pen.

Recognition of the forms of letters: The letters of the alphabet are cut in sand paper and pasted on cardboards. The children are asked to place their fingers over these letters. As they are doing so, they gradually learn to hold a pencil. This type of exercise is then practised several times with closed eyes. In this way a child can recognise the forms of the letter.

Learning of phonetic sounds: The teacher should tell the sounds of letters while the pupils trace them out. Then he should ask the pupils to reproduce the letters and prepare them for reading. In this way the phonetic sounds are taught in three stages namely association, recognition and recall.

Manipulation of pen: This is the third step of exercises through which the students are taught to use the pen. The pupils are asked to place the metal frame on a piece of paper and draw a line round it with a coloured chalk. This type of exercise is repeated by placing the metal inset. As a result, two figures are produced on the paper. Then the intervening figure is filled up with another piece of chalk. Pupils are not allowed to move pencil or chalk outside the outline when they make upward and downward strokes. Thus, this exercise enables the child to learn the necessary manipulation of the pen effectively.

Teaching of Reading

In the words of Montessori, "Reading is the interpretation of an idea from written signs and not merely looking at print. Until the child receives a transmission of ideas from the written word, he does not read". Her reading material consists of papers or cards on which the names of the familiar objects are written and pasted. The child is provided this paper or card and asked to translate the writings slowly into sounds and then read them faster. After some practice, the child is able to pronounce the word correctly. Then the teacher should ask the child to place the card under the object, whose name has been mentioned on it. In the same way sentences and describing action should be written on paper or card, and the child should be asked to select a card or paper, read it and do the action mentioned in it.

Teaching of Arithmetic

After the teaching of writing and reading, Montessori wants to teach the child the four fundamental rules of arithmetic. That is, the children are taught addition, subtraction, multiplication and division. There is no originality in the method of teaching arithmetic. She follows the old procedure of teaching by means of coloured beads, numerical rods, wooden spindles, sand paper numbers, simple boxes, printed shells and other attractive materials. She uses a "Long stair" to teach numbers. It consists of a set of ten rods varying in length, from one to ten decimeters. Each rod is divided into parts, painted red and blue alternatively. Then the child is taught to arrange the rods on the basis of length and to count the red and blue divisions and number the rods as one, two, three etc. Count the rods from the shortest to the longest as piece number one, piece number two; always going back to one in the counting of each rod and starting from the same end. The graphic signs for the numbers are cut in sand paper and the pupil is taught to associate the names of the numbers with their graphic forms. The graphic signs are then related to the quantity represented. In this way, Montessori method teaches arithmetic.

ROLE OF TEACHER IN MONTESSORI METHOD

The teacher occupies a very important role in the Montessori method. It is true that the success of the Montessori method depends on the efficiency of the teacher and the spirit with which he undertakes the task. He should not be a dictator but he should be a sympathetic guide having instinctive understanding of the needs and difficulties of the children. He should allow the children maximum educative freedom to secure their intrinsic and spontaneous growth. In the words of Robert R. Rusk, "The Montessori Method necessitates the employment of teachers who are possessed of a training in child psychology and in its application to young children". The teacher should be patient, loving children and identifying himself completely with children. He should neither be rigid nor dogmatic in his approach. He should help the child to cultivate a sense of real discipline which should grow from within and not imposed from outside by the authority of his teacher. Montessori methods require teachers who possess a training in child psychology.

Functions of Teacher

Teacher as gardener: Montessori assigns a unique place to the teacher. She believes that the soul of the child is pure and sensitive and requires the utmost care. The teacher, therefore, should care for the child like a gardener who cares for the plants. This type of care brings out natural growth and development in the child harmoniously.

Teacher as the directress: Montessori replaces the word 'teacher' by the word 'directress'. This is so because she thinks that the primary duty of the teacher is to direct and not to teach the child. She insists that the teacher should have extensive knowledge in child psychology and laboratory techniques to be a successful directress in the Montessori method.

Teacher should have knowledge of child: It implies that the teacher should have an intimate knowledge of the mind and character of each child. She should maintain the psychological records of each child's development in order to have a proper knowledge of his pupils. The psychological records should include the information about the pupil's weight, height and other measurements.

Teacher as doctor, scientist, missionary: Montessori says that the Directress (teacher) should be partly a doctor, partly a scientist and a completely religious missionary. She is of the opinion that like a doctor, the directress should avoid scolding to avoid the worst situations. Like a scientist she should wait patiently for the result and conduct experiments with her materials; like a religious lady, she should serve the child.

Teacher as believer in child: Montessori emphasises the condition that the directress should have faith in the personality of the child. The directress should allow the child to grow according to his inner law. In this regard, her primary duty is to provide the children with a suitable environment so that they think for themselves.

Teacher as the protector of child's soul: Montessori is of the view that "The child is God". Hence, the soul of the child is pure and sensitive and requires the gentlest handling. It is on the part of the directress that she should protect and direct the soul of the child in a proper way.

Teacher as man of moral: Montessori wants the directress to have moral qualities and she must be a lady of patience, love and humility. She must banish anger which is a great sin that prevents her from understanding the child. So, she must possess moral qualities and develop them to undertake the task of teaching in the Montessori method.

DISCIPLINE IN MONTESSORI METHOD

Montessori believes that discipline cannot be attained by way of commands, by sermons, by any of the disciplinary methods universally known. Therefore, she suggests that discipline should be fostered in the child indirectly by developing activity in the spontaneous work. In this way each child is expected to learn how to control himself by his own efforts and through calm, silent activity which is directed towards no external aim but is meant to keep alive that inner flame on which his life depends. In the words of Montessori, "In truth, the 'good' are those who move forward towards the goodness which has been built up by their own efforts".

MERITS OF MONTESSORI METHOD

Montessori method is an outstanding method of education that emerged as an outcome of Montessori's profound love, affection, keen sensitiveness, artistic imagination and exceptional sympathy for the mentally challenged children. It has given a new touch to the educational theory and practices which are meant for the ordinary child's education in general and the mentally challenged children's at the nursery stage in particular. Let us bring out the chief merits of the Montessori method.

Reverence for the child: Montessori says that the child is God, her school is temple and the duty of the temple is the essence of childhood. She further remarks, "Today there stands forth one urgent need—the reform of methods in education and instruction, and he who struggles towards this end is struggling for the regeneration of man". Thus, Montessori method gives great importance to the child in the educational process.

It is a boon to the deficient children: Montessori method is meant for the education of small children at the nursery stage. This method provides sensory and muscular training to the mentally challenged children so that they can learn writing, reading and arithmetic. In fact, this method is a boon to the mentally deficient children.

Scientific method of teaching: Montessori is a physician and scientist. So, her method is based upon scientific grounds. She applies scientific principles based on experience and observation gained out of her infant school. Hence, this method is very useful and applicable everywhere.

Individualised teaching: Montessori recognises the physical and mental differences of the individuals. So, she opposes collective or group teaching which crushes the individuality of the children. The concept of individualised teaching is the hallmark of the Montessori method.

Freedom for children: The heart of education is man making. Freedom is essential for acquiring knowledge through education. Montessori is against the interference of teacher and allows full freedom so that the child can learn according to his own interest and speed. She suggests that the spontaneous development of the children can be achieved through full liberty.

Education through sense training: Like Rousseau and Froebel, Montessori is of the view that senses are the gateways of knowledge. So, the Montessori method aims at educating the children through sensory training. It uses the sensory apparatus to train up the senses and develop them for effective learning.

Unique method of reading writing: Montessori Method of education provides special attention to the learning of writing. She lays great emphasis on the muscular movements of the child for learning to write. Thus, she gives properly graded and correlated exercise for writing and reading, in order to bring the names and objects to the child's mind.

Learning through practical exercises: Through Montessori method, many practical exercises relating to life are provided in her school which enables the child to learn good habits of cleanliness and order. As a result, the students learn self-help by attending to their needs themselves.

Putting the teacher in the right place: Montessori assigns an important place to the teacher. The teacher is called the Directress. She occupies a vital role in the educative process.

Self or auto-education: Montessori method encourages auto-education or self-education based on the psychological aspects of the child's development. The chief merit of this method is that it enables the child to learn according to his own interest and at his own speed. Didactic apparatus is used in order to facilitate self-education.

DEMERITS OF MONTESSORI METHOD

Though the Montessori method is widely used throughout the world and it has had a great impact in the field of education for small children at the nursery stage, yet it is not free from certain limitations.

Mechanical and artificial nature: Great importance has been provided to the didactic apparatus in the Montessori method, which is mechanical, artificial and unnatural. The apparatus handcuffs both the teacher and the pupil. They are expected to do different types of exercises with the help of this apparatus. Hence, it limits the free expression of the children and the work of the teacher. Moreover, this method requires too much time to impart some knowledge to children.

More emphasis on biological aspects: It is the duty of the teacher in Montessori method to maintain the records of the height, weight, skull and limbs of each child. As a result she pays little care to observe the psychological aspects of the child.

Belief in transfer of training: Montessori believes that the training given for particular faculties through particular senses makes it possible to make use of that training in other life situations. For example, sense training is given to learn writing before reading. This idea of Montessori has been disapproved by the modern psychologists.

Neglects training of imagination: Montessori feels that fairy tales affect the development of child and take him away from the real world. So, she opposes the inclusion of such stories in the curriculum. But fairy tales used in a proper way help to develop the imaginary as well as creative power of the child.

Lack of suitable teachers: The successful function of the Montessori method depends on the quality of teachers. In fact, they are required to possess extensive knowledge of child psychology and laboratory procedure. The availability of such qualified teachers is insufficient in relation to its demand. So, this method is not suited to Indian conditions.

Little scope for projects and correlation: Since the Montessori method depends on the mechanical apparatus, there is very little scope for projects and correlation. It is against the present tendency to teach all subjects together in the form of projects.

Very expensive to set up Montessori school: Montessori school requires a lot of money to set it up. This is because the functioning of such a school depends on the quality of the teacher and the didactic apparatus. The cost incurred on the mechanical apparatus is very high. Moreover, the trained and experienced teachers need to be paid high wages.

Neglects social values: She has ignored the development of social qualities in the child through education. She gives more importance to individual development and neglects group activities and cooperation.

Neglects sports and games: The Montessori method of education aims at teaching language and arithmetic only. It has neglected play activities which are essential for the physical development of the child.

No scope for religious life: Montessori method is devoid of religious and spiritual aspects of life. Hence, Montessori's method of education may make the children materialistic and lead them to neglect the spiritual values.

CONTRIBUTION OF MONTESSORI TO MODERN EDUCATIONAL THEORY AND PRACTICES

Dr. Maria Montessori, the Italian lady doctor, became a world famous educationist. She is one of the greatest pioneers of the education of the mentally challenged children of the preschool age. Her work has considerably influenced modern educational theories and practices especially in the case of nursery school stage. Montessori system of child education has become so popular that the word 'Montessori' has become synonymous with 'child'. Thus, today 'Montessori' is related to 'child'. Moreover, her gospel of love, respect, patience and humility for the child has been accepted all over the world.

Scientific approach to education: Montessori is a physician and educationist. She formulates her method of teaching in the light of her observation, experience and experiments. She applies scientific methods in education. The scientific approach to education has been accepted and put into practice in modern education.

Psychological approach to education: Montessori accepts that every child has a peculiar interest, aptitude, capacities and endowments. The child, therefore, can learn according to his own interest, rate and speed. Hence, the physical and mental differences of the individual must be recognised and collective method of teaching or group activities which crush the individuality should be shunned. In this regard, she advocates individualised instruction based on the interest and ability of the child. This concept of Montessori has been accepted by the modern philosophers.

Learning through exercises: The most significant contribution of Montessori is the didactic apparatus. She uses this mechanical and artificial device for imparting sensory training, muscular coordination and instruction in 3 R's. Learning through practical life exercises is a notable contribution of Montessori in the field of child education especially that of mentally challenged children.

Special role of teacher: In the Montessori system of education, teachers are regarded as directresses. The primary task of the directress is to direct and guide the movements of children. She is a real guide and friend who inspires faith in them, motivates them, guides them when they confront any difficulty and leads them to constructive and purposeful activity. So, the teacher must have love, sympathy, patience and humility for the child. According to Montessori, "The teacher is a doctor cum scientist cum a missionary". Thus, she has to play a different role altogether. R.R. Rusk says that instead of the facility of speech, she has to acquire the power of silence, instead of teaching, she has to observe; instead of the proud dignity of one who claims to be infallible, she assumes the vesture of humanity.

Method of teaching writing: Montessori pays due attention to the muscular movements and exercises needed in the process of writing. Therefore, the exercises suggested by her for writing and reading are properly graded and correlated with one another. She insists that the child should be taught the art of writing before he learns the art of reading. Her attention to muscular movements and exercises in the process of writing is a unique contribution to modern education.

Emphasis on self or Auto-education: Montessori emphasises the child's development from within through his own efforts. For this, she advocates auto education in an atmosphere of freedom, joy and activity. There should be no strain or effort on the education of children. The children are placed in an educationally rich and aesthetically attractive environment so that they can learn naturally by their own experiences and observation. Such type of learning will be more effective. The child gets joy and satisfaction out of self-education.

Reverence for small children: Montessori is ranked among the foremost of the educators who stresses on an environment of freedom, love, sympathy, and respect for the children. In her own words, "The child's soul which is pure and very sensitive requires our most delicate care". For her, child is God, her school is the temple and the duty of the temple is the essence of childhood. The profound love for children forced her to travel from one corner of the world to another to establish institutions for them. With this purpose she came to India (1937–1951) and conducted a number of training courses for teachers in her method of child education.

Rationalised discipline: Montessori believes that true discipline grows from within the child and not imposed from outside. Discipline can be developed through self-control and self-directed activity. So, it should come from the child himself. The needs of children and their interests should be kindled, and education should be child centred to secure good discipline. This view of Montessori has had a great impact on the modern educational theory and practices.

Training for teachers: Montessori conducts training courses for the teachers in her system of child education especially pre-primary or nursery education. Teachers from several parts of the world came to her for getting training in the Montessori system of education. It is due to her influence that a large number of nursery schools for children have sprung up in almost all countries of the world.

Free and compulsory education: Montessori lays emphasis on the personality development of each child. As a result, the idea of free and compulsory mass education has found currency. Hence, proper education of the handicapped and mentally challenged children is considered necessary both on human and social grounds. In this way Montessori is regarded as a humanist and a great thinker whose contribution is everlasting in the field of child education.

COMPARISON OF FROEBEL AND MONTESSORI

Aim of education: The aim of education, according to both Froebel and Montessori is the growth and development of small children for the well-being of man.

Philosophy of idealism: Both Froebel and Montessori believe in the philosophy of idealism. They recognise child as divine and pure. To Montessori, child is God, while Froebel wishes education to lead man to unite with God.

Function of education: They regard education as the development of the inner nature of the child. According to them, the function of education and the educator is to draw the inner power of the child out.

Congenial environment: They stress on a congenial environment for the child. A healthy and conducive environment is essential for the growth of the inner nature of the child in a suitable manner.

Reverence and affection for the child: Froebel and Montessori have greatly emphasised the fact that there should be an environment of love, affection, sympathy and humility for the child.

Place of teacher: They have given more importance to the teacher and consider him as a guide in the learning process.

Sense training: Both Froebel and Montessori are in favour of sense training for sharpening the intellect of children. They have devised an apparatus for training the senses of children.

Self-education: Froebel and Montessori have recommended self-education on the part of the child with his own efforts.

Freedom for the child: Freedom, joy and peace are salient characteristics of kindergarten and Montessori methods of education.

Nursery education: Froebel and Montessori have organized a scheme of education for preschool children on a psychological basis. Both have brought about a revolutionary change in the concept of education at the nursery school stage. The differences between these two methods can be seen in Table 28.2.

TABLE 28.2 Difference Between Kindergarten and Montessori Methods

Sl.No.	Froebel's Kindergarten	Montessori Method
1.	**Philosophical background:** Kindergarten is based on philosophical background and it is the outcome of the thinking of a philosopher.	**Scientific background:** Montessori Method is based on scientific background and it is the outcome of the thinking of a doctor and a scientist.
2.	**Scope for imagination:** Froebel recommends story telling for the development of imaginary power in the child.	**No scope for imagination:** As there is no place for fairy tales, no scope for the development of imaginary power in the child.
3.	**Social development:** There is a scope for social development by encouraging the children to work in groups.	**Individual development:** Since individual work is encouraged in this method, individual development is possible.
4.	**Classroom teaching:** Classroom activities and instruction form an important place. A fixed time table is followed.	**Individual learning:** This is an individualistic method in which students are free to learn according to their tastes. There is no fixed timetable to be followed.

(*Contd...*)

TABLE 28.2 Difference Between Kindergarten and Montessori Methods (*Contd...*)

Sl.No.	Froebel's Kindergarten	Montessori Method
5.	**Sense training through Gifts:** Sense training is provided to the child through gifts. Each child is assigned an occupation with the gifts.	**Sense training through apparatus:** Didactic apparatus is used for the training of senses which are essential for learning 3 R's –reading, writing and arithmetic.
6.	**Scientific background:** Montessori Method is based on scientific background and it is the outcome of the thinking of a doctor and a scientist.	**Self-corrective apparatus:** Apparatus is provided to the child and it can be used in a specific way. There is a little scope for play.
7.	**No scope for imagination:** As there is no place for fairy tales, no scope for the development of imaginary power in the child.	**Stress on daily life activities:** Daily life activities like cleaning, dusting, sweeping, washing, dressing and undressing, brushing tooth, nail cutting, combing hair, keeping home tidy etc. are emphasised.
8.	**Individual development:** Since individual work is encouraged in this method, individual development is possible.	**Teacher as directress:** Teacher is called as a directress. Her function is to provide apparatus to the child and work like a spectator and watch from a distance, and help whenever needed.
9.	**Individual learning:** This is an individualistic method in which students are free to learn according to their tastes. There is no fixed timetable to be followed.	**Indispensability of apparatus:** It is impossible for a school to function without an elaborate and costly apparatus.
10.	**Sense training through apparatus:** Didactic apparatus is used for the training of senses which are essential for learning 3 R's –reading, writing and arithmetic.	**Detailed system:** This is a detailed as well as a suitable system for the teaching of reading, writing and arithmetic.

CONCLUSION

Dr. Maria Montessori has revolutionised the concept of child education. Her impact on educational thoughts and practices is universal. In fact, the Montessori system of education has come to stay in all progressive countries. She ranks among the foremost of the educators who stand for an environment of love, freedom and sympathy for the child. In the opinion of Robert R. Rusk, "The permanent elements of her method are more likely to be practical activities and the exercises subsidiary to the didactic apparatus". Sir John Adams attributes to Montessori, the credit of sounding the death knell to class teaching. The most significant feature of the system is the individualisation of instruction. Today, the word 'Montessori' is freely associated with schools meant for very young children.

CHAPTER 29

IVAN ILLICH
1926–2002

INTRODUCTION

Ivan Illich is a great educator, enlightened intellectual thinker and a great revolutionary in the field of education. He thought critically about the present system of education. In fact, he analysed the impact of school and education on the society and concluded that a new social order can be achieved through disestablishment of schools. He believed that schools have not done anything good to the society. In his famous works, *School: The Sacred Cow and Deschooling Society*, he highlighted the evils of schools and advocated de- schooling to produce an educated society. He also felt that alternative institution should be built in order to achieve the goals of universalisation of education and remove illiteracy from the masses of the world. He recommended establishing the Educational Resource Centre as an alternative way to provide education outside the school. His concept of deschooling has drawn the attention of many educationists like Ivan Lister, Everett Reimer, John Holt, Neil Postman, Charles Silverman, Paul Goodman and Palo Frier, and developed a new thinking in the world of education.

LIFE OF ILLICH

Ivan Illich, father of de-schooled education, a revolutionary educationist and former Vice-Chancellor of Ponce Catholic University, was born in Vienna in 1926. He attended a religious school for ten years from 1931 to 1941. He received general education from Florence University in Italy. After studying theology and philosophy at the Gregorian University in Rome, he obtained a doctorate degree in history from the University of Salzburg.

He served as a priest from 1951 to 1956. After ordination as a Roman Catholic Priest and some years of advanced studies, he was assigned to do pastoral work in the Pureto Rico Community in New York. Then he was the Vice-Chancellor of the Ponce Catholic University in Pureto Rico for sometime. He established a Centre for Intercultural Documentation to train the American priests and make them serve in Latin America. His proposals for deschooling society were developed at the Centre for Inter Cultural Documentation (CIDOC) in Mexico. Illich developed his aversion for schooling after he had met Everett Reimer in Pureto Rico in 1958. As he says, "Until we first met in Pureto Rico in 1958, I had never questioned the value of extending obligatory schooling to all people. Together we have come to realize that for men the right to learn is curtailed by the obligation to attend school".

Illich published his principal works in the field of education in between the late 1960s and the mid 1970s. His writings were reproduced in many languages and were distributed worldwide. The most famous article *School: The Scared Cow* was published in 1968 in which Illich criticised public schooling for its centralisation, internal bureaucracy, rigidity and the inequalities that it harbours. In 1970, he published his most important work *Deschooling Society* in English and Spanish languages which created a great impact on the society. Ivan Illich, the founder of *Deschooling Society*, passed away in 2002.

MEANING OF DESCHOOLING

The term 'Deschooling' was first coined when Illich's *Deschooling Society* was published in 1970. Deschooling is a modern concept which emphasised "Separation of Education from Schools' and that "Schooling should be abolished altogether". The concept of deschooling society was advocated and expounded by Ivan Illich, Ivan Lister, Paul Goodman, John Holt, Paulo Frier, Everett Reimer, Charles Silverman and Neil Postman. They expressed the idea of deschooling society at the CIDOC Conference in 1974. The basic assumption of deschooling society is that universalisation of education through schooling is not feasible. Illich, therefore, feels that alternative institution should be built in order to achieve the goals of universalisation of education and to remove illiteracy from the masses of the world. Population explosion and poverty are the two main evils which retard the progress of the world.

PRINCIPLES OF DESCHOOLING

Ivan Illich has developed the concept of deschooling society based on the following principles:

1. Education and schooling are not one and they are different from one another.
2. The rejection of schools would bring about a radical change in the society.
3. The prescriptive and compulsory nature of schooling discourages learning.
4. As children possess an innate ability to learn, they can acquire knowledge from their social environments.
5. The creation of a new social order requires the prior deschooling of society.

REASONS FOR DESCHOOLING OR EVILS OF PRESENT SCHOOL

Ivan Illich is the father of deschooling. He attacks the present system of schools on the grounds that they have not done anything good to the society. Teaching is not all learning. According to Illich, "There is nothing important to learn in the schools but everything is learnt in the school of life. The evils of schools are many, namely, knowledge belongs to school, knowledge forms a particular authority and knowledge dominates the society". Illich is against the present system of school and he is in favour of deschooling due to the following reasons:

- Learning is a complex and life-long process. Therefore, it must be entrusted only to the specialist who has the proper training and experience in teaching.
- These specialists need to have certificates to show their educational competence. They need to be paid highly.
- Since learning is a complicated and continuous process, the learners, both child and youth, will have to spend a long period of time in schools and colleges.

- The school is a coercive, discriminatory and destructive agency of society.
- Education or learning through school is expensive.
- Monopoly of the school over education, and compulsory attendance forcing the child and youth to attend school would not promote learning.
- The monopoly of school leads to consumer society and not service society.
- Education has become a commercial product. Students should invest more but achieve little.
- The school attempts to monopolise education, which has made learning complicated and costly.
- Inequality exists even though the governments implement free and compulsory primary education.
- The curriculum formulated in schools and colleges is not suitable for the fulfillment of the needs of the child and society.
- The schooling system does not develop real knowledge, or reasoning capacity, creativity, social awareness etc. among the students.
- Nowadays, schools are converted into shopping centres for earning much profit by selling books, notebooks, pen, pencil, uniforms, shoes, bags etc.
- The cost incurred on education increases every year but the standard of education is not raised.
- Now the aim of education is only lecturing and providing certificates. This is almost like a mass superstition that has seized society.
- School imposes strict and violent rules on the child developing a fear in his mind.
- School uses its rights in a wrong way over children and it makes them depend on teachers and the educational system again and again.
- The attempts to reform schools are futile and they should be abolished, and education should be separated from the school.
- If schools were eliminated, education could be open to all and it could become a genuine instrument of human liberation.
- The universalisation of education is not possible through school. Hence, alternative institutions should be built to achieve the goals of universalisation of education and remove illiteracy from the masses of the world.

CHARACTERISTICS OF SCHOOLS

Ivan Illich says, "Schooling—the production of knowledge, the marketing of knowledge, which is what the school amounts to—draws society into the trap of thinking that knowledge is hygiene, pure, respectable, deodorized, produced by human heads and amassed in a stock. I see no difference between rich and poor countries in the development of these attitudes to knowledge". Illich has pointed out the three main characteristics of the present day schools.

Institutionalisation: In the name of service, we open more hospitals and find more patients, more police result in more thefts, we open more schools and we find more students, and we get more degeneration. It is a kind of package of goods; however, package of knowledge is more important.

Standardisation: Everywhere we find standardisation. For instance, standard companies for medicines. We want the standardised things in every walks of life. Schooling is also a standardised form for studies.

Certificates: The knowledge of a person is measured in terms of certificates. More certificates and degrees mean more knowledge. A degree from foreign countries is considered as a sign of more knowledge and more qualified persons.

CHARACTERISTICS OF DESCHOOLING

Illich criticised schools for being just traditional institutions which have been imparting education through ages and have practically monopolised the sources of knowledge. Schooling has been made compulsory, mechanical, expensive, dead and dreary. Therefore, a revolution has been started for a deschooling society which has the following features.

Against institutionalisation: Illich stands against any type of institution as it becomes the cause for physical pollution which results in degeneration of the society. In his words "All over the world, the school has an anti-educational effect on society. School is recognized as the institution which specializes in education. The failures of school are taken by most people as a proof that education is very costly, very complex, always arcane and frequently almost an impossible task".

Against schooling: Illich holds that schooling confuses process and substance. The pupil is schooled to confuse teaching with learning, grade and achievement with education, a diploma with competence and fluency with the ability to say something new.

Anti-schools: Deschooling is anti-school and rests on three unquestioned premises, that is, children belong to school, children learn in school and children can be taught in the schools. Illich defines a school as the age specific, teacher specific, attendance specific, curriculum specific, and place specific. Schools group pupils according to age.

Anti-teacher: Learning is the result of teachings. Illich says, "Everyone learns how to live outside the school". We can learn to speak, to love, to feel, to play, to discourse, and to work without the interference of a teacher. Children learn mostly from peer groups, from comics, from observation and participation. According to Illich, "School creates jobs for school teachers no matter what their pupils learn from them". He also remarks that teachers have made a poor showing in their attempts to increase learning among the poor and that poor parents who want their children to go to school are less concerned about what they will learn than about the certification and the money they will earn. Illich also says that middle class parents send their children to school to prevent them from learning what the poor learns on the streets.

Anti-full-time attendance: Illich says that schools enforce full-time compulsory attendance. The teacher becomes a custodian, a moralist and a therapist for the child. Deschooling opposes this tradition of schools.

Anti-certification and standardisation: Illich is neither in favour of certificates nor standardisation. He does not agree that valuable learning can be measured by grades and certificates. He says that no certificate, grade, or class should be emphasised and all media and methods based on experience, interest and initiative should be utilised for effective and efficient education.

Modern technology: Deschooling system uses modern technology to make free speech, free assembly, and a free press truly universal and fully educational.

IVAN ILLICH ON LEARNING

As a revolutionary educationist, Illich attacks the myths of schooling. At the same time, he advocates deschooling and asserts his ideas on learning that:

- It is a continuous process.
- It takes place when people seek solution to their problems.

- It is not confined to school walls.
- It occurs when people pursue their interests and seek to fulfil their needs.
- It would be more without school and teachers.

NON-SCHOOLING ALTERNATIVES

Illich is of the view that a new social order can be achieved through the disestablishment of schools and development of new educational opportunities outside the school. He says that learning occurs when a person gains a new skill or insight. In place of schools, Illich recommends four learning webs or network to facilitate the public's access to educational objects, persons and situations through which people can acquire learning.

Educational objects: Ivan Illich suggests various educational objects in which and by which people learn most. Such educational objects are tool shops, industries, libraries, laboratories, gaming rooms, print shops, museums, art galleries, hostels, hospitals, park, zoo, botanical garden, studio etc., in fact any collection of objects or tools and any place that has learning possibilities in them.

Peer matching: Learning takes place through communication among the peer groups when they wish to engage in a particular activity. The network provides information regarding the activity, place and time. It assists the people to promote their learning by keeping in contact with the peer groups.

Skill exchange: This enables the interested learners to receive training in skills at public expense. In this process, those who are competent in a particular skill such as foreign language teaching, swimming computer programming, automobile repairing, and who wish to teach that skill would be listed in the exchange. The individuals who wish to learn such skills would make specific arrangements with the skill teacher who provides the required training.

Educators at large: Educators are persons who have educational competence as administrators, pedagogical counsellors and intellectual initiators. The administrators create and operate educational exchanges; the pedagogical counsellors serve as advisers to parents, and to students. They provide assistance to them in using the networks. The educational initiator acts as a leader who points the way to new ideas and seeks to create new intellectual standards.

EDUCATIONAL RESOURCE CENTRE

Ivan Illich recommends Educational Resource Centre as an alternative way to provide education outside the school. In this regard, he has given the following suggestions:

- Education Resource Centre should be opened in every village.
- Public should use these centres irrespective of their age.
- Mass media such as radio, television, journals and newspaper should find a place in the centre.
- Library facilities should be provided in it.
- Create voluntary learning groups according to their own interest.
- People of almost the same age should gather in the centre and share their talents among themselves.
- Education Resource Centre maximises free choice for learning.
- It is free from the compulsory and the prescriptive nature of schooling.
- It makes education informal, incidental and life long.
- It is meant for people of all categories and is free from any interference.

Merits of Deschooling

1. It creates awareness in the present schooling, which makes education a commercial product.
2. It is a non-expensive method of learning and it has no interference from outside.
3. It reduces inequality in education.
4. People can get education at any time as they wish.
5. It makes education informal, incidental and life long.

Demerits of Deschooling

1. Illich's deschooling system leads to irregularity and indiscipline in education.
2. It is not suited for the backward and poor people.
3. Learning of writing and reading is difficult without teachers.
4. It is not a regulated method of learning and makes the purpose of education meaningless.
5. It does not develop social qualities and democratic feelings among the students.

NON-CLASSROOM LEARNING

The idea of non-classroom learning was born out of Ivan Illich's idea of deschooling society. But the concept of non-classroom learning was introduced by John Holt. He says that apart from school reforms, we try to examine the bases of education and see whether school is the best way to provide real education or find what are the other alternatives. In school, the freedom of the student is restricted. The excessive rules and regulations, and authority develop a sense of slavery and fear in them. Non-classroom learning liberates the students from the grip of the school.

Learning by using the community resources is called non-classroom learning. The non-classroom learning is based on the practical method of learning acquired from outside the school.

Methods of Non-classroom Learning

Non-classroom learning occurs when the students come into contact with environment through travel, training, service, self-experience and experience gained from others.

Travel: By undertaking travel, an individual can learn about culture, civilization, language, climate, art and geography of different places and its people.

Vocational training: This is the simplest way of learning for job training. People can acquire practical knowledge and skill when they have vocations in hospital, hotels, bakery, tailoring shop, industry, tool shop, studio, print shop, etc.

Voluntary service: Services like laying roads, cleaning streets, wells, parks and ponds, helping the needy people etc. by which an individual can learn better and develop social qualities.

Informal survey: This type of learning takes place in the individual when he observes and comes into contact with the activities of other people.

Self-experience: Self-experience is the outcome of one's own activities. It is also gained from role play, social drama, reading books, watching television, and getting experience from others. An individual can learn better through self-experience.

Merits

- This is non-expensive and an informal education.
- This type of learning makes education a life-long process.
- Learning takes place in human life without any interference.
- It is not subjected to time, place and age.
- This kind of learning requires a minimum period and plays a vital role in the development of the individual.

Demerits

- This is irregular method of learning as against the formal education based on rules and regulations.
- This is not a suitable method for learning 3 R's—reading, writing and arithmetic.
- It is not suitable for mentally and physically challenged children.
- This kind of learning takes place in the individual only when he comes into contact with the environment.
- This is one of the ways by which man acquires knowledge and skill for which no certificate is given.

However, we cannot deny the fact that non-classroom learning prepares and develops the individual to survive successfully and trains him to adjust with the varying environments of the modern world.

CONCLUSION

It is not good to take away the school from the society. But it is better to propose some new strategies and reform the schooling system. It is clear that it is not good to burn the home to kill the insect. The disestablishment of school cannot succeed in practical life. Let us reform the schools and make education available to all. The entire school system should be revamped and re-organised to suit the individual needs and aspirations. Piveteau has rightly remarked, "Illich is not the enemy of the school but of the school system". Thus, attempts maybe made not to 'deschool' but to 'reschool' the society by making education meaningful, lively, free and interesting. Today Illich's ideas and thoughts on education influence a considerable number of educators.

CHAPTER 30

KARL MARXIAN EDUCATION

INTRODUCTION

Karl Heinrich Marx is one of the most influential men in the social, political, philosophical, economic and educational thoughts of modern society. He was a revolutionary political thinker, philosopher, economist, sociologist, effective reader and writer. He became very popular in the social, political and economic world through his powerful theories about capitalism and communism. He is regarded as originator of Marxism which has brought about a revolutionary change in politics and society. The socio-economic doctrines of Marxism has a dramatic and powerful influence over all aspects of education in the West of the world. In fact, Marxism has transformed the economic conditions of bourgeoisie and social relations in the Soviet Union (Russia), republic of China and many parts of the world. As such, Marxism is considered as an educational tool to bring about revolutionary change in the society. The Marxian theory and practice are an educational experience born out of the dialectic of enlightenment. Karl Marx did not write anything about education but his influence on writers, thinkers and academicians brings forth educational thoughts. Marxian education is understood not as the accumulation of facts and knowledge but as the experience of the oppositions and contradictions to the capitalist society.

LIFE OF KARL MARX

Karl Heinrich Marx, a German philosopher, intellectual thinker, prolific writer and humanist, was born on 5th may 1818 in Trier, Prussia, Germany. His father Heinrich Marx was a successful lawyer and a man of enlightenment devoted to Kant and Voltaire who took part in the occupations for a constitution in Prussia. His mother Henriette Pressburg was native of Holland. They were Jewish but converted to Christianity and took baptism in the Evangelical Lutheran Church. Karl Marx was baptised in 1824 at the age of 6. However, he was influenced less by religion than by the critical and radical social policies of the Enlightenment. The Jewish background exposed him to prejudice and discrimination that may have led him to question the role of religion in society and contributed to his desire for a social change.

Marks was educated from 1830 to 1835 at the high school in Trier. His writings during this period exhibited a spirit of Christian devotion and a longing for self-sacrifice on behalf of humanity. He was matriculated at the University of Bonn in 1835 and enrolled at the University of Berlin in 1836 to study law and philosophy.

Karl Marx arrived to Berlin in 1836 matriculating in the faculty of Law. He attended the lectures of Eduard Gans who elaborated the progressive stand point of Hegelian on rational development in history emphasising libertarian aspects and of Karl Von Savigny who, represented the historical school of Law. He studied Law but was fascinated by philosophy. He looked for a way to combine law and philosophy and believed that without philosophy nothing could be accomplished in the society. So he became interested in German philosopher Georg Wilhelm Friedrich Hegel whose ideas widely debated among Euopean philosophical circles.

He joined the Doctor's club, a student group which discussed Hegelian ideas and thus became involved with a group of radical thinkers known as the young Hegelians in 1837. He made a close friendship with Ludwig, Feuerbach, Bruno Bauer and Adolf Rutenberg, who were the critical of Hegel's metaphysical assumptions but adopted his dialectical method to criticise the established society, politics and religion from a left-wing perspective. Marx's father Heinrich breathed last in May, 1838 which diminished income of the family. He wrote fiction, non-fiction, and novel (Scorpion and Felix), a drama (Oulanem) and a number of love poems dedicated to his lover Jenny von Westphalen. His early writings were not published during the lifetime. However, the love poems were published posthumously in the "Collected Works of Karl Marx and Frederick Engels: Volume 1. Later, he abandoned writing fiction for the study of English and Italian, art, history and the translation of Latin classics. He with the co-operation of Bruno Bauer, edited Hegel's Philosophy of Religion in 1840. He wrote doctoral thesis on the difference between the Demorcritean and Epicurean Philosophy of Nature in 1841. It was described as a daring and original piece of work in Marx set out to show that theology must yield to the superior wisdom of philosophy. As it was controversial, among the conservative professors of Berlin University, Marx submitted his thesis to the liberal university of Jena, its faculty awarded him doctoral degree in April 1841. Karl Marx and Bauer became atheists and began a journal entitled Atheistic Archives. They failed in their efforts and both took a trip to Bonn (from Berlin) where they scandalised their class by getting drunk , laughing and galloping on donkeys in the streets.

He was seeking an academic career but his path was barred by the opposition of governments to classical liberalism and the young Hegelians. As a result, Marx moved to Cologne in 1842 and became a journalist and writer of Rhinaland News expressing his views on socialism and his interest in Economics. Marx criticised the right-wing European governments and figures in the liberal and socilist movements. This is because he believed that it is an ineffective or counter productive one. Marx's news paper drew the attention of the Prussian government censors who checked throughly every issue seditious material before printing. This declaration made Marx to lament as "Our news paper has to be presented to the police to be sniffed at, and if the police nose smells anything non-Christian or non-Prussian, the news paper is not allowed to appear".

Karl Marx married political activist Jenny von Westphalen in 1843 in a Protestant chruch and they had seven children of whom three daughters and four sons. His life combined independent scholarship, political activity and insecurity. He had to spend three successive periods of exile in the capital cities of France, Belgium and England. He became the co-editor of a new, radical left-wing Parissian news paper—German-French Annals which was set up by the German activist Arnold Ruge bringing German and French radicals together. Therefore, Marx and his wife moved to Paris in October 1843. He contributed two essays "Introduction to a Contribution to the critique of Hegel's Philosophy of Right" and "On the Jewish Question". But only one was published and it was relatively successful. He began to write only for the non-censored German language radical news paper 'Forward' which was connected to the League of the Just. Marx refined his views on socialism based upon Hegelian and Feuerbachian ideas of dialectical materialism but criticising liberals and other socialists operating in Europe. Marx met German socialist Friedrich Engles at the Cafe de la Regence on August 28, 1844.

They became very close and had a life-long friendship. Engles showed Marx his published paper, "The Condition of the Working Class" in England in 1844. It convinced Marx that the working class would be the agent and instrument of the final revolution in history. Marx and Engles criticised the philosophical ideas of Bruno Bauer. It was published in1845 as The Holy Family. Marx had an intensive study of political economy of Adam Smith, David Ricardo and John Stuart Mill, the French socialism and the history of France. The study of political economy influenced Marx to pursue the rest of his life and prepared for the major economic work in three Volumes called Das Kapital. Thus, Marxism is based on the influences of Hegel's dialectics, French Utopean Socialism and English Economics.

However, an outline of Marxism definitely formed in 1844. He needed to write down the details of his world view to clarify the critique of political economy. Accordingly, Marx wrote The Economic and Philosophical Manuscripts espousing scientific socialism required to build up of a thoroughly developed materialistic view of the world. It contains Marx's criticism of materialism. Marx moved from Paris to Brussels in 1845 and continued his critical study of capitalism and political economy. In order to stay there, he had to pledge not to publish anything related to contemporary politics. Marx and Engles left Brussels in July 1845 and went to England to meet the leaders of the Chartists, a working class movement in Britain. He used this opportunity to analyse the economic resources available for study in various libraries in London and Manchester. He developed a close relationship with many Chartists. He wrote 'The German Ideology' in collaboration with Engles. They completed their philosophy based on materialism as the sole motor force in history. It was written in a humorously satirical form but not saved from censorship. So, it was not published in his lifetime. After completing the German Ideology, Marx intended to clarify his own position in the revolutionary proletarian movement operating from the standpoint of a scientific materialist philosophy. This work was intended to show the distinction between the utopian socialists and Marx's own scientific socialist philosophy. The utopian believed that people must be persuaded one person at a time to join the socialist movement, the way a person must be persuaded to adopt any different belief. But Marx believed that people would tend to act in accordance with their own economic interest on most occasions. Thus, appealing to an entire class (working class) with a broad appeal to the class's best material interest would be the best way to mobilise the broad mass of that class to make a revolution and change society. Karl Marx considered this book a new planning but the government censors called it The Poverty of Philosophy and offered it as a response to the "petty-bourgeois philosophy" of the French anarchist socialist. Pierre Proudhon expressed it in his book. 'The Philosophy of Poverty.'

The writings of Karl Marx and Engels commonly known as The Communist Manifesto. Marx, while residing in Brussels in 1846, continued his association with the secret radical organisation League of the Just. He thought that this organisation is needed to spur the working class of Europe toward the mass movement that would bring about a working-class revolution. However, organise the working class into a mass movement the League ceased its secret or underground orientation but the operate as the open political party. This new open political society was called the Communist League in 1847. Marx and Engels planned the programme and principle of the new Communist League. They wrote programme of action for this League in 1847 and published as The Communist Manifesto in 1848. Marx stated the aims and intention of the opening lines of the pamphlet that "The history of all hitherto existing society is the history of class struggles between the bourgeois (capitalists) and the proletariat (industrial working class). The Manifesto argued for why the Communist League than hiding itself. Marx remarked in the opening lines of the pamphlet set forth the principal that the history of all hitherto existing society is the history of class struggles. It is struggles between the bourgeois (wealthy capitalist class) and the proletariat (industrial working class). Thus, the manifesto presents the argument for why the Communist League opposed the other socialist and liberal political parties, and acting in the interests of the proletriat to overthrow capitalist society and replace it with socialism. The clashes made Europe to undergo a series of protests, rebellions and violent causing the revolution of 1848. This revolution overthrow the monarchy and established French second republic in France.

Marx moved to London in 1849 and spent his rest of life. He also transferred the Communist League to London. A split took place in the Communist League when began agitating Karl Schapper and August Willich for immediate uprising. They believed that the initiation of uprising the Communist League would join the entire working class from across Europe spontaneously and create revolution. But Marx and Engels opposed that the unplanned uprising of the Communist League would be adventuristic and suicide for the league. The uprising recommendation Schapper and Willich group was easily crushed by the police and the armed forces of the reactionary governments of Europe. Marx believed that this would spell doom for the league itself, and argued that changes in society are not achieved overnight through the efforts and the will power of a hand full of men. So, they brought about through a scientific analysis of economic conditions of society by moving toward revolution in different stages of development. The stages of development-defeat the uprisings across Europe in 1848, the Communist League should encourage the working class to unite with progressive elements of the rising bourgeois and defeat the feudal aristocracy demanding governmental reforms such as constitutional republic with freely elected assemblies and universal suffrage. It emphasised the working class to join with bourgeois and democratic forces so as to bring about the succesful conclusion of the bourgeois revolution before stressing the working class agenda and its revolution. This idea of Marx made Schapper/Willich group to leave the Communist League. At the same time, Marx became heavily involved with the socialist German Workers' Educational society. This society conducted a meeting in Great Windmill Street, Soho, London. This organisation was racked by an internal struggle between its members some of whom followed Marx whereas others followed the Schapper and Willich faction. Marx lost the fight with Schapper and Willich faction within the German Workers' Educational Society. He resigned from the society on 27 September 1850.

Karl Marx and his family lived in extreme poverty. He reached his audience, the working classes through his own news paper. Marx and Engels published six papers from England, the United States, Prussia, Austria and South Africa. So, his principal earnings came from his work as European correspondent for the New-York Daily Tribune and from producing articles for bourgeois news papers. He became involved in the International Working men's Association known as the First International. The most important political event of the International was the Paris Commune of 1871 when the citizens of Paris rebelled against their government held the city for two months. He wrote the pamphlet 'The Civil War' in France as a response to the bloody suppression of rebellion. Marx accumulated over 800 pages of notes and short essays on capital, landed property, wage labour, the state and foreign trade and world market. He published A Contribution to the Critique of Political Economy in 1859. He also wrote Das Kapital in three volumes of which the first was published during his lifetime and other two after his demise. The first volume analysed the capitalist process of production. It described the labour theory of value. The work Das Kapital and the Theories of Surplus value discussed and critiqued the theoreticians of political economy. The theories of Surplus Value was published as fourth volume of Das Kapital in 1963 in London highly appreciated by the classical economists. It was also published in Moscow in 1971.

Marx's life was full of sufferings and losses. He dedicated his life and family to the uplift of economically poor sections especially working classes. He wanted to establish a socialistic society against inequality and capitalism. His highly commandable golden philosopy is "From each according to his ability , to each according to his need". Marx's health declined and he became incapable of the sustained effort during the last decade of his life. The untimely death of his wife Jenny in December1881 affected him severely. He had catarrh which made him ill health for the last 15 months. It eventually brought on the bron chilies and pleurisy that stopped the breathing of Karl Marx. The socially glorious humanist left the world on 14, March 1883. Family and friends buried him in Highgate Cemetery London on 17 March 1883 in an area reserved for agnostics and atheists (close to George Eliot's grave).

The experience of extreme poverty, deep thoughts and prolific effective writings have made him an imperishable thinker, socialist, communist in the international level.

Philosophy of Karl Marx

Karl Marx has mentioned very important ideas to be quoted as philosophical thoughts.

- Religion is the sigh of the oppressed creature, the heart of a heartless world and the soul of soulless conditions. It is the opium of the people.
- Revolutions are the locomotives of history.
- Last words are for the fools who haven't said 'enough'.
- History repeats itself, first as tragedy, second as farce.
- Reason has always existed, but not always a reasonable form.
- The theory of communism abolishes all the private properties.
- Workers of the world unite: you have nothing to lose but your chains.
- The production of too many useful things results in too many useless people.
- Everyone should contribute what they can and everyone should get what they need.
- The history of all previous societies has been the history of class struggles.
- Necessity is blind until it becomes conscious. Freedom is the consciousness of necessity.
- The philosophers have only interpreted the world in various ways. The point, however, is to change it.
- The last capitalist we hang shall be the one who sold us the rope.
- Surround yourself with people who make you happy. People who make you laugh who help you when you are in need. People who genuinely care, they are the ones worth keeping in your life.
- The tradition of all dead generations weighs like a nightmare on the brains of the living.
- Time is everything, man is nothing. He is at the most time's carcass.
- Men make their own history.
- The increase in value of the world of things is directly proportional.
- Nothing have value without being an object of utility.

CONCEPT OF MARXISM

Marx's Political and philosophical thoughts have enormous influence on subsequent intellectuals, economic, political and educational history. Marxian critical theories about society, economics and politics collectively known as Marxism. Believing that human societies develop through class conflict in the capitalist mode of production. Thatmanifests it in the conflict between the ruling classes that control the means of production and working classes (proletariat) who sell their labour for wages. Thus, Marxism constituted a general view about the world and the human society. In other words, it was developed as a protest against the idealist conception of man and the world. As such, it contains social economic doctrines meant for a revolutionary change in the society. Karl Marx is the originator of Marxism with the collaboration of his friend German thinker Friedrich Engles. However, the concept of Marxism developed from the idealistic view of Hegel.

Karl Marx was influenced by Hegelian dialectical idealism, French socialism and English Economics. That is why, Marxism is a fundamental and total philosophy of life based on social and political Theory. So it is a scientific plan for complete social change and revolution. General characteristics of Marxism are:

- Reality exists in the materialistic philosophy of life.
- It has no faith in spirituality or idea.
- It interprets human history from reality (matter)to spirituality.
- It is also known as dialectic materialism believing that this real world is the only true reality.
- There can be no existence of mind without body physical existence is real one.
- Man is a productive machine or animal.
- He has no personal or individual freedom. But his freedom exits in the collective will of the people.
- The working class should seize the power and abolish all private ownership in order to create a classless society that is equality.
- All the people will own all the natural resources without any discrimination or inequality.
- Religion is considered as the opium of the people.

MARX AND MODERN SOCIALISM

Karl Marx is the founder of modern scientific socialism. He analysed the forces and impulses which govern the human nature and mould its environments. He turned socialism into a philosophy and gave a new direction with dynamic force through his communist manifesto which described in 1848. So it has been regarded as the birth cry of modern socialism. He believed that the evolution of history is the result of economic changes brought about by the changing method of production of wealth. According to him, a social revolution would lead to the dictatorship of the proletariat. His book Das Capital has become the Bible of all socialists in the world. In fact, it heralded revolution in the realm of ideas and become the gospel of a new faith. Thus, Marx has brushed aside all the earlier socialistic theories which were vague and unscientific one. This is because they ignored the operation of certain immutable laws which determine the cause of history. So, he declares that the future state cannot be the product of intellectual ingenuity or the device of a reformer. However, the future is determined by the past; it is the inevitable product of certain forces and tendencies which are irresistible in their operation. Hence, the business of social philosophy is to discover these forces but not to describe panaceas.

ECONOMIC INTERPRETATION OF HISTORY AND CLASS STRUGGLE

Karl Marx gave an economic interpretation of history and arrived at the conclusion that all history is a record of class struggles. According to him the fundamental impulse of human life is economic factor. He also holds that the course of history has always been determined by economic factors. For example, those who control the means of production dominate the society and perpetuate their social and political prominence. As a result, it arises the division of the society into those who control and those who are uncontrolled, the haves and the have-nots. It is from this division of society into two antagonistic sections that cause class struggles.

He also points out that the present society has been evolved gradually out of many class struggles in the past. Infact, History is a record of class struggles between Freeman and slave, lord and serf, the landed aristocracy and the bourgeoisie. It is also a record of how one class has gained wealth and political power only to be over the throne and succeeded by another class.

It is seen that industrial revolution has destroyed the power and political influence of the old aristocracy and magnified those of the bourgeois, the middle class capitalists but it has also created a class of wretched wage owners, the proletarians who are being mercilessly exploited by the capitalists. Hence, these two classes are set in mutual hostility but the result that a severe conflict between them is quite inevitable. This would be the final struggle leading to a terrible revolution which would establish the dictatorship of the proletariat in a classless society. Karl Marks in his Communist manifesto makes a strong appeal to the people in the ringing words: Let the ruling classes tremble at the communist revolution. The proletariats have nothing to lose but their chains they have a world to win. "Working men of all countries unite".

CAPITALISM AND THEORY OF SURPLUS VALUE

Economic interpretation of history and class struggles or the two main principles of Marxism. Karl Marx directed his attack upon capital through the economic theory of surplus value. Accordingly, all wealth is the product of labourers, and labour is the only measure of value. Hence, labourers have the right to the whole produce of Labour. The walk-man should work longer and harder than the wages he receives. Warrants, and the surplus above what he actually receives is the source of the income of capitalists. According to him, capitalism is digging its own grave. Its inevitable tendency is the progressive concentration of wealth in the hands of increasingly few men. The big capitalists swallowing up the little ones, the result of this tendency would be to increase the number of the proletariat. So, the society would be composed of two classes differentiated by increasing wealth and increasing misery.

VALUES IN MARXISM

- Marxism emphasise is some values which should be observed in the personal and social life.
- Marxist should dedicate to the welfare of the state or country
- He should respect the public properties.
- He should develop a respect for authority.
- Welfare of the state or country is more important than individual.
- Respect parents, elderly people and all labourers.
- Common good occupies an important position in Marxism.
- There is no existence of private property in the Marxist state or country.
- Discipline is important value in the public life.
- It attaches highest importance to the value of Labour.

KARL MARX AND EDUCATION

Marx is a great educationist and intellectual thinker but he never wrote any thing on education. However, his influence on writers, academicians, intellectual and educators has turned his powerful ideas into educational thoughts. In fact, Marxian views have a great impact on education, philosophy, politics and society whether we accept or oppose it. Karl Popper, one of the fierce opponents of Marxism has rightly stated, that all modern writers are indebted to Marx, even if they do not know it. Hence, an attempt is made to analyse the educational thoughts found in Marxism. Marxian Education stresses the indoctrination of ideas and practises. So, education should aim at developing Marxist attitudes and values. According to Marx, the state should be strengthened through the creation of classless society. He believed that the proletariat would dominate the state. So education would not be limited to a handful of people and it should be provided to all sections of the society. In short, he wanted the Universalization of education to establish a classless society and inculcate Marxian values. Hence, Equalisation of educational opportunity is the principle of Karl Marx. Thus, Marxian education aims at maximum good to the maximum people. He also believed that social advancement can be ensured through education because he considered education as the greatest instrument of social change. But the intellectual education cannot achieve this goal. So, he emphasised vocational and technical education. He wanted all educands to know the true character of social development. History and economics should be taught in proper perspective. The student should also learn the fundamental principles of science. Labour and work or considered as an integral part of Marxist education. A Walkman cannot work properly unless he poses a sound health. Hence, physical development is considered as an important aim of Marxist education.

Meaning of Education

Karl Marx says education is meant for five things namely intellectual, physical, cultural, vocational and aesthetic development. According to Lenin, education is an integral part of culture. Both culture and education are shaped by socio-economic conditions. But Labour is the basic source of all cultural advancements. Thus, Labour occupies an important place in Marxist education.

Marxist Principles of Education

There will be no discrimination in respect of educational opportunities.

- Education should be provided to all sections of the people irrespective of caste, creed, sex and socio-economic status.
- Common education should be provided to men and women. So, co-education is accepted in the society.
- Education should be made universal and compulsory one.
- There is no discrimination made among schools.
- Establishment of common school system should be the goal of the state.
- Education of the child depends on the education of mother.
- Education should not be confined within the four walls of the school.
- Learning through the personal experience of the child.
- Marxism emphasises group activity instead of individual one.
- Marxist education intends to promote co-operative spirit instead of competitive spirit among students.
- Education should be combined with productive work.
- Marx advocates secular education.
- There will be only state agency to provide education. Private agency is banned in Marxist educational administration.

Marxist Aims of Education

Generally the notable Marxian aim of education is state welfare and establishment of a classless society. He opposes privatisation of education and capitalism but advocates universalization of education and make it free and compulsory for all. The specific objectives of Marxian education are:

- Propagate Marxian attitudes and values.
- Create creative productive and faithful citizenship.
- Develop the mind of child through scientific studies.
- Establish a classless society and equality.
- Strengthen the state in all aspects.
- Prepare the child to sacrifice everything for the welfare of the state.
- Provide vacation or production oriented education.

Marxist Curriculum

Marxist philosophy and doctrines should be taught at all levels of education on compulsory basis. Hence, curriculum should include those subjects which make the students conscious about Class divisions, unequal distribution of wealth, exploitation of the working classes by the capitalists.

- Curriculum should contain those subjects and knowledge which develop the skills and abstract knowledge and experiences.
- It should include work experience as an integral part of education.
- The curriculum should include the socially useful subjects such as science, mathematics, geography, life science, geology, astronomy and history.
- It should also contain the history of communist movement and political economy.
- Karl Marx advocated the study of mother tongue at the primary level and foreign language at the secondary level.
- It should give due importance to creative work and co-curricular activities such as physical exercises, music, painting, drawing, games and sports.

Marxist Method of Teaching

- Practical aspect of education is more important than the theoretical one.
- Marxist education is based on the principle of learning by doing. Itemphasises learning through personal experience of the child.
- Students should be encouraged to work in agricultural forms and factories so as to develop vocational efficiency and respect the dignity of Labour.
- It emphasise group activity instead of individual activity because Marxist education should promote co-operative spirit instead of competitive spirit among students.
- Education should not be confined within the four walls of the school. The natural environment and community will also serve as great books and teachers.

Role of Teacher in Marxist Education

The role of the teacher is very important and crucial in Marxist education. He must be fully equipped not only with the content of education but also the Marxist methodology of teaching and objectives of education. Hence, a Marxist teacher must entirely be different in attitude and temperament from a bourgeois one. This is because the teacher should teach Marxist philosophy. Therefore, he must be an active member of Marxist social order. Lenin rightly remarks, "A best Marxist worker can only be a best Marxist teacher". So, he must be a true Marxist in thought and actions. Moreover, he should not have only mastery on the content of education but also have consciousness about life, social environment and communist ideology. Above all, he should have sound health, respect the cultural heritage, deep practical sense, socialistic bent of mind and true patriotism.

Contribution of Marxism to Education

Sociological based education: Marxist education is sociological based one which aims at universalization of education and building up of a classless society. Thus, it has a social purpose of service of the state. In short, all are for the state and the state for all.

Opposes capitalism: Marxist education strongly opposes the existence of capitalism and its exploitation. Which widens the inequality. It makes rich richer and poor poorer. It works for the welfare of the individual not for state. There is a private ownership of properties. It is just against socialism or Marxism.

Production-oriented education: According to Marx, education should be combined with productive work. He appreciated the work of a British factory owner Robert Owen for initiating this idea to increase the efficiency of Labour. Marx remarks, "As Robert Owen has shown the jump of education of the future in the case of every child should combine productive Labour with instructions and gymnastics not only as one of the methods of adding to the efficiency of production but as the only method of producing fully developed human beings".

A comprehensive curriculum for life: Marxist curriculum emphasises the teaching of productive works and practical activities of life. It encourages the study of history scientifically to understand the class struggle and establish a classless society.

Develop vocational efficiency: Marxist education stresses the development of vocational efficiency through group works and respect for the dignity of Labour. As such, it gives very importance to labourers because they produce goods and services.

Group work and activities: Marxism encourages group works and activities for the welfare of the state and develop co-operation among the different people. This would mitigate the competition and make the child to feel that he is a unit in the society and he has a duty to the state.

Emphasises the role of state: Marxist education always emphasises the role of state in all activities. It considers the state as the sole agency of education and production. In other words, it has the power to control all educational institutions. As such, there is no decentralisation of educational administration or planning or curriculum construction. It means that there is no part of private agency but the state should control and administer the methods of teaching textbooks and evaluation system.

Universalization of education: Marxism always advocates the provision of free and compulsory education at the school level.

Equalisation of educational opportunities: Marxism is strong in the universalization of educational opportunities to all children irrespective of their caste, creed, sex and socio-economic status. As such, there is no discrimination in education which is essential to establish equality and classless society.

Limitations of Marxist Education

It is very difficult to apply Marxist education in the profit-oriented materialistic society. However, there are few shortcomings found in it.

Neglects individual differences: Marxist education has failed to highlight individual differences while advocating child-centred education.

Little scope for state: It emphasises the state to control and administer the educational institutions. No private agency is allowed to run educational institution. But it is very expensive and difficult to provide and control all educational institutions, the state can play a limited role in the educational system.

Lack of freedom for teachers: In Marxist education there is no freedom provided to the teachers in the academic environment. This is because it stresses child centred education.

Students are machines: Marxism follows a very rigid discipline which affects the normal growth and development of the child. Students are treated as machines in the educational institutions.

Impossible of achieving the goal of education: The ultimate aim of Marxist education is to strengthen the state and bold up a classless education. As long as people are still in the darkness of ignorance, superstition, poverty, unemployment and money mindedness, it is not possible to achieve the Marxist aim of education.

Develop narrowism: Marxism develops narrowism of capitalism and communism and struggle between them. As such, it creates conflicts in the people and wide gap between the capitalist and working class. There is no place for human values but prepare the people to fight against capitalism. So, it is applicable until the particular section of people get equality or social justice.

CONCLUSION

Karl Marx is one of the living personalities in politics, economics, philosophy, psychology and education. He approached the whole range of psychological issues of development, feelings, neurosis, pathology, personality and character. There is no short line between social and individual development. However, his powerful ideas penetrate deeply into psychology and educational theories. In fact, his approach to education is constructivists, emphasises activity, collaboration and critic rather than a passive emulation of elders and conformism; education is student-centred rather than teacher-centred one. But he recognised that education cannot transcend the problems and capabilities of the society. There is no doubt that Marxian thoughts have a global impact on the modern education, politics, economics, philosophy, literature, psychology and sociology. Marxian Education has changed the aims, curriculum and method of teaching of various subjects and activities. It provides more importance to activity centred education than theoretical one. It encourages self-learning from work experiences and prepare the people for state welfare. We can conclude that the role of Marxian education is very important in man and nation making in the materialistic society. Karl Marx was a fighter-willing to sacrifice anything in the battle for his conception of a better society. So, he is regarded struggle as the law of life and existence. Engles declared that Karl Marx has made two great discovers that is law of development of human history and law of motion of bourgeois society. He was the best hated and most calumniated man of his time. But he died a beloved, revered and mourned by the millions of revolutionary fellow workers.

UNIT IV

EDUCATIONAL SOCIOLOGY

CHAPTER 31

MEANING AND SCOPE OF EDUCATIONAL SOCIOLOGY

INTRODUCTION

Man is a social animal. He is born and brought up in society. He spends his whole life in society. Human history is a standing proof of his social nature, social feelings and social behaviour. In short, he is a part and parcel of the society. Hence, we cannot think of a human life without a society. Social interaction among individuals is a constant process which develops fellow-feeling, friendship, relationship and social elements. Sociology, according to Duncan, is the scientific study of dynamic processes of interaction of persons and the patterns. These form a relation with biological, psychological and cultural influences. In the words of Merrill and Eldridge, the field of study of sociology is 'human relationships'. According to E. Durkheim, "Sociology is the science of collective representation".

MEANING OF SOCIOLOGY

Before discussing the term "educational sociology", it is necessary to understand the meaning of the word 'sociology'. Auguste Comte, the well-known French philosopher, used the word 'Sociology' for the first time in his lecture in 1837. He coined the word 'Sociology' by combining the Greek word *Societus* meaning society and the Latin word *Logos* meaning 'Science' 'or' 'Study'. He recognised sociology as a fundamental science which deals with the application of scientific method to study the relationship between society and the individual. Since Comte advocated the scientific study of society for the first time, he is considered as the Father of sociology. According to him, sociology is the synthesis of all sciences and as such it should be effectively used in the reformation and reconstruction of society. Hence, sociology is the scientific study of society or it maybe called the science of society. In short, sociology is the science of the nature and growth of society. The teaching of sociology started in 1876 in the United Nations; in 1889 in France; in 1907 in Great Britain, after the World War I in Poland and India; in 1925 in Egypt and Mexico; and in 1947 in Sweden. Hence, sociology is the youngest of social science.

DEFINITIONS OF SOCIOLOGY

Alex Inkeles: "Sociology is the study of systems of social action and their inter relations".

Comete, Ward, Blackmar, Gilonin, Giddings: "Sociology is the science of society".

Gillin and Gillin: "It is the study of interactions arising from the association of living beings".

MacIver, Page, Abel: "Sociology is the study of the nature of social relationships".

Max Weber: "Sociology is a science which attempts the interpretative understanding of social action".

Green: "Sociology is the synthesizing and generalizing science of man in all his social relationships".

Parson, Merton: "Sociology is the study of social action".

John Madge: "It is the study of the interacting groups of which all societies are composed".

Morris Ginsberg: "Sociology is the study of the conditions and consequences of human inter-action and inter-relations".

Kimball Young: "Sociology is the study of human behaviour in groups".

J.F. Cuber: "Sociology may be defined as a body of scientific knowledge about human relationships".

Fair Child: "Sociology is the study of the relationships between man and his human environments".

It is clear from the given definitions that the central theme of sociology is social interaction. Social interaction includes interaction with cultural and other institutions such as family, play groups, peer groups, religious, economic and educational institutions. It studies the customs and traditions that grow out of these interactions, the institutions that crystallise these basic human interests and the changes that occur in these institutions. Thus, in the study of sociology different forms of human inter-relations are involved. In the words of Robbins, "Sociology deals with the whole man in relation to all the social, cultural and bio-physical backgrounds". We may define Sociology thus "Sociology is the study of human relationship and behaviour in the social environments".

MEANING OF EDUCATIONAL SOCIOLOGY

Educational sociology is a branch of sociology which has come into existence as a synthesis between Education and Sociology. E. George Payne is regarded as the father of educational sociology. According to him, "Educational sociology is the applied science in the field of sociology". It emphasises that the aims of sociology should be achieved through educational processes. Thus, educational sociology is that science which studies social activities, human groups, social institutions and agencies which fulfil the needs of education. It concerns itself with the development of individuals and society. It is, therefore, necessary to study the working of various social institutions, customs and traditions, social rules, codes and norms of behaviour which affect human progress and development through various educational activities and experiences. Educational sociology is a branch of sociology which deals with the problems of the relationship between society and education. It is the application of sociological principles to education for the sake of the improvement of educational programmes in the schools. Educational sociology is an important division of sociological studies like criminal sociology, industrial sociology, medical sociology, occupational sociology, rural sociology, social stratification sociology and urban sociology. The theme of educational sociology is preserving and modifying the society. Thus, educational sociology is a separate subject which has been developed by prominent educationists and sociologists such as Auguste Comte, George Payne, John Dewey, Ottaway, David Snedden, Allen Cook, George Counts, Hilda Taba, Emile Durkheim, Max Weber, Oris Herod Clarke, Karl Mannheim, MacIver, Morris Ginsberg, Davis, Frédérick Lepay, Moore, Dollard and Merrill.

DEFINITIONS OF EDUCATIONAL SOCIOLOGY

The term 'educational sociology' has been defined by different educationists and sociologists in the following manner:

George E. Payne: "Educational Sociology is a science which describes and explains the institutions, social groups, and social processes or social concerns, that is, the social relationship in which or through which the individual gains and organizes his experiences".

Ottaway: "Educational Sociology is the scientific study of the relationship between education and society".

Brown: "Educational Sociology is the study of interaction of the individual and his cultural environment including other individuals, social groups and patterns of behaviour".

Robinson Smith: "Educational Sociology is the application of the scientific methods and principles of sociology to the study of education".

Good: "Educational Sociology is the scientific study of how people live in social group especially in the study of education that is obtained by living in the social groups, and education that is needed by the members to live efficiently in social groups".

Alvin Good: "Educational sociology is the study of education which is obtained by man in social groups and the education that is needed by the member to live efficiently in the social groups".

Roucek: "Educational Sociology is sociology applied to the solution of fundamental educational problems".

D.W. Dodson: "Educational sociology is particularly interested in finding out how to manipulate the educational process to achieve better personality development".

Carte: "Educational sociology is the study of those processes of sociology that are significant for the educative process".

Cook and Cook: "Educational Sociology is the study of human factors in the educative process, with the aim to improve teaching and learning in all types of educational systems".

From the given definitions, it is discerned that educational sociology is the study of the relationship between education and society. Hence, we may define the term "educational sociology" as the branch of sociology which scientifically deals with the impact of society on education and education on society, their relationship in solving problems related to them. In short, educational sociology through the medium of education socialises human beings and links man with society.

NATURE OF EDUCATIONAL SOCIOLOGY

Educational sociology is an important division of sociology which has the following characteristics:

- Educational sociology is a theoretical study of the interaction between the individual and the society.
- Educational sociology is also a practical study of the forces of interaction between the individual and the society.
- Educational sociology regulates and controls the interacting forces of individuals and society.
- It is an educational method to develop one's personality.
- It establishes the relationship between society and education.

NEED FOR EDUCATIONAL SOCIOLOGY

The combined approach of education and sociology is necessary in order to foster social feelings among the people to achieve better human relationship. Educational sociology is considered necessary for the following reasons:

- The larger aims of sociology cannot be achieved without integrating the process of education into it.
- Without making a micro study of social problems through education, we cannot think of a macro solution.
- Educational sociology studies social processes and interactions very objectively. It is essential to find solutions for educational problems.
- It is needed to foster social attitudes among the people through education and to improve human relationship.
- Educational sociology studies social activities and social institutions in the context of future social needs also. It is, therefore, very helpful for the progress of education.
- Educational sociology gives equal weightage to the development of the individual as well as the society.
- Education and sociology are interrelated and interdependent. Sociology without education is like a body without a soul and education without sociology is like a vehicle without wheels. Hence, the combination of education and sociology, that is, educational sociology is necessary for cultural and social development.

IMPORTANCE OF EDUCATIONAL SOCIOLOGY

- Man should be socialised to lead a group life. So, he should learn and understand the significance of social adjustment at school. For this purpose educational sociology recognises the social nature of man and plans accordingly.
- It emphasises the belief that all men are equal. In fact, the influence of educational sociology guarantees every man the right to have education according to one's needs, aptitude, interests and ability. There is no bar such as race, caste, creed, colour and sex for any individual to develop more and more to the utmost extent.
- It protects and promotes the progress of culture. It fosters those cultural qualities which promote international understanding and welfare.
- It formulates rules and procedures which establish and develop social growth among individuals and make them active participants in social activities.
- It secures for an individual self-reliance and self-development.
- It tries to secure and promote happy life for all individuals. It makes people to understand their welfare and strive to achieve social good for all.
- School is an integral part of the society. It is the reflection of society. Hence, any change we want to bring about in the society requires its foundation to be laid in the school. It is because small and immatured representatives of the society will lead the society in future when they are matured.
- Educational sociology helps the educationists in constructing the curriculum keeping in view the socio-economic tendencies and demands of society.
- It helps us to provide sound social bases for educational researches. In fact, sociological researches in education have special significance.

- It analyses the causes of social and group conflicts and helps to remove them by imparting suitable education.
- It prepares and develops the child for living independently in the society.
- It studies the social elements which affect the individual objectively, and apply them in the educational environment of the school.

SCOPE OF EDUCATIONAL SOCIOLOGY

The scope of educational sociology is a wide and comprehensive subject. This is because it deals with the influences of educational process on sociology and the effects of sociological process on education. It deals with the impact of the total cultural milieu in which and through which experience is required and organized. In fact, anything under the sun which concerns society is the theme of sociology. Hence, the scope of educational sociology includes the following factors:

- Mutual relationship among students and their impact on education.
- Mutual relationship between teachers and students and their impact on teaching-learning process.
- It includes how culture is handed over to coming generations through agencies like the school, the home, the religious organisation and the play and peer groups.
- It includes how socialisation takes place in the child as a result of social interaction.
- It includes the role of the school, the press, the radio, the television and the cinema in the educational process.
- It includes how education serves as a means of social change and social control.
- The impact of sociological thinking on the meaning, aims, and functions of education, the curriculum including co-curricular activities, social organization and the methodology of teaching.
- The place of the teacher in the society.
- Social aspirations, needs and problems and their impact on education and life.
- Interrelationship of education and sociology.
- Social organisation and their role on education and school administration.
- The place of school in the society and its relationship with society and other small organizations.
- Effects of social patterns and culture on education.
- Progress of democratic values in educational institutions.
- Role of education in socialisation and social change.
- Social life in the school.
- Promotion of social feeling in the students.
- Curriculum and the needs of the society.
- Equalisation of educational opportunities.
- National integration.
- New world order and its impact on education in future.
- School and community.
- Role of the mass media in education and social progress.
- Use of group and cooperative methods of teaching.
- Terrorism and fundamentalism in relation to social change.

OBJECTIVES OF EDUCATIONAL SOCIOLOGY

Prof. Harington has suggested a few objectives of educational sociology. They are:

- Acquire knowledge about the school work in relation to society and social progress.
- Gain knowledge about the role of the teacher in relation to the society and social progress.
- Acquire knowledge about the effects of social elements on the individual.
- Construct a curriculum fully understanding the economic and cultural tendencies of the society.
- Gain knowledge about the democratic values or ideologies.
- Study the effects of the individual on social elements.
- Employ research techniques for achieving the aims of educational sociology.

RELATIONSHIP BETWEEN EDUCATION AND SOCIOLOGY

Sociology and education are mutually interrelated and they are interdependent on each other. They are interrelated disciplines like philosophy and education and psychology and education. Sociology of education is the scientific study of the analysis of the social progress and social patterns involved in the educational system. Sociology without education is like a body without soul and education without sociology is like a vehicle without wheels. Hence, we may analyse the interrelationship between sociology and education.

Sociological basis and meaning of education: The meaning of education is considerably influenced by sociology. According to the educational sociologists, education is a social process which socialises the child and causes certain changes in his behaviour. In defining education the sociologists have stressed its social aspects. From the sociological point of view Brown says, "Education is the consciously controlled process whereby changes in behaviour are produced in the person and through the person within the group. Educational sociology focuses upon the social forces through which the individual is developed and the social relations by which the individual gains experience".

Sociological basis and aim of education: According to the educational sociologists, the aim of education from the sociological point of view is to develop those social qualities and social feelings in the child which will enable him to grasp his responsibilities in the society and the nation, and to become an ideal citizen of his country. Thus, the aim of education is to enable the individual to live as a member of his society. Educational sociology brings about a change in the habits, skills, interests and attitudes. Sociological knowledge and abilities develop a person into a socially accepted personality, who is adjusted with his environment and socially responsible. We can include the following aspects in the aim of education from the sociological points of view:

- Education for social service.
- Education for citizenship.
- Education for social efficiency.
- Education for emotional integration
- Education for national unity.
- Education for nationalism.
- Education for patriotism.

Sociological basis and functions of education: Educational sociologists have stressed the social functions of education. From the sociological point of view, Munroe has laid down the following functions of education:

Diffusion of more and more knowledge: The first function of education is to provide various kinds of knowledge to the child. Spread of knowledge develops the mind of the child, without which other developments are not feasible.

Education as a means of social control: Social control through education eventually gives self-control to the child. Hence, in every society, school instils the elements of social control into the younger generation through the process of education.

Protection and transmission of social heritage: Education is an important medium of protecting and transmitting social heritage and culture from one generation to the next. It is through education that the new generation is taught to adopt the culture of our ancestors. The new generation makes its own contribution to this heritage and passes it onto its successor.

Education as a means of social development: Individual development is not possible in the absence of social development. The school is considered as a miniature society. Therefore, the educators try to create an ideal social environment with a view to inculcate the best possible picture of society in the minds of the educands.

Development of constructive and creative outlook of the individual: After leaving the school, the educand retains the ideal social environment of the society in his mind and tries to recreate it in reality. Through education the individual develops a constructive and creative outlook required for the ideal members of the society.

Sociological basis and curriculum: Educational sociologists have given valuable suggestions in relation to the reorganization of the curriculum which reflects the quality and quantity of education. From the sociological point of view, the primary concern of the curriculum is the development of 'we feeling'. Brown, Moore and Cole have pointed out the principles of constructing school curriculum from the point of view of educational sociology:

- Curriculum should be based on conditions, problems and needs of society.
- It should be based on the real concerns and problems of pupils.
- It should reflect the basic cultural values of the society it serves.
- It should be an agent in the transmission of the highest value of the culture.
- It should prepare the child for the world society.
- It should be conducive to the development of responsible citizenship.
- It should prepare socially efficient individuals.
- It should develop healthy attitudes regarding human relations.
- It should be flexible and changeable for the effective realisation of socially determined objectives.
- It should lead to the development of genuine "we feeling", a feeling that the student belongs to the society and has a spirit of social interaction.
- It should treat with dignity all worthwhile vocations and services in the community life.
- It must function in relation to adult living and concurrently be adapted to the level of the development of the child.

Sociological basis and method of teaching: From the sociological point of view, only those methods are good which will develop the democratic outlook, social behaviour and social values in the child. The effectiveness of learning for social competency depends on the suitability of motives and procedures. Educational sociologists suggest some methods of teaching such as the Dalton method, project method, group discussion, problem-solving, socialised techniques and constructive thinking. The principles of sociologically based method of teaching are given below:

- The methods of teaching should enable the pupil to acquire those skills and knowledge in the classroom which are helpful to him in his adjustment to social situations.
- The methods of teaching must seek to utilise the social forces operative in the social life with a view to develop the capacity for social adjustment.
- The methods of teaching should develop problem-solving and constructive thinking.
- The methods should promote democratic feelings, ideals and values.
- The socialised techniques, the project and the group methods, by and large should replace the lecture and recitation method.

Sociological basis and school: According to the sociologists, "School is regarded as a miniature society". But in the modern times, a school is like a living organism. It is because the school brings into being various useful social activities and experiences which promote the development of social qualities in the individuals. In fact, school becomes a social being where all- round personality development is possible and the child develops its internal and external qualities.

Sociological basis and teacher: Dr. S. Kothari, Chairman of Indian Education Commission, says that the destiny of a nation is shaped in its classroom. It is, therefore, the teacher who is a very important instrument in moulding that destiny. Hence, it is very necessary that the teacher must become conscious of his role towards the society. His personality should reflect the characteristics of good citizenship. The teacher himself must be exposed to the concepts of freedom, equalitarianism, dignity of the individual rights and duties. The educational sociologists consider the teacher as a social engineer who can plan an important role in social reconstruction. Therefore, the teacher is expected to possess a right attitude of social behaviour and give due regard to the dignity of the pupils.

Sociological basis and discipline: Educational sociologists stress on the view that education should inculcate social discipline. Discipline should come through participation in group activities and social service activities. Social discipline should naturally emerge in the educand so that he may not indulge in activities that are harmful to the individual or society. In this way community feeling and social discipline can be developed.

Sociological basis and child education movement: From sociological point of view, developed countries began a movement for the education of infants. For instance, many infant schools were established in America and in many European countries which aimed at providing education to the children of poor labourers.

Sociological basis and monitor method: Dr. Andrew Bell has introduced the monitor method on the basis of sociological tendency. This method indicates that children of senior classes teach the children of junior classes. As a result one single educator could teach a large number of educands. Many monitorial schools have been established in a number of countries on the basis of this monitor system.

Sociological basis and adult education: The sociological influence on education insists upon the fact that no individual in the society should be left uneducated. As a result many movements for adult education have been established and classes are conducted during evenings and nights. Great attention has been given to adult education in India.

Sociological basis and social education: The sociological tendency has a great impact in the field of social education. Social education acquaints the individual with every aspect of his environment and trains him to fulfil his responsibilities as a citizen. This type of education aims not only at the complete development of the individual but also at evolving social unity in him. The agencies of social education are lecturers, exhibitions, meetings, debate, drama, tour etc.

Sociological basis and responsibility of state: Educational sociologists stress that it is the responsibility of the state to provide education. Hence, it is for the state to make every individual capable of earning his livelihood and develop his personality to fulfil his social duties. Proper education of the masses is very essential without which democracy can never be a success. As a result, the state provides primary, secondary, university and professional education. The different levels of education produce better citizens and build a powerful nation.

CONCLUSION

Today, we can hardly afford to think of education in isolation. That is, education without sociology is like a vehicle without wheels. In fact, sociology shapes education as a vital force in the entire framework for social, political and economic changes. As a consequence, the whole structure of education depends on social forces, needs and demands. The expectations and aspirations of a changing society are reflected through the educational system of a country. Educational sociology also emphasises that the individual alone is nothing.

He is a part of the society and he owes his importance to the society. So, his goal of life should be the progress of society. Clarke has rightly stated that no writer on education, however, much he strives for universal thought can wholly shake himself free from the influence of time and place. Society is dynamic and it grows and changes. Social changes must be reflected in education. Hence, we come to the conclusion that both education and sociology are inter-related and inter-dependent, and they change in relation to time.

CHAPTER 32

EDUCATION AND SOCIAL MOBILITY

INTRODUCTION

Social mobility refers to the movement of an individual in a social structure. It maybe taken as a movement from one social status to another. It does not mean the physical movement of a person or group from one place to another. Similarly, material change from poverty to prosperity is not social mobility. So, mobility means the transformation in the social status of an individual or a group. This change in a social status is called **social mobility**. For instance, if a poor Dalit child becomes an IPS or an IAS officer, according to his desire and efforts, his social status will definitely change. The social position, status and economic conditions of people change from time-to-time. In fact, in many cases, social status and economic standard of a person changes due to hard work or higher education or super intellect. Better education and better service lead to social mobility. Travelling from Kanyakumari to Madurai or Chennai or New Delhi is physical mobility, whereas, the promotion from the post of a clerk to that of a teacher or headmaster or lecturer is social mobility.

DEFINITIONS OF SOCIAL MOBILITY

P.A. Sorokin: "Social mobility is either horizontal or vertical. Horizontal mobility is the process of making changes on the same status level, while vertical mobility is the process of changing from one status to another, either to a higher or lower level".

S. Bogardus: "Social mobility is any change in social position such as occupational changes where persons move up or down the occupational scale or relation to office whereby a follower becomes a leader or a leap from a low economic class to a high one or vice-versa".

Kimball Young and Raymond W. Mack: "By social mobility we mean movement within the social structure".

Havighurst and Neugarten: "The term social mobility means movement from one social position to another involving the consolidation of the various elements of the new social position, new friends, and new organisational membership".

Wallace and Wallace: "Social mobility is the movement of a person or persons from one social status to another.

In the modern society, we may define social mobility as "the up or downward movement of the individual from existing social position to another either in profession, occupation, leadership or responsibilities due to his ceaseless efforts or any other criteria".

TYPES OF SOCIAL MOBILITY

Sorokin has divided social mobility into two categories in accordance with the direction of movement of the people in the society.

- Horizontal social mobility
- Vertical social mobility

Horizontal Social Mobility

Horizontal social mobility refers to the change of occupations, without any change in social status. For instance, a headmaster leaves one school and works in another. Here, only the social group of teacher changes, but his social position or status remains the same. When the transformation of a person takes place within the group, it is called **horizontal social mobility**. Social status of a person does not change here, or this change is insignificant in society. Here, the working place of a person may change but his salary, grade, prestige, privileges etc. remain unchanged. We can make this clear with the help of a suitable example. It is similar to the transformation of a professor of Madurai Kamaraj University transferred to University of Madras or University of Delhi with the same social and economic status.

P.A. Sorokin has also discussed various forms of horizontal social mobility.

Inter-group mobility in race, sex and age group: There is no mobility among the people of the same race, sex and age groups. The reason is that nobody can change his race, sex and age by his own efforts. For example, no man can become a woman even if he desires so. But when these groups grow and develop as social groups due to interactions, horizontal mobility will be seen among them.

Occupational mobility: The change from one occupation to another of the similar nature, status, conditions and circumstances is called occupational mobility. For instance, if a tailor changes his occupation and opens a showroom or tea stall, it will not increase his status in the society. In closed societies even this mobility is not easily possible because of the restrictions imposed by the society. Sometimes a particular class of the society is associated with its occupation so firmly that it is not willing to change. On the other hand, in open societies occupational mobility gets an impetus during crisis or economic prosperity.

Religious mobility: The conversion from one religion to another is called religious mobility. This type of mobility is more seen in men than women, in urban population than in rural, and in educated class than uneducated one. This mobility becomes horizontal when a section of the population which is highly discriminated against, in his own community, embraces the religion of those who give him equal status in the society and the community. The conversion of Dalits to Islam or Christianity is the example of religious mobility.

Political mobility: Leaving one political party for another is political mobility. In India, several people change their party loyalties because of self-interest, allurements, political instability, lack of moral character and personal reason. Generally, it does not bring out any change in their social status. But when an ordinary member of the central or state legislative council joins a ruling party and occupies a ministry, this becomes vertical mobility. This type of mobility is very common in India. People raise their social status in this way.

Family and kinship mobility: This type of mobility takes place in a society because of marriage, remarriage, adoption of child or divorce.

Territorial mobility: Leaving of a particular territory by a group of people and entering another territory for residing is called territorial mobility. This kind of mobility is more frequent among the youngsters who reside in towns and work in government institutions or private industries. Territorial mobility occurs very rapidly at the time of harvest failures, epidemics, wars, riots, and critical circumstances, in order to get security and safety. But, the migration of villagers to cities for jobs is not included in this territorial mobility.

International mobility: International mobility takes place when people migrate from under-developed countries to developed countries for better prospects of life. Indians migrating to Gulf countries and other developed countries such as America and England is an example of international mobility. This type of mobility increases when people of one country migrate to other countries where they are welcomed and find better position. International mobility is more economic oriented than social. This kind of mobility is also very high when the number of educated unemployed increases.

Vertical Social Mobility

In vertical social mobility, the individual may move up and down in the social position. All social groups are not equal in social status. Some of them are considered high and some are low with respect to social prestige. The achievement of higher status and prestige by an individual or a group of lower status and in the same manner degradation of an individual or a group from higher status and prestige to lower status is called **vertical mobility**. That is, vertical social mobility implies achieving higher to lower or lower to higher social status and prestige in the society. For instance, in India, zamindars enjoyed a very high position in the society but the rise of the new industrialist groups have pushed them down. Dhirubhai Ambani can be cited here. He started his career as a worker in a petrol pump in Yaman, but achieved very high social status by establishing the Reliance Group in India. This vertical social mobility refers to both achieving higher or lower status in the society. In the words of Sorokin, "By vertical mobility, I mean the relations involved in a transition of an individual from one social stratum to another".

Further, Sorokin has categorised vertical social mobility into two sub-parts.

Ascending mobility: It refers to the movement of an individual from lower to a higher position. Promotion of a clerk to an officer or promotion of a school teacher to a headmaster or promotion of a professor to a Vice-Chancellor of University are the examples of ascending vertical mobility. Thus, ascending vertical mobility means the entry of persons from lower strata and prestige to higher status and prestige groups. Persons belonging to the lower stratum of the society do achieve higher status. For instance, Dalits and backward classes have had upward mobility and influenced national policies and programmes.

Descending mobility: Descending mobility means the going down of a person from the higher prestige and status to lower ones. It may occur due to political changes, economic depression and crisis, behavioural changes etc. This type of mobility is also caused due to lack of initiative and efforts on the part of the people and moral turpitude. Downward social mobility takes place in government and private organization. It is, generally, the outcome of inefficiency or acts of criminal tendencies of the individual.

DIMENSIONS OF SOCIAL MOBILITY

Lipset and Zitterberg have mentioned certain areas of social mobility.

Occupational ranking: Society is stratified on the basis of occupations and economic status. Some occupations are given high social status and some others are considered low. For instance, rikshaw pulling is considered as an occupation of low status as compared to that of a vendor. Because of these two different natures of occupations, horizontal as well as vertical mobility is seen simultaneously. Persons who are engaged in comparatively less prestigious occupations strive to move towards occupations comprising greater prestige and social distinction. The entry of a skilled worker in the white collared jobs or occupations is called **occupational mobility**. Here, income is not the criteria for this stratification. For example, many occupations of low social prestige can fetch larger incomes than those with high social prestige.

Social class: Society maybe divided into rich, poor and middle classes. It is very difficult for any one to shift from one social class to another. But any person can go to higher social classes if he is able to increase his income to that level. Thus, vertical social mobility is not impossible here. But it is essential to note that people of elite sections of society do not associate with persons of inferior social status.

Consumption ranking: Lipset and Zitterberg have stressed that there is a difference between occupational status and economic status. Business status of different individuals is ranked according to the income that they earn whereas economic status of persons is determined on the basis of their consumption volume and pattern. Consumption is positively correlated to the standard of living. Society is also divided on the basis of their standard of living. The standard and style of living also depend on education. If the person is educated, his standard of living maybe high despite the fact that his income is comparatively low. An uneducated rich man may adopt a very low standard of living. Social mobility is not difficult in this situation. Anybody can change his status according to his will and effort.

Caste ranking: Ranking of the people on the basis of their caste or sub- caste is so rigid that social mobility becomes very difficult here. The system of ranking the people on the basis of caste is characteristic of the social system. Only horizontal mobility is possible through marriages.

Power ranking: The powers maybe social or political or both. Groups belonging to ruling class are generally given high status in the society. This power division is not of permanent nature in social or political system. Hence, social mobility is not difficult here.

FACTORS AFFECTING SOCIAL MOBILITY

There are many factors that affect social mobility in positive as well as negative ways.

Structure of the society: The structure of society powerfully influences the process of social mobility. Societies maybe of two types—closed societies and open societies. People in closed societies have very backward and narrow thinking. They weigh everything on the basis of their birth, tradition and old customs. In such societies they do not get opportunities for requiring ascending and descending vertical social mobility. Thus, the chances of social mobility are very low in such societies. On the other hand in open societies individuals have full freedom and opportunities to do or adopt anything as they like. For example, any person belonging to any caste or creed can marry any woman of any caste or creed. No one in the society cares who marries whom. Thus, open society is better than closed society which is not conducive to social mobility. Urban societies are somewhat open societies where social mobility is possible. But in India rural societies are very closed in structure where social mobility is very difficult. This rigidity is being slowly loosened up through education and promotion of progressive democratic ideas.

Economic prosperity: There are three groups of people known as the poor, the middle class and the rich. Their standard of living is different. Rich people are highly respected in the society because of their prosperity. This is an inducement for the people belonging to poor and middle class to try to earn more money so as to rise to the level of the rich people. Thus, to a large extent economic prosperity influences social mobility from one group to another in the Indian society.

Industrialisation, liberalisation and globalization: Industrialisation increases social mobility because it creates employment opportunities and thereby raises the standard of living of the people. Liberalisation and globalization become the cause for social mobility because people belonging to different countries of the world come into contact with one another. The income of the people also determines social mobility. If income of the people increases, their social status and prestige also increases and such people automatically move from one social group to another.

Religion and superstition: Anything which is associated with religion becomes rigid. For example, the status of Mullah, Bishop or Pundit is ranked high because of beliefs. Social mobility is very difficult in case of people who follow unscientific religions. People who undertake pilgrimages and participate in many superstitious rituals find social mobility difficult. But scientifically interpreted religion increases social mobility.

Demographic structure: Social mobility is closely associated with diffusion of population, its size and density. Birth rate and migration of village folks towards towns and cities increase social mobility because of the open environment and better future prospects there. Thus, more and more people of the villages are migrating to towns and cities and industrial centres with a view to taking up jobs in educational and religious institutions, government services, factories and mills etc. This attitude gently promotes social mobility.

Political Factors: Political factors influence social mobility to a large extent. In fact, social mobility will increase if a person has freedom to run any business or adopt any trade and profession. A peddler, a farmer, an actor or a clerk can become the Prime Minister or Chief Minister or any Minister if he wins the election in a democratic country like India where social mobility is possible in a high degree. For example, Dev Gowda and Guntu Rao in Karnataka, M.G Ramachandran (M.G.R) and Jayalalitha in Tamil Nadu, N.T Rama Rao in Andhra Pradesh, Laloo Prasad Yadav in Bihar became the Chief Ministers. In fact, opportunities for social mobility in democratic society are greater than despotic or authoritarian society. Political equality and equal educational opportunity removes untouchability in society.

Education: Education plays a most important role in increasing social mobility. The people who receive more and more education can achieve higher and higher social status. A layman, a man of the street or clerk can become an engineer, a teacher, a lecturer or a doctor after education. Thus, his social status will automatically go up. In fact, teachers who earn less than a businessman or other industrial workers are given high social status only because of their education.

Level of aspiration: There is a direct and close relationship between the level of aspiration of the people and social mobility. Social mobility will be high in the society where people are more ambitious to raise their status. Some people are ambitious by nature and some are inspired and encouraged to achieve higher positions of status, which promotes social mobility. This ambitious or aspiration level of the people depend on the trend prevailing in the society and achievement level of certain groups. There will be no social mobility in the absence of ambitions and aspirations, and all sections of the society will be economically and socially stagnant.

Occupational status: All the occupations in the society do not get the same respect. Some professions carry higher social status and prestige in comparison to other professions. For instance, IAS, IPS officers, doctors and scientists are considered to be better than the engineers, lawyers and teachers. Hence, people engaged in occupations of lower status and prestige try to achieve occupations and positions of higher social status and prestige. This aspiration of the individual accelerates social mobility in a developing country like India.

Intelligence factor: It is seen in the modern industrialised society that the inherited positions have become less and less because the person occupying the chair cannot always give the same to his son or daughter due to his/her intelligence factor. Thus, the social position held will be changing from one generation to next. Social mobility takes place as a result of variation in the intelligence level of the people.

RELATIONSHIP BETWEEN EDUCATION AND SOCIAL MOBILITY

Education plays the most predominant role in promoting social mobility. An educated person gets recognition, position and prestige everywhere in the society. In fact, education abolishes the rigidity of social structure, removes untouchability and destroys discrimination based on birth and eradicates rigid stratification. It is true that education develops ability and capacity in the individual to gain higher social status and thereby it makes social mobility effective. Thus, education and social mobility are closely related.

- Education raises individual status in the society. An educated person receives recognition, prestige, honour and position in the society because of his education.
- Education provides employment opportunities and thereby income and standard of living of the people will be very high.
- Education brings out the latent qualities and potentialities of man and enables him to understand 'himself' and the environment surrounding him.
- Education makes the people so liberal and broad minded that they cross their caste barrier and help dismantle the caste based society.
- Education is a dynamic process through which values continuously change and new values and ideas are formed which change the criteria of social status.
- Education abolishes rigidity of social structure and removes discri- mination based on birth, sex or ethnicity. Once the bonds of social stratification are loosened, social mobility automatically goes up.
- Education motivates the people to change their occupations and earn more. When it occurs, social mobility will appear in the society.
- Higher education helps in gaining higher income. It is an important means for upward social mobility.
- Any person can occupy any position in the society with the help of education. Even a poor student can qualify for IAS, or IPS or IES and achieve a high status in society. Thus, education helps the students belonging to lower strata to attain high social position in a society.
- Mass media—the specialised branch of education has increased the rapport among the people. It is the prerequisite of all social mobility.
- Education from primary to university level is also stratified. As a result an individual will gain vertical social mobility according to his level of education.
- Those individuals who engage in research studies, inventions and discoveries are rated high in the society. The higher the academic achievement, the greater will be the social mobility.

- Different subjects have different importance and value. Subjects like engineering, medicine, and technology are rated higher in comparison with humanities (history, political science and sociology). Therefore, the person having knowledge of science gets higher social status and prestige. Hence, there is a relationship between the type of subjects and social mobility.
- Education helps the people to prepare themselves for self-employment which influences social mobility.
- All schools, colleges and universities are not equal in educational standards. Some of them are rated high by the people of the society. So, the selection of a good college or university for higher education increases social mobility. Students of such institutions of higher prestige can get jobs easily. University of Madras, Allahabad, Varanasi, Calcutta (Kolkata) and other universities in India, and Oxford and Cambridge Universities in England are famous for higher education.
- Education promotes the social status of women. Educated women achieve a high social status and prestige in the society which encourages the social mobility of the women.
- Medium of instruction in education affects social mobility. In fact, adopting regional language as a medium of instruction in school hinders spatial mobility of both teachers and students. For them, both horizontal and vertical social mobility is not within easy reach.
- Education promotes the social status of teachers belonging to the lower caste and becomes the cause for upward social mobility.
- Education breaks off shackles of caste, class or colour when people acquire higher level of education. It influences social mobility.
- Non-formal education system also plays an important role in influencing social mobility. This system of education improves the quality of people and motivates them to be involved in various services leading to social mobility.

MERITS OF SOCIAL MOBILITY

Social mobility

- Helps the individual to achieve full and wholesome development.
- Increases income and standard of living of people.
- Raises the social status and prestige of the individual.
- Helps to achieve higher position for deserving persons.
- Develops social efficiency and social progress.
- Promotes national solidarity in the face of danger.
- Leads to social and economic development.
- Instigates the individual to do their best to achieve higher social status and prestige in the society.
- Makes the society dynamic and develops positive thinking among the individuals.
- Breaks down the rigid social stratification.

DEMERITS OF SOCIAL MOBILITY

Social mobility

- Leads to disorder in rural and urban societies.
- Creates an attitude of pride and snobbery in individuals.

- Widens the gap between the haves and the have nots.
- It may create a constant discontentment among individuals with the social order.
- Develops the lust for higher income and social status which may cause people to engage in illegal activities for increasing their social status.

CONCLUSION

Today's world is more materialised, more industrialised and more competitive. As it is more dynamic as well as progressive, social mobility has become quite natural. People get education as much as possible to raise their social position. Thus, education and social mobility are going on hand-in-hand and they establish a positive relationship between them.

CHAPTER 33

EDUCATION AND SOCIAL STRATIFICATION

INTRODUCTION

We can make it clear that all people are different in society. They maybe ranked or stratified on the basis of their age. Some are old, some are young, some are adult and some are children. Further, they can be classified as rich and poor, upper caste people and lower caste people and male and female population etc. Thus, they can be ranked on the basis of age, caste, colour, sex, education, language, politics, location, culture, wealth and occupations. The ranking of people in the society on the basis of some particular charac- teristics is called **social stratification**. In other words, all societies arrange their members in terms of superiority, inferiority and equality. The vertical scale of evaluation, this placing of people in strata or layers, is social stratification. People who are in the top stratum would have more power, privilege and prestige than those who are in the low stratum.

MEANING OF SOCIAL STRATIFICATION

The word 'stratification' has been derived from the word 'strata' means 'layers'. It is like the geological layers or layers of rock. By social 'stratification' we refer to various groups or categories of people ranked in some order. For example, in a caste society like India, people are ranked or stratified on the basis of caste or class that is from higher to lower or upper to lower. The process of defining such categories is social stratifications. It is simply a process of differentiation whereby some people come to be ranked higher than others.

DEFINITIONS OF SOCIAL STRATIFICATION

Gilbert: "Social stratification is the division of society into permanent groups or categories linked with each other by the relationship of superiority and sub-ordination".

Murray: "Social stratification is a horizontal division of society into higher and lower social units".

Sutherland and Woodward: "Stratification is simply a process of differentiation whereby some people come to higher rank than others".

Kimball Young and Raymond: "In most societies people classify one another into categories, and rank these categories from higher to lower. The process of defining such categories is social stratification".

Lundbert: "A stratified society is one marked by inequality, by differences among people that are evaluated by them as being lower and higher".

Ogburn and Nimkoff: "The process by which individuals and groups are ranked in a more or less enduring hierarchy of status is known as social stratification".

Melvin M. Tumin: "Social stratification refers to arrangement of any social group or society into a hierarchy of positions that are unequal with regard to power, property, social evaluation and/or psychic gratification".

Today, by social stratification we may mean that "it is a process of grouping or ranking the people of a society based on any criteria which determines their socio-economic and political status". In other words, a stratified society is one where people are grouped or ranked as one superior to other.

SOCIAL STRATIFICATION IN INDIA

Since men differ from one another in many respects, human society is heterogeneous. Their intellectual, moral, philosophical, mental, economic, religious, political and other aspects are different. In fact, no two individuals are exactly alike. Diversity and inequality are inherent in society. Hence, human society is everywhere stratified. Social inequality is the basis of social stratification. All the constituents of social stratification namely, community, wealth, urban and rural, income, education, occupation, political power etc. which existed in the British period are very much seen now. Let us see how people have been stratified in Indian society.

Sex stratification: Sex is an important criteria on the basis of which human population is stratified in India. They are categorised as male and female population. Males are considered as superior to female. In our culture women are occupying an inferior status to men in all walks of life. This tendency is gently changing with the development of women education.

Caste stratification: Caste is the most pervasive principle governing social stratification. In fact, Indian society is a caste based society where all people are stratified on the basis of their caste. Now, in most of the villages and towns people belonging to the upper caste are considered to be having high social status and prestige whereas people belonging to the most backward, Schedule Caste and Scheduled Tribes enjoy low social status and prestige.

Religious stratification: Ours is a secular country where all religious beliefs are accepted. In this regard, religion is said to be an important criterion on the basis of which people of our country are stratified. People belonging to different religions are stratified as Hindus, Muslims, Christians, Buddhists, Jains, Sikhs etc.

Rural and urban stratification: This is another characteristic on the basis of which stratification is made. It is seen that people of our country is stratified according to the status of the place where they live. That is, total population is divided into urban and rural population. People living in cities are considered to be superior to those living in rural areas. On the basis of areawise stratification, nearly 80 per cent of our population resides in rural areas and 20 per cent in urban areas. People living in rural areas depend mainly on agriculture and allied activities and cottage industries whereas people in cities are engaged in trade, offices, educational institutions, banks, hospitals, factories etc. The standard of living of urban population is higher than that of the rural population.

Social status or social class: Social class means people are differentiated and categorised in terms of privilege, prestige, power and opportunity. The criteria by which social class is determined includes amount of education, occupation, amount of income, place of residence, kind of residence, religion and caste etc. The members of our society can be classified into three distinct classes, namely, upper class, middle class and lower class. This type of social stratification is made on the basis of wealth and annual income of the family.

Upper class: Upper class is the highest social class based on the combination of economic, legal and family factors. People belonging to this class comprise less than 5 per cent of the total population. The size of the family is small, usually consisting of the parents and one or two children. Divorce is firmly condemned among the upper class people. Their sources of income are rents, royalties, and dividends from stock market rather than salaries. They have two or three expensive cars and other vehicles. They enjoy political influence to control political organization so as to escape from heavy taxes. They receive higher monthly income and enjoy high social status. Generally, they are highly paid professionals. They do not engage in agricultural activities. Most of the youngsters belonging to this category attend college.

Middle class: People belonging to the middle class have limited resources. But they nurse aspirations for a luxurious and comfortable life like the upper class people. The middle class people are white collared workers. They live in the best residential communities and virtually all own their homes. Law, medicine, dentistry, engineering, ownership business and salaried positions enable this group to earn the top rank incomes. The size of their family is larger than that of the upper class. They give vital importance to education. Children's achievement motivation is high. Incomes from wages and salaries are moderate with one third of wives working as teachers, clerks and secretaries. Few fathers have been graduated from colleges and only a few mothers hold a college degree.

Lower class: People of lower class will have inferior social prestige. They resent the attitudes of the upper classes and avoid contact with them. The lower class people include migrant workers, slum dwellers and the poverty stricken inhabitants of rural areas. The educational achievement of parents is very low. People belonging to this category are agricultural and industrial labourers, low paid employees and daily wage earners. One third of the mothers are engaged in non-prestigious jobs outside the home and, in addition, bear heavy household burden. They often suffer from poverty, powerlessness, illiteracy, disease, hunger, superstition and exploitation of various kinds. In rural areas people of this class live in small huts. In towns and cities their homes are near the rail road track or the swampy river bank. Divorce is rare but separation and desertion are found in this class. People spend their leisure time in gambling, gossip, listening to radio, attending cheap theatres and drinking.

CRITERIA OF SOCIAL STRATIFICATION

Society has been divided into different classes at different times. In fact, different principles or criteria have been followed from time-to-time in order to determine the status of the individuals in a society. We place a person higher or lower in a status scale according to characteristics such as occupation, wealth, birth, race, religion, education, language and political powers.

Criteria of birth: The status of the individual was fixed by birth during feudal and early medieval times. There were slave and slave-master, the noble and serf. Thus, the class structure becomes rigid and integrated. As a result, social mobility is impossible. The attitude of members of each class tends to become habitual and quasi-automatic.

Criterion of wealth: The 'middle class' was responsible for revolutionising the feudal system and secured a new definition for social status in terms of wealth. Under the feudal system, the principal form of wealth was the land. Thus, the whole system of feudal relationship was based on land ownership. The idea of subservience, loyalty, duty and honour depended on the size of the land that one had. In fact, only big landlords were regarded as superior to others. But land was subordinated to the new forms of money and credit because of the progress of industrial revolution and commercial, financial and factory production enterprises. Thus, the status of individuals came to be defined in terms of wealth. Wealth penetrated all social divisions and provided a universal and significant basis for social stratification. On the basis of wealth, individuals were demarcated as upper class, middle class and lower class.

Criterion of occupation: There is an intimate relationship between the social class and the occupation it follows. Occupation indicates the status of individuals. For instance, agricultural and agriculture related occupation, industrial occupation and white collar jobs had each specific status. Thus, occupation is one of the criteria for ranking the status of individuals.

Criterion of education: Social stratification is made on the basis of education that individuals possess. The children of wealthier class can get better education while the poor youth cannot afford to meet the expenses of higher education. Here, individuals are ranked according to their education. See for instance how persons are stratified into tenth or below tenth standard, higher secondary class, degree in arts, degree in science, degree in engineering, degree in medicine, degree in law, postgraduate degrees etc.

Criterion of politics: In an aristocratic political system there was a belief that some were born to rule and others to be ruled. In every society, rulers lead a luxurious life and enjoy higher status. It is seen in democracy also that the legislators and ministers enjoy a higher prestige though some of them may even be illiterate. Thus, the individuals are stratified as ruling and non- ruling polity.

Criterion of religion: People of the society is ranked or stratified according to the religion they belong to. We can say that Indian society is stratified as Hindus, Sikhs, Muslims, Christians etc. on the basis of religions.

Criterion of caste: Our society is a caste based society where people are stratified as forward class, backward class, most backward class, Scheduled Caste and Scheduled Tribes. This system of stratification implies that people belonging to one class is superior to other classes.

Criterion of sex: On the basis of sex, the total population is stratified into male and female population by which the sex composition of people could be clearly made out.

Criterion of age: This is another criterion by which social stratification can be made. It helps to understand the size of dependent population and independent population. It is that those who are below the age of 15 and above 60 are treated as dependent population. Moreover, age groups are recognised as infancy, childhood, adolescence, adulthood and old age.

Criterion of location: People of Indian society are stratified on the basis of the place where they reside. On the basis of the dwelling area, people can be stratified into rural and urban population.

CHARACTERISTICS OF SOCIAL STRATIFICATION

M.M. Tumin has mentioned the five attributes of social stratification. Let us explain them here.

Ancient: Social stratification system is quite old. According to historical and archaeological records, stratification was present on the basis of sex and age. Differences between the rich and poor, powerful and humble, freemen and slaves existed in almost all the civilizations. Plato and Kautilya were deeply concerned with social, economic and political inequalities.

Universal: The stratification system is a worldwide phenomenon. Difference between the rich and the poor or the haves and the have-nots is evident everywhere. Stratification is very much present even in the non-literate societies.

Social: Stratification is social. It does not represent biologically caused inequalities. Statuses are distinguished on the basis of factors such as strength, intelligence, age and sex. For instance, the manager of an industry attains a dominant position not by his physical strength and age but his education, skills, experience, personality and character. Tumin has pointed out that the stratification system is intimately connected with the political, familial, religious, economic, educational and other institutions.

Diverse forms: Stratification system seems to be much more complex in the civilized societies. It has never been uniform in all societies. For example, the ancient Aryan society was stratified in two four Varnas: The Brahmins, Kshatriyas, Vaishyas and the Shudras; the ancient Greek society into freemen and slaves; the ancient Chinese society into the mandarins, merchants, the farmers and the soldiers; the ancient Roman society into two strata: the patricians and the plebians. Class, caste and income seem to be the general forms of stratification found in the modern world.

Consequential: The stratification system leads to two kinds of consequences: (i) life chances and (ii) lifestyles. Life chances refer to such things as infant mortality, longevity, physical and mental illness, childlessness, marital conflict, separation and divorce. Lifestyle implies the mode of housing, residential area, education, means of recreation, relationship between the parents and children, the kind of books, magazines, and TV shows to which one is exposed, mode of conveyance and so on. Life chances are more involuntary while lifestyle reflects differences in preferences, tastes and values.

FUNCTIONS OF SOCIAL STRATIFICATION

According to Wilbert Moore and Kingsley Davis, stratification system came to be evolved in all societies due to functional necessity. H.M. Johnson has noted certain things about the functional necessity of the stratification system.

Encourages hard work: It is known that occupations are ranked high if their functions are highly important and the demand for personnel is very high. Hard work, prolonged training and heavy burden of responsibility are associated with such occupational positions. Thus, the function of stratification is to induce people to work hard.

Ensures circulation of elites: When a high degree of prestige, comforts and other rewards are offered for certain positions, there will be some competitions for them. This process of competition helps to ensure that the most efficient people are different, and are able to rise to the top, where their ability can best be used.

Serves as economic function: Economic function helps to ensure the rational use of the available talent. It is functionally necessary to offer differential rewards if the positions at the top are largely ascribed as it is in the case of caste system. Even in the caste system, the people at the top can lose their prestige if they fail to maintain certain standards. Hence, differential rewards provide the incentives for the upper classes to work at maintaining their position.

Prevents waste of resources: The stratification system prevents the waste of scarce resources. The men in the elite class actually possess scarce and socially valued abilities and qualities. It becomes functionally beneficial for the society to make use of their talents without being wasted. For example, pouring the resources of the society into the training of doctors and engineers would be a waste if they are made to work as peons and attendants. The selection of individuals and training them for difficult positions would be a waste when there is enough manpower.

Stabilises and reinforces the attitudes and skills: More intimate relationships are mostly found between the fellow class members. Even this tendency has its own function, it tends to stabilise and reinforce the attitudes and skills that maybe the basis of upper class position. Those who have similar values and interests tend to associate comfortably with one another. Their association itself confirms their common values and interests.

Helps to pursue different professions: The values, attitudes and qualities of different classes do differ. This difference is functional for the society to some extent because society requires both manual and non-manual workers. Many jobs are not attractive to highly trained or refined people for they are socialised for certain other jobs. The influence of family and society makes the individuals imbibe certain values, attitudes and qualities which will influence their selection of jobs.

Social control: Lower class cultural characteristics are essential to the society. The classes are functional. In fact, mutual antagonism between social classes is also functional. To some extent upper class and lower class groups can act as negative reference groups for each other. Thus, they should act as a means of social control.

Controlling effect on the shady world: In the 'shady' world of gamblers and in the underworld of lower criminals, blackmarketeers, racketeers, smugglers etc., the legitimate class structure has got respectability. They know that money is not a substitute for prestige but only a compensation for renouncing it. Hence, instead of continuing in a profitable shady career, such people want to gain respectability for their money and for their children. They try to enter legitimate fields and become philanthropists and patrons of the arts. Thus, the legitimate class structure continues to attract the shady classes and the underworld. This attraction exerts a social control function.

EDUCATION AND SOCIAL STRATIFICATION

The provision of universalisation of education in the form of formal and non- formal modes of education determines the wealth, power and status of individuals, and helps bring about a new social structure in the society. Education facilitates a rapid change in the base of social stratification as it trains the people in engineering, medicine and technical skills. Thus, education is the most important instrument for bringing a change on the basis of social stratification in our Indian society. In our present day life, we often notice the fading away of the rigidity of the social stratification when an individual is educated. For instance,

- When educated women take up higher jobs or professions and draw good monthly salaries, their status will change for the better.
- It is also possible that when a rural youth completes his higher education and gains employment, he will earn more wealth or income. This atmosphere not only changes his lifestyle but also becomes a cause for change in social stratification.

- When the children of agricultural labourers from the villages receive higher education, they would get good employment. Jobs with good income lead to change in social stratification in our Indian society.
- Education improves the quality and efficiency of workers so that production could be increased and the income of the workers may be increased paving the way for social stratification changes.
- As a result of equalisation of educational opportunities, people belonging to most backward class, Schedule Caste and Scheduled Tribes get opportunities to join various courses so that they may attain better positions, such as collectors, doctors, engineers and scientists. In this way, education influences social stratification. In fact, education is the cornerstone of social and economic development, and it breaks down the rigid social stratification in our society.

CONCLUSION

Since human society is heterogeneous, people are stratified or ranked on the basis of a number of characteristics such as caste, sex, age, education, occupation, income, wealth, language, region, religion and politics. This kind of stratification is common in the Indian society. Education plays a most important role in bringing about changes in the pattern of social stratification. In fact, education increases the productivity of goods and services and income of the people, which raises their social and economic status in the society. As a result, people may shift from lower class to middle or upper class. Moreover, education prepares the lower castes to follow the religion, politics and culture of the upper castes in order to raise their social status within the caste hierarchy. In fact, education turns the poor into the rich, and sanskritises the lower castes and raises their social status. Thus, education not only reduces the inequalities found in the names of socio-economic and cultural factors but also raises the status of people belonging to lower castes. This kind of change in social stratification can be seen in the present society.

CHAPTER 34

SCHOOL AND COMMUNITY

INTRODUCTION

School is one of the most important, active, direct and formal agencies of education. The word 'school' has been taken either from the Greek word *Skhole* or Latin word *Schola* meaning 'leisure'. The history of ancient civilizations of India, Greece, China and Egypt reveals that material prosperity increased as a result of which the people belonging to the upper class found leisure time. They developed special institutions to educate themselves, and spent their leisure time profitably. The institution that developed out of surplus economy is known as **school**. In ancient India, we had schools like Guru Ashram, Gurukula, the Vihar, the Sangha, the Pathsala and the Vidhyapitha which preserved and promoted the rich cultural heritage of our country. We called school in the name of Maktabs and Madrasas during the medieval period. The modern school system developed with the advent of the British to our country.

Today, school has been used as an important instrument to preserve and strengthen the cultural heritage of our society. It also plays a very significant role in discovering and moulding the innate capacities, attitudes, habits and ideas of the children with a view to producing well-balanced personalities, who are aesthetically rich, culturally refined, emotionally stable, mentally alert, morally good, physically strong, socially efficient and spiritually enlightened. Thus, it aims at a comprehensive programme for the physical, intellectual, moral, religious, cultural, aesthetic, social, vocational, domestic and recreational needs of the children to bring about their all-round development.

MEANING AND DEFINITIONS OF SCHOOL

School is a place where teachers, under a preplanned curriculum and examination system, provide specific doses of knowledge and experiences to the children (students) under a fixed timetable. Once this process is over, students are evaluated by examination to certify the degree of success that they achieved from the school. The word 'school' has been defined by different thinkers, educationists and sociologists in different ways.

John Dewey: "School is a special environment where a certain quality of life and certain types of activities and occupations are provided with the object of securing the child's development along desirable lines".

Ottaway: "School may be regarded as a social invention to serve society for the specialized teaching of young".

J.S. Ross: "Schools are institutions developed by civilized man for the purpose of aiding in the preparation of the young to be well-adjusted and efficient members of the society".

K.G. Saiyidain: "The school is a centre of vigorous life. It is in direct intimate contact with the realities of life around, reflecting the best and worthiest of its features which are simple enough to appeal to the child".

CHARACTERISTICS OF SCHOOLS

- It is a special environment for teaching–learning process.
- It is an institution by which direct contact between educators and educands is created.
- It provides life related activities and experiences to students that make the quality of life better.
- It develops the child along a desirable line with the help of social activities and experiences.
- It establishes civilized societies by preparing young children and adults to get adjusted in the society.
- It makes the students efficient and productive members of the society.
- It imparts knowledge to all students regardless of their caste, religion, sex, place, economic conditions etc.
- It works on the lines of the general welfare of the people.
- The role of school and its aims change with the change and demand of time.
- It is a social institution established by the society for the society. Its fundamental character is determined by the society.

NEED AND IMPORTANCE OF SCHOOL

Growth of knowledge: Knowledge is growing very fast due to the growth of researches, inventions and discoveries in modern times. The fast growth of knowledge should be preserved, transmitted and promoted from one generation to the other in order to strengthen our cultural heritage. In this regard, schools and colleges perform their functions very effectively.

Enhances the life of people: People are unable to spare time for social work (NSS, NCC, RCS, Scout etc.) because they become busy in their economic and political activities. Therefore, schools and colleges are necessary to carry out various kinds of social work.

Vocational and technical knowledge: Only a specialised and fully trained person can perform the job of spreading vocational and technical knowledge to increase the productivity of our nation. Hence, schools and colleges are required to produce persons of special knowledge in scientific, technical and agricultural fields.

Mass education: Education is the birthright of all citizens. It is not the privilege of the rich and the well to do or upper class people. It should be provided to all citizens irrespective of their ethnicity, culture, race or sex etc. Hence, an organized system of education is necessary in schools and colleges to fulfil this purpose.

Bridges family and society: The values and ideals taught to children in the family are practised in the society through the schools first. The child comes in contact with so many children belonging to different families. He learns new values and ideals. It is the school that should prepare the child to accept only those values and ideas which are useful.

Special environment: To face the modern needs and challenges of the society, we have to prepare the child for specialised jobs. For this purpose, schools provide special environments in a preplanned and a well-organized manner.

Harmonious development: School is the most important organization which brings about harmonious development in the child by inculcating intellectual, physical, moral, spiritual and social values.

Cultural pluralism: School develops the emotions of sympathy, cooperation, tolerance, respect for others etc., among children belonging to different culture, creed, caste, place and economic status. It is possible in the school where they learn to mix up with each other in a friendly manner to achieve the common goals.

Citizenship training: Schools are the best place to train children for an ideal citizenship. They learn their rights and duties, social norms, political values and ethics through various activities and experiences.

Economic and social significance: It is the duty of the school to prepare the children to earn their living after education. Moreover, the child develops social qualities through the school.

Place for learning: The school atmosphere is conducive for learning because of its preplanned physical and social environments. It is a place where co-curricular and extra-curricular activities are organized so that the child learns better. The progress of learning can be facilitated with the assistance of pedagogue.

Cheap education: School reduces the cost of education and wastage of time by providing education to a large number of children collectively.

Finds solutions to social problems: School is important to discuss and find solutions for various social problems like population growth, casteism, communalism, AIDS, environmental problems and the need for secularism, national integration and international understanding in the modern world.

FUNCTIONS OF SCHOOL

School is the most important institution which makes the society rich in all aspects. Its functions are very useful to mankind to lead a fruitful life. Let us discuss some important functions of school:

Develops mental power: The first function of school is to develop the mental powers of the child so that he is able to think freely, clearly and logically. The mental faculties of the child are developed in school through knowledge, activities and experiences. School performs this function according to the interests, abilities and needs of the children.

Cultivates dynamic and adaptable mind: The second function of school is to cultivate a dynamic and an adaptable mind. Such mind is resourceful and is able to create new values for future life. It is seen that the physical and social environment is fraught with dangers for living organisms. Humans are always taught to be ready for the struggle for survival. In this regard, school makes their lives easy, adaptable and useful to the environment.

Conservation and transmission of social life: Maintaining the continuity of social life is one of the important functions of the school. This function can be performed by transmitting the traditions, experiences, values, beliefs and customs of the society from one generation to the other, through the medium of education.

Promotion of culture and civilization: It is the duty of the school to promote culture and civilization. The school trains children in such a manner that they enrich and modify their cultural heritage through their participation. It helps in the establishment of a better and a happier society. Prof. D.J.O. Cannon says, "If each generation had to learn for itself what has been learned by its predecessors, no sort of intellectual or social development would be possible and the present state of society would be little different from the society of the old stone age". In this way school performs the function of continuous reorganizing and reconstructing of human experiences for the promotion of culture and civilization.

Physical developments: Physical development is essential for mental and intellectual development. This function is performed by the school by means of games and sports, gymnastics and co-curricular activities such as NSS, NCC etc. Thus, school helps the children to use their energy for constructive work and accomplishes the famous dictum of "a sound mind in a sound body".

Moral development: The school develops moral values and provides capable citizens to the society. As a result of it, people can eradicate immorality and recreate the faith of the people in moral values. This performance has become an important function of the school in modern times.

Spiritual development: Religious education has been an integral part of general education taught at schools and colleges. Man is different from beast and his soul will remain as the ultimate reality. School makes him think about the purpose of his existence on this earth. Schools bring about spiritual development by conducting prayers and religious functions.

Emotional development: The school develops human qualities lying dormant in the child. It fosters in the child the feelings of love, cooperation, honesty, truthfulness, respect for one another. Thus, it trains the child to control his emotion so that his behaviour may remain balanced.

Vocational development: The school provides that education and training to the child which makes him self-reliant and enables him to stand on his own feet and helps him get employment after education. In the words of John Dewey, "We send children to school to learn in a systematic way the occupations which constitute living". The development of vocational education and training prepares the child to be professionally competent. In order to perform this function, the school includes several programmes and activities like work experience and vocational subjects. Gandhi has stated that true education ought to be a kind of insurance against unemployment.

Social efficiency: The promotion of social efficiency is necessary in modern democratic society. Therefore, the child should be trained for effective participation in democratic government. Cultivation of a balanced sense of rights and duties is an important function of the school. To perform this function effectively, the school should have a clear concept of democratic ideals and then direct the educational programme, accordingly.

Reconstruction of society: Society is always changing as time changes. As a result, a number of new problems are created and solved. In this way a society is reconstructed. Schools actively participate in the reconstruction of society by solving various problems such as illiteracy, ignorance, environmental conservation, poverty, family welfare programme etc. Proper education enables the students to criticise evils or social problems and find solutions. As a result, certain modification and reconstruction take place in the social life.

Leadership quality: School trains the leaders of tomorrow. In fact, schools train the students to understand their role in society and enable them to make proper use of their rights and duties. They also foster the leadership quality in the children to lead in all socio-political spheres. The children get training for leadership in schools by taking leadership in various co-curricular activities. Such leadership helps them to become leaders of our country in future.

Higher values of life: The inculcation of higher values through moral and religious education has been the responsibility of school in recent times. Joint family system is degrading and religious institutions are losing their hold over the people. It is, therefore, the role of the school to develop in the children a sense of true appreciation of truth, goodness and beauty.

Character formation: Life has become busy today due to social or political or economic activities. As a result of it, parents may not find time to look after their children. Some parents maybe illiterate and ignorant and may fail to mould the character of their child. It is the school which takes this responsibility and special attention is given to build the character of the child on ethical or social lines.

Modification of child behaviour: Many delinquents and truants are moulded in schools. The ideals of the teacher modify the behaviour of the child. Thus, it is school that brings about desirable changes in children and makes them acceptable to the family and the society.

Develops secularism: School is an important place where the feeling of secularism is developed among the children of different faiths and beliefs. For this purpose, school celebrates all religious festivals and organizes cultural programmes so as to inculcate in the students respect for all religions. They should learn that "God is Love" and "Love is God". Religious leaders are invited to the school to deliver special talks on the important aspects of different religions. Moreover, school arranges programmes in which students are encouraged to take part and develop a secular feeling. Such programmes develop love, sympathy, friendship, tolerance among the students. These qualities are essential to form a secular country.

National integration: The school develops in the children feelings of national integration through the curriculum, the co-curricular and extra-curricular activities. In order to perform this function, school celebrates national days, national leader's days, various religious festivals and organizes cultural programmes, exhibition, study tours etc.

International understanding: School prepares the children for world citizenship. It is the school that teaches the necessity of international understanding through inculcating the fact that no country in the world can stand alone. For developing international understanding the school encourages the students to learn foreign languages and culture, celebrates international days (ILO, WHO etc.) anniversary days of international leaders, celebrates independence days of foreign countries, organizes international tours etc.

Post-school adjustability: A child spends more than a decade of his life in school. After completing his school education, he has to adjust himself with the society outside the school to the best of his knowledge and capacity. So, one of the functions of the school is to turn out of its portals such young men and women as may adjust themselves with their social groups and lead successful lives. Prof. Brown remarks, "The school has a direct responsibility of preparing the individual child for post school adjustments". In the words of John Dewey, "We send children to school to learn in a systematic way the occupations which constitute living".

Spirit of cooperation: School performs this function through developing an environment of cooperation and harmony among the staff members. As a result, students also imbibe the attitude of cooperation among themselves and foster it in their social life. In the words of S. Balakrishna Joshi, "A well conducted school is a happy home, a sacred shrine, a social centre, a state in miniature form and bewitching Brindavan, all beautifully blended into a systematic structure".

COMMUNITY

The word 'community' is the combination of two words 'Com' and 'Munis'. While 'Com' means 'together', 'Munis' means 'To serve'. Hence, community means to serve together. The term "community" is frequently mixed up with caste, religion, class, profession, language, etc. As a result of this erroneous usage, we come across phrases such as the Brahmin community, the Muslim community, the Hindu community, the Christian community, the teacher community, the student community, the urban community etc. Some people use the term 'society' and 'community' as synonyms in both oral and written communication. This usage is also erroneous. In fact, "society" is an abstract concept that elucidates the network of social relations. Community is a concrete concept that manifests this abstract notion. Society is an abstract concept; a group of individuals is not called a society. Social relations are the basis of society; society is the network of human relations. Community is a concrete social organization constituting a group of individuals located in a specific geographical area. The members of this group have a common lifestyle, language, objectives and occupations. It is a cluster of people living within a small area and sharing a common way of life to a considerable extent.

Definitions of Community

K. Davis: "A community is the smallest territorial group that can embrace all aspects of social life".

Ginsberg: "By community is to be understood a group of social beings living a common life including all the infinite variety and complexity of relations which result from common life or constitute it".

Ogburn and Nimkoff: "A community may be thought of as the total organization of social life within a limited area".

MacIver and Page: "Whenever the members of any group, small or large, live together in such a way that they share, not this or that particular interest, but the basic conditions of a common life, we call the group a community".

Bogardus: "A community is a social group with some degree of "we feeling" and living in a given area".

Ottaway: "A community is everybody—adults and children, social and non-social persons living in a certain territory where all share a mode of life".

Brownell: "By community is meant a small diversified group of people, male and females with different skills and abilities living together as kin— neighbours".

Alvin Good: "A community is a primary group resulting from social contacts, largely direct of those residing in a small area".

Technically, community is a group of people either living together on a geographical place of land or tied with each other with common ideals and ways of living to achieve the common objectives. A community maybe big or small depending on the number of people joining the group ranging from four or five persons to hundreds. Thus, villages, towns, cities, Muslims, Hindus, Christians, Buddhists, Jainists, Sikhs, Indians, Americans, Europeans, Russian, British, consumers, producers are all communities in their circles.

Characteristics of Community

Definite geographical area: The word community is applicable to the people living in a particular geographical area. It evolves a sense of belonging among the members. Hence, residence in a particular territory is an essential characteristic of a community.

Human group: A community is a concrete concept. So, it is a definite human group. The term can be applied only to that human group which occupies a particular geographical area.

Common culture: The beliefs, customs, style of life—dietary habits, housing— are common.

Common language: This human group occupying a specific geographical area has a common language used by all its members.

Sense of identity: The members of this human group exhibit a clear sense of identity or oneness which helps to strengthen the feeling of belonging to a particular community.

Common ideals and aspirations: This human group shares common ideals and aspirations and consequently, the members also have similar goals of life.

RELATIONSHIP BETWEEN SCHOOL AND COMMUNITY

School is an important place for educational process, which is established by the community. A good school cannot function in isolation. It has to develop a close link with the community in which it is located by relating its programme to the community service. Therefore, there is a close relationship between school and community. Franklin is of the opinion that there is a two-way traffic between the school and the community. The community conveys its problems to the school for guidance and solution. School analyses the problems and feeds back the searched out, experimented knowledge to the community. A community lags behind in development if it does not get feedback process from its school as guidance and probable solutions. Thus, the school and the community are closely related. They are mutually interdependent upon each other for their progress.

IMPACT OF SCHOOL ON COMMUNITY

School has a great influence on community. Let us discuss them here.

Fulfil needs of community: The community has its own needs which changes the form of the school. The school moulds and transforms its activities so as to meet or fulfil the needs of community in political, social, economic and other spheres of life. It is because school is the centre of the community life.

Problems of community: School identifies the problems of community and tries to find solutions to the problems. It also conveys the earned knowledge together with the conclusions of experiments as tentative solutions to the problems of the community.

Culture of community: Each community has its own cultural heritage. School preserves this cultural heritage and develops and transmits the same from one generation to the other. For this purpose, the school organizes various activities which enable the children to understand and practise the cultural values of the community.

Standard of living of community: The standard of living of a community is determined by the styles and standard of living of individuals. School improves the standard of living which influences the whole community. Education improves the skills and ability of children. As a result, economic growth and standard of living will go up. Thus, school plays an important role in determining the standard of living of a community.

Vocational and industrial progress of community: School influences the vocational and industrial efficiency of a community. School prepares the children to be self-reliant and economically well-off by providing training in crafts or modern techniques of production.

Citizens of community: Children of a community receive education from the school. They are greatly influenced by the philosophy of the school and its aims and curriculum. More and more children receive education and become useful citizens which raise the greatness of the community.

Reformation of values of community: The school conveys to children the aim, ideals and values of the community. Children mould and purify ideals and values by their own practice and experimentation. Then they feed them back to the community which reforms and inspires itself in the light of that feedback from the schools.

Bringing change in community: Every community needs progressive change and reformation according to the changes in times and circumstances. To achieve such changes, it is necessary to change the minds of children. In this regard, school provides the directions to bring about changes in children.

Reconstruction of community: School plays an important role in the reformation and reconstruction of a community. It is school where the blind beliefs, useless customs, traditions and harmful doctrines prevalent in the community are critically examined and reconstructed, in the light of new aims, ideals and values, according to the changing circumstances.

Policy of state: The school criticises and evaluates the policy of government and tries to improve the administration and change the policies to suit the welfare of the individuals and the state. Moreover, schools send their representatives to the legislatures and parliament. In this way, the school influences the policy of the state to a great extent.

Environment of community: A school is able to build neat, healthy and controlled environment. It becomes an example for a community to follow and provide the same environment for all the members of the community.

IMPACT OF COMMUNITY ON SCHOOL

A community establishes schools for the fulfillment of its needs. Therefore, it wields a great influence on schools. We may discuss them here for a vivid understanding.

Ideals and traditions of community on schools: Each community has its own ideals, traditions and cultural values. These values should be transmitted and developed from generation-to-generation. A community opens schools to perform this task. The school provides activities and experiences to the children in order that they inherit the cultural heritage and lead the community to the higher levels of development.

Impact of community on schools: The needs, problems, cultural heritage and religious beliefs of a community exert a powerful impact upon schools. The development of the community depends on the education which the people receive in schools. According to time and situations, the needs of a community may change and they also change the philosophy, aims, curriculum and methods of teaching to suit the community. These changes are reflected in schools also.

Values of community on schools: The good and bad factors of a community directly influence the working of schools. Evils like corruption, drinking, smoking etc., prevalent in a community, are found to have their impact upon school life. At the same time, the good values of a community purify school life and influence the attitudes, character and behaviour of the teachers and students.

Economic impact of community on schools: The economic impact of industrial revolutions on craze for advertisement and new inventions influence the school to a great extent. In fact, such revolutionary changes have brought significant changes in the aims, curriculum and methods of teaching. It is also seen that a greater demand for more vocational, technical, professional, agricultural and other types of education promote the earning capacity of the individuals. Thus, the economic conditions of a community have a great influence on schools.

Political set-up of community on schools: The political set-up of a community directly influences the schools. It is because the political setup of a nation determines the educational setup of schools. In a totalitarian setup, education is centralised. A school inculcates the ideals of unquestioning obedience, absolute loyalty, rigid and controlled discipline in order to develop the sense of duty, devotion, service and sacrifice to the state. On the other hand, under a democratic set-up education is decentralized. Schools promote self-discipline, free growth and development according to one's interests, aptitudes and natural tendencies. In short, in a totalitarian setup, schools suppress the individuality of children by indoctrinating their minds to dance according to the tunes of the State. On the contrary in a democratic set-up, schools respect the individuality of a child. They provide a clean, conducive and progressive environment for children's development to the fullest extent.

COLLABORATION: SCHOOL AND COMMUNITY

Education is a life-long social process and it can become active only in the community. Educational process is not possible without its base, the community. This is because a school has an important place in the educational process, desired and promoted by the community. It reveals that there is a close relationship between school and community. In fact, both school and community are dependent on each other for their existence and development. That is, the school and the community influence each other. It is the school which reflects the ideal life of the community whereas the community serves as a laboratory for the children to test the knowledge and skills learnt in the school. In this way, a good community is formed from good schools and good schools are formed from good communities. It is said in the report of the Ministry of Education, "A good school cannot function in isolation. It has to develop a close link with the community in which it is located by relating its programme to community service". That is why, John Dewey remarks "School is a miniature society". Today school is not only a miniature of the society, but it is also a mirror of the society which reflects the programme of the community. The following are ways and means through which a cordial relationship between school and community can be established to make the school a centre of community life, to bring about reforms in education and community life and to make educational programmes popular. Let us see the cooperation between school and community under two headings:

- Community in school
- School in community

Community in School

- We should understand the problems of community. The problems should be studied in order to bring the community nearer to schools. Students should be made perceptive to these problems and they would find solutions for the same. This would increase the stature of the school in the eyes of community and they would appreciate such awareness on the part of the school. In this way, mutual cooperation between community and school can be increased.

- Teacher's Association should be established. Its meetings should be conducted in the school from time-to-time. The guardians of the children should be intimated about the progress and performance of their wards through this association. Thus, the association helps to exchange the views between the teacher and the parents and find solutions for the problems of students. The teachers reveal their interests in the child. Thus, cooperation between the two is established.
- Parents day should be celebrated in the schools. During this occasion parents should be invited and welcomed to the school. This would create co-operation between the community and the school.
- School should invite eminent people and specialists in various fields belonging to the community or employment officers in order to provide vocational knowledge and directions to the students. The students should be encouraged to select the vocation according to their interests. It increases the cooperation between the community and schools.
- School should use the services of retired professionals like doctors to give knowledge related to health, educationists to provide knowledge related to subjects, social reformers to acquaint students with social evils, military men to explain about NCC to the students. In this way retired professionals can be utilised for the benefit of the students. It would strengthen the relation between the school and eminent members of the community.
- School can provide its building, furniture and playgrounds etc. to the community for public programmes—such as cultural programmes, fairs, debates, marriages, adult education, distance education, polling booth, shelter during emergencies like, flood, earthquake, tsunami etc. The school can also provide its grounds for games, sports, meetings etc. This increases the relationship between the community and the school.
- The school should invite the leaders and members of the community to its various cultural programmes, celebrations, games and sports etc. This attitude can create friendliness between the school and the community.
- School should act as the centre of community life. In this regard, it should organize adult education programmes, sewing and embroidery classes, screening of films, literary and medical camps during holidays for the benefit of the community. It would develop the spirit of cooperation between the two.
- School should also organize entertainment programmes like debate, drama, music, dance, skit, competitions, exhibitions etc. for the community. In this way, a school develops and transmits our culture and strengthens its cooperation with the community.
- School may provide facilities of library and reading room liberally to the community. Books and journals can be given to the members of the community to develop their reading habits. It opens an avenue to build cooperation between the community and schools.
- School should invite the leaders and members of the community during seminars, science exhibitions, NSS, NCC etc. organized by it. It would increase their interest in the field of education and the school would get an effective cooperation.
- The school should give due representation to the members of the community in its managing committees. It would increase their direct participation in schools, and they can provide suggestions for further development of the school. In this way, community establishes a better cooperation with the schools.

School in Community

- The school should send its teachers and students into the community to study its social, economic, political and religious situations. It strengthens the contact between the school and the community.
- The school should send its teachers to the residence of the students so that teachers learn about the individual students—their strengths and weaknesses and provide special attention in educating them. It also creates the opportunity to exchange views about the students with their guardians. This leads to a happy atmosphere between the school and the community.
- The school should take part in the various social, religious and cultural programmes organized by the community as fairs, festivals and marriages. As a result of this participation, cooperation between the school and the community is developed and their relationship is strengthened.
- The school engages in community services such as cleanliness, building of roads, afforestation, harvesting, adult education and help during droughts, flood, earthquake and tsunami. Through these activities the school fulfils a few objectives of the community. This builds the relation of the school closely with the community.
- The school conducts educational tours to the places of historical, natural, religious, industrial, scientific and educational importance in the community. It would give knowledge about the community and what it does, and what we should do for it. In this way a relationship is built between the two.
- The school provides knowledge and entertainment to the students by presenting educational and cultural programmes in the community. It would help to solve the prevalent problems of the community.
- The school can organize cultural programmes in the community to infuse the spirit of patriotism during national emergencies.
- During natural calamities such as floods, droughts, epidemics, tsunami and earthquake the school collects funds and provides medical facilities and financial assistance and awakens the spirit of cooperation.
- A school may adopt a village and organize programmes of cleanliness, afforestation, building of roads, healthy environment, literacy movement etc. It leads to an all-round development of the village and strengthens the relationship between the school and the adopted village (community).
- The school can make available free books, notes and uniforms to the backward and poor children. This activity attracts the community towards the school.
- School can help with the inherent maladies of the community by organizing NSS, NCC Red Cross society, Scouts and camps.
- School can make use of community resources such as library, museums, art galleries, places of pilgrimages, historical places, trade, industry, agriculture, banks, post office etc. to educate its students in a practical way. In this way, school and community can build better relationship.

ABSENCE OF RELATIONSHIP BETWEEN SCHOOL AND COMMUNITY IN INDIA

The gulf between the school and community is widening more and more. Both are incapable of fulfilling the obligations towards the development of the individual and progress of the community. Let us see the cause for the absence of relationship between the school and the community.

Causes of Absence Relating to Schools

- The aims of Indian education are more comprehensive. Moreover, objectives of education are changing and growing as time changes. As a result, objectives are indefinite and they fail in their mission.
- Indian schools do not fulfil the needs of the community.
- Indian schools do not help in the progress and development of the community.
- Teachers do not discharge their obligation.
- The problems of a community become the concern of the school only in principle. But practically Indian schools are unconcerned and indifferent to these problems.
- The growing indiscipline in school keeps the community away from them.
- The increasing number of educated unemployed population plagues the welfare of the community. They become the cause for social evils.
- The growth of English medium schools changes the social environment which is far removed from the expectations of the community where it functions.
- The present school aims at generating profit and produces a non- service minded generation, which minimises its contact with the community.
- School provides education to the children and issues certificates on payment of huge amounts.
- The quality of the school and its relationship with the community largely depends on the quality of teachers who work in it. Both are declining qualitatively due to various reasons. As a result, the school is losing its respect in the community.
- Indian schools are quite indifferent towards the community. Hence, there is a gap between the school and community.

Causes of Absence Relating to Community

Lack of education: Most of the members of Indian community are illiterate and ignorant regarding the functions of schools. They keep themselves away from the school thinking that the school is a government institution and that they need not cooperate in its development.

Poverty: India is a country where most of the members of the community are extremely poor. They are not able to fulfil their own essential needs. Hence, they are not able to pay even the meagre expenses for the education of their children.

Traditions: The British government created the gulf between the school and the community. This atmosphere makes most of the members of the community afraid even to enter the school campus. We see this among the village people in general and the illiterate in particular.

Lack of interest: It is common to all whether the members of the community are poor or rich and literate or illiterate. They do not have any interest in the development of schools. It is a pity that even the rich and educated members of the community keep themselves off the school and its activities.

Rules and regulations: The educational rules and regulations formulated by the managements inhibit voluntary community participation in school life. For example, in our country, caste and religion oriented schools do not permit others to take interest in the working of the school.

However, the school has become an integral part of the community life and the community has become the mainstay of school life. M.P. Muffat says, "The school is an important social agency and will play an even greater part in the future of community. An informed and interested public can assist in meeting the problems and needs of both our schools and community". Thus, the existence of school and community would be secured only with mutual cooperation. This mutual relationship is necessary to achieve the social and economic progress of our nation.

MEANING OF COMMUNITY SCHOOL

A community school is a community centred, child centred, mini society which prepares the children for community development. We can explain the term 'community school' in a comprehensive way as "A community school is a school which is directly related to the life of the community, whose aim is to bring about the comprehensive and best possible development of the community in which it is located, whose curriculum conforms to the needs and life of its community, which functions as a centre of community activities, which makes use of the resources of the community for its own development, and which employs its own human as well as material resources for the development of the community". This type of school is called **Community School**.

The conception of community school has emerged due to innovations in the field of education in modern times. Education is a social process and a means of social progress and development. It is linked with the life of society and community. Community school means that it is a school which develops the characteristics of the community in the children and prepares them for social progress.

Characteristics of Community School

- It educates the children about the development and proper use of the resources of the community.
- It serves for the entire community.
- It functions as the agent of the community and for the welfare of the community.
- It creates a suitable school environment.
- It is a life-centred school.
- Its buildings, equipment, apparatus, playground, library are constructed in such a manner that children, youth and adults can be given experiences.
- It has faith in change.
- It provides services to the students in the school and conforms to the needs of the community.
- It prepares and develops instructional materials suited to its needs.
- It makes its curriculum flexible and comprehensive with a view to fulfilling the objectives of the community.
- It adopts a democratic behaviour pattern in the relationship between students and teachers, and between teachers and administrators.
- It adopts modern techniques of education.
- It is an integral part of the community and it cannot be separated from the society.
- It strives for bringing about reforms in the community.
- It uses human and physical resources.
- The attitude of its teachers is liberal and democratic.
- It provides adequate opportunities to all members of the community to provide them learning experiences, and it cooperates with all other related agencies.

However the differences between a traditional and a community school can be seen in Table 34.1.

TABLE 34.1 Difference Between Traditional and Community School

Subjects	Traditional School	Community School
Aim	Passing examinations and child's development	Progress in community life. Development of both community and individual life.
Curriculum	A few traditional subjects on the basis of traditional knowledge.	Flexible, based on the community's needs, interests and capacities. Central place given to community experiences and activities related to life.
Teaching methods	Lectures, discussions, debates and other methods suited to particular subjects.	Principle of activity and social experience project method, problem-solving method.
Teachers living	Professionals	Professional and specialists within the community.
Development	Related to child's intellectual development	Concerned with the development of the entire community.
Management	Government or private managing committee or bodies. Buildings, materials etc. of Government or private bodies.	Management by the whole community. Use of the entire materials and human resources of the community.
Discipline	Imposed from outside	Cooperative discipline, democratic atmosphere prevailing in the school.

Programmes of Community Schools

Knowing the community: A community school should get knowledge of the social, economic, political, religious and cultural situation of the community.

This helps to bring about reforms in the community life and for the best development of the community. A community school gets knowledge of the physical and human resources of the community so as to use them in education. The physical and human resources such as public service institutions, industrial institutions, historical places and buildings, museums, local geographical environment, social institutions, population, health services, customs, standard of living, diverse occupations, agriculture, forest resources, minerals, transportation and residential facilities, scientific and technical places, informed agencies of radio, television, press, religious institutions, family, state journals and family situation etc., are used in order to bring about the maximum development in the community.

Plan: Community school prepares a plan to execute its programmes so that it may achieve the objectives through the medium of available resources. It brings about changes in the curriculum, co-curricular activities, teacher's behaviour and administration. It starts the plan to bring the community into the school and school into the community through co-curricular activities.

Implementation: A coordination committee is formed to implement the community school plan. The committee determines the constitution, membership, system of working and posts of officials. All classes of the community take part in the committee to implement the programme successfully. The school leads to the all-round development of the child and gives the community every type of help.

In this way mutual relations between school and community become more and more cordial. In fact, we cannot live as a lonely island in the community. School would have to become a community centre for the service of the community.

CONCLUSION

School and community are the sides of a coin, which serve as the most important sources of education. They are closely related to each other and inter-dependent for their existence and development. In fact, the role of school and community is important in bringing about an all-round personality development in the child. School is an effective formal agency which educates the child to achieve intellectual, moral, cultural and physical development. On the other hand, community is an informal agency that also educates the child to make him fit for society. Thus, school and community act together in educating the child differently. But they aim at both, in man making and society making.

CHAPTER 35

EDUCATION AND SOCIAL CHANGE

INTRODUCTION

The world is dynamic in nature. Hence, change is the eternal law of nature and the law of life. Whenever there is a change, there is life. Thus, there is a close relationship between natural life and change. The ancient Greek philosopher Heraclites has said that we cannot dive in the same water of the river twice, because by the time we come out of the river after diving, the water would have moved forward with its flow. We do not know what would be the form of change in the next moment because nothing is permanent in this world; whatever was being seen yesterday, is not to be seen today and what we see today, may not be seen in the succeeding days. We, therefore, can conclude that nothing is permanent in the dynamic world except change.

MEANING OF SOCIAL CHANGE

The concept of social change came into being with the publication of W.F. Ogburn's book *Social Change* in 1922. Social means concerning the society and change means deviation from the existing pattern. Thus, social change is the combination of 'social' and 'change' meaning change in the structure and functions of the human society. This changing process maybe rapid in some societies and slow in others, but no society in the world can escape from change. In our Indian society, the things that we use today the different types of machines, gadgets, vehicles of transport, medicine, computer, television, cell phone and other entertainment devices were never even dreamt of by our forefathers. Human beings are now confronting new problems and challenges in all fields of life and the human mind is endeavouring to find solutions for them through researches, investigations and up-to-date inventions.

In fact, the styles of living are changing fast today. So, it is difficult to keep pace with the changing ideas, beliefs, lifestyles and material pursuits for human welfare. Such changes in social structure are known as social change. Any alteration, difference or modification that takes place in a situation or in an object through time can be called **change**. The term 'social change' is used to indicate the changes that take place in human interactions and inter-relations. Thus, a social change is the change that occurs in the social structure and social relations. The process of social change can be depicted as:

Change in the experiences of individuals

↓

Change in the attitude of individuals

↓

Change in the thought pattern of individuals

↓

Change in the social interactions

↓

Change in social relations
(social change)

↓

Change in the social structure

FIGURE 35.1 Process of social change.

Thus, social change refers to the alteration in the pattern of social organization or activity. The following examples indicate the concept of social change:

- Highly educated parents like to have only one child.
- The craze for foreign degrees and courses induces the foreigners to start their courses in our country.
- The establishment of university for women encourages women to undertake research studies.
- The unemployed husband of employed wife looks after domestic work and the child at home.
- Social institutions like schools are changing into commercial institutions or money-making industries.

DEFINITIONS OF SOCIAL CHANGE

Sociologists of different places and times have defined the term 'social change' differently which make the concept yet more clear.

M.E. Jones: "Social change is a term used to describe variations or modifications of any aspects of social process, social interaction or social organization".

Kingsley Davis: "By social change is meant only such alterations as occur in social organization, that is, structure and functions of society".

MacIver and Page: "Social change is a process responsive to many types of changes, to change in the man-made condition of living, to change in the attitudes and beliefs of men, and to the changes that go beyond human control to the biological and the physical nature of things".

B. Kuppuswamy: "Social change is the change in social behaviour and social structure, norms, roles, cultural values and personality of individuals".

Harry Johnson: "Social change maybe defined as modification in the ways of doing and thinking of the people".

Fairchild: "Social change means variations or modifications in any aspect of social process, patterns or forms".

Gillin and Gillin: "Social changes are variations from the accepted modes of life whether due to alterations in geographic conditions, in cultural equipment, composition of the population or ideologies and whether brought about by diffusion or invention within the group".

Morris Ginsberg: "By social change I understand a change in social structure, in the size of society, the composition or balance of its parts, of the type of its organization".

Miller: "Social change refers to a pattern of social relationship in a given social setting, which exhibits changes over some definite period of time".

Listerward: "Social change is related to change in social aims and aspirations of the individuals".

S.P. Ruhela: "Social change implies changes in social attitudes, behaviour, customs, habits, manners, relations and values of people, in social institutions and structures in the ways or styles of living".

Mazumdar: "Social change may be defined as a new fashion or mode, either modifying or replacing the old, in the life of people or in the operation of a society".

From the above definitions, we may conclude that social change refers to the modifications which take place in the life patterns of people. In other words, it means variations of any aspects of social process, social patterns, social interactions or social organization. It is a change in the institutional and normative structure of society. Today, the term "social change" has become a very common and comprehensive concept. This is because it is an endless and rapid process of inclusion of all changes occurring in individual as well as social life. Therefore, we may define it thus, "Social change is process of any variation whether desirable or not in the existing social structure, social behaviour and cultural values occurring as a consequence of the explosion of scientific and technical knowledge followed by new inventions and discoveries".

SOCIAL CHANGE AND CULTURAL CHANGE

According to the famous sociologists namely Brown, Gillin and Gillin, Chopin, Spencer, Listerward, Malinowski, Ogburn and Ruth Benedict, there is no difference between social change and cultural change. For them both are same and interrelated in the sense that cultural change is an important part of social change. In the words of Brown, "Social and cultural changes are the same thing, cultural change is a sizeable part of social change". But some sociologists are of the view that social change and cultural change are not the same in meaning. These are different from each other. The distinction between social change and cultural change can be explained with the help of an example. Previously, untouchability was in vogue in our country. Upper caste and lower caste were different from each other and they could not live together. They used separate wells to draw water and temples to worship. But today people belonging to all the castes sit together at public places, travel together in trains and buses, study together in schools, college and universities, work together in offices, banks, factories, educational institutions etc. The relation between the upper class and untouchables comes under social change. Cultural change takes place when caste differences totally disappear and even matrimonial relations start taking place.

The term "cultural change" according to Kingsley Davis, "embraces all changes occurring in any branch of culture including art, science, technology, philosophy etc. as well as changes in the forms and rules of social organization". Thus, cultural change is broader than social change and social change is only a part of it. All social changes are cultural changes, but all cultural changes need not necessarily be social changes. Cultural changes can be called social changes only when they affect human relations and the social organizations and cause some variation in them. For instance, changes in the musical styles, painting styles, rules of writing poetry and drama, pronunciation of words etc. represent cultural changes. These are cultural changes and they cannot be called social changes because they do not affect the existing pattern of human interactions, social system and social organization. But the rise of organized labour in the capitalistic society and the introduction of communism in place of democracy represent social change. These two changes may cause a series of changes in human relations and social organization. They represent a basic alteration of relationship between the employer and employee and the rulers and the ruled. Thus, cultural change is broader than the social change.

Social change is the change that takes place in social structures and social relations. But cultural change is the change, which occurs in the way of life of the people. In the words of Mc Gee, "Cultural change refers to the changes in the normative, cognitive or material culture". The examples of cultural changes are:

Using new vehicles: People of today make use of cars, buses, trains, aeroplanes for travelling. Structures of such vehicles are changing and new models enter the scene.

Using new media: As we see, today, television, computer and cell phones are being widely used as media for communication. Likewise, new types of media will be discovered and used in the course of time.

Using new vocabulary: Our people are adopting a number of new terms such as "social forestry", "capitation fee", "tree plantation", "educational industry", "water harvesting", "mother milk bank", "environmental awareness", "globalization" and "tsunami".

New moral values: Youngsters select their life partner without the consent of their parents. Faith in religions has been declining in the modern scientific world.

New dimension in arts: Modern poetry, disco dance and Western music have become very popular among the people.

New avenue for women progress: Today, there is no field without women. They are competing with men. They have entered the police department and we have women police stations.

Women in men's Clothes: It is now common in towns and cities as women start to wear fashion pants and shirts like men. It is the current fashion and has become a part and parcel of the present culture.

FORMS OF SOCIAL CHANGE

The concept of social change is very wide. It has been described in some of its forms.

Economic form: It includes changes in the production of industries, agriculture, trade etc. Lust, theft and corruption have encouraged an economic form of social change.

Political form: It includes political power changes in the state and changes in the administration. The examples of such changes are adopting the values of secularism, equality, justice and freedom.

Religious form: Religious changes are those which have their impact on gurudwaras, churches, and temples etc. Their importance in the present age has decreased because of the development of science and technology.

Moral form: It includes the changes in values and thoughts. In the ancient time co-educational system was considered as immoral. Now it has been accepted without any reservation. Youngsters selecting their life partner are a recent social change.

Scientific and technological form: Such form of social change takes place due to the invention in science and technology or their development.

International form: Social change can take place in the form of international relations. International relations or globalization have improved in the modern age. Indian and foreign matrimonial relations are an example of the international form of social change.

Legal form: It includes changes that take place as a result of the law practised in the country. Sometimes the law protects institutions such as prostitution, birth control, divorce, abortion etc. Birth control and abortion affecting the birth rate is an example of legal form of change.

Social form: Many changes occur in social forms. Social customs like purdah system, child offering, child marriage, devdasi system, sati, and prohibition of widow remarriage etc. affect the society in numerous ways. These rituals have been changed in the modern age.

Location form: People living in urban areas procreate less than those living in rural areas. Moreover, death rate is higher in urban areas due to the existence of slums, insanitary condition and lack of fresh air and sunlight. The urban people practise birth control methods which reduce the birth rate. This change occurs in the urban form.

NATURE OF SOCIAL CHANGE

Let us discuss the nature or characteristics of social change.

Universal: Social change is a universal phenomenon and it occurs in all societies. No society can escape from social change. The population changes, science and technological progress, material equipment changes, ideologies and values take on new components and institutional structures and functions undergo reshaping. The speed and extent of change may differ from society-to-society.

Continuous: It is true that social change is a continuous process. Society is undergoing endless changes that cannot be stopped. Society cannot be preserved in a museum to save it from the ravages of time. In fact, from the dawn of history, society has been in a state of continuous flux.

Temporal: Social change is temporal in the sense that it denotes the time sequence, innovation of new things, modification and renovation of the existing behaviour and the discarding of the old behaviour patterns. Thus, social changes are taking place through times.

Community change: Social change does not refer to the change in the life of an individual or individuals. It is a change which occurs in the life of the entire community.

Not uniform: The speed of social change is not uniform. In most societies social change occurs slowly while it takes place in some other societies rapidly. We can see such social change occurring in urban areas faster than in rural areas.

Environmental change: Social change is an environmental change. It must take place within a geographical or physical and cultural context. These contexts have a great impact on human behaviour. In fact, social changes never take place in vacuum.

Human change: The sociological significance of the change involves the human aspect. Thus, social change refers to social interaction and social relation of people, that is, it is about human change.

Related to time: The nature and speed of social change is affected by and related to time . Social change is faster today than before 1947. The reason is that the factors which cause social change do not remain uniform with the change in times. Before 1947, there was less industrialisation and fewer educational institutions and no scientific and technological development. As a result, the speed of social change after 1947 is faster than before 1947.

Planned and unplanned change: The direction and rate of social change is the law of nature. Social change may occur either in the natural course (unplanned) or as a result of planned efforts. Some changes are conditioned by human engineering. Plans, programmes and projects maybe launched by man to determine and control the rate of direction of social change. Unplanned changes refer to changes resulting from natural calamities such as famines and floods, earthquakes, volcanic eruptions, tsunami and droughts.

Prediction of change is not possible: It is not possible to make any prediction about the exact forms of social change. We may say that on account of the social reform movement, untouchability, child marriage, child offering and sati etc., will be abolished. Such changes may take place due to the laws passed by the government. Industrialisation will increase the speed of urbanisation and deforestation. But we cannot predict the exact forms which social relationships will assume in future. Likewise, it is not possible to predict what shall be our attitudes, ideas, norms and values in future.

Create chain reaction: Change in one aspect of life may lead to a series of changes in its other aspects. For example, equalisation of educational opportunities has resulted in a series of changes in people belonging to most backward classes, Scheduled Class and Scheduled Tribes. We may note that industrialisation has destroyed the democratic system of production. The destruction of the domestic system of production brought women from the home to the factory and office. The employment of women reveals their independence from the bondage of men. It has brought about a change in their attitudes and ideas. It means that a new social order for women has come and it is reflected in every part of the family life. It has also led to social, cultural and economic change.

Interaction of number of factors: Social change is the consequence of a number of factors, such as physical, biological, technological, cultural and political factors. This is due to the mutual interdependence of social phenomenon. The combination of these factors may produce particular social changes.

Short-run and long-run changes: Any change in the society takes time. Some social changes may bring about immediate results whereas some others take years to produce results. Time alone can place the events of the day in their true perspective.

Objective terms: Social change is an objective term. According to the sociologists, social change should be neither moral nor immoral, it is amoral. The study of social change is no value-judgement. One can study change with an ethically neutral mind within the value system without being for or against the change.

Changes are modification or replacement: Social changes maybe categorised as modifications or replacements. It maybe modifications of physical goods or social relationship. Bullock carts have been replaced by lorry. Horses have been replaced by automobiles. Similarly, old ideas have been replaced by new ideas. The old authoritarian family has become the small egalitarian family. Our ideas about adult education, women education, human rights, secularism, co-education and globalization have been modified in the recent years. The form of food we take has changed into ready-to-eat cornflakes, breads, omlettes, cakes etc. These substituted for the form of food that we had earlier. In the post-modern world democracy has replaced aristocracy in many countries.

FACTORS OF SOCIAL CHANGE (CAUSES)

Social change is brought about by a large number of causes or factors. Sometimes just one cause or factor becomes responsible for social change. At other times, some factors jointly act as the cause for social change. Idea and ideologies of great leaders like Jesus Christ in the world, Karl Marx in Germany, Rousseau in France, Lenin in Russia, Mao Tse Tung and Dr. Sun Yat Sen in China, Mahatma Gandhi in India, Abraham Lincoln in America and Nelson Mandela in South Africa have played an important role in social changes. The thought- provoking ideas of Rousseau like 'Liberty' 'Equality' and 'Fraternity' gave birth to the French Revolution which immensely changed the French society. Indian freedom movements and the American War of Independence were the outcome of social, political and economic changes. The independence of India and America brought about revolutionary changes in the social life of the people of these countries. Let us see the main factors which cause social changes in the modern age.

Educational factors: Education is the most important factor for creating social changes. It is education that transforms the child from a young animal into a rational human. Education improves the quality and skill of the individuals. Thus, it modifies behaviour in a desirable way and brings about new values and ideas. It is the cause for the invention of new things and also for social, political and economic changes.

Time factors: Time itself is an important factor for social change. Man gets bored of old values, ideas, or culture with the passage of time. So, modifications and alterations are sought. This is possible in the long run. Thus, time is considered to be one of the causes of social changes in the present context. Child marriage, devdasi system, sati, untouchability and prohibition of widows' re-marriage have become old customs.

Biological factors: Social change maybe related to the qualitative aspect of population that is, the powerful and great men in the society. For instance, Jesus Christ, Buddha, Rousseau, Froebel, Lenin, Karl Marx, George Washington, Abraham Lincoln, Mao Tse Tung, Mohamed Nabi, Mahatma Gandhi, Guru Nanak, Martin Luther King, Dr.Sun Yat Sen and Nelson Mandela have played a vital role in social changes.

Environmental factors: Environmental factors like geographical factors influence social change. For instance, excessive rain, floods, tsunami, drought, famine, hurricanes, earthquakes and have a significant effect on social relationships. Thus, social change takes place as a result of the impact of geographical environment upon human society.

Cultural factors: The culture of a country plays an important role in bringing about social change. The basic elements of culture like language, literature, religion, philosophy, religious epics, poetical works and faith give speed and direction to social change. Culture is more effective and powerful. It determines the limits for social change. According to Max Weber, "Social change takes place along with cultural changes".

Psychological factors: Human beings come across a number of new problems everyday. They think and act in divergent ways in order to solve these problems. Thus, the psychology of people itself is the cause for social change. They happen to deviate from the existing pattern by trying to discover new things in every sphere of life.

Technological factors: The style of living also changes due to science and technological development. Ogburn says, "Technology changes our society by changing our environments to which we in turn adapt". This change is usually in the material environments. However, it also changes often our customs and social institutions. The society changed as a result of the inventions of electric, steam and petrol driven machines for production and as the means of transport and communication. In fact, a single invention may have innumerable social effects. For example, television has influenced our entertainment, education, politics, sports, literature, attitudes and knowledge. Thus, there is a close relationship between technological development and social change.

Demographic factors: The demographic factors like the birth and death rate influences social change. When a country faces population growth to the point of overcrowding, social relationships change both within that society and with surrounding societies having fewer people. Changes in the quality and size of the population have an impact upon the social organization as well as customs and traditions. As a result, the joint family system has totally failed and it causes the emergence of a new family system called nuclear family.

Ideological factors: Social change occurs in the society because of ideas and ideological factors. For instance, philosophical, sociological and political ideas such as liberty, fraternity, equality, socialism, democracy, secularism and community feeling and scientific ideas like health is wealth and prevention is better than cure, have led to major social changes in the modern age. Social change is also influenced by the doctrines of Buddhism, Christianity, Islam, Hinduism, Jainism and Sikhism.

Communication factors: Communication among various societies brings about a social change. Changes will be possible and high in the society which keeps in contact with other societies and it will be difficult in case of an isolated society.

Political factors: The Government itself maybe a cause for social change. The establishments of women university and women police station have changed the lifestyle of women. Equality in education, human rights, secularism, adult education, family welfare programme etc., implemented by the government, have also had a great impact upon social changes. Thus, any activity undertaken by the government leads to social changes.

Social factors: Social problems such as caste, communalism, prostitution, unemployment, poverty, beggary, dowry, illiteracy, ignorance, superstition etc., involve a good deal of social conflict in society. These problems have become a major cause for social change.

Revolutionary factors: Revolutionary factors like the American Revolution, the French Revolution, the Russian Revolution and the American War of Independence took place due to several factors such as liberty, exploitation, hunger, tyranny, unemployment, corruption, famine, inflation and low wages. These revolutions have brought about far reaching social changes. War is another factor which upsets the whole structure of the society by destroying the established conventions and inter-personal relations.

Social and non-social environment: Soil erosion, deforestation, exhaustion of mineral resources, business cycle, migration, military invasions, peaceful immigration, trade etc., have a great impact upon social change.

Economic factors: The change in economic aspect necessarily influences social changes. Due to the influence of Western culture, the use of machines in production process on a large scale has been started in India. Moreover, economic factors like employment, saving habits, income, production, profit etc. determine social changes.

METHODS OF SOCIAL CHANGE

Prof. S.P. Ruhela has mentioned the most important process of social change. Let us explain them under ten headings here.

Westernisation: The Western culture, customs, ways of living, values, and technology influence the Indian society. In fact, we not only adopt their technology but also follow their habits, ways of eating, living style, social relations, recreation, marriage and values.

Indianisation: This is the process of social change in which people of different faiths tend to identify themselves with Indian culture. It is observed in several catholic churches that nuns wear Indian dresses—sarees and blouses. Worship is also done in the Indian style. Lamps, candles, incense, prasad are used in churches. It is also seen that instead of English, regional languages are used in religious songs and prayers.

Industrialisation: Industrialisation is the process of social change. It has given rise to crimes, prostitution, drinking, trade union activities, growth of slums, growth of educational and banking institutions, business centres, strikes, corruption etc. which have great impact on society.

Urbanisation: Urbanisation has led to continuous migration of people from rural areas to towns and cities. It also increases the number of town and industrial cities. Deforestation, environmental pollution and social problems such as corruption, cheating, thefts, socio-economic inequality etc., are the consequence of urbanisation.

Modernisation: Modernisation has brought about many positive changes in the social, economic, cultural, moral and religious outlook of the people. It is in the interest of people to become conscious of their rights and duties. Cultivation of a scientific outlook has made them put an end to bad customs like sati, child marriage, casteism, anti-widow re-marriage, superstitious and religious rituals. Thus, modernisation has led to the adoption of modern ways of life and values.

Politicalisation: Politicalisation is the process of social change through the spread of knowledge about political ideologies, parties and leaders, rights and duties, regional, national and international relations. Such knowledge helps the people become aware of their rights and responsibilities, so that democratic citizenship can be formulated.

Social mobility: This is the process of social change in which people move from one social group to another. It increases their status and prestige. Social mobility is of two types, viz., horizontal and vertical. In horizontal mobility there is no change in the social position of the individual. For instance, the movement of a school clerk from one school to another is horizontal mobility. Vertical social mobility refers to the movement of the individual from a lower to a higher social status or higher to lower social status. For example, a clerk becomes a teacher, that is, the person moves from a lower status (clerk) to a higher status (teacher). Here, the social position of the individual has been changed.

Secularisation: Arya Samaj and Brahma Samaj have promoted the process of secularisation. The real meaning of secular is logical. It means religious tolerance, impartiality, broad outlook and unorthodoxy. Thus, it is a process of change which considers events, things and ideas from a rational point of view.

Sanskritisation: This is the process of social change in which people belonging to the Hindu lower castes or tribes attempt to change their customs, habits, ideologies, rituals, style of living, to be in tune with those of the upper castes. This leads to a great change among lower caste people.

Hinduism: This process of social change consists of the attempts of many tribal communities to enter the broad field of Hindu social structure. Such attempts are made to popularise Hindu beliefs, customs and way of life among the tribes of India.

FACTORS RESISTING SOCIAL CHANGES

Social change is universal, continuous and permanent. But the social and cultural functions do not change 'overnight' even in the most dynamic, industrialised, urbanised and modernised society. It means that certain resistance to social change is everywhere. As a result of it, no society welcomes all the changes. It maybe due to the fact that the upper crest of the society facilitates social change while the middle and lower classes are not generally in favour of change because of their illiteracy, ignorance, poverty, customs, beliefs etc. Here we list the factors which resist social change.

Lack of new inventions: The invention of new objects, techniques, thoughts, devices and plans influence social change to a great extent. According to Ogburn and Nimkoff "The main reason of restraint is the relative absence or shortage of inventions". Hence, changes will take place only if the people have the strong craving for new things. Lack of new invention and interest in invention cannot create a favourable atmosphere for social change.

Rejection of new inventions: The non-acceptance of new technology, beliefs, ideas, values etc. will not bring any change in the society. In short, no change is possible when people reject the new inventions. Dr. William Harvey's blood circulation theory and Galileo's the planetary system and the movement of earth were opposed in the beginning. The British parliament opposed the use of steam energy in British Naval ships.

Fear about novelty: Man not only has love for the past but also fears new things. It is in the nature of man to distrust novelty. According to Ogburn and Nimkoff, "Most of the people show a tendency to stick to traditional routine life and are therefore averse to gaining anything new for fear that these new elements may turn to be harmful and injurious to them". Man is directed by his old customs and traditions. Indians once had been distrustful of British medicines, English education and even sea voyages.

Social circumstances: Social change is resisted by social circumstances prevalent in Indian society. In fact, Indians are bound by casteism, religiosity, ancient traditions and conservatism. For example, Hindus are not willing to convert to Christianity or Islam and vice versa because of rigidness of casteism. Inter-caste marriage is also not accepted in our society due to social inhibitions.

ignorance: The ignorance and superstition of the people keep them away from accepting new inventions or changes. They take a long time to grasp the importance of new discoveries, For instance, the iron plough was not accepted easily in America. It took many years to find acceptance with the farmers. This is due to their ignorance. Such attitudes of the people may stand against social change.

Political conditions: Many times political conditions have become obstacles in the process of social change. The kings and the big landlords of our country opposed social equality among the people.

Economic conditions: Economic distress among the poor is an important obstacle in the process of social change. The poor people do not think of anything except bread. Excessive surplus money makes the rich lazy. Such people will obstruct good changes. In fact, people who are suffering from various economic problems are not prepared to accept changes because they are incapable of accepting new changes.

Vested interest: Individuals who feel that social change endangers their interests are likely to oppose it. They used to fight against every proposal. Such persons may organize themselves as opposition groups when their rights are threatened. Likewise, people oppose changes if their self-interests are endangered. For example, capitalists oppose progressive labour legislation. Social reforms have been opposed by the traditionalist section of the Indian society.

Isolation: In fact, some people refuse to come into contact with persons of other cultures. They remain in isolation and insulated from other influences. These people resist any kind of social change. For example, the most backward communities and tribal groups resist any outside contacts apprehending danger to their self-centred narrow spheres of life. When a social group is isolated from a group or community, it feels that it is isolated from the other communities, cultures and countries as well. As a result of it, the flow of knowledge is stopped from one social group to the isolated group or community.

Cultural condition: Cultural condition refers to the blind beliefs, customs and traditions which come down to us from our forefathers. The cultural conditions such as 'sati', 'devdasi', child marriage, child offering and purdah system etc. were regarded as sacred and indelible. This rigid, conservative and narrow outlook makes us static and develops aversion to any change.

Religious inclination: Religious customs are hurdles in the process of social change. People belonging to certain religions resist divorce, higher education for women, family planning, test tube babies etc. On the other hand, the people who are in favour of purdah system, child marriage do not show interest in change of these aspects.

Romantic attachment to the past: Some people do not change themselves according to the changing social environment. They rigidly stick to their romantic past customs, such as resistance to widow re-marriage, inter-marriage, higher education for women and favour of child marriage and untouchability etc. This is because people are emotionally and sentimentally bound to the old and traditional practices, things and ideas. This traditional attitude of the people will not allow them to accept new things.

THEORIES OF SOCIAL CHANGE

Sociologists, philosophers, historians and social anthropologists have propounded a number of general theories explaining the phenomenon of social change. The theories of social change have been grouped into four main categories: evolutionary, cyclical, conflict and functional theories.

Evolutionary Theory

The evolutionary theory of social change was highly influenced by Charles Darwin's theory of 'Organic Evolution'. A number of thinkers like Spencer, Hobbhouse and MacIver have tried to make the people grasp the evolution theory. The elucidation of this theory has been given by Herbert Spencer, a British sociologist. He has stated that the whole world is making efforts to move towards perfection and every living being tries to become complete in order to maintain its existence and if he is not able to do so, his very existence would come to an end. According to the evolutionary theory, social change is not linear and not like the growth of a plant. Many branches come out from the stem of a plant during its growth and they go in various directions. Spencer is of the opinion that society has been gradually progressing towards a better state. He further argues that it has evolved from military society to the industrial society. This type of change is an example of evolutionary change.

Cyclical Theory

Oswald Spangler, Ian Robertson, Toynbee and Pitirim Sorokin are considered as the champions of this theory. In the words of Ian Robertson, "Cyclical theory of social change focuses on the rise and fall of civilizations attempting to discover and account for these patterns of growth and decay". According to this theory, the motion is like that of the pendulum of a clock and various states are repeated again and again. According to Spangler and Sorokin "Society is like a cycle as the birth of child, childhood, adolescence, period of youth, old age, and finally death". Similarly, we can say that there is the birth, development, downfall and the end of civilization. The same thing can be said about fashions. Spangler has mentioned four stages of the civilizations in his book "Decline of the West". He has compared the stages of civilizations with the four seasons—spring, summer, autumn and winter. Prof. Sorokin has stated three types of civilizations in his book *Social and Cultural Dynamics*. The civilizations are sensory, idealistic and rationalistic. Our present civilization strives for sensory pleasures but also makes efforts to enter the second stage. As a result of it, we are facing the crisis of values.

Degradation Theory

Albert Schweitzer is the profounder of the deterioration theory of social change. He has mentioned the degradation of the civilization of the whole world in his book *Philosophy of Civilization*. As far as nineteenth century is concerned, material and moral powers developed side by side. Schweitzer says, "The fall of world civilization is possible because of the unlimited growth of physical powers and loss of moral powers. Man does not have the capacity to use his own power properly". Now it is seen that the moral values are degrading day by day and the material values are strengthening more and more. In fact, we are living in "kaliyuga".

Conflict Theory

Conflict theory highlights the forces producing instability, struggle and social disorganization. Rolf Dahrendorf, a German sociologist, says that the conflict theory assumes (i) every society is subjected at every moment to change. Hence, social change is ubiquitous; (ii) every society experiences at every moment social conflict, hence social conflict is ubiquitous; (iii) every element in society contributes to change; (iv) every society rests on constraint of some of its members by others.

Karl Marx, a famous German social thinker and philosopher, has asserted that individuals and groups with opposing interests are bound to be at conflict. There are conflicts where there are two social classes, that is, the rich and the poor, or capitalists and labourers or employer and employee. History is the story of conflicts between the exploiting (rich) and the exploited (poor) classes. This conflict continues until capitalism is overthrown by the workers and a socialistic state is created. It is believed that "the existing conditions in any society contain the seeds of future social changes".

George Simmel says "Conflict is a permanent feature of society and not just a temporary event". It is a process that binds people together in interaction. Moreover, conflict encourages people of similar interests to unite together to achieve their objectives. Continuous conflict keeps society dynamic and ever-changing.

Dynamic or Equilibrium Theory

Talcott Parsons and his followers and a number of American Sociologists advocated the dynamic or functional theory of social change in the middle decades of the twentieth century. They have shifted their attention from social dynamics to social static or from social change to social stability. Parsons has stressed that society has the ability to absorb disruptive forces while maintaining overall stability. He considers change "not as something that disturbs the social equilibrium, but as something that alters the state of the equilibrium so that a qualitatively new equilibrium results". According to Parsons, "Changes may arise from two sources, that is, from outside the society, through contact with other societies and from inside the society, through adjustments that must be made to resolve strains within the system". He speaks of two processes that are at work in social change. The family, for example, a single undifferentiated institution performs reproductive, educational, socialising, economic, recreational and other functions. On the other hand different institutions such as schools, churches and factories may take over some of the functions of the family. Thus, new relationship between school and home is established.

Deterministic Theory

Deterministic theory is based on geographical, cultural and industrial factors. Karl Marx is the supporter of the deterministic theory of social change. He has stated thus "The production of material things influences social, political, cultural and spiritual activities". In short, we can say that economic elements are the causes of social change. Modern sociologists are advocating this theory with different views. Some of them say that economic factors are important while others are of the view that it is cultural factors which influence social change to a large extent. Thus, different factors have different roles in the deterministic theory of social change.

Spiritual Theory

Arnold Toynbee, a British historian with sociological insight, puts forward the spiritual theory of social change. He has elucidated this theory in his book, A Study of History. After studying the history of various civilizations, he has come to the conclusion that the spiritual aspect is very important in human life. The lack of development of spiritual and moral aspects leads to various social evils. It is the reason that man has become enemy of man and dissipates human values. In the words of Toynbee, "The disintegration of spiritual values causes the down fall of civilization. According to Waver, "Religion starts the process of social change".

Unilinear Theory

The unilinear theory of social change refers to the change that takes place in a straight line. This theory suggests that the society moves ahead towards a fixed aim by means of social change. Here, the aims of social change are determined beforehand. Its nature has already been predestined with specific purposes. For example, education to all, education to women, employment to women, women in politics, women in economic development etc. is a straight line. Moreover historical events help in this change of society, for instance, Indian freedom movement, independence, political change, planning, economic development and social change. Thus, change takes place in a straight line.

Great Men Theory of History

The great men theory of history of social change has been formulated from the history of great men. It means that social change is influenced by great men of the society. In the words of Carlyle, "The history of the world is the biography of great men". In fact, the history of the whole world is full of the names of great men who were instrumental in bringing about not only changes in the society but even revolutions in it. The inspiring thoughts, ideas, words and deeds of great men have had a great impact on every aspect of the society. For instance, Jesus Christ in the world, Buddha in India, Japan and Srilanka, Rousseau in France, Mohammed in Gulf countries, Kamal Basha in Turkey, Karl Marx in

Germany, Abraham Lincoln in America, Lenin in Russia, Mahatma Gandhi, Swami Vivekananda, Raja Ram Mohan Roy, Indira Gandhi in India, Mao Tse Tung and Sun Yat Sen in China and Nelson Mandela in South Africa have brought about revolutionary changes in the society.

Technological Progress Theory

The technological progress theory of social change has been enunciated by Ogburn. He has propounded this theory in his book *Social Change*. In the words of Ogburn, "Social change is the result of technical influence". He has found out the relationship which exists between technical progress and social change. He has also established the fact that inventions have an important place in bringing social change. According to him, "Every invention and discovery in the field of science has its impact in our social life; development of the means of transportation and communications have changed our lives". For instance, Ogburn has counted 150 impacts as a result of the invention of radio in the society.

ROLE OF EDUCATION IN SOCIAL CHANGE

We cannot even imagine social change without education and in the same manner education is not possible without society. Thus, there is mutually very close relationship between education and social change. They are regarded as the two sides of the same coin which cannot be separated. In fact, education is a creator of social change and it is influenced by social change. According to Samuel Koenig, "Education a process whereby the social heritage of a group is passed on from one generation to another". In the words of Francis J. Brown, "Education is a process which brings about changes in the behaviour of society". We can see this relationship functions in three ways.

- Education as a condition of social change.
- Education as an instrument of social change.
- Education as a result of social change.

According to Prof. Ottaway, "Educational change tends to follow social change". These social changes are brought about through the process of education and social changes also influence changes in the educational structure. Munroe, in his book, *Brief Course in the History of Education* cites "Social control, propagation of culture and civilization and encouragement of social progress in addition to knowledge as the function of education".

Prof. Ottaway has remarked, "In a democratic society education can prepare for change in society, and that is part of its creative function. It prepares children for changes by encouraging permissive and critical attitudes, but it can only do this because these are already sufficiently accepted values of the society".

John Dewey says, "Education is fostering, a venturing and a cultivating process. All of these words mean that it implies attention to the condition of growth". Education is that effective and powerful means which is fully helpful in the social development of man.

Let us point out the role of education in social change:

Imparts knowledge: The knowledge pertaining to various social changes taking place can be transmitted to the people through the medium of education. For instance, national integration is in danger in the present situation. At this juncture awareness among the people about the oneness of "my country and my people" should be developed and their cooperation can be solicited. An educated man could develop the national feeling and prevent the factors which vitiate the integration of our nation. The transmission of this knowledge to the people would be very difficult in the absence of education.

Protects eternal values: Every society has some eternal values which stabilise and consolidate it. The society begins to decay and degenerate where eternal values lose their hold due to social change. In such a situation, education protects the eternal values and saves them from the pernicious effects of social changes. Though, social changes are taking place in our society, people keep faith in the eternal values of moral and spiritual nature. Education protects, propagates and promotes these eternal values.

Helps to analyse changes: Education helps to analyse each and every change that takes place in the society. It provides knowledge to the people about good and bad changes. For example, people oppose women education and family welfare programmes in the villages. It is education that makes them conscious towards positive changes and realises that such change is necessary for the betterment of the society.

Promotes capacity tc welcome changes: Education prepares the minds of people to welcome and adopt desirable social changes easily and gladly. People will welcome and adopt any change (technique or pattern) only when they become convinced of its utility and desirability. It is education that creates conducive environment among people so that they welcome and accept social changes.

Removing obstacles: Vested interests among the people retard the march of social change. For instance if the government is inclined to pass legislation on family planning which maybe against the interests of certain sections of the society, they throw obstacles in the way of implementing it. It maybe due to their superstition, ignorance, illiteracy, customs etc. But education can help them overcome these obstacles by enabling the people to understand the consequence of population explosion and convince them about the importance of a small family. Thus, education helps to eliminate the mental recreational complexes of the people which curb the progress of social change.

Spread of knowledge: Spread of knowledge is the main cause of social change. Education helps the individuals to increase their areas and scope of knowledge. As a result of it, people do researches in different areas of knowledge which bring about desirable changes in the material and non-material aspects of culture. More knowledge leads to more changes because every human being is a philosopher.

Mother of new changes: Education is known as the mother of the eradication of caste system and untouchability and the development of new thoughts. In fact, education produces skilled people like, scientists, doctors, engineers, and scholars etc., who usher in changes through the medium of inventions. For instance, education produces scientists and engineers because of whom we can travel in rails and buses. As a result, the rich and the poor and the people belonging to different classes can be seen sitting side by side. The same situation is seen in schools, offices and industries where different caste people are working together as the result of equalisation of education.

Democratic values: When the students indulge in negative changes such as strike, burning of buses and destruction of building, education counsels them that freedom does not mean they could tread wrong path. In this way, democratic values like, equality, freedom, fraternity, secularism, tolerance, non-violence etc., are stabilised through education.

Aids new social changes: Education removes social evils, old customs and blind traditions through social reformation, political movements and social service schemes. It brings about the required social changes and reforms. Public movements and agitations against child marriage, caste insulation, untouchability and social injustice have resulted in desirable social changes.

Transmission of culture: Transmission of culture from generation-to-generation is one of the functions of education. In this sense, education is the creator, generator and director of all social changes. In fact, education is a conservative, consolidating and stabilising force. Prof. Ottaway says, "The function of education is to transmit the social values and ideals to the young and capable members of society".

Unity and integration: Education solves conflicts which arise between various groups and sections of a society through its thoughts and feelings, and brings about unity in diversity. Education prepares the people to rise above petty caste, rivalries, communal feuds, linguistic conflicts and regional discords, and tries to achieve national integration and national glory.

Maintains human relations: The progress of new techniques and devices in an industrial society leads to social laxity, disunity and discord among the people. Education strives to maintain and consolidate good human relations.

Evaluates social changes: It means that education lays down the required standards and criteria to evaluate the values effectively. On the basis of evaluation, the desirable social changes are adopted and propagated while the undesirable ones are discarded.

Improves standard of people: It is education that improves the quality of the individuals and raises the standard of living which naturally brings about social changes. In fact, education increases the working efficiency of human capital leading to more production and more income. When the standard of living improves, social changes take place automatically.

ROLE OF TEACHER IN SOCIAL CHANGE

A teacher has to play an important role in bringing about social change. In a sense, teacher and social change are like the body and soul. Body without soul is futile and soul without body is ineffective. In the same way, any social change without a teacher is a mere myth. A teacher is like a sun which provides light to the students. A teacher is a gardener who brings perfection and tends the garden. A teacher is a sailor who takes the students ashore safely. Teachers are social engineers who have to perform a double task to bring about social change. That is, he would have to give constructive suggestions to bring about changes in every direction and make arrangements to remove obstacles that come in the way of the execution of those suggestions. Edmund W. Gordon has rightly stated, thus, "It is the task of the teacher to educate for change, to educate through change, to educate for orderly planned revolution, and if necessary to educate through more disruptive revolutionary action". That is why, H.G. Wells has rightly remarked, "The teacher is the real maker of History". Once the principal of a school in Moscow said, "The prime duty of the Soviet teacher is to train our younger generation for the work of building communism". But in the democratic countries, our younger generation is trained to believe that, "The state is for man, not man for the state". Now the teacher is looked upon as a social engineer, ambassador of social change and nation builder of the future. Hence, the role of the teacher in social change is quite inevitable.

Let us see the role of the teacher in bringing about changes in the Indian society.

Believer in social change: The duty of the teacher is not only teaching but also he is to lead in bringing about social change. This is possible only when he considers himself fit and worthy of it. In fact, he should have faith in positive change. He should encourage the students to use radio, television, films etc., to increase their own knowledge so that social changes can be brought about in the society.

Give suggestions for change: The teacher should not hesitate to provide suggestions which are needed to bring about social change. He should be like the sun that yields light. He is a gardener who sacrifices his soul to beautify the garden. He is a sailor who rows the boat safely. Thus, it is a teacher who has to bestow positive and constructive suggestions to bring about social changes for the benefit of the society.

Welcomer of change: Teacher should welcome new social changes like, adult education, women education, education of Scheduled Caste and Scheduled Tribes, social forestry, blood donation bank, population control measures etc. He should actively participate in these activities which bring about social change that is needed for the progress of our nation. He must emphasise the importance of human values, national and international integration and secularism in the school as well as in the society.

Remover of obstacles in change: The duty of the teacher is to remove and help to eradicate the obstacles which impede changes. When the government wants to bring social change by ensuring educational opportunities to all or family planning or reservation for women in employment etc., the teacher should welcome these activities of government and help to break down the resistance of people. They should make the people realise the importance of such schemes by providing necessary suggestions to overcome the hurdles.

Opposer of undesirable changes: It is the responsibility of the teacher to analyse the various schemes implemented by the government and oppose undesirable changes. He has to speak against and resist the undesirable change which can curb the development of our nation.

Preserver of values: The teacher is not only the follower of human values and culture but he also has to protect and propagate them among his students so that the coming generation maybe able to understand the importance of values and, thereby, lead a fruitful life. The preservation of values is most important to save human lives from degradation.

Approacher of social problem: In our Indian society a large number of social problems like dowry system, population explosion, environmental pollution, unemployment, poverty, communalism etc., have cropped up. These problems take the human race to the brink of destruction. So, it is an essential duty of the teacher who should approach these problems and create awareness in order to protect the society from the dangers and evils of these problems.

Sower of the seeds of integration: We are talking of national integration and unity in diversity so as to strengthen our nation. But divisive elements and disintegrating forces have been increasing in our country. In this situation, the teacher should explain to the students the importance and necessity of national integration and how our national leaders struggled and suffered to get freedom. This will prevent the students from falling a prey to the elements which vitiate our unity. In this regard, the teacher should behave as one who sows the seeds of national unity and be a backbone of national integration.

Remover of illiteracy for change: The social changes can be brought about through the medium of education. It is possible only when people accept such changes. Hence, illiteracy and ignorance of the people should be removed. Illiteracy is harmful to the nation and is against social changes. So, the teacher should organize literacy campaigns in the villages to conduct cultural programmes. This programme develops awareness among the educated people. The teacher should utilise his students by involving them in social services in order to remove illiteracy among the people.

Promoter of global thinking: Globalization is one of the social changes that has a great impact on social and economic development in these days. It shows that all countries of the world have converged into a global village. In fact, no nation of the world can remain independent. It has to depend on others because problems like earthquakes, tsunami, famines, flood etc., faced by one country affect the whole world. It is, therefore, the responsibility of a teacher to prevent the students from developing narrow nationalism and foster global fraternity in them.

Supporter of modernisation: Teacher should support modernisation in our country according to the progress of science and technology. It is regarded as the social responsibility of the teacher to teach the values which are useful for the development of human race. These values are helpful in utilising scientific inventions and technological improvements. The teacher should develop an attitude among the younger generation to use cookers, biogas plants, computer etc. He should advise the people to utilise iron and other metals instead of timber so as to protect the environment.

ROLE OF SCHOOL IN SOCIAL CHANGE

School is a social institution that plays a major role in moulding the ideas, habits and attitudes of children with a view to producing well-balanced personalities—physically strong, mentally alert, emotionally stable, culturally sound and socially efficient. There is no place better than school to bring about social change. Hence, the future of mankind depends on the education imparted in schools. In the words of K.G. Saiyidain, "The school is a centre of vigorous life. It is in direct intimate contact with the realities of the life around, reflecting the best and worthiest of its features which are simple enough to appeal to the child". The Indian Education Commission under the Chairmanship of Dr. S. Kothari (1964–66) explains the significant role of the school in social change. According to Kothari Commission, "The destiny of India is now being shaped in her classroom". It emphasises that school is the most important and active formal institution. Hence, it can play a very important role to bring about social changes.

Reflection of social order: The size, form, nature and organizational setup of a school depends on the prevailing social order. That is, the aims, the ideas, values, customs and traditions of society are reflected in the functioning of the school. If some changes occur in the social system, the school changes its programmes accordingly. This means that school works according to the social order. Hence, the school is bound to reflect the social changes that occur in the society.

Reflection of national policy: The policies framed by the nation are reflected in the school system. School adopts the national policy and implements it; so our national objectives, needs and aspirations can be achieved. For example, if national policy is to create environmental awareness, AIDS awareness, increase the production of goods through education or equalisation of educational opportunities, the school should include those subject matters related to these policies in the curriculum.

Training in live together: School activities such as community service, NSS, NCC, scout and guides, cultural programmes, sports and games, discussion method etc., provide proper training to the students in the art of living together. In other words, school is a social institution which trains the students to live together regardless of their caste, religion, place of birth, culture and economic status. This is a considerable social change brought about by the school.

Contact wide environment: The school provides its pupils a rich, pleasant and stimulating environment which make life a matter of joyful experience. The environment of a school is wide and varied in comparison with the limited environment of a family. In fact, school brings its pupils into contact with the wide environment by its diverse activities.

Scientific outlook: The development of scientific temper has been emphasised on all school programmes. When such an attitude is sown in the minds of the students, social changes are brought about in a scientific way.

Preservation of culture: School preserves and transmits our cultural heritage. It is the school through which social and cultural heritage can be propagated from one generation to another and it promotes the culture of our society.

Glorious future: A school strives to plan for a very bright and glorious future of society. For this purpose, it preserves the glories of the past, and tries to make society achieve greater heights of glory and fame in the ensuing days.

Employment education: School runs professional and technical courses in order to increase the productivity and to raise the standard of living of the people. Those who complete such courses can get employment. Thus, the school prepares the child to stand on his own legs. It also helps to increase his earning and improves the quality of life. The high standard of living is conducive to social change.

Speed of change: It is seen that whatever inventions or discoveries take place in the society has its foundation in the school. Thus, school identifies and selects creative and talented children, with a view to preparing them to contribute something to material culture. They should be given proper educational environment. This helps to increase the speed of social changes.

Meeting economic needs of society: Education promotes the economic efficiency of individuals who achieve their own economic prosperity. Thus, school meets the economic needs of individuals. It brings about the prosperity of society and social changes.

Simplify socio cultural patterns: The socio-cultural patterns are varied and often complex in our Indian society. School tries to simplify and categorise the bewildering variety of socio-cultural patterns and preserves them for use, and enables the children to understand them better.

Minimise the resisting factors to change: Many factors like blind beliefs and old tradition resist social changes. School minimises their role by changing the attitude of the people. This can be done by the modification of the curriculum and active participation of teachers and students. In fact, school prepares the mind of the child in such a way that he can overcome the resisting factors and accept those changes willingly.

CONCLUSION

We come to understand that education, teacher and school play a predominant role in bringing about social changes. In fact, without education, the knowledge of social change is impossible and it cannot be preserved and promoted. Hence, education is the means through which all progress in the society is made. It brings about changes in the thoughts, ideals, habits and attitudes of the members of the society. Charles A. Elwood, has rightly remarked, "Education is the chief means to which society must look for all substantial progress." According to John Milton, "I call therefore, complete and generous education that which fits a man to perform justly skillfully and magnanimously all the offices, both private and public, of peace and war". Some great teachers in their individual capacity have given us new ideals in the field of education and social change. We cannot deny and forget the contributions of Jesus Christ, Buddha, Mohammed Nabi, Guru Nanak, Confucius, Socrates, Mahatma Gandhi, Tagore, Swami Vivekananda, Radhakrishnan, John Dewey, Rousseau, Montessori, Froebel and Pestalozzi, who have brought about new thoughts, ideas and values. They have brought social changes which have a great impact on education. That is why, John Dewey says, "Teacher is a representative of God in society. School inspectors are not to criticize the work of the teacher but to help him in improving his work through sympathetic suggestion and advice". In this way, education brings changes in the society and social changes bring changes in education. In short, the cycle of "social change through education" and "education through social change" always goes on in a progressive society.

CHAPTER 36

EDUCATION AND CULTURE

INTRODUCTION

'Culture' is one of the most important concepts used in education, psychology, sociology, political science and economics. The study of human society immediately and necessarily leads us to the study of its culture. The study of society becomes incomplete in the absence of an understanding of the culture of that society. It is because both culture and society go together. Hence, they are inseparable in any circumstances.

MEANING OF CULTURE

The word 'culture' has been derived from the Latin word *cultura* which means to cultivate or cultivating the mind. It is also said that the term has been taken from the verb 'cultivate' and its noun 'cultivation'. In this way, culture means to refine or to civilize the individual as well as the society. Thus, culture is a very broad term that includes our walks of life, our modes of behaviour, our philosophies and ethics, our morals and manners, our customs and traditions, our religious, political, economic and other types of activities. It includes all that man has acquired from his individual and social life. Actually human beings are born with a cultural environment that consists of:

- Tools, buildings, equipments, machines, and other material objects, which man has made out of his physical environments for his comforts and use.
- The meanings which are attached to things and their various qualities together with the knowledge, institutions, social practices, symbolic systems and all other creations of man.
- Beliefs, customs, attitudes, mutual association and all religious or social organizations.
- Style of living, dressing and participation in various social sub-systems.

Education and culture are closely related to each other. In other words, to be cultured means to be educated and to be educated means to be cultured, balanced, sweet and enlightened. Thus, culture and education go hand-in-hand.

DEFINITIONS OF CULTURE

Though it is a difficult task to define the term 'culture', different writers have defined it in different ways. The definitions that make the meaning of culture more clear have been given here.

E.B. Taylor: "Culture is the complex whole which includes knowledge, belief, art, morals, law, custom and other capacities and habits acquired by man as a member of the society".

MacIver: "Culture is the expression of our nature in our modes of living and of thinking in our everyday intercourse in art, in literature, in religion, in recreation and enjoyments".

Robert Bierstedt: "Culture is that complex whole that consists of everything we think, do and have as members of society".

Ottaway: "The culture of a society means the total way of life of a society".

Sutherland and Woodward: "Culture includes anything that can be communicated from one generation to another. The culture of people is their social heritage which includes knowledge, belief, art, morals, laws, techniques of food, fabrication and use, and modes of communication".

Gandhi: "Culture is the foundation, the primary thing ... It should show itself in the smallest detail of your conduct and personal behaviour."

Jawaharlal Nehru: "Culture is the widening of the mind and of the spirit".

H. Rugg: "Culture means the total life of the people that goes on with these groups, what the people in a given society do, think, feel, believe, desire, fear".

Mathew Arnold: "Culture is the way of life, the habits, the manners, the very tone of voices, the literature, the things which give pleasure to community, the words, the thoughts which make the furniture of their minds".

K.M. Munshi: "Culture is the characteristic way of life inspired by fundamental values in which people live. It is the sum total of the values, expressed through art, religion, literature, social institutions and behaviour, the overt acts of individuals and mass action inspired by collective urge".

Ellwood: "Culture includes on the one hand the whole of man's material civilizations, tools, weapons, system of industry and on the other, all the non- material or spiritual civilization such as language, literature, art, religion, morality, law and government".

F.J. Brown: "Culture is the total behaviour pattern of the group conditioned in part by the physical environment, both natural and man made, but primarily by the ideas, attitudes, values and habits, which have been developed by the group to meet the needs".

Leonard Broom: "Culture refers to a social heritage that is all knowledge, beliefs, customs, and skills that are available to the members of a society".

CHARACTERISTICS OF CULTURE

Culture is learnt or acquired: Culture is not inherited biologically but learnt socially by man. The new born baby is like a clean slate. When it grows, it acquires different ideals, attitudes, values, skills, beliefs, traditions and style of living and thinking in social contacts. Shaking hands or saying namaskar or thanks, touching feet or kissing check as a gesture of affection, shaving, dressing, combing hair, driving, singing, wearing ornaments, wearing white sarees at mourning, walking bare-footed, eating food from plate or leaf, reading newspaper, singing, dancing, worshipping etc., are the examples of learnt culture. Thus, culture is a system of learnt behaviour shared by and transmitted among the members of a group or society.

Culture is social: Culture is a product of society. It originates and develops through social interaction. Man cannot acquire culture in the absence of association with other human beings. Culture helps man to develop human qualities in the social environment.

Culture is distinct entity: Different societies of the world have different patterns of culture. It is because of difference in beliefs, material and social progress, geographical conditions and physical environment which establish the different identities of different nations. Culture itself distinguishes the societies.

Culture is shared: The culture of man such as customs, traditions, beliefs, ideas, values and morals are all shared by people of a group or society. For example, the philosophical works of Confucius, Swami Vivekananda, the literary works of Tagore, Bharathi, Kalidasa, Vallathol, Thakazhi Siva Sankara Pillai, Premchand are being shared by a large number of people.

Culture is transmissive: Culture is transmitted from one generation to the next. Parents pass on cultural traits to their children and they in turn give them to their children, and so on. Language is the main vehicle of culture and through its forms like reading, writing and speaking culture is transmitted from one generation to another. Transmission of culture may take place by imitation as well as instruction. In the words of Ellwood, "Culture is transmitted socially, that is, by communication and gradually embodies in a group tradition of which the vehicle is language".

Culture is continuous and cumulative: Culture exists as a continuous process. It is a growing whole which includes the achievements of the past and the present and makes provision for the future achievements of mankind. Culture is cumulative. History of mankind is the history of culture.

Culture is gratifying: Culture provides proper opportunities and prescribes the means for the satisfaction of our needs and desires. Our needs for food, shelter, clothing (biological) and our desire for status, name, fame, money, mates (social) are all fulfilled according to the cultural ways. In fact, culture is defined as the process through which human beings satisfy their wants. Culture also meets the recurring demands of mankind. For instance, the demands of reproduction, of nursing an infant to maturity and finally the disposal of the dead, all are met by culture from generation-to-generation.

Culture is dynamic: Culture changes as society changes. Some cultures change rapidly while some others do so slowly. In fact, a living culture is ever changing when we compare it with the culture of the Vedic times.

Culture is adaptive: Culture has an adaptive quality. It also intervenes in the natural environment and helps man in his process of adjustment. Contest of two or more cultures takes place and this interaction tends the adaptive quality to culture.

Culture is integrated: Different parts of culture join hands to form a whole or integrative culture. For instance, the value system of a society is closely connected with its other aspects such as morality, religion, customs, traditions, beliefs and so on.

Culture varies from society to society: Every society has its own culture which differs from society-to-society. Cultures are not uniform. Cultural elements such as customs, traditions, morals, ideals, values, ideologies, beliefs, practices, philosophies, institutions differ from society-to-society. Ways of eating, dressing, speaking, greeting, entertaining and living are also not uniform everywhere. Thus, culture varies from time-to-time and society-to-society.

Culture has utility: A culture is good if it has some utility to the individual and society. If a culture has no utility, it will decay and die in the long run. In fact, cultural fanaticism and snobbery promotes conflict and chaos. Therefore, we should adopt the excellent world cultures. This attitude can promote the development of world culture which leads to international brotherhood.

Culture is idealistic: Culture is based on some ideals. Ideals are the real foundations of culture. Every society considers its culture as an ideal. It is intrinsically valuable. The people are also aware of their culture as an ideal one. They are proud of their cultural heritage.

Culture is necessary: Culture is necessary for man because it shapes the individuality of a man. It has direct impact on the social, mental, physical and spiritual development of a man. It helps to divide the society into different castes, classes, religion, politics and social status.

Culture is the sum total of man's life experience: The knowledge and experiences a man acquires in life is his culture. They are manifested in social contacts.

Culture is man made: Most part of human culture is made by man himself for his social and economic life. It is man who is the greatest biotic organism, and is the cause for all inventions and discoveries, including culture also.

CULTURE AND CIVILIZATION

The terms 'Culture' and 'Civilization' represent two broad fields of human activity and experience. Let us explain the distinction between these two terms to make them clear for our understanding.

Civilization has a precise standard of measurement but not culture: The products of civilization can be measured quantitatively on the grounds of efficiency. For example, we can say that a tractor is superior to a hand plough, currency system is superior to the primitive barter system and bullock cart is superior to bus. Here we can measure civilization quantitatively. But we can measure the cultural products such as values opinions, ideas, morals, customs, beliefs, fashions etc., we can only assess these cultural products by our personal judgement. For example, we may say that the literary works of Kalidasa are better than those of William Shakespeare. We cannot prove or disprove it. But we can agree or disagree with that statement.

Civilization is always advancing but not culture: Civilization always marches on if there is no break of social continuity. Every generation adds its own achievements to the already stored up energy and intelligence. Thus, every technical achievement is an improvement on the past. Once an instrument is discovered, man goes on improving it: change from mud road to tar road, and then to cement and concrete road, from bow and arrow to the machine gun and then to atom bomb. Thus, the progress of civilization is assured; culture is not always advancing. Our ancestors had developed and transmitted good cultures of values, ideals, beliefs etc. Now these cultures have been changing with the development of science and technology. For example, the height reached by Gautama Buddha, Swami Vivekananda, St. Paul, Shankaracharya and Mohammed Nabi in the field of religion and spirituality had not been reached by their followers. In the same way Kalidasa, Bharavi and Bhasa of the Sanskrit literature still retain their supremacy.

Civilization can be communicated than culture: The products of civilization are open to all. Civilization can be passed on very easily and without much effort. For example, millions may use radio, television, telephone, computer, camera, different types of vehicles etc., without understanding their techniques and mechanism. On the other hand, the products of culture can be communicated only between the like minded. For example, those who have poetic talent alone can appreciate poetry. In the same way, the work of an artist is only for a man with artistic appreciation.

Civilization is borrowed without loss or change but not culture: People can borrow the products of civilization very easily. In fact, technical services and plants can easily be borrowed or transferred. For example, it will be easy for an Indian to borrow a scientific technique invented in the west. Similarly, many of the Eastern countries have borrowed Western technology. But it will be difficult for the foreigners to borrow the Indian culture. Hence, civilization is far more widespread than culture. Though we have had some cultural borrowings like dress style, speaking style, fashions, food habits, entertainment etc., from foreigners, they are insignificant compared to the borrowings of civilization.

Civilization is external and culture is internal: Civilization is external, mechanical and utilitarian in character. It caters to the external needs of man. Civilization is means. It reflects the material wealth of mankind. Culture is something internal. It refers to the intrinsic values. It is the expression of our modes of living and of thinking, in behaving and in acting, in art and literature, in philosophy and religion, in morality, in recreation and enjoyment, in dance, drama, music etc. Kant, a famous philosopher, says, "Civilization is the matter of outward behaviour whereas culture requires morality as an inward state of man". In the words of MacIver and Page "Civilization is what we have, culture is what we are".

Culture reveals nature of individual or society or nation but not civilization: In the realm of culture, an artist or a poet or a painter can express his love of beauty, his admiration for literature, his fascination towards art by means of his artistic, literary or painting works. On the other hand, an engineer or a scientist cannot express his personality, his love, or beauty, his likes and dislikes, his morals and values by means of machines, discoveries or inventions.

Civilization reveals economic status but culture reveals social status of individual or society or nation: It is clear from the words of MacIver and Page that "Civilization is what we have, culture is what we are". Civilization indicates standard of living of individual or society or nation in terms of material things. Culture indicates the standard of living of the individual or society or nation in terms of non-material products by which we can measure the quality of people in the society.

TYPES OF CULTURE

Individual and common culture: Individual culture includes interests, attitudes, likes, dislikes and thinking behaviour which differ from person-to-person. Common culture is the result of religious faith, customs and traditions.

National or local culture: National cultures include laws, values, ideals, thinking and living. Local culture is restricted to a particular locality influenced by geographical climate, local belief, tradition and standard of living of people in that area.

Material and non-material culture: Material culture includes man-made, physical objects such as vehicles, clothes, buildings, food items, machines, equipments, means of transports and communication. Non-material culture includes beliefs, traditions, customs, values, ideals and language. They are accepted and followed by at least one sizeable section of the society.

Universal and particular culture: Universal culture includes truth, honesty, cooperation, sympathy, love for children. They are adopted by all members of the society across the world. Particular culture is that culture which is adopted by a particular section of the society. It is because of the existence of different castes and religions in a particular society. Therefore, a particular culture differs from caste-to-caste and religion-to-religion. This type of culture is prevalent in the Indian society.

Optional form of culture: It is neither universal or particular. It is optional in the sense that it is not adopted by many people. The person who adopts more optional elements of culture is said to be more cultured. This is necessary for the progress of human civilization.

FUNCTIONS OF CULTURE

Culture elevates mankind from the level of animal to the heights of a rational man. Man cannot survive as a man without culture. In fact, culture represents the entire achievements of mankind. Culture serves the following functions:

Treasury of knowledge: Culture provides knowledge for the physical, social and intellectual existence of man. They help him to adapt himself with the environment. Culture has made modification possible and easier by providing man the necessary skills and knowledge. It helps to preserve and transmit knowledge from generation-to-generation.

Defines situation: Culture defines social situation for us. It also determines what we eat and drink, what we wear, when to laugh, weep, sleep, love, to make friends with, what work we do, what God we worship, what knowledge we rely upon, what poetry we recite and so on.

Defines attitude, values and goals: This is another important function of culture. Attitudes refer to the tendency to feel and act in certain ways. Values are the measure of goodness or desirability. Goals refer to the attainments which our values define as worthy. Culture conditions our attitudes towards religion, morality, marriage, science, family planning, prostitution and so on. Our values concerning private property, fundamental rights, representative government, romantic love etc., are influenced by our culture. Our goals such as winning the race, understanding others, attaining salvation, being obedient to elders and teachers, being loyal to husband, being patriotic etc., are set forth by our culture.

Decides our career: What career we are likely to pursue is largely decided by our culture. For instance, whether we like to become a politician, a social worker, a doctor, an engineer, a policeman, a farmer, a religious leader, a teacher, and so on is decided by our culture. Individuals may develop, modify or oppose the trends of their culture but they always live within its framework. But only a few can find outlet in the culture.

Provides behaviour pattern: Culture directs and confines the behaviour of an individual. It assigns goals and provides means for achieving desirable behaviour. In fact, we see, dream, aspire, work, strive, marry, enjoy according to the cultural expectation. Culture controls and liberates human energy and activities. As a consequence of it, we can say that indeed man is a prisoner of culture.

Moulds personality: Culture has a great impact on moulding and developing individual personality. In the absence of a cultural environment, no child can develop human qualities. It is culture that alone prepares man for group life and provides him the design of living. Ruth Benedict has remarked, "Every culture will produce its special type of personality". The same view has been stressed by an American anthropologist Margaret Mead thus, "Culture shapes the character and behaviour of individuals living in it". In fact, culture provides opportunities for the development of personality and sets limits on its growth. But the impact of culture on the individual is not always identical in every case as he differs from others in ability, aptitude and learning. He meets other person outside the culture. As a result, travelling, books, radio, cinema, television, newspaper etc. have brought about influence outside the culture. Thus, biological and sociological factors bring about the uniqueness of the individual in any culture.

RELATIONSHIP BETWEEN EDUCATION AND CULTURE

The educational system of any society has a clear impact on its culture. Education and culture are closely related to each other. In fact, true education is incomplete without cultural heritage. For example, if the cultural pattern of a society is materialistic, then its educational pattern will be shaped for the attainment of material values which promote material comforts. It is clear that a society devoid of any culture will have no definite educational organization. Hence, the culture of a country has a very powerful impact on its educational pattern. In short, the destiny of any educational system is shaped by the cultural patterns in which the system lives. In the words of S.P. Chaube and

A. Chaube, "Culture is closely related to education. The bases of the educational system of a society are its needs and impact on its culture and they are fulfilled by education. Culture has its impact on education".

INFLUENCE OF CULTURE ON EDUCATION

Education and culture are intimately and integrally related. Education has great influence on culture. In the same way, culture influences education. Let us analyse the relationship between education and culture.

Aims of education: The cultural ideals, values and patterns of a society determine the meaning and aim of education. Culture helps the individual in refining the physical, intellectual and moral aspects of his personality. Thinking and pattern of behaviour of the people and their standard and style of living will also play an important role in determining educational aims.

Curriculum construction: Curriculum is the medium through which the aims of education are achieved. The cultural needs of society such as philosophy of life, ethics, values and traditional practices are realised through the curriculum in every system of education. As the aims of education are determined according to the culture of society, the curriculum is also conditioned according to the culture of society.

Method of teaching: There is an inter-relationship between culture and methods of teaching. It is a fact that culture of a society determines the behaviour of the teacher and his method of teaching. Whether education will be teacher centred, curriculum centred or child centred will depend on the cultural pattern of society. It is seen that the methods of teaching followed in an autocratic society are different from the methods followed in a democratic society. The teacher will teach the students according to their needs, interests, and aptitude if the society follows a democratic culture. If it is totalitarian, the behaviour of the teacher will be very rigid. Moreover, in ancient times, education was teacher centred and specific knowledge was taught in disregard of the child's natural interests and needs. In modern times, education has become child centred and the subjects are taught according to the interests, attitude, and needs of the child. Thus, cultural and social needs condition the methods and techniques of teaching in a very powerful way.

Discipline: The concept of discipline is influenced by the cultural values. Generally, the problem of indiscipline is seen in those societies where education is not given priority by the people. Rigid discipline was followed in ancient authoritarian rule. But, the modern psychologists lay stress on self-discipline. The democratic society emphasises social discipline which is accepted all over the world.

Teacher: Culture influences the philosophy of life, cultural ideals and values of teacher. The teacher has a very significant part in the educational system. He is not only the architect of future culture but also the conserver and transmitter of it. Hence, it is the duty of the teacher to build up the capacities of the children through education, so that they could adjust themselves the cultural needs of the society. In short, a teacher can modify and transform the culture of his students by his own behaviour. That is, he himself is a model to the child.

Textbooks: The whole system of school education is influenced by culture. Curriculum is constructed on the basis of the culture of the time. Textbooks have been prepared according to the curriculum based on the culture of the society. It means that the cultural values of the society are taken into consideration while writing textbooks in order to foster and promote our cultural values and ideals.

School system: John Dewey, a well known pragmatist as well as educational thinker, says that a school is a miniature of society. The total activities and programmes of the school should be organized according to the cultural ideas and values of the society. In this way a school functions as a centre for promoting, moulding, reforming and developing the cultural pattern of the society.

Development of art, music and literature: The culture of a particular age is reflected in its arts, music and literature. We can study the culture of the past on the basis of these things and can relate them to the present in order to predict the future. Thus, culture binds the past, present and future into a single time unit.

Reconstruction of education: The culture of a society always changes with the change of time. Such changes are taken into consideration while formulating educational plans. In fact, education and its plans are reconstructed in the light of changing culture.

Co-curricular activities: Cultures are not meant for preservation. They have to be developed and transmitted to the next generation. In this regard, various literary, cultural and games activities are organized in the school campus. Thus, the basis of co-curricular activities is the culture of that time. Prof. A.N. Whitehead rightly says, "Education should produce men who possess both culture and expert knowledge. Their expert knowledge will give the children the ground to start from and culture will lead them as deep as philosophy and as high as art".

ROLE OF EDUCATION IN CULTURE

Culture influences education in the same way as education influences the culture of a country. The culture of any society should be preserved for the benefit of the coming generation. It should be transmitted properly from generation-to-generation. If culture is not conserved and promoted and then transmitted, all the human knowledge and experiences will be lost to the successive generations. Moreover, culture should be developed by dropping a few old elements and incorporating a few new elements according to the changing needs and demands of the society.

PRESERVATION AND TRANSMISSION OF CULTURE (ROLE OF EDUCATION IN CULTURAL DEVELOPMENT)

The school and the teacher can play an active role in the preservation, transmission and development of culture.

Preservation of culture: The most important function of education is to preserve the culture of society. It is the school that has to consolidate the spiritual strength of a society or nation and maintain its historical continuity and secure its past achievements. Preservation of culture through education keeps the society alive.

Transmission of culture: The process of preservation of culture is undertaken with a view to transmitting it from one generation to another. Prof. Ottaway has remarked thus, "The function of education or school is to transmit the social values and ideals to the young and capable members of society". The traditions of the society cannot be preserved in the absence of cultural transmission. Hence, both preservation and transmission of culture should go hand-in-hand for the benefit of society. Preservation of culture is meaningless unless it is transmitted to the ensuing generation. Education is the only tool through which such a function can be carried on effectively.

Promotion of culture: The function of education is to bring about the needed as well as desirable changes in the cultural pattern, ideals and values for the progress and continuous development of society. Social progress will stratify and come to naught if there is no promotion of culture in the society. In other words, education civilizes individuals, modifies cultural progress by research and deeper investigations into all areas of human requirements. D.J.O. Cannon remarks, "If each generation had to learn for itself what has been learned by its predecessors no sort of intellectual or social development would be possible and the present state of society would be little different from the society of the old stone age".

Continuity of culture: The continuity of cultural condition is an essential condition for the survival of the nation. It is because culture is the life blood of a society. In fact, without culture, a society is bound to decay and die today or tomorrow. Education upholds the continuity of culture through its diverse activities and programmes. For this purpose, children are motivated to learn more from cultural interaction among various cultures and develop the qualities of tolerance, adjustment together with mutual give and take.

Development of personality: Education has a very significant role in shaping the personality and character of the child. It helps to foster diverse cultural patterns of thinking and behaviour of children in order to ensure social, physical, mental and emotional development.

Cultural reforms: Culture is dynamic in nature. As a result of it, many new things are added to culture everytime. But all cultures are not desirable for the good of the society. Education analyses the cultures scientifically and brings out all those undesirable elements which are not conducive for their development.

Removing cultural lag: Material culture grows at a faster rate due to scientific researches and technological advancements; whereas non-material culture consisting of ideals, values and norms lags behind creating a gulf between the two. It creates ideological conflicts in man through his internal behaviour. Education redefines the concepts, beliefs and ideals according to the changing needs of the society. In short, education bridges this cultural lag by its activities and programmes of development. Thus, cultural lag is removed.

Teaching the way of life: The teacher should help the students to understand about their meals, dress, home, neighbourhood, and respect to elders. This is the best way by which a teacher can transmit his cultural values to his students.

Celebrating national days, festivals and leaders days: The teacher has an important role in cultural progress and its transmission. National days such as January 26 and August 15, the birth anniversary of Gandhi, Nehru, Guru Nanak, Tilak etc., and festivals like Pongal, Deepavali, Christmas, Ramzan etc., should be celebrated in the school campus. It is the responsibility of the teacher to explain the importance of and the need for such celebrations.

Cultural activities: The teacher should organize diverse cultural activities and programmes to inculcate in the students our cultural values. Cultural activities such as dramatic performance, debate, talent performance, talent shows, musical and dance performances should be organized periodically.

Curriculum: The curriculum should provide a place for teaching Indian History, Indian Literature, Sociology, Geography etc., with a view to transmitting our culture to the younger generation.

Organization of fairs and programmes: Organization of fairs and other programmes like NCC, NSS, Scouting, Red Cross Society etc., in the school fosters the spirit of our culture of courtesy, tolerance and balance. They develop social qualities in the child.

Creative activities: Teacher may guide and encourage students to invent things and repair appliances. Students maybe encouraged to write short stories, verses and plays to develop their culture.

Teaching methods: Teacher may adopt those methods of teaching which reflect and develop culture. For example, play-way method, group activity, role play etc., can help develop and transmit our culture.

Teacher as model: Teachers can themselves act as personal models in the preservation and transmission of culture. He who loves a systematic life under rules and discipline and obedience to every legitimate authority is capable of imparting to his students the knowledge of well-refined customs and traditions of our society.

EDUCATION AND CULTURE: INDIAN VIEWS

Dr. S. Radhakrishnan says, "The more Indian culture changes, the more it remains the same. The power of Indian spirit has sustained us through difficult times. It is the tangibles that give a nation its character and vitality".

Shriman Narayan says, "The youth of India should be enabled to imbibe the spirit of our composite culture and be familiar with the glorious history of our freedom movement in which all the communities and religious groups participated with a sense of purpose".

Jawaharlal Nehru says, "One of the miracles of history has been the continuity between the past and the present of India. Even through the dark of India's political fragmentation, she always kept hold on her common culture. Although India must break up with the past, she should not discard the core and cream of her past culture and heritage. She should not forget the magnificent achievements in art, literature and culture. The core of Indian cultural heritage is love of beauty and truth, spirit of tolerance, capacity to absorb other cultures and work out new synthesis. Education must help in preserving the vital elements of our heritage. Education must help in washing away the dirt and dust of the ages that cover India's beauty, and significance. Education must regenerate the youth of the country so that they may keep themselves in tune with the present".

The Indian Education Commission has stated thus, "The most important and urgent reform needed in education is to transform it, to endeavour to relate it to life, the needs and aspirations of the people and thereby make it a powerful instrument of social, economic and cultural transformation, necessary for realization of national goals".

CONCLUSION

Culture is any things which an individual acquires or follows and practice in the social environment. As man is a social animal, he is influenced by the society. Culture may be desirable if it is useful to the society, for example, practice of human values—compassion, sympathy, kindness, affection, brotherhood, co-operation, secularism, democracy, etc. It may be undesirable one when falls in drinking, smoking, illegal sex, homo marriage, raping, adulteration, killing, robbering causing social pollution. The present generation is behaving worst because of cultureless obsence-violence mass media and corruptive society. Moreover, characterless education is produce useless human society. Culture has become meaningless in complicated materialistic society. Education, religion and politics have failed to fostering socially acceptable culture, but they pollute the social environment. Too much emphasise on money cause human values meaningless, and useless. Only good parents, teachers, friends, governments alone can foster desirable culture in the society which is very essential for man-making.

CHAPTER 37

EDUCATION AND HUMAN RESOURCE DEVELOPMENT

INTRODUCTION

Human Resource Development is a comprehensive word which implies the creation of appropriate manpower for taking up jobs and occupations in accordance with the needs of a country. It also means increasing the knowledge, skills and attitudes of the manpower to the optimum level. A well-known Chinese saying points out–

If you are planning for one year, plant grains.
If you are planning for ten years, plant trees.
If you are planning for a hundred years, plant men.

In education, human resources include teachers, headmasters, supervisors, administrators and other workers of education. Generally speaking, the meaning of human resource development differs from country-to-country. For instance, in developed countries such as Italy and Canada, human resource development means how to increase population. In USSR, it is to improve upon the quality and quantity of human resources. But in developing countries like India, human resource development is the process of increasing knowledge, the skills and the capacities of all people in the society. In economic terms, human resource development may mean the accumulation of human capital and its effective investment in the development of economy. In political term, human resource development means preparing the people for effective participation in democratic political process. From the social and cultural points of view, human resource development helps people to have a happy life.

MEANING OF HUMAN RESOURCE DEVELOPMENT

The term 'human resource' refers to total knowledge, skills, creative abilities, talents, aptitudes, attributes as well as values of the population of a country. In the words of F.H. Harbison, "The human resources are the energies, skills, talent and knowledge of people which potentially can be applied to the production of goods or the rendering of useful services". Alfred Marshall considered "the investment in human beings as the most valuable of all capital". The word 'development' refers to actualisation of implicit potentiality present in human beings. The actualisation of human potential can be considered analogous to a "seed that grows into a tree". When the seed germinates, actualisation process is triggered in the seed. The seed finally develops into a tree. Similarly, the human beings have innate biological, psychological and sociological capacities. These potential capacities should be developed and brought out to be productive. The process of developing these competencies in people is termed as *Human Resource Development* (HRD).

DEFINITION OF HUMAN RESOURCE DEVELOPMENT

Human resource development (HRD) maybe defined thus "It is that process through the medium of which the workers and members of the organization get continuous and planned cooperation". Human resource development is a process by which the people in various groups are helped to acquire new competencies continuously so as to make them more and more self-reliant and simultaneously develop a sense of pride in their country. According to Shashi Agarwal, "Human resource development refers to the relationship of one's self and with society. Human resource development also refers to factors in the individual which determine the personality, attitude and professional skills". The United Nations Development Programme (UNDP) defines the term human resource development as "Those policies and programmes that support and sustain equitable opportunities for continuing acquisition and application of skills, knowledge and competencies which promote individual autonomy and are mutually beneficial to individuals, the community and the larger environment of which they are a part". This definition refers to many dimensions of development including, physical, intellectual, emotional, social, moral, political and spiritual and all other forms of development in people.

SYMBOLS OF HUMAN RESOURCE DEVELOPMENT

The most important indicators of human resource development fall under four headings. They are as follows:

From educated people: The educated class can surely give necessary information about human resource development. This is because educated people are capable of discussing human resource development. Expansion of primary, secondary and higher education indicates that human resource development is actually taking place in the country.

Expansion of literacy: In countries like India, a vast number of people are becoming literate year by year. It means that human resource development is taking place in developing countries.

Skilled workers: From the population point of view, if the number of skilled workers like scientists, engineers, educationists, managers, doctors, teachers etc., are high in relation to the working population in a nation, then the country is considered developed. That is, the number of skilled workers is an indicator of human resource development.

Social and economic awakening: Social and economic awakening is also a symptom which indicates that human resource development is taking place. The development of socio-economic awakening and the inclination towards solving social and economic problems are an indication of the human resources of the nation.

OBJECTIVES OF HUMAN RESOURCE DEVELOPMENT

The objectives of human resource development are as follows:

- Develop the prospective powers of every worker.
- Foster his capacities according to the nature of his present work.

- Develop the capacity of workers related to their work according to their expectations.
- Create cordial relations between employers and employees.
- Develop every group and organization in an effective manner.
- Develop the spirit of mutual cooperation among the different units of organizations and groups.
- Provide opportunities to the officials of the organization and groups for self-reforms.
- Provide opportunities for complete health that may develop the capacities of the employees.

BASIC FACTS OF HUMAN RESOURCE DEVELOPMENT

- Man is the best living being.
- The nature of man is pious.
- All men are valuable capitals in one form or the other.
- Every individual has the capacity to foster himself.
- Man can be motivated to march forward by providing him suitable and healthy environment.
- The development of man is possible at any time.
- Every individual is productive and more production can be achieved by providing right direction to his innate powers.
- Individual differences in the interests and aptitudes of the individuals are unavoidable.
- The value of man cannot be measured and the ability to work cannot be separated from him.
- The efficiency of man decreases with increase in the age.

NEED AND IMPORTANCE OF HUMAN RESOURCE DEVELOPMENT

The most important sources of the development of a country is its human resources. Out of three M's—man, money and material, man is the most important key to all development. In order to achieve the goals of national development in terms of goods and services, manpower needs to be assessed, located, trained and harnessed. Human resource has been accepted as a very powerful means for the increase in productivity and income. It constitutes human capital as distinguished from physical capital. Human capital refers to investment in education, training, health and recreation of human beings. Investment in human capital is a precondition for growth and development of a nation.

An end in itself: The adoption of science based technology is the most distinctive feature of modern society. It helps the developing societies to increase their production and get ready to catch up with the developed societies. The developing countries need physical resources as well as human resources to become a developed one. Physical resources can be developed through the modernisation of agriculture and rapid industrialisation. But we require organized programmes of education for human resource development. The development of human resource is an end in itself and without it development of physical resources is not possible.

Economic endeavour: Human resources, in terms of trained and skilled manpower are the most important factors in any economic endeavour. Prof. A.K. Ghosh rightly remarks "Most of the backward countries are backward not because of inadequate supply of physical and financial resources but because of acute shortage of skilled personnel and techniques". The need and importance of human resource development is justified by its contribution to the Gross National Product, skillful handling of the machines and strengthening the durability of capital assets. Education supplies trained human resources who can get easily adjusted to the new technology.

Sustaining development: We need the development of human resources because it is a vital factor in sustaining the process of development. In the words of Paul Holffman, "The underdeveloped countries need high level manpower just as urgently as they need capital. Of all the resources required for economic development, high talent manpower requires the longest "lead time". The power station, textile factories and steel mills can be constructed in a few years, but it takes ten to fifteen years to develop managers, engineers, and administrators to operate them. The existence of such manpower is essential, if the countries are to achieve self-sustaining growth".

Building modern nation: Human resource development is a vital factor in building a modern nation. Harbison and Mayers have rightly stated that the building of modern nations depends on the development of people and the organization of human activity. Capital, natural resources, foreign and international trade, of course, play important roles in economic growth but none is more important than manpower. The Indian Education Commission has also emphasised the role of education in building the destiny of our nation.

Realising country's aspirations: Human resource development plays the most important role in the realisation of the aspirations of a country. It involves changes in the knowledge, skills, interests and values of the people that are the basic foundations of socio-economic development. In order to achieve self-sufficiency in food the farmers must be educated to adopt science based technology.

FACTORS ENCOURAGING HUMAN RESOURCE DEVELOPMENT

Great attention has been paid to the development of human resources since the closing years of the twentieth century. Dr. V.K.R.V. Rao has said, "It is the man who makes use of these equipments of production. So long as he does not have the knowledge of the necessary skills and is not motivated to play his whole role in the production, till then the development facilities would not be able to be used with economical capacity". The motivating factors of human resource development are explained as follows:

Technical skill: Technical skills are now universally recognised as the most important aspect of human resource development. This skill is very essential for technological efficiency. To achieve this skill, people should have cent percent functional literacy. Study material should be made available in simple language. Such kind of literature should also be made available at the doorstep of the functional adult. These activities facilitate the availability of technical skill for the development of the technical efficiency of the workers.

Motivation: Motivation should be given to the officials related to the groups and organizations for the positive use of the skills. It is because an employee or official could make maximum use of his capacities and skills for more and more production. In short, motivation induces the workers to work more and utilise their skills to the maximum level.

Management: Good management by a good manager is helpful in increasing the work efficiency of the organization and group in a well-mannered way. It motivates a right person to work in the right direction. Able and efficient individuals are appointed under a good management. A good employer establishes direct contact between the officials and workers and motivates them. Direct contacts enable the employees to take quick decisions and execute them promptly.

Utilisation of human resources: More utilisation of human resources, brings about more progress in the individuals, society and the nation. Underemployed and unemployed manpower block the progress of the country. Therefore, employment opportunities must be provided to those who are educated and technically trained unemployed people. Self-employment should be encouraged by providing economic help. Banks and industries can play a powerful role in order to utilise such human resources in all possible ways.

Planning: Planning techniques constitute the technology of better utilisation of human resources. It means that human resources should be utilised in a planned manner. In our country we have sufficient natural resources in the form of raw materials. They can be useful to the nation only when there is a correct and detailed survey related to human resources and natural resources. Through proper planning of techniques, creation of necessary pre-condition for accelerated economic growth, surveys of natural resources, transmission of technical knowledge of developed countries and application of science, logic and economics and natural resources can be put to good use.

ROLE OF EDUCATION IN HUMAN RESOURCE DEVELOPMENT

The development of a country is determined by its human resources, whereas the development of human resources depends on the rate of literacy and the quality of education that are available in that country. Man is ignorant and indolent by nature. It is education that makes him transformed into manpower. Education acts as an important and powerful instrument for developing human resources.

A challenging task before education: Man's intellect is getting nourished and nurtured in a right manner in the right process of education. Education makes him familiar to new things and accessible to real values and virtues of life. Thus, education tries to perform a noble and challenging task by broadening the inner structure of human mind and widening of outlook in terms of human spirit.

Revolution in technology: Education has become the cause for the revolution in communication technology, knowledge explosion, new inventions and discoveries and changing patterns of work and learning. They are essential for human resource development. On the other hand, such revolution in science and technology is impossible in the absence of education.

Education is a potential instrument: Education is a potential instrument of national development and one of its tasks is human resource development. It is the powerful channel through which our cultural heritage is transmitted from one generation to the other. Thus, it preserves our cultural values that are essential for the development of human resources. Education is a means of promoting "individual excellence". According to Prof. T.P. Nunn, "It is due to such immense importance that education has been enunciated as one of the fundamental rights". Education is directed to the full development of the human personality.

Education refines sensitivities: Education refines human sensitivities and perceptions which contribute to national cohesion, scientific temper and independence of mind and spirit. Ultimately it reaches the goals of secularism, socialism and democracy in our country.

Education develops manpower: Education makes man into manpower and produces trained and skilled persons for the agricultural, industrial and tertiary sectors of an economy. Ultimately, it guarantees national self-reliance. The National Policy on Education (1986) stated that education is a unique investment in the present and the future.

Education as a means of economic development: Education guarantees jobs or self-employment and leads to economic development by providing ways and means to improve the standard of life. Theodore Schultz and Alfred Marshall have outlined the close relationship between economic development and education. Developed countries spend more on educational development that leads to human resource development. Thus, there is a direct relationship between education and between human resource development and between human resource development and economic development.

Education an investment: Human resources are considered as human capital. So, any expenditure incurred on human capital is called investment. The Greek philosopher Plato rightly stated, "Education has an economic value as a considerable part of the wealth must be invested in education". Thus, the acquired knowledge and skill that adds to the productive capacity of an individual is taken as capital from the economic point of view.

KOTHARI'S VIEWS ON EDUCATION IN HUMAN RESOURCE DEVELOPMENT

The report of Kothari Education Commission (1964–66) highlights the role of education in human resource development. The commission says, "One of the major programmes in national reconstruction is the development of our human resources and in this there can be no limit to the education to be provided". It means that all educational endeavours have to be directed towards the development of human resources. The report of International Commission on the development of education aptly stated, "Education is no longer the privilege of an elite or the concomitant of a particular age; to an increasing extent, it is reaching out to embrace the whole society and the entire life span of the individual".

Education can play a very important role in the human resource development. Let us analyse the functions of education in bringing about human resource development.

Development of awareness: Development of awareness is the basic function of education. It is very necessary for every individual to be awakened to the individual, social and national interests. Education makes him realise that he is linked with the main stream of the country. Therefore, he should have an appropriate knowledge of his rights and duties. Education fosters positive attitudes in the individual so that he will perform his duties.

Change in behaviour: The behaviour of an individual influences the development of a society and a nation. Education nourishes human qualities by motivating him to adopt the desirable behaviour. It develops social qualities in the individuals so that socialised human resources can be produced for the betterment of nation.

Socialisation: The development of social qualities in the child is one of the functions of modern education. By socialisation we may mean that the individual and the child play a major part in social activities. As a result, he can exchange his views with other members of the society. Every child is endowed with social qualities. School is an important place where socialisation of the child can be developed.

Education imparts knowledge: Education gives us knowledge. Knowledge increases the will power of the individual and makes them mentally conscious and awakened. It is a fact that knowledge is the third eye of man through which he acts rationally with farsightedness, and in an experienced manner. Acquisition of knowledge is very important to perform every type of function, vocation and employment. For this purpose, education should make a man practical, so that he is able to make his life economically prosperous and become a useful member in the society.

Basic skills and training: It is necessary that one should have knowledge, skills and training in language. Similarly, he should have basic knowledge skill and training in vocation so that he can undertake any job or occupation to improve his social and economic status and to lead a better life.

It is education that develops human resources from every point of view by providing knowledge and training in different skills. Proper knowledge and training in different skills in different occupations make the individuals successful. This is the function of education that should be provided at the school level. In fact, it is education that makes human resources the biggest capital of the nation. In this way, a close relationship between education and economic development has been established.

Educated manpower: Education produces highly educated citizens such as able men, professors, doctors, scientists, technologists, engineers, industrialists and agriculturists etc. They are the good and powerful human resources of a nation. Education transforms a man into manpower and helps him in his vocation and vocational development. Man is successful in getting certificates or diplomas or degrees through formal and non-formal education. Highly educated persons are powerful human resources through whom changes and developments take place in the society.

Research and development: Education is a dynamic and social process which goes on continuously. It is an endless process, that is, the end of learning is giving more experience and the end of education is getting more knowledge. Research and development activities are important aspects of education to bring about human resource development. They produce individual discoverers who help to improve the other individuals, society and nation. The quality of research and development activities determines the development of human resources.

CONCLUSION

The development of human resources is very necessary for all countries. This is because human resource is now accepted as the prime mover in both the mechanics and dynamics of development. Education alone can bring about development in the intellectual, emotional, moral, material, social, spiritual, political and economic aspects of society. The wheels of history have turned a full circle and have placed man on top. Thus, man is the most powerful natural resource on the earth. He can create a new heaven and a new earth with the help of the powerful weapon called **education**.

CHAPTER 38

EDUCATION AND ECONOMIC DEVELOPMENT

INTRODUCTION

We are living in the new world of education. As a result of it, economics of education, education and economic growth, education as Investment, educational planning and manpower planning, education and human resource development and so on, have emerged as the latest concepts in the field of education. The concept "economics of education" has been developed by modern economists like Streemelin (America), John Vaizy (England) and Michael (France) in recent years. They have established a close relationship between economics and education. But we cannot deny the fact that classical economists like Adam Smith, T.R. Malthus, F.A. Walker, J.B Say, Alfred Marshall etc., had already laid the foundation of "economics of education". Education seeks the help of economics to achieve its aims of national development in all fields of national life including economic prosperity and national security. In fact, the development and reconstruction of any country depends on the quality of its citizens. The quality of its citizens depends on the quality of education which they obtain from different sources. It follows that there is an intimate relationship between education and economics. In modern times education and economics are so integrally correlated that they are like the two sides of a coin.

MEANING OF ECONOMICS

The term 'Economics' has been derived from two Greek words, *Oikos* and *nemein*. *Oikos* means a 'household' and *nemein* means 'management'. It came to be called **Oikonemia** meaning **house management**. Thus, the term 'Economics' is derived from the term *Oikonemia.* Different economisits have defined the term 'Economics' in different ways. However, it has been defined as "Science of man in relation to his wealth getting and wealth-spending activities".

Adam Smith: Father of Economics defines, "Economics is the science of wealth".

Lionel Robbins: "Economics is the science which studies human behaviour as a relationship between ends and scarce means which have alternative uses".

Alfred Marshall: "Political Economy or Economics is a study of mankind in the ordinary business of life, it examines that part of individual and social action which is most closely connected with the attainment and with the use of material requisites of well-being".

Paul Samuelson: "Economics is the study of how men and society choose, with or without the use of money, to employ scarce productive resources which could have alternative uses, to produce various commodities overtime and distribute them for consumption now and in the future among various people and groups of society".

According to the present trend, we can define thus, "Economics is the science which deals with the utilisation of scarce natural and financial resources in alternative ways to produce various goods and services over a period and distribute them for consumption now and in the future among the individual or groups and the measures taken for the welfare of each and every citizen of the country". In other words, Economics is the science of all problems related to the utilisation of alternative resources and maximization of human welfare.

MEANING OF NATIONAL DEVELOPMENT

The term "National Development" is a very wide concept indicating a harmonious and balanced development of all economic, social, cultural, religious and political aspects. If we ignore any one of these aspects, development will remain incomplete. Economic development is an important part of national development. The Kothari Commission has stated national development as "Self sufficiency in food grains, economic development, national integration, social reconstruction, development of political values and establishment of religious and cultural values etc." John Vaizy says, "National development is the total effect of all citizen's forces and additions to the stock of physical human resources, knowledge and skill". According to the United Nation Expert Committee, "National development is not only economic growth but growth plus change in turn in social, cultural and institutional as well as economic". It is concerned with both qualitative as well as quantitative improvement of the variables. Thus, national development is the development of all aspects of the nation.

MEANING OF ECONOMIC DEVELOPMENT

The meaning of economic development of a country is the increase in national income in terms of money. In the words of Prof. C.L. Anand, "Economic development means the proportion of national income that is devoted to physical investment". According to John Vaizy, "Economic development comprehensively is the total effect of development of the labour force, the accumulation of physical capital and addition to the stock of knowledge and skill available in the community". Mayer and Baldwin have defined it as, "Economic development is a process whereby an economy's real national income increases over a long period of time".

EDUCATION OF ECONOMIC VIEWS

Education as an economic good: It means that education is regarded as an economic good. It is a good that satisfies human wants and its availability is limited. Education is a non-material good. It is service rendered that satisfies human wants. It is limited and capable of being allocated to the individuals. Education is a producer's good. It can be used in the process of producing other goods and services. It helps in the production of more goods and services. As a producer's goods, education produces a teacher, an engineer, a scientist, a doctor, an industrialist, an agriculturist etc., who produce both material and non-material goods. Education is a consumer's good. It can be used by a consumer to satisfy his wants. It enriches the life of the consumers by increasing their capacity to use and enjoy the available resources, which maximise their satisfaction.

Education as an industry: Education itself is an industry producing skilled and capable persons, and prepares them to undertake various jobs in different sectors of the economy. Government spends its national income in agriculture, industry and education. The expenditure on education is increasing every year because it is a "growth industry" which creates employment opportunities. Thus, it helps to solve the problem of unemployed educated youths. Moreover, education produces material and non-material goods which satisfy our social and economic needs. In fact, they are necessary for human welfare.

Education as an important factor: We know that production is the combination of four factors such as land, labour capital and organization. Labour occupies the most important role in the process of production without which production becomes impossible. In fact, the most important factors in economic growth and development in the modern world is not based on capital formation, but human resources. The development of human resources is possible only through education, training, development of knowledge in science and technology and health improvement.

Education as a human capital: Education is the most important and valuable capital which directly promotes the quality and capacity of human beings. In short, it is the key to the production of more goods and services. Any increase in goods and services means increase in national income, and it leads to economic development and growth. Today, economists consider human beings as the most important form of capital due to three reasons. They are:

1. There are costs associated with the development and formation of human capital.
2. The costs of skilled human resources add incrementally to the national product.
3. Expenditure on human resources increases the national product and the national wealth.

Education as investment: Money spent on education is now regarded as investment. It changes man into manpower. Factors affecting human capital formation are investment in formal education, improved health, on job training, manpower rehabilitation, migration etc. Formal education increases the economic value of the human capital by developing the earning power. It also increases the current asset value of human beings. H.G. Wells says, "Investment in education has a unique importance to any nation because the effect of under investment in this field can never be fully recovered". Edward F. Denison has remarked, "Education is far from being a consumption item, it is, instead a vital item of capital formation on which the future productivity of the economy depends". Alfred Marshall has also emphasised the importance of education as, "a national investment". According to him, "The most valuable of all capitals is that which is invested in human beings". Adam Smith boldly includes all of the acquired and useful abilities of all the inhabitants of a country as part of capital.

IMPACT OF ECONOMICS ON EDUCATION

Aim of education: Economics determines the aim of education. For example, if we want to increase national income with the increase in productivity and make the nation move forward towards economic development, the aim of education should be predetermined and craft-centred. For this purpose, it gives more importance to science education, work experience and vocationalisation of education. Thus, the role of economics in determining the aims of education is very important.

Importance of education: Economics explains the need for and importance of education. In fact, the economic growth of a country is entirely based on its educational development. There is a close relationship between the growth of a nation and the development of education. In short, more education means more economic development.

Education as the means: Economics is a normative science that teaches man to be a better producer. It is meant for his personal good and for the good of the country. Thus, economics acts as the means for that end.

Education as an investment: In economic terms, education is itself an investment. Education helps to eradicate ignorance and poverty and produce skilled labourers. It creates awareness among the people to lead a better living. H.G. Shaffer makes a study of the relationship between the number of years spent in education and the income got after education. He finds that financial returns after education are proportional to the investment in education. Thus, educational expenditure is not consumption expenditure but investment expenditure.

Education as an economic security: Educational qualification determines the professional values of different individuals. It helps to determine the wage structure and guarantee for economic security of the people.

Education and economic status: Economic status of a person in a society or a nation is highly influenced by his education. It means that there is a direct relationship between education and economic status. In short, more education means more economic status. The highly qualified persons can possess good earning power and lead a good economic life.

Education and economic prosperity: Economic development and reconstruction of the country depends on the quality of its citizens. The quality of citizens depends on the quality of education. Quality education leads to the improvement of the standard of living of the people. Thus, economic prosperity of the country is directly proportional to the educational development of the people. The educational development in science and technology is a must without which economic prosperity cannot be attained in the modern age.

ROLE OF EDUCATION IN ECONOMIC DEVELOPMENT (VIEWS OF ECONOMISTS)

Economists believe that economic development of a country depends on its natural resources. But countries like Israel, Holland, Norway, Switzerland, Denmark and Japan are highly developed countries possessing scarce natural resources. At the same time, the Gulf countries and Brazil are underdeveloped countries though they have rich oil resources and mineral wealth. From this fact, the opinion of earlier economists has been disproved. In fact, countries rich in natural resources are poor and countries poor in natural resources are rich. It has been proved beyond doubt after a prolonged analysis that educational development of a country is the most potent factor of its economic development.

Adam Smith (1776) and Karl Marx (1867) have accepted the contribution of education to economic development. Alfred Marshall (1890) has stated that the expenditure upon education is 'national investment'. Joseph Schumpeter (1911) has called education a very important factor in economic development. Prof. John Vaizy (1962) has mentioned three functions of education and described the relationship between education and economic development as chicken–egg relationship. Herbinson and Mayers (1964) have indicated that education is both the seed and the flower of economic development. Bertrand Russell has pointed out the influence of different economic systems on education. Schultz has proved that education is an essential factor in economic growth and that the money spent on education is, in fact, investment in education. In India Dr. Atmananda Misra (1962), J.P. Naik (1965), Dr. V.K.R.V. Rao, D.P. Chaudhri (1968), J.V.J. Tilak and others, have conducted a number of studies to establish the relationship between education and economics. D.P. Chaudhri has proved the existence of positive relationship between the educational level of farmers and their productive capacity in many states. J.V.J. Tilak has also found a very high level of positive correlation between the educational expenditure and the national income in India.

Views of Great Thinkers

John Vaizy: "Education has become a major source of skills and trained skills. Indeed, from one point of view, this is education's critical role".

Schultz: "Fewer steel mills and other big plants should be built in the so- called under developed countries and more invested in the people of these countries".

J.K. Norton: "The effect of investment in physical capital depends in a large measure on the intelligence and the skill of the people who use this capital".

Don Adams: "The wisdom distilled from the last two decades of international focus on the developing areas of the world suggests that the educational factor is of crucial importance in attaining even modest goals of economic and social development".

H. Combes: "Today, it is clear that industrialization and whole modernisation process cannot proceed without the development of human resources, and for this a major investment in education is required".

V.K.R.V. Rao: "Let us not think that education is just a consumption of welfare activity, some think that it can be postponed in preference to investment in irrigation, power, steel mills or more salaries for government officers who will administer these programmes. The sooner this is recognized by influential persons in this country, the better would be India's chances to achieve the high rate of economic growth which we all desire".

National policy on education (1986): "The country has reached a stage in its economic and technical development when a major effort must be made to derive the maximum benefit from the assets already created and to ensure that the fruits of change reach all sections. Education is the highway to that goal".

From the given analysis and the views of thinkers, it has been made vivid that human resources are more important than natural resources in determining the economic development of a country. The history of the world is also a witness to the fact that countries such as, Japan, England, China, Russia, America, Germany, France, Holland, Switzerland, Norway, Denmark, Israel etc., have attained an all-round progress through the medium of education. In fact, the industrially advanced countries have almost cent percent literacy. The quality of education is also very high. On the other hand the underdeveloped and undeveloped countries have very low rate of literacy and the quality of education is also poor.

ROLE OF EDUCATION IN ECONOMIC DEVELOPMENT

Economic development of a country is largely determined by its human resource development. The development of human resources depends on the rate of literacy and the quality of education. Let us bring out the role of education in economic development.

Education as a material wealth: The role of human resources in the economic development of a country is more important than its natural resources. Education changes a man into manpower.

According to Alfred Marshall, "education produces a man more intelligent, more ready and more trustworthy in his ordinary work; it raises the tone of his life in working hours and out of working hours; it is an important means towards the production of material wealth. Education is universally accepted as a very useful productive activity to produce material wealth which promotes national prosperity and welfare in all fields.

Education develops occupational skill: Education creates able workmen, administrators, teachers, doctors, scientists, engineers, lawyers, industrialists, etc. It means that education prepares the people to work in various fields such as agriculture, science, industry, banking, business, transportation, medicine, law, engineering, construction work etc. In short, education increases the quality of manpower and develops occupational skills which lead to increase in production and national development. In this way education determines the economic development of a country.

Education is job-oriented: Education guarantees some sort of employment or self-employment to the individual. Mahatma Gandhi introduced basic education in which he emphasises craft education rather than academic education with a view to preparing the individual to stand on his own leg. Indian Education Commission stresses on productivity as one of the goals of education.

The new structure of education 10+2+3, guarantees to the individual, thousands of trades and professions in the field of agriculture, industry, business, commerce, defence etc. Work experience and vocationalisation are the two factors needed for job-oriented education. It has been proposed that work experience should be an integral part of the curriculum prescribed for school education. Moreover, vocational courses should be introduced at the 11th and +2 levels. Thus, vocationalisation of education means making education job oriented and producing self-sufficient human beings.

Education increases productive efficiency: We know that education is an investment and the economic development of a country depends on the productive efficiency of the individuals. Illiterate people cannot cooperate with the government in the campaigns of increased production. For example, our five year plans could not function properly because out of 600 million people, about 400 millions were illiterates. But the comprehensive scheme of adult education, women education, distance education and non-formal education have increased skill and proficiency of millions of people. Mass media like, newspapers, television, radio programmes help in this regard. Thus, the emphasis on adult education, in service and on the job training facilities, distance education and non-formal education for productive efficiency can help to raise the country above the poverty line. It is the power of education that forces the country to move towards economic prosperity.

Education and planning educational expenditure: The economic prosperity of a country depends on the size of finances spent on educational development. It has been proved that the developed countries spend more than 10% to above 25% of the national income on education. But the underdeveloped and developing countries like India and Brazil spend hardly 2% of the national income on education.

Economics explains two major principles on the basis of which educational expenditure should be planned:

1. There should be an optimum level of investment (a good proportion of national income) in education and it must be raised from the present meagre outlay. The plan and non-plan expenditure on education in public and private sectors need to be enhanced considerably.
2. Any future planning of educational expenditure should take its consideration the economic aspects of the society. It implies that we have to spend more on polytechnics, industrial schools and colleges, agricultural courses, engineering courses, distance education, non-

formal courses and on vocational courses in order to increase the skill of the earners whose contribution is immense in the economic development of the country.

Education and cost benefit analysis: Both economists and educationists have conducted researches to establish the relationship between the cost incurred on education and the benefit obtained out of such costs, and determine the future benefit of increasing an investment in the field of education. It has been proved that money invested in education of a child guarantees far more dividends than money spent in the business and industry. For example, investment made on a child enabling him to become a doctor brings an enormous income in future and this benefit is far greater than the benefit got from the same investment in teaching profession. Educated parents are conscious of this phenomenon. As a result of it, a career in IAS, IPS, IES, medicine, engineering, science and technology, banking is more preferred than one in teaching, ITI, nursing etc. Economics teaches one to be a physician or a surgeon than a dentist or radiologists. It is because education determines the economic status of an individual. A head-nurse does not have the same status as a junior house surgeon. In this way, education determines the economic status of the people and economic development of a country. A developed country is one where the quality of education is very high and where there will be plenty of doctors, engineers, scientists and technologists.

Education and manpower planning: Human resources are plenty in our country. Hence, it needs proper direction so that the available resources are utilised to an optimum level to achieve the goal of our country, that is, economic development. Such direction is called manpower analysis. The aim of manpower analysis is to have a clear picture of the human problems of India and forecast trends in the inter-relationship between these problems and their causes. Education helps and solves various problems relating to human resources through manpower analysis. Let us see them here:

- It determines the shortages in the requirements of skilled workers. It points out the reasons thereof.
- It indicates the surplus of trained workers and also the reasons thereof.
- It indicates the future needs for trained workers in different sectors of the economy.
- It plans educational courses and vocational courses in such a manner that there would be no surplus or shortage of workers in any field.

There should be no unemployment or overemployment, either among the educated or the uneducated. The human resources should be fully utilised in the country.

In the absence of manpower planning, human resources cannot be utilised in the best possible manner and economic development is not possible. Education provides the people proper training and skills to undertake various economic activities and to raise their income that determines the economic development of a country.

Education–population Control and economic development: Growth of population spoils the economic growth of a country. T.R. Malthus has stated that the rise in population growth, results in exhaustion of the natural resources. In fact, there is a negative correlation between growth of population and economic development. It is essential that to achieve economic development, population explosion should be controlled. In this regard, education is a powerful instrument in reducing the size of population and bringing about the desirable changes among the people. It is population education which should be taught in the schools, colleges and non-formal institutions in order to foster awareness about the growth of population and its consequences. It also teaches how to control population growth and suggests various measures for it. Thus, education has become an effective means of economic development through controlling the size of population.

Education and prosperity: Education improves the quality and working capacity of the individuals. It helps them to find jobs and it enables them to be independent. An educated person increases production according to his abilities and skills. Education increases his income, raises his standard of living and saving capacity etc. It brings about economic prosperity to the nation. In short, education enables man to earn his living and ensure his welfare and prosperity.

Education and infrastructural facility: Education is closely associated with economic development. It produces a number of scientists, technologists and engineers who engage in inventions and discoveries. New transportation and communication systems have been created to make human life very simple. The inventions and discoveries in the field of infrastructure can bring about economic development in a society.

Education—social mobility and economic development: Education increases the efficiency of workers and encourages them to try for better position. This tendency leads to social mobility and physical mobility of workers. The movement of a person from lower status to higher status improves his quality of life. Similarly, movement of a person from rural to an urban area increases his income and standard of living. Thus, both social mobility and physical mobility become the cause for economic development. This is only because of job oriented education and training.

Education—national integration and economic development: Education fosters the feeling of national integration, international understanding and globalization. This kind of feeling is very essential in modern times so that a country can make a move towards economic prosperity. Moreover, international understanding and globalization increase investment opportunities across the world.

Education—democracy and economic development: Education can make the people democratic in attitude and behaviour. Democratic behaviour can usher in social peace. Such peace is essential for economic growth. Thus, education modifies human behaviour in such a way that it develops social justice in wealth distribution and equalisation of educational opportunities.

Education—medicines and economic development: Education improves the health of the people by discovering new medicines to cure diseases. It helps the people to protect their health by propagating preventive measures before they get affected. Education also brings about awareness in consumers to use fresh materials and protect themselves from exploitation of any kind.

Education—machines and economic development: Education helps in the invention of new types of machines and equipments. As a result of it, modern methods of production are followed in agricultural, industrial and tertiary sectors that produce more goods and services. The production of goods and services determines the economic development of a country. In other words, all the inventions and discoveries take the country in the path of economic development.

CONCLUSION

Education acts as a powerful instrument and it creates a proper environment for economic development. In fact, education contributes to the economic development of the country through training and developing skills required for efficient and improved production. The developed countries of the world also prove that economic development takes place only as a result of the development of education. We cannot disagree with the views of Herbison and Meyers that education is the seed and flower of economic growth.

UNIT V

EDUCATION AND SOCIETY

CHAPTER 39

SOCIALISATION OF CHILD

INTRODUCTION

The purpose of education is not only teaching the child to read, write, speak and think, but also making him a social being to emerge as a responsible being for himself and the society. Man is an animal by nature, but his behaviour and activities like selfishness, cheating, eve-teasing, raping, ragging, human trafficking, back biting, swindling, stealing, murdering, committing suicide, printing fake certificates and currencies, dishonesty, corruption, communal riots, regionalism and lust over wealth, make him worse than animals. So, socialisation of the child is one of the most important aims of education. In fact, education is a process of man-making and nation-making. Socialisation with desirable character formation is very essential, especially in the materialistic society.

MEANING OF SOCIALISATION

Socialisation is a process of making an individual a social being. It is a process through which society develops an individual according to the ideals, beliefs and traditions. It also bestows recognition to him in the society. In other words, it is the process of enabling an individual to interact with other individuals, and learn social values and behaviour. Such learning makes himself well-adjusted with his family, neighbours and other social groups. According to Kimball Young, the whole process of socialisation falls within the scope of interaction or the social act.

DEFINITIONS OF SOCIALISATION

- **J.S. Ross:** "Socialisation is the development of 'we feeling' in association and the growth in their capacity, and will to act together."
- **Havighurst and Newgarton:** "Socialisation is the process by which children learn the ways of their society, and make these ways a part of their own personality."
- **Bogardus:** "Socialisation is the process whereby persons learn to behave dependably together on behalf of human welfare, and in doing so, experiences social self-control, social responsibility and balanced personalities."

Thus, we may define socialisation as training or instructing the child to adjust himself and live amicably with the varied cultured people of a society or nation.

FACTORS OF SOCIALISATION

The following are the factors, which play a vital role in making the child a social being.

Family of the child: The nature of upbringing of a child plays an important role in socialising him. The child is born and brought up in a family. He initially comes in close contact with his parents, brothers and sisters. The way in which the parents bring up the child, and the atmosphere in which he is brought up, moulds him to become social or anti-social individual in the society. Hence, love, sympathy, tolerance, co-operation, adjustments, honesty and non-violence are essential for social life. It is from the family that such values should be inculcated in the child. Improper upbringing of a child leads to the formation of anti-social tendencies in him. So, a healthy and proper upbringing of the child is essential to make him/her a good social being.

Friends and neighbours: Relatives, friends and neighbours play important role in socialisation of the child. In fact, children living in the same locality interact with above people and develop affection, fellow-feeling, brotherhood, kindness, compassion, helping, and responsibility. Bad friends and neighbourhoods, and so on, spoil the desirable development and socialisation of the child. So, people belonging to good families prefer to live with good friends and neighbours.

School: School is an important center for socialisation of the child. In fact, it is a place where children belonging to different socio- cultural economic backgrounds meet, learn and play together. Such interaction inculcates social feeling, adjustment, vselfish-less, affection, kindness, co-operation, and sacrifice in children.

Games and sport: Games and sports lead to more effective interaction than organised teaching in the class. In fact, they help the child socialise through developing the social qualities, such as selfless service, sacrifice, co-operation, team spirit and fellow-feeling.

Scouts and guides: Scouts and guids also play important role in socialising a child. It aims at serving the society. Thus, it motivates and inspire the child to involve in various social service-oriented projects and programmes through co-operative efforts, sacrifice, sympathy, fellow-feeling, and discharge various social responsibilities.

Religion: Religion plays vital role in socialisation of the child. In fact, each religion has its specific virtues, rituals, dogmas cosmologies, philosophies, faiths and beliefs, which have great impact on the personal as well as social life of the child. For instance, the religion inculcates values, such as respecting the elders, honouring the parents, loving the enemies, helping the poor, co-operating, being honest, adjusting, tolerant and selfless sacrifice.

Teachers: Like parents, teachers also hold an important place in socialising the child. It is one of the responsibilities of the teachers. They can make the child socialise through social teaching and life.

Imitation: Imitation is found as a natural character in the child as well as social life. It is one of the ways of learning in the social environment. It prepares the child for social life.

FACTORS RESISTING SOCIALISATION

Negative attitude of family: Right parenting is necessary to build up the future of a child. In the present times, parents are seeking for a short-cut and easy ways to bring up their kids for their own benefit. Most of the parents are selfish in nature. They do not know how to treat their children. Lack of parental affection, tolerance, non-violence, selfishness, favouritism, divorce, or separation or widowed have great impact on socialisation of the child. In fact, these elements curb the child from socialising in the materialistic world.

Undesirable culture: Casteism, religionism, and regionism affect the socialisation of the child. In fact, caste distinction, social disparities, religious prejudices, social status, snobberies, superiority and inferiority affect the socialisation of child.

Practical experiences: Bad experiences with friends, relatives and neighbours such as sufferings, hardships, insult, envy-less of life or properties, injustice, despondency, desperation, receipt, cheating, dishonesty and lust for wealth have adverse effects on socialisation.

Economic conditions: Unemployment, poverty, low income, indebtedness and inequalities in income distribution affect the process of socialisation.

Materialistic development: The real spiritual development has been declining whereas materialistic development dominates the whole human society. The lust for wealth and money reduces the social attitude towards social responsibility.

Commercial world: This is a commercial world in which every activity whether religious or irreligious is measured in terms of money. In fact, almost all services are profit-oriented and works are wage-centred. It turns man-making process of socialisation of child into money-making.

Narrow outlook: "I-feeling" and selfishness, caste-, religious- or region-based politics develop narrow mindedness which also affect the development of social attitudes in the child.

Social factors: Lack of literacy, drinking habits, ignorance, disease, social immobility, corruption and lack of adjustment and cooperation also have adverse impact on socialisation.

NEED AND IMPORTANCE OF SOCIALISATION

Social being: Man is a social being and individual life is not possible on earth so he should socialise for the betterment of his personal as well as social life.

Materialism: Every individual considers that money is more important than man. So, he gives utmost importance to money- making. This tendency affects socialisation of the child. He is prepared to accept that man is more important than money.

Aimless man: A number of people in the society lead aimless life. Such people spend their time only in chatting, smoking, drinking, chewing tobacco, gossiping, gambling and any other anti-social and personal matters. They live a filthy life. So, socialisation of the child is very important in a globalised society.

Selfishness: Most of the people are selfish in all respects. It is not good for a healthy human life and society. Hence, every child needs to socialise from its childhood through people, education, training and guidance.

Broad outlook: The present education and practical life fail to shun narrowism in most of the people with respect to caste, religion and regionalism. In fact, we are staying in a globalised society and this earth is meant for human existence. The formation of regional groupism in the name of caste, religion and language not only vitiate the co-operation and operation of the people and but also weaken them. Groupism makes it a meaningless one. Hence, socialisation of the child is very essential to make him come out of narrowism and prepare for social life.

ROLE OF TEACHER IN SOCIALISATION OF CHILD

Teachers are parents in the school and parents are teachers in the family. The child should follow and practice the lifestyle and ideas, and belief of his teacher. So teacher's role is very important in the socialisation of a child.

Teacher-parent co-operation: The teacher should come into close contact with the parents of the child and know his interest, aptitudes and tendencies. Then he should provide suitable facilities for the maximum development of social qualities in the child.

Transmission of culture: It is teacher who should convey to the child about the cultural heritage in the form of customs, traditions, ideas, values and patterns of behaviour in effective and meaningful way. Such cultures will lead to the development of valuable and desirable social outlook in the child.

Social ideas: Teacher should instill social ideas in children not only in classrooms but on the playground and in the cultural and social functions and in all academic activities. Above all he should be role model and have social qualities and responsibilities in such a way to make the child socialise gradually.

Group work: Teacher should organise team for group work, where children work jointly with natural co-operation, love, sympathy, fellow-feeling and adjustments. The inculcation of team spirit leads to socialisation of the child.

Inter-cultural programme: Generally, children of different cultures learn and play together. So, the teacher should develop inter- cultural feelings in children. Such efforts enable them to accept and respect their culture along with others.

Human relation: A healthy human relationship plays a significant role in the socialisation of a child. In this regard teacher should build healthy human relations with other children, teachers, parents and society will provide such healthy social environment which will help in socialisation of the child.

Teachers' practices: Every teacher should have clean habits and be impartial in words and deeds. He should be socialist, sacrificer, succour and at least man of good qualities and aim at socialisation of the child.

CONCLUSION

This is a monetary world where parents seek for the economic benefits for their children. Teachers aim to get promotion, increment and transfer (near to their houses), and achieve academic achievement of their students and the governments seek the welfare of the people by encouraging the production and marketing of intoxicants. So, the society is full of drunkards, smokers, tobacco chewers, corrupt, dishonest, groupist, narrow mindedness and characterless people. Moreover, the present education is not meant for man-making but it is a source of employment or income for standard of living or degrees. Thus, socialisation of the child is difficult in the commercial, principle-less political and characterless world. However, every child should socialise for personal, social and national development from the socio, cultural and economic point of view. This is possible only through effective and efficient government, good parents, good teachers and good society. So, teachers and students should bring a change in themselves to be a model to ensure a better generation in all respects.

CHAPTER 40

EDUCATION FOR NEW SOCIAL ORDER

INTRODUCTION

Education is not only meant for employment and income generations but also most important and useful tool to bring about new social order. In the words of George S. Counts "Education as a force for social regeneration must march hand in hand with living and creative forces of the social order". For this purpose, the teacher must bridge the gap between school and society. Infact, the process of education cannot go in isolation from the changing social order. That is why the British rulers considered education as the most important medium to establish a social order in the Indian society so Lord Macaulay laid the foundation for British system of education in India, that is we must be at present do our best to form class of persons. Accordingly, Indian in blood, and colour but English in taste, in opinion, in morals, and in intellect. After the independent of India, the national leaders felt that the existing social order needed radial changes Accordingly the concept of the new social order of aspirations, ideals and values found expression in the India constitution on 26th January 1950.

MEANING OF NEW SOCIAL ORDER

New social order is anything which governs and activates the society in the right direction in which all people enjoy freedom, equality and secularism. It emphasises internationalism, multi-lingualism, unity of whole human races and avoiders the separations of people in terms of languages caste and religious. Thus social order is the order in which the society is for individual and the individual for society. So everyone should enjoy the life in the natural and social environments.

Aspirations Ideals and Values of New Social order: The values for social order are based on the cultural, Philosophical spiritual and social traditions of India. It emphasises the democratic principles such as freedom, equality, tolerance, ability to adjust and work together. It also includes socialistic principles such as respect for and commitment to equality in opportunities and status and equitable distribution of wealth. And the secular principles such as freedom of workshop, respect for all religious and readiness to manage civil affairs with secular outlook.

The preamble of the constitution states the social order as,

- Justice in social economic and political life.
- Liberty in expression, belief, faith and worship.

- Equality in opportunities and status.
- Fraternity in dignity of the individuals and integrity of nation.

PRESENT SITUATION OF HUMAN LIFE

The present position of human affairs is profoundly disturbed in all respects. It is seem that civilisation changes the social structure which is the greater turning points in personal and social life. As a result, a few enjoy the life and they dare to assert that we live in an age of sanity, decency and enlightment. However, the present man is confronted with challenging situation in political economic social cultural and religious activities. Infact he comes across the great changes taking place in everyday life let us examine deeply the challenges that the existing social order poses in the Indian society.

According to Dr S Radhakrishnan, the present man is a source of pride, bewilderment and alarm. It is a matter of pride that the present generation has developed science and technology which enable them to dominate the skies reach out to the stars and expand to the ends of the world. It is a strange that while the world is shrinking, the narrow society is extending out of its limits to become a world society consequently nationalism is now being understood in terms of inter nationalism. And the whole mankind is advancing rapidly towards a new social integration.

The present world is also a source of bewilderment Dr Radhakrishnan observes "We are bewildered that human efforts to establish a world order on the principles of equality and freedom through international organisations and have not been successful. Though the world is one that, in spite of political, national and racial divisions the fortunes of every one of us are linked to those of others even though we know it- we do not feel it in our bones. Even today the devils such as war, violence, poverty, unemployment, inequality, terrorism corruption, greedy, jealous, ignorance, illiteracy, selfishness, egoism, casteism, religious fundamentalism, prostitution murdering and intoxication destroy the future dream and retard the development of mankind. So the dream of building a new social order based on happy life and cooperative living is still in the darkness.

Moreover the well advanced countries are not ready to change their ways, of dealing with others. So the present generation is not only bewildered but also alarmed in the competitive market economy. The intimacy has been forced upon nations. But, the enforced intimacy intensified differences and increased the possibilities of friction. Dr Radhakrishnan observes that we are baffled by the problems because the leadership of advanced countries are failing us.

NEED AND IMPORTANCE OF NEW SOCIAL ORDER

The formation of new social order is very essential in the market economy where everything is more important than man. However we may state the following factors which emphasise the need and importance of new social order is the globalised society.

- Inequality in economic life and injustice to women in social life have been increasing and have a great impact on the social environments.
- Family is a basic unit in social order but there is a vast disintegration in it. It is one of the causes of neglected social goods and damaging social order.
- The cooperation between home, school and society is fast disappearing at present. So life has became extremely complex in which man is ever busy in getting and spending for goods and services.

- This is an industrialised society where man is huge machine and life is all mechanical. Moreover there seems to be a fundamental contradiction between the individual's freedom and actual opportunity under conditions of mass production.
- There has been a fast growth of middle class people in the Indian society. It struggles to survive but slips down in the socio- economic ladder.
- The existing social order is fast crumbling under the heavy weight of moral degradation which rises to conflicts in the economic order. Profit motive has become common in the materialistic market economy. In fact, profit making at the cost of the weaker has been the order of the day.
- Political corruption has become a social culture found in almost all fields. It is a process of buying and selling votes for money. The public in its turn caught in a private gain will disregard public welfare continue to vote straight and thus maintain the machine in Power. The corruptive officials invite the dishonest business. This is an endless vicious circle which has a great impact on the ordinary life and social environment.

NEW SOCIAL ORDER FOR 21ST CENTURY

The objective of establishment of new social order for 21st century may be listed as,

- Love the country and develops patriotism.
- Realise man is more important than anything in the earth.
- Establish and strength equality, justice and freedom to all either rich or poor and male or female.
- Foster the feeling of everything for man but not man for everything.
- Eradicate poverty, illiteracy and socio-economic disparities.
- Ensure social welfare and happy life.
- Put an end to the production and consumptions of those products which affect the health and mislead man to involve in illegal sex, corruption, murdering, suicide, divorcé, and anti-social activities.
- Avoid the exploitation of population in the name of regional language caste, gender, principles mushroom politics.
- Enable the individuals to understand himself and reality of uncertain life.
- Turn animal man into rational one to be useful himself others and society and prepare him for better life.
- Train the people develop those qualities which prepare them for co-operative life and work.
- Establish a corruption, terrorism and violence free and peaceful society.

Thus the objectives of social order emphasise to bring about social changes in the social environment for equal right and happy life and to shun social discrimination and contemptible or undesirable human activities.

SOCIAL ORDER AND FUTURE VISION

The government should frame social orders and implement them further betterment of middle class and low groups and socially back ward people. This is because every child is born free but he is chained everywhere. So, the future vision of new social order is to free the individual from the grip of harrow mindedness and develop a secular based democratic outlook and happiness irrespective of discriminating the people.

The small nations break off the chain of political subjugation and relieve themselves from the political, economic mental and emotional strain. Every man and woman are conscious of his/her rights and the values of justice equality and opportunity. Thus, the new social order emphasises the provision of equal opportunities in education, employment and income. Moreover, peace at home and abroad is the future hope and expectation of every individual.

The ideal of the new social order proposes to shifts the political power to these who are to be governed in a real democratic way. Exploitation of capitalists at any cost should not be allowed Barriers of castes, colour, creed, religion, region and language and economic conditions should be broken and the antinationalistic out look should be included in all towards the path of progress and happy life. The false pride, competitive spirit, lust for wealth and political corruption should give social bliss and happiness which make life worthless. The socio-cultural values such as brotherhood, tolerance, forgiveness, sacrifice, co-operation and selflessness are to be fostered and the intellectual values of thinking, judging, understanding criticising and reasoning capacity should be developed through providing right learning atmosphere. The individuals and the society should develop together that is live and let live for peaceful co-existence is the vision of future. Prof. K.G. Saiyidain says "Social order should be an order which would exploit the resources and possibilities of modern scientific technology to eliminate all avoidable poverty and in security which afflict mankind today. Striving for a miserable and insecure livelihood. The social order to which we pledge our loyalty must attempt to control the productive activities of scientific industry in the interests of society as a whole. It must secure real equality of opportunity for individuals and groups and bring about a fairer distribution of the good of life, both materials and cultural. It should reject the claims of the acquisitive instinct and incentive as the only powerful and stable motive force of human conduct".

EDUCATION AND SOCIAL ORDER

Education is the only remedy for the implementation of social order. It helps in the creation of the new social order in the materialistic society. In fact, education should inculcate democratic way of life and internationalism . Moreover, it bridges the gap between 'haves' and 'have-nots'. So, education for children and adult should be made free and compulsory Education should eradicate social discrimination and establish new social order for better and happy life.

ROLE OF TEACHER

The stupendous task of the teacher is creating a new and better world through right education. Hr should treat the school as the social institution where pupils should be trained for co-operative work and life. So the teachers should discharge their duties and responsibilities honestly and sincerely. They should take care of intellectual, physical social, economic, cultural and emotional development of the child. Mark or grade is not a matter of man making but it is one of the ways for higher education and employment. Above all, students should be trained to accept, respect, and recognise the individuality of every child and fight against anything which separate the unity of mankind. But the present teachers do not teach the values but insist the students to memorise the study materials for mark scoring the study materials for mark scoring. So there will be no difference between literate and illiterate in character and deeds. In fact, lust for materialism, selfishness, laziness and lack of quality teachers make them worse than the students. However, man can alone teach man so teacher should prepare selves to be fit for teaching and man making. It is mostly deplorable that they do not worry about the growth of anti-social activities and production of intoxicants which pollute the social environment but worry about their transfers, promotions, increments and higher salary. They should stand against caste, color, creed, corruption terrorism, violence, production of obscene-violence based mass media and intoxicants and work for the progress of society and nation. Education can be effective for new social order only if teachers are dedicated for students, society and welfare of the country.

GOVERNMENT AND SOCIAL ORDER

It is mostly true what Bacon says, "it would be futile thinking to analyse a situation and then to do nothing about it. The role of government is more important than education and teachers. The government is strong enough to enact the social order for the betterment of middle class and socially backward groups. In fact, it is difficult to know whether it encourages materialisation of education in the image of English or cheating the public using mother tongues as a medium instruction. For political advantage it makes the people fool, and uses mother tongue, religion caste and money as the weapon to win in the state/Central election. It widens the gap between haves and have-nots in economic distribution but also in educational aspects. So, freedom, equal opportunities, justice, brotherhood and cooperation have become verbal and not practical. The success of social order and provision of better life to all depend on effective government teachers and education. Obscene films, indecent communication in television, production of intoxicants, corruptions and terrorism spoil the whole social environments in which expectation of best men and better life is not possible. In fact, opportunities should reach the people who live in slums bus stand, railways stations and road sides. The government should know that increase in the salary of employees in government departments and educational institutions does not improve the efficiency of workers but cause inflation and inequality which vitate social order and happy life of the mass.

CONCLUSION

Social order is very essential to make the human life happy and meaningful. In fact, freedom, justice, equal opportunities co-operation and equality make the people enjoy the life peacefully. But, the ineffective government and teachers and selfishness and narrow mindedness make the social order meaningless. However, freedom and equality in opportunities prepare the people for co-operative work and life. Education is one of the means by which a little changes can be brought about in the society. Best government best teachers and best education can alone help the implementation of social order in a better and effective manner in the complicated Indian Society.

CHAPTER 41

EDUCATION AND POLITICS

INTRODUCTION

There is a close relationship between politics and education. Politics plays important role in the welfare of the state and social life. In fact, a welfare state whether capitalists or socialist or mixed one should provide the basic necessities like education, medicine, and food to all or needy ones. So, one of the important functions of the state is to provide free and compulsory education upto secondary level or free education on the basis of merits. Thus education has become one of the subject of state control, guidance and assistance from pre-primary education to research levels. Education produces different types of human resources to be employed in various fields to produce goods and services which determine the economic development of the country. So, a country whether developed or under developed or undeveloped one reserve a fund for educational development. It has been proved that education is the back bone of economic, social and cultural developments. Thus, politics and education are integrally co-related and mutually complementary and supplementary. This is also because both aim to bring out the full development of individuality and society. It is seen that the present politics or state is believed to aim at welfare of the citizens. So, it is the responsibility of the state to provide the best possible kind of education at all levels.

STATE AND EDUCATION

In the ancient times, the aim and function of the state were to protect the people and country from foreign aggression and natural hazards. Thus, it was a police state not welfare one. So, people established educational institutions in the residential places and separate ones on voluntary basis to teach reading, writing, arithmetic and protect from animals. So, the state had nothing to impart education and uplift the society. However, charitable institutions and religious associations provided education in the middle age period. They opposed the interference of state in their field of educational activities. But the people began to welcome the interference of state or government in education. So the politics or state came to control and provide education to all in the end of 19th century. The political philosophers like Fitche and Hegel emphasized and advocated control of state over education and centralized it. Moreover, the social transformation and gradual complication of cultural and civilisational behavior created the necessity of state control on education. It is also proved that no force is strong enough to meet and solve the every growing problem of the people. In fact, state is the only powerful organization which alone can meet the educational and material needs of the people.

POLITICS ON EDUCATION

The whole educational process remained under the control of monarchy or despotic rules in the despotic state. Education is used to bolster up consolidating the rule of the monarchy. So, education is centralized by the state government. On the other hand, democratic state decentralizes the educational process for the benefits of the individuals and society. The constitution of democracy empowers the state to take up the responsibility of providing education to all children irrespective of caste, religion, creed and economic status. The state governments control educational institutions by means of financial aids and supports. It also supervises the privately managed institutions by means of great-in-aid and recognition. It guides controls and supervises the fields of aims, curriculum, textbook and examinations at various levels of education through various agencies and boards. It has administrative control in the field of appointment of principals, headmasters and teachers as per the qualification and experience prescribed by educational authorities. The privately owned aided and non-aided institutions also fall in line and work according to the direction of state government.

Education in Monarchy: An individual cannot even dream of his progress and freedom in a monarchial government. But he is expected to sacrifice his all, even his life for the welfare of the society. As such, the aim of education is not formulated in the interests and needs of the child but it aims to achieve and foster the welfare of society. As a result, education becomes a very formal and dull process which remains quite indifferent towards the development of the child. Therefore, the monarchial state lays down the pre-determined pattern of education. As such the matters included in the curriculum are indoctrinated rigidly into the minds of children, which foster the qualities such as self-discipline, obedience, tolerance, service and sacrifice. These qualities help the monarch to achieve its own welfare. As such, education is meant for state welfare not for individual ones.

Education is Aristocracy: The government in aristocracy fosters the welfare of the powerful few who enforce absolute obedience and service among the masses. As such, education is meant a few not for all people. So, the aim of education is to promote the good of the chosen few and neglect the welfare of ordinary people. However, the qualities of tolerance, obedience, service and self-sacrifice are inculcated through educational processes.

Education in Democracy: The democratic state provides importance to education for all. So, it decentralized the educational system in order to develop the individuals and society as far as possible. This is because such government is based upon the principles of equality, fraternity and liberty, focusing the formation of co-operation, fellow-feeling, brotherhood, tolerance,, understanding, adjustment, service and sacrifice. As such, each individual is provided with maximum opportunities to develop himself/herself to the possible extent according to his/her interest, inclinations, aptitudes, capacities and needs. So, the democratic curriculum is formulated on the basis of principle of diversity to suit the needs of all children. Therefore, a democratic teacher should provide best possible guidance to develop the child and prepare him for all aspects of life.

Education in Socialistic State: A socialistic state emphasizes the growth and development or welfare of society. It is not meant for individual development. In other words the development of country is very important. So, agricultural, technical and vocational education is imparted on scientific lines. Moreover, the educational opportunities are provided to all in order to develop them according to their needs, interests, aptitudes and capacities. It raises the standard of living up which contributes to the welfare of the country.

Education in Welfare State: The welfare state is believed to be aim at the welfare of people. Such state should provide best possible kind of education which enables the people to achieve balanced development. The state should step in and fill the vacuum where educational opportunities are not available. In fact, it is desirable that the state should retain some control over education in order to achieve the welfare of the people. For instance, it should compel the parent to send their children to educational institutions. For this purpose, the states should arrange universal and compulsory education upto secondary level. Moreover, it should provide textbooks, uniforms and meals to the students. The state may impose taxes upon the people to collect funds for educational purposes. It also determines the syllabi for state institutions as well as institutions controlled by private individuals.

EDUCATIONAL FUNCTIONS OF POLITICS/STATE

MacIver and Page have rightly pointed out that there are certain functions which the state alone can perform, others which can be performed by others but not so efficiently as by the state, and yet others which are best left to other agencies, apart from those which the state does not have the ability to perform. The provision of education falls into the first and second of the above four categories, because not only is the state the best equipped for this task, it is in fact the only agency capable of coping with the educational problems of populations of remarkable size. So, it is believed that the state alone can provide universal and compulsory education to a large number of people especially in developing countries. The functions of democratic state government in the sphere of education have been mentioned below.

Establishment of Educational Institutions: The most important function of the state in the democratic country is provision of schools, colleges and universities to meet various levels and types of education for socio-economic life. It is not feasible to provide educational facilities in the rural and backward areas. But, the state government takes up this responsibility to maintain equality in the sphere of education.

Providing Free and Compulsory Education: This is another remarkable function of the state provide equal opportunity in education by making it free and compulsory for all irrespective of socio-economic status. This function encourages the poor parents to send their children to school for education which removes the darkness of ignorance and superstitions.

Financing Educational Institution: This is regarded as one of the most important functions of the state. In this regard, the state plans and provides finance for education, scholarships and financial assistance to very poor and intelligent students at all stages. It provides adequate financial assistance to the schools, colleges, universities established either by the state government or run by religious/ private individuals.

Supply of Efficient Teachers: The provision of universal, free and compulsory education requires a number of competent and efficient teachers. So the state government opens teacher training institutions/colleges to train up the students and turn into capable teachers to provide quality education and experiences useful to achieve the development of the child.

Provision of Military Education: The role of state government is to open school/college for military education in order to protect the country from foreign attacks/invasion. Such educated/trained people are necessary to save lives and properties during emergency and natural hazards.

Control and Guidance of Education: One important function of state in the sphere of education is control, inspection and guidance of educational institutions run by the governments and private individuals. Such activities of the state improve the quality of teachers and education.

Construction of Curriculum: The state/central government officials plan and construct the curriculum for various levels of education according to the needs and interest of the child with the help of educationists and well experienced teachers or experts in the educational field.

Provision of Standard Books: The quality of education depends upon the availability of good and standard text books for teaching and learning. In fact the quality text books should contain exercises for creativity, self-development and develop research attitudes in the learners. Moreover, the state pursued authors and publishers to produce good and standard text books of reasonable price.

Organisation of Educational Boards: It is state which organizes the Boards and committees for determining the aims, curriculum, methods and examination system and relevant activities concerning education for the development of individuals and society.

Appointment of Educational Commissions: The laudable function of state in the sphere of education is the appointment of commissions and committees to review and modify the educational systems in the light of science and technological advancements. It also removes the drawbacks found in the current educational systems and renew it with remarkable changes to be done for the benefits of the pupils living in the complicated society.

Provision of Scholarships: In a democratic and welfare state, the government provides scholarships, stipends and awards to many talented, gifted and intelligent students of indigent means who cannot pursue their education properly or go ahead further. It also provides such financial assistance to the needy and deserving ones without any discrimination of colour, caste, creed and sex.

Construct National Scheme of Education: A democratic state appoints a committee to construct a national scheme of education based on the multifarious needs of the children. The committee consists of educationists, educational philosophers and government officials (Ministers). After the construction of a comprehensive scheme of education, it is scrutinized and executed in such a way that no one is discriminated on the basis of colour, caste, sex and socio-economic status. It means that each child should get equal opportunities to grow and develop in the democratic state.

Training in Citizenship: The progress of a state depends on the ability, capacity, strength and character of people. So, in the sphere of education, one important function is to train the young man and woman in political, social, cultural, scientific and economic life. For this, the state should create art galleries, cultural committees, scientific exhibitions, libraries, zoos, clubs, industrial and agricultural (vocational) oriented training. Such training and programmes/activities enable the citizens to grow into dynamic, resourceful and national minded ones and to serve the society with sincerity, zeal and devotion. It is seen that the state sends cultural delegations to other countries and helps the international exchange of teachers and students which are necessary to maintain a healthy levels of social being with all round personality developments. National Cadet Corps, National Service Scheme, Scouting and Guiding, Red Cross Club, train the young people to serve the society, country and world, political training on principles, aims and ideas is provided by means of free film shows, military demonstrations, radio, magazines, newspapers, television and various social mass media, which acquaint the people with the latest progress taking place in political, economic and social thinking. Such knowledge develops leadership qualities of the citizens. Thus, all aspects of education and training depend entirely upon the co-operation of the state.

Organisation of Refresher and Orientation courses/programmes: This is also said to be an important function of state. It undertakes and organize various refresher or orientation programmes/courses to improve the efficiency of faculties working in colleges/universities. Moreover, it also organizes adult education for the illiterate adults and uneducated who are interested in education. It reserves a huge find to conduct adult education and refresher courses. It may fail to bring about desirable results in the teaching faculties in India. However, it may provide an opportunity to develop the quality of resource person who share their knowledge and experiences in the programmes.

Encourage Educational Researcher: The modern education is project or research oriented especially in science and technology. Most of the researchers in the Indian society undertaken for certificate or degrees to get employment in higher educational institutions. However, there are plagiarisms or duplicate or old one in the new jackets due to meet the requirements of appointments. Anyhow, the state encourages research activities to solve social issues and expand the area of various subjects. Indian researchers suffer a lot due to lack of efficient guides and poor quality of research scholars. Moreover, it leads to corruption and favouritism in the educational fields.

EDUCATION ON POLITICS

It cannot be denied that education has a great impact on politics or state. In fact, education enables the people to analyse and understand different political parties and elect the best one for the betterment of individual and society. But, this is not possible in Indian society where democracy is misused by a lot of principleless political parties which cannot face or contest the election individually. This is the weakness of Indian Politics. So well educated people who are thinking rationally avoid polling votes to any political party. Moreover, Indian politics are caste, religion, profit and corruption centred where character and efficiency of politicians are immaterial. Votes for cash, caste or religion is the slogan of present politics. Hence, education is very important to make the people understand various socio, economic and political issues which retard the progress of individuals and country and foster a secular – democratic outlook and broad minds in the younger generations. We may point out the remarkable impact of education on politics in many countries.

- Education produces learned people in political field who dedicate them for individual and national developments.
- It makes the people to understand socio-economic cultural problems and elect the right politicians to face the challenges and issues.
- It develops leadership qualities and empower the politicians to establish good and healthy governments.
- It helps the voters to cast their votes to the candidates whom they intend to elect at central or state level.
- Education establishes good government at the state and central levels (This is not true in India).
- True education and rational thinking prepare the ruling parties and opposite to accept and adjust one another for nation-making but not treating as enemies in India.
- It never develops selfishness, narrow minds and insecular and non democratic outlook in the state government.
- Educated persons never try to cast the votes of other in the assembly or parliamentary elections.

MERITS OF STATE ON EDUCATION

The role of state is very important in the field of education. We can justify in the following grounds.

- Universalisation of education for all people of all categories in all places.
- Provision of free and compulsory education to illiteracy and poverty.
- State alone can provide better education and training and work for the welfare of the individual and society.
- Equality in education provided in the schools run by the state.
- It meets the educational requirements of needy and poor.

DEMERITS OF STATE ON EDUCATION

- It causes the entry of politics in education.
- Its policy of liberalization and privatization reduces the quality of education.
- It creates inequality in education by permitting different boards of education at regional, state and central levels.
- It cheats and exploits the society in the name of medium of instructions. The narrow minded people also support to the state. There must be opportunities for learning any language.
- It causes education a corruption centred for appointments, promotion and transfer of staff and authorities.
- Vice-Chancellors and educational authorities appointed on the basis of corruption, caste and politics in Indian society.
- It insists to the school to produce cent percent results in the public examination which sport educational qualities and character of the students.
- Teachers working in state school neglect their duties and responsibilities. They involve illegal sex, drugs or intoxicants and many antisocial or undesirable activities.
- It compels the Ph.D. Degree for recruitment in college and universities. As a result most of the candidate misuse of researches and submit duplicate/qualityless thesis.
- The state and characterless teachers/officials pollute education and make it to the extent that illiterate is better than literate in character.
- The Indian educational philosophers emphasise national system of education with uniform curriculum. But there is no equality, uniformity and freedom in education.
- Everything is thrown in winds, but not practice that is the weakness of Indian society.

CONCLUSION

Education has become one of the basic necessities of human beings in the personal, social and global life. So, it should be provided to all irrespective of creed, caste, religion, sex, colour and economic status. Education is a costly goods in the materialistic society. So, it is not feasible for all especially economically backward ones. At this juncture, it is the responsibility of the state which showed to provide it upto a certain levels so that illiteracy, poverty and child labour can be eradicated to a certain extent and welfare of the people and society can be maintained in the country. The state should provide uniform education and abolish different boards of education which exploit the society for money-making. In other words, there should be one curriculum and education in the country. However, regional matters may be given due importance in a separate subjects or paper. So that the students can grasp their society. The state should impart vocation education and training after the secondary education and value education for man and nation making which is very essential in the monetary world. Moreover, the state should recruit the educational officers based on their academic and personal qualities and experience in the relevant field not on caste or corruption. It should advise the committee to construct the curriculum according to social and economic needs of the child. They may think or feel that big curriculum would improve the quality of education. But it is never so, because education is meant for life in all aspects. The poor quality of committee in character and deeds construct a very curriculum due to their ignorance. Such one never keeps in mind the ability, interest and needs of the children. They simply sitting and talking unnecessary matters or consuming intoxicants and construct aimless curriculum which develops aversion over education. The state and educationists or committee should understand that curriculum whether big or small must contain those subjects and activities which should lead to desirable character formation and develop socio-democratic outlook in the teachers and learners. Further, the state should not stress the head master, or teacher to produce cent percent results in the public examination at secondary and higher secondary levels. Such a situation produces lakhs of unemployable graduates and post graduates who may engage in many filthy activities and increase the expenditure of the governments. The state government should realize that education is not only received from the educational institutions but from the obscene violence based mass media, and society. The society is full of intoxicants, illegal sex and corruption which spoil the children. As such, education has become meaningless in the man-nation making process. So the welfare state should be careful to avoid intoxicants and anti-social or undesirable activities such as divorce, poverty, suicides, illegal sex, raping, killing, printing fake certificates and currencies diluting painted effigies in water resources and crack firing in the festivals which cause social and environmental pollution. Lack of efficient governments and quality educationists, the system of education is not related to life but creates problems.

CHAPTER 42

RELIGIOUS EDUCATION

Man is the most powerful living species in the earth. He behaved like animals and had no rational thinking. He killed human beings and animals. He had many wives and a woman had many husbands. No human relationship is maintained in the family and society. At the same time, antisocial/ undesirable activities such as illegal sex, prostitution, killing, unkindness, disrespecting parents and elders, polygamy and polyandry telling lies, lust for wealth and greedness pushed him into darkness life. As such there was no difference between man and animals in deeds and behavior. However, he learned to protect him from animals and natural hazards. Such learning transferred from old and experienced one to young ones. Thus learning or education modified and changed his behavior and developed rational thinking which helped him to invent many machines, tools, equipments and apply them for protection. Shelter and production of food and cloths met his basic necessities. However, the ancient generation lived in fear of harmful animals, natural hazards, illness, untimely death and complicated problematic society. So he believed in the super natural power, life after death and the existence of evil spirits. Consequently, he started to worship the nature and gods. The great people like Socrates, Gautam Buddha, Jesus Christ, St. Paul, Sri Narayana Guru, Swami Vivekananda, Mohammed Nabi, Confusious, Gurunanak and various idealists, philosophers, preached and practiced ethical principles and doctrines to lead the human beings in the right path. For instance, Do not kill, Do not lie, Honour parents, Respect elders. As a result the idea or concept of religion emerged in the ancient time. And people have different beliefs, faiths, rituals and ceremonies, to please their gods – Sun, rivers, Cobra, Banion Trees and Idols or supreme power of nature. The present generation enjoys technological, scientific and materialistic life on the one hand and believes in god, heaven, blessings, and life after death on the other hands. Thus, man's life has become a pendulum between materialism and spiritualism. In fact, about 89 per cent of the people cannot be separated from religious faiths, beliefs and rituals. Today, there are gods in different names, forms and colours at local, regional, national and international levels. Jesus Christ is entirely different from all other idols worshipped as gods due to superstition and ignorance, but he is only one who preached and practiced everything for human beings.

MEANING OF RELIGION

The word 'Religion' is a combination of two Latin words that is, '*Re*' and '*Legere*' which refer to bind back or establish connections between man and God. Accordingly, religion signifies those moral bonds of love, sacrifice, kindness and social service which hold the human community together. As such, the essence/core of true religion is love, affection, kindness, sympathy, empathy, co-operation, tolerance, fellow-feeling, brother-hood, sacrifice, forgiveness and other moral and spiritual values which shape and modify the behavior and deeds of human beings in a desirable way.

Gisbert has rightly remarked as, "Religion establishes a double bond one between man and God and the other between man and man as children of God". In the narrow sense, religion is a blind belief in some rituals, religious ceremonies and ways of worship. However, the real concept is much wider than mere rituals that is attending the temples, reciting incantations, performing Hindu rituals or going to the church, listening the word of Jesus Christ, singing hymns and praying to God. Broadly speaking religion signifies the purity of heart, love, helping, good, feelings and actions together with spiritual development. It is the inculcation of a feeling of good to others and stimulation of a spirit of service towards humanity.

Accordingly, religion/worship of God is not confined to any specific precincts but embraces our actions everywhere and throughout the whole life. So, religion consists of all noble ideas, ideals and values which specify the relation between man and God together with a mission of service, devotion and dedication to human welfare. In other words, religion is not merely an intellectual imagination but it is the sum total of all the desirable social, moral and moral values embodied in our conduct and character. The true religion enables to realize all the highest desirable social, moral, ethical and spiritual values which prepare the man for better life. We may say that religion is a set of principles doctrines and ethics of human values formulated with different faiths and beliefs on God or divinity which make human life happy, healthy and peaceful in the materialistic and problematic society. Religion preaches many moral values which strengthen and purify our heart, body and mind and establishes heavenly life in the earth.

DEFINITIONS OF RELIGION

Dawson: "Whenever and wherever man has a sense of dependence on external powers which are conceived as mysterious and higher than man's own, there is religion"

Kant: "Religion is the recognition of all our duties as divine commandments".

Harald Hoffding: "The essence of religion is faith in the conversation of values".

A.N.White: "Religion is a vision of something which stands beyond, behind and within".

Gisbert: "Religion is the dynamic belief in and submission to God or Gods on whom man feels dependent".

Oxford Dictionary: "Religion is the belief in and worship of a super human controlling power, especially a personal god or gods".

Thus, different scholars define religion in different ways but everything centred around gods, divinity, moral values and ethics which makes human life happy and peaceful. Therefore we may define as "Religion" is a faith and worship of people in different names of gods made of clay or metal with ritual ceremonies (pouring milk, bathing with turmeric water, organizing chariot procession with a effigy of gods and elephants to please them for healing, blessing and solving problems of life". The religious books preach values, ethics and principles/doctrines to be practiced for man-making and happy life.

RELIGIOUS-ORIENTED HUMAN VALUES

The role of religion is very important in modifying the behavior of human beings. As it emphasizes both human and spiritual values, it fosters desirable characters in the child. Religion is important and useful tool which help man to enjoy a peaceful life in complicated society. At the same time superstitious activities like procession with elephant, dissolving effigy of Vinayaka (Ganesh) in water resources using loud speakers, pulling chariots, pouring milk over idols, firing crackers reduce spiritual development, pollute socio-natural environments, creates conflicts, and wasting time, money and energy. As such religious activities and undesirable deeds of pastors, poojaris, priests and moral vies, and offering-centred prayers, threatening the innocent people in the names of witches, evil spirits, heaven and hell. Moreover, people worship their grandfathers/mothers or ancestors with rituals. It also reduces faith on gods. However, religious principles and doctrines inculcate values which are basically essential for man-making.

Hindu Scriptures: Hindu scriptures contain value-oriented thoughts which humanizes the mankind. Do the good to humanity. Enjoy your own wealth and covet not the wealth of others. Earn wealth in a righteous way. The Hindu scriptures shun crookedness and make the people live in a spirit of friendliness with all. Noble qualities give peace of mind; widespread fame and add to one's greatness. Bhagavad-Gita says that we should discharge duties diligently and honestly and fight for justice and right cause. It also emphasizes the development of self-reliance, self-confidence, self-effort, self-control and courage. Death is certain so one should not lament over the inevitable. Do good, avoid bad and fight against evils.

Taoism: Three jewels of Taoism are: (1) Compassion, kindles, love, gentleness, tenderness and mercy (mother's qualities), (2) Simplicity, moderation, frugality and economy teach moral life, (3) Humanity and modesty to avoid premature death. Ethics of Taoism is concerned less with doing good acts than becoming a good person who lives in harmony with all things and people. It teaches moral values against killing, steeling, lying and sexual misconduct. Return anger with goodness.

Judaism: Treat others with respect, be tolerant of differences, be honest and reliable. Kindness to the needy, benevolence, faith, compassion for the sufferings. Tension and conflict result in destructive behavior. Anger causes strife and destruction. Share your bread with hungry, and take the poor into your home, when you see the naked clothe him and do not ignore your own kin God made all men brother and they should live together as brothers at all times.

Sikhism: It emphasizes the human values which makes human life happy and peaceful. According to this religion, truth is higher, but higher still is truthful living. There can no worship without good action. God's eye of mercy falls on those who take care of lowest. The life of speaking god's grace is not to be of idle mysticism but of active service done in the midst of worldly relations. Anger is fire that burns us. Get together my brothers and remove all misunderstanding through regard for each other.

Buddhism: One should not give way to anger, but control it. God loves sincere man. Works determine one's place the world. One should have right understanding, right thoughts, right concentration and right effort. Suffering is caused by desire. The suppression of desire leads to the extinction of suffering. Buddhism leads to life which is very simple and pure.

Jainism: It believes in non-violence/non-injury to beings. Liberation is obtained through right philosophy, right knowledge and right conduct. Right conduct refers to not to lie, not to steal not to strive for luxury, and not to strive for possessions, not to be unchaste and not to injure any livng organism. Treat all men as brother at all times. Reach the goal of good life by pious works.

Confucianism: Confucius, a Chinese philosopher, preached human values such as avoid hatred and anger. Friendship and brotherhood are the cordinal virtues. Heaven will help the man who is sincere. Work in the mark of a good man not ease. Friendly towards everyone. When you see a man of worth, think of how you may emulate him. When you see one who is unworthy, examine your own character. Father should be father, son should be son and king should be king to form good life and governments.

Christianity: Jesus Christ is the father of human values which enable the people to lead a happy, healthy and peaceful life. In fact, there is a everlasting life in His powerful words. Honour the father and mother. Respect the elders. Do not kill, Do not commit adultery. Do not steal. Don't bear false witness against neighbours. Do not covet neighbour's wife and goods. Bless those who curse. Love your enemies. Endure in brother's love. Do not commit sin. Forgive other's mistakes/sins. Love thy neighbours as love thyself. Thus, he is the symbol of love, simplicity and kindness.

Islam: Islam also emphasizes values such as be honest in exchange of things. Do not acquire other's substance wrongfully. Do not sell inferior and low-quality things. Do not be unjust to others. All men are brothers and should live as such. Secrets of progress lies in self sacrifice. Every Muslim should expend all his / her effort and energy for the society. Greedy people are not successful and suffer loss. Work for global solidarity struggle against injustice and for the protection of human rights, sincerity, help the deserving people, compassion towards disasters, poverty and unjustice.

RELIGION AND EDUCATION

The aim of contemporary education is to achieve the mental, physical, economic, social, cultural, moral and spiritual development of the individual. As such the modern educationists stress the importance of moral and religious education at school and college levels. According to Swami Vivekananda, "Religion is the basis of education". There is a very intimate relation between religion and education. In the words of E.D. Burton, "Religion and education are close and real friends. Both are related to spiritualism in contrast to physical and material phenomenon. Both try to free the human being not from his physical surroundings but try to free from the slavery to physical environment". Education broadens the human outlook and modifies his behaviour according to those ideals and values recognized by different religions. Mahatma Gandhi believed that morals, ethics and religion are convertible terms. So, a moral life without reference to religion is like a house built upon sand. In the opinion of Ross, "It is through religion that the youth can be set on the road to the pursuit of three absolute values that is truth, beauty and goodness. In fact, man cannot have faith in truth, beauty and goodness in the absence of moral character which depends on religious education. The religious faiths and beliefs assist the individual to face all kinds of adverse conditions. This is because religion provides confidence and courage to solve the problems / difficulties irrespective of darkness outlook.

According to Ryburn, "Religion plays an important part on the lives of people that the work of school for democracy will be facilitated through it". It is true that religion inculcates those moral qualities which mould the educational system on democratic lines. The democratic and secular policy which aim at providing equal opportunities for all the citizens is rightly based on the religious principles. Moreover, religion inculcates in the child a spirit of self-confidence, self-discipline, sense of duty, responsibility and humanity. So that he / she can work for the welfare of others with a spirit of love, kindness, devotion and dedication. In the opinion of E.A. Pires, "Harmony in education brings out the necessity of religious education for harmony in educational philosophy or system". In fact, there is a harmony among philosophy, religion and education. The triangle relationship has a great impact on human life. Therefore, the curriculum which incorporates philosophical and cultural values in the educational system naturally give due place to religious values and ideals. It is also important to note that naturalism and pragmatism cannot preserve the moral and spiritual values of life in the complicated materialistic society. So, the need of the day is that philosophy and education should lead man higher towards achieving the noble and immortal ideals of truth, beauty and goodness for making life happy and peaceful through the realization of God. This is possible by incorporating the philosophy of idealism in education which serves as a sound basis for noble ideals and values derived from religions. As such, education and religion aim at the fullest development of human personality including moral and spiritual aspects. That is why religion has been an integral part of education since ancient times. Moreover, we cannot deny the views of Prof. Kabir, "Religion is one of the greatest forces in the librating and uplifting the human beings from the bondage of selfishness. Since it is during adolescence the mind is most ready for identification with a higher cause and willing to sacrifice everything for its sake, it is necessary that pupils must not be denied the liberating influence of religion in this widest aspect. Short of dogma and ritual will express the great ideals and values which form universal ethics for all men. Unless students are brought into contact with the great ideals, their lives with remain improverished and meaningless". Moreover, the role of religious values cannot be underestimated in the man-making process at any cost in the complicated materialistic society.

AIMS OF RELIGIOUS EDUCATION

Religious education should be imparted in school and college levels so as to modify the behavious of the educands. It should be taught as an integral part of general, vocational and professional education and training. Such education should be purposeful and aim at achieving desirable changes good personal, social and national life.

Moral Development: Naturally, man is a type of animal who should be humanished with desirable character and conduct. He should be disciplined one in all aspects of life. All religion teach good virtues and values which are essential for moral development. It enables the child to follow whatever is good and keep away bad ones.

Refinement of Human Values: Religious education distinguishes divine or spiritual world from materialistic one. It refines human values and puts him on the path to higher values which make him happy, healthy and peaceful. It also aims at fostering divine qualities and values which shift the man from the bondage of darkness of ignorance and superstitions to free light of divinity and humanity.

Character Formation: This was one of the most important aim of education in the idealistic society. But it is neglected in the scientific and materialistic society. As a result, Man becomes characterless and inhuman–disrespect elders and teachers, dishonouring parents, addicting to smokes and drugs and obscene–violence mass media. As a result, raping, killing, robbering, prostitution, illegal sex, corruption, suicides, accidents and intoxicants are increasing. Man becomes machines, life becomes use and through one. This tendency should be changed through character formation which depend on religious education and social behavior. According to Madden Ward, "Religious strength of character includes humility, which recognizes one's inevitable fallibility and submits to the correct process of group thinking and co-operative action".

Development of Democratic Outlook: This is one of the important aims of religious education in the post-modern society. It develops a democratic outlook among the school children and college students, so that they realize importance of equal rights and opportunities. They respect one another in the social environment. Religion establishes relation of man to God and man to man, and society. Swami Vivekananda says, "See God in human faces". Aringer Anna Durai (Chief Minister of Tamil Nadu

1967–1969) says, "See god in the smile of poor". Jesus Christ says, "Love your enemies" and "Forgive others". The basis of democracy is liberty fraternity and equality. These values develop a democratic outlook so that we can live as the children of God.

Social Development: Generally man is selfish one but he should be socialized by religious education. Jesus Christ says, "One should not look into one's matters but concern for others". Proverb and Sirach books of Bible and other religion emphasis the self-renunciation but sacrifice the self and serve the society. In short, man should forget his own interest to think of humanity at large level.

Develop Broad minds: This remarkable aim of religious education is to develop a broad mind/ wider outlook in the child. It requires a higher thinking and divine qualities which can be gained from religious studies. In fact, man should give up narrow outlook on language, caste, religion and region but develop a broad mind to adjust to live in the varied socio–cultural environment. Here, 'we' feeling is more important than 'I' feeling. Religion develops proper attitude which helps the child to achieve complete development. Such development ensures independent, self-reliant and self-confidence and enables to face the problems of life.

Spiritual Development: Religious education is a source of spiritual development. Naturally people have faith on life after death. Man is a spiritual being and it should be developed by religious rituals and ceremonies or worship/prayers. Moreover, spiritual development is very essential to have right thoughts and action. Hence, religious education is meant for spiritual development and spiritual life.

Cultural Development: Generally, culture differs from religion to religion. As a result, people have different culture followed in personal, cultural and spiritual life. Dr. S. Radhakrishnan has stressed the contribution of religious education to the cultural development of the child. In fact, good habits, dressing and life style are influenced by religion. For instance, Islam prefers to non-vegetarians whereas Hindus prefer vegetarian. Thus, role of religion of important in the preservation of culture.

Scientific Development: Religion is not only meant for spiritual development but also for scientific and rational development. As such, religion consists of the reality of life. Take medicine to heal illness and pray to God for your sin. Patients need doctors and medicine (The Bible). Do whatever is good but do not expect its consequences. As death is certain to that which is born, avoid lament over the death (Bhagavad-Gita). Man's days are seventy or eighty years depend on his strength (The Bible). Lust for money / wealth is the root cause of all sins (The Bible). Thus religion inculcates the scientific outlook and reality of human. There is no salt in the yolk of egg and life exists in the blood of living organism (The Bible). Similarly, a number of truth and scientific values can be gained from religious books. Hence, scientific development can be considered as one of the aims of religious education in the modern world.

Sublimation of Instincts: Child is the outcome of obscene activities. So, it is born with undesirable instincts which make it less than animals. However, it is socialized in social environments. There are inborn instincts which sprout in the childhood and developed in the adolescence period. Such instincts may be socially desirable or abrogable one. But it should be sublimated and rediverted in a useful way. It is religious education which purifies and sublimates the raw instincts of children into desirable channel of behavior or it turns undesirable instincts into useful and important one for man-making and nation-making.

METHODS AND FORM OF RELIGIOUS EDUCATION

The importance of religious education can be justified from the religion oriented human values and the role of religion in the man-making process. Now, the question is how religious education can be important and what should be its subject matter. This is because religion is acquired, not taught for it is not a subject to be learnt but to be realized and translated into life. However, lecture method, discussion method, assignment method, seminars, conference and project method can be used to impart religious education at school and college levels.

Lecture Method: This method is useful to explain the basic principles of different religions. It can also be used to teach human and spiritual values. Moreover, religious based stories can be explained through lecture method. The teacher who are interested in teaching religious education should be permitted to impart such education because it can be realization of life. This method is very simple and useful at school and college levels.

Discussion Method: This methods provides equal opportunities in teaching and learning religious education. In short, both teacher and educand take part in discussion method. As such, this is a students centred learning. Teacher and student discuss the basic principles, ideals and values of different religions. It provides a comprehensive ideas of every religion. The method of teaching can be very effective because students belong to different religions can share / discuss their religious thoughts for moral and spiritual development. Accepting the strength and weakness of religion leads to secularism and democracy. All students can have opportunity to share their religious thoughts, experience and knowledge gained in personal and social life.

Assignment Method: This method may be effective at high and higher secondary school level. The teacher should prepare list of topics from different religions and distribute them among the students for writing assignments in 5 or 10 pages. He should collect the assignments and share the core points of every religion, so that students can get the knowledge about various religions. Students may also be demanded to produce assignment on religious leaders and their contribution to the society. Such topics develops desirable qualities in the students.

Seminars and Conferenes: There are hearing techniques used in college and university levels. Students are asked to organize seminars / conferences at regional, national and international levels. It should be done under the guidance and supervision of teachers/profession. Topics should be selected based on the needs of the society to highlight moral and spiritual values and develop secular outlook to shun communal riots and conflicts. Moreover, biography and contribution of great men like, Confucius, Buddha, Jesus Christ, Mohamed Nabi, Guru Nanak, Sri Narayana Guru and Swami Vivekananda to the society may be selected as topics for seminars and conference. Such methods enable the educand to comprehend the reality of life and achieve fullest personality development - tolerance, adjustment, cooperation, brother-hood, wider outlook.

Project Method: This is also known as learning by doing method followed at college / university levels. The titles such as comparative religious studies, religious oriented moral and spiritual values, origin of religion, values of Hinduism, Thoughts of Buddhism and Impact of Religion on society may be selected as major topics for analytical studies. It encourages self-learning and develops analytical minds. It enables to find answer/solution to communal riots/conflicts. It also helps to develop leadership qualities.

FORMS OF RELIGIOUS EDUCATION

Since ancient times, the religious and moral principles have been influencing the aims, curriculum and techniques of education. In those times, religion held sway in almost all the western countries. It was only through religious education that people were taught to live in unity, peace and co-operation.

The reformation movement in England had left the work of education on churches and other religious institutions. Gradually the concept and practice of secular education began to hold the field and replaced religious education and monopolized by a particular sector mission in the 19th century. The religious school movement in America replaced the old pattern of education by general and liberal education under the policy of religious neutrality in the 20th century.

Education has been religious in India and other Eastern countries since ancient times. Mc Donell remarks, "Indian education bears the imprint of religion since very early ages of human history. It is true that in those days religious people were used to be teachers who taught moral and religious values. Moreover, education maintained its religious character and form during Muslim rules. But religious neutrality was practiced during the British Rule. However, the religious neutrality policy was opposed by Indians. As a result, denominational schools began to be established in the country. The Hindu insisted firmly that education devoid of religion would destroy their religion and culture. Hence the Hunter Commission, The Punjab University Commission and other Commissions and Committees recommend some sort of religious education to be included in the various system of education in India. Thus, the study of religious aspect has become an integral part of education and it is being imparted in form at school and college levels.

- Religious education is provided weekly once / twice in the last school / college hours.
- It is imparted in two forms that is moral instruction (MI) and religious instruction (RI).
- Religious and moral values are taught with examples to be followed in the practical life.
- Short stories and skits are used to inculcate religious values in the students.
- Religious / social leaders or workers are invited to deliver religious and moral values on special occasions.
- Religious / moral instructions / scriptures are displayed in libraries or school / college premises so that students / teachers can listen them.
- Such education / values are insisted through morning prayers / singing hymns and thoughts for the day.
- Religious festivals are observed with special functions so as to make the student happy and peaceful.

PROBLEMS OF RELIGIOUS EDUCATION

There are many religions or gods in the world with different faiths, beliefs, rituals, ceremonies and performances. So, it is not possible to unite them into one in the complicated society. Moreover, children born in a religious family may not acceptor adjust to other religions because of the existence of superstitious faiths and deeds. However, people of different religions can be integrated or united through right thinking of life realty and virtues. Generally, all religions have four components that is virtues, dogmas, rituals and cosmology. Virtues may be positive and negative commendments which can be imparted through religious education. The inculcation of rituals, dogma and cosmologies in the child would lead to narrow views and evil consequences. In fact, teaching of religious education itself involves some problems.

Bigotry and Narrow Mindedness: Narrow and rigid religious education trains the child in fanaticism and blind following of dogmas and rituals of a particular religion. It develops narrow communal outlook which leads to strife, discard and conflicts to the detriment of national unity.

Neglecting Present Life: Most of the religious education aims at preparing the child for the unknown super natural world that is life after death. As such it separates him / her from the present life and hampers the whole development of personality.

Unhealthy Atmosphere: A dogmatic and blind communal education spoils the mental health of the child. This promotes narrow outlook and chauvinism which cause discord and conflicts. It creates an unhealthy atmosphere against liberal outlooks and attitudes at national and international levels.

Create Objection: Narrow bigoted religious education creates many problems in almost all spheres of life. Teaching of one religion in a community / minority school / college may be opposed / protested / objected by other religious children / society. It is against secularism and democracy.

No Solution for Problems: Religious education may overlook and neglect the pressing problems such as poverty, unemployment, drugs, dowry, corruption and a number of undesirable deeds which the individual and society faces today. As schools serve the society and as such type of education imparted by them should tackle the problems of the individual and society. No religious education removes the inequality and narrow minds of castes and religionisms.

Mental Conflicts and Confusions: Religious education creates mental conflicts and confusions in the minds of children. For instance, the concepts of truth, and falsehood, virtue and vice, materialism and spiritualism, seven births, life after death, heaven and hell, create a sort of tension in the problematic society.

Lack of Faith and Confidence: Scientific, technical and materialistic development and undesirable behavior and activities of religious workers reduce faiths and beliefs on religions. However, illness, chronic diseases, physical feebleness fearness and thinking of unknown eternal life push the people into religious realm. That is why people use god's names to tobacco products, tea stalls, intoxicants and vehicles.

Lack of Teachers and Money: Teaching of education requires capable teachers to handle the sensitive issues. They should be good in behavior and models in all respects. But, it is very difficult to find such religious persons in the monetary and obscene-violence centred world.

Misinterpretation of Religion: The present generation use religion for blessings and not for character formation and good deeds. It is used as a source of employment and income. So, the aims of religion is shifted from human values to money values in terms of offerings. Hence, religious education is not much effective in materialistic society.

PRECAUTIONS IN RELIGIOUS EDUCATION

There are private or aided schools and colleges established in the names of gods and religious leaders or religion in the Indian Society. As such, religion has become an integral part of life and education. Hence, religious education, moral instructions, prayer, singing religious songs and hymns, worship, ritual performance and religious ceremonies are given due importance in schools and colleges. Therefore, we should keep in mind the precautions given here to make it successful in the multi-religious countries.

- Narrow religious education spoils the natural development of the child. So, healthy principles and virtues of all religions should be incorporated in the education which enables the child to avoid fanaticism, bigotry and blind beliefs.
- School environment should be conducive to impart the moral and spiritual values of all religions.
- The indoctrination of dogmatic education should not be made compulsory or allowed at all, because, it misleads the child.
- No child should be compelled to receive any kind/particular religious education as it causes communal riots or superstitious faiths and beliefs and develops narrowism in him/her.

- Generally, religious education should be imparted only to those students who opt it with the consent of their parents/guardian.
- Moral stories and life of great personalities should be included in the religious education in order to imbibe and foster human values, patriotism, democratic outlook and secularism.
- Critical outlook of the adolescents should be developed through moral and religious values so that they can avoid blind beliefs and rationalize their faiths and actions.
- The activities of school/college should reflect all the higher moral ideals and values to be implemented in the practical life.
- The teacher should be example/model to the students in words and deeds based on moral and spiritual values.
- Unity of all religions should be emphasized to integrate students of different religious principles and values in the man-making process. In fact, every one should remember the words of Mahatma Gandhiji, "the fundamental principles of ethics are common to all religions. These should be certainly taught to students".

RELIGIOUS EDUCATION FOR SECULARISM

The development of secular outlook is very important in the country of diverse religions one to avoid communal riots and terrorism. It strengthens the unity and integrity of the nation. Secular based religious education not only removes the fanaticism and blind beliefs but also broadens the minds of students which prepar them to work and live together. In fact, any kind of narrow, bigoted and communal education would create divisions and dissensions in a country or in the world. Hence, a separated ideal of secular liberal education should be imparted to the students for man-making and nation-making. The defects of religious education cause India to emphasize secular ideal. According to Article 19 of Indian Constitution, all citizens are free to follow any creed or section and no tax is imposed on them. According to Article 22 no religious education can be imparted in government schools. Even in other schools, there is no compulsion on any child who does not like to opt for that education. As such the country or state has no religion. It is committed to democratic ideal beliefs and human values.

Moreover, rationalists believe that man is more important than religion and god. This is because religion is made of man, by man and for man make his life happy and peaceful. He frames principles, values and ideals for better life. The symbols of his extraordinary imagination is the creation of gods in different shapes, size and colour. But Jesus Christ is worshiped and considered as God because of His affirm human values, love, devotion and dedication until death and for the concern over the poor and sick. His powerful preaching and deeds influence the people like St. Pauls, St. Therase, Ida Scudder, Francis Assisi and foreign missionaries who served the society. Swami Vivekananda, a great practical Saint rightly remarks If I belonging to Eastern nations worship, Jesus Christ as Good. There is no doubt that He the divine qualities and deeds found in Him. The present pastors and priests exploit in the words of evil spirits, witching, heaven, hell, blessing and healing for money making. As such, religion has become offering entertainment and film centred one. So, faith spiritualism has gone and finance materialism has come in the monetary world. But everything whether good or bad happens according to one's fate, faith, thoughts and deeds. However, one can reprise the divinity of God in the service, sacrifice, dedication, spotless love, justice, kindness, sympathy and sharing of wealth to uplift the needy and downtrodden people. Otherwise, religion is useless and meaningless in the materialistic society. Jesus Christ asked the people to be the slat and light to the world. Accordingly, religion is not to be taught at any price but practiced them at any costs for socio-spiritual development which is more essential in humanizing the man than anything in the complicated society.

CONCLUSION

There are culturally, socially, rationally, economically, academically, professionally and religiously different types of people in the world. Most of them whether rich or poor, literate or illiterate, young or old, doing filthy or socially undesirable deeds have faiths and beliefs in gods and religions. Some of them belong to any religion but do not have faiths and beliefs. Few of them belong to any religion but have strong faith in divinity and religious rituals. A very few of them, whether belong to religion, have rationalistic and secular outlook. However, many of them are religious and still in the darkness of ignorance and superstitions. Jesus Christ affirmly remarks, "know the truth which will make you free". Nobody wants to know the reality/truth but proud of his/her religion and performing rituals and worshiping idols. But not ready to practice the moral and spiritual values in the real life. Religion was used for man-making through education by religious teachers. Now, it is used for money making in temples and churches. Jesus Christ may be considered as god because He is the symbol of love and truth. Other gods are idols made of imagination of human beings. However, the religious values and principles are essential in making life happy and peaceful in the obscene–violence materialistic society. Covid 19 (Corona Virus) destroyed crores of lives in a few months in 2020–2021. People blamed gods and religious faiths. In fact, there is no relation between Jesus Christ and Covid-19 or other gods. Everything happens artificially or naturally and we have to love and help others at the time of needs and hazards so that the existence of divinity can be realized through man.

Whatsoever may be religious education should be imparted to the students at all levels of education and training. Human value based stories, biographics of great people and spiritual leaders should be taught with examples of life experiences. At the same time, all religion should be given due importance to avoid impartialism and develop secular outlook. The younger generation lives in corruptive, raping, violence-obscene centred intoxicated materialistic society. So they become dreamless and hopeless in life and treat it as use and throw one. Hence, teacher should be a person of moral and ethical values and reflect all values in the school activities. As such schools can be turned into temples, churches, mosques and gurudhwar and students into gods where there is happiness and peaceful always.

CHAPTER 43

UNIVERSALISATION OF ELEMENTARY EDUCATION

INTRODUCTION

After the achievement of independence, free and compulsory elementary education has been given prime importance. The framers of the constitution of India recognised the need and importance of such an education. In fact, when the constitution of India came into force on January 26, 1950, education received added importance, and it became the responsibility of the people. Therefore, high priority was given to the programme of universalisation of primary or elementary education. As a result, every boy and girl in this country should receive a minimum standard of education.

MEANING

Free and compulsory education—Article 45 of the Indian Constitution states, "The state shall endeavour to provide within a period of ten years from the commencement of this constitution, for free and compulsory education for all children until they complete the age of fourteen years". In other words, we are committed to universal, free and compulsory elementary education. Universalisation of elementary education in India means making education available to all children in the age group from 6 to 14 or in the classes from I to VIII. The word 'state' which occurs in Article No. 45 is defined as, "The Government and parliament of India and the government and the legislature of each of the states and all local or other authorities within the territory of India or under the control of the government of India". Thus, we notice that the responsibility for elementary education lies with the Central Government, the State Governments, the local bodies and voluntary organizations.

The concept of universalisation of elementary or primary education signifies that education is for all and not for a selected few. Thus, it implies that education is the birth right of every child and it should be made free and compulsory upto the age of 14. Therefore, the State should provide elementary education to all children irrespective of their caste, colour, creed, sex, language, religion, socio-economic status and place of birth or living. Thus, all children of the country, whether rich or poor, living in rural or urban areas and in remote places should be provided with the facilities of elementary education.

NEED FOR FREE EDUCATION

Education should be free for all boys and girls between the age of six or seven and fourteen because it is the birthright of all the human beings. Gandhiji believes that primary education should be available to all. He observes "I think we can postpone the question of higher education for sometime, but the problem of primary education cannot be postponed even for a minute". Thus, the important prerequisite of basic education is to extend the torch of knowledge to all. This is because India is a poor country where all parents cannot afford the cost of education. Some parents cannot even afford to send their children to school. Education, therefore, should be made available free of cost. If it is so, parents will not consider it a burden. Moreover, in a democratic society, education of the masses becomes necessary to ensure its success and progress.

NEED FOR COMPULSORY EDUCATION

Education is regarded as the third eye of human beings which gives light. It is the remover of illiteracy, ignorance, superstition and poverty. But the majority of the people do not realise the real value of education. Some do not admit their children in schools due to their ignorance, illiteracy and poverty. Therefore, education should be made compulsory for every child. Children should be admitted to schools under the system of compulsory education. Some psychologists have proved that the minimum age required for education is six years. There is an apparent coordination in the physical organs of the child. Therefore, a duration of eight years makes education a complete entity or a terminal stage. This will make the child self-sufficient after the completion of eight years of education. For all these reasons education should be made free, compulsory and universalised for all children from 6 to 14 years regardless of their socio-economic conditions. Compulsory school education has become a part and parcel of the civilized world.

UNIVERSALISATION OF ELEMENTARY EDUCATION

Universalisation of elementary education may be defined as the provision of primary education to all children in the age group from 6 to 14 years or in the classes I to VIII. This also means that all children of the country either rich or poor, living in towns or rural areas are to be provided with the facilities of primary education. At present, we may think that universalisation of elementary education is a free education upto the primary stage. In developed and advanced countries free education means no fees, free books, and stationery, free mid-day meals and free school transport. But in our country free education means education "free of tuition fees" and other facilities free of cost.

IMPORTANCE OF UNIVERSALISATION OF ELEMENTARY EDUCATION

Primary education plays an important role in laying the proper foundation for the child's cultural, emotional, intellectual, moral, physical, social and spiritual development. It produces children with sound and balanced personalities. The development and progress of a country depends solely on the universalisation of primary education. In the words of J.P. Naik, "The progress of primary education is an index of the general, social and economic development of the country as a whole". That is why Article No. 45 of the Indian constitution stresses on free and compulsory education for all children, until they complete the age of fourteen.

1. Elementary education is a fundamental right of every citizen. In 1993, the Supreme Court of India declared, "The citizens of the country have a fundamental right to education. Every citizen of this country has a right to access free education until he completes the age of 14 years.
2. In 1945, Mahatma Gandhi in his letter to Nehru pleaded for the villages to be the focal point of free India's political structure, economic and developmental policies. But Jawaharlal Nehru replied him, "Indian villages are intellectually and culturally backward from where no progress could be made". It is a fact that developmental policies do not reach the villagers who constitute nearly 60 per cent of the total population of our country. The basic reason for this failure is that most of the people have not received elementary education. Therefore, universalisation of elementary education is important for:
   (a) Eradication of poverty
   (b) Fostering economic progress
   (c) Managing the growth of population
   (d) Creating a clean and healthy environment
3. There cannot be effective empowerment of our Indian people without universal elementary education.
4. J.P. Naik, an eminent educationist of our country has rightly stated, "The progress of primary education is an index of the general, social and economic development of the country as a whole".
5. Primary education plays an important role in laying the proper foundation for a child's cultural, emotional, intellectual, moral, physical, social and spiritual developments.
6. Primary education contributes to the national development. Countries which have made proper provision for primary education are far ahead than those without adequate provision for primary education.

STAGES OF UNIVERSALISATION OF PRIMARY EDUCATION

There are three stages for universalisation of primary education:

Universalisation of provision: This means that primary education should be provided to all children between the age group of 6–14 years in the country. The location of the primary school should be within a walking distance (1 km) from the house of every child. During the first five year plan, primary schools were established so as to provide primary education within a distance of one mile from the residence of a child. It enables and encourages the parents to send their children to schools.

Universalisation of enrolment: This means that all children of the desired age group (6 years old) must be enrolled in the school. It is essential that all eligible children should be enrolled compulsorily by the school. The Kothari Commission feels that the problem of enrolment in class I is of great significance. Different states have enacted compulsory education acts their purpose. But the desired targets have not been achieved due to the ignorance of parents, isolation from school and local community and financial difficulties.

Universalisation of retention: This means that every child enrolled in Class I must continue in the school till he completes class VIII. That is, after the enrolment of the students in school is over, it is essential to see that they progress regularly from year-to-year. There should be no stagnation in the school. Again we should see that the child does not leave the school before the completion of the course so that there is no wastage. Kothari Commission has pointed out that wastage at the lower stage is very large. About 56 per cent of the boys and 62 per cent girls give up education at this stage. Hence, it is important schools to provide all assistance to enroll the children in the age group 6–14 and it is important to retain the children in the schools in order to complete their primary education without wastage.

PROBLEMS OF UNIVERSALISATION OF ELEMENTARY EDUCATION

Problem of finance: Lack of financial resources has been a major hurdle in the expansion of elementary education.

Problem of priority: The universalisation of education depends on priority basis. During the First Five Year Plan 50 per cent of the total educational budget was spent on primary education. But it was 31.9 per cent in the Fifth Five Year Plan.

Problem of population explosion: Tremendous increase in population frustrates all efforts to bring every child under the roof of schools. In spite of overall planning for the enrolment of vast number of children in schools, the explosion of population does not allow us to improve their condition.

Problem of poverty: Due to poor economic conditions, parents are forced to keep their children away from school. Instead of sending them to schools, parents send them to work and live on the labour of their children. The female children are engaged in domestic work due to poverty.

Problem of illiterate parents: Illiterate parents do not realise the importance of education for their children. They are indifferent to education due to their ignorance.

Problem of unattractive school: Our primary school programmes are dull and boring, because they follow traditional and uninspiring method of teaching. The courses of study are unrelated to the lives of the students.

Problem of wastage and stagnation: Wastage and stagnation stand in the way of universalisation of primary education. It was nearly 40 per cent in the class I itself. But now wastage and stagnation have been controlled.

Problem of girls' education: Some people do not like girls' education due to ignorance, superstition and poverty. Such parents do not like to send their daughters to school. Moreover, the girls are more useful at home. Therefore, instead of sending them to school, they are engaged in domestic work.

Problem of small and scattered habitation: There are more than 3,00,000 habitations of less than 100 people in each. Small habitations which are in inaccessible areas like dense forests, prevent the establishment of primary schools there.

Problem of scarcity of teachers: Universal, free and compulsory education at the elementary stage need a large number of teachers and adequate equipments. The paucity of teachers and other equipments particularly in rural areas, curbs the universalisation of primary education.

Problem of education of backward class: Like scheduled class and scheduled tribes, backward groups also do not bother about education because of different values of life and their social setup. In educationally backward areas like Bihar, Odisha, Rajasthan, Kashmir, Madhya Pradesh and Himachal Pradesh the number of people belonging to these groups is very high.

Problem of fictitious enrolment: Practice of fictitious enrolment is also seen in many elementary schools due to the pressure of parents who do not want to send their children to school.

Problem of education of the handicapped: Due to the non-availability of special teachers and financial resources for the education of disabled children, their education stands against the universalisation of primary education.

Problem of contact between teacher and parents: There is a lack of healthy contact between the parents and teachers, which also impedes the universalisation of primary education.

Problem of enforcing Compulsory Primary Education Act: The Compulsory Primary Education Act has not been properly enforced in the country. It is also a problem in the universalisation of primary education.

SUGGESTIONS FOR UNIVERSALISATION OF ELEMENTARY EDUCATION

Introducing programme of education for all: The programme of education for all should be introduced in hilly areas, rural areas, slum areas, sparsely populated areas and tribal areas where the number of drop-outs among girls is quite high and in these areas most of the people belong to the deprived section of the community.

Educating the parents: Parents should be educated so that they can realise the value of education. Educated parents send their children to schools.

Financial incentives: Financial incentives should be given to the needy parents.

Free books and uniforms: As the parents are poor, it will be difficult for them to send their children to schools. So, children should be given books, uniforms, transport facilities, healthcare and mid-day meals free of cost.

Separate schools for girls: Separate schools should be established for girls. Parents should be persuaded to send their daughters to co-educational schools where separate schools cannot be established for a small number of girls. Lady teachers should be appointed with proper training in the rural areas.

Control population explosion: Due to high birth rate, it is not possible to admit 100 per cent children of the age group of 6–14 in the primary schools. To solve this complicated problem, family planning should be enforced in the country.

Managing financial resources: The total educational expenses devoted to primary schools are much less than that of the secondary and university education. So, both the central and the state governments should see that primary education gets its proper share out of the total expenditure on education. The cost of primary education should be lowered and for this purpose: (a) class size maybe a bit large; (b) double shift system maybe introduced; simple and durable buildings should be provided; (d) the equipment in the schools should be efficiently and economically used.

Participation of parents: Participation of parents in the educational programmes maybe encouraged to create awareness and interest regarding the utility of the education of the children.

Lessening wastage and stagnation: To avoid wastage and stagnation, a system of automatic promotion should be adopted. No student should be asked to repeat a class even if his performance is not up to the mark. The teaching in primary schools should be made efficient and attractive in order to decrease wastage and stagnation.

Broadening objectives of primary education: The qualitative improvement of education at primary level should be broadened. J.P. Naik says, "The objectives of teaching should be 3 R's, good manners, healthy habits, some skills with hands, general knowledge about the physical and social environment of India, level land people and the building up of some essential qualities like sense of responsibility, cooperativeness, discipline and patriotism".

Suitable curriculum for the school: The curricula of primary education should not be rigid and bookish. They should be activity- and experience- centred related to the natural and social life of the children. They should enable the children to develop their individual potentialities and lead a corporate life in the school.

Provision of audio-visual aids: Provision of audio-visual aids for the development of education of children is very essential. This will attract the attention of the children towards education.

Improvement of elementary teachers: The conditions of the primary school teachers should be improved for the qualitative improvement of primary education. For instance, the teachers posted in tribal areas should also acquire the knowledge of tribal dialects.

Parental cooperation: Enlisting parental cooperation and community mobilisation in the education of the child lead to the universalisation of primary education.

Reforms in educational administration: The educational administration should be decentralised so that the powers and functions of administrative authorities at the village level, district level and state level can function more effectively.

It should be free from political interference for smooth administration. It should also keep in touch with the latest developments in primary education and should readily help the teachers accordingly.

REALISATION OF UNIVERSALISATION OF ELEMENTARY EDUCATION

Provision of school facilities: Several attempts were made for the universalisation of elementary education and quantitative expansion of elementary education by increasing the number of primary schools. For example, the number of primary schools increased from 2,10,000 in 1951 to 5,58,392 in 1991. But we failed to universalise elementary education in some schools as there were no buildings, sufficient teachers, and in some cases they existed without any enrolment or with very poor enrolment.

Universal enrolment: Attempts were made to enrol all children in the age group of 6–14. Such attempts include enrolment drive and public awareness programme through mass media such as the radio, the television, the newspapers, posters and pamphlets. Even though these attempts were taken, universalisation of elementary education (UEE) failed because of the following factors:

- Low enrolment ofgirls.
- Low enrolment of children belonging to SC, ST and backward communities.
- Low enrolment of disabled children.
- Low enrolment of children belonging to linguistic and religious minority groups.
- High rate of wastage and stagnation.

Universal retention: Attempts were made to ensure universal retention so that all children in the age group of 6–14 would continue in the school until they complete the elementary education. This means that children would not dropout from the school before completing class VIII. For the purpose of universal retention, the government has taken the following measures:

- Adoption of 'No Detention Policy'.
- Free supply of uniforms to girls and other children of backward communities.

- Attendance scholarship for girls and SC/ST children.
- Provision of mid-day meal.

In spite of these measures UEE failed because of the high rate of stagnation and wastage.

Universal achievement: Attempts were made to reduce the rate of stagnation and to ensure universal achievement. This means all children in the age group of 6–14 would achieve success in relation to Minimum Levels of Learning (MLL). Universal achievement necessitates two conditions—equal opportunity to learn and qualitative improvement of elementary education. The government adopted several measures to provide equal opportunities to all children in the age group of 6–14 and to bring qualitative improvement of elementary education. Such measures are:

- Provision of minimum two classrooms in primary schools.
- Provision of minimum two teachers in primary schools.
- Supply of black boards and teaching aids to primary schools free of cost.
- Renewal of primary education curriculum.
- Identification of minimum levels of learning.
- In-service training of primary school teachers for ensuring qualitative instruction in the classroom.
- Introduction of workbooks for children.
- Introduction of teachers handbook in different subjects.

Several schemes and projects were implemented in different states to bring qualitative improvements in elementary education. They are:

- Primary Education Curriculum Renewal (PECR)
- Operation Blackboard (OB)
- Project Mass Orientation of School Teachers (PMOST).
- Survey on Educational Backwardness of Girls (SEBG).
- Centrally Sponsored Scheme of Integrated Programme (CSSIP).
- Education for Disabled Children (EDC).
- Early Childhood Education and Care (ECEC).

ATTEMPTS MADE AT PRESENT FOR UEE

Attempts are being made at present in our country to improve the quality of elementary education and to realise the goal of universalisation of elementary education. District Primary Education Programme (DPEP) is being implemented in different states with assistance from the World Bank. In order to realise the goal of UEE, the DPEP focuses on the following:

- Attainment of minimum levels of learning (MLL).
- Updating and reorganising the primary education curriculum and the textbooks.
- Emphasis on child-centred approach.
- Emphasis on activity-based approach to teaching–learning process.
- Shift of emphasis from teaching to learning.
- Joyful learning.
- Multigrade teaching.
- Provision of infrastructure facilities in primary schools.
- Community participation in education.

- Care of special group of underprivileged children, disabled children, girls and first generation learners.
- In-service education for primary school teachers for the enrichment of their content and upgradation of their skills.
- Preparation and utilisation of low cost and no cost aid in teaching and learning.
- Continuous and comprehensive evaluation in the context of minimum level of learning.
- Enlisting parental cooperation and community mobilisation in the education of the child.

The DPEP is ultimately meant to lead to greater achievement among all children in the age group of 6–14. This means that children should find it worth coming to school and staying there long enough. For this, the school should become an attractive place where:

- the education offered is able to cater to the children's needs;
- effective and feasible teaching practices are available;
- they have good materials to learn from;
- their learning is constantly monitored and supported; and
- their teachers support them when they need help.

A National Elementary Education Mission (NEEM) is being set up in the country. The chief objective of NEEM would be to expedite, resolve and take concerted action in partnership with state and local bodies, such as the panchayat samiti and the village education committee, teachers and NGOs. In addition to this, a number of submissions would be established to deal with the critical aspects of elementary education.

RECOMMENDATIONS OF SAIKIA COMMITTEE

The Supreme Court of India (1993) declared, "The citizens of the country have a fundamental right to education ... every child of this country has a right to free education until he completes the age of 14 years". Therefore, the government of India appointed a committee to consider the implications of the proposal to make elementary education a fundamental right under the Chairmanship of Muhi Ram Saikia (Saikia Committee, 1997). The Saikia committee has recommended:

- Amendment of the constitution to make the right to free elementary education up to 14 years of age—a fundamental right in the Indian constitution.
- Provision of free textbooks for all primary school children up to the upper primary level.
- Provisions of essential stationery to all children in the primary classes.
- Exemption from tuition fees.
- Continuance of mid-day meals.
- Provision of other incentives such as free school uniforms, cash incentives, scholarships depending on the economic capacities and priorities of the states.
- Provision of minimum infrastructure and teachers to all schools.
- Quality teacher training, quality textbooks and minimum levels of learning (MLL).

The Committee felt that there would be no need to enact a central legislation making elementary education compulsory. States should either amend their existing legislation or enact a fresh legislation in this regard. Governments and parents have joint responsibilities for compulsory education. Government should be required to provide accessible schooling facilities to all, and parents should treat it as their fundamental duty to send their children to schools.

SARVA SHIKSHA ABHIYAN (SSA)

Sarva Shiksha Abhiyan is an effort to universalise elementary education. It is a response to the demand for basic education all over the country. It realises the importance of Early Childhood Care and Education and provides useful and relevant elementary education for all children upto the age of 14 by 2010. Objectives of the Sarva Shiksha Abhiyan are:

- All children should be in school, Education Guarantee Centre, Alternate School, Back to School Camp by 2003.
- All children should complete five years of primary schooling by 2007.
- All children should complete eight years of elementary schooling by 2010.
- Focus on elementary education of satisfactory quality with emphasis on education for life.
- Bridge all gender and social category gaps at the primary stage by 2007 and at the elementary education level by 2010.
- Universal retention by 2010.

OPERATIONAL STRATEGY OF SSA

The scheme of Sarva Shiksha Abhiyan was evolved from the recommendations of the State Education Minister's Conference held in October 1998 that is during the Nineth Five Year Plan (1997–2002) for the achievement of Universali- sation of Elementary Education in a time bound manner as mandated by the 86th amendment of the consitution of India, making free and compulsory education to the children of 6 to 14 ages. This scheme is executed by the Government of India with the full cooperation of the State Government in 11 lakhs villages for the benefit of 20.5 crore children in 2011 as a fundamental right. As a result, it covers the entire country with a special focus on educational needs of girls, scheduled castes and scheduled tribes and other children in difficult circumstances. For this purpose, the scheme seeks to open new schools in those habitations which do not have schooling facilities and strengthen existing school infrastructure through provision of additional classrooms, toilets, drinking water, and school improvement grants. It strengthens the capacity of teachers by extensive training. It provides grant for developing teaching learing materials and strengthening the academic support structure at block and district level. The financial assistance for the programmes of SSA is on 85:15 sharing arrangement during the IXth plan, 75:25 in Xth plan and 50:50 thereafter between the central and the state governments. However, the distribution of scholarships and uniform should be funded under the state plan, which will not be funded under the SSA programme.

ACTIVITIES OF SSA

- Enrolement of all school age (6–14) children in schools.
- Stoppage of drop-outs or wastages.
- Providing quality education at elementary level.
- Appointing at least two teachers in each school.
- Establishing school or Education Guarantee Scheme within a radius of one kilometer.
- Setting up a separate office room for the headmaster.
- Building new schools or maintaining damage buildings through Village Education Committee.
- Allotting ₹ 10,000 to SSA primary schools in order to purchase teaching-learning materials.
- Allotting to ₹ 50,000 to SSA with a view to upgrade middle schools and purchase teaching-learning materials.

- Allotting ₹ 5,000 per year to each primary school for its maintenance purposes.
- Providing ₹ 500 to each teacher and ₹ 2000 to each school for the preparation of teaching-learning materials (TLM).
- Providing 20 days in service training to each teacher in order to improve his/her capacity in the teaching learning process.
- Giving a days training to community leaders in matters related to school activities.
- Providing integrated education to the physically challenged children for physical, mental and vocational development.
- Setting up block resource centres and cluster resource centres for providing quality education.

CONCLUSION

Universalisation of primary education has now become a challenge before the educationists, teachers, social reformers, political thinkers and leaders and social activists in India. To achieve their targets, we will have to overcome many different problems such as, financial resources, physical resources and human resources. In fact, various efforts have been taken for the last five decades for the universalisation of elementary education. In this context, the National Policy on Education (1986) and Programme of Action (1992) gave priority to the achievement of Universal Elementary Education. Sarva Shiksha Abhiyan (SSA) was introduced during the Ninth Five Year Plan (1997–2002). It provides a wide convergent framework for the implementation of elementary education. However, it is time for us to face all challenges and build the emerging Indian society into a learning society, where education will be for all. Let us conclude with the words of Swami Vivekananda, "Awake, Arise and Stop not till the goal is reached".

CHAPTER 44

EDUCATION FOR DEMOCRACY

INTRODUCTION

After the achievement of independence, India has become a democratic country. In order to make democracy successful in India, education should make the people mentally prepared. Indira Gandhi says, "Education is a liberating force, in our age it is also a democratizing force, cutting across the barriers of caste and class, smoothing out inequalities imposed by birth and other circumstances". In fact, education is the weapon of democracy and without good education for all, democracy will not be successful. Democracy is incomplete without the expansion and propagation of education. It can be inculcated in the people only through education and a healthy philosophy of life. Educational system through its aims, curriculum, methods of teaching, students, teachers and schools can provide democracy in a formal form. Democratic philosophy of education is not only to adopt education to democracy, but to make democracy itself 'safe' for education. Therefore, education should be democratically oriented in its ideology, methods and its organization, so that it will develop the basic qualities such as love, cooperation, justice, equality, non-violence, brotherhood, and secularism, These are very essential for the successful functioning of a democratic life in India.

MEANING

The term 'democracy' has been derived from two Greek words, namely *Demos* which means 'the people' and *cratic* meaning power. Thus, the literal meaning of the combined word 'democracy' is power of the people or power of the public. Abraham Lincoln, the former president of America says, "Democracy is a government by the people, for the people and of the people". In its common and more accepted sense, democracy means "a form of government in which the supreme power is vested in the people collectively".

DEFINITIONS

Following definitions give the meaning of 'democracy' clearly:

Aristotle: "A government by the many".

Seeley: "Democracy is a government in which every body has to share".

Lord Bryce: "Democracy is a form of government in which the ruling power of the state is legally vested not in any particular individual or class but in the member of the community as a whole".

Mazzine: "True democracy refers to—the progress of all through all under the leadership of the wisest and the best".

Bode: "Democracy is a way of life and a way of life means a determining influence in every area of life".

Abraham Lincoln: "Democracy is a government by the people, for the people and of the people".

Dr. S. Radhakrishnan: "Democracy is a way of life and not a mere political arrangement. It is based on the principle of equal freedom and equal rights for all its members, regardless of race, religion, sex, occupation or economic status".

THREE INTERPRETATIONS OF DEMOCRACY

The word democracy can be interpreted in three ways, namely:

- Political democracy
- Social democracy
- Economic democracy

Political Democracy

This form of democracy implies the government by the people, for the people and of the people. It is established when all its men and women participate in the state affairs through their votes. In other words, political democracy is a formal structure of government which stands on the shoulders of the elected representatives of people. The laws of the state are applicable to all citizens irrespective of colour, caste, creed and sex. In a political democracy, the administration is run by the people for their own welfare and through their own freely elected representatives. The chief characteristics of this democracy are:

1. Political power is not in the hands of a single despot or a few. But it is in the hands of the people elected through voting.
2. Every citizen of the country has equal right to caste his vote, which has equal weightage.
3. The laws of the state are equally applicable to all the citizens irrespective of caste, community, sex, religion and colour.
4. Accountability is maintained at every step of power-sharing. An executive is responsible to the legislature and the legislature is accountable to the public and so on.
5. Political power changes with the change of values and expectations.

Social Democracy

This form of democracy abolishes all distinctions of colour, caste, creed, sex, language, region and economic status. It is the spirit of understanding, sympathy and cooperation. It is the way of life upholding the ideal of sincere compromise with the essential freedom of the spirit. The chief characteristics of this democracy are:

- Equality is maintained at all costs by abolishing the distinction based on caste, community, colour or sex. For instance, none can deny a Dalit to draw water from the public well.

- Equal educational opportunities are provided for all children. It is the responsibility of the government to impart education for children.
- Maximum freedom is allowed to the people in order to develop themselves according to their interests and abilities.
- Fraternity, universal brotherhood, cooperation, equality and freedom are maintained by justice in the society.
- Individuals are allowed to form their own organizations so that they can develop as a group.

Economic Democracy

This form of democracy implies that all individuals have economic power. The main characteristics of economic democracy are:

- Every citizen rich or poor will equally benefit from the fruits of the production and distribution of goods and services.
- Every citizen shares the economic prosperity of the nation and participates in his own way in the economic development of the country.
- All hands are provided work of their choice, profession, trade or job on the basis of their interests and abilities.
- Equal opportunities are provided to all citizens along with the supportive schemes for weaker sections, so that poverty can be reduced.
- The problems of unemployment and exploitation are reduced by various welfare schemes and by adopting preventive measures.
- Economic organizations are made cooperative without compromising their competitiveness.
- Goods and services are produced and distributed by the people for the welfare of all the people.

PRINCIPLES OF DEMOCRACY

Freedom: Freedom is the basic principle of democracy. It implies freedom of thought, expression, belief, faith and movement. This kind of freedom is essential for every individual to develop his personality in every possible way that he is capable of. In fact, complete freedom allows an individual to think in his own way, to speak out what he wishes, to discuss, to advise and to criticise freely and he develops his personality to the maximum extent. Democracy in education gives academic freedom along with academic justice. Thus, it provides a free atmosphere to the individual to find a true outlet.

Equality: A democratic philosophy of life makes for equality of opportunities for all, irrespective of their caste, creed, sex, location, linguism, politicalism, and economic status. This implies that every child should receive equal opportunities to develop his personality according to his abilities, aptitudes and interests. In a democracy, equality of educational opportunity means education should be given to all children equal to their inborn capacities.

Fraternity: Democratic philosophy of life develops the feeling of brotherhood and group living. In a democracy each individual receives proper respect in the society, not as a Hindu, Muslim, Christian, Buddhist, Sikh or a Jain. He has a right to contribute his best to the development of the society. Group living, fellow feeling and brotherhood of man are the pillars of democracy. Prof. V.R. Taneja says, "Another essence of democracy is that all individuals must cooperate. Prosperity and progress lie in co-operation rather than in cut throat competition".

Justice: Justice is a must for the success of democracy. According to this principle, all social, economic, political and other institutions bestow equal consideration and provide equal opportunities to all individuals regardless of their caste, colour, creed or sex. When justice prevails in the society an individual need not suppress or repress his self-consciousness. All are free to enjoy and exercise their own rights and duties for the welfare of the whole community. It emphasises that all are equal before the eyes of law and the rules of the state.

DEMOCRATIC VALUES

True democracy lies in the hearts of the people and manifests in their attitude and behaviour.

Respect the dignity of individual: Each individual is an integral part of the society and he is capable of contributing something to the welfare of the society. Hence, he should be respected by others for his capacities and powers and allowed to flourish without any hindrance from other individuals.

Toleration: This is an essential element of democratic citizenship. A true democrat should always be ready to differ and tolerate differences with humility and cordiality. That is, 'live and let live' should be the gospel of his life, accepting all kinds of differences. In a democracy, nobody should think that he is right and others who do not consent with him are wrong. Hence, all sorts of political, economic, social, cultural, religious, physical and mental differences should be tolerated.

Middle path: Middle path is a fundamental reality of democracy. In the absence of consensus through discussion and dialogue the opinion of the majority is (more than 50 per cent people present and voting in the state election) followed without disregarding the minority votes. For this purpose the middle path is adopted.

Faith in peaceful methods: Democracy rejects violence and discrimination and it establishes a peace-loving society. It solves all problems through peaceful methods of mutual discussion, understanding and social welfare instead of violence.

Faith in change: A true democracy is dynamic in nature and it always changes in social, political and economic aspects. A democrat has a scientific attitude towards life and believes in change for developing a better society based on equality, fraternity, freedom and toleration.

Change through persuasion: A true democrat believes in change, but he never likes to bring any change by force. Persuasion is the cause of change in public opinion.

Social service: A true democracy lives in and through individual's active participation in civic life. Thus, democracy develops the spirit of social service which is the essence of individual development. In the words of Ryburn, "Democracy is a system whereby the members of a community live together, so that each member can render the maximum service to the community and the community can give maximum service to each individual member".

Individual and social progress: In a democratic society, the individual and the society are mutually interdependent and contribute to each other's development and welfare. Thus, both the individual and the society develop together side by side to achieve total development and maximum welfare. In short, the individual is for the society and the society in turn promotes the good of the individual.

Good citizenship: The survival and success of a democracy depends on its good citizenship. A democratic citizen should have certain qualities such as intelligent behaviour towards men and rational mindedness. Good citizenship is an essential condition for a true democracy.

Universal brotherhood and cooperative living: Universal brotherhood and cooperative living through progress, peace, toleration and free interplay with other persons are the ultimate values of democracy. In fact, unity of human soul is real and unity of soul with the divine soul is real knowledge and the practice of this unitary idea is of real value.

NEED OF EDUCATION FOR DEMOCRACY

The democratic principles and values have entered the field of education in recent times. Democracy cannot be thought of in isolation from education. This is because democracy is the result of education. Therefore, there is a functional relationship between democracy and education. Education has always stood as a great force behind democratic ideals and a democratic society all over the world. In fact, democracy without education is a contradiction in terms. On the other hand, the democratic forces all over the world have been strengthened by the progressive trends in education.

It has been universally recognised that the strength of democracy depends on the character and intelligence of all its citizens. Bernard Shaw highlights the value of education in a democracy in his characteristically satirical fashion, thus: "Democracy implies election of the corrupt few by the ignorance of many. Their education is the major means to enrich the strength and overcome the weakness of the people. It is also a powerful means for the widespread diffusion". The University Education Commission has rightly observed, "Education is a great instrument of social emancipation by which a democracy establishes, maintains and protects the spirit of equality among its members". It has further added, "Democracy affirms that each individual is a unique adventure of life. The function of education is the guidance of this adventure for the realisation of the potentialities of each individual in the face of the actual world of men and things". The American educationist John Dewey has emphasised that in a democratic society, educational planning should be done in such a way that each individual member is made capable to shoulder social responsibilities efficiently and discharge them effectively and profitably. Thus, democratic education prepares every individual to participate in the continuous construction of improvement and enrichment of the patterns of individual and of group life. Hence, more emphasis is laid on free, compulsory and universalised education in almost all democratically ruled countries.

Education in Democracy: Implications

- The right to education becomes a fundamental right in a genuine democracy.
- Education is essential to a citizen to function as a voter and a legislator.
- Education is essential to enable voters to comprehend and intelligently discern the programmes of parties.
- Education is necessary to enable citizens to prepare themselves for securing the means of livelihood.
- Education is essential for participating intelligently in the social and other processes, which require attitudes, orientation, skills and emotional integration.
- Education is essential for a citizen to comprehend the laws of the land.
- The right to vote and the right to participate intelligently in shaping the policies of the state, demand not merely the right to education but the right to education in the language of the people.

PRINCIPLES OF DEMOCRATIC EDUCATION

Equal opportunities for all: Equal opportunities are made available to every individual in the country to receive education for his fullest development. Economic, social and political hindrances are removed so that each child will receive proper support to develop his individuality according to his interests, aptitudes and capacities. Democratic education stands for equal educational opportunity for all regardless of intelligence, race, religion, location, language, sex, politics and economic status.

Free education: Education should be provided to all children free of cost upto a certain level. As education is regarded as the birthright of every individual, free education should be made available to all citizens irrespective of colour, creed, community, sex, language or region.

Compulsory education: Since education makes the people more conscious of their rights and duties, and removes their ignorance, it should be made compulsory to all its citizens at least upto the elementary or the secondary stage. The principle of universal and compulsory education involves free education upto a certain stage in almost all democratic countries. In a democracy the ruling power remains in the hands of the people. Therefore, all should be brought under the scheme of universal and compulsory education so as to develop themselves as responsible and dynamic citizens conscious of their rights and duties.

Welfare for All: The central purpose of democratic education is the maximisation for welfare for all the people irrespective of their caste, creed, colour, sex, region, language or politicalism.

Recognition of individual differences: The principle of individual difference is given proper recognition in democratic education, so that each child receives proper support according to his interests, aptitudes, and capacities to develop his individuality to the fullest extent.

Child-centred education: The child is always supreme in a democracy. Hence, the curriculum, the method of teaching, discipline and textbooks are determined on the basis of the child's interests, attitude, inherent powers and needs. Thus, democratic education has become child centred.

Adult education: The provision of adult education, women's education and education of the mentally retarded and physically handicapped have been emphasised under the influence of democratic tendency in different countries. In order to provide education for these people, right schools, short-term courses, one day schools and distance education are being introduced throughout the country.

Community-centred education: All education takes place in a social setting, which provides due importance to the community. It is related to the social environment. Community-centred education is essential for the success of democracy in a country.

Methods of teaching: In democratic education, teaching methods such as seminars, lectures, workshops, symposium, discussions and debates are encouraged. These methods pave the way for free participation of students. Self-learning devices are encouraged in order to motivate children to pay much attention and learn by their own efforts.

Individual attention: Each child receives individual attention in a democratic education. His family background, interests, abilities, attitudes, inclinations and needs are taken care of in all plans of educational development. Such educational development helps the child to achieve the maximum development of his personality.

Social service: Democratic education develops the 'feeling of working together' through various social service activities. That is why proper attention is being paid to social, cultural and co-curricular activities such as tree planting, road construction, deepening of ponds and wells, keeping the environment free from pollution and cleaning the streets and parks which bring about more and more social experiences in the children.

Education for disabled: Democratic education lays stress on equalisation of educational opportunities to all children. Therefore, special provision is made for disabled people, who cannot be accommodated in the normal setting of education, and special facilities are provided to them either in normal or in special schools.

Political training: This type of training is given to students through students' union, Student Welfare Association, Students Council, group activities and clubs. Such a training helps the students to become balanced, dynamic, efficient and socially motivated personalities. They are trained for future leadership and democratic living, which is the cornerstone of democracy.

Consultation with students: In order to carry out the school functions effectively, teachers should consult students before taking a decision. This tendency develops democratic qualities in the students and improves their performance in school activities.

Respecting teacher's personality: Democratic philosophy of education respects the teacher as a very dynamic and effective agency of social change for social progress. Hence, his participation in curriculum construction, educational planning, administration and conducting researches in the field of education is encouraged in a democratic society.

Education for national integration and international understanding: Democratic education inculcates the qualities of good citizenship among the students. Such qualities are essential for national integration and international understanding, because the world has become a single unit. A feeling of international understanding among students is created through democracy. In this regard, school is a miniature society.

School administration: Democratic education welcomes participation of students in actual educational and school administration so as to inculcate in them the sense of self-discipline and self-administration.

Intelligence test: Intelligence and diagnostic tests are conducted to evaluate the mental capacity, growth and achievement of children. If there is no problem in the student and yet he fails, he must take the full responsibility for his failure.

Physical and health education: In a democratic school, games and sports, gymnasia, medical tests and medical help are provided freely to promote the physical well-being of children in order to save the country from despots.

Decentralised educational organization: The basis of democratic education is the decentralisation of various educational organizations. This will lead to the proper functioning of an educational institution at local, district and state level.

Knowledge for democratic agency: Democratic education equips citizens with the materials of knowledge needed for democratic efficiency.

Promotes loyalty to democracy: Democratic education promotes loyalty to democracy by stressing on positive understanding, appreciation and by summoning youth to serve a great cause.

Respect for humanity and occupational efficiency: Democratic education helps in self-realisation, creates respect for humanity, encourages attitudes of friendship and tolerance, makes for occupational efficiency through occupational adjustment and creates a sense of civic responsibility in every individual.

Cultural basis of education: Culture is the best that has been thought and known. Democratic education has cultural basis so that the future citizens of a country will be in a position to lead a happy life.

Cooperation between agencies of education: All agencies of education cooperate actively for the development of children in a democratic setup. Hence, schemes are being formulated to establish cooperation among family, school, community, church and state.

DEMOCRACY AND EDUCATION

Aldous Huxley has pointed out that if your aim is liberty and democracy, you must teach people the art of being free and of governing themselves. In the words of University Education Commission Report "Education is the great instrument of social emancipation by which a democracy establishes, maintains and protects the spirit of equality among its members". In fact, democracy can never be successful without education. Democracy immensely influences education in terms of its aims, curriculum, method of teaching, discipline, role of teacher and school administration.

Democracy and Aims of Education

The success of a democracy does not exist in educational institutions but it exists in the hearts of men and women. Democracy without education is a figment of the imagination. Therefore, the main aim of democratic education is the creation of democratic personalities through the inculcation of democratic values and a democratic way of life. According to Prof. K.G. Saiyidain, "Education must be so oriented that it will develop the basic qualities of character which are necessary for the functioning of democratic life. These basic qualities are a passion for social justice and quickening of social conscience, tolerance of intellectual and cultural differences in others, a systematic cultivation of critical intelligence and the development of deep and true love for the country". The chief aims of democratic education are:

- Develop worthy membership of home and society on the basis of love, cooperation and reconciliation.
- Develop professional or vocational efficiency and professional ethics.
- Provide training for leisure to employ it gainfully to the best advantage of recreation and self-progress.
- Promote physical and mental health education.
- Train the intellect and the intelligence.
- Provide training in discipline and leadership in various fields through co-curricular activities.
- Build character and inculcate positive discipline in the children.

The Secondary Education Commission under the chairmanship of Dr. A.L. Mudaliar emphasised the importance of development of democratic feeling because India has got rid of slavery with difficulty. In order to foster democratic feeling among the citizens, the commission has given the following aims of education:

Development of democratic citizenship: The prime aim of democratic education is to promote in children a sense of devotion to democratic values which makes them democratic citizens. The development of democratic citizenship requires the qualities of: (i) clear thinking; (ii) receptivity to new ideas; (iii) clarity in speech and writing; (iv) art of living in a community; (v) passion for social justice; (vi) tolerance; (vii) true patriotism; (viii) inter-nationalism; (ix) consciousness of one's rights and duties; (x) development of economic efficiency; and (xi) sense of service and sacrifice. In order to develop these qualities, children should be provided with opportunities to practice democratic norms and standards of behaviour. Hence, the whole educational process aims at developing democratic citizenship to lead a democratic way of life.

Development of vocational efficiency: Democratic education aims at developing vocational efficiency in children, so that they are able to become self-reliant and serve the nation as much as possible. The Secondary Education Commission recommends diversified courses to suit various aptitudes, interests and attitudes, which promote a healthy attitude to work and improve technical skill and efficiency.

Development of personality: The aim of democratic education is to develop the individuality of a child into a balanced and harmonious personality. To achieve this, the teacher organizes various cooperative activities in the school. Curriculum includes subjects like art, craft, music, dancing and the development of other hobbies which are helpful in the development of the personality.

Development of leadership: Democratic education instils in children the leadership qualities from the very beginning. This type of education enables them to shoulder the multifarious duties and responsibilities in the social, political, industrial, agricultural, educational, cultural, and technical field.

Development of internationalism: The aim of democratic education is to develop in children the sense of ardent nationalism and devotion to international brotherhood. All nations of the world are mutually interdependent and no nation can exist in isolation. Hence, education should foster the sense of interdependence, international goodwill and fellow feeling, which are the basic foundations of world peace and prosperity.

Development of democratic values: Democratic education aims at the development of democratic values, so that the child can learn to live democratically. That is why the whole educational setup of present schools reflects the values of democratic philosophy.

Development of worthy interests: The famous educationist Herbert has insisted upon the fullest development of diverse interest. As a consequence, democratic education provides with various and varied opportunities to participate in diverse activities and programmes in all fields of human life. The large number of interests that are developed in children make them happy, well balanced and efficient citizens.

Development of sound habits: The aim of democratic education is to develop good habits in children from the very beginning. The success and survival of the democracy of a country is determined by the good habits of its citizens.

Development of thinking power: Democratic education aims at making the children think clearly and take decisions confidently. The development of thinking power in a child is very essential to face the problems in social, political and economic fields.

Development of social outlook: The aim of democratic education is the inculcation of a social outlook in children. Development of social outlook prepares them to live and die for their nation. This sense of service and sacrifice makes them learn the sacredness of obligations and duties for the welfare of the country.

Democracy and Curriculum

Curriculum includes the totality of experiences that a child acquires in the classroom as well as outside the classroom. Hence, in democratic education, curriculum includes only those subjects, activities and programmes which promote democratic values and permit an all-round development of an individual's personality according to his potentialities. So, the ultimate target of the curriculum is to enable the students to live a successful democratic way of life. Democratic curriculum has been constructed on the basis of the following principles:

General curriculum: General education upto a certain level is essential so that every citizen in the society can acquire some fundamental tit-bits of knowledge. This is because each and every citizen cannot be taught everything. For instance, in India, a general curriculum is adopted up to X standard. Every student has to study every subject.

Broad-based curriculum: Curriculum should be broad based including manifold activities in order to achieve democratic aims. It provides every pupil the totality of experiences through studying various subjects and participating in manifold activities and programmes in the classroom, in the library, in the laboratory, in the playground and in the study tour.

Diversified curriculum: Interests, abilities, aptitudes and needs of children are different. Therefore, diversified curriculum (different options) should be followed to suit the needs of all children. For instance, arts, science, commerce, mathematics or management, and a number of co-curricular activities are organized for this purpose.

Flexibility: Democratic curriculum should be varied and flexible to satisfy the interests and needs of the individual and the society. This is because needs of the individual and the society change with the change of time. Hence, a core curriculum is made compulsory and diversified subjects are made optional for children to choose according to their interests and aptitudes.

Need and environment based: Democratic curriculum should be constructed on the basis of local needs and availability of resources according to the changing needs of the environment. It is a curriculum which is directly related to the realities of life, needs, and aspirations of the people which differs from time-to-time and place-to-place.

Vocational needs: The purpose of democratic education is to enable the individuals to face their economic needs. Therefore, democratic curriculum is vocationalised to encourage economic uplift of the individual and the society. As a result of this, vocational subjects are included in the curriculum after class X. This enables the country to develop economically.

Equal weightage to all subjects: In democratic education, no specific stream of subject is given preference to other streams. Equal weightage is given to humanities, science and social sciences to develop social, political and economic awareness. Thus, different subjects, experiences and activities are integrated.

Activity centred: Democratic curriculum stresses on the principle of 'learning by doing'. This enables the children to search for truth through their own experiments and experiences. This is real learning which develops confidence, foresight, and farsight. It prepares the children for the future life.

Secular curriculum: Democratic curriculum is not in favour of any religion. It treats all religions equally. In fact, no religious education is imparted in government institutions.

Ensure total development of personality: Democratic curriculum brings about physical, mental, social, economic, emotional and aesthetic development in the individual's personality. Such development prepares him for the larger world in which he can find a place for himself.

Democracy and Methods of Teaching

A democratic school introduces radical methods of teaching, based either upon the nature of the subject matter or the psychology of learning process. It follows certain ways to present the lesson material that attract the interest and holds the attention of pupils. Different democratic methods that are followed in different democratic countries of the world are Montessori method, heuristic method, laboratory plan, Dalton plan, experimental method and problem solving. These methods allow maximum freedom to the students to learn by their own efforts, experiences and experiments. They further develop the insight and foresight of the students and make them confident and self-reliant.

Learning by doing: All education in a democracy takes place through learning by doing. Activity, experiences and experiments are preferred to acquire knowledge. For this purpose, laboratory and experimental methods are used.

Self-learning: Children are motivated to go through self-learning under the guidance of an able teacher. Montessori method, heuristic method and Dalton plan are commonly used in this regard.

Problem solving: In this method, students learn to solve life related problems. They find solution to various problems by discussions or experiments. It enables the student to think independently and judge rationally.

Discussion method: Each child is free to express his views and discuss subject matters. For this purpose, discussion and debate are followed in the classroom and the conclusion is arrived at. This encourages active participation and cooperation in the educative process.

The democratic education adapts new, dynamic and progressive methods of teaching at all stages to develop the intelligence of children to the fullest extent. Children are assigned difficult problems and are required to exercise their thinking power and capacity to solve them. This capacity makes them confident and reliant, so that they are able to solve national and international problems in all areas and in all spheres of life. "Programmed learning" is the latest development in the democratic method of teaching. Education in Indian society adopts "child-centred method" in order to safeguard democracy.

Democracy and Discipline

Since discipline is the cornerstone of democracy, democratic education advocates self-discipline, democratic discipline and social discipline through impression and experiences for the maintenance of discipline.

Self-discipline: Democratic discipline is self-discipline based on love, sympathy, cooperation and human relationship. To develop social discipline, students are fully permitted to run their unions and clubs and to participate in various co-curricular activities in the school. Moreover, curriculum should include those programmes and activities according to the needs and interests of students, which develop self-discipline among them.

Discipline through freedom: Democratic methods provide maximum freedom to the children to learn by their own efforts, experience, and experiments. Mdm. Montessori once remarked, "To obtain discipline, give freedom". In democratic schools full freedom is given, and opportunities are provided for each child to develop his individuality to the fullest extent. In order to develop democratic discipline, students are encouraged to participate in the administration and management of the school.

Social discipline: Social discipline in the people can be developed through the joint activities of the school. In democratic schools, the sense of rights and duties is instilled in children through social service and social consciousness. In this way discipline becomes social discipline. According to John Dewey, "Social discipline means the cultivation in the pupils of social attitudes, habits and ideals of conduct through the conjoint activities of the school which has been organized as a community".

Democracy and Teacher

Teacher is the pivot of the whole system of education. Success or failure of a democracy largely depends on his attitude and outlook on life. He should create necessary conditions for the development of the children's personality. Tagore remarks, "They only deserve to be teachers who are patient and tolerant". He further says, "Only he can teach, who can love. The greatest teachers of men have been lovers of mankind. The real teaching is a gift. It is a sacrifice. It is not a manufactured article of routine work and because it is a living thing, it is the fulfilment of knowledge of the teacher himself".

In democratic schools, the teacher is expected to possess the following qualities:

- The teacher is devoted whole-heartedly to the ideals and values of democracy. He should impart the same ideals to children through affectionate rapport.
- The principals, the headmasters, the teachers and the administrators should not behave like police officers.
- They should be friends, philosophers, guides in the school and they should mould the behaviour of children through their friendly and affectionate behaviour.
- They solicit maximum cooperation from the guardians, parents and other social agencies for the development of children and the society.
- Their democratic behaviour plays an important role in maintaining discipline. Hence, instead of teaching 100 words, a single behaviour of the teacher is enough to bring about the desirable discipline in children.
- They should be fully conscious of their rights and duties towards the society, and they should instil the same sense of responsibility in children to make them capable and intelligent citizens of tomorrow.
- Each teacher should be well-versed in his subjects and have full academic competency to develop the children physically, mentally, morally, emotionally, socially and spiritually, so that they can discharge national and international responsibilities.

Democracy and School Administration

In a democracy, school administration is decentralised administration based upon democratic principles and values. Democratic administration develops children into capable and responsible citizens and also trains them as future leaders of social, political and economic activities.

- School organization is based upon democratic spirit. The headmaster, the teachers, the clerical staff, the administrators and the students work together as a team to run and develop the school successfully.
- The headmaster and the management should develop the initiative of teachers who receive constant appreciation and reward for their good and devoted work.
- There should be mutual relations of teachers, supervisors, parents, guardians and social workers based upon democratic philosophy.
- The headmaster and the teachers should plan, discuss and decide all school activities and carry them out with the full cooperation of all. They should function as one group of dedicated workers.

- The supervisors, administrative officers and management personnel may criticise the work of teachers in a constructive spirit of cordiality and beneficial evaluation, which encourages teachers to do better and develop their competency more.
- The democratically administered school provides adequate rights and freedom to teachers in framing the school policy and programmes.
- The school becomes a community and functions as a social organization with a democratic environment.

Education for Democracy: Ways and Means

Education is the weapon which plays an important role in the success of democracy. Thomas H. Briggs writes, "The school is truly the guardian of democracy". In fact, schools have an important role in educating children for democratic living by strengthening the democratic values. In the words of Ross, "The true function of a school in a democracy therefore is to provide for the enrichment of individual life for the child as he is and to secure it for him when he grows up. It is a prepared environment in which he may best blossom; its main function is to discover the good for each pupil and to device means of attaining it".

The Secondary Education Commission has remarked, "A passion for social justice based on sensitiveness to the social evils and the exploitation which corrupts the grace of life must be kindled in the heart and mind of our people and the foundation for it should be laid in the school". In this regard, the Commission has stressed, "the secondary school must make itself responsible for equipping the students adequately with civic as well as vocational efficiency and the qualities of character that go with it so that they may be able to play their part worthily and competently in the improvement of national life".

Dr. K.L. Shrimali writes, "The school should set up situations which provide constant practice in social and cooperative living. It must encourage activities through which the child can make a personal contribution in group enterprise, cooperative instead of competitive individualism".

T.M. Greene stated, "To describe the school as a community is to emphasize the corporate, social character of education". In the words of Kilpatrick, "The effective school in a democracy must give its pupils an intelligent understanding of the issues of democracy, make them well disposed towards democracy as a way of life, and make them skilful in the co-operative activities through which democracy must function".

According to Harold Rugg, "The school is an enterprise in living both social and personal". Education in a democracy both within and without the school, should develop in each individual, the knowledge, interests; ideals and powers whereby he will find his place and use that place to shape both himself and society".

The school performs threefold functions to inculcate democratic values and principles in children.

- Convey to the students the meaning of democratic values, ideas, and principles and their implications for conduct in the various life situations.
- Enable the students to incorporate these values, ideas and principles in their daily conduct, in and out of school.
- Democratic school introduces radical changes in respect of methods, discipline and administration.

In order to perform these functions, the school adopts the following ways and means:

Respect for individual personality: Since individual is the heart of a democratic philosophy of life, the individuality of the child is given due respect. The recognition of the individuality of the staff and students enables them to understand the value of democracy. J.S. Mill says that out of 100 persons 99 maybe wrong and one maybe right. Hence, recognition and development of the individual personality is in the forefront.

Universalisation of education: For recognising the worth of the individual, education should be provided to all children regardless of their colour, caste, creed, region, language and economic status. It has been made as a fundamental right of every citizen including the physically handicapped, the mentally retarded, and the socially and economically backward children in India.

Recognising individual differences: Democratic school gives due consideration to individual differences. The gifted, the average and the mentally retarded or backward children are recognised on the basis of their interests, aptitudes, abilities and needs.

Diversified courses: In a democratic school, diversified subjects activities and programmes are taught and practicals are conducted to suit different aptitudes, tastes and interests, capacities and needs of students. Only then a democratic system of education can be formed and developed by which democratic values can be inculcated in students so that they can enjoy the democratic way of life.

Mother tongue as medium: Language is the most powerful tool for an individual to express his feelings and thoughts. In fact, no tool is better than one's mother tongue. So, in a democratic school, mother tongue should be the medium of instruction.

Encouraging creative thinking: School should provide opportunities for the students to think and discuss matters on controversial problems. Individual creative thinking should be encouraged to develop democratic behaviour in the child.

Promotion of self-expression: Activities such as debates, poetical recitation, declamation contests, symposiums, seminars, sports and games should be organized in the school. These activities develop relative thinking which enable the children to express themselves effectively.

Democratic method of teaching: The democratic schools should adopt various teaching methods like, learning by doing, montessori method, project method, dalton plan, heuristic method, laboratory or experimental method, socialised techniques etc.

Introducing house system: All students of the school should be divided into three or four houses. Each house should consist of students from all classes. This will bring co-operation, fellow feeling and other desirable personal and social qualities. According to Prof. V.R. Taneja, "The more varied and the more frequent the activities of the students, the greater chance they have to develop desirable personal and social qualities".

Organizing group activities for group living: Today, the society is torn by mutual jealousies, internal division and narrow sentiment. These elements stand against democracy. Therefore, training for human relationship is necessary, for an effective democracy. It is the school, that must organize group living through community activities such as games, excursions, debates, discussions, dramas and social service activities. These activities enable the students to live and work together. In this way, the school can promote the habits of cooperation, fellow feeling, tolerance, love, sympathy, social sensitiveness and adjustments. These qualities are very necessary for democracy and human welfare.

Highlighting interdependence of man: The responsibility of a teacher is that he should highlight the interdependence of man upon man. While teaching, he should impart a rational knowledge about the subjects such as civics, history, political science and other social sciences. Teaching of these subjects would enable the students to understand the social environment in which they live and interdependence of man upon man to improve their life.

Residential schools: Residential school plays a vital role in bringing out a democratic way of life. In fact, such schools can provide effective training in human relationship through various activities and programmes.

Social services: Social work will bring the students into direct contact with the community and enable them to understand its problems. This work makes them social beings and prepares them for democratic life.

Training for character building: A country may have rich resources and a proud history, but if it does not have men of integrity and character, it cannot stand the blasts of the present day world. Emerson says, "Not gold but men can make a nation great and strong". As character development is the aim of a democratic society, the school should develop children's character. The school can inculcate in the pupils the habits of truth, goodness, independent and unbiased thinking and judgement, leadership qualities, and broad mindedness.

Developing vocational efficiency: Poverty, disease, unemployment and dishonesty affect a democracy. To overcome these enemies, craft education is very helpful. Therefore, work experience must be an integral part of all education. In this regard, Kothari commission suggests that the youth should be trained to exploit the country's resources and they must be taught the dignity of manual work. The Commission stresses on agricultural and technical education because vocationaliation of education leads to the eradication of unemployment. To improve vocational efficiency, education should be oriented to science, technology and industrialisation.

Democratic oriented educational administration: School should become the centre of democracy. It should work out its programmes through democratic organizations and administration. Democratic principles in the organization of pupil's activities, student self-government, clubs, classroom procedures, timetable construction and other similar school activities should be applied to school administration and organization.

Visits to legislatures: The schools should allow and encourage students to visit legislatures. Such visits provide the students with first hand opportunities to see for themselves the working of democracy.

DEMOCRACY AND EDUCATION IN INDIA

Education is regarded as the most important tool and dynamic agency to achieve the values of democracy. After the independence of India on August 15, 1947, she transformed herself into a democratic country based on the principles of freedom, equality, fraternity and justice. The constitution of India was adopted on January 26, 1950 and it guarantees the fundamental rights to each citizen. That is, each citizen has the right to equality, right to freedom, right against exploitation, right to freedom of religion, cultural and educational rights, right to property and right to constitutional remedies. To translate the declaration of the constitution into a reality, the government provides all kinds of education to all the children irrespective of their socio-economic conditions. Greater attention is being paid for the education of the mentally retarded and the physically handicapped children. More and more universities, colleges, technical and medical institutions are being established to meet the needs of the nation in all areas and in spheres of education.

Both the central and the state governments are doing their best to instil and promote unity and fellow feeling of oneness in the citizens of the land, irrespective of colour, caste, creed, sex, language, region and economic status through education which has been made free and compulsory under

Article 45. Even then, the prevailing system of education is completely devoid of democratic values. Therefore, we need an appropriate educational setup based on our socio, economic, political, religious and cultural conditions. In this regard, education must be a great force to make democracy work as a practical creed. The devotion of democracy to education is a familiar fact. Education for democracy must become creative and practical; it must make possible free and full development of each man and woman in India.

CONCLUSION

Education is a powerful weapon for democracy. No country can claim to be democratic unless it permits political liberty, freedom of conscience, economic justice, social prosperity, faith in the dignity of the individual and opportunity for a peaceful and orderly life. Education for democracy must become creative and practical, and it must strive to inspire students with a burning passion for social justice, to break down the barriers of caste, creed, colour and sex, to deepen cultural understanding and sympathy and broaden their intellectual outlook, to instil a love for honest work and an attachment to national culture. There is a close relationship between democracy and education. We conclude with the words of Prof. K.G. Saiyidain who states, "A democratic education then, as I visualize it, will be dedicated to the training of a generation of men and women who will be tolerant and broad-minded in their outlook, who will strive for the cause of social justice and not rest content till it has been achieved so far as it is humanly possible, who will have their intelligence so disciplined that they will be able to understand the complex fabric of modern life, to see what role they should play in it, who will have the will power to do with courage and persistence".

CHAPTER 45

EDUCATION AND SECULARISM

INTRODUCTION

India is a democratic and secular country. It means that our country does not discriminate against the followers of a particular religion. All Indians—Hindus, Muslims, Sikhs, Buddhists, Jains and Christians have freedom to practise their own religion. As we follow a democratic educational system, secularism has been the unique gift of the Indian society. An eminent educationist and saint like Vinoba Bhave once remarked, "The days of religion and nationalism are gone, the days of science and spirituality have come". Therefore, in our multiracial and multireligious society, spirituality and good conduct must be taught in the centres of learning. For this purpose, our classroom instruction should not be based on one's own religion. It means that when we teach the Bhagavad Gita, we should also teach The Bible and The Quran. This will develop the feeling among the students that they are living in the temple of humanity and bow down their heads before all the great teachers and preachers of the world and forget all their differences. They will also realise the meaning of "the fatherhood of God and the brotherhood of mankind". This is the brief meaning of education for secularism.

MEANING OF SECULARISM

The term 'secularism' has been derived from the Latin word, *Seculum* meaning "this present age" or "this present generation". George Jacob Holydake was the first man who used the word secularism in the nineteenth century to restructure a pluralistic society based on democracy and tolerance where equal opportunities were to be given to all, irrespective of their caste, creed, colour, race or culture. The real concept of secularism is that the state shall not impose any religion on people and it should pay equal respect to all religions. Strictly speaking, secularism implies an attitude of accepting all religions rather than rejecting any or all religions. According to Holydake, "Secularism may be defined as a system which seeks the development of the physical, moral and intellectual nature of man to the highest possible point as the immediate duty of life, which inculcates the practical sufficiency of natural morality apart from atheism, theism or the Bible, which selects as its methods of promotion of human improvement by material means". He evolved secularism as a social and ethical system based on the following principles:

- Emphasis on the material and cultural improvement of human beings.

- Respect and search for truth, whatever be its source, which can be tested in experience leading to human betterment.
- Concern for 'this present age' or world and its improvement.
- Liberal, permissive, progressive and tolerant social and moral order.
- It is a state of harmonious coexistence of various religions.
- It is equality of all religions in a society.
- Independent, rational morality, unbiased and positive attitude of life which is not based on a single divine faith and commandment.

Bradlaugh, a successor of Holydake says, "Secularism is hostile to religion and maintained that either secularism or religion should survive".

WESTERN SECULARISM

According to the Western view, "All political and social life should proceed without the involvement of the religious institutions". They advocate the separation between religion and politics or between the church and the state. This view can be seen in different dictionaries. According to Chamber's Dictionary, "Secularism is the belief that the state morals, education etc. should be independent of religions". According to Oxford Dictionary, "Secularism means the doctrine that morality should be based solely on regard to the well-being of mankind in the present life, to the exclusion of all considerations drawn from belief in God". According to Webster's Dictionary, "Secularism is a system of doctrine and practices that rejects any form of religious faith and worship". According to the Encyclopaedia Britannica, "Anything non-spiritual, having no connection with religion or spiritual matter, anything that is distinctly opposed do not connect with religious or ecclesiastical thing temporal as opposed to spiritual or ecclesiastical".

Prof. **Donald Smith** states, "The secular state is a state which guarantees individual or corporate freedom of religion, deals with individual as a citizen irrespective of his religion, is not constitutionally connected to a particular religion nor does it seek to promote or interfere with religion".

Dr. **K.R. Bombwall**, "In a secular polity, the state as such is neither religious nor irreligious, nor anti-religious but is wholly detached from religious dogmas and activities and is, thus neutral in religious matters".

Brubacher says, "Secularism has no religious point of view while it has a theory of moral education. If the secularist has any religion at all it is likely that scientific doctrine constitutes the pre-supposition of that religion and that scientists are its high priests".

According to the pluralistic view, "Secularism is an attitude of accepting all religions rather than rejecting any or all religions".

INDIAN CONCEPT OF SECULARISM

India feared that religious fundamentalism would pose a great threat to national unity and integrity. As a result secularism has been made one of the basic elements of the structure of the Constitution of India since 1976.

Mahatma Gandhi: "The soul religion is one but it is engaged in a multitude of forms. Wise men will ignore the outward crust and see the same soul living under a variety of crusts". He further says, "My veneration for other faith is the same as for my own faith. We believe in Sarvadharmasamabhava having equal regard for all faiths and creeds". Then in 1928 he remarked, "After long study and experience, I have come to the conclusion that

- All religions are true.
- All religions have some errors in them.
- All religions are almost as dear to me as my own Hinduism".

S. Radhakrishnan: "Secularism does not mean anything irreligious or atheism or even stress on material comforts, rather it lays stress on the universality of spiritual values which may be obtained by a variety of ways".

B.R. Ambedkar: "All that secular state means is that this parliament shall not be competent to impose any particular religion upon the rest of the people".

Dr. Rajendra Prasad: "There are some who think that because we are a secular state, we do not believe in religion or spiritual values. Far from being so, it really means that in this country all are free to profess or preach the faith of their liking and that we wish well of all religions and want them to develop in their own way without hindrance".

Pandit Jawaharlal Nehru: "Secularism means that not religious narrowness but religious broadness". Religion is the free choice of the individual, the family or the group. He further says, "Secularism means while religion is completely free, the state including in its wide-fold various religions and cultures, gives protection and opportunities to all and thus brings about an atmosphere of tolerance and cooperation".

The idea of secularism is one of the fundamental aspects of the Indian society. India has no national religion and it provides all religions with equal opportunities. Articles 25, 28 and 30 of the Indian Constitution emphasise the concept of secularism. Article 28 states, "No person attending any educational institution recognized by the state or receiving state funds shall be required to take part in any religious instruction that may be imparted in such institution or to attend any religious worship that may be conducted in such situation or any premises attached thereto unless such person is a minor or his guardian has given his consent thereto". According to Article 28 of the Indian Constitution, any institution which operates completely on government funds, religious education cannot be given. But those institutions whose control is in the hands of the government can provide religious education according to the needs. If a student is studying in a recognised and financially aided institution he cannot be forced to receive the education of any religion. Similarly, a state cannot discriminate for and against any institution in the name of religion. Grants should be provided without any discrimination. Therefore, education should inculcate such habits and sacraments in students that they give respect to all religions and learn their good principles or doctrines. Thus, religious instruction in government schools and colleges has been considered as a taboo. Article 30 states, "All minorities whether based on religion or language shall have right to establish and administer educational institutions of their choice. The state shall not discriminate against any educational institution in respect of grant in aid on the ground that it is under the management of a minority; whether based on religion or language".

CHARACTERISTICS OF SECULARISM

- It treats all religions equally, though their paths of realising their goals maybe different.
- It gives freedom to every individual to practise his own religion.
- It implies freedom of worship.
- The perfect toleration of understanding is to be maintained in the field of religion.
- It encourages rational thinking and understanding.

- No one should be politically or socially disqualified for his religious views.
- It encourages moral and spiritual values.
- It develops freedom from dogmatic ideas.
- It does not mean a negation of religion but accepts that all religions have equal value.
- It implies that no religion is superior or inferior to other religions.
- Mutual co-existence of all religions without any hatred or bias against anyone.
- Emphasis is given to the material and cultural upliftment of the individual and the society.
- Progressive and scientific attitude of people towards the aspects of life, free from superstitions and rigid beliefs.
- Equality of all religions in the state and the state is almost at the irreligious level.
- Equal opportunities in education, employment, business and economic benefits irrespective of religion.

SECULARISM IN EDUCATION

Secularism in education means making public education free from any religious dominance, especially in its learning environment. Those institutions which impart pure religious education should be brought to the national mainstream by adding new scientific and technological knowledge to the curriculum of these institutions. That is, whatever religious tenets are taught to students, they are judged on a scientific basis.

Need for Secular Education in India

Education is the most powerful instrument and with its help secularism can be improved in India. We need secular education in the emerging Indian society due to the following reasons:

- India is a multireligious and culturally varied society. People have different religions, faiths and beliefs. Most of them are uneducated and narrow minded. At this juncture secular education is necessary to inculcate that all religions are equal.
- Fanaticism, communalism and regionalism are on the increase. In fact, Ram Janmabhoomi and Babri Masjid issue caused a great struggle between the two communities. To overcome this problem, secular education is needed and it may make people realise the importance of national unity and emotional integrity.
- Equality, liberty, fraternity, national outlook and international understanding need to be propagated. Scientific outlook also needs to be developed in the fast growing and developing generation.
- We need secular education in India where there is erosion of values, narrow mindedness, selfishness and quarrels over petty religious matters. Corruption, dishonesty, cheating and disbelief are rampant. The suitable weapon for this is education. D.E. Smith says, "Secularism's best hope for future in India lies in its classrooms".
- To train the youth to be good citizens and play their part effectively in the social reconstruction and economic development.
- To inculcate in the youth social, moral and cultural values in accordance with the secular nature of our constitution.
- To strengthen secularism and human relationship in India.
- To fulfil the needs and requirements of democratic India.

- The Secondary Education Commission says, "The educational system must make its contribution to the development of habit, attitude and qualities of character which will enable its citizens to counteract all those fissiparous tendencies which hinder the emergence of a broad, national and secular outlook".
- The National Policy on Education (1986) says, "In our culturally pluralistic society, education should foster universal and eternal values, oriented towards the unity and integration of our people. Such value education should help to eliminate obscurantism, religious fanaticism, violence, superstition and fatalism".

Characteristics of Secular Education

If secularism is introduced in education, education should possess certain characteristics. For example, India's present educational system promotes secular attitudes and values through its broad based aims, curriculum, enlightened teachers and appropriate activities, all emphasising open-mindedness, progressivism, rationality, freedom from bigotry and superstition and equal respect for all religions. Let us see the characteristics of secular based education in the Indian society.

Secular aims: The aim of the educational system is secular. Such an aim develops India into a rational, democratic, progressive and modern state. The secular aim of education is guided by the philosophy of humanism. The goal of India's educational system is the well-being of all its citizens.

Organization of educational institutions: Most of the Indian educational institutions have been organized on the basis of secular principles. Secular, democratic and rational criteria in appointments, promotions and admissions are necessary.

Multiple curricula: The educational curricula at all levels stress on the promotion of secular values. Textbooks should be free from religious bigotry and prejudice but the good ideas and values, emphasised in different religions, are to be presented in appropriate forms. The cocurricular activities which aim at promoting harmony and cooperation among different social groups and respect for each other's culture are encouraged and included. It avoids condemnation or undue praise of any particular religion. All schools, colleges and universities celebrate fairs, festivals and birth anniversaries of different religions. Moral education has given equal importance to different faiths and beliefs.

Science teaching: Secular education stands for scientific rationalism. Such an education stresses on logical thinking and abhors superstitions and irrational things. That is why, Indian education gives much attention to science teaching in a practical manner. The spirit of science with emphasis on enquiry, experimentation, proof and critical outlook influences the attitudes and values of the pupils. Thus, secular education promotes scientific values of rationality, objectivity and open mindedness.

Enlightened teachers: In the secular education, teachers are expected to treat their educands without nepotism. Therefore, the teachers should eschew the feeling of caste, community or economic status when they deal with their students. Equal respect is given to all pupils and to all religious groups.

Moral outlook: Secular education is the foundation for the development of moral outlook. Moral development inculcates in pupils—humanity, truthfulness, tolerance, honesty, courtesy, sympathy, spirit of service and sacrifice which form a noble character in man and develop his personality.

Development of a wider vision: Secular education makes a man dynamic and enlightened. This type of education develops in him a wider vision towards life and it turns him towards social service by sacrificing his selfishness. It prepares him to face the problems of life and solve them to the best of his efforts and intelligence.

Pluralistic outlook: A pluralistic outlook is the very essence of democracy. Secular education leads to the emergence of a healthy pluralistic outlook which fosters the growth of science, art, philosophy and religion. The universality of pluralism is accepted and due respect is given to individual differences.

Democratic value: Secular education helps man in developing democratic values such as liberty, equality, fraternity and cooperative living. It treats every person as an end and never as a means. It also stresses on the dignity of the individual and the sacredness of the human personality.

Cultural development: Secular education gives emphasis to cultural development. It preserves and reinforces culture. In this way both secularism and culture go hand-in-hand and influence each other. Such an education develops in man the scientific spirit which releases him from the bondage of blind faith and beliefs.

Synthesis of spiritual and material: Secular education glorifies material needs and promotes reverence for earthly life, without disregarding spiritual progress and spiritual values. It looks upon science as a means of material progress but, it looks upon spiritual values as a quest for truth and a search for harmony with nature.

Humanitarianism: Secular education stands for peace, goodwill, understanding, brotherhood of man and the unity of the world. The absence of such an education leads to exploitation, corruption, disaster, selfishness, aggression and hatred, chaos and disorder. It exalts man to a high level by encouraging the policy of "live and let live". It replaces hatred by love, selfishness by self- sacrifice and violence by non-violence. It leads to happiness, order and contentment in society by cultivating faith in truth, beauty and goodness. The betterment of society depends on secular education. Thus, secular education provides the basis for true humanitarianism.

WAYS AND MEANS OF PROMOTING SECULARISM THROUGH EDUCATION

We have already seen the need and importance of secular education in the emerging Indian society. Now let us turn our attention to how we can make our country a secular one. Secular education would be the answer for this problem. Therefore, we should make special efforts in the field of education to make India a really secular state. For this purpose, aims and curricula of education in modern India have to be redesigned to foster tolerance, love, sympathy and respect for the beliefs and faiths of all religions. The methods which we follow in teaching should promote the feeling of secularism and national integration. Teachers should be trained in such a way that they themselves must be secular in their attitude towards life and education. They should not have any bias towards students on the basis of caste, creed and colour. In order to make India a secular country, our Education Commissions have put forward various suggestions.

University Education Commission (1948–1949)

1. All educational institutions start work with a few minutes of silent meditation.
2. In the first year of degree course, lives of great religious leaders like Jesus Christ, Gautham Buddha, Confucious, Zoroaster, Mohammed Nabi, Kabir, Guru Nanak, Ramakrishna Paramhamsa, Swami Vivekananda and Shri Narayana Guru are taught.

Secondary Education Commission (1952–1953)

This Commission believed that, "Healthy trends with regard to religious or moral behaviour spring from three sources".

1. The influence of the home which is the dominant factor.
2. The influence of the school through the conduct and behaviour of the teachers themselves and life in the school community as a whole.
3. The influence exercised by the public of the locality and the extent to which public opinion prevails in all matters pertaining to religious or moral codes of conduct.

The Secondary Education Commission says, "The educational system must make its contribution to the development of habits, attitudes and qualities of character which will enable its citizens to counteract all those fissiparous tendencies which hinder the emergence of a broad, national and secular outlook. Therefore, the Commission has recommended religious instruction or moral instruction as, "One of the methods adopted in some schools is to hold assembly at the commencement of the day's session with teachers and pupils present, when a general non-denominational prayer is offered. Moral instruction in the sense of inspiring talks given by suitable persons selected by the headmaster and dwelling on the lines of great personages of all times and of all climes will help to drive home the lesson of morality. In view of the provision of the construction of the secular state, religious instruction cannot be given in schools except on voluntary basis and outside the regular school hours. Such instruction should be given to the children of the particular faith and with the consent of the parents and the management concerned".

Sri Prakash Committee (1959–1960)

Sri Prakash Committee (1959) was constituted to suggest a programme for religious and moral education. Let us see the salient features of the programme.

Elementary Stage

1. The school assembly should be held for a few minutes in the morning for group singing.
2. Simple and interesting stories about the lives and teachings of prophets, saints and religious leaders should be included in the syllabus for language teaching.
3. Audio-visual material connected with the major religions of the world should be there, especially in teaching geography.
4. In the school programme, two periods a week should be set aside for moral instruction. Dogmas and rituals should be excluded from moral instruction.
5. Physical education and all forms of play in the school should contribute to the building of character and the inculcation of the spirit of true sportsmanship.

Secondary Stage

1. The morning assembly should observe two minutes silence followed by readings from the scriptures and classics. Community singing should also be encouraged.
2. The essential teachings of the great world religions should be studied as part of the curriculum pertaining to social studies and history. Simple texts and stories concerning different religions maybe included in the syllabus.

3. One hour in a week should be assigned to moral instruction. Suitable speakers maybe invited on this occasion.
4. Organized social service during holidays and outside class hours should be an essential part of the school programme. This will be very helpful in teaching the dignity of manual labour, love of humanity, patriotism and self-discipline. Participation in games and sports should be compulsory. Physical education and sex education should form a normal part of the school programme.
5. Qualities of character and behaviour of students should form an essential part of the overall assessment of a student's performance at school.

University stage

1. Silent meditation should be encouraged.
2. General study of different religions should be an essential part of the general education course in degree classes.
3. There should be a separate department in universities for the comparative study of religions.
4. A fairly long period of social service should be introduced by all universities.

Prakash committee remarks, "The many ills that our world of education, and our society as a whole, is suffering today, are mainly due to the gradual disappearance of the hold of the basic principles of religions on the hearts of the people. The old bonds that kept them together are fast loosening and the various new ideologies that are coming to us are increasingly worsening the situation. The only cure that seems to us is the deliberate inculcation of moral and spiritual values from the earliest years of our lives. If we lose them, we shall be a nation without a soul".

Indian Education Commission (1964–1966)

The commission has made a strong recommendation in favour of religious and moral education in the country. According to the report of the commission, "Religion has a great motivating force and is intimately bound with the formation of character and the inculcation of ethical values". The commission has put forward the following programmes to establish a secular state:

1. Arrangements should be made for compulsory and free education from 6–14 years (as per Article 45).
2. Arrangement should be made for social education and adult education.
3. Educational opportunities should be provided to all without any distinction of creed, race, colour, sex, language and region.
4. Democratic-secular and scientific outlook should be developed.
5. The quality of leadership should be developed in the students.
6. Education should be imparted through modern technology.
7. Education should be made employment oriented.
8. National integration and international understanding maybe developed in order to develop the feeling of brotherhood.

National Policy on Education (1986)

Change in curriculum: The erosion of essential values and cynicism in society needs re-adjustments in the curriculum in order to make education a forceful tool for the cultivation of social and moral values.

Universal and eternal values: Education should foster universal and eternal values in the culturally pluralistic society towards the unity and integration of our people. Value education helps to eliminate obscurantism, religious fanaticism, violence, superstition and fatalism.

Positive content: Value education should have a profound positive content based on our heritage, national goals and universal perceptions.

ROLE OF SCHOOL AND TEACHER IN SECULAR EDUCATION

It is the need of the hour in a multireligious country like India to prepare an ideal scheme for imparting religious education to our students. In this regard, the role of the school and the teacher can help in imparting secular education in the following ways:

- A well-planned syllabus containing essential moral values like love, sacrifice, compassion, fellow feeling and tolerance should be prepared.
- Teaching of literature, history and social studies, should be done effectively with a view to promote human values.
- Respectable teachers of high learning should be asked to impart religious instruction. The personalities of such teachers in themselves will be good examples for the students to follow them as models for dedication, love, affection, cooperation and sacrifice.
- Every school should celebrate religious festivals pertaining to different religions. At least one function of each religion must be celebrated in the institution. Students belonging to different religions should be encouraged to associate in the celebration of each religious function. The school authorities should ensure that all religious festivals are given equal importance.
- One or two periods in a week should be set aside in the school time- table for instruction of moral and spiritual values.
- The school authorities should organize declamation contests on topics related to all religions. The teachers in-charge of declamation
- contests should make all efforts to maintain that the central string of all religions is one.
- In the school programme, a particular religious faith should not be emphasised. Students should not feel that one religion is superior to another one. They should be broadminded and should develop a sense that all religions are equal.
- Extension lectures on topics of comparative religious study maybe organized in the schools. Eminent scholars of different religions maybe invited for giving lectures to students on comparative study of different religions.
- Spiritual education should be imparted to the students. The textbooks used for such education should contain questions from all religions of the world—Buddhism, Christianity, Hinduism, Islam, Jainism, Sikhism etc. There should be a provision for the comparative study of different religions.
- The students maybe taken on tours and trips to different centres of religious study. For instance, Guru Gobind Singh Bhawan in the Punjab University, Patiala, is the centre of different religious studies and it unites all and ultimately shows oneness which will have a great impact on the personality of the child.
- Many qualities such as love, compassion and social service are common in different religions. At the time of celebrations, sacrifice and service to humanity maybe highlighted in the schools. The students maybe encouraged to take up such activities so that they can realise the dignity of social service, which will have an everlasting impact on their personalities.

- Every school should create an atmosphere in which students should get an opportunity to cooperate with different religious communities.

IMPACT OF SECULAR EDUCATION

- Secular education develops in the child the spirit of love, tolerance, discipline, cooperation, equality, sympathy and fraternity.
- Education is free from specific religions.
- Education becomes an active and independent process by which the teacher can develop broad mindedness among students.
- It develops moral and spiritual qualities among the students in an unbiased form on the basis of secularism.
- It is helpful in maintaining internal peace which strengthens national unity and national integrity.
- Secular education shuns communalism, sectarianism, provincialism, traditionalism and language controversies.
- Secular education is based on the principles of "unity in diversity" and "diversity in unity".
- This type of education accepts all religions equally and develops the sense in the child that no religion is superior or inferior to the others.
- Secular education makes the attitude of the teacher liberal so that he can develop the spirit of religious tolerance among the students.
- Secular education protects the child from becoming a prey to the superstitious faith and beliefs and develops him as a rational human being.

LIMITATIONS OF SECULAR EDUCATION

India is a country of many religions, castes, customs, traditions and cultures. Therefore, the principle of secularism cannot be fully implemented here. It is regretted that even 60 years after the attainment of independence the ugly monster of communalism is still destroying the peaceful coexistence of people. According to Norman D. Palmer, "Officially India is fully dedicated to the concept of a secular state as it was when it was led by the great champion of secularism Pt. Jawaharlal Nehru, but this dedication is constantly being threatened by some of the most deeply rooted forces in Indian society". It is vivid that secularisation of education in India is facing a lot of difficulties.

Educational institutions related to religion: There are some provisions in the Indian constitution for starting schools and colleges related to religion if they do not receive any grant. As a result denominational schools and colleges like Pathshalas, Shia schools, Catholic schools, Catholic colleges, Hindu Vidyalayas, Vaish schools, Ahir schools, Kayastha institution, DAV schools, Jain schools, Jain colleges, Muslim schools and Muslim colleges are allowed to function with a lot of freedom. These institutions admit children and appoint teachers of the respective communities or castes. Education in these institutions is not provided on the basis of secularism. As a result, secularism cannot be developed among the students through education.

Use of religion as a political tool: In Indian society, religion is being used as a powerful political tool. It is a great hindrance on the way of promoting secularism through education. This is the pathetic condition of India where different political parties contest elections, and selections are not made on the basis of merit but on the basis of religion and race. It indicates that starting a new political party in the name of religion and caste is easier than developing secularism through education in our country.

Lack of toleration: It is our bitter experience that the religion-based political system and religion-based private educational institutions foster religious feeling and reduce toleration among the people of varied faiths and beliefs. Such activities give a severe blow to secular education in a country like India.

Narrow outlook: It is an undeniable fact that the establishment of schools and colleges by various communities, religious groups and the people of different castes have developed a narrow outlook towards other communities. Moreover, Indians are very narrow minded in faith and culture. So, it becomes very difficult for them to recognise other faiths.

Teachers are not secular: The most shocking thing in India is that even the teachers are not secular. In fact, appointments of teachers are made, in private schools and colleges, on the basis of their community/caste/creed. Therefore, teachers are narrow minded and they are also infused with the spirit of religionism and casteism. Hence, we cannot expect secular education from them.

Feeling of religious superiority: The feeling of religious superiority among people who establish schools and colleges is common. Such people give more importance to their own religion and neglect all other religions. This attitude develops religious conflict. Such conflict cannot inculcate the secular outlook among the students. This is a major limitation of our education in promoting secularism.

Emphasis on theoretical learning: Our present system of education lays more stress on its theoretical learning than on its practical application. Very little effort is made to change the values and attitudes of education. Therefore, many ills like caste, creed, 'gotras', dowry, lack of tolerance and courtesy, and ill-treatment of women, the poor and the old have entered into our society which retard the secular outlook of the pupils. As marriage is arranged and solemnised on the basis of socio-economic and cultural backgrounds, the highly educated parents of boys demand huge dowry. Education has failed to eradicate such evils and has developed an anti-secular outlook among our students.

Negligence of secular celebrations: The remarkable drawback of Indian schools is that holidays are given in schools and colleges on the occasion of important religious fairs, festivals and birthdays of great men. These days are not celebrated properly giving due importance to the person or festival concerned. In fact, mass media like the television, the radio and the newspapers are utilising these days for commercial benefit by telecasting film based programmes, which corrupt and spoil the minds of youth. Thus, the very purpose of declaring holidays in the name of festivals and political and religious leaders is defeated. As a result, the students do not get enough opportunities to understand the importance of these days and lives of great men, which are essential to imbibe secular values in them.

Negligence of group activities: Educational institutions do not encourage group activities and social service programmes. They neglect group activities and group methods of teaching and learning. This is one of the hindrances in the way of promoting secular ideas and values.

Social inequalities and illiteracy: The unfair attitude of the government officials and their discriminatory behaviour towards certain groups stands against secularism. For example, the people of low castes are the victims of social exploitation in their actual life even today. Illiteracy is entrenched in rural areas and they are not ready to leave their conservatism. Therefore, it is very difficult to teach them secularism.

CONCLUSION

Whatsoever maybe the limitations, no doubt that our country is secular and we are expected to believe in secularism. But it is regrettable that religion is gradually getting politicised and used as an instrument by the politicians to achieve their own selfish ends. The state assembly and parliament elections are witnesses for religion being used as a vote-catching device. That is why, many people feel that introduction of religious education may bring struggle for power in the school campus. We are committing a mistake by avoiding religion in the name of secularism. In the words of Prof. M. Ruthna Swami, "Religion holds people together while secularism is divisive, religion is constructive while secularism erodes, religion inspires while secularism criticizes, religion builds while secularism dissolves, religion unites the people while secularism makes people to look at one another with doubt if not suspicion". However, let us try to remove the hindrances mentioned earlier in order to realize the dream of our great patriots and make India a secular state both in words and deeds. Pt. Jawaharlal Nehru has remarked, "Let us, pursue our path to industrial progress with all our strength and vigour and at the same time, remember that material riches without toleration and compassion and wisdom may well turn to dust and ashes". People are ready to sacrifice even their lives for the sake of religion without understanding what it means, but they are not ready to apply at least a little bit of their religious doctrines in their deeds and practical life. This is the present trend of the Indian society.

CHAPTER 46

EDUCATION AND MODERNISATION

INTRODUCTION

The word 'modernisation' has been echoing around the world since the dawn of the twentieth century. Modern age is the age of material science and technology. During this age, emphasis is being given to modernisation in every aspect of human life and it has become quite inevitable. That is why modernisation is considered as the biggest gift of the modern society. In fact, all of us want to be modern. Therefore, all individuals take untiring efforts to be modernized. The craze for modernity is to be witnessed in all the aspects of human life and in all areas. For example, a housewife decorates her kitchen with modern gadgets and uses modern methods to prepare food items. Similarly, a doctor wants to furnish his hospital with all the modern facilities. As we have already mentioned, education is a dynamic process which is subject to change in relation to the time and needs of the society. Thus, when fast changes are taking place in all the areas, education cannot remain unchanged and untouched by the impact of modernisation.

MEANING OF MODERNISATION

The term 'modernisation' has acquired different meanings which differ from time-to-time and person-to-person. As a result, we have different meanings of modernisation. For a common man, it is the use of modern means for a happy and comfortable life, through industrialisation and automation. The economists use this term as another word for economic growth through the application of science and technology in the productive process. The political scientists look at it as the process of how governments increase their capacity to change and cope with social conflict. The psychologists emphasise self-reliance and achievement motivation essential to modernity. To the educationists, it implies a new approach not only to the aims and process of education but also to the totality of its entire programmes so as to relate it to the development, needs and aspiration of the nation.

In general, modernisation is a process of change from the traditional and quasi-traditional order to a desired type of technology. These changes take place in values, social structure and achievements of the pupils. In the words of William E. Moore, "Modernisation is a revolutionary change leading to the transformation of a traditional or pre-modern society into the type of technology and associated social organization that characterize the advanced economically prosperous and relatively politically stable nations of the Western world". Thus, modernisation refers to the changes in material elements and also the belief of the people, their values and way of life as a whole. The process of modernisation aims at bringing about desirable changes in the social structure, values and social norms. According to S.N. Eisentadt, "Historically, modernisation is the process of change towards those types of social, economic and political systems that have developed in Western Europe and North America from the seventeenth century to the nineteenth and have been spread to other European countries and in the nineteenth and twentieth centuries to the South American, Asian and African countries".

A modernised society is one which adopts a new way of life according to the changing environments and does not remain at the level of the tenth century society. People who follow the traditional lifestyle will not use watches, trains, buses, planes, televisions, radios, calculators, computers, refrigerators and other modern gadgets. Modernisation means neither industrialisation nor Westernisation, but it brings about qualitative and quantitative improvement to produce such citizens who are educated and efficient and have faith in the progress of the nation. It is the process of economic, technological, industrial, social and cultural changes. In other words, it is the process of transforming the old traditional societies and nations with the objective of bringing about radical changes in the fields of economic, educational, industrial, social and technological advancement.

MAIN FEATURES OF MODERNISATION

Inkelz has mentioned some characteristic features of modernisation in his book, *Becoming Modern*. They are:

New ideas: Modernity is meant to become progressive and to adopt new thoughts or ideas which give a positive direction to the society. After a good deal of thinking and critical analysis, new ideas or thoughts are put into practice.

New knowledge: The modern age is the age of materialism and science and technology. The development of science and technology is the cause of the explosion of knowledge. As a result, there is a lot of curiosity to acquire new knowledge which modernises the society.

Emphasis on the present: Modern age does not permit us to stick to dogmas bound with ancient values, faiths, beliefs, customs and traditions. We try to give a new direction to our thinking by which we become modernised and forget the past.

New techniques and methods: We use those methods and techniques which are being used in the developed countries. For example, in the place of bullock carts we use cars, trains and buses, in the place of the wooden plough we use the tractor. Thus, we adopt those methods and techniques that are suitable to the situation of our country.

Faith in equal justice: Modernisation reduces the gulf between the haves and the have-nots or the lower and the higher classes by maintaining equal justice. The opportunities for the demonstration of talent are given to all without any discrimination.

Practical and realistic attitude: This is another feature of modernisation with a practical and realistic attitude rather than a theoretical attitude. Such an attitude is very important to decide what to accept and what to reject.

Rapid socio-cultural change: Modern society is fast moving and socio- cultural changes take place rapidly. This is the most important feature of the present age.

COMPONENTS OF MODERNISATION

There are certain components which prove helpful in bringing out the modernisation process. Lerner, Coleman, Mc Leland, Willebt and Dubey have identified the following factors or components of modernisation:

(i) empathy; (ii) mobility; (iii) high participation in social, political and professional life; (iv) interest in articulation towards achieving one's goals and infuse rationality discipline and foresight into his modes of thought and attitude; (v) interest aggregation; (vi) institutionalised political competition; (vii) achievement orientation; (viii) rational ends; (ix) new attitudes to wealth, work and risk taking; (x) faith in the desirability and possibility of change; (xi) socio-economic and political discipline; (xii) postponement of immediate, short-run satisfactions for higher satisfaction in the long run.

Let us explain the various components which bring about the modernisation process directly or indirectly.

Scientific attitude: Scientific attitude keeps an individual away from blind faiths, beliefs, superstitions, ignorance and ritualism and makes his mind liberal. As a result, his thinking becomes logical and critical. He arrives at a conclusion only after observation and full investigation.

Faith in change: Change is the law of nature. The individual who has faith in modernisation welcomes change. If not, there will not be modernisation. Changes take place in all aspects of life such as social, cultural, scientific and technological areas.

Change by persuasion: Change can be brought about by making others realise that it is for their good and betterment. Democratic efforts are made to bring about changes. This is because there is a close relationship between modernisation and democracy. No force should be used to bring about changes.

Rational thinking: As man is the best creation of God, he has the power of rational thinking which enables him to distinguish between good and bad. It can provide speed to the modernisation process.

Faith in materialism: In the modern age, man loves to enjoy material comforts in order to lead an easy life. The love for materialism leads him to modernisation.

Democratic attitude: The democratic attitude of the individuals or a society helps to bring about changes. This is because people have freedom to discharge their duties and rights. In countries like India, democratic attitude accelerates the process of modernisation.

Explosion of knowledge: Knowledge is expanding fast in the individual and social life due to the increase of the thinking power. It speeds up the expansion of communication through various methods. As a consequence, modernisation has become a natural process.

Emphasis on secularism: Secularism develops a new attitude among the people towards religions. It makes the individual tolerant and liberal. Religious freedom gives a boost to the process of modernisation.

Industrialisation: In the modern age, industrialisation is increasing rapidly. It changes the attitude of the people towards science and technology as a result of its new inventions and discoveries. Industrialisation changes the lifestyle of the people, their habits of eating and drinking. Society has undergone a change and it turns the present age into a mechanical one. In this way, industrialisation accelerates the process of modernisation.

Urbanisation: Growth of population, increasing unemployment and demand for quality education force the rural people to migrate to urban areas. Such a movement to cities and towns brings about a change in the life of the rural people. Thus, migration expands urbanisation and it is helpful in the process of modernisation.

Computerisation: This is the age of computerisation. In fact, the computer occupies a vital place in every aspect of life. Its use in various vocations, government offices, banks and private factories has been increasing day by day. It not only brings novelty in the working process but also modernises the society.

Respect the individual: In a democratic country like India, everybody should be given equal respect without any discrimination. An individual should be respected as an individual. This attitude of humanism is very helpful in the expansion of modernity. It is said, "Man should not be idealized nor he should be demoralized, he is a human being and should be humanized".

Desire of modern living: Leading a modern life is the desire of every individual and it changes the lifestyle of the people. The wealthy people use modern gadgets like cooking gas, mixer, pressure cooker, television, car, refrigerator, grinder, washing machine etc. But the people who have limited means also strive to change their lifestyle and become successful to some extent in their effort. In this way people modernise their day-to-day life.

Removing superstitions: The expansion of education, advancement of science and technology, industrialisation and urbanisation play a positive role in removing superstitious and conservative views, which hinder modernisation.

Emphasis on the present and the future: We should forget the past in order to relieve us from worries and mental tension. To make our present life happy, we should take efforts to make the present better and the future successful. This kind of thinking and efforts modernise the human society in a better way.

Accept mechanisation: The use of machines in the modern age has made our life simple. That is why, machines are being increasingly used in all the aspects of human life. The use of machines as the means of transportation, trade, information and production helps in the process of modernisation.

National and international outlook: The term nationalism should be used in a broad sense. An international outlook is essential to accelerate the speed of modernisation. It is because no country can stand on its own for meeting its requirements. The occurrence of earthquakes, flood, drought, famine and tsunami in a particular place affects all the parts of the world. Thus, we are living in an age where no individual is a citizen of his own country, but he is a citizen of the whole world. The development of an international outlook modernises our attitudes.

Universal brotherhood: The worldwide feeling of brotherhood is a mirror of modernisation in the present age. The creation and development of amity, mutual love, cooperation, sympathy, understanding the woes of others, and fellow feeling modernise the human values and human life.

Independent thinking: Independent thinking and rational judgement enhance individual knowledge and remove his conservative life, blind faiths and beliefs and traditional activities. Independent thinking and rational judgement is very important to bring about modernisation.

Social justice: Justice, equality and liberty are actively helpful in modernizing the society. Therefore, everybody should be entitled to receive justice, equality and liberty from the Panchayat level without any discrimination. Justice should be given in a very short time. "Justice delayed means justice denied". It modernises the world more dynamically by bridging the gulf between the high and the low class people.

ROLE OF EDUCATION IN MODERNISATION

Education is an effective and powerful means for modernisation. According to Yogendra Singh, "Education has been one of the most influential instruments of modernisation in India. It has led to the modernisation of people's aspiration for nationalism, liberalism and freedom. It alone has been responsible for the growth of an enlightened intelligential which carried forward not only a movement for independence but also a relentless struggle for social and cultural reforms". Thus, there is a close relationship between education and modernisation. The Education Commission (1964–1966) states, "The progress of modernisation, will therefore, be directly related to the pace of educational advance and the one sure way to modernize quickly to spread education, produce educated and skilled citizens and train an adequate and competent intelligential". Modernisation is the process of bringing change. Education is the only medium through which the traditional men and institutions can be modernised in an advanced way. In the words of Thomas, Mahatma Gandhi, Jawaharlal Nehru and other reformers have attempted to build up a new India. They have succeeded in reducing the importance of traditional institutions. Perhaps a first step in moving towards the establishment of a new social order, which is already in process". In education, modernisation means a new approach not only to the aims and process of education but also to the totality of its entire programmes so as to relate it to the national development, national needs and national inspiration.

Aim of education and modernisation: The aim of education in modernisation is imparting knowledge or the preparation of a finished product, awakening of curiosity, the development of proper interests, attitudes and values and the building up of such essential skills as independent study and the capacity to think and judge for oneself and to become a responsible member of a democratic society.

Science based education: Science education has become an integral part of school and college education. The study of science has also become a part of all courses in humanities and social sciences at the university level. The purpose of science teaching is to develop problem solving, analytical skills and the ability to apply them to the problems of the material environment and social living and to promote the spirit of enquiry and experimentation.

Vocationalisation of education: Greater attention has been given to the vocationalisation of education. Such education is provided in schools in the names of 'manual work' or 'work experience' to produce scientists and technical workers. It is based on Gandhi's Basic Education, which prepares the students to stand on their own feet.

Mass education: The proportion of persons who receive education has been increasing in order to produce educated and skilled citizens. They train an adequate and competent intelligential who modernise the society rapidly.

Education for national integration: Education plays a vital role in developing and strengthening national integration. Social and national integration has been an important problem of the modern society. It is education that shuns all hindrances by advising the young men to have a judicious mixture of zeal and understanding to play an active role in the process of nation building.

Development of skilled manpower: Modernisation in agriculture industry, trade and commerce is impossible in the absence of education. It is education that produces able men, scientists, industrialists, agriculturists, officers, managers and engineers. They are required for modernising agricultural, industrial and the tertiary sectors of an economy.

Dynamic method of teaching: Education modernises the methods of teaching by applying new techniques such as the project method, problem solving, play-way method, Dalton method etc. Moreover, audio-visual aids and mass media are applied in the teaching process.

Harmony between science and spirituality: The concept of the mingling of science and spirituality is of special significance in Indian education. Vinoba Bhave has described the present age as "the age of science spirituality". Education shuns the blind faith and beliefs and develops science and spirituality in the students.

Study of foreign language: The present education encourages the study of foreign languages like Russian, French, German, Japanese, Spanish and Chinese, besides English. These languages are important for communication all over the world. They are also required for the preservation and promotion of knowledge and culture. Their role is very important in modernising society.

Develop democratic values: Education develops democratic values and qualities in the students. It also helps to clarify the differences between the traditional and modern values. By providing knowledge of the modern values, education can accelerate the pace of modernity.

Develop secularism: The spirit of secularism can be developed in the students by removing fanaticism. This is possible only through the medium of education.

Develop rational thinking: Education develop rational thinking and judgement among the students. It makes them wise by removing conservatism and blind faith. The rational decisions give boost to modernisation.

We may list the role of education in modernisation briefly as follows:

- Education and equalisation of educational opportunity.
- Education and removal of illiteracy and ignorance.
- Education and social, political and cultural awakening.
- Education and emphasis on science and technology.
- Education and democratic values.
- Education and secularism.
- Education and development of national integration.
- Education and international understanding.
- Education and synthesis between scientific and cultural values.
- Education and increased production and economic prosperity.

MODERNISATION ON DIFFERENT ASPECTS OF EDUCATION

We have seen how far education brings about modernisation. Now let us turn our attention to the impact of modernisation on different aspects of education.

Aims of education: As we are moving forward towards modernity, the aims of education also have to be modernised in the right direction. For example, the aim of education is justified in the following ways for bringing about modernity:

- Inspire the boy and girl students through teaching.
- Develop rational thinking among the students.
- Foster the creative power of the students.
- Develop leadership qualities.
- Train them to earn their livelihood.
- Develop scientific and optimistic attitude.
- Develop democratic values.
- Inculcate patriotic feeling and secularism.

- Strengthen national integrity and international understanding.
- Develop social, moral and spiritual qualities.
- Speed up the process of modernisation.
- Bring out an all-round development.
- Develop the spirit of world brotherhood and healthy cooperation.
- Make the students efficient citizens so as to discharge their responsibilities and rights.
- Develop character and promote human values.

Curriculum: As the aim of education is to modernise the society, the curriculum should also be modernised. Therefore, the curriculum should be comprehensive in accordance with the aims of education based on modernity.

- The basis of the curriculum should be scientific and technical.
- The curriculum includes vocational skill in order to increase the productivity of the country.
- The curriculum comprises social service, National Service Scheme.
- The curriculum should include those subjects and activities which develop patriotic feeling, national integrity and secularism.
- It should also include health education and environmental education.
- There should be diversified subjects in the curriculum.
- The curriculum should be organized in order to develop international understanding and world brotherhood.

Method of teaching: Modernity is related to science and technology. Therefore, methods of teaching should be used to develop the scientific attitude among the students. In this regard, heuristic method, inductive method, demonstration method and experimental method should be used. Television, radio, computers and audio-visual aids can also be used in order to make the teaching process more effective and attractive.

Role of the teacher: Education is the most powerful instrument by which desirable changes can be brought about in the society. It is the teacher who plays a predominant role in modernising the society. The teacher should be dynamic and active with faith in modernity. There should be a coordination in his thoughts, speech and deeds. He should give clear information about the need and importance of modernisation to his students and tell them as to how they can make their contribution in the process of modernisation. For this purpose the teacher should use scientific methods of teaching.

Discipline: Modernisation is not in favour of giving any type of corporal punishment to the students. As students are the future citizens of the country, modernity allows limited freedom to them. Hence, the teacher should present an ideal personality in order to inspire the students for self-restraints. This is essential for democracy and modernisation.

Let us list the role of modernisation in the educational sphere:

- Universalisation of free and compulsory education.
- Equalisation of educational opportunities to everyone.
- Establishment of a common school system.
- Multifaceted curriculum.
- Education is related to economic development.
- Education and training for democracy.
- Maximum importance to science and technology.

ROLE OF THE TEACHER IN MODERNISATION

The process of modernisation has its roots in industrialisation based upon the infusion of science and technology. Therefore, the teacher should make use of science and technology in the routine activities of the school. He should develop a rational, curious, thoughtful and scientific attitude in his students by encouraging debate and discussion. He should try to root out blind faith and superstition. He should promote the sentiment of liberty, equality and fraternity by providing appropriate freedom to students in the classroom and outside. He has a critical role in generating the school's atmosphere to speed up the process of modernisation. He should develop the sentiment of secularism and respect all religions by respecting the saints of all religions and reading various sacred texts as part of the morning prayers. In this way, he can play a crucial role in promoting the process of modernisation in India.

HINDRANCES IN THE MODERNISATION IN INDIAN SOCIETY

The modernisation of Indian society is not an easy task, because our society is suffering from many hindrances and obstacles, which curb the progress of modernisation in all aspects of individual and social life.

Lack of unity: Our country is a country of varied religions, cultures, languages, castes and communities. Therefore, a comprehensive progress of modernity of the country is not feasible in the absence of unity.

Communalism: Communal feelings become very strong on account of diversities leading to violence, skirmishes, arson and looting. Their thoughts are very narrow and limited. This becomes a hurdle to modernity.

Religion: People who have a narrow attitude towards religion cannot be liberal. The feeling of fundamentalism creates extremists who become very dangerous for the individual, the society and the nation. Such citizens stand against the progress of their nation.

Ignorance: The majority of the population of India has been enveloped in the darkness of superstition and ignorance. This leads them to blind faith and beliefs which retard the process of modernisation.

Illiteracy: This is another factor which plays a considerable role in curbing the progress of the nation. The illiterates do not know the need and importance of modernisation. They stick on to their traditional culture and customs. Such attitudes affect the process of modernisation adversely.

Poverty: The majority of the population in India cannot afford even two meals per day. This is not conducive for creative thinking and rational attitudes. Economic prosperity is essential for the people to modernise the society.

Social and cultural lag: Most of the people in India are much attached to the traditions of their culture, faiths and traditions. Such people will not accept any change. Though they adopt any change that takes in material aspects of life, they are not ready to accept the change in the non-material aspects of life. This tendency becomes an obstacle in the process of modernisation.

Gap between ideals and reality: There is a lot of difference between words and deeds in many aspects of life. Such gaps impede the process of modernisation.

CONCLUSION

In order to modernise the present society, Indian education should transmit the culture to the new generation and transform the outlook of the young towards life in the light of the past, in the context of cross-cultural influences and in the light of the future requirements of the individual and the society. The emerging Indian society can move rapidly towards modernisation through an ideal system of moral, social and spiritual education combined with general and vocational education. The Indian Education Commission (1964–1966) has given the following suggestions to bring about modernisation through the medium of education.

- Education should be related to increase production.
- Education should inspire social and national integration.
- Education should be dynamic to bring about changes in the process of modernisation.
- Education should develop social, moral and spiritual values in order to develop and modify individual character.

Thus, in all respects the role of education is important in modernising the Indian society.

CHAPTER 47

VALUES IN EDUCATION

INTRODUCTION

Education has become materialistic and an undue emphasis is given to knowledge-oriented education. The intellectual development of the pupils has become one sided. Such an education leads to the development of lopsided personalities and it pushes back the religious, moral, and spiritual values of our great tradition. As a result there is no harmony between the outer life of actions and the inner life of emotions in the modern man. Because of this situation, we find the crisis of character and the deterioration of values in social, economic, cultural, moral, and religious spheres of human beings. The growing erosion of essential values and the increasing cynicism in society stress the need for value education. Education should foster universal and eternal values like compassion, courage, honesty, tolerance, peace and truthfulness to develop balanced individuals and to create a better human society. In other words, the main function of education is to develop physical, mental, emotional, social and spiritual aspects of the individuals by laying stress on the development of healthy habits, traits, right attitudes, values, skills and interests. In the words of Dr. Rawat, "If education in our country has to fulfil the above urgent need, then it is absolutely essential to promote value oriented education in our schools in order to make them training centres of democratic citizenship which catalyse social transformation, promote economic growth and accelerate our progress towards democratic socialism".

MEANING OF VALUE

Friedrich Nietzshe (1844–1900), a German philosopher, used the word 'values' in 1880 in the plural to denote moral attitudes and beliefs that were personal and subjective. But in modern democratic societies, values include all important religions, beliefs, moral attitudes, philosophy of life and political ideologies. Etymologically, value means the quality of an individual or thing which makes an individual or thing important, respectable and useful. Thus, value is anything (person, object, activity or condition) that men regard as worthwhile or preferable to other things. A value can be defined as an endeavour which satisfies the need system, psychological as well as physiological. The same thing maybe quite useless and of no value to another individual. From the philosophical standpoint, a value is directly related to a view point or thought. For instance, keeping silence before elders is considered as a value in some societies, but in many societies frankness in attitude and behaviour is considered necessary and useful, and father and sons share wine from the same bottle. In the same way, the preachers and spiritualists, the economists, educators, humanists, philosophers, political leaders, psychologists, social reformers, sociologists and thinkers have given different meanings and dimensions to the concept 'value' but all of them stress on the significance of values at personal, national and global levels.

DEFINITIONS OF VALUE

Values are part and parcel of the philosophy of a nation and its educational system. They are the guiding principles of life which are conducive to all- round development. The concept 'value' has been defined by different philosophers, educationists, thinkers and scholars in the following manner:

N.T. Ramji: "A value is what is desired or what is sought. Values may be operationally conceived as those guiding principles of life which are conducive to one's physical and mental health as well as to social welfare and adjustment and which are in tune with one's culture".

John Dewey: "The value means primarily to prize, to esteem, to appraise and to estimate. It means the act of cherishing something holding it dear and also the act of passing judgement upon the nature and amounts as values of compared with something else".

C.F. Kluckhon: "Value is a conception, explicit or implicit, distinctive of an individual or characteristics of a group of the desirable which influence the selection, from the available means and ends of action".

S. Brightman: "In the most elementary sense, value means whatever is actually liked, prized, esteemed, desired, approved, or enjoyed by anyone at any time. It is the actual experience of enjoying a desired object or activity".

N. Torralba: "Values can be defined operationally to include norms of right conduct and good intellectual and moral habits".

P.N. Kirpali: "Values may be defined as (i) what we believe—professed values, (ii) what we practise—operational values and (iii) what we learn from experience in order to adapt and renew traditions received from the past— traditional values". He proposes for a fresh enunciation of human values which can be shared by all and made operative in order to build human solidarity for greater justice and higher quality of life.

Kane: "Values are the ideals, beliefs or norms which a society or the large majority of a society's members hold".

Cuber: "Values are the ideas and beliefs which people cherish. These ideas contain or express the judgement which people have, of the relative importance of thing".

Henderson: "It has been pointed out that man acts to satisfy his wants, anything which satisfies a human want becomes thereby a value. To say that our conduct is motivated by our value is another way of saying that we act to satisfy our wants".

Seshadri: "Value refers to objects that human beings consider desirable and worthy pursuit in their thoughts, feelings, and actions. These objects may be material or abstract qualities and states of mind and heart like truthfulness, happiness, peace, justice. In any case, they function as ideals and standards and govern human actions".

M.P. Hunt: "As a judgement concerning worth of an object, person, group or situation. Value judgement contains evaluative rating terms, such as good, bad, moral, immoral, beautiful and ugly etc".

R.K. Mukherji: "Values are socially approved drives and goals that are internalized through the process of conditioning, learning or socialization and that becomes subjective preferences, standards and aspirations.

Rokeach: "Value is an enduring belief, a specific mode of conduct or end state existence along a continuum of relative importance".

T.W. Hipple: "Values are conscious or unconscious motivators and justifiers of the actions and judgement".

D.W. Prall: "Value is precisely the term applied in common usage to objects which stand at the outer end of the relation called liking, the inner end of which is a human mind that likes".

R. Borsodi: "Values are emotional judgements generated by feelings not cognition. They are emotional, not intellectual judgements".

N.K. Dutt: "A value is defined as an endeavour which satisfies need system, psychological as well as physiological needs. Almost, all human beings have the same physiological needs but differ in their psychological needs, hence differ in their values and styles of life".

Manheim: "A value is anything which is believed by an individual or society to be important and to have meaning to be desirable and to be worthy of serving as a guide for people's thoughts, aims and behaviours".

E.B. Hurlock: "Values are concepts heavily weighted with emotions. They are concepts of the desirable which influence the child's selection from available modes, means, and ends of action. Because they are primarily subjective, they are stronger predispositions of behaviour than concepts with less heavy emotional weighting".

Committee on religious and moral instruction: "Anything that helps us to behave properly towards others is moral value" and "Anything that takes us out of self, and inspires us to sacrifice for the good of others or for a great cause is spiritual values".

NATURE OF VALUES

- Values are standards or guidelines for an individual's life.
- Values are the guidelines for a nation that guide its policies.
- Values are learned and acquired in many ways.
- Values are influenced by an individual's experiences, desires and specific situations.
- Values are created and developed in the society through the inter- relationship of its members.
- Values steer our life's journey.
- Values are not static and they change with time.
- Values are socially shared and transmitted, and accepted by all members of the society.
- Values energise the individual to action.
- Values can be structured and restructured through the processes of reflective thinking.
- Values are influenced by emotions.
- Value of a thing or person has the power to satisfy its/his desires.
- Values are derived from several sources (church, school, family etc.)
- Anything which has utility is a value.
- Values are hierarchical in nature.
- Values are helpful for survival.

- Values involve emotions and people often sacrifice and even enter into conflict to uphold them.
- Values frequently represent alternatives.
- Values possess both cognitive and effective dimensions.
- Values represent wants, preferences, and opinions about what is right, fair, just or desirable.

CLASSIFICATION OF VALUES

Values are influenced by social, religious, political, technological, psychological and moral factors. As a result, values mean different things to different people. Therefore, they are classified differently by different scholars.

Swami Vivekananda's Classification of Values

- Cultivation of heart
- Fearlessness
- Non-injury
- Personal purity and social purity
- Self-sacrifice
- Service to others

Mahatma Gandhi's Classification of Values

- *Ahimsa* (Non-violence)
- *Satya* (Truth)
- *Astayans* (Non-thriving)
- *Brahmacharya* (Purity)
- *Aparigraha* (Non-acquisitiveness)
- *Sharirshram* (Physical work)
- *Aswada* (Control of palate)
- *Sarvatra Bhavjavarjana* (Fearlessness)
- *Sarva Dharma Sambhava* (Looking up at all religions equally– toleration)
- *Swadeshi* (Patriotism)
- *Sparsha Bhavana* (Abolition of untouchability)

Values Emphasized at the National Seminar Held at Ramakrishna Mission

- Cleanliness
- Community service
- Compassion
- Dignity of labour
- Dutifulness
- Faith in God
- Orderliness
- Patriotism
- Punctuality
- Respect for elders

- Respect for all religions
- Self-discipline

Dr. Karan Singh's (Vice-Chancellor, J.N. University) Classification

Family values (respect for elders, helpfulness, cooperation and affection)

Social values (courtesy, consideration to strangers, punctuality, cleanliness and co-operation)

Environmental values (develop an awareness of the importance of preserving and improving the environment)

Inter-religious understanding of values (accepting multiple paths to the divine)

Spiritual values (prayer, meditation, yoga, zen etc.)

Global values (we need shared values for the emerging global society) through a worldwide programme of education.

List of Values as Compiled by NCERT

1. Abstinence
2. Anti-untouchability
3. Appreciation of cultural values of others
4. Citizenship
5. Concern for others
6. Consideration for others
7. Cooperation
8. Cleanliness
9. Compassion
10. Common cause
11. Common good
12. Courage
13. Courtesy
14. Curiosity
15. Democratic decision making
16. Devotion
17. Dignity of the individual
18. Dignity of manual work
19. Duty
20. Discipline
21. Endurance
22. Equality
23. Friendship
24. Faithfulness
25. Fellow feeling
26. Freedom
27. Forward look
28. Good manners

29. Gentle manliness
30. Gratitude
31. Honesty
32. Helpfulness
33. Humanism
34. Hygienic living
35. Initiative
36. Integrity
37. Justice
38. Kindness to animals
39. Leadership
40. Loyalty to duty
41. National consciousness
42. National integration
43. National unity
44. Non-violence
45. Obedience
46. Patriotism
47. Peace
48. Proper utilisation of time
49. Punctuality
50. Purity
51. Quest for knowledge
52. Regularity
53. Resourcefulness
54. Respect for others
55. Reverence for old age
56. Secularism and respect for all religions
57. Self-confidence
58. Self-control
59. Self-discipline
60. Self-duty
61. Self-help
62. Self-reliance
63. Self-respect
64. Self-restraint
65. Self-support
66. Sense of discrimination between good and bad
67. Sense of social responsibility
68. Simple living
69. Sincerity
70. Socialism
71. Social justice
72. Social service
73. Solidarity of mankind
74. Spirit of enquiry

75. Sympathy
76. Team spirit
77. Team work
78. Tolerance
79. Truthfulness
80. Universal love
81. Universal truth
82. Value for national and civic property

Jangira Classifies Values into Two Groups

Core values: Mutual trust, faith in the goodness of man, mutual respect, pursuit of excellence in work, appreciation of aesthetics, supporting the just cause and truthfulness.

Ethical values: Hard work, regularity, punctuality, respect for teachers, concern for the prestige of the institution, avoidance of telling lies for petty gains, smoking, drinking, gambling, stealing and copying.

V.S. Mathu Lists the Following Values

1. Avoiding extremes
2. Receptivity to learn
3. Spiritual approach to life
4. Taking a comprehensive view of life
5. Tolerance

V.K. Gokak's Classification Values

1. Truth
2. Love
3. Righteous conduct
4. Non-violence
5. Peace

Plato's Classification of Values

1. Truth 2. Goodness 3. Beauty

Walter G. Everett's Classification of Values

1. Economic values : Market price, purchaseable things
2. Bodily values : Health efficiency, beauty of physical life
3. Recreation values : Values of play and leisure life.
4. Association values : Friendship, family life to worldwide relationship
5. Character values : Justice, benevolence, self-control and truthfulness
6. Aesthetic values : Beauty of nature, works of art and literature
7. Intellectual values : Values of knowledge and quest for truth
8. Religious values : Worship, devotion and commitment

Parker's View of Values

1. Biological values
2. Economic values
3. Affective values
4. Social values
5. Intellectual values
6. Aesthetic values
7. Moral values and
8. Religious values

Harry S. Broudy's Classification of Values

1. Economic values
2. Health values
3. Recreational values
4. Associational values
5. Aesthetic values
6. Moral values
7. Religious values

S.J. Dackawish in Analysis of Values of Modern Age Midwerbarn Community, Sociology and Social Research has Mentioned the Following Twelve Basic Values

1. Fairness
2. Genuineness
3. Happiness
4. Humanity
5. Impulsive control
6. Integrity
7. International skills
8. Love of people
9. Mentality
10. Religion
11. Respect for dignity
12. Sobriety

White House Conference on Education Emphasises the Following Values

1. Appreciation of our democratic heritage.
2. Ability to think and evaluate consistently and creatively.
3. Ethical behaviour based on a sense of moral and spiritual values.
4. Wise use of time, including constructive leisure pursuit.
5. An awareness of our relationships with the world community.

Berelson and Salter have Divided Values into two Categories

Values of heart: Adventure, affection, idealism, independence, justice and patriotism.
Values of mind: Domination, economic success, personal success, power, problem solving, competence and social security.

Thomas has Classified Values into Six Groups

1. Aesthetic values
2. Humanitarian values
3. Intellectual values
4. Associational values
4. Material values
5. Religious values
6. Power values

Roheach has Classified Values into two Categories

Instrumental values	*Terminal values*
1. Ambitious	1. Beauty
2. Broadminded	2. Comfortable life
3. Capable	3. Equality
4. Cheerful	4. Exciting life
5. Clean	5. Equity
6. Courageous	6. Family security
7. Forgiving	7. Freedom
8. Helpful	8. Happiness
9. Honest	9. Inner security
10. Imaginative	10. National security
11. Independent	11. Self-respect
12. Intellectual	12. Sense of accomplishment
13. Logical	13. Social recognition
14. Loving	14. True friendship
15. Obedient	15. Wisdom
16. Polite	16. Responsible
17. Self-control	

Hunt's Classification of Values in the Modern Age

1. Concern for egalitarianism
2. Concern for free speech
3. Concern for peaceful resolution of disputes
4. Concern for participatory democracy
5. Concern for freedom in personal lifestyle
6. Disdain for traditional political interests
7. Concern for natural human environment
8. Concern for natural human values

Spranger's Classification of Values

1. Theoretical values
2. Economic values
3. Aesthetic values
4. Social values
4. Social values
5. Political values
6. Religious values
8. Religious values

Modern and Traditional Values

1. Modern democratic values and traditional colonial values.
2. Modern socialist values and traditional capitalist values.
3. Modern secular values and traditional religious values.

4. Modern scientific values and traditional spiritual values.
5. Modern global values and traditional national values.
6. Modern material values and traditional moral values.

Graphical Representation of Human Values

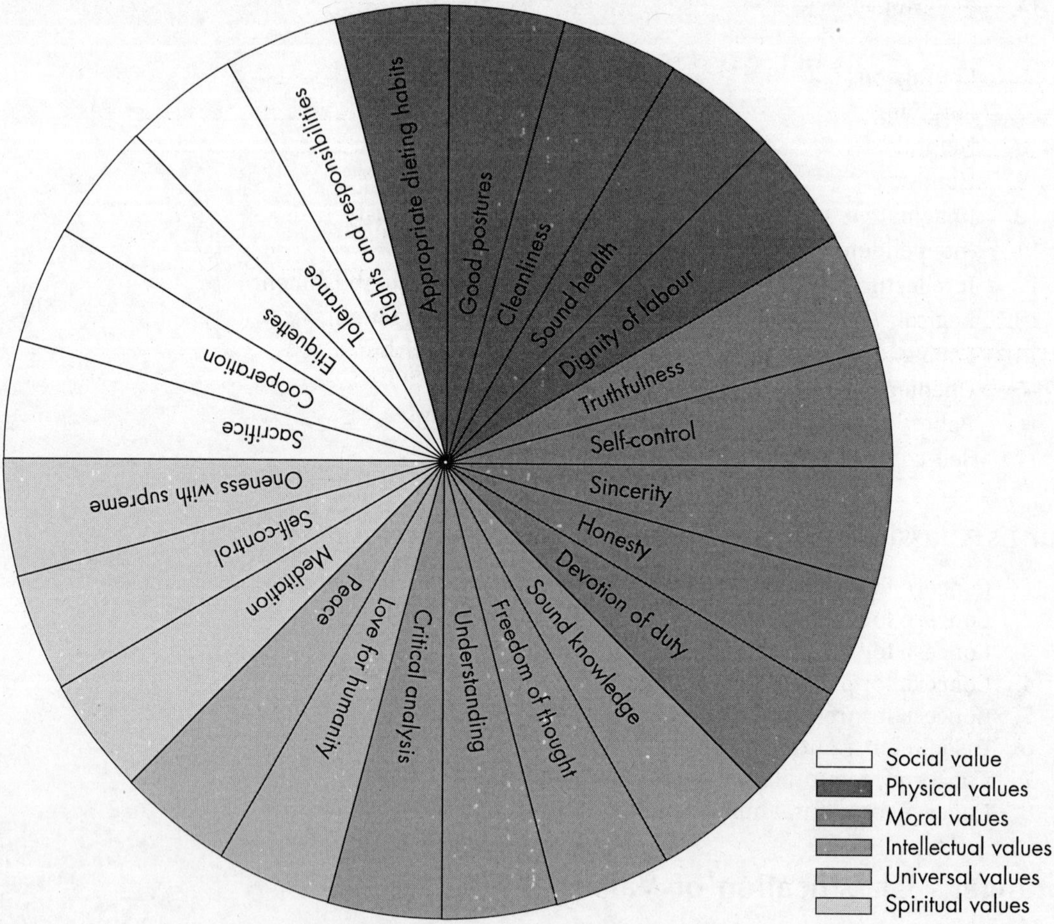

FIGURE 47.1 1 Human values.

SOURCES OF VALUES

Religion

Religion is the basis of many of our moral principles and human values. It binds and unifies the people. Christianity, Islam, Hinduism, Buddhism, Sikhism, Jainism and other religions of the world emphasise a particular way of life based on their respective religious doctrines and principles. Bertrand Russell says, "Religion is the source of the sense of social obligation". According to German philosopher Kant,

"Religion is the recognition of all our duties as divine commandment". Mahatma Gandhi writes, "For me morals, ethics and religions are convertible terms. A moral life without religion is like a house built on sand". According to Dr. S. Radhakrishnan, "True religion is in the heart of man, not in the man-made creeds". If you become merely a 'Sakasra'—literate man—and you do not have the moral principles and you do not cultivate wisdom. What will happen to you? You will become a 'Raksasa'— an evil person". Ross says, "It is through religion that the youth can be set on the road to the pursuits of the absolute values—truth, goodness and beauty". Thus, religion is the main source of social, moral and spiritual values such as love, cooperation, sympathy, pity, companionship, well-being, renunciation, social service, service to humanity, tolerance, forgiveness, simplicity, peace, universal brotherhood, high ideals, dignity of labour and love of justice.

Value-oriented thoughts from religions

Hindu (Yajur Veda)

1. Do good to humanity.
2. Enjoy your own wealth and covet not the wealth of others.
3. Earn wealth in a righteous way.
4. Shun crookedness.
5. Live in a spirit of friendliness with all.
6. Noble qualities give peace of mind, widespread fame, adds to one's greatness; practice of truth gives ease; and concentration of mind gives strength.
7. Perform noble deeds, develop your intellect and purify your mind.

Manu

1. Cultivate the firmness of mind and contentment.
2. Cultivate the spirit of forgiveness under all circumstances.
3. Devote your mind to virtues and observe abstinence from the entertainment of sinful thoughts.
4. Do not be dishonest by taking a thing without the permission of its owner through fraud, hypocrisy, or breach of faith or by teaching falsely.
5. Keep mental purity by freeing yourself from inordinate love or hatred from prejudice or injustice.
6. Follow the path of rectitude and freedom from sin.
7. Develop your intellect by seeking the company of the noble and the learned.
8. Harmonise your thoughts, words and deeds.
9. Cultivate peace of mind and calmness.

Christianity

1. You shall honour your father and mother.
2. You shall not kill.
3. You shall not commit adultery.
4. You shall not steal.
5. You shall not bear false witness against your neighbour.
6. You shall not covet your neighbour's wife.
7. You shall not covet your neighbour's goods.

Islam

1. Be honest in the exchange of things.
2. Do not acquire another's substances wrongfully.
3. Do not sell inferior and low-quality things.
4. Do not bribe.
5. Do not be unjust to others.

Sikhism

1. Truth is higher but higher still is worthful living.
2. There can be no worship without good action.
3. God's eye of mercy falls on those who take care of the lowest.
4. The life of speaking God's grace is not one of idle mysticism but of active service done in the midst of worldly relations.

Buddhism

1. Have right understanding.
2. Have right thought.
3. Have right speech.
4. Do right action.
5. Earn right livelihood.
6. Do right effort.
7. Have right information.
8. Cultivate right concentration.

Jainism

1. Have right faith
2. Have right knowledge
3. Have right conduct.

Philosophy

All the philosophies relating to education have thrown light on the values of education. There are varying philosophies of life and education. Idealistic philosophy recommends higher and fundamental values of life such as truth, goodness and beauty. These values are eternal and everlasting. Naturalistic philosophy discusses the values related to the physical or material life. Pragmatic philosophy recommends the values of life such as cooperation, fellow feeling, social service and service of humanity.

Literature

There is a close relationship between society and literature. Literature has its impact on the minds of the individuals and the society. This is because almost all literature in the form of poetry, novel, drama, one act play and story are related to humanity and society. For instance, Mumshi Premchand in most of his novels and stories has depicted the social problems and social values. The national poets like Bharathiyar and Rabindranath Tagore have expressed in their poems the values of patriotism and national integration. The study of literature is very much related to the life character of the individual, which creates and develops the appropriate attitudes, interests and positive feelings, and emotions in the individual. Literature determines and develops the following types of values:

1. Literary values
2. Material values
3. Scientific values
4. Vocational values
5. Cultural values
6. Moral values
7. Social values
8. Human values
9. Aesthetic values
10. National values
11. Democratic values
12. Secular values
13. Spiritual values
14. World brotherhood values

Social Customs

Social customs play a very significant role in influencing our value pattern and living pattern to a great extent. In fact, social customs and traditions have been the basis of our values since the ancient times. Today, they direct the individual as well as the society towards the desirable ways. Social customs reflect a number of values such as social regulations, social activities, social beliefs, cultural heritage, manners, thoughts and conducts, rituals, ways of worship, hospitality to guests, place of woman in the society, system of marriages, births and deaths, joint families and nuclear families, language, vocation, skills, arts, music, dance, painting and spiritual and material values.

Science

Science is a source of values and it has made a very deep impact on all the aspects of human life. It plays an important role in the life of an individual and society. The knowledge gained through science can be harnessed by man to enrich his own economic, social and cultural life. The means of transportation and communication have reduced distance between nations. On account of science and technology, we talk of world 'brotherhood' "world citizenship" and "globalization'. In the words of Bertrand Russell, "The effects of science are various and of different kinds. There are direct intellectual effects, the dispelling of many traditional beliefs and the adoption of others". Thus, science changes not only the material, but also the non-material aspects of culture, including religion, philosophy education and beliefs. In fact, science influences the whole life of a society and its value system. Brubacher has mentioned some values such as rationality, utilitarianism, universalism, individualism, and progressivism and meliorism (betterment of the world through human efforts), which are favourable for science. In this way, science has become an important source of values.

MEANING OF VALUE EDUCATION

Value education is related to those activities, which are good, useful and valuable from the educational point of view and considered as educational values or values in education. Learning values for the pleasure of the individual and the welfare of the society is called **value education.** It is education which develops a sense of discrimination between the good and the evil. This discrimination is based on values. The search for what is right and what is wrong is value education. In this sense, education is a much wider concept than teaching. As Adam says education is a bi-polar process which has the "educator pole" teacher and the "educated pole" (student). Hence, education has for its aims to modify the nature of the educand, and not merely to supply a certain amount of knowledge. In the words of Ruskin, "Education does not mean teaching people to know what they do not know, it means teaching them to behave as they do not behave". Therefore, the teacher employs only those activities which are educationally useful and valuable in order to mould and modify the behaviour of the child. Thus, the teacher and the child participate only in those activities which they regard as educationally useful and valuable. As Cunningham says, "Educational values become the aims of education". Therefore, John S. Brubacher says, "To state one's aim of education is at once to state his educational values".

CHARACTERISTICS OF VALUE EDUCATION

1. Value education is a comprehensive process.
2. Value education is a process of direct as well as indirect inculcation of proper habits, the development of proper attitudes, sensibilities and characters of the learners.
3. Value education is related to the good of 'every' learner and of 'whole' learner to serve as a powerful instrument of social and national reconstruction.
4. The process of value development is influenced by a host of environmental factors—home, school, peer group, community, the media and the general ethics of the society.
5. Value education covers all-round personality development in aesthetic, intellectual, social, political and spiritual aspects.

VIEWS ABOUT EDUCATIONAL VALUES

The educators have expressed two views about educational values. They are:

(a) Internal and subjective, and
(b) External and objective.

Internal values: Some educationists claim that values depend on personal ideas and experiences. According to them, value is born out of a mind's power of imagination. They hold the view that whatever is useful to human beings is good and valuable, and whatever good is useful. In other words, a thing which is useless, becomes valueless also. They determine their values according to their utility. Thus, educational values are internal and subjective in nature.

External values: The educationists who support external values hold that values are inherent in objects and activities. According to them, the social environment influences the quality or the value of an object. In other words, all educational activities are not connected with the individual but with the social environment.

It is clear from the above discussion that there is a controversy between values as internal and as external. It should be borne in mind that either of them is one sided and reveals only one side of the truth. For instance, when we accept internal values, we become interested only in the interests, aptitudes and capacities of the child at the cost of the external social environment. In fact, the internal and external values are essential for an effective and wholesome process of education. Therefore, educational values should be created taking into consideration the nature of the child together with the nature of the objects and activities. In short, a synthesis between the internal and external values is very essential.

KINDS OF EDUCATIONAL VALUES

Brubacher has divided educational values into immediate values (related to likes) and remote values (related to intelligent likes). Further these values are divided into—instrumental and intrinsic values aesthetic absolute values.

Immediate values: These values fulfil the biological and psychological needs of children. For instance, a child having an interest and liking for fine arts, shall be able to satisfy his artistic taste by practising artistic activities only. The values of this type is related to immediate needs.

Remote values: These values are closely related to intelligent and rational needs. It is a matter of common experience that each programme of the school satisfies the diverse needs of the teachers and the children. But all these needs are not likely to be satisfied. Therefore, each individual has to make an intelligent selection out of all these needs and try to achieve maximum advantage from all the activities of the school. Hence, these values are related to intelligently selected likes and needs.

Instrumental values: Brubacher says that instrumental values are values that are good for something. These values are subjective in nature and are based on the principle of utility. They change according to change in circumstances. Pragmatists like John Dewey advocate these values. For instance, if a child wants to become a musician, knowledge of 'taal' and 'swar' will be useful for him to realise his chief objective. This knowledge of 'swar' and 'taal' is an instrumental value for some higher values. These instrumental values are subjective and change according to circumstances. But these values are of no use in other vocations and professions.

Intrinsic values: In the words of Brubacher, "Intrinsic values are values, which are judged good, not for something else, but in themselves". These values are inherent, self-contained and complete in themselves. They do not depend on anything external. For example, 'truthfulness' is a value whether someone likes it or not. The values like, truth, beauty and goodness are inherent values. They do not depend on anything else. The idealistic philosophy emphasises intrinsic values.

Aesthetic values: Aesthetic values like truth, beauty and goodness give us pleasure and happiness. Some educationists delimit these values upto the domain of fine arts only. But other educationists hold that pleasure and happiness maybe derived from other subjects besides fine arts. Hence, various curricular as well as co-curricular activities should be organized in schools in order to develop the aesthetic values more and more.

Absolute values and relative values: Some values are basic to the life of the individual and for social life. They are common to the human race. They do not differ from nation-to-nation and time-to-time. These values are absolute values, which are important for the overall development of the individual and the society. Love, truth, beauty, honesty, courage, generosity, friendship, politeness, industry, perseverance, justice, freedom, tolerance, self-respect, independence, duty consciousness, sense of cooperation, sense of gratitude, discipline and sense of justice are examples of these values.

Some values are useful for the life of the individual and the nation. They are subjected to change from time-to-time and nation-to-nation according to the social, cultural, political and economic needs of the society. Relative values are essential for the peaceful coexistence along with time. New Educational Policy (1986) has emphasised some relative values that students must learn for the welfare of the nation. They are Indian cultural traditions, equality, democracy, fraternity, equal rights for women, protecting the environment, removing social barriers, concept of small family, scientific temper, secularism, peaceful coexistence, purity of action, national integration, international understanding and globalization.

NEED FOR VALUE EDUCATION

The modern materialistic world raises our standard of living but declines our standard of life, i.e., the value of life. On account of population explosion, knowledge explosion (science and technology) and material explosion, man has started moving towards the wrong path by considering the material comforts of the world as the real happiness. In fact, from the nineties we see man going downhill due to the erosion of human values at all levels and everywhere in the present society, "leading to the spread of greed, self-aggrandizement, gross injustice, abuse of human rights, pervasion of power, callousness, insensitivity, depravity of taste and behaviour, pettiness, waste and plunder, deceit, dishonesty, thefts, bribery, smuggling, corruption, exploitation, craftiness and man's wallowing in the low and dark dimensions of his consciousness". As a result, there is no peace of mind in him and every structure of our society is facing the downfall of the social, moral, cultural, emotional, religious, spiritual, intellectual and political values. Religion and morality are being throttled, and the power of man is being misused. The growing influence of the negative aspects of the Western culture on the younger generation is stranded on the crossroads. It is very necessary to dispel this pollution spreading in the society, so that we can preserve and maintain the advanced position of our country. In this juncture, education is the only powerful weapon which can be used to overcome all these evils and make us rational human beings. Hence, it has become necessary for us that the future citizens should be given value education and the darkness of materialism should be removed. Value education prepares and develops the minds, hearts and hands of children to engage in forming their own character to know what is good, love 'good' and do 'good'.

The unprecedented explosion of population, knowledge and human desires, lead to a continuous downfall in the social cultural, religious, political, emotional and spiritual life. Such a life pushes the modern man into a life of mental pressure and tensions and he is engrossing himself in the dazzle of materialism. In order to redeem the modern man from the above maladies, the concern of value education is quite imperative. Value education is the best means to inculcate values such as truth, justice, affection, sympathy, cooperation, fellow feeling tolerance, non-violence, peace and universal brotherhood, which can make an individual a good citizen.

Albert Einstein, one of the greatest scientists of the world has observed, "A positive aspiration and effort for an ethical and moral configuration of our common life is of overriding importance. Here no science can save us. I believe, indeed, solely the practical and theoretical approaches in our education have led directly, to the importance of ethical values". In the words of our first Prime Minister, Pt. Jawaharlal Nehru, "Let us pursue our path to industrial progress with all our strength and vigour and at the same time remember that material riches without tolerance and compassion and wisdom may turn to dust and ashes:" Dr. S. Radhakrishnan says, "Education is not limited to the imparting of information or the training in skills. It has to give the educated a proper sense of values". It is regrettable to state that values and qualities which differentiate and exalt man from all creatures are being lost because of his increasing selfishness and lust for material welfare. In fact, he is ready to do any filthy and wrong deeds in order to maximise his satisfaction and become richer. As a result, values of the educated, that is workers in educational and religious institutions and politics have been declining in the present days. This tendency indicates that they are not better than the uneducated and the economically backward people. Hence, though it is difficult, preservation and development of human values is important to make man's life meaningful. It can be achieved only through teaching value education, which is a panacea for raising human values.

From the views of scientists, national leaders and educationists we can say that good education is unthinkable if it fails to inculcate essential values to good life and social well-being. Let us see the need and importance of education based on values.

Moral development: Education based on values is needed for fostering moral qualities such as humility, truthfulness, honesty, respect for elders, tolerance, courtesy, spirit of service and sacrifice, affection, sympathy, love and cooperation among the younger generation.

Cultural development: Education based on values is fully helpful in the development of culture. Values make the culture dynamic. The values and culture mutually affect each other. Therefore, value education is given due importance in the curriculum for the cultural development.

Social development: Value education helps in developing the positive and social attitudes by creating awareness among the younger generation about the ills of the society. Such an education enables them to raise their voice against the dowry system, corruption, red-tapism, traditional religious rituals, superstitions and child marriage.

All-round development: Value-based education is very essential in these days for the all-round development of the youth. This is because the present day curriculum is full of technical data which consists of facts, figures, theories and law, and it has no scope for the youth to take part in the finer things of life.

Development of wider outlook: Education based on values develops the outlook of the boy and girl students by providing a new direction to their thinking which brings consciousness and awakening in them. This education thus prepares them to sacrifice their personal interest for the welfare of the society. Such an outlook enables them to lead a life of "plain living and high thinking".

Development of democratic qualities: Education based on values develops democratic qualities such as dignity of the individual, social and individual justice, equality, brotherhood, cooperation, freedom and sympathy among the students. These democratic values are essentially needed for the success of democracy.

Solving conflicts: There are some conflicts between the traditional views and the modern views in the name of caste, creed, religion, region, culture and customs. Such conflicts affect the progress of the society. Hence, it is necessary to eliminate the conflicts for the growth of the society. Value education inculcates the feeling of respecting others by teaching tolerance, peace, love and patience, cooperation, fellow feeling and secularism.

Sublimation of instincts: Value-based education is essential to prepare and develop the individual to control his instincts, emotions and sexual urges. Such an education enables him to utilise his power in the social welfare activities. This leads to the development of both the individual and the society.

Cooperative living: Education based on values inculcates a sense of cooperation and fellow feeling. This education leads to a peaceful life by cooperating with one another. It gives inspiration that one should live for all and all should live for one.

Humanising effect: "True education must humanize the person". Therefore, humanism has become the basis of value education and all educational activities are related to the welfare of the community. This type of education gives a message of world peace and brotherhood of mankind. It also develops the feeling of quality and inspires all the people of the world to adopt the policy of "Live and let live".

IMPORTANCE OF VALUE EDUCATION

Man and values are inseparable. Education makes a man strong. Values make his life wholesome and perfect. Prof. N.K. Dutt says, "Life without values is reduced to a series of meaningless activities". We give importance to values because they distinguish man from animals. Modern man is found unhappy. Value education enables him to lead a personally satisfying and socially constructive life. Hence, teaching of value education in school has become important in the modern society.

Value erosion: Due to the explosion of population, knowledge and human desires, we find erosion of values in social, spiritual, cultural, economic, political and religious fields. In order to preserve and maintain values, value education is very important.

Knowledge-oriented education: Present educational system gives importance to knowledge-oriented education. It prepares the students for examinations and it does not create a desirable character. As a consequence, educated persons commit crimes and indulge in barbarious activities. To redeem people from evil actions, value education is inevitable.

Violent culture: The youth of today lead a reckless life. Dowry system, corruption, bribery, dishonesty, violence, casteism, religionism and regionism play a very important role in the modern Indian society. These undesirable violent aspects take the place of values, which affect our individual and social life adversely. This critical situation is not desirable for the progress of a country. Hence, value education plays an important role in rooting out violent culture from the society.

Social indifference: People of the present day are self-centred. They do not have concern for others. In fact, they are not willing to sacrifice anything for the welfare of others and the country. It reflects social discomfort as well as social disintegration. Therefore, we should give importance to value education.

Indifference towards national interest: The new generation is devoid of cultural qualities like patriotism, national interest, sense of sacrifice, national integration, international understanding, fellow feeling, cooperation, sympathy, affection and compassion. These values are very important for the successful and smooth functioning of the society. As a consequence, value education has become an important part of general education.

OBJECTIVES OF VALUE EDUCATION

National Policy on Education (1986)

It has mentioned the following aims of education based on values such as non-violence, truth, love, cooperation, justice, tolerance, coexistence, democratic and scientific attitude and a healthy critical thinking.

- Develop the physical, mental, intellectual and aesthetic aspects of the individual.
- Inculcate a scientific attitude and create democratic, moral and religious values.
- Develop firm determination for the solution of the problems.
- Make the individual conscious and awakened relating to material, social, technological, economic and cultural environment.
- Develop respect for the individual dignity of labour and a healthy and positive attitude.
- Dedicate towards the unity and integrity of the country and to provide a firm pace to the development of the country.
- Remain firm on secularism and social justice.
- Develop international understanding.

These objectives have been given in a document named "Challenges of Education", published in 1985.

UNESCO (1980) Lists the Following Objectives of Value Education

- Full development of the child's personality in its physical, mental, emotional and spiritual aspects.
- Inculcation of good manners and creation of responsible and cooperative citizenship.
- Developing respect for the dignity of the individual and sanctity of the fundamental human rights.
- Inculcation of a spirit of patriotism and national integration.
- Developing a democratic way of thinking and living.
- Developing tolerance towards and understanding of different religious faiths.
- Developing a sense of brotherhood at the social, national and international level.
- Helping children to have faith in some supernatural power and order that is supposed to control this universe and human life.
- Enabling children to make decisions on the basis of sound moral principles.

Central Board of Secondary Education, Delhi

It has identified 50 values based on school climate in a conference on value education (1986)

- Respect for individual
- Education for service rather than competition
- Openness, freedom, flexibility
- Human relationship
- Participation with maximum
- Sensitivity and awareness involvement
- Concern for each other
- Scientific attitude and scientific temper
- Honesty and integrity
- Value of time
- Mature self
- Self-acceptance, self-awareness, self-confidence
- Understanding leading to forgiveness
- Relationship with God
- Individual yet socially responsible
- Work ethics
- Dignity of labour
- Trust
- Fearlessness
- Moral courage
- Tolerance/acceptance of differences
- Practice before preaching
- Compassion
- Use of head, heart and hand
- Accumulation
- Patriotism
- Communication
- Environment preservation

- Justice
- Exposure to world and international understanding
- Integrated development
- Staff development
- Pastoral care
- Team spirit
- Parent teacher relationship
- Developed potentials
- Optimism, faith and hope
- Vision and sense of purpose
- Life-long learners
- Innovativeness and resourcefulness
- Creativity and initiative
- Sense of belonging
- Sense of pride
- Risk taking
- Sense of adventure
- Dedication and commitment
- Simplicity and austerity
- Ability to set standards and stick to them.
- Adaptability
- Attention to details.

J.C. Verma Suggested the Following Values in "Education for Self-development" (1983) to be Inculcated in Schools

1. Care for public property
2. Cleanliness
3. Cooperativeness
4. Consideration of others
5. Freedom
6. Hard work
7. Honesty
8. Love of one's country
9. Justice
10. Non-violence
11. Scientific temper
12. Secularism
13. Self-discipline
14. Service to people
15. Team spirit
16. Truth

V.M.T. Ramji has suggested the following values in "Value-oriented School Education" to be inculcated among the students.

1. Cleanliness
2. Courage
3. Courtesy
4. Dignity of Manual Work
5. Joy
6. Peace
7. Purity
8. Service
9. Truth
10. Universal love

METHODS OF IMPARTING VALUE EDUCATION

- Examples should be taken from day-to-day life situation.
- Extracts from the sayings of great men should be explained.
- Incidents and problems which develop value judgement should be taken up.
- Inspirational dialogues, dramas, poems, stories and materials from religious scriptures could form the major part of the content of value education.
- Biographies of great personalities should form an important source of value education.
- Personal, neighbourly and community values should be taught in the classroom and thoroughly discussed with the students.
- Yoga and other activities that develop self-discipline among students should be included.
- Group activities like cleaning the school campus, visiting slums, service camps, visits to hospitals and visits to places of worship of different faiths, should form a part of content in value education.
- Discourses on the lives of national and spiritual leaders can bring out values like self-sacrifice, collective happiness, love for truth and ultimate values of life for which the great leaders lived.
- Prayer, meditation and *shramadan* should form an integral part of the content of value education.
- Celebrating the birthdays of great national and spiritual leaders.
- A variety of learning resources such as biographies, scriptures, proverbs, hymns and sayings of great persons can be used for value education.
- A spirit of cooperative work and mutual help should be organised in the entire functioning of the school.
- Arrange picnics and excursions to give opportunities to the students for moving among different people and seeing the monumental achievements in the country for broadening their outlook and understanding humanitarian values.
- Training in drawing, painting and dancing should be arranged in order to develop aesthetic values.
- Encourage women students to organize mass-cooking, mass-knitting of woolen equipment, and visit orphanages to do voluntary services like washing and bathing them.
- Encourage students to engage in minor construction works such as repairing and laying roads, building houses and digging wells and tanks.

ROLE OF SCHOOL IN VALUE EDUCATION

Morning Assembly: Before starting the teaching work in the schools, it is necessary to hold a morning assembly for 15 to 20 minutes. There should be prayer, religious discourses, patriotic songs and moral lectures in the assembly to develop values such as punctuality, faith in God, team spirit, orderliness, patriotism and discipline.

Compulsory subjects: Moral education should be taught as a compulsory subject. This education should contain the substance of all the religions. At least two periods in a week should be reserved for this subject in the time- table. Moral education develops the values such as truthfulness, cooperation, love and compassion, peace, non-violence, courage, equality, justice, tolerance, dignity of labour, common brotherhood of man, and scientific temper.

Re-designing of curriculum: Some changes should be made in the curriculum keeping in view the social, moral, cultural and national values. The subjects like history, geography, social studies, science, languages, literature and arts, should be included in the curriculum as they inculcate the values such as cooperation, unselfishness, desire to serve, national spirit, international brotherhood, truthfulness, hospitality, leadership qualities, social justice, sharing, courage, faith in God and serving the poor.

Extension lectures of scholars: National and spiritual leaders should be invited to the institution from time-to-time to express their views on the subjects of human interests.

Declamation contest: Declamation contest should be organized in the school on the subjects or titles relating to educational values. The students should be encouraged to take part in these contests. Such contests develop national spirit, love, sympathy, universal brotherhood, fellow feeling, secularism, service to humanity and intellectual thinking.

Skits and dramas: The subject matter of skits and dramas organized in the school should be related to moral, social and cultural values.

Celebration of birthdays: The birthdays of great men like Jesus Christ, Buddha, Mohammad Nabi, Guru Nanak Dev, Guru Gobind Singh, Sri Nayayana Guru, Mahatma Gandhi, Nehru, Indira Gandhi, Dr. Radhakrishnan, K. Kamaraj (former Chief Minister of Tamil Nadu), Swami Vivekananda, Abraham Lincoln, Karl Marx, Thomas Alwa Edison, Michael Faraday, Albert Einstein, Abdul Kalam, Mother Teresa, Joan of Arc, Rani of Jhansi, Sarojini Naidu, Martin Luther King and Nelson Mandela should be celebrated in the schools and their ideals should be presented to the society. Such celebrations develop the values, such as secularism, equality, patriotism, national spirit, scientific temper, honesty, truthfulness, dignity of labour, love, compassion, cooperation, leadership qualities and social service in the students.

Celebration of national and international days: The national days like Independence Day (August 15), Republic Day (January 26), Gandhi Jayanthi (October 2), Teachers' Day (September 5), Children's Day (November 14) and the international days like World Peace Day (September 21), Human Rights Day (December 10), World Environmental Day (June 5), World Health Day (April 8), Labour Day (May 1), World Red Cross Day(May 8), International Youth Day (August 12) and World Day Against Child Labour (June 12) should also be celebrated in the schools. The celebration of these important days develops the values such as national spirit, patriotism and world brotherhood among the students.

Use of mass media: Maximum use of the mass media should be made to provide value education in the schools. The mass media such as newspapers, journals, radio and television can be used to develop social, moral and cultural values among the students.

Special camps: The spirit of social service and national service can be inculcated in students through the medium of special camps like National Cadet Corps (NCC), National Service Scheme (NSS), and International Voluntary Service for Peace (IVSP). These camps develop cooperation, fellow feeling, national spirit, love, sympathy, serving mind, secularism and equality in the students.

School magazine: Magazines which are published by the schools should contain articles related to value oriented education. Such magazines enable the students to get value education, which develop desirable values in them.

Co-curricular activities: Schools should provide activities like debates, and discussions on the issues and problems of our country, mock parliament and mock panchayats and mock assemblies in order to inculcate proper civic values and attitudes.

ROLE OF THE TEACHER IN VALUE EDUCATION

The teacher has to play a very important role in the inculcation of value- oriented education in the new generation. This is because the twenty-first century has seen remarkable development in science and technology explosion in population and in human desire. If we run too much after science and technology and materialism it is said, "One day there will be no tomorrow". That is why, R.C. Lahoti, the Chief Justice of India (2005) in his convocation address rightly remarked, "Be a man of value than a man of success". So, a teacher of the present time should have the following principles:

- He must have faith in the basic human values.
- He should cultivate the basic human values in students.
- He should develop faith in democratic, socialistic and secular values.
- He should help in the conservation of environmental resources and preservation of the cultural heritage.
- He should cherish high human values in the global context.
- He should create an atmosphere of love, trust and security in the school.
- He should relate value education to concrete situations so that a young child can distinguish between a lie, fantasy and truth. For instance, a child should understand the concept of property to make a sense that stealing is wrong.
- He should organize value education through different co-curricular and extra-curricular activities.
- He should not get away from the fact that he is a value educator (whatever be the subject that he teaches in class).
- "Example is better than precept". The teacher should practise the values that he teaches.
- He should encourage students to organize pen-friend clubs in the entire state and inter-district.
- He should establish a sincere and friendly relation among the students to impart deliberate value education cautiously.
- He should provide facilities and experiences to develop higher values in students.
- He should explore strategies of developing higher values in children.
- He should assist in fostering and promoting national unity by organizing excursions to places of historic, religious and cultural importance.

ADVANTAGE OF VALUE EDUCATION

Value education helps the individual and the society in the following ways:

- It develops a healthy and balanced personality.
- It enables the child to earn his livelihood.
- It develops vocational efficiency.
- It enables the individual to acquire material prosperity.
- It fosters the character and morality of the children.
- It makes the children ideal citizens.
- It helps for the reconstruction of experiences.
- It enables the child to adjust to his environment.
- Value education promotes social efficiency in the child.
- It inculcates ideas about national integration.
- Value education develops cultural values.
- It enables the child to use his leisure profitably.

CONCLUSION

The environment in different educational institutions depends on value systems being followed. Decline in value systems leads to decline in educational standards. We see the effects of declining values in our schools, colleges and universities. We have to follow values that may contribute to the proper functioning of our educational institutions. Peaceful environment and its development depend on the value system being followed in a particular family. We, generally, find that there are disputes among family members. This is due to the erosion of values. Respect for each other in the family is generally lacking cooperation, sympathy, affection, fellow feeling and tolerance. We, generally, observe that people are least concerned about the neighbours in big cities and towns. Hence, it is the need of the hour to make all possible attempts to inculcate value-oriented education in the centres of learning. It is the duty of the educators, the educational administrators and the people that they should support value-based education and devote their time, energy and resources to make this education a success.

CHAPTER 48

POPULATION EDUCATION

INTRODUCTION

Population education is the latest arrival in the educational scenario of the world. The study of population is more urgent and important than any other matter, because population explosion has become almost a global problem. The growth of population began to accelerate from two billion in the year 1930 to three billion in 1960. It has become four billion within a period of just 15 years (1976). Many problems have emerged in the economic and social aspects due to the growth of population. It is population education through which we can check the growth of population by developing the right attitude among the vast population. The national seminar on population education held in Mumbai in 1969 opined that a population education programme should enable the students to understand that family is controllable and the population limitations can facilitate the development of a higher quality of life.

MEANING OF POPULATION EDUCATION

Population education is related to population and it deals with the ill effects of the increasing population, ways and means to form healthy attitude about limited families, and lead a happy life in the society. Thus, we may discern that such an education develops the basic consciousness relating to population among students. It also creates a basic consciousness about the dynamic direction and the development of the nation. In short, population education is 'education' about fertility, mortality, sex ratio, age group, the working and the non-working, the literate and the illiterate, the urban, the rural and migration. It also deals with the problems of individuals, families, community, nation and the world.

DEFINITION OF POPULATION EDUCATION

We may define population education as "It is an education through which the basic consciousness is formed about the problems of population and it creates a co-operative disposition towards a small planned family through the school".

R.C. Sharma: "Population education is the study of human population in relation to his environment with a view to improve his quality of life without adversely affecting the environment".

Taylor, Daniel: "Population education has a double task. It is both motivational (encourage people to adopt family planning) and instructional (teach people about population problems), its probable consequences and what the possible alternatives are".

Burbson: "Population education is an exploration of knowledge and attitude about population, the family and sex. It includes population awareness, family living, reproduction education and basic values".

Viderman: "Population education is a process by which a student investigates and explores the nature and meaning of population process, population characteristics, the causes of population change and the consequences of these processes, characteristics and changes for himself and his family, his society and the world".

Gopal Rao: "Population education may be defined as an educational programme which provides for a study of the population phenomenon so as to enable the students to take rational decision towards problems arising out of rapid population growth".

Dr. V.K.R.V. Rao: "Population education should not be treated merely as a quantitative phenomenon or just an essay in numbers. It is the quality of population that is more relevant both as a factor of growth and an end product of growth and numbers have to be treated in terms of the effect they have in quality either by way of deterioration or improvement. Population education, therefore, is essentially related to human resource development. Thus, population education is not only concerned with population awareness but also with developing values and attitudes so that both quality and quantity are taken care of".

Massials: "Population education is the teaching and learning of reliable knowledge about the ways of inquiring into the nature of human population and the natural and human consequences of population change".

UNESCO: (Regional workshop on population, family planning and life education held at Bangkok in 1970), "Population education is an educational programme which provides for a study of the population situation of the family, community, nation and world, with the purpose of developing in the students rational and responsible attitudes and behaviour towards that situation".

Population Reference Bureau1 Washington (1971}: "Population education is an attempt to create a deep, universal, action guiding perception of the consequences of demographic change. It seeks to bring about a realization of the individual family, social and environmental effects of the explosive increase in human population, the rapid shifts in the concentration and distribution of people, the implication of changing age and other demographic patterns and the conceivable options that may be open to mankind to cope with the consequent problems. It is focused primarily on students who will become the principle, child bearers within one or two decades".

ISCOMPE: (International Study of the Conceptualization and Methodology of Population Education), "Population education is an educational activity which is part of a total social learning process; is problem centred; derives its content from population studies; is concerned primarily with the population- related interactions of individuals, families communities, societies and nations; is aimed specifically at improving the present and future quality of human life".

NATURE OF POPULATION EDUCATION

- Population education is a new arrival in the field of education.
- It studies the impact of the increase in population of different age groups.

- It studies the impact of the total population on the economic development of a country.
- It helps the students to investigate and explore the interaction between population and the environment.
- It enables the students to be aware of the process and consequences of the population growth on the quality of our lives.
- It enables the students to describe the causes and consequences of population increase at the local, the national and the global levels.
- It provides solutions to population problems and makes human life happy.

NEED AND IMPORTANCE OF POPULATION EDUCATION

India is the second populous country in the world. The population of India was 36 crores in 1951 and the number increased to 102 crores in 2001. As a consequence we have had an average increase of more than one crore people per year. The population explosion has adversely affected the quality of life. Population problem gives birth to a lot of other problems. It is estimated that by the year 2050 India will have about 153 crore people. The number of people will be greater in India than in China. The unprecedented growth of population affects our nation adversely and places it among the under-developed countries though it has taken various efforts such as economic planning, educational planning and family planning. Hence, the study of population explosion and its consequences and solutions are important as far as the underdeveloped countries like India are concerned. The knowledge of the rate of growth of population is very important for individuals for effective planning and family welfare. Let us list the need and importance of population education in India.

Controlling population explosion: The most important need for population education is to develop an awareness among the students about the rate of growth of population and the necessity of having a small sized family.

Ensuring quality of life: Population education is essential to control population explosion, so that it can ensure a better quality of life.

Optimum use of natural resources: Population education is needed to maintain an optimum population or balanced population. Optimum population alone can utilise the natural resources effectively. It creates full employment and there is no avenue for wastage of natural resources.

Maintaining and improving health: Maintaining and improving health is the basis for a happy life. Population education provides knowledge to the students about the ways and means to maintain and improve their health in order to lead a better life.

Checking under-nourishment: Population education is needed to check under- nourishment, which affects the growth of the individual adversely. It enables the people to understand the cause for under-nourishment and the solutions to overcome it.

Preparing young people for life: It prepares the young people for a better life by teaching sex education, and the importance of a small family.

Creating healthy skills and attitudes: Population education has become an important factor in socio-economic studies to develop healthy skills and attitudes among the students.

Giving impetus to family planning: Population education develops an awareness among the people towards population explosion and gives an impetus to family planning.

Developing appropriate reproductive behaviour: In fact, population education reduces the number of children and maintains three or five years' gap between two children.

Establishing equality of sexes: Population education inculcates in the students that the male child and the female child are equal. No male child is superior or inferior to the female child.

Increasing national wealth: Unless the growth of population is checked, national development is not possible. Population education helps to control population explosion and increases the national wealth as well as per capita income.

Controlling environmental degradation: Population education has become quite inevitable in modern times. Growth of population is the most important reason for environmental pollution, deforestation and environmental crisis. To overcome these environmental problems, such an education is essential.

NEED FOR POPULATION EDUCATION IN THE INDIAN SOCIETY

We need population education to check many problems which emerge as a consequence of population explosion in the Indian society.

Low per capita income: India is a poor country. Its per capita income is very low. The growth of population reduces the availability of income per head. Population education controls the rate of growth of population and increases the per capita income.

Low rate of capital formation: Since the per capita income is very low, people live in a very pitiable condition. They cannot save anything out of their income. As saving is very low, the rate of capital formation is very poor. In order to increase saving and investment, population education is essential.

Unemployment and underemployment: A large number of unskilleds workers face the problem of underemployment in rural areas. There are skilled workers who face the acute problem of unemployment and under-employment in rural as well as urban areas.

More pressure on land: India is an agricultural country where 60 per cent of the total population depends on agricultural and allied activities for their livelihood. Growth of population creates heavy pressure on land by producing many agricultural labourers.

High density of population: The number of people living (405) per square kilometer in India is comparatively higher than that (320) of developed countries. The growth of population increases the density of population. Population education helps to reduce the size of family and the density of population.

Poverty and subsistence level: Since the per capita income is very low, people are unable to get the basic necessities of life. That is why a vicious circle of poverty has been an important characteristic of our society.

Low standard of living: The standard of living is low and housing conditions are very poor. The standard of hygiene and quality of nutrition are also low, which lead to health problems. Population education tries to improve the standard of living of the people.

Unfavourable balance of payments: This situation takes place when our imports exceed our exports due to more demand for foreign goods and services to meet the needs of the growing population.

Growth of slums: Slum areas emerge near rail road tracks of cities or the swampy river banks due to uncontrollable explosion of population and poverty.

Undernourished population: The quality of nutrition is very low in India. There is shortage of nourishment especially balanced diet in the developing countries.

Growing pollution: The pressure of transport, water supplies, sewage, and refuse disposal grow and create problems. Smoke and chemical effluents from factories produce air and water pollution. Traffic congestion and industrial growth produce noise pollution.

High ratio of dependent population: The explosion of population produces an uneven age structure of the population. That is, the percentage of 0–15 years of age group who depend on their parents for their subsistence is higher than the other age groups.

Depletion of natural resources: The natural resources are being depleted due to population explosion. It is seen that the forest area is encroached for non-agricultural purposes. Trees are cut for construction and fuel purposes.

Unhygienic living: Growth of population creates shortage of medical facilities, lack of financial resources, poverty, ignorance and illiteracy leading to unhygienic living conditions.

Unhealthy economy of the country: Though we have taken various steps to attain economic development, we have not succeeded in our efforts. This is because the growth of population absorbs the goods and services produced in our country.

Illiteracy: There has been an increase in the number of illiterates in the country. The increasing population is the cause of this pitiable state of affairs.

Urbanization: The ever-growing population increases the area of towns and cities and creates new towns. The highly productive agricultural lands are encroached by houses, roads and industries.

Slow growth of the industrial sector: In underdeveloped countries like India, Pakistan and Srilanka the industrial sector is not very strong. The poor industrial base, lack of capital, and poverty of the people create a vicious circle and the growth of industries is hampered.

Subdivision and fragmentation: Population explosion leads to the subdivision and fragmentation of lands. This makes the small size of land holding which is not suitable for the application of modern methods of cultivation.

Inflation: The growth of population increases the demand for goods and services. The increase in demand for goods and services would raise their price, causing inflation.

Inadequate transport facility: There is a lot of rush and over crowding seen in trains and buses. People have to wait for hours at the bus stops. Getting seats in the bus are difficult as a result of population explosion.

Social stagnation (fatalist attitude}: The society is darkened with casteism and communalism. These social evils have made our social system poisonous. Therefore, stagnation is still prevalent in the society. This problem has become serious due to population explosion.

Public debt and deficit financing: This society is a welfare society. Hence, Government expenditure is increased day-by-day to meet the necessities of the people. Sometimes it maybe forced to borrow money from within the country or abroad. When the expenditure of the government exceeds its revenue there is deficit finance. This is due to population explosion.

Migration: Population explosion creates poverty, diseases and unemployment. As a result people migrate from the rural to the urban areas or the urban to the urban areas with a view to find employment.

Lack of accommodation: Population explosion has created the problem of accommodation especially in cities. The concentration of population in the cities leads to congestion and increase the rate of rent. The working class hardly gets any accommodations in the cities. They have to pay a high amount for renting dirty and unhealthy rooms in the slum areas.

OBJECTIVES OF POPULATION EDUCATION

The main objective of population education is to make the students understand that a small family is an ideal one. The standard of living can be made good in a small and ideal family. Population education, thus, aims at maintaining the health and welfare of the members of the family.

According to Stephen Viderman, "The purpose of population education is to develop awareness and understanding of the relations between population growth and national development in short and long run and to develop an understanding of the consequences of individual decisions in the important area of reproductive behaviour".

Prof. Bhatia has mentioned six primary objectives of population education.

- Understand population dynamic including the growth rate and structure of population in the country in the context of world population.
- Appreciate the significance of population characteristics for the present and the future quality of life including economic develop- ment and the attainment of a high level of health education, diet, housing and other amenities of life.
- Realise that the size of the family can be easily planned for the betterment of individual families and that of large families are not necessary in the present day.
- Understand the health risks involved for the mother and the child.
- Appreciate the fact that small family is a setting in which a high quality of life for each person is more likely to be attained.
- Understand the governments family welfare programmes in relation to the country's needs.

General Objectives of Population Education

Knowledge and understanding: The objective of population education is that the learner should get an opportunity to acquire knowledge, skills, attitudes and values necessary to understand the concept of population.

Evaluation and judgement: The purpose of population education is to enable the learners to evaluate the prevailing population situation, and its effect on the present and future welfare of their families, communities, societies, nations and the world.

Decision making: The aim of population education is to enable the learners to make conscious and informed education after understanding and evaluating the scheme of population education.

Response to the programmes: The objective of population education is to enable the learner to respond to population situations and problems in a conscious and informed manner either by an intention to act or by an action itself.

Specific Objectives of Population Education

1. Provide knowledge and understanding of the prevailing population situation.
2. Provide knowledge about the present population trends.

3. Acquaint the learner with a knowledge of the national population policy.
4. Help the learners to understand how rapid urbanisation affects their lives.
5. Explain the learner the reasons for the government's efforts to manage population growth rates.
6. Provide the learner with the necessary skills to evaluate the impact of population change on the society.
7. Teach the pupils the importance of a small family.
8. Create an awareness among the students about population issues.
9. Provide information about the measures to be taken to control the growth of population.

SCOPE AND CONTENT OF POPULATION EDUCATION

The National Council for Educational Research and Training (NCERT) conducted a workshop on population education in New Delhi in July 1970. The workshop has accepted the following areas as the curriculum:

- The population growth.
- Population and economic development.
- Population and social development.
- Health, nutrition and population.
- Biological factors—family life and population.
- Population programmes—national and international levels.

Dr. Gopal Rao has suggested the following as the content of population educations:

- The history of population growth—world in general, India in particular, causes, trends and implications.
- An introduction to demography with particular reference to India: components of population growth, population distribution and its composition.
- Effects of rapid population growth on economic, social, cultural and political aspects of rational development.
- Effects of rapid growth of population on individual and family life, and standard of living.
- Effects of rapid growth of population on the physical environment, food, natural resources and quality of life.
- An elementary knowledge of the physiology of reproduction wherever feasible.
- The population policies and programmes of the world in general.

POPULATION EDUCATION PROGRAMME

Population education is a continuous process and it should be provided to the growing children. In fact, population education should be given at all levels of education. i.e., from the kindergarten level to the university level, in order to inculcate appropriate attitudes in the students and to create a deep impact on their minds. The Population Education Cell has developed a draft syllabus on population education at the school and college levels. Population education is not to be treated as a separate subject in the school curriculum but it should be integrated with other subjects.

OBJECTIVES OF POPULATION EDUCATION IN SCHOOLS

- Develop among the students a keen insight into the inter- relationship between population change and the process of socio- economic development vis-à-vis the individual, the family, the society, the nation and the world.
- Create among the students and the teachers an awareness of the population situation in the country and the strategies adopted to face this critical situation.
- Create an awareness in children that the present population explosion in our country is due to the steady birth rate as against the rapidly falling death rate over the past few decades.
- Develop desirable attitudes and behaviour in the students and the teachers as well as in the community at large towards the population issues so as to enable them to arrive at a rational decision about the quality of life that suits them best.
- Impress upon the children the truth that the use of science and technology has helped us in bringing down the death rate and that the same can help us in bringing down the birth rate as well.
- Help the children realise the socio-economic burden involved in bringing up large families usually resulting in deterioration in the quality of living.

Population Education at the Elementary Level

- Growth of population in rural and urban areas
- Over-crowded situation
- Population and economic development
- Population and social development
- Importance of health
- Factors responsible for personal hygiene
- Life in slums
- Control of diseases
- Basic food groups
- Biological factors and population

Population Education at Secondary Level

- Population growth
- Economic development and population growth
- Comparisons of national graphs—development and population
- Social development and population growth
- Health, nutrition and population growth
- Biological factors and population
- Stages of growth

Population Education at Higher Secondary Level

- Population growth
- Economic development and population growth
- Health, nutrition and population growth

- Social development and population growth
- Biological factors and population

CURRICULUM OF POPULATION EDUCATION

Population education should be introduced and continued upto the university level. It should be an integral part of the curriculum at all the levels. In this way the schools and colleges can play an important role to challenge the horrible dangers of population explosion. The curriculum of population education includes the following headings:

- Meaning of population education.
- Population education and economic development.
- Population explosion and economic development.
- Population explosion and social development.
- Population explosion and the health of the people.
- The policies and programmes of the government relating to population.
- Situation of the population in India and the world.
- Comparison of population explosion in India with that of other countries.
- Population explosion and increasing crimes.
- Population explosion and human values.
- Population explosion, social stagnation and terrorism.
- Growth of population and cost of living.
- Growth of population and size of land holding.

Population education maybe introduced and integrated with the following subjects:

Languages: Population education in the form of stories, essays and poems can be incorporated in the language textbooks in the mother tongue, regional language and the national language (mother tongue, Hindi, English).

Social studies: Statistics on population education and material on the impact of population on socio-economic development of the nation can be included in the studies.

Science and health education: Population education can be incorporated with science subjects. For instance, problems relating to fertility, reproduction and family planning can be studied in science and health education.

Mathematics: Population education can be taught more effectively with the help of percentages and bar graphs.

Arts: Drawing cartoons, pictures and diagrams related to the problems of population explosion can be used for teaching population education.

TEACHING METHODS OF POPULATION EDUCATION

Correlation method: This method of teaching can be done effectively through statistical representation. In this method, population of different countries can be compared and various problems can be correlated with population explosion. For example, population explosion and economic development, population explosion and inflation, population explosion and the standard of living.

Direct and indirect method of teaching: Population education can be taught directly by explaining the impact of population explosion on socio-economic development. It maybe taught indirectly indicating the causes of inflation and the degradation of human values.

Co-curricular activities: These activities should be organized in the school to impart population education. Such activities include, drawing, music and sports.

Extra-curricular activities: These activities should be organized outside the classroom to impart population education. Such activities include conducting tours and excursions to the thickly populated areas to analyse the consequences of population explosion.

Discussion: Declamation contests, debates, seminars, symposium and essay writing competition on the impact of population explosion on socio-economic development should be organized.

ROLE OF THE TEACHER IN POPULATION EDUCATION

The role of the teacher is of utmost importance in population education. This is because the impact that the teacher has on his students cannot be achieved by any other agency. Therefore, all teachers are expected to be involved in the activities and programmes related to population education. For this, he should have a healthy and scientific attitude towards the size of the family.

The teacher can play a powerful and effective role in providing population education to the students. To teach population education, the teacher can adopt the following ways:

- The teacher should make an in-depth study of population education. He must be fully conversant with the knowledge related to this subject.
- He should have a perfect knowledge of the socio-economic situation of the country.
- He should always be ready to play a very effective and powerful role for bringing about a social change.
- He should be endowed with the qualities of being progressive, tolerant, cooperative, skilled, creative and far sighted.
- He should have a full knowledge of the important areas related to population.
- He should take an active interest in population education.
- He should actively contribute to the family welfare programmes.
- He should act against the population explosion with self-confidence and a scientific attitude.
- He should present his own idea for providing population education to his students.
- He should have stability and integration in his thoughts, words and actions.

LEARNING EXERCISES FOR POPULATION EDUCATION

- Children with the help of parents or elders may prepare the "family tree" to depict information about the past generations and their births, deaths and causes of deaths. Such information may help them to draw some inferences about the population trends of the past and the present.
- Children may find out what medicine or treatment is available for certain diseases during their time, and the childhood of their ancestors. They may discuss this in their classes and arrive at their inferences.
- Children may also compare the health and medical facilities available in urban and rural areas and arrive at their inferences after discussing the fact.
- Children may collect census figures of their village or town for the past few decades and draw a graph depicting the trends of population.

- Children may also collect figures of school enrolment for the past few decades to draw their inferences.
- Children may collect figures about the area and population of countries like the Soviet Union, Japan, China, the United States of
- America, Canada, Brazil, Australia and India and compare them in terms of population, area, average density of population and per capita income.
- Similar exercises can be done for a few states in India such as Tamil Nadu, Kerala, West Bengal, Bihar, Uttar Pradesh, Rajasthan, Maharashtra and Gujarat. They may arrange them as per the average density of population.
- Children may draw pictures of an average Japanese family and an Indian family and compare them in terms of their size and living conditions or standard of living.
- Children may compare two families; one with an earning member and five dependents and another with two earning members and only two dependent young children.
- Budgeting one's pocket expenditure (in urban situation).
- Presenting two or three imaginary monthly budgets of people drawn from lower middle class families with somewhat equal incomes but with varying family size (children may collect data).
- Working out per head income of families with equal income but varying sizes.
- Finding out broadly the food requirements of our country after 30 years when its population is likely to be doubled. Holding debates and discussions on how and at what cost this can be achieved.
- Finding out how many additional primary school teachers would be required if every year additional 10 million students join the primary school.
- Finding out if population remains steady and no new class is required to be opened in their schools, how the amount, which was otherwise spent on new classes, could be utilised under the new situation.
- Finding out the total number of doctors we would need in a district at the rate of one doctor for every 500 people.
- Finding out what happens when one new job is created in the school or a village or what happens when a person loses his job against his wish.
- Comparing life in various respects in two families, one with a working woman and the other with a housewife.
- Finding out the advantages of a family when the mother is educated and the size of the family is small.
- Comparing the standards of living in advanced and developing countries. Finding out probable causes that account for the vast differences between the two.
- Children may collect information on four or five families they know with regard to their basic needs of food, clothing and shelter.

(*Source:* Adapted from 'Population Education': A conceptual framework, NCERT, 1979).

PROBLEMS OF POPULATION EDUCATION

Confusion of the concept: As the concept of population education is quite new, it does not have a satisfactory definition. Therefore, it becomes very difficult on the part of the teachers and the educationists to have a clear-cut idea about its aims, curriculum and method of teaching. This weakness makes them remain in darkness. Seminars and symposia should be organized to explain the aims and curriculum of population education to the parents and teachers from time-to-time.

Inadequate curriculum: The construction of curriculum plays a vital role in implementing any new educational programme. Though population education is a new subject, we have not developed a suitable curriculum for the in- school and out-of-school programmes. The NCERT, SCERTS and allied organizations should take up this problem and prepare guidelines for the use of the teachers at various stages.

Lack of materials and new technology: This is another impediment that is faced in implementing the programmes of population education. In fact, the inadequate development of teaching materials like textbooks, audio-visual aids, instructional materials, shortage of literature for mass media like radio, television, newspapers, films and film strips affect the propagation and implementation of population education adversely.

Lack of trained teachers or qualified personnel: Population education is a new arrival in the domain of education in India. Our teachers of both the primary and the secondary schools are not adequately equipped with the right type of subject matter to be dealt within the area of population education. NCERT should produce suitable literature for teachers in this connection. Population Education Centre, M.S. University, Baroda has brought out a publication A Handbook of Information for Teachers, Parents, and Students. The syllabus both for B.Ed., and M.Ed., should be revised and it should include the area of population education.

Education of parents: Parents should be educated about the necessity of the introduction of population education in schools, so that they will realise that all the socio-economic ills of poverty, spiraling prices, shortage of food and consumer goods are chronic due to the unprecedented growth of population in underdeveloped countries like India. Moreover, they will think of birth control devices. This is an urgent need that parents should be enlightened about the real objectives and contents of population education.

Lack of variety of language and dialects: Language is the main vehicle for communication by which the new ideas can be propagated among the people. Ours is a multi-lingual nation having 15 official languages and 1652 dialects. The people living in distant places, speaking their own dialects fail to grasp the programmes broadcast through the radio in the official language. So, the authorities face difficulties to propagate ideas about population education throughout the country.

Lack of planning and coordination: As population education is comparatively a new area in the field of education, it requires proper planning and coordination at every level. But, due to lack of proper planning and coordination it becomes difficult to implement the programmes of population education.

Lack of resources: We need trained teachers, teacher educators, directors and material resources, like instructional material, textbooks and teacher's guides to propagate and implement the new education. But the lack of the aforesaid resources makes the programme unsuccessful.

Lack of transport and communication: As a large portion of our country is covered with hills and rivers, proper transport and communication facility is not available there. As a result, it becomes very difficult to establish the centres for propagating and implementing population education. Teachers and authorities are not interested to work in those areas due to lack of transport and communication. Thus, lack of communication works as a principal impediment for the progress of this new education.

Social and religious taboos: The social and religious taboo is another barrier responsible for the slow progress of population education. For instance, Muslims and Roman Catholics are against the family planning programme. Such religious people believe that having many children is the blessing of

God. Even many people who are illiterate, ignorant, superstition and traditional become hostile to the new education. Because of this, we consider social and religious taboos as one of the reasons for the slow progress of population education.

Problems of integration: We face problems in finding integration among the different areas of population. There are three types of integration namely interdisciplinary integration, contextual integration and curriculum integration which should be encouraged to implement the programme of this education effectively.

Lack of research: Lack of research has now become a major barrier to implement the programme of population education. As this area of education is new, it requires adequate research work. Three types of researches, namely, synthetic research, basic research and action-oriented research should be undertaken to implement the programme successfully. But, we have failed in the field of conceptualisation and methodological development of population education.

POPULATION EDUCATION PROGRAMME IN INDIA

The Ministry of Education launched a Population Education Programme in April 1980 to tackle the problem of the growing rate of population. It introduced population education in the formal education system. The underlying purpose of the programme was to create in the younger generation, an adequate awareness of the population problems and its impact on the socio-economic development of the country.

Population Education Programme is a planned scheme in the central sector of the Ministry of Education. It has been developed in collaboration with the United Nations Funds for Population Activities (UNFPA) and with the active involvement of the Ministry of Population Education.

At the state level, population education programme is being implemented by the state government according to an approved plan. The National Council of Educational Research and Training provides the technical assistance. A National Steering Committee has been set up under the Chairmanship of Education Secretary with over-all authority for coordination as well as implementation of the programme. This committee held its first meeting in December 1980. The states, namely, Bihar, Chandigarh, Gujarat, Haryana, Karnataka, Madhya Pradesh, Maharashtra, Punjab, Rajasthan and Tamil Nadu joined the programme in April 1980. Nine states, namely, Andhra Pradesh, Assam, Delhi, Himachal Pradesh, West Bengal, Jammu & Kashmir, Kerala, Odisha and Uttar Pradesh joined the programme in April 1981. Some leading universities of India like Madras University, Sri Venkateswar University and Tirupati are carrying out different plans and programmes for the propagation and implementation of this education.

At present the population education department has taken the following steps to implement the programme successfully:

- Preparation of context books, handbooks and publications.
- Preparation of teaching materials.
- Publication of a monthly magazine.
- Establishment of libraries and information centres.
- Issue of teaching materials to schools at low prices.
- Preparation of kits for population education.

FUTURE PROGRAMME

Our population annually increases by 13 millions, which is equal to the entire population of Australia. It is at present about 140 crores (May 2022), and it is estimated that by the year 2050 our population will be about 164 crores (approx.). In order to solve the problem of the future, we may adopt the following programmes:

- Department of education should make arrangement for in-service training, research and programme implementation.
- Departments of universities should conduct research and prepare desirable literature.
- Departments of science should conduct factual experiments on the evil consequences of rise in population.
- Programmes of population education should be implemented through seminars, discourses, exhibitions and debates.
- Population education should be made an integral part of general education at every level.
- The United Nations Fund for Population Studies has been set up at Mumbai with the cooperation of the World Health Organization and the United Nations for the purpose of combating the problem of education at the international level.

We may hope that these programmes will check the increasing population and save our future generation from the spectre of a gigantic problem.

CONCLUSION

Population explosion is the only reason for a country to be an underdeveloped one. This is because the unprecedented growth of population affects the socio-economic development of the country adversely. Therefore, population education has become quite inevitable to solve the problem. The purpose of population education is to develop an awareness of population problems and discern the relationship between the growth of population and socio-economic development of the nation. In order to create population awareness and to prepare the people and the society to lead a happy life, an effective programme of population education is a must for the present-day world.

CHAPTER 49

EDUCATION FOR PEACE

INTRODUCTION

Jesus Christ is the man of great personality whose birth has been declared as peace unto the earth. He is the father of peace, love and simplicity. He also emphasized *peace*. This is because there is fear, peaceless, tension, war, conflicts, violence and terrorism in the earth. Peace of mind is very essential for keeping life happy, healthy and successful in the materialistic and complicated society. Modern technology has made our life very easy and comfortable, but lack of peace affects our mind and body and causes many illness or suicide or untimely demises. In fact, the present generation seeks peace but they could not find it. Peace is health and health is wealth. That is why the king of poem Kannadhasan (South India) wrote, "Where is Peace? Where is Peace? There I want a place". Every individual whether rich or poor, literate or illiterate, man or woman wants peace. But, it is very difficult to keep our mind peaceful in the complicated materialistic society where greed for wealth, tension, conflicts, misunderstanding, lack of adjustment, incurable diseases, inequality, inflation, corruption killing, raping of innocent girls and women accidents, wars, violence, loss of money and life, terrorism, illegal sex, divorce, disobedience of children, attack of wild animals, threats and vitiate our peaceful life. Above all, the present life is more and more complicated and peaceless causing tension, frustration and despondency. Hence, education for peace is very important to promote peace among the present and future generation. In other words peace education should be taught as an integral part of general and professional education at all levels.

MEANING OF PEACE EDUCATION

In the ordinary sense, peace refers to the state of mind free from any disturbance. But, every individual is disturbed by any one or more of the matters such as conflicts, tension, revolt, fear, divorce, separation untimely loss of children, or parents, incurable diseases, illegal sex, poverty, unemployment, war, violence, terrorism, raping, murdering, lack of understanding and a lot of contemptible activities. As such no man is found peaceful in the personal as well as social life. So, peace is the obverse of tumult, revolt, mutiny, tension, conflicts, and violence and war. Broadly speaking, peace is mind related satisfactory life. It is a state where every problem is regarded or treated as simple and easy. Hence, we should understand the nature of life and learn to adjust or overcome the difficulties and problems which we come across in the social environments.

Peace education can be defined as the creation of mind free from anything which makes peaceless. It is that education by which skills, knowledge and experience, provided to prepare child for a peaceful life. It teaches various subjects and experiences with examples to make the life healthy, happy and peaceful. In other words, it is that education which creates and promotes peace in the complicated minds of people. As such, it includes those activities, knowledge and experiences which maintain a peaceful life as for as possible.

DEFINITION OF PEACE EDUCATION

Education is meant for peace making is called peace education. It may be defined as, "Peace education is one which prepares the mind of the individual to live peacefully". In other words it is that education prepares for life free from all challenges and problems vitiating the people. Broadly speaking that education which makes man free from mental agony, worries, tension, fearness and conflicts or anything disturbing peaceful life. In short, peace education develops and promotes happiness and peacefulness.

OBJECTIVES OF PEACE EDUCATION

- Identify those activities or challenges which cause peacelessness.
- Strengthen the Mind of people to overcome or adjust the challenges.
- Develop those skill and knowledge which prepare the people for peaceful life.
- Enable the people to comprehend the uncertainty of human life.
- Find out the solution for various challenges faced in the ordinary business of life.
- Make human life simple, easy and happy with limited sources and unlimited wants.
- Relate the philosophy of human life to peacefulness.
- Develop the reading culture for transformation of mind.
- Avoid those activities which vitiate peaceful life.
- Provide education and training for peace making in the dynamic business oriented life.

FACTORS OR CHALLENGES CAUSE PEACELESSNESS

There are challenges and problems which make human life peaceless, unhappy and unhealthy. As a result, a number of diseases and undesirable or contemptible activities are increasing in the aimless materialistic life. We point out a list of matters which pollute the mind and body.

- Excess demand for goods and services.
- Inflation affects more unemployed and poor than employed and rich.
- Poverty and unemployment.
- Inequality in income distribution.
- Stresses and conflicts due to unnecessary thinking and worries.
- Lack of adjustment and understanding.
- Incurable or chronic diseases.
- Mentally and physically challenged children.
- Lack of understanding of man and social environment.
- Cash centered education, religion and politics.
- Narrow mind of family, caste, religion, language and region.
- Corruption and bribes.

- Untimely demise of children and parents.
- Violence, terrorism and war.
- Lack of leadership quality and humanity.
- Lack of secularism and democracy.
- Excess of competition in politics, education and religion.
- Illegal sex, polygamy and polyandry.
- Suicide, Killing and loss of wealth.
- Raping, Prostitution and accidents.
- Addiction of drugs and intoxicant substances.
- Divorce, separation and denial of family responsibility.
- Imitation of others and obscene–violent based mass media.

NEED AND IMPORTANCE OF PEACE EDUCATION

Jesus Christ always says to His disciples and people "Peace on the earth, peace unto you", Be peaceful, I offer you my peace because I am simple and humble, learn from me. Even after His resurrection, He appeared in the closed room and said to the disciples that peace be unto you. This is because they were afraid of Jews, stress and peaceless. He also insists the human beings let not your heart be troubled. His words are very powerful giving courage, confidence and peace. But our contemptible activities or undesirable deeds pollute us and society so that there is no peace in the individual, social and global life. The great saint and practical philosopher Swami Vivekananda says, "No one can be happy unless others are happy". In fact, accidents, raping of children, corruption, Killing, suicides, consumption of intoxicants and obscene–violent based mass media make us unhappy and peaceless. Moreover, the present education and religion have failed to promote 'peace' in the challenged life. Instead, both also pollute the people in many ways. However, peace is very important to avoid diseases and make life happy and healthy. One can justify the need and importance of human life in t he following grounds.

Present Education: The present system of education, instead of man-making, widens the inequality gap between the poor and rich in terms of English and regional language education based on various syllabus. Moreover, it has failed to create peaceful citizens, but itself causes peaceless. In fact, mark scoring, higher cost of education, frequent tests and examination, torture of teachers and parents vitiate the peace of students and parents. Further, privatization of education develops competition among schools for admission and results. So, students study for examination and not for understanding the subject matters. There is no freedom in the learning environments, and not for understanding the subject matters and preparing students for peaceful life. Frequent tests, restless works and higher fees make the learning environment peaceless, tension and stress. There is no freedom in the learning environments and chance for peacefulness. Hence, we need a peace based education at all levels.

Present Religion: Once, people had faith on God, heaven, hell and devils. Such faith and beliefs have declined due to the development of advanced science and technology, undesirable activities of religious workers and rational thinking. However, many people have faith on God for blessings, recovery from chronic diseases and wealth. No one understands the meanings and principles of religions and practice them in their life. But, religion is used for income and employment, and to exploit the weaker sections and pollute the society. As such, it has also failed to foster peace among the people. Therefore, peace education is required separately to teach the ways for peace development.

Politics: Present politicians not only lack of leadership qualities but also develop enmities among them. The government is in favour of government employees and neglect the working classes or non-government employees. Moreover, it causes in equality by increasing the salaries and other monetary benefits given to workers in the government departments. It is the center of corruption, bribes, irresponsibility, laziness and misuse of national wealth. So, it has also failed to maintain peace among various groups of people. Moreover, the present government is not a welfare one but kill-ware promoting the business of intoxicants. This also requires for peace education to create a peaceful mind in politicians, governments and national leaders.

Social Hazards: Social hazards are more powerful than the nuclear hazards in making people peaceless. This is because corruption, addiction to drugs, mobiles, internets, illegal sex, stealing, murdering, obscene-violent based mass media push the man down to hell and make him peaceless, stress and tension. In fact, drunkards never satisfy their families and causes their wives suicide, separation or divorce, ultimately demise of children, become destitute ones leading a characterless and peaceless life. Thus, the whole families suffer. Similarly, those who misuse and addict to mobiles and internets spoil their life and become burden to the family and society. In this, situation, a meaningful peace oriented education is very important to lead the children in right direction and peaceful life.

Fast Life: Man becomes a restless machine. He always engages in any type of mental or physical activities. Restless work and stress for poor wage or salary makes life placeless. Bible says that life is like a running of postman. It is like flowers and grasses, King David says, "I have finished my life like a story". In fact preparing food, sending child to school, washing clothes and utensils and cleaning houses keep the mother very busy. Such busy life causes stress, tension and peaceless. At this juncture, everyone should learn to maintain a peaceful life.

E-Philosophy: The present generation is led or guided by the three E-philosophy of life that is Earn, Enjoy and Empty(die). Such philosophy forces man to earn either by working hard or using various tricks such as producing intoxicants, prostitution, corruption, printing fake currencies and certificates, stealing, robe ring and swindling etc., In other words, earn maximum and enjoy maximum and leaving or quite(die) the world. So, no one can be happy and peaceful. There is no place for human values and life becomes materialistic, aimless and hopeless. In fact, most of the people have failed in their attempt. Finally, they commit suicide or are subjected to many diseases. So , everyone needs peace for which peace education is very indispensible in materialistic society.

Ignorance of Real life: Education for peace is very essential to comprehend the nature, meaning and purpose of human life in the complicated world. More than 90 per cent people do not know what life is. Such people should understand that naturally, the sexual contact cause the birth of children who do not know the quality of parents, castes, religion, region, language and social environments. Later on, they understand everything. Here it is very important to note that no parents think of children but enjoy maximum pleasure at the time of conjugal. As a result, the children are born unfortunately and unexpectedly. As such, our children are not our children and it is the flow of sperm and ovum of men and women from one generation to another. So every child should be brought up with maximum freedom proper guidance and socially acceptable characteristics. In this regard, parents should be good, role model and intelligent in all respects. Above all they should understand the reality of human life. Life is a gap between birth and death, which may be short or long, happy or unhappy and rich or poor but make it useful in the social environments. A peaceful mind is necessary to comprehend the nature of human life. So, education for peace is quite unavoidable one in the problematic society.

Accidents and Demises: The number of road accidents increases day by day due to over speed, over take of other vehicles, tension and unaware of traffic rules. As a result, there is loss of life which causes the victim's family peaceless and unhappy. It is seen that youths drive the vehicles very fast and violate the traffic rules and cause many accidents and demises. As it affects, the peaceful life, an integrated peace education should be included in the curriculum. That is, everyone must learn that minimize the speed of vehicles to maximize the duration of life.

Challenged Children: The physically and mentally challenged children vitiate the peace of the parents. In fact, the whole family suffers because of such children. The provision of peace education with life oriented activities may comfort and help to adjust themselves to the varying socio-natural environments. Hence, education for peace is felt necessary to prepare the mentally and physically challenged children for a peaceful life. It is possible through fostering human values in the neighbours, friends and relatives for making such families peaceful.

Create Better Generation: The present generation uses various tricks, social hazards, discoveries, intoxicants and obscene violent mass media for entertainment and happy life but which make them characterless, peaceless and unhappy. Education for peace teaches the ways for the creation of better generation. This is free from contemptible activities. We think and use of high yielding varieties of seeds and plants to increase the agricultural productivity or modern technology to increase industrial production and services. At the same time, we have failed to produce good children and men. In fact we decorate bridegrooms and brides as much as possible with costly cosmetic products and ornaments, but totally fail to remember the facts that they create a new one (child) in the earth. This is because many of us do not care about the behavior of the children. We should understand that physical and mental strength and behavior of the child are created, carved, shaped and formed in the mother's womb. In this regard, the Indian philosopher Osho (Rajanish) rightly remarks, "children are the outputs of obscene-based sex". So, sex is not only meant for pleasure but also for creation of child. So, the present generation should be very careful otherwise we produce children whose quality is less than animal in behavior. Swami Vivekananda says, "Everything is in child bring it out through proper education". Therefore, the married couple whether poor or rich, literate or illiterate, employed or unemployed should maintain amicable relationship between them. Husband and wife must avoid quarrel, conflicts, sex, unnecessary talk and anything which affect, peaceful life of their children. Pregnant women must avoid watching obscene-violent based mass media, develop good thinking, and read holy books and materials related to great national and spiritual people. Jesus Christ rightly said to the people of Jerusalem "Die in your sin" For this purpose, we need a peace education which includes the ways and means of producing better generations.

Develop Rational Thoughts : We may be proud of saying that man is a supreme creature, better than animals. But his deeds like homosexual, homo marriage, raping of girls, rape to death, excess greed for wealth, comparing and envying, back biting, consumption of intoxicants and illegal sex prove that he is not better than animals. Bible says that man is not better than animal. Whatsoever, it may be, man is more important than God, religion, languages and money. He is born to live, then why should he die before his time of death. Everyone should understand that peace is psychological and it is determined by the internal and external factors. Internal factors those which we take seriously that is one's mind related. It is because of mental and physical weakness, undesirable character, misbehavior of children lack of adjustments, misunderstanding, lack of patience, excessive expectation and negative thinking. On the other hand, external factors, are those which affect the family, society, nation or globe. For instance murdering, raping, kidnapping, hijacking, loss of life and wealth corruption, terrorism, violent, war, and natural hazards. Thus, man's peace is disturbed by socio-natural hazards. As such, no one is free from disturbances and difficulties. Hence, if want peace, we have to take easy and simple. And learn to satisfy needs with what is available but don't be greedy for anything. Illiterate, physically challenged, unemployed, poverty stricken, chronic diseased people, destitute women and children are surviving where as why can't you? Nothing anything to be exposed, so let us live as it is without much expectation, you can marry more than one, you can buy more and more land, you can acquire wealth more and more, can you be happy or satisfied and peaceful what of you today may of others tomorrow. This is the law of human life .So, don't worry for anything but adjust yourself in the ever changing social environments. Hence, this kind of education is necessary to turn the people in to rationalists and peaceful life.

Overcome Challenges: Education for peace is not only meant for peaceful life but also overcome the challenges like, conflicts, violence, terrorism, war, poverty, unemployment, inflation, diseases, loss of life and properties, spiritual desolation, illegal sex, raping of girls, corruption murdering and environmental destruction. As these challenges affect the individual, families, societies and countries, efforts should be taken to overcome them at all levels. Therefore, a world-wide transformation from disunity, conflict and inequality to unity, peace and equality, from war to peace, violent and terrorism to peace through right education and guidance. Hence, peace education aims to create a culture of peace, adjustment, healing, understanding and excellent in families, societies and countries.

EDUCATION AND PEACE

The present education makes the students restless and peaceless. It is materialistic oriented and provides certificates and degrees to be produced for employment. There is no place for man-making and peacemaking. However, education is the most powerful tool by which anything can be inculcated in the minds of children and people. Peace is more essential than anything for keeping life happy. In fact, peace is health and wealth. Absence of peace or mental disturbances cause conflicts, tension, pressure and many other diseases. Hence, an attempt should be taken to provide peace as an integral part of general, professional and vocational education. It should promote and develop this culture of peace and health among the masses. The International Education for peace is non-profit research, training, community development and service agency. It organizes and conducts various programmes for the creation of peace within the context of oneness of humanity, at national and international levels.

AIMS

The main objectives are:

- Education the students based on the universal principles of peace.
- Understand the nature and dynamics of peace from individual, national and international levels.
- Lay foundation of sustainable and universal peace to respond the challenges and opportunities.
- Comprehend the nature and purpose of life and human relationship.
- Educate the children and youth to become peace makers.
- Create peace based leaders at local, regional, national and international levels.
- Provide training and skills to prevent conflicts, violent, terrorism and war.

Curriculum

It is based on three premises as given bellow.

- Unity in human relationship
- Modify the behavior of individuals and groups
- Unity based on peace.

According to the curriculum, it includes four major areas for peace education.

- Peace based family
- Peace based education
- Peace based leadership and
- Peace based conflict resolution.

However, the present E F P curriculum comprises eleven volumes including a wide range of peace related issues.

PROGRAMMES OF EFP

Peace based Education (PBE): The international education for peace (EFP) institution organizes various peace based progremmes (known as peace for education, (EFP) to create a culture of peace, healing and excellence with the help of teachers, parents and students. The culture of peace refer to mutual trust, unity in diversity, practice the principles of human rights, democracy and prevent violence and resolve conflicts in such a way to create a peaceful environment. The culture of healing refers to the development of ability to overcome the trauma which affects, the school community (students, teachers, administrator, and supportive staff). The culture of excellence refers to an environment in which critical thinking about intellectual, emotional, social and moral and spiritual life is encouraged and realized in the practical life.

Peace based Leadership and Governance (PLG): It is also known as leadership for peace. This programme is designed for the leaders of society, government agencies, departments, community organizations religions organizations and social institutions. The leader faces socio-economic and political problems, interpersonal–intergroup conflicts, grievances, rivalries and various challenges. Hence, the task of leadership is difficult and it requires enlightened, progressive and effective leader to integrate the manifold and complicated demands of the communities. As such, PLG is designed suitable for the public, service, civic and business leaders and elected government representatives at the local, state and national levels.

Peace based conflict Resolution (PBCR): It is also known as conflict free conflict resolution (CFCR). It is a peace oriented, non-adversarial, consultative process of decision making for resolving conflicts. It provides an integrative and unique approach to prevent and resolve conflicts and violence based on unity. CFCR introduces the concept, conflict in the absence of unity and conflict resolution in the process of unity building. It offers the participant, new insights and tools to facilitate peace-oriented decision making processes and face the conflicts. Thus it develops new approach to administrate the human affairs.

Peace based Family or Unity Based Family: This is a family development programme which aims to:

- Create unity based families,
- Provide learning experiences for creating healthy married families.
- Give learning experiences on unity-based programme for preventing the highly conflicted world.
- Explores how to create unified and harmonious family relationships.
- Help to grasp the movement from a power orientation to a love orientation.
- Learn skills to practice gender equality in marriages and families.
- Learn to deal with every conflict effectively and peacefully.
- Make the family an abode of peace and children as peaceful and peace creating citizens.

Youth Peace Building Network (YPN): This is a part of the education for peace (EFP) programme, It is a network of youth mobilizing peers with a goal of creating violence-free, peaceful schools, neighbor hoods and communities. It trains them in the concepts of peace making conflict transformation and violence prevention. The participants lead the peers in exploring the funds, wanted ideas, world views and actions that promote the culture of peace. It also organized in a few schools in North America and implemented at schools in Bermuda and several hundred schools in Bosnia and Herzegovina The purpose of this programme is to produce many YPN groups around the world. The local and national YPN groups were formed to undertake a wide range of activities mentioned below:

- Organize and conduct peer workshops on peace based world views.
- Develop the attitudes and skills for peace making.
- Undertaking peace-building conflict resolution projects in the communities and schools.
- Provide training to the YPN groups.
- Present the youth peace-builders network activities to the leaders of the societies.

EDUCATION AND TRAINING

The EFP institute has been offering wide range of education and training in universities, schools and institutions for higher learning to create the culture of peace, healing and excellence in families, societies and countries (Since 1997). Moreover, training has been given to educators, peace-building professionals, policy–makers and peace researchers.

- ***Laudegg International University*** provides M.A Degree in conflict resolution peace Education, and leadership and governance. And it also provides certificate and diplomas on a variety of peace based issues.
- ***European Peace University (Austria)*** provides graduate level on site course in peace education, peace building and conflict resolution.
- ***World Peace Academy (Switzerland)*** also conducts online graduate level courses on peace education, peace building, peace leadership and conflict resolution.
- ***EFP Internship:*** The EFP in Bill provides internship to undergraduate, graduate, and post-graduate students from North America, Europe, Australia, Asia and Africa.

The International Institute of EFP arranges peace-based programmes in Mexico, Columbia, Bermuda, Canada, Malawi, America, Europe, Africa, Turkey, Greece, Cyprus, China, India and Israel.

HOW TO CREATE PEACE

Now the question before every individual is how to create peace in the polluted world. It is very difficult question to be, answered when there is peaceless. At the same time, it is very easy and simple for those have adjustable mind, and take everything easy. It is important to note that no education, no religion or no politics is not strong enough to make human life happy and peaceful in the market economy of competitive world and this is centered life in the polluted society. In fact education is not meant for man making but for money making, in the names of qualities, facilities and English. Religion is not for peace-making but for exploiting the society in the name of god, prayer and offerings. Politics is not meant for peace-building but for widening the gap between haves and have nots, promoting the production and sales of intoxicants. Moreover, a number of social hazards pollute the family and society and vitiate happiness and peaceful life. What so ever it may, we want peace to make our personal, social, economic, cultural, spiritual and political life happy and successful.

Peace is mind centered which should free from worries or disturbances. Hence we should understand and practice the ideas mentioned below.

- Mental peace is the most important source of healthy, wealthy and happy life.
- Peacelessness cause conflicts, tension, sufferings, disease, unhappy life ultimately, untimely death or suicide
- Do not allow the mind for unnecessary worries, and excess demand for goods and services.
- Peace is internal mind centred, maintained it with peace centred skill, knowledge and experience.
- Socially be flexible and smile gently to make others happy and healthy, and create conducive environment for, personal and social life .
- Always free from social hazards such as corruption, prostitution, illegal sex, blue film, intoxicant, raping, murdering, robbing, swindling stealing, cheating, backbiting, terrorism, conflicts, and avoid anything which pollutes the mind, and body and make life peaceless and unhappy.
- Develop and follow good thoughts, good word, and good deeds. Life is short, uncertain, and hopeless but take everything positively and make it successful.
- Don't let your heart be troubled in the mechanical life and learn to treat the loss as gain and unhappy as happy.
- Don't hurt others in words and deeds, but create peace.
- Help and comfort the physically and mentally retarded children and their parents as for as possible to make them peaceful and happy.
- Avoid sexy or transparent dress showing upper breast, which pollutes and instigates the lads to rape and kill the innocent girls and women.
- Share your wealth to the needy and poor who are your neighbors, relatives and friends.
- As Jesus Christ said, "You are the temple of God". Swami Vivekananda said, "See God in human faces'. So turn your house in to a temple or mosques or church, if so you will be 'God'. As such, "God is man and man is God".
- Let not our heart to be troubled in socio-natural hazards. When we be free from social hazards such as corruption, lust, prostitution, illegal sex, murdering, raping of innocent girls and women, drinkins drugs, and other contemptible activities. We can escape from unnecessary worries, economic burden, suicides and chronic diseases.
- There is an end for everything and change is permanent so need not worry about anything which happens and affects peace and happiness.
- Let us learn to live as a man of values not man of success.
- Avoid fast driving to avert accidents and untimely demises. We should keep in mind the words of Saibabha "Start early, drive slowly and reach safely".
- Pregnant women must avoid watching obscene violence centred mass media, Instead, read good books about great people at international level to become a mother of best child.
- Parent should inculcate human values and peace in the minds of children.
- Parents must avoid sex quarrels, divorce, illegal sex before children which cause them peaceless and characterless.
- Parents should create peaceful atmosphere in the family so that children will be peaceful.
- As for as possible maintain a cordial relationship with neighbours, friends, and relatives and love enemies.
- Avoid wearing sexy or transparent dresses exhibiting the upper breast of ladies which instigate the lads and old to rape and kill the innocent girls and women causing peaceless life.
- Don't compare you with anybody because nobody is like you. But you should be a model and example to all.

- The government should prohibit the production of all intoxicant substances which make the family and society peaceless and characterless.
- The government should reduce or not increase the salary of government employees as it causes, inequality and inflation, and poor become poorer.
- Teachers and parents should not force the child for study and make scoring but they should deal with them politely for healthy and peaceful life.

CONCLUSION

Peace is the gift of life. It is related to the mind. So learn to keep the mind free from all troubles or disturbances. It is in us. So, we should be peaceful in all situations whether best or worst take everything simple and easy. Avoid worries, conflicts, undesirable and contemptible activities. Prepare for satisfactory life within available income in the honest way. Don't rely on anybody but trust on you and lead a life with faith, confidence, courage and hope. Whether we live or die, be happy and peaceful. In fact, whatever the education, religion, employment and income may be, try to live peacefully. No one in practical life, no one is happy or unhappy permanently. Everything changes in course of time. No doubt that we live in the polluted, social and natural environments where all are good and all are bad. So it is better to learn to lead a satisfactory life with peace. Finally let us observe the widely known Christian prayer of St. Francis of Assisi:

O Lord, make me an instrument of your peace:
Where there is hatred, let me sow love:
Where there is injury, pardon
Where there is discord, union:
Where there is doubt, faith:
Where there is despair, hope:
Where there is darkness, light: and
Where there is sadness, joy.

O Divine master
Grant that I may not so much seek.
To be consoled, as to console;
To be understood, as to understand.
To be loved, as to love;

For it is in giving that we receive,
It is in pardoning that we are pardoned;
And it is in dying that we are born again to eternal life.... Amen.

Sing the song and remember always (Author's song)

Peace is strength
Peace is courage
Peace is Happiness
Peace is Health
Peace is Wealth

Let us enjoy peaceful life with the prayer of Jesus Christ

. . . Give us this day our daily bread
And forgive us our trespasses
As we forgive them that trespass against us
And lead us not into temptation
But deliver us from evil . . . A men

Let me conclude that no one whether rich or poor, literate or illiterate, strong or weak, male or female is free from problems or difficulties or scarcities of resources. But the flow of kindness, help, sympathy, spotless love and smiling from one individual to another makes human life happy, healthy and peaceful.

CHAPTER 50

WOMEN'S EDUCATION

INTRODUCTION

Women play a prominent role in the cultural, social, political and economic life of a country. In fact, women's education was encouraged in ancient Indian society. That is why, they are given due respect and have equal rights to receive education. According to the Vedas, women should have the opportunity to attain knowledge of the Vedas. Separate organizations had been set up to provide education to the women during the Buddhist period. But no importance was given to women and their education during the Muslim period. Women were sent behind the "purdah" (veil) under the Muslim influence and this tradition spread among the Hindus also. Evil traditions like child marriage, sati and devdasi system were also prevalent during this period. This culture developed different attitudes towards women's education. But by the end of the nineteenth century, some progressive Indians and Englishmen like Raja Ram Mohan Roy, Ishwar Chandra Vidyasagar, Gandhiji, David Hard and Annie Besant worked for making women aware of education. They established many schools to encourage women's education. After independence the national government considered the expansion of women's education as its sacred duty. As a result, the progress of women's education has been continuing and the girls belonging to remote areas, rural areas and SC/ST are being encouraged to receive education.

MEANING OF WOMEN'S EDUCATION

The provision of all facilities and opportunities to women for education is called **women's education**. Our constitution gives great importance to the equality of status and opportunities for men and women. The state shall not discriminate against any citizen on the grounds of religion, caste, sex or place of birth. Thus, educational facilities and opportunities are provided to women regardless of their caste, religion or location at par with men.

NEED AND IMPORTANCE OF WOMEN'S EDUCATION

Women's education becomes very essential when we accept that the mother is the first teacher of her children. In fact, a good mother is better than the teachers. But there is a wide gap between the education of men and women in our country. This is because of illiteracy, child marriage, purdah system, economic backwardness, traditional outlook and ignorance of parents. These factors discriminate in the provision of education to the boy and the girl. Several attempts were made before and after independence to remove this discrimination. However, the need and importance of women's education was realised in free India.

Swami Vivekananda has emphasised, "If you do not raise the women who are living embodiments of the divine mother, don't think that you have any other way to their social and economic status". Gandhi has stated the importance of women education in these words, "I am strongly of the opinion that women should have the same facilities as men even special facilities where necessary". Pundit Jawaharlal Nehru has very rightly observed, "Education of a boy is the education of one person but education of a girl is the education of the entire family". It is accepted that a mother occupies the central point in the family.

Dr. S. Radhakrishnan (University Education Commission 1948–1949) states, "There cannot be educated people without educated women. If general education has to be limited to mere men or women, the opportunity should be given to women, for then it would most surely be passed on to the next generation". Similarly, the Kothari commission (1964–1966) has rightly remarked, "For full development of human resources, the improvement of human beings and for moulding the character of children during the most impressionable years of infancy, the education of women is of great importance than that of men". In other words, the education of the women is more important for the development of human resources, improvement of homes and character development in the impressionable years of childhood. Realising the need and importance of women's education, the National Policy on Education (1986) states, "The education of women should receive emphasis not only on grounds of social justice, but also because it accelerates social transformation".

Women play a predominant role in the social, cultural, economic, religious and political life of a country. A mother is better than the teachers. This is because from birth to school stage, the home environment and association of other members of the family play a significant role in developing the proper attitude of a child. It is proved that the pass percentage of girls in school, college and university examinations and their share in prizes and scholarships are greater than that of the boys.

Let us mention the need and importance of women's education in India based on the views of the Indian educationists, philosophers, and political leaders.

- The cooperation of women is necessary for the progress and prosperity of the country.
- An educated woman produces an educated family and an educated society.
- An educated woman makes the home happy and healthy.
- An educated woman can mitigate the economic difficulties of the family.
- An educated woman knows the importance of having small family and how to bring up her children.
- A woman can become an ideal mother only when she receives education.
- An educated woman participates in social, cultural, political and economic activities.
- An educated woman produces better citizens whose role is very important to strengthen the democracy.
- An educated woman helps to develop national integration, world peace and international understanding.
- There is a positive relationship between education and economic development. Educated women increase the production of goods, services and national income.
- An educated woman knows the importance of saving which is basic for capital formation and economic development.
- To produce great women in different walks of life like science, literature and various disciplines of studies in the universities and in social and political life of the country.

- An educated woman can help in removing social evils, and save the society from old beliefs and customs which adversely affect the progress of our society.
- Women have the same rights to receive education as in the case of men. So, women cannot be discriminated on the basis of sex, as far as education is concerned.
- Swami Vivekananda says no expectation of the progress of a family or a country can be achieved where women are not educated, and are leading a pitiable life. To him, welfare of the country is not possible until the condition of women is improved. Therefore, their educational uplift is of utmost importance.

OBJECTIVES OF WOMEN'S EDUCATION

The unit of National Council for Educational Research and Training (NCERT) for women's education has formulated the following objectives of women's education:

- Promote the education and the development of girls.
- Undertake and promote research in the area of girls' education and development.
- Develop and apply concepts and methods of women's studies.
- Suitably intervene in the areas of policy planning, curriculum and teacher education for removing gender bias and disparities.
- Act as a catalyst in promoting innovations and programmes of girls' education in the country.
- Act as a national resource centre on girls' education and development.
- Provide consultancy services in the areas of girls' education and development.

FUNCTIONS OF WOMEN'S EDUCATION

To fulfil the objectives of women's education, women's education unit of NCERT became a full-fledged department of women's studies in 1990 with the following functions:

- Awareness generation action.
- Re-designing curriculum and educational programme.
- Orientation of curriculum developers and textbook writers.
- Inculcation of positive self-image in the girl child.
- Promotion of research and innovative action projects.
- Inputs into teacher education.
- Data bank.
- Work in close collaboration with National Institute of Educational Planning and Administration (NIEPA), Ministry of Human Resource Development (MHRD), Women's Universities and other international bodies.
- Mobilisation of women and community.
- Interacting with the media.

PROBLEMS OF WOMEN'S EDUCATION

Conservatism: Most of the people of India feel that educated girls become morally depraved. The purdah system among Muslim girls and early marriage among Hindus have been great hindrances in the expansion of women's education. The traditional prejudices still operate in backward and rural areas to some extent. In fact, the lower and poor sections of the society fall an easy prey to these superstitions and traditional prejudices.

Poverty: The poor economic condition of parents is the greatest obstacle in the way of the development of women's education in underdeveloped countries like India. Education has become a costly affair. Hence, it is not an easy task for poor parents to make suitable arrangements for the education of their daughters.

Illiteracy: This is an undeniable fact that most of the parents of our country are illiterate and ignorant. Such parents do not know the need and importance of education. Due to the illiteracy and ignorance of parents, they fail to send their daughters to educational institutions. They discourage women's education.

Lack of schools: The number of schools imparting education are located either in urban areas or at distant places. Therefore, the girls have to walk long distances for attending schools. Moreover, the number of schools meant for girls is very few. This factor curbs the expansion of women's education.

Lack of lady teachers: There is shortage of qualified women teachers in our country. The available lady teachers do not like to go to village schools because facilities of life are absent. Absence of lady teachers discourages girls' education.

Lack of transport in rural areas: There are some rural areas, hills and remote places, where no transport facility is provided. Women teachers and girl students cannot go to schools located in these areas. Thus, it is the main hurdle in the progress of women's education.

Lack of physical facilities: Lack of hostel and transport facilities or hostels without proper security measures affect the expansion of women's education. In fact, many parents do not admit their daughters at distant schools and colleges due to lack of physical facilities.

Indifference of government: The government spends a huge amount on the education of boys and the amount spent on the education of girls is comparatively very low. It does not provide special emphasis for the popularisation of girls' education.

Unsuitable curriculum: At all stages of education, boys and girls have the same curriculum. But the physical, social, cultural and emotional needs of girls are different. In our country women are compelled to take up courses and jobs which are similar to men's. As a result parents do not feel enthusiastic to send their girls to schools.

Problem of co-education: Though it is advisable, it is difficult on the part of the government to open separate schools for girls at different stages of education. Co-education can be encouraged at the elementary level, but it is not advisable to open co-educational schools particularly in a country like India, where adolescents do not possess sufficient emotional stability.

Problem of wastage: We find a lot of wastage in the education of girls. It maybe owing to the negative attitude of parents towards the education of girls, or capitation fee and increasing unemployment problem.

Lack of incentives: The lack of adequate incentives and proper supervision and guidance to girls and parents discourage the expansion of women's education in India.

RECOMMENDATIONS OF COMMISSIONS AND COMMITTEES ON GIRLS' EDUCATION

Our national and social leaders feel that no national development can take place without women's education. Therefore, education of women has been regarded as a major programme in India. In fact, after the independence of our country the central government, state governments and non-government institutions have been taking all efforts to encourage women's education. Preference has been given in the five year plans of India for the expansion and development of women's education. In order to minimise the existing gap between the education of boys and girls and to expand and develop women's education, the government of India has appointed commissions and committees. Let us look at the recommendations put forth by different education commissions and committees.

University Education Commission (1948–1949)

The University Education commission is popularly known as **Radhakrishnan Commission**. This commission analysed the problems of women's education at the college and the university level and made the following recommen- dations:

Amenities of life: The ordinary amenities of life should be provided for women in colleges originally planned for men but to which women are being admitted in increasing numbers.

Educational opportunities: There should be no curtailment in educational opportunities for women but rather a substantial increase in them.

Educational guidance: There should be an intelligent educational guidance by qualified men and women to help women to get a clear view of their real educational interests and to provide good education according to their needs and capacities.

Normal place in society: Women should be helped to find their normal place in society, both as citizens and as women.

Cultural and social responsibility: Men should be encouraged to extend right courtesy and social responsibility in mixed colleges.

Equality in co-educational institutions: In co-educational institutions, due weightage should be given to women.

Equal salaries: Women teachers should be paid the same salaries as male teachers for equal work.

National Committee on Women's Education (1958)

Education panel of the Planning Commission recommended in July 1957 that, "A suitable committee should be appointed to go into the various aspects of the question relating to the nature of education for girls at the elementary, secondary, and adult stages and to examine whether the present system was helping them to lead a happier and more useful life". This was placed before the conference of the State Education Ministers. They agreed that a special committee should be appointed to examine the whole question of women's education. Accordingly, the government of India appointed the National committee on women's education under the chairmanship of Smt. Durgabai Deshmukh. The committee made the following recommendations:

Universal enrolment: The attempts for expansion of girls' education should aim at universal enrolment of girls in the age group 6–11 by 1979 and in the age group 11–14 by 1981.

Improvement programme: The recommendations made by the Central Advisory Board of Education for the improvement of women's education should be implemented and for this purpose cent per cent assistance should be provided. The programmes include: (i) construction of teachers' quarters; (ii) provision of school teachers; (iii) provision of rural allowance for the lady teachers working in the villages; (iv) provision of hostels; (v) provision of crèches (vi) provision of school uniforms; (vii) provision of mid-day meals; (viii) construction of sanitary blocks.

Facilities in isolated and backward areas: The girl students of backward, hilly and isolated areas should be provided with facilities such as free transport and free residential accommodation to encourage them to get education.

Publicity programme: Publicity programmes should be launched to awaken the people towards the need of women's education. For this purpose, documentaries and films concerning women's education should be prepared and displayed.

Facilities for continuation class: Some girls are forced by the social and economic circumstances to leave the school. For such girls, continuation classes should be started.

Education for adult women: Central Social Welfare Board should start condensed courses to give suitable education to adult women.

Assistance to voluntary organization: Voluntary organizations working for the expansion of women's education should be given assistance towards the building of hostels, libraries and laboratories.

Scholarships: There should be provision for an adequate number of scholarships to encourage the girls to continue their education.

Encouragement to co-education: Where it is difficult to start separate schools for girls, co-education should be encouraged.

Close up the gap: The gap between the education of men and women should be filled as fast as possible.

Securing cooperation: Cooperation of semi-official organizations, local bodies, voluntary organizations and teachers' organizations should be secured for the development and expansion of women's education.

National council for women's education: National Council for Women's Education should be set up for studying the needs and problems of women education at the national level.

State council for women's education: At the state level, State Council for Women's Education should be set up.

Women's education in five year plan: Women's education should get an important place in five year plans and the planning commission should make an estimation for women's educational requirements.

Suggestions of Durgabai Deshmukh Committee (1959)

- The central and the state governments should give priority to the education of girls.
- In the central ministry of education, a department of women's education should be created.
- For proper education of girls, a director of women's education should be appointed in each state.
- Co-education should be properly organized at the higher level of education.
- The University Grants Commission should specify a definite amount for the education of girls.
- In the first phase of development, provision of free education should be made for girls upto class VIII.
- Facilities in the choice of optional subjects should be made available for girls.
- Girls should get training facilities on a liberal basis.
- Education of girls should be given due encouragement in rural areas.
- A large number of seats in various services should be reserved for them.
- Programmes for the development of adult women's education should be properly initiated and encouraged.

Recommendations of Hansa Mehta Committee (1962)

National Council of Women's Education appointed Hansa Mehta Committee in 1962 to suggest measures for the improvement of women's education. It made the following recommendations:

- Co-education should be adopted and encouraged at the primary stage.
- Separate primary schools or middle schools for girls should be started where there is such demand and where there is adequate enrolment.
- Separate and co-educational institutions can be started at secondary school and college stages. Parents should send their daughters to the institutions they like.
- Number of women teachers should be increased in primary schools. Women teachers should also be appointed in all institutions at the secondary and college stages which are meant for boys, but where girls are also admitted.
- There should be a common curriculum for boys and girls at the primary and middle stages.
- Home science is a useful subject for girls at the higher secondary level.
- Girls should be encouraged to study science and mathematics at the higher secondary stage. Sex education should be provided at this stage by matured, competent and well-trained teachers.
- Special needs of girls should be kept in view while constructing the curriculum at the university stage.
- Girls should be provided with necessary facilities such as scholar- ship, free transport and stipends
- Women should be given adequate representation in textbook committees.
- There should be the provision of vocational schools at the end of secondary education so that girls are trained for different vocations.
- Music, drawing, painting, tailoring and fine arts are the subjects of interest for girls. Therefore, proper facilities should be provided in educational institutions.

Recommendations of Bhaktavatsalam Committee (1963)

The National Council for Women's Education endorsed the suggestions made by the Union Education Minister that a small committee should be appointed to look into the reasons for the lack of public support, particularly in rural areas for women's education and enlist public cooperation. Accordingly, the Chairman of the National Council for Women's Education appointed a committee in May 1963 under the Chairmanship of Shri. M. Bhaktavatsalam, the then Chief Minister of Tamil Nadu, to suggest ways and means of achieving substantial progress in this field. The committee submitted its report in 1964 and the report was published in 1965. The following recommendations were made by this committee:

Fields of public cooperation: Direct public cooperation should be encouraged in the fields such as; (i) establishment of private schools; (ii) construction of school buildings; (iii) contribution of voluntary labour in constructing school buildings; (iv) rendering help in the maintenance of school buildings; (v) giving help in the provision of suitable accommodation for teachers and students, particularly in rural areas; (vi) helping in popularisation of co-education at the elementary stage; (vii) creation of public opinion in favour of teaching profession and giving greater respect to the teachers (viii) popularising teaching profession for women; (ix) giving encouragement to married ladies to get part-time education in village schools and work as school teachers (x) undertaking necessary educative propaganda to break down additional prejudices against girls' education; (xi) organization of school betterment committees and improvement conferences; (xii) provision of mid-day meals; (xiii) provision of uniforms to the poor and needy children; (xiv) provision of textbooks and writing materials to the needy children.

State's responsibility: State should take up the responsibility of creating public opinion in favour of women's education. For this purpose it may adopt: (i) seminars; (ii) radio talks; (iii) school improvement; (iv) audio-visual aids and distribution of information pamphlets; (v) organization of enrolment drives; (vi) assistance to various organizations engaged in the field of women's education.

Schools in all areas: Schools should be set up in all areas howsoever small they may be. It is the responsibility of the state to provide primary schools in each habitation with the population of 300. There should be a middle school in each habitation with a population of 1500 and above within a radius of three miles and there should be provision of secondary schools to meet the needs of those who leave middle schools after the completion of the course. There should be at least one secondary school within the radius of five miles.

Provision of pre-primary schools: It is essential that pre-primary schools should be attached with primary schools, particularly in the rural areas. These schools will help the children to get accustomed to schooling at an early stage.

Good school building: Buildings which are not suited to school functions should be changed and good school buildings should be provided to meet modern educational needs.

Women teachers: More and more women teachers should be appointed in primary schools. In co-educational institutions, the number of female teachers should be more than that of male teachers. Such a provision will create confidence in parents and they will feel encouraged to send their girls to schools.

Good working conditions: Working conditions of teachers should be good and inspiring. Financial incentives should be given to the teachers who are made to work in hilly and isolated areas.

Part-time appointment: Some women leave the teaching profession after marriage. They should be encouraged to continue teaching and offered part- time appointment.

Education for adult women: To educate adult women, particularly in rural areas, condensed courses should be organized.

Relaxation in age-limit: Age limit for the married and unmarried women teachers should be relaxed. This relaxation will help in attracting women to the teaching profession.

Posting of women teachers near their homes: Every possible effort should be made to post women teachers in or near their own villages.

Preference to women candidates in admission: Women candidates, particularly in rural areas, should be given preference in admission to training courses.

Training facilities: More training facilities should be given to women candidates to meet the increasing demand for additional teachers.

Hostel facilities: Adequate hostel facilities are essential for the enrolment of girls. So, it should be one of the main objectives of the plan of states to provide financial assistance for the construction of hostels.

Residence for women teachers: Women can be attracted to the teaching profession by providing them with residential quarters near the school. So, teachers' quarters should be built to enable the teachers to live near the school.

Sound inspection: Well-qualified and competent inspecting staff should be appointed for the improvement in girls' education. Sound and improved inspection will also help in reducing wastage.

Adult education: While organizing programmes for adult education, every effort should be made to liquidate illiteracy among rural women.

National Council for Women's Education (1964)

National Council for Women's Education was set up in 1959 by the Central Ministry of Education. It was reconstructed in 1964 and consisted of the Chairman, the Secretary and 27 members. The main functions of the council are:

- Advise the government on the education of the girls at school level and the education of adult women.
- Suggest and fix programmes, targets and priorities for the improvement and expansion of girls' and women's education.
- Suggest suitable measures for creating public opinion in favour of girls' and women's education.
- Create awareness in the society with regard to the importance of women's education.
- Organize seminars, surveys and other research works for the improvement of girls' education in the country.
- Make periodic evaluation for the progress of women's education.

Kothari Education Commission on Women's Education (1964–1966)

Kothari Commission has given a lot of importance to women's education. According to this commission women's education is very important and helpful in reducing the birth rate. Regarding the education of girls, this commission states, "In our opinion the strategy for the development of the girls and women will have to take two forms. The first is to emphasize the special programmes recommended by the National Committee on Women's Education and the second is to give attention to the education of girls at the states in all sectors as an integral part of the general programme for the expansion and improvement of education". It is of the opinion that in the coming times, the progress of women's education should be very effective. The present differences in the male and female education should be removed as much as possible. It has made the following recommendations regarding women's education:

- The gap between men's education and women's education should be closed by considering women's education as a major programme in education for some years. Moreover, determined and bold efforts should be made to face the difficulties involved in the expansion of women's education.
- Special plan should be prepared for this purpose and the funds required for them should be provided on a priority basis.
- There should be a special administrative machinery to look after the education of girls and women.
- The education of girls requires special attention at the primary stage. So, more and more ancillary services should be provided. Special measures should be taken to check the undesirable growth of wastage among girls.
- Efforts should be made to accelerate the expansion of girls' education. At the secondary level, the development of the education of girls should be increased. The ratio of male and female education should come to 2 : 1 from 3 : 1 in 20 years.
- Emphasis should be placed on establishing separate schools for girls, provision of hostels and part time and vocational courses.

- The present proportion of women students and men students (1:4) should be increased to about 1:3 at the university stages in order to meet the requirements of women in different fields.
- At the graduate level separate colleges for women maybe established if there is a local demand. Courses in home science, nursing and social work need to be developed as these have attraction for a large number of girls.
- Research units should be set up in one or two universities to deal specially with women's education.

Recommendation of National Policy on Women's Education (1986)

National Policy on Education plays a positive role in order to provide powers to the women. In this regard, its recommendations are as under:

Status of women: Education will be used as an agent of basic change in the status of women.

Improvement of women's education: There should be improvement of women's education through re-designed curricula, textbooks, training and orientation of teachers and decision making on administration.

Provision of various courses: Various vocational and professional courses will be provided for the promotion of women's studies.

Promotion of women studies: Various courses such as home science, music, fine arts, tailoring and embroidery, cooking and Needlework will be provided for the promotion of women's studies.

Removal of illiteracy: Highest place would be given to eradicate women's illiteracy. The obstacles that come in the way of primary level of education should be put to an end.

MEASURES FOR POPULARISATION OF WOMEN'S EDUCATION

- Opening of more schools—a primary school for 300 pupils, a middle school for 1500 pupils within the radius of 3 miles and a secondary school within a radius of 5 miles.
- Appointment of more women teachers.
- Special incentives for teachers in rural areas.
- Provision of quarters for women teachers.
- Free education to girls.
- Gaining community support for girls' education.
- Enforcement of Compulsory Education Act.
- Flexibility of curricula and school hours.
- Separate schools for girls.
- Educating the parents through adult education programmes
- Inspectresses for schools even at the elementary level.
- Part-time employment to girls.

PRESENT POSITION OF WOMEN'S EDUCATION IN INDIA

After independence, the progress of women's education has been satisfactory. The girls belonging to remote areas, rural areas and weaker sections of society are being encouraged to receive education.

From the increasing number of women's educational institutions and girl students from the primary level to the university level, we come to know that India is marching forward towards the progress and development of women's education. This is an undeniable fact that the enrolment of women is increasing day-by-day in all levels of education, both in formal and non-formal educational institutions. Government of Tamil Nadu has given priority to women's education. The number of girl students is higher than that of boys from primary level to university level. This is the present position of Tamil Nadu and Kerala, and it is the same condition in almost all towns and cities of India.

CONCLUSION

The women of today are very conscious of their social, economic, intellectual, mental and spiritual development. Their role, both within the home and outside the home, has become an important feature of the social and economic life of the country. It will become more significant in the years to come. Therefore, they cannot be deprived of education at any cost and greater attention should be paid to the problems of training and development of women. It maybe pointed out here that there cannot be educated men without educated women. If a chance has to be made between education of men and education of women, in that case only women should be given opportunity to receive education because in this way education will easily reach the next generation. Hence, the education of girls should be emphasised not only on grounds of social justice, but also because it accelerates economic and social transformation, and above all to achieve cent per cent literacy.

CHAPTER 51

ADULT EDUCATION

INTRODUCTION

India achieved political freedom, but social and economic freedom is yet to be achieved. Social and economic freedom is not possible unless we achieve cent per cent literacy. This is so because illiteracy is the root cause for all ignorances and superstitions, and all social, cultural, political and economic backwardness. In other words, it retards individual, social and national progress and development in all aspects. Moreover, illiterate parents produce illiterate children. Therefore, the state and the central governments have taken various efforts to eradicate illiteracy. As a result, eradication of illiteracy is one of the most important objectives of the Indian Education Commission (1964–1966) and it has become most inportant problem of India. In the words of Prof. K.G. Saiyidain, "There is hardly any social problem in India, which is more urgent in its significance and wider in its scope than that of tackling liquidation of illiteracy". However, adult education programme is the vital instrument to eradicate illiteracy in the contemporary Indian Society.

MEANING OF ADULT EDUCATION

The literal meaning of the term 'adult education' is the education of grown up men and women, who could not get formal education in the early years of their lives. It has some other connotations such as adult literacy, functional literacy and social education. Functional literacy means ability or that level of literacy which enables a person to function as a literate in his social and professional life. It also means mastery of the 3 R's (reading, writing and arithmetic) and the ability to acquire knowledge and information independently. It also means the ability to discharge multifarious civic duties and responsibilities in an efficient manner. Social education is adult education. Maulana Abdul Kalam Azad says, "By social education we mean an education for the complete man". In the words of M.K. Gandhi, "Social education is education for life and not for the sake of literacy. It includes everything". Thus, it is adult education for a desirable social change and for the betterment of the individual's social, economic, political and moral life. Education enables the community to assume direction for its own development. It is education for better work, better rest, better use of leisure and better recreation. Thus, it can be concluded that the wider concept of adult education is renamed as **social education**.

Adult education is given to adults in the age group of 15–35 in an informal setting and on a part-time basis concurrently with work and the earning of a living and for helping them to acquire functional literacy, professional or work efficiency and personal and social development. Thus,

- It is meant for adults in the age group of 15–35.
- It is given in an informal way.
- It is a part-time education.
- It is learning while earning. That is, a person who works in the factory, field, farm, trade or in any organization can receive this education.
- It is given to the individual for his functional literacy, work efficiency and social development.

DEFINITIONS OF ADULT EDUCATION

The term adult education is defined by different scholars in different ways.

Morgan, Holmes and Bundy: "Adult Education may be thought of as the conscious effort of a mature person to learn something new".

Byron: "Adult education includes all activities with educational purpose carried on by people, in the ordinary business of life, who use only part of their energy to acquire intellectual development".

S.N. Mukerji: "Adult education may be defined broadly as to include all instructions, formal or informal imparted to adults. In India it has two aspects (i) education of those adults who never had any schooling; (ii) continuation of education of adults".

Reense, Fensler and Houle: "Adult education may be concerned with any or more of three aspects of an individual's life—his work life, his personal life or his life as a citizen".

Earnest Baker: "Adult Education is given on a part-time basis and given concurrently with work and the earning of a living".

AIMS OF ADULT EDUCATION

The aims of adult education can be classified as: (i) Individual aims and (ii) Social and national aims.

Individual Aims

It is essential for every individual to keep himself abreast with the latest developments. Otherwise, it will be very difficult for him to adjust himself properly in the ever-changing world. It is adult education that keeps him up- to-date in new needs and new trends in various fields of human activities. Let us point out the individual development aim of adult education.

Remedial measures: Adult education aims at providing education to those adults who could not receive education during their early days.

Eradication of iiliteracy: The individual aim of adult education is to eradicate illiteracy and ignorance of the masses.

Physical health: The adult education programme aims at educating the adults about the principles of health development and the prevention of diseases. Through adult education, individuals are made to understand the methods of combating ill health, eradicating various diseases, keeping the surroundings clean and solving nutritional problems within his available resources.

Vocational skills: This is the age of advanced science and technology. So, traditional skill will not provide vocational satisfaction. But adult education makes the individual conversant with new skills concerning his vocation.

Social skill: The development of social skill in the adults is the aim of adult education. It enables them to make effective advancement in life and make their family life happy by developing harmonious relationships with their friends, relatives, neighbours and people at large.

Cultural development: The aim of adult education is bringing about cultural development in the adults. It is adult education that shuns the blind faith and beliefs by developing rational thinking. It also teaches them how to use their leisure usefully, through various recreational programmes.

Self-development: The individual aim of adult education is to bring about self-development and self-expression through the training of the creative faculties so that adults can get the opportunities to develop their philosophy of life.

Social and National Aims

As man is a social animal, he has to develop himself in social and environmental surroundings. Society helps him in the development of his personality and also expects such help from him. Therefore, social aim of adult education is essential for social and national development.

Development of civic sense: Every individual should have ample civic sense to discharge his duties and responsibilities towards the society for the development of a democratic the society. So, it is essential that adult education should help in inculcating and developing civic sense in the people.

Development of social unity: The social aim of adult education is to promote social unity in diversity. This aim helps to reduce individualism that exists between different groups speaking different languages, the urban and the rural groups, the educated and the uneducated, the rich and the poor, the capitalists and the labourers etc. It creates and develops common bonds between people and a common culture acceptable to all situations.

Improvement of natural resources: Adult education aims at making people realise the necessity of conserving and improving natural resources available in our country. It teaches them how the natural resources can be used for the purpose of advancing rural economy, raising economic standards and increasing production in industry and agriculture.

Development of social and national consciousness: The development of social and national consciousness is essential for an all-round national progress. In this regard, adult education aims at preparing people to subordinate their private welfare to the welfare of the society and the nation. The continuation of education enables people to learn and realise the ideology of tolerance, brotherhood, emotional integration, nationalism and service to mankind.

Development of co-operative institution: The aim of adult education is to develop cooperative movement for national progress. It helps in building up cooperative societies for studying collectively various problems and solving them with cooperative efforts and actions.

We may list out the aims of adult education in India in the following lines:

- Removal of illiteracy and ignorance in adults and expand literacy programmes.
- Improve vocational efficiency.
- Promotion of the ideas of mutual tolerance.
- Development of a balanced sense of rights and responsibilities.

- Developing scientific and rational attitude in life.
- Improving the quality of leadership in the villages.
- Developing democratic values and secularism.
- Acquainting the adults with the benefits of new knowledge.
- Imparting knowledge of the basic essentials of a healthy civic life.
- Enabling to appreciate the need for the preservation and promotion of cultural heritage.

NEED AND IMPORTANCE OF ADULT EDUCATION

For a long time, our country suffered from a very low percentage of literacy because about 48% of our population was illiterate as per 1991 census. Prof. K.G. Saiyidain, a leading educationist of India has rightly lamented, "If some one to prepare a literacy map of the world and colour the illiterate areas of the earth black, India will, to our shame, look like a dark continent". Realising the importance of adult education, Dr. V.K.R.V. Rao says, "Without adult education and adult literacy, it is not possible to have that range and speed of economic and social development which we require. A programme of adult education and adult literacy should, therefore, take a front place in any programme for economic and social development". The Indian Education Commission has stated, "Adult education to provide every adult citizen with an opportunity for the education of the type which he wishes and which he should have for his personal enrichment, professional advancement and effective participation in social and political life". Dr. V.K.R.V. Rao stresses on the same view in his words, "From the point of view of either economic development or national integration or social cohesion or cultural advancement or preservation of democracy it is essential, therefore, that we should achieve a hundred percent literacy among our people". Let us point out some of the reasons for which we need adult education in India.

Remove illiteracy: Adult education brings a new hope for the illiterate masses who failed to get education during their school years. About 50 per cent of our people still live in the darkness of ignorance and illiteracy. In this situation adult education is essential to remove illiteracy and ignorance.

Save adults from exploitation: Adult education is needed to educate adults so as to enable them to understand the meaning of the rights and duties provided by the constitution of free India. It will save them from exploitation and maltreatment.

Widen the intellectual horizon: There is a large number of partially illiterate adults. It is essential to educate these half-illiterate persons and complete the process begun in the past. These efforts will widen the intellectual horizon of all such adults and thus give them training to grasp the real meaning of things.

Make a happy and joyful life: The programmes of adult education help the Indian masses to develop the habit of a joyful life by removing dullness and uninteresting environments.

Make the adults politically conscious: Political freedom is meaningless without economic, social, moral and spiritual freedom. The real political awakening depends on proper education. In fact, education is a powerful tool by which India's most urgent needs in social, political and economic aspects, and national unity can be achieved. So, we also need adult education as it enables the great masses to be conscious in selecting the right candidate for the right place in a right way. It is essential to strengthen a democratic country.

Help the adults in cooperative living: The adult education programme tries to remove classism, groupism, casteism etc. It helps for the unity of the nation by providing training in cooperative living.

Bridge the gap between the educated and the uneducated: Adult education is needed to remove the widening gap between the educated children and the uneducated adults. In fact, it is not wise to educate the children and throw adults in the midst of the ocean of ignorance.

Continue education: Education is a life-long process and it never ends. So, people who have already completed their education can once again receive fresh knowledge from the adult education centres. Hence, we need adult education in order to make education a life-long process.

Ensure national development: Adult education is directly linked with the economic, social, cultural and political regeneration of our country. It is not possible to have the range and spread of economic and social development in the absence of adult education. Therefore, a programme of adult education should find a prime place in any programme for economic and social development.

Ensure national security: Educated adults can contribute effectively to national security. The Education Commission has rightly remarked, "No nation can leave its security only to the police and army: to a large extent national security depends upon the education of citizens, their knowledge of affairs, their character and sense of discipline and their ability to participate effectively in security measures".

Make democracy successful: If the education of children is important for the future welfare of the state, education of adults is also necessary for the very existence of democracy. The slogan of Gladstone is "Educate Your Masters". In the words of J.B. Harold Laski, "Without educated voters democracy becomes monocracy". Lenin has rightly remarked, "Socialism cannot be successful with illiterate masses". The function of adult education is needed to eradicate the stumbling blocks like casteism, communalism, provincialism, population explosion, poverty and mass illiteracy.

Ensure advancement of family: The advancement of a family depends on the adult members. Educated adults can contribute effectively to population control in the family, the society and the nation. Population education should be given to adults in order to create awareness among them about the causes and consequences of population explosion and to maintain small families so that they can lead a happy life.

Live a decent living: Adult education is important because it enables adults to have personal enrichment, professional advancement and social efficiency, to find an honourable place in the society and to live a decent life.

Implement government schemes: Adult education is essential to implement the goal of universalisation of elementary education, family welfare programmes, to control environmental degradation and to awaken an appreciation of the five year plans.

Modernise the society: To make education a powerful instrument for rapid modernisation of society, adult education is quite inevitable. Adult education transforms the adults from blind faith and beliefs to develop rational thinking in them. Such changes are needed for rapid modernisation in socio- economic aspects.

Improve vocational efficiency: Adult education is important to improve vocational efficiency in the adults by acquainting them with the modern technology. This helps to increase their productivity.

Promote economic development: Adult education prepares and develops the adults to undertake any sort of jobs by which they can earn. It improves the quality of the workers and increases their productivity leading to more income. When income increases, savings also increases and it leads to capital formation which is the determinant of economic development in the Indian society.

The need for adult education maybe summed up in the words of Prof. Humayun Kabir, "Educated workers would make for increased production and thus make for increased prosperity for both industry and trade. The benefits would not however, be confined to business alone, increased education would lead to an addition in the national wealth and create the basis for an expansion of necessary social services. Education alone can create the material basis for an improvement in the standard of life of our people. It is also the necessary condition of the training of mind and character, which will permit the people to make a creative use of their leisure. Social education (adult education) is thus the foundation on which alone free India can build up a welfare state which will recognize the claims of both the individual freedom and social security".

PROBLEMS OF ADULT EDUCATION

Educating the millions of illiterate masses has been one of the most significant problems since the dawn of independent India. To overcome this problem our country has adopted the adult education programme. This programme faces concomitant problems. Let us point out some obstacles which retard the progress of adult education in India.

Non-cooperation of adult masses: Adults belonging to rural areas are not enthusiastic about education. They show apathy to adult education programme and do not cooperate with adult education workers. They feel that it is of no use to learn at a ripe old age. For them economic relief has greater importance than education. Moreover, blind faith, beliefs and ignorance, lack of motivation, lack of leisure, lack of peace of mind, lack of physical comfort and family burden have been the reasons for the non-cooperation of the adults.

Defective policy of adult education: The policy of adult education adopted in this country is vague and undefined. So, we do not exactly understand the meaning of adult education and its purpose. The programme is not successful as it is meant only for rural people.

Problem of adult education workers: Lack of professional and vocational skills in adult education programme is a great stumbling block in the success of adult education. In fact, most of the adult workers entrusted with this programme are not trained and do not possess the professional and vocational skills so as to motivate the illiterate adults. They are neither conversant with adult educational psychology nor competent to teach with the help of the available material. Adults are not interested to be taught by untrained teenagers.

Lack of equipment: Most of the adult education centres lack the proper equipment such as textbooks, audio-visual aids, charts, models, workshop, libraries and reading rooms which adversely affect the progress of adult education.

Problem of social backwardness: People in most of the rural as well as urban areas still suffer from social backwardness. The social backwardness in the name of casteism, sex and location is the stumbling block in the way of promoting adult education. For example, scheduled caste people are not allowed to attend the classes with others.

Lack of suitable literature: Proper literature is not available for neo-literates who want easy and interesting books for self-study. Prof. K.G. Saiyidain says, "Adult education is greatly handicapped both at its literary stages and in the wider sense by paucity of suitable reading materials. There is an urgent need for producing a large number of booklets, folders, charts, journals, newspapers, wall posters and other illustrated material which will capture adult's interests".

Lack of vocational training: Adult education workers are not proficient in the vocation of teaching the adults. As a result an illiterate farmer knows more of agriculture than the adult education worker himself. Such workers do not promote the progress of adult education. In fact, adult education held by teenaged and inexperienced teachers was one of the reasons for its failure in Punjab.

Lack of finance: The finance invested by our government for adult education is quite inadequate. As a result, many schemes of adult education have failed in our country. It will not create a positive attitude to open more and more adult education centres. Priority is not given to the adult education programme.

Lack of proper planning: Proper planning is essential for the success of adult education programmes. The progress of adult education is not satisfactory due to the lack of proper planning.

Lack of proper curriculum: We do not have a systematic curriculum to implement the adult education programme. While designing it, the needs, interests and capacities of adults are not taken into consideration. Hence, it becomes impossible to meet the educational needs of the adults and it does not attract them.

Problem of teaching methods: Proper methods of teaching is essential for the success of adult education. But, in the prevailing adult education programme we do not have the help of the radio, the television, stories, diagrams, charts and maps to make the teaching-learning situation interesting and lively.

Problem of teachers: We do not have trained teachers meant for imparting education to the adults. We use primary school teachers who are not competent enough to teach them and do not know how to deal with the adults in getting education.

Lack of proper administration: Lack of efficient and proper administration is also an important reason for the failure of adult education in India. This is so because adult education is an additional duty of the Education Minister. Hence, adult education programme is implemented at different places in various manners.

Solutions to the Problems of Adult Education

- Organize national campaign for understanding adult education programmes.
- Involve students in literacy programmes.
- Provide adequate radio and television programmes for adult education.
- Open more public libraries and reading rooms.
- Provide more community centres.
- Utilise the services of voluntary organizations.
- Provide dynamic methods of training to adult education workers.
- Increase the expenditure on adult education programmes.
- Formulate condensed courses for adults.
- Constitute adult education rewards.

The Ministry of Education of the Government of India has given the following suggestions for the success of adult education programmes in India:

- Primary schools should arrange classes of two hours each at least three or four times a week for the children of 13 or 14 years. It should be done apart from the regular teaching programme of these schools.

- Teachers should be trained by the following programmes for imparting education to the 14–15 age groups.
- Regular classes should be arranged for men and women over a five month period.
- The teacher should educate a group of people in his neighbourhood.
- A home class movement must be initiated for the education of women. It can be made an integral part of the Rural Education Programme.
- Teacher training establishments should formulate and implement programmes of adult education in their respective communities.
- Voluntary organization should organize adult education schemes.

NATIONAL POLICY STATEMENT ON ADULT EDUCATION (1977)

The national policy statement on adult education provides, "While determined efforts must be made to universalise elementary education upto the age of 14 years, educational facilities must be extended to adult population to remedy their educational deprivation and to enable them to develop their potentialities. Indeed, universalisation of elementary education and adult literacy are mutually inter-dependent".

According to the policy statement, the adult education programmes should be:

- that illiteracy is a serious impediment to an individual's growth and the country's socio-economic progress.
- that education is not co-terminus with schooling but takes place in most work and life situations.
- that learning, working and living are inseparable and each acquires meaning only when correlated with the others.
- that the means by which people are involved in the process of development are at least as important as the ends and that the illiterate and the poor can rise to their own liberation through literacy, dialogue and action.

NATIONAL ADULT EDUCATION PROGRAMME (NAEP)

The National Adult Education Programme was launched on October 2, 1978. It aims at eradicating illiteracy among adults of the age group 15–35. The objectives of the programme are:

- Promotion of literacy skills of persons belonging to economically and socially deprived sections of the society.
- Creation of awareness in helping them overcome their helplessness and to achieve self-reliance.
- Raising functional capabilities in their occupation and skills of management to their own advantage as a group.

Features of National Adult Education Programme

Need-based programme: This programme is linked with the conditions and realities of the lives of adults. Its curriculum, teaching and learning materials will be need-based to arouse sufficient interest in the learners.

Priority to weaker sections: Priority is given to the needs of most illiterate women and of most illiterate persons belonging to the scheduled castes in setting up adult education centres.

Honorarium: A centre is to be organized by an instructor who is paid an honorarium of ₹ 50 per month. He is assisted in his work by all the field level government functionaries.

Duration: The period during which the learners participate in the adult education centre would be 300 or 350 days or 9–10 months.

Approach: The programme is organized to give literacy with assured follow- up, conventional and functional literacy, literacy with learning-cum-action group, literacy for conscientisation and formation of organizations of the poor and functional literacy supportive of a dominant development programme.

Training: Special importance has been given in national adult education programme for training adult education functionaries. It includes: (i) key functionaries at the national and state levels; (ii) professional and experts in specific areas such as curriculum construction, preparation of teaching-learning materials, training evaluation etc.; (iii) functionaries at the district, project and block levels; (iv) field level supervisors; and (v) adult education centre instructors.

Agencies: The various categories of persons should be assigned with instructional responsibilities which include: (i) school teachers; (ii) students voluntary involvement; (iii) unemployed village youth; (iv) ex-servicemen and other retired personnel; (v) field level government and other functionaries such as village health worker, gram sevika, bal sevika functionaries of cooperative societies and village panchayats; (vi) voluntary social workers who are willing to make their contribution to community development.

Follow-up activities: The post literacy and follow-up activities are essential for those who go through a programme of adult literacy. Before the conclusion of the programme, preparations have to be made for the organization of a continuing education centre. These centres provide library and reading room facilities, training courses for functional development as well as group action and group organization activities.

Organization and administration: The government of India decided to launch a well-planned programme of adult education in order to make people literate. Proper planning is essential both at the centre and the state levels. The National Board of adult education has been established under the Chairmanship of the Union Education Minister to periodically appraise the progress and implementation of NAEP and advise the government on various matters. There is a State Board of Adult Education and a State Adult Education Officer with supporting administrative and professional staff. At the district level, the responsibility rests with the District Collector, who is assisted by a District Adult Education officer and advised by the District Adult Education Committee.

International co-operation: NAEP should have international cooperation with UNESCO and other international institutions to formulate and implement it in the right direction.

The programme is implemented through various agencies such as the State Governments, Union Territories, voluntary agencies, universities, colleges, Nehru Yuvakendra etc. and a number of centres (92,045 in 1984) are being run by different agencies with or without the financial assistance of the government of India. In our country, adult education in the form of extension of education has been developed mainly by agricultural universities. These universities have agricultural communication centres to provide technical knowledge to the rural people through the media of mass communication. The centres take decisions and print educational materials for cultivators and homemakers through which a good deal of knowledge having practical implications is disseminated in order to make life more useful, productive, comfortable and regulated. These universities organize job oriented training courses for functionaries at different levels in order to increase their efficiency by the help of the latest technical 'know-how' and 'do how'.

CONCLUSION

It is high time for our country to get rid of the darkness of ignorance by the help of the adult education programme. Dr. V.K.R.V. Rao has rightly remarked, on this red letter day in the history of adult education, "I would like to appeal to my friends here and country men to realize the gravity of the situation and to take up the task of liquidation of illiteracy in India and lend them support in items of their time, energy and other resources. Let me make sure that light spreads throughout the length and breadth of this country. Then only we can breathe a really fresh air at hope and fulfilment and thus usher in real freedom to our country". We can make people literate and keep them literate through formulating and implementing the adult education programme.

CHAPTER 52

DISTANCE EDUCATION

INTRODUCTION

Dr. S. Radhakrishnan Commission says, "Education must be universalized and equal opportunities for all be given. Each and every citizen be given education irrespective of his caste or creed, social or economic status, motivation or aptitude". Formal education in schools, colleges and universities cannot help to achieve the goals of universal education. It creates a distance between the haves and the have-nots by serving the privileged few. The great masses have had a little or no schooling. The Government of India, therefore, prepared a blueprint for opening new schools which offer non-formal education for the universalisation of education. Thus, the tremendous need for open learning through distance education system has made education a life-long process. Distance education system meets the educational needs of all the people of our country by breaking all socio-economic barriers.

MEANING OF DISTANCE EDUCATION

The concept of distance education system has been universally accepted as an alternative mode for receiving higher education, professional education and technical education. Distance education is the method of learning at one's own pace, in one's own time, without the boundaries of the formal classroom and without the formal presence of a teacher. It is based on the philosophy that the learner is an active and self-directed agent who makes choices, takes decisions, directs the process qualitatively and quantitatively and assumes the responsibility for all. But it does not remain confined only to the postal service between the universities or institutions and the taught. It is a non-formal system of education utilised for supplementing and enriching the formal system of education. In distance education all the problems and difficulties of the students are solved through correspondence. Supply of books and journals, establishment of radio and television programmes, personal contact programmes and the use of audio-visual aids are the chief features of this programme.

In short, the term distance education implies a form of education in which there is usually a long physical distance between the teacher and the learner and the distance is being shortened by the rapid means of communication. The concept distance education is denoted by a number of terms such as:

1. Continuing education
2. Correspondence education

3. Correspondence learning
4. Correspondence course
5. Correspondence school
6. Correspondence teaching
7. Distance education
8. Distance learning
9. Distance teaching
10. External degree programme
11. External studies
12. Extra-mutual system
13. Home study
14. Home tuition
15. Independent learning
16. Independent study
17. Life-long education
18. Non-formal education
19. Off-campus study
20. Open education
21. Open learning
22. Open schools
23. Open university
24. Out of school education
25. Postal courses
26. Teach yourself programme
27. Tele university
28. University of air
29. University without walls
30. School of distance education.

DEFINITIONS OF DISTANCE EDUCATION

Peter: "Distance education is a method of indirect instruction implying geographical and emotional separation of the teacher and the taught, whereas in main stream of education, the relationship between a teacher and students in the class-room is based upon social norms, in distance education it is based upon technological norms".

Dohmen: "Distance education is a systematically organized form of self-study. It is made possible at a distance by means of media which can cover long distances. The opposite of 'distance education' is 'direct education' or 'face-to-face education': a type of education that takes place with direct contact between lecturers and students".

Borge Holmberg: "Distance education covers various forms of study at all levels which are not under the continuous, immediate supervision of tutors present with their students in lecture rooms or on the same premises, but which, nevertheless, benefit from the planning, guidance and tuition of a tutorial organisation".

Keegan: "Distance education describes those forms of education in which teacher and learner carry out their essential tasks apart from one another".

Borah: "Distance education is a system of education in which there is no face-to-face relationship between the teacher and taught but they are linked through correspondence, radio talk or voice and TV appearance".

CHARACTERISTICS OF DISTANCE EDUCATION

On the basis of meaning and definition, we can discern and point out the following features of distance education:

Absence of direct contact: The first characteristic of distance education is the absence of face-to-face contact between the teacher and the learner. It is done either visually through video recording or the television or through impersonation at the time of personal contact programme.

Distance gap: There is a gap between the teacher and the taught. For example, a number of learners throughout India are pursuing their degree and postgraduate degree courses through distance education conducted by Annamalai University, Tamil Nadu.

Non-formal education: Distance education is a non-formal system of education given like correspondence education, open learning, open university etc. The classroom teaching is not essential or compulsory.

Postal courses: Distance education is quite innovative and flexible as reading materials are sent to the student's address by post.

No fixed class room: The universities that conduct correspondence courses or distance education would arrange personal contact programmes for a few days but these institutions do not have fixed lecture rooms.

Cheapest method of learning: Distance education is less expensive than the formal system of education that requires social, political pressures, capitation and donation.

Wide coverage: Distance education enjoys a wide coverage of learners. For instance, Annamalai University of Tamil Nadu possesses learners throughout India. Learners from remote areas and hills can benefit from learning through distance education.

Effectiveway: Distance education is psychologically as well as sociologically sound and effective, because the learner is not imposed by outside forces. He can learn according to his ability, interest and convenience.

Democratic education: Distance education is democratic education in nature because all the people of the country, whether rich or poor, forward class or scheduled caste, urban or rural, are able to fulfil their academic aspirations and satisfy the unfulfilled desire for knowledge and degrees.

Flexible: Distance education follows flexible norms regarding the date of admission, number of enrolment and place of admission. There is no age limit and percentage of marks obtained in previous studies is not considered.

Programmed instruction: The courses of distance learning are sequenced according to the principles of programmed instruction that are beneficial for the learner who can learn according to his own pace.

No compulsion of attendance: In distance education, attendance of learners in the personal contact programme is not compulsory except for a few courses like psychology, science subjects and other practical oriented courses.

Use of mass media: Distance education makes use of mass media like the radio, the television and the newspapers. It also provides printed lessons.

Close contact: There is one kind of close relationship between the teacher and the pupils as contact courses (practical oriented subjects) and study centres are provided in the correspondence education.

Part-time based education: Distance education is on a part-time basis. One can go on earning while one learns. The contact classes are conducted either during the vacation or the calendar holidays for the benefit of the learners.

OBJECTIVE OF DISTANCE EDUCATION

The Indian Education Commission has pointed out, "There must be a method of taking education to the millions who depend upon their own effort to study, whenever they can find time to do so. We consider that correspondence or home study courses provide the right answer for these situations". Distance education is necessary not only for eradicating mass illiteracy but also for meeting the ever-increasing demand for higher education. This system of education has become successful due to the effective utilisation of various media, methods and materials by the educationists, curriculum planners and researchers. The notable objectives of distance education are given below:

- Provide an effective and alternative way for higher education.
- Provide educational facilities to all who wish to receive higher education and degrees.
- Provide a less expensive system of education.
- Provide opportunities to students who discontinued their formal education due to various reasons such as poverty, family conditions or sickness.
- Make higher education available to geographically remote and hilly areas.
- Help socio-economically backward students to receive higher education.
- Satisfy the educational aspiration of people who engage in socio-economic activities for livelihood.
- Create a deschooling society, that is, taking teaching–learning process out of the school.
- Open the doors of education to people who want to be aware of the modern advancements in their fields.
- Make available the recent technological advancements and innovative developments to various fields so that ordinary people can increase their knowledge that will help them to adjust to their physical and social environment.

NEED FOR DISTANCE EDUCATION

The National Policy on Education 1986 says, "Life-long education is a cherished goal of the educational process. This pre-supposes universal literacy. Opportunities will be provided to the youth, housewives, agricultural and industrial workers and professionals to continue the education of their choice, at the pace suited to them. The future thrust will be in the direction of open and distance learning". Hence, distance education is the imperative need of the present day society which has undergone unimaginable change with the explosion of scientific knowledge. The following factors have necessitated distance education:

Population explosion: The unprecedented growth of population results in the corresponding increase in the number of students. Though the number of schools and colleges is increasing, they are unable to accommodate the increasing number of students. Hence, students are admitted in schools and colleges on the basis of merit. Students, who are not able to get admission in the regular stream, will seek an alternative for the continuation of their education. Distance education is the only source by which such students can fulfil the desire for higher education.

Knowledge explosion: This is the age of knowledge explosion. The rate at which knowledge has been growing is stupendous. As a result, the knowledge acquired in schools and colleges becomes outdated. It also widens the gap between the educated and the uneducated people. In this case, distance education helps people in providing them with up-to-date knowledge and helps them to adjust to the changing environment.

Varied needs of varied clients: Education has been regarded as a sound national investment. It makes man into manpower by which goods and services can be produced. The country needs varied groups with varied knowledge for its progress. This requirement cannot be fully faced by the formal system of education. It calls for the need of distance education or correspondence courses.

Earn while learn: Distance education helps to improve the quality of the workers and enables them to apply modern technology in the productive process. The knowledge related to modern devices and communication can be acquired by education which is not possible to get while earning. In this situation they need evening or part-time courses through distance education.

Improve qualification and skills: The educational requirements of various jobs have changed and new demands have come up owing to the increased complexity of all the aspects of modern life followed by new inventions and discoveries. This atmosphere forces the individual to improve their qualification and skill in order to compete in the modern world. Distance education is the only source by which they can improve their qualification and skills.

Mobility of modern life: Modern life is mobile in the business and industrial world. In order to find a better position, people are moving from place-to-place. This movement makes it difficult for many people to stick to regular educational institutions to acquire academic degrees and diplomas. Institute of correspondence course and continuing education becomes a better source to satisfy the educational requirements of such people and makes them fit in the modern life.

Independent learning: Correspondence courses are required for those who are interested in studying at home, at their own time schedule and at their own pace. This type of non-formal education helps the people to utilise their leisure usefully. Thus, it encourages independent learning.

Democratic education: Education is the birthright of every citizen. It should be provided to all people regardless of their sex, caste, religion, language, location and socio-economic status. Dr. G.S. Dillon, the former speaker of the Lok Sabha pleaded in favour of correspondence course that "If we cannot increase the seats in a classroom for the simple reason that it is walled up on all other four sides, or if we cannot increase the number of institutions of higher learning because it entails formidable expenditure, then the only way out is to remove the walls of the classroom and do away with the necessity of opening a college in every village or small town. The correspondence study programme augments, expands and strengthens the universal character so inherent in the very concept of a university".

Universal literacy: Universal literacy is the ambitious goal of our country. But it is not possible to achieve this goal unless the government imparts education through distance education or correspondence courses which is more economical than teaching in regular schools and colleges.

Arrest socio-economic and geographical isolation: We need distance education to meet the educational requirements of people who reside in remote and hilly areas, people who are unable to study at regular schools and colleges due to economic backwardness and people who are not willing to attend the regular courses because of their castes and creeds.

MODE OF DISTANCE EDUCATION

The practice of distance education is being carried through: (i) Correspondence courses, (ii) Open university, (iii) Open school, and (iv) Mass Media.

Correspondence Education

The practice of correspondence studies or education involves printing the study material and sending it to the aspiring candidates for home study. The postal study material is supported by personal contact programmes. Provision is made for correcting students' response sheets, library facilities, study centres and audio-visual aids.

Study material: The study material sent to the students is prepared by specialists in the field. It should be relevant, interesting and suitable for self-learning.

Despatch of study material: Despatching the study material to the student as per the roll is the key administrative function. The dispatch should be regular and in perfect accordance with the schedule.

Response sheets: At the end of each lesson or unit, there are some questions or answer sheets which serve as an assignment for the students. Students should construct the answer sheets or response sheets properly and send them to the institution concerned for correction. They should be returned to the candidates after correction pointing out the mistakes with comments.

Personal contact programme: This programme is necessary in correspondence education in order to create interest in the students. It is a process of establishing direct contact between the educators and the educands. This programme provides classroom lecturing, guidance and tutorial assistance. The period for personal contact program is 15 to 20 days.

Study centres or information centres: Study centres have been fixed for the benefit of students. They should be kept open during vacations, evenings or on holidays. Application form and other information can be obtained from these centres.

Examination: Institute of correspondence course and continuing education conducts examinations at the end of every academic year. Supplementary examination is held during November for those who have failed in the previous examination.

Certificates and degrees or diplomas: The candidates who have completed their courses successfully are eligible to apply for degrees or diplomas.

Open University

Open university is the latest innovation in the field of distance education programmes. It is known by different names such as 'university of the air', 'tele university', 'university without walls', 'correspondence universities', etc. The idea of open university has been adopted by the University of Mysore and Madurai Kamaraj University. Andhra Pradesh open university is the first open university opened in 1982. The principle of open university is life-long and individual need-based learning. It keeps its doors open for those who have the desire to learn and acquire academic qualification. In short, this is a university for all.

The idea of open university was born in England in 1963. The open university of England was established in 1969. Many countries like China, Thailand, Pakistan, Korea, Sri Lanka, Indonesia, Japan, Spain, Netherlands and India have open universities. In Japan, it is known as university of air. The Indira Gandhi National Open University (IGNOU) is the first National Open University established in 1985. Besides IGNOU, there are 10 Open universities in the country (2003). Tamil Nadu Open University is the 10th state open university established in 2003. A number of universities such as Annamalai University have started courses under open university system.

Objectives

- Provide higher educational opportunities to a large number of people at the graduate and the postgraduate level.
- Provide quality education to all, regardless of their age, caste, creed, region or formal qualification.
- Promote and develop the distance education programme.
- Provide educational opportunities to drop outs as well as to those who could not study in the regular stream due to some reasons.
- Satisfy the people who desire to have up-to-date knowledge or to improve their educational qualification whether they are in service or not.
- Provide need-based academic programmes related to professional and vocational orientation.
- Put new educational technology in order to make the learning programmes effective.
- Make education a life-long process and help the people to utilise their leisure time fruitfully.
- Maintain the standard of distance education by attempting to compete with the educational efforts of the existing universities but, not to compete with them.
- Fulfil the educational requirements of those who fail to join in full time courses due to reasons such as limited number of seats, fees, distance or remote areas, disability/handicapped or lack of time.

The National Policy on Education 1986 states that, "The open learning system has been initiated in order to augment opportunities for higher education, as an instrument of democratizing education and to make it a life-long process. The flexibility and innovativeness of the open learning system are particularly suited to the diverse requirements of the citizens of our country, including those who had joined the vocational stream. The Indira Gandhi National Open University, established in 1985 in fulfillment of these objectives, will be strengthened. It would also provide support to establishment of open universities in the state".

Educational system in open university: Open university adopts a special system of distance education in order to achieve its objectives so that higher education will be accessible to the maximum number of people and different groups in the country. It conducts its programmes through postal tuition, personal contact programmes and audio-visual programmes. Any person who has completed 18 or 20 years of age is eligible to apply for the graduate courses. If the candidate has not passed intermediate examination or higher secondary examination, he has to qualify for the course by passing the eligibility test of the university. Those who have attained 25 years of age can pursue postgraduate degree course in Madurai Kamaraj University under the scheme of open university.

Open School

Open schools and open universities are playing an important role in providing distance education. Open school is one of our efforts to eradicate illiteracy and to expand educational facilities all over the nation. This school is open to all who have the minimum qualifications for admission. The enrolled students can pursue their studies according to their convenient time and in their own manner. It is not compulsory to remain present in the classroom regularly. National Open School and other Regional Open Schools are examples for this category. These schools fulfil the demand for providing education at the secondary level.

The Director of NCERT appointed a working group in August 1974 to examine the feasibility of setting up an open school in Delhi and offer education to the students in their homes. In connection with the establishment of open school, a series of meetings were held between 1975 and 1978 between NCERT, CBSE and Ministry of Education, Government of India. As a result of this discussion, a blue print of the open school was prepared, which was approved by the Ministry of Education. Subsequently the central Board of Secondary Education set up an open school in New Delhi, in 1979. It provides educational opportunity to

- school drop-outs, who have completed VII or VIII class.
- working adults and women who do not have any formal education.
- unemployed adults and housewives.
- students of economically weaker sections who cannot afford to continue formal education.
- those who failed in class X and XII.
- those who wish to pursue continuing education.
- students desiring to undertake life-enrichment courses.

Need and importance of open school: We need open schools because eradication of illiteracy has been the main aim of a democratic country like India. Let us point out the importance of this school.

Education for all: Open school is important to achieve the goal of education for all. Education is the birthright of every citizen. It is not possible to provide educational facilities to all through formal education in the over- populated and economically backward countries like ours. In fact, open schools are inevitable to mitigate the problem of illiteracy.

Need for secondary education in future: Enrolment in primary level is increasing continuously. The primary students will reach the secondary level. But owing to economic crisis the state may not be able to run secondary schools for them. Open schools will substitute the secondary schools in future.

Educate the deprived and the backward children: Open schools provide opportunities to people who are deprived of receiving formal education due to various reasons and people belonging to scheduled castes, scheduled tribes, backward class and minority communities, and some people who are engaged in different occupations, to get education upto the secondary level.

Educate women and disabled people: Women, disabled and handicapped children may not get formal education. They can easily get education upto the secondary level through the open schools.

Mass Media

Many information and communication technologies are arranged for the benefit of the learners of distance education.

Satellite: Satellite plays an important role in telecasting educational programmes. It is praised as "Teacher in the sky", and "Education, rising star". Education satellite (EDUSAT) is used to telecast programmes that can reach the learners living in distant places of the hilly areas, deserts and sea shores. Indira Gandhi National Open University is engaged in this task.

Broadcast: Radios are widely used as mass media to broadcast the lessons. The learners of distance education listen to the radio programmes. It is popular in Tamil Nadu. For example, Madurai Kamaraj University broadcasts lessons for the benefit of correspondence course students everyday at 10.30 P.M.

Audio cassettes: Lectures, lessons and explanations of efficient professors are recorded on audio cassettes and they are played before the students. Annamalai University in Tamil Nadu prepares audio cassettes and distributes them to the correspondence course students.

Television: Television has been functioning as a means of distance education since 1972. It plays an important role in removing illiteracy and providing education in almost all subjects. The UGC programmes are telecast through televisions for the students of regular colleges and universities. Indira Gandhi National Open University telecasts educational programmes for the students of distance education from 6.30 to 7.00 A.M.

Video cassettes: The explanation through oral communication of ideas is converted into visual images in a video cassette. Complicated and minute scientific ideas and explanations are recorded on a video cassette and they are played in the classroom.

Computer-based programmes: Computer is used for teaching in distance education. More than 300 computer-based programmes have been prepared for distance education.

Study centres and counselling centres: Study centres are opened at the district level for the students of distance education for their easy access. Students can make use of libraries and get information related to their studies. Annamalai University and Madurai Kamaraj University have their study centres in Tamil Nadu. Generally, the distance education universities conduct counselling classes and personal contact programmes on Saturdays, Sundays and summer holidays.

ADVANTAGES OF DISTANCE EDUCATION

- This is a very flexible system of education which is not limited by age, place, sex, creed or time.
- A learner can progress at his own time and pace.
- It fulfills the educational needs of people who are unable to pursue their education in the regular stream.
- It reduces pressure on the formal system of education.
- It makes the learner more self-reliant and confident.
- It makes education a life-long process.
- It encourages learning while earning.
- It reaches the learners who live in remote areas, hills, deserts and sea shores.
- It is an economic method of learning without any donation or capitation fee.
- It is useful to spend the leisure time fruitfully.
- It helps to improve knowledge and skill in the field of interest.
- It prepares the people to be competent in the modern society.
- It is useful to in-service personnel, housewives, disabled/handicapped, under-privileged and school drop-outs.

- It encourages people who are socially and economically backward to get education and degrees.
- It is relevant to the over populated and the ever-increasing educa- tional needs of a developing country like India.

DISADVANTAGES OF DISTANCE EDUCATION

- It will lead to deterioration of the academic standards.
- The courses become stereotyped gradually.
- The scope of practical experience is limited/negligible.
- The provision for study centres and book bank is very meagre.
- Students are given extensive written material by post but the same is not suitably supplemented by discussion on the radio or the television.
- Students hardly get opportunities for co-curricular activities.
- Human values such as love, sympathy, cooperation and fellow feeling cannot be fostered through distance education.
- Generally, weightage is not given to degrees obtained through distance education.
- Students cannot clarify their doubts.
- It prepares the students for writing examinations and getting degrees and diplomas.
- It is not possible to provide education related to science, engineering, technology and medicine through distance education.
- It is one of the reasons for the increase in number of unemployed graduates and postgraduates in underdeveloped countries.
- It has limited scope for making people aware of the cultural change and social development.

PROBLEMS AND SUGGESTIONS FOR THE PROGRESS OF DISTANCE EDUCATION

- Need-based courses should be selected and imparted through distance education.
- The course material should properly be edited by the experts.
- Study materials should be prepared in regional languages.
- Printing of material should be well organized with reasonable quality.
- Study material should be dispatched in time.
- The response sheets or assignments sent by the students should be evaluated regularly.
- Personal contact programme should be held at regular intervals and at suitable centres (in all districts).
- Proper boarding and lodging arrangements should be made for outstationed students.
- Appropriate guidelines should be issued.
- Study centres should be suitably equipped with libraries and other facilities.
- Subject experts and experienced professors should be appointed to conduct the personal contact programmes.
- Electronic media should be used on a large scale and made available in most of the distance learning centres.
- Separate radio and television channels should be used for the use of distance education.
- The notion of second-rate education should be removed by strengthening face-to-face teaching in distance learning to gain full acceptance.
- The cost of distance education should be minimised and adequate practical training should be given wherever necessary.

CONCLUSION

Distance education is a new innovation in the process of imparting education. This system will be helpful to solve our educational problems and minimise the pressure of population over the traditional system of education. It is an alternative to formal education through which crores of people can get education and fulfil their dream of higher education. National policy on education (1986) states thus, "Distance education is a cherished goal of educational process. It pre-supposes universal literacy. Opportunities will be provided to the youth, housewives, agricultural and industrial workers, and professionals to continue the education of their choice at the pace suited to them. The future thrust will be in the direction of open and distance learning". Nobody denies that it is an effective media of life-long education, which is essential for the progress of our nation.

CHAPTER 53

HEALTH AND PHYSICAL EDUCATION

INTRODUCTION

Great attention should be paid to the study of health and physical education as an integral part of general education, because it is necessary for every individual to know and follow the rules of healthy living from the cradle to the grave. Health education is an integral part of general education and professional education. Aristotle has rightly remarked, "A sound mind in a sound body". This is true for all ages and all human beings. Regarding the importance of health, Ben Johnson has stated "O Health! Health! the blessings of the rich! The riches of the poor! who can buy thee at too dear a rate, since there is no enjoying this world without thee". Hall has very emphatically observed, "A ton of knowledge bought at the expense of an ounce of health which is the most ancient and precious form of wealth and worth costs more than its value". From these sayings, we may discern that the study of health as well as physical education is quite inevitable in the context of education in the emerging Indian society.

MEANING OF HEALTH

The word health first appeared in English (approximately in 1000 A.D.) as a means of referring to the quality of soundness and wholeness of the body in a very broad sense. However, the term has different meanings with different people. According to the old English term "Health is a condition of being hale, that is safe and sound". A physician defines it as the normal functioning of the body organs and systems. The Encyclopaedia of health states that "it is a state in which the individual is able to mobilize at his resources— intellectual, emotional and physical—for optimum daily living". In the words of J.F. Williams, "Health is the quality of life that enables an individual to live most and serve best". According to the World Health Organization (1947), "Health is a state of complete physical, mental and social well-being and not merely the absence of disease or infirmity".

MEANING OF HEALTH EDUCATION

Health education inculcates healthy habits among the students to make them healthy individuals from the physical and mental point of view. It maybe defined as education concerning the protection, preservation and promotion of health through self-care behaviour. In the words of Sophe, "Health Education is concerned with the health related behaviour of people. Therefore, it must take into account the forces that affect those behaviour, and the role of human behaviour in the promotion of health and the prevention of disease". As a profession, it uses educational process to effect change or to reinforce health practices of individuals, families, groups, organizations, communities and larger social systems. Its intent is the generation of health knowledge, the exploration of opinion for behaviour change, their consequences, the choice of the course of action open and acceptable to those affected. According to Dr. Thomas Wood, "Health education is the sum of experiences in school and elsewhere that favourably influence habits, attitudes and knowledge related to individual, community and racial health". In the words of Ruth E. Grout, "Health education is the translation of what is known about health into desirable individual and community behaviour patterns by means of the educational process". In other words, anything that educates anyone in the matter of health is health education. Thus, health education is the study of the good life of the individual and promoting and maintaining good community health.

OBJECTIVES OF HEALTH EDUCATION

The aim of health education is to engage people actively in programmes and services which are organized for the solution of health problems, that is, to help people learn to do things themselves for their own health improvement. According to WHO Expert Committee on Health education (1954), "Health education aims at creating such a quality of life as may enable an individual to live most and to serve best". The objective of health education is to lead the students in the knowledge and development of all the aspects of his personality that is to acquaint them about the ill effects of bad habits and to eradicate those habits. Health education is related to the balanced development of the personality of the individual which enables him to harmonise in the society in the right way and lead to social development and building up of the nation along with his individual development. We have different objectives of health education put forth by different health educationists.

Ruth E. Grout has laid down the following specific objectives of health education:

- Optimum development of the individual with special reference to physical and emotional development.
- Betterment of human relationships, particularly from the standpoint of health.
- Application of health facts and principles in respect of economic efficiency in the production and consumption of goods and services.
- Civic responsibility especially in respect to health.

Anderson has highlighted the following objectives for the physical, emotional and social health of the students:

- Examine the health of every boy and girl student.
- Understand the needs of students related to health and meet them.
- Know all the diseases and defects obstructing health and cure them.
- Make efforts to improve the health of every boy and girl student.
- Know the need, importance and advantages of good health.
- Develop the spirit of self respect among the students.
- Develop healthy dispositions among students.
- Give knowledge of First-Aid.
- Save the nearby environment from pollution.

C.E. Turner in his book, *UNESCO Source Book* stated the following objectives of health education.

- Maintain a healthy environment in the schools.
- Develop such habits which are good for health.
- Seek measures to safeguard from infectious diseases.
- Develop cooperation among school, home and society for attaining better health.
- Examine physical diseases and cure and prevent them.
- Develop knowledge and dispositions among students for their personal health.

GENERAL OBJECTIVES OF HEALTH EDUCATION IN SCHOOL

- Make the students realize the necessity of having good health.
- Provide information regarding health rules.
- Inculcate health habits among children.
- Provide skills concerning health, e.g., training in first aid/food preparation and care of a sick child.
- Enable the students to understand the educative value of sanitation, cleanliness and healthy living.
- Foster better human relationship in matters concerning health.
- Acquaint them with the cause and remedies of common diseases.
- Take interest in adopting new methods for the development of health.
- Have experience in democratic solutions of health problems in school, home and community.
- Enable the students physically, mentally and emotionally.

IMPORTANCE OF HEALTH EDUCATION

Three things are very necessary for a man to lead a meaningful life in the earth namely, health, wealth and education. Health is the basis for education and wealth. Without health nothing can be achieved by man and his existence in the society becomes futile. In fact, when health is absent, wisdom cannot reveal itself, art cannot manifest, science cannot develop, strength cannot fight, wealth becomes useless and intelligence cannot be applied. It is through health education that we can develop a healthy awareness and scientific attitude towards healthy life. It cannot be achieved by taking one or two pills everyday and by observing a few restrictions. But it is possible only by understanding what health is, on what it depends and then applying this knowledge in everyday life. The care of the body regarding food, cleanliness, exercise, rest and protection against disease are essential for the preservation of sound health. Health is life and life is for living. We cannot enjoy the fruits of joy, pleasure and freedom without health. Hence, optimum health is the right of every individual to keep him emotionally balanced when associated with people who hold different opinions. If an individual does not have good health and knowledge of health problems and the ways to cure or prevent them, his life becomes a burden to the society.

The child is like the clay that can be moulded and shaped in a desirable way to attain healthy habits and attitudes. Health programmes cannot be implemented without the help of a school. The efforts taken in school regarding health have a direct bearing on the community and whatever happens in it will have its effect on the school. This is because the students discuss with their parents, friends or relatives whatever they learn about health in school. In this way, health knowledge can be multiplied through schools, parents and community. At present, school is the only agency to impart health education. The headmaster or principal and teachers can provide a programme of health education to their students. This method enables the students to know the ways and means of maintaining good health. It is expected that many physical challenges such as those involving hearing, sight, posture and nutrition which develop during childhood can be prevented at large by intelligent health behaviour and development through health education.

PRINCIPLES OF HEALTH EDUCATION

Health education brings together the art and science of medicine, and principles and practice of general education. At present the programmes of health education have been organized on the basis of certain principles given below:

Principle of everyday living: Health education is concerned with everyday living as it affects the individual, his family and his community. It deals with the present and future health problems of the individual and those of the family of the pupil, the school, the community and the nation.

Principle of heredity and environment: Heredity and environment are equally important in determining the health of students. In spite of having the same type of food and environment in respect of playing, health is not the same for two individuals. Hence, health education should be provided on an individual basis.

Principle of needs of the people: Health education programmes should be related to the interest of people. The public does not like the health slogan like "be healthy" or "eat good food". Therefore, health education must find out the real health needs of the students.

Principle of individual difference: Health education programme of the school should be provided on an individual basis. This is because the same type of medical facilities is not suitable for all the students. Therefore, giving individual attention to the health of boy and girl students is required in order to make the health programmes meaningful and powerful.

Principle of participation: The participation of physicians, visitors, ENT specialists, dentists and physical education teachers should be necessary. As we are now living in an age of specialisation, we need physicians to proceed with the health programmes smoothly.

Principle of cooperation and direction: In order to make the health education programme powerful and meaningful, there should be cooperation between the school and home. The officials of the school should be aware of health education so that they are able to direct the health programmes effectively.

Principle of objective information: Health education is based on objective information about the pupils' health status, physical and mental attitudes, knowledge and interests based on their needs.

Principle of a five pronged attack: Health education attempts to improve mental and physical health of the students, erase the pseudo information and misconceptions, promote health practices and healthy attitudes. Such attitudes applied in everyday life can strengthen the individual's health and stimulate interest in health education.

Principle of teacher's enthusiasm and interest: Success of health education programmes depends on the teacher's enthusiasm and interest. Health education cannot accomplish its purpose unless the instructor is interested in it.

Principle of specific facts: This principle indicates that health education deals with specific facts based on the results of experimentation, research and conclusion of various branches of science, medicine, dentistry, public health, nursing, nutrition and pharmacy. It provides reliable factual evidence such as relation between smoking and lung cancer so that the students can have a positive opinion.

METHODS FOR IMPARTING HEALTH EDUCATION

Personal cleanliness: The daily morning inspection of the cleanliness of the students should be undertaken by the teacher. This is very helpful in enforcing personal cleanliness.

Consuming fresh air: The need of fresh air should be stressed especially while sleeping. The students should be advised not to cover their mouth at night. They should also be taught to breathe through their noses.

Training in first-aid: The students should be provided training in first aid habits. This will enable them to give immediate attention to cuts and bruises.

Vaccination and inoculation: Precautionary measures should be suggested at the time of epidemics, so that people can be vaccinated and inoculated.

Hygienic feeding: The students should be taught to take the right type of food in a suitable quantity. They should be asked to avoid overeating and eating sour food, and advised to take plenty of water.

Suitable physical exercise: A number of physical activity programmes should exist in a school. The students may choose any activity of their interest.

Good classroom: The classroom should have proper facilities to accommodate the students who are admitted. It should have proper ventilation, furniture, light and air.

Better human relation in health matters: The child should be asked to make it a point to do his best for the betterment of the health of friends, relatives, neighbours and the whole community.

Medical inspection: Medical examination should be thorough and the follow- up action should be taken seriously.

Health education activities: Health project weeks maybe celebrated. Films, posters and audio-visual aids maybe used to impart health education. Health clubs maybe organized for this purpose.

TEACHER AND HEALTH EDUCATION

The main burden of the education of the students is on the teacher. He, therefore, plays a powerful role in taking care of the health of his students. In this regard, the job of the teacher is to develop the intellect of the students and provide them with knowledge pertaining to health. Hence, the teacher should pay attention to the health of the students right from the beginning. This is because the school environment is very important and suitable for the students in getting training to become ideal citizens. They should be taught to understand the diseases that spoil their health. It is the teacher who should play an important role by creating a healthy environment for a healthy life by paying attention to their seating arrangements, provision of air, water and light in the classroom. It is also the duty of the teacher to examine the unhealthy symptoms among the students and remove them. The following points help us discern the role of the teacher for the development of health education:

- Make in-depth surveys of the environment of all students relating to their physical, mental, emotional and social aspects.
- Provide them with lessons for keeping themselves healthy and clean.
- Get the health of the students examined by experienced physicians.
- Try to rectify the postural deformities among the students.
- Arrange recreational activities related to health and physical education among the students and society.

- Present his ideals relating to health education before the students.
- Make provision for mid-day meals for the students with a view to save them from the ill effects of malnutrition.
- Make efforts to safeguard the students against infectious diseases.
- Make proper lighting and fresh air arrangements in the classroom.
- Make proper arrangements for games and sports, food, accommodation and potable water in the school.
- Make the students healthy, periodical medical check-up and guidance should be provided.
- Make the students understand the problems related to health and to prevent or cure them with medical help.

PHYSICAL EDUCATION

The modern age is an age of space adventurism and technological giganticism that have made the human beings an active machine. Therefore, the modern thinkers in education emphasise that the best individual is one who is physically fit, mentally sound and sharp, emotionally balanced and socially well adjusted. In fact, every individual should have all the necessary neuromuscular mechanisms that enable him to run, walk, throw, bend, manipulate fingers, swing a stick, swim in a river or climb mountains. It is physical education which prepares and develops the individual to act so. That is why, physical education is considered as an integral part of total education which enhances and integrates the physical, social and psychological aspects of an individual's life through direct physical activity. Physical education refers to an educational process concerned with activities which develop and maintain the human body. It is education through physical activities for the development of the total personality of the child to its fulfilment and perfection in body, mind and spirit. In other words, it includes all forms of physical activities and games which promote the development of the body and mind.

DEFINITIONS OF PHYSICAL EDUCATION

The term "physical education" has been defined by different educationists in different ways in different times.

Charles A. Bucher: "Physical education is an integral part of total education process, is a field of endeavour which has its aim the development of physically, mentally, emotionally and socially fit citizens through the medium of physical activities which have been selected with a view to realizing these outcomes".

A.R. Wayman: "Physical education is that phase of education which has to do with the development and training of the whole individual through physical activities".

Nixon and Cozen: "Physical education should be defined as that phase of the whole process of education which is concerned with vigorous muscular activities and related responses and with the modifications in the individual resultant from these responses".

D. Obertcuffer: "Physical education is the sum of those experiences which come to the individual through movements".

J.B. Nash: "Physical education is that phase of the whole field of education that deals with big muscles activity and their related response.

Brown Hill and Hagman: "The accumulation of wholesome experiences through participation in large muscles activities that promote optimum growth and development".

Ministry of Education: "It is education through physical activities for the development of the total personality of the child to its fullness and perfection in body, mind and spirit".

R. Cassidy: "Physical education is the sum of changes in the individual caused by experiences centred in motor activity".

Secondary Education Commission: Physical education is an indispensable part of all health programme. Its various activities should be so planned as to develop the physical and mental health of the students, cultivate recreational interests and skills and promote the spirit of teamwork, sportsmanship and respect for others. Physical education is, therefore, much more than mere drill or a series of regulated exercises. It includes all forms of physical activities and games which promoted the development of the body and mind".

Indian Education Commission: "Physical education contributes not only physical fitness but also physical efficiency, mental alertness and the development of certain qualities like perseverance, team spirit, leadership, obedience to rules, moderation in victory and balance in defeat".

NEED AND IMPORTANCE OF PHYSICAL EDUCATION

Physical education has been accepted as an integral part of education. In fact, it is that part of education which proceeds by means of, or predominantly, through physical activity; it is not a separate or partially related field. Its contribution can be more to the goals of general education than that of any other subject. Mahatma Gandhi has stated "By education, I mean, an all-round drawing out of the best in child and man—body, mind and spirit". It implies physical, mental and social development of the individual. It is proved that physical education plays an important role for the all-round development of the child. In the words of the renowned educationist Froebel, "If we wish to develop the whole being, we must exercise the whole human being". Swami Vivekananda has stressed on the importance of physical education as "what India needs today is not the Bhagavad-Gita but the football field". W.M. Rybun remarks, "We need in Indian education a general philosophy physical education. We need a conception of education in which physical education takes its rightful place in which its vital importance is recognized".

Our Secondary Education Commission 1952–1953 emphasized the importance of physical education as, "The physical welfare of the youth of the country should be one of the main concerns of the state. Any departure from the normal standards of physical well-being at this period of life may have serious consequences". The report of the Indian Education Commission said "Physical education is of the utmost importance for the physical abilities and skills, mental consciousness and some qualities related to the development of character". Physical education generates energy in the individual and gives boost to his self power. Such an education inspires the boy and girl students to become players par excellence.

From the given views we may point out the importance of physical education in the following manner:

Physical well-being: Regular physical exercises develop and maintain a healthy, well-functioning circulatory system and efficient functioning of the organic systems of the body. In fact, the sedentary worker is more prone to various diseases than the active one. Low back pain is much more prevalent in the sedentary persons than in the physically active.

Good health: Dr. Paul Dudley White has written, "Proper exercise is as essential to good health as eating and sleeping".

Control of obesity: Physical inactivity, overeating and excess weight are important reasons for obesity. Fat is more susceptible to thick bodies than the thin ones. It is physical activity that controls obesity and weight by consuming energy and burning calories.

Mental alertness: Physical fitness is closely related to the mental alertness of the child. It is true that a person's general potential for a given level of intelligence is increased or decreased with his degree of physical fitness.

Personal and social adjustment: Physical education enables the pupils in personal and social adjustment. Studies prove that boys having strength tend to be well-adjusted socially and psychologically and weak boys show tendencies in social difficulties, maladjustment and inferiority complex.

Healthy instinctive expression: Physical education offers opportunities for the healthy instinctive expression of original tendencies of human beings. For instance, the basic urge to kick, throw, jump or run is satisfied in football, volleyball and athletics.

Sportsmanship: Physical education provides ample opportunities for training in sportsmanship. Sportsmanship is that quality of honour that desires always to be courteous, fair and respectful. It is termed as players, spectators, coaches and school authorities.

Mental relaxation: Physical education as well as physical activities provide mental relaxation by keeping off the child's mind from worries and troubles and help in better concentration.

Adrenaline secretion: Emotional stress and strain are high during adolescence because of contractions in one's own thinking and the thinking of others. It develops anger or fear in youth causing more secretion of adrenalin. Physical education helps to get rid of these products through vigorous activity.

Development of character: Physical education class provides opportunities to discuss character education theory. It helps to develop the character of the pupils.

Good citizenship: Physical education produces good citizenship by inculcating the laws and rules of games to be obeyed and penalties imposed for any infringement of the rules.

Use of leisure: Physical education helps the child to utilise his surplus energy and make the best use of his leisure time. It prevents him from involving in anti-social activities.

Economic value: Physical education raises the economic value of people who participate in games and athletics. In fact, today many people make their living by teaching, coaching and taking part in physical activities. It increases one's efficiency in work and economic values.

Overall development: Physical education provides overall development such as intellectual, spiritual social, character, economic development. Thus, it develops the whole man.

Creativity: Physical education provides for leadership training, healthy expression and creativity.

SCOPE OF PHYSICAL EDUCATION

The scope of physical education is very wide and it is not limited to drill, games, sports and physical training. It is made of a deep study and is an important part of general education. However, the total physical education programme consists of the following aspects:

Service programme: It includes instructional programmes that provide each child with the minimum essential physical education.

Intramural programme: It is concerned with the provision of competitions for all students within the school. It provides opportunities to all students to develop skills in athletics and other games.

Extramural or inter-school programme: It includes the main aims and objectives of physical education, that is, physical training, physical culture, gymnastics, group games and sports according to the tendencies of the students and mass drill and folk dance.

AIMS OF PHYSICAL EDUCATION

The main aim of physical education is the physical, mental, emotional and social development of the students and to develop such qualities which may make them efficient citizens and enable them to lead a happy life and perform their duties in the right manner.

It is difficult to explain the aims of physical education because various physical educators have listed them differently.

According to J.F. Williams, "Physical education should aim to provide an opportunity for the individual to act in situations that are physically wholesome, mentally stimulating and satisfying and socially sound". "Physically wholesome", means that the activity given to the children must be good for them to produce physiological results of exercise, growth and development of the human body. "Mentally stimulating and satisfying" means that the activity must make the child think and give him satisfaction. "Socially sound" means that the activity should do service to the present society and to the future generation like truthfulness, honesty, loyalty and obedience which develop moral and social values.

According to Jackson R. Sermon, "The aim of physical education is to influence the experiences of persons to the extent that an individual within the limits of his capacity may be helped to adjust successfully in society to increase and improve his wants, and to develop the ability to satisfy his wants". The report of physical and recreational educational plan of Education Ministry states, "The aim of physical education must be to make every child physically, mentally and emotionally fit and also to develop in him such personal and social qualities as will help him to live happily with others and build him up as a good citizen".

Book Walter says, "The aim of physical education is the optimum development of physically, socially and mentally integrated and adjusted individuals through guided instruction and participation in selected body sports, rhythmic and gymnastic activities conducted according to social and hygienic standards".

Cowell and Schcahn have classified the aims of physical education into, six groups.

1. Development of organic power.
2. Development of the ability to maintain adaptive efforts.
3. Neuromuscular development.
4. Personal and social adjustment.
5. Intellectual development.
6. Emotional responsiveness.

J.B. Nash has listed four developmental aims of physical education. They are: (i) organic development; (ii) neuromuscular development; (iii) interpretive development and (iv) emotional development.

Wood and Cassidy have listed two general aims:

- Harmonious development during childhood which includes interest, capacities and abilities
- Harmonious development for useful adult life which includes interests, ideals and habits; seven specific objectives
  - Muscular growth
  - Organic Vigour
  - Nervous vitality
  - Good health habits
  - Correction of defects
  - Good health service
  - Supervision of mental hygiene.

American Association for health, physical education and recreation has listed the following objectives of physical education:

- Help children move in a skilled and effective manner in all selective activities in which they engage in the programme of physical education.
- Develop an understanding and appreciation of movements in children and youth, so that their life becomes meaningful.
- Develop an understanding and appreciation of certain scientific principles concerned with movements.
- Develop through games and sports better interpersonal relationships.
- Develop various organic systems of the body, so that they respond in a healthy way to the increased demand placed on them.

GENERAL OBJECTIVES OF PHYSICAL EDUCATION

- Development of the whole man—neither soul nor body, but the whole man.
- Balanced development of the individuality of the child.
- Conservation of health for the development of well-built bodies.
- Develop democratic, social and moral qualities in the child.
- Develop qualities like endurance, self-control, courage, cooperation, fellowship and leadership.
- Develop regular habits of exercise, play and health habits.
- Create physically, mentally and socially healthy citizens.
- Develop the feeling of dignity of labour among the students.
- Save the students from mental tensions and pressures, and use their leisure fruitfully.
- Train students by encouraging them to take part in games, sports and other physical activities.

PHYSICAL EDUCATION PROGRAMME

Before planning a programme of physical education, it is necessary to know the physical and psychological characteristics of children at different age levels.

Nursery Level: It is a period of growth. The child does not develop strength and his bones are soft. He can develop curvature easily. Psychologically he enjoys imitating or copying others. He wants a quick change in activities. He likes free play, he wants to jump, run and play hide and seek. He likes stories and songs with actions. Sex difference is insignificant.

Activities

Rhythmics: Motion stories, action songs, marching folk dances.

Mimetics: Elephant walk, bear walk, frog jump, bird hop, ox walk, crouch walk, lame dog.

Hunting games: Cat and mice, lion and sheep, circle ball, hide and seek.

Free play: Running, jumping, hopping, skipping, climbing and balancing.

Primary Level: It is a period of slow and steady physical growth. A child has a better control over his large muscles and soft bones. Psychologically, the child likes team games. Leadership responsibility is developed. Sex is significant.

Activities

Rhythmics: Action songs, marching, motion stories, social dances, singing games, light apparatus, drill like tipri, lezium.

Exercises: Calisthenics, flag drill, mass physical training with or without music, gymnastic,

Yoga exercises

Dancing: Folk dance, group singing, imitation.

Natural activities: Running, jumping, throwing, skipping, athletics, minor games, cub masters, blue birds, relay, swimming.

Middle School Level: It is a period during which the child wants group activities, develops leadership feeling and interests in competitions. He loves to play most of the time with increased muscular strength. Boys and girls want to have their own respective groups. They follow rules:

Activities

1. Competitive athletic skills, running, jumping, throwing and walking.
2. Games of low organization, minor games and relays.
3. Team sports: kabaddi, kho-kho, volleyball, football, basketball, hockey cricket and hunting games.
4. Yoga
5. Gymnastics
6. Folk dances
7. Swimming

High School Level

At this stage, students are matured physically. Girls pass through rapid growth. Some boys have rapid growth and others have little. Their hearts are capable of strenuous activities. Their interests are narrow and they have the tendency to specialise, self-confidence and strong hero worship and they are highly competitive. But girls have the liking for passive activities. There is a strong desire for the opposite sex.

Activities

Team games: Basketball, volleyball, football, softball, netball, kho-kho, kabaddi and wrestling.

Dual games: Tennis, table tennis, badminton, ring tennis, boxing, judo, lathi fight and daggar fight.

Individual activities: Athletics, weight lifting.

Sports: Cycling, canoeing, shooting, riding, skating, running, long jump, throwing, mountaineering and biking.

Rhythmic: Folk dances, group and individual dances.

Gymnastics, yoga
Aquatics: Swimming, diving, and life saving.
Boys scouting, girls guiding and NCC
Special activities: Demonstrations, ceremonial parades, singing the National Anthem, flag salutation, practical projects and citizenship training.
Outdoor activities: Excursions, tours and trips.

ROLE OF TEACHERS IN PHYSICAL EDUCATION

Teachers have an important role to play in the organization and management of physical education.

- The senior physical education teacher should be a member of the school committee.
- All teachers should extend their cooperation for the smooth organization and management of physical education.
- Teachers should discharge their duties and responsibilities in connec- tion with intramural competitions and annual athletic meet.
- Each teacher must see that students under his charge attend physical education classes regularly.
- Each teacher must try to encourage group competitions and individual competitions among students. He must ensure a healthy interaction and relationship among students of various classes.
- Teachers should participate and join in competitions meant for them in the annual athletic meet of the school. For example, field events, yogasans and musical chair.
- One teacher of the school may conduct the minimum programme of physical education.

ROLE OF PHYSICAL EDUCATION TEACHERS

- Physical education teachers are specialists in one particular physical educational activity. They should plan their activities very carefully in order to achieve the objectives of physical education.
- He should choose activities in keeping with the maturational level and interest of the students.
- He should allow students to explore and discover activities for themselves.
- He should organize indoor and outdoor activities, individual and group competitions, activities for boys and girls.
- Physical education teacher is the right person to identify the talented students and recommend them for their further education and achievement. He should maintain up-to-date records of individual talented students and help them to receive advance coaching and participate in various competitions.
- He should manage intramural and inter-school programmes by conducting inter-school athletic competitions in which highly skilled students participate. He should organize district competitions.
- He should help the headmaster to maintain order and discipline in the school by attending to punctuality, sincerity, regularity, cooperation, tolerance, sensitivity to others, problems and difficulties, discipline and gentleness of students through physical education programmes and show these behaviour in all walks of their school as well as social life.
- He should seek the cooperation and assistance of other teachers in organizing various programmes of physical education.

CONCLUSION

Health is the most important wealth of the people and power of the nation. This is so because the aim of life and education cannot be achieved until and unless health of the people is maintained. In fact, ignorance and negligence of health and physical education is the cause of many evils such as weakness, diseases, sloth, poverty, peaceless, tension and frustration. Health is basic to lead a happy life and it prepares the individual to involve in social, cultural, spiritual, political and economic activities. Swami Vivekananda, the champion of physical education, stresses the importance of such education. According to him, "Power is life and weakness is death". He, therefore, advises the youth to make their muscles iron and nerves steel. For this purpose, he recommends football playing instead of studying the Bhagavad-Gita. In his words "What India needs today is not the Bhagavad-Gita but the football field". As health is the cornerstone of all-round development and all activities of human beings, health and physical education should be taught and practised from the very childhood. And also it should be included in the curriculum as an integral part of education at all levels for the welfare of individuals and society.

CHAPTER 54

EQUALITIES IN EDUCATIONAL OPPORTUNITIES

INTRODUCTION

The inspiring concept of 'egalite', derived from the French Revolution, has been rightly enshrined in the constitution of democratic India. The survival and success of a democracy is based on the widest provision of educational facilities for all its members irrespective of caste, religion, creed, language, sex, location or economic status. It means that all children should be provided with uniform education and similar learning opportunities. Regarding the equalisation of educational opportunity, the report of the Indian Education commission (1964–1966) states, "One of the important social objectives of education is to equalise opportunity, enabling the backward or under-privileged classes and individuals to use education as a level for the improvement of their condition. Every society that values social justice and is anxious to improve the lot of the common man and cultivate all available talent must ensure progressive equality of opportunity to all sections of population. This is the only guarantee for the building up of an egalitarian and human society in which the exploitation of the weak will be minimized".

MEANING OF EQUALISATION OF EDUCATIONAL OPPORTUNITIES

Equal opportunity implies that the rich and the poor alike should have equal access to the educational system and programme without any hindrance. It means all material barriers should be removed. Caste, colour, creed, location or sex, should not put any check on an individual to pursue the course of education in accordance with his ability and aptitude. In short, equality in education means equalisation of individual differences among the learners.

New education policy of 1986 states, "Equality of educational opportu- nities means the provision of standard education from primary education to university education to all the students irrespective of caste, religion, creed, residence or sex, and providing opportunities for students to attain success in education".

According to Dr. S. Radhakrishnan, "Equality in education means providing educational opportunities to everyone to develop their innate potentialities to the maximum level". All children should be given the uniform education and similar learning opportunities.

NEED FOR THE EQUALISATION OF EDUCATIONAL OPPORTUNITIES

- Education is the birthright of every individual. So, it must be provided to all children regardless of caste, religion, region or sex.
- No child, who is physically and mentally fit, should be allowed to go uneducated on any excuse.
- Education is a social emancipation by which democracy establishes, maintains and protects the spirit of equality among its members.
- Equality in education is a must for the development of the innate potentialities of children belonging to all classes of people.
- Equality in education provides an opportunity to the children of lower classes and girls to receive education so that social justice is maintained.
- Equalisation of educational opportunities lays the foundation for the formation of an egalitarian society.
- To minimise the exploitation of the socially and economically disadvantaged people of the society.
- Education is considered as the third eye of human beings which removes poverty, ignorance, illiteracy and superstition.
- Equalisation of educational opportunity is required to improve the country economically, socially, politically and make it morally strong.
- Cent per cent literacy is essential for developing national integration and international understanding among the masses.

Every individual should get equal and suitable opportunity to cultivate his talent and receive education according to his needs, abilities and aptitudes. In fact, equalisation of educational opportunity is the basis of democracy.

CAUSES FOR INEQUALITY IN EDUCATION

There are many barriers in providing equalisation of educational opportunities in an underdeveloped country like India. The Indian Education Commission (1964–1966) has mentioned the following causes which are responsible for inequality in education.

Lack of educational facilities: There are many places and areas in our country where primary, secondary and higher educational institutions do not exist. At present there are glaring imbalances of educational development in different parts of our country. For example, the number of educational institutions and facilities are greater in Kerala than in Bihar.

Poverty of parents: Children from poor families fail to attend educational institutions where the cost of education is very high. This is also due to the poverty of the families. On the other hand, children from affluent families get all levels of education which they need. Thus, poverty of the parents is one of the major causes of inequality in educational opportunities. This critical situation is still prevalent in the Indian society.

Differences in the educational standards: Differences in the standards of schools and colleges lead to educational inequality. For instance, the standard of education of the urban educational institutions and the standard of education of the rural educational institutions are entirely different.

Differences in home environment: A child from a rural household or an urban slum having illiterate parents does not have the same opportunity which a child has from an upper class home with highly educated parents.

Disparity in education of boys and girls: There is a wide disparity between the education of boys and girls at all stages and in all sectors of education. The enrolment of the male students is higher than the enrolment of the female students at all levels of education. And the additional educational opportunities which are available for male students are not available for female students.

Disparities among the social status: This is another factor that leads to inequality of opportunity in education. Differences can be identified in educational and cognitive development of children belonging to upper castes, most backward classes and scheduled tribes.

High private cost of education: The costs of education required for textbooks, uniforms and co-curricular activities have increased very substantially in recent years and this amount is higher than that of the tuition fees. Therefore, parents have to incur a very heavy expenditure for educational purpose. This is one of the reasons for inequality in education.

Inequality in management: Many educational institutions are under the control of the Central Government, the State Government and private sectors. The education given in these institutions is not of the same type. According to the educationist Dr. K. Venkata Subramaniam, "In India there is education of Kerala, education of Maharashtra, education of Bengal, but there is no education of India".

Inequality within the state: The availability of educational opportunities is different from place to place within the state. For instance, educational facilities available in the district headquarters are not available for the children of the rural areas.

Economic disparities: The inequalities among the economic status of the people are reflected in the educational opportunities available to the children. For example, when the children of the rich people study in the public school in Delhi, the children of the poor people study in the government schools. This is because people think that quality of education in a public school is comparatively better.

METHODS OF EQUALISATION OF EDUCATIONAL OPPORTUNITIES

After the independence of our country, it has taken adequate steps for equalisation of educational opportunities. Let us list them here along with the role of the Central Government and the Government of Tamil Nadu in providing equality in educational opportunities.

Equality of education at primary stage: Primary education is the basic education of the child. It caters to the most fundamental needs of all men and women. Without this education, the individuals cannot qualify themselves for social life. Therefore, Article 45 of the constitution of India declares, "The State shall endeavour to provide . . . for free and compulsory education for all children until they complete the age of fourteen years". In order to provide equal opportunity to all children primary education has been made free, compulsory and universal. It has been decided that primary education should satisfy the basic universal needs of all men and women without any kind of discrimination.

Equality of education at secondary stage: Equality of education at secondary level is important for the survival of a democratic society like India. At the secondary level, equality of educational opportunity implies provision of diversified curricula to suit the different needs and interests of individuals. In fact, students differ from each other on the basis of their unique interests, abilities, and attitudes. Therefore, a good system of education should include a diversified course in order to meet the needs of different individuals.

Educational progress of SC/ST students: The inequalities in educational development among educationally backward communities have been minimised by special efforts. Teachers have a special role towards the education of the children of Scheduled Castes and Scheduled Tribes. They have a role to sensitise the parents and community members of the SC/ST to motivate them to educate their children. The school staff should seek, provide and ensure non-discrimination between the children of Scheduled Castes and Scheduled Tribes and other communities. Use of caste names while calling roll calls or naming children should be avoided. Teachers should lead all the children equally to participate in the curricular and co-curricular activities of the school. Frequent meetings between the staff, school teachers and parents of the children of Scheduled Castes and Scheduled Tribes should be arranged. It must impress them to continue the education of their children.

Equal opportunity of education to women: The National Policy on Education for women's equality states, "Education will be used as an agent of basic change in the status of women. The National Education System will play a positive, interventionists role in the empowerment of women. It will foster the development of new values through redesigned curricula, textbooks, the training and orientation of teachers, decision makers and administrators and the active involvement of educational institutions. Women's studies will be promoted as a part of various courses and educational institutions encouraged to take up active programmes to further women's development". The removal of women's illiteracy and obstacles inhibiting their access to, and retention in elementary education will receive priority through the provision of special support services. It is necessary to provide adequate attention to the education of girls at all stages for the purpose of ensuring national development, social justice and a healthy family life.

Equal opportunity of education to disabled children: Special provision should be made for the education of handicapped children. There are ten officially recognised categories of disabled children requiring special educational facilities—(i) children who are blind; (ii) Partially sighted; (iii) Deaf; (iv) Partially hearing; (v) Educationally abnormal; (vi) Epileptic; (vii) Maladjusted; (viii) Physically handicapped; (ix) Affected by Speech defects; and (x) Delicate. Special education is given to the disabled and gifted children in the modern days. Webster defines, Special as distinguished by some unusual quality, uncommon, not worthy, extraordinary, additional to regular, extra or employed for a certain purpose in addition to the ordinary, unless the disabled children get equal opportunities for education we cannot achieve our national goal. Therefore, the National Policy on Education (1986) states, "The objective should be to integrate the physically and mentally handicapped with the general community as equal partners, to prepare them for normal growth and to enable them to face life with courage and confidence". The education of children with motor handicaps and other mild handicaps will be common with that of others. Special schools with hostels will be provided for the severely handicapped children. Teachers' training programmes will be reoriented to deal with the handicapped children. Vocational training will be given to the disabled children. Voluntary effort for the education of the disabled will be encouraged in every possible manner.

Nationalisation: Nationalisation of all educational institutions is an important step to provide uniform educational facilities throughout the country.

Common school system: Equalisation of educational opportunity necessitates the adoption of a common school system in the primary and secondary stages. All children should rub shoulders with each other and they should be admitted regardless of their caste, religion, creed or language.

Removal of inequalities among the states: To bring about equality in education, inequalities in education among the states must be removed. For instance, Kerala allots more financial resources for education, whereas Bihar and Odisha allot less amount. The central government should remove such inequalities and allot special funds for the backward states.

Removing inequalities in rural and urban areas: More schools should be opened in rural areas, and quality education should be ensured in rural schools.

Fair and just admission: In order to equalise educational opportunities admission in educational institutions should be based on merit.

Free education: Free education should be given at all levels of education. This country should never lose the talented students just because they are unable to pay the tuition fees for education.

Reduction in other costs: Parents have to incur a heavy indirect expenditure on the education of their children. The indirect expenditure includes the costs incurred by parents on textbooks, uniforms and co-curricular activities. Therefore, free textbooks and uniforms at the primary stage should be given. A programme of book banks should be developed in secondary schools.

Scholarship: Government should provide financial assistance and scholarships to the poor, the talented and the intelligent students.

Compulsory education: Education should be compulsory for all children upto the higher secondary course.

Transport facilities: Adequate transport facilities maybe provided in rural areas so that students are encouraged to attend the educational institutions.

Education of the backward sections: The Education Commission has stressed, "The education of the backward classes in general and of the tribal people in particular is a major programme of equalization and of social and national integration".

Meeting the needs of slow learners: The average and dull students need individual attention, special remedial help and modified curriculum to suit their rate of learning. Guidance and counselling services have an important role to play in the education of such children.

Reservation of seats: In order to equalise educational opportunities, seats should be reserved for the Scheduled Caste and Scheduled Tribe students in schools, colleges and universities.

Higher professional education: At the stage of higher education and professional education, emphasis should be placed on individual capacity or merit and maintenance of quality and standard.

Correspondence education: Distance education can play a vital role in equalising educational opportunities. It makes education cheaper and will be convenient for those who cannot attend regular courses due to lack of finance, time and non-availability of educational institutions in rural areas.

ROLE OF CENTRAL GOVERNMENT IN EQUALISATION OF EDUCATIONAL OPPORTUNITIES

After independence, our government has been taking various efforts to provide equal opportunities in education. It has organized three important education commissions, two national education policies and various councils of teacher education for making education available to all children and improving the quality of education.

- Central Government is keen on providing free, compulsory and universal education to all children from 6 to 14 years.
- The Indian Education Commission recommended the implementation of the general pattern of education 10+2+3 throughout the country. Now this pattern of education has been implemented.

- The Indian Education Commission has recommended the opening of "common schools" to all children irrespective of caste, creed, community, religion, economic and political condition in order to achieve the national goal of equalisation of educational opportunities.
- Nowadays, schools have been opened for the talented rural children. One such vidyalaya has been set up in each district during the Seventh Five Year Plan. It has been opened to serve the objectives of excellence coupled with equity and social justice and provide opportunities to talented rural children from different parts of the country to live, and learn together as Indians breaking the traditional social, regional, and economic barriers.
- According to the new education policy, textbooks based on the uniform pattern of curriculum known as **core curriculum** are written and followed throughout the country.
- Non-formal education for the drop outs and "multiple-point entry" system enable the students to pursue their education. This kind of education has been emphasised by the government so as to reduce the inequalities found in educational opportunities.
- The government opens more and more schools, colleges, and universities to provide easy access to all children in getting education. Steps are taken to open primary schools at least within two kilometers in each village.

ROLE OF NATIONAL POLICY ON EDUCATION (1986) IN EQUALISATION OF EDUCATIONAL OPPORTUNITIES

- The National Policy of Education (1986) calls for providing equality of educational opportunities to all in terms of access as well as in the conditions for success.
- Special attention will be given to the participation of women in general, vocational, technical and professional education.
- Special emphasis will be given on the education of Scheduled Caste and Scheduled Tribe children at all stages and all levels in all areas and dimensions.
- For the education of SC and ST children, incentives should be given to them at all stages of education.
- Adequate facilities should be provided in unreserved, rural, hilly, remote and inaccessible areas.
- Minority communities should be allowed to set up and administer their own educational institutions.
- Education of handicapped children should receive due attention. The education of children with motor handicaps and other mild handicaps should be the same as that of others. Special schools with hostel facilities should be provided at district headquarters for the severely handicapped children. The objective should be to integrate the physically and mentally handicapped with the general community as equal partners, to prepare them for normal growth and enable them to face life with courage and confidence.

EQUALITY OF EDUCATIONAL OPPORTUNITIES IN TAMIL NADU

Systematic and concrete steps are being taken by the government of Tamil Nadu to expand the equalisation of educational opportunities:

Uniform standard of education: Government schools are opened in each village throughout Tamil Nadu to maintain the uniform standard in education. Government arts colleges have been opened at least in each district. The Government of Tamil Nadu has been publishing uniform textbooks from the first standard to the twelfth standard.

Improvement of women's education: There are government schools, higher secondary schools and colleges exclusively for women to improve women's education. Colleges in rural areas have been instructed to admit 10 per cent women students in men's college where there is no college for women. Mother Teresa University for Women has been started at Kodaikanal in order to improve the educational status of women. The government of Tamil Nadu has ordered to appoint only women teachers in all the primary schools upto the fifth standard. Moreover, in order to encourage women's education, the government has sanctioned Rs. 5000 for the marriage of the poor women who have completed the eighth standard.

Removal of the economic barriers: Free education is given to the children belonging to de-notified tribe, most backward class and the disadvantaged groups. Tuition fees and examination fees are not collected from them. Separate hostels have been constructed for their free stay. The differences due to poverty are eliminated through schemes such as uniform, scholarship and mid-day meals. Free bus pass facility is available to all the students upto the twelfth standard.

Removal of the community and caste barriers: Seats are allotted for the students belonging to backward class, de-notified tribes, Scheduled Caste and Scheduled Tribes in the universities, colleges, technical colleges and medical colleges in Tamil Nadu. Talented students of these communities are coming to the forefront through their education. Coaching and training classes are conducted free of cost for these students for the union public service examinations.

Equal opportunity for the physically handicapped: Special schools are functioning in Tamil Nadu for providing education to the physically handicapped children. Seats are also reserved for the physically handicapped students in both education and employment. Besides, government financial assistance such as loans and scholarships are available for them.

CONCLUSION

Equalisation of educational opportunities is a social justice. So, it is the responsibility of the government to provide uniform educational opportunities to all its citizens. Equalisation of educational opportunities is a long, social journey, which is very essential for national integration, international understanding and socio-economic development of every citizen of the country. Hence, in this journey, the state and central governments should go hand-in-hand to reach the destination, which is far away.

CHAPTER 55

EDUCATION FOR NATIONAL INTEGRATION

INTRODUCTION

National integration is a powerful feeling of 'oneness' which should be sown like seeds in the hearts and minds of people to sprout and grow into "One nation", "One people" as branchless trees. In other words, though we are stratified by caste, creed, religion, region, language, politics and other socio-economic aspects, we have to unite and bind ourselves together by a powerful feeling of "We are One—Indians and Live for India—our Nation". India is a very vast democratic country with many sided diversities. This is because she touches the countries like China, Russia, Pakistan, Tibet and Burma. The people of these countries have diverse customs and traditions. They speak different languages which have their own beauty, style and traditions. They believe in different religious faiths and ideas. In fact, India is a country of many races, religions, politics, castes, community, languages and ethnicity. Indian philosophers and saints recognised the blessing of this diversity and tried to unite Indians in one nation, keeping intact the character of diversity. Thus, from the earliest times it has been recognised by all that the cultural traditions of our country is characterised by unity in diversity. Pandit Jawaharlal Nehru remarked, "Like the ocean so received the tribute of thousand rivers, and though she was disturbed often by storms ranged over the surface of her waters, the sea continued to be the sea. It is astonishing to note how India continued successfully this process and assimilation and adoptions. It could only have done so if the idea fundamental unity were so deep rooted as to be accepted even by the new corner and if her culture were flexible and adoptable to changing conditions".

Thus, there has always been diversity of thought, action and outlook among our people. As a consequence of these diversities, we are facing the challenges of communalism, narrowism, casteism, provincialism and linguism. Therefore, after independence national integration has become a problem for us. Nehru pointed out, "Political integration has already taken place to some extent, but what I am after is something much deeper than that —an emotional integration of Indian people so that we might be welded into one nation and into one strong national unit maintaining at some time all our wonderful diversity". National integration is one of the important tasks that India has after independence. In fact, our free democratic country depends on the unity and strength of our country. But India is still faced with many disintegrating forces and narrow loyalties which have posed a major threat to our national solidarity. Moreover, the foundation of national life is common citizenship, unity in diversity, freedom of religion, secularism, equality, justice and fraternity among all communities. This foundation can be laid only through education.

MEANING OF NATIONAL INTEGRATION

National integration means national unity, that is unity in diversity. The expression "national integration" consists of two words—'national' and 'integration'. The word 'National' implies a country. The word integration means the fusion of the people into one. Thus, national integration means unifying all the forces in the country so as to produce the idea of "One Nation". It also implies social, political, economic, linguistic and cultural unity. It is the negation of all differences of caste, creed, religion, language, communities, beliefs, provinces and traditions. National integration is also known as **nationalism**. The protagonists of nationalism assert that the individual is for the nation and the nation is for the individual. Hence, every individual is duty bound to uphold the integrity and strength of his nation and offer his cooperation in its advancement. In short, nationalism means full-hearted devotion to the nation, sense of duty together with obligation and unquestioning faith in its glorious future based on its present well-being and prosperity.

DEFINITIONS OF NATIONAL INTEGRATION

Brubacher: "Nationalism ordinarily indicates a wider scope of loyalty than patriotism. In addition to ties of lace, nationalism is evidenced by such other factors as race, language, history, culture and traditions".

Humayun Kabir: "Nationalism is that which depends on we feelings towards the nation".

National Integration Conference 1961: "Nationalism or National Integration is a psychological and educational process involving the development of a feeling of unity, solidarity and cohesion in the hearts of the people, a sense of economic citizenship a feeling of loyalty to the nation".

Kothari Education Commission: "National Integration includes a confidence in Nation's future, a continuous rise in the standard of living, development of feeling of values and duties, a good and impartial administrative system and mutual understanding".

Dr. Bedi: "National integration means bringing about economic, social, cultural, and linguistic differences among various states in the country within tolerable range and imparting to the people a feeling of the oneness of India".

From the given definitions of nationalism or national integration, we can understand that national integration is the mental maturity of the people who can free themselves from the tendencies of partition, communal hatred and religious fanaticism. Such tendencies endanger the very foundation of national unity and commitment and involvement in the national unity and progress of the nations. In short, it is a feeling among the people to share certain aims and objectives, purposes and ideals, and giving them priority over minor sectional considerations. It means a feeling of oneness to pervade all the spheres, it may be religion, caste, language, colour, province, belief, dress, food, habits and economic variation. In the words of Pandit Jawaharlal Nehru, "We should not become parochial, narrow minded, provincial, communal and caste minded because we have a great mission to perform. Let us stand up right, with straight backs and look up at the skies, keeping our feet completely and firmly planted on the ground and bring about this synthesis of integration of the Indian people". Therefore we may define national integration thus "It is a feeling which unites the people of different cultures and prepare them to think and act for the oneness and progress of nation".

The following ideas come to our mind whenever we talk of national integration or nationalism:

- A feeling of brotherhood in the minds of the people.
- A feeling of oneness though people differ in all spheres of life.
- A feeling of cohesion.
- A feeling of harmony in thoughts and actions.
- A feeling of loyalty to the country.
- A feeling of solidarity.
- A feeling of patriotism.
- A feeling of unity of the country.
- A feeling of tolerance with others ideas and beliefs.
- A feeling of 'we' and 'I'.

NATIONAL INTEGRATION AND EMOTIONAL INTEGRATION

National integration is not possible without emotional integration. In fact, emotional integration is the basis of national integration. Practically, there is a close relationship between emotional integration and national integration. Generally, these two terms are treated as a single term. But both emotional integration and national integration differ in meaning.

National integration: It is a psychological and emotional process involving the development of a feeling of unity, solidarity and cohesion in the hearts of the people, a sense of common citizenship and a feeling of loyalty to the nation. It includes social, political, economic, linguistic and cultural unity.

Emotional integration: It means the unity of thoughts and feelings of all the citizens of a country or nation. It prepares the people mentally for national integration. It also prepares a line of defence for national integration in the minds and hearts of the people. It leads nationalism to national pride, national loyalty and national welfare. Emotional integration in an individual means a completely satisfied personality whose personality, urges, aspirations and emotions are sufficiently sublimated and directed towards healthy and fruitful channels, and who should have been sufficiently trained in the creed of temperance and toleration.

MEANING OF EMOTIONAL INTEGRATION

Emotional integration is a feeling which ties into one whole all the diverse caste, creeds and various groups of persons by raising them above narrow differences and divisions. It may imply several things like emotional integration of personality of an individual, family emotional integration, caste emotional integration, linguistic emotional integration, regional emotional integration and national emotional integration. Pandit Jawaharlal Nehru had emphasised the emotional integration for bringing about national integration. He says, "By emotional integration, I mean the integration of our minds and hearts, the suppression of feeling of separation". Thus, emotional integration is a feeling among people to share certain common objectives, purposes or ideals and give them higher places. It is a feeling of oneness which transcends all groups of cultural differences and synthesizes the different religions, castes and linguistic communities, into a compact one. The Emotional Integration Committee (May 1961) under the Chairmanship of Dr. Sampurnanand explains, "The composite structure of Indian culture and the need to prepare unity and diversity by cherishing and respecting equally the various cultural stands which enrich Indian civilization".

The terms of reference are as follows:

- To study the role of education in considering and promoting the process of emotional integration in national life and to examine the operation of tendencies which come in the way of their development.
- In the light of such a study to advise on the positive educational programmes for youth in general and students in schools and colleges in particular to strengthen in them the process of emotional integration.

NEED FOR NATIONAL INTEGRATION

India is a land of diverse castes, races, religions, politics, languages, cultures, faiths, customs and traditions. As a result, the integrity of our nation is in danger. In the words of the emotional integration committee, "One of the hardest problems before us today is the building up of a national mind by curbing the religious, linguistic and communal conflicts which tend to disunite us". Jawaharlal Nehru observed that national integration would weld Indian people into one and make India into "one strong national unit maintaining at the same time all our wonderful diversity". According to Dr. Kanungo, "Every country at every time needs national integration but India needs it most". This means that there is a unity in the country in all the matters. The need for unity is not only at the time of wars but it is needed at all the times so that it makes the people to get knowledge of social and cultural situations of the country, to eradicate the evils prevalent in the country. In fact, the success of a nation entirely depends on the extent of the development of a feeling of nationalism in its citizens.

Develop national character: The present society shifts from the spiritual to the material world where there is a lack of national character. It is true in the scientific and technological age that people seek short routes to become rich and make life happy and comfortable. Man mars his values in individual and social life. Corruption, has become an integral part of people's life. We have sold our honesty for money. We are ready to engage in any evil deed in order to satisfy our needs and desires which may work against freedom. Democratic values and national interests are sacrificed for the sake of a meal. At this juncture, it is very essential to build the national character in the child in order to make the nation powerful. In the absence of the feeling of nationalism or national integration, national character cannot be formed among the people.

Protect from foreign aggression: The clouds of war are threatening and hovering over India in the form of Pakistan, China or from any part of the world. Globalization and liberalization create tensions and economic dangers at the international level. National integration is vital for India's survival especially at a time when the country is under the perpetual threat of foreign aggression, as well as the internal centrifugal forces of regionalism, communalism, linguism, racialism and politicalism.

Bring unity in diversity: Every country requires national integration to bring about unity in diversity but, India needs it most. Stressing on the need for national integration, Nityanand Kanungo says, "National unity is essential for any country at any time. It is doubly so far India in view of varied compositions of her population the vast distances that separate her different parts, the vastly varying climate, and physical features that condition the daily lives and occupations of the people and above all, because of the period of rapid change—social, political, economic and technological—through which she is passing to discover her bearings in the modern world".

Hold democracy: National integration is the basic foundation for democracy. In fact, our free democratic country depends on the unity and strength of our country. Dr. C.D. Deshmukh says,

"National integration is the prerequisite for the fulfilment of our democracy". Otherwise, the fissiparous tendencies in the country may lead to serious consequences. Our democracy will disappear and decay if there is no nationalism or national integration.

Face the present challenges: National integration is quite inevitable to face the increasing social economic and external challenges in the present times. A nation is a nation because its people passionately and unanimously believe themselves to be so. Therefore, national unity must be maintained at all cost. Once Jawaharlal Nehru remarked, "The time has surely come when every Indian must look within and ask for himself whether he is with the nation or with a particular group". This is the challenge of our time that every man, woman, and child come out of their shells to push back the aggression of the selfish forces.

Control narrow tendencies: National integration is a must to check the unprecedented growth of narrow tendencies like casteism, linguism, religionism, politicalism and provincialism. All these factors retard the very vitals of our nation. So, if we fail to control them, we will have to lose our freedom.

Create internal peace: National integration is essentially needed to maintain peace and harmony among the people of India. Internal peace and harmony enable them to lead a disciplined life and contribute actively and effectively to the democratic country.

Develop Indian culture: We all are one, though we live in different patterns and we speak different languages. We have our own literature. National integrity is essential to develop national culture, language and literature and promote them to the next generation through education. This type of cultural development and transformation is possible in the country only if there is national integration.

Economic progress: The rise and fall of a nation depends on the extent of the development of a feeling of national integration in its citizens. National integration fosters in the people of India the sense of duty the sense of service to the nation and the sense of sacrifice for the sake of the country. It also helps in the development of trade and industry which brings economic efficiency among the people. Internal peace creates an atmosphere for saving, investment and employment which are the backbone of economic progress.

Establish world peace: India is to contribute to the establishment of world peace through its ideal of "unity in diversity". Establishment of world peace is impossible unless a country enjoys the fruit of national integration. In fact, national integration is necessary for a country to contribute its role in the establishment of world peace.

Achieve scientific and technical progress: We need national integration to achieve a prestigious place in the field of science and technology at international level. Science and technology will develop only if there are national spirit, secularism, equality, justice and fraternity among all communities. These factors will improve the quality of the people towards intellectual and scientific thinking.

Achieve social progess: National integration is the only way by which broad mindedness can be developed among the people. National integration makes the country economically and socially strong and progressive. Moreover, national integration inculcates in the people of India a sense of duty, service and good culture, which makes the country socially strong.

OBSTACLES TO NATIONAL INTEGRATION

India is facing a number of problems after her independence. Attainment of national integration is one of the most important problems, for which she has been struggling with a number of obstacles that tend to undermine national unity and hamper national progress. Let us examine the fissiparous and separatist tendencies which impede our social and economic progress and national integration.

Provincialism: For the purpose of effective and smooth administration, our country has been divided into certain regions on the basis of languages. As a result, many provinces or regions or states have been formed like Punjab, Haryana, Maharashtra, Karnataka, Andhra Pradesh, Kerala, Tamil Nadu etc. It leads to the problem of interstate demarcation of boundaries, particularly, in newly created provinces. For example, dispute between Punjab and Haryana over Fazilka and Abohar, and between Maharashtra and Karnataka over Belgaum. An ugly tendency of forming senas to perpetuate the separatist tendencies is also causing a lot of anxiety. For instance, Lachit Sena in Assam and Shiv Sena in Maharashtra. Anti-North, anti-Hindi and anti-Brahman tendencies have been built up in Tamil Nadu. People think of themselves as Malayalis, Gujaratis, Marathis, Bengalis, Punjabis or Tamilians and they do not think themselves as Indians. Thus, provincialism is turned into extremism and terrorism which disintegrate the country.

Linguism: India is a land of many languages. There are about 18 regional languages spoken in this country with countless differences in dialects. Unfortunately, the provinces of Andhra Pradesh, Tamil Nadu, Odisha, Punjab, Maharashtra and Assam have been formed in the name of languages. Our national language is Hindi but people are not prepared to accept it at the intellectual level. The boards written in Hindi and Hindi movies are burnt in Tamil Nadu. In fact, most of the Tamil schools can tolerate English which is a foreign language but not Hindi which is a national language. There are some politically motivated persons in different parts of the country who obstruct the development of a national language which makes national unity real and effective. Thus, linguism retards our national integrity.

Casteism: This is another obstacle which curbs the unity of our nation. The people of India belong to different castes like the Brahmins, the Kshatriyas, the Vaishyas and the Sudras and a number of subcastes. People belonging to a particular caste think that they are superior to the people of other castes. Most of the elections in India are fought on caste-lines. In fact, political leaders are selected on the basis of either their religions or castes. Exploitation on the basis of caste is successful because people are illiterate and they only know their castes. The people who cast their votes in the name of caste fail to elect the right man to the right post. Therefore, undesirable as well as incapable persons capture the seats of power. It is dangerous for a democratic country. Casteism has become a chronic evil which plays a vital role in vitiating the integrity of our nation.

Communalism: India is a very vast democratic country. Its length is more than 2500 kms from the North to the South and its width is about 1500 kms from the East to the West. Its people belonging to different religions like the Hindus, the Muslims, the Sikhs, the Buddhists, the Christians and the Jains have lived together for many centuries. People belonging to a particular religion think that their religion is superior to all other religions. The existence of different religions becomes the cause of communal riots which engulf the lives of many people. Dr. A.L. Srivastava says, "Today the main problem of unity is, the adjustment of proper relationship between the Muslims and the non-Muslims". The history of India proves that many conflicts and riots burst out because of communalim. Terrorism in Punjab, Jammu and Kashmir, Andhra Pradesh, Bhagalpur, Kota, and the Babri Masjid–Ram Janmabhumi controversy are some examples of communal clashes. Political parties encourage such conflicts and exploit them for their advantage and political gain. Whitehead says, "There is no country in the world where religion plays a more important part in the daily life of the people than it does in India". Communalism affects our social progress and curbs national integration.

Classism: India's cultural tradition is the most ancient one in the world's history. It is a country of people of different castes. On the basis of occupations and income, people of our country have been stratified as forward class, backward class, most backward class, scheduled castes and scheduled Tribes. Such a classification was useful for the Government to take efforts in order to uplift the people who were economically backward. Now classism itself has become harmful to national integration. People belonging to the forward and backward classes agitate against the government for declaring them as backward and most backward class in order to obtain more economic benefits and employment opportunities. This tendency creates communal riots and political clashes which are against national integration.

Inequality: The structure of Indian society is not egalitarian and it is marked by socio-economic inequalities. Our late Prime Minister Mrs. Indira Gandhi remarked, "A serious danger to national integration and perhaps one of the great menaces is the persistence of inequality". In fact, inequality is found in educational, economic, political and social spheres. Socio-economic inequality widens the gap between the rich and the poor. Social discrimination against the minorities affects the internal peace of our country. Existence of inequality in the political, religions, economic and social spheres makes it difficult to build national integration. Though socialism has been declared as our coveted goal, no serious attempt has so far been made to alleviate these inequalities.

Political parties: The existence of different political parties is essential in a democratic country to create political consciousness among the masses to form the public opinion and to run the government efficiently. But the present political parties are not organized for the formation of a healthy government and the welfare of the nation. They are organized in the name of community, religion, language and province which are a serious threat to national integration. They always aim at propagating communalism, casteism, regionalism and linguism. They fail to foster the powerful feelings such as "one nation" and "one people" in the minds of the present citizens. The political parties started in the name of caste, or religion seriously disrupt other castes and religions and create communal riots or political clashes for their benefit. Thus, political parties are acting against national integration.

Unemployment: Unemployment among the intelligentsia blunts the feeling of national integration. It develops disappointment, frustration, conflict and tension. The educated, but unemployed youth becomes easy victims to anti- social and anti-national ideas and activities. At present unemployment has become a cause of the evils of restlessness, characterlessness, corruption and suicide among the educated lads. Unemployed engineers, teachers and graduates become a burden to their families as well as to the society. They pollute the glory of our country by their evil deeds, and there will be no national feeling and national integration. A frustrated youth is the country's worst enemy. Thus, national integration becomes a meaningless concept in the minds of the unemployed youth who look to God for bread.

Economic disparities: India is one of the under developed countries of the world where more than one third of the population live below the poverty line. Such people have to work hard for their daily needs. Therefore, national unity or national integration is meaningless for them. Inequality in the distribution of wealth, unemployment and the size of the family force majority of the people into poverty and widen the gap between the haves and the have-nots. It becomes a threat to national integration and it can be removed to some extent through proper planning.

Social disparities: There are various religious groups like the Hindus, the Muslims, the Christians, the Sikhs, the Jains and the Buddhists in our country. Every religion has its own customs, traditions, and modes of behaviour. As a result, we have different and distinct customs, traditions and modes of behaviour. Such discrepancies lead to conflicts in the social life which adversely affect our national consciousness and ultimately national integration.

Lack of social sense: In modern India, it is difficult to find social feeling among the present generation which is an obstacle to national integration. Prof. V.R. Taneja remarks, "It is unfortunate that in this country, we lack, what may be called, social sense". We are self-centred and do not realise that we have duties to discharge for the welfare of the society. Naturally, we insist on 'I' instead of 'We' and develop narrow-mindedness which is harmful to national integration.

Lack of leadership: National integration is impossible unless social, political and religious leaders develop broad-mindedness. They should be above narrow selfish interests and understand their responsibilities towards the nation and its progress and prosperity. The leadership at the lower level in our country fosters the feeling of casteism, communalism, provincialism and linguism, among the masses, which vitiate national integration. Good leadership is essential for an efficient working of the democracy which depends on the unity and strength of our country. It is regrettable that most of our present leadership aims at self-development and ignores national development and national integration.

Lack of national character: When wealth and health are lost, we lose something but when the character is lost we lose everything. Character determines the quality and value of an individual. In the scientific world, we do not have anything as character. At every step, destructive tendencies such as corruption, dishonesty, adulteration, prostitution, bribery, black marketing, betraying of trust, treachery and smuggling are rampant in social, political and spiritual lives. Educational institutions are no exemption to this. Thus, lack of character has become a great obstacle to national integration.

Foreign languages: Importance of English, German and French and their rich literature encourage some people to adopt any one of these languages as the medium of instruction and expression which has resulted in the disintegration of people. In fact, the people who have a longing for English have a different character which keeps them away from the people whose medium of instruction is an Indian language. English language widens the gap between the educated and the uneducated people. Those who are educated through the English medium think themselves superior. This tendency is not good for national integration.

Defective education system: Education is the most important means of developing national integration. It is a sad fact that our system of education has no such vision and it has not done anything practically. Our late Prime Minister Mrs. Indira Gandhi rightly stated on January 1979 in Gandhigram, "One of the biggest mistakes we made when we gained independence was not to have overhauled thoroughly our educational system and structure, we are paying for it now". In fact, our educational system has not been linked with the national life and fulfilled our needs and aspirations. Kothari Commission remarks, "Instead of promoting social and national integration and making an active effort to promote national consciousness, several features of the educational system promote diverse tendencies". Thus, the lack of vision in education has been against the national interest of one country.

EDUCATION FOR NATIONAL INTEGRATION

The unity of our nation is passing through a crisis due to the disintegrating factors such as casteism, communalism, classism, religionism, provincialism, politicalism, linguism, economic and social disparities and unemployment. Unless we overcome these disintegrating forces, we cannot find the integrity of our nation. The rise or fall of a nation depends on the extent of the development of a feeling of nationalism in its citizens. Hence, the feeling of nationalism should be developed and strengthened in every individual by all possible ways and means. Education is the most powerful and effective means to carry out this great task successfully. World history proves that Sparta, Germany, Italy, Russia, China and Japan shaped their education in such a way that those nations have become powerful in the world. In modern times, Russia and China inculcate communism in the children's mind so as to make them to be dynamic and fanatic devotees of communism.

Education for national integration means using education as a powerful instrument to inspire a sense of love and devotion in the hearts of young boys and girls towards their country. Dr. K.L. Shrimali writes, "The process of national integration must continue and be strengthened, if we are to preserve and enrich our hard-won freedom". Education is the only effective process, through which the seeds of unity can be sown in the beginning so that we can slowly overcome all obstacles which threaten the unity of our nation. In the words of Dr. S. Radhakrishnan, "National integration cannot be built by bricks and mortar, it cannot be built by chisel and hammer, it has to grow silently in the minds and hearts of men. The only process is the process of education".

Objectives of Education for National Integration

- Foster the emotionally integrated personality of the child.
- Develop the spirit of sacrifice and tolerance among the students.
- Make the students realise the importance of unity in diversity.
- Make the students realise that they have duties and responsi- bilities for the progress of the country.
- Acquaint the students with the different aspects of our culture.
- Encourage the students to involve in those activities which develop national integration.
- Inculcate democratic values like equality, sympathy, fellow feeling and faith in change.
- Inspire the sense of love and devotion towards one's country.
- Develop patriotism and nationalism by teaching about our great leaders.
- Develop democratic citizenship and leadership qualities in the students.

Role of Education in National Integration

Each nation formulates its aim of education and organizes its educational structure according to its own needs and requirements and with the definite goal of developing the feeling of national integration in its citizens. Education plays a very significant role in India to bring about unity in diversity.

National system of education: We must have a national system of education to bring educational uniformity which plays an important role in establishing integration in the country. Unfortunately, unreasonable diversities exist in the system of education in different states. This is because education is a state subject. Effective coordination between the Centre and the states is needed to evolve an effective national policy of education. Kothari Commission had the same view that national integration cannot become a reality unless the arrangements are made to provide uniform education throughout the country. Therefore, the Government has announced 10+2+3 system of education in order to develop national integration in the country. Prime Minister Rajiv Gandhi was in favour of introducing uniform educational system in the country to produce national integration. The uniform educational system can solve the problems concerning admission, recognition of institutions, scholarships and other problems.

Re-designing curriculum: Curriculum is the means to achieve the aim of our nation. It includes all those knowledge, experiences and activities which a child acquires in school, classroom, library, laboratory, playground and study tour. Therefore, curriculum should be redesigned in such a way that it should include various subjects and activities to promote national integration. The school and college curriculum should be reoriented to suit the needs of a secular state which aims at national integration.

Primary level: At the primary stage, stories, poems folklores, social studies, national anthem and other national songs should be taught to develop a sense of love and devotion towards the country. Daily morning prayer has been recommended.

Secondary level: At the secondary stage, language, and literature, social studies, moral and religious and co-curricular activities are included in the curriculum.

University level: At the university level, social sciences, languages and literature, culture and art, and the exchange of teachers and students have been emphasised to develop national integration.

Re-designing textbooks: Textbooks should be re-designed at the national level. Textbooks on important subjects like history, geography, social studies, civics and languages should lead the students to appreciate the historical, social, economic, cultural, religious and linguistic solidarity of the people of this land of scholars and poets, saints and seers, warriors and benevolent rulers, scientists, artists, leaders and peace lovers. The materials which obstruct national integration should be removed and the materials which foster national integration should be incorporated. All textbooks should be nationalised. In the preparation of textbooks, special care has to be taken to see that the facts are not misinterpreted, distorted, or exaggerated to cause prejudice and national disintegration.

Teaching of social sciences: Social sciences include the study of geography, history, civics and economics. The subject history should be reorganized and reoriented in such a way that the facts included in it should foster national integration. Special importance should be given to the histories of Ashoka, Akbar, Guru Nanak, Mahatma Gandhi, and Swami Vivekananda as they worked for the welfare of the humanity at large. History of freedom fighters and national freedom movements should be emphasised and little importance should be paid to the study of historical men like Hitler, Mohammed Ghazini, Zia-ul-Haq and Mussolini. Through the study of geography, we come to understand the interdependence of people of one area upon the other. For example, we depend on Bengal, Bihar and Odisha for their mineral resources and we rely on Punjab, Haryana and Uttar Pradesh for food grains. The knowledge of geography makes us conversant with the lifestyles of people inhabiting different areas. The interdependence of one area upon the other helps the students to realise the importance and necessity of national integration. Teaching of civics inculcates a sense of duty and responsibility to the nation by which national integration is strengthened. Teaching of economics makes the students to realize that the economic development of the nation depends on her states' interdependence and cooperation.

Teaching of mathematics and science: The study of mathematics leads to exactitude of mind, which is vital for national integration. This is because no person with a sane mind will think of disruption, diversion and disintegration.

Similarly, the study of science takes us away from narrow-mindedness which disintegrates the unity of the nation. Knowledge of science, on the other hand, opens our inner eyes and broadens our intellectual thinking which will not stand against national integration. Scientific knowledge which led to the nuclear explosions in Hiroshima and Nagasaki during the World War II, should be quoted as examples to avoid destruction.

Teaching of languages: Students should be taught and encouraged to learn as many languages as possible. This will strengthen the unity of our nation. Learning of many languages keeps the students above narrow-mindedness. In the words of Mr. C. Chugla, "In India there are different languages and each language is rich and full of potentialities for development and that knowledge of different languages was essential for national integration and consolidation of national unity". Therefore, every Indian language should be given adequate freedom to develop in order to avoid misconception and to promote national integration.

Teaching of art, literature and music: The role of art, literature and music cannot be under estimated in the development of national consciousness and national integration. Art, literature and music broaden our outlook and remove narrowism. Jawaharlal Nehru remarks, "Art Galleries and Museums in a great city are like windows which look out in the broader, richer and deeper things of life". Literature is an important means of national integration. It is a mirror which tells the story of the rise and fall of the society. Literature possesses the power not found in the common sword or bomb shots. It is the expression of a nation's mind in writings imbued with patriotism. Emphasising upon the integrating qualities of literature, Dr. S. Radhakrishnan once indicated, "Literature works for togetherness, fellowship, love of neighbours and reconciliation of people. Compassion and mercy are the qualities exacted by literature, not hatred and oppression". Music is the means to develop emotional integration. Once a layman remarked "Though physically East and West Bengal have been separated, the part of both sides will feel one, as belonging to one community till the day Ravindra Sangeet is sung in the streets of Bengal". Today, Rabindranath Tagore's music is sung and enjoyed in the East and the West, in every nook and corner of the country, and it is not confined to Bengal alone.

Teaching of moral education: No religion in the world teaches violence and hatred. But our history stands testimony to the fact that more blood has been shed in the name of religion than anything else. So, appropriate religious and moral education should be provided to the students to inculcate moral character like tolerance, honesty and truthfulness. Religious harmony is especially necessary for multi-religious countries like India. Moral education should be included in the curriculum to develop national character, which is a must for national integration.

Adult education: Illiteracy and ignorance are the important forces in underdeveloped countries like India which weaken the unity of the nation. It is not possible to develop national integration when the adults are illiterate and ignorant. So, every adult should be given education. In fact, there should be cent per cent literacy among the adults to enable them to understand the need of national integration. Dr. V.K.R.V. Rao, says, "From the point of view of the either economic development or national integration or social cohesion or cultural advancement or preservation of democracy, it is essential that we should achieve 100 per cent literacy among our people". Therefore, adult education is essential and its programmes should be organized on the basis of national integration.

Medium of instruction: English should not be encouraged as a medium of instruction, because it widens the gap between the educated and the uneducated people. This is not good for national integration. So, regional languages should be made mediums of instruction at all stages of education. Our culture can effectively be transmitted through regional languages, which promote the feeling of national integration.

Role of Educational Institutions in National Integration

The destiny of India is being shaped in her classrooms. In fact, the aims of our life and nation are turned to the aims of our education, which are framed in the form of the curriculum. The curriculum includes all subjects and activities according to the aims of education, which are executed in school. Therefore, the role of the school is very important in bringing national integration. The school performs the following functions to shape the destiny of our nation and national integration.

Co-curricular activities: A number of co-curricular activities can be effectively organized in the school to promote national and emotional integration. These activities include common observance and celebration of festivals and events of national importance, sports, educational excursions, tours and picnics, military training like NCC, ACC, scouts and guides, students camps, debates, dramatics and youth festivals. These co-curricular activities help in the growth of a well-balanced and well-adjusted personality and create a group feeling of oneness and brotherhood, broaden the outlook and develop a catholicity of spirit and tolerance which are the basic foundations of national integration.

Special stress on social studies: For national integration, social subjects should be emphasised at all levels of education to impart knowledge of the geographical, historical and cultural background of the country. Books on social studies should include the history of the lives and works of the great men of India and of the world. They should also include the stories from the ancient books like the Ramayana and the Mahabharata.

Textbooks on history: It is the responsibility of the school to see whether books are prepared in a way to promote national integration. Schools should teach those facts which inculcate a feeling of nationalism in the students and avoid distortion or exaggeration to create prejudice. Textbooks used at primary levels should contain pictures and illustrations of great leaders so as to create interest in the child.

Language and scripts: Roman scripts maybe permitted in certain areas to enable the students to improve their acquaintance with Hindi. Throughout India the international numerals must be used. Hindi maybe learnt in the non-Hindi areas. Hindi books in the Roman scripts and dictionaries in Hindi—other languages, also in the Roman script maybe published in order to popularise the study of Hindi in non-Hindi areas. Hindi books maybe published in the regional languages and Hindi dictionaries should be encouraged. Hindi and English should be effectively taught at the university level to shun the creation of intellectual isolation. In short, Hindi should be taught in all schools throughout the country to strengthen the unity of the nation.

Uniforms: Common uniform for all the Indian school children is not necessary. To inculcate the feeling of unity and oneness, schools may have their own preference with regard to colour and pattern. Uniform system reduces the gap between the rich and the poor.

National days: Every school should celebrate the national days—January 26, August 15, September 5, October 2 and November 14 and give the— children lectures on the importance of these days to motivate their feeling towards their country. These days should be celebrated with the full participation of the teachers, the students and the community.

Birthday of greatmen: Birthdays of great men of this land should be celebrated. The celebration of the birthdays of Guru Nanak, Guru Govind Singh, Mahatma Gandhi, Sri. Naranaya Guru, K. Kamaraj (Chief Minister of Tamil Nadu), Pandit Jawaharlal Nehru, Swami Vivekananda, Radhakrishnan and Abdul Kalam help the young children to learn much from the lives of these great men. On this occasion great persons maybe invited to deliver lectures on our national and religious leaders and the students maybe asked to follow the lives of great men to become good citizens so that they may discharge their services to the unity and welfare of the nation.

Reverence for the national flag: The teachers and the students should respect the national flag. Students should be told the history of the national flag at the very earliest stage to show reverence for the national flag. The students and teachers should salute the flag out of deep respect.

National anthem: It is very important that all functions in the school should end with the singing of the national anthem. Students should be taught the meaning and importance of the national anthem. They should be taught to sing the national anthem in unison and behave in a disciplined way when they sing it.

National and patriotic songs: Patriotic songs of Mahakavi Bharathiyar, Bankim Chandra Chatterji and Rabindranath Tagore should be collected and sung on different occasions to express the feeling of oneness and the glory of our country. The students should be given training in schools to sing patriotic songs properly and meaningfully.

Special talks on the unity of nation: Special meetings should be held in the school assembly on different occasions; in which the speakers should be asked to give talks on topics developing the feeling of national and emotional integration and insisting on its need and importance in the present age.

Taking the national pledge: Students should be asked to take the pledge and repeat it twice a year dedicating themselves to serve their countrymen. A draft of the following pledge should be given to the children in English:

> *India is my country, all Indians are my brothers and sisters.*
> *I love my country and I am proud of its rich and varied heritage.*
> *I shall always strive to be worthy of it.*
> *I shall give my parents, teachers and all elders respect and treat everyone with courtesy.*
> *I shall be kind to animals.*
> *To my country and my people, I pledge my devotion. In their well-being and prosperity alone lies my happiness.*

This pledge inspires the students to develop a sense of love and devotion towards their country.

Celebration of festivals: Schools should celebrate the festivals of all important religions which makes the students happy and strengthens religious harmony. Celebrating Holi, Deepawali, Ramzan, Bakrid and Christmas in schools will bring different groups of students closer together and share their happiness with others.

Inter-state games: Planning of inter-state games leads to unity in diversity. Schools and colleges should organize such games once or twice a year so that regional feelings can be turned to national feeling.

Organizing camps: Students' camp in the name of NCC, NSS, Scouting, Girls guiding and social service should be organized to cut across states and regions and foster the feeling of brotherhood which is essential for national integration.

Open-air dramas: Open air dramas should be staged four times a year by every school. At least one or two plays should be based on themes of secularism and the history of our freedom fighters or the idea related to the importance of national integration.

Educational excursions: Educational tours should be organized to cut across narrow provincialism. The inter-state visits do much to acquaint both the teachers and the children with the different parts of the country. "With the change of place, we change our ideas, our opinions and feelings".

Admissions: Admission in schools, colleges, universities and other educational institutions should be made only on the basis of means and merits. Caste, religion and region should not be taken into consideration at the time of admission. It enables the educational institutions to admit the right students in the right course without racial or social discriminations.

Recognition of institutions: Recognition should be given to the educational institutions which are located in places where people are illiterate. It should not be given to institutions where divisive tendencies are encouraged.

Scholarships: Scholarships should be given to the students only on the basis of merit.

National greetings: The school should follow a common form of welcome or national greeting acceptable to all. The students should be trained to use suitable greetings like 'Jai Hind'. They should discard religious greetings as they suggest separation.

No inter-state restrictions: Domiciliary restrictions with regard to migration of students between one state and the other should be removed. Such a tendency encourages the students to conduct study tours to enhance their knowledge. Students of one state should be allowed to study in other states without any restriction. This will eliminate state feeling and develop national feeling.

Respecting national symbols: Next to the national flag and the national anthem, students should be trained in the schools to respect national symbols like the Taj Mahal, Ashok Chakra, Lotus, Tiger and Peacock.

All India award: Students should be asked to write poems, essays or stories about the importance of national integration. An all India award should be given for the best poem or essay.

Bulletin board: Good things from every religion should be written on the blackboard. Such a bulletin board should be placed in front of the assembly hall. It will bring religious harmony which is essential for national integration.

Setting up clubs: Clubs maybe organized on an inter-state basis, so that the children may correspond with each other on different topics of national importance.

Exchange of teachers and students: Exchange of teachers and students on the inter-state basis will bring about mutual understanding among the teachers and students of different states. It helps to understand the various cultures of different people and trains them to adjust with the environment.

Community living programmes: Schools should organize community living programmes to create social harmony among the students belonging to different religions, castes and regions. Community living in the school hostels provides opportunities to the students to live together eat together and share joys and sorrows together, which develops the spirit of national and emotional integration.

School projects: The schools may conduct several projects to promote national integration on topics like 'know your country' or 'analyse state wise literate and illiterate population', 'agricultural production in india', 'problems of population explosion' and 'environmental degradation'. When they undertake such projects, students may share the collection of information about all the states and union territories in India. Thus, projects improve their general knowledge of the country. Such a knowledge makes them to realise the need and importance of national integration.

School libraries: Library is the heart of education. So, the libraries of educational institutions should be strengthened with the right types of books. That is, only those books which inculcate the feeling of nationalism irrespective of religions, castes and regions should be kept in the library.

All India youth council: At the university and college levels, All India Youth Council should be set up to coordinate all the youth programmes taken up by the central and state governments. This activity strengthens the feeling of nationalism.

National science exhibitions: Every year students of different states should assemble and conduct science exhibitions. The birthdays of Indian scientists must be celebrated in schools. Special talks maybe given on the importance of national integration for scientific development.

Role of the Teacher in National Integration

A teacher should be the symbol of national unity because no programmes which create the feeling of national integration can succeed in educational institutions unless the teacher himself is above casteism, communalism, provincialism, politicalism and narrow mindedness. It is the responsibility of every teacher that he should play a vital role in developing the values of national integration among the students.

- Teachers should see national integration through their democratic behaviour, ways of thinking and doing things.
- The teachers should maintain the atmosphere of national unity in the school environment by presenting historical facts in an impartial and objective manner.
- Teachers should not discriminate against students on the basis of caste, colour, language, region and religion.
- They should be alert in checking the wrong tendencies of the students towards casteism, linguism, regionalism and narrow mindedness.
- They should implement the directions and programmes of the government for developing national integration in schools.
- They should encourage the students to read newspapers and books which develop the feeling of nationalism.
- They should lay balanced stress on the achievements of great leaders belonging to different communities and regions.
- All possible efforts should be taken to inculcate an attitude of national integration in the students.
- Teachers should organize community dinners, camps, educational excursions and tours once a year so that the students get opportunities to appreciate the concept of unity.
- Students should be involved in organizing various school progra- mmes like science exhibitions and national projects.
- Teachers who teach language and literature should emphasise those poems, proverbs, tit-bits and essays which develop national integration. They should give such literature to their students for reading during the leisure time.
- Teachers teaching science subjects must inculcate openness in the minds of students. They should teach them to arrive at a final decision only after observation and verification. It is possible only when they are above narrowism.
- Teachers teaching history should explain the demerits of communal riots, racialism, provincialism and linguistic fanaticism. They should also explain our heritage, the constitution of India, the history of India's freedom struggle and the sacrifice of our national leaders. They should teach the needs and importance of unity in diversity.
- Geography teachers should imbibe in the minds of students that no state can stand on its own feet for meeting its requirements. This is because each state differs from another in natural

resources and fertility. In this way he should guide his students to realise that unity in diversity is very essential.

- Teachers teaching economics should explain the needs and importance of national integration and its role in the economic development of the country. They should also insist that there would be low capital formation, unemployment, low production and low income in the absence of nationalism.

Role of Kothari Education Commission in National Integration

The Indian Education Commission was appointed by the Government of India under the Chairmanship of Dr. S. Kothari in 1964–66. It submitted its recommendation in 1966. It explains the meaning of national integration as:

1. A confidence in the nation's future.
2. A continuous rise in the standard of living for the masses which includes reduction in unemployment.
3. A deep sense of values and obligations of citizenship and growing identification of the people, not with national loyalties but with the nation as a whole.
4. Assurance of good and impartial administration, equal treatment for every citizen.
5. Mutual understanding and respect for the cultural traditions and ways of life of different sections of the people.

Steps for Promoting National Integration

Kothari Education Commission has mentioned four steps for promoting national integration.

Common school system: The Commission says, "If the educational system is to become a powerful instrument of national development in general and social and national integration in particular we must move towards the goal of a common school system of public education which will be opened to all children irrespective of caste, colour, creed, community, religion, economic or social status". According to this view, a common school system should be established for national integration.

Social and national services: The Commission criticised the existing educational system as it increases the sad gulf between the educated and the uneducated classes between the intelligentsia and the masses. So, it recommends "as some form of social and national services should be made obligatory for all students and should form an integral part of education at all stages". It suggests to organize the following services:

- Enabling and encouraging students to participate in the community life of the school or the college.
- Creating opportunities for the students to participate in the works of national and social service development.

Development of appropriate language policy: The commission suggests to follow three language formula to bring about national integration. National language (Hindi) at the National level, regional language (Kannada, Telugu, Oriya or Tamil) at the regional level and administrative language (English) at the administrative level and other issues should be followed to strengthen the unity of the nation.

Promotion of national consciousness: The commission feels that promotion of national consciousness is very important to promote national integration. National consciousness can be promoted through: (i) re-evaluation of our cultural heritage by a well-organized teaching of languages, literature, philosophy, religion, history and other allied subjects, (ii) creation of faith in the future, and (iii) a programme for inculcating democratic values.

Role of New Education Policy (1986) in National Integration

New Education Policy of 1986 has suggested various programmes for the improvement of the educational system of India and national integration.

National system of education: The new education policy of 1986 insists on the concept of the national system of education to provide education upto a given level to all students, irrespective of caste, creed, location, sex or economic status. This policy believes that national integration cannot succeed unless all citizens are educated.

Common educational structure: The national policy on education envisages an educational structure of 10+2+3. There will be primary education of 5 years, upper primary (secondary) education of 3 years followed by 2 years of high school. +2 indicates 2 years of higher secondary education. +3 implies 3 years of education leading to BA, BSc, BCom, or BBA, degrees. This structure has been accepted in all parts of the country.

National curriculum: The national system of education is based on a national curricular framework containing flexible common core along with other components. The common core includes the history of India's freedom movement, the constitutional obligations and other contents. These cores have been designed to promote national values such as our cultural heritage, democracy and secularism, equality to the sexes, protection of the environment, removal of social barriers, observance of the small family norm and inculcation of the scientific temper. These elements are essential to develop the feeling of nationalism.

International understanding: India stands for world peace. For this purpose, she works for understanding between nations, and treats the whole world as one family. In this regard, education should play an effective and powerful role to strengthen this worldview and motivate the younger generations for international cooperation and peaceful coexistence. This aspect cannot be neglected in bringing about unity in the national level.

Equal opportunities: The national policy on education lays special emphasis on the removal of disparities and equalising educational opportunities in order to create national integration in the country. Special attention should be bestowed to attain the goal of equalisation in educational opportunity for bringing about national integtrity.

Education for women's equality: Education should be used as an agent to bring about the basic change in the status of women. Therefore, curricula should be re-designed, according to the needs and interests of the women. The training and orientation should be organized to promote women's studies and status. Educational institution should be encouraged to take up active programmes to further women's development. Women's participation in vocational, technical and professional education should be emphasised at different levels.

Education of scheduled castes: The national policy on education emphasises the importance of education of Scheduled Caste people to create national integration. The central focus in the Scheduled Caste educational development is their equalisation with the forward, backward and most backward people at all stages and levels of education. In this regard, the new education policy contemplated the following measures:

1. Incentive to families to send their children to school upto the age of 14.
2. Pre-matric scholarship schemes for children of families engaged in occupations such as scavenging, flaying and tanning should be made available from class I onwards.
3. Special steps to provide non-formal education for the drop-outs.
4. The recruitment of teachers from Scheduled Castes.
5. Location of school building, balwadies and adult education centres should be set up in such a way as to facilitate full participation of the Scheduled Caste.
6. Provision of hostel facilities at district quarters for SC students.
7. Find new methods to increase the participation of the Scheduled Castes in the educational process.

Minorities: The new education policy pays more attention to the education of the educationally deprived or backward groups. This is essential to maintain equality and justice, which promote national integration.

Handicapped: The new policy on education proposes to integrate the physically and mentally handicapped with the general community as equal partners. It prepares them for normal growth and enables them to face life with courage and confidence. This is needed to develop the feeling of nationalism among the physically challenged people.

Adult education: The new policy on education has suggested a vast programme of adult and continuing education in the age group of 15–35 through various ways and channels.

1. Centres should be established in rural areas for continuing education.
2. Programmes of distance learning.
3. Establishing libraries and reading rooms.
4. Need- and interest-based vocational training programmes.
5. Radio, television and films as mass and group learning media

Understanding of cultural and social systems: Proper understanding of diverse cultural and social systems of the people living in different parts of the country will create national integration among the students. Therefore, steps should be taken at each stage of education to foster among students an understanding of the diverse cultural and social systems of the people living in different parts of the country. The translation of books from one language to another and publication of mutilingual dictionaries and glossaries promote the feeling of nationalism among the youngsters.

Research and development: Special emphasis on research and development in science and technology establishes network arrangements between different institutions in the country. It helps to pool their resources and participate in various projects of national importance, removes narrowism and creates national integration.

Understanding universal character of universities: The inter-regional mobility of students should be encouraged in higher education in general and technical education in particular. This is possible by providing equal access to all Indians regardless of his origin, socio-economic status, location and sex. The universal character of universities and other institutions of higher education should be understood for promoting unity in diversity.

National support for implementing programmes: The new policy on education emphasises that the nation as a whole should assume the responsibility of providing resource support to implement programmes of educational transformation, reducing disparities, universalisation, elementary education, adult literacy and scientific and technological research.

Life-long education: The new education policy cherishes a life-long educational process. Opportunities are bestowed to the youth, housewives, agricultural and industrial workers and professionals to continue the education of their choice. The direction of open and distance learning makes education life-long process, which paves the way for national integration in our country.

MERITS OF EDUCATION FOR NATIONAL INTEGRATION

Education is a powerful and effective means which is fully helpful to develop the feeling of national integration in the real sense among the citizens of the nation. Let us discuss various merits of education for national integration:

Political unity: Education for nationalism develops political unity among the people. Such an education inspires the people with higher ideals of national unity, so that they will be above the differences of casteism, communalism, politicalism regionalism, linguism and other social disintegrating factors. This sense of unity and oneness bestows the nation great strength.

Social progress: Education for nationalism removes bad traditions, blind beliefs and evil ways of living, which carry the nation to decay and destruction.

On the other hand, it carries the nation towards the heights of greatness and prosperity. Such a national progress and prosperity is positively correlated with the progress and development of the society.

Economic progress: The rise and fall of a country depends on the unity of that country. Education for national integration stimulates the development of industry, trade, vocations and various professions. Such an education enables all citizens to become hardworking, laborious, self-reliant and prosperous. As a result, production, income, saving and investment increases. These are the basic determinants of economic development.

Development of culture: Education for national integration preserves, develops and transmits the cultural heritage of the nation from one generation to another. Such activities display the glory of the country and exalt its fame at the international level.

Eradication of hindrances: Education for nationalism eradicates corruption and obstacles which hamper and obstruct the progress of the nation by inspiring a sense of national honour among its citizens. In fact, this type of education cultivates honesty, truthfulness and uncorruptedness which are powerful factors in creating national integration.

Development of self-sacrifice: Education for national integration inculcates in the citizens a higher sense of love, devotion and service to others and self-sacrifice for the sake of the nation. These qualities lead to the development and prosperity of the nation.

Development of national language: Education for nationalism promotes the development of the national language. The use of a particular language unifies the different units of the society. This tendency develops a national language which reveals the thinking and sentiments of the whole nation.

Powerful nation: Education for nationalism develops a feeling of oneness in various cultured people. Such a feeling of oneness makes the nation powerful and it protects the nation from external forces.

Good citizens: Education for nationalism carries the citizens of the country away from casteism, religionism, provincialism and linguism. It develops the sense of love, devotion and service towards their nation. Such a sense creates good citizens.

Development of leadership: Education for nationalism, develops leadership qualities in the citizens of the country. Such an education produces broad- minded people, who can have efficient leadership qualities, which is essential for a democratic country.

DEMERITS OF EDUCATION FOR NATIONAL INTEGRATION

Education for national integration plays a vital role in bringing about national unity and national development. Though this type of education is a must for countries like India, it has some limitations and drawbacks which are common when it emphasises too much on nationalism.

Develops narrowism: Education for nationalism stresses to develop the feeling of "My country, right or wrong". This type of narrow and chauvinistic outlook leads to feuds and conflicts in the international sphere. Bertrand Russell is of the opinion that this type of education teaches children to believe that their first devotion and duty is to obey the dictates of their government. The state teaches them false and cooked up history, politics and economics, which enable them to criticise the blind beliefs and blind obedience to government politics and programmes.

Ignores individual freedom: This type of education may achieve unity among the diversities of caste, colour, creed, sex, region, language and other factors, but, it neglects the individual freedom and development, which is unpsychological and militates the ideals of democracy.

Develops bigotry: Education for national integration leads to bigotry and chauvinism. The people who hold the strings of political and religious supremacy indoctrinate and brainwash the individuals. Such bigotries change the individuals to become blind to the evils and drawbacks of their own country.

War psychology: When education insists on nationalism, it leads to the narrow die-hard nationalistic attitudes, which make the individuals intolerant and hateful to others. Citizens of a despotic country become self-conceited. They regard all others as inferior to them. This attitude leads to widespread miseries, war and destruction.

Develops the spirit of isolation: The emphasis on education for nationalism develops the spirit of isolation in the citizens against the conditions of citizens belonging to other nation. Such an education makes them self-conceited and egotistic. So, they never mind about the people of all other countries of the world.

Encourages self-interest and immorality: This type of education teaches love for one's own country. So, the feeling of envy and jealousy over other countries are developed. It leads to blind beliefs, narrow self-interests, exploitation and even try to attack other countries of the world. The feeling of 'my country, right or wrong' has become the war slogan. This feeling became the cause of India–Pakistan war and India–China wars.

Develops hate and fear: Education for nationalism creates evil feelings of hatred for others and fear from the strength and greatness of other nations. Dr. Saiyadain says that education for nationalism creates mutual envy and hatred, disbelief in others, neglect of higher aspirations to make human life happier and also provides such circumstances in which the very existence of nations is jeopardized. According to Bertrand Russell, "There is object that the teaching of hatred which is a necessary part of nationalistic education is in itself a bad thing".

Obstacle to civilized life: This kind of education leads to the denial of human qualities, which are essential for human civilization and culture. At the same time, such education develops in the individual ill feelings and unhealthy attitudes that militate against cultural living.

Develops provincialism: Education for nationalism, instead of national integration develops provincialism, for the sake of politicalism or regional feeling is greater than national feeling because of lingualism. Aversion to other states has been increasing in connection with water resource sharing between or among the states of India. It can be seen between Tamil Nadu and Kerala, Karnataka and Tamil Nadu.

Corruption and selfishness: We may believe that education for nationalism eradicates corruption in all the fields of life and that it inspires in the individual a sense of sacrifice and services. In fact, such an education does not remove corruption from the society. It does not develop a sense of sacrifice in the people. It is seen in the post-modern society that income and standard of living of the educated is higher than that of the uneducated, but the educated are not better than the illiterate and the economically backward in character. This is the trend of the present Indian society.

CONCLUSION

National integration is nothing but achievement of unity in diversity. It includes political, economic, social, cultural and emotional integration. Therefore, the citizens of an integration nation should have mutual understanding, tolerance and respect for the culture, traditions and ways of life of the different sections of people in the country. In fact, we should have common national ideals, common objectives, common interests and above all a profound confidence in the future of the nation. Pandit Jawaharlal Nehru says, "The journey to achieve national integration is far away. In this journey, we should not get drowned in narrow feelings, provincialism, communal diseases and casteism, but we must progress". As national integration is vital for India's survival, the country must mobilise all its resources to evolve a concrete national programme involving every significant section of our society in purposeful action to combat in every town, village and street the dark forces which seek to disintegrate the very fabric of our social, political and economic existence. The question of national integration has to be studied calmly. We have to fight all that leads to injustice, inequality and discrimination. In this way, we should not degrade the very name of Indian citizenship. Let us join our hands, heads and hearts to build up national integration, which fulfil our dreams of making a stronger nation.

CHAPTER 56

EDUCATION FOR INTERNATIONAL UNDERSTANDING

INTRODUCTION

Jesus Christ is the first human personality who revealed and developed the powerful feeling of internationalism through His sound advice to the people of the whole world that "Thou shalt love thy neighbour as thyself". But this world failed to recognise Him and the importance of His sound advice due to a number of reasons such as selfishness, ignorance, illiteracy, poverty and lust for the material world. That is why, the concept "international understanding" or 'internationalism' is regarded as an idea of very recent origin and it has drawn the attention of all the people of the earth. This is the most important new tendency and powerful feeling that has emerged out of the consequences of the two World Wars. We are living in an age of "space travel" and "nuclear energy". New discoveries and inventions have made the different countries of the world to shrink and become a global village. In fact, development of science and technology has reduced the boundaries of the world. No country can be absolutely autonomous and can act on its own. Each and every nation is dependent on other nations for trade, economic needs, educational development, food, health, scientific and technological development, and new inventions and discoveries. For these reasons, all the progressive countries of the world are trying their best to bring the world closer together, that is, to create a "world society". Therefore, we must learn to live together by developing constructive cooperation among the countries. This is the alternative to save the world and humanity from total destruction. We should also know that though the world is separated by the oceans, there is a need for people to act together for world goodwill. This is because war, riots, earthquakes, floods, droughts, and tsunami which occur in one part of the world affect people all over the world. In the words of Prof. K.G. Saiyidain "We can no more isolate ourselves from what is happening in the world around us than we can isolate ourselves in our homes when virulent epidemic is raging in our neighbourhood".

MEANING OF INTERNATIONAL UNDERSTANDING

International understanding or internationalism or inter-cultural understanding refers to the development of that insight and attitude in the individuals who, rising above their own selfish and narrow interests, find out the really valuable items in all other cultures, besides their own. Acquisition of knowledge, understanding and feeling about world nations, world cultures, world societies, world arts, world poems, and world's natural resources is said to be world mindedness or international understanding. In short, international understanding means, a sense of world citizenship. Such a sense emphasises that all human beings are members of the world family. Thus, internationalism is the feeling that the individual is not only a member of his country, but also a citizen of the world. Internationalism indicates love, sympathy and cooperation among all the people of the world. Dr. S. Radhakrishnan says, "The greatness of a nation is to be measured not by its material power and wealth but by the inter-cultural relationship of its people". The following views of educationists and thinkers provide us with a comprehensive meaning of international understanding:

Dr. Radhakrishnan: "It is essential for us not to live apart but to live together, understanding one another's fears and anxieties, aspirations and thoughts. We must work for the racial harmony. We may be German, we may be American, we may be Russian, but we are essentially human beings. Let us learn to live in a world community".

Dr. Walter H.C. Lewis: "International understanding is the ability to observe critically and objectively and appraise the conduct of men everywhere to each other, irrespective of the nationality or culture to which they belong". To do this one must be able to observe all nationalities, cultures and races as equally important varieties of human beings inhabiting this earth.

Oliver Goldsmith: "Internationalism is a feeling that the individual is not only a member of his state, but a citizen of the world".

Klausmeier: "Inter-cultural understanding implies how individuals and groups within a community, state or nation are alike discovering and discussing differences which exist and applying democratic ideals to solving problems which groups meet".

General Education Board (evaluation committee): "Prejudices are dispelled and attitudes of understanding and appreciation of various cultures are built up through inter-cultural understanding".

Panda, S.N.: "International understanding implies adequate and proper understanding and appreciation of the life, culture and contributions of different societies and nations. It also suggests interdependence among nations, a broad outlook and identification with the whole of mankind".

Mishra, A.N.: "International understanding refers to friendship and harmony amongst different nations of the world and also includes co-operation amongst them, and each one maintaining the identity and sovereignty as usual".

Ledge, H.C. (Director General to UNESCO): The term international understanding refers to that human ability which allows the individual to interact truly with others. It is also inevitable for the individual to liberate himself from his own civilisation and nationalism. He must also learn to regard all men and women as equal in the world. It is very important to obtain the maximum possible understanding about other nations. This is possible only through the medium of education. Thus, Internationalism inspires the people of the world to live together in peace with one another as good neighbours, to take effective measures for the removal of areas of differences and to develop friendly relations among nations.

From the given views, we discern that "international understanding is the highest thinking through which all countries are seen as one family, its men of West and East learn to live and work together for the progress of the whole world". Broadly speaking, "international understanding is the way of thinking and feeling developed in the West and East by which relationship is established, culture is transmitted and promoted, scientific and technological knowledge is expanded, war is prevented and peace is maintained, trade is strengthened, economic assistance is increased and poverty and unemployment are decreased in and among the countries not only for the progress of a country but also for the whole world."

NEED FOR INTERNATIONAL UNDERSTANDING

History of the past reveals that all nations have moulded and shaped their educational system in such a way as to teach their children, "my country right or wrong" or "my country is at the top of all other countries". This type of education creates in the children a sense of narrow nationalism. Narrowism became one of the causes of the two World Wars, which not only crushed human rights and civil rights of citizens but also made the whole humanity to suffer unbelievable miseries and cruelties. Hence, all the leaders of the world firmly realise the need and importance of better understanding and friendship in all the nations of the world. Romain Rolland has remarked, "The two global wars, with their terribly devastating results, have at least established the fact that the narrow bonds of sordid and aggressive nationalism must be smashed through an un-walled, un-hedged federation of mankind and should be brought into being for fostering human relation on the plane of love, pity and sympathy".

We need international understanding because modern scientific means of rapid communication have removed the barriers of time and space. So, the entire world has become one indivisible unit and there is interdependence among various nations for socio-economic reasons. As a result, a famine is now a world famine, a war is a world war, an earthquake is a world earthquake and a tsunami is a world tsunami. In the words of K.G. Saiyadain, "A war starts in Europe and three million people die of famine in Bengal and millions find themselves uprooted from their homeland, cut off from their natural occupation and deprived of all that makes life pleasant, gracious and meaningful". The war between Iran and Iraq exploded into world tension and economic crisis with serious worldwide repercussions. Therefore, all the nations of world—big and small realise that the world should fall or stand together. In the words of Dr. S. Radhakrishnan, "If human race is to survive, we have to subordinate national pride to the international feeling". In short, international understanding is needed to inculcate in the people that they should live and die together. We list the following needs for international understanding in the modern scientific and technological world:

- Ensure world peace.
- Prevent World Wars.
- Promote human welfare.
- Promote mutual understanding and interdependence.
- Strengthen faith in democratic principles.
- Maintain one's sovereignty.
- Promote international trade and commerce.
- Promote economic and scientific development.
- Create a helping tendency among the nations at the time of emergencies.
- Transmit and promote cultures.
- Remove narrow mindedness and create world citizenships.
- Eradicate poverty and unemployment.

ARGUMENTS FOR INTERNATIONAL UNDERSTANDING

Whole human race is one: This world consists of many nations having the people of different colours, races, languages, politics, economic status, religions, but the inner spirit or soul is the same in all. The only difference is that the people living in India are called the Indians, the people residing in Germany are considered as the Germans and the people dwelling in Japan are known as the Japanese. In the same way, people belonging to America, Russia and Pakistan are designated as the Americans, the Russians and the Pakistanis, respectively. Thus, the whole human race is one and the whole world is also one unit. To inculcate the feeling of oneness among the varied people, the development of international understanding is essential.

Human welfare: The modern world has made all nations to come closer to one another. The events occurring in one nation have their direct impact upon the life of other nations as well. The emotion of fear develops in all against the onslaughts of the other and each nation prepares feverishly for defence and offence. It leads to the diversion of more and more money and other resources towards military preparations. Today's scientific development is also exploited for human destruction. Hence, a sense of international understanding should be developed in all the people of the world to utilise their natural resources for the welfare of humanity.

Scientific world: Modern scientific inventions like the radio, the television, the wireless, the jet planes and the rocket have annihilated the formidable barriers of time and place. Therefore, no country can feel secure in isolation. In fact, a rapid rise in the means of transport and communication has made the whole world a small "world society". This closeness has been increasing day-by-day in the scientific world. In this regard, international understanding is very essential to maintain a cordial relationship among all nations.

Self-sufficiency: No nation in the modern world can boast of its self-sufficiency and self-reliance unless it depends on each other economically, politically and culturally. The success of a nation in agricultural and industrial sectors depends on the raw materials imported from other nations. Every small nation tries to form an alliance with one of the big nations for political purpose. The culture of a nation also invades the culture of other nations. As a result, a world culture is gradually coming into being. All these elements vividly prove that international understanding is essential to build international brotherhood and fellow feeling, which are the basis of self-sufficiency.

One world and one family: International understanding is a must for inculcating a feeling that all nations belong to one world. All nations whether backward or advanced belong to one family. In short, one world and one family—the world family. It is just like all the members of a family, all nations of the world should feel dutiful and morally obliged for promoting the welfare of all others. The nations maybe weak, backward or advanced, but the feeling should be one world and one family.

Nature of human beings: Love, sympathy, compassion, affection, cooperation and friendship are the desirable qualities of each human being. These laudable human qualities cannot be controlled by the geographical boundaries of a country. The political and spiritual ideologies of citizens of different nations may vary but the desirable qualities of humanity are the same everywhere in all nations at all times. This attitude should lead us towards international fellow-feeling, international cooperation and international understanding.

Development of democracy: The development of international understanding is essential to achieve success in democracy. Democracy allows the people freedom to think, speak and write clearly and critically prepares them for community living with true patriotism and tolerance. In this way, democracy promotes human values and international brotherhood. Hence, internationalism is needed in order to strengthen democracy for the welfare of all men in the world.

Development of nation: The development of international understanding has an immense value in our country. India has attained political freedom, but she needs peace in the world to develop herself in all spheres. In this regard, Nehru remarks, "Isolation means backwardness and decay. The world has changed and old barriers are breaking down, life becomes more international. We have to play our part in this coming internationalism".

Development of trade and commerce: As we know, no nation in the present world can stand on its own feet for its varied needs and requirements. Therefore, exports and imports of goods and services have been done at the international level. The word 'globalization' has become very popular in the field of commercialisation. For this, international understanding is essential.

Peace and prosperity of the world: The whole world is considered as one family, in which there are the poor, the weak and the backward nations. Therefore, the affluent and developed nations should try to improve the conditions of the economically backward countries. This will develop mutual love and friendship among all the nations resulting in peace and prosperity throughout the world. Thus, international understanding is the basic foundation for the development of the world.

PRINCIPLES OF INTERNATIONAL UNDERSTANDING

The general conference of UNESCO held in 1974 recommended the following guiding principles of international understanding:

International dimension: An international dimension and a global perspective in education at all levels and in all its forms.

Respect for all people: Understanding and respect for all people, their cultures, civilizations, values and ways of life including domestic ethnic cultures and cultures of other nations.

Awareness of interdependence: Awareness of the increasing global interdependence between people and nations.

Communication: Ability to communicate with others.

Rights and duties: Awareness not only of the rights, but also of the duties incumbent upon individuals, social groups and nations towards each other.

Necessity: Understanding the necessity for international understanding, solidarity and cooperation.

All-round participation: Readiness of the individual to participate in solving the problems of his community, his country and the world at large.

BARRIERS IN DEVELOPING INTERNATIONAL UNDERSTANDING

There are many problems, which retard the progress of a country towards international understanding such as the following:

1. Secrecy about the nuclear strength of nations.
2. Inequality of countries in size, resources, income, scientific and technological progress.
3. Racial prejudice is one of the strongest barriers in developing internationalism.
4. Lack of national solidarity due to the existence of regionalism, communalism, casteism, politicalism and lingualism.
5. Narrowness owing to illiteracy, ignorance, poverty and internal problems.

GOALS OF EDUCATION FOR INTERNATIONAL UNDERSTANDING

- Enable the students to feel that the world functions for the merits of humanity and other living and non-living organisms.

- Enable them to understand how people live in other countries and their cultures, natural resources, scientific and technological development.
- Enable students to feel that they are responsible for world peace.
- Inculcate the sense of 'oneness' and "one land" in the students.
- Realise the fact that every country is to be dependent on other nations for trade and commerce, and economic prosperity.
- Develop the helping tendency among the students at the time of natural calamities like drought, tsunami, flood or fire.
- Shun narrowism in the students and teach them to discharge their duties and responsibilities as world citizens.
- Make them to realize the necessity of internationalism as a powerful way to protect the nations from wars and foreign aggression.
- Enable students to discern that no scientific and technological development will take place in the absence of internationalism.
- Enable students to understand that internationalism uplifts the economically and socially backward countries.

NEED FOR EDUCATION IN INTERNATIONAL UNDERSTANDING

Education is a meaningful, powerful and progressive means for achieving the high ideal of intercultural understanding. Therefore, we should provide such wholesome educational experience and programmes which develop international understanding. Education for international understanding is essentially education for peace, love, cooperation, cooperative living, brotherhood feeling and world citizenship. This type of education is based on the idea that the whole of mankind is one and the whole world is one single unit. Such an education promotes, "Understanding, tolerance and friendship among all nations having varied colours religions and races". Klausmeier says, "Intercultural education is concerned with helping students to understand the difference and likenesses of individuals who comprise our society and the world". The war minded world is a serious challenge to the peace and happiness of mankind. Therefore, education for international understanding is the crying need of our age. The publication of UNESCO has rightly remarked, "one of the chief aims of education today should be to prepare boys and girls, to take an active part in the creation of a world society". It indicates that development of internationalism or international understanding is more urgent today than in any other period in the history of education. Education should be directed to the full development of the human personality and for strengthening respect for human rights and fundamental freedom. It shall promote understanding, tolerance and friendship among all nations, racial, or religious groups and shall further the activities of the UNO for maintenance of world peace.

Education for international understanding is the vital need of the present generation for the propagation and development of the feelings of internationalism or world fraternity. Let us list the need of education for international understanding in the modern society.

Remove wrong emphasis on nationalism: Education for international understanding is needed to counteract the wrong emphasis on "my country, right or wrong". This is because our Secondary Education commission Report (1953), points out that "There is no more dangerous maxim in the world today than "my country, right or wrong" The whole world is now so intimately interrelated that no nation can or dare live alone. The development of a sense of world citizenship has become just as important as that of a national citizenship. Therefore, such an education is essential to remove the narrow-mindedness and to develop internationalism.

Emphasise on interdependence: Every country is dependent on others for its various needs and requirements. As a result, all nations come into contact with each other through trade and commerce. This closeness and nearness makes the modern world a knit world and there is more interdependence and intimate relationship between people here and there. Many agencies like CENTO, ECM, SAARC, WHO etc., symbolise this interdependence. P.E. James says, "If it is to survive, it must draw upon all the world's resources and all the world's people must share its benefits". Today no country can remain free from any tilt in the international economic balance. Hence, this aspect of interdependence of all countries of the world should be emphasised by the educational organization of all nations and their governments.

Cultivate independent thinking: Education for international understanding is essential to develop internationalism in the youth because, it develops in them the power of independent thinking and decision making. Such an education enables the children to go deep into the matter and decide for themselves what is wrong and what is right. Such cultivation in the youth not only develops the power of independent thinking, but also promotes an urge in them for international goodwill and cooperation.

Train the young men to use their knowledge: This education provides training to the youth to use their knowledge properly and profitably. Such an ability enables them to make use of their knowledge for solving the problems which they face in their daily lives. Prof. K.G. Saiyidain says that people of a country cannot even dream of denying bread to their own people when all the people of an enemy country die of starvation. This narrowness of attitudes and behaviour can only be removed by training the young men to use their knowledge through moral and spiritual education for the welfare of the humanity.

Educate for democratic ideals: The modern world is governed by democratic forces. The democratic ideals express the slogans such as "World Government", "World Society", "One World", "Globalized Society" etc. In order to activate these forces and prepare the young minds to adopt them, education related to international understanding is needed.

Correct the meaning of patriotism: Education for international understanding is essential to correct the meaning of patriotism by removing its narrow and selfish way of behaviour such as envy, jealousy, a constant fear of others and my country and my people. In fact, narrowness promotes self-conceit and a false sense of superiority over all others. Such aggressive attitudes create the feeling in the individuals and they try to subdue others. Hence, the meaning of patriotism should be corrected and developed in such a way that it should lead to internationalism and world outlook.

Eliminate fear from individual and social life: In the modern scientific world, education for international understanding is needed to inculcate in children of all nations the sense of fellow-feeling, brotherhood, sympathy, love, cooperation and tolerance. The inculcation of such a sense removes all apprehensions and fear from the minds of all children and citizens. This facilitates the seeds of love, tolerance, cooperation, brotherhood and mutual goodwill, to sprout and grow into international goodwill and amity.

Promote international living and sociability: The world is more important than a country. So, the promotion of international living, social consciousness and its development is very essential. To achieve this, education for international understanding should be organized, which promotes sociability, spirit of social service and a sense of social responsibility at the international level. The sense of national service for national welfare will develop the great ideal of international service and international cooperation, which are so essential to the welfare of the whole humanity.

Educate for human prosperity: The whole world is shaped in the school. Therefore, the future prosperity of the total human race depends much on the type of education which we provide in our schools. In fact, mankind stands at the crossroads of human prosperity and human extinction. Education shapes the world for a prosperous and happy life. In this regard, education for international understanding is very essential. "For any system of education which refuses to concern itself with world peace, is shutting eyes to the stark fact that, if world peace is not maintained, there must come a time when there will be no one left to educate".

Save the world from nuclear war: This type of education is essential in the present world, because every nation strengthens itself with nuclear weapons to show its power over other nations. A nuclear war implies total annihilation. The threat of a nuclear war is haunting every nation and especially those who are ignorant of nuclear war technology. Therefore, such an education is quite inevitable in the scientific world. John F. Kennedy, the former president of the United States of America remarked in 1962 in his first presidential address that, "We should abolish the weapons of war before they abolish us". There is a need for the nuclear nations to guarantee the non-proliferation of nuclear weapons and the security of non-nuclear nations.

Promote human civilization: We see that there has been tremendous progress in all spheres of life. In fact, man has progressed from paleolithic and neolithic ages to the nuclear and space age, from cow dung and bullock cart to computer technology, from dictatorship to communism and democracy, from aristocracy to republican forms of governments in values and beliefs, from Adam and Eve to origin of species, from slave trade to equality and from tyranny to liberty. Besides, there has been progress in mathematics, medicine, agriculture, oceanography, metallurgy and all walks of life. It proves that education for international understanding is essential for the progress of human civilization.

Synchronise world culture: There is no cent per cent American, Indian, Pakistani, Englishman or Frenchman at present. Bernard Shaw remarks, "A cent per cent American (original, native, Red Indian) is ninety nine per cent a fool". Both the East and the West have influenced each other. It is true that the ideas of Rousseau's liberty equality and fraternity consciously felt in the French revolution have brought about a great impact on the world. Educational thoughts of Rousseau, Froebel, Pestalozzi, John Dewey, Swami Vivekananda and Mahatma Gandhi have influenced the world of thinking. Moreover, the remedy for dreadful diseases, population problems, pollution, nuclear, non- proliferation, unfortunate episodes like tsunami, earthquakes and floods has become world problems. Therefore, the solutions for these problems should be analysed at the international level, for which such an education is essential. The world becomes a melting pot of all cultures when two more men from different countries meet one another for trade or any other economic or non-economic purposes.

Acquire the world knowledge: The people of the world have different standards of living, ways of living, eating and drinking, patterns of behaviour, customs, traditions and occupations. If we do not have knowledge about these attitudes, we will remain indifferent to any specific thing, individual society or nation. In this regard, education for international understanding is essential for getting more world knowledge, which enables us to come out of narrow and limited circle of knowledge.

EDUCATION AND INTERNATIONAL UNDERSTANDING

The philosophers, educationists, thinkers, politicians, scientists and social reformers of the world are of the view that the development of international understanding is the vital factor in international growth and development, which can be achieved by an effective instrument of education. Education makes our world safe and peaceful by developing an international outlook and international understanding. To make education a powerful instrument for developing international understanding, it should be re-organized in the following aspects:

Curriculum: Curriculum should be re-designed in the light of the guiding principles of a programme for international understanding. The re-designed curriculum should enable the students:

- Learn that the earth is the home of man and other living things.
- Acquire knowledge about the world we live in—its people, their similarities, and differences, the variety of their modes of life, and its reasons.
- Inculcate respect for all the major religions of the world.
- Learn how to promote better understanding of the interdependence of the people of the world.
- Know something about the strength of mankind to replace conflict with cooperation.
- Discern all international welfare programmes and higher achievements of all nations in all fields of human activity.
- Learn language, literature, music, and art creations of all the nations of the world.

Instruction in various subjects: A spirit of international understanding can be developed by the instruction of various subjects in school. All subjects and programmes included in the curriculum should have a social content which will help the pupils to lead from nationalism to internationalism.

Literature: This should be viewed as an expression of the noble and creative urges of the individuals of the different countries of the world. A UNESCO publication states, "Extracts from the works of writers such as Charles Dickens, Gorky, Tolstoy, Tagore and Ibsen can be used to illustrate stages in social progress, in emancipation of women in religious freedom, and in the struggle for human rights in other domains". Therefore, literature which emphasises the humanistic spirit should be interpreted to bind humanity into a common fraternal bond.

Language: This is an effective vehicle of international understanding. So, emphasis should be placed on the learning of an international language. Pupils should be encouraged to study the language of other countries. In the words of C.F. Strong, "The social purpose of languages and the vital part they have to play in peaceful intercourse of the people of the world require emphasis. Here, perhaps with less strain than in any other branch of the curriculum, we may harness an academic exercise to the beneficent purposes of international understanding. For a language is at once the expression of the way of life of the people who speak it as their native language and means by which people of other nations may more surely comprehend the spirit of the society, which has evolved it".

Science: This does not belong to a particular nation, race, creed colour or religion. During the course of teaching science subjects, it maybe emphasised that a man of science belongs to the whole world. Students should be taught that scientific discoveries and inventions must be made use of for the betterment of human civilization. The study of science is based on experimentation and verification of facts and it rejects prejudice, superstition and propaganda. We should stress that great scientists such as Copernicus, Galileo, Michael Faraday, Thomas Alwa Edison, Isaac Newton, Albert Einstein, Abdul Kalam, Subash Chandra Bose and C.V. Raman belonged to different nations but they worked for the whole world.

History: This is an important subject which should be re-oriented towards an international objective. To develop international understanding in all the children, human history depicting the struggles of the whole people, their common weal and sufferings should be related to the children. The real history of man consists of the history of the lives of the prophets and teachers, artists and men of letters, scientists and investigators, peasants, labourers, craftsmen and builders. Prof. K. G. Saiyidain has pointed out very lucidly that we should re-orient our history teaching towards a higher and nobler objective and bring through it re-education of people's ideas and emotions. History is wide enough to enable the students to cultivate international outlook. While teaching history, the following points maybe observed to inculcate in the child the feeling of internationalism:

- History of the countries should be taught objectively with a cultural bias.
- The impact of technological and scientific techniques on the lives of the different countries of the world should be stressed in the teaching of history.
- The interdependence of the different countries of the world should be explained in concrete terms.
- Selected stories from The Bible, The Quran, and The Bagavad Gita, and of the great personalities like Abraham Lincoln, Sun Yat Sen, Akbar, Bismark, Ashoka, Buddha, Mohammed Nabi, Mahatma Gandhi, Nelson Mandela, Martin Luther King, Mother Terasa and Guru Nanak should be included.
- Students should be encouraged to read newspaper, journals, magazines, and textbooks to increase their knowledge about the contemporary world events. The lessons in the history textbooks which spoil international harmony should be omitted.
- Students should be told about the needs and importance of international understanding and agencies like the UNO, the UNESCO, the WHO and IMF.

Geography: The teaching of geography enables the students to have a vivid global concept of the world. It also enables them to understand the inter- dependence of the people in the different parts of the world for their varied necessities of daily life. Geography teaches the students how geographical situations have affected the environment and course of history of the different countries of the world. Thus, the teaching of Geography can have a humanising influence on the pupils and it will develop the ideal of "one world".

Civics: The teaching of civics should be re-oriented in such a way that it aims at the training of children not only as citizens of their own countries or nations but also as the citizens of the world. The teacher should organize the teaching of civics in order to make the children aglow with the citizenship through songs and stories, facts and statistics, charts and pictures, festivals, celebrations and exhibitions. Thus, the teaching of civics impresses upon the students the ideas of human freedom, dignity of the individual and equality and brotherhood of men of the world. These ideas develop in the students an acceptance of the differences and an appreciation of the reason for cultural diversity, which promotes international understanding.

Philosophy: Philosophers, scholars and thinkers throughout the history of the world have been stressing mental peace and happy life as the human goal. Such environments may inculcate the feeling of internationalism in the students.

Psychology: Naturally human behaviour everywhere is guided by man's innate tendencies. Psychology brings about a desirable change in the individuals' behaviour. So, the feeling of internationalism can be inculcated in the students by modifying human behaviour.

Music: Music has its own international language. Singing classes should be organized and students should be provided with opportunities to listen to recorded or broadcast music. When the child learns the words and tunes of songs from other countries, he begins to have a sense of the variety or differences in traditional songs and folk music. Students will have to rely on foreign tape-recorder or discs and other devices in order to learn the music of other countries.

Drawing, painting, modelling and handicrafts: These subjects represent the unity of human feelings and thought. Therefore, these arts should be encouraged with the aim of rousing the pupil's interest in international cooperation. Different visual aids, objects for exhibitions, properties and costumes for dramatics should be organized in the secondary schools so that the students involve in them personally. This kind of activity provides the students with an experience in cooperation. Education for international understanding is a planned programme which involves several subjects and it has the greatest impact. It is likely to have the greatest effect in orienting the whole life of a school towards a world outlook.

Teaching about United Nations: To develop internationalism in some countries, the directives have been given to the heads of primary and secondary schools to include some teaching about the United Nations in the curriculum. In some countries some passages on the work of the United Nations have been included in the textbooks. In this way, teaching about the United Nations has become inseparable from teaching about international understanding.

Teaching about human rights: The principles of the Universal Declaration of Human rights (UDH) proclaimed by the General Assembly of the United Nations of December 10, 1948 are essential. Article 55 of the Charter reads, the creation of conditions of stability and well-being are necessary for peaceful and friendly relations among nations based on respect for the principle of equal rights and self-determination of people, the United Nations shall promote:

1. Higher standard of living, full employment and conditions for economic and social progress and development.
2. Solution of international economic, social, health and related problems, and international cultural and educational cooperation.
3. Universal respect for, and observe the human rights, and fundamental freedom for all without distinction as to race, sex, language, nation, colour or religion.

The subject of human rights has several branches of study. At the secondary stage, it includes the historical background against which the Universal Declaration was drafted and the interpretation of the Declaration, was in terms of human relations in the schools, the family, the community, the nation and the world as a whole.

ROLE OF EDUCATIONAL INSTITUTIONS AND INTERNATIONAL UNDERSTANDING

Educational institutions such as school, college and university can play a vital role in developing international understanding among the students through various cocurricular activities.

Celebration of birthdays: The birth anniversaries of great political and religious leaders of different communities, thinkers, scientists and social reformers of all lands like Buddha, Mohammed, Guru Nanak, Swami Vivekananda, Mahatma Gandhi, Pandit Jawaharlal Nehru, Karl Marx, Lenin, Abraham Lincoln, Guru Gobind Singh, Tagore, Rousseau, Froebel, Pestalozzi, Bertrand Russell, Marconi, Edison, Michael Faraday and Abdul Kalam should be celebrated in the schools by the students.

Celebration of world days: An annual day of international importance such as the UN Day, the Human Rights Day and World Health Day should be celebrated in the educational institutions and special talk should be given about the importance of these days.

Celebration of independence days: International week and independence days of other countries like America, Indonesia, etc. should be celebrated and the history of such countries maybe discussed.

Clubs and study groups: Voluntary clubs and study groups of young people are organized specifically to study international affairs. These clubs and study groups should be organized at the school level to inculcate in the children a feeling of internationalism.

Organization of UN societies: Organizing and running United Nations societies and international clubs promotes international understanding.

Bulletin boards and wall news sheets: Maps, charts, diagrams and albums having the cultural heritage of other countries and the work of the UNO and its various branches maybe designed by the pupils themselves or cut-out of newspapers or magazines and they should be placed in a prominent position in the school.

Assemblies: A wide knowledge of world problems can be developed in the students. Assembly meetings, inter-class debates, panels, symposium and similar activities enable the various school groups to develop their knowledge in international understanding.

Special discussion: Teachers and students should discuss in the class natural resources, culture, arts, heritage and science and technology of the different countries of the world. Video programmes on these aspects maybe shown in the school. A news board must be placed in the assembly hall of the school to indicate world records and accomplishments.

Model assemblies: A model meeting of the United Nations Assembly maybe organized in the educational institutions at least once a year for lectures, dramatic performances, concerts and other such activities. Pupils may study the work of some parts of the United Nations and present a model assembly of the Economic and Social Council or Trusteeship Council, in which they become participants.

Libraries: Internationally popular encyclopaedias such as 'Americana', 'Britannica', World Hand Book, History of other countries should be made available in the libraries. Besides, famous international magazines like The Courier, Soviet Russia, The Span etc., should be placed in the school library.

Pageants and festivals: Plays, dances, pageants and festivals can be used to present the United Nations dramatically. Schools should select subjects in the folklore, music, literature and traditional drama of other countries so that students can learn to appreciate and understand the culture of other countries.

Discussion with foreigners: Foreigners visiting our country on tour or any other purpose maybe invited to the school and have discussion with students. This will remove narrowness and broaden their outlook.

Educational tours: To develop the feeling of internationalism, students should be encouraged, whenever possible to visit other countries to have a wide knowledge about them. In the words of Hazlitt, "With the change of place, we change our ideas, nay our opinions and feelings".

Special lectures: Teachers, researchers, businessmen, reporters, experts, political and religious leaders who have visited other countries should be invited to the school and made to deliver special talks on various aspects of the countries which they had visited.

International youth service camps: Organizing international camps for students and teachers will break the cultural barriers and create mutual unity and international accord. In fact, students who occasionally participate in re-constructional projects and international youth service camps can get direct experiences of coming into touch with the people of other lands. This kind of participation in services and projects will develop the feeling of internationalism.

International colleges: Establishment of educational institutions of international character promotes international understanding. Therefore, every country may have at least one international college like the International People's College in Elsimore, Denmark, in order to promote international understanding.

Fund collections: Students must be encouraged to subscribe to the funds raised in aid of foreign countries which suffer from natural calamities like tsunami, earthquake, floods, droughts and mishaps.

Collection of stamps and pictures: Students maybe encouraged to collect the pictures of writers, leaders, scientists and philanthropists of different countries who had worked for world peace and international understanding and hang them on the walls in the classroom. They may also be encouraged to collect stamps and coins of various countries of the world. This activity develops the interests of the students in other lands.

Pen friendships: Organizing pen friendship with children of other lands maybe useful for inculcating international feeling.

Exchange of teachers and students: Exchange of teachers and students among different countries of the world develops international understanding. In the words of Dr. C.D. Deshmukh, "This international exchange of persons will not only facilitate transmission of knowledge, skills and experiences, but will also encourage free and frank discussions of differences in such a way as to minimize the area of misunderstanding and to maximize that of cooperation".

ROLE OF TEACHER IN INTERNATIONAL UNDERSTANDING

The role of the teacher is very important in developing international under- standing. He is the creator of the future world. The success of this noble task depends on his ideals, faiths, understanding, farsightedness, sense of duty, tolerance and dedication. Therefore, the teacher should inspire his students with a sense of international goodwill by trying to develop the sense of internationalism by organizing various activities. In this regard international get-togethers and conferences maybe organized. The teacher is called the **ambassador of international understanding**. He develops the attitudes favourable to internationalism among his students.

Faith in world society: The teacher should himself have faith and enthusiasm in the world society and the value of international understanding and cooperation. Only then he will be able to infuse international spirit in the minds of his students.

Link the subjects at international level: The teacher should emphasise not merely the contents of the various school subjects. But he should try to link the subject at the international level to develop the spirit of world fraternity and cooperation among the students.

Conditioning pupils' mind for international spirit: The teacher should condition the pupils' mind for international spirit. "War begins in the minds of men". So, the teacher should be more concerned with the healthy development of his pupil's body and mind to enable him to appreciate the unity of mankind. In short, according to the prevailing conditions, students should be trained to develop international spirit.

Inculcate internationalism through motivation: The teacher can motivate the students in his direction by preparing them through the medium of various activities from the emotional point of view towards international understanding. He should also encourage them to make pen friends and celebrate important international days.

Effective teaching: The teacher should promote the sense of international understanding in the children through his effective teaching. He should kindle the interest of the pupils to know more about other lands and their people and create an emotional background by teaching subjects like history, geography, civics, political science and economics.

Visits to other lands: The teachers should be encouraged by giving leave of absence and financial aid to travel to other countries and study there. Such visits acquaint the teachers with the culture of foreigners so that they can share their experience and knowledge with their students, which promotes international understanding.

Through adult education: A teacher has sufficient spare time after school time. So, he can make use of this spare time to educate the adult society, instil in them the spirit of internationalism and encourage a peaceful way of life and mutual coexistence.

Research in international concepts and attitudes: The teachers maybe encouraged to undertake research on international concepts and attitudes in the field of international understanding. They try to learn the attitudes of the students towards other races and cultures in order to determine the extent of training for each student so as to foster international thinking.

Discussion: The teachers can discuss with their students the natural resources, culture, arts, heritage and science and technology of the different nations of the world in the classroom. In this way, teachers' role in fostering international understanding among their students is quite inevitable.

Special lectures: It is the responsibility of the teacher to invite eminent scholars, scientists, leaders or teachers who visited foreign countries in order to explain to the students about the various cultures of the countries that they had visited.

Radio and television: Teachers should encourage the students to watch telecasts from foreign countries and listen to chief radio programmes. This will enable the students to identify with the developments of those countries.

International magazines: The teacher should encourage the school authorities to purchase foreign magazine such as The Span, The Courier, Soviet Russia, and place them in the school library. He should also motivate the students to make use of such magazines as, World Hand Books, Encyclopaedia, Americana and Britannica.

Pictures of world leaders: Teachers can develop the sense of internationalism among the children by asking them to collect the pictures of religious and political leaders and scientists who worked for world peace and international understanding.

News bulletins and albums: The teacher should encourage students to prepare news bulletins and albums having the cultural heritage of different countries.

World record news board: The teacher should take steps to place a news board in the school to write world records and achievements which develop the interests of the students in learning about foreign countries.

Thus, teachers can play an important role in promoting international understanding. In the words of Leonard S. Kenworthy "A world minded teacher is an integrated individual, skilled in the art and science of human relations, and conscious of the wide variety of behaviour patterns in the world to which we may have to adjust–clear in his mind about the goals of education for international understanding".

ROLE OF UNESCO IN DEVELOPING INTERNATIONAL UNDERSTANDING

UNESCO is one of the specialised agencies of the United Nations. Its structure and operation are determined by its constitution drawn up by the members of the London Conference in 1945. It is an outcome of the enlightened leadership and efforts of a group of scientists, artists, thinkers, educationists and men of culture belonging to more than three dozen nations. According to K.G. Saiyidain, "These distinguished people realized, the rather obvious truth that peace and international understanding could not be built up only on the basis of political and economic treatises and plans. The prevention of war and the establishment of peace is as much a psychological problem as a political problem and, it is therefore, necessary to provide an educational, cultural and psychological background for the political and economic organizations that were being set up to ensure political and economic security".

After the two global wars, it was seriously thought by eminent leaders of the world that the need of the time was to develop goodwill and cooperation among the different nations of the world. To establish peace in the world, an international organization like the United Nations Organization was established.

Aims of UNESCO

The purpose of the organization is to contribute to peace and security by promoting collaboration among the nations through education, science and culture in order to further universal respect for justice, for the role of law and for human rights and fundamental freedom which are affirmed for the people of the world, without distinction of race, sex, language or religion, by the character of the United Nations". The main purpose of this organization is found in its preamble as "Since wars begin in the minds of men, it is in the minds of men that the defense of peace must be constructed ... the wide diffusion of culture and the education of humanity for justice and peace are indispensable to the dignity of man and constitute a sacred duty ... a peace, based exclusively upon the political and economic arrangements of Governments would not be a peace which could secure the unanimous lasting and sincere support of the people of the world and it must therefore, be founded, if it is not to fail upon the intellectual and moral solidarity of mankind".

Functions of UNESCO

UNESCO strives for world peace by doing the following activities:

- It tries to remove fear and disbelief in the nations by promoting fellow-feeling and goodwill among the various countries of the world.
- It tries to get rid of illiteracy and ignorance from the backward nations of the world and promote internationalism
- It brings culture, art, science and literature of one country within reach of other countries.
- It gives financial aid to research scholars to promote their work.
- It undertakes useful project technology in different countries of the world.
- It translates classical literature and organizes art exhibitions.
- It organizes study circles to know the needs of other nations and establishes an international university to discuss their common problems.
- It organizes an international exchange of the teachers, students, scientists and thinkers among various countries which enable them to discuss individual and common problems and find out solutions for them.

- It provides financial aid for opening schools in poor and backward countries. Such an activity reduces the gap between the developed and the undeveloped countries.
- It advises nations about the scrutiny and the preparation of books, re-organization of curriculum and promoting translation of higher standard books for the use of those who need translations with an international outlook.
- It organizes exhibitions of periodicals, magazines, books and art creations on an international scale, to promote international understanding.
- It encourages international tours of students to stimulate goodwill and fellow-feeling among students of different nations.
- It tries to propagate the ideals of fellow-feeling and brotherhood among the different nations of the world through television, press, wireless and other published material for international welfare.
- It organizes international seminars and symposiums on world educational problems. Experts from various countries come together and discuss the issues and crisis in promoting global education.
- It organizes international camps where students of different nations would meet each other and exchange their views.
- It strives for world peace by the re-organization of the press, the radio and the cinema for international welfare.
- It involves more than fifty countries to experiment the innovations in education, natural science, social science, mass communication education and cultural activities of the world.
- It fosters international understanding through the improvement of curricula and experimental activities in teacher-training institutions.
- It prepares history books with an international outlook and expands libraries and museums.
- It tries to rehabilitate the devastated countries culturally.

The UNESCO has been doing a useful work for providing a proper environment for the success of UNO. Dr. S. Radhakrishnan has rightly stated, "There is nothing national with regard to education. The different countries are provinces of a common republic of culture. There is no such thing as Proletarian, Mathematics or Nazi Chemistry or Jewish Physics. Culture is international and science is cosmopolitan in its essence and reality".

CONCLUSION

Education is a powerful instrument which can be used as a peerless device to make our children internationally alert. The curriculum should be reconstructed and it should include various activities so that education brings about change in ideas and feelings of the pupil and they can inculcate international outlook in them. In fact, education is the root cause of all inventions and discoveries which shrinks the world into one land. It prepares the people of different countries to forget all their differences and live amicably. It also enables people to accept the same God with several names. Today, the whole world has become one land, one family. Therefore, the study of international understanding is more important than any other problem which we face in the present world.

CHAPTER 57

GLOBALIZATION AND EDUCATION

INTRODUCTION

The modern world is not only confined to modern science and technology, but it is also marching towards the process of liberalisation, privatisation and globalization (LPG). As a consequence, relations are being established among science and technology, globalization and liberalisation. In fact, the slogan "Think globally and act locally" has become popular everywhere in the world. We see that the unprecedented scientific and technological advancement has made time and space shrink the distance between the nations. Liberalisation, privatisation and globalization (LPG) are the three important phenomena which we hear throughout the world during and after the 1980s. The Government of India adopted these phenomena during and after the 1990s. These new policies have brought about several changes in the Indian education society, world trade and economy. So, the actions and interactions that are taking place in different areas in different countries across the geographical limits, and all the countries of the world are coming closely to one another, leading to globalization. Thus, globalization is a new technique of establishing recognition of man, society and the nation. It brings about a healthy attitude in the actions and interactions among the nations. In fact, globalization develops interest among different nations towards one another for their mutual actions and interactions, and the economic development of the different countries.

MEANING OF GLOBALIZATION

The term 'Globalization' means integration of economics and societies through cross-country flows of information, ideas, technologies, goods, services, capital finance and human resources. This is a multidimensional cross border integration including cultural, social, economic and political dimensions. The International Monetary Fund (IMF) defines globalization as "the growing economic interdependence of countries worldwide through increasing the volume and variety of cross-border transactions in goods and services and of international capital flows and also through the more rapid and widespread diffusion of technology". Charles Hill defines 'globalization' as "the shift towards a more integrated and interdependent world economy. Globalization has two components—the globalization of markets and the globalization of production".

MEANING OF GLOBALIZATION OF EDUCATION

The commercialisation, privatisation and capitalisation of education at the international level is called as **globalization of education**. In other words, educational services will progressively be commercialised, privatised and capitalised at the international level. Therefore, globalization of education means making educational services as goods that can be bought and sold. It is nothing but making education a business and it is considered as a profit- making activity. After 1990, private people in India took over schools, colleges, and universities with a view to make them business centres for generating profit. That is, educational services have become profitable goods which can be bought and sold at the international level for monetary benefits.

Anthony Giddens, a sociologist and Director of the London School of Economics defines globalization of education as "a decoupling of space and time stressing that with instantaneous communications knowledge and culture can be shared around the world simultaneously". Globalization of education leads to sharing of 'knowledge'. For a nation like India sharing of knowledge is very important because knowledge is universal and its creation and dissemination cannot be confined to national boundaries.

GLOBALIZATION OF HIGHER EDUCATION

Globalization of higher education depends on liberalism. This is because liberalisation is a base of globalization of education. Let us mention the basic things that are related to liberalisation of education.

- Higher education is not related to only bringing about awakening in some specific nation. But it aims at bringing about universal awakening at the world level.
- Higher education tries to bring about uniformity in the development of human values in the nations.
- There would be an improvement in the character of human life at the international level by the globalization of higher education.
- Through activities and interactions between the cultures of the nations; the development of these cultures would be facilitated.
- The participation of the different nations would facilitate the broader studies, research and experiments. This would lead to economic development and qualitative improvement.
- There would be improvement and development at a very fast speed by the mutual cooperation, exchange; and healthy scientific and technological attitude in the economy at world level.
- Higher education leads to economic progress of the country and from the vocational point of view, skilled citizens can be prepared.

NEED AND IMPORTANCE OF GLOBALIZATION

The development of science and technology, knowledge explosion, population explosion, increasing material aspiration and industrialization have made man's life difficult and complex. In order to face such difficulties in life and to make it easy and simple, we have to change our way of thinking, not at the national level only, but at the world level. This way of thinking and acting is the need of the time in the modern competitive society. The following reasons have made the globalization of education quite unavoidable in the present world:

- There has been tremendous improvement and unprecedented development, both internally and externally, in the process of transformation and communication.

- Due to the expansion of mass media like the newspaper, radio and television all the countries of the world have come nearer to one another.
- It has become necessary for us to discover new resources for the fulfilment of our needs which have increased much due to the explosion of population, urbanisation and industrialisation.
- The development of science and technology has become important with a view to increase production and maintain its quality.
- The nations of the world have been developing owing to trade at the world level in agriculture, industries, minerals and defence.
- Globalization has been a very important factor for developing international understanding.
- All the nations of the world have been forced to give a thought on international platform in order to find a solution to the cleanliness and purity of the environment, natural calamities, AIDS, population explosion, poverty and unemployment.
- Globalization has become inevitable to change the theoretical conception of world citizenship into a practical one.
- It has become essential in the sense that wars, riots, earthquakes, flood, tsunami, and drought occurring in one country affect all other countries of the world.
- In the modern competitive society, no country can be absolutely autonomous and can act on its own resources. In fact, each and every country is dependent on other nations for trade, economic needs, educational planning and development, food, medicines, machines and defence.
- It is urgent and important to prepare and develop the individual personality, and create awakening in him at the national and world level, so that he might be a useful world citizen.
- It is also essential that higher education be the best means by which knowledge is related to health, medicine, science, engineering and technology that can be expanded at the world level.

GLOBALIZATION OF INDIAN HIGHER EDUCATION

The entry of the World Trade Organization (WTO) and the inclusion of educational services under the General Agreements on Trade and Tariffs (GATT) have given a boost to the internationalisation of education or globalization of higher education. In order to globalize higher education, the representatives of all the Indian universities were invited to convene a meeting in Mysore. In this round table conference, Indian as well as international educationists, planners, and the representative of developing countries gave a serious thinking to the issue of internationalisation of education through exchange of views. The main issue of the exchange was the utopian principle of Globalization. The views were:

1. Internationalisation and development of Indian Higher Education.
2. To divide the international education programme at three levels among the groups in selected universities of India.
3. To prepare an international programme at the world level.
4. To determine the policy of making reforms in the structure of education relating to management.
5. Educational reconstruction.

The Mysore conference has accepted the notion that internationalisation of education is the complete need of the age of knowledge and it has remarked, "By feeling that internationalisation would bring about improvement in the level of education, develop Indian culture and civilization in the foreign countries, that would create credibility and understanding and provide economic gains. It has to make it understand that in order to expand the activity of teaching and learning and for the improved kind of research, it is necessary to have partnership and network". On the basis of this statement and faith in internationalisation of education, Indian government has been given certain suggestions; that is, the educational institutions and the associate institutions of Indian universities should be motivated to develop the level of higher education at the international level.

SUGGESTIONS TO THE INDIAN GOVERNMENT

In order to fulfil the dream of internationalisation of education, the Mysore conference has given the following suggestions to the government of India:

- Steps should be taken to upgrade Indian education in foreign countries.
- In order to open centres overseas, reform should be made in Indian export, education and rules of University Grants Commission (UGC) 1956 and those of other councils.
- Efforts should be made to rationalise the process of the present legal structure in the registration related processes in the needs of entrance tests, to give no objection certificate and, similarly, in the process of providing visas.
- The government through its Indian embassies and High Commission set up in foreign countries should play an important role in providing facilities related to higher education available in India.
- There is a need for adopting an open policy of private investment for the students.
- The international research scholars doing research in the related fields should be provided with the facilities in order to strengthen figures and knowledge.
- The government should provide more elasticity to the private management in the establishment of overseas centres and admitting foreign students in higher institutions, UGC and universities.
- A task force should be constituted to settle all accounts through a single window in giving admission to the students in different vocational courses.
- The government should think of establishing an economic structure like that of International Development Bank for International Education (IDBIE) .
- The government should create the system suggested by the foreign companies for maintaining the level of education.

RECOMMENDATIONS TO EDUCATIONAL INSTITUTIONS

- The process of admission for the foreign students should be simple. It is possible only through the process of single window process.
- Those universities and other educational institutions where there are a large number of foreign students should be built up in the right manner and good facilities should be made available to these students.
- These institutions should be developed in some specific areas in order to attract foreign students.
- Social structure should be strong and prone to changes so that students do not have to face any difficulty.
- A network should be established in developed or developing countries whereby the Indian universities with the cooperation of foreign universities can pay more attention to the development of international programmes.

- Emphasis should be given to create an educational structure in the universities in the matter of selection of courses, semester system, continuous internal evaluation and credit system.
- Curriculum should be renewed and internationalised.
- Foreign students who have a poor knowledge of English should be given full cooperation to learn this language.
- Special educational programmes should be developed by the Indian universities for the foreign students so that they would get the knowledge of the cultural heritage, diversities in natural resources, languages and the technology of the country.
- The special educational programmes developed for students who seek admission from foreign countries should be completed in one semester.

OBJECTIVES OF HIGHER EDUCATION AND GLOBALIZATION

In the changing scenario of the world, new developments are taking place in the modernisation of technology, science, agriculture, commerce, space knowledge, intellectual knowledge, health, healthy environment, information technology and social sciences. In order to bring about the rapid changes in the above fields, and achieve the goals of self-sufficiency, national development at international level, we need globalization of the educational system. The objectives of higher education related to modernisation and globalization are listed here:

- Acquaint the students with the completely new areas of knowledge.
- Use new techniques of instructions to provide higher education.
- Discover new attitudes regarding maintaining discipline for the acquisition of education.
- Develop international understanding through the medium of higher education.
- Develop the feeling of world citizenship.
- Develop human values and world culture.
- Have an exchange of the knowledge of science, technology and economic development of all the countries and to get the benefit of the experiences of one another.
- Prepare the students to compete with the scholars of developed countries in the global market.

GLOBALIZATION AND CURRICULUM OF HIGHER EDUCATION

The courses related to the new areas should be included at the graduate and postgraduate levels according to the explosion of knowledge and the growing needs of the people at national and international levels. The curriculum of higher education related to globalization are:

- Macro electronics and optoelectronics.
- New content and techniques concerned with peculiar feelings.
- Workable techniques and equipment.
- Strong powerful techniques from environment point of view.
- Space techniques.
- Techniques based upon life science.
- Extension and communication system.
- Social and cultural studies.
- Management system.
- Health and medicines.

A broad curriculum that has faith in diversities of courses can lead a healthy and positive development of social, cultural and educational environment in both the developed and developing countries. We are in need of deep studies, extensive experience, skill and specialisation to structure the courses according to the needs of international students.

METHODS OF TEACHING: HIGHER EDUCATION AND GLOBALIZATION

The age of today is not merely an age of science, technology and computers but it is an age of modernisation and globalization. Hence, the methods of teaching determined for higher education and globalization should be Utopian. In other words, the course that we teach at the world level should have the most modern methods discovered through world level efforts. New techniques have to be used to teach the various subjects. The novel methods should be based on research, observation and new experimentation. These methods should be result-oriented and helpful in removing the doubts of the students.

DISCIPLINE: HIGHER EDUCATION AND GLOBALIZATION

Discipline is of utmost importance to accomplish any task, activity and process successfully. By discipline in the globalization of higher education we mean that there should be such coordination between the teacher and the student, so that the teacher is successful in giving that knowledge to the students who are desirous to get that knowledge quite easily and naturally.

ROLE OF TEACHER IN GLOBALIZATION OF EDUCATION

The role of the teacher is very important in modernisation and globalization of education. He should have faith in modernisation and should be cooperative in the exchange of different cultures. His attitude should be liberal. He should have a wide knowledge and interest in the new techniques of teaching while teaching a particular course or subject he should be dedicated towards his duties and be an expert in adopting the new techniques of experimentation, observation and supervision. He should be capable of developing the spirit of world citizenship among his students.

IMPACT OF GLOBALIZATION ON EDUCATION

Let us look at some of the effects of globalization in the field of education:

- Globalization of education is the direct consequence of economic reforms and economic globalization.
- Students of our country can learn the courses of foreign universities.
- They may get dual degrees—one from within the country and the other from a foreign country.
- Indian universities may conduct the classes on information technology with the consent of private organizations.
- Some courses conducted in Indian universities have been accepted and awarded degrees by the foreign universities.
- Foreign universities make use of the organizations that are functioning in India to propagate their educational practices.
- The representatives of foreign universities organize conferences and seminars in order to attract the attention of Indian students.

- The craze for foreign degrees and courses, and vying of foreign institutions to start their courses in our country can affect the popularity of Indian courses.
- The uncontrolled privatisation of education may affect equity, quality and social relevance. Transparency is gradually lost and commercia- lisation get established. The theory of 'survival of the fittest' may give way to money power and various kinds of social evils.
- It creates the trend of "state minimalism and market maximalism".
- The craze for English medium schools increases and even primary education costs much. The system of capitation fee starts from the LKG level. Therefore, the have-nots suffer a lot and they are denied opportunities for quality education.
- The cost of higher education goes beyond the fiscal capacity of the average and the poor people. For instance, more than one lakh rupees was collected from each candidate for B.Ed. course (2005–2006) in Southern India. Thus, higher education has become a
- commercial product in the hands of private institutions. But the introduction of B.Ed. course (since 2008) through distance learning by a few universities reduces the cost of such course offered in private educational institutions.
- This is a present trend that the more you get educated, the more you become corrupt and non-service minded.
- The LKG process leads to the mushroom growth of the unaided professional institutions. As a result, the entry depends not on merit or competence but mostly on money power. This will decrease social obligations and service mentality.
- There is a positive correlation between education and corruption. Even teachers will not be an exemption to this phenomenon. Hence, the future is likely to be gloomy.
- There will be no scope for value education and social interaction. Knowledge-centred education is giving way to market-centred education.
- It takes the people from 'knowledge-ware', 'skill-ware' and 'software' to 'cash-ware'.
- It favours computers and teaching machines and it may dislodge teachers. As a consequence, the sanctity of the teaching profession and the human side of education will get neglected.
- It develops a new trend that professional courses like medicine, engineering and technology are preferred and social science subjects are neglected by most parents and students. This trend may affect the future of the country as a whole.
- It shifts the aim of education from physical, intellectual and spiritual development to prepare and develop the personality of the individual to undertake a task.
- It encourages privatisation of education which increases cost of education and number of degree holders but diminishes the quality of education and human values.

SUPPORTERS OF GLOBALIZATION OF EDUCATION

The strongest proponents of globalization of education believe that this process must go on concomitantly with the process of economic globalization. They are in favour of globalization of education on the following grounds:

- The job opportunities and the needs of the economy are the driving forces for the globalization of education.
- Knowledge, skill and competency required for the vocations and professions in demand are the major focus of the globalization of education.
- All jobs, vocations and professions will acquire the same character worldwide demanding similar skills, professional competencies and knowledge.

- Success in career or profession is the ultimate aim of human life.
- The educational packages offered by foreign universities and colleges, being only job related, have neutral value and as such cannot have negative socio-cultural and psychological implications.
- Human beings are essentially self-centred and are motivated to work only for personal gain.
- It helps to undertake needed research to create socio-economic models on the basis of freedom, democracy and social justice, which are suitable to each and every country of the world.
- It induces to respect the rights of world people.
- It assists to foster international understanding and world citizenship.
- Our university courses change in accordance with the foreign university courses.

OPPONENTS OF GLOBALIZATION OF EDUCATION

In the process of globalization of education, a problem may arise with reference to the incompatibility between the national goals of the host country and the aims and objectives of the educational packages of the foreign universities and colleges. This conflict can be resolved when the national goals of the host country match the national goals of the country in which the foreign educational institution is headquartered. The opponents of the globalization of education stand against this process having the following opinions.

- The national goals of the foreign educational institutions and the host countries invariably are different and they may lead to a conflict of values. Secular countries cannot have goals that are common to theocratic countries. Similarly, dictatorships cannot share the goals of democracies.
- Value systems and beliefs vary across cultures.
- Western education may lead to unforeseen social disorganization, conflict and serious disruption of culture.
- Education is integrated to culture and foreign educational packages may prove to be disruptive in another culture.
- Students who receive education through the process of globalization of education may prove to be misfits in their own culture resulting in serious psychological repercussions.
- It promotes competition and this will be dysfunctional in a culture and society that seeks greater social harmony, community spirit and social advancement. These are based on the belief that human beings are essentially social and not individualistic, seeking each other's company and support and willing to eschew self-interest in the common interest of the community.
- It transforms the educational institutions into profit-generating institutions. Education has become a commercial product which is being sold and bought for profit.

REGULATION FOR GLOBALIZATION OF EDUCATION IN INDIA

As a consequence of the globalization of education, a number of foreign universities and colleges are making intensive effort to enhance their presence in India by offering alluring packages of academic programmes for the gullible Indian students who have a craze for foreign degrees. But many of these universities and colleges are not accredited in their own countries. In order to check this problem, the All India Council for Technical Education (AICTE) has decided (September 2003) to regulate the entry of foreign universities into India. Some standard foreign universities are cheating thousands of students in the country. The parent bodies of these foreign universities refuse to recognise the degrees awarded by them stating that the courses are not equivalent to their courses. Therefore, the AICTE stipulated that no foreign university could start a programme in India without its approval. As a result, the franchisees offering these programmes must get approval from the AICTE for continuing their programmes within six months. Taking advantage of the Indian students' craze for foreign degrees, some of the universities based in the USA, UK, Canada and Australia are appointing franchisees in India. The franchisees are offering courses, charging huge amount of money. This situation forces the AICTE to frame a new regulation for foreign universities. As per this regulation, every university intending to set up a centre in India should get the approval from their embassies and must be accredited by their country's regulating authority. Besides, the universities should either set up their own campuses in India or must collaborate with an AICTE approved college. The AICTE has not decided to allow any foreign university to run the courses through franchisees.

EVALUATION

It is said that in 1999 there were 48 lacs learners in the world, out of which 17 lacs were in Asia. On the basis of this estimation, it is believed that in future this number would be 159 lacs at the world level and 87 lacs in Asia. There are three main countries namely, USA, UK, and Australia which are providing higher education at the world level.

CONCLUSION

As a result of globalization, we could achieve international standards in education. It would be for the good of the country. But foreign education that results from the globalisation of education, however innocuous it may appear to be, certainly transmits culture. This may ultimately lead to homogenization of the society. Hence, we may have to ignore our social, cultural and moral values at the risk of world peace, social harmony, world citizenship, disappearance of community feeling and of course, diversity. In the words of Mahatma Gandhi, "I do not want my house to be walled on all sides and my windows to be stuffed. I want the culture of all the lands to be blown about my house as freely as possible. But I refuse to be blown off my feel by any".

CHAPTER 58

EDUCATION FOR HUMAN RIGHTS

INTRODUCTION

Jean Jacques Rousseau was the first man who brought about remarkable changes in the social, political and educational structures of many countries through his ideas such as liberty, equality, fraternity, rights of man and rights of childhood. These ideas have had a profound influence on the social, cultural and political life. In fact, all societies and cultures have developed the concept of human rights and principles. The struggle for the recognition of human rights against political, economic, social and cultural oppression, injustice and inequalities has been the integral part of human life. Human rights are the fundamental rights, which are possessed by all human beings irrespective of their colour, caste, religion, sex, politics, language, region and economic status. United Nation Organisation, established in October 1945, took special interest in protecting the Human Rights. The United Nation Human Rights Commission (UNHRC) started functioning from 1946 and released the Universal Declaration of Human Rights (UDHR). This declaration gave emphasis to 'Rights to Life'. Human Rights cannot be taken away by any legislature. The General Assembly of the United Nations adopted and proclaimed the Universal Declaration of Human Rights on December 10, 1948.

MEANING OF HUMAN RIGHTS

Human rights are a generic term that embraces civil rights, civil liberties and social, economic and cultural rights. Therefore, the rights that all people have by virtue of being humans are human rights In other words human rights are the rights conferred to the human beings in the society, politics, culture, citizenship, freedom, religion, employment and law. A UNESCO publication Human Rights (1946) explains the term human rights as "Human beings are born equal in dignity and rights. These are moral claims, which are inherent in all human individuals by virtue of their humanity alone. These claims are formulated in what we today call human rights. These have been translated into legal rights, established according to the new creating processes of societies, both national and international". In fact, they stress those values of 'dignity' and 'equality' of all human beings, which we can call human rights found almost in every religion and philosophy. Thus, it is the rights for a peaceful, happy and healthy life. The right to life itself and the necessities of food and clothing are considered as fundamental human rights. However, they refer to fundamental or basic rights, inherent rights, natural rights and birthrights. Thus, the idea of human rights is bound up with the idea of human dignity. So, the rights which are essential for the maintenance of human dignity may be called human rights.

DEFINITION OF HUMAN RIGHTS

Human rights refer to the "basic rights and freedoms to which all humans are entitled". It has been defined in different ways as given below. According to Bennet, "Human rights include those areas of individual or group freedom that are immune from governmental interference or that, because of their basic contribution to human dignity or welfare, are subject to governmental guarantee, protections or promotion". The world Conference on Human Rights held in Vienna in 1993 stated in the Declaration that all human rights derive from the dignity and worth inherent in the human being, and that the man is the central subject of human rights and fundamental freedom. D.D. Basu defines human rights as "those minimum rights which every individual must have against the State or other public authority by virtue of his being a member of human family, irrespective of any other considerations".

NEED FOR HUMAN RIGHTS

All human beings are born free and equal in dignity and rights. They are endowed with reason and conscience and should act towards one another in a spirit of brotherhood and humanity. Moreover, human rights are essential for all-round development of the personality of the individuals in the society. Hence, these should be necessarily protected and be made available to all the individuals. The need for the protection has arisen because of inevitable increase in the control over men's action by the governments, which by no means can be regarded as desirable. The consciousness on the part of the human beings as to their rights has also necessitated the protection by the states. The function of all the laws should be to protect human rights in the interest of the humanity. As the vast majority of legal scholars and philosophers agree that every human being is entitled to some basic rights, there is universal acceptance of human rights in principle in domestic and international plane. Human rights are the birthrights of all individuals irrespective of their caste, creed, religion, sex and nationality. They provide suitable for the material and moral uplift of the people. In fact, they are conducive to physical, moral, social, cultural, spiritual and economic welfare. Let us list out the factors which emphasise human rights most.

- People were treated as slaves from the prehistoric period.
- The slaves built the pyramids of Egypt.
- The Brahmins treated the Sutras as slaves.
- Slaves were auctioned as inanimate things in the African seashore. They were led in the lower chambers of the ship and the diseased were thrown into the sea.
- The low caste people were denied entry into the temple to worship God. They were prohibited to draw water from the wells owned by upper caste people. Education was denied to the poor and low caste people.
- Hitler killed six million Jews in concentration camps in Germany.
- The United Nations exploded atom bombs in Hiroshima and Nagasaki causing the massacre of thousands of people and properties in 1945.
- The women were denied to enjoy the ancestral property.
- Sati, child marriage and dowry were against the progress of women.
- No case was charged against the rich and upper caste people when they burnt, hit or raped the low caste people.

- Human rights are the birthrights which should be enjoyed by all individuals irrespective their caste, creed, colour, sex, religion, region, economic and political status.

Human rights embody the fundamental values of human civilizations. In fact, people are different in dressing, language, religion, tastes and in food habits. However, all people have a common attribute that is; all are human beings – nothing more and nothing less. In other words, all cultures embrace certain common principles.

No culture tolerates the exploitation of human beings.
No religion allows the killing of the innocent.
No civilization accepts violence or terror.
Torture is appalling to the human conscience.
Brutality and cruelty are appalling in every tradition.

These common principles shared by all civilizations reflect our fundamental human rights. Therefore, they are respected and cherished by everyone, everywhere. It shows that the Universal Declaration of Human Rights is needed universally, applicable to both the west and the east.

KINDS OF HUMAN RIGHTS

All human rights are equal importance and are inherent in all human beings. In fact, human rights are indivisible and interdependent. Therefore, there cannot be different kinds of human rights. This is also because the Universal Declaration of Human Rights has not categorized the different kinds of human rights, but it simply enumerated them in different article. However, the subsequent development made in the human rights under the United Nation System makes it clear that there are two kinds of human rights namely Civil and Political Rights and Economic, Social and Cultural Rights. Let us see them briefly.

Civil Rights

Civil rights are related to the protection of the rights to life and personal liberty. Such rights are very essential for a person to have a dignified life. Human rights of this category include right to life, liberty and security of persons, right to privacy, home and correspondence right to own property, freedom from torture, inhuman and degrading treatment, and freedom of thought, conscience, religion and freedom of movement.

Political Rights

Political rights allow the person to participate in the government of a state to vote, right to be elected at elections, right to take part in the conduct of public affairs directly or through a chosen representative.

Generally, civil and political rights are inter-related and interwoven. As a result, there is one covenant covering both Civil and Political rights that is International Covenant on Civil and Political Rights. Civil and Political Rights may be termed as negative rights in the sense that a government is required to abstain from doing those activities that would violate them. These rights protect the citizens from the act of murder, torture, cruel and unusual punishment, ex-post facto legislation, the denial of bribe as corpus and imprisonment without due legal process.

Economic, Social and Cultural Rights

Economic, social and cultural rights are related to the guarantee of minimum necessities of life to human beings. The very existence of human beings is endangered in the absence of their rights. For instance, their rights include the right to adequate food, clothing, housing, and adequate standard of living and right to work, right to social security, right to physical and mental health and right to education. These rights are included in the International covenant on economic, social and cultural rights. Economic, social and cultural rights are based fundamentally on the concept of social equality. Hence, these rights are called the rights of second generation.

The United Nations has recognized civil and political rights and economic, social and cultural rights in two separate covenants. But there is a close relationship between them. In fact, civil and political rights can have no meaning unless which are accompanied by social, economic and cultural rights. Therefore, all rights are equally important and where civil and political right does not exist, there cannot be full realization of economic, social and cultural rights. Moreover, the International Human Rights Conference held in 1968 recognized such relationship. The U.S. General Assembly in 1977 reiterated that all human rights and fundamental freedoms are indivisible and inter dependent and equal attention and urgent consideration should be given to the implementation of promotion and protection of both civil and political rights and economic, social and cultural rights. Moreover, the resolution stated that civil and political rights are the means to the economic and social rights of the people. The Vienna Conference of 1993 also emphasized that there is no difference between the two sets of human rights, and it stated that all human rights are universal, indivisible, and interdependent and inter related to one another.

We classify the human rights into eight broad categories. Let us see them briefly.

Classification of Human Rights – No.1

(1) Civil Rights
(2) Cultural Rights
(3) Economic Rights
(4) Educational Rights
(5) Legal Rights
(6) Political Rights
(7) Social Rights
(8) International Rights

Civil Rights – Articles, 1, 2, 3, 4, 5, 9, 12, 13, 15, 17.
Cultural Rights – Articles 24 and 27
Economic Rights – Articles 16, 23 and 25.
Educational Rights – Article 26.
Legal Rights – Articles 6, 7, 8, 10, 11.
Political Rights – Articles 18, 19, 20, 21 and 30.
Social Rights – Articles 22 and 29.
International Rights – Articles 14 and 28.

Classification of Human Rights – No.2

(1) Political Rights (Articles 3 to 21)
(2) Economic, Social and Cultural Rights (Articles 22 to 27)
(3) Universal Rights (Articles 28 to 30)

Classification of Human Rights – No.3

- (1) Civil and Political Rights (Articles 3 to 21)
- (2) Economic, Social and Cultural Rights (Articles 22 to 27)
- (3) Universal Rights (Articles 28 to 30)

Classification of Human Rights – No.4

- (1) First Generation Right
- (2) Second Generation Rights
- (3) Third generation Rights

First Generation Rights

These are primarily concerned with civil and political rights of individuals. They include (i) Right to life, liberty, security, freedom from torture and slavery, political participation, right to property, marriage, fundamental freedoms of opinion, expression, thought, conscience and religion, freedom of association and assembly.

Second Generation Rights

They are also termed as 'security' oriented rights. They provide social, economic and cultural security. They are considered more positive in nature because they make it the duty of the state to ensure that these rights are realized.

Third Generation Rights

These rights emerged recently based on international consensus. These include cultural, developmental and environmental rights. They relate to groups rather than to individuals. They are especially the concern of the developing countries.

It may be remembered that since several human rights overlap and they cannot be divided into watertight compartments.

Characteristics of Human Rights

- (1) Universality
- (2) Individuality
- (3) Paramount
- (4) Practicability
- (5) Enforceability

According to Macfarlane, they are universal in the sense that they are "rights of all people at all times and in all situations." The U.N. Declaration also professes a statement of human rights irrespective of the type of social and political order under which people happen to live.

Secondly, the human rights are individualistic because the concept of human right is derived from the acceptance of man as free and equal in dignity and rights. He is endowed with reason and conscience, and capable of moral choice and free activity. Where the worth of the individual is not recognized, there is no place for rights.

Thirdly, the human rights are paramount in the sense that 'no one can be deprived of human rights without a grave affront to justice.' Human Rights represent certain freedom which are sacred and which should never be invaded. The State should not override them at any cost and they can be exercised in spite of the law of the country.

Fourthly, the human rights are practical n the sense that they are the claims, which are not physically impossible to be realized. Moreover, they can be extended to the majority and should not be restricted to a small minority. It does not mean that everybody can be made equal, but he has a claim to an adequate livelihood, basic economic and social needs with minimum basic rights to existence.

Lastly, these rights are enforceable, because, otherwise, their fruits cannot reach the people. National Commission on Human rights has been set up to ensure their implementation.

SIGNIFICANCE OF HUMAN RIGHTS

Meaning of Inspiration: The Declaration serves as a great source of inspiration to the millions of people especially who are oppressed and remained for long under colonial regimes.

Instruments of Maximum Welfare and Happiness of the Individual: The implementation of the human rights would go a long way to provide a happy, healthy and satisfying life to millions of individuals.

Recognition of Elements of Dignity and Equality: Keeping in view this factor, states and societies, take several measures towards the fulfillment of this ideal.

Basic for Human Life: It is recognized that human rights are basic for the optimum development of the individuals. They indicate the basic needs and demands of the individuals, which must be fulfilled. Without the fulfillment of these, a human being cannot remain a human being in the true sense.

Inclusion in the Constitutions: Keeping in view the importance of the human rights, states incorporate these in their constitutions, which mirror their hopes, ideals, aspirations and values.

HUMAN RIGHTS UNDER THE U.N. CHARTER

Several delegates at the San Francisco Conference expressed that the United Nations should establish an International Bill of Rights. They realized that it should be the obligation of the international community to cooperate in prompting and respecting human rights as an integrated part of the U.N. Charter. The U.N. Charter contains a number of provisions for the promotion and protection of human rights and fundamental freedoms in the preamble and in Articles 1, 13(1) (b), 55, 56, 62 (2), 68 and 76 (c) as given below:

Preamble

The preamble of the charter lays down that . . . we the people of United Nations determined to reaffirm faith in fundamental rights, in the dignity and worth of the human person, in the equal rights of men and women and of small and large nations.

Para 3 of Article 1

The article provided the achievement of international cooperation in promoting and encouraging respect for human rights and for fundamental freedoms for all without distinction as to race, sex, language or religion shall be one of the purposes of the United Nations. It is a general agreement that all human beings are entitled to some basic rights. Thus, it marked the birth of the international and universal recognition of human rights. The achievement of maximum freedom and dignity of the human beings are the aims of the United Nations.

Article 13

The General Assembly, Economic, and social Council were given the task for the realization of the promotion of human rights and fundamental freedoms. The article 13 empowers the General Assembly to initiate studies and make recommendations for assisting in the realization of human rights and fundamental freedom for all without distinction to as to race, sex, language or religion.

Article 55

The United Nations shall promote (a) high standards of living, full employment and conditions of economic and social progress and development (b) Solutions of international economic, social, health and related problems and international cultural and educational cooperation; and (c) universal respect for and observance of human rights and fundamental freedoms for all without distinction as to race, sex, language or religion.

Article 56

It provided that the members of the United Nations pledged themselves to joint and separate action in cooperation with the organization for the achievement of the purposes set forth in article 55.

Article 62

It authorized the Economic and Social Council to make recommendations for promoting respect for, and observance of human rights and fundamental freedoms for all.

Article 68

It directed the council to set up commissions in economic and social fields and for the promotion of human rights and such other commissions as may be required for the performance of its functions. The commission on Human Rights and the Commission the status of women are the subsidiary bodies of the Economic and Social Council.

Article 76

It stipulated that one of the basic objectives of the trusteeship is to encourage respect for human rights and for the fundamental freedoms for all without distinction as to race, sex, language or religion, and to encourage recognition of the interdependence of the people.

The U.N. Charter emphasized the concept of fundamental rights, the dignity and worth of the human beings, equal rights, justice, social progress and fundamental freedom. The human rights and fundamental freedoms have become one of the basic principles of international law.

UNIVERSAL DECLARATION OF HUMAN RIGHTS

The General Assembly of the United Nations adopted and proclaimed the Universal Declaration of Human Rights on 10th December 1948. The list of Human Rights elaborated in the declaration provides a common standard of achievement for all people and all nations.

Preamble of Human Rights Declaration

- Recognition of the inherent dignity and of the equal and inalienable rights of all members of the human family is the foundation of freedom, justice and peace in the world.
- Disregard and contempt barbarous acts, which have outraged the conscience of mankind. The human beings shall enjoy freedom of speech and belief and freedom from fear and want has been proclaimed as the highest inspiration of the common people.
- It is essential if man is not to be compelled to have recourse as a last resort, to be rebellion against tyranny and oppression, that the law should protect human rights.
- It is essential to promote the development of friendly relationships between nations.
- The people of the united nations have in the charter reaffirmed their faith in fundamental human rights, in the dignity and worth of the human beings and in the equal rights of man and women and have determined to promote social progress and better standards of life in larger freedom.
- The member states have pledged themselves to achieve in corporation with the United Nations, the promotion of Universal respect for and observance of human rights and fundamental freedoms.
- A common understanding of these rights and freedoms is of the greatest importance for the full realization of this pledge.

The General Assembly

The Universal Declaration of Human Rights proclaims a common standard of achievement for all people and all nations. It shall strive by promoting the respect for the human rights and freedoms and by progressive measures, national and international, to secure their universal and effective recognition and observance among the people of member states and territories under their jurisdiction.

Article 1: All human beings are born free and equal in dignity and rights. They are endowed with reason and conscience and should act towards one another in a spirit of brotherhood.

Article 2: Everyone is entitled to all the rights and freedoms set forth in this declaration, without distinction of any kind such as race, colour, sex, language, religion, political or other opinion, national or social origin, property, birth or other states. Furthermore, no distinction shall be made on the basic of the political, jurisdictional or international status of the country or territory to which a person belongs, whether it be independent, trust, non-self government or under any other limitation of sovereignty.

Article 3: Every one has the right to life, liberty and security of person.

Article 4: No one shall be held in slavery or servitude; slavery and the slave trade shall be prohibited in all their forms.

Article 5: No one shall be subjected to torture or to cruel, inhuman or regarding treatment or punishment.

Article 6: Everyone has the right to recognition everywhere as a person before the law.

Article 7: All are equal before the law and are entitled without any discrimination to equal protection of the law. All are entitled to equal protection against any discrimination in violation of this Declaration and against any incitement to such discrimination.

Article 8: Everyone has the right to an effective remedy by the competent national tribunals for acts violating the fundamental rights granted him by the constitution or by law.

Article 9: No one shall be subjected to arbitrary arrest, detention or exile.

Article 10: Everyone is entitled in full equality to a fair and public hearing by an independent and impartial tribunal, in the determination of his rights and obligations and of any criminal charge against him.

Article 11: Everyone charged with a penal offence has the right to be presumed innocent until proved guilty according to law in a public trial at which he has had all the guarantees necessary for his defence. No one shall be held guilty of any penal offence because of any act or omission, which did not constitute a penal offence, under national, or international law, at the time when it was committed. Nor shall a heavier penalty be imposed than the one that was applicable at the time the penal offence was committed.

Article 12: No one shall be subjected to arbitrary interference with his privacy, family, home or correspondence, or to attacks upon his honour and reputation. Everyone has the right to the protection of the law against such interference or attacks.

Article 13: Everyone has the right to freedom of movement and residence within the borders of each State. Everyone has the right to leave any country, including his own, and to return to his country.

Article 14: Everyone has the right to seek and to enjoy in other countries asylum from persecution. This right may not be invoked in the case of prosecutions genuinely arising from non-political crimes or from acts contrary to the purposes and principles of the United Nations.

Article 15: Everyone has the right to a nationality. No one shall be arbitrarily deprived of his nationality nor denied the right to change his nationality.

Article 16: Men and women of full age, without any limitation due to race, nationality or religion have the right to marry and to found a family. They are entitled to equal rights as to marriage, during marriage and as its dissolution. Marriage shall be entered into only with, free, and full consent of the intending spouses. The family is the natural and fundamental group unit of society and is entitled to protection by society and the State.

Article 17: Everyone has the right to own property alone as well as in association with others. No one shall be arbitrarily deprived of his property.

Article 18: Everyone has the right to freedom of thought, conscience and religion; this right includes freedom to change his religion or belief, and freedom, either alone or in community with others and in public or private, to manifest his religion or belief in teaching, practice, worship and observance.

Article 19: Everyone has the right to freedom of opinion and expression; this right includes freedom to hold opinions without interference and to seek, receive and impart information and ideas through any media and regardless of frontiers.

Article 20: Everyone has the right to freedom of peaceful assembly and association. No one may be compelled to belong to an association.

Article 21: Everyone has the right to take part to public service in his country. The will of the people shall be the basis of the authority of government; this shall be expressed in periodic and genuine elections, which shall be by universal and equal suffrage and shall be held by secret vote or by equivalent free voting procedures.

Article 22: Everyone, as a member of society, has the right to social security and is entitled to realization, through national effort and international cooperation and in accordance with the organization and resources of each State, of the economic, social and cultural rights indispensable for his dignity and the free development of his personality.

Article 23: Everyone has the right to work, to free choice of employment, to just and favourable conditions of work and to protection against unemployment. Everyone, without any discrimination, has the right to equal pay for equal work. Everyone who works has the right to just and favourable remuneration ensuring for himself and his family and existence worthy of human dignity, and supplemented, if necessary, by other means of social protection. Everyone has the right to form and to join trade unions for the protection of his interests.

Article 24: Everyone has the right to rest and leisure including reasonable limitation of working hours and periodic holidays with pay.

Article 25: Everyone has the right to standard of living adequate for the health and well-being of himself and his family including food, clothing, housing and medical care and necessary social services, and the right to security in the event of unemployment, sickness, disability, widowhood, old age or other lack of livelihood in circumstances beyond his control. Motherhood and childhood are entitled to special care and assistance. All children, whether born in or out of wedlock, shall enjoy the same social protection.

Article 26: Everyone has the right to education. Education shall be free, at least in the elementary and fundamental stages. Elementary education shall be compulsory. Technical and professional education shall be made generally available and higher education shall be equally accessible to all based on merit. Education shall be directed to the full development of the human personality and to the strengthening of respect for human rights and fundamental freedoms. It shall promote understanding, tolerance and friendship among all nations, racial or religious groups, and shall further the activities of the United Nations for maintenance of peace. Parents have a prior right to choose the kind of education that shall be given to their children.

Article 27: Everyone has the right freely to participate in the cultural life of the community, to enjoy the arts and to share in scientific advancement and its benefits. Everyone has the right to protection of the moral and material interest resulting from any scientific, literary or artistic production of which he is the author.

Article 28: Everyone is entitled to a social and international order in which the rights and freedoms set forth in this Declaration can be fully realized.

Article 29: Everyone has duties to the community in which alone the free and full development of his personality is possible. In the exercise of his rights and freedoms, everyone shall be subject only to such limitations as are determined by law solely for the purpose of securing due recognition and respect for the rights and freedoms of others and of meeting the just requirements of morality, public order and the general welfare in a democratic society. These rights and freedoms may in no case be exercised contrary to the purposes and principles of the United Nations.

Article 30: Noting in this Declaration may be interpreted as implying for any state, group or person any right to engage in any activity or to perform any act aimed at the destruction of any of the rights and freedoms set forth herein.

A GLANCE OF UNIVERSAL HUMAN RIGHTS

This abbreviated version of the 30 Articles of the Universal Declaration of Human Rights provides an overview of the principal rights and freedoms that are every person's birthright.

The first two articles are fundamental principles underlying all human rights. Articles 3 to 21 comprise civil and political rights. Articles 22 to 27 refer to economic, social and cultural rights. The last three articles provide a framework of solidarity safeguarding the universal enjoyment of all human rights.

Article 1	Right to freedom and equality in dignity and rights.
Article 2	Freedom from discrimination
Article 3	Right to life, liberty and security of person
Article 4	Right to freedom from slavery and servitude
Article 5	Right to freedom from torture or degrading treatment
Article 6	Right to recognition as a person before the law
Article 7	Right to equal consideration before the law
Article 8	Right to remedy through a competent tribunal
Article 9	Right to freedom from arbitrary arrest or exile
Article 10	Right to face trial or public hearing
Article 11	Right to be considered innocent until proven guilty
Article 12	Freedom from interference with privacy, including home, family and correspondence
Article 13	Right to freedom of movement and residence in one's own country and to leave and return at will
Article 14	Right to asylum
Article 15	Right to a nationality and freedom to change it
Article 16	Right to marriage and protection of family
Article 17	Right to own property
Article 18	Freedom of belief and religion
Article 19	Freedom of opinion and information
Article 20	Right to peaceful assembly and association
Article 21	Right to participate in government and in free elections and to equal access to public service

Article 22	Right to social security
Article 23	Right to work and fair pay for work
Article 24	Right to rest and leisure
Article 25	Right to adequate standard of living for health and well-being
Article 26	Right to education
Article 27	Right to participate in the cultural life of the community
Article 28	Right to social order assuring human rights
Article 29	Responsibility to community essential to free and full development of the individual
Article 30	Right for protection of these rights from State or other interference.

UNORGANISATIONS FOR HUMAN RIGHTS

The United Nations Commission on Human Rights

A major United Nations body working to promote and protect human rights is the 53-member United Nations Commission on Human Rights, which was established in 1946 by ECOSOC (Economic and Social Council). The Commission provides overall policy guidance, studies human rights problems, develops and codifies new international norms and monitors the observance of human rights around the world. The Commission provides a forum for states, intergovernmental organizations and NGOs to voice their concerns about human rights issue. Made up of 53-Member States elected for three-year terms, the Commission meets for six weeks each year in Geneva.

Human Rights Committee

The International Covenants (1968) established an 18-member Human Rights Committee, which considers reports submitted by parties on measures taken to implement the Covenants' provisions. The Committee makes specific recommendations to the parties, based on its study of their reports. The Committee also makes general comments on the scope and meaning of certain provisions of the Covenant, which are designed to help states parties to implement the provisions.

The High Commissioner for Human Rights

The post of High Commissioner for Human Rights was created in 1993 to strengthen the coordination and impact of United Nations human rights activities. Appointed for a four-year term, the High Commissioner is charged with many tasks, including: promoting international cooperation for human rights; stimulating and coordinating action on human rights in the United Nations system; and assisting in developing new human rights standards and promoting ratification of human rights treaties. The High Commissioner is also mandated to respond to serious violations of human rights and to undertake action to prevent violations.

The Office of the High Commissioner for Human Rights (OHCHR)

This is the focal point for United Nations human rights activities and serves as the secretariat for the Commission on Human Rights, the treaty bodies (expert committees monitoring treaty compliance) and other United Nations human rights organisation. In addition to the regular budget, some of its activities are financed through voluntary or trust funds.

Centre for Human Rights

The centre for Human Rights is located at Geneva in Switzerland. Since 1955, the Centre for Human Rights has administered a programme of advisory services and technical assistance, which aims to foster a climate conducive to respect for human rights.

The programme encompasses wide range of activities from the training of public officials and law enforcement personnel to the translation and dissemination of human rights instruments and information. Governments are provided with expert assistance in a number of crucial areas including election procedure, legislative and constitutional drafting and the development of effective and accessible legal system.

UN CONTRIBUTION TO HUMAN RIGHTS

The great achievement of the United Nations is the creation of a comprehensive body of human rights law, to which all nations subscribe. The UN has created effective mechanisms to protect and promote human rights.

- The UN created the first global Bill of Human Rights: the 1948 Universal Declaration of Human Rights and the two 1966 International Human Rights Covenants (on civil and political rights and on economic, social and cultural rights), which make many of the declaration's provisions legally binding on states.
- The UN has helped negotiate more than 80 international treaties fostering political, civil, economic, social and cultural rights.
- The UN has been instrumental in securing universal recognition of crucial rights: for instance, the rights of women and the right of all people to development.
- Many peacekeeping operations include provisions for protecting the human rights of the population.
- The UN High Commissioner for Human Rights seeks to prevent violations, investigates abuses in specific countries and engages in dialogue with governments.
- The UN Secretary-General and the High Commissioner confidentially raise human rights concerns with government's items such as the release of prisoners and the commutation of death sentences.
- By investigating and reporting on complaints of violations, the UN Commission on Human Rights helps focus world attention, generating international pressure on governments to improve their human rights practices.
- UN human rights experts monitor the human rights situation in a specific country, or widespread violations such as torture, alerting the international community to human rights abuses.
- A 24-hour fax hotline to report violations is in operation at the UN Office in Geneva.
- The UN Centre for Human Rights assists in all the above efforts; it also helps governments to fulfil their human rights responsibilities by providing technical assistance in matters such as the training of police, the drafting of laws and the improvement of legal systems.

HUMAN RIGHTS FOR DIFFERENT SECTIONS

End of Apartheid and Racial Discrimination

- In 1952, when the General Assembly took up the issue of apartheid in South Africa, the United Nations placed itself at the forefront of international efforts to end this "crime against humanity".
- Constant vigilance and pressure over the years resulted in the dismantling of the apartheid system in South Africa in 1994.
- The fight against racism continues around the world. The United Nations strives to raise awareness to combat this social injustice. The years 1993–2003 had been proclaimed the Third Decade to Combat Racism and Racial Discrimination.

Women's Rights and Human Rights

- Respect for human rights will not be universal until women's rights are recognized and protected.
- The Convention on the Elimination of All Forms of Discrimination against Women was adopted by the General Assembly in 1979 and has now been ratified by over 160 countries. The Committee on the Elimination of Discrimination against Women (CEDAW) monitors compliance.
- UNIFEM, the UN Development Funds for Women, has a special programme, which works to promote and protect women's rights.
- But around the world, cultural and traditional forces continue to subject women to secondary status. Too often violations remain hidden and silent. The global women's movement, a new cultural force, is working to break the silence and demands that rights for women everywhere be respected and upheld.

The Rights of Indigenous People

- Throughout history, the world's indigenous people—an estimated 300 million in more than 70 countries—have suffered at the hands of colonizers and others seeking territory and riches.
- The United Nations Working Group on Indigenous Populations, which has been meeting since 1982, works to promote indigenous people's rights. Members have drafted a Declaration on the Rights of Indigenous Peoples, which, if adopted, will represent a major step forward.
- The General Assembly's proclamation of 1993 as the International Year of the World's Indigenous People and 1995–2004 as the International Decade of the World's Indigenous people was an effort to strengthen international cooperation for solving the problems faced by indigenous communities.

The Rights of the Child

- Respect for human rights begins with the way society treats its children.
- On 20 November 1989, the UN General Assembly adopted the historic Convention on the Rights of the Child. Till date it has been ratified by 191 countries.
- But where they seek improved living standards, many migrant workers find discrimination and abuse.
- In 1990, following 10 years of negotiations, the General Assembly adopted the International convention on the protection of the Rights of All 5.

Migrant Workers and Member of Their Families

- However, the treaty has not yet entered into force because it needs ratification by 20 Governments and as of May 1998 had only been ratified by nine: Bosnia and Herzegovina, Cape Verde, Colombia, Egypt, Morocco, Philippines, Seychelles, Sri Lanka and Uganda.

Human Rights of Disabled Persons

- Often marginalized in society, disabled persons constitute ten per cent of the world's population.
- They are frequently denied the most basic educational opportunities. Physical restrictions bar them from public buildings and transport. Social attitudes exclude them from cultural life and normal relationships. Prejudice and ignorance often lead to unnecessary institutionalization.
- In striving for a consensus on the protection of the rights of disabled persons, the General Assembly in 1993 adopted the Standard Rules on the Equalisation of Opportunities for Persons with Disabilities.
- The rules offer an instrument for policy-making in the quest for a "society for all" which recognizes the development of the human potential of each person.

Human Rights, Development and Democracy

- Full human dignity means not only freedom from torture, but also freedom from hunger. It means freedom to vote and the right to education. It means freedom of expression and the right to health. It means the right to enjoy all rights without discrimination.
- In 1986, the UN General Assembly adopted the Declaration on the Right to Development, which states that:
- "The human person is the central subject of development and should be the participant and beneficiary of the right to development".
- However, despite international efforts, over one billion people nearly one sixth of world population today live in absolute poverty on less than $1 a day.
- Good governance, democracy and popular participation are increasingly viewed as key agents in the quest for economic and social development, as are equitable trade terms and debt relief.

Human Rights and Humanitarian Assistance

- Around the world, human rights are an integral part of situations in which humanitarian assistance is required. Victims might be refugees, displaced people or other civilians caught up in internal conflicts. Still, their plight is the same. Their human rights are likely to have been violated and they need protection and assistance.
- "Human rights violations are a major cause of refugee flows," says Sadako Ogata, the UN High Commissioner for Refugees. Refugees also suffer a range of abuses once they leave their homes, from piracy and rape to arrest, detention, torture and discrimination in the country to which they have escaped.
- The international community is increasingly focusing on preventive action to address problems before they become humanitarian emergencies.

Human Rights and International Criminal Court

- High hopes have been raised by the June 1998 conference in Rome to establish an international criminal court, which would form a vital part of a merging system of international human rights protection.
- For nearly half a century, the United Nations has recognized the need to establish an international criminal court to prosecute and punish persons responsible for crimes against humanity.
- In the absence of such a court, two *ad-hoc* criminal courts have been set up to judge war crimes in the former Yugoslavia and in Rwanda.

INDIAN CONSTITUTIONAL PROVISIONS AND HUMAN RIGHTS

The task for preparing the Constitution of India was entrusted to the Constituent Assembly, which met for the first time on December 9, 1946, i.e., before India became a Dominion. The Assembly appointed various Committees to draft the different articles of the Constitution. The reports of these Committees formed the basis on which a draft of the new Constitution of India was prepared in February 1948. Its final shape was given on November 26, 1949, and it came into force on January 26, 1950. The Preamble of the Indian Constitution declares India to be a 'sovereign, socialist, secular, democratic republic'. The Constitution laid down the implementation procedure in Parts III and IV known as 'Fundamental Rights' and Directive Principles of State Policy respectively. While the former guarantees certain rights to the individuals, the latter gives direction to the State to provide some other rights to its people in specified matters. Directives, though not enforceable before the courts, are not to be regarded inferior to the fundamental rights. The Constitution under Article 37 lays down that the provisions contained in this Part shall not be enforceable by any Court, but the principles laid down therein are nevertheless fundamental in governance of the court and it shall be the duty of the State to apply these principles in making laws. It may be stated that fundamental rights and directive principles, together constitute the conscience of the Constitution.

MEANING OF FUNDAMENTAL RIGHTS

The constitution provides a number of rights to individuals in Part III, which have been termed as 'fundamental rights'. The expression 'fundamental' denotes that these rights are inherent in all the human beings are essential for the individuals for blossoming of the human personality and soul. These rights represent the basic values of a civilized society and the Constitution makers declared that they shall be given a place of pride in the Constitution and therefore they elevated them to the status of 'fundamental' rights. These rights are therefore calculated to protect the dignity of the individuals and create conditions in which every human being can develop his personality fully. Fundamental rights differ from ordinary rights in a sense that the former are inviolable. No law, ordinance, custom, usage or administrative order can abridge or take them away. Any law, which is volatile to any of the fundamental rights, is void. These rights are binding on the legislature as well as on the executive. The founding fathers of the constitution thought it necessary to incorporate them for the welfare of the people.

Fundamental rights are those legal rights, which are framed not by the Legislature but are provided in the Constitution of India.

- The rights are fundamental because of four reasons.
- First, they are included in the Constitution, which is known as the 'Fundamental Law of the Land'.

- Second, they are justifiable. The Supreme Court and the High Courts have the power to enforce whenever these rights are violated.
- Third, the rights are held to be belonging to all citizens, irrespective of caste, creed, race, religion, sex etc.
- Fourth, they are indispensable to the all round development of the personality of an individual.
- In the words of Dr. S.C. Kashyap and Vita Prakash, "Whereas the ordinary rights can be changed by legislature through simple law making process, the fundamental rights cannot be changed easily".

SIGNIFICANCE AND NEED FOR FUNDAMENTAL RIGHTS

- Justice Gandragadkar has described the inclusion of fundamental rights in our Constitution as "the very foundation and cornerstone of the democratic way of life ushered I this country by the Constitution" (Sajan Singh vs. State of Rajasthan, AIR 1965 SC 845).
- In the words of Justice Bhagwati, "These fundamental rights represent the basic values cherished by the people of this country since the Vedic times and they are calculated to protect the dignity of the individual and create conditions in which every human being can develop his personality to the fullest extent. They weave a 'pattern of guarantee' in the basic structure of human rights and impose negative obligation on the state not to encroach on individual liberty in its various dimensions. (Menaka Gandhi vs. Union of India, AIR 1978, ACT 597)
- Dr. S. Radhakrishnan considers the fundamental rights "as a pledge to our people and a pact with the civilized world".
- Justice Patanjali has said, "The whole object of Part III of the constitution is to provide protection for the freedoms and rights mentioned therein against arbitrary invasion by the State (State of West Bengal vs. Subodh Gopal Bose, AIR 1954, SC 1992".
- Dr. B.R. Ambedkar described fundamental rights as "the heart and soul of the Constitution".
- The importance of these rights is brought out as under:

Necessary for the Optimum Development of Individuals: The rights such as right of equality, freedom of religions etc. help in the development of the inherent strength of an individual in a democratic country like India.

Essential in a Democratic Set-up: In a democratic set-up, people choose their own government. For fair reflection of opinion, people need to have certain freedoms which are granted to them through the fundamental rights.

Essential for a Multi-cultural and Multi-Religious Society: India is a vast country having people belonging to different religions and cultures. For national unity, it is required that all people should be free to profess the religion of their choice. There should not be any discrimination on the part of government on grounds of religion, race, sex etc. The fundamental rights available ensure this to the citizens.

Check on the Arbitrary Power of the Executive and Legislature: The inclusion of fundamental rights in the Constitution protects the citizens on the arbitrary power of the government.

Establishment of Social Democracy: Articles 15 and 16 prohibit discrimination on the grounds of religion, race caste, sex or birth.

Protection of the Interest of the Minorities: The fundamental rights provide for safeguarding the language, script and education of the minorities.

Promotion of Education: Education is considered as an instrument of peaceful revolution in different areas of life of the individual as well the society. Realising this, 'Right to Education' has been included as Fundamental right by the Eighty-Sixth Amendment to the Constitution introduced in 2002 under Article 21A.

Fundamental Unity of India: By providing the same liberties, irrespective of social status, wealth, race, caste, sex and place of birth to all the Constitution emphasises the national unity of India.

ORIGIN AND DEVELOPMENT OF THE CONCEPT OF FUNDAMENTAL RIGHTS

In India, the plea for granting Fundamental Rights to the Indian by the British rulers was first made by Dadabhai Navaroji (1825–1917), one of the foremost reformers of all kinds—educational, political, religious and social and who became the president of the Indian National Congress three times, in 1886, 1894 and 1906. The Karachi session (1931) of the Indian National congress drafted the model for Fundamental Rights. However, the dream materialized only when India achieved its independence and the Constitution included Fundamental Rights.

NATURE AND MAIN FEATURES OF FUNDAMENTAL RIGHTS

- The rights form an integral part of the Constitution.
- Fundamental rights are justifiable. In case of violation, one can seek protection.
- These rights are available not only to citizens, but in certain cases to the foreigners living in India too; for instance right to religion.
- The rights are not absolute. Each right is given under certain limitations and reasonable restrictions are provided for.
- Some rights are positive in nature like right to liberty or religion.
- Some rights are negative in nature, e.g., abolition of untouchability.
- Fundamental rights can be amended or even deleted. For this, an elaborate process is needed.
- Rights are liable to suspension. During emergency, fundamental rights can be suspended.
- Fundamental rights are comprehensive in nature.
- Fundamental rights differentiate between citizens and persons. For instance, freedom of speech and expression, freedom of movement are secured only to citizens while the rights relating to the protection of life and personal liberty are granted to every person irrespective of his or her being a citizen of India.
- Fundamental rights definitely stand on a higher pedestal than the ordinary laws.
- Fundamental rights put restrictions on the powers of the State also. If the State violates these rights, the citizens can seek redressal through the courts.
- Rights limit the authority of the Government.

CLASSIFICATION OF FUNDAMENTAL RIGHTS AND THEIR DESCRIPTION

- Right to equality
- Right to Freedom
- Right against Exploitation

- Right to Freedom of Religion
- Cultural and Educational rights
- Right to Constitutional Remedies

Articles: Constitution of India and Articles Relating to Fundamental Rights

Part III of the Constitution of India entitled 'Fundamental Rights' includes 24 Articles–12 to 35. Article 12 relates to the definition of the word 'State' and Article 13 to Laws inconsistence with or in derogation of the Fundamental Rights. Article 34 provides for restrictions on rights while martial law is in force. Article 35 deals with legislation to give effect to provisions of this part.

Right to Equality

Equality before Law

The state shall not deny to any person equality before the law or the equal protection of the laws within the territory of India.

Prohibition of Discrimination on Grounds of Religion, Race, Caste, Sex or Place of Birth

- The State shall not discriminate against any citizen on grounds only of religion, race, caste, sex, and place of birth or any of them.
- No citizen shall, on grounds only of religion, race, caste, sex, place of birth or any of them, be subject to any disability, liability, restriction or condition with regard to –
  - access to shops, public restaurants, hotels and places of public entertainment; or
  - use of wells, tanks, bathing ghats, roads and places of public resort maintained wholly or partly out of State funds or dedicated to the use of the public.
- Nothing in this article shall prevent the State from making any special provision for women and children.
- Nothing in this article or in clause (2) of Article 29 shall prevent the state from making any special provision for the advancement of any socially and educationally backward classes of citizens or for the Scheduled Castes and the scheduled Tribes.

Equality of Opportunity in Matters of Public Employment

- There shall be equality of opportunity for all citizens in matters relating to employment or appointment to any office under the state.
- No citizen shall, on grounds only of religion, race, caste, sex, descent, place of birth, residence or any of them, be ineligible for, or discriminated against in respect of any employment or office under the State.
- Nothing in this article shall prevent Parliament from making any law prescribing, in regard to a class or classes of employment or appointment to an office (under the government of, or any local or other authority within, a State or Union territory, any requirement as to residence within that State or Union territory) prior to such employment or appointment.

- Nothing in this article shall prevent the State from making any provision for the reservation of appointments or posts in favour of any backward cases of citizens, which, in the opinion of the State is not adequately represented in the services under the State.
  - Nothing in this article shall prevent the State from making any provision for the reservation of appointments or posts in favour of any backward class of citizens, which, in the opinion of the State is not adequately represented in the services under the State.
  - Nothing in this article shall prevent the State from considering any unfilled vacancies of a year which are reserved for being filled up in that year in accordance with any provision for reservation made under clause succeeding year or years and such class of vacancies shall not be considered together with the vacancies of the year in which they are being filled up for determining the ceiling of fifty per cent, reservation on total number of vacancies of that year.
- Nothing in this article shall affect the operation of any law, which provides that the incumbent of an office in connection with the affairs of any religious or denominational institution or any member of the governing body thereof shall be a person professing a particular religion or belonging to a particular denomination.

Abolition of Untouchability

- "Untouchability" is abolished and its practice in any form is forbidden. The enforcement of any disability rising out of "Untouchability" shall be an offence punishable in accordance with law.

Abolition of Titles

(i) No title, not being a military or academic distinction, shall be conferred by the state.
(ii) No citizen of India shall accept any title from any foreign State.
(iii) No person who is not a citizen of India shall, while he holds any office of profit or trust under the State accept without the consent of the President any title from any foreign State.
(iv) No person holding any office of profit or trust under the state shall without the consent of the President, accept any present, emolument, or office of any kind from or under any foreign State.

Right to Freedom

Protection of Certain Rights Regarding Freedom of Speech, etc.

- All citizens shall have the right -
  - To freedom of speech and expression;
  - To assemble peaceably and without arms;
  - To form associations or unions;
  - To move freely throughout the territory of India;
  - To reside and settle in any part of the territory of India; and
  - To practice any profession, or to carry on any occupation, trade or business.
- Nothing in sub-clause (a) of clause (1) shall affect the operation of any existing law, or prevent the State from making any law, in so far as such law imposes reasonable restrictions on the exercise of the right conferred by the said sub-clause in the interests of the sovereignty and

integrity of India, the security of the State, friendly relations with Foreign States, public order, decency or morality, or in relation to contempt of court, defamation or incitement to an offence.

- Nothing in sub-clause (b) of the said clause shall affect the operation of any existing law in so far as it imposes, or prevents the State from making any law imposing, in the interests of the sovereignty and integrity of India or public order, reasonable restrictions on the exercise of the right conferred by the said sub-clause.
- Nothing in sub-clause (c) of the said clause shall affect the operation of any existing law in so far as it imposes, or prevents the State from making any law imposing, in the interests of the sovereignty and integrity of India or public order or morality, reasonable restrictions on the exercise of the right conferred by the said sub-clause.
- Nothing in sub-clauses (d) and (e) of the said clause shall affect the operation of any existing law in so far as it imposes, or prevents the State from making any law imposing, reasonable restrictions on the exercise of any of the rights conferred by the said sub-clauses either in the interests of the general public or for the protection of the interests of any Scheduled Tribe.
- Nothing in sub-clause (g) of the said clause shall affect the operation of any existing law in so far as it imposes, or prevents the State from making any law imposing, in the interests of the general public, reasonable restrictions on the exercise of the right conferred by the said sub-clause, and, in particular, nothing in the said sub-clause shall affect the operation of any existing law in so far as it relates to, or prevents the State from making any law relating to,
  - The professional or technical qualifications necessary for practicing any profession or carrying on any occupation, trade or business, or
  - The carrying on by the State or by a corporation owned or controlled by the state, of any trade, business, industry or service, whether to the exclusion, complete, partial, of citizens, or otherwise.

Protection in Respect of Conviction for Offences

- No person shall be convicted of any offence except for violation of a law in force at the time of the commission of the act charged as an offence, nor be subjected to a penalty greater than that which might have been inflicted under the law in force at the time of the commission of the offence.
- No person shall be prosecuted and punished for the same offence more than once.
- No person accused of any offence shall be compelled to be a witness against himself.

Protection of Life and Personal Liberty

- No person shall be deprived of his life of personal liberty except according to procedure established by law.

A. Right to Education

- The State shall provide free and compulsory education to all children of the age of six to fourteen years in such manner as the State may, by law, determine.

Protection against Arrest and Detention in certain Cases

- No person who is arrested shall be detained in custody without being informed, of the grounds for such arrest nor shall he be denied the right to consult, and to be defended by, a legal practitioner of his choice.
- Every person who is arrested shall be detained in custody shall be produced before the nearest magistrate within a period of twenty-four hours of such arrest excluding the time necessary for the journey from the place of arrest to the court of the magistrate and no such person shall be detained in custody beyond the said period without the authority of a magistrate.
- Nothing in clauses: (1) and (2) shall apply—
  - To any person who for the time being is an enemy alien; or
  - To any person who is arrested or detained under any law providing for preventive detention.
- No law providing for preventive detention shall authorize the detention of a person for a longer period than three months unless—
  - an Advisory Board consisting of persons who are, or have been or, are qualified to be appointed as, Judges of a High Court has reported before the expiration of the said period of three months that there is in its opinion sufficient cause for such detention.
  - Provided that nothing in this sub-clause shall authorise the detention of any person beyond the maximum period prescribed by any law made by Parliament under sub-clause (b) of clause (7); or
  - Such person is detained in accordance with the provisions of any law made by Parliament under sub-clausues (a) and (b) of clause (7).
- When any person is detained in pursuance of an order made under any law providing for preventive detention, the authority making the order shall, as soon as may be, communicate to such person the grounds on which the order has been made and shall afford him the earliest opportunity of making a representation against the order.
- Nothing in clause (5) shall require the authority making any such order as is referred to in that clause to disclose facts which such authority considers being against the public interest to disclose.
- Parliament may by law prescribe—
  - the circumstances under which, and the class or classes of cases in which, a person may be detained for a period longer than three months under any law providing for preventive detention without obtaining the opinion of an Advisory Board in accordance with the provisions of sub-clause (a) of clause (4);
  - the maximum period for which any person may in any class or classes of cases be detained under any law providing for preventive detention; and
  - The procedure to be followed by an Advisory Board in an inquiry under sub-clause (a) of clause (4).

Right against Exploitation

Prohibition of traffic Human beings and Forced Labour

- Traffic in human beings and beggar and other similar forms of forced labour are prohibited and any contravention of this provision shall be an offence punishable in accordance with law.

- Nothing in this article shall prevent the State from imposing compulsory service for public purposes, and in imposing such service, the State shall not make any discrimination on grounds only of religion, race, caste or class or any of them.

Prohibition of Employment of Children in Factories, etc.

- No child below the age of fourteen years shall be employed to work in any factory or mine or engaged in any other hazardous employment.

Right to Freedom of Religion

Freedom of Conscience and Free Profession, Practice and Propagation of Religion

- Subject to public order, morality and health and to the other provisions of this Part, all persons are equally entitled to freedom of conscience and the right freely to profess, practice and propagate religion.
- Nothing in this article shall affect the operation of any existing law or prevent the State from making any law—
  - Regulating or restricting any economic, financial, political or other secular activity, which may be associated with religious practice;
  - Providing for social welfare and reform or the throwing open of Hindu religious institutions of a public character to all classes and sections of Hindus.

Explanation I: The wearing and carrying of kirpans shall be deemed included in the profession of the Sikh religion.

Explanation II : In sub-clause (b) of clause (2), the reference to Hindus shall be construed as including a reference to persons professing the Sikh, Jain or Buddhist religion, and the reference to Hindu religious institutions shall be construed accordingly.

Freedom to Manage Religious Affairs

Subject to public order, morality and health, every religious denomination or any section thereof shall have the right—

- to establish and maintain institutions for religious and charitable purposes;
- to manage its own affairs in matters of religion;
- to own and acquire movable and immovable property; and
- To administer such property in accordance with law.

Freedom as to Payment of Taxes for Promotion of any Particular Religion

- No person shall be compelled to pay any taxes, the proceeds of which are specifically appropriated in payment of expenses for the promotion or maintenance of any particular religion or religious denomination.

Freedom as to Attendance at Religious Instruction or Religious Worship in Certain Educational institutions

- No religious instruction shall be provided in any educatioinal institution wholly maintained out of State funds.
- Nothing in clause; (1) shall apply to an educational institution, which is administered by the State but has been established under any endowment or trust, which requires that religious instruction shall be imparted in such institution.
- No person attending any educational institution recognized by the State or receiving aid out of State funds shall be required to take part in any religious instruction that may be imparted in such institution or to attend any religious worship that may be conducted in such institution or in any premises attached thereto unless such person or, if such person is a minor, his guardian has given his consent thereto.

Cultural and Educational Rights

Protection of Interests of Minorities

- Any section of the citizens residing in the territory of India or any part thereof having a distinct language, script or culture of its own shall have the right to conserve the same.
- No citizen shall be denied admission into any educational institution maintained by the state or receiving aid out of State funds on grounds only of religion, race, caste, language or any of them.

Right of Minorities to Establish and Administer Educational Institution

- All minorities, whether based on religion or language, shall have the right to establish and administer educational institutions of their choice. In making any law providing for the compulsory acquisition of any property of any educational institution established and administered by a minority, referred to in clause (1), the state shall ensure that the amount fixed by or determined under such law for the acquisition of such property in such as would not restrict or abrogate the right guaranteed under that clause.
- The State shall not, in granting aid to educational institutions, discriminate against any educational institution on the ground that it is under the management of a minority, whether based on religion or language.

Saving of Laws Providing for Acquisition of Estates etc.

Notwithstanding anything contained in Article 13, no law providing for—

- the acquisition by the State of any estate or of any rights therein or the extinguishment or modification of any such rights, or
- the taking over of the management of any property by the State for a limited period either in the public interest or in order to secure the proper management of the property, or
- the amalgamation of two or more corporations either in the public interest or in order to secure the proper management of any of the corporations, or

- the extinguishment or modification of any rights of managing agents, secretaries and treasurers, managing directors, directors or managers of corporations, or of any voting rights of shareholders thereof, or
- the extinguishment or modification of any rights accruing by virtue of any agreement, lease or licence for the purpose of searching for, or winning, any mineral or mineral oil, or the premature termination or cancellation of any such agreement, lease or licence, shall be deemed to be void on the ground that it is inconsistent with, or takes away or abridges any of the rights conferred by Article 14 or Article 19.

Right to Constitutional Remedies

Remedies for Enforcement of Rights Conferred by this Part

1. The right to move the Supreme Court by appropriate proceedings for the enforcement of the rights conferred by this Part is guaranteed.
2. The Supreme Court shall have power to issue directions or orders or writs, including writs in the nature of habeas corpus, mandamus, prohibition, *quo warranto* and *certiorari*, whichever may be appropriate, for the enforcement of any of the rights conferred by this Part.
3. Without prejudice to the powers conferred on the Supreme Court by clauses (1) and (2), Parliament may by law empower any other court to exercise within the local limits of its jurisdiction all or any of the powers exercisable by the Supreme Court under clause (2).
4. The right guaranteed by this article shall not be suspended except as otherwise provided for by this Constitution.

Power of Parliament to Modify the Rights Conferred by this Part in Their Application to Forces, etc.

Parliament may, by law, determine to what extent any of the rights conferred by this Part shall, in their application to:

1. the members of the Armed Forces; or
2. the members of the Forces charged with the maintenance of public order; or
3. persons employed in any bureau or other organization established by the State for purposes of intelligence or counter intelligence; or
4. persons employed in, or in connection with, the telecommunication systems set up for the purposes of any Force, bureau or organization referred to in clauses (a) to (c), be restricted or abrogated so as to ensure the proper discharge of their duties and the maintenance of discipline among them.

Restriction on Rights Conferred by this Part While Martial Law is in Force in Any Area

Not withstanding anything in the foregoing provisions of this Part, Parliament may by law indemnify any person in the service of the Union or of a State or any other person in respect of any act done by him in connection with the maintenance or restoration of order in any area within the territory of

India where martial law was in force or validate any sentence passed, punishment inflicted, forfeiture ordered or other act done under martial law in such area.

Legislation to give effect to the provisions of this Part

Notwithstanding anything in this Constitution-

(a) Parliament shall have, and the Legislature of a State shall not have, power to make laws—
   (i) with respect to any of the matters which under clause (3) of Article 16, clause (3) of article 32, Article 33 and Article 34 may be provided for by aw made by Parliament; and
   (ii) for prescribing punishment for those acts which are declared to be offences under this Part, and Parliament shall, as soon as may be after the commencement of this Constitution, make laws for prescribing punishment for the acts referred to in sub-clause (ii);

(b) Any law in force immediately before the commencement of this Constitution in the territory of India with respect to any of the matters referred to in sub-clause (i) of clause (a) or providing for punishment for any act referred to in sub-clause (ii) of that clause shall, subject to the terms thereof and to any adaptations and modifications that may be made therein under Article 372, continue in force until altered or repealed or amended by Parliament.

CONSTITUTION OF INDIA AND HUMAN RIGHTS

The Constitution of India incorporates the fundamental values as contained in the UN Declaration of Human Rights. There are several Articles in Part III of the Constitution entitled 'Fundamental Rights', which are parallel to the Declaration. Likewise, Part IV 'Directive Principles of State Policy' contains several provisions similar to human rights.

Article 14 of the Constitution provides: 'The State shall not deny to any person equality before law." This provision reflects the spirit of Article 2 of the UN Declaration of Human Rights. Article 19 of our Constitution gives every Indian the right to move freely, settle and reside in any part of India. This is commensurate with the Article 13 of the Declaration, which provides for freedom of movement and residence. Other provisions in our Constitution which are parallel to the Declaration of Human Rights include Right of Freedom of Worship and Propagation of Religion (Article 25), right of Conservation of One's Language and Culture (Article 29); Right of Equal pay for Equal Work for both Men and Women (Article 39) and Right to have Free and Compulsory Education up to the age of 14 (Article 21A).

ENFORCEMENT OF HUMAN RIGHTS

One of the purposes of the United Nation is the promotion and encouragement of respect for and observance of human rights and fundamental freedoms. The role and scope of UN action in promoting and protecting human rights have tremendously increased in the last sixty-five years. The term promotion of human rights may mean setting of international standard of human rights, education and dissemination. The Charter of UN mentions the term promotion of human rights seven times but does not refer to 'protection' of 'human rights'. The prime responsibility for the promotion of human rights rests in the General Assembly under the UN Charter. It is usually accepted the sustainable achievement of the three agreed global priorities of peace, development and democracy could not be achieved without enforcing human rights. Enforcement of human rights can assure the rights of political choice and association, of opinion and expression, and of culture the freedom from fear and from all forms of discrimination and prejudice, freedom from want and the light to employment and well-being. However, billions continue to live in poverty and there is huge disparity between the rich and the poor. Moreover, there have been violent ethnic conflicts. Communities have been uprooted because of violation of human nature. Consequently, millions have been forced to leave their place of residence. Political extremism and terrorism have targeted countless civilians. Unemployment, discrimination and social exclusion bedevil all societies.

UN WAYS TO PROTECT HUMAN RIGHTS

UN has adopted several covenants declaration and instruments, which are legally binding on the members, and they are obliged to respect the procedures for their implementation. The covenants elaborate the rights identified in the Universal Declaration of Human Rights.

The Covenants form part of the Bill of Human Rights. The United Nations strives to create a culture of human rights around the world. The broadest legally binding human rights agreements negotiated under UN auspices are the International Covenant on Civil and Political Rights and the International covenant on Economic, Social and Cultural Rights. Both were adopted in 1966 and entered into force in 1976. They take the Universal Declaration a step further by making provisions legally binding. A majority of the world's countries are parties to the two conventions, thereby opening the door to international monitoring of their human rights practices. Along with the Universal Declaration, they comprise the International Bill of Rights. Consensus was reached in 1966, and the United Nations General Assembly adopted the International Covenant on Economic, Social and Cultural Rights and the International Covenant on Civil and Political Rights that year. The preambles and articles 1, 2, 3 and 5 are virtually identical in both International Covenants. Both Preambles recognize that human rights derive from the inherent dignity of human beings. Article 1 of each Covenant affirms that all peoples have the right of self-determination and that by virtue of that right they are free to determine their political status and to pursue their economic, social and cultural development. Article 2, in both cases, reaffirms the principle of non-discrimination, echoing the Universal Declaration, while Article 3 stresses that States should ensure the equal right of men and women to the enjoyment of all human rights. Article 5 of both Covenants echoes the final provisions of the Universal Declaration, providing safeguards against the destruction or undue limitation of any human right or fundamental freedom. Two Optional Protocols elaborate certain provisions of the Covenant on Civil and political Rights, one providing for complaints by individuals, the other advocating the abolition of the death penalty.

PROMOTION AND PROTECTION OF HUMAN RIGHTS BY THE UNITED NATIONS

One of the purposes of the United Nations is promotion and encouragement of respect for and observance of human rights. The term promotion of human rights may mean setting of international standard of human rights, education and dissemination. Under the U.N. Charter the prime responsibility for the promotion of human rights rests in the General Assembly, in the Economic and Social Council and its, subsidiary body—the Commission on Human Rights. The General Assembly has adopted treaties setting standards. It socializes into those standards. It holds conferences and seminars to spread the message of human rights values found in international documents.

Enforcement is the authoritative application of human rights. Among the United Nations agencies, only the Security Council and the International Court of Justice can engage in enforcement action. They alone have the competence to pass a binding resolution or issue a binding judgment. The Security Council can threaten or vote sanctions in relation to its own previous actions or that of the Court.

Implementation efforts include passing non-binding resolutions about specific problems of States. When a U.N. agency approves a resolution calling on a specific State to take specific human rights action, it generates political pressure on the target. This is an effort at protection, not just promotion.

UN WAYS TO PROTECT HUMAN RIGHTS

1. Human Rights Consciousness: The United Nations has made the people and the States conscious of the human rights and fundamental freedom. It has set a pace in establishing minimum standards of acceptable behaviour by states. The proclamation of the Universal Declaration of Human Rights containing the universal code of human rights is the first step towards the promotion and protection of human rights.

2. Codification of the Law of Human Rights: The United Nations has codified the different rights and freedom for all sections of the people such as women, child, migrant workers, refugees and stateless persons. The prohibition of genocide, apartheid, racial discrimination and torture have been brought within the international rule of law.

3. Monitoring of Human rights: Treaty bodies, Special Reporters and Working Groups of the Commission of Human Rights prescribe procedures and mechanisms to monitor compliance with conventions. They investigate allegations of human rights abuses. Termed as U.N. Treaty Organs a number of expert committees established under particular treaties are not subsidiary organs of the United Nations, but autonomous. Their resolutions on specific cases carry a moral weight that a few Governments are willing to defy. U.N. Human Rights monitors have been sent to many countries including EI Salvador and Cambodia. They have also worked as part of peacekeeping operations in Haiti, Rwanda, Guatemala and the former Yugoslavia.

4. Procedure for Individual's Complaints: Many human rights treaties permit individuals to make petition before the appropriate international bodies. The First Optional protocol to the International Covenant on Civil and Political Rights, the International convention on the Elimination of All Forms of Racial Discrimination and Convention against Torture, permit individuals to make petitions against their States that have accepted relevant international legal procedures. The Commission on Human Rights, its Sub-Commission on Prevention of Discrimination and Protection of Minorities and their Working groups, hear numerous complaints annually submitted by individuals as well as by non-governmental organizations (NGO). The Commission on Human Rights may discuss human rights situations anywhere in the World. It may examine information from individuals, NGOs and other sources.

5. Resolution 1503: In 1970, The Economic and Social Council adopted a Resolution entitled 'Procedure for Dealing with Communications Relating to Violations of Human Rights and Fundamental Freedom' commonly known as '1503 Resolution' wherein individuals and non-governmental organizations (NGO) were allowed to make a communication to the commission concerning "situations which appear to reveal a consistent pattern of gross and reliably attested violations of human rights". A communication, i.e., a complaint is sent to the Office of the UN High Commissioner for Human Rights in Geneva. The Commission has focused the 1503 procedure mainly on civil and political rights using reporters and working groups in specific countries and specific problems. Individual petitions help to provide some check on governmental violations of human rights as they provide a source of information to international organizations.

6. Compilations of Information on the Violations of Human Rights: Commission on Human Rights examines situations where massive violations of rights appear to be taking place has been complemented by a new function. It compiles information on the incidence of certain kinds of violations, or violation in a specific country through Special Reporters / Representative or Working Groups. These gather facts, keep contacts with local groups and government authorities, conduct on-site visits and make recommendations on how human rights institutions might be strengthened.

7. Examination of Human Rights Situations: The Commission on Human Rights may ask the Secretary–General to intervene or send an expert to examine human rights situations in any State to prevent flagrant violations. The Secretary-General himself in the exercise of his good offices may perform such tasks. This may establish the U.N.'s legitimate concern and curb abuses. The Secretary-General or his special representative and the High Commissioner for Human Rights, confidentially raise human rights concerns with member States, including items such as the release of prisoners, commutation of death sentences and other issues.

8. Coordination of Human Rights Activities: In 1993, the post of High Commissioner for Human Rights was created for strengthening the coordination and impact of UN Human Rights activities. All charge him with promoting and protecting the effective enjoyment of all human rights. He maintains a permanent dialogue with the member States.

9. Providing Advisory Services: The Centre for Human Rights provides advisory services to Governments seeking to improve their human rights performance. Assistance may be given to draft a constitution, to improve electoral laws, establish or upgrade human rights institutions, prepare new criminal codes, or overhaul the judiciary.

Thus, the United Nations has been performing a variety of functions to promote and protect human rights.

(i) It has promoted global culture of human rights through education and awareness. Regarded as a matter of domestic jurisdiction of the States. Human Rights have acquired an international character, vis-à-vis, international human rights. International human rights are increasingly a well-established issue area of international politics,

(ii) States are increasingly obligated to respect human rights norms, and

(iii) Individuals have increasingly obtained legal personality, in the form of partial subjectivity, with regard to human rights matters.

Limitations/Result of UN Action

1. The impact of the U.N. activities on international human rights issues has been indirect and long term. All of its promotion efforts and most of its protection attempts entail considerable time to have an impact.
2. Human rights continue to be widely violated around the globe. Fundamental rights of individual's life, liberty and physical security, right to health, housing and work as well as cultural rights continue to be threatened by forces of repression, ethnic hatred and exploitation.
3. Torture, cruel and inhuman punishment for seemingly minor crimes to spousal and child abuse have led to the description of societies and ethnic, religious and other conflicts. The

United Nations has to intervene in cases of massive human rights violations. It has to work with the cooperation of the member States to strengthen the commitments of promoting and protecting human rights.

HUMAN RIGHTS ABUSES AND PREVENTION

Over the years, the United Nations has developed different methods to investigate human rights abuses and to press for remedial action. Experts known as special reporters of representatives gather facts, visit prisons, interview victims, and make recommendations on how to increase respect for human rights. They investigate situations in specific countries and conduct thematic studies on such issues as torture, religious intolerance, racism, the sale of children and violence against women. Each year they send thousands of urgent cables to Governments requesting the release of prisoners, the commutation of death sentences or other vital action. Working groups have been established to investigate such issues as involuntary disappearances and arbitrary detention. Their reports highlighting human rights violations help to mobilize international attention.

- Human rights agreements depend on the cooperation of Governments and people. The United Nations offers technical assistance to Governments in the following areas to promote human rights:
- Supporting democratization and advising on electoral procedures.
- Assisting in the drafting of national laws and preparation of national reports.
- Strengthening national and regional institutions, such as courts and school systems.
- Training criminal justice personnel—judges, lawyers, prosecutors and police.

COMMISSION ON HUMAN RIGHTS

Establishment

The establishment of a Commission on Human Rights was recommended in 1945 by the Preparatory Commission of the United Nations in order to deal with those human rights issues, which could not be resolved during the original drafting of the U.N. Charter. A principal organ of the United Nations 'The Economic and Social Council (ECOSOC)' was most directly concerned with the question of human rights. Under Article 68 of the U.N. Charter, the Council was empowered to set up commissions for the promotion of human rights. Accordingly, it appointed a Commission on Human Rights, which was approved by the General Assembly on February 12, 1946. It was composed of 18 members and elected by ECOSOC. Each State member selected its own representatives. In 1962, the membership increased to 21, and in 1966 to 32. Since, 1990, the Commission has 53 member Government. It meets annually in Geneva for six weeks beginning in March. It reports to ECOSOC, which, in turn, reports to the General Assembly. The Commission was directed to prepare recommendations and reports on the following items:

(i) International bill of rights;
(ii) International declarations and conventions on civil liberties, the status of women, freedom of information and similar matters.
(iii) Protection of minorities.
(iv) Prevention of discrimination on grounds of race, sex, language or religion.

Functioning

The Commission began its work in January 1947 under the chairmanship of Mrs. Franklin D. Roosevelt. In its First session, it established the Sub-Commission on Prevention of Discrimination and Protection of Minorities, a body of independent experts. In the same session, it appointed a committee known as Drafting Committee for the preparation of the draft of an International Bill of Rights. The Committee drafted the Universal Declaration of Human Rights adopted by the General Assembly on December 10, 1948. Using the Declaration as the basis, the Commission prepared in 1966, International covenant on civil and Political Rights and International Covenant on Economic, social and Cultural Rights. In 1967, the Commission set up an *ad hoc* working group of experts on South Africa. It has since established working groups on Chile; Situations revealing consistent Pattern of Gross violations on Human Rights; Disappearances and the right to development.

- The Commission has set up elaborate machinery and procedures, country oriented or thematic to monitor compliance by States with international human rights law and investigate alleged violations of human rights. It has acted mainly be dispatching fact-finding missions to rich or poor, developing or developed countries in all parts of the World. In 1994, the Special Report on Religious Intolerance visited China Special Report on Contemporary Forms of Racism visited the United States of America.
- In 1990s, the Commission increasingly turned its attention to provide advisory services and technical assistance to the needy States so that they may overcome the obstacle in securing the enjoyment of human rights by all. More, emphasis has been put on the promotion of economic, social and cultural rights, including the right to development and the right to an adequate standard of living. Increased attention is being given to the protection of the rights of vulnerable groups in society, including minorities and indigenous people and to the protection of the rights of the child and of women.

Centre for Human Rights

Located at Geneva to coordinate activities, the Centre provided staff for the Commission, the Sub-Commission, the Human Rights Committee, the Committee on the Elimination of Racial Discrimination and other policy–making or investigate bodies. It prepared studies, reports and publications and provided advisory services and technical assistance to governments. The Centre implemented the different aspects of the programme entrusted to the United Nations. When the General Assembly adopted a programme of action relating to human rights, such as, the Programme for the Second Decade for Action to Combat Racism and Racial Discrimination in 1983.

Recommendations

The Vienna Declaration and programme of Action adopted by the World Conference on Human Rights in 1993 stressed the importance of str4engthening the Centre for Human Rights. It stated that the Centre should play an important role in co-coordinating system-wide attention for human rights. The focal role of the Centre can best be realized if it is enabled to cooperate fully with other United Nations bodies and organs. The Centre should be assured adequate means for the system of thematic and country reporters, experts, working groups and treaty bodies. Follow-up on recommendations should become a priority matter for consideration by the Commission on Human Rights.

Achievements

- The Centre always remained at the disposal of victims of human rights violations, their relatives and non-governmental activities, to allow them to contact the Centre for Human Rights.
- It provided, on request, technical assistance in the field of human rights such as assistance in drafting new constitutions and laws in the line with human rights, conventions.
- Assistance has been given to Bulgaria Malawi and Mongolia. Provided assistance in the drafting of national laws and preparations of national reports.
- Regional and sub-regional training courses have been held in Africa, Latin America and the Pacific.
- The Centre has also provided assistance to institutions in various countries to strengthen human rights protection and promotion activities.

UN HIGH COMMISSIONER FOR HUMAN RIGHTS

- In 1997, the Centre for Human rights was consolidated with the UN High Commissioner for Human Rights with a single office of the United Nations High commissioner for Human Rights (OHCHR).
- UN High Commissioner for Human rights seeks to promote and protect the effective enjoyment by all of all civil, political, economic, social and cultural rights.
- The office of the High commissioner is located at Geneva with a branch office in New York. The Secretary – General as the first High Commissioner, nominated Jose Ayala Lasso of Ecuador.

Responsibilities

- Promote and protect the effective enjoyment by all of all civil, cultural, economic, political and social rights, including the right to development.
- Provide advisory services, technical and financial assistance in the field of human rights to States that request them.
- Co-ordinate United Nations education and public information programmes in the field of human rights.
- Play an active role in removing the obstacles to the full realization of human rights and in preventing the continuation of human rights violations throughout the world.
- Engage in a dialogue with Governments in order to secure respect for human rights.
- Enhance international co-operation for the promotion and protection of human rights.
- Co-ordinate human rights promotion and protection activities throughout the United National system.
- Rationalize, adapt, strengthen and streamline the United Nations machinery in the fields of human rights in order to improve its efficiency and effectiveness.
- Report annually to the Commission on Human Rights and through the Economic and Social Council to the General Assembly.
- Carry out the 'good offices' function in the field of human rights on behalf of the Secretary-General.
- Promote and protect human rights for all and maintain continuing dialogue with Member States.

In 1997, the Office of the UN Commissioner for Human Rights was consolidated along with the Centre of Human rights into a single Office of the United Nations High commissioner for Human Rights (OHCHR).

Human Rights 'Hot Line'

In 1994, the United Nations High Commissioner for Human Rights established a Human Rights Hot line, a 24 hours facsimile line that will allow the Office of the High Commissioner for Human rights in Geneva to monitor and react rapidly to human rights emergencies. The Hot line is available to victims of human rights violations, their relatives and non-governmental organizations. It is valuable to those wishing to establish urgent, potentially life-saving contact with the Special Procedures Branch of the Office of the High Commissioner for Human Rights.

Office of the United Nations High Commissioner for Human Rights (OHCHR)

On September 15, 1997 the Office of the UN High Commissioner for Human Rights and the Centre for Human Rights were consolidated into a single Office of the United Nations High Commissioner for Human Rights (OHCHR). Located at Geneva OHCHR maintains a liaison office in New York as well as numerous country officers around the world. A High Commissioner with the rank of Under-Secretary-General heads the office.

Responsibilities

- The High Commissioner is responsible for all the activities of the Office of the United Nations High Commissioner for Human Rights.
- He carries out the functions specifically assigned to him or her by the General Assembly in its resolution 48/41 of December 20, 1993, i.e., the resolution that created the post of the High Commissioner for Human Rights.
- He advises the Secretary-General on the policies of the United Nations in the area of human rights.
- He ensures that substantive and administrative support is given to the projects, activities, organs and bodies of the human rights programmes.
- He represents the Secretary-General at meetings of the human rights organs and at other human rights events.
- He also carries out special assignments as decided by the Secretary-General.

Deputy Commissioner

In the performance of his or her activities, the United Nations High Commissioner for Human Rights is assisted by a Deputy to the High Commissioner who acts as officer-in-charge during the absence of the High Commissioner. The Deputy also carries out specific substantive and administrative assignments as decided by the High Commissioner. The Deputy is accountable to the High Commissioner.

State Office

The OHCHR has a State Office headed by a chief accountable to the High Commissioner. It assists the high Commissioner in the overall direction and supervision of the activities of the human rights programme. It also assists the High Commissioner in the formulation, communication, implementation and evaluation of policies, practices and activities for the promotion and protection of human rights. It assists the High Commissioner in maintaining relations with Governments, other United Nations agencies and entities, international organizations, regional and national institutions, non-governmental organizations, the private sector and academic.

New York Office

The OHCHR maintains an office at the Headquarters called New York office headed by a Director accountable to the High Commissioner. The Director performs a number of functions including the representation the High Commissioner at Headquarters, at meetings of policy-making bodies, with permanent missions of Member States. The New York office also provides advice and recommendations on substantive matters to the High Commissioner.

Administrative Section

A Chief who is accountable to the High Commissioner heads the Administrative Section. The core functions of the Administrative Section are to advise the High Commissioner on the budgetary; financial and personnel matters relating to the human rights programme and to assist him and provide appropriate staff in the discharge of their financial, personnel and general administrative responsibilities and administering the associate report and internship programmes.

Functions of OHCHR

- It promotes universal enjoyment of all human rights by giving practical effect to the will and resolve of the World community as expressed by the United Nations.
- It plays the leading role on human rights issues and emphasizes the importance of human rights at the international and national levels.
- It promotes international cooperation for human rights.
- It stimulates and coordinates action for human rights throughout the United Nations system.
- It promotes universal ratification and implementation of international standards.
- It assists in the development of new norms.
- It supports human rights organ and treaty monitoring bodies.
- It responds to serious violations of human rights.
- It undertakes preventive human rights action.
- It promotes the establishment of national human rights infrastructures.
- It undertakes human rights field activities and operations.
- It provides education, information, advisory services and technical assistance in the field of human rights.

Difficulties in Implementation

1. The International Court of Justice is open to States only. It implies that individuals have no access to the Court. Thus, it has always refused to entertain the petitions and requests, which have often been addressed to it by individuals.

2. The jurisdiction of the International Court of Justice depends upon the consent of the States involved, and few States to dispute involving human rights have done this.
3. Even if In-ternational Court in a few cases is able to render judgments against the State, which violates human rights, there is no international police to enforce the decisions of the Court. No doubt, the Security Council has been empowered to enforce the decisions of the Court against a party to a case, which has failed to perform the obligations under a judgment of the Court, if the aggrieved party brings the matter before it. But it is regarded as a political body and its recommendations are sometimes motivated by political considerations. If the barrier of veto is not crossed, the Council becomes incompetent to take any decision against the State, which has failed to comply the decision of the Court.
4. Although the International Law of Human Rights has fostered a growing political and legal support for the protection of human rights, many States still regard that enforcement of human rights is an interventionist act. Consequently, implementation of International Human Rights Law depends largely on voluntary compliance by the States. Security Council, of course, can take collective action against a State if it decides that violations of human rights by a State are likely to endanger international peace and security.

Need of Domestic Laws

The most effective way to implement human rights vests within the legal systems of the different States. Domestic law of a State is required to provide an effective system of remedies for violations of international human rights obligations. International Human Rights Law has not become that strong to enforce and implement human rights violations committed by a State.

INDIAN LAWS RELATING TO HUMAN RIGHTS

The following is a list of some of the important national statutes, which have a bearing on the promotion/ protection of Human Rights.

1. **Constitution of India (Preamble Parts III, IV and IVA, Articles 226, 300A, 325, 326).**
2. **Protection of Human Rights Act, 1993.** 'The act provides for the constitution of a National Human rights Commission, State Human Rights Commissions, and Human Rights Courts for better protection of human rights'.
3. **National commission for Scheduled Castes and Scheduled Tribes.** 'Article 338 of the Constitution requires constitution of the National Commission for Scheduled Castes and Scheduled Tribes for better protection of the rights of the members of the Scheduled Castes and Scheduled Tribes'.
4. **National Commission for minorities Act, 1992.** It is an Act to constitute a National Commission for Women for better protection of the rights of women.
5. **National Commission for Women Act, 1990.** It is an Act to constitute a National Commission for Women for better protection of the rights of women.
6. **Protection of Civil Rights Act, 1955.** 'Under Article 17 of the Constitution, un-touchability is abolished and its practice in any form is forbidden. By this Act, enforcement of any disability arising out of un-touchability has been made in offence punishable in accordance with the relevant provisions'.

7. **Scheduled Castes and Scheduled Tribes (Prevention of Atrocities) Act, 1989.** It is an Act to prevent the commission of atrocities against the members of the Scheduled Castes and the Scheduled Tribes, for constitution of special courts for trial of such offences, and to provide relief and rehabilitation to the victims.
8. **Employment of Manual Scavengers and Construction of Dry Latrines (Prohibition) Act, 1993.** 'Fraternity, assuring the dignity of the individual is one of the objects proclaimed in the Preamble to the Constitution. Article 47 requires the State to raise the standard of living and improve the health of the people. This Act has been enacted to achieve those objectives. It provides for the prohibition of all manual scavengers as well as construction or continuance of dry latrines and for the regulation of construction and maintenance of water-seal latrines'.
9. **Immoral Traffic (Prevention) Act, 1956.** 'Article 23 of the Constitution prohibits traffic in human beings. On 9 May 1950, India ratified the International Convention for Suppression of Immoral Traffic in Women and Girls. This is an Act to give effect to the same'.
10. **Indecent Representation of Women (Prohibition) Act, 1986.** It is an Act to prohibit indecent representation of women through advertisements or in publications, writings, paintings, figures, or in any other manner'.
11. **Dowry Prohibition Act, 1961.** 'This is an Act to prohibit the evil practice of giving and taking of dowry'.
12. **Commission of Sati (Prevention) Act, 1987.** 'Sati or burning or burying alive of widows or women is revolting to the feelings of human nature and is nowhere enjoined by any of the religions of India as an imperative duty. This is an Act for effective prevention of the commission of Sati and its glorification'.
13. **Maternity Benefit Act, 1961.** 'This is an Act to provide maternity benefits, etc. and to regulate employment of women in certain establishments for certain periods before and after child birth'.
14. **Child Marriage Restraint Act, 1929.** 'This was enacted with a view to preventing child marriages, namely, a marriage to which either of the contracting parties is under the specified age'.
15. **Children (Pledging of Labour) Act, 1933.** It is an Act to prohibit the pledging of the labour of children and the employment of children whose labour has been pledged.
16. **Orphanages and Other Charitable Homes (Supervision and control) Act, 1960.** It is an Act to provide for the supervision and control of orphanages, homes for neglected women or children and other like institutions and to penalize criminal activities indulged in such institutions.
17. **Children Act, 1960.** It is an Act to provide for the care, protection, maintenance, welfare, training, education and rehabilitation of children and for trial of delinquent children in the Union territories.
18. **Child labour prohibition and Regulation) Act, 1986.** 'The Act bans employment of children in specified occupations and processes, lays down a procedure for inclusion in the schedule of banned occupations and processes and regulates the conditions of work of children in employments where they are not prohibited from working'.
19. **Juvenile Justice Act, 1986.** It is an Act to provide for the care, protection treatment, development and rehabilitation of neglected or delinquent juveniles and to provide a specialized approach for the juvenile justice system.

20. **Young Persons (Harmful Publications) Act, 1956.** 'Pictorial and other publications containing stories of crime, violence, cruelty or incidents of repulsive or horrible nature would tend to corrupt a young person and incite or encourage him to commit such acts. The Act seeks to prevent the dissemination of publications, which are harmful to young persons'.
21. **Caste Disabilities Removal Act, 1950.** 'The Act provides that when in a civil suit the parties belong to different persuasions, the laws of the religions of the parties shall not be permitted to operate to deprive such parties of any property which but for the operation of such laws, they would have been entitled'.
22. **Mental Health Act, 1987.** 'The Act regulates determination of lunacy, reception, care and treatment of mentally ill persons'.
23. **Bonded Labour (System) Abolition Act, 1976.** 'Article 23 of the Constitution prohibits "beggar" and other similar forms of forced labour and further provides that any contravention of the said prohibition shall be an offence punishable in accordance with law. The Act provides for the abolition of bonded labour system to prevent the economic and physical exploitation of the weaker sections of the people'.

NATIONAL HUMAN RIGHTS COMMISSION

The National Human Rights Commission was constituted in October 1993 under the Human Rights Ordinance of 28 September 1993, which was soon after enacted as the Protection of Human Rights act, 1993 (No. 10 of 1994) (hereinafter referred to as 'the Act'). It is a fully autonomous body; its autonomy derived out of the method of appointment of the members, their fixity of tenure, and statutory guarantees thereto, the status they have been accorded; the manner in which the staff responsible to the Commission would be appointed and would conduct themselves; as also the autonomy it enjoys in terms of its financial powers.

Composition of the Commission

- The Act envisages that the Commission shall consist of:
  1. A chairperson who has been a Chief Justice of the Supreme court;
  2. One Member who is or has been, a Judge of the Supreme court;
  3. One Member who is, or has been, the Chief Justice of a High Court;
  4. Two Members to be appointed from amongst persons having knowledge of, r practical experience in, matters elating to human rights.
- The Chairperson of the National Commission for minorities, the National Commission for the Scheduled Castes and Scheduled tribes and the National Commission for Women shall be deemed Members of the Commission for the discharge of certain functions.
- There shall be a Secretary-General of the rank of the Secretary to the Government of India who shall function as the Chief Executive Officer of the Commission.
- The Headquarters of the Commission shall be at Delhi and there is an enabling provision in the Act to establish offices at other places in India with the previous approval of the Central Government.
- The method of appointment envisaged in the Act is unique in as much as it is made by the president on the recommendations of a high-powered Committee consisting of the following:

(a) The Prime Minister - Chairperson
(b) Speaker of the House of the People - Member
(c) Minister-in-charge of the MHA in the Government of India - Member
(d) Leader of the Opposition in the House of the People - Member
(e) Leader of the Opposition in the Council of States - Member
(f) Deputy Chairman of the Council of States - Member

- However, no sitting Judge of the Supreme Court or a sitting Chief Justice of a High Court shall be appointed without consultation with the Chief Justice of India.
- The Chairperson or any other Member of the Commission can only be removed from his office by an order of the President on the ground of proved misbehaviour or incapacity after the Supreme Court has, on an inquiry held in this behalf recommended such removal.
- The term of office of the Chairperson and members will be five years from the date of assumption of office or until the age of 70 years, whichever is earlier. On ceasing to hold office, the Chairperson and Members shall be ineligible for further appointment under the Government of India or under the Government of any State.

Officers and Other Staff of the Commission

- The Act provides that besides the Secretary–General, the Central Government shall make available to the commission such police and investigative staff and an officer not below the rank of Director General of Police and such other officers and staff as may be necessary for the efficient performance of the functions of the Commission. The Commission may appoint other administrative, technical and scientific staff considered necessary in conformity with the Rules made by the Central Government in this behalf.

Functions of the Commission

The following functions devolve in the Commission under the Act:

(a) Inquire, on its own initiative or a petition presented to it by a victim or any persons on his behalf, into complaints of:
  (i) Violation of human rights or abatement thereof; or
  (ii) Negligence in the prevention of such violation, by a public servant.
(b) Intervene in any proceeding involving any allegation of violation of human rights pending before a court with the approval of such court;
(c) Visit under intimation to the State government, any jail or any other institution under the control of the State Government, where persons are detained or lodged for purposes of treatment, reformation or protection to study the living conditions of the inmates and makes recommendations thereon;
(d) Review the safeguards provided by or under the constitution or any law for the time being in force for the protection of human rights and recommend measures for their effective implementation;
(e) Review the factors, including acts of terrorism that inhibit the enjoyment of human rights and recommend appropriate remedial measures;

(f) Study treaties and other international instruments on human rights and make recommendations for their effective implementation;
(g) Undertake and promote research in the field of human rights;
(h) Spread human rights literacy among various sections of society and promote awareness of the safeguards available for the protection of these rights through publications, the media, seminars and other available means;
(i) Encourage the efforts of non-governmental organizations and institutions working in the field of human rights; and
(j) Such other functions as it may consider necessary for the promotion of human rights.

Procedure for Dealing with Complaints

- The complaints are expected to be self-contained. They may be in Hindi, English or in any language included in the eighth Schedule of the Constitution. No fee is charged on complaints. The Commission may ask for further information and affidavits to be filed in support of allegations whenever considered necessary. The Commission may, in its discretion, accept telegraphic complaints and complaints conveyed through FAX.

Nature of Complaints not Entertained

Ordinarily, the Commission does not entertain complaints of the following nature:

(a) About events which happened more than one year before the making of the complaints.
(b) With regard to matters which are sub-judice;
(c) Which are vague, anonymous or pseudonymous;
(d) Which are of frivolous nature;
(e) Those which are outside the purview of the Commission; and
(f) Which pertain to service matters?

Powers Relating to Inquiries

The Commission is vested with the wide-ranging powers relating to inquiries and investigation under the Act. While inquiring into complaints under the Act, the Commission could exercise all the powers of a civil court trying a suit under the code of Civil Procedure, 1908, and in particular in respect of the following, namely:

(a) Summoning and enforcing the attendance of witnesses and examining them on oath;
(b) Discovery and production of any document;
(c) Receiving evidence on affidavits;
(d) Requisitioning any public record or copy thereof from any court or office;
(e) Issuing commissions of the examination of witnesses or documents; and
(f) Any other matter, which may be prescribed.

Investigation Staff

The Commission has its own investigating staff for investigation into complaints of human rights violations. Under the Act, it is also open to the Commission to utilize the services of any officer or investigation agency of the Central Government or any State Government. In addition, the Commission envisages the association in appropriate cases of outsiders as Investigators or Observers.

Inquiry into Complaints

The Commission, while inquiring into complaints of violations of human rights, may call for information or report from the Central Government, any State Government, or any other authority or organization subordinate thereto within such time as may be specified by it. If the information or report is not received within the time stipulated by the Commission, it may proceed to inquire into the complaint on its own; on the other hand, if, on receipt of information or report, the Commission is satisfied either that no further inquiry is required or that the required action has been initiated or taken by the concerned Government or authority, it may not proceed with the complaint and inform the complainant accordingly.

Steps after Inquiry

The Commission may take any of the following steps upon the completion of any inquiry:

1. Where the inquiry discloses the commission of violation of human rights or negligence in the prevention of violation of human rights by a public servant, it may recommend to the concerned Government or authority the initiation of proceedings for prosecution or such other action as the Commission may deem fit against the concerned person or persons;
2. Approach the Supreme Court or the High court concerned for such directions, orders or writs as that Court may deed necessary;
3. Recommend to the concerned Government or authority for the grant of such immediate interim relief to the victim or the members of his family as the Commission may consider necessary;
4. Subject to the provisions of (5) below, provide a copy of the enquiry report to the petitioner or his representative;
5. The Commissioner shall send a copy of its inquiry report together with its recommendations to the concerned. Government or authority and the concerned Government or authority shall, within a period of the month, or such further time as the Commission may allow, forward its comments on the report, including the action taken or proposed to be taken thereon, of the Commission;
6. The Commission shall publish its inquiry report together with the comments of the concerned Government or authority, if any, and the action taken or proposed to be taken by the concerned Government or authority on the recommendations of the Commission.

Procedure with Respect to Armed Forces

The term 'armed forces' for purposes of the Act means the naval, military and air forces and includes any other armed forces of the Union. The act envisages the procedure with respect to armed forces, which is at variance with the procedure set out for complaints of violations of human rights by any other public servant.

1. The Commission shall, notwithstanding other provisions of the Act, adopt the following procedure while dealing with complaints of violations of human rights by Members of the armed forces.
   (a) It either may, on its own motion or on receipt of a petition, seek a report from the Central Government.
   (b) After the receipt of the report, it may either not proceed with the complaint or, as the case may be, make its recommendations to that Government.
2. The Central Government shall inform the commission of the action taken on the recommendations within three months or such further time as the Commission may allow.
3. The Commission shall publish its report together with its recommendations made to the Central Government and the action taken by that Government on such recommendations.
4. The Commission shall provide a copy of the previously mentioned report to the petitioner or his representative.

Responsibility of the Central Government/State Government/Authority to which report/recommendation have been sent

The Central Government/State Government/Authority have to indicate its comments/action on the report/recommendations of the Commission within a period of one month in respect of general complaints and within three months in respect of complaints relating to armed forces.

Annual and Special Reports of the Commission

- The Commission is required to submit an Annual Report to the Central Government as well as the State Governments concerned. Besides, the Commission may at any time submit Special Reports on any matter, which, in its opinion, is of such urgency or importance that it should not be deferred until submission of the Annual Report.
- It is enjoined on the Central Government as well as the concerned State Government to lay before each House of Parliament or the State Legislatures respectively the Annual and Special Reports of the Commission along with a memorandum of action taken or proposeod to be taken on the recommendations of the Commission and the reasons for non-acceptance of the recommendations, if any.

STATE HUMAN RIGHTS COMMISSION

Structure

- There is an enabling provision in the Act for State Human Rights Commission to be constituted by the respective State Governments. The State Commission shall consist of:
  (a) A Chairperson who has been a Chief Justice of a High Court;
  (b) One Member who is, or has been, a Judge of a High Court;
  (c) One Member who is, or has been, a District Judge in that state;
  (d) Two Members to be appointed from amongst persons having knowledge of, or practical experience in, matters relating to human rights.

- There shall be a Secretary who shall be the Chief Executive Officer of the State Commission and shall exercise such powers and discharge such functions of the State Commission as it may delegate to him.
- The headquarters of the State Commission shall be at such place as the State Government may, by notification, specify.

Constitution of the State Commission

The Chairperson and other Members of the Commission shall be appointed by the Government after obtaining the recommendations of a committee consisting of:

(a) The Chief Minister	Chairperson
(b) Speaker of the Legislative Assembly	Member
(c) Ministry-in-charge of the Department	Member
(d) Leader of the Opposition in the Legislative Assembly	Member

Where there is a Legislative Council in a State, the Chairman of that Council and the Leader of the Opposition in that Council shall also be members of the committee. No sitting Judge of a High Court or a sitting District Judge shall be appointed except after consultation with the Chief Justice of the High Court of the concerned State.

The term of office of the Chairperson or Member will be five years from the date of assumption of office or at the age of 70 years, whichever is earlier. A Member is, however, eligible for reappointment for another term of five years subject to the age limit of 70 years. On ceasing to hold office, the Chairperson or a Member is ineligible for appointment under the Government of the State or under the Government of India.

Officers and Staff of the State Commission

The concerned State Government shall make available to the State Commission an officer not below the rank of a Secretary to the State Government who shall be the secretary of the State Commission and such police and investigative staff under an officer not below the rank of an Inspector General of Police and such other officers and staff as may be necessary for the efficient performance of the functions of the State Commission. The State Commission may appoint such other administrative, technical and scientific staff, as it may consider necessary.

Functions of the State Commission

A State Commission may inquire into violations of human rights only in respect of matters relating to any of the entries enumerated in List II (State List) and List III (Concurrent List) in the Seventh Schedule of the Constitution. However, if the National Commission or any other Statutory Commission is already inquiring into any such matter, the State Commission shall not inquire into the said matter. Subject to this, the powers, the procedure of investigation, inquiry and steps to be taken thereafter are comparable to those of the National Commission.

Annual or Special Reports of the Commission

The State Commission shall submit Annual Report to the respective State Governments and may, at any time, submit Special Reports on any matter, which in their opinion is of urgency or importance. It is enjoined on the State Governments to cause to lay on the Table of the respective State Legislature the Annual and Special Reports of the State Human Rights omission.

Human Rights Courts

The Act envisages that for providing speedy trial of offences arising out of violations of human rights, State Governments may with the concurrence of the Chief Justice of the Concerned High Court specify for each District Court of Sessions to be a Human rights Court to try such offences. For every Human Rights Court, the State Government shall specify a public prosecutor or appoint an advocate of at least seven years standing as a Special Public Prosecutor for conducting cases in that Court.

Finance, Accounts and Audit

The Central Government and the concerned State Government shall, after due appropriation made in this behalf, pay to the National Commission and the concerned State Commission respectively by way of grant necessary funds for being utilized for purposes of the Act. The accounts of the Commission will have to be maintained in an appropriate form devised in consultation with the Comptroller and Auditor General of India and are subject to audit by the latter or any person appointed by him. The accounts of the Commission as certified by the Comptroller and Auditor General or his appointee together with the Audit report shall be laid before each house of Parliament by the Central Government in the case of National Commission and before the appropriate State Legislature by the concerned State Government in respect of the State Commission.

Miscellaneous

- The National Commission as well as the State Commission shall not inquire into any matter, which is pending before a State Commission or National Commission as the case may be, or any other statutory Commission.
- If the Government considers it necessary, it may, notwithstanding anything contained in any other Law, constitute one or more special investigation teams consisting of the requisite police officers for purposes of investigation and prosecution of offences arising out of violations of human rights.
- The Central Government as well as the State Government concerned may make rules to carry out the provisions of the Act. The Rules so made are required to be laid before each House of Parliament for a total period of 30 days as regards the National Human Rights Commission and appropriate State Legislature in respect of the State Commission.

HUMAN RIGHTS EDUCATION

All human rights documents stress the importance of education in promoting human rights. In fact, a part of the Vienna Declaration reproduced in Section II, is devoted to Human Rights Education. Moreover, the General Assembly of the United Nations proclaimed this Universal Declaration of Human Rights in the end that every individual and every organ of society shall strive by teaching and education to promote respect for human rights and freedom. Similarly, many Articles in the Convention on the Rights of the child are concerned with various aspects of the right to education and the content of education including among others, "that the education of the child shall be directed to . . . the development of respect for human rights and freedoms."

HISTORY OF HUMAN RIGHTS EDUCATION

In 1974, the General Conference of UNESCO adopted the "Recommendation concerning Education for International Understanding, Cooperation and Peace and Education relating to Human Rights and Fundamental Freedom" that has gained very large acceptance and has inspired teachers, students and educational authorities as well as peace and human rights activists, individuals and associations, all over the world in their work. In 1978 and 1987, UNESCO held international congresses on human rights teaching, information and documentation in Vienna and Malta resulting in long-term actions of the Organisation. In March 1993, the third congress in their series was organized in Montreal, Canada, where a World Plan of Action on Education for Human Rights and Democracy was adopted as a common strategy of all those committed to these aims. The United Nations World Conference on Human rights (Vienna, June 1993) commended as the basis for relevant actions in the future.

- In 1994, the United Nations Decade (1995–2004) was proclaimed.
- In April 2004, the Commission on Human Rights adopted resolution 2004/71 in which it took note of the need to continue a global framework for human rights education beyond the Decade.

SIGNIFICANCE OF HUMAN RIGHTS EDUCATION

- The United Nations considers education as the key to development, as a fundamental human right and as a prime means in the promotion of human rights. The Universal Declaration of Human Rights Article 26.2 states "Education shall be directed to the full development of the human personality and to the strengthening of respect for human rights and fundamental freedoms. It shall promote understanding tolerance and friendship among all nations, racial or religious groups and shall further the activities of the United Nations for the maintenance of peace."
- In the words of the General Assembly resolution establishing the Decade of Human Rights Education, human rights education is intended to be "a life-long process by which people at all levels of development and in all strata of society learn respect for the dignity of others and the means of ensuring that respect in all societies." In this sense, human rights education significantly contributes to promoting equality and sustainable development, preventing conflict and human rights violations and enhancing participation and democratic processes, with a view to developing societies in which all human rights of all are valued and respected.
- According to UNESCO Director–General Koichiro Matsuura, "Human rights education is indispensable for every individual to fully enjoy and claim a life of security and dignity. It is indispensable for public officials to give effect to human rights commitments by the State. Finally, it is indispensable for the entire society to develop and nurture a human rights culture as a prerequisite of harmonious and peaceful development".
- The 1993 Vienna Conference—a landmark in human rights education confirmed that human rights education, training and public information were essential for fostering mutual understanding, tolerance and peace among communities.
- Human rights education implies that education which enables an individual to understand his rights.
- Important aspects of human rights are given below:
    - Learning about human rights as an important element of the preparation of all young people for life in a democracy.
    - The historical struggle for human rights to be a topic in curriculum.

- The teaching of human rights has to face the problem of the reemergence of racist attitudes and has to teach the recognition and acceptance of differences.
- Human rights education, to take into account the internatioinal dimension of the problem.
- Human rights education may have to face the problem of the ideological and political dimension of the human rights debate.
- Human rights education focuses on instances of progress in the protection of human rights in order to avoid the feeling of discouragement when confronted with the violations of human rights.

AIMS AND OBJECTIVES OF HUMAN RIGHTS EDUCATION

Education for Human Rights should aim at imparting knowledge, inculcating right attitudes and values and developing the skills of the students.

A.	Knowledge	Concepts	(i)	Historical development
			(ii)	Infringements/violations of Human Rights in one's own and other countries
			(iii)	Concept and scope of Human Rights
			(iv)	Problems of under-developed/ developed countries on Human Rights, their obligations and responsibilities
		Understanding of development process	(i)	Understanding of the environment and Human rights over a period of time
			(ii)	Internatioinal understanding and the cultural heritage of humanity
			(iii)	The united Nations System
			(iv)	Universality of Human Rights
B.	Attitudes and Values	Attitudes		Attitude formation is more important than knowledge acquisition. It includes:
			(i)	Self-respect
			(ii)	Respect for others
			(iii)	Commitment to peace and justice
		Values		Procedural values are considered more important than social attitudes. These include:
			(i)	Fairness and respect for truth
			(ii)	Tolerance, freedom and open mindedness
C.	Skills	Intellectual skills		Problem solving, critical thinking and communicative competence
		Action skills		To be able to participate and communicate in human rights

Knowledge

(1) Historical Background Student should know the major "sign posts" in the development of human rights. Significant examples in history of the denial of rights should be studied (e.g., political domination, slavery, persecution of the Jews, etc.)

(2) Infringements of Human Rights within one's Own Country: Students should appreciate that no country has a clean reputation. The observance of human rights is a matter of degree. Some ways in which the Indian National Commission monitors violations of human rights, for example for Human Rights, should be dealt with.

(3) Violation of human Rights in Other countries: Students should make aware of all kinds of inequalities and injustices including the results of gender bias and racism.

(4) Knowing about Other People and Groups: Students should develop the ability to approach people of different backgrounds confidently and without arrogance.

(5) Equality of People: Students should develop an understanding of the principles of democracy and quality, which underlie a belief in the equality of all peoples, and the right of all people to life, freedom and self-determination.

(6) Maintenance of Peace: Students should develop an understanding of the nature of negative and positive peace, of difference types of war and their causes and effects, of the importance of cultural, economic and political relation between countries, and, of the importance of international law and collective security in maintaining peace.

(7) Understanding of Rights: Students should develop an understanding of their rights or responsibilities as citizens of local, national and global communities and of the need to eliminate discrimination and other threats to human rights from various sources.

(8) Development: Students should develop an understanding of the need for balance between economic growth and social development in the interests of the sustainable development and the overcoming of poverty and social justice. They should learn about forms, approaches and stages of development and causes of poverty.

(9) Environment: Students should be familiarised with the significance of ecological balance, effects of environmental degradation and destruction, and the need to balance economic growth and conservation through a process of sustainable development.

(10) Understanding of the International Cultural Heritage: Students should develop an understanding of cultural diversities as well as universality of human culture, which give quality to life and contribute to world cooperation and peace.

(11) The United System: Students should develop an understanding of the roles of the United Nations, its efforts to protect human rights and to solve international problems.

(12) Universality of Human Rights: Students should understand the concept of universality of human rights.

Attitudes and Values

More importance should be given to attitude formation than knowledge acquisition.

1. Respect: In order to give due respect to other students, students should develop respect for themselves. Students should have respect for others especially for those with cultural, family and national backgrounds different from their own.

2. Ecological Concern: Students should have respect also for the natural environment and the overall place, which they hold in the web of life. Also, they should have a sense of responsibility for both the local and global environment.

3. Commitment to Peace and Justice: Students should value genuinely democratic and peaceful principles and processes and should be ready to work for a more just and peaceful world at interpersonal, local, national, regional and international levels.

4. Open-mindedness: Students should be willing to approach different sources of information, people and events with a critical and open mind.

5. Empathy: Students should be able to imagine sensitively the viewpoints and feelings of other people, particularly those belonging to groups, cultures and nations other than their own.

6. Solidarity: Students should develop a genuine interest in and commitment to common concerns and the search for solutions to problems, beginning at the local level.

7. Toleration: Students should be aware of their own prejudices and develop attitudes of toleration, mutual understanding and respect among all social groups.

Skills

1. Critical Thinking: Students should be able to approach issues with an open and critical mind and be willing to change their opinions in the face of new evidence and rational argument. They should be able to recognize and challenge bias, indoctrination and propaganda.

2. Multi-disciplinary: Students should be able to use a multi-disciplinary approach to solving problems.

3. Cooperation: Students should be able to appreciative the value of cooperating on shared tasks and be able to work cooperatively with other individuals and groups in order to achieve a common goal.

4. Imagination: Students should be able to develop images of what a better world might look like, not only in their own communities but also in other communities and in the world as a whole.

5. Assertiveness: Students should be able to communicate clearly and assertively with others, avoiding aggression, which denies the rights of others, and avoiding passivity, which denies their own rights.

6. Controversial thinking: Students should study controversial issues using a critical analysis of all points of view and avoiding dogma and values relativism. In evaluating, alternative viewpoints and evidence, they should exercise and develop thinking skills and clarify their own values and opinions.

7. Conflict Solution: Students should be able to analyse different conflicts in an objective and systematic way and be able to suggest a range of solutions to them. Where appropriate, they should be able to implement solutions themselves.

8. Tolerance for Ambiguity: Students should develop a capacity to realize that not all problems can be immediately solved while simultaneously being optimistic about their eventual solution.

9. Participation: Students should be developing an ability to influence and participate in decision-making within their local community, and at national, regional and international levels.

10. Communicative Competence: Students should be able to communicate in at least one language other than their own to facilitate their contact with people of other countries and their understanding of other cultures.

CURRICULUM OF HUMAN RIGHTS EDUCATION

Curriculum should include the following elements:

1. Main concepts Associated with Human Rights—Different Human Rights
2. Manifestations and Phenomena
3. Dimensions of Human Rights—Discrimination, Violence, etc.
4. Perspectives and Levels of Human Rights—Individual Rights
5. Role of UNO and Its Agencies in the Promotion of Human Rights
6. Mechanism for checking violation of Human Rights
7. National Human rights Commission
8. Rights of Deprived Sections and Their Safeguards
9. Constitutional Provisions Relating to Human Rights

1. Inclusion of Main concepts Associated with Human Rights

1. Children's Rights
2. Civic Rights (and sometimes Civil Rights, Civil Liberties)
3. Cultural Rights
4. Economic Rights
5. Human Rights
6. Legal rights
7. Minority rights
8. Natural Rights
9. Political rights
10. Social Rights
11. Welfare Rights
12. Women's Rights

2. Manifestations and Phenomena

1. Discrimination
2. Conflict
3. Environmental Protection
4. Equality (and quality of treatment)
5. Fairness
6. Freedom (freedom to and freedom from)
7. Genocide
8. Injustice
9. Justice
10. Oppression
11. Peace
12. Self-determination
13. Toleration
14. Welfare
15. Violence (and Structural Violence)

3. Dimensions of Human Rights

Life		Liberty		Security	
		From		To	
		Political – Legal		Economic-Social-cultural	
		Slavery, exile, arbitrary, arrest, retroactive laws, punishment	Speech, assembly, participation in government, fair trials	Work, just remuneration, reasonable standard of living, social security	
Individual	Preservation of life	Discrimination according to race, religion, sex	Nationality, religion, marriage, movement, privacy, property	Life of dignity, rest and leisure, free education for development of personality, enjoyment of cultural life	Against torture and degrading treatment
Group/ Country	Against genocide	Discrimination	Existence self-determination		

4. Perspectives and Levels of Human Rights

Individual rights	♦ Rights are possessed by individuals ♦ Rights are opposed to the state ♦ Rights are enforced through individuals' claim against the state ♦ Rights are observed through the absence of interference by individuals and institutions
Social and collective rights	♦ Rights are held by groups or classes ♦ Rights are defined and activated through the state ♦ Rights are enforced through administrative action ♦ Rights are achieved through actions by institutions and the state
European rights	♦ Continuous development of rules for communal life which reflect and encourage a gradual convergence of national laws ♦ The European Court of Human Rights ♦ The European convention on Human Rights ♦ The Case Law of the European commission
International rights	♦ Human Rights violations as a result of the political and economic relationship between the First and the Third World and the Western and Eastern hemisphere
Global rights	♦ Idea of an indivisible world ♦ Consciousness of the "interlocking-crises" ♦ Idea of the unity of humankind ♦ Rights must be extended to all human beings and all human groups and peoples

MAIN ENTRIES ON CURRICULUM IN THE 'ENCYCLOPEDIA OF HUMAN RIGHTS' (1989)

- Abortion
- Affirmative Action
- Aggression
- Amnesty laws
- Apartheid
- Armed Conflict

- Assembly and Association
- Bonded Labour
- Centre for Human Rights
- Chemical Weapons
- Conscientious Objection to Military Service
- Constitutional Councils
- Council of Europe
- Earth Threats
- Debt Bondage
- Derogation
- Domestic Violence
- Drug Abuse
- Education
- Environment
- Equality
- Food
- Forced Labour
- Foreign Dept.
- Freedom of Information
- General Assembly
- Genocide
- Health
- Holy See
- Homelessness
- Hostages
- Illiteracy
- International Bill of Rights
- International Court of Justice
- International Labour Organisation
- Judiciary
- League of Nations
- Legal Aid
- Mentally Ill Persons
- Migrant Workers
- Nationality
- OAS
- OAU
- Permanent Court of Arbitration
- Persons Born out of Wedlock
- Political Rights
- Poverty
- Privacy
- Property
- Public Emergency
- Refugees
- Remedy

- Right to Development
- Right to Leave any Country (including One's Own), and to Return to One's Own Country
- Right to Life
- Right to Organise
- Science and Technology
- Self-Determination
- Shelter
- Social Security
- Standard of Living
- State of Emergency
- Thought, Conscience and Religion
- Torture
- Transsexuals
- UNESCO
- UNICEF
- UN-Charter
- UN-Development Fund for Women
- UN-Environment Programme
- Un-High Commissioner for Refugees
- UN-Institute for Training and Research
- UN-University
- Universal Declaration Human Rights
- World Food Council
- World Health Organisation
- World Intellectual Property Right

HUMAN RIGHTS EDUCATION AS THE CORE OF THE SCHOOL CURRICULUM

Human rights as the core of the school curriculum is illustrated in the following Figure.

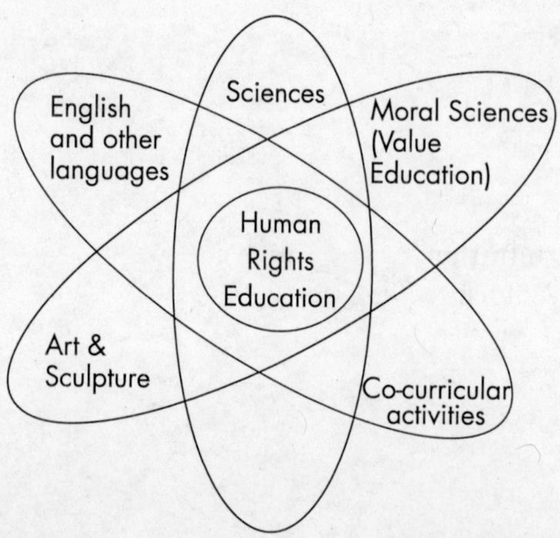

FIGURE 58.1 Human Rights Education as the Core of the School Curriculum.

TEXTBOOKS ON HUMAN RIGHTS RESEARCH

Major contents of the textbooks should cover are illustrated in the following Figure.

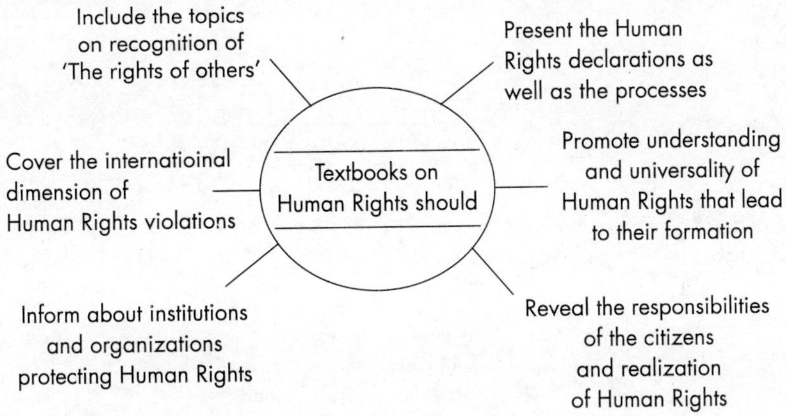

FIGURE 58.2 Textbooks on Human Rights.

GENERAL METHODS AND ACTIVITIES OF TEACHING HUMAN RIGHTS

Important methods of teaching human rights are:

1. Promotion of Cooperative Practices: The process of teaching and learning should promote cooperative practice is between teachers and students and among students in the classroom.

2. Active Methods: Teaching and learning methods, which are active and process-based, should be used to involve students in the investigation of issues and concerns and formulation of solution.

3. Learning Needs and Interest of Students: Content organization and teaching methods should be matched to different learning needs and interests of students of different ages and abilities.

4. Oral Exposition: The students to be helped to acquire and develop a language for discussion of human rights issues and to master the concepts associated with Human Rights.

5. Questioning: Questions should be used as an invitation to students to express their views on an issue to pose questions, and to exchange views with each other, to encourage students to consider sympathetically views, which they themselves do not hold, to express their opinions openly and clearly and to pose questions, which invite further exploration of an issue.

SPECIAL METHODS AND ACTIVITIES OF TEACHING HUMAN RIGHTS

1. Frontal teaching
2. Discussions
3. Drama and Role-Play
4. Practical activities – organization of adult education centres, community service etc.
5. Projects
6. Workshops
7. Visits to orphanages, old age homes

8. Organising human rights days
9. Collecting documents on human rights
10. Displaying human rights materials on bulletin boards
11. organizing debates

Methodology

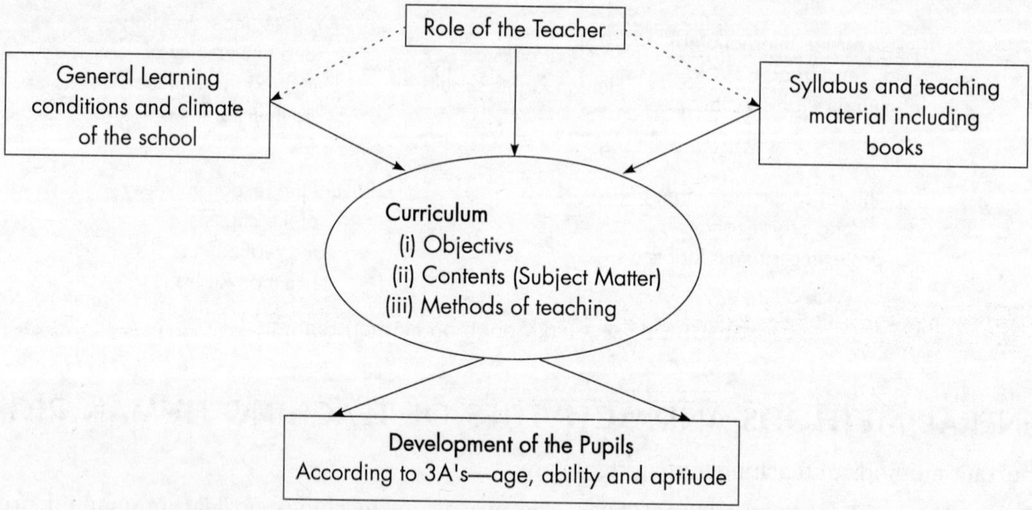

FIGURE 58.3 Contents and Methodology of Teaching Human Rights.

OBSTACLES TO HUMAN RIGHTS EDUATION

- Ignorance of historical processes, which shape and change one's awareness of human rights.
- Incompetence as far as the citizens' chances of and the responsibilities for the protection of human rights are concerned.
- Indifference arising from such incompetence and the feeling of powerlessness.
- Imbalance in the perception of human rights violation and implementation.
- Instrumentalisation of human rights as a means of legitimizing power interests.
- Intolerance through fear, the lack of self-esteem and improper and inadequate readiness.

UNITED NATIONS DECADE FOR HUMAN RIGHTS EDUCATION (1995-2004)

- By its Resolution 49/184, adopted on 21 December 1994, the United Nations General Assembly proclaimed the ten-year period beginning on 1 January 1995 the United Nations Decade for Human Rights Education.
- The objectives of the Decade (1995–2004) have been spelled out in the Plan of Action. These include:

  1. The assessment of needs and the formulation of effective strategies for the furtherance of human right education at all school levels, in vocational training and formal as well as non-formal learning.

2. The building and strengthening of programmes and capacities for human rights education at the international regional, national and local levels.
3. The coordinated development of human rights education materials.
4. The strengthening of the role and capacity of the mass media in the furtherance of human rights education.
5. The global disseminatioin of the Universal Declaration of Human Rights in the maximum possible number of languages and in other forms appropriate for various levels of literacy and for the disabled.

- The General Assembly appealed to all governments 'to contribute to the implementation of the Plan of Action and to step up their efforts to eradicate illiteracy and to direct education towards the full development of the human personality and to the strengthening of respect for human rights and fundamental freedom' and urged governmental and non-governmental educational agencies to intensify their efforts to establish and implement programmes of human rights education, in particular by preparing and implementing national plans in this field.
- The United Nations High Commissioner for Human Rights was requested to coordinate the implementation of the Plan of Action. The Centre for Human rights of the Secretariat, and the Commission on Human Rights in cooperation with Member States, human treaty-monitoring bodies, other appropriate bodies and competent non-governmental organizations, was asked to support his efforts. Specialised Agencies and United Nations programmes were invited to contribute, within their respective spheres of competence, to the implementation of the Plan of Action.
- The General Assembly called upon international, regional and national non-governmental organizations, in particular those concerned with women, labour, development and the environment, as well as all other social justice groups, human rights advocates, educators, religious organizations and the media, to increase their involvement in formal and non-formal education in human rights.

SUGGESTIONS FOR STRENGTHENING PROGRAMMES FOR HUMAN RIGHTS EDUCATION

The United Nations High Commissioner for Human Rights, in its mid-term global evaluation of the progress made towards the achievements of the objectives of the United Nations Decade for Human Rights Education (1995–2004), submitted to the UN Secretary General made recommendations under the following heads:

(i) Overall Recommendations. These cover:
   1. Rights Education: Concepts and Methods.
   2. Content of Human rights Education.
   3. Programmes on Human rights Education.
   4. Evaluation, Research and Monitoring.
   5. Mass Media and Freedom Information
   6. Resources.

(ii) National Level Recommendations.

(iii) Regional Level Recommendations.

(iv) International Level Recommendations.

I. Overall Recommendation

Set out below are overall recommendations directed at all principal actors and for implementation at all levels.

Human Rights Education: Concepts and Methods

1. Value-oriented human rights education alone is insufficient. Human rights education should refer to human rights instruments and mechanisms of protection, and to procedures for ensuring accountability.
2. Creative participatory teaching methods that are relevant to people live should be used, and human rights should be introduced as a holistic framework.
3. Gender sensitivity should be emphasized in all educational activities.
4. An enabling environment for human rights educators (including the provision of information, training, facilities, equipment and protection from harassment) should be ensured.
5. Priority should be given to sustainable approaches (i.e. training of trainers, integration of human rights into all relevant training and education curricula etc.).

Content of Human Rights Education

Activities for human rights education should address the following issues:

1. Economic, social and cultural rights;
2. Good Governance;
3. Impunity, and international criminal tribunals to deal with crimes against humanity;
4. Human rights defenders (and the related United Nations declaration), racism and discrimination.
5. The link between development and human rights should be stressed.
6. The universality and indivisibility of human rights should be emphasized.

Programmes on Human Rights Education

1. Sufficient attention should be paid to ensure that the human rights education needs of children and young people, as well as of adults, are met.
2. Interaction among children and youth belonging to different ethnic communities should be promoted. Human rights education should be fostered within and outside school curricula.
3. Human rights education should be promoted in all educational initiatives aimed at adults.
4. Human rights education efforts aimed at the following targets should be increased:
   (a) local government officials, community leaders;
   (b) legal and paralegal service providers;
   (c) rural populations and illiterate people;
   (d) women and girls;
   (e) vulnerable groups, such as people with HIV/AIDS, people with disabilities, minorities and the elderly;
   (f) Non-state actors, such as multinational corporations, trade and financial organizations (World Trade Organisation, World Bank, International Monetary Fund etc.).

Evaluation, Research and Monitoring

Evaluation, studies, and research of long-term impact should be undertaken in order to better understand which approaches work best and why, and in order to elaborate evaluation criteria. Every project on human rights education should incorporate the development of indicators to evaluate qualitative impact.

Mass Media and Freedom of Information

1. Mass media strategies that would effectively promote human rights should be developed. Such strategies might include the following elements:
   (a) Media focus on human rights monitoring;
   (b) Increasing the use of the media by non-governmental organizations;
   (c) Training of media professionals on mechanisms for human rights protection;
   (d) Involvement of the community of artists;
   (e) Use by the media, when appropriate, of techniques of social marketing.
2. Law reform policies and practices that improve access to information and strengthen mechanisms that facilitate the flow of information and freedom of the press and other media should be promoted and implemented more vigorously. Human rights education should focus on such law reform policies and practices.
3. The possibilities offered by new information technologies in furthering human rights education should be better exploited, and access to such technologies should be increased. Existing programmes supporting the online development of projects on human rights education should be strengthened and new programmes implemented.

Resources

- Good practices for human rights education should be identified, compiled and disseminated.
- Organisational capacity building in human rights education should be fostered.
- Funding for human rights education should be increased.
- Research on issues related to human rights education should be enhanced in academic institutions and human rights institutes.
- When appropriate, alliances with the business sector should be developed in support of human rights education.

II. National Level

- Governments should reaffirm the commitments and obligations that they have already made in respect of human rights education and accelerate their pace of implementation to realize significant achievements by the end of the decade.
- Governments should promote the development of national strategies for human rights education which are comprehensive paticipatory, effective and sustainable. Such strategies could be embodied in a national plan of action for human rights education.
- Human rights education should be included as a component of national development plans and of other relevant national plans of action.
- All governmental and non-governmental actors recognize, in a spirit of mutual respect, each other's potential and capacities in furthering human rights education. Partnerships should

be established where cooperation is furthered. Maximum use should be made of existing programmes, materials and resources.

- Systems for better coordination of effort and greater cooperation among the various governmental agencies should be developed.
- Non-governmental organizations should develop and implement strategies to encourage Governments to fulfil their obligations to integrate human rights education into all forms and levels of education for children, youth and adults, and should monitor those strategies.
- International resources and materials should be adapted to local linguistic and cultural contexts.

III. Regional level

- Key regional human rights education organizations, institutions, agencies and networks should be supported to develop further the human rights education capacity within regions, including support for regional meetings, training of trainers, online networking, sharing of region-specific materials etc.
- Region-specific programmes or coordination systems to maximize the participation of national entities in programmes on human rights education should be developed. Such region-specific programmes can be linked to existing regional programmes supported by the United Nations.
- Strategies should be developed for the wider distribution of materials on human rights education through regional networks.
- Links should be established with regional mass media, social development and other groups to encourage the inclusion of human rights in their training programmes.
- Existing regional intergovernmental organizations should be encouraged to integrate human rights education into their programmes and to allocate additional resources in that regard within the framework of the Decade.
- Work with regional, education-related intergovernmental organizations should be enhanced in order to promote human rights education.

IV. International Level

- United Nations institutions should adopt a system-wide approach. An effective coordination system should be developed and the role of the Office of the High Commissioner for Human Rights in such a system should be strengthened.
- Effective human rights training should be undertaken for all United Nations Staff.
- Human rights education should be included in the agenda of the special session of the General Assembly on the follow-up to the World Summit for Children, 2001.
- The Office of the High Commissioner, as requested by the General Assembly, should monitor the developments in human rights education that take place during the decade. In this regard, Governments should provide adequate means to enable the office to fulfil that role.
- UNESCO, through its network of national commissions, should play an active part in encouraging Governments to develop human rights curricula for formal education and to take steps to ensure that school environments are conducive to human rights education.
- United Nations treaty bodies should emphasise the obligations of States parties with regard to human rights education by actively seeking detailed information during their review of the reports of State parties. Inadequacies in addressing priority target audiences should consistently be identified by treaty bodies as an area of concern. In addition, treaty bodies

should perform a clearing-house role by sharing with Governments approaches and strategies that have proved successful elsewhere, and should keep the Office of the High Commissioner informed of major national developments in human rights education.

- The capacity for human rights education of national presence of intergovernmental organizations (United Nations resident coordinators, field presences of the Office of the High Commissioner for Human rights, United Nations information centres, national and local offices of United Nations agencies etc.) should be strengthened so that they can provide technical support to national and local activities for human rights education.
- Intergovernmental organizations should facilitate collaboration between governmental institutions and non-governmental organizations at the national level.
- Educational materials developed by international organizations should be made easily accessible, distributed free of charge and translated into local languages.
- The potential support and contribution to human rights education by non-state actors, including the business community, as well as development, trade and financial organizations, should be explored.

CONCLUSION

Human rights embody the fundamental values of human civilization. All human beings are born free and equal in dignity and rights. So, every individual is entitled to enjoy his/her rights freely irrespective of caste, creed, colour, religion, region, sex and economic status. Human rights provide opportunities to an individual in the society to develop his/her personality. They are essential for human existence. Therefore, human rights are called sometimes as fundamental rights or birth rights or natural rights. Harold J. Laski says, "Rights are necessary conditions of social life without which no one could become best, to be himself". In fact, rights are absolutely essential as they are concerned with their freedom and dignity and are conducive to the physical, moral, social and spiritual welfare. Moreover, human rights education is an important strategy for achieving several ends, empowerments, participation, transparency, accountability, prevention of conflict, and peacemaking and the effective protection and realisation of human rights for all.

CHAPTER 59

EDUCATION FOR SOCIAL POLLUTION

INTRODUCTION

The term 'social pollution' is of recent origin. It has been developed from the undesirable characteristics of human beings in the ordinary business of life. As it spreads from one person to another in the social environment, it may be termed as 'social pollution'. It is a new area of study concerned with the anti-social activities and undesirable behaviour of human beings and the remedies to prevent the people from such pollution. Environmentalists study only the cause and effects of air, water, soil, marine, thermal, noise, nuclear and food pollution, pesticide and plastic pollution, and suggest the ways and means for controlling such environmental pollution. However, the humanologists study the causes of social pollution and its impacts on education, religion and politics. They also highlight various consequences of social pollution and suggest the ways for controlling such pollution. The study of social pollution cannot be neglected, as it is the basis for all types of pollution found in the human environment. The modern technological world has made it difficult to find a man of character or a family without tension and conflict. In fact, changes in philosophy from spiritualism (Idealism) to materialism (pragmatism) have modified the aims of education and life. Consequently, social services like education, religion and politics have been changed into economic services. In other words, commercialization of education, religion and politics has changed the behaviour of every individual in social, spiritual, moral, cultural, political and economic life. Moreover, man applies various tricks and techniques such as corruption, prostitution, printing fake currencies and certificates, kidnapping and murdering for fiscal development and comfortable life. In short, he is ready to do any filthy deed for income and pleasure. Such an attitude pollutes the man and the society. For instance, production and consumption of drugs, cigarettes and tobacco affect the health of the users and their family and society. Similarly, corruption and prostitution change the behaviour of the people and encourage them to lead a dishonest life. Thus, production of intoxicants, obscene and violent movies, corruption and dowry, pollute the whole human society. Hence, an attempt is made here to study the nature of social pollution and its impact on the individual and the society comprehensively.

MEANING OF SOCIAL POLLUTION

Social pollution refers to the people becoming corruptive, dishonest, selfish, unkind and anti-social activists such as killers, cheaters, kidnappers, rapists, eve teasers, addictors to drugs and smoke, tobacco producers and creators of caste or religious based groups or politics. Nature never pollutes the man but he pollutes himself because of his ignorance, foolishness, and the lust for materialism. In other words, any person who engages in anti-social activities which cause social pollution is known as social pollution. The activities and products, which cause social pollution, are known as social pollutants. It is seen in the Bible that God created everything good but man has chosen various tricks and techniques in order to make his life happier and more comfortable than ever before. Consequently, he engages in many filthy deeds such as plagiarism, printing fake currencies and certificates, kidnapping, killing, raping, cheating and eve teasing, organizing caste and religion-based groupism or politics and producing intoxicants.

DEFINITION OF SOCIAL POLLUTION

Social pollution may be defined as "the concentration of any socially undesirable character and deed in man causing value crisis". The concentration of anti social activities in man decreases the personal and social values. Social pollution refers to the concentration of undesirable activities and habits in man, which affect the health and wealth, and decrease his values in the society. Thus, polluted man is one who is corruptive, dishonest, unkind, selfish, deceiver, killer, rapist, drunkard, smoker, tobacco chewer and he lacks character and good deeds. In short, the polluted man is a burden to the society and nation.

SOCIAL POLLUTANTS

Any activity or object, which causes human value crisis, is known as social pollutant. A number of man-pollutant has been found in the modern technological world. Let us point out the following objects, activities and circumstances, which cause social pollution.

TABLE 59.1 Social Pollutants

Adulteration	Non-cooperation
Backbiting	Obscene sex
Blue Film	Partiality
Bribery	Politics
Cheating	Poverty
Cigarettes	Printing fake currency
Corruption	Prostitution
Dishonesty	Raping
Disrespect	Regionalism
Dowry	Religion
Egoism	Robbery
Eve-teasing	Slavery
Homosexual	Theft
Jealousy	Tobacco products
Kidnapping	Unemployment
Killing	Unkindness
Liquor	Violence

Sins of Humans

TABLE 59.2 Social Sins

Education without character	Religion without love
Worship without humbleness	Divinity without humanity
Relationship without affection	Friendship without truthfulness
Politics without principles	Science without rationality
Teaching without dedication	Degrees without quality
Commerce without purity	Preaching without practice
Work without honesty	Wealth without charity
Leadership without personality	Unity without integrity

Figure 59.1 shows that smoking not only affect the smokers but also pollutes air, and society.

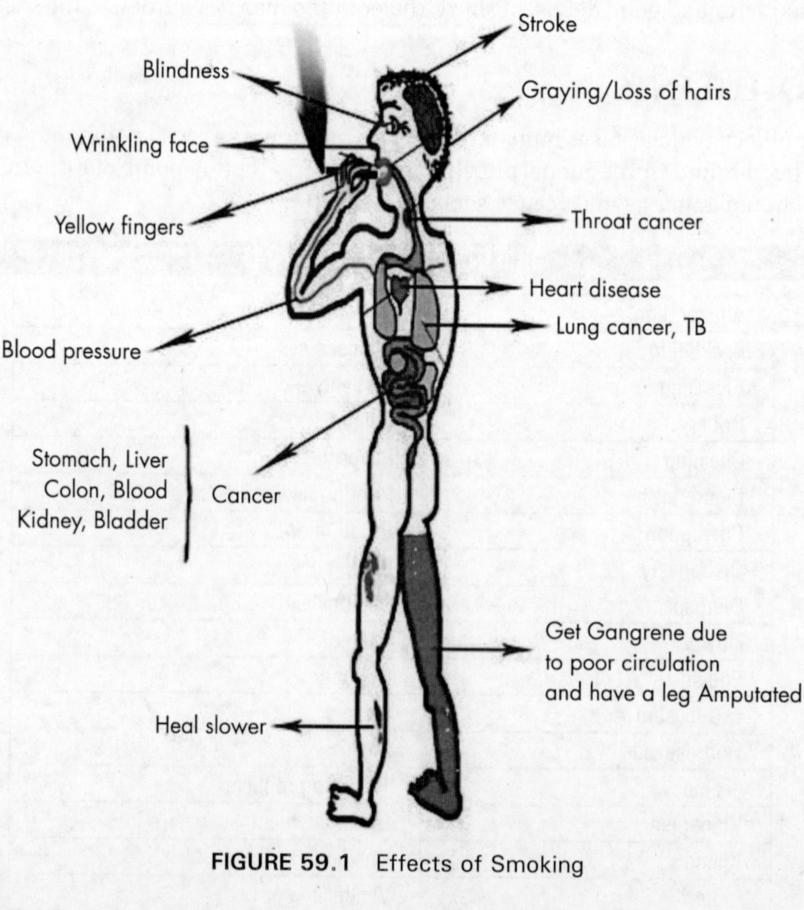

FIGURE 59.1 Effects of Smoking

TABLE 59.3 Centre of Human Life and Activities

Man is creation-centred	Education is cash-centred
Politics is caste-centred	Religion is offering-centred
Office is corruption-centred	Relationship is status-centred
Friendship is time-centred	Marriage is dowry-centred
Festival is cinema-centred	Cinema is obscenity-centred
Health is wealth-centred	Work is wage-centred
Service is profit-centred	Sex is lust-centred
Puberty is emotion-centred	Youth is strength-centred
Old age is weak-centred	Body is disease-centred
Mind is pollution-centred	Life is dream-centred

Ten-Combined Contradictions of Human Activities

- Flattering in the presence and backbiting in the absence
- Blessing in the lips and cursing in the hearts
- Cheering in the faces and cheating in the minds
- Speaking holy words and doing filthy deeds
- Holding mobile and driving vehicles
- Taking intoxicants and discharging responsibilities
- Remembering God in sickness and forgetting Him in smoking
- Tea in one hand and cigarette in the other hand
- Neglecting parents and observing death anniversary
- Polluting the environment and organising students' processions

Objectives of Studying Social Pollution

The main objectives of studying man pollution are to prevent or control man from profit-oriented filthy deeds and prepare him for a happy and healthy life.

- Prevent the individual from filthy deeds and prepare him to lead an honest life.
- Prevent the people from sudden demise and chronic diseases.
- Prepare the individual for a peaceful and comfortable life.
- Study the factors which cause man-pollution and suggest the ways and means to overcome them.
- Develop awareness among the people about value crisis and its impacts on social environment.
- Highlight the disguised democracy system in the Indian society.
- Establish a casteless secular and democratic society.
- Produce people of good character and deeds that is a better generation and a better society.
- Study the impacts of family, school, government, mass media, religion and politics on social environments.
- Foster humanism, national integration and international understanding in the students.
- Shun narrow mindedness and lust for materialism from the people.
- Develop rational thinking and social efficiency in the people.
- Create awareness about corruption and dowry and their impacts on society and family.

- Prevent the commercialization of education, religion and politics.
- Arrest and crush terrorism and antisocial activities.
- Suggest the government to lay down effective policies and constitutional acts for eradicating the social evils and social pollution.

NEED FOR SOCIAL POLLUTION STUDY

After the invention of money, expansion of education, development of science and technology, modernization of agriculture, industry and transport systems, and commercialization of educational, religious and political activities, remarkable changes have taken place in the social, cultural, spiritual, political and economic life. Such changes and developments have made human life very busy and comfortable. In other words, standard of life is high but quality of life is low. In fact, the terms 'character' and 'culture' have lost their meanings in the modern society. This is because people seek various tricks and techniques that are socially undesirable and apply them to make their lives happier and more comfortable. Consequently, the numbers of people who engage in filthy and inhuman activities have been increasing un-precedentally. For instance, the number of criminals in the name of corruption, dowry and sexual harassments, fake currency, raping, kidnapping, eve teasing, robbing, stealing, murdering, breaking boundaries, prostitution and adulteration is increasing day by day due to the lust for physical and fiscal pleasure and materialism. Such activities cause human value crises and reduce the difference between literates and illiterates in character and deeds. It cannot be denied that if wealth is lost, nothing is lost, if health is lost, something is lost and if character is lost everything is lost. That is why, the great saint Swami Vivekananda wants education by which character is formed Education is a meaningless process unless it differentiate the literates from the illiterate not in reading, writing and speaking but in character and deeds. Hence, we need a separate study on social pollution and its causes, effects and ways to control them in the mechanized society. Following factors state the need for studying social pollution in the Indian society.

Human Values Crisis

Man is the supreme creation of nature. He creates values, which serves as guidelines for his fruitful life and strengthen his relationship with others. Human values such as love, sympathy, kindness, adjustment, tolerance, non-violence, selfless sacrifice, compassion, faithfulness, dedication, devotion, punctuality, honesty, justice equality, patriotism and cleanliness exalt and differentiate him from all other living organisms. These values are the bases for the formation of society and development of social efficiency. The change in the aim of life from spiritualism to materialism and changes in the aim of education from man making to moneymaking cause value crisis. This is because the number of profit oriented filthy activities has been increasing due to the lust for materialism and ignorance. As a result, character is lost in the air and cash is caught in the hands. This policy makes man lack character which is more important than health and wealth. Hence, human values should be preserved and promoted for a better life and values are very essential in the processes of man and nation making.

E-Philosophies of Human Life

Man's life is always guided by the existing philosophy, which changes from place to place, time to time, and even person to person. However, a philosophy guides every individual in his personal as well as social life. The development of science and technology, and demand for materialism have modified the life style of religious workers and created crisis in spiritual values. Therefore, most of the people give importance to the present and immediate future and neglect the life after death (their generation). In fact, such people are guided and directed by 3E's philosophies that are Earn, Enjoy and Empty (die) the world. In other words, people consider their life as "use and throw". People have become machines in the mechanized world. They believe that material prosperity, health and happiness are the real blessings. This kind of faith develops narrowism in them. It cannot be denied that people have only a short period of life and their generation should continue the life circle. Therefore, they should be trained to realize the nature and uncertainty of life and shape them to be more useful in the society.

Superstitious Faith: Man seeks the guidance of God at the times of need, illness, and last moment. Such faith and habits make his life a pendulum between spiritualism and materialism. He gives more importance to the accumulation of wealth even at the cost of his health. At the same time, he believes that every individual has seven births or there is a life after death. This superstitious faith has created a great impact on most of the people due to their ignorance and fear about the future after death. Is it a meaningful faith? Is it under the control of man? Is there any evidence for such life or rebirth? Who prepares himself for it in the problematic and materialistic word? When and where does it begin? Moreover, what is the importance of it? Like these, a number of questions arise in our minds about life after death. Now our question is, why should we think about it when it is beyond the power of our imagination? However, a life without human values such as affection, compassion, sympathy, cooperation, tolerance, adjustment, equality, justice and freedom irrespective of caste, religion, region and economic criteria is meaningless and hopeless. At this juncture, why should we emphasis life after death? This is a superstitious faith and if it is real, the religious leaders and workers would have a simple, humble and holy life and be the models to the whole human society. There is no room for such rebirths and eternal life unless we realize and taste that experience when we are in the earth. Moreover, who can imagine life after death, when he engages in anti-social activities. Therefore, it is not necessary to think of such a life when we lead an honest and simple life with love and sympathy. Man cannot live both in the spiritual and material world at the same time. In this circumstance, we need a study on social pollution to help the individual understand himself and the purpose of his life.

Unholiness of Holy Places: The meaning and importance of spiritual values are flying in the air in this scientific as well as materialistic world. It is seen that holy places lose their holiness due to the complicated mind of the people. In fact, holy places are turned into place for entertainment and commercialization. For instance, Sabarimala in Kerala, Thiruppathi in Andhra Pradesh, Kasi in Uttar Pradesh, Annai Velaankanni in Tamil Nadu, Golden Temple in Amirstar and Mecca in Saudi Arabia are the important holy places, which are polluted by the filthy deeds of the pilgrims. Churches are the places of commercialization and advertisement for offerings and prayers. The undesirable activities of a few priests, pastors and poojaris pollute the human society. Bhakthi (deity) has been turned into bombastic decoration of churches, temples and mosques, which is imitated and transmitted from one religion to another. Religious rituals, celebrations, and offerings in the name of God lead to extravagance and meaningless deeds like procession with effigies and elephants, which develop competition between religions and curbs, transport and vitiate the peaceful life. The atmosphere of religious places is not conducive for spiritual development but the place for entertainments. Holiness of the churches, temples, mosques and gurudhwars should be preserved for the spiritual development of the people. Hence, we need a special study on social pollution to save man from value crisis and maintain the holiness of holy places for spiritual development.

Power of Money: Money is the most important and powerful tool that makes the business transaction very fast. It has been invented and controlled by man but now it measures and controls him. In other words, the quality and quantity of man is measured not by his education and character but by money. Too much need and importance of money forces the people to seek profit-oriented filthy deeds such as corruption, dowry, production of drugs, cigarettes and tobacco products, organize groups in the name of caste and religion, stealing, murdering, kidnapping, robbing and printing fake currencies. In fact, man is ready to do anything, which fetches him more income. Life is unthinkable in the absence of money, but it cannot be the end of life. In fact, money alone cannot give man a peaceful and happy life. It is so because the lust for money has been increasing even in the minds of rich people. It exploits humanism, spiritualism, secularism and nationalism and pollutes the whole human society. Hence, a study of social pollution is needed for developing a rational attitude among the people in relation to man and money.

Failure of Education

Education aims at money-making rather than man making. In fact, education has failed to produce a man of character and culture and developed casteism, religions, and narrow-mindedness. There is no difference between literates and illiterates in words and deeds but educated are more human pollutants than the uneducated. This statement can be made clear with negative views of education.

> *"We thought the student wanted education, but all that they wanted was a degree"*
>
> *"We thought they wanted a degree, but all that they wanted was a job"*
>
> *"We thought they wanted a job, but all that they wanted was a work"*
>
> *"We thought they wanted a work, but all that they wanted was money"*
>
> *"We thought they wanted money, but all that they wanted was money through fair or foul means"—Anon,*
>
> *Erich Fromn says, "Education makes machines, which act like men and produces men who act like machines".*
>
> *F. D. Roosevelt says, "A man who has never gone to schools may steal from a freight car, but if he has university education, he may steal the whole rail road".*

In fact, more education leads to more corruption, more laziness and more selfishness. The number of degree holders increases, but the quality of education and greatness of human values decrease. Moreover, privatization and commercialization of education inculcates selfishness, narrow mindedness and money making in the youth. We cannot expect a secular and casteless society as long as privators are encouraged to establish educational institutions in the name of their caste and religion. It is the greatest tragedy that the educated like teachers, engineers, doctors, lawyers, professors, scientists and scholars are unconscious about the production and consumption of liquor, cigarettes and tobacco products, which pollute man and society. It is also seen that educated people demand more dowry and are immersed more in corruption than the uneducated. There is a direct relationship between education and corruption, between dowry and peaceless life, between corruption and tension and between corruption and consumption of liquor. Though some people know the injurious effects of such products, they still consume them. Moreover the warnings such as 'smoking cigarettes is injurious to health', 'chewing tobacco causes cancer', 'drinking liquor is injurious to life, family and society', 'Dowry brings peaceless life' and 'Prostitution causes AIDS' and 'corruption mars character and causes curse' never change the habits of people. Thus, the complicated and anti-social activities of man cause the production of many human pollutants, which pollute him further. Hence, we need a separate study on social pollution to develop rational thinking and humanism in the educated minds and prevent the production of goods, which degrade the quality of human beings.

Vicious Circle of Unconsciousness (Complicated minds)

Lack of rational thinking and understanding arrests the people in the vicious circle of complicated mindedness. In fact, man has lost the capacity to foresee the consequences of his activities. He holds a cigarette at his right hand and a teacup at his left hand and consumes both. The parents of bridegrooms demand high dowry, and never think whether the bride will look after them and how long their son lives. Women stand against women in insisting on dowry, more jewels, and cash and emphasize rituals related to the cannibal matter. Some people consider corruption as one of the sources of income and a happy life. Most of the anti-social activities and evils are justified and regarded as culture due to the ignorance and complicated minds of people. For instance, smoking, drinking, prostitution, club dancing, homo marriage, divorce and corruption are socially accepted as culture. These habits develop unconscious (complicated) mind and create a gloomy society because such habits are transmitted from parents to children quickly. Therefore, the future generation will not be in a position to distinguish between what is culture and what is not. Thus, the social environment encourages them to accept everything as culture even if it hurts him and others. However, he seeks the grace of God and His forgiveness for his deeds at the time of physical feebleness or at the last moments. This is due to his fear of the unknown future and imagination of heaven and hell. In this way, man's life is centred on the vicious circle of unconsciousness doing filthy deeds for money and seeking grace of God for forgiveness and blessing. This is like swallowing iron and drinking water or smoking cigarettes and drinking boiled water, drinking and driving, sitting while teaching, driving and holding cell-phones. These are meaningless activities. People cannot be redeemed from the grip of this vicious circle of unconsciousness unless they understand themselves and the nature of life and death. The study of social pollution develops an awareness, which will enable them to lead a better life.

Cine Based World

This is a cine world, which is reflected in almost all programmes organized in educational and religious institutions. Even religious days and birthdays of spiritual, political and national leaders are celebrated and entertained with cine-based programmes. It shows that cine-world is more important than the purpose of celebrating such functions. Cinema displays programmes, which pollute the youth, and make their life gloomy. In fact, most of the movies teach the people violence rather than human values. Moviemakers show many filthy deeds as entertainment for money but they ignore the impact of giving importance to violence, sexual scenes, kidnapping, raping, using abusive words, disrespecting teachers, police departments, officers and ministers in the movies. However, such programmes pollute the youngsters and destroy their life. It is highly regrettable that governments and public are silent over the exaggeration of violence and obscenity which have a great influence on the personal and social life of the individuals. For instance, the criminals quote the name of movies as the examples for their evil deeds or anti-social activities.

Explosion of Filthy Deeds

As population increases, the number of filthy deeds and criminals increases in the modern society. In fact, people of the present age never bother about the consequences of their deeds and do anything which fetches them income and pleasure. The number of people who involve in anti-social activities have been increasing due to poverty, unemployment, ignorance, and exploitation. The study of social pollution prevents the youth from falling a prey to the filthy deeds and becoming victims to the intoxicant products.

Social Cancer

Like cancer affects the victim and the family, social cancers such as corruption, dowry, prostitution and illegal sexual contacts will affect the human society. These activities of the people are considered as social cancers because they destroy the human beings and they spread from one person to another. For instance, the off-spring of anti-social elements cannot have a happy and comfortable life in the womb of time. In fact, the person who engages in these social evils will have to suffer from mental conflicts, frustration and illness. Consequently, they and their generations may lose their lives and properties or even commit suicide in the end. Hence, we need a study of social pollution in order to prevent the people from social cancers and prepare them for a honest and happy life.

Growth of Criminals

The number of criminals increases as population increases in the modern society. It shows that more education leads to more criminals. In fact, the number of criminals who are arrested has been increasing. As criminals escape unpunished, others are encouraged to engage in such activities. As a result, the number of criminals who engage in antisocial activities has been increasing due to unemployment, poverty, ignorance and lust for money. The study of social pollution is necessary to produce better human resources.

Narrow Minds

Narrowism is the general characteristic of the present generation that affects the development of social efficiency and secularism. Therefore, one's caste, religion, and region occupy a very important place in all thoughts and deeds. This kind of pollutant acts against secularism, equality, national integration, international understanding and the progress of human society. Hence, narrowism should be destroyed for the development of the country through right education that needs the inclusion of a study on social pollution at the international level.

IMPORTANCE OF STUDYING SOCIAL POLLUTION

The study of environmental pollution will be incomplete unless we study the nature of social pollution and its impacts on social and natural environment. We give importance to other pollution but fail to think that man pollutes himself in different ways. In fact, he is more interested in speaking about the weakness of others rather than knowing himself and his weak points. It is the greatest tragedy that he has forgotten his background and the sufferings of parents in bringing him up and he fails to understand himself and his death. He considers that his present life is very important and gives more importance to the physical pleasure and accumulation of wealth. He selects only those seeds and plants that yield him more output. He also selects and buys only those goods and services that are good, useful and beautiful.

Nevertheless, he never thinks that he should be good, and produce the generations of good character and deeds for the benefit of the individual and the society. Moreover, we may get pure air, water and land but it is very difficult to find out men of character in the polluted world. Therefore, the study of social pollution is more important than that of natural environment because the latter can be protected when man's activities do not have adverse effects on it. Such a study develops rational thinking and helps to understand the matters related to life and environment. Hence, the study of social pollution should be emphasized at any cost and at all levels for man and nation making. Let us see the importance of studying social pollution in the World society.

Protection of Human Values

Modern science, technology, transport, and communication systems have raised the standard of life but reduced the quality of life. For instance, selfishness, lust for materialism, ingratitude, disrespect, intolerance, lack of love, lack of sympathy, lack of cooperation, lack of adjustment, lack of fellow-feeling, lack of patriotism, lack of responsibility and lack of duty consciousness and dishonesty have become the common characteristics of most of the people. The crisis in human values adversely affects the personal, social and national development. In fact, human value crisis makes man characterless and cultureless. Education becomes a meaningless process in the attempt of man-making. Hence, these values should be preserved and developed for the well-being of human society. It is the need of the hour to protect the human values from their destruction due to the commercialization, privatization and profitisation of social activities.

Eradication of Social Evils

The social evils such as corruption, prostitution, eve teasing, dowry, castism, raping, production and consumption of intoxicants, adulteration, commercial riots, principle less politics and organization in the name of caste and religion spoil the quality of people. These activities further widen the unconsciousness and ignorance in both educated and uneducated people. In fact, the number of educated people who engage in social evils are more than the illiterates. As a result, the whole human community will suffer from their unconscious deeds (most of the people do not know what they do at the time of tension in the complicated life). Therefore, right teachers under the supervision of spotless scholars and selfless social activists should eradicate the social evils that affect the progress of man through right education. The study of social pollution highlights how man is polluted and the ways that make him a man of rational thinking and useful to the family and society.

Establishment of Democratic Society

We cannot establish a democratic society or government due to the existence of more than two political parties. India is not a pure democratic country but a disguised democratic society where we can cast our votes to any party or any candidate whom we want to select as our M.L.A. or M.P. in the State and Central elections. But the elected candidate may join another political party (which may be the opposition party) to form the government. Thus, the purpose and desire of the voters cannot be fulfilled when a number of political parties join without principles and establish a government at the state or centre. For instance, some people cast vote in favour of a candidate from Janata Dal, some people vote for a candidate belonging to Jana Morksha and another group votes in favour of Rashtrya Janata, but these candidates from different parties elect a person as a Chief Minister or Prime Minister who belongs to Bahujan Samaj Wadi or Ahalidal. This is known as disguised democracy in which real democracy is latent or concealed. Thus, the meaning and purpose of democracy is defeated and such a democracy increases the number of principle less political establishments, different functionaries based on caste, religion and region, which creates and develops conflicts, brawls and quarrels among the politicians. It is not good for the development of national integration, international understanding and economic development. The study of social pollution changes the attitudes of principle-less politicians who are the backbone of disguised democracy and suggest the ways to establish a democratic society.

Formation of Secular Society

Man is more important than religion and gods. Destruction of lives and properties in the name of religions is more than what occurs in war. Generally people have different faiths, beliefs and rituals which differ from religion to religion, time to time and even place to place. As a result, people belonging to one religion may think that their religion and rituals are superior to those of others. Such a tendency leads to communal riots and terrorism that vitiates the integrity of people and the development of secular outlook. Religion is a meaningless process unless we love and treat others as our brothers and sisters. In fact, we may be Hindus, Sikhs, Muslims, Jains or Christians but these titles or stratifications become meaningless when we reach the age of seventy and above. Moreover, religion divides the people but secularism unites them. In fact, secularism is very essential for a peaceful and happy life and better human relationship. The study of social pollution enables the people to shun their superstitious faith and ignorance and develop in them a rational outlook, which prepares them for understanding, tolerance and adjustment with one another.

Establishment of Casteless Society

Everything changes and is modernized in the dynamic world. However, we still separate the people in the name of caste, which is a great sin. There are two castes by birth male and female but they are stratified into a number of castes and are grouped into forward, backward, most backward and scheduled caste/tribe people. We can say that such classification is quite unavoidable for providing economic and employment opportunities in our society. Such classifications might have been done based on occupation or economic and social factors. But, is it necessary now? Are all people who have been categorized under forward communities rich? Are all people who have been classified under most backward and scheduled communities poor? People belonging to all communities or castes get education and employment. One may be a Brahmin or a non-Brahmin but what is his character? Anti-social elements are found in all communities and all castes. Hence, human population should be classified based only on family income and the place for caste and religion in the application forms for education and employment should be deleted. It is the worst situation that, some people including politicians, officers and ministers demand caste-based census. Emphasising castes means polluting the human society. In fact, politicians use caste as a device for getting votes and people establish caste-based politics not for the benefit of the society but for the welfare of the particular candidates. There is a controversial opinion in Tamil Nadu about castes. That is, the national poet Mahakavi Subramonia Bharathi of the 20th century says, "there is no caste baby. Saying caste is a sin" (chathikal illaiyadi papa) but ignorant politicians demand caste based census in the twenty first century. If it is so, where is society and nation? Man is a social animal who is born empty and leaves the world empty and who can be proud of his caste and community above the age of sixty or at the time of sickness and feebleness. Moreover, casteism is a meaningless structure or system, which pollutes the social environment. For instance, the government compels the people to produce community certificate for education and employment but such certificate issuing office is the centre of delay and corruption. People who demand certificates have to waste their time, energy and money. It is a meaningless burden falling on the shoulders of authorities and the public. Therefore, future generations must be redeemed from the grip of castes and community and all efforts should be taken to create a casteless society. Hence, a special study on social pollution is very important.

Establishment of Corruption Free Society

What we need today is not scientific and technological development but the establishment of a casteless secular and corruption free democratic society. Corruption has become a chronic disease like cancer, which decays the whole human society. Consequently, it is known as social cancer. It is born at home, brought up in religious institutions, spreads to education and society, and is strengthened by politicians. It is the shortest route for becoming rich. It is a painless gain causing many diseases and curses. In fact, it pushes the man to lead a dishonest life and pollutes the social environment. The pain derived out of corruption is greater than the gain obtained out of it. Moreover, there is a close relationship between corruption and the consumption of drugs. Corruption develops an unquenchable thirst for money and reduces the quality of officers, politicians and educational authorities. It starts and continues from birth (When we demand birth and death certificates we should pay a sum of rupees other than fee) to death. Corruption increases wealth but decreases health and produces and ruins the character of human beings. Therefore, a corruption free society should be established for a happy and peaceful life. For this purpose, the study of social pollution is very important to indicate the effects of corruption and suggest the ways and means for establishing a corruption free society.

FIGURE 59.2 Exhibiting Drunkard's Behaviour

Man and Nation Making

According to Swami Vivekananda, "The end of all education and all training should be man making". Therefore, the goal of education should be man and nation making. Nevertheless, the privatization, commercialisation and politicalisation of educational activities change the aims of education from man-making to money-making. In fact, present education does not aim at character formation but cash accumulation by preparing the individual for any sort of employment. Consequently, man becomes selfish, dishonest and indulges in anti-social activities. Moreover, he engages in many filthy deeds, which fetch him fiscal power and physical pleasure. Thus, present education has failed to produce an honest citizen and a better society. Hence, the study of social pollution should be included at all stages and all types of education. In other words, the study of social pollution is very important in the process of man and nation making.

Prevention of Intoxicants

The number of manufacturers of drugs, cigarettes, beedi, tobacco, ganja, toddy and illicit arrack are increasing based on the increase of consumers. Educated people are addicted to the consumption of these products. In fact, ignorance engulfs the rational thinking of most of the people. The consumption of intoxicants spreads from father to son and from son to his friends. It is highly deplorable fact that school going boys have become victim to the consumption of intoxicants. The government is recognising the production of intoxicants for increasing the income. But the consumption of such products affects the health, wealth and character of younger generations who are the pillars of the nation. The encouragement of the production of intoxicants may cause many accidents, death, divorce, quarrels, suicides, peaceless and unhealthy life and poverty. Moreover, environmental pollution cannot be controlled unless social pollution is prevented. For instance, more and more plastic products are used in the wine shops. Plastic pollutes the soil whereas liquor pollutes the man. Therefore, the government should take immediate efforts with the cooperation of the public to prevent the production of those products that cause environmental and social pollution.

Achievement of Balanced Development

The balanced development of the child is highly influenced by both natural and social environments. All-round development of the child includes the physical, mental, spiritual, cultural, social and aesthetical aspects. Such a development depends on the availability of natural factors like air, water, food and climate and social factors such as character of parents, teachers, friends and relatives and their examples. For instance, polluted natural and social environment adversely affects the balanced growth of the child in all aspects of his life. Just as fruitful trees yield good fruits, good parents and teachers produce a better generation. This responsibility firmly lies on them. The study of social pollution facilitates the child and man to achieve a balanced development.

Making Life Happy and Peaceful

A man does not live for a long time but he has to live a happy and peaceful life as long as he is on the earth. Such a life is a blessed one that is determined by the natural and social environments. The modern society has turned the man in to a machine and he is busy always. In fact, most of the educated and employed people do not have a peaceful and happy life due to social pollution. Corruption and lust for material and physical pleasure make him to lead a filthy life causing tension, frustration, despondency, loss of money, property and lives, diseases and death. Such incidents and happenings make human life unhappy and unhealthy. Hence, the study of social pollution is very important to prepare the people for a happy and peaceful life.

Development of Quality Personnel

The development of quality personnel depends on the quality of parents, teachers, educationists, religious workers, social activists and politicians. They should be improved through proper guidance and counselling. Most of the people do not understand their qualities and how they cause pollution in social and natural environments. It is because materialism, drugs, ignorance and filthy deeds pollute these people. Only good parents, teachers, religious, social and political leaders can develop quality personnel and prevent social pollution. Therefore, they should study the causes and effects of social pollution and improve themselves to be the models for future generations.

FACTORS CAUSING SOCIAL POLLUTION

The child is pure and sensitive in nature. He is born free but he is chained everywhere in the stratified society. In fact, children are stratified under categories of caste, religion, language, region, community and economic status. Moreover, a number of social, political and economic factors pollute them. For instance, the factors such as parents, teachers, education, religion, caste, politics, mass media, poverty, unemployment, intoxicants producers and consumers and lack of punishment are the causes of child pollution. As a result, it is difficult to establish a better human society. In fact, a better human society can be established only when the government, the religious leaders/pastors, the politicians, the teachers, the parent and the children play their roles. If there is any deviation or crisis in their relationship, a better human society and a better government cannot be established in a country. Hence, an attempt is made here to study the factors that cause human value crisis or pollution in the present society.

Parents

Parents are the first and the best teachers and models from whom their children learn, develop and prepare themselves to live as social beings. Only a good parent can be the model to his/her children. In our society, about 83 percent of the marriages are arranged based on age, wealth, health, beauty, education and family backgrounds of the bridegrooms and brides. They never think that their children should be like Jesus Christ, Buddha, Mahatma Gandhiji, Mother Teresa, Abraham Lincoln, Swami Vivekananda and at least the men of great personality in character and deeds. It is found that more than 68 percent married couples are not running their family life smoothly due to poverty, unemployment, lack of affection, misunderstanding, inferiority or superiority complex, diseases and undesirable character of husband/wife. In fact, the parents who are addicted to drugs, smoking, and chewing tobacco and who follow polygamy or polyandry system or illegal sexual relations and who divorces before and after the childbirth may not bring up their children in a better way.

About 92 percent parents do not know how to treat their children in the social environments. The parents who are corrupt, dishonest, immoral, drunkards, smokers, rapers, killers, thieves, kidnappers and print fake currencies cannot expect their children to be better than themselves. Such parents play a very important role in producing a bad generation and polluting the human society.

Teachers

Teachers are social engineers whose places are very essential in man making and nation-making. Once, they were considered as 'guru' or 'asan' and in modern days, they are called as philosophers, friends, guides and counsellors. But today their role in the development of human society is declining due to their lack of character and quality, privatization and commercialization of education. However, they take the place of parents in the school and help them to achieve intellectual, social, cultural, physical and economic development. But the teachers who consume drugs, cigarettes and tobacco products and expect money or materials from students for internal assessment or for any favouritism cannot be the role models for the students. Teaching does not mean sitting and reading the textbooks prescribed for study but it is meant for developing or formulating good characters in the student. It is regrettable to emphasise that the teachers have lost their social status, but instead of that, they have gained their economic status. In fact, some of the of the teachers are sitting and using cell phones and leave the classroom before the class is over. The invigilators of public/university examinations are found to be chatting outside the exam halls. (The author had seen such bitter experience on 21 November 2009 in an aided college near Nagercoil, South India.) Some teachers use the students for their personal gain. For instance, cleaning their vehicles and purchasing things. A few teachers use their students in valuing the class test papers and entering the marks in the progress card. Such undesirable activities of some teachers reduce the quality of teachers and but also develop the habit of copying from other's answer scripts, cheating, lying, laziness and dishonesty in the students. In fact, the irresponsible attitudes of the teachers pollute the students who may develop and practise such activities in their social life. It is also seen that some teachers discriminate their students based on their colour, caste, religion, economic status and location.

Most of the teachers have gone to the extent of forcing or advising their students to respect them. Moreover, the observation of teacher's day in educational institutions (September 5) is misused in the recent years. The teachers who do not know the academic and professional quality of Dr.S.Radhakrishnan demand the poor students for gifts. Every teacher must know that students are not earners and they depend on their parents for all. The real observation of this day lies not in insisting the students for gifts but making themselves effective teachers. In this way, teachers not only neglect their responsibilities to the society butalso pollute the student communities who are the sons of the nation.

Educational Institutions

The purpose of educational institutions has been changed from knowledge development to fiscal development. Consequently, remarkable changes have taken place in social, cultural, spiritual, political and economic life. In fact, privatization, commercialization and politicalisation of education not only decrease the quality of the education but also increases the cost of education offered in private educational institutions. For instance, admissions are not made on the basis of merit, but on money in most of the private educational institutions. Appointments in aided and non-aided schools and colleges are also made on the basis of caste, religion, politics and location. Moreover, it is seen that most of the students choose various academic and professional courses not on the basis of their interest, ability, intelligence and skill but only on the basis of educational facilities available in nearby institutions and employment opportunities. Consequently, teachers lack quality and character. Age is the only factor that differentiates the teacher from the student. In fact, both teachers and students are living in the same social environment and watching the same television programmes and their family atmosphere also is almost the same. Students are exploited and squeezed in terms of money in the name of different fees. Sundays and holidays are also working days in most of the private educational institutions. Strict discipline, punishments, lack of freedom, over-work , nepotism and favouritism have developed laziness, selfishness, dishonesty and lust for materialism in the students. The role of the educated in social pollution is higher than that of the uneducated. In fact, caste and religious based private educational institutions give importance to the development of their religion and fail to foster secularism in the students. Further, such institutions have become the business centres for stationeries, textbooks, bags and uniforms.

It should be noted that more education leads to more corruption, laziness, selfishness and materialism. In fact, the habit of corruption, socio-economic based favouritsm and printing fake certificates have been the characteristics of some higher educational institutions in India. For instance, a few Lectures of the southernmost Indian university in Tamil Nadu collected ₹ 5000 from B. Ed. students 2010–2011 (Distance Education System) for teaching practice observation and internal evaluation (The University allotted ₹ 600/per student for this purpose). This undesirable behavior of the lecturers pollutes the minds of teacher trainees, which is spread to the society. Therefore, role of privatization and commercialisation of education cannot be neglected in social pollution.

Casteism

Human population is stratified into different castes, communities and economic groups. Consequently, a number of castes exist in the Indian society, and further they are grouped into Forward, Backward, Most Backward and Scheduled Caste and Scheduled Tribe Communities. Based on economic status, they are categorized into upper class, middle class and lower class people. As a result, people belonging to the forward community request the government to declare them as backward and people belonging to backward community may demand to be declared as most backward community for getting concession in education and employment. This kind of demand develops a feeling of 'our caste and our community' in all people, that affects their integrity. In fact, casteism develops groups among the people and it is used as a powerful weapon for getting votes in the assembly and parliament elections. Some politicians establish caste-based politics that causes riots, quarrels and commotion at the time of election. In short, it creates a wide gap among the castes that pollutes the human beings in different ways.

Politicians

Ours is a democratic country where too much of freedom encourages the people to establish a number of political parties on the basis of caste, religion and region. Consequently, there are many political parties without principles. In fact, the principle-less politicians make alliance with different political parties in order to face the election and get monetary benefits. Politicians offer attractive posts to the students in the party and spoil their life. Existence of many political parties commercialises vote. That is, votes are bought and sold for money. This symptom is not good for a healthy democracy. Moreover, politicians protect and help the anti-social elements or any accused from punishment and seek their help at the time of election. In short, commercialization of political activities is one of the reasons for social pollution. The selection of candidates for the election is not done on the basis of character and academic qualification, but on the basis of health, wealth, local popularity and political alliance. Therefore, inefficient persons are elected as M.L.As or M.Ps in the elections which is not good for the development of the country.

Religion

Religion is the source of spiritual and moral development. But, the modern society has turned it into economic services. Therefore it is regarded as one of the factors that pollutes the human society. In fact, privatization and commercialization of medical and educational services has changed the churches, mosques, temples and gurudwaras into profit -making industries. It is also seen that there is a firm relationship between the quantity of money and the quality of prayer. In other words, quality and quantity of prayer depend on the quality of the person and quantity of money. Moreover, scientific development and the undesirable activities of some pastors, priests, poojaris, hazarath and religious leaders and commercialization of religious activities have decreased the spiritual and moral values. It is also seen that politicians seek the help of religions for votes and religion seeks the help of politicians for publicity. However, people worship gods like Vinayagar, Siva, Krishna, Murugan, Durga, Saraswathi and Kali with different faiths and rituals. In Christianity, there are many denominations such as Roman Catholics, Malankara Catholics. Syrian Malabar Catholics, Church of North India , Church of South India, Methodist, Jacobites, Mar Thomas, Baptists, Lutheran Churches, London Mission Society, Seventh Day Adventists and Evangelical church of India, and a hundreds of independent Pentecostal denominations. Consequently, people give more importance to the denominations and celebrations of family gods and their development than the spiritual development and holy life. It cannot be denied that church politics, money-centred spiritualism, commercialization and politicalisation of religious activities, treating other denominations as enemies, utilization of loud speakers in public places and conducting processions and disturbing transport, dissolving crores of painted effigies of Vinayagar on the occasion of Vinayagar charthurthi, and throwing colour powder on Holi festival pollute both social and natural environments.

Mass Media

Mass media is the centre of knowledge development and the source of entertainment of 89 percent of the people. In those days, movies were meant for the development of personal, social and national values and people of all ages could enjoy them with family. But most of the present movies emphasise sexual and violent scenes and they are unfit to be seen by the family members together. The movies that highlight sex, violence and indecent dialogues pollute the human society. In fact, most of the criminals found in raping, kidnapping, printing fake currencies, murdering, stealing, , ragging, eve-teasing and robbing cite the names of movies as the examples for their activities. Sex inducing acts, and the way that actors used to steal, cheat, kill, kidnap and escape from punishment have a great impact on the thoughts and behaviour of the criminals and influence the younger generations. Moviemakers display many obscenities that are not related to the story for money-making which spoil the youth. For instance, kissing, bathing, raping, semi-nude and violent scenes are not necessary to inculcate cooperation, fellow feelings, patriotism, national integrity, secularism, casteless society and democracy. We may think movies are only entertainments. But we cannot neglect their great impact on younger generations. Is it fit to be seen by father and daughter together? Is it useful for value education? What does a movie emphasise in the society? Nobody think s of its evil effects on the society. Who can say that this or that movie is good for the development of family or society? Moreover, cine-based programmes are arranged for celebrating religious festivals and national days. Hence, the purpose and importance of such celebrations have become meaningless. We cannot deny the fact that the present mass media is one of the causes of social pollution.

Poverty and Unemployment

It is the outcome of rapid growth of population and under-utilization of natural and human resources. These factors play an important role in social pollution. In fact, poverty and unemployment prevent the people from leading honest lives and instigate them to engage in filthy deeds. For instance, people engage in prostitution, adulteration, stealing, cheating and doing any other deeds like being brokers or commission agents that fetch them income. Consequently, the human values such as honesty, love, kindness, faithfulness, cleanliness, un-selfishness, sacrifice, patriotism, cooperation and fellow-feeling may not be found in the personal as well as social life of the poverty-stricken and unemployed people. Such people justify their deeds even if they are socially undesirable. Moreover, child labour, child marriage, bonded labour, labour exploitation, stealing, robbing, deceiving and human trafficking have been the consequences of poverty and unemployment. Most of the rich and educated people are not leading a good life. How can we expect such life from the poor and unemployed people?. Hence, the role of poverty and unemployment in social pollution cannot be ignored in the Indian society.

Negligence of Governments

The role of governments is very important in preserving the social and natural environments. For this purpose, it should give much attention to the health of people and the sustainable development of nature. But, it concentrates on the sources of revenue, plans expenditure, and maintains its sustainability. Consequently, it does not care for the production and consumption of liquor, cigarettes, tobacco and betel nut products, and movie that focus on the sexual and violent scenes, which is spoiling the health, and duration of one's life and degrade the social as well as natural environments. In fact, all intoxicants are poisons that affect the body and mind. Thus, the production of intoxicants is not only a cause of the social pollution, but also degrades the environment. For instance, most of the intoxicants are packed up in plastics that spoil the fertility of the soil. Moreover, a few drunkards throw the empty wine bottles at the government bus that break its glasses and some pieces fall under the bus tyres that may cause puncture and cause inconvenience to the passengers. (The author had such a bitter experience at Chidambaram Bus Stand near Chennai at 10.40 P.M. on 19.07.2010). The government should have prohibited the production of intoxicants and punished the producers. The intoxicants have the label which read as follows. "Smoking is injurious to health", "Chewing tobacco causes cancer" and "Drinking is injurious to life, family and nation". If so, why should people produce such products and pollute the human society? Is it the way to fulfil the dream of the former president Dr. A.P.J. Abdul Kalam? No doubt, the governments have failed to foresee the ill effects of such products on the health of people and considered them as one of the sources of its revenue. It is very dangerous that school-going children are inclined to the consumption of intoxicants that impede balanced development and create problem in maintaining relationship with family and society. Hence, we cannot deny that the government is also one of the factors of social pollution.

Liberalisation of Punishment

Liberalisation or freedom from punishment is one of the most important causes of social pollution in the Indian society. It can be seen that the person who steals, hijacks planes and trains, prints fake currencies and certificates, receives bribes, takes dowry kills, eve teases, kidnaps, human traffics, cheats and engages in any anti-social activity escapes punishment. For instance, the culprits are being arrested and imprisoned for a few days, months or years and released with or without a little fine. Even if he is sentenced to life imprisonment or death, he will escape from the sentence due to the influence of money, support of politicians or the influence of higher authorities. Consequently, stealing, robbering, swindling, cheating, printing fake currencies, and certificates, corruption, dowry harassment, raping, kidnapping, human trafficking, vengeance, eve teasing, suicides, bomb blasting and rail track-cut are the experience of the present life. In fact, any one of these incidents is the headline of every newspaper and it is an important news in televisions and radios. Thus, the mass media highlight every crime with evidences and states that the culprit is arrested and remanded for fifteen days and the case is under police investigation. Finally, crimes are exposed and criminals are escaped. In other words, whatever may be the severity of crimes, the punishment will be over by one or two years with a fine of thousands rupees. But, the accused who are financially weak, and do not have the influence of politicians or higher authorities will have to be in jail for a few more years. This nature of punishment strengthens and encourages the people to do any crime for physical pleasure and monetary benefit.

EFFECTS OF SOCIAL POLLUTION

Explosion of Criminals: Social pollution increases the number of criminals in proportion to the increase in population. As a result, it is very difficult to identify who is honest and who is a criminal. Even the character of man changes from time to time and place to place due to the concentration of human pollutants. For instance, corruption of one person may tempt others to be corrupt in the absence of punishment. Likewise, a drunkard or a smoker may encourage or help others to turn into his ways in the social environments. Such habits may instigate them to lead dishonest lives. Thus, social pollution increases the number of criminals.

Values Become Invalid: One of the important effects of social pollution is value crisis. In fact, love, sympathy, compassion, selfless sacrifice, adjustment, tolerance, cooperation and brotherhood are the important values that differentiate man from animals. But human pollutants such as lust for money, corruption, dowry, raping, kidnapping, cheating, stealing and dishonesty throw the values into air. Crisis in human values makes life materialistic, peaceless and unhappy.

Declining Spiritualism: This is also one of the undesirable effects of social pollution. In fact, materialization of spiritualism, scientific and technological development, politicalisation of religions and undesirable activities of a few pastors, priests, poojaris, moulvi and the examples of religious leaders have reduced the importance of spiritualism, and faith on rebirth or the life beyond this world.

Growth of Terrorism: Social pollution leads to the development of terrorism. It is seen that a group of people or region may be neglected due to political and social reasons. And the existence of casteism, religion, unemployment, poverty, ignorance and illiteracy have developed narrow mindedness in the minds of many people that give birth to emergence and development of terrorism. Consequently, the vicious circle of violence crosses throughout the world. Terrorists may have positive planning to be implemented for the welfare of a group of people or region. But it may be against the government or the society. However, their activities cause heavy loss of lives and property. Therefore, terrorism is considered as one of the ill effects of social pollution.

Accidents and Demise: Social pollution causes the occurrence of many accidents and demises. This is because people who are addicted to the consumption of the intoxicants lose their capacity for controlling the activities of their body and mind. It is seen that drinking, smoking and chewing tobacco have become the acceptable characteristics of the present generation. These habits change the manner and speed of driving bikes, cars, buses and lorries. In fact, the activation of intoxicants accelerates the mood of drivers causing many accidents and death. It is calculated that more than 78 percent of the road accidents occur because the drivers are drunkards. The warnings such as "Don't drink while drive', 'Don't drive while drink' and 'Don't use mobile while drive' have failed in bringing about desirable changes in the habits of many drivers. Hence, accidents and death are considered as the serious effects of social pollution.

Chronic Diseases: The diseases like cancer, AIDS and jaundice are caused by the consumption of liquor, smoking cigarettes, chewing tobacco and sexual relationship with harlots. In fact, drinking, smoking, chewing intoxicants affect the lungs, kidney, liver, heart, eyesight, and nerves, causing tuberculosis, cancer, jaundice and kidney failure. Moreover, illegal contact with prostitutes and polyandry or polygamy causes AIDS. It has been proved that sexual contact with prostitutes is the cause of AIDS and consumption of tobacco is the cause of cancer. Likewise, corruption and anti-social activities breed incurable diseases and cause death or heavy loss of money and property.

Corruption is the Centre of Activity: This is the worst effect of social pollution found from sweepers to superintendents. Commercialisation of education, religion and politics pollute the whole human society. Even if a person is against corruption, he will have to bribe for getting things done in the private and government departments. The movement of files or application form depends on giving bribes. In fact, most of the activities in the government departments have become corruption-centred and nobody can escape from this social cancer in the future. For instance, a hundred rupee note should be attached to the application form when we apply to the taluk office for a community, nativity, or income certificate. In short, corruption is the starting point of birth certificate and the ending point of death certificate and this is the experience of an ordinary citizen. It is highly deplorable that corruption policy flies in the air with the two wings—politics and education. For instance, the education minister and the Vice-Chancellor demand the correspondent ₹ 10 to 15 lakhs for the renewal of the continuation of college affiliation (B.Ed.) to Tamil Nadu Teacher Education University in 2014. This practice instigates the correspondent to raise fees for such course and exploit the students. Thus, politics and education strengthen and justify the corruption policy in the Indian society. Thus, corruption will be a bitter as well as acceptable experience of the future generation. Consequently, the statement "Bribe brings victory" takes the place of "prayer brings victory". It will be true unless the practice of corruption is eradicated from the society.

Prosperity and Poverty: It is practically seen that people engage in anti-social activities in order to bring about financial prosperity quickly. But the financial prosperity through such filthy deeds cannot last long and they push the people in to poverty in the course of time. It means that prosperity for a few years is turned to poverty for many years. For instance, prostitutes, corruptive, producers of intoxicants and thieves become very rich shortly, but they lose their health, wealth and family status, after a certain period. This is the experience of many people who become rich through such activities. They have become poor and have physically or mentally retarded children. This is the law of nature which is applicable to all those who pollute themselves and the human society.

Unhappiness and Peacelessness: This is one of the worst outcomes of social pollution. The lust for materialism encourages some people to apply various tricks and techniques that make them rich very quickly. Moreover, some people are addicted to the consumption of liquor, chewing tobacco and smoking cigarettes causing the loss of health and wealth. In fact, the shortcut method of becoming rich and consumption of intoxicants develop in-humanism, conflicts, tension and despondency in most of the people. Consequently, the life of the poor and the rich is enveloped with the feeling of sorrows and peacelessness. Moreover, we may think that corruption, prostitution, adulteration, liberalization of punishments of criminals and consumption of intoxicants could make the people financially sound and physically happy. But the statement 'you will reap what you sow' never fails in anybody's life. Our generation and we cannot escape from the reward or punishment for our every deed that may be good or not. In fact, when a person is found in corruption, prostitution, murdering, printing fake currencies and certificates may commit suicide or disguise himself due to fear and shame, or to escape from punishment. Thus, their life is full of sorrows and peacelessness.

Environmental Pollution: Social pollution itself is a factor for environmental pollution. There is a relationship between human and environmental pollution. In fact, most of the human pollutants such as drugs, tobacco and betel nuts are packed up in bottles and plastics. After the consumption of such products, bottles and plastics are thrown in the open air that pollutes the cities and the bus stands. The broken bottles and thrown plastics damage the bus tyres, injure the feet of pedestrian, and affect the fertility of the soil. Moreover, smoking cigarette and beedi pollute the air directly. As intoxicants affect both man and nature, social pollution is directly related to the environmental pollution.

Crisis in Family Life: This is also one of the ill effects of social pollution in the present society. Lack of love, understanding, adjustments, inferiority or superiority complex, addiction to drugs, keeping illegal contacts and polyandry or polygamy affect the family relationship and cause the formation of characterless generation. In fact, the number of divorce cases registered in the court has been increasing and at the same time, the number of husbands and wives living separately has been increasing in these days. This is mainly due to the character of either husband or wife or both. The lust for money, intoxicants and illegal sexual relationship pollute the character of husbands and wives. Consequently, divorce or separation of family will be the outcome of social pollution that may cause suicides, agony, poverty and unhappiness affecting the balanced development of their children.

Tumultuous Parliament: This is the bitter experience faced in Indian politics, number of political parties join without principles at the times of parliament and state assembly elections. Consequently, wealthy, healthy and characterless persons will be elected as M.P's and M.L.A's. Most of them use their influence for personal gain. A few of them do not know Hindi, the national language or English, the international language and act like deaf and dumb people in the parliament. Alliance among political parties commercialises politics for getting M.P. or M.L.A. seats and votes. As a result, no government at the centre or the state can be established without the support of alliances. Thus, democracy is in the hands of M.P and M.L.A. not in the hands of the people. They demand caste-based censes, reservation for education, employment and scholarship. In fact, the declaration of forward as backward and backward as most backward that develop communal riots, terrorism and narrowism in the ordinary course of life. Above all, commercialization of politics leads to corruption, selfishness and liberalization of punishments for criminals, inflation and inequalities. For instance, various political parties make alliance to contest in the election and establish a hung parliament and demand for the post of ministers based on caste or religion or region. Sometimes, M.L.A's and M.P's are bought and sold for lakhs of rupees to prove the strength required for forming the central or state governments. Thus, selling and buying of votes and M.L.A's and M.P's pollute the human society. In fact, politics is without principles, politicians are without character and politics is commercialized for money. The 12th February, 2014 is the black day in the history of Indian parliament because a barbarian congress MP L. Rajagopal, sprayed pepper powder in the parliament assembly demanding the separation of Telangana from Andhra Pradesh. This shows the poor quality of the present MPs. The misbehaviour of one MP collapse the whole atmosphere of the country. Non-violence is the culture of Indian society. So every MP should remember the dedication, scarifies and struggle of the great Indian leaders. Hence, parliament or assembly is the place for tumultuous action s like beating, breaking furniture and howling and impeachment of opposite parties and vice-versa and discussing about anti-social activities have become the habitual activities of politicians that is the practical effect of social pollution.

Declining quality of Education and Research: This is one of the most evil effects of social pollution caused by the politicalisation, privatization and commercialization of education. Educational institutions have become profit-making industries. The aim of education was man-making but it is now money-making. In other words, quality of education depends on the quantity of money. For instance, students who obtained 900/1200 marks at higher secondary level have been admitted in medical colleges, 700/1200 in engineering colleges, 500/1200 in arts and science colleges. Students who obtained third class marks at degree courses are admitted in the college for education. The liberalized valuation of answer scripts at B.A., B.Sc. and B.Ed. level increases the number of passed students and decreases the quality of education. For instance, when the author valued answer-scripts of hundred trainees, only 33 or 34 trainees got pass marks in the model examination, but it was 97 or 98 percent when other lecturers valuated the B.Ed. answer scripts in the Tamil Nadu Teacher Education University during the academic year 2009–2010. It shows the very poor valuation of present lecturers who are interested in counting the number of answer scripts and calculating the remuneration rather than the performance of the trainees. Consequently, teachers of poor quality are found in almost all schools. They do not know how to teach but how to punish and speak about the weakness of the students. Moreover, they think that they are better than students in character and knowledge. Moreover, as per the norms of University Grants Commission a candidate should have Ph.D. Degree for the consideration of lectureship in college and University level. Consequently, students who are not interested in research and are poor in subjects and language, join M.Phil., and Ph.D., Degrees. It increases the number of researchers and the cost of research but reduces the quality of research. In fact, the demand for such degrees for employment leads to plagiarism. Thus, liberalization of examination valuation and compulsion of Ph.D. make education and research a meaningless process that pollute the human society and educational environment.

Indisciplined Generations: This is the present trend of the new generation due to the impact of social pollution. In fact, most of the children are disobedient and do not give due respect to their elders, parents, teachers and relatives. The undesirable character of parents and teachers, sex and violent scenes of mass media and movies, liberalization of punishment and commercialization of politics, education and religion and intoxicants foster bad character in the present generation. For instance, parents who are addicted to intoxicants, keep illegal sexual relationship, engage in prostitution and adulteration are criminals marring the character of their children. Consequently, there is a crisis in the relationship between teacher and students, between parents and children and between students and society. In fact, more than 30 percent of the criminals arrested are between the age of 13–20 found in the case of murdering, stealing, kidnapping, rapping, robe ring, eve teasing, ragging and sex harassment and destroying lives and property. Hence, the undisciplined characteristics of new generations are regarded as a dangerous effect of social pollution.

Gloomy World: The impact of social pollution is more dangerous than that of environmental pollution in making the world gloomy. It is a world in which there is no difference between literates and illiterates, between spiritualism and materialism, between religion and politics and between teacher and students in knowledge and character. Moreover, what were considered and neglected as anti-social activities will be the acceptable culture of the future generations. Education is not meant for knowledge, but for employment and moneymaking. Laziness, wasting energy and water, chatting, corruption, stealing and postponing the work will be the general characteristics of most of the people working in government departments. However, selfishness, commercialization and profitisation of social services, backbiting, dishonesty and flattery are the general features of people working in the private institutions. All religious functions and celebrations are centred around film show based programmes. Likewise mass media and cinema emphasize sexual and violent scenes for the sake of money.

WAYS FOR CONTROLLING SOCIAL POLLUTION

The quality of a country is determined by the quality of its people that depend on social and natural environments. We believe that education and religion will mend, shape and improve the quality of people in a desirable manner and produce better man and nation. It is needless to say that both education and religion have failed in their attempt due to the commercialisation of such factors. However, some of us may deny this fact and say that education and religion are very important factors in bringing about economic and spiritual development. Hence, the role of governments, politicians, teachers, moviemakers, broad-casters, religious activists and parents is very essential in preventing social pollution. For this purpose, the quality of these people should be modified and improved by adopting and implementing the following suggestions as the ways and means for protecting man and environment from pollution.

Role of Government

The role of central and state governments is very necessary for the removal of vanishing social pollution from the Indian society. They may implement or adopt the following suggestions for strengthening themselves and preventing social pollution.

- A strong government should be established at the centre and the state without any alliance or support of any other political parties. For this purpose, there should be two political parties—ruling and opposition both should aim at the welfare of the people and the development of the country and they should not clash or dispute with each other.
- Election alliance among various political parties should strictly be prohibited and each party should face the parliament or assembly election independently. It will stop the establishment of hung parliament or government and mushroom growth of political parties without principles.
- Commercialisation of votes should strictly be arrested and those politician or parties asking for votes for monetary benefits should be punished severely and may be imprisoned for ten years.
- Government should appoint various officers irrespective of their political influence, caste, religion and region but based on their education, character and social efficiency to scrutinize the activities of M.L.As., M.Ps., and government Officers.
- Government should delete the place for caste and religion or community in the applications for admission in education and employment to strengthen the unity and integrity of nations. If not there should be a column for secularists so that people can fill it in the application for certificates, education and employment.
- Government should consider the economic status of the people as the criterion for concession in education, employment and scholarships.
- Government should strictly prohibit the caste or religion based politics or organisations since they develop narrow mindedness and selfishness and vitiate national integrity and may lead to the formation of terrorism.
- Government should not encourage the production of intoxicants at any cost and punish the people who produce such products severely as they spoil the character and health of younger generations.
- Government should punish the criminals such as rapists, eve teasers, kidnappers, murderers, prostitutes, stealers, fake currency and certificate producers, plane and train hijackers and corruptive and terrorists within a week or month. If necessary, the criminals should be sentenced to death. No gain without pain should be the policy of punishing the criminals.

- Government should not recognise the production of intoxicants as the source of its revenue for increasing the salary of workers in its department and providing free television, cooker and dress for seeking political favouritism of the illiterate and the poor.
- Government should pass an Act in the parliament to prohibit the dissolving of the painted effigies in the water resources and it should declare, "Worship God and Protect Nature" and Observe Festivals without Pollution". For instance, Holi festivals may be celebrated without throwing colour powder, as it pollutes human body (eyes, nose and mouth) and the air and the celebration of Vinayagar chathurthi is directly related to marine pollution and communal riots causing loss of aquatic living organisms, human beings and government properties.
- Government may increase the salary of workers once in five years according to its fiscal capacity but note that any increase in salary without increase in agricultural production causing inflation and inequalities that affects the people who are working in private institutions. The salary of government employees should be enough to maintain themselves.
- Government should provide national awards for the top-most producers of sugar, paddy, wheat, plantain, fruits, and vegetables at village, district, state or national level to encourage the farmers to increase agricultural production and economic prosperity. However, awards to actors, musician and players do not bring economic development.
- Government should keep an eye on the privatization of education and recognize only those institution having adequate facilities, fees structure and qualified staff. The service of the educational institutions should be confirmed for the welfare of the students.
- Government should appoint Vice-chancellors and higher educational authorities irrespective of politics, caste, religion and region but based on talents, honesty, and experience.
- Government should not expect or compel the schools to produce centum results as it liberalises the valuation of answer scripts and reduces the quality of education.
- Government should prohibit the movies exposing sexual and violent scenes as they mar the character of students and provide tax concession to those movies that develop social, spiritual and moral values in the students and society.
- Government should appoint a group of social thinkers and scholars to scrutinize whether the movie is useful to the individual and society.
- Government should constitute higher educational committees of talented, honest and well-experienced persons to scrutinize the function of schools, colleges and universities.
- Government should not emphasise state language for political favouritism as it develops narrowism. Language is the only factor that differentiates the people from region to region, state to state and even country to country. Hence, the study of Hindi, English and any one language spoken in other states or in other countries should be taught to every child for international understanding.
- The government should understand that languages are the media for expressing our thoughts and feelings. Therefore, opportunity to learn any language should be provided and encouraged at school and college levels. In fact, opportunities should be provided to study mother tongues, the national language Hindi and the international language English. Apart from this, people may be encouraged to learn any other foreign languages. The state should not discriminate its citizens in providing Hindi at school and college levels as long as it is the part of India. What benefit does the state government of Tamil Nadu get by neglecting Hindi? But, learning such a language develops nationalism. Moreover, the state governments need not bother about the study of any language because people who are born in America and England speak English, the

French speak French and Indian speak Hindi and the people of Tamil Nadu speak Tamil and the people of Andhra Pradesh speak Telugu.

- Government may avoid conducting by-elections on account of the demise of M.P. or M.L.A. as it leads to corruption and proves the power of the ruling party in terms of money and commercialization of votes. In this situation, a person belonging to the political party of the deceased M.P. or M.L.A. may be selected based on his education, social efficiency and character instead of conducting a by-election or the responsibility of the M.P may be entrusted to the district Collector and that of the M.L.A to the Thasildhar.
- Government should supervise the performance of the M.P s. and at the central and M.L.A.s, and guide them to keep their hands free from corruption and filthy deeds.
- Opposite party should cooperate with the government for the development of the country and suggest ways and means for eradicating poverty and increasing employment opportunities and work for the economic development of the country.
- Governments should not increase the salary of workers beyond their quality, work and basic needs. The wage of workers in the business is ₹ 3000–7000 whereas, it is ₹ 50,000–1,00,000 and above per month in colleges and in government departments. This variation causes inflation, inequality, crimes (officers and professors are killed for money and properties) and the development of capitalism.
- Government should cancel the Faculty Improvement Programme (FIP) to pursue the research programmes leading to PhD degree. It is treated as Family Improvement Programme. The expenditure on these programmes increases the burden of the government. In fact, most of the research programmes are only plagiarism and useless but wasting money and time.

Role of Politicians

As politics is one of the important factors for social pollution, the quality of the politicians should be improved through the following ways.

- Politicians should be men of character, socially efficient ready to do, selfless sacrifice and be examples to others in personal, social, moral and political life.
- They should avoid drinking, smoking, chewing, corruption and supporting those who engage in anti-social activities.
- They should avoid the establishment of any organization or political party based on their caste, religion and region.
- They should not involve the students in politics because it would affect their studies and responsibilities.
- They should dedicate themselves and their families for the development of the nation.
- They should face the parliamentary and state elections independently, and never seek alliance for money or becoming M.P. and M.L.A.
- They should realize that more than two political parties cannot establish a democratic government at the centre and the state.
- They should not consider politics as one of the sources for profit making business.
- They should avoid keeping cutouts and banners along the roads to welcome the political leaders and ministers on their visit and thus avoid dissipation of lakhs of rupees, time and energy. But, it should be used for productive purposes.
- They should fight against the production of intoxicants and social evils .They should not strive for personal development but for the welfare of the country.

- They should not support the criminals and help them escape from punishment and thus decrease the number of crimes and enable the people to live happily.
- They should not seek advertisement but work without publicity.
- They should not sell their principles for designation and monetary benefits.
- Politicians should not appoint their sons, daughters, or family members as their successors in politics. They should avoid nepotism in order to earn the hatred of the public and other political parties.

Role of Religious Workers

Religion is one of the factors for man making. It is the source of spiritual and moral development that prepares the man to lead an honest, happy and peaceful life. The purity and development of religion depend on the religious leaders, workers, pastors, priests, poojaries and bikshus and moulvies. Nobody can make others holy but his dedicated and sacrificial life may bring about desirable changes in the personal life of the individual. However, religion teaches many principles to be practiced for a healthy and happy life. Hence, the role of religious workers is very important in controlling social pollution. But, it is not possible for them unless they change their character and deeds. For this purpose, the quality of pastors, or priests or poojaris should be improved. They should set themselves as examples to all other human beings. The following suggestions may shape and mould them:

- Religious workers should always wear cassocks and rosary or the dress prescribed for them, that differentiates them from other people and keep them holy and honest.
- They themselves should understand whether they deserve such a designation and are the source of spiritual and moral development.
- They should not consider religion as a source of income and employment for their comfortable life. But, it is for the uplift of the poor, needy, and downtrodden.
- They should lead humble and simple lives with high thoughts and dedication.
- A pastor or priest must keep himself off from drinking, smoking or chewing tobacco and nuts.
- They should fight against all anti-social activities such as terrorism, corruption, untouchability, dowry, homo-marriages, raping, and production of intoxicants.
- They should not dilute religion with politics and avoid politicalisation and commercialization of religion.
- They should practice what they preach in churches, temples, mosques and gurudwaras.
- Fasting, meditation and yoga should be the characteristics and practices of all religious workers.
- They should be men of love, kindness, sacrifice, dedication, devotion, faithfulness and divinity.
- They should contract their intestines and expand their minds and souls for intellectual, spiritual and moral development.
- They should avoid the establishment of different denominations like business centres. They should not consider their God as superior to other gods but they should be better than others in character and deeds.
- They should not deceive the people in the name of religion and God but they should differentiate them from atheists in character and deeds.
- They should have genuine concern for the poor, destitute, orphans and the physically and mentally challenged people.
- They should not aim at their monetary development but spiritual and moral development, which is essential for man-making.

- They must differentiate themselves from all other human beings and be the reflection of God and divinity.
- They should not incline to any filthy deeds or lose their quality for monetary benefits. They should keep themselves off from 3w's—wealth, women, wine as they spoil their personal, social, moral and spiritual life.
- They should love and help all people irrespective of caste, religion, region and economic status.
- They should not cause any type of environmental pollution, communal riots and superstitious deeds. For instance, religious rallies, elephant processions and worshipping and dissolving gods in the water resources should be avoided.

Role of Teachers

The teacher is the moulder of human society. He/she takes the place of parents in the school or college, which is the mini society for intellectual, physical, moral and social development. We cannot deny the impact of teachers on their students and society. His role is very important in man making and protecting him from social pollution. For this purpose, every teacher should be a role model in character and deeds. In fact, most of the students reflect the behavior of their teachers. Hence, the quality of teachers should be improved by adopting and implementing the following ways and means for shaping and moulding their behavior in a desirable manner.

- Teaching is a noble profession and noble men should do it.
- Teachers should be men of love, affection, sympathy, compassion, intelligence, honesty, sincerity, dedication and punctuality.
- They should stand or walk in the class and keep an eye on every student and avoid sitting while teaching. If the teacher sits, students will not sit in the class. (They will not concentrate on studies.)
- They should be effective learners and know each student by his/her name.
- They should treat the students impartially and see them as the noble creation of God or nature irrespective of colour, caste religion, location and economic status.
- They should not use the students for their personal gains like asking them to buy food or stationery items and cleaning their vehicles and houses.
- They should be present the classroom in time and not leave it before the bell rings.
- They should not leave the class when they conduct class tests and other examinations and avoid peeping outside and chatting with adjacent classroom teacher. It may encourage the student to copy from the neighbours' scripts or book. Students learn the irresponsibility of the teacher.
- They should avoid using cell phone, taking tea or coffee and eating fruits in the classroom because most of the students studying in government and aided schools would be poor and hungry. Moreover, the above habits will demoralize the students as well as teachers.
- They should be models to the students in character and deeds and they should be free from the consumption of drugs, smoking cigarettes and chewing tobacco in and out of the school.
- The teacher should enter the marks obtained in the class-tests or examinations and not entrust the work to the students. Moreover, the teacher should do the valuation himself. If not, students learn the laziness and dishonesty of teachers and they may enter high marks instead of the actual marks obtained in the examination.
- The teacher should not demand or expect money or material for internal assessment and for favouritism.

- They should advise the students to switch off lights and fans that are not required and close the water taps after use. This will train them to lead an economic life.
- The teachers should keep in their mind that they are not better than the students but age is the only factor that differentiates them from students. This is because; both the teacher and student watch the same movies and read the same news and are living in the same environment.
- The teachers should always think of their past academic achievements whenever they scold or punish the students who are weak in studies.
- He should not expose the weakness of his students with others (co-workers and headmaster) and try to solve the problems without the interference of other teachers or the head of the institution.
- He should provide necessary guidance and counselling to the slow learners for their academic achievements.
- He should treat the students with affection and avoid punishment or take the matter seriously when a student is found in love affairs and using any intoxicants and advise them effectively by sharing his experiences and never leave the matter to be worsened that affect the student and the school.

Role of Parents

Parents are the first and the best teachers or architects in shaping and moulding the behavior of their children. As good trees yield good fruits; parents with good character can yield good children. Hence, the role of parents is very important in protecting the children from social pollution. For this purpose, parents may implement the following suggestions for making good children and society.

- Parents should treat their children with love and limited freedom.
- They should encourage them in studies, co-curricular activities and in keeping amicable relationship with relatives, friends and neighbours.
- They should keep an eye on their children when they leave for school/college, play and work and watch their behavior.
- They should train them to limit the expenditure to their income and if possible to meet all requirements. Urgent needs must be met immediately and others later.
- They should treat their children impartially and avoid scolding and beating them when they commit any mistake or are disobedient and correct them through right advice.
- They should reserve or spare time to spend with their children to discuss the problems related to travel, studies, food, clothing, relationship with teachers and their future plans.
- They should give importance to watch television for acquiring information and knowledge related to scientific and technological development, important episodes happening in different parts of the world.
- Fathers should be role models in running the family smoothly and sweetly. They should not be addicted to any bad habits in order to foster good habits and behaviour in their children.
- The father should be a man of love, affection, honesty, sympathy, sacrifice and patriotism.
- He should avoid scolding, criticizing or beating his wife in the presence of his children.
- Parents should lead a blameless life and avoid illegal sexual contact and polygamy or polyandry for the character formation in their children.
- They should praise their children in their success or efforts taken for their development and avoid treating them negatively.

- They should not give a place for frustration or despondency even if the children fail in the examination or efforts taken for employment or loss of money or properties, but encourage them by narrating the experience of great leaders, scientists and scholars and their failures and achievements in various fields.
- The father should avoid sexual talk or contact in the presence of children.
- He should not compel or beat his children to get first mark or rank and compare them with other students or neighbours in studies but train and advise them to be the best.
- Parents should not support or encourage their children when any complaint is charged against them, but they should look into the issue and find a good solution.
- They should not separate themselves or divorce under any circumstance but live together for the balanced development of their children.
- They should advise their children to close the water taps and switch off fans and lights whenever they are not in use, in the place where they live and work. Such habits will train them to lead an economic life.
- They should be cautious and vigilant over their teenage children because they may fall in infatuation or be addicted to drugs, smoking and other social evils. This matter should be dealt with amicably without making the situation worse. It may be nipped in the bud through counseling. Parents can illustrate the ill effects of love marriage or marriage before the completion of their studies and drugs, smoking and chewing tobacco. Parents need patience, affection, cooperation and adjustment according to the situation.
- They should not expect their children to become doctors or engineers, but qualify them and make them useful to the family, society and the nation.
- They should not spoil the married life of their children for the sake of dowry.

Role of Educational Institutions

The role of educational institutions cannot be neglected in preventing social pollution. In fact, educational institutions are social institutions or mini societies where man and nation are shaped. Therefore, the quality of educational institutions should be improved for the balanced development of the students. In this regard, following suggestions may be implemented for the development of the institution and creation of a better society.

- The private educational institutions should have all facilities for the intellectual, physical, social and moral development of the students. It means that the institution should be well-furnished and have a good library, playground, laboratories, seminar hall, classroom facilities, auditorium and well-qualified and experienced staff.
- Attendance register should be properly maintained for students as well as staff. Attendance for students should be compulsory and irregular students should not be permitted to appear for the examination.
- The institution should collect fees uniformly. No student should be discriminated in tuition fees. It makes education as vegetable in the market. But, fee reduction may be made on the basis of marks obtained in the previous examinations.
- Generally, retired schoolteachers or headmasters should not be appointed as teachers or lecturers in private colleges for monetary benefits as they sit and chat in the class. That does not motivate or create the atmosphere for learning.
- Recruitment of teachers or lecturers in private educational institutions should be made based on merit, but not on the basis of caste, religion and economic status.

- Academically and professionally qualified candidates should be appointed according to the rules of the Board of Education or University Grants Commission.
- The fresh candidates may be appointed as probationers for one year from the date of joining. During that period skill, efficiency and character of the candidate should be assessed by direct observation and enquiring the students.
- Salary for the staff should be paid on the last working day of every month or the first working day of the next month. Delay in disbursement of salary should be avoided as it affects the enthusiasm and efficiency of the teachers.
- The correspondents of private institutions should aim at the quality of education and facilities available in the institutions rather than the collection of money.
- He should visit the college once a week or twice a month and arrange a meeting for discussing matter s related to the problems and development of the institution.
- The co-curricular and extra-curricular activities should be organised in the institution not for profit making but for socializing the students by providing them direct experience and learning resources. Hence, tour and camps should be conducted for refreshment without exploiting the students.
- Internal assessment should be made based on the performance of students and not on the basis of caste, colour, religion or economic status.
- The commission or government officials should avoid getting bribery when the Government or Education Board sends them for evaluating the strength and weakness of the institutions or granting recognition for new colleges.
-
- Appointment of drunkards, smokers and chewers without moral character should be avoided in educational institutions as they mar the character and habit of the students.
- Private educational institutions should observe all holidays and the aim of national days should not be defeated at any cost. The national and religious days should be used for inculcating value and moral education for man making and not money-making.

PUNISHMENTS FOR CONTROLLING SOCIAL POLLUTION

The statements such as 'No gain No pain' and 'You reap what you sow' never fail in our experience of life. It cannot be denied that reward and praise increase academic achievements of the students and improve the quality of teachers. However, punishment reduces the number of criminals and crimes. In the absence of punishment, we cannot think of character formation or cultural development in the Indian society. Hence, the role of punishment is a must for bringing about desirable changes in man and society. The following criminals should be punished without procrastination. The government should be strict and public should cooperate for the execution of punishment. The person who rapes, murders, prints fake currencies and certificates, eve teases and kidnaps should be imprisoned or sentenced to death. It should be remembered, "Death of a man can save the lives of many". This policy should be implemented to control social pollution.

- The teacher who smokes, drinks and chews should not be promoted and increment should be stopped or may be terminated for two years in order to make them role models to the students and society.
- The teacher, who rapes the students, engages in sexual matter and prints fake currencies should be sentenced to death or terminated from service and imprisoned for double life imprisonment.

- The man who manufactures intoxicants and gives room for prostitution should be given life imprisonment.
- Recognition of colleges and schools that do not fulfil the minimum requirements of the Board of education and University Grants Commission should be cancelled straight away without any notice.
- The movie producers who emphasise sexual and violent scenes that spoil the youngsters should be imprisoned for ten years or the release of such movies should be prohibited.
- Any religious leaders or workers found in swindling or sexual matters or in anti social activities should be given life imprisonment without any consideration to shape them for the betterment of the society.
- Adulterators, harlots and caste and religion based organizers should be punished severely.
- Any person charged in corruption case, should be terminated from the service and criminal action should be an example for all generations.
- Terrorism should be eradicated at the beginning itself.

Thus, all criminals should be punished with a view to correct them. Absence of punishment encourages the people to do any filthy deed or engage in anti-social activities. Consequently, even ordinary people cannot have a peaceful and happy life. Therefore, punishment must be given to criminals severely and uniformly irrespective of their politics and socio economic status.

CONCLUSION

Every child is pure, sensitive and noble in character. However, the artificial stratification based on socio-economic status, and the undesirable behaviour and activities of parents, teachers, religious workers, politicians and professionals spoil its body, mind and soul at different stages of development causing human and environmental pollution. It is a highly deplorable fact that the uncertainty of life, chronic diseases, accidents, sudden demises and natural hazards do not have a great impact on human society in eradicating its undesirable behaviour and activities. The study of undesirable behaviour and activities should be given more importance than any other subjects in the postmodern society. Hence, the study of social pollution and its impact on social and natural environments should be taught as an integral part of all types and in all stages of education. However, a number of questions may arise in our minds about the inclusion and implementation of such a study in general education and practical life. For example, Is it to be included as a part of environmental education? Is it possible to control social pollution? Can it be possible to keep the man free from the consumption of liquor, smoking cigarettes and chewing tobacco, corruption, killing, kidnapping, eve-teasing, printing fake currencies and certificates, raping, stealing, prostitution, adulteration, dowry, sex harassment and production of intoxicants? Who can take efforts to control social pollution? Could the governments prohibit the production of intoxicants and the movies that expose sexual and violent scenes, which are the sources of income and employment for a large number of people? In addition, what is the role of parents, teachers, politicians, religious activists and governments in controlling social pollution? We may find it difficult to answer these questions and neglect the study of social pollution. However, it is the need of the hour that we may postpone the study of environmental pollution for some years but we cannot procrastinate the study of social pollution for a few days. In fact, a balanced and sustainable development of man and nature cannot be achieved in the absence of such a study. Hence, the study of social pollution and environmental pollution should go together like the two parallel rail tracks to reach the destination of creating better men and better environment. The central and state governments should punish the criminals and prohibit the production of all intoxicants and should not consider them as the sources of income, employment, and getting votes or political favouritism but think of the health and welfare of human resources and the development of the country. We cannot deny that the destruction of human society is greater through sexual and violent scenes and intoxicants than through environmental pollution and nuclear bombs. Once Swami Vivekananda the great saint of India remarked, "The end of all education and all training should be man making". Today we can say that the end of all activities and all efforts should be the end of prohibiting anti-social activities and production of intoxicants, and punishing the criminals, eradicating poverty and unemployment, and establishing a casteless, secular and democratic environment for forming a real human society. We should keep in our mind that today our children depend on us for everything, but tomorrow we depend on them. This is an eternal law of human life.

REFERENCES

Aggarwal, J.C., *Theory and Principles of Education*, Vikas Publishing House, New Delhi, 2002.

Aggarwal, J.C., *Landmarks in the History of Modern Indian Education* Vikas Publishing House, 2004.

Aggarwal, J.C., *Development and Planning of Modern Education*, Vikas Publishing House, New Delhi, 2005.

Aggarwal, J.C., *Education for Values, Environment and Human Rights*, Shipra Publications, New Delhi, 2006.

Aggarwal, J.C. and S. Gupta, *Great Philosophers and Thinkers on Education*, Shipra Publications, New Delhi, 2006.

Aggarwal, Somnath, *Philosophical Foundations of Education*, Authors Press Publishers, New Delhi, 2007.

Ansari, M.S., *Teacher in the Emerging Indian Society*, International Publishing House, Meerut, 2005.

Bharathi Vijaya and Rao, *Educational Philosophy of John Dewey*, Discovery Publishing House, New Delhi, 2006.

Bharucha, E., *Textbook of Environmental Studies*, Universities Press, Hyderabad, 2005.

Bhatia, K.K. and C.L. Narang, *Philosophical and Sociological Bases of Education*, Tandon Publication, Ludhiana, 2004.

Bhatia, K.K. and C.L. Narang, *Principles of Education*, Tandon Publication, Ludhiana, 2006.

Bhatnagar, S. and Anamika Saxena, *Development of Education in India*, Surya Publication, Meerut, 2004.

Bhushan Vidya and Sachdeva, *An Introduction to Sociology*, Kitab Mahal, Allahabad, 1992.

Brubacher, J.S., *Modern Philosophies of Education*, Surjeet Publications, New Delhi, 2007.

Chada, S.C., *Teacher in Emerging Indian Society*, International Publishing House, Meerut, 2005.

Chakraborthy, A.K., *Principles and Practice of Education*, Surya Publications, Meerut, 2004.

Chandra, Anil, *Sociology of Education*, Book Enclave, Jaipur, 2004.

Chandra, S.S. and Sharma, R.K., *Philosophy of Education*, Atlantic Publishers, New Delhi, 2004.

Chandrasekhran, P., *Environmental Studies* (Tamil), T.K. Publication, Pudukkottai, 2004.

Chaube, S.P. and Akhilesh Chaube, *Educational Ideals of the Great in India*, Neelkamal Publications, New Delhi, 2007.

Chaube, S.P. and Akhilesh Chaube, *Ideals of the Great Western Educators*, Neelkamal Publications, New Delhi, 2002.

Chaube, S.P. and Akhilesh Chaube, *Western Educational Thinkers*, Concept Publishing Company, New Delhi, 2002.

Chaube, S.P., *Recent Philosophies of Education in India*, Concept Publishing Company, New Delhi, 2005.

Chauhan, C.P.S., *Modern Indian Education*, Kanishka Publishers, New Delhi, 2004.

Dash, B.N., *A New Approach to Teacher Education in the Emerging Indian Society*, Neelkamal Publication, New Delhi, 2006.

Dash, B.N., *Education and Society*, Dominant Publishers, New Delhi, 2004.

Dash, B.N., *Principles of Education*, Neelkamal Publications, New Delhi, 2006.

Dash, B.N., *Theories of Education and Education in the Emerging Indian Society*, Dominant Publishers, New Delhi, 2004.

Dash, B.N., *Trends and Issues in Indian Education*, Dominant Publishers, New Delhi, 2004.

Dash, M., *Education in India*, Atlantic Publishers, New Delhi, 2004.

Durant, W., *The Story of Philosophy*, Pocket Books, New York, 1961.

Gopal Dutt, N.H., (Ed.) *Environmental Pollution and Control*, Neelkamal Publications, New Delhi, 2007.

Gupta, P.K., *Population Education*, Surya Publication, Meerut, 2004.

Gupta, S., *Education in Emerging India*, Shipra Publications, New Delhi, 2005.

Johri, P.K., *Foundations of Education*, Anmol Publications, New Delhi, 2005.

Kaur, M. and R.C. Sharma, *Health Education and Physical Education*, Tandon Publications, Ludhiana, 2005.

Khanna, S.D. and V.K. Saxena, *et al.*, *Education in the Emerging Indian Society*, Doaba House, New Delhi, 1985.

Krishnamacharyulu, V., *School Management and Systems of Education*, Neelkamal Publication, New Delhi, 2006.

Madhukar Indira, *Impact of Globalization on Education*, Authors Press Publishers, New Delhi, 2005.

Mehta, D.D., *Development of Education System in India*, Tandon Publications, Ludhiana, 2003.

Mohanty, S.B., *Theory and Practice of Integral Education*, Manu Publications, Pondicherry, 2007.

Moore, B.N., and K. Bruder, *Philosophy: The Power of Ideas*, Tata McGraw-Hill Publishing Company, New Delhi, 2005.

Mukherjee, R., *Environmental Management and Awareness Issues*, Sterling Publishers, New Delhi, 2002.

Murthy, S.K., *Philosophical and Sociological Foundations of Education*, Tandon Publications, Ludhiana, 2003.

Murthy, S.K., *Teacher and Education in Indian Society*, Tandon Publications, Ludhiana, 2005.

Nanda, V.K., *Education in Emerging Indian Society*, Anmol Publications, New Delhi, 2005.

Naqi Mohammed, *Modern Value Education*, Anmol Publications, New Delhi, 2005.

Nunn, T.P., *Principles of Education*, Discovery Publishing House, New Delhi, 2003.

Odum, E.P., *Fundamentals of Ecology*, W.B Saunders Company, USA, 1971.

Pandit, K.L., *Educational Sociology*, A.B.D. Publishers, Jaipur, 2003.

Panneerselvam, A. and R. Mohana, *Environmental Science Education*, Sterling Publishers, New Delhi, 2005.

Prasad, Janardan, *Education and Society*, Kanishka Publishers, New Delhi, 2006.

Pruti, R.K., *Education in Modern India*, Sonali Publications, New Delhi, 2005.

Rai, Amarnath, *Distance Education*, Authors Press Publishers, New Delhi, 2005.

Ramesh Ghanta and B.N. Dash, *Foundations of Education*, Neelkamal Publications, New Delhi, 2004.

Rao, D.B., *Education for Women*, Discovery Publishing House, New Delhi, 2004.

Rao, V.K., *Emerging Trends of Education*, Rajghat Publications, New Delhi, 2004.

Rather, A.R., *Theory and Principles of Education*, Discovery Publishing House, New Delhi, 2004.

Saxena, N.R. and B.K. Mishra, *et al.*, *Teacher Education*, Surya Publication, Meerut, 2004.

Saxena, Swarup, N.R. and Shikha Chaturvedi, *An Encyclopaedia of Philosophical and Sociological Foundations of Education*, Surya Publications, Meerut, 2006.

Saxena, Swarup, N.R. and Shikha Chaturvedi, *Teacher in Emerging Indian Society*, Surya Publications, Meerut, 2004.

Saxena, Swarup, N.R., *Philosophical and Sociological Foundations of Education*, Vinay Rakheja Publications, Meerut, 2006.

Shaida, B.D. and R.N. Safaya, *Modern Theory and Principles of Education*, Dhanpatrai Publishing Company, New Delhi, 2004.

Shankar Rao, C.N., *Principles of Sociology*, S. Chand Company, New Delhi, 2005.

Sharma, Aditi, *Environmental Studies*, Surjeet Publications, New Delhi, 2005.

Sharma, D.L., *Education in the Emerging Indian Society*, Surya Publications, Meerut, 2005.

Sharma, Lalit, *Environmental Science*, International Publishing House, Meerut, 2007.

Sharma, R.A., *Economics of Education*, Surya Publication, Meerut, 2007.

Sharma, R.C., *Population Trends, Resources and Environmental: Handbook on Population Education*, Dhanpatrai Publishing Company, New Delhi, 2002.

Sharma, S.R., *Principles of Education*, Mohit Publications, New Delhi, 2003.

Sharma, V.S., *Environmental Education*, Anmol Publications, New Delhi, 2005.

Sharma, Y.K., *Doctrines of the Great Indian Educators*, Kanishka Publishers, New Delhi, 2004.

Shrivastava, K.K., *Environmental Education*, Kanishka Publishers, New Delhi, 2004.

Singh, U.K. and A.K., Nayak, *Modern Education*, Common Wealth Publishers, New Delhi, 2004.

Sivarajan, K., *Education in the Emerging Indian Society*, Calicut University, 2006.

Taj Haseen, *Current Challenges in Education*, Neelkamal Publications, New Delhi, 2006.

Taneja, V.R., *Educational Thought and Practice*, Sterling Publishers, New Delhi, 2004.

Tilak, J.B.G. (Ed.), *Education, Society and Development*, APH Publishing Corporation, New Delhi, 2003.

Trivedi, P.R. and Gurdeep Raj, *Environmental Ecology*, Akashdeep Publishing House, New Delhi, 2002.

Trivedi, P.R., *Environmental Education*, APH Publishing Corporation, New Delhi, 2004.

Trivedi, R.N., *Environmental Sciences*, Anmol Publications, New Delhi, 2001.

Wadhwa, S.S., *Education in Emerging Indian Society*, Tandon Publications, Ludhiana, 2003.

Wangoo, M.L., *Population Education*, Tandon Publications, Ludhiana, 2002.

Yadav, H.S. and S. Yadav, *et al.*, *Education in the Emerging Indian Society*, Tandon Publications, Ludhiana, 2004.

Yogendra, K.S., *Foundations in Sociology of Education*, Kanishka Publishers, New Delhi, 2004.

NAME INDEX

SUBJECT INDEX